Twentieth-Century Literary Criticism

Guide to Gale Literary Criticism Series

When you need to review criticism of literary works, these are the Gale series to use:

If the author's death date is:	You should turn to:
After Dec. 31, 1959 (or author is still living)	**CONTEMPORARY LITERARY CRITICISM** for example: Jorge Luis Borges, Anthony Burgess, William Faulkner, Mary Gordon, Ernest Hemingway, Iris Murdoch
1900 through 1959	**TWENTIETH-CENTURY LITERARY CRITICISM** for example: Willa Cather, F. Scott Fitzgerald, Henry James, Mark Twain, Virginia Woolf
1800 through 1899	**NINETEENTH-CENTURY LITERATURE CRITICISM** for example: Fedor Dostoevski, George Sand, Gerard Manley Hopkins, Emily Dickinson
1400 through 1799	**LITERATURE CRITICISM FROM 1400 TO 1800** **(excluding Shakespeare)** for example: Anne Bradstreet, Pierre Corneille, Daniel Defoe, Alexander Pope, Jonathan Swift, Phillis Wheatley
	SHAKESPEAREAN CRITICISM Shakespeare's plays and poetry

Gale also publishes related criticism series:

CONTEMPORARY ISSUES CRITICISM

Presents criticism on contemporary authors writing on current issues. Topics covered include the social sciences, philosophy, economics, natural science, law, and related areas.

CHILDREN'S LITERATURE REVIEW

Covers authors of all eras. Presents criticism on authors and author/illustrators who write for the preschool to junior-high audience.

ISSN 0276-8178

Volume 16

Twentieth-Century Literary Criticism

**Excerpts from Criticism of the
Works of Novelists, Poets, Playwrights,
Short Story Writers, and Other Creative Writers
Who Died between 1900 and 1960,
from the First Published Critical Appraisals
to Current Evaluations**

**Dennis Poupard
James E. Person, Jr.
Editors**

**Thomas Ligotti
Associate Editor**

**Gale Research Company
Book Tower
Detroit, Michigan 48226**

STAFF

Dennis Poupard, James E. Person, Jr., *Editors*

Thomas Ligotti, *Associate Editor*

Lee Fournier, Marie Lazzari, Serita Lanette Lockard, *Senior Assistant Editors*

Sandra Giraud, Paula Kepos, Sandra Liddell,
Claudia Loomis, Jay P. Pederson, *Assistant Editors*

Lizbeth A. Purdy, *Production Supervisor*
Denise Michlewicz Broderick, *Production Coordinator*
Eric Berger, *Assistant Production Coordinator*
Robin Du Blanc, Kelly King Howes, *Editorial Assistants*

Victoria B. Cariappa, *Research Coordinator*
Jeannine Schiffman Davidson, *Assistant Research Coordinator*
Kevin John Campbell, Leslie Kyle Schell, Filomena Sgambati,
Valerie J. Webster, *Research Assistants*

Linda M. Pugliese, *Manuscript Coordinator*
Donna Craft, *Assistant Manuscript Coordinator*
Colleen M. Crane, Maureen A. Puhl, Rosetta Irene Simms, *Manuscript Assistants*

Jeanne A. Gough, *Permissions Supervisor*
Janice M. Mach, *Permissions Coordinator*
Susan D. Nobles, *Assistant Permissions Coordinator*
Patricia A. Seefelt, *Assistant Permissions Coordinator, Illustrations*
Margaret A. Chamberlain, Sandra C. Davis, Mary M. Matuz, *Senior Permissions Assistants*
Kathy Grell, Josephine M. Keene, *Permissions Assistants*
H. Diane Cooper, Dorothy J. Fowler, Yolanda Parker, Mabel C. Schoening, *Permissions Clerks*
Margaret Mary Missar, *Photo Research*

Frederick G. Ruffner, *Publisher*
James M. Ethridge, *Executive Vice-President/Editorial*
Dedria Bryfonski, *Editorial Director*
Christine Nasso, *Director, Literature Division*
Laurie Lanzen Harris, *Senior Editor, Literary Criticism Series*

Since this page cannot legibly accommodate all the copyright notices,
the Appendix constitutes an extension of the copyright notice.

Copyright © 1985 by Gale Research Company

Library of Congress Catalog Card Number 76-46132
ISBN 0-8103-0230-6
ISSN 0276-8178

Computerized photocomposition by
Typographics, Incorporated
Kansas City, Missouri

Printed in the United States

Contents

137713

Preface

It is impossible to overvalue the importance of literature in the intellectual, emotional, and spiritual evolution of humanity. Literature is that which both lifts us out of everyday life and helps us to better understand it. Through the fictive lives of such characters as Anna Karenin, Jay Gatsby, or Leopold Bloom, our perceptions of the human condition are enlarged, and we are enriched.

Literary criticism can also give us insight into the human condition, as well as into the specific moral and intellectual atmosphere of an era, for the criteria by which a work of art is judged reflects contemporary philosophical and social attitudes. Literary criticism takes many forms: the traditional essay, the book or play review, even the parodic poem. Criticism can also be of several types: normative, descriptive, interpretive, textual, appreciative, generic. Collectively, the range of critical response helps us to understand a work of art, an author, an era.

Scope of the Series

Twentieth-Century Literary Criticism (TCLC) is designed to serve as an introduction for the student of twentieth-century literature to the authors of the period 1900 to 1960 and to the most significant commentators on these authors. The great poets, novelists, short story writers, playwrights, and philosophers of this period are by far the most popular writers for study in high school and college literature courses. Since a vast amount of relevant critical material confronts the student, *TCLC* presents significant passages from the most important published criticism to aid students in their location and selection of criticism on authors who died between 1900 and 1960.

The need for *TCLC* was suggested by the usefulness of the Gale series *Contemporary Literary Criticism (CLC)*, which excerpts criticism on current writing. Because of the difference in time span under consideration *(CLC* considers authors who were still living after 1959), there is no duplication of material between *CLC* and *TCLC*. For further information about *CLC* and Gale's other criticism series, users should consult the Guide to Gale Literary Criticism Series preceding the title page in this volume.

Each volume of *TCLC* is carefully compiled to include authors who represent a variety of genres and nationalities and who are currently regarded as the most important writers of this era. In addition to major authors, *TCLC* also presents criticism on lesser-known writers whose significant contributions to literary history are important to the study of twentieth-century literature.

Each author entry in *TCLC* is intended to provide an overview of major criticism on an author. Therefore, the editors include approximately twenty authors in each 600-page volume (compared with approximately sixty authors in a *CLC* volume of similar size) so that more attention may be given to an author. Each author entry represents a historical survey of the critical response to that author's work: some early criticism is presented to indicate initial reactions, later criticism is selected to represent any rise or decline in the author's reputation, and current retrospective analyses provide students with a modern view. The length of an author entry is intended to reflect the amount of critical attention the author has received from critics writing in English, and from foreign criticism in translation. Critical articles and books that have not been translated into English are excluded. Every attempt has been made to identify and include excerpts from the seminal essays on each author's work. Additionally, as space permits, especially insightful essays of a more limited scope are included.

An author may appear more than once in the series because of the great quantity of critical material available, or because of a resurgence of criticism generated by events such as an author's centennial or anniversary celebration, the republication of an author's works, or publication of a newly translated work or volume of letters. A few author entries in each volume of *TCLC* feature criticism on single works by major authors who have appeared previously in the series. Only those individual works that have been the subjects of vast amounts of criticism and are widely studied in literature classes are selected for this in-depth treatment. Henrik Ibsen's *The Wild Duck,* James Joyce's *A Portrait of the Artist as a Young Man,* and D. H. Lawrence's *Sons and Lovers* are the subjects of such entries in *TCLC,* Volume 16.

Organization of the Book

An author entry consists of the following elements: author heading, biographical and critical introduction, principal works, excerpts of criticism (each followed by a bibliographical citation), and an additional bibliography for further reading.

- The *author heading* consists of the author's full name, followed by birth and death dates. The unbracketed portion of the name denotes the form under which the author most commonly wrote. If an author wrote consistently under a pseudonym, the pseudonym will be listed in the author heading and the real name given in parentheses on the first line of the biographical and critical introduction. Also located at the beginning of the introduction to the author entry are any name variations under which an author wrote, including transliterated forms for authors whose languages use nonroman alphabets. Uncertainty as to a birth or death date is indicated by a question mark.

- The *biographical and critical introduction* contains background information designed to introduce the reader to an author and to the critical debate surrounding his or her work. Parenthetical material following many of the introductions provides references to biographical and critical reference series published by Gale. These include *Children's Literature Review, Contemporary Authors, Dictionary of Literary Biography, Something about the Author,* and past volumes of *TCLC.*

- Most *TCLC* entries include *portraits* of the author. Many entries also contain illustrations of materials pertinent to an author's career, including holographs of manuscript pages, title pages, dust jackets, letters, or representations of important people, places, and events in an author's life.

- The *list of principal works* is chronological by date of first book publication and identifies the genre of each work. In the case of foreign authors where there are both foreign language publications and English translations, the title and date of the first English-language edition are given in brackets. Unless otherwise indicated, dramas are dated by first performance, not first publication.

- *Criticism* is arranged chronologically in each author entry to provide a useful perspective on changes in critical evaluation over the years. All titles by the author featured in the critical entry are printed in boldface type to enable the user to ascertain without difficulty the works being discussed. Also for purposes of easier identification, the critic's name and the publication date of the essay are given at the beginning of each piece of criticism. Unsigned criticism is preceded by the title of the journal in which it appeared. When an anonymous essay is later attributed to a critic, the critic's name appears in brackets at the beginning of the excerpt and in the bibliographical citation.

- Important critical essays are prefaced by *explanatory notes* as an additional aid to students using *TCLC.* The explanatory notes provide several types of useful information, including: the reputation of a critic; the importance of a work of criticism; the specific type of criticism (biographical, psychoanalytic, structuralist, etc.); a synopsis of the criticism; and the growth of critical controversy or changes in critical trends regarding an author's work. In many cases, these notes cross-reference the work of critics who agree or disagree with each other. Dates in parentheses within the explanatory notes refer to a book publication date when they follow a book title and to an essay date when they follow a critic's name.

- A complete *bibliographical citation* designed to facilitate location of the original essay or book by the interested reader follows each piece of criticism. An asterisk (*) at the end of a citation indicates that the essay is on more than one author.

- The *additional bibliography* appearing at the end of each author entry suggests further reading on the author. In some cases it includes essays for which the editors could not obtain reprint rights. An asterisk (*) at the end of a citation indicates that the essay is on more than one author.

An appendix lists the sources from which material in each volume has been reprinted. It does not, however, list every book or periodical consulted in the preparation of the volume.

Cumulative Indexes

Each volume of *TCLC* includes a cumulative index to authors listing all the authors who have appeared in *Contemporary Literary Criticism, Twentieth-Century Literary Criticism, Nineteenth-Century Literature Criticism,* and *Literature Criticism from 1400 to 1800,* along with cross-references to the Gale series *Children's Literature Review, Authors in the News, Contemporary Authors, Contemporary Authors Autobiography Series, Dictionary of Literary Biography, Something about the Author,* and *Yesterday's Authors of Books for Children.* Users will welcome this cumulated author index as a useful tool for locating an author within the various series. The index, which lists birth and death dates when available, will be particularly valuable for those authors who are identified with a certain period but whose death date causes them to be placed in another, or for those authors whose careers span two periods. For example, F. Scott Fitzgerald is found in *TCLC,* yet a writer often associated with him, Ernest Hemingway, is found in *CLC.*

Each volume of *TCLC* also includes a cumulative nationality index. Author names are arranged alphabetically under their respective nationalities and followed by the volume numbers in which they appear.

A cumulative index to critics is another useful feature in *TCLC*. Under each critic's name are listed the authors on whom the critic has written and the volume and page where the criticism may be found.

Acknowledgments

No work of this scope can be accomplished without the cooperation of many people. The editors especially wish to thank the copyright holders of the excerpted criticism included in this volume, the permissions managers of many book and magazine publishing companies for assisting us in securing reprint rights, and Jeri Yaryan for assistance with copyright research. We are also grateful to the staffs of the Detroit Public Library, the Library of Congress, University of Detroit Library, University of Michigan Library, and Wayne State University Library for making their resources available to us.

Suggestions Are Welcome

In response to various suggestions, several features have been added to *TCLC* since the series began. Recently introduced features include explanatory notes to excerpted criticism that provide important information regarding critics and their work, a cumulative author index listing authors in all Gale literary criticism series, entries devoted to criticism on a single work by a major author, and more extensive illustrations.

Readers who wish to suggest authors to appear in future volumes, or who have other suggestions, are cordially invited to write the editors.

Authors to Be Featured in *TCLC*, Volumes 17 and 18

James Agee (American novelist and journalist)—Agee's *Let Us Now Praise Famous Men* and *A Death in the Family* are harshly realistic treatments of the moral crises and moral triumphs of mid-twentieth-century America. In addition, Agee's film criticism is recognized as the first serious consideration in English of film as a modern art form.

Hilaire Belloc (English poet and essayist)—One of turn-of-the-century England's premier men of letters, Belloc has been the subject of renewed critical and biographical interest in recent years.

Arnold Bennett (English novelist)—Bennett is credited with introducing techniques of European Naturalism to the English novel. Set in the manufacturing district of the author's native Staffordshire, Bennett's novels tell of the thwarted ambitions of those who endure a dull, provincial existence.

Christopher John Brennan (Australian poet)—Considered one of Australia's greatest poets, he introduced many of the techniques and themes of twentieth-century European literature to the literature of his homeland.

Hermann Broch (Austrian novelist, poet, and essayist)—Broch was a philosophical novelist whose works are considered profound reflections upon the social and moral disintegration of modern Europe. His major works, which include his masterpiece *The Sleepwalkers*, have been compared to James Joyce's *Ulysses* and *Finnegans Wake* for their contribution to the Modernist exploration of language.

Stephen Crane (American novelist)—Author of *The Red Badge of Courage*, Crane was one of America's foremost Realist writers and is credited with establishing American literary Naturalism.

Anne Frank (Dutch diarist)—Composed while its author was in hiding from the Nazis in Amsterdam, *The Diary of Anne Frank* is one of the most enduring and widely read documents of the Holocaust, as well as a testament to the suffering and creative talent of its young author.

Rémy de Gourmont (French critic, novelist, and dramatist)—Gourmont was one of the most prominent French men of letters of the modern era. Displaying an encyclopedic range of learning, his critical writings were extremely influential among early twentieth-century English and American critics.

Thomas Hardy (English novelist)—Hardy's novel *Tess of the d'Urbervilles* was controversial in the late nineteenth century for its sympathetic depiction of an independent female protagonist. *TCLC* will devote an entire entry to the critical reception of this classic work of English fiction.

O. Henry (American short story writer)—O. Henry (William Sydney Porter) was one of America's most popular short story writers. His stories, known for their inventiveness and characteristic surprise endings, are widely anthologized and often compared to the works of Guy de Maupassant.

Julia Ward Howe (American poet and biographer)—A famous suffragette and social reformer, Howe was also a popular poet who is best known as the composer of "The Battle Hymn of the Republic."

William Dean Howells (American novelist and critic)—Howells was the chief progenitor of American Realism and the most influential American literary critic of the late nineteenth century. Several of his early novels have been recently reissued, and discussion of his work is growing.

T. E. Hulme (English poet)—A major influence on the work of T. S. Eliot, Ezra Pound, and other important twentieth-century poets, Hulme was the chief theorist of Imagism and Modernism in English poetry.

James Weldon Johnson (American novelist and poet)—One of the most prominent black public figures of his time, Johnson is also regarded as the principal forerunner of the Harlem Renaissance. His novel *The Autobiography of an Ex-Colored Man* was one of the first works of fiction to explore the complexity of race relations in America and profoundly influenced such writers as Ralph Ellison and Richard Wright.

Rudyard Kipling (English short story writer and poet)—Best known for such works as *Kim, Captains Courageous,* and *The Jungle Book,* Kipling is one of the most popular authors of this century and one of the finest short story writers in world literature.

T. E. Lawrence (English autobiographer)—Lawrence is more popularly known as Lawrence of Arabia, a sobriquet received for his campaign against the Turks during World War I. His chronicle of this period in what has been described as "perhaps the strangest, most adventurous life of modern times" is contained in *The Seven Pillars of Wisdom. TCLC* will present excerpts from the entire range of criticism on this classic modern work, along with commentary on Lawrence's diary, his letters, and *The Mint,* an account of his experiences following his enlistment as a private in the Royal Air Force.

Ludwig Lewisohn (American novelist and critic)—An important man of letters during the first quarter of the twentieth century, Lewisohn made a notable contribution to modern literature through his critical works and his translations of the works of German and French authors. Many of Lewisohn's later works of fiction and nonfiction reflect his concern for the plight of European Jews during the 1930s and 1940s.

Detlev von Liliencron (German poet)—The author of works in several genres, Liliencron is most renowned for his lyric poetry, which is praised for its forcefulness and vivid detail.

George Meredith (English novelist and poet)—A prolific author and an associate of England's most famous Victorian literary figures, Meredith ranks among the outstanding writers of his era.

Rainer Maria Rilke (German poet and novelist)—Rilke's *The Notebooks of Malte Laurids Brigge,* a loosely autobiographical novel that explores the angst-ridden life of a hypersensitive man in Paris, is considered the author's most accomplished prose work. To mark a new translation of this novel, *TCLC* will devote an entire entry to critical discussion of this important work.

Ole Edvart Rölvaag (Norwegian-American novelist)—Born in Norway, Rölvaag emigrated to the United States in his twentieth year, and subsequently depicted in his seven novels the experience of Norwegian immigrants in America. Both as a novelist and as a teacher at Saint Olaf College in Northfield, Minnesota, Rölvaag attempted to preserve among Norwegian-Americans the European values that had become obsolete in their new homeland.

Jacques Roumain (Haitian novelist, poet, and essayist)—One of the most militant and influential Haitian intellectuals of this century, Roumain was the author of the novel *Masters of the Dew,* which was widely praised for its haunting stylistic beauty as well as its powerful social message.

John Ruskin (English critic)—Most renowned for his critical writings on art and architecture, particularly *Stones of Venice* and the five-volume series *Modern Painters,* Ruskin was also an important social critic. His advocacy of various reforms and his association with the Pre-Raphaelite circle of artists, writers, and thinkers place him at the intellectual and cultural center of Victorian England.

Lincoln Steffens (American journalist and autobiographer)—Steffens was one of a group of writers in the early twentieth century who were described as "muckrakers" by President Theodore Roosevelt. Steffens's call for radical reforms in American government and society forms the substance of his best works, including *The Shame of the Cities* and *The Struggle for Self Government,* and serves as the background to his highly readable *Autobiography.*

Leo Tolstoy (Russian novelist)—His *Anna Karenin* is considered one of the greatest novels in world literature. *TCLC* will devote an entire entry to the critical history of this work.

Mark Twain (American novelist)—Twain is considered by many to be the father of modern American literature. Breaking with the genteel literary conventions of the nineteenth century, Twain endowed his characters and narratives with the natural speech patterns of the common person and wrote about subjects hitherto considered beneath the consideration of serious art. He is renowned throughout the world for his greatest novel, *Huckleberry Finn. TCLC* will devote an entry solely to critical discussion of that controversial work. Included will be works of criticism written from the late nineteenth century

through 1985, the centenary year of *Huckleberry Finn's* American publication and the one hundred-fiftieth anniversary of Twain's birth.

Robert Walser (Swiss novelist and short story writer)—Considered among the most important Swiss authors writing in German, Walser was praised by such major figures of German literature as Franz Kafka and Robert Musil. His fiction is distinguished by a grotesque imagination and black humor suggestive of the Expressionist and Surrealist movements.

Beatrice and Sydney James Webb (English social writers)—Prominent members of the progressive Fabian society, the Webbs wrote sociological works significant to the advent of socialist reform in England and influenced the work of several major authors, including H. G. Wells and Bernard Shaw.

H. G. Wells (English novelist)—Wells is best known today as one of the forerunners of modern science fiction and as a utopian idealist who foretold an era of chemical warfare, atomic weaponry, and world wars. *The Time Machine, The Invisible Man, The War of the Worlds, The Island of Doctor Moreau,* and several other works among Wells's canon are considered classics in the genres of science fiction and science fantasy. *TCLC* will devote an entire entry to Wells's accomplishments as a science fiction writer.

Owen Wister (American novelist)—Considered the founder of modern fiction about the Old West, Wister is best known as the author of *The Virginian,* a novel that established the basic character types, settings, and plots of the Western genre.

Andrei Zhdanov (Soviet censor)—As Secretary of the Central Committee of the Soviet Communist Party from 1928 until 1948, Zhdanov formulated the official guidelines for all writing published in the Soviet Union. He was instrumental in establishing the precepts of Socialist Realism, which for decades severely circumscribed the subjects deemed suitable for Soviet literature.

Emile Zola (French novelist, dramatist, and critic)—Zola was the founder and principal theorist of Naturalism, perhaps the most influential literary movement in modern literature. His twenty-volume series *Les Rougon-Macquart* is one of the monuments of Naturalist fiction, and served as a model for late nineteenth-century novelists seeking a more candid and accurate representation of human life.

Stefan Zweig (Austrian biographer and fiction writer)—Through extensive translation of his works, Zweig's biographical studies of such important figures as Leo Tolstoy, Marie Antoinette, and Sigmund Freud, as well as his dramas and stories, are well known to English-language readers. Zweig stated that his works, both fiction and nonfiction, have as their focus "the psychological representation of personalities and their lives," which was his "main interest in writing."

Additional Authors to Appear
in Future Volumes

Abbey, Henry 1842-1911
Abercrombie, Lascelles 1881-1938
Adamic, Louis 1898-1951
Ade, George 1866-1944
Agustini, Delmira 1886-1914
Akers, Elizabeth Chase 1832-1911
Akiko, Yosano 1878-1942
Aldanov, Mark 1886-1957
Aldrich, Thomas Bailey 1836-1907
Aliyu, Dan Sidi 1902-1920
Allen, Hervey 1889-1949
Archer, William 1856-1924
Arlen, Michael 1895-1956
Austin, Alfred 1835-1913
Austin, Mary 1868-1934
Bahr, Hermann 1863-1934
Bailey, Philip James 1816-1902
Barbour, Ralph Henry 1870-1944
Barreto, Lima 1881-1922
Benet, William Rose 1886-1950
Benjamin, Walter 1892-1940
Bennett, James Gordon, Jr. 1841-1918
Benson, E(dward) F(rederic) 1867-1940
Benson, Stella 1892-1933
Berdyaev, Nikolai Aleksandrovich
  1874-1948
Beresford, J(ohn) D(avys) 1873-1947
Bergson, Henri 1859-1941
Binyon, Laurence 1869-1943
Bishop, John Peale 1892-1944
Blackmore, R(ichard) D(oddridge)
  1825-1900
Blake, Lillie Devereux 1835-1913
Blum, Leon 1872-1950
Bodenheim, Maxwell 1892-1954
Bosschere, Jean de 1878-1953
Bowen, Marjorie 1886-1952
Byrne, Donn 1889-1928
Caine, Hall 1853-1931
Campana, Dina 1885-1932
Cannan, Gilbert 1884-1955
Chand, Prem 1880-1936
Churchill, Winston 1871-1947
Coppée, Francois 1842-1908
Corelli, Marie 1855-1924
Croce, Benedetto 1866-1952
Crofts, Freeman Wills 1879-1957
Crothers, Rachel 1878-1958
Cruze, James (Jens Cruz Bosen) 1884-
  1942
Cunninghame-Graham, R.B. 1852-1936
Curros, Enriquez Manuel 1851-1908
Dagerman, Stig 1923-1954
Dall, Caroline Wells (Healy) 1822-1912
Daudet, Leon 1867-1942

Davidson, John 1857-1909
Day, Clarence 1874-1935
Delafield, E.M. (Edme Elizabeth Monica
  de la Pasture) 1890-1943
Deneson, Jacob 1836-1919
DeVoto, Bernard 1897-1955
Douglas, Lloyd C(assel) 1877-1951
Douglas, (George) Norman 1868-1952
Dovzhenko, Alexander 1894-1956
Drinkwater, John 1882-1937
Drummond, W.H. 1854-1907
Durkheim, Emile 1858-1917
Duun, Olav 1876-1939
Eaton, Walter Prichard 1878-1957
Eggleston, Edward 1837-1902
Erskine, John 1879-1951
Fadeyev, Alexander 1901-1956
Ferland, Albert 1872-1943
Feydeau, Georges 1862-1921
Field, Rachel 1894-1924
Flecker, James Elroy 1884-1915
Fletcher, John Gould 1886-1950
Fogazzaro, Antonio 1842-1911
Francos, Karl Emil 1848-1904
Frank, Bruno 1886-1945
Frazer, (Sir) George 1854-1941
Freud, Sigmund 1853-1939
Froding, Gustaf 1860-1911
Fuller, Henry Blake 1857-1929
Futabatei, Shimei 1864-1909
Futrelle, Jacques 1875-1912
Gladkov, Fydor Vasilyevich 1883-1958
Glaspell, Susan 1876-1948
Glyn, Elinor 1864-1943
Golding, Louis 1895-1958
Gosse, Edmund 1849-1928
Gould, Gerald 1885-1936
Gray, John 1866-1934
Guest, Edgar 1881-1959
Gumilyov, Nikolay 1886-1921
Gyulai, Pal 1826-1909
Hale, Edward Everett 1822-1909
Hall, James 1887-1951
Harris, Frank 1856-1931
Hawthorne, Julian 1846-1934
Hernandez, Miguel 1910-1942
Hewlett, Maurice 1861-1923
Heyward, DuBose 1885-1940
Hilton, James 1900-1954
Hope, Anthony 1863-1933
Hudson, W(illiam) H(enry) 1841-1922
Huidobro, Vincente 1893-1948
Hviezdoslav (Pavol Orszagh) 1849-1921
Ilyas, Abu Shabaka 1903-1947
Imbs, Bravig 1904-1946

Ivanov, Vyacheslav Ivanovich 1866-
  1949
Jacobs, W(illiam) W(ymark) 1863-1943
James, Will 1892-1942
Jammes, Francis 1868-1938
Jerome, Jerome K(lapka) 1859-1927
Johnson, Fenton 1888-1958
Johnson, Lionel 1869-1902
Johnston, Mary 1870-1936
Jorgensen, Johannes 1866-1956
Kaye-Smith, Sheila 1887-1956
Khlebnikov, Victor 1885-1922
King, Grace 1851-1932
Kirby, William 1817-1906
Kline, Otis Albert 1891-1946
Kohut, Adolph 1848-1916
Korolenko, Vladimir 1853-1921
Kuzmin, Mikhail Alexseyevich 1875-
  1936
Lamm, Martin 1880-1950
Lawson, Henry 1867-1922
Ledwidge, Francis 1887-1917
Leipoldt, C. Louis 1880-1947
Lemonnier, Camille 1844-1913
Leverson, Ada 1862-1933
Lima, Jorge De 1895-1953
Lindsay, (Nicholas) Vachel 1879-1931
Locke, Alain 1886-1954
Long, Frank Belknap 1903-1959
Louys, Pierre 1870-1925
Lucas, E(dward) V(errall) 1868-1938
Lyall, Edna 1857-1903
Maghar, Josef Suatopluk 1864-1945
Manning, Frederic 1887-1935
Maragall, Joan 1860-1911
Marais, Eugene 1871-1936
Martin du Gard, Roger 1881-1958
Masaoka Shiki 1867-1902
Masaryk, Tomas 1850-1939
McClellan, George Marion 1860-1934
McCoy, Horace 1897-1955
Mirbeau, Octave 1850-1917
Mistral, Frederic 1830-1914
Molnar, Ferenc 1878-1952
Monro, Harold 1879-1932
Moore, Thomas Sturge 1870-1944
Morley, Christopher 1890-1957
Morley, S. Griswold 1883-1948
Mqhayi, S.E.K. 1875-1945
Murray, (George) Gilbert 1866-1957
Nansen, Peter 1861-1918
Nathan, George Jean 1882-1958
Nobre, Antonio 1867-1900
Nordhoff, Charles 1887-1947
Norris, Frank 1870-1902

Obstfelder, Sigborn 1866-1900
O'Dowd, Bernard 1866-1959
Ophuls, Max 1902-1957
Orczy, Baroness 1865-1947
Owen, Seaman 1861-1936
Page, Thomas Nelson 1853-1922
Papini, Giovanni 1881-1956
Parrington, Vernon L. 1871-1929
Peck, George W. 1840-1916
Peret, Benjamin 1899-1959
Phillips, Ulrich B. 1877-1934
Pickthall, Marjorie 1883-1922
Pinero, Arthur Wing 1855-1934
Pontoppidan, Henrik 1857-1943
Prem Chand, Mushi 1880-1936
Prévost, Marcel 1862-1941
Quiller-Couch, Arthur 1863-1944
Quiroga, Horacio 1878-1937
Randall, James G. 1881-1953
Rappoport, Solomon 1863-1944
Read, Opie 1852-1939
Reisen (Reizen), Abraham 1875-1953
Remington, Frederic 1861-1909
Renard, Jules 1864-1910
Riley, James Whitcomb 1849-1916
Rinehart, Mary Roberts 1876-1958
Ring, Max 1817-1901
Rohmer, Sax 1883-1959
Rolland, Romain 1866-1944

Roussel, Raymond 1877-1933
Rozanov, Vasily Vasilyevich 1856-1919
Saar, Ferdinand von 1833-1906
Sabatini, Rafael 1875-1950
Saintsbury, George 1845-1933
Sakutaro, Hagiwara 1886-1942
Salinas, Pedro 1891-1951
Sanborn, Franklin Benjamin 1831-1917
Santayana, George 1863-1952
Sardou, Victorien 1831-1908
Schickele, René 1885-1940
Seabrook, William 1886-1945
Seton, Ernest Thompson 1860-1946
Shestov, Lev 1866-1938
Shiels, George 1886-1949
Skram, Bertha Amalie 1847-1905
Smith, Pauline 1883-1959
Sodergran, Edith Irene 1892-1923
Solovyov, Vladimir 1853-1900
Sorel, Georges 1847-1922
Spector, Mordechai 1859-1922
Spengler, Oswald 1880-1936
Squire, J(ohn) C(ollings) 1884-1958
Stavenhagen, Fritz 1876-1906
Stockton, Frank R. 1834-1902
Subrahmanya Bharati, C. 1882-1921
Sully-Prudhomme, Rene 1839-1907
Talev, Dimituv 1898-1966

Thoma, Ludwig 1867-1927
Tolstoy, Alexei 1882-1945
Trotsky, Leon 1870-1940
Tuchmann, Jules 1830-1901
Turner, W(alter) J(ames) R(edfern) 1889-1946
Vachell, Horace Annesley 1861-1955
Van Dine, S.S. (William H. Wright) 1888-1939
Van Doren, Carl 1885-1950
Van Dyke, Henry 1852-1933
Vazov, Ivan Minchov 1850-1921
Veblen, Thorstein 1857-1929
Villaespesa, Francisco 1877-1936
Wallace, Edgar 1874-1932
Wallace, Lewis 1827-1905
Walsh, Ernest 1895-1926
Webb, Mary 1881-1927
Webster, Jean 1876-1916
Whitlock, Brand 1869-1927
Wilson, Harry Leon 1867-1939
Wolf, Emma 1865-1932
Wood, Clement 1888-1950
Wren, P(ercival) C(hristopher) 1885-1941
Yonge, Charlotte Mary 1823-1901
Zecca, Ferdinand 1864-1947
Zeromski, Stefan 1864-1925

Readers are cordially invited to suggest additional authors to the editors.

Akutagawa Ryūnosuke

1892-1927

(Born Niihara Ryūnosuke) Japanese short story writer, novelist, poet, translator, and critic.

Akutagawa is widely known to readers and critics for the short story "Rashōmon," which, with another of his stories, "Yabu no Naka" ("In a Grove"), was adapted in 1950 by Kurosawa Akira for the noted film *Rashōmon*. He is considered one of the foremost authors of Japan's modern era, a period that began in 1868 under the rule of the Emperor Meiji. His works contributed greatly to his generation's thoughtful consideration of such issues as the function and merits of different literary genres and the artist's role in contemporary Japanese society; they also proved instrumental in extricating Japanese literature from what critics consider the morass of gossip and tedious didacticism into which it had fallen before the Meiji Restoration. In his works, Akutagawa drew upon elements of both Eastern and Western literary forms to create a distinctively modern form of Japanese literature.

Within the relatively brief span of approximately forty years, from Meiji's accession in 1868 until the Russo-Japanese War of 1904-05, Japan underwent a period of profound change, shaking off an isolationist past and energetically embracing a wide spectrum of elements of Western culture. While the Japanese were quick to assimilate industrial and scientific advancements, they were less eager to adopt Western thought and values. For a time, attempts were made to incorporate Western technology into a society still predominantly Eastern in its spiritual character. This desire was not only impossible to fulfill, but it also inspired a sense of conflict between Japan's traditions and the new Western ways. An additional source of conflict was the deep interest shown by Japanese writers in contemporary European literature. What began in the 1880s as a mere trickle of Western literature into Japan became a torrent by the end of the century. Translation of European authors assumed monumental importance, acquainting the reading public with a totally unfamiliar body of writing and inspiring many Japanese writers to break away from traditional forms that they believed had grown sterile. From this passion for European literature emerged a revived interest in Japan's past, for many authors came to see their heritage as the only precious thread of continuity in a world filled with ominous change. Akutagawa was acutely aware of these conflicts, and throughout his career he sought to utilize the modern, realistic techniques of European literature as well as elements of Japan's past, attempting to revive Japanese literature by exploring the promising resources of both Western and Eastern cultures.

Akutagawa was born in Irifunecho, a district within Tokyo. His father was the enterprising owner of five dairies by the time Akutagawa was born. Shortly after Akutagawa's birth his mother, a woman of tenuous mental health, lapsed into a schizophrenic state from which she never recovered, although she lived for another ten years. Remembrance of his mother's insanity and the resulting fear that he might have inherited her mental condition preyed upon Akutagawa all his life; he later bitterly satirized tainted heredity, as well as capitalism, traditional morality, and other aspects of contemporary Japanese society, in *Kappa*, a novel in which the protagonist finds himself transported, like the hero of Jonathan Swift's *Gulliver's Travels,* to a world where alien creatures comport themselves with all the shortcomings and foibles of human beings. After his mother's death, Akutagawa was adopted by his mother's elder brother and his wife, who gave the boy their family name, Akutagawa. His adopted parents had remained largely untouched by Western culture, and they instilled in him a reverence for Japanese traditions, particularly in literature. Akutagawa developed a fondness for ancient legends and tales of the grotesque, both of which later figured significantly in his work. However, he was a voracious reader, and by the time he reached middle school he was reading the works of Henrik Ibsen, Rudyard Kipling, and Anatole France, among others, sharing in his country's wave of interest in European literature. He attended Tokyo Imperial University, where he excelled in his studies of English literature, translated many Western works, and became quite active in publishing a student-produced literary periodical, as well as regularly participating in a discussion group conducted by the renowned novelist Natsume Sōseki.

Some of the short stories for which Akutagawa is most widely known had already appeared in periodicals by the time he graduated in 1916, and he was widely acclaimed as one of the brightest newcomers on the literary scene. He accepted a part-time teaching position at the Naval Academy at Yokosuka, meanwhile strengthening his reputation during 1917 by publishing his stories in various magazines and in two collections. In 1918 Akutagawa married the niece of a friend he had known since childhood; in the same year, he also entered into a contract with a Japanese newspaper to publish his fiction. This enabled him to resign his post at the Naval Academy and devote himself entirely to his writing.

In 1921, Akutagawa was sent by his newspaper to China as an "overseas observer," an assignment which proved to be a turning point in his life. Never having enjoyed sound health, he suffered during his travels from a number of debilitating illnesses that left him weakened, depressed, and helpless to combat a developing mental illness brought on by fears of a deterioration similar to his mother's. His writing, which up to this point was firmly rooted in history and legend, grew introspective and autobiographical. Akutagawa's fear of madness became obsessive, and he sought temporary respite from both psychological and physical troubles through the use of drugs, toying with the idea of suicide. Following the mental breakdown of a close friend, Akutagawa took his own life with poison in 1927.

While Akutagawa did not confine himself to any particular genre during his career, his greatest work was done in the short story form. He consistently attempted to examine predictable and universal patterns of human behavior, and to depict those natural aspirations and illusions that transcend barriers of space and time. Conflicts between the natural inclinations of human beings and the demands imposed by ordered societies, as well as humanity's struggle with baser propensities, are echoed throughout Akutagawa's works. For example, "Rashōmon," which has come to be synonymous with its author's name, candidly and symbolically confronts the moral dilemma of a servant for whom convention and prosperity have been effaced by misfortune. Set in twelfth-century Kyoto, a locale rife with plague, violence, and anarchy, "Rashōmon" depicts the moral collapse of a man driven to assault and thievery by the horror he witnesses in a society which has itself collapsed and lives by the savage morality of expediency; the sight of an old crone squatting in a roomful of dead epidemic victims, matter-of-factly denuding the corpses of their hair to make a wig she can sell, destroys the man's last compunctions. In this story Akutagawa portrayed the psychological drama of humanity caught in the confrontation between circumstantial chaos and structured morality, an approach unceasingly fascinating to him, in one of the ancient settings he had always found so effective as dramatic background. His commitment to presenting life in even its most unsavory aspects led him to depict subjects which, though often offensive to his critics, were essential to providing the proper perspective for character development, as exemplified in a story such as "Rashōmon." Somewhat less grim, but not without the author's unvarnished appraisal of human nature, "Kumo no Ito" ("The Spider's Thread") deals allegorically with one man's pervasive egoism, a flaw that proves fatal both to himself and to others. A robber, Kandata, has been banished to hell after his death, and the all-merciful Buddha, who would deliver him from eternal agony, recalls that he once spared the life of a spider that crossed his path. Buddha, therefore, causes the spider to spin a single thread that extends far down into hell. Kandata begins to climb this thread, but soon notices that other sinners are likewise employing this means of escape. Fearful lest the thread break under their weight, Kandata summarily orders the others to relinquish the salvation he is convinced was intended only for himself, and at that moment the thread breaks, plunging all, including Kandata, back into hell, and Buddha into inestimable sadness over human selfishness. While Akutagawa's subjects here, as elsewhere, constitute faithful representations of both the grim and the foolish aspects of human behavior, they are not always devoid of humor. "Hana" ("The Nose"), for example, addresses egoism by relating the predicament of a Buddhist monk who has succeeded in shortening his enormous nose, the bane of his existence and, as he sees it, the impediment to his social acceptance; his resulting vanity is then penalized by coldness from peers who before had been quietly solicitous of his feelings. Many critics have noted in this and other stories Akutagawa's unpretentious treatment of human behavior revealed in insights edged by dry wit, and astute characterization effected in a word, gesture, or expression.

Although Akutagawa wrote with great speed, he was an exacting stylist, and it is probably this facet of his writing, more than any other, that has been most widely discussed. The author, who had always evinced a passion for poetry, once affirmed: "Human life cannot compare with a single line by Baudelaire." He himself wrote poetry and, although far better known for his short stories, often insisted both upon referring to himself as a poet and being recognized as one. Indicative of his poetic influences are his concern with the precise word and his method of portraying characters through subtle characteristics rather than explicit statement. Some commentators have praised Akutagawa's stark, spare prose as an appropriate vehicle for illuminating human foibles and misfortune and for judiciously keeping the narrator's presence unobtrusive. Others have found his style conspicuous for its lack of description, and note that it often obscures the very subject matter that the author sought to emphasize. Similarly, many critics have debated whether Akutagawa regarded his stories as anything more

than a mere vehicle to exhibit his verbal dexterity. While Akutagawa's distinctive style has been the source of critical controversy, and while the author's devotion to matters of technique has been well documented, the content of his work was never deliberately subordinated to method of expression. In fact, Akutagawa believed that it would be a grave mistake to assume the primacy of either form or content, both of which were to him inseparable, and the marriage of which he considered essential to the attainment of high artistic achievement.

As well as being an artist, Akutagawa was a literary theorist. In addition to his carefully considered position on form and content, the pursuit of aesthetic perfection was of extreme importance to him, insofar as this ideal could be realized by the artist during the creation of any one work, and notwithstanding the artist's inherent fallibility. Akutagawa was also adamant in his unwillingness to divorce criticism from other realms of artistic endeavor. Opposing what he considered the cowardice of contemporary critics, whose accomplishments, for the sake of expediency, had become superficial, and the half-heartedness of those fellow-artists who took up criticism as a hobby, Akutagawa maintained that criticism was no less an art form than any other. His directness and genuine desire to see a serious, comprehensive body of critical theory restored to Japanese literature gained Akutagawa the universal respect of his literary peers, despite their frequent opposition to his views.

One of the most famous of these critical debates occurred in 1927, when Akutagawa argued in print with the noted novelist Tanizaki Junichirō over the necessity of plot in the novel. The debate was launched when Akutagawa questioned the artistic value of plot, referring explicitly to Tanizaki's recent works, in which strange stories and complicated plots, departing as far as possible from mundane reality, were characteristic features. Tanizaki's own innovations were the result of his efforts to break away from the scrupulously candid autobiographical "shishōsetsu" or "I-novel," with which he had been highly dissatisfied, a feeling shared in many Japanese literary circles where keen interest was quickly aroused by the ensuing controversy. Tanizaki asserted that his attention to plot constituted interest in the novel's structure and, therefore, in its architectural beauty. He further maintained that the novel, by virtue of its form, was capable of the greatest structural beauty of all literary genres. Akutagawa, in turn, argued that in terms of structural aesthetics, drama must be said to have the greater structural beauty, and, moreover, that the value of a novel is determined by its "poetic spirit," a term he went on to define as lyrical in the broadest sense of the word: that is, literature that is not subject to the criteria of entertainment and vulgar interests. Tanizaki affirmed that he considered it useless and meaningless to try to present an absolute standard of artistic value for the novel, for art, he believed, like human history, develops and progresses. He contended that Japanese literature had to be rescued from the lingering influences of Naturalism and its preoccupation, among Japanese artists, with the mindless recording of human nature at its most mundane or sordid by a return to novels with plot. Akutagawa finally conceded, barring his insistence that a pure "poetic spirit" determines a novel's artistic value, to the validity of Tanizaki's points. Ironically, throughout his career Akutagawa had consistently practiced many of Tanizaki's literary tenets, to which his scrupulous detachment and bizarre subjects bear testimony. Some commentators believe that his years of unstinting productivity, coupled with conflicts between his family and career had, by the time of his debate with Tanizaki, brought Akutagawa to a creative impasse, and had caused him to challenge some of his former tenets and techniques.

After his death Akutagawa was largely neglected in Japan by critics who considered his style affected and his poetic approach overly refined—as evidenced, for example, in his subtle characterization. But for the lively interest of a Western audience, which was removed from Japanese literary debate and which found in his work a fresh Eastern perspective on dilemmas long familiar in Western literature, Akutagawa might have been completely forgotten. The history of Akutagawa's reception is far more complex; due to a neglect by Western readers of the later stories, and a tendency in Japan to range the author's efforts purely in terms of personal preference, more comprehensive critical estimations of Akutagawa's career have been largely nonexistent. However, commentators have found that Akutagawa's stories are skillfully written and demonstrate scope unrestricted to his own time and culture, and for that reason widened the dimensions of their genre and helped make it a more important part of Japanese literature. Through his early work as a translator and his later concern with important critical issues, he helped introduce and foster the tradition of the European novel in his own country where, according to some critics, the novel form might otherwise have degenerated. Far from being dismayed by the differences between East and West, Akutagawa utilized them as sources for both the content and spirit of his work; the result was a significant achievement in the development of modern Japanese literature.

PRINCIPAL WORKS

Rashōmon (short stories) 1916
  [*Rashomon, and Other Stories*, 1948]
Tobaku tu akuma (short story) 1917
"*Shuzanzu*" (short story) 1920
  ["An Autumn Mountain" published in *Modern Japanese Stories*, 1961]
Tales Grotesque and Curious (short stories) 1930
Kappa (novel) 1947
Hell Screen (Jigoku Hen), and Other Stories (short stories) 1948
"*The Nose*" (short story) 1955; published in journal *Japan Quarterly*
Japanese Short Stories (short stories) 1961
Exotic Japanese Stories: The Beautiful and the Grotesque (short stories) 1964

———————

GLENN W. SHAW (essay date 1930)

[*In the following excerpt, Shaw gives an account of Akutagawa's influences and development as a short story writer.*]

[Akutagawa's] graduation thesis was entitled, *Wiriamu Morisu Kenkyū (A Study of William Morris).*

He was like Morris in his surrender to the fascination of the Middle Ages, but he had none of the practical reforming tendencies of that artist socialist. He has been more aptly compared to Flaubert for the seriousness with which he took his art and the preciousness of his style. And the post-bellum point of view has been expressed by a Japanese social worker who, at his death, compared him, as a man with a keen sense of humor

and knowledge of human nature and "an arbiter of elegance in the vicious society in which he lived," to Petronius.

He says of himself while at the University that he did not attend classes very well and was an idle student, but we may take this for the expression of a sincere wish to be more like some of his hardier classmates, for Kikuchi Kan, one of them and to-day the literary Crœsus of Japan, says that Akutagawa went to his classes faithfully and had the confidence of his professors. (p. ii)

Kikuchi first came to admire Akutagawa when, with a few others at the University, they began in 1914 the publication of the third series of the magazine *Shinshichō*. His maiden effort appeared in the first issue, attracting no particular attention. But in the following year he published in the magazine *Teikoku Bungaku* two stories, the second of which, "**Rashōmon**," became the title story of his first volume . . . and is now always associated with his name. It is a gruesome thing concerning the old two-storied south gate of Kyōto in the days when that landmark was falling into decay with the rest of the ancient capital toward the end of the twelfth century. By way of lame extenuation, this much, at least, may be said for the story (which is the fourth in this volume), that in other tales, Akutagawa has written with even more disgusting realism of this truly distressing period.

In December, 1915, while still at the University, Akutagawa became a disciple of the preëminent writer of the day, Natsume Soseki, who probably had a greater influence than any other man on his literary life. Mori Ogai, the versatile army surgeon, who tried his hand at so many things in the literary field during the periods of Meiji and Taishō, has been credited with having had the next greatest influence on him.

In 1916, in a fourth revival of the magazine *Shinshichō*, Akutagawa published "**Hana**" ("**The Nose**"), the second story in this book, which drew from Natsume the highest praise. He told his young disciple that if he would write twenty or thirty more stories like it, he would find himself occupying a unique position among the writers of his country, a prophecy which came true. Out of old material, with the greatest attention to detail and to the atmosphere of the period of which he wrote, Akutagawa had produced a grotesquely amusing thing, writing into it some modern psychology and the little lesson that ideals are precious only so long as they remain ideals. This new way of treating historical material in Japan attracted the attention of his countrymen and became characteristic of much of Akutagawa's work. Of this sort of tale, "**Lice**" and the Chinese story, "**The Wine Worm**," go one step further in grotesquery, while "**The Pipe**" turns to lighter and more wholesome humor.

In 1917, when Akutagawa published his second volume of short stories, ***Tobako to Akuma (The Devil and Tobacco)***, he had already established himself as one of the foremost writers of the day. The title story of the volume is the opening story in this book. In it we see an Oriental saturated with western literature playing with an old theme in a highly amusing and clever way. (Incidentally Akutagawa was himself an inveterate cigarette smoker.) It is one of the many stories he wrote about the early Catholic missionaries of the sixteenth century, one of them so cleverly that it fooled Japanese students of the period into believing that it was a translation from an old Latin text, non-existent, but called by Akutagawa *Legenda Aurea*. (pp. iii-v)

[There] can be no doubt that he had more individuality than any other writer of his time and has left in Japanese literature a mass of artistic work, often grotesque and curious, that, while it undoubtedly angers the proletarian experimenters who now hold the stage and fight with lusty pens and a highly developed class consciousness against all that he stood for, will continue to live as long as men go on treasuring the fancies their fellows from time to time set down with care on paper. (p. vii)

> Glenn W. Shaw, in an introduction to Tales Grotesque and Curious by Akutagawa Ryūnosuke, translated by Glenn W. Shaw, The Hokuseido Press, 1930, pp. i-vii.

W.H.H. NORMAN   (essay date 1948)

[In the following excerpt, Norman offers introductory remarks on several of Akutagawa's works, affirming that the author is worthy of a wider audience.]

Some occidental friends who have read my translation of "Jigokuhen" and "Jashūmon" have professed themselves puzzled by the novels, and suggested I should write some paragraphs in the introduction "explaining" them. This in turn I find puzzling, for the stories seem to me straightforward tales by a consummate artist. I believe them worth translating, not only for the pleasure their reading affords, but also because "Jigokuhen" is—or used to be—extremely popular in Japan. By Japanese critics it was rated as one of Akutagawa's masterpieces, and a dramatized form was given as "Kabuki" at the Tokyo Theatre in 1935. Sadanji, one of the greatest Kabuki actors took the part of Yoshihide.

"Jigokuhen" is the story of an artist with a dominant passion for his ambition in painting. The brief tale in the "Uji shūi Monogatari" is so bald as to suggest that it is based on fact. Akutagawa, like Shakespeare, takes a story from an ancient source, and makes high drama out of it: to what limits would an artist go who delighted to watch his house burn because it showed him how to paint the flames of hell? But Yoshihide was not a complete monster of ambition and art; he had one human trait, his love for his daughter, and the climax, that last terrible scene, is brought about by the struggle between the two passions in his heart.

"Jigokuhen" evokes our "pity and terror", and yet lacks the dimensions of great tragedy. There is something peculiarly Japanese about the whole story. Akutagawa's erudition and historical imagination guarantee the accuracy of the customs and psychology of feudal Japan depicted in "Jigokuhen" and its sequel.

"Jashūmon" was prompted by the success with which "Jigokuhen" was received. The title, literally "false religion", was one of the terms formerly used in Japan for Christianity. It opens with an account of the death of the Daimyō of Horikawa, and goes on to tell of "the only remarkable event which took place in the life of his son, the young Daimyō." Indeed we read of many remarkable events and of a character quite as demonic as Yoshihide. Unfortunately we never reach the climax which constitutes "the only remarkable event." It is not surprising that Akutagawa was unable to finish the story: after the build-up he gave the two chief characters, any clash between the two could only result in an anti-climax.

The interest lies in the character of the Young Daimyō and the picture of feudal Japanese aristocracy. The "Mary priest" is an incredible character, but the Young Daimyō, the æsthete, is real, and some of the scenes in which he appears are unforgettable in their romantic beauty. The supernatural element reflects the part that superstitions played in Japanese life until recent times. (pp. 10-12)

"The General" is a debunking of General Nogi. Westerners who have read this translation have said that the satire is not savage enough. Surely, however, Akutagawa's hatred of cruelty, militarism and prudishness are obvious enough. Though there was a reaction against militarism in Japan at the time the story was written, General Nogi already held a high place in the military pantheon, he was the beau ideal of the militarists, and Akutagawa did not dare mention him by name in the story. (p. 12)

Mr. Shaw's remarks on Akutagawa [see excerpt dated 1930] . . . suggest the writer in the ivory tower, but Akutagawa is more than that. He was a satirist moved to indignation by cruelty, insincerity, and the hollow pretensions of nationalism. "Kappa" has recently been translated; it reminds us of the "sæva indignatio" ["savage indignation"] of Swift, and certainly refutes the notion that the Japanese are incapable of perceiving their own faults. Akutagawa is a writer that deserves wider introduction to the west. (p. 13)

> W.H.H. Norman, in an introduction to Hell Screen ("Jigoku Hen") and Other Stories by Ryūnosuke Akutagawa, translated by W.H.H. Norman, The Hokuseido Press, 1948, pp. 1-13.

HOWARD HIBBETT   (essay date 1951)

[In the following excerpt from his introduction to Rashōmon, and Other Stories, Hibbett defends Akutagawa's style, frequently considered affected, as the means by which the author was able to most effectively illuminate those social issues and human foibles that interested him.]

[Akutagawa's] stories have a dazzling and perhaps deceptive sheen. Superficial critics called Akutagawa precious, or decadent, or dismissed him as a fatiguingly clever dilettante. Unprepared for the strength of his later satires, they supposed him to care only for the superb texture of his prose. Translation protects us from the seductions of this style, yet encourages a similar error, since the nuances of Akutagawa's prose are what convey the essence of his thought. Like Natsume Sōseki and Mori Ōgai, whom he admired, Akutagawa used his language delicately, precisely, and with a richness enhanced by a knowledge of several literatures. It is significant that his first published writings were translations of Yeats and Anatole France. He remarked once that words must yield more than the bare dictionary meanings; he had a poet's feeling for their shapes and flavors, as well as their ambiguities, and he combined them with such freshness and economy that his phrasing never lacks distinction. Like Picasso, Akutagawa often varied his style, but always, whatever the particular blend of vernacular and mandarin, he controlled it with scrupulous precision. A master of tone, he gave his stories a cool classic surface, colored but never marred by the wit and warmth underlying that perfect glaze. The composure of his style is undisturbed even by vivid accents of the sordid or the bizarre.

Detachment was a key strategy to Akutagawa. As a narrator, he liked to be unseen, impersonal; he cultivated the oblique glance. When he did enter his stories, it was usually in the slight role of the observer or the suave self-effacing compiler. Old tales and legends, historical settings of the remote Heian Period or the feudal ages which followed—these he used not to turn his elaborate erudition to account, but to enrich and extend the implications of his themes, and to maintain aesthetic distance. The early era of Christian conversion in Japan, in the sixteenth century, was a favorite of his; in *Hōkyōnin no shi (The Martyr)* he exploited it to the point of hoax by supporting an archaic style with a source reference which, after an interval for learned controversy, he acknowledged to be fictitious. It suited his ironic taste to play the illusionist who leaves his audience staring blankly into a mirror.

But Akutagawa did more than deceive scholars and baffle the unwary: he antagonized ruling critical opinion. His attention to style, his preference for techniques of indirection and restraint, his indifference to current dogma—such attitudes were heresy to both the leading literary schools. The Proletarian writers, flourishing in the '20's, found nothing in common between Akutagawa's subtle stories and their own carefully chosen but grossly cut slices-of-life. The Naturalists, their rivals, had moved toward romantic individualism, forgetting Zola's concept of social inquiry. Dominant since the Russo-Japanese War, they sanctioned only the literary method to which, in the name of the first-person-singular *shishōsetsu*, their successors still adhere. This was the Confession, ranging from the sentimental memoir to the clinical report of an author's sexual life. Despite the exhaustion of the autobiographical form of fiction after Proust, these novelists went on eagerly probing their wounds and laying themselves open to reproach; while Akutagawa, unmoved by the exhibition of so many tedious egos, went his own way. A few of his stories suggest maliciously that confession itself may be false. *Yabu no naka (In a Grove)*, for example, converts an old melodramatic tale into a series of conflicting statements which undermine our prosaic confidence in distinguishing between subjective and objective, truth and fiction. Even the dark testaments which he left before suicide contain flashes of mockery to perplex the straight-forward reader.

There are enough Swiftian touches in Akutagawa to show his hatred of stupidity, greed, hypocrisy, and the rising jingoism of the day. But Akutagawa's artistic integrity kept him from joining his contemporaries in easy social criticism or naive introspection. If, too often, his finely enameled miniatures seem cold, over-subtilized, worn thin by an obsessive critical sense, still they are never merely decorative. What he did was to question the values of his society, dramatize the complexities of human psychology, and study, with a Zen taste for paradox, the precarious balance of illusion and reality. He developed a variety of techniques—from realism to fantasy, symbolism to surrealism—and used all of them in the search for poetic truth. Akutagawa was both intellectual and artist, and it was the quality of his artistry that enabled him to explore these difficult problems as deeply as he did, and to give his perceptions such exquisite and durable form. (pp. 11-15)

Howard Hibbett, in an introduction to Rashōmon and Other Stories *by Ryūnosuke Akutagawa, translated by Takashi Kojima, Liveright Publishing Corporation, 1952, pp. 11-15.*

JAMES KELLY   (essay date 1952)

[*In the following excerpt from a review of* Rashōmon, and Other Stories, *Kelly distinguishes Akutagawa's vigorous, moralistic art from the gentle and delicately wrought oriental style most familiar to Western readers.*]

One thing is certain. Akutagawa does not belong to the jade-and-peonies school of oriental writing. In the spare, textured prose of [*Rashōmon, and Other Stories*], he brings us clear-

eyed glimpses of human behavior in the extremities of poverty, stupidity, greed, vanity. If lotus blossoms appear at all, they are firmly rooted in the background vegetation.

A muscular moralist, working in a small framework, Akutagawa believes that Man is a poor thing who almost always reacts badly. A satirical writer with a delicate, Chaplinesque quality (in which illusion and reality are blended in a kind of fairy-tale surrealism), he is drawn first to the fictional possibilities of pretense and hypocrisy. To find a comparison the reader must go to the paintings of his countryman Kuniyoshi, in which the colors are somber, the palette limited, and the detached social comment unmistakable.

Few American readers had heard of Akutagawa (who was a suicide in 1927 at the age of 35) before last year when his story **"In a Grove"** was named as the source of "Rashomon," a prize-winning Japanese film. Here is story-telling of an unconventional sort, with most of the substance beneath the shining, enameled surface. For some, it will seem too superficial, too artful and "clever." Few will deny the tension or psychological focus of the themes.

James Kelly, "No Jade, No Peonies," in The New York Times Book Review, *November 30, 1952, p. 47.*

IVAN MORRIS   (essay date 1955)

[*In the following excerpt, Morris compares the stylistic achievements of the short stories of Akutagawa and his contemporary Shiga Naoya.*]

It is customary in comparing Shiga Naoya and Akutagawa Ryūnosuke to emphasize the differences between them. Indeed any juxtaposition of these two important writers is bound to reveal more contrasts than similarities in their general outlooks on life as well as in their literary work. . . . Shiga's approach has from the outset of his career been positive, secure, self-confident; Akutagawa, on the other hand, was increasingly plagued by doubts concerning his own artistic abilities, by bitter pessimism over the state of mankind and by what he himself described as a "vague uneasiness" that led eventually to his suicide. These diametrical differences were inevitably reflected in the two writers' work.

At the same time Shiga and Akutagawa have certain significant points in common. They both attached predominant importance to the creation and development of a literary style, specifically to the use of language. In this respect Shiga Naoya must be considered the pioneer. (p. 452)

In the case of Akutagawa, absorption in style caused his work frequently to be criticised as precious or even decadent; the vehicle seemed too fine and elaborate for the content which it was designed to convey. In even his simplest, least "literary" writing, Akutagawa was painstaking in his choice of words and in his construction of sentences. However trivial or banal the ideas in some of his less important stories, his brilliant use of language ensures their being read and admired. (pp. 452-53)

Because of its relative brevity, the short story, like the poem, is undoubtedly one type of writing in which style or form plays the greatest part. An indifferently-written novel may impose by the ingenuity of its plot, by the evocation of some unusual scene or atmosphere or again by the vivid portrayal of a character, but a badly-written short story is almost bound to fail, regardless of its subject-matter. This may be the underlying reason why the stylists Shiga Naoya and Akutagawa Ryūnosuke lent themselves particularly to the writing of short stories. With very few exceptions, their short stories are not simply short pieces of fiction, but carefully constructed units with a development and a climax, one or two main characters and a single central idea. Their skill as short story writers can be judged by examining the economy of their selection, the rapid development of their characters and the care with which they plan their endings. (p. 454)

"The Nose" was Akutagawa's first published short story and it immediately launched him on his successful literary career. It is typical of its author in many respects, for instance in the exotic setting (a medieval Buddhist monastery), in the fascination with grotesque details verging on the disgusting, and at the same time in the beauty of description, as in the final scene in the cold morning sun. Typical also are the bitter humour, the profound disenchantment about human nature and the complete absence of sentimentality. One weakness that may strike some Western readers is that the theme of the story is explicitly stated ("The human heart harbours contradictory feelings.."). This type of didactic explicitness recurs in many of Akutagawa's early stories, but disappears in his later writing, which, if anything, may seem to err on the side of obscurity.

"The Painting of an Autumn Mountain" is one of Akutagawa's most beautiful, but at the same time most difficult stories. Unlike the greater part of his writing, it has about it something very positive and, with the final paragraphs in mind, one might almost say sanguine. The theme is the essential subjectivity of beauty—in other words, the idea that a work of art exists primarily within the observer's mind. To present this aesthetic theme, Akutagawa has evoked a classical atmosphere *par excellence:* two aged Chinese sages are described discussing paintings many centuries ago by the flame of a copper lamp. At the end of the story they laugh and clap their hands with delight as they realise the significance of the elusive painting, and this happy image of the two serene old men is often mentioned by admirers of Akutagawa. For this strange and significant writer, in whose mind human nature and life came to bear an increasingly gloomy aspect, aesthetic values alone seemed to retain any value or meaning. Hence his preoccupation up to the very end with the perfection of his style, and hence the words in his suicide letter, "Nature now seems to me more beautiful than ever before . . . During this final period, the beauty of nature is constantly in my eyes." (p. 455)

Ivan Morris, in an introductory note to "The Nose" and "The Painting of an Autumn Mountain," in Japan Quarterly, Vol. II, No. 4, October-December, 1955, pp. 452-55.

JOHN McVITTIE (essay date 1961)

[*In the following excerpt from his introduction to Akutagawa's* Japanese Short Stories, *McVittie explores the use of the predominantly Eastern concept of contentment through self-detachment in several of Akutagawa's short stories.*]

The doctrine of *sokuten kyoshi*—self-detachment in pursuit of heaven—was taught by the famous writer, Natsumé Soseki, to his students at the Imperial University of Tokyo in the early years of the Taisho era (in the years of World War I). Happiness exists only in contemplation and imagination, suggested Soseki,—a contention which fascinated his brilliant and extremely sensitive young student, Akutagawa Ryunosuké, who had already admired the detachment evident to some degree in the styles of Prosper Merimée and Anatole France. (p. 14)

Apparently spurred on by Soseki's research into the intellectualism of 18th century England, the Neo-Intellectuals [of whom Akutagawa became a leader] set about providing some solution to the problem of suggesting an ethical system worthy of Japanese life and consistent with the age. Akutagawa sought the solution in attaining self-detachment through his art, a simple solution that did not satisfy his author associates.

This ethical dilemma is evident in the story entitled **"Otomi no Teiso"** (**"Otomi's Virginity"**). It is a story of pride in chivalry and the preservation of personal dignity and honor. There is some inspiration felt in the act of a person of humble origin who, presumably lacking in moral training, is faced with the choice of safeguarding the honor and dignity of her mistress or of maintaining her own; she loves her mistress, and she loves "Pussy"; instinctively she decides what to do according to the situation in which she is placed; and instinct proves a wise judge. The story is a masterpiece in the study of individualism, a monument to Oriental evanescence. Naturalists would clamor for the fulfillment of desire, but the reader of this story, like Otomi as Shinko's carriage passes by, feels relieved of care,—a moment of self-detachment.

Akutagawa's outlook, however, is not as egotistic as Japanese literary critics like to quote one another in contending. **"The Tangerines,"** (**"Mikan,"** in Japanese) is one of the many stories that indicates he was willing to admit the influence of others' actions in assisting, unconsciously, the individual in achieving some measure of detachment. The country girl who is the heroine of **"The Tangerines"** was a symbol of "vulgar realities in human shape . . . the symbol of an unintelligible and wearisome life . . . but within a few minutes I felt life welling up within me . . . I completely forgot I was bored, I became oblivious to the apparent absurdity of my meaningless life." **"The Tangerines"** reminds me of the *haiku* poetry of Japan—the few brief syllables of poetry in which the Japanese, with skill varying according to intensity of feeling, are inclined to enshrine the ecstasy of the moment, the succinctness of Zen. (pp. 23-4)

"Yonosuke no Hanashi" (**"The Story of Yonosuke"**) embodies this "touch on life," and has a theme as old as human life, a theme which is epitomized in one of the briefest but most dynamic words in the English language,—"sex." This story serves to illustrate Akutagawa's position that the ecstasy is in the expectation, not in the fulfillment. In ancient Rome it was said that the anti-climax upon fulfillment is the annihilation of the thrill of nature's inducement. "My story begins at the moment my knee touched hers . . . Was she feeling as I felt? . . . I enjoyed her clear eyes . . . I enjoyed the delicate shades of her eyelashes slightly moving on her fresh cheeks. I enjoyed the charm of her fingers flexing on her lap . . . The rest I leave to imagination." This is where Akutagawa's story ends, and where the reader's really begins; it begins with what is unspoken, with what is unwritten; it is the delicate realm of self-detachment. (pp. 24-5)

[**"Ikkai no Tsuchi"** (**"A Clod of Soil"** . . .)] is reminiscent of the *haiku.* Hiroji, the little boy, is content to amuse himself with a sprig of cherry blossom,—not to be interpreted only as a sign of his lack of playthings, but as typical of some intangible quality of Japanese life. Moreover, grandmother Osumi's smoking of cigarette butts is no confession of extreme poverty; "she had carefully collected the cigarette butts left by her (dead) son"; it is an innate habit among the lowly classes of Japan—even in this period of national prosperity, to use and re-use to exhaustion everything usable; it would not be an over-statement to interpret this habit as an unconscious virtue in the Buddhist pilgrimage towards zero. Hiroji's mother died, and the grandmother, Osumi, lay awake thinking that her daughter-in-law's death ''had brought her great happiness . . . Her memory vividly recalled a certain night nine years before; on that night she had sighed in the same way; that had been the night after the funeral of her only son . . . She heard the clock strike four; the sleep of the weary fell upon her. At the same time the sky over the thatched roof was bathed in the first chill grey streaks of dawn from the eastern horizon.'' Osumi's attitude is puzzling to the Western mind, but Akutagawa understood it, not as the callousness which Western ideals must assume it to be, but as the Oriental relief experienced upon the elimination of some of life's problems in the vacuum of nothingness.

If we realize this, then we can comprehend why at the early age of thirty-five years, Akutagawa chose to enjoy that experience himself. He had gone as far as he could in his pursuit of self-detachment through creation of literary works; the only step forward was in the direction of death through self-annihilation. When he took this step, the public widely grieved, and his fellow writers—the leader among whom was the illustrious Kikuchi Kan, wept bitterly with Akutagawa's wife and three boys; and yet because they were Japanese, they understood. (pp. 26-7)

> *John McVittie, ''A Sprig of Cherry (Introduction),''*
> *in* Japanese Short Stories *by Ryūnosuke Akutagawa,*
> *translated by Takashi Kojima, revised edition, Liv-*
> *eright Publishing Corporation, 1962, pp. 13-28.*

JOHN McVITTIE   (essay date 1964)

[*In the following excerpt, McVittie discusses a number of Akutagawa's short stories as expressions of the distinctive cultural mores and practices of Japan, including the Japanese concept of ''belief,'' adherence to tradition, and search for ultimate enlightenment.*]

Nothing in Japan may be done directly; to the Japanese, life is not direct but is as circuitous as it possibly can be, so he does not bother to learn the elements of logic in an attempt to establish a standard way of thinking. We, too, can begin our pilgrimage through these stories [in *Exotic Japanese Stories*] indirectly with an act of *belief* which Akutagawa anticipated might startle the reader—the belief that badgers can change their form. Why should it be so difficult to convince modern man that badgers can change their form? He can believe that an inverted basket or a lamp shade becomes a hat when used by a woman *as a hat,* but he cannot believe that the man next door could be a badger which has changed its form; he will even use a table knife for a screwdriver, but will scorn the idea that the barman at his club could be a badger. (pp. 14-15)

So naïve, so formal a study as ''**The Badger**'' presents one of the most satisfying—though sometimes one of the most cruel—aspects of the Japanese mind. The Japanese has still not lost the capacity to *believe*. . . . There is something enlightened about the Japanese contention that we cannot discern much distinction between what *is so* and what is *believed to be so*.

With respect to badgers, it is not so much, submits Akutagawa, that the badger came to bewitch people, as that it was *believed to bewitch*. Yet, between bewitchment and belief in bewitchment there would not be much distinction.

The author's assurance that this is not only confined to badgers is more provoking to thought; he asks—is it not that any *existence* is but what we *believe it to be?* (pp. 15-16)

Akutagawa was aware of some superiority in the Japanese sense of values when he wrote ''**The Dolls.**''

The dolls of this story were not the ''ordinary'' dolls little girls carry about in all countries of the world. They were dolls for display on or about March 3rd, during the festival that has been popular in Japan for over three centuries.

Sometimes this quaint festival is referred to as *Jômi no Sekku*, the Girls' Festival. On March 3rd, tasty food and *shiro-zaké* (a sweet saké) are prepared for the dolls, but the little girls themselves visit the houses of their friends and enjoy an adequate share of the delicacies on that day. It is a day when little girls—with their magnificent dolls displayed in the alcove reserved for the display of family treasures—can feel important; and even in the most ''modern'' households of Japan the place of the daughters is overshadowed by the far loftier importance of the sons.

Soon after Japan was reopened to intercourse with the West (1868), and the Meiji Emperor began his historic encouragement of Western ways and thought, many of the finest families of Japan, impoverished directly and indirectly by the collapse of the feudal system, began to dispose of their Japanese treasures; this to some extent was in their attempt to survive financially, and to some extent because traditional things were inconsistent with their new way of life and inhibited their enlightenment. It can well be imagined that one of the family heirlooms disposed of might have been the set of *Hina-matsuri* dolls.

''**The Dolls**'' embodies an expression of the author's failure to find satisfaction in his own studies of Western ideals. In all of his works there is no more boorish a creature than the young man who in ''**The Dolls**'' compares the brightness of the new kerosene lamp to the brightness of the ''new learning.''

When mother is ill, O-Tsuru is as dutiful a child as any Japanese daughter should be. Only when mother is feeling more comfortable does she give some voice to her own suppressed desires. She wants to see her dolls once more before they are sold. Her entreaty is in vain; but she does have her reward in a singular way; she learns that in her uncompromising father there is still a yearning for the elegance of old Japan—a yearning that he must suppress in ''modern times'' for the material welfare of his family. O-Tsuru's revelation can never be proven, but she has gained a lifetime of spiritual comfort from her *belief* that it is so.

For the Western reader, ''**The Dolls**'' is a humbling story; it makes us feel awkward and unrefined. We feel that the Japanese could never learn anything of enlightenment from us who are such unenlightened people.

We have been prepared to give to Japan but not to receive. Okakura Kazuo, in ''**The Book of Tea,**'' points out that the Christian missionary, too, has gone to Japan to give, but not to receive. It is not enough to read these stories in a spirit of curiosity and tolerance; if you are not prepared ''to receive'' you should lay aside this book.

In this volume there is a Japanese who feels impelled to help the Westerner towards some interpretation of Japanese culture. Most educated Japanese prefer to be silent on matters pertaining to their own culture, either because they are afraid of the ridicule of people who cannot fully appreciate them, or because their attempts to reconcile the somewhat incompatible elements of Japanese and Western culture usually lead to confusion.

The Professor in **"The Handkerchief"** has long dreamed of being "a bridge between East and West." Presumably he found some outlet for his ambition by marrying an American woman who had a passion for Japanese culture. "It was safe to surmise that the fancy lantern, suspended from the ceiling of the veranda, did not represent the Professor's taste, but was rather an expression of his wife's enjoyment of the things of Japan."

Professor Haségawa in **"The Handkerchief"** is really a portrait of Dr. Nitobé Inazo who sprang from a samurai family which so well understood the principles of bushido that his work entitled "Bushido" is considered a standard text and has been published in several languages.

It was his belief that if this bushido could be revived in the existing current of Japanese thought, it would be advantageous in facilitating mutual understanding between the European-American peoples and the Japanese people. Or, it would be a means of advancing international peace.—He himself had long dreamed of becoming such a bridge spanning East and West. The principles of bushido—loyalty, sincerity, courage—could be emphasized because of their universal acknowledgement as virtues.

But it was Professor Nitobé's awareness of how bushido could become a mere *mannerism*, empty of understanding, that is the burden of **"The Handkerchief."** . . . And in contemporary Japan there is the sad fact that the Japanese are fast losing their faith in their own traditions.

Propriety is a mild term for some of the great acts of sacrifice perpetuated under the name of "obligation" that are to be found recorded in Japanese history. Sometimes the fulfilment of obligation can be ironic, and even sometimes terrible, as it is in **"Gratitude."**

After twenty years' separation, destiny has once more brought together a notorious thief and a renowned merchant. The extreme predicament in which the merchant, Yasoêmon, is placed, demands quite naturally of Jinnai, the robber, an acknowledgement that he must satisfy his debt of gratitude.

Quietly the steaming kettle sets the atmosphere of impending tragedy. Jinnai, who evidently understood the significance of "tea," would have felt this mood—a difficult mood for the reader to sense if the reader be uninitiated into the philosophy of tea. Okakura in **"The Book of Tea"** contends that the average Westerner, in his sleek complacency, will see in the tea ceremony but another instance of the thousand and one oddities which constitute the quaintness and childishness of the East. It will surely be a serious affair when many of Japan's heroes are understood to have partaken of tea with their intimate friends before they have committed *seppuku* (better known in the West under the more vulgar term *harakiri*).

As the story progresses, we wonder how the author can resolve the dilemma between the conscience of Yasoêmon, a Christian, accepting money that would surely be stolen, and the Japanese demand for the fulfilment of obligation. Akutagawa's genius is equal to the task, and his story, **"Gratitude,"** consequently becomes one of the really great short stories of the world.

Jinnai, one of Japan's most notorious villains, becomes a noble being as he hurries with all possible dispatch along the snow-covered road, his wicker umbrella-hat glimmering in the moon-light. As to who is the hero of the tale—that is for the reader to decide; perhaps it is the man who has been shamed into remembering his own debt—his filial duty—who finds such contentment as occurs only once in a lifetime. Could this contentment be the resignation that comes from enlightenment? (pp. 20-4)

Yet, neither enlightenment nor resignation can ever come to a person in his capacity as citizen of a state. It can come to him only in his capacity as an individual. So, although he must serve his state, he must never lose his individuality.

Confucius, whose life was devoted to expounding his views on the place of the individual in society, has been a source of much inspiration to China and Japan for two and a half thousand years. If Confucius had been born in the China of today he would by now be in prison. In the "Great Learning," a Confucian classic, we read: "The men of old who wished to spread complete virtue throughout the world ordered well their own society. Wishing to order well their society they organized the affairs of their families; wishing to organize the affairs of their families, they cultivated their own persons; wishing to cultivate their own persons, they rectified their hearts. . . ."

In the background of Akutagawa's stories there is evidence of this process of rectification. If we were able to ask Akutagawa himself why he wrote a certain story, he would probably say that he had no end in mind, but that his stories were his own personal interpretation of life as he understood it to be. In writing **"The Robbers"** he had no idea in mind of pointing a moral, but if we were to nominate a story which illustrates how individuals "rectified their hearts" (though the rectification was far too mediæval for current approval) we would suggest **"The Robbers."**

"The Robbers" is set in an age when might was law; provided a man were strong enough there was little inhibition—killing, praying, mating, eating—every desire was satisfied provided the man was strong enough. But, if in those remote times one were not strong enough—then there would be little chance of survival to inflict one's weaknesses on the succeeding generations, or to be a burden on one's fellow men. . . . In the history of the human race, power has always been an idol. "Power is the grim idol that the world adores" (Hazlitt). The preoccupation of man, whether primitive or civilized, has been at all times a struggle for "the idol."

In present times we have learned to be subtle enough to conceal "the idol" lest others discover our treasure and covetously deprive us of it. In the era in which **"The Robbers"** of Akutagawa's story were active in the capital of Japan, there was no subtlety attached to the possession of power, and there was constant battle for it between rival clans and between honest warriors and rascals—the distinction between an honest man and a rascal not always being clear. (pp. 25-7)

[Coarse] as she might have been, any young wench would nevertheless have been sufficiently desirable to the hardy men of the times. It is around such a raw theme that **"The Robbers"** revolves, the passion of one generation devolving on the next. The things about us change sometimes beyond recognition to those who see them after a long absence; but the nature of lust does not change. (p. 28)

[Under] heat of day, in moments of treacherous intrigue, the plans have been made for the robbers' assault on the mansion of Judge Tô. Action that has been painfully slow under the summer sun, promises to be swift as the night darkens. There are a few moments of suspense while the robbers gather at the appointed place. (p. 29)

The scenes of the bloody skirmish that follow, belong to a long past age; but the human principles involved are ageless. There is a moment of treachery when a youth and a girl, planning a murder, "feel the awful will to agree." Fortunately for man's feeling of security, there is not so much homicide in modern times as there was in feudal ages, but there is something less despicable in the murder of a man than in the present-day compromise—the murder of his reputation. There is a moment when we peer on a dead face and feel ashamed that, in the normal order, a human face in death should appear holier than a living face.

"The Robbers" has a satisfying denouement in that two characters in whom our interest is aroused, though utterly confused by the intrigue around them, were able, either from conscience or instinct, to "rectify their hearts." Here we have a pleasant contrast to much of Japanese fiction and drama which assumes that man is not good by nature, and that where the forces for good and evil are matched together the latter more often prevails. (pp. 29-30)

It is inspiring to read a story in which men have "rectified their minds." (p. 30)

One of the most elusive stories in Japanese literature is **"Withered Fields,"** which is rather in the mood of a confession than a story. (p. 44)

Bashô's disciples have come even from remote places to pay their last respects to their Master. There is a sympathy apparent between all those present, as all had learned to rely upon the Master.

Among the adherents of Buddha, death marks the transmigration of the soul into either a higher or a lower stratum of existence, ultimately the soul's shuffling off the edge of life into nirvâna, eternal bliss. Those who have some feeling of obligation towards the deceased are fastidious about the last rites which must be carried out with appropriate dignity and sincerity.

The atmosphere of which we are conscious in **"Withered Fields"** reminds me of the solemn atmosphere of tea ceremony. There is the same restraint of movement, and the silent acknowledgement of the spiritual presence of the living Buddha. If we are aware of conscience, it will be most transparent in those spiritual moments. If you have never instinctively been conscious of a spiritual presence at any time, be it a baptismal, nuptial, communion or funeral ceremony, or when left alone with the stars at night, or in the sunshine on the summit of a mountain clad in snow, or been privileged to witness and be moved by an act of benevolence—if you have never instinctively felt that presence, neither Akutagawa nor I myself could explain the elusive "something" of this story, for you have been born without the capacity to experience spiritual existence; and if you have been born blind, of course, none can ever adequately explain what beauty the eye can see. (p. 45)

Akutagawa, to the last degree, analyzes the introspection of the disciples attending the last rites of Bashô. They are all accomplished writers of *haiku* (seventeen-syllable verse), and therefore accustomed to introspection and critical observation of life. The degree of honesty inspired in each of the disciples by the spiritual atmosphere in the room where Bashô lay dying provides some further indication as to how one should go about rectifying the mind in preparation for enlightenment. (p. 47)

"Absorbed in Letters" is especially interesting for those who wish for a more intimate knowledge of Akutagawa himself. It was suggested that Bakin had no knowledge of current affairs, that he was an incorrigible fellow who could not make any money from pursuits of any worth, that when he was writing he would be oblivious to all other things.

For all Akutagawa's self-detachment, his works were created in "the mental state of being absorbed in letters," so we must assume that his self-detachment is an actual one and not a literary device. Therein lies the difference between Akutagawa and other writers, East and West, who are acclaimed as being "objective." In his writing he is oblivious to any misgivings about adverse criticism, though he did entertain such misgivings in his non-creative hours.

When Akutagawa wrote that Bakin had towards his readers always felt goodwill, he was surely enlarging on his own attitude. With Bakin such goodwill did not influence his evaluation of the people who read his works; hence at the one time he was able to feel both contempt and goodwill.

Perhaps, like Bakin, Akutagawa had not the courage to be too introspective. He hid from the public his own uncertain attitudes. There is some indication that, as with Bakin, there had always existed in him the insoluble problem of reconciliation of *himself as a moralist* and *himself as an artist*. He deplored the affectation of writers who sought to satisfy the public artistically and morally.

We must not, he contends, assume that the writing of mere fiction is easy to achieve. Right mind and right setting are as important to fiction writing as are knowledge and experience. Akutagawa's brush has all these advantages behind the mind that propels it, and like Bakin's brush, it sometimes zealously slips down the pages, writing of itself, as though it writes in veneration of some god.

In the story **"Absorbed in Letters"** there is a recurrence of the theme, the acquisition of "right mind." To Bakin, neither conceit about his ability to write *haiku* if he chose, nor his preoccupation with his readers' criticism could induce a state of mind satisfactory for his writing. The hot water of the public bath was evidently relaxing, and assisted in diverting his mind sufficiently to bestir his imagination, but it is only a temporary indulgence, and his attention is soon arrested by the "bathhouse critic" who addresses an acquaintance close by him in the foggy atmosphere.

". . . It can be said of all Bakin's works that in writing them Bakin uses only the tip of his brush. His works have no substance. When his works do have anything to convey, it is just as if he were a (history) master of a temple school. . . ."

Reflecting on such criticism, Bakin decided that an author who drew only from the prevailing taste of the time would fall into the peril of failing to express his own sentiments in his works, and would write only in response to the taste of his readers.

Izumiya Ichibê, the publisher, endeavors to persuade Bakin to write "in response to the tastes of his readers," but Bakin is as contemptuous of the idea as he is of Izumiya himself. (pp. 48-50)

[It] will come as no surprise to [the reader] when Bakin calls his maidservant and asks if Izumiya's shoes (left at the door of the Japanese house) have been turned, as is the custom, towards the street, ready for his departure.

Then Bakin, "the possessor of a liberal area of warm sunshine," turns to the garden to assuage his wrath. "When ten minutes later Sugi, the maidservant, came to inform him that his midday meal was prepared, he was leaning vacantly against a veranda post, still altogether enwrapped in dream."

"Until a short while ago, it had been my aim to write a great work which had no rival in this land. But there again, in that, too, perhaps there existed the kind of vainglory common to all men. . . ." His strong *ego* had filled him with passion too ardent to allow him the refuge of *enlightenment* and *resignation*.

But Bakin was to gain spiritual satisfaction from the unexpected and simplest of sources, as such satisfaction may often be gained.

In the evening when he settles down in his study to write, "a power that would shatter the stars, was flowing swiftly through his mind, infusing him moment by moment with strength, urging him onwards. In his eyes there was neither advantage nor disadvantage, neither love nor hate. The flowing torrent in his mind had washed away the dregs of life, and life glowed resplendent like a new ore."

We leave Bakin completely "absorbed in letters," seated with legs cushioned beneath him, upon the *tatami* (matting) of his room, one arm on the low-set desk, writing. Outside his study the crickets are chirping to acclaim the autumn.

Akutagawa assumed that, allowing for the influence of heredity, destiny could be said to be a compromise between faith, environment, and chance—to which three entities, through decades of painful and pleasurable experience, we learn to be resigned, and through resignation to be comforted. *Chance* is the romantic, the unexpected element in life. *Environment* is just where one happens to be. *Faith* is, as is written in the Epistle of St. Paul to the Hebrews, "the evidence of things unseen," or, we might say for consistency of style, "the evidence of what is believed to be so;" and all life can be said to be no more than what is believed to be so.

We cannot always be sure whether another man is *resigned* or whether he is not. If he be a soldier he might be resigned, but if he be agitating for an aggressive war, then he is not resigned. If he be a social agitator demanding more and more material benefits from life, he is not resigned, for he is under the misapprehension that impetuosity is strength and that material advantages strengthen rather than weaken a man. Unlike Yasukichi of **"The Greeting,"** a man who is resigned does not live for yesterday and tomorrow, but for today—conscious that life and death, yesterday and tomorrow are swift, but that the present instant is eternity. The man who is resigned will enjoy the tranquillity of the crescent moon either above the pine forest or above the restaurant roof, or through the bathroom window; beauty has no special place to be seen or not to be seen.

May we pray that these stories respond to the search for inspiration and of themselves suggest the ways in which, if need be, the reader may "rectify his mind." To be enlightened the human mind should be disciplined as a garden is pruned, swept and watered. And is enlightenment to be found in the process of such discipline? Buddha was careful to rebuke those who were too devoted to their own style of discipline. "The beauty," he said, "is *not* in the *discipline* of the garden." . . . (pp. 50-2)

[The] beauty—the inspiration—of the garden is not in the discipline of the garden, but in what grows in the garden by virtue of it. (p. 53)

John McVittie, "A Sprig of Wild Orange (Introduction)," in Exotic Japanese Stories: The Beautiful and the Grotesque *by Ryūnosuke Akutagawa, edited by John McVittie and Arthur Pell, translated by Takashi Kojima and John McVittie, Liveright Publishing Corporation, 1964, pp. 13-53.*

PATRICIA M. LEWIS   (essay date 1971)

[*In the following excerpt, Lewis discusses Akutagawa's integration of setting and symbolism in the short story "*Rashōmon.*"*]

In **"Rashomon,"** a short story by Ryunosuke Akutagawa, the central theme—the destruction of conventional morality—is skillfully conveyed primarily through patterns of imagery and the setting. Through a combination of casual events and psychological justifications, the protagonist shatters the facade of noble principles that would eventually result in his death by his realization that his resurgent doubts about the immorality of stealing in order to live are merely symptomatic of a harsher reality—that principles are only fabrications of social convenience with little validity when measured against survival itself.

The author constructs and embellishes this theme by establishing the setting in conventional symbols and images: it is a cold, rainy evening, and the servant has taken refuge from the weather (and his plight) in the Rashomon, the deserted gate in Kyoto's outer wall, itself symbolic of the decline of ancient values. The physical features of the setting are vehicles, both on a literal, causal plane and also on the symbolic level, of the destruction of the servant's traditional views of honor and morality. This tradition is emphasized by the fact that the protagonist has been released from his function as the servant of a samurai, the literal and symbolic figure of traditional Japanese life and custom. The old order has been disrupted: the servant has been discharged, and the time-honored code of morality has been displaced. On a larger scale, the decaying Rashomon is representative of the declining prosperity of Kyoto, and it is this decline that has resulted in the servant's dismissal. Thus, it is subtly significant that he should take refuge in an edifice that is suffering, as he is, from the effects of economic pressures. These pressures precipitate his confrontation with his own moral precepts just as they precipitate the desecration of the Buddhist images which are sold as firewood. The setting at the gate is also important because it is on the perimeter of the city and opens out to the unknown, the significance of which will be discussed later in this paper.

But the decaying state of the Rashomon is not the only symbolic indication of future realizations. The deathly ominous red sky "in the afterlight of the departed sun," the depressing effect of the rain, the "howling wind in the evening dusk," and the presence of the "white droppings of crows" dotting the crumbling stones, all contribute to the realistic setting of the story, but also operate on a symbolic level to portend the transformation of the servant into an absurd hero devoid of metaphysical anchorage. The symbolic death of metaphysics is intensified by the ghostly aura created by the presence of the unwanted corpses as well as by the image of "a fat black cloud impal[ing] itself on the tips of the tiles jutting out from the roof on the gate."

It is the presence of the bodies in the surreal flickering light which magnifies his receptivity to the nightmarish confusion of reality with appearance: "He caught sight of a ghoulish form bent over a corpse." This confusion is paralleled by his vacillation between the alternative of death and good or the alternative of life and evil, but the confusion is subliminally negated by the red, festering pimple which, like his final commitment to evil, is resolutely emerging. But the conventional view of evil as the absence of good is torturously inverted. For the servant, good becomes the absence of evil, or at best, a superfluous construct of appearances superimposed on a reality that makes no distinctions. It is therefore his commitment to reality instead of appearance that supplants his original conflict. And it is his realization of this distinction expressed in the "certain courage [which] was born in his heart," that designates his emergence as an absurd figure. (pp. 867-69)

The motif of appearance and reality is further exemplified by the old woman stealing from the corpses hair that will be made into wigs. Not only does the initially apparent desecration of the bodies serve to horrify the servant and thus act as catalyst to his epiphany, but the idea of wig-wearing also carries with it overtones of artificiality, subterfuge, a deliberate attempt to mask reality with an artifact of appearance. And it is ironic that the old woman's words, "... I pull out the hair ... to make a wig ...," banish the unknown—the realm of appearance.

This same motif is apparent in the depiction of the bodies: "Some of them were women, and all were lolling on the floor with their mouths open or their arms outstretched showing no more signs of life than so many clay dolls. One would doubt that they had ever been alive, so eternally silent they were. Their shoulders, breasts, and torsos stood out in the dim light; other parts vanished in shadow." The fusion of clay dolls with shadow again juxtaposes appearances and reality, inducing them to merge in the bizarre, surrealistic, limbo-like setting. It is in limbo that life and death are no longer dichotomous.

Perhaps the most complex image and symbol pattern lies in the recurrence of "the unknown." The first instance where this occurs is when the servant is climbing the broad lacquered stairs leading to the tower over the gate. He is halfway up the stairs when he sees a flickering light in the tower. "What sort of person would be making a light in the Rashomon ... and in a storm? The unknown, the evil terrified him." The second instance occurs after the servant has stolen the old hag's clothes and disappeared into the night: "Shortly after that the hag raised her body from the corpses. Grumbling and groaning, she crawled to the top stair by the still flickering torchlight, and through the gray hair which hung over her face, she peered down to the last stair in the torch light. Beyond this was only darkness ... unknowing and unknown."

The images are inverted: the servant, in a state of moral conflict, sees the light in the tower as he climbs the stairs and fears an unknown that awaits him; the hag, who has resolved, or perhaps denied moral conflict, looks down the stairs into the darkness. And there lies the unknown for her. Because the images are inverted, their symbolism must likewise be inverted. As the servant transcends the unknown by his metamorphosis to the absurd and his implied commitment to life (conveyed by the light imagery, ghostly though it may be), the old hag, now faced with the consequences of her amoral "noncode" turned back upon her, must undergo a reversal of the servant's metamorphosis from conventional morality to valueless existence. She is no longer detached from a code of values because her encounter with the servant has altered her perception of reality. For her, the darkness beyond the stairs is death. And therein lies the despair of this story.

Although a congruity of theme, action, character and imagery exists within the story proper, the entire incident is beyond the confines of rational or normal experience. But the bizarre seems less so when placed in a nebulously remote time. Like the servant's pimple, the author has established a festering poetic truth that is not contingent on a believeable, or rather, mundane setting. (pp. 869-71)

> *Patricia M. Lewis, "Akutagawa's 'Rashōmon': The Development of Theme through Setting and Symbolism," in* Literature East and West, *Vol. XV, No. 4, December, 1971 & Vol. XVI, Nos. 1 & 2, March & June, 1972, pp. 867-71.*

BEONGCHEON YU (essay date 1972)

[*In the following excerpt, Yu examines several of Akutagawa's literary theories in relation to the development of the author's career, and enumerates Akutagawa's major contributions to modern Japanese literature.*]

[Akutagawa] took every opportunity to clarify his [literary] intent: to go his own way as best he could—the only sure way of growing. In reply to the question, "Why do you write?" he said he wrote neither for money nor for the public but because something vague and chaotic within himself demanded a certain form which was at once clear and precise. Declaring that art is, first of all, expression, he challenged the general critical assumption that a writer starts with content and then frames it in some sort of form, as though there were two separate and separable processes. The common critical clichés, "stylistic obsession," "too deft" or "too dexterous," were meaningless to Akutagawa. Form, he said in effect, does not wrap content in a neat package; form lies in content, and *vice versa*. To one who cannot understand this basic truth, art will forever remain another world. Art begins and ends in deliberate expression. Write with your soul or with your life—all these gilded sermons had better be addressed to high school students. All creative activities, even those of a genius, are conscious; he is perfectly aware of what effect his single touch, his single stroke will create; if not, then he is no better than an automaton.

In Akutagawa's view, then, it would be a mistake to assume the primacy of either form or content. In the same reflections on art he in fact warned that stressing form would be equally harmful, and that in practice it might be even more harmful than stressing content, a warning apparently against a typical Japanese tendency toward the decorative or a refined preciousness. The point here is Akutagawa's passion for perfection. . . . The artist, in Akutagawa's view, must strive to perfect his work; otherwise his devotion to art amounts to nothing. For moral exaltation the reader might as well turn to sermons, but for aesthetic pleasure he must go to a work of art. And to secure this pleasure the artist must pursue his dream of perfection. It was in this vein that Akutagawa also wrote: "There is in the kingdom of art no room for the unperfected"; "A work of art, when perfected, becomes timeless"; and "In the religion of art self-reliance is the only key to salvation."

"One who has a correct view of art does not necessarily create a better work. Such a reflection makes me sad. Am I the only one in this? I pray this is not the case"—so Akutagawa wrote in **"Art, etc."** The truth is that Akutagawa not only had a "correct" view of art but also wrote "better" works because of it. In reference to Poe's "Philosophy of Composition" he observed that the American poet wrote his poems and stories just as a brick layer would go about his job. Then turning to his own manner of writing, Akutagawa said in the preface to *Tobacco and the Devil:*

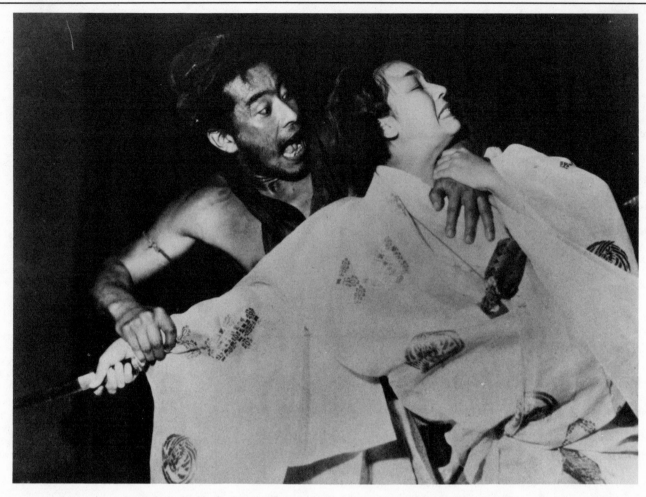

Scene from the film Rashōmon, *directed by Kurosawa Akira. Courtesy of Janus Films.*

To speak of my feelings while I am at work, it seems like growing rather than making something. Every phenomenon, human and otherwise, follows its own unique course of development in that it happens in the way it must. So as I write I proceed from point to point, from moment to moment. If I miss one step, then I am stuck. I can not go even one step further. If I force myself, something is bound to go wrong. I must always be alert. No matter how alert, it often happens that I miss it. That is my trouble.

This, according to Akutagawa, explains why a work of art in progress sometimes refuses to follow the artist's own plan, however well calculated, "just as the world may have gone out of God's hands, much as he tried to adhere to his original plans of creation." Thus, despite his insistence on conscious intelligence, Akutagawa recognized that the artist was fallible, but this human frailty was no excuse for not striving for perfection. (pp. 19-20)

The first period of Akutagawa's career was one of glory and splendor that reminded his contemporaries of Pegasus' flight to the sacred Parnassus. Ever eager to explore new fields of the imagination, afire with passion for perfection, and driven by fear of repetition, he wrote some seventy stories, a little less than half of his total output, in a span of three years or

so. But what may have seemed Pegasus' flight was actually a strenuous uphill climb, a conscious revolt against the contemporary literary world.

Armed with the conviction that every literary revolt, even when against oneself, deserves sympathy, Akutagawa carried out his revolt in two ways. First, he opposed the tradition of the *shish-osetsu* [the I-novel] which, subordinating art to life, had in effect caused their confusion. Rejecting this cult of life he upheld the autonomy, the superiority, of art. Second, he opposed the three major schools which divided the contemporary literary scene. Acutely aware of the dark forces in human nature, he could not accept the idealist position that free cultivation of individuality would automatically lead to a better world; painfully sensitive to life's suffering, he could not partake of the sensual orgy of the aesthetic school, however alluring; and deeply committed to rigorous intellectual discipline, he could not share the naturalist capitulation to the lawlessness of human instincts. While criticizing each of these schools Akutagawa nevertheless sought to harmonize their ideals in his own kind of art.

If his emphasis on perfect intellectual control was what made his conquest of Parnassus possible, it also made him experience a peculiar sense of loneliness. As Akutagawa said:

As we strive toward artistic perfection, there is something that stands in our way. Is it possibly our indolence? No, nothing of the sort. It is of stronger nature—difficult to define. It is like what grips the heart of a man who, the higher he climbs the mountain, feels the more nostalgic toward the world below the clouds. Whoever cannot understand what this means, must remain a stranger forever as far as I am concerned.

Perhaps this sense of isolation, this yearning for the world was also present when Akutagawa declared: "I am an artist for art's sake, and at the same time I am not. Life is too vast." Most certainly, it was his instinctual love of life which in a moment of frenzy he had disdained as not being worth a single line of Baudelaire, and from which he had turned to books in emulating his early literary master France. (Indeed, he took special note of Renoir's advice: If you want to learn painting, go to museums.) There was also his increasing self-doubt as to whether or not in his dedication to artistic perfection, he had somewhere been led astray from the path of his own being which demanded a total, not partial, fulfillment for its own survival. This danger of transcending life, or rather of bypassing life, Akutagawa had already expressed in **"The Holy Man"** . . . and **"The Wine Worm,"** . . . and was now expressing in **"Tu Tzuch'un"** . . .—all with one recurring theme: You cannot help being what you are: and living honestly as a human being is the best way you can be faithful to your destiny.

While scaling his Parnassus, Akutagawa no doubt remembered his youthful dreams of "great horizons." Now standing on the lonely summit and gazing at the great horizon unfolding far below and beyond, he wondered whether or not he had really achieved something that would make him equal to those great masters who seemed to have succeeded eminently in harmonizing art and life, a harmony which enriched both. As he again heard the nostalgic call of life, his doubts about himself—his life and art—inevitably darkened his vision.

Self-doubt resulted in artistic impasse which occurred soon after **"The Hell Screen."** . . . As if he had instinctively sensed this impasse, Akutagawa turned away from the short story to the novel. In the next year or so he tried the latter form twice in **"Heresy"** . . . and **"On the Road"** . . .—the one set in his favorite Heian period, dealing with the early confrontation between the native way of life and the Christian (featuring as hero a son of that Grand Lord of **"The Hell Screen"**), and the other set in the contemporary period depicting the world of young Japanese intellectuals. Neither was completed, however, and he tended to blame his publishers. He felt that he could write a novel if only they would forget, and let him forget, his reputation as a short story writer. Yet, he may have suspected that the novel, the conventional novel form, suited him least. For this reason perhaps, speaking later of the unfinished **"Heresy,"** he declared, in effect, that the artist's mind, like a mountain stream, could not turn back.

In the meantime Akutagawa kept writing short stories. Following **"Heresy"** he turned out **"Mr. Mori,"** **"Those Days,"** . . . and other pieces, set in the contemporary world. In April 1919 he wrote two pieces, **"The Marshland"** and **"The Dragon."** The former portrayed a painter who lost his mind because he was unable to create the kind of work he dreamed of, a pathetic contrast to that willful genius Yoshihide. The latter portrayed a vindictive monk who, by duping people to believe that a dragon would rise from a lake, avenged himself on those who ridiculed his big nose. **"The Dragon,"** which in conception and execution is an imitation of his earlier pieces, **"The Nose,"**

"Lice," and **"Yam Gruel,"** indicates that Akutagawa had reached the point where all he could do was repeat himself. Of **"The Dragon"** he wrote several months later: "In the realm of art there is no such thing as pause. 'No progress' means regress. When an artist regresses, there always begins a sort of automatism; that is, he turns out the same kind of stuff. Once this automatism sets in, the artist is clearly on the verge of death. When I wrote **'The Dragon'** I faced such an artistic death."

Artistic death, in Akutagawa's case, signified his crisis as a man. Since the trouble stemmed from his deliberate alienation from life, and life alone could offer a satisfactory solution, if he was to survive as an artist, the only alternative was to return to it. Apparently in a hopeful mood and in spite of failing health Akutagawa, at the request of the *Osaka Mainichi*, undertook a four-month visit to China. His account of this visit, however, showed no tangible signs that the journey helped him. At this point a trip to Europe might have been more helpful—an idea his friends suggested but his family turned down in fear that it might aggravate his undermined health. A leisurely journey through his literary homelands, as his old friend Tsuneto Kiyoshi pointed out, might have had a salutary effect on his creative career and his inner life, and forestalled his later suicide. He remained at home, however, and had to fight his way through this crisis without whatever benefit a journey to Europe might have afforded him. Thus began his descent from Parnassus. (pp. 43-6)

Some fifteen years after Akutagawa's death, Furuya Tsunatake, evaluating his critical writings as a whole, found them trivial in quality and devoid of any sense of reality. Superb craftsman and brilliant intellectual that he was, Akutagawa the critic showed few signs of maturity in other respects, a striking contrast to the contemporary naturalist and idealist writers. For Furuya, those very qualities which made Akutagawa's art appear so intellectual, refreshing and unique in the eyes of his contemporaries turned out to be fatal weaknesses. Here, however, Furuya seems to combine the two critical principles, of partial and total negation, which Akutagawa once denounced through the mouth of Mephistopheles. The principle of total negation is to deny the artistic merits of a given work by its very merits; to condemn, for instance, a tragedy for its terror and pity or for its lack of felicity and gaiety. Since this procedure is too patently biased, Mephistopheles urges the alternative principle of partial negation: This work is written intelligently, to be sure. But that's all there is to it.

What Akutagawa chides through Mephistopheles is the cowardice of contemporary critics playing safe for the sake of expediency, as well as the half-heartedness of fellow-artists taking up criticism as a hobby. Unlike them, he firmly believed that criticism as an act of self-expression is indisputably a form of art. If art is immortal, then criticism is also immortal, for man will forever ask: What is art? Criticism is thus a response to this most basic question. Yet Akutagawa was too much of an artist to suggest the separation of art and criticism. Criticism or critical appreciation, as he took it, is really an act of collaboration between artist and critic in that the latter attempts his own creation on a given work of art as his subject. (This is one of the themes of his story **"An Autumn Mountain."** . . .) Akutagawa wholeheartedly subscribed to Baudelaire's statement that every poet has a critic within himself, if not always *vice versa*. "A genuine critic," said Akutagawa,

> will take up his critical pen to sift rice from
> husks. More often than not I too experience

such a messianic urge within me. Most of the time I take up criticism for my own sake—in order to sing myself intellectually. Thus criticism, as I understand it, in no way differs from writing novels and haiku.

As an act of self-expression criticism is a form of art. With this conviction Akutagawa took criticism as part of his artistic activity, always eager to discuss his own trade, write reviews and prefaces, and ponder the problems of art and criticism. With the artist and the critic within himself challenging each other, he produced a great deal—enough to be collected in three volumes. By virtue of his intelligence, insight, erudition, and passion, much of his criticism is still worth reading, especially in connection with his creative writing. (pp. 75-7)

The reasons for Akutagawa's sudden rebirth are not difficult to surmise. Many Western readers are surprised, as with **"Kappa,"** to discover something so familiar in the least expected quarters. Those who have long been accustomed to a stereotyped exotic Orientalism suddenly find in Akutagawa a writer haunted by his daemon and intensely tragic in his view of life. Thousands of miles away from Japan, they are in a better position to meet Akutagawa's own demand: Do not look at me. Look at my work. By comparison, the Japanese are less fortunately situated in that their very familiarity with Akutagawa makes it difficult to separate him from his art. Mishima was quite right when he said unfortunate is the writer whose personality rather than his art is still discussed long after his death. This difficulty of distinguishing works from their author is all the greater in Japanese literature due to its peculiar tradition of the *shishosetsu* which tends to emphasize the intimacy between life and art, man and artist. (p. 120)

Akutagawa is far more complex than his legend often leads us to believe. Throughout his three-stage career he underwent a significant change, and his works also reflect his developing view of art and life. Because it is based primarily on his early stories, the image of Akutagawa among his Western readers, refreshing as it is, is by no means whole and complete. Although free of this delimited view of Akutagawa, Japanese critics do not fare any better. Because of the many problems Akutagawa's suicide raises, they are constantly tempted to read his life back into his art. When dealing with various stages of his career, they tend to evaluate his works simply in terms of personal preference. Consequently, those who prefer his last period stress his later work at the expense of the earlier; likewise, those who are interested mainly in his middle period often disparage the work of his other periods. This fragmented judgment by personal preference inevitably makes it difficult to see Akutagawa's writing in its totality. Perhaps it is time for us to seize on the recent change in the climate of opinion, and by tracing Akutagawa's career through its varied stages, re-adjust our view to the complex drama of his inner world. Only by a renewed effort to view his life and art in proper perspective can we do justice to Akutagawa.

From the present inquiry it is apparent that Akutagawa has earned his place in modern Japanese literature for several reasons. First, by opposing naturalism he aligned himself with the intellectual tradition of Ogai and Soseki and developed it further. Convinced that literature is primarily a form of intelligence, he both broadened the function of the latter and enriched the quality of the former, thus re-affirming their greater intimacy. Second, by challenging the peculiar Japanese tradition of the *shishosetsu* he helped to foster the great tradition of the European novel in Japan where the novel might otherwise

have degenerated into a form of popular entertainment. This he accomplished by virtue of his thorough training in modern Western literatures and also by his firm grasp of the basic relationships between form and content, art and life. Third, by his intelligence, imagination, and passion he demonstrated the artistic possibilities of the short story, and by exploring its dimensions and limits, helped make it part of modern Japanese literature. Finally, through his dedication to his chosen task, he reminded his contemporaries that literature is a very serious and vital part of life, and thereby he affirmed the dignity and worth of artistic pursuit.

Because his art was born out of the very confrontation of East and West, Akutagawa's significant achievement in modern Japanese literature gives him a rightful claim to a niche in world literature as well. Nurtured by the best of both traditions, his work suggests that the continuing interaction of those traditions may yield yet finer fruits. If, as he himself said, Japanese literature is a new fabric whose warp is native and whose woof is Western, it also characterizes the nature of his own art, which is at once Japanese and Western. Viewed in this light, there may be a time when Akutagawa will stand side by side with some of his better-known fellow writers—Poe, Mérimée, Baudelaire, Maupassant, Chekhov, and Kafka.

Akutagawa once said: "I often think—what I have created would have been written by someone, even if I hadn't been born." Perhaps so, though it is doubtful. The best of Akutagawa's work has the indelible mark of his personality and many of his stories will undoubtedly continue to fascinate the reader with their peculiar *frisson nouveau.* "The world is overcrowded with immortal works," wrote Akutagawa. "If a writer can leave ten pieces worth reading thirty years after his death, then, we may call him a master. If he can write five of the same worth, he is still entitled to the Hall of Fame. And, even if only three, he can pass as a writer." Judged by his own standards, Akutagawa is a master. Over half of his some 150 stories are still readable more than thirty years after his death, and unless chance plays one of its unpredictable pranks, most of his best stories will remain. In their own way they are masterpieces with windows open toward various vistas of life, to apply one of his own criteria for distinguishing excellence from mediocrity. To be sure, none of his best stories are very long, but as he warned, "To confuse massiveness with excellence is critical materialism." He was at heart a poet, a pure poet, as he wished to be. Because this is so his stories will continue to send forth their fiery purple sparks, imperishable sparks struck from life that offer their precious glimpse of the human soul. (pp. 120-22)

Beongcheon Yu, in his Akutagawa: An Introduction, *Wayne State University Press, 1972, 148 p.*

YOSHIHIKO MUKOYAMA   (essay date 1975)

[*In the following excerpt, Mukoyama examines the influence of works by Robert Browning and Oscar Wilde upon Akutagawa's short story "In the Woods."*]

In studying Akutagawa's **"In the Woods"** it is first necessary to take at least a brief glance at the composite elements in the manner of narration to appreciate Akutagawa's emphatic points in that story. We first notice that the statements of the seven witnesses are given mainly in an objective manner of narration. Nowhere in this story is the subjective disposition more in evidence than in the following lines of the bandit's outcry against the existing order of his society.

Why, to me slaying a man is not a matter of so much consequence as you might think. Man must be killed anyway when his woman is to be plundered. When I slay a man I use a sword I wear at my side, but when you kill a man you don't use your sword. You kill him, not with your sword, but with your power, with your money, or sometimes with a flattering word. In your way no blood is shed, it is true, and he is still alive in good health, but all the same you have killed him. Judging from the depth of sinfulness, I don't know who is worse sinner, you or me. [His ironical smile.]

This is a witty criticism of his society, a fine piece of *jeu d'esprit* out of his conviction, and more so since none of the other witnesses speak in protest against the existing order of society or criticise it.

We are less likely to read Akutagawa's **"In the Woods"** as criticism against the order of society, and more likely to find in it "the lesson, that our human speech is naught, our human testimony false, our fame and human estimation words and winds." Yet a critical study of this story cannot omit these passages spoken out by the outlaw criticising the prevailing injustice of his society. If the significance in these lines is overlooked, the core of the business will be missed.

Yasuo Yasuda noticed for the first time in 1958 . . . the importance of the passages in question. He suggests that Akutagawa may have obtained the idea of social criticism from reading the following remark in Lafcadio Hearn's commentary on [Robert Browning's] *The Ring and the Book:*

He [the Pope] sends word to the prison that the Count must be executed immediately. So justice is obtained, at least so far as the punishment of murder can be called justice. But what becomes of the money? The nuns of the convent in which Pompilia died, they get the money by very discreditable means, and they keep it. The terrible Franceschini family cannot try to get the money from the convent; for the convent means the power of the Church; and the power of the Church is even more terrible than the power of the Franceschini. Of course the Pope knows nothing of this whole matter. The Pope is the finest character in the whole story.

Yasuda observes that Akutagawa may have had these cynical remarks against the Church in mind when he conceived the criticism which the bandit dares to speak to the police commissioner. This connection of Akutagawa to Hearn is valid inasmuch as the criticism against the power of society is found in both instances. It is the contention of this writer, however, that a much truer connection may be drawn to "The Ballad of Reading Gaol" by Oscar Wilde.

The evidence which supports this view is found in the following lines of the 7th and 8th stanzas of the "Ballad":

Yet each man kills the thing he loves,
    By each let this be heard,
Some do it with a bitter look,
    Some with a flattering word,
The coward does it with a kiss,
    The brave man with a sword!

Some kill their love when they are young,
    And some when they are old;
Some strangle with the hands of Lust,
    Some with the hands of Gold.
The kindest use a knife, because
    The dead so soon grow cold.

The relationship between Akutagawa and Wilde is in part explained on the one hand by the similarity of the language used, and on the other hand by the emphatic tone sympathizing with the social outcasts in their protest against the injustice in the existing order of society.

Similarities in the language are found in such instances as "sword," "blood," "flattering word," "money-gold." Besides these similarities, it must be noted that a line "Some do it with a bitter look" corresponds to the episode of the bitter look of the husband's eyes in the story by the wife.

The connection between the two works is not explained only by the parallel use of the language, but is also noticed by the manner in which Akutagawa reproduced a word he borrowed from Wilde. The word in question is "flattering" which is used in both stories for the same effect. The present writer's translation of the line with that word is simply "Sometimes with a flattering word," while the same line in the published translation by Takashi Kojima is "Sometimes you kill them on the pretext of working for their good." This difference is accounted for by Akutagawa's elaboration in trying to reproduce the same word. Akutagawa was probably deeply impressed or excited by the idea of killing "with a flattering word," so when he translated it in Japanese he used elaboration, choosing the word "otame-gokashi" instead of other simpler, easier to understand words such as "oseji," "kangen," or "hetsurai," etc. It is true that "otame-gokashi" is a plain, common Japanese word familiar to most Japanese, yet it carries a note of elaboration if used in the narration of a conversational style, as in the case of **"In the Woods."** An example of this is the difference the reader notices if, instead of **"In the Woods,"** some other title like "In a Woodsy Glen" is used for this story, with the latter carrying a note of elaboration. Kojima's translation is faithful to Akutagawa's elaborated word, and the present writer's is the original word from Wilde.

Another connection of Akutagawa's story with Wilde's "Ballad" is in the symbolic use of blood and wine:

He did not wear his scarlet coat,
    For blood and wine are red,
And blood and wine were on his hands
    When they found him with the dead,
The poor dead woman whom he loved,
    And murdered in the bed. . . .

In Akutagawa, "a single sword-stroke had pierced the heart. The fallen bamboo blades around the body looked as if they had been dipped in sappan dye juice." Akutagawa could not borrow the blood-wine symbol because his story was set in a period before red wine was known in Japan. In the place of wine Akutagawa used dye juice of sappan tree [Judas' tree], borrowing the word from one of the stories in Vol. 27 of *Konjaku Monogatari*.

A comparison of the emphatic tone in the outcasts' criticisms of social injustice in both stories also reveals the similarity. In Wilde's "Ballad" there is a symbolic repetition of "He does not. . . ." in the first lines of each successive stanza from the

9th to the last of part I, while, in Akutagawa's story, there is a cynical outcry of the outlaw philosophizing his conviction of social injustice:

> In your way no blood is shed, it is true, and he is still alive in good health, but all the same you have killed him. Judging from the depth of sinfulness, I don't know who is worse sinner, you or me.

In addition to this comparison of emphatic tone, it is no less important to note the corresponding emphasis in the outcry of Akutagawa's outcast and in Wilde's declaration of "By each let this be heard."

Wilde's "The Ballad of Reading Gaol" is in essence an excellent expression of sympathy with the social outcast. In Akutagawa's story, likewise, the outcast received the sympathy. A brief consideration of Akutagawa's life and works indicates that he very often contemplated himself as a suffering victim of the social régime of his time. (pp. 66-70)

On the weight of these internal evidences alone, it could be effectively argued that there is a relationship between Akutagawa's story and Wilde's "Ballad." More significant, however, is the circumstantial evidence which supports this connection.

The matrix for the connection of Akutagawa's story with Wilde's "Ballad" is found in Hakuson Kuriyagawa's short commentary on Wilde's "Ballad" given as supplement at the end of his critical study of Browning's "Porphyria's Lover" in the 15 August, 1921, issue of *Eigo Seinen [The Rising Generation]*, pp. 297-99.

In his excellent critical study of "Porphyria's Lover," Kuriyagawa gives line by line explanations for the readers to avoid any possible mistakes in a grammatical understanding of the lines of this poem. Kuriyagawa, at the conclusion of his study of "Porphyria's Lover," gives the following supplementary note for a better appreciation of the poem:. . .

> A man kills a woman he loves—to get satisfaction! Should this be interpreted, in the view of abnormal sexual psychology, as a case of sadism that takes delight in blood from the opposite sex, or as a case of sex motivated killing (as termed Lustmord in German)? It calls to my mind "The Ballad of Reading Gaol" by Oscar Wilde with its repetition of the following stanza:
>
> > Yet each man kills the thing he loves,
> >   By each let this be heard,
> > Some do it with a bitter look,
> >   Some with a flattering word,
> > The coward does it with a kiss
> >   The brave man with a sword!
>
> If a man slaps, twists, scratches, or beats his love, it does not matter so much as a sin. On the contrary, it is by no means rare that a man kills a woman with gold, with a flattering word, with a kiss, or with an embrace. Perhaps only a brave man can kill his woman with a cold steel, or by strangling her with her hair.

This commentary of Browning's "Porphyria's Lover" by Kuriyagawa appeared in *The Rising Generation* four months before Akutagawa wrote his **"In the Woods."** From this it can

fairly be justified to assume that this note of Kuriyagawa on "The Ballad of Reading Gaol" exercised an immediate influence directly instrumental in molding the idea for the cynical criticism against the injustice of the existing order of society uttered by the outcast bandit.

The following table of the words used by the three respective writers shows a close adherence to each other in their use of the languages.

(Wilde)	(Kuriyagawa)	(Akutagawa)
A bitter look	— — — — —	A bitter look
A flattering word	A flattering word	A flattering word
A kiss	A kiss	— — — — —
A sword	A sword	A sword
Hands of Lust	Embrace	— — — — —
Hands of Gold	Gold	Gold
Blood shedding	Sadism	Blood shedding
Brave-Coward	Brave-Coward	Brave-Coward

A reason for the absence of the word "kiss" from Akutagawa is simply because it was not known to the Japanese at the time of this story. The coinage of the Japanese counterpart of this word belongs to the rather recent past.

We cannot fail to notice the significant connection of four men of letters of England and Japan—Browning, Wilde, Kuriyagawa, and Akutagawa, joined together by *The Rising Generation*. This relationship may seem only accidental, but this writer contends that this relationship is significant because it not only substantiates the possible Akutagawa-Kuriyagawa-Browning-Wilde relationship but also reveals some aspects of Browning study in Japan against the background of the history of English studies in Japan. In regard to the question of the significance of this relationship of these four men of letters there is one answer which deserves some careful analysis.

While there is no way of knowing how Akutagawa's interest in Browning first originated, it is the belief of this writer that it was due to the influence of Lafcadio Hearn and the tradition of his school of English studies in Japan. (pp. 71-3)

We are not sure if Akutagawa read *The Ring and the Book* in its text, but we are certain that he had read Hearn's detailed comments on that poem. (p. 77)

This study was conducted, on the bases of the foregoing internal and circumstantial evidences, to show the source of immediate influence on Akutagawa for his **"In the Woods."** If the evidences for this view are questioned, there is still another strong support for this view from Akutagawa himself. This is the letter Akutagawa wrote in 1923 to Takeshi Kimura, one of the active literary critics at that time, and himself a Browning scholar. In his article in the November, 1925 issue of *Shincho* (a literary journal), Kimura pointed out the influence of Browning's *Dramatic Lyrics* on Akutagawa's recently published **"Repayment in Gratitude,"** one of Akutagawa's masterpieces written in the form of dramatic monologue. In reply to Kimura, Akutagawa admitted the influence from Browning. He said, "You are right in your argument for the influence I received from Browning's *Dramatic Lyrics*. I tried Browning's method not only in my **'Repayment in Gratitude'** but also I tried it in my **'In the Woods.'**" It is not necessary to say that "Porphyria's Lover" was originally in *Dramatic Lyrics*, before the new grouping of 1863.

The present writer has tried to show Akutagawa's interest in Browning, but it must be noted with equal emphasis that Akutagawa was a great student of *fin de siecle* decadent literature.

His graduation thesis was on William Morris. In the early period of his career in 1916 he wrote a short story **"A Handkerchief,"** in which Akutagawa made specific reference to Wilde's "De Profundis" and "Intentions," and later in 1925, two years before his death, he compiled the *English Reader in 8 Volumes* for the use of college level students for which he selected Wilde's two works, "Selfish Giant" and "Happy Prince." It is significant that his career as a writer began in 1914 with the translation of Anatole France and W. B. Yeats.

Akutagawa started his career as a student of the art-for-art school, and generally remained so until his death, but in him there had always been the realization that men cannot live by aesthetics alone and became more aware of his own sensitive feeling for humanity. One of his masterpieces, **"Mandarin Oranges,"** a story about a Pippa-like girl, written in 1919 from personal experience, shows him to be a man of sensitivity for suffering humanity.

The Taisho Era is commonly called a time of democracy and peace, but in spite of this good appellation given Akutagawa's time, the people in mass were compelled to eat the most expensive foods in the world. And the "warped souls and bodies" were crying for more foods for less price while numberless young girls, "with thin lips on tremble, lashless eyes inveterately tear-shot," worked in the mills under conditions no better than those for Pippa herself. Under such social conditions, Akutagawa's art-for-art school literature began losing its stage to the rising tide of the so-called proletarian literature movement in the 1920's.

Throughout his career, Akutagawa had a conflict in his dichotomy between idealistic aspiration and aesthetic morbidity. His idealistic side was strongly inspired from the influence he received from Browning while his aesthetic side was enhanced from Oscar Wilde. (pp. 78-80)

It may be best to conclude that . . . Akutagawa's **"In the Woods"** is the result of what may be termed the cumulative effect of the influences from varied sources. It may be that the great writer makes in this way increment of the past and present, the foreign and native, as Robert Browning had earlier done for the literature of his own country. This point of Akutagawa's erudition has been touched on not to eulogize him, but to show the place he stands in the history of Browning study in the line of tradition of Lafcadio Hearn's school of English literature in Japan. (p. 80)

> *Yoshihiko Mukoyama, "Ryunosuke Akutagawa and Browning Study in Japan," in* Studies in Browning and His Circle, *Vol. 3, No. 2, Fall, 1975, pp. 63-80.**

NORIKO MIZUTA LIPPIT (essay date 1980)

[*In the following excerpt, Lippit discusses the emergence of the I-novel as a major development in Japanese literature, but one which compelled such writers as Akutagawa and Tanizaki Junichiro to overcome the inherent limitations of the genre with their own innovations. Lippit considers Akutagawa's almost exclusive reliance on other works as source material for his stories, in conjunction with his use of the author as narrator, an attempt to bridge the dichotomy between art and life.*]

Following in the path of Mori Ogai and Natsume Sōseki, writers whom he especially admired, Akutagawa Ryūnosuke . . . started his writing by rejecting the confessional self-revelation and open self-search which characterized Japan's I-novelists, including the naturalistic writers like Katai and the idealistic

Shirakaba writers. Akutagawa, who was also strongly influenced by Western fin-de-siècle literature, chose the short story as his form from the start, and studied Poe, Anatole France, de Maupassant, Gautier, and Merimée, among others.

Although the short story has been the dominant form in modern Japanese literature, it was often—particularly in realistic works—meant only to be a short form of the novel. In fact, the Japanese term *shōsetsu* is used to refer to both the novel and the short story. Such writers of the I-novel as Shiga Naoya (who wrote major novels) and Kajii Motojiro (who wrote short fiction exclusively) excelled in using the short-story form to present situations which led to the height of the author's or protagonist's perception and to a moment of profound realization in his daily-life experiences. Precisely for this reason, however, precisely because they used the short-story form to explore openly the self and life, centering on the protagonist-author's self-search and self-expression, the form of their short stories was no different from that of the novel, except in length. For writers pursuing self-growth, the novel is definitely a more suitable form, and even Kajii, who was devoted to the genre of the short story, turned to the novel just before his untimely death.

Akutagawa, on the other hand, approached the short story in a manner completely different from the I-novelists. First of all, the short story for him was a modern form of storytelling and had to center around the story element (the lack of which characterizes the work of the I-novelists). Second, the stories had to present a self-sufficient world of their own. The art of the short-story writer, therefore, had to concentrate on creating in the works a perfectly autonomous "architectural structure," to borrow Tanizaki's phrase. . . . (pp. 39-40)

The most characteristic feature of Akutagawa's short stories is the fact that they are based almost exclusively on other stories: classical tales, foreign tales, the works of other writers, and so forth. In other words, Akutagawa's short stories do not usually deal with human reality directly, but with materials which have already been fictionalized in tales or stories. On the rare occasions when he dealt with situations in his own experience, they were almost invariably limited to those in his childhood. He did deal with historical situations, learning much from Mori Ogai, but even there his interest was not in dealing with the actual human experience, but in the use of stories which had already been told in history.

The borrowing of old stories or the use of someone else's stories, immediately and on a superficial level, frees the writer from having to confront the epistemological question of how to know, grasp and present reality, a question which has been vital to modern fiction. The reality in Akutagawa's works is one or two steps removed from the reality of the author and the reader, and the reality in his twice-told tales is replaced by the "story," temporarily solving the problem of the relation between reality and art. Moreover, the story element, which he made central, helps to create the structure of the works and to make them self-contained. Their perfection can be evaluated in terms of the narrative structure, that is, by the art of storytelling and the extent to which the story presents a world complete in itself.

The borrowing of old stories also exempts the author from confronting directly the question of self-expression in his works. He is a storyteller, one whose business is to mediate between the readers and the story. Not only does the story give shape and boundaries to the world of his works, but it also defines the author's identity in relation to his works as a storyteller, both inside and outside the works. Akutagawa was amazingly unconcerned with the question of the relationship between the author and the work. He often appears openly as a narrator in his works (as in **"Rashomon"**), and the author as narrator is surprisingly free from self-consciousness in his intrusion into the world of the story.

Thus, the use of existing stories, particularly old stories, whose credibility the author did not have to defend, enabled Akutagawa to circumvent dealing directly in his works with the two vital problems of modern fiction, reality and self, and to avoid the deadlock which the I-novelists reached in dealing with these problems. In Akutagawa's short stories, the question of reality and fiction and that of their relation to the search for the self in literature are temporarily suspended because of the dominance of the story itself. In that world of story, the questions of reality and the self are converted into technical or aesthetic problems of narration.

This does not mean that Akutagawa lacked concern with the problems of reality and self or that he tried to avoid dealing with them. By borrowing stories and taking the reader away from the immediate reality, Akutagawa sought to present symbolic situations relevant to all human reality. A self-avowed literary cosmopolitan, Akutagawa was confident of the universal validity of his works, confident that his works transcended the particular time and place in which they were set. Most of Akutagawa's works deal with complex psychological situations that exist in human relations, and they often reveal his fundamental skepticism about human life and belief in the relativity of human relations. In other words, Akutagawa's borrowing of the stories was a device for dealing with the modern human situation and psychology. The borrowed story provided the distance of time and space which helped give universality to the situation with which he was dealing. In this sense, the story provided only a convenient framework.

Moreover, Akutagawa's consistent use of old stories, stories twice or thrice told, reveals his belief in or reliance on archetypal literary themes and patterns of human life. Often in his stories, the narrator evades the responsibility even for being the witness or providing firsthand information on the story. By relying on the archetypal patterns of his stories, Akutagawa was able to expand his imagination to present his own story. In fact, his short stories are characterized by the exceptional integration of storytelling with the presentation of modern psychological reality.

In depending on earlier literary works, Akutagawa was certainly not alone among Japanese authors; such dependence has been one of the major techniques of Japanese (and Chinese) literature. Japanese fiction in particular, including the *monogatari*, *setsuwa* and short fiction of Saikaku and Ueda Akinari, has relied extensively on the use of earlier works as source materials. In utilizing earlier works, therefore, Akutagawa was only revitalizing a deep-rooted tradition of Japanese fiction, and in doing so, he countered the dominant trend of his time which treated the short story as a form of direct self-search and self-expression or as the presentation of a slice of life, a form without a story. (pp. 40-2)

Furthermore, Akutagawa was far from indifferent to the question of self-expression or the author's ego. Indeed, he admired and envied Shiga Naoya and Goethe, both of whom openly exposed their internal lives as the materials for their literature and the subject of their literary pursuit. Considering himself a poet, Akutagawa was strongly inclined toward the pursuit of self-exultation and self-transcendence. His persistent concern with egotism, particularly the egotism of the artist, was reflected in various ways in his works, but most often in the recurring theme of conflict between the decadent pursuit of art and beauty and the humanistic acceptance of the self as part of humanity. **"Jigokuhen"** (**"The Hell Screen"** . . .) is the most brilliant dramatization of the conflict. By assuming the role of a storyteller, therefore, Akutagawa was only wearing a mask which would hide the author's ego in the archetypal drama contained in the stories. In fact, it can be said that the development of modern fiction is the history of the authors' search for the appropriate masks in which to confess.

Mishima Yukio, who is the proper successor to Akutagawa in this respect, reveals plainly the mechanism of the confession of a mask. Unlike Mishima, however, Akutagawa was never successful in dramatizing the self in different personae; not only was the short-story form decidedly unsuitable for it, but also the narrative structure in which the narrator assumed the role of storyteller imposed inherent limitations on such dramatization.

The plot controversy between Akutagawa and Tanizaki, which took place in the last year of Akutagawa's life, sheds considerable light on these issues. In this dispute, Akutagawa, almost negating his entire literary achievement, advocated the writing of stories without a story and the expression of the author's "poetic spirit" as the purpose of literary expression rather than the creation of an autonomous world of fiction with architectural beauty. The dispute took place at a point when Akutagawa's confidence as a storyteller was deeply shaken and he had come to doubt whether storytelling was an adequate form to provide the mask for the search for the self and the meaning of life. . . . Although it would be too simple to take his last work, **"Aru ahō no isshō"** (**"A Fool's Life"** . . .), as a straight confessional, autobiographical work, the change of his literary stance and form of expression, the open and direct dealing with himself at the time of his mental crisis, only impresses us the more with his earlier effort to hide his vulnerable self under the mask of a storyteller.

Such critics as Saeki Shōichi have pointed out that Akutagawa's failure as a storyteller in his later years was due mainly to his failure to clarify the relation between the narrator and the author himself. Such modern writers as Henry James, Mauriac and Jean-Paul Sartre have long cast doubt on the ontological legitimacy of the author assuming the role of narrator, and in contemporary fiction, the narrator has become nothing but a fictional character. Akutagawa's turning to the story without a story, therefore, was only the result of his doubt about having the author assume the role of narrator and of his recognition of the problems which became acutely felt in the modernist era. Akutagawa was thus anticipating, in his later years, the direction which modern fiction itself would take.

In this sense, Akutagawa's early works present a happy union of storytelling and the presentation of the psychological or inner reality of human beings, a union between the architectural beauty of a self-sufficient, artificial world of art and the human condition. In other words, Akutagawa found in his stories, his twice-told tales which borrowed from earlier works, a means of overcoming the dichotomy between art and life, a dichotomy which was the major literary and aesthetic concern of the fin-de-siècle writers. (pp. 42-4)

Akutagawa's **"Toshishun"** has a clear message for the reader: To learn the value of being human is the meaning of life; to be human means to be true to one's feelings and to accept the life of emotions. The humble recognition of joy and sorrow, and submission to love as the substance of human life is what saved Toshishun from the life of decadence and inhuman immortality. The *sennin* in the story is a moral teacher. Among art, immortality and life (humanity), humanity receives the highest value. When he wrote "**Toshishun,**" Akutagawa had just finished writing "**The Hell Screen,**" whose central theme is the conflict between art and life. The painter in the story sacrifices love and human life for the sake of art. The work of art which was produced through this negation of humanity, however, stands as a brilliantly true work of art. Akutagawa condemns the artist as a human being, but never dismisses the value of his art, which demands perfection and purity in the sacrifice of human emotion. In "**The Hell Screen,**" therefore, the dichotomy between art and life is left unsolved. In "**Toshishun,**" the conflicts presented are among the selfish pursuit of beauty (art), the transcendence of life (immortality), and humanity (life). Akutagawa clearly states that the aspiration for humanity is more valuable than the other two.

Akutagawa was torn between art and life throughout his life. Unlike Tanizaki, who chose to live in a way that would serve his art, and Shiga Naoya, who used art to attain a higher realization of life, Akutagawa despaired of life in human society from his early years and wished to live the condensed life of a line of poetry, while remaining aware of and torn by the sacrifice of humanity such a life would demand.

In one of his later works, "**Shūzan zu**" ("**The Autumn Mountain**" . . .), Akutagawa even considers art to be an illusion; a masterpiece of art is certainly the product of man's imagination dreaming of the ideal, perfect beauty, but the actual work may not exist at all. The conflict between art and life presented in the case of "**The Hell Screen**" no longer exists here. Art is meaningful not because of itself but because man aspires for it. The question of realism Akutagawa raised in "**The Hell Screen,**" the question of the artist's need to see reality in order to paint it, is also dismissed here. The significance of art is reduced to the point of denying art, for art without visible work is no longer art. "**Toshishun**" reflects Akutagawa's turning toward life, moving away from his belief in art for art's sake.

The central theme of "**Toshishun**" is indeed a theme in Akutagawa's own life as an artist. In the place of realism and confession, Akutagawa used an old tale to dramatize his own search. He thus converted the classical Chinese tale into a short story which contained his own quest and his own clear message. By confining the work clearly within the framework of the ancient tale and directing it to young adults, Akutagawa was able to avoid being didactic despite the existence of a moral. In "**Toshishun,**" Akutagawa successfully combined brilliant storytelling with the presentation of a symbolic situation in which the quest of modern man can be dramatized. In his search for a method to dramatize his quest for reality and self, Akutagawa revived the tradition of storytelling in fiction, a tradition which had been lost in the era of modern realism and naturalism. (pp. 53-4)

Noriko Mizuta Lippit, "From Tale to Short Story: Akutagawa's 'Toshishun' and Its Chinese Origins," in her Reality and Fiction in Modern Japanese Literature, *M. E. Sharpe Inc., 1980, pp. 39-54.*

DONALD KEENE (essay date 1984)

[*An American critic and educator, Keene is one of the foremost translators and critics of Japanese literature. In the following excerpt, he traces the various stages of Akutagawa's career, with particular emphasis on the historical periods which Akutagawa used as sources for his works, and on the contemporary writers who influenced him.*]

The most striking literary figure of the fifteen years of the Taishō era was Akutagawa Ryūnosuke. . . . He established his reputation early in his brief career, and even when his style and manner had greatly changed he retained his hold on the mass of readers. His short stories, especially those of the early period, have acquired the status of classics, and are read in the schools and frequently reprinted. (p. 556)

[Akutagawa's early style] was in fact more distinguished than that employed by most translators at the time. His first original story, "**Rōnen**" ("**Old Age**" . . .), which . . . appeared in *Shinshichō,* already suggested the crisp, precise style of his major works. (p. 558)

"**Rashōmon**" appeared in the November 1915 issue of *Teikoku Bungaku (Imperial Literature),* [a] Tokyo Imperial University literary magazine. Akutagawa's friends were merciless in their criticism; one even wrote him a letter, urging Akutagawa to give up writing altogether. Such criticism induced him to make various alterations in the manuscript, mainly deletions in the interest of concision, but it is extraordinary that Akutagawa's closest friends should have been so insensitive to what became one of his most popular and admired stories.

The description of the Rashōmon gate in *Konjaku Monogatari,* the twelfth-century collection of tales from which Akutagawa had derived his basic material, is extremely brief, only a dozen or so lines; he augmented it from other sources. The setting of "**Rashōmon**" is Kyoto in the twelfth century, when the great buildings of the capital were sometimes broken up for firewood, and desperate men turned to banditry or even murder in order to stay alive in a time of disorder and violence. (pp. 558-59)

The story is given its effectiveness by the vividness of Akutagawa's evocation of the age, as much as by the details he found in *Konjaku Monogatari.* He borrowed also from the descriptions in *Hōjōki (An Account of My Hut)* of the famine and other disasters of the time, but it is apparent on examination that his story owed comparatively little to such borrowings; the psychology of the man and the overtones of the story owe more to Akutagawa's readings in European literature. Akutagawa some years later explained why he had set such works as "**Rashōmon,**" which are essentially modern in outlook, in the distant Japanese past:

> Supposing I have thought of some particular theme and decide to write a story about it. In order to express this theme as artistically and strikingly as possible, I must include unusual incidents. The more unusual the incidents, the harder it will be to describe them convincingly as events of present-day Japan. If an author nevertheless insists on making a modern story out of such events, it generally seems unnatural to readers, and the result is that his carefully chosen theme drops by the wayside. A short story, unlike a fairy tale, has certain requirements peculiar to the genre; the author simply cannot write "once upon a time" and let the background go at that. In practice this means that something akin to restrictions of period are established, and it becomes necessary therefore

to introduce social conditions of the time, at least to the degree of satisfying the requirement that the story seem natural and plausible. Stories of this kind can be distinguished from "historical novels" in that they in no sense aim at a re-creation of the past. I might mention in this connection that—as the reader will easily guess from the above—I feel no great yearning for the past even when I write about distant times. I am far luckier to have been born in present-day Japan than in the Heian or Edo periods.

Most of Akutagawa's popular stories were set in the past. His favorite historical periods were the twelfth century, when Kyoto was wasted by disasters; the late sixteenth century, when Christian influence was at its height in Nagasaki; and the beginning of the Meiji era, when European culture was uncritically adopted, especially in Tokyo, the new capital. Akutagawa was always at pains to create an impression of verisimilitude by supplying details—often harsh or cruel—drawn directly from accounts in such works as *Konjaku Monogatari.* Sometimes his fondness for unusual effects (suggested by the passage quoted above) induced him to indulge in sensationalism. When this method was successful, as in **"Rashōmon"** and a dozen other stories, Akutagawa created unforgettable vignettes of the past, as filtered through the mind of a modern Japanese who knew Western literature well. Sometimes he tried too hard. One of his longest stories, **"Chūtō"** (**"The Bandits"** . . .), is set in the same period as **"Rashōmon,"** and opens with the description of a sultry summer day in Kyoto:

> The tracks of an ox-cart that had passed by not long before wound off into the distance. A small snake, run over by the cart, for a time had twitched its tail, the flesh of its gaping wound turning green, but now it lay motionless, not a scale stirring, its greasy belly exposed. If there was one spot of moisture visible on this dusty street, under the burning sky, it was the raw-smelling, putrescent liquid oozing from the snake's wound.

The snake, a symbol of the city of Kyoto, mortally wounded and festering, recurs again and again in the story, together with another symbolic figure, a sick woman, apparently a victim of the epidemic, who lies more dead than alive in a wretched hut, her body marked by toothmarks from ravenous hounds. Some children find the snake lying in the dust, and a mischievous little boy slings it into the sick woman's hut. "The greenish, greasy belly slapped against the woman's cheek, and the tail, wet with putrescent liquid, slid over her face."

The reader is sooner or later numbed by the reiteration of such details, and the rest of the story is on the same level. . . . Akutagawa's inability to make something more impressive of his longest story suggests his limitations as a writer, and clearly demonstrates that a mere accumulation of the kind of details that made **"Rashōmon"** memorable was not enough to make a work succeed.

Not all of Akutagawa's early stories are in this ghastly vein. His first popular success, in fact, was scored with **"Hana"** (**"The Nose"** . . .), an amusing story of a priest whose nose is five or six inches long, and of his efforts to shorten the nose. (pp. 559-61)

"The Nose" was also derived from *Konjaku Monogatari,* and there may have been influence from Gogol's story "The Nose" (1835). But the composition as a whole owes much to Akutagawa's ability to combine the grotesque and the humorous without being too obvious. Natsume Sōseki read the work in *Shinshichō* and was so impressed that he wrote Akutagawa a letter expressing his admiration. (pp. 561-62)

Sōseki's letter, written in February 1916, praised the novelty of the materials, the skill of his terse style, and Akutagawa's ability to be humorous without forcing. He urged Akutagawa to write more stories in the same vein, cautioning him that he must not worry even if **"The Nose"** failed at first to attract much attention. Sōseki predicted that if Akutagawa could write twenty or thirty such stories he would establish an absolutely unique reputation. He urged Akutagawa to follow his own path without taking into account the possible reactions of the mass of readers. (p. 562)

Critics have claimed to detect resemblances between Sōseki's late works and those stories by Akutagawa that deal with the problem of egoism. In **"Karenoshō"** (**"Withered Fields"** . . .), for example, Akutagawa described Bashō's disciples gathered around the bedside of their dying master in these terms:

> Even as they were watching over the last moments of their teacher, each was absorbed with thoughts of possible repercussions of the master's death on other schools, the advantages and disadvantages to his own pupils, and similar calculations of self-interest that were not directly related to their master, now in his last moments. . . . The disciples were grieving not for their teacher but for themselves, for having lost their teacher.

Such analyses of self-interest had preoccupied Sōseki, but egoism as a theme need not have been learned from Sōseki: no writer has gone beyond La Rochefoucauld in detecting the base considerations that influence people even when they seem to be acting in the most disinterested or noble manner. Clearly Akutagawa had his own personal interest in the problem of egoism, but it may have been because of Sōseki that he continued to emphasize it as a theme of his writings. (pp. 562-63)

Akutagawa was more conspicuously influenced by Mori Ōgai. The style of his early works is so indebted to Ōgai's that one critic believed it would be more accurate to speak of imitation, rather than of influence. This critic, the novelist Nakamura Shin'ichirō, went on to state:

> Akutagawa Ryūnosuke's special virtue as a new writer lay, more than in anything else, in his dry, intellectual manner of dealing with his subjects. The strongest influence Mori Ōgai exerted on Akutagawa, in fact, was embedded in the very foundations of Akutagawa's creative formation as an author. It may be detected, for example, in the way he preserved his distance from his subjects. If this analysis is correct, it means that Ōgai handed over to Akutagawa the key for unlocking the secrets of modern literature, and that *Ōgai created Akutagawa.* In that case, this event brought about an important advance in the stages of the Japanese absorption of Western literature.

Letters from Akutagawa to his friends written as early as 1913 plainly reveal with what special interest he read Ōgai's historical fiction. The attitudes the two men adopted with respect to historical materials were, however, fundamentally quite dissimilar. Ōgai's historical fiction, even at its freest, never ignored historical fact, but Akutagawa used the past mainly as the springboard for elaborations and inventions, and he was attracted to distant times and places because of the possibilities they afforded to treat the unusual, the supernatural, or the miraculous. His art has been compared to that of the waka poets of the past who, borrowing some theme familiar from earlier poetry, imparted to it their distinctive, modern sensibility.

The success of **"The Nose"** encouraged Akutagawa to write other historical works with comic overtones. The most popular was **"Imogayu"** (**"Yam Gruel"** . . .), the first work he wrote after his graduation from Tokyo Imperial University. Like so many other early stories, **"Yam Gruel"** had its origins in *Konjaku Monogatari (Stories of Times Now Long Ago)*, but Akutagawa's ironic attitude toward his materials owed little to this source. This is the story of Goi, a scruffy, minor official who normally eats mainly the leavings from the banquets of his superiors. Goi's dream is to eat his fill of yam gruel, a dish that was probably more appetizing than it sounds. Another official, a rough and powerful man, promises to provide Goi with all the yam gruel he can eat. The two men travel a great distance to the other man's estate where, as promised, an immense quantity of yam gruel is prepared for Goi's delectation. But the sight of so much yam gruel quite takes away Goi's appetite; as so often in Akutagawa's stories, the realization of a dream brings not satisfaction but disillusionment.

Akutagawa was obviously not interested in presenting a convincing portrayal of life among the petty officials of the late Heian period. Goi is a not unfamiliar figure in contemporary society, and his disillusion is described in the literary works of every country; no doubt it was this universality that so appealed to Akutagawa in the theme. Sōseki wrote Akutagawa his impressions of **"Yam Gruel"** not long after it appeared. He found the plot "too labored," and the style overingenious. But he praised Akutagawa's techniques, saying they were second to no writer's. Akutagawa's mastery of the short story won him an exceptionally large following for so young a writer, but he was most often admired for his faults: the overingenuity that Sōseki criticized, his seeming inability to resist adding a surprise ending where none was needed.

Another, more crucial weakness was Akutagawa's lack of originality. He was likened, even by admiring critics, to a mosaicist, piecing together fresh masterpieces out of the materials gleaned from many books. Sometimes the list of "sources" for a single story, as uncovered by diligent scholars, is so extensive that one can only marvel that any author could fuse together so many disparate elements. . . . Akutagawa relied more on books than on his imagination or his personal experiences when writing the short stories of this period. Later in his career a seeming inability to invent materials forced him to draw on even the most trivial incidents of his life. One critic went so far as to suggest that despair over his lack of imaginative resources may have been an important cause of Akutagawa's suicide.

Too much should not be made, however, of Akutagawa's reliance on foreign sources. Even when a scholar has identified to his own satisfaction the origins of some section of an Akutagawa story, there is generally no question of direct imitation.

Shimada Kinji, for example, believed that the climactic scene in Akutagawa's story **"Jigokuhen"** (**"Hell Screen"** . . .)—the burning alive of a beautiful woman in a court carriage—was inspired by the novel by D. S. Merezhkovski, *The Forerunner, the Romance of Leonardo da Vinci*. Shimada's arguments are persuasive, but even if a Japanese translation of Merezhkovski's novel inspired Akutagawa, his central theme—that the artist must personally experience what he describes, though this may entail the most terrible sacrifices—was surely Akutagawa's conviction anyway. The apparent identification of the author with Yoshihide, the painter in **"Hell Screen,"** gives this story a moving quality absent from most other works of this period, however skillfully constructed or stylistically distinguished. (pp. 563-66)

Another important group of historical stories is set in Nagasaki during the period of greatest Christian influence, at the end of the sixteenth century. **"Death of a Martyr"** is written in a style closely modeled on that of a version of *The Tale of the Heike* published at that time by the Jesuit Mission Press. Akutagawa attempted to convey with this style the compelling innocence of the legends of the saints. The young Lorenzo, who has mysteriously appeared at the Church of Santa Lucia in Nagasaki, revealing nothing of his past, is accepted as a monk and leads a life of conspicuous sanctity. One day, however, a girl of the town, also a Christian believer, declares that Lorenzo is her lover. He denies this, but when the girl reveals she is pregnant, no one believes his gentle protestations. Lorenzo is ordered to leave the church and takes shelter in a wretched hovel nearby, scorned and detested by all. Some months later a fire breaks out in the house where the unmarried girl and her baby live. In the confusion she forgets the baby. Another priest, a man of unusual strength, braves the flames, intending to rescue the baby, but the blazing heat forces him back. Suddenly Lorenzo appears and, dashing into the flaming house, retrieves the baby. The contrite girl now reveals she has lied—Lorenzo is not the father of her child. But her confession comes too late. Lorenzo is dying, badly burned. As people gather around him, marveling at his fortitude and self-sacrifice, his tattered garment falls apart, revealing a woman's breasts. All cry out in astonishment at this unanswerable proof that Lorenzo was unjustly accused and punished, and they kneel before the dying woman. With a smile on her lips she breathes her last, confident in her salvation.

The reverence with which Akutagawa treated Christian materials contrasts with the cynicism he often displayed toward Japanese heroes and paragons of samurai behavior. He found something especially appealing in beliefs that transcended the realm of ordinary human virtue, about which he had grave doubts, and envied people of the Middle Ages whose religion enabled them to make sense of the seemingly irreconcilable elements in ordinary daily life. Egoism could be transcended through divine grace, but not by a careful observance of any code of etiquette. (pp. 568-69)

Akutagawa's third variety of historical fiction treated the Japan of the early Meiji era. These stories are colored by a nostalgia for what seemed to be a remote age, though it was only forty or fifty years before. During the 1870s and 1880s fashionable Japanese ladies and gentlemen built themselves homes modeled on Victorian domestic architecture, dressed in Western-style clothes, chatted knowingly about European fashions, and prided themselves on their associations with titled foreigners. In Akutagawa's day, however, the Japanese lived in Japanese-style homes with perhaps one foreign room, tended to wear kimonos, and had very few social contacts with Europeans. The extreme adulation of the West of the early Meiji era had come to seem picturesque, and Akutagawa described it with almost the same sense of distance as in his accounts of sixteenth-century Nagasaki. **"Kaika no Satsujin" ("A Murder During the Age of Enlightenment"** . . .) was the first of his stories set in this period. It is absurdly overplotted, reminiscent of the early Izumi Kyōka, and cannot be taken seriously as a work of literature.

"Butōkai" ("The Ball" . . .) is more successful. Akiko, who has just turned seventeen this year of 1886, is taken by her father to a ball at the Rokumeikan. She has learned some French, knows ballroom dancing, and wears her elegant Western gown with assurance. A young French naval officer asks permission to dance with her. When she has tired they sit outside talking. He remarks that the ball at the Rokumeikan is exactly like one in Paris, or anywhere else. As they talk, they see fireworks, a part of the evening's entertainment. The young Frenchman, watching the skyrockets cascade, compares their brief moment of brilliance to human life itself. In the concluding section of the story a young novelist meets Akiko, now Mrs. H, in the autumn of 1918, and she tells him about that night at the Rokumeikan. He asks if she remembers the name of the French officer. "Indeed I do," she says, "his name was Julien Viaud." "Then, he was Loti, the author of *Madame Chrysanthème.*" "No," Mrs. H replies, "his name was not Loti. He was called Julien Viaud."

Akiko is uninterested in the historical fact that Viaud and Loti were the same person. He has lived so long in her memory as Julien Viaud that it is of no significance to her that the Viaud she knew later became the famous novelist Loti. Akutagawa's manner of treating the past was similar; his aim was always poetic truth, rather than historical accuracy. The young French officer's comparison of human life to fireworks also represented one of Akutagawa's convictions. He used the image of fireworks again and again as a simile for human life, especially in his late works, and otherwise expressed his belief that a whole life may be contained in one perfect moment. Elsewhere he stated, "Human life cannot compare with a single line by Baudelaire." (pp. 570-71)

["Yabu no Naka" ("Within a Grove")] demonstrated that Akutagawa retained his skill at handling historical materials. Once again he turned to the *Konjaku Monogatari* for the basic story, but he gave the materials depth and freshness by arranging them in the form of testimony from various persons concerning an event in which three of them—a samurai, his wife, and a bandit—had directly participated. The accounts differ widely, each person naturally describing his actions in the most favorable manner. It has been suggested that Akutagawa's technique of narrating a single story from several viewpoints was inspired by Robert Browning's *The Ring and the Book*. But even if this work influenced the conception of **"Within a Grove,"** Akutagawa's contribution can hardly be disputed. The most striking of the seven accounts of the crime is given by the dead samurai who, speaking through the mouth of a medium, relates how he was tricked by the bandit, trussed, then forced to watch as the bandit violated his wife. He accuses the wife of having not merely been a willing victim but of having urged the bandit to kill him. He finally describes how the bandit ran off, appalled by the wife's inhumanity, and how he himself committed suicide with the dagger his wife had dropped, unable to endure the humiliation. (pp. 571-72)

The stories written [after Akutagawa's assignment in China, and the onset of his ill health] are in a distinctly different vein from his earlier fiction. **"Torokko" ("The Hand Car")** is the deceptively simple story of a boy who helps some railway workmen push a hand car. At first he is exhilarated by the ride, especially when the car coasts downhill, but after they have traveled a considerable distance the two men reveal that they are not making a return trip and they leave the boy. Bewildered, he is assailed by such loneliness and fear that he all but bursts into tears as he makes his way home alone in the gathering darkness. **"The Hand Car"** is strikingly like Shiga Naoya's short story "Manazuru" (1920), which tells of two small brothers who have gone to a nearby town to buy presents for themselves and are overtaken by darkness on the way home. Both stories are set on the Izu Peninsula, and surely it was no coincidence that Akutagawa chose a theme so similar to Shiga's. (pp. 572-73)

The stories that immediately followed **"The Hand Car"** included two set in the past, the Heian period and the early Meiji era, but these were Akutagawa's last mining in familiar veins. **"The Hand Car,"** on the other hand, was the forerunner, especially in its quiet, undramatic manner, of a series of autobiographical stories, which were no doubt influenced by Shiga's success with his "I novels." In these stories Akutagawa called himself Yasukichi, and he related mainly his experiences as an English instructor at the Naval Engineering College in Yokosuka from 1916 to 1919. **"Yasukichi no Techō kara" ("From Yasukichi's Notebooks"** . . .) is typical of the series, an almost plotless work that is awkwardly constructed and generally uninteresting. Why, we may wonder, should a master of the short story have produced such a dreary work? Probably his poor health had taken its toll: Akutagawa seems to have been too exhausted to attempt to work with more imaginative materials, and writing about himself may have been the one way out of what was otherwise a hopeless impasse. (pp. 573-74)

The Yasukichi stories are occasionally moving, but they do not possess the unique overtones of Shiga's works. Akutagawa could not follow in Shiga's footsteps, but the neurotic "I novels" of his last period are almost unbearably affecting. Even the brief **"Kyō" ("Ill Omens"** . . .), scarcely a page in length, is unforgettable because of Akutagawa's incredibly evocative descriptions of three apparitions that have filled him with dread. (p. 576)

Most of Akutagawa's remaining stories were openly autobiographical. The chief exception is the novella ***Kappa,*** a satire rather in the vein of Anatole France's *Penguin Island*. The mistakes and hypocrisy of human society are ridiculed by the distorted or exaggerated forms they take in a nonhuman world. The kappa, a kind of water sprite, figures prominently in Japanese folktales. Despite their grotesque appearance—part human, part bird, part reptile—they are sufficiently human to seem plausible when fulfilling the roles of artists, capitalists, students, and so on in Akutagawa's imaginary world. Some passages are amusing, making telling thrusts at current mores, but on the whole ***Kappa*** is a depressing work, not only because its humor is so joyless, but because it betrays a lack of resourcefulness that would have been unthinkable in the earlier Akutagawa. (p. 580)

Akutagawa's stories were translated into European languages even during the long arid period from the early 1920s to the mid-1950s, when hardly any modern Japanese literature was translated, and his name was known abroad. His early stories do not always stand up to repeated readings, but their effectiveness, even in translation, is undeniable. The works of the middle period, as yet little translated, are often hardly more than sketches brought to life by a single haunting touch, an unforgettable observation, or a devastating association. But it is the autobiographical works of the late years that are probably Akutagawa's most enduring testament, though they lack the brilliance of the earlier works. No one can read them without recognizing in Akutagawa a quality at once peculiarly modern and peculiarly tragic. In his last works he surrendered the skills that were his birthright and gained with his death a lonely immortality. (pp. 588-89)

> *Donald Keene, "Akutagawa Ryūnosuke," in his* Dawn to the West: Japanese Literature of the Modern Era, Fiction, Vol. 1, *Holt, Rinehart and Winston, 1984, pp. 556-93.*

ADDITIONAL BIBLIOGRAPHY

Morrison, John W. "Intellectuals and Independents: Akutagawa, Kikuchi, Yamamoto." In his *Modern Japanese Fiction*, pp. 88-101. Salt Lake City: University of Utah Press, 1955.*
> Compares the works of Akutagawa, Kan Kikuchi, and Yuzo Yamamoto, three Japanese authors who chose to perfect style and technique rather than build consistent philosophies in their writings.

Yamanouchi, Hisaaki. "The Rivals: Shiga Naoya and Akutagawa Ryūnosuke." In his *The Search for Authenticity in Modern Japanese Literature*, pp. 82-106. Cambridge: Cambridge University Press, 1978.*
> Details the differences between the authors' literary styles as well as their accomplishments as short story writers.

Randolph S(illiman) Bourne

1886-1918

(Also wrote under pseudonyms of Max Coe, Aurelius Bloomfield, and Juvenis) American essayist and critic.

Bourne was one of the twentieth century's most astute and visionary critics of American life and letters. During his brief career his writings established him as a leader of the youth movement that swept across American college campuses in the decade preceding World War I and which transformed New York's Greenwich Village into a mecca for modern artists and avant-garde intellectuals. In such works as *Youth and Life*, Bourne's eloquent defense of the youth of his era from the attacks of an older generation—which was dismayed by a growing trend toward religious agnosticism, Whitmanian exultation of personality, and a search for liberation from many traditional elements of American life—made him a hero to many of his contemporaries. From his platform at *The New Republic* and other progressivist publications, Bourne spoke out with authority and insight in favor of social justice, educational reform, and a new, pragmatic American culture. When confronted with the tragedy of the First World War, Bourne broke with many of his fellow liberals by strongly opposing American involvement in the conflict on the grounds that the war would benefit only the industrialists and militarists, while undermining American democracy and disrupting the nation's cultural and social growth. In the years since Bourne's death, his courage in opposing what he perceived to be an unjust and unmitigatedly destructive conflict, the depth of his critical insights, and the prophetic nature of many of his writings on American culture have combined with his unusual personal history to make him a legendary figure in the history of American dissent.

Bourne was born in Bloomfield, New Jersey, in 1886. His mother, Sarah Barrett Bourne, was descended from an old New Jersey family of puritan ancestry, while his father, Charles Rogers Bourne, was also from an established family with deep roots in the Bloomfield area. Bourne, the oldest of their four children, was badly deformed at birth through the carelessness of the attending physician, whose mismanagement of a forceps delivery resulted in the twisting of Randolph's face and ear. When he was four years old, Bourne contracted spinal tuberculosis, which left him dwarfed and hunch-backed. Bourne's physical afflictions were compounded by his family's difficult circumstances. After suffering several severe setbacks in business, Bourne's father approached his well-to-do brother-in-law, Halsey Barrett, for financial assistance in 1896. Barrett agreed to support his sister and her children on the condition that Bourne's father leave and never return. After Charles Bourne consented to these conditions, the family split apart, and Bourne saw his father only rarely after this time. His father's disgrace and failure to live up to the strict standards of Bloomfield's Victorian middle class affected Bourne deeply, and his disenchantment, in later years, with America's puritanical "business civilization," in which economic failure was often equated with moral weakness, was partly founded on this bitter childhood memory. Throughout his childhood, Bourne endeavored to live normally in spite of his handicaps. He attended public school, where he studied Latin and Greek along with literature and the sciences and learned, through torturous efforts, "to

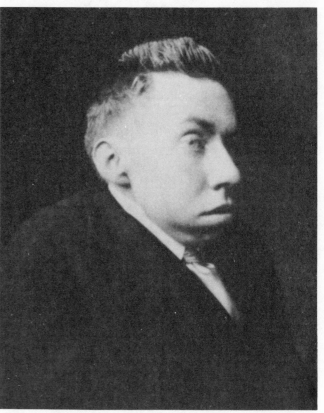

skate, to climb trees, to play ball." He was a talented pianist, and was well enough liked by his schoolmates to be elected president of his high school class.

In 1903 Bourne passed the entrance exams for Princeton University, but his uncle viewed a college education for a handicapped man as a wasteful extravagance, and refused him any further support. Consequently, instead of going on to Princeton, Bourne set out to find a job. For the next six years he worked wherever he could obtain employment, though people were often reluctant to hire him because of his disabilities. His experiences during this period with an unfair employer in a shop that made sheet music for player pianos deepened his sympathy with laborers who lived at the mercy of the piecework system, and provided the basis for one of his best-known essays, "What is Exploitation?"

In 1909 Bourne received a scholarship to Columbia University. There he came under the influence of such well-known scholars and philosophers as Charles Beard, James Harvey Robinson, John Dewey, and Frederick P. Keppel. Dewey, in particular, impressed Bourne with his philosophy of instrumentalism, which was a branch of Pragmatism, a philosophy developed by William James that stressed practical consequences as the most important criterion in determining the meaning, truth, or value of an idea. Instrumentalism similarly stressed the importance of practical consequences, but Dewey's approach centered more on active problem solving and human progress. Bourne was greatly excited by Dewey's ideas, seeing instrumentalism as a welcome liberation from the Protestant absolutism that he had grown up with in Bloomfield, and adopting it as if it were a "new American religion." Bourne believed strongly that instrumentalist philosophy held the key to social progress, and many of the ideas he later expressed in works such as *Youth and Life* and *Education and Living* were derived directly from Dewey, and reflected his desire to help popularize Dewey's thought.

Bourne's career at Columbia was extremely successful. While there he was elected to the Phi Beta Kappa society, joined several student literary organizations, and was awarded the university's Gildern Fellowship, which provided him with money for a year of study and travel abroad. His essay "Impressions of Europe, 1913-14," is based on the papers he presented to the Columbia faculty upon his return, and it reflects his enthusiasm for the social and intellectual reform movements that he found engaging the interest of young people all over Europe. Bourne also began his professional writing career while at Columbia. In 1910 he became a regular contributor to the campus magazine, the *Columbia Monthly,* and in 1911, at the request of Dean Frederick Woodbridge, he submitted an article to the prestigious *Atlantic Monthly* in reply to an attack on youth that had recently appeared in that publication. Bourne's article, "The Two Generations," was well received, and *The Atlantic* published seven more of Bourne's essays over the next two years. These pieces, together with material gleaned from his *Columbia Monthly* columns, formed the basis for his first book, *Youth and Life,* published in 1913.

Youth and Life established Bourne as the champion and chief spokesperson of the younger generation. In it, Bourne introduced two themes that recur constantly in his later works: the conflict of generations as a sociological force, and moral relativism. In *Youth and Life* Bourne described the power struggle between youth, whom he saw as the incarnation of reason and the scientific attitude, and an older generation steeped in rigid traditions and moral inertia. Bourne addressed his message to "radical youth," whom he distinguished from the "traditional" youth who sacrifices adventure and spiritual awareness for the sake of security, bidding them to put their desire and vision to work to regenerate the social order. The new society that Bourne envisioned as a result of youth's victory would not only benefit "the weak and exploited," but would fulfill the desire of youth for a "healthy, free, social life," and its "artistic longing for a society where the treasures of civilization may be open to all," as well as its "desire for an environment where we ourselves will be able to exercise our capacities, and exert the untrammeled influences which we believe might be ours and our fellows'." This idealistic portrayal of youth and its aspirations was well received even by conservative critics, who recognized elements of the philosophies of Henry David Thoreau and Ralph Waldo Emerson in Bourne's writings. Recent critics continue to view *Youth and Life* as a remarkably insightful and stirring work which is still capable of arousing the spirits of youth today. For example, Sherman Paul has noted that Bourne "anticipated or confirmed the advanced thought of men like Ortega, Erikson, and Paul Goodman, for he recognized the concept of the generation and its historical, social, and psychological components." However, the most revolutionary aspect of Bourne's book was not his conception of the conflict of generations, but his moral relativism, which grew out of his admiration for James's philosophy of Pragmatism.

In *Youth and Life* Bourne extended the Pragmatist doctrine into the moral realm and proposed a relativistic approach to moral questions. He believed that both individuals and society would benefit if people would concern themselves only with those evils that human interests and ideals could correct, and dispense with the burdensome and insoluble problem of "metaphysical evil" altogether. Bourne believed that the older generation was obsessed with the notion of personal sin at the same time that it tolerantly endured every type of social injustice, and he exhorted his generation to reverse this situation by utilizing the principles of Pragmatism in combination with its superior social conscience. As Vitelli points out, there is an implicit challenge to the American ideal of progress in Bourne's position, as well as an unspoken condemnation of the American "business civilization" with its emphasis on personal gain. Bourne's genuinely radical suggestions, aimed at eliminating the cowardice and complacency that he saw undermining American democracy, were overlooked and underestimated by some of his earliest critics. However, they are important to note if one is to understand Bourne's antiwar stance and his intellectual position in such later writings as *The History of a Literary Radical.*

Bourne published only two other books in his lifetime: *The Gary Schools* and *Education and Living.* In writing the essays collected in *The Gary Schools,* Bourne fulfilled an assignment for *The New Republic,* which had asked him to report on an experiment in education conducted by William Wirt in the schools of Gary, Indiana. Wirt's plan for providing children with an individualized educational experience—one grounded in the belief that children are not "empty vessels to be filled by knowledge" but are, rather, "pushing wills and desires and curiosities . . . living growing things"—was based largely on the instrumentalist principles advanced by John Dewey, and in *The Gary Schools* Bourne endorsed Wirt's approach enthusiastically. However, critics of Wirt's plan soon pointed out many inequities in it that Bourne had overlooked, and it never received wider implementation. Nevertheless, *The Gary Schools* and the later *Education and Living,* in which Bourne applied the same sorts of educational principles to a discussion of issues connected with colleges and universities, did much to popularize Dewey's theories, and to make his educational philosophies known. It is on the basis of these two books that Bourne is sometimes regarded by critics as being primarily an exponent of Dewey's theories, despite the fact that a disillusionment with Dewey is obvious in his later writings, particularly in his essay "The Twilight of Idols," published in the journal *The Seven Arts* in 1917. Although Bourne also wrote literary criticism, critics agree that his judgments in this field were largely colored by his social concerns, a fact which diminishes the value of these works for those who accept the principle of "art for art's sake." Nevertheless, the wit and insight in these essays, many of which appeared in *The History of a Literary Radical,* make them interesting and instructive, according to many critics.

Bourne's mature writings, collected after his death in *The History of a Literary Radical* and *Untimely Papers,* represent his most important contribution to American culture. Many of these essays first appeared in such periodicals as *The Dial, The New Republic, The Atlantic,* and, in the case of the *Untimely Papers* essays, *The Seven Arts,* a journal which ultimately lost its financial backing and folded as a consequence of having published Bourne's antiwar essays during World War I. By 1915, Bourne had begun commenting in these various periodicals on the spectacle of the war in Europe, attacking in the process such popular American myths as the theory of "the melting pot.'' Bourne's purpose in this was to inspire his readers to look beyond the narrow-minded nationalism that had led to the outbreak of the European war, and to adopt instead a cosmopolitan ideal that would enable the United States to develop into a nation where people of various ethnic backgrounds could retain their own ''living and potential cultures,'' but still work together to produce a vigorous, diverse, and uniquely American culture. Although this statement describes an approach to American culture that is widely popular today, it was regarded as shockingly radical by many of Bourne's contemporaries, who viewed the wave of immigrants who came to the United States early in this century with fear and dislike. Bourne's writings from this period abound in ideas of this type, leading essayist Henry Fairlie to designate Bourne as ''the prophet of solutions only now being tried.''

By 1916, Bourne noted that many of his colleagues, including John Dewey and *New Republic* editor Herbert Croly, had begun to write about the war in terms of a great moral crusade, and to portray American intervention in the conflict as inevitable. Bourne responded to this with a series of essays in which, as Fairlie has observed, ''the fierceness of the conviction still scorches.'' Bourne objected strongly to American involvement in the war on the grounds that the existence of a war state was detrimental to democracy. He believed that the propaganda and the nationalistic emotion generated during a war stifled dissent and clouded legitimate social issues, thus benefiting the militarists and the wealthy classes. Angered by what he considered a betrayal by American liberals, some of whom held that they had themselves guided America into war and that they could control the progress, outcome, and aftermath of the war through the force of their collective enlightened opinion, Bourne flared back at the very idea of ''an intellectual class, gently guiding a nation through sheer force of ideas into what other nations entered only through predatory craft or popular hysteria or military madness.'' These views and the outspoken acerbity with which he expressed them cost Bourne his influential position at *The New Republic,* to which he had regularly contributed since the magazine's inception in 1914, and much of his popular support as well. Despite the angered claims of his opponents on both the American left and the right, Bourne was neither a socialist nor a communist, but, in his own words, an intellectual radical, who believed that the role of the intellectual in society was to remain aloof from political and economic concerns, and to keep the public informed on the meaning of events in these sectors by criticizing them from a detached vantage point. Thus Bourne believed that the intellectual class, in supporting the war, had betrayed not only its moral responsibility as leaders and teachers of American society, but the deeper principles of pragmatism, which Bourne had always interpreted as a philosophy concerned with just ends, and not just a shallow method for achieving the efficient mastery of means. This explains Bourne's deep disillusionment with Dewey, who not only became one of the chief apologists for the government's war policy, but profited personally by conforming to this position, as did many others. Bourne joined with the rest of America in celebrating the Armistice of November 1918, declaring that, with the war over, even the air in America seemed ''blither and freer.'' But he died less than two months after the war's end, stricken during the nationwide influenza epidemic of 1918—an epidemic believed to have been caused, ironically for Bourne, by the homecoming of infected American soldiers.

Of all Bourne's writings, it is primarily his essays on war that remain of interest today because of the gift that Bourne evi-

denced for penetrating the propaganda and emotional confusion of his era, and for correctly identifying issues that are still debated by contemporary scholars and philosophers. For while the liberals of Bourne's era argued that only by taking an active role in such things as politics and economics can one hope to manipulate them, Bourne raised the deeper question of values. He maintained that the abandonment of one's values in an effort to manipulate events brings with it the danger of being caught up and overwhelmed by the stream of circumstances. Considering his war essays, critics note that Bourne addressed major issues which have reechoed throughout the history of the twentieth century: in Dwight Eisenhower's warning about the ''military-industrial complex,'' in the criticism of the Vietnam war, and in concern over increased military growth. Critics consider it astonishing that in 1917, at the birth of the modern era, Bourne was able to correctly identify and examine so many of the issues that have plagued numerous societies throughout the century.

PRINCIPAL WORKS

Youth and Life (essays) 1913
The Gary Schools (essays) 1916
Education and Living (essays) 1917
Untimely Papers (essays) 1919
The History of a Literary Radical, and Other Essays
    (essays) 1920
War and the Intellectuals: Collected Essays 1915-1919
    (essays) 1964
The Letters of Randolph Bourne (letters) 1981

THE DIAL (essay date 1913)

[*In the following excerpt, an anonymous critic favorably reviews Bourne's first book,* Youth and Life, *praising it as a promising start for a new figure in the field of American letters. For a more in-depth discussion of* Youth and Life, *see the excerpt by James R. Vitelli (1981).*]

[In] his sober and thoughtful book of essays, ***Youth and Life*** . . . Mr. Randolph S. Bourne, a Columbia graduate student, has attempted something of a philosophic interpretation of youth. His temperament and training have led him to dwell upon the higher and more permanent aspects of youthfulness,—those which ought to be preserved throughout life. Chief of these is the *naïveté* of intellectual outlook which means absolute truthfulness, a spiritualized scientific conscience. The moment we substitute policy for this clearness of vision we violate our intellectual integrity. Youthfulness means, therefore, a continual warring of reason against tradition, a conflict of two generations. ''Old men cherish a fond delusion that there is something mystically valuable in mere quantity of experience. Now the fact is, of course, that it is the young people who have all the really valuable experience. It is they who have constantly to face new situations, to react constantly to new aspects of life, who are getting the whole beauty and terror and cruelty of the world in its fresh and undiluted purity.'' To sustain it, this wisdom of youth needs an enthusiastic idealism and a tremendous capacity for resistance and sacrifice. The pressures of society are all in favor of tradition. And so, ''few men remain quite true to themselves. As their youthful ideals come into contact with the harshnesses of life, the brightest succumb and go to the wall. . . . Youth rules the world, but only when it is no longer young. It is a tarnished, travestied youth that is in the saddle in the person of middle age. Old age lives in the delusion that it has improved and rationalized its youthful ideas by experience and stored-up wisdom, when all it has done is to damage them more or less—usually more. And the tragedy of life is that the world is run by these damaged ideals. . . . It is the young only who are actually contemporaneous; they interpret what they see freshly and without prejudice; their vision is always the truest, and their interpretation always the justest." As an essayist, Mr. Bourne has dared erase "Whim" from his lintel. But his style, although restrained, abounds in illuminating epigram and characteristic touches of charm. It is a book of much promise, which marks the arrival of an essayist who can deal with the larger themes with something like finality.

A review of "Youth and Life," in The Dial, Vol. LIV, No. DCXLVI, May 16, 1913, p. 420.

HARRIET MONROE (essay date 1918)

[*As the founder and editor of* Poetry, *Monroe was a key figure in the American "poetry renaissance" which took place in the early twentieth century.* Poetry *was the first periodical devoted primarily to the works of new poets and to poetry criticism, and from 1912 until her death Monroe maintained an editorial policy of printing "the best English verse which is being written today, regardless of where, by whom, or under what theory of art it is written." In the following excerpt, Monroe takes issue with Bourne's essay "Traps for the Unwary" (1918), in which he asserted the need of modern artists for a "new criticism" to save them from the trap of the "genteel tradition."*]

Mr. Randolph Bourne, in a recent issue of *The Dial*, utters a solemn warning about **"Traps for the Unwary."** At first, in passing, he shows the unwary artist the open and obvious traps set by such intemperates as the "philistine" W. C. Brownell and Stuart P. Sherman on one side of the road, and the "blustering" H. L. Mencken on the other. Both extremes, he says, are products of the smothering "genteel tradition," for both represent a "moralism imperfectly transcended." By a process of cancellation, he gently persuades them "to kill each other off."

Their traps, being quite conspicuous with teeth and springs on edge, have ceased, he thinks, to be a menace—even the halt and the blind can avoid them. The real danger is a less evident trap in the dusty middle of the road, a trap set once more, but more beguilingly, by that same "genteel traditon":

> Let us look for the enemy of the literary artist in America today not among the philistines or the puritans, among the animal-obsessed novelists or the dainty professors who make Mr. Mencken profane. . . . For the deadly virus of gentility is carried along by an up-to-date cultivated public—small perhaps, but growing—who are all the more dangerous because they are so hospitable. The would-be literary artist needs to be protected not so much from his enemies as from his friends. Puritan and professor may agree in their disgust at the creative imagination at work in America, but it is not their hostility which keeps it from being freer and more expressive. The confusing force is rather an undiscriminating approval on the part

of a public who want the new without the unsettling. The current popularity of verse, the vogue of the little theatres and the little magazines, reveal a public that is almost pathetically receptive to anything which has the flavor or the pretention of literary art. The striving literary artist is faced by no stony and uncomprehending world. Almost anyone can win recognition and admiration. But where is the criticism that will discriminate between what is fresh, sincere, and creative and what is merely stagy and blatantly rebellious?

There we have it—the "literary artist in America" can escape traps only by putting himself under guidance—the wary guidance of the sound and superior critic: "A new criticism has to be created," etc.

Far be it from us to deny the value of sound criticism. Mr. Bourne, though somewhat over-weighted with glittering generalities, is strictly in order in keeping a watchful eye out for traps, and Miss Lowell's book on *Tendencies,* which he praises, is valuable, whether we agree with her conclusions or not, as an effort to clear the road and set American poetry in its proper array. The only trouble with Mr. Bourne is a natural overemphasis of the critic's importance. The critic *is* important, perhaps over-important, to the public—Mr. Bourne's pathetically hospitable or pathetically contemptuous public which likes to be told what it should think: but he is not very important to the artist, that "desperate spiritual outlaw with the lust to create" whom Mr. Bourne almost intemperately longs for, with—to use his own phrase—"a sort of joyful perversity."

To the artist, I repeat, the critic is not very important, especially the professional critic who would soundly and sanely guide him past all manner of traps. What *is* important to the artist is his chance to be seen or heard, his chance of a frugal living while he is doing his work, his chance of admission to the society of his peers, whoever these may prove to be among the dead or living. These three things the artist must have if he is not to starve physically, mentally or spiritually; and the most well-meaning and highly intellectualized criticism, though proceeding from the Delphic seat of the oracle, cannot give him one of them.

With all due deference to Mr. Bourne, are not "the little theaters and the little magazines," which he so gently deprecates, doing more to supply the essential needs of the poet and the playwright than any amount of "the new criticism" could? We have heard, during the last five years, a chorus of voices uttering criticism new and old, trained voices with every right to competence; but we have yet to hear that any of this clamor has either influenced, or especially served or hindered, any poet or playwright in doing his work. (pp. 90-2)

There is much truth in what Mr. Bourne says of the danger for the artist which lurks in pink-tea adulation and "the impeccable social tone" of certain quasi-literary groups. No one can deny that our good-natured American hospitality sets "an insidious trap—the terrible glamor of social patronage which so easily blunts idealism in the young prophet." Perhaps, however, it is a weak grade of idealism that is so easily blunted, and the true prophet will survive tea and toast as of yore he survived cakes and ale, or sesame seed and Falernian.

In Mr. Bourne's terrors there may be just a hint of that ancient, deep-seated prejudice in favor of penury for a poet. With a few exceptions, the precedents would seem to be against its being an advantage. Few of the great poets of all nations had the bad luck to starve, and most of them endured without quailing "the terrible glamor of social patronage" from kings and courts, millionaires and great ladies. In fact, it is doubtful if the modern American poet or artist runs any more danger from intemperate social influences than Chaucer did, or Holbein, Shakespeare or Sophocles, Phidias or Li Po or Leonardo da Vinci.

Mr. Bourne ends his article with a definition of the kind of man who is to give us "a literary art which will combine a classical and puritan tradition with the most modern ideas." Maybe his rather formidable array of qualities hits off the prodigy—I wouldn't venture to say, because a five-years' intimacy with poets makes me hesitate to affirm or deny anything about them. But I feel quite sure that the prodigy, once achieved, will not worry his mind about getting "intelligent, pertinent, absolutely contemporaneous criticism which shall be both severe and encouraging." That, in spite of Mr. Bourne, is not "the problem of the literary artist," nor will his problem be solved "when the artist himself has turned critic and set to work to discover and interpret in others the motives and values and efforts he feels in himself." He will have more important things than this to do. His problem will be, as it always has been, to get himself expressed in his art, and to get his art before his public. And the only aid which he will recognize is that which forwards these ends. (pp. 93-4)

Harriet Monroe, "Mr. Bourne on Traps," in Poetry, *Vol. XII, No. II, May, 1918, pp. 90-4.*

RANDOLPH BOURNE   (essay date 1918)

[In this excerpt from a thinly disguised autobiographical fragment, Bourne, in the guise of the character Miro, states his objections to "classical" education and discusses what he considers to be the proper role of literature in modern society.]

[Miro] had come from school a serious boy, with more than a touch of priggishness in him, and a vague aspiration to be a "man of letters." He found himself becoming a collector of literary odds-and-ends. If he did not formulate this feeling clearly, he at least knew. He found that the literary life was not as interesting as he had expected. He sought no adventures. When he wrote, it was graceful lyrics or polite criticisms of William Collins or Charles Lamb. These canonized saints of culture still held the field for Miro, however. There was nothing between them and that popular literature of the day that all good men bemoaned. Classic or popular, "highbrow" or "lowbrow," this was the choice, and Miro unquestioningly took the orthodox heaven. In 1912 the most popular of Miro's English professors had never heard of Galsworthy, and another was creating a flurry of scandal in the department by recommending Chesterton to his classes. It would scarcely have been in college that Miro would have learned of an escape from the closed dichotomy of culture. Bored with the "classic," and frozen with horror at the "popular," his career as a man of culture must have come to a dragging end if he had not been suddenly liberated by a chance lecture which he happened to hear while he was at home for the holidays.

The literary radical who appeared before the Lyceum Club of Miro's village was none other than Professor William Lyon Phelps, and it is to that evening of cultural audacity Miro thinks he owes all his later emancipation. The lecturer grappled with the "modern novel," and tossed Hardy, Tolstoi, Turgenev, Meredith, even Trollope, into the minds of the charmed au-

dience with such effect that the virgin shelves of the village library were ravished for days to come by the eager minds upon whom these great names dawned for the first time. "Jude the Obscure" and "Resurrection" were of course kept officially away from the vulgar, but Miro managed to find "Smoke" and "Virgin Soil" and "Anna Karenina" and "The Warden" and "A Pair of Blue Eyes" and "The Return of the Native." Later at college he explored the forbidden realms. It was as if some devout and restless saint had suddenly been introduced to the Apocrypha. A new world was opened to Miro that was neither "classic" nor "popular," and yet which came to one under the most unimpeachable auspices. There was, at first, it is true, an air of illicit adventure about the enterprise. The lecturer who made himself the missionary of such vigorous and piquant doctrine had the air of being a heretic, or at least a boy playing out of school. But Miro himself returned to college a cultural revolutionist. His orthodoxies crumbled. He did not try to reconcile the new with the old. He applied pick and dynamite to the whole structure of the canon. Irony, humor, tragedy, sensuality, suddenly appeared to him as literary qualities in forms that he could understand. They were like oxygen to his soul.

If these qualities were in the books he had been reading, he had never felt them. The expurgated sample-books he had studied had passed too swiftly over the Elizabethans to give him a sense of their lustiness. Miro immersed himself voluptuously in the pessimism of Hardy. He fed on the poignant torture of Tolstoi. While he was reading "Resurrection," his class in literature was making an "intensive" study of Tennyson. It was too much. Miro rose in revolt. He forswore literary courses forever, dead rituals in which anaemic priests mumbled their trite critical commentary. Miro did not know that to naughtier critics even Mr. Phelps might eventually seem a pale and timid Gideon, himself stuck in moral sloughs. He was grateful enough for that blast of trumpets which made his own scholastic walls fall down. .

The next stage in Miro's cultural life was one of frank revolt. He became as violent as a heretic as he had been docile as a believer. Modern novels merely started the rift that widened into modern ideas. The professors were of little use. Indeed, when Miro joined a group of radicals who had started a new college paper, a relentless vendetta began with the teachers. Miro and his friends threw over everything that was mere literature. Social purpose must shine from any writing that was to rouse their enthusiasm. Literary flavor was to be permissible only where it made vivid high and revolutionary thought. Tolstoi became their god, Wells their high priest. Chesterton infuriated them. They wrote violent assaults upon him which began in imitation of his cool paradoxicality and ended in incoherent ravings. There were so many enemies to their new fervor that they scarcely knew where to begin. There were not only the old tables of stone to destroy, but there were new and threatening prophets of the eternal verities who had to be exposed. The nineteenth century which they had studied must be weeded of its nauseous moralists. The instructors consulted together how they might put down the revolt, and bring these sinners back to the faith of cultural scripture.

It was of no avail. In a short time Miro had been converted from an aspiration for the career of a cultivated "man of letters" to a fiery zeal for artistic and literary propaganda in the service of radical ideas. One of the results of this conversion was the discovery that he really had no standards of critical taste. Miro had been reverential so long that he had felt no preferences. Everything that was classic had to be good to him. But now that he had thrown away the books that were stamped with the mark of the classic mint, and was dealing with the raw materials of letters, he had to become a critic and make selection. It was not enough that a book should be radical. Some of the books he read, though impeccably revolutionary as to ideas, were clearly poor as literature. His muffled taste began to assert itself. He found himself impressionable where before he had been only mildly acquisitive. The literature of revolt and free speculation fired him into a state of spiritual explosiveness. All that he read now stood out in brighter colors and in sharper outlines than before. As he reached a better balance, he began to feel the vigor of literary form, the value of sincerity and freshness of style. He began to look for them keenly in everything he read. It was long before Miro realized that enthusiasm not docility had made him critical. He became a little proud of his sensitive and discriminating reactions to the modern and the unsifted. (pp. 10-15)

When Miro and his friends abandoned literary studies, they followed after the teachers of history and philosophy, intellectual arenas of which the literary professors seemed scandously ignorant. At this ignorance Miro boiled with contempt. Here were the profitable clues that would give meaning to dusty literary scholarship, but the scholars had not the wits to seize them. They lived along, playing what seemed to Miro a rather dreary game, when they were not gaping reverently at ideas and forms which they scarcely had the genuine personality to appreciate. Miro felt once and for all free of these mysteries and reverences. He was to know the world as it has been and as it is. He was to put literature into its proper place, making all "culture" serve its apprenticeship for him as interpretation of things larger than itself, of the course of individual lives and the great tides of society. (pp. 17-18)

> Randolph Bourne, "History of a Literary Radical," in his History of a Literary Radical and Other Essays, edited by Van Wyck Brooks, B. W. Huebsch, Inc., 1920, pp. 1-30.

FLOYD DELL   (essay date 1919)

[*An American novelist and dramatist, Dell is best known today as the author of* Moon-Calf *(1920), a novel which captures the disillusioned spirit of the Jazz Age. For several years, he was a member of the Chicago Renaissance group of writers, which also included Carl Sandburg, Ben Hecht, Theodore Dreiser, and several others, who established the American Midwest as a source of artistic material and achievement. A Marxist during his early career, Dell moved from Chicago to New York in 1914, and served as editor of the leftist journal* The Masses *and its successor,* The Liberator, *for ten years. During the 1920s, Dell was associated with the bohemia of Greenwich Village and, in a series of novels and one-act plays, became known as a spokesman for society's rebels and nonconformists. His socialist sympathies softened over the years, though he remained an outspoken leftist throughout his career. One of the founding editors of* The New Republic, *Dell was a close personal friend of Bourne. In the following excerpt from his eulogistic tribute to Bourne, Dell describes Bourne's special qualities as "restless curiosity undeterred by sentiment and never recoiling in cynicism; the mood of perpetual inquiry, and the courage to go down unfamiliar ways in search of truth." Dell sees these as the special characteristics of his generation, but maintains that they were expressed most nobly and fully by Bourne, whom he describes as "the promise of our special contribution to American life."*]

Those who are not in some sense of the younger generation will hardly realize what poignancy there is for us in the news of the death of Randolph Bourne. It is not only that with his death a literary career of startling brilliancy and peculiar value has been cut short; it does not suffice to say that American literature has lost what would have been one of its most notable figures. . . . [Beyond] the bounds of respect for an extraordinary talent, and beyond even our personal affection, we have here the sense of special misfortune. Randolph Bourne belonged to us, and stood for us, in a way which he perhaps did not fully know, but which we now very keenly feel.

It was the quality of his mind which gave him this place among us, the range of his sympathies, the clear force of his thinking, the candor and vigor of his expression, but more than all, the happy union of these traits in an intellectual prsonality which had for all its force a singular and captivating charm. He was of us because he had a restless and relentless curiosity, undeterred by sentiment and never recoiling in cynicism: the mood of perpetual inquiry, and the courage to go down unfamiliar ways in search of truth. These are traits of our generation: but in many of us they show themselves for the most part as anxious hopes and stubborn fears, violent and apparently perverse disloyalties to accustomed ideals, wanton or whimsical followings of private and inexplicable fancy. In literature, in art, in politics, in all departments of life, there has been an alienation of the younger generation from traditional modes of action; and the newer, untraditional activities have seemed unformed, fantastic or half-hearted—even insincere. Randolph Bourne was a part of this revolt, its blood pulsed in him, he breathed its air. But, of a happier nature than most of us, in him the intellectual tendencies of an intelligentsia which was crudely and blunderingly engaged in finding itself, had already finely flowered. It seemed that he had the qualities toward which our defects aspired. But so it was that his achievement seemed to us not only significant of his powers, but of our own; he was the promise of our specific contribution to American life.

It may be said that all those who have felt themselves in obscure and yet irreconcilable conflict with the repressions which in literature, in art and in politics alike are our heritage from the past, felt understanding, sympathy and help in the personality of Randolph Bourne; and all these, too few as yet and too scattered to feel other than lonely, will be lonelier because of his death. He could speak for them, he was their voice, and their rebellion became through the clear candor of his prose, "clarified and transfigured." It was an accident, though a hugh and inescapable accident, that this revolt should in the last few years have had to take the form of hostility to the dominant political tendencies of the time. And yet this accident was one which could more perhaps than anything else try him and prove if his was indeed the lonely courage which our hearts had acclaimed in him. There are few avenues of expression for protest, however sane and far-seeing, against the mood of a nation in arms; and one by one, most of these were closed to him as he went on speaking out his thought. It is one of the more subtly tragic aspects of his death, a misfortune not only to a fecund mind that needed free utterance, but to a country which is starved for thought, that he should in these last years have been doomed to silence. He who should have spoken for them—and who might still have spoken for them—went down to the grave voiceless. . . .

His career was ended before he had to any degree accomplished the things of which he was capable. He was at the beginning of a great career. But in what we have from him, in his articles and books on education, and his contributions during the last few years to the *Seven Arts*, the *New Republic* and the *Dial*, we have what will serve to stimulate us to our task of understanding the forces which are not so much disintegrating an old world as creating a new. We cannot have his help in that task any more, but we can have the memory of him to enhearten us.

> *Floyd Dell, ''Randolph Bourne,'' in* The New Republic, *Vol. XVII, No. 218, January 4, 1919, p. 276.*

WALDO FRANK   (essay date 1919)

[*Frank was an American novelist and critic who was best known as an interpreter of contemporary civilization, particularly that of Latin America. A socialist and supporter of various radical groups in the United States, he was a founding editor of* The Seven Arts *(1916-1917), a leftist, avant-garde magazine of literature and opinion. One of Frank's most significant works of criticism,* Our America *(1919), derides the ''genteel tradition'' in American letters and is considered an influential work for its support of realism in the nation's literature. As the founding editor of* The Seven Arts, *Frank boldly published Bourne's antiwar writings long after other periodicals, such as* The New Republic, *had severed their connections with him. Frank's support of Bourne eventually led to the withdrawal of financial backing by the patroness of* The Seven Arts *and the collapse of the magazine. In the following excerpt from* Our America, *Frank claims that Bourne's work and life represented the joining of the best in the new political and cultural currents in American life.*]

Randolph Bourne was the essayist of our time whose future must have been most worthy to stand with that of [Van Wyck] Brooks. In his college days, Bourne was a pragmatist—an intellectual. He sat at the feet of Professor Dewey. But the war, which drove all the world including Dewey mad, drove Bourne sane. The crisis which set and fixed the master, freed Bourne and made him fluent. He who had sat among the rationalists now turned to destroy them. Better than another, he knew the blandishments of this practical philosophy. He saw the lack of desire, the lack of life, understood what catalepsy of the spirit Pragmatism meant to a groping nation. And while the American State moved with the dead precision of a machine along the track of its pioneer exploiters—a machine oiled by the intellectuals who were nothing but its slaves—Bourne rose to the attack.

Such essays as **''Below the Battle,'' ''War and the Intellectuals,'' ''Twilight of Idols''** marked the literary voice of young America, stirring at last against the iron course upon which the old America had bound it. Bourne found himself a leader of tens of thousands. But they whom he led were silent and were scattered: they whom he opposed were the Herd, with all the machinery of the world behind them. (pp. 198-99)

The best significance of Randolph Bourne lies in the joining, through his work, of the political and the cultural currents of advance. Brooks holds aloof from the transience of affairs. Our most sensitive poets and novelists do likewise. The crassness of the American world is too much for them. Unlike the European lands, where all the activities of life and thought are fused into that integer called Culture, Life in America is still a secluded, almost a romantic thing. The world is a Machine. To find the Life on which the artist feeds, he must withdraw from the Machine. He has done so. And conversely, the propagandist, the political rebel whose immediate concern is the Machine, withdraws from Life, from its immediate expressions

which are religious and artistic. Bourne, almost alone, embraced the two. More than any of our fellows, he pointed the path of fusion which American leadership must take. His political discussions were actually lit by a spiritual viewpoint. They took into account the content of the human soul, the individual soul, the values of *being*. Through him, men who had lost touch with the spiritual base of life were led in its direction, since his discussions upon actual events, his discussions of the Machine, furnished a channel they could follow.

It is a deep pity Randolph Bourne is dead. Our ranks were scant enough and straggling before he left them. Now, the political field is once more clearer to the pat materialist, the shallow liberal, the isolated radical whom he despised, and whom, eventually, his power of irony must have shamed. With him gone, the political and artistic columns of advance—Life and the Machine—are again severed. (pp. 199-200)

> *Waldo Frank, ''New York,'' in his* Our America, *Boni and Liveright Publishers, 1919, pp. 171-201.**

HAROLD J. LASKI   (essay date 1920)

[*A controversial figure with strongly held Marxian views, Laski was a noted English political scientist and author who, as a popular lecturer and teacher, maintained a large following of students throughout his career. In addition, he was an outspoken and active participant in the British Labour Party, advocating labor reforms that were in line with his socialist thought. While lecturing at several universities in the United States, he became an astute observer of the American social and political scene, as reflected in his works* The American Presidency *(1940),* American Democracy *(1948), and* Reflections on the Constitution *(1951). In an assessment of Laski, Edmund Wilson stated that he was ''not only a well-equipped scholar and an able political thinker but a fighter for unpopular ideals whose career as a whole is an example of singularly disinterested devotion.'' In the following excerpt, Laski praises* Untimely Papers *as at once a ''superb cry of anger'' against war and a work that is flawed by Bourne's effete libealism. For further discussion of* Untimely Papers, *see the excerpt by C. E. Bechhofer Roberts (1923).*]

[In *Untimely Papers*] Mr. Bourne's friends have collected the papers written by him in war-time which, collectively, form the protest of his liberalism against the results of war. They are courageous papers in that they represent an unwincing defence of an attitude which can never have been at all popular. They are turned from protest into positive statement by a long andunfinished essay on the State, in which Mr. Bourne was clearly searching to vindicate the ultimate rights of personality against the demands of authority outside. His liberalism, at bottom, is akin to the protest of William Godwin against the encroachment of political power. It has obviously been deeply influenced by the attractive anarchism of Tolstoy and Kropotkin. Even more, I think, it is an unconscious revolt against that impotence to which the vast machine of war reduces the individual. Bourne seems to have felt engulfed by a moral cataclysm; and his answer to its annihilating effort was the assertion of uncompromising defiance. He hated war; the state was an engine of war; therefore he hated the state. Bourne exhausts the vocabulary of rhetorical vituperation to record his conviction that political authority must be made impotent before the demand of conscience. He views the state as a great Moloch devouring its victims, and without the virtue of thinking in terms of their pain. The whole essay is a superb cry of anger against a tyranny which he felt to be grinding.

Yet I venture to think that the essay is in fact largely devoid of realistic basis. It has a specialized motivation which makes it valuable as the record of a personal experience, but impracticable as a contribution to political science. Those who did not fight in the war took refuge from its claims in one of two ways. Either, like Mr. Archibald Stevenson, they sought to compel a uniformity of outlook which should prevent the emergence of inconvenient and disturbing thoughts; or, like Bourne himself, they resented what was basically the destruction of the positive effort of their personality. It was not, in Bourne's case, a mere shrinking from the hideous nature of war. It was a half conscious recognition that they could neither be themselves nor do what it was in them to achieve if so ghastly an intrusion could find its justification.

That, I take it, is where liberalism such as Bourne's parts company with the more complex attitude of not less genuine liberals like Herbert Croly and Walter Lippmann. They had, equally with Bourne, a genuine hate of war. Not less genuinely they realized that civilization was impeded in its forward movement by the inevitable consequence of conflict. But they seem to have felt that a denial of its validity, however passionately brilliant, is not a positive contribution to its destruction. They sought, therefore, to capture the war for purposes of which, equally with themselves, Mr. Bourne approved. Admittedly, they failed. Yet I think that no one can look back upon the period since America entered the war and doubt that their hypothesis was nearer to success as a summary of the facts than Bourne's. If America had kept out of the war, Germany might well have been successful; and most students of international affairs would agree that the results of her success would have been more irremediably tragic than is the case with the relentless and stupid cruelty of the peace of Versailles. And even if we grant that the Allies would have been successful without America, the peace which would have resulted does not loom up more fairly. Neutrality in the modern conflict of nations is an unthinkable attitude. The business of the world is the business of the world. We can not stay at Armageddon to philosophize upon the abstract injustice of war. Bourne's attitude, I think, comes perilously near to that manoeuvre.

His liberalism seems, moreover, to suffer from a second defect. The individualism he preaches is one in which the single person stands as an Athanasius against the world. I do not doubt he should; and it is for that reason that I should urge that conscientious objectors, like Stephen Hobhouse and Roger Baldwin, were among the bravest men revealed to us by the war. But this world, after all, is a complex world; and those who postulate their individual effort as the ultimate are not likely to turn it from its ancient ways. It is a world in which institutions have transcended the character and power of men, and only organized corporate effort can make a definite impression upon it. The deduction is that the main need of liberalism is a technique of organization. Or, if we choose to use the paradox of Rousseau, it is the problem of how men may surrender their whole rights to the community and yet remain free as before. Mr. Bourne's freedom is the freedom of a lonely vagabond whose soul does not dwell in the common haunts of men. It is possible in a frontier civilization where one's chief commune is with the birds and beasts, or for some stout, itinerant preacher who yearly braves the terrors of an uncharted wilderness to proclaim the love of God. (p. 237)

No one, I think, could read Bourne's eloquence without something of the thrill that comes in reading the superb defiance of Thoreau, fifty years ago, to a state which condoned slavery.

But the eloquence must look beyond the soul that expresses it to institutional form. Philosophers may no longer seek kingship that their wise despotism respite our sufferings; and the penalty for a republic is the patient study of an infinite process of details in which the elimination of our personal bias is the essential starting-point of hope. (p. 238)

> *Harold J. Laski, "The Liberalism of Randolph Bourne," in* The Freeman, *Vol. 1, No. 10, May 19, 1920, pp. 237-38.*

VAN WYCK BROOKS (essay date 1920)

[*An American critic and biographer, Brooks is noted chiefly for his biographical and critical studies of such writers as Mark Twain, Henry James, and Ralph Waldo Emerson, and for his influential commentary on the history of American literature. His career can be neatly divided into two distinct periods: the first, from 1908 to 1925, dealt primarily with the negative impact of European Puritanism on the development of artistic genius in America. Brooks argued that the Puritan conscience in the United States, carried over from Europe, produced an unhealthy dichotomy in American writers and resulted in a literature split between stark realism and what he called "vaporous idealism." During this early period, Brooks believed that in reality America had no culture of its own, and that American literature relied almost exclusively on its European heritage. After 1925, and his study on Emerson, Brooks radically altered his view of American literary history. He began to see much in America's past as unique and artistically valuable, and he called for a return in literary endeavors to the positive values of Emerson, as opposed to the modern pessimism of such writers as T. S. Eliot and James Joyce. Despite the radical difference in these two critical approaches, one element remained constant throughout Brooks's career, namely his concern with the reciprocal relationship between the writer and society. Brooks knew Bourne well from working with him while on the staff of* The Seven Arts. *In the following excerpt, he discusses Bourne's goals and philosophy, including his aspirations for an American "super-culture" drawn from the best of all European cultures, and his desire for an alliance of the intelligentsia and the proletariat which would create an "economically democratic, but intellectually aristocratic" society.*]

[Bourne's interests were] almost universal: he had written on politics, economics, philosophy, education, literature. No other of our younger critics had cast so wide a net, and Bourne had hardly begun to draw the strings and count and sort his catch. He was a working journalist, a literary freelance with connections often of the most precarious kind, who contrived, by daily miracles of audacity and courage, to keep himself serenely afloat on a society where his convictions prevented him from following any of the ordinary avenues of preferment and recognition. It was a feat never to be sufficiently marvelled over; it would have been striking, in our twentieth century New York, even in the case of a man who was not physically handicapped as Bourne was. But such a life is inevitably scattering, and it was only after the war had literally driven him in upon himself that he set to work at the systematic harvesting of his thoughts and experiences. He had not quite found himself, perhaps, owing to the extraordinary range of interests for which he had to find a personal common denominator; yet no other young American critic, I think, had exhibited so clear a tendency, so coherent a body of desires. His personality was not only unique, it was also absolutely expressive. I have had the delightful experience of reading through at a sitting, so to say, the whole mass of his uncollected writings, articles, essays, book reviews, unprinted fragments, and a few letters, and I am astonished at the way in which, like a ball of camphor in a trunk, the pungent savor of the man spreads itself over every paragraph. Here was no anonymous reviewer, no mere brilliant satellite of the radical movement losing himself in his immediate reactions: one finds everywhere, interwoven in the fabric of his work, the silver thread of a personal philosophy, the singing line of an intense and beautiful desire.

What was that desire? It was for a new fellowship in the youth of America as the principle of a great and revolutionary departure in our life, a league of youth, one might call it, consciously framed with the purpose of creating, out of the blind chaos of American society, a fine, free, articulate cultural order. That, as it seems to me, was the dominant theme of all his effort, the positive theme to which he always returned from his thrilling forays into the fields of education and politics, philosophy and sociology. One finds it at the beginning of his career in such essays as **"Our Cultural Humility,"** one finds it at the end in the **"History of a Literary Radical."** One finds it in that pacifism which he pursued with such an obstinate and lonely courage and which was the logical outcome of the checking and thwarting of those currents of thought and feeling in which he had invested the whole passion of his life. *Place aux jeunes* might have been his motto: he seemed indeed the flying wedge of the younger generation itself. (pp. x-xii)

One divined him in a moment, the fine, mettlesome temper of his intellect, his curiosity, his acutely critical self-consciousness, his aesthetic flair, his delicate sense of personal relationships, his toughness of fiber, his masterly powers of assimilation, his grasp of reality, his burning convictions, his beautifully precise desires. Here was Emerson's "American scholar" at last, but radiating an infinitely warmer, profaner, more companionable influence than Emerson had ever dreamed of, an influence that savored rather of Whitman and William James. He was the new America incarnate, with that stamp of a sort of permanent youthfulness on his queer, twisted, appealing face. You felt that in him the new America had suddenly found itself and was all astir with the excitement of its first maturity.

His life had prepared him for the rôle, for the physical disability that had cut him off from the traditional currents and preoccupations of American life had given him a poignant insight into the predicament of all those others who, like him, could not adjust themselves to the industrial machine—the exploited, the sensitive, the despised, the aspiring, those, in short, to whom a new and very different America was no academic idea but a necessity so urgent that it had begun to be a reality. As detached as any young East Sider from the herd-unity of American life, the colonial tradition, the "genteel tradition," yet passionately concerned with America, passionately caring for America, he had discovered himself at Columbia, where so many strains of the newer immigrant population meet one another in the full flood and ferment of modern ideas. . . . Intensely Anglo-Saxon himself, it was America he cared for, not the triumph of the Anglo-Saxon tradition which had apparently lost itself in the pursuit of a mechanical efficiency. It was a "trans-national" America of which he caught glimpses now, a battleground of all the cultures, a super-culture, that might perhaps, by some happy chance, determine the future of civilization itself.

It was with some such vision as this that he had gone abroad. If that super-culture was ever to come it could only be through some prodigious spiritual organization of the youth of America, some organization that would have to begin with small and highly self-conscious groups; these groups, moreover, would

have to depend for a long time upon the experience of young Europe. The very ideas of spiritual leadership, the intellectual life, the social revolution were foreign to a modern America that had submitted to the common mould of business enterprise. . . . [Bourne] was in search, in other words, of new ideas, new attitudes, new techniques, personal and social, for which he was going to demand recognition at home, and it is this that gives to his **"Impressions of Europe 1913-1914"**—his report to Columbia as holder of the Gilder Fellowship—an actuality that so perfectly survives the war. Where can one find anything better in the way of social insight than his pictures of radical France, of the ferment of the young Italian soul, of the London intellectuals. . . . Two complex impressions he had gained that were to dominate all his later work. One was the sense of what a national culture is, of its immense value and significance as a source and fund of spiritual power even in a young world committed to a political and economic internationalism. The other was a keen realization of the almost apostolic rôle of the young student class in perpetuating, rejuvenating, vivifying and, if need be, creating this national consciousness. No young Hindu ever went back to India, no young Persian or Ukrainian or Balkan student ever went home from a European year with a more fervent sense of the chaos and spiritual stagnation and backwardness of his own people, of the happy responsibility laid upon himself and all those other young men and women who had been touched by the modern spirit. (pp. xiii-xix)

The New Republic had started with the war, *The Masses* was still young, *The Seven Arts* and the new *Dial* were on the horizon. Bourne found himself instantly in touch with the purposes of all these papers, which spoke of a new class-consciousness, a sort of offensive and defensive alliance of the younger intelligentsia and the awakened elements of the labor groups. His audience was awaiting him, and no one could have been better prepared to take advantage of it. (p. xx)

He saw that we needed, first, a psychological interpretation of these younger malcontents, secondly, a realistic study of our institutional life, and finally, a general opening of the American mind to the currents of contemporary desire and effort and experiment abroad. And along each of these lines he did the work of a pioneer.

Who, for example, had ever thought of exploring the soul of the younger generation as Bourne explored it? He had planned a long series of literary portraits of its types and personalities: half a dozen of them exist (along with several of quite a different character!—the keenest satires we have), enough to show us how sensitively he responded to those detached, groping, wistful, yet resolutely independent spirits whom he saw weaving the iridescent fabric of the future. He who had so early divined the truth of Maurice Barrès' saying, that we never conquer the intellectual suffrages of those who precede us in life, addressed himself exclusively to these young spirits: he went out to meet them, he probed their obscurities; one would have said that he was a sort of impresario gathering the personnel of some immense orchestra, seeking in each the principle of his own growth. He had studied his chosen minority with such instinctive care that everything he wrote came as a personal message to those, and those alone, who were capable of assimilating it; and that is why, as we look over his writings today, we find them a sort of corpus, a text full of secret ciphers, and packed with meaning between the lines, of all the most intimate questions and difficulties and turns of thought and feeling that make up the soul of young America. He re-

BY RANDOLPH BOURNE

HISTORY OF A
LITERARY RADICAL
AND OTHER ESSAYS

EDITED WITH AN INTRODUCTION
BY VAN WYCK BROOKS

"To write in favor of that which the great interests of the world are against is what I conceive to be the duty and the privilege of the intellectual."

PADRAIC COLUM

NEW YORK   B. W. HUEBSCH   MCMXX
INC.

vealed us to ourselves, he intensified and at the same time corroborated our desires; above all, he showed us what we had in common and what new increments of life might arise out of the friction of our differences. In these portraits he was already doing the work of the novelist he might well have become,—he left two or three chapters of a novel he had begun to write, in which "Karen" and "Sophronisba" and "The Professor" would probably have appeared, along with a whole battle-array of the older and younger generations; he was sketching out the rôle some novelist might play in the parturition of the new America. Everything for analysis, for self-discovery, for articulation, everything to put the younger generation in possession of itself! Everything to weave the tissue of a common understanding, to help the growth and freedom of the spirit! (pp. xxiv-xxvi)

The task of the thinkers, of the intelligentsia, in so far as they concerned themselves directly with economic problems, was, in Bourne's eyes, chiefly to *think*. It was a new doctrine for American radicals; it precisely denoted their advance over the evangelicism of fifteen years ago. "The young radical to-day," he wrote in one of his reviews, "is not asked to be a martyr, but he is asked to be a thinker, an intellectual leader. . . . The labor movement in this country needs a philosophy, a literature,

a constructive socialist analysis and criticism of industrial relations. Labor will scarcely do this thinking for itself. Unless middle-class radicalism threshes out its categories and interpretations and undertakes this constructive thought it will not be done. . . . The only way by which middle-class radicalism can serve is by being fiercely and concentratedly intellectual."

Finally, through Bourne more than through any other of our younger writers one gained a sense of the stir of the great world, of the currents and cross-currents of the contemporary European spirit, behind and beneath the war, of the tendencies and experiences and common aims and bonds of the younger generation everywhere. He was an exception to what seems to be the general rule, that Americans who are able to pass outside their own national spirit at all are apt to fall headlong into the national spirit of some one other country: they become vehement partisans of Latin Europe, or of England, or of Germany and Scandinavia, or, more recently, of Russia. Bourne, with that singular union of detachment and affectionate penetration which he brought also to his personal relationships, had entered them all with an equal curiosity, an impartial delight. If he had absorbed the fine idealism of the English liberals, he understood also the more elemental, the more emotional, the more positive urge of revolutionary Russia. He was full of practical suggestions from the vast social and economic laboratory of modern Germany. He had caught something also from the intellectual excitement of young Italy; most of all, his imagination had been captivated, as we can see from such essays as **"Mon Amie,"** by the candor and the self-consciousness and the genius for social introspection of radical France. And all these influences were perpetually at play in his mind and in his writings. He was the conductor of innumerable diverse inspirations, a sort of clearing-house of the best living ideas of the time; through him the young writer and the young thinker came into instant contact with whatever in the modern world he most needed. And here again Bourne revealed his central aim. He reviewed by choice, and with a special passion, what he called the "epics of youthful talent that grows great with quest and desire." It is easy to see, in his articles on such books as "Pelle the Conqueror" and Gorky's Autobiography and "The Ragged-Trousered Philanthropists," that what lured him was the common struggle and aspiration of youth and poverty and the creative spirit everywhere, the sense of a new socialized world groping its way upward. It was this rich groundnote in all his work that made him, not the critic merely, but the leader. (pp. xxviii-xxx)

Bourne, whose ultimate interest was always artistic, found himself a guerilla fighter along the whole battlefront of the social revolution. He was drawn into the political arena as a skilful specialist, called into war service, is drawn into the practice of a general surgery in which he may indeed accomplish much but at the price of the suspension of his own uniqueness. Others, at the expiration of what was for him a critical moment, the moment when all freedom seemed to be at stake, might have been trusted to do his political work for him; the whole radical tide was flowing behind him; his unique function, meanwhile, was not political but spiritual. It was the creation, the communication of what he called "the allure of fresh and true ideas, of free speculation, of artistic vigor, of cultural styles, of intelligence suffused by feeling and feeling given fiber and outline by intelligence." (pp. xxxii-xxxiii)

We have had no chart of our cultural situation to compare with his **"History of a Literary Radical,"** and certainly no one has combined with an analytical gift like his, and an adoration for the instinct of workmanship, so burning an eye for every stir of life and color on the drab American landscape. I think of a sentence in one of his review: "The appearance of dramatic imagination in any form in this country is something to make us all drop our work and run to see." That was the spirit which animated all his criticism: is it not the spirit that creates out of the void the thing it contemplates? (p. xxxv)

He was a wanderer, the child of some nation yet unborn, smitten with an inappeasable nostalgia for the Beloved Community on the far side of socialism, he carried with him the intoxicating air of that community, the mysterious aroma of all its works and ways. "High philosophic thought infused with sensuous love," he wrote once, "is not this the one incorrigible dream that clutches us?" It was the dream he had brought back from the bright future in which he lived, the dream he summoned us to realize. And it issues now like a gallant command out of the space left vacant by his passing. (p. xxxv)

> *Van Wyck Brooks, in an introduction to* History of a Literary Radical and Other Essays *by Randolph Bourne, edited by Van Wyck Brooks, B. W. Huebsch, Inc., 1920, pp. ix-xxxv.*

C. E. BECHHOFER [PSEUDONYM OF C. E. BECHHOFER ROBERTS] (essay date 1923)

[*In the following excerpt from one of the few unfavorable assessments of Bourne's career, Roberts attacks* Untimely Papers *as a work that evidences little understanding of the issues surrounding World War I, a myopic obsession with America's stake in that conflict, and "a contempt for 'reality'." For further discussion of* Untimely Papers, *see the excerpt by Harold J. Laski (1920).*]

[Were] it not for the reverence with which he is regarded by his friends, one would hardly think to pay much attention to the work of the late Randolph Bourne; as things are, however, he is symbolical of so much in the young movement in American thought that it is necessary to consider him with attention. . . . His range of interests and knowledge was extensive, and his friends are engaged to-day in the republication of his work under various heads. One volume contains his writing on political subjects, under the title of *Untimely Papers*, edited with an introduction by Mr. James Oppenheim, one of the editors of the *Seven Arts*; the other, edited by Mr. Brooks as *The History of a Literary Radical*, contains his literary essays. Reading these volumes through, one cannot help feeling that it would have been kinder of Bourne's friends to have celebrated his very remarkable human qualities in some other way than by collecting his writings and transferring their admiration to them. But, however, here the books are; and their significance is not least in their defects.

The seven essays reprinted as *Untimely Papers* were written during the War, and are concerned with it in greater or less degree. It is significant of the barrenness of the outlook of an *intelligentsia* that Bourne rarely shows in them any real comprehension of the issues of the European conflict. He is always thinking locally—of the repercussion of the War upon American life, of the muddled and often exaggerated partisanship that preceded the entrance of America into it, and the hysteria that followed this. He writes in the same evangelical spirit that inspires his butts among the ruling class; with all his open contempt for excessive American pretensions, we find him naïvely regretting that 'we have not even retained the demo-

cratic leadership among the Allies.' He is as contemptuous of the intelligence of the Old World as any vote-catching politician in the backwoods. He declares, for example, that

> there are probably not a dozen men fighting in Europe who did not long ago give up every reason for their being there except that nobody knew how to get them away.

He proclaimed also that America was a rudderless nation that was being exploited by her cunning Allies, to whom her independence and her resources had been supinely surrendered. 'With the arrival of the British Mission our "independent basis" became a polite fiction.' His general attitude towards the War is expressed in this sentence:—

> The American intellectuals, in their preoccupation with reality, seem to have forgotten that the real enemy is War rather than imperial Germany.

This contempt for 'reality,' so characteristic of the man, perhaps explains how, in August 1917, Bourne could enunciate the statement that 'Revolution, impossible while the Fatherland is in danger, becomes a practicable issue as soon as war is ended,' a fallacy which had already been exposed by the Russian Revolution in March 1917, and was to be still further discredited by events in Russia and Germany in the following twelve-month. There is no need to delve further into his war writings; he was wrong as often as he could be, although he wrote with a messianic pen. And yet Mr. Brooks can say of him that his was 'one of the fullest, richest, and most significant lives of the younger generation.' Full and rich it clearly was not; but it was significant in the highest degree of a contempt for 'reality' and an exaggeration of personal values that are reminiscent of the old Russian *intelligentsia*.

Bourne's literary papers remain to be mentioned. The essays in *The History of a Literary Radical* contain nothing that necessitates a revision of the criticism of his political writings; rather they confirm it. (pp. 15-19)

> *C. E. Bechhofer [pseudonym of C. E. Bechhofer Roberts], in a chapter in his* The Literary Renaissance in America, *William Heinemann Ltd., 1923, pp. 14-41.*

LEWIS MUMFORD (essay date 1930)

[*Mumford is an American sociologist, historian, philosopher, and author whose primary interest is the relationship between the modern individual and his or her environment. Influenced by the works of Patrick Geddes, a Scottish sociologist and pioneer in the field of city planning, Mumford has worked extensively in the area of city and regional planning, and has contributed several important studies of cities, including* The Culture of Cities *(1938),* City Development *(1945), and* The City in History *(1961). All of these works examine the interrelationship between cities and civilization over the centuries. Also indicative of much of his work is Mumford's concern with firm moral values to assure the growth of civilization. Writing for the* Saturday Evening Post, *Mumford noted that: "The test of maturity, for nations as well as for individuals, is not the increase of power, but the increase of self-understanding, self-control, self-direction, and self-transcendence. For in a mature society, man himself, not his machines or his organizations, is the chief work of art." In the following excerpt, Mumford separates Bourne's writings from what Bourne himself came to represent, and praises him for his contribution to the betterment of American culture.*]

[Bourne] had died at thirty-two, or was it thirty-three? on the brink of maturity; and there had been nothing precocious about his development: indeed, if I remember rightly, his physical handicaps had retarded it a little, and he left the university at a somewhat later age than most young men of equal intelligence.

What had Bourne done? He had written a series of commentaries upon life and letters in "The New Republic," "The Seven Arts," "The Dial": he had begun a novel, he had written an opening draft for a book on the State. The essays had been collected in three volumes, and in addition there was an interpretative study of the Gary system in education. All of this work represented the very first quality in the journalism of ideas, but for the most part, it was still journalism. His view of life was maturing, deepening, not yet ready for rounded expression, it was still a promise: a cool luminous dawn was spreading across the skies, but the landscape was still in silhouette, and one could only guess what shapes, what vistas, what living creatures it might show and what inviting roads might lead away through it. Randolph Bourne was precious to us because of what he was, rather than because of what he had actually written: how could his especial significance be made clear to later *lustra* merely by putting within fresh covers his little heap of writings? More than once I had inquired about Bourne's letters, with a view to their publication in "The American Caravan"; it appeared that they were too meager in content to give any sufficient clue to his mind. One must perhaps therefore be content that his four slender volumes should diminish to one, which should hold the quintessence of his spirit, so far as he had yet expressed it: to keep that one book alive would be better than to let all four remain in the discard, forgotten by all except some curious mole, delving through the literature of 1910-1920, in search of a doctor's thesis. One volume is a small pledge of immortality, but it is some consolation to remember that personalities like Socrates, who have profoundly disturbed and affected mankind, left nothing behind them at all—nothing except their image of candor and virtue and sweetness and light. That, in a precious degree, was what Randolph Bourne left to his contemporaries. He will never occupy the place of a great teacher, but one feels that potentially he had exactly that office, and that in ten years, in twenty years, he would have distilled out of such pain and frustration as only a crippled man can know, a new image of beauty and perfection. Is it due to some callowness in our spirit, some raw jealousy or irreverence, that no poet has sought to embody the image of Randolph Bourne, if one except a commemorative poem by Mr. James Oppenheim, and his appearance as an incidental character in a novel by Miss Babette Deutsch. We want more than this. Just because his works are, when sifted and counted by time, so sparse in their own message, one wants someone to seize the proper magnitude of Randolph Bourne, and to give him, as a living image and symbol, some more durable means of existence. It was the good fortune of American society to produce this man. We must not toss that luck away. (pp. 151-52)

*Lewis Mumford, "The Image of Randolph Bourne,"
in* The New Republic, *Vol. LXIV, No. 825, September 24, 1930, pp. 151-52.*

MAX LERNER (essay date 1941)

[*Lerner is a political scientist, educator, author, and nationally syndicated columnist. His career as a social commentator began in 1927 as an editor for the* Encyclopedia of Social Sciences;

from 1936 to 1939 he served as editor of The Nation, *and since 1949 he has worked as a columnist for the* New York Post. *Throughout his career, Lerner has also interspersed academic work with his writing. Of his political philosophy, he states: "My political convictions are on the left, although I belong to no party. I feel that my energies must lie with the movement toward a democratic socialism." Lerner's numerous works include the popular* It Is Later Than You Think *(1938), a study of contemporary politics, and what he considers his most ambitious work,* America as a Civilization: Life and Thought in the United States Today *(1957). Lerner is one of the most insightful writers on Bourne and his ideas. In the following excerpt, he examines Bourne's antiwar essays and the unfinished fragment on "The State" from the perspective of a liberal observer of the world writing during World War II. Lerner observes that many of Bourne's pacifistic principles simply did not apply in the case of the conflict with the Nazis.*]

[Bourne] tended to approach problems of social theory as an essayist—through indirections, through tracing in one essay after another a personal psychograph. To get at the structure of his thinking one must piece it together, block by block, from his essays and letters, all surcharged with an intensely personal emotion. Yet the structure, what there is of it, is there.

It has, for its base, three principal lines of thought. One is Bourne's cultural outlook. Here his code phrase is one taken, as if by a special ironic twist, from the *New Republic*'s Herbert Croly—"the promise of American life." But while the phrase is Croly's, the content is Bourne's, taken from the whole odyssey of Bourne's life and thought, his travel in Europe fused with his hope for America. The second is Bourne's class vision—a growing proletarianism which made him feel that the struggle to fulfill the American promise was wholly an internal struggle within American life; that it was a struggle between the possessing classes and the functional classes; and that it could be carried on without a primary concern for what happened in Europe. The third is Bourne's theory of the relation between war and the state.

This theory Bourne expressed most fully in his **"Unfinished Fragment on the State,"** written in the winter of 1918 just before his death. It was written as a treatise rather than as another essay. Its form is rigid and severe. "Government," it starts, "is synonymous with neither State nor Nation. It is the machinery by which the nation, organized as a State, carries out its State functions." It was as if Bourne, isolated and frustrated, finding his anti-war essays ineffective, had given up the attempt at month-by-month persuasion and protest, and had decided to dig deep into political theory in preparation for the long struggle to come after the war. Yet I am inclined to think that the impulsions of this treatise were more personal than its outward form would indicate. I cannot help feeling that Bourne was dissatisfied with the level on which his thinking had rested. Up to 1917 he had accepted Dewey's philosophy. It had failed him. But his protests against it would be ineffective unless they came from a counter-philosophy as deep and integrated as Dewey's own. And here Bourne could find no one to lean on, even if he had wished to. No one but himself. He could draw on Veblen's *Imperial Germany and the Industrial Revolution*. He could draw on Simon Patten's *Culture and War*. He could draw on Beard's *Economic Interpretation of the Constitution*. But he would have to use them for his own purposes, and the final product would have to be his own.

What Bourne might have achieved in this respect if he had lived we can only guess at. The **"Fragment"** is a brilliant beginning in what John Chamberlain has called ironically "grand political theory.'' But only a beginning. Bourne's whole train-ing had scarcely fitted him for grand political theory. His natural language was the language of literary and social criticism. When it comes to political concepts he handles them as a brilliant amateur, but still an amateur. Bourne was groping toward a Marxian theory of the state as an expression of the class relations of production, but there is no evidence of any intimate acquaintance with the Marxian literature, on either economic theory or state theory. He was dealing with material involving the clash between idealist and materialist theories of politics, yet there is no indication that he knew the work of either Engels or T. H. Green. He was dealing with the nature of power, force, and violence, yet there is no mention of the tradition that had wrestled with these problems in the modern state from Machiavelli to Sorel. He was dealing with the knotty question of why men fought and what fighting did to them, yet there is no indication that he was acquainted with the work that had been done on mass psychology. Bourne's **"Fragment"** has insights that go deeper than the work of the formal academicians. Yet as it stands those insights are not integrated.

But even as it stands Bourne's **"Fragment"** must be regarded as one of the notable American attempts at a theory of the state. It is part of a tradition that began with Madison's papers on class theory in the *Federalist,* and that extends through Turner's theory of the frontier and the work of J. Allen Smith, Charles Beard, Herbert Croly, Walter Weyl, Vernon Parrington. Which is to say that Bourne sought his theory of the state in a study of American history and an attempt to discover the shaping forces that produce a politics and a culture. There can be little doubt that it was Beard's *Economic Interpretation of the Constitution* that gave him his starting-point, for the larger part of the book is an attempt to apply Beard's class approach to the later reaches of American history.

But if Bourne is giving us Beard, it is Beard with a decided difference. And that difference is contained in Bourne's emphasis on the strength of the state. Here was something not to be found in Marxian theory, which has always underscored the viability of economic rather than political constructions. Nor was it to be found in the thinking of the American progressives on which, in the main, Bourne drew. It was related rather to a strain in contemporary German thought. We know that Bourne had read John Dewey's *German Philosophy and Politics,* and Thorstein Veblen's *Imperial Germany.* He may have read, or perhaps only dabbled, in some of the contemporary German thinkers whom the war had for the first time revealed to Americans. But there can be little doubt that he saw, more clearly perhaps than any other American except Thorstein Veblen, the toughness of state power, once granted its roots in class interest and tenacity, in traditional acceptance, in psychological allegiance. One of the revealing passages in the **"Fragment"** deals with the attack, in the decade of 1904-1914, upon the capitalist control of the American state—an attack made by T.R., by the muckrakers, by the Wilsonian idealists.

> These [the possessing] classes actually had little to fear. A political system which had been founded in the interests of property by their own spiritual and economic ancestors, which had become ingrained in the country's life through a function of 120 years, which was buttressed by a legal system which went back without a break to the early English monarchy, was not likely to crumble before the anger of a few muckrakers, the disillusionment of a few

radical sociologists, or the assaults of proletarian minorities.

The propertied classes, Bourne continues, bided their time until ''the exigency of a war, in which business organization was imperatively needed.''

> The mass of the worried middle classes, riddled by the campaign against American failings, which at times extended almost to a skepticism of the American State itself, were only too glad to sink back to a glorification of the State ideal, to feel about them in war the old protecting arms, to return to the old primitive robust sense of the omnipotence of the State, its matchless virtue, honor, and beauty, driving away all the foul old doubts and dismays.

Here in these passages one gets the essential quality of Bourne's state theory. The reverence for the state was a primitive tribal feeling. The state itself, rooted in this feeling and buttressed by legal institutions, was an instrument of class power. That instrument had been challenged in America by a nascent proletarian and agrarian democracy. Upon that democracy the dominant class had imposed a Constitution, formulated in its own interest; and it had fortified itself by a party system it could manipulate and corrupt. Its own failure as an economic ruling class, however, made the prestige of its state a shaky affair. When war broke out, therefore, this class welcomed it for reasons of class interest, just as the middle class welcomed it because of (here Bourne delighted to use a phrase of L. P. Jacks) ''the peacefulness of being at war.'' Thus the state was again strengthened. ''For war is,'' Bourne repeatedly asserts, turning the German conservative thought to ironic use, ''essentially the health of the state.''

It is a melancholy experience to read the **"Fragment"** today— melancholy because so much of it is profoundly right and profoundly disturbing. There can be little doubt that Bourne and Veblen, almost alone of their generation in America, saw the roots of totalitarianism in the modern state. Bourne set those roots in a psychological soil of what he called the ''gregarious impulse.'' In terms of contemporary psychology that now sounds archaic, and one must remember that Bourne wrote before the reception of Freudianism in America. Yet if one overlooks the terminology there still remains a residue of validity in his analysis.

> Just as in modern societies the sex-instinct is enormously over-supplied for the requirements of human propagation, so the gregarious impulse is enormously over-supplied for the work of protection which it is called upon to perform. . . . All human progress . . . must be carried against the resistance of this tyrannical herd-instinct which drives the individual into obedience. . . . There is in the feeling towards the State a large element of pure filial mysticism. . . . The chief value of the state in wartime is the opportunity it gives for this regression to infantile attitudes.

But Bourne does not stop with this psychological analysis, however faulty. He goes on to a class analysis of the state in wartime.

> War becomes almost a sport between the hunters and the hunted. The pursuit of enemies within

outweighs in psychic attractiveness the assault on the enemy without. . . . A white terrorism is carried on by the Government against pacifists, Socialists, enemy aliens, and a milder unofficial persecution against all persons or movements that can be imagined as connected with the enemy. War, which should be the health of the state, unifies all the bourgeois elements and the common people, and outlaws the rest.

Is this true, as Bourne sees it, only of a particular type of state? Here his answer is difficult, but I shall try to present it. War is, as he sees it, the inevitable function of a *state-system*. (pp. 133-37)

What Bourne seems to be saying is that war is an integral part of the Western system of dynastic states, including the capitalist democracies. (p. 137)

Bourne alone, of those who opposed America's entrance into the war, did so as part of a reasoned analysis that sought to pierce to the heart of the problems of psychology, class relations, and political power that were involved. I do not propose here to inquire how valid Bourne's reasoning was for his time. . . . If . . . I emphasize my points of difference, it is partly because I have already by implication indicated my sympathy for many of the positions he took with respect to his own generation. (pp. 137-38)

What has intervened between Bourne's generation and ours is a change of world perspective so complete as to make the earlier outlines unrecognizable. The state, whose power Bourne feared so, has multiplied its power many times. The dynastic state has become the totalitarian state. And the totalitarian state has fed not upon the readiness of its opponents for war, but upon their unreadiness. Bourne made the ghastly error of thinking so completely in absolutes that he lumped all states together with respect to the nature of their power. I say "ghastly" advisedly, since the absolutist tendency shared by Marxian and liberal schools alike to think of the state as a single abstraction left us unprepared for the emergence of totalitarian states, the range of whose powers went far beyond that of even the most illiberal democracies. And because men did not see how different in kind was the totalitarian state from our own, they were unprepared either to see its threat or to resist it. Bourne, as I have said earlier, foresaw the psychological basis of totalitarianism; and he foresaw also that it could grow out of the tensions of the Western state-system. What he could not see—what even most of our own generation did not see—was that there were two lines of direction in the Western state-system: that one was in essence anti-democratic and anti-humanist (Veblen saw this in his *Imperial Germany*); and that the other would become so only by not fighting (as Belgium, Holland, Norway), or fighting too late and badly (as France).

And because Bourne was an absolutist, he was misled in his class analysis, arguing that the worst fate that could befall the working-class in a capitalist democracy was war. Actually the destroyed working-classes in the former European democracies would be alive today if they had understood that not to wage a war against an anti-proletarian as well as anti-humanist enemy like Nazism was the surest way to destruction. (pp. 140-41)

Bourne, in his hatred of war and his insistence on viewing it only as "an upper-class sport," failed to take account of the possibility that in the Western state-system the fate of the lower and functional classes might be just as surely tied up with the use of war as a defensive instrument as the fate of the possessing

classes. And by premising a one-to-one correspondence between the control of state machinery and the control of economic power, Bourne left out of account the continuing fight that the functional classes in a democracy have been making to gain and retain control of the state machinery. There is nothing in his thinking that would prepare us for the administrative revolution that has already taken place in the American state, and the rise of a new bureaucracy whose allegiance is not given primarily to the owning classes.

It is in his affirmations that Bourne's abiding importance will lie—his affirmation of the necessity for safeguarding liberty of expression and cultural variants, whatever the internal pressures toward centralized power. Bourne's writings will serve to remind us how easy it is for a democracy at war to turn its ferocity inward, against the friends rather than the enemies of the culture. This happened in France at the outbreak of the present war; yet the current example of England shows that it need not happen generically in a democracy at war. (pp. 141-42)

Bourne did not think through to the utmost reaches of his problem. Who in his time did? Who has in our own time? He thought in many respects, I venture to say, further than anyone in his generation. His has been called the "lost generation" because the war came athwart its promise and its unfolding. We may or may not accept Bourne's conclusions for our day. But if we learn from him that the question of war or no war cannot be accepted negatively, that it must ultimately be referred to the question of what will preserve and extend the creative groups in American life, ours will not be called the lost generation. (p. 142)

> *Max Lerner, "Randolph Bourne and Two Generations," in his* Ideas for the Ice Age: Studies in a Revolutionary Era, *The Viking Press, 1941, pp. 116-42.*

ALFRED KAZIN   (essay date 1942)

[*A highly respected American literary critic, Kazin is best known for his essay collections* The Inmost Leaf *(1955) and* Contemporaries *(1962), and particularly for* On Native Grounds *(1942), a study of American prose writing since the era of William Dean Howells. Having studied the works of "the critics who were the best writers—from Sainte-Beuve and Matthew Arnold to Edmund Wilson and Van Wyck Brooks" as an aid to his own critical understanding, Kazin has found that "criticism focussed many—if by no means all—of my own urges as a writer: to show literature as a deed in human history, and to find in each writer the uniqueness of the gift, of the essential vision, through which I hoped to penetrate into the mystery and sacredness of the individual soul." In the following excerpt, Kazin declares that Bourne, in retrospect, seems "less a writer than the incarnation of his time," explaining that Bourne believed wholeheartedly in a future established on such pre-World War I ideals as the preeminence of art, pragmatism, reason, European social democracy, and the experimental school, and that his life and career, in many ways, reflect the failure of many of these hopes.*]

Bourne owed less to Brooks, perhaps, than he did to John Dewey and a certain literary idealism in the Progressive period which he personified, but Brooks gave his interest in criticism a direction and influenced it by his technique. Above all Bourne was the perfect child of the prewar Enlightenment; when its light went out in 1918, he died with it. Afterward his story seemed so much the martyrology of his generation that the writer was lost in the victim. Yet even when one goes back to Bourne's books—not merely his bitter and posthumously published collections of essays, but his early studies of contemporary youth, education, and politics—it is not hard to see why Bourne must always seem less a writer than the incarnation of his time. For from his first book, *Youth and Life,* to the *Impressions of Europe* which he wrote on a fellowship abroad and his books on education and the Gary schools, Bourne proved himself so inexpressibly confident of a future established on the evangelicisms of his period, so radiant in his championship of pragmatism, art, reason, European social democracy, and the experimental school, that he now seems a seismograph on which were recorded the greatest hopes and fiercest despairs of his time. No other critic in his period wrote so little about himself, or had, as it were, so little interest in himself. His books were always selfless; they were reports on the great developments of the day. He was not a great writer; he died too young to be even a complete writer; but carried along by his ardent belief in the modern spirit, he made himself an extraordinarily keen and sympathetic observer. Everywhere, as it seems on reading his *Impressions of Europe, 1913-1914,* he found men as eager, as open-hearted, as himself; everywhere he saw "the sense in these countries of the most advanced civilization, yet without sophistication, a luminous modern intelligence that selected and controlled and did not allow itself to be overwhelmed by the chaos of twentieth-century possibility."

Youth alone, he had written in his first book, *Youth and Life,* has all the really valuable experience, for it is youth which has constantly to meet new situations and react to new aspects of life. "It is only the interpretation of this first collision with life that is worth anything." He protested against those who would make youth too humble, who would bind it to conventional traditions; and he protested in the same spirit against those who were so absorbed in their own careers that they missed the gaiety of life and what seemed to him, despite his own crippled body and his poverty, its great promise. "I always have a suspicion of boys who talk of planning their lives. I feel that they have won a precocious maturity in some illegitimate way." When he went to the *New Republic,* he wrote, out of the sublime faith of the instrumentalism that John Dewey had burned into his mind, that "genuine opinion is scientific hypotheses to be tested and revised as experience widens." Two years later the Randolph Bourne who died amidst the fusillades of war, bitterly opposed to what seemed to him the defection of the intellectuals from their own standards, cried "War is the health of the state." But it was not of the state that he was writing with such terrible bitterness at the end; it was the decline and fall of the Progressive ideal. He described in terms of his own experience the fate of the Progressive idealist in a world overrun by war, a world of which the high hopes of 1910-17 had given no warning, a world to which reason and art and the experimental school alone could give no clue. He had spent his life seeking the American promise as his education had prepared him to understand it; and when the war came it seemed to him that his education had betrayed him. (pp. 183-85)

Alfred Kazin, "The Joyous Season," in his On Native Grounds: An Interpretation of Modern American Prose Literature, *1942. Reprint by Harcourt Brace Jovanovich, Inc., 1963, pp. 165-85.**

LOUIS FILLER (essay date 1943)

[*In the following excerpt from his biography of Bourne, Filler commends him for his courage and idealism, but argues that*

Bourne made a grave error when, disillusioned with society, he assumed that democracy "required more criticism than defense." For a reply to Filler's conclusions, see the excerpt by Dwight MacDonald (1944).]

[During the 1920s] Bourne's life attracted respect because it presented so purposeful a pattern. Readers of postwar literature were frequently reminded that but a few years ago there had been a dissident who had seen his conclusions through to the end. That Bourne came again into influence as a legend, rather than as a living force, was evident in that *only* the fact that he had been a social rebel was remembered. His crusade for peace was not reviewed in all its aspects, his services to education were not recalled, the reformist and humanistic elements in his thought were not acknowledged. Bourne received the casual respect of iconoclasts who would probably have been shocked, if not disillusioned, by actual acquaintance with his work. (p. 132)

Bourne's own generation had done well to remember the individual in the machine age and to recognize that culture was not a luxury but rather a necessity of civilization. But culture was not all of civilization. In the 1930's, it became less and less possible to forget this fact. A radical-minded young man could criticize his government, but he could not deny its importance in his affairs. The New Deal did much to bring about a closer relationship between the younger generation and the state. The relationship, however, remained uneasy—possibly because events seemed to point to a life and death struggle between communism and fascism. When, in 1941, it became impossible for youth to ignore its responsibilities to the state, the youth movement, as conceived by Bourne and those who followed him, disappeared.

Here, then, was the dead-end of Bourne's crusade. He could be viewed as having been a prophet of the 1920's and one could even consider him to have been a prophet of the 1930's. But he cannot be viewed as a prophet of the 1940's. A cycle had played itself out.

However, one could at last take the sum of Bourne not merely in terms of his personality and ideas, but in the more balanced terms of what he had accomplished in the course of his career.

Carl Roberts, an English critics, in one of the few unsympathetic analyses made of Bourne, pointed out that his friends would have done better to write about "his very remarkable human qualities," [see excerpt dated 1923] rather than collect his writings as a tribute to his memory. But Roberts failed to see that it was the faith of Bourne's friends in his work which suggested the need for reviewing it. It represented a body of material exhibiting a basic integrity of purpose which had appealed to a considerable number and variety of people. It cannot be said that the ideals he expressed had been ungenerous. Nor could his writings be dismissed as unsound. Bourne was a romantic, and Irving Babbitt, who analyzed the dangers implicit in romanticism, had himself agreed that it contained virtues as well.

Yet Roberts was not wrong in calling attention to Bourne's "very remarkable human qualities." His independence of thought, his transparent honesty, and his single-minded determination to realize the ideals of his generation distinguished him from many of his contemporaries who were merely brilliant. Alfred Kazin has noted the peculiar spirit of selflessness in which Bourne wrote [see excerpt dated 1942]. And yet he had impressed few of his contemporaries—few even of those who firmly disagreed with his viewpoint—as a fanatic. His charm of personality, his ability to move freely among social elements, his interest in others, marked him through most of his career. (pp. 133-34)

It was, however, because of the intensity of Bourne's desire for a freer and more satisfying life that he fell into tragic errors. In believing as he did that the defects of American society could be best corrected from an outside vantage point, he assumed that society would be receptive to his criticism. But he maneuvered himself into a position which isolated him from the public he hoped to influence. Especially in his peace crusade, Bourne revealed himself as totally unable to accept America for what it was or (though he had emphasized the "promise of American life") to operate within its framework. The philosophic anarchism implicit in his last essays vividly demonstrated this contradiction in his thought.

There was a second error which flowed from his assumption that democracy required criticism more than defense. This error is illustrated by Professor Joseph Ward Swain's striking reminiscence of Bourne's European tour. While in Paris, Bourne had been impressed by a volume which depicted the young Frenchmen of the day as turning from the skepticism of Renan and Anatole France towards more constructive attitudes. The book revealed what would in later years have been termed fascist trends, but, as Professor Swain recalls, "Randolph did not see it that way; he saw only a 'youth' movement, young men revolting and improving their elders, and he was properly enthusiastic. I suppose it never occurred to him that *Giovinezza* [Youth] could be fascist."

Bourne would certainly have found fascism a false and revolting social development. But the reminiscence suggests that he had placed too high a premium on mere dissatisfaction with the *status quo* of society. He had not sufficiently discriminated between idealists and the ways and means which idealists selected to express their attitudes and inclinations. Bourne had condemned pragmatism as being a philosophy for opportunists, but it apparently never occurred to him that idealism as well as pragmatism could serve irresponsible people; that it was the *use* to which pragmatism or idealism was put that determined its value.

His basic belief in a democratic society rescued him from the more dangerous shoals of idealism. Even at the last, he did not turn against society; he became disillusioned with it. And even while disillusioned, he began a fresh attempt to influence America for the better. He thus demonstrated that it was not his concrete plans for higher living, educational and social, which had most profoundly concerned him; it was the *need* to modernize social institutions which he had tried to make clear. To this extent, Van Wyck Brooks was justified in his opinion that Bourne's unique function had not been political but rather spiritual [see excerpt dated 1920].

It is, finally, the loyalty with which Bourne maintained his ideals, and the courage with which he defended them, which entitle him to great respect. He was our equivalent for Bertrand Russell and Romain Rolland. He wished to serve the country and his appeal was entirely to reason. His fight for free thought was wholly creditable, however much his arguments can be debated.

Bourne takes a natural place among those dissidents who have helped leaven the thought and character of America. As with Thoreau, there is a flavor and moral tenacity in his work which should continue to attract students of the American scene. They will, it is true, concern themselves with social relations which

Bourne himself never anticipated. They will, nevertheless, continue to cope with problems of free speech, individualism, and social injustice—problems to which Bourne gave his best thought. Those who take up the gauntlet as he did can find profit as well as challenge in his experience. In doing this they may reconcile him with his America. (pp. 135-37)

> *Louis Filler, in his* Randolph Bourne, *American Council on Public Affairs, 1943, 158 p.*

DWIGHT MacDONALD   (essay date 1944)

[*An American essayist and critic, Macdonald was a noted proponent of various radical causes from the mid-1930s until his death in 1982. Founder of the journal* Politics *(1944-49), which welcomed "all varieties of radical thought," he pursued Trotskyism, anarchism, pacifism, and anti-communism before eventually settling on "conservative anarchism"—a humanistic libertarian ethic of which Thoreauesque civil disobediance is a part—as his personal ethic. In the following excerpt, Macdonald strongly criticizes both Louis Filler's biography of Bourne and Max Lerner's introduction to it, contending that both critics erred in designating as Bourne's chief faults the very qualities that made him a significant figure: his ruthlessly uncompromising respect for truth, and his willingness to follow to the logical end the consequences of his analyses.*]

[Louis Filler, in his biography of Randolph Bourne] lacks the sensitivity and imagination to understand Bourne's personality; he is respectful, but respect is never enough in such matters. . . .

It is a pity because a good biography of Bourne, the intellectual hero of World War I in this country, was never more needed than today in the midst of World War II. The story of Bourne's stand in the last war, even as it is refracted through Mr. Filler's muddy prose, is a moving one. While practically all American intellectual leaders, from John Dewey on down, were accepting the war as a just crusade against Prussian autocracy, Bourne stood out to the last against it. Although he had no independent income and was entirely dependent on his writing for a living, his criticism of American war policy became more and more uncompromising. (p. 35)

There was little political in Bourne's rejection of the war; he belonged to no party. He was really alone. Sustained by no party comradeship or loyalty to a definite set of political principles, Bourne reacted simply as a thoughtful and humane individual, which makes his stand all the more heroic, in a sense. Although he called himself a socialist and was one in a general kind of way, he never developed—except in his unfinished last fragment on the state—much beyond an American liberalistic position. He showed such slight political insight as to edit in 1916 a pacifist symposium, *Toward an Enduring Peace,* put out under the sponsorship of the American Association for International Conciliation, one of those window-dressing "peace" groups with which respectable people amuse themselves between wars. But when the war caused the Association, whose directorate included such peace-lovers as Nicholas Murray Butler, to fold up its tents and silently steal away, and when even John Dewey, his intellectual leader, came out for the war and conscription, Bourne broke with them and went his own way. Or rather, he continued along the way they had all been following until the war began. By holding fast to the values of liberalism, Bourne in the war found himself brought into increasingly sharp conflict with most liberals. This process, in its turn, led him to scrutinize liberalism more closely, and in the last years of his life, from which most of the work for which he is today remembered dates, his whole system of values was changing, becoming more critical of bourgeois society, more penetrating and tragic.

It is one of the oldest ironies that when the rebel dies he is memorialized by the very people he would have despised while living. Randolph Bourne has been especially unfortunate in this respect. The introduction to Mr. Filler's book is by Bourne's most assiduous contemporary chronicler, Max Lerner, whose own career and personal temper offer a painful contrast to Bourne's. Messrs. Lerner and Filler deplore, like two maiden aunts clucking over a beloved but wayward nephew, precisely the qualities which made Bourne a significant figure: his ruthless, uncompromising respect for the truth, and his willingness to follow out to the logical end the consequences of his analysis.

"If there was a fatal flaw in Bourne as a social critic," writes Lerner, "it was that he allowed himself to be pushed into the position of too consistent fault-finding with the institutions of his day and ultimately as Mr. Filler points out—to be alienated from the main sources of strength in American life, the people themselves." This totalitarian mystique of "the people" is simply a way of protecting the oppressors of the people from the criticism of men like Bourne. And Bourne's remarkable and uncomfortable essay on the state—"War is the health of the state"—is to Lerner "catastrophically wrong". The catastrophe is there, all right, but it involves Lerner's own totalitarian liberalism, which aims at a strong state—and no nonsense from the fascist-Bukharinist-Trotskyist enemies of the people! Bourne's analysis of the state represents the organic completion of his whole intellectual development, and if he was "catastrophically wrong" there, then his whole thinking was askew.

It is a curious process, a way of immunizing liberalistic thought against the destructive acids generated by a mind like Bourne's: utmost respect for the style of thinking and none at all for the conclusions reached. The trick is to wallow to one's heart's content in sentimental glorification of Bourne the rebel and fighter and thinker, without abandoning the philistine values of those against whom he rebelled, fought and thought while he was alive. Mr. Filler believes that Bourne was a prophet for the 20's "and even the 30's". "But he cannot be viewed as a prophet of the 40's". That is to say, the only good prophet is a dead one. But Bourne is very much alive today, let me assure his biographer, and there still exist those who are not at all disturbed by the "error" Mr. Filler finds in Bourne's social thinking, namely: "his assumption that democracy required criticism more than defense". (pp. 35-6)

> *Dwight MacDonald, "Randolph Bourne," in* Politics, *Vol. 1, No. 2, March, 1944, pp. 35-6.*

CHARLES A. MADISON   (essay date 1947)

[In the following excerpt, Madison briefly discusses each of Bourne's books.]

In 1913, while still at Columbia, Bourne published *Youth and Life,* a collection of essays. The imprint of instrumentalism was on almost every page of the book. The social ferment of the time—the vigorous reform movements, the attacks on the Victorian-Puritan morality, the cultural awakening, the enthusiasm of the Progressives at Armageddon—helped to confirm him in his determination to fight for the right of each child to a free and friendly development. Written with force and fluency, his challenging book became a fresh and compelling voice in American literature, articulating clearly and convincingly the rebellious idealism of the younger generation. (p. 424)

The pages of *Youth and Life* glow with passion and excitement. The writing is easy and forceful, at times even brilliant, but it is not subtle or seasoned. Bourne's intense conviction animates every essay. He despised hypocritical and pretentious people—"pseudos" was his name for them—those who prized conformity and glossed over the evils vitiating their conventional morality. Armed with his greater knowledge of man's achievements, possessed of "a truly religious belief in human progress," he set about to discomfit the forces of the status quo and to array against them the youth of the land. His criticism of the older generation tended to be sweeping and extravagant. Whatever seemed antagonistic to it he praised as worth while and desirable—and all the more so if it reflected favorably on youth. His agitation for social change, however, remained on the literary level. For all his sympathy with the struggle of labor and reformers, he was still the student, brilliant and bold, but not yet the independent and active radical. (pp. 426-27)

To him socialism was essentially applied Christianity. He favored "a Religion of Socialism, moving towards an ever more perfect socialized human life on earth." (p. 427)

Bourne's investigations in and reflections on education are to be found in *The Gary Schools,* a brief volume published in 1916, and in *Education and Living,* a collection of essays that appeared a year later. An ardent admirer of John Dewey, he took a professional interest in the newer developments in the public schools. He gave his support to the current clamor for more progressive methods of teaching, and for a closer coordination between the schools and the practical world. He envisioned a future in which children in school would acquire not merely intellectual tools but the training for a democratic, rich, and wholesome life.

The public schools he visited pursued the timeworn methods and activities which he had experienced in childhood. Deeply concerned for the well-being of the child, he wrote scathingly of this stultifying atmosphere. He insisted that a child could not be confined to mental activity for five hours a day without injury to its normal growth; that a stimulating and salutary education must also include play, constructive work, socialization, and other non-intellectual activities. He advocated the classroom study of the daily newspaper, greater emphasis on the democratic way of life, the intelligent and intensive use of psychological tests and educational measurements, equal stress on study, work, and play, and the training of all children to the limit of their individual capacities. In 1915 these measures were, if not revolutionary, truly radical. (p. 430)

The History of a Literary Radical, the posthumous collection edited by Van Wyck Brooks, contains some of Bourne's best-known writings on American culture. The title essay, a vividly sketched self-portrait, traced his literary development from adolescence to maturity and stressed the radical changes in cultural attitudes between the old generation and the new. Ironically enough, his first introduction to the great modern European writers came not in his college studies but at a popular lecture by Professor William Lyon Phelps. He discovered a new world of literature. One book led to another, and all of them produced in his mind a rebelliousness against the dead classics which he had been taught to revere. With other literary radicals he shared the joys of new discoveries, new standards, a new appreciation of America's capacity for cultural greatness. (p. 432)

Bourne's enthusiasm for our cultural progress led him to examine the then vexing problem of Americanization. In **"Trans-National America,"** an essay of seminal significance, he took a bold stand against the anti-alien intolerance which had become accentuated in 1916, when the article appeared in *The Atlantic Monthly.* Our vociferous chauvinists, he argued, in their insistence upon conformity with American tradition were in truth demanding the assimilation of millions of our population to our Anglo-Saxon way of life. This claim was as unjust as it was unreal. (p. 433)

[America's] transnational character [according to Bourne] is our great contribution to civilized society. If we are to be true to our destiny we must treasure our cosmopolitan heritage; not confine our culture to the narrowness of the melting pot but broaden it to the variegated vastness of a transnational society.

Meantime Bourne watched with increasing dread as the United States drifted towards intervention in Europe. He believed that our participation in the carnage would be catastrophic. "The war—or American promise: one must choose. One cannot be interested in both. For the effect of the war will be to impoverish American promise." He had no choice. He hated war—the antithesis of everything that was dear to him. So he fought it openly and desperately. Whoever favored war—for whatever reason—he attacked without quarter.... To the end of his brief life in December 1918—he fell victim to an attack of pneumonia—he fought for the American promise with a courage and conviction that placed him with the eminent pacifists of his time.

One of his first major essays against war, appearing in *The New Republic* in July 1916, presented a persuasive, if idealistic, moral equivalent of universal military service. Compulsory militarism, he explained, was a complete negation of true Americanism. In its stead he proposed an application of William James's "conception of a productive army, finding in drudgery and toil and danger the values that war and preparation for war had given." He would have all boys and girls of sixteen enlisted in a universal educational service that would train them for both work and citizenship by setting up as the enemy "our appalling slovenliness, the ignorance of great masses in city and country as to the elementary technique of daily life." For our need, he pleaded, was to learn how to live rather than how to die, how to create rather than how to destroy. Here he was of course the poet, nurtured in nineteenth-century humanitarianism, and not the pragmatist adapting himself to practical situations; but by this time he was done with pragmatism.

The intellectual pacifists, from John Dewey down, who had favored war in 1916 in their zeal to safeguard democracy, received his severest lashings. In a series of passionate and provocative papers in *The Seven Arts,* which James Oppenheim later collected in **Untimely Papers,** he pilloried these teachers and friends for their rationalized apostasy. He was not fooled by their make-believe assertions that they were deliberately leading the nation into "a war that will secure the triumph of democracy and will internationalize the world." No new world order, he declared, could be "built out of the rotten materials of armaments, diplomacy and 'liberal' statesmanship." The deluded intellectuals, pathetically allying themselves with the ruling reactionary groups for the sake of democracy, were certain to be ignored and scorned by them once the war was won. Yet they might have prevailed earlier, when the people were still pacifist and amenable to reason, if they had spent their time and thought in clarification and education, in devising other means than war for carrying through American policy. Instead they had unwittingly become tools of the jingoes. "The intellectuals have still to explain why, willing as they are now to use force to continue the war to absolute exhaustion, they were not willing to use force to coerce the world to a speedy peace." For all their presumed realism they "have forgotten that the real enemy is War rather than imperial Germany." (pp. 434-36)

Bourne's unfinished study of the state, begun shortly before his death, is probably the most important of his writings. An iconoclastic, emotional, almost mystical criticism of the state power, it is in a true sense a development of the earlier attacks by the extreme Abolitionists and individualist anarchists, and particularly that by Thoreau. His chief contention was that the state perpetrated war and fed upon the death of its subjects. "For war is essentially the health of the State," was his ironic refrain. The state began as "the organization of the herd to act offensively and defensively against another herd similarly organized." It served to stress man's gregarious impulse in a time of social crisis, when the individual needed to feel behind him the full power of the community. Symbolizing at once communal strength and parental shelter, the state in time arrogated to itself the power to deal politically with other states. And throughout civilized history such dealings have always ended in war.

The state, Bourne insisted, was not at all the equivalent of the nation. The latter was synonymous with the people and served their intrinsic welfare. Nations never warred with one another, since their interests were never in conflict. States, on the contrary, existed for the sole purpose of waging war and becoming strong at the expense of vanquished states. Governments were their agents and served them by declaring war without consulting the people who did the fighting and the dying. "It is not too much to say that the normal relation of the States is war. Diplomacy is a disguised war, in which States seek to gain by barter and intrigue, by the cleverness of wits, the objectives which they would have to gain more clumsily by means of war."

War is therefore the health of the state in that it unifies the people and completely subjugates them to the will of the government. (pp. 438-39)

From a pragmatic standpoint Randolph Bourne was a tragic failure. In possession of all the intellectual qualifications for leadership, well on his way towards a position of power and influence, he deliberately rejected the world at a time of crisis and assumed the role of an outcast crying in the wilderness. (p. 440)

[He] belongs not with the politicians but with the prophets. What matters in his case was not his reaction to daily events nor his judgment of temporal affairs but his energetic stimulation of minds and his vision of the good life. Few Americans possessed his enthusiasm for the deepening and enrichment of our indigenous culture. He early sought to remove the layer of rust and rot which crusted the minds of many Americans. He vigorously assailed the smugness with which this retarding condition was accepted and called upon youth to discard the stiff and prim ways of their elders. Proud of our potential greatness in art and letters, he was impatient with our subservience to Europe. He exhorted us to "turn our eyes upon our own art for a time, shut ourselves in with our own genius, and cultivate with an intense and practical pride what we have already achieved against the obstacles of our cultural humility." His energy, enthusiasm, and sympathy injected into his writing the dynamic appeal which activated and enriched the renascence then in progress.

Together with a more vital cultural growth he sought greater social justice. He believed our continent was rich enough to provide abundantly for all the people, and he wanted everyone to receive his rightful share. Oppression and exploitation, slums and poverty and ignorance—these scabs of inequality offended his soul and he cried out against them with righteous indignation. Culture and justice became the two pillars adorning the edifice of his American promise. . . . Nor should it be forgotten that he was still in the process of becoming, still in the first flowering of his artistic and intellectual powers, when the war struck at the roots of his being and the "flu" epidemic snuffed out his life.

It was his passionate eagerness for the richer and freer life of the American promise that made him oppose the war so desperately. He knew that war was inimical to culture; that in fighting Prussianism we would expose ourselves to a similar militarism. Because he saw no good reason for our joining a war that did not really concern us, he regarded the efforts of the pro-war liberals as criminal folly. Having no alternative but to oppose them, he did so with all the fierce anger of a visionary at bay. He readily suffered the loss of his reputation, his income, and many of his friends. He continued his Jeremian criticism even after ostracism had driven him into the wilderness. For zeal had sublimated his pacifism into prophecy. His dissenting voice rose accusingly against the moral myopia of the mob and gave expression to a patriotism far nobler than

A drawing of Bourne's death mask. The Granger Collection, New York.

that of the war leaders: a love of country that held fast to the ideal of the ultimate good at a time when practical citizens were concerned solely with matters of immediacy. Paul Rosenfeld well said: "Bourne was the great bearer of moral authority while America was at war. He was our bannerman of values in a general collapse." It was this nobility of vision—so irritating to men of action in times of crisis and yet so vital to the moral health of society—that places Randolph Bourne among the true, if minor, prophets of America. (pp. 441-42)

Charles A. Madison, "Randolph Bourne: The History of a Literary Radical," in his Critics & Crusaders: A Century of American Protest, *Henry Holt and Company, 1947, pp. 419-42.*

JOHN ADAM MOREAU (essay date 1966)

[*In the following excerpt, Moreau examines Bourne's writings on the American educational system. For further discussion of Bourne's essays on education, see the excerpt by Joseph Featherstone (1982).*]

[The] themes of needless waste in American schooling and of what the future held pervade most of Bourne's writing on education. He expressed the sentiments—if not through facts and specifics, then in general terms—of progressive educationists and their supporters. The older generation, he felt, had always hidden the unpleasant things of life and had preserved a conspiracy of silence about them. Education had been no exception. It had encouraged a rigid and therefore useless morality unrelated to real life. The older generation was as responsible for the need and growth of progressive education as were population increase and industrialization. For, as Randolph said in another context, "educated men still defend the hoariest abuses, still stand sponsor for utterly antiquated laws and ideals. This is why the youth of this generation has to be so suspicious of those who seem to speak authoritatively. He knows not whom he can trust, for few there are who speak from their own inner conviction."

As one who cherished the Socratic method, he maintained it was just this speaking from conviction which was crushed by traditional education. His first school article for the *New Republic* was based on a visit to his hometown high school. Only the year before, a shiny, expensive building was completed in Bloomfield. Inside, however, he found an unreality of curriculum and a cranky rivalry between teacher and student which he supposed unfolded daily in thousands of American schools. Although the business at hand presumably was ideas, an artificial silence was imposed on students.

Only when class adjourned did the pupils show interest in anything. Socrates would have been amused by this training school for incipient legislators, he commented. The only thing the Bloomfield classroom resembled, he said with Mencken-like dismay, was a state legislature. It is a platitude, Bourne observed, that those who succeed in life are those who express themselves and whose minds are flexible and responsive to others. Thinking cannot be done without talking. But the classroom shuts off such intercourse.

Randolph admitted he might be overly intellectual about the matter, and acknowledged the problems of cost, equipment, time, and space. Still, the difficulty was that—unlike cotton looms—massed children compose a social group, and personality can be developed only by free stimulation of minds. "Is it not very curious", he asked, "that we spend so much time on the practice and methods of teaching, and never criticize the very framework itself? Call this thing that goes on in the modern schoolroom schooling, if you like. Only don't call it education.''

He believed he knew why the school was out of harmony with 20th century America. To him pedagogy was just learning that you can put a child in school but he will not profit unless he is fed well, his physical defects cared for, and particularly unless he grows naturally. The child's energy must be harnessed to interesting and fruitful activity. Indeed, the case against the conventional school was blacker than the worst muckraker could conceive. The next generation, he predicted, ''will rank the pseudo-pedagogy which had directed the physical conditions of school life with the black magic of the Middle Ages.''

American education had become a morass because the nation's educators traditionally had seen the world divided into two radically different groups, adults and children. While adults went about their work, off in a separate sphere, children idled, waiting to take their places in the world. Book knowledge, because it was a badge of success and seemed the key to achievement—it was the sign of the enviable leisure class—had become the stock of the school. ''We came,'' he said, ''to think of ourselves as cupboards in which were laboriously stored bundles of knowledge. We knew dimly the shape of the articles within. But we never expected to see the contents until we were grown, when we would joyfully open our packages and use them to the infinite glory of our worldly success and happiness. But it was a slow child who did not begin to suspect, long before his shelves were full, that most of his adult friends had lost no time, when their schooldays were over, locking their cupboards and leaving their bundles to the dust and worms.''

If parents and teachers now recognized this they generally still insisted that discipline is the ability to do painful things. Adults still distrusted a world in which children do joyfully what interests them. This doing the interesting was the trend of the new education, Randolph contended. It was the transformation from the unconscious school to the self-conscious school. That change was the very kernel of the excitement of the new education.

What had happened in American education, it appeared, was that a democratic education had been achieved in the sense that common schooling was practically within the reach of all. But in another sense education was not democratic because it did not give equal opportunity to each child of finding in school the life and training he peculiarly needed, that is, of finding himself. Such education still had to be worked for, and this meant transforming the American school from an institution into a life-like situation.

Education had presumed, he said, that children were empty vessels to be loaded with knowledge. They are neither that nor machines for the teacher to wind and set running. They are ''pushing wills and desires and curiosities.'' As growing things, they need places to grow. Children live full lives more than older people do; and they cannot become minds and only minds for four or five hours a day without stultification. It was clear, Bourne continued, ''that education has grown up in this country in a separate institutional compartment, jealously apart from the rest of the community life. It has developed its own techniques, its own professional spirit. Its outlines are cold and logical. It is far the best ordered of our institutions. Its morale is the nearest thing we have to compulsory military service. There is something remote and antiseptic about even our best

schools. They contrast strangely with the color and confusion of the rest of our American life. The bare class-rooms, the stiff seats, the austere absence of beauty, suggest a hospital where painful if necessary intellectual operations are going on.''

Compartmentalizing of American education had resulted in ''puzzle education,'' Bourne maintained. This constituted a rote memorization of facts, seldom related to the main current of life. This was nothing more than a ''riddle-curriculum,'' and one's genuine education, that is, his familiarity with the world, came after getting out of school. He declared that such a system was demonstrably futile. . . . (pp. 83-5)

Foolishness in education or elsewhere always was fair game, but he had an un-Menckenesque approach to his carping, and he believed his criticism just. He admitted that education resented outside criticism, and that there were few able administrators who did not believe they were doing the best with the resources they had. Naturally pedagogues felt that criticism should come only from the profession and were resentful and hurt when arraigned in the light of the product turned out by the schools.

Yet, an almost pathetic confidence in ''expert'' overhauling had not been justified, he argued. Alleged experts really did not have the magical power attributed to them, and as much as educators complained that their problems are financial, a student of the subject could not be convinced—in a wealthy nation like the United States where the prestige of education was extraordinarily high—that money was the crux of the matter. The problem was one of more intelligent use of resources, less ostentatious concern with buildings and frills, and higher teacher salaries.

The difficulty, in short, was to Bourne not predominantly mechanical, but psychological; and the public in sensing that it was psychological, was demanding more and more that as much attention as had been given to organization and system be given to the conscious and spiritual side of learning and teaching. The result of preoccupation with organization and system, he said, was an unnecessary emphasis on routine which created the ''wasted years.'' This was the period of intellectual leakage. The child first learned the basics of the three R's, but instead of using them to move into other disciplines and awaken intellectual curiosity, he rehearsed from primary school to high school. Paradoxically the more excellent became the primary methods, the poorer became the schools' product at the end of the system.

The question facing Americans who wanted to create effective school systems before population overran buildings and swamped trained personnel was, to him, evident. The nation was pushing against old barriers which had thwarted it in leading the full life it was capable of. The issue was, What kind of school do we want? To decide that would determine the kind of society Americans wanted. About the future of American education, he was both guarded and hopeful. All the revolutionary strivings of the past, he said, were away from institutional authorities toward greater freedom. (pp. 86-7)

Bourne might have continued theorizing abstractly about education, had the *New Republic* not sent him in March 1915 to inspect the Gary, Indiana, school system, then famous for its innovations. The Gary Plan convinced him that the embryonic community life type of school had been effected. Followers of Dewey, he wrote, saw in the Gary system, as the master himself did, the ''most complete and admirable application yet attempted, a synthesis of the best aspects of the progressive 'schools of tomorrow'.''

The father of the Gary plan was William Wirt, a Deweyite who already had attracted attention for similiar pioneering innovations as superintendent in his native town of Bluffton, Indiana, before Gary hired him in 1907. Wirt had tried 50 different programs for what he called ''work-study-and-play'' schools, but Gary was a special challenge. The town was recently established and a school system had to be formed from scratch. (p. 87)

[In articles in the *New Republic, Scribner's,* and in a book, *The Gary Schools,* Bourne described] how the school related study to real life. The print shop produced the office supplies. The commercial course worked on the school's financial records. Home economics prepared the meals and served them at cost, and the chemistry class—taught by the municipal chemist—analyzed local food, candy, and water supplies. The session was lengthened an hour to 4 p.m., but teachers and students had no homework. Classes were designated slow, normal and rapid, aimed at graduating students in 10, 12, and 14 years. Voluntary Saturday classes were packed, 6,000 adults attended night school, and a long summer school, intended to keep children off streets and creatively busy, had proved its worth. In fact, Gary authorities believed they could not afford to have their schools idle. Randolph also depicted how teachers of manual courses were craftsmen who incidentally were good teachers. Part of their salary was for keeping the buildings and grounds in shape, tasks at which their students assisted.

The Gary system could have been the most stupendous laboratory in creation, yet if it lacked social pertinence he would not have looked twice. But in a nation where perhaps only one-fifth of school children reached high school, here was a chance to change the situation. The special activities were not mere trimmings on the three R's, but neither was the latter neglected in favor of the former, Bourne explained. (pp. 88-9)

When antagonists charged that the system was an intricate method of making things easy and encouraging unruliness Bourne became angry. On this major point he cited Dewey. It was wrong to consider that an interesting school with little formal discipline like Gary unjustifiably simplified things. The point, he contended, is that interesting things are not necessarily easy. They may be hard, but when there is interest, the difficulty is overcome or at least lessened and prepared for a later effort. It is in the overcoming that the moral value lies. Moreover, there is an implicit geometric progression: interest means more and more acquired skill and therefore a more intense effort. Bourne called it ''willed skill.'' A side effect was that interested busy children seldom were troublesome. (p. 89)

As much moral value lay in what he called the democracy of the Gary plan. The school not only had become intimately part of the lives of Garyites, but had destroyed traditional barriers separating book learning from vocational training and manual work. Nothing seemed more delightful about the Gary schools than the absence of cant. (p. 90)

''It is true that there is probably not a single idea operative that is original with Mr. Wirt. Probably there is not a single idea that is not being applied in some school in the country. The novelty is the synthesis, and the democratic spirit that motivates it.''

Randolph also viewed the Gary school as a combination preventative and rescue operation where the child's development

was concerned. Previously and still in 1915, the vocational school touched the child too late in life, sometimes not until high school, he complained. By then the child's interest very likely was dulled. When the student was then put to work, he often found pure drudgery. The Gary plan, however, tried to lead the student early to what suited him. Neither books nor tools was paramount. More important, machines were not ends, but means.

The public school in the United States generally turned out low-grade specialists, despite a fancy liberalized curriculum, Bourne maintained. Industrial training had made no effort to produce the type of mind most needed—the versatile machinist, the practical engineer, the mind that adapts and masters a mechanism. Such resourcefulness, inventiveness, and pragmatic judgment of a machine by its product—the sense of machinery as a means, not an end—are precisely what society demands of every profession and trade in the 20th century. ''The Gary school,'' he remarked, ''is the first I have seen that promises to cultivate this kind of intelligence. It frankly accepts the machine not in the usual sense of the vocational schools, as an exacting master that the child is to learn docilely to obey, but as the basis of our modern life, by whose means we must make whatever progress we may will. The machine seems to be a thing to which society is irrevocably pledged. It is time the school recognized it. In Gary it is with the child from his earliest years. It is the motive of his scientific study.'' (pp. 90-1)

[Bourne's] articles on education were generally temperate, and he consciously tried to make his writing sober in *The Gary Schools.* But if his articles on the new education were felicitous in style, they also were occasionally marked by a characteristic intemperateness toward what he rejected. And he forgot that reform sentiment could run ahead of the community.

What stands out in Bourne's writing about the new education, particularly the Wirt plan, is his unquestioning espousal of it, although he did realize that no prudent person could declare that the Gary plan was a panacea. And he was keenly aware of practical problems ranging from politician educators to a lethargic citizenry. His *The Gary Schools* was well received generally, but it gave many the impression expressed in a sympathetic reception in the December 1916 *Education Review:* ''He thinks the problem solved.'' (p. 92)

Although the Wirt system—or what it became—took a beating in a special report published in 1955 for the Gary board of education, there is no denying its extensive influence on American schools. (p. 93)

[Bourne] consciously acted as a gadfly, bringing the tidings of the new education and often trying to sting the public into concern for something he believed vitally important to the welfare of America. Mindful of the relatively few persons, even among the articulate, informed, and educated whom the *New Republic* reached—and mindful of widespread reaction against the Gary Plan—one must not claim too much for him. He and the Gary plan had opponents as evidenced by a piece such as Paul Shorey's ''The Bigotry of the New Education'' which appeared in the *Nation* for September 6, 1916. Yet his *The Gary Schools* was generally well received. So was his *Education and Living* . . . in which all but one of 28 essays were *New Republic* contributions.

Max Lerner wrote in 1940 that, ''It is hard for us, in these days when John Dewey's reputation is embalmed in jubilee volumes, to think ourselves back to a time when his educational ideas were living and—it seemed—revolutionary weapons. Yet that was true, and to no small measure as a result of Bourne's ardent discipleship." Lerner overstated the case for Bourne. Most assuredly, it was the force of Dewey's ideas which was responsible for the impact Dewey had on American life. Had Randolph never appeared on the scene, Dewey's ideas would have had their hearing. (pp. 93-4)

Dewey was the original thinker; Bourne's significant effort, principally aimed at the literate informed public, was as publicist. For he took Dewey's—and Wirt's—ideas and phrased them in meaningful, human, day-to-day terms. So well did he write, that the new education under his treatment took on fresh mundane significance.

The Reader's Guide for the years 1910-21 lists 105 articles about Wirt or Gary schools or by Wirt. A sampling gives the impression that no article or combination of articles surpassed his handling of Dewey's ideas and the new education. For Randolph realized that the new education was not only the pedagogical ramification of progressivism but also of efficiency innovations in American life, especially those initiated and encouraged by Frederick Taylor. As Bourne saw it, science had jumped the barriers of subject matter and spread through the school system.

"Science means that nothing must be wasted," he had written, and now he understood perfectly that efficiency was what industrial America wanted—the best use of time, space, and all other resources of its schools. Randolph saw Taylorism in the Wirt plan and it was that insight which contributed to the vividness of his writing on education. He was publicist of the new education.

The new education meant a firmer America. A public school, Bourne said in words which struck the heart of the progressive education movement and which ring true today, "is a mockery unless it educates the public. It cannot make the rarefied and strained product at the top the test of its effectiveness. And the public is not ideally educated unless its individuals—all of them—are intelligent, informed, skilled, resourceful up to the limit of their respective capacities. Life itself can no longer be trusted to provide this education; the school must substitute. The Gary school deliberately sets such an ideal." (pp. 94-5)

John Adam Moreau, in his Randolph Bourne: Legend and Reality, *Public Affairs Press, 1966, 227 p.*

JAMES R. VITELLI   (essay date 1981)

[*In the following excerpt, Vitelli discusses the importance of* Youth and Life, *closely examining Bourne's point of view in an effort to determine if his ideas were really as "radical" as Bourne himself often declared them to be.*]

A man's "spiritual fabric" is almost completely woven by the time he is into his twenties, according to Bourne. True or not, his own ideas and ideals had been pretty well formulated by the time, aged twenty-eight, he left Europe and returned to America to start living beyond youth. Those ideas and ideals may not have been so radical as he supposed, or at least as he declared them to be, but the way he had formed and expressed them, and the ways in which he proceeded to apply them made him seem radical to others of his generation. They too thought of themselves, self-consciously and proudly, as rebellious and revolutionary. They may not have been very radical either, as some historians of the Progressive era have suggested, but that is how, partly under Bourne's guidance, they perceived themselves. It may be worthwhile . . . , therefore, to attempt a

summary of the ideas and ideals which made up the spiritual biography of his generation that Bourne gave to them in his *Youth and Life.*

First and foremost was his concept of youth. Nearly all else that he addressed himself to is suffused with that ideal and the special burden of meanings he poured into it. It is an all-embracing term, virtually equated with the second word in his book's title, "life." He defined it and used it in such a way as to take it beyond meaning merely a stage of personal growth; it was for him a state of being, a state of consciousness of being alive. Hence it followed that a life truly lived was the life of perpetual youth, a life that preserved the initial consciousness of the wonder of life that is first fully experienced in youth. Thoroughly romantic, it is Bourne's equivalent to the nineteenth-century concept of the "self," only more perilously poised, having no absolute existence, only a relative one defined by time and how it appears to those no longer young. "Youth," he said, "seems curiously fragile. Perhaps it is because all beauty has something of the precarious and fleeting about it." Youth is a state of heightened awareness of life. Life's "wistfulness and haunting pathos" is especially real only to youth, for "it feels the rush of time past it," and is haunted by the sense of change, not simply "the feeling of past change," the false wistfulness of middle and old age, but also "by the presentiment of future change."

Under Bourne's use of it, the concept of youth has a way of melting and merging with other concepts: life, reality, change—all positive values, of course. Or it takes on positive coloration by being contrasted with its opposition—middle age, old age, the older generation. The concept of the generation is a necessary corollary to that of youth, but these are not defined by chronological gaps between them any more than youth is defined by age—though twenty-five is the magic symbolic age used by Bourne in these essays. The "older generation" consists of those who are running the world with damaged ideals, or ideals become dogma, fixed by tradition, by dead tradition. Hence if youth and the younger generation equal life, reality, change, truth, idealism, then that which is dead, fanciful or unreal, static or immovable, false and sentimental, is the older generation. Once one has gotten the clue to this Manichaean world the rest can be an amusing little game: youth is to democracy as the older generation is to———? Or, "In this conflict between youth and its elders,———is the incarnation of reason pitted against the rigidity of tradition."

This may not be altogether fair to Bourne's portrait of youth, risking a reduction of it to caricature. But caricature and the idealized sketch have in common a simplicity of content, even an oversimplification, and depend for their effectiveness on manner and style; the line between them may very well be a brush stroke turned up instead of down. What I wish to emphasize here is that Bourne's achievement was one of style: his brush strokes are consistently up, and the idealized youth that emerges from his book is a charming, forceful, and persuasive champion for the young in heart of all ages, and this achievement is less a triumph of argument by idea than of persuasion by rhetorical skill.

Bourne's most effective rhetorical device, what makes for the oversimplified division of his world between the forces of good and the forces of evil, when reduced to outline, is the balanced, parallel construction. What happens in the sentence is matched by what happens in the paragraph, most often constructed on the principle of comparison and contrast; and similarly, from essay to essay, there is balance and matching and overlapping, the book, like each essay, developing in Emersonian fashion in a spiraling rather than linear progression. One effect, already remarked upon, is that of one concept almost imperceptibly becoming identified with another, less through direct comparison or connection than through a repeated common rhetorical locution. The interconnectedness of all things, the organic universe Bourne valued so highly, is thus intimately manifest in his style and expresses that principle of growth and of awareness which is at the heart of his concept of youth. (pp. 66-8)

In ["**The Mystic Turned Radical**"] where Maeterlinck is used by Bourne as "the best of modern mystics," we learn that it was Maeterlinck from whom Bourne learned that "an excess of radicalism is essential to the equilibrium of life." Society's habit, Maeterlinck had said, is always to think in terms less reasonable than are required. We learn that "with the instinct of the true radical, the poet [Maeterlinck] had gone to the root of the social attitude." But this radical who is a poet is also youth. In ["**For Radicals**"] the birth of youth was described as follows:

> Youth has suddenly become conscious of life. It has eaten of the tree of knowledge of good and evil.
>
> As the world breaks in on a boy with its crashing thunder, he has a feeling of expansion, of sudden wisdom and sudden care. The atoms of things seem to be disintegrating around him. Then come the tearings and the grindings and the wrenchings, and in that conflict the radical or the poet is made.

Youth is thus made into the true radical and poet by his titanic struggle with the world's conditions (but also, for the achievement of perpetual youth, he must struggle with "inner spiritual ones"). Still later (in "**The Life of Irony**") we will learn that what makes the youth into a radical and a poet is also what accounts for his being an ironist born (not made) and whose passion for comprehension is what in turn makes youth as an ironist "a person who counts in the world."

As the "incarnation of reason" youth actually adopts "the scientific attitude," that is, a remorseful questioning of all that is old, and a daring willingness to experiment. And as with radicalism, Bourne argued in "**The Adventure of Life**," not less but more was needed: "Not less science but more science do we need in order that we may more and more get into our control the forces and properties of nature, and guide them for our benefit." Whether more radicalism or more science, more irony or more mysticism or more poetry, they are needed for "control," for insuring youth's "command" of the world when its turn comes. This recurring exhortation makes *Youth and Life* a kind of manual of power, a series of rhetorical calisthenics proposed as preparation for the assumption of power. They are exercises for the individual but designed to insure a social and collective end. They are proposals for the development of personality, for only "the most glowing personality" is assured of influence, of exercising power. The rationale for this lies, of course, in youth's consciousness of being alive: "We are alive, and we have a right to interpret the world as living; we are persons, and we have the right to interpret the world in terms of personality." This is, moreover, a religious consciousness—a good transcendental awareness, as it turns out—the sense that there is "the humble fragment of a divine personality" in youth's own. And so we come full circle from

youth to the mysterious core of life itself which is contained in the personality that is youth.

"Desire," as we have seen, is a crucial word in Bourne's world. Hardly an idea, not quite susceptible to being an ideal, it points rather to a fact of experience, something Bourne felt acutely and attributed to all youth. It is part of the paradoxical figure of Bourne's youth that he can be that supreme ironist, cool, detached, scientific, capable of getting outside himself, and also very much possessed by all sorts of desires and passions that sway him almost beyond control. Bourne's radical youth sought to capitalize upon the strength of youth's desires, releasing them from the restraints imposed on them by social custom and tradition, and directing them to noble fulfilling ends. At bottom, as I have suggested is evidenced in Bourne's correspondence, especially that with Bligh, Bourne recognized youth's desire as a sexual force. Sex is given explicit recognition in *Youth and Life* as one of youth's "supremest and most poignant of adventures," the other being death, "the one the gateway into life, the other out of it." But it is implicitly present behind the masking defenses of an abstract language, a language that throbs with feeling. On the one hand Bourne's diction makes intense the felt wishes and hopes Bourne attributes to the young; on the other, his figurative language emphasizes the frustrating constraints and inhibitions working against the fulfilling expression of youthful personality. Often he takes off on metaphors of battle: "To get command of these arch-enemies [sex and death] is an endeavor worthy of the moral heroes of today. We can get control, it seems, of the rest of our souls but these always lie in wait to torment and harass us." Youth thinks of itself only as the "master of things," never as a mere "soldier in the ranks," but as the leader, "leading the cohorts to victory . . . bringing in some long-awaited change by a brilliant *coup d'etat* or writing and speaking words of fire that win a million hearts at a stroke." (Bourne's youthful warrior often turns out to be that poet whose weapons are words, as with the ironist, too, whose armor is almost impregnable against "the shafts of fortune and blows of friends or enemies" for "he knows how to parry each thrust and prepare for every emergency.") The "enemy" or the barriers, the obstructions, provoke in youth an "intolerant rage" or a "passionate despair" as youth "collides" with them, against the "inertia" of older men, and the "moral hedges" that surround life; or as he struggles to throw off the "weight" of dead tradition, or the "fetters" of a puritan code. When it is not battle that youth is waging, he is contending against some poison, sickness, or festering sores for which "youth is the drastic antiseptic." Yet running throughout this world of conflict or plague is a persistent thread of exuberant hope sparkling with youth's desire, which is also "passion" or "enthusiasm" or both at once, generally "turbulent," or burning in youth's "furnace" or "crucible."

And there is little doubt about youth's eventual triumph. "It is the glory of the present age that in it one can be young," Bourne trumpeted. "Our times give no check to the radical tendencies of youth. On the contrary, they give the directest stimulation. A muddle of a world and a wide outlook combine to inspire us to the bravest of radicalisms. Great issues have been born in the last century, and are now loose in the world. There is a radical philosophy that illuminates our environment, gives us terms in which to express what we see, and coordinates our otherwise aimless reactions." Precisely what the "great issues" were he did not say, presuming his audience would know them, of course—which is another reason why succeeding generations have been able to fill in the blanks with their own notions of the "great issues." Pragmatism is presumably the radical philosophy he alludes to, but nowhere in *Youth and Life* is there any mention of William James as, indeed, there is a paucity of direct reference to any proper names to illuminate the issues which youth is going to bring to some triumphant culmination.

Broadly, very broadly, his words sweep up all the melioristic spirit of the early Progressive era and place youth on the crest of its still moving wave. "The great social movement of yesterday and today and tomorrow has hit us of the younger generation hard." This sentence, opening his essay **"For Radicals,"** leaps beyond history as does much that immediately follows: "Many of us were early converted to a belief in the possibilities of a regenerated social order, and to a passionate desire to do something in aid of that regeneration. The appeal is not only to our sympathy for the weak and exploited, but also to our delight in a healthy, free, social life, to an artistic longing for a society where the treasures of civilization may be open to all, and to our desire for an environment where we ourselves will be able to exercise our capacities, and exert the untrammeled influences which we believe might be ours and our fellows'." All this had for "the disinterested and serious youth of to-day" the powerful attraction of "a practicable ideal." It was this marriage of the ideal with the efficient that made youth "gloriously hopeful" for the future, and this hope "is the lever of progress,—one might say, the only lever of progress."

More than any other feature of the book, this optimistic faith in youth's victory, linked as here with the idea of progress and that in turn dependent upon the marriage of the ideal and the practical, made Bourne appear far less radical than his other words declared his youth to be. As Henry May has pointed out, a belief in progress was one of three main articles in the dominant American faith, and not simply the nineteenth century's belief in an inevitable evolutionary improvement, but in one that men could shape, as Bourne argued that it was youth's special mission to do. Moreover, the average American considered himself, like Bourne's youth, an idealist, but also like Bourne's youth, a "practical idealist," a phrase, May says, that most Americans happily subscribed to, finding it sanctioned by no less an authority than Harvard's philosopher Josiah Royce—one of Bourne's idols at this stage, and whose name he sometimes included in his pantheon of the American geniuses who spoke the ideals of adventurous democracy.

Though Bourne spoke as if his youth were the only practical idealist on the horizon, there were in fact many in his American audience who identified themselves with him, including many in that older generation Bourne was inclined to dismiss with contempt. Indeed, there was some truth in the charge leveled at him by one of his older critics (in rebuttal to an *Atlantic Monthly* essay that appeared after *Youth and Life*) that in his enumeration of tasks the younger generation had to fulfill Bourne cited lessons the older generation had already taught. His book, moreover, was well received, generally praised, and in conservative organs at that—the *Dial* reviewer, for instance, welcoming the arrival of an essayist "who can deal with the larger themes with something like finality" (and noting, too, the paradox of his using "so reflective a form of literary art" as the essay to express the turbulent energies of youth) [see excerpt dated 1913].

With some justification, therefore, historians like Louis Filler have concluded that much of Bourne's radical thinking in this book was only a "facade of idealism"; the abstract nature of

his rebellion made him "stimulating," perhaps, but nevertheless "acceptable to the calm-browed reader of the *Atlantic Monthly*. Still, *Youth and Life,* and not just Bourne's subsequent radical postures, as toward the war, for instance, established him in the eyes of his contemporaries as a radical spokesman, and it is still capable of stirring young readers into making radicalism their cause. The facade is deceptive, or a facade at all only if behind it we expect to find specific issues of time and place—and there are none, or few so specific as to have a particular historical identity. The issue is only one, the big one of life itself, of life in America. *Youth and Life* is therefore little dated by its content. But it was and remains a truly radical book, and some genuinely explosive challenges were imbedded in the cottony abstractions of its language, needing only the events of history, in Bournes' own time and since, to set young readers aglow with a sense of radical defiance of their elders.

To begin with, though his apparent endorsement of the idea of progress posed no challenge to one of the three received doctrines of nineteenth-century America, Bourne's thoroughgoing moral relativism did challenge another. May speaks of it as first in importance and in its widespread acceptance: "the reality, certainty, and eternity of moral values," and the corollary belief in the applicability of moral judgments in all areas of expression and behavior, in art and literature as well as in politics and social conduct. Most Americans, as May said, agreed that right and wrong were most important categories, that all good citizens knew one from the other and would act properly given a choice between them. "Whatever challenged this set of assumptions," according to May, "was genuinely revolutionary."

To be sure, there had been a moment during Bourne's undergraduate years when he betrayed a still lingering allegiance to the demon of the absolute. In a *Columbia Monthly* review of Professor Joel Spingarn's published lecture, *The New Criticism,* he had attacked Spingarn's Crocean views because they ruled out "all that savors of the ethical," and denied the "humanistic" vitality of the art of the past. Bourne had expressed his preference instead for "the sane and healthy message" of Harvard's Professor Irving Babbitt. (In appreciation, Babbitt wrote to Bourne that he was encouraged "to see younger men . . . take up and continue what seems to me the good fight.") But it was not long after this that Bourne began to revise his understanding of Spingarns' views and to shift toward a position that would eventually have him joining in the attack on the humanism of Babbitt and Paul Elmer More and their disciple, Stuart Sherman. *Youth and Life* amply anticipates that attack in its persistent sniping at the dogmas of the past and at puritanic codes of morality. What had intervened in the meantime was Bourne's growing interest in psychology, on the one hand, with its attention to the unconscious aspects of men's behavior, and on the other hand his interest in social and economic issues, like those of women's rights and the rights of workers, both of which groups seemed denied justice under old notions of right and wrong.

He became suspicious of the "Sane and healthy message" of Irving Babbitt with its stress on rationality. "It is good to be reasonable," he wrote in *Youth and Life,* "but too much rationality puts the soul at odds with life." "The old rigid morality," he said, had "riveted the moral life to logic" and "neglected the fundamental fact of our irrationality." In a passage that May might have cited in support of his own description of that moral faith Bourne went on: "It believed that if we only knew what was good we would do it. It was therefore satisfied with telling us what was good, and expecting us automatically to do it. But . . . we are creatures of instincts and impulses that we do not set going. And education has never taught us more than very imperfectly how to train these impulses in accordance with our worthy desires.''

Elsewhere in *Youth and Life* he wrote that ''social morality'' was not something to be taught, to be inculcated in children, for instance—as he had said in his critique of Spingarn that ''the common sense of the centuries'' testified to—but rather something that could only be built up by each individual ''out of a vast store of experience.'' A child could not get ''the relish of right and wrong until he has tasted life, and . . . [t]hat taste comes only with youth,'' and youth, as we have seen, is a relative stage of consciousness. Yet it was only with youth Bourne asserted, ''that the moral life begins, the true relish of right and wrong,'' and, moreover, this ''must be a relish of social right and wrong as well as individual.''

If it was genuinely revolutionary simply to question the old assumptions, it was more so to make youth virtually the creator of moral life, forged moreover out of youth's desires, or, as he put it, out of the hot ''crucible of passion and enthusiasm'' and tested in ''the furnace of youth's poignant reactions to the world of possibilities and ideals that has been suddenly opened up to it.'' A hot metaphor appropriately conveyed a hot idea. And to insure its enthusiastic reception by those he had in mind, Bourne limited this moral life to the elite among youths. Not those victimized by the old morality; they would suffer from the ''imposed priggishness,'' would have their vision of the whole life permanently distorted, or would be stupidly ''oblivious of the spiritual wonders on every side.'' But for those who had somehow escaped? Bourne's rhetoric persuaded them of the virtues of being revolutionary. . . . (pp. 68-75)

Bourne's moral relativism, with its emphasis . . . upon the practical, was a feature of his pragmatism, of course, that revolutionary philosophy so inspiring to others of his generation. He was quite consistent in extending it to every other reach of life. In so doing he sounded the really revolutionary note in his book, one that challenged his own apparent commitment to the reigning faith in progress and which anticipated the ironic abridgment of hope he contended with in his final years.

May speaks of ''the hinge'' which joined the belief in eternal morality with the belief in progress as ''the central and most vulnerable point in the American credo of the early twentieth century.'' In the essay **''Seeing, We See Not''** Bourne betrayed the fragile nature of his own commitment to progess, raising the questions that would shortly unhinge those joined faiths for himself and others of his generation. This essay, paradoxically, is the most quiet, meditative one in the collection, and it casts a subtle shadow of doubt over the optimism of the rest of the book. Moreover, though Bourne did not confront directly and challenge the third article in the standard American credo, as May enumerates them—the belief in culture—until after his return from Europe with a new sense of a national culture, there is also the faint hint that the hinge which joined a belief in culture to the other faiths was also weak.

The essay is a meditation on historical relativism, taking off with an allusion to Maeterlinck again—one of *Youth and Life*'s favorite touchstones. It expresses a position that Bourne's Columbia teacher, Charles A. Beard, would champion at a later time. It also anticipated his friend Van Wyck Brooks who would seize the same notion and, forging a new hinge, would

connect it to the new ideas of culture and argue the need for ''creating a usable past.''

''History is peculiarly the creation of the present,'' Bourne wrote, agreeing with Maeterlinck that it was mere superstition to suppose anything about the past was irrevocable. ''On the contrary, we are constantly rearranging it, revising it, remaking it.'' It is only the past we do make, he said, and tradition was nothing more than the ''artistic creation of a whole people or race.'' But this perception led to the depressing thought that we had less to do with making the present than we supposed, and that we could not see what was distinctive or imperishable in our own time. In a series of observations and questions Bourne then pointed out the transitory and possibly deceptive nature of the signs of progress, the doubts that after centuries of man's being ''in transition'' some kind of ''crystallization'' or absolute achievement had occurred. ''We are weeding out our culture, and casting aside the classical literature that was the breeding ground for the old ideas,'' he said—a positive achievement for Bourne—but he had misgivings about the little that was taking its place. He was looking for a ''robust and vital'' grasping of life, but to him most of modern literature, art, and music seemed feverish, morbid, and only a restless groping so far. Was the socialistic state coming into being? Was religion doomed, or simply being transformed? ''Will our age actually be distinctive as the era of the Dawn of Peace, or will the baby institution of arbitration disappear before a crude and terribly reality? Are we progressing, or shall we seem to have sown the seeds of world decay in this age of ours, and at a great crisis in history let slip another opportunity to carry mankind to higher social level?''

In this meditation on time he expressed youth's special sense for the rush of time, for the haunting feeling of past change, but also for the ''presentiment of future change.'' Are we progressing? It was a radical question then, in the 1910s, with all the public emphasis upon progress; but it remains a radical question, always putting the older generation on the defensive as responsible for the past and the present, and making for apprehension about future possibilities to which the young are committed and determined to control when the future arrives.

The special radicalism of youth contained in *Youth and Life* cannot be fully assessed in some historical context alone. Even more that Lippmann's *Drift and Mastery*, which Bourne wished he had written, and with which *Youth and Life* corresponds in so many ways—the common antipathy to absolutes and stasis, to puritanism; the shared faith that science or the scientific attitude could serve desire intelligently, and that control or mastery of progress could be achieved; all these common positions expressed in comparable prophetic tones and with a similar quality of abstraction, even the self-conscious labeling of them all by Lippmann as ''the rebel program''—it transcends its contemporary aims. What historical significance it possesses lies in its announcing and containing, almost for the first time, that ''new'' stage of life called youth; but it provides in its style, tone, and point of view not so much and historical as a mythical model for dissenting youth. *Youth and Life,* unlike *Drift and Mastery* and unlike another ''manifesto'' of the younger generation of the 1910s, *America's Coming-of-Age*, both of which more consciously issued a call for action in a particular historical moment, is a kind of fiction going on outside of time, the idealized autobiography of a character called ''youth.''

''The world is in need of true autobiographies,'' Bourne said in his book, and he argued that ''the best autobiographies are still the masters of fiction, those wizards of imaginative sympathy, who create souls and then write their spiritual history, as those souls themselves, were they alive, could perhaps never write them.'' Bourne may not have exactly created youth, but his imaginative sympathy, sharpened by his unique condition, enable him to write its spiritual history in advance of the ''psychohistorical'' analyses we have of youth now, which seem simply, but uncannily to confirm his insights.

Kenneth Kenniston's compressed, ''schematic'' summary of the themes of youth [in *Youth and Dissent*]—*his* ideal type or model—for instance, is a virtual abstract of the themes in *Youth and Life*. Greatly simplifed, Kenniston's major themes of youth are these: the central conscious issue during youth is the *tension between self and society*, characterized by youth's pervasive *ambivalence* toward both self and society, involving a ''characteristic stance'' toward both self and society in an effort to reconcile them, a stance Kenniston calls ''the *wary probe*'' but which resembles Bourne's ''life of irony''; phenomenologically, youth is a time of alternating *estrangement and omnipotentiality*, leading to another characteristic, the *refusal of socialization*, Bourne's ''dodging of pressures,'' and a paradoxical relationship to history, often involving an attempt to reject history but in its own way (by creating a more ''usable'' or relevant past, for instance); there occurs in youth the emergence of *youth-specific identities*, inherently temporary, but involving a deep commitment for whatever the duration to the positive advantages of simply being youthful; another special issue during youth is ''the enormous value'' placed upon change, with the consequent abhorrence of stasis, often part of a heightened *valuation of development* itself (Bourne's life as adventure and experiment); *fear of death*, as in all stages, takes a special form in youth for which it is simply the cessation of all vitality, the end of all movement, progress, and promise (''Death I do not understand at all. . . .[It is] a perpetual warning of how much there is to be known and one in the way of human progress and development''); this in turn affects the youthful view of adulthood (Bourne's older generation) which is equated with stasis and death; and the desire for perpetual youth proceeds therefore from an assumption that to ''grow up'' is the cease to be alive. Finally, youths tend to band together into *youthful countercultures*, for youth is a time when solidarity with other youths is important (Bourne's making friendship so important for his youth, his tendency to think of youth as ''in league,'' or in his collective notion of ''young America'').

There is more in *Youth and Life* and the rest of Bourne's story than just this outline of his themes. He did more that observe and record and report. He created a spokesman; his voice spoke the words of youth, in the tones and accents of the young practical idealist. (pp. 75-8)

> *James R. Vitelli, in his* Randolph Bourne, *Twayne Publishers, 1981, 195 p.*

JOSEPH FEATHERSTONE   (essay date 1982)

[*In the following excerpt, Featherstone discusses Bourne's interest in education, positing that it was his most characteristic concern, and one which probably arose from his ''fascination with the intersection of politics and culture.''*]

The legend of Bourne and the war is true enough as far as it goes—truer than most legends—yet it makes us forget that his fascination with the intersection of politics and culture led him to write mainly about education. . . . Bourne was our first serious educational critic: the three books published in his lifetime were all on education. Of course a long line of philosophers,

journalists, writers, reformers and radicals turned education into one of the liveliest intellectual topics of the eighteenth and nineteenth centuries. Education, childhood, and the family were among the major topics in the great Western debates on politics and modernization. (p. i)

Bourne was operating in an old and durable tradition, and he knew it. He was trying something quite new, however, something that even the Europeans had never done—with the exception of Tolstoy. He was trying to give the ever-neglected world of classrooms and pedagogy sustained critical attention, to take the day-to-day issues of learning and teaching seriously, to write about the classroom as a world in which a thoughtful observer could find certain of the major issues facing the culture and some of the central drama of life itself. I like to think that Bourne was trying to pay pedagogy the kind of probing attention that Edgar Allan Poe as a critic tried to give the feeble dawn of American literature. Poe was determined to take literature seriously—to review books as though they were life and death matters—in a country where most writing was either pirated or junk, and cultivated readers few and far between.

Bourne took advantage of two developments in the new public for intellectual writing, and the new interest in education. That period of our history we loosely call the Progressive era: as a working journalist on the staff of Herbert Croly's *New Republic,* he discovered that the news about schools is that they are windows on American life. At Columbia John Dewey taught Bourne that the allied subjects of education and esthetics were the great challenges for a modern philosophy. Dewey himself had first made his name as a popularizer of what was called the New Education. It was Bourne, however, who tried to cover pedagogy, classrooms and school reform. The genre of writing he was attempting doesn't have a definite name. You can call it criticism and you can call it journalism. It was the sort of enterprise that Shaw made out of his London theatre criticism in the '90's, and that Edmund Wilson later attempted in his chronicles on the literary scene from the '20's to the '40's. (pp. i-ii)

Whether we call it criticism or journalism, the stance is that of a critic: someone who tries to look at a given realm and interpret it to contemporaries in the light of wider fundamental issues. The critic tries to say what's significant, to point out bad and promising developments, to take sides and make enemies and mistakes in pursuit of that moving target the spirit of the times. The real critic differs from lesser figures mainly I suppose, in the depth of the question he or she asks. Bourne went to education to look at certain cultural themes that were, at the time, mainly the concerns of the literary and intellectual avant-garde. The conflict between the green promise of youth and the rigidity of formal institutions had, for example, developed as one of the key myths of the older generation of Progressive cultural radicals, like Dewey, and younger literary figures like Sherwood Anderson.

In fact, Bourne's work may be seen as continuing a line of radical, neo-romantic culture radicalism that began with Progressives like Dewey, Thorstein Veblen and Theodore Dreiser in an earlier generation and which got taken up by younger writers in Bourne's time. The line included Van Wyck Brooks in his earlier phases, Lewis Mumford, the great and now-forgotten sociologist of education, Willard Waller, the cultural Marxists of the '30's and '40's, the novelist James Farrell, the late Paul Godman, and a host of more recent figures. Despite many quarrels, generational feuds, and differences in outlook, the cultural radicals shared a common enterprise: they were out to splice culture and politics in the name of a utopian vision of human nature and American possibility. Whether they knew it or not, the secular patron saint of their line was Jean-Jacques Rousseau. The line of thought they all shared with Rousseau involves a psychological approach to people and institutions. This is its strength and its weakness. The cultural radicals' discovery of psychology led to the exploration of new realms: education, childhood, the family, relations between men and women, art—and raised novel perspectives on American life and culture. Yet the characteristic weakness of the cultural radicals who follow in Rousseau's footsteps is their reluctance to square psychology with what might be called "structural" issues of class and power.

Some time ago, the historian Christopher Lasch described Progressive cultural radicals like Bourne as "New Radicals," and criticized them for their frequent confusion of psychology and politics. Lasch had a point: like Dewey, Bourne sometimes spoke as though a single change in psychology—a new attitude, say—would do the work that only politics could actually accomplish. The assumption that a new cooperative psychology was sweeping America in the years leading up to World War I was one of the central implicit ideas of the cultural radicals. It was linked to something which nearly everyone shared in the period Henry James called the "fool's paradise" of the prewar years—the faith in inevitable progress. A second weakness of the cultural radicals was their penchant for thinking that relatively dependent and subordinate institutions—like schools—could pull off major political and cultural changes all by themselves. (pp. ii-iii)

Bourne lacked a good structural analysis, but he was right to see that schools were the intersection of social forces and autonomous human beings. Our scholarship on the schools today suffers from the thinly veiled predestinarianisms of both sociology and marxism. Figures like Dewey and Bourne had a guiding, mythic vision of human nature that led them to make mistakes, but also made their commitments and presuppositions clear. Much of today's work on education is limited by its lack of clarity concerning implicit assumptions about human nature and how society works.

Mentioning Bourne and Dewey together in this fashion may seem odd to some, since part of the Bourne legend is his dramatic repudiation of Dewey's pragmatism as a philosophy of arrival and survival, unequipped to deal with catastrophes like the war. In the great crisis, pragmatism seemed to Bourne a philosophy of technique, lacking any vision, and thus a doctrine of expedience. In his famous essay **"Twilight of Idols,"** Bourne wrote:

> . . . it never occurred that values could be subordinated to technique.
>
> (p. iv)

Bourne was especially astute in seeing that war was an opportunity for intellectuals; the educated elites, seemed to have been made for the war, as the war was made for them. In describing the war intellectuals, Bourne gave a marvelous portrait of the essentially administrative outlook of the brightest and best among the Progressive elites.

He was also showing how the war opened a chasm between the cultural radicals in education and other realms and the administrative Progressives. In the genial climate of prewar reform, radicals and reformers had banded together, each group assuming that the goal would in the end be the fulfillment of all the respective private utopias.

Now the pressure of war was unravelling all the old coalitions, and the administrative Progressives were proving to be quite different from the cultural radicals and their allies in education, the child-centered Progressives.

Bourne had a point. As a disciple of James and Dewey, he was saying that prewar pragmatism had only articulated part of a whole philosophy of life, not the complete thing, that a complete philosophy would have to make a central place for poetry, vision, and the depths of extremity and despair. Dewey's prewar pragmatism exalted the scientific method as a technique, implying at times that facts could somehow replace values. The idea that science as an institution could serve many masters—any master at all—was not something Dewey appreciated. There was an astonishing hopefulness bordering on complacency in the pre-war Dewey's outlook: he never examined his major, inarticulate premise, that history was progressing. He assumed that the new collective and corporate institutions of American life were automatically producing a cooperative new American social character to replace the selfish old individualism. He thought that historical events were things you could shape and guide to rational social purposes. And in his exaggerated respect for efficiency he had put forth a vision of education that was in some crucial respects Philistine.

Bourne was right to see that the outlook was inadequate. Yet its inadequacies were those of almost all the pre-war reformers and radicals including Bourne himself. Dewey had the advantage over Bourne of living on for three decades, and he shifted his emphasis, if not his basic ideas. It is an interesting fact that Dewey's post-war career is much closer in style to Bourne's mode of radical prophecy than his own earlier role as the Progressive sage of science and efficiency. The late Dewey took much more of an interest in the visions and values that ought to underlie our techniques—*Art as Experience* is a radical and Romantic utopian critique of what today we would call the quality of life under industrial capitalism—and he struggled, with mixed success, to deepen his own philosophy.

I don't want to be misunderstood as saying that ultimately Dewey worked out all the answers. He didn't. Today he seems less useful to us as an answer-man than a figure who grappled with some of the basic and enduring dilemmas of education. To ask what Dewey in the end made of science, value, and the possibilities of democracy and education in America is to ask ourselves what we make of them today.

My point is that Bourne's wartime critique of pragmatic liberalism was in part an attack on himself as well as Dewey. He was saying that the whole spectrum of prewar reform had important blind spots. He was not necessarily saying that pragmatism was wrong, only that its incompleteness made it terribly vulnerable to the reigning forces in American life. Dewey, I think, came to agree with him, moving much closer to Bourne's own critical stance toward the reigning institutions.

Bourne's weakness as a prewar reformer-radical comes out in . . . the strange case of the Gary, Indiana schools. Both Dewey and Bourne were much impressed by the package of reforms put together by Gary's school superintendent, William Wirt. Wirt shrewdly blended together the values of administration Progressivism—economy, efficiency, double use of the plant—with the values of the child-centered Progressives—learning by doing, projects, self-management. In Gary, at least, the mix sounded good; both Dewey and Bourne were impressed at all the lively things that were going on. When the "Gary

Plan'' was exported to New York City as a model for the city's schools, however, the meaning of the ''reform'' changed dramatically. Without new funds or necessary facilities, the Gary Plan was in effect a way to water down education by doubling the number of children in the same plant: it was later peddled around the country as ''the platoon system.'' The teachers and principals in the New York schools were naturally opposed, and weren't consulted in the first place. Immigrant Jewish parents thought the plan—which involved good deal of manual training—was a capitalist plot to give the children a working caste education. The Gary plan became a powerful symbol in the political battles between Tammany Hall and the immigrants on the one hand, and the new Progressive municipal elites, on the other. ''Reform'' in this case meant an attempt to impose an elite business outlook on the city's educational system, and New York's ethnic voters were right to throw the reformers out in the stormy election of 1917. An alliance of Tammany, immigrants, and traditional education won out; two cheers for democracy.

The episode ought to be studied as a classic instance of how a set of educational reforms is never pure ideas or pure pedagogy alone, but rather takes its meaning from its constituencies and the political context in which it operates. Dewey, I think, came to see that reforms pushed down the throats of teachers and parents are not real reforms at all, though he never suspected how basically flawed and elitist American traditions of school reform can be. The Gary episode showed that Bourne was right about the uncritical character of pre-war educational thought. Discussions of pedagogy without context of class and power were risky.

The Gary school war illustrated once again the chasm between child-centered Progressivism in education and the essentially administrative outlook of the mainstream educational Progressives. Dewey and Bourne thought for a time they were the vanguard of educational history, whereas in fact they were expressing a distinctive minority point of view about education. It's a point of view that has continued to gain in significance over the years, although it has scarcely swept the field. This point of view holds out a high Romantic vision of human nature: insisting that people mediate between reason and feeling in making their meanings and symbols. Its sovereign value is growth; it argues for a developmental view of human life. It says that education has to serve a plurality of values, and that school is life itself, as well as preparation for life. The outlook questions the traditional tendency of schools to treat children as passive objects of education and teachers as passive conduits of curriculum and policy. (pp. v-vii)

We need Bourne today, to show us that life in classrooms is in fact an invaluable mirror of our society and its problems. We need his interest in structural issues and his sense that teachers and children, too, participate in the battles of the time. (pp. vii-viii)

In his day, John Dewey was a friendly, but severe critic of what was called ''progressive education.'' I suspect Bourne would have been too. What would he have made of the 1960's? He might have spotted the weaknesses in his own generational bias—''Youth is never wrong, age never right'' is pretty dumb, if you think about it, but Bourne would have kept reminding us that the quality of the lives of the young is a basic test of any civilization. Like Dewey, Bourne would have probably have been impatient with many features of the cultural scene of the 60's and after: the low, irrationalist Romanticism, the anti-intellectualism, the lack of confidence in legitimate adult

authority, the perennially mistaken notion that new educational ideas automatically invalidate all traditional practices and standards. Bourne might have watched for what was promising in the best classroom work to come out of the recent ferment in education: the emphasis on active learning, helping children to think, the hope that schools can serve as cooperative communities of adults and children, the emphasis on children's uniqueness and diversity, and the sense that childhood is a time of intellectual construction, when children fashion models of the world out of their encounters with experience.

I like to think that Bourne would have stayed with the schools. His great interests besides education were literary criticism, the ''transnational'' possibility of a pluralistic American culture, and the problem of modern war and the modern state. All bear on education, and I like to think that Bourne would have gone back and forth from these other interests to education, and that he might have been one of those who articulated a tough-minded and sober progressivism. It's a wonderful thought, like imagining the sort of figure Dewey might have cut had he been able to stay with his model elementary school at the University of Chicago; American education, which has by and large undervalued the realm of practice, would have had the voice of at least one prominent practitioner to remind the public about teachers and children. And with Bourne as a critic, American education might now have a better sense of its traditions—to rebel against, but also to draw on. Bourne's example might have helped the inhabitants of the United States of Amnesia to overcome their bad habit of starting up in each generation from scratch instead of building on the past in a cumulative way.

In elaborating a program of tough-minded progressivism, Bourne, like Dewey, would no doubt have made explicit something that the prewar cultural radicals generally concealed: their dissent from an essentially economic view of education. The administrative Progressives—whose heirs still preside over many of our schools—were busily intent on reordering schools along managerial and corporate lines. Schools were to sieve kids out according to their future jobs. This, I'm certain, Bourne would have denounced, with his gift for humor and his love of precise analysis. He was a radical at heart, but unlike many subsequent radicals, he felt that the first task of middle class radicalism was to be passionately and singlemindedly intellectual. (pp. viii-ix)

> *Joseph Featherstone, in a foreword to* Randolph Silliman Bourne: Education through Radical Eyes *by Thomas N. Walters, Mercer House Press, 1982, pp. i-ix.*

HENRY FAIRLIE (essay date 1983)

[*An English free-lance writer and frequent contributor to the liberal journal* The New Republic, *Fairlie has written extensively on the state of twentieth-century American politics. In the following excerpt he surveys Bourne's wartime essays, arguing that Bourne's principal interest lay in defining the proper role of the liberal intellectual in American society.*]

What was [Bourne's] influence on his own generation? What then made him a legend? Why did his reputation fade? Most important, why should we read him now? (p. 26)

By his own intellectual generation, after he died, he was elected a martyr; and in [the] simple facts of his life there lay, indeed, the stuff of which legends are made. The conquering of his hideous deformities, and of his early frustrations and bitterness;

the spokesman but also the critic of his generation of rebellious youth who, perhaps, best clarified their impulses and aspirations; the young man who turned his back on Europe, discarding it like a worn-out coat, to proclaim "the promise of American life," to interpret it and try to energize it anew—and then. . . . Then, the lonely, unflinching opposition to America's entry into the war; the desertion of almost the entire generation that he had led; the sacrifice of his career, the wracking poverty he endured. (His own apartment was not even properly heated when he caught influenza.) When the armistice at last came, he was ready, his friends tell us, to sing the songs of America again. But he died. Of his writing and example during the war, *The Nation* said in 1920 that he had left "the cleanest picture of ourselves when we were not ourselves." It is still one of the cleanest pictures of ourselves.

Let us begin at the end, with his opposition to the war. On the central issue his position was rather awkward. He was not a pacifist. He did not deny that war might sometimes be justified; he avoided saying that World War I was an absolute evil. In an article in *The Dial* in September 1917, which does not appear in the collections of his writings, he explicitly detaches himself in his first paragraph from the evangelism of the conscientious objector. As he put in *Seven Arts* at the same time, "We can be apathetic with a good conscience." Because of his handicaps, he would not be drafted. This placed him in an uncomfortable position, which privately he did not altogether face. There is something unsatisfactory in his advice: "Let us compel the war to break in on us. . . . When we are broken in on, we can yield to the inexorable. Those who are conscripted will have been broken in on. If they do not want to be martyrs, they will have to be victims." This is scarcely a ringing call to oppose the war. If he had been drafted, would he have gone? We cannot tell.

But it was not really the war in itself that interested him; at no time did he consider the occasions that led to the war. He was least satisfactory when he argued in **"The Collapse of American Strategy"** (August 1917) that America should have remained neutral so that it could continue to be the arbiter. So what did interest him? "There is work to be done to prevent this war of ours"—not Germany's, mind you—"from passing into popular mythology as a holy crusade." He was one of the very few intellectuals in 1917 who did not buy the notion that America was entering the war for selfless reasons to make the world safe for democracy. "There must be some irreconcilables left who will not even accept the war with walrus tears." But that gives only a hint of his insight or his impulse.

In his opposition to the war, he was cutting far deeper. One can disagree with him about the war—as I do—and still be thankful for the position he took. He was shocked by an unsigned editorial in *The New Republic* on April 14, 1917, which contained a remarkable passage at which one still rubs one's eyes. Denying that "the bankers or capitalists" had taken America into the war, it claimed the credit (no less a word) for the intellectuals.

> The effective and decisive work on behalf of war has been accomplished by an entirely different class—a class which may be comprehensively described as the 'intellectuals'. . . . The American nation is entering the war under the influence of a moral verdict reached after the utmost deliberation of the more thoughtful members of the community.

Bourne was never again to write a really political article for the magazine. Two months later his answer to the editorial appeared in *Seven Arts:*

> A war made deliberately by intellectuals! A calm moral verdict, arrived at after penetrating study of the inexorable facts!. . . . An intellectual class, gently guiding a nation through sheer force of ideas into what other nations had entered only through predatory craft or popular hysteria or military madness.

The pages burned with his scorn.

Bourne had found the theme that held together everything else he said: not simply the guilt of his own intellectual generation, but the betrayal by the "intellectual class"—which its representatives at *The New Republic* had so clearly and loftily identified—of its vocation and its responsibility to American society. He pursued the theme in a series of essays—which should be together, and each in its entirety—in which the fierceness of the conviction still scorches. If they have an unyielding moral force, as is often said, it lies in an unyielding intellectual commitment. The criticisms that have been made in our own time of "the best and the brightest" for their responsibility for American involvement in the Vietnam War seem scarcely more than a form of higher gossip when contrasted with Bourne's criticisms of the nature of the intellectuals' participation in World War I. We may still see through his prism. We must.

No one recognized more clearly at the time that something new had happened. For the technical organization and management of modern war, governments required the collaboration of the intellectual class. He saw the intellectuals—many of them his friends and colleagues—give this collaboration in 1917-1918. "It has been a bitter experience to see the unanimity with which the American intellectuals have thrown their support to the use of the war-technique." He wrote of "the coalescence of the intellectual classes in support of the military programme"; and one may recall in passing, for it is usually forgotten, that Eisenhower included the intellectual class in the military-industrial complex. When Bourne says of 1917 that "Our intellectuals consort with war-boards," we can count how many intellectuals today have launched their public careers from war boards. "War is the health of the state," he was later to proclaim. War had become the profit of the intellectual.

As he drove wider and deeper with his theme, his voice carries with it an edge to our own time. He warned that this intellectual collaboration must lead "toward the riveting of a semi-military state-Socialism on the country." He pointed to "the undemocratic nature of this war-liberalism." He said that

> the old radicalism has found a perfectly definite level, and there is no reason to think that it will not remain there. Its flowering appears in the technical organization of the war by an earnest group of young liberals, who direct their course by an opportunist programme of State-socialism at home and a league of benevolently imperialistic nations abroad.

We may wish to qualify some of the harshness of his judgments, but we cannot deny that, writing in 1917 and not in 1968, he anticipated much of the course of American liberalism in this century, and many of the dangers, still not met, of a permanent war-state to the health of democracy. The size of today's defense budget is not just an economic but a political threat.

For he pushed yet deeper, wherever it took him. John Dewey had been his mentor since his days at Columbia. As late as March 1915 he had idolized him in *The New Republic:* "... the most intensely alive, futuristic philosophy..., some of the wisest words ever set to paper." In an essay in *Seven Arts* in October 1917, **"Twilight of Idols,"** he expressed the depth of his disillusion. Again he reaches to our own time. For when he turned on Dewey for his support of American participation in the war, finding "a slackening in his thought for our guidance and stir, and the inadequacy of his pragmatism as a philosophy of life in this emergency," he was anticipating the criticisms that must be made of the "pragmatic liberals" of our own time. He attacked the pragmatic intellectual liberal realists for believing that they could control events by giving their services to the very interests and forces that had created the events.

> The realist thinks he at least can control events by linking himself to the forces that are moving.... But if it is a question of controlling war, it is difficult to see how the child on the back of a mad elephant is to be any more effective in stopping the beast than is the child who tries to stop him from the ground. If the war is too strong for you to prevent, how is it going to be weak enough for you to control...?

In the nuclear age, that question is a hundred times more disquieting.

Almost half a century later this was my criticism, in *The Kennedy Promise*, of the intellectuals who served John F. Kennedy:

> The pragmatic liberal, acting within a "consensus" that he seeks both to foster and to manipulate, frees himself from political values, only to find that he has bound himself to react pragmatically to events as they occur, able to judge only their urgency, and not their importance.

(We now even have a phrase for it: crisis management.) The genius of Bourne was that he recognized this type as soon as he first arrived in Washington from the universities. (pp. 26-8)

We are again brought sharply into our own time when he says that this younger intelligentsia has been trained to be

> immensely ready for the executive ordering of events, pitifully unprepared for the intellectual interpretation or the idealistic focusing of ends.... They have absorbed the secret of scientific method as applied to political administration. They are liberal, enlightened, aware. They are touched with creative intelligence toward the solution of political and industrial problems. They are a wholly new force in American life, the product of the swing in the colleges from a training that emphasized classical studies to one the emphasized political and economic values.... Practically all this element, one would say, is lined up in the service of the war-technique.

He wonders "what scope they would have had for their intelligence without it." We know the answer each year in June when there come from the great universities to Washington, in their droves, those who have

no clear philosophy of life except that of intelligent service, the admirable adaptation of means to end..., vague as to what kind of society they want, or what kind of society America needs, but ... equipped with all the administrative attitudes and talents necessary to attain it.

The law schools now feed them to Washington, as interchangeable as disc jockeys. Every administration, liberal or conservative, must endure them.

> The war—or American promise; one must choose. One cannot be interested in both.... The conservation of American promise is the present task for this generation of malcontents and aloof men and women.

This was another note he struck—"the effect of the war will be to impoverish American promise"—and in it sounded his earlier writing. He did not change, he followed through. Herbert Croly, the first editor of *The New Republic*, had published *The Promise of American Life* in 1909, when Bourne went to Columbia. In looking to the fulfillment of the promise, Croly placed much of the emphasis on technical and organizational efficiency, a reflection of the time at which he wrote. Bourne uses the phrase, "the American promise," again and again, and surely deliberately, to give it his own meaning. He broke with the "new republicans," as he called them, on a deeper issue than the war. (p. 28)

The most famous of Crowly's fellow editors, Walter Lippmann, wrote *Drift and Mastery* in 1914. It echoed the promise of which Croly had written five years before. Man's scientific knowledge now enabled man to escape from the "jungle of disordered growth." Man could now master himself and his environment; change had become "a matter of invention a deliberate experiment." The scientific spirit made possible "the discipline of democracy, the escape from drift, the outlook of a freeman." Simon Patten, in another key book of the period, had written: "The final victory of man's machinery over nature's is the next logical step in evolution." This was the intellectual credo of the Progressive era, and from the start Bourne would have none of it. When he spoke of "the American promise," he spoke of something that was still open, not closed and finishing: not a technique or system.

In July 1916 he wrote a remarkable article for *The Atlantic*. It was called **"Trans-National America."** Later that year he adapted it for *The Menorah Journal*, where it appeared as **"The Jew and Trans-National America."** Only those who know how fearful was the alarm and how fierce the dislike with which the mass immigration at the beginning of this century was met—even by cultivated men; one may almost say, especially by them—can have any idea of how unusual was the welcome that Bourne gave to this transformation of America and how unbounded the vision he had of its future.

> America is a unique sociological fabric, and it bespeaks poverty of imagination not to be thrilled at the innumerable potentialities of so novel a union of men.... It is for the younger generation to accept this cosmopolitanism, and carry it along with self-conscious and fruitful purpose.

This was not only imaginative sympathy; it was also intellectual acuteness.

"We must perpetuate the paradox that our American cultural tradition lies in the future. It will be whatever we make out of this incomparable opportunity of attacking the future with a new key." He never wrote more remarkable sentences than these:

> Just in so far as our American genius has expressed the pioneer spirit, the adventureous, forward-looking drive of a colonial empire, is it representative of the whole America of the many races and peoples, and not of any partial or traditional enthusiasm. And only as that pioneer note is sounded can we really speak of the American culture. As long as we thought of Americanism in terms of the 'melting pot', our American culture lay in the past. It was something to which the new Americans were to be moulded.

He was "beyond the melting pot" almost half a century before Moynihan and Glazer. "The failure of the melting pot"—this in 1915, one must recall—"far from closing the great American democratic experiment, means that it has only just begun."

It has been said that Bourne was in this, as in so much else, the prophet of solutions only now being tried. The endurance of ethnicity even in the now unhyphenated American; the attempt to create or recover the intermediary associations by which people may more securely and even enthusiastically govern themselves; and above all, the unceasing effort to give to American nationality a particular meaning, then and now: again and again at the beginning of this century, he pointed the radicals of his generation to the truths, to the possibilities, which the liberals of this century then conceded to the conservatives. As he warned against the riveting of state-Socialism on America in the war, he was already far ahead of the flabby efforts of liberals now to reinvigorate their creed.

I have said that he was not really interested in the war itself. If we do not understand this, we will not understand his uniqueness. "For many of us, resentment against the war has meant a vivider consciousness of what we are seeking in American life," and he preserved the hope "that in the recoil from war we may find the treasures we are looking for." A malcontent? But how generous a one. Aloof? But how wedded to America. His biographer is not being cheaply sentimental when he says of Bourne's death that "America lost a son who loved her as much as any who had been in the trenches." He belonged to a generation of rebels and, from the publication of his undergraduate essays in *Youth and Life* in 1913, became its "clear-minded leader and critic." No other name of that rebellious youth has survived so strong and unstained. (pp. 29-30)

From where, in Bourne, did it come? Every subsequent writer on Bourne seems to find it necessary to deal first with the legend, the election to martyrdom, and even canonization by his generation after the war, as if to get them out of the way. But Bourne was one of those writers from whom, if we are to appreciate his work, we cannot strip either his life or the legend. We need a term of Christian theology to describe his example. Witness. To bear witness is to testify by words and deeds, or through the goodness of one's life and work, to a personal acceptance of the Christian faith. Bourne was not a Christian—he left open the question of whether there is a God—but we may use the term. Men may become martyrs by their deaths—and Bourne's early death left his generation stricken—but the witness of their lives also counts.

To this personal witness we may then add his sense of the role of the intellectual in public affairs. While he was deeply, even intensely, engaged in the social and political issues of the time—he touched on almost all of them, and almost always with the same clarity—he nonetheless believed that the intellectual should stand in his own realm and from there criticize the political or the economic realms. Thus, the growth of his corporations in his day bothered him, and his criticisms of the corporate system are acute, but he did not waste his time thinking that one could bust the trusts, and he certainly placed little faith in regulating them under government supervision. This was why he saw no need to be a socialist or a conservative. If *the rest* of American society was kept vigorous and alert—including the intellectual realm—then it was a large and open enough society to contain, in the end, any overweening power. The struggle was unending—there was no complacency in him—but if the intellectual remained on his own ground, refusing to collaborate, he would play his role, and, however pitifully in his case, earn his keep.

One of Bourne's earliest essays—he was only twenty-five at the time, and still an undergraduate at Columbia—appeared in *The Atlantic* in September 1911. It was called **"The Handicapped—By One of Them."** It has, as far as I can judge, one fault. He was both handicapped *and deformed*. He does not make it clear that he is writing as someone who was not only disabled, but also so facially deformed that a sensitive man could say that his appearance was without a redeeming feature. But this said, the piece is astonishing. For there comes a point in reading it when, as he talks of "the handicapped," one thinks not of him but of oneself. Who is not handicapped? Bourne's sympathy is almost imperceptibly translated to all of suffering humanity; and as he grows more explicit, one's own sympathies deepen.

> What one does get sensitive to is rather the inevitable way that people, acquaintances and strangers alike, have of discounting in advance what one does or says. The deformed man is always conscious that the world does not expect very much from him.

Where does that differ from the remark that a young leader of the Oglala Sioux once made to me as he talked of the policies of the Bureau for Indian Affairs: "We are not given the chance to fail"? . . .

At the age of twenty-five, Bourne is pushing, from his own experience, to the social philosophy that sustained him:

> It makes me wince to hear a man spoken of as a failure, or to have it said of one that "he doesn't amount to much." Instantly I want to know why he has not succeeded, and what have been the forces that have been working against him. . . . [My] experience has made my ideal of character militant rather than long-suffering. . . . The Stoics depress me. I do not want to look on my life as an eternal making of the best of a bad bargain. . . . Of one thing I am sure . . . : that life will have little for me except as I am able to contribute toward some such ideal of social betterment, if not in deed, then in word. . . .

Undergraduate writing? Well yes, some of it, undergraduate writing. But what does one say of a man who then goes on to live and write, suffer and fight, for it all under the severest of test? . . . One cannot ignore the fact that, after writing as a professional journalist for only three years, Bourne had emerged by the age of thirty-one, as the most independent, defiant, thoughtful, courageous exemplar of his profession. The writing cannot be separated from the example of the life. For he met even his easy allies with his criticism.

He was not only the leader but the *critic* of his generation. That is the testimony that we can read from the members of his generation. The early essay on **"The Handicapped"** had already included a criticism of youth, and it is perhaps here that we may discover why the "radical" youth of the 1960s did not adopt him. As he wrote of the feeling that his handicap and deformity, when he was young, made him "truly in the world, but not of the world," he went on to say: "The world of youth is a world of so many conventions, and the abnormal in any direction is so glaringly and hideously abnormal." As the editor of his most recent collection of essays puts it: "Bourne was at no time merely the prophet of a youth cult. . . . Youth does not guarantee a new beginning but merely its possibility." It was in two articles for *The Atlantic*—**"The Two Generations,"** . . . and **"Youth"** . . .—that he made himself the leader of his generation. But not even in them did he concede any particular virtue to youth itself.

This is a rare discrimination in a writer of any age. Where was the censor within him? We have already seen that, in his opposition to the war, it was the intellectuals' betrayal of their vocation, more than the horror of the war, which really troubled him. (One can find in his writing barely a reference to the slaughter.) What he conceived to be the role of the intellectual is the key to his authority even now. He never called himself a "socialist." He was a "radical," an American radical. In a book review for *The New Republic* in 1916, he made himself clear, so clear that many middle-class radicals today may squirm.

> The real trouble with middle-class radicalism in this country today is that it is too easy. It is becoming too popular. . . . The ranks are full of the unfocused and the unthinking. . . . *The only way by which middle-class radicalism can serve is by being fiercely and concentratedly intellectual* [my italics]. . . .

There then comes this vital disassociation: "Intellectual radicalism should not mean repeating the stale dogmas of Marxism." He was to repeat this from the beginning to the end: ". . . much of Marxism is doctrinaire and static in its concepts"; he said that what he called "the old solution of State ownership and control" was not valid as an American solution. He said it then, and he said it again and again. He tested everything against his one touchstone, his vision of America and its possibilities. That is why they make a movie about John Reed and not about Randolph Bourne. Reed is not a threat, since he spoke no truth; the Bournes are threats.

Most people who write about him ask what he would have become if he had lived. It is a foolish question, not because we cannot know, but because he answered it. The timeliness which we find in his writing even today, seventy years later, tells us how little he would have had to shift his fundamental position in order to meet, one by one, all the alarms and excursions of this century. The man who so clearly rejected Marxism in 1917 would not have followed so many of the writers of the 1920s into the Communist camp in the 1930s. The man who was the critic of his own generation of rebellious youth, even as he was its leader, would have had no truck with the

intellectual laxity and dishonesty of the New Left. Yet just as he did not have to reach to a political conservation in his own times, so he would not have had to reach to it later. He would have had no need to become a neo-anything in order to make his position clear.

For *clear* it was. The words that Lewis Mumford [see excerpt dated 1930] used about him in *The New Republic* twelve years after his death merely echo the words that are always used by those who have studied him: "His view of life was maturing, deepening, not yet ready for rounded expression, it was still a promise; a cool luminous dawn was spreading across the skies." And what is astonishing is that even now it is like a cool luminous dawn that the freshness of his writing still touches us—almost, one may say, touches our cheeks. Mumford was writing of how, even then, Bourne seemed to have been set aside, and he protested: "It was the good fortune of American society to produce this man. We must not toss the luck away."

What is it, then, that stays in his writing? This was a radical who believed more in America than any Rotary speaker or sponger off the media. The man who had so clear a vision of transnational America was the same man who believed that the East Coast was still Europe and that only West of the Alleghenies did America begin. Yet he could believe all this without a page falling into the trap of a conservatism that is just one long grouch at the twentieth century. America must be kept open—no technique, no system, no ideology, must be allowed to close it down. There was his inspiration. He was—for try any other name against his—the last man who believed in America. (pp. 30-2)

> *Henry Fairlie, "A Radical and a Patriot," in* The New Republic, *Vol. 188, No. 8, February 28, 1983, pp. 25-32.*

ADDITIONAL BIBLIOGRAPHY

Abrahams, Edward. "Randolph Bourne on Feminism and Feminists." *The Historian* XLIII, No. 4 (May 1981): 365-77.
Biographical and critical article. Using previously undiscovered archival materials, Abrahams examines Bourne's attitudes toward radical feminism and the basis for those attitudes.

Bourke, Paul F. "The Status of Politics 1909-1919: *The New Republic*, Randolph Bourne and Van Wyck Brooks." *The Journal of American Studies* 8, No. 2 (August 1974): 171-202.*
Analysis. Using the writings of Bourne and Van Wyck Brooks, and considering the changing style of *The New Republic*, the critic attempts to demonstrate the effect of war on the making of political decisions.

Brooks, Van Wyck. "The Younger Generation of 1915." In his *The Confident Years: 1885-1915*, pp. 491-512. New York: E. P. Dutton and Co., 1952.*
Lengthy discussion of Bourne and his work.

———. "Randolph Bourne." In his *Fenollosa and His Circle: With Other Essays in Biography*, pp. 259-321. New York: E. P. Dutton & Co., 1962.
Biographical sketch. Brooks also summarizes Bourne's philosophy, quoting extensively from his best-known essays.

Cather, Willa. "Escapism: A Letter to the *Commonweal*." In her *On Writing: Critical Studies on Writing as an Art*, pp. 18-29. New York: Alfred A. Knopf, 1949.
Letter to the editor of *The Commonweal* in which Cather eloquently disputes the claim of such critics as Bourne that art which does not raise social consciousness is mere escapism.

Curtis, Tom. "Bourne, MacDonald, Chomsky, and the Rhetoric of Resistance." *The Antioch Review* XXIX, No. 2 (Summer 1969): 245-52.*
    Comparative study. Curtis examines the antiwar writings of Bourne and compares his assessments of American liberalism and the failure of the liberal intellectuals in World War I, to similar protests in later eras by Dwight MacDonald and Noam Chomsky.

Dreiser, Theodore. "Appearance and Reality." In *The American Spectator Yearbook*, edited by George Jean Nathan, Ernest Boyd, and others, pp. 204-09. New York: Frederick A. Stokes Co., 1934.
    Brief appreciation of Bourne's character and writings.

Filler, Louis. "Randolph Bourne: Reality and Myth." *The Humanist* X, No. 5 (September-October 1950): 198-202.
    Brief discussion of Bourne's career and of the legend that has grown up around him. Filler concludes that Bourne was not necessarily a great original thinker, but that he was a great publicist and communicator of the original ideas of others.

Oppenheim, James. "The Story of *The Seven Arts*." *The American Mercury* XX, No. 78 (June 1930): 156-64.
    Brief history of the magazine that published seven of Bourne's antiwar essays and was closed down in consequence. Oppenheim writes, in tribute to Bourne: "His coming was the greatest thing that happened to *The Seven Arts* though in the end it was the main cause of our shutting down."

Sillen, Samuel. "The Challenge of Randolph Bourne." *Masses and Mainstream* 6, No. 12 (December 1953): 24-32.
    Discussion of Bourne's career from a socialist perspective. Sillen sees in Bourne's writings on literature and American society a challenge to modern-day liberals and socialist intellectuals.

Teall, Dorothy. "Bourne into Myth." *The Bookman*, New York LXXV, No. 6 (October 1932): 590-99.
    Analysis of the myths that have grown up around Bourne and his writings since his death in 1918.

Mikhail (Afanasevich) Bulgakov

1891-1940

(Also transliterated as Michael and Mixail; also Afanas'evich, Afanasievich, Afanasyev, and Afanasyevich; also Bulgakof) Russian novelist, short story writer, dramatist, biographer, essayist, and translator.

Considered one of the foremost satirists of post-revolutionary Russia, Bulgakov is best known for his novel *Master i Margarita (The Master and Margarita)*, which is recognized as one of the greatest Russian novels of the century. Many of Bulgakov's works concern the adjustment of the Russian intellectual class to life under communist rule. Heavily influenced by Nikolai Gogol, he combined fantasy, realism, and satire to ridicule modern progressive society in general and the Soviet system in particular. His works celebrate the nonconformist, and often portray an artist or scientist in conflict with society. Due to official censorship of his manuscripts during his lifetime, Bulgakov's best works remained unpublished until after his death.

Bulgakov was born in 1891 into a Russian family of the intellectual class in the Ukrainian city of Kiev. Music, literature, and theater were important in the family life of the young Bulgakov, as was religion. His father, a professor at the Kiev theological academy, instilled in his son a belief in God and an interest in spiritual matters that he would retain throughout his life. Bulgakov attended Kiev's most prestigious secondary school, where he earned a reputation for playing practical jokes and inventing stories. He continued his education as a medical student at the University of Kiev and graduated with distinction in 1916. Assigned to noncombat duty in the Russian army during World War I, Bulgakov worked for several months in frontline military hospitals until he transferred to a remote village, where he served as the only doctor for an entire district. His trials as an inexperienced doctor working under primitive conditions, and the difficulties he faced as an educated man among the ignorant, superstitious peasants, are recorded in the autobiographical stories of *Zapiski iunogo vracha (A Country Doctor's Notebooks)*. Upon his discharge in 1918 Bulgakov returned to Kiev in time to witness the Bolshevik Red Army, the anti-Bolshevik White Army, German occupation forces, and Ukrainian nationalists struggling for control of the city, which experienced fourteen violent changes of government in two years. Bulgakov's first novel, *Belaia gvardiia (The White Guard)*, deals with the life of a family in Kiev during this period.

In 1919 Bulgakov published his first story, and the following year he abandoned medicine to devote his time to writing feuilletons for local newspapers and plays for local theaters in the Caucasian city of Vladikavkaz. In 1921 he moved to Moscow, where he struggled to support himself and his first wife by editing and writing for various newspapers, a task which he described as "a flow of hopeless grey boredom, unbroken and inexorable." With the partial publication in 1925 of *The White Guard* in the magazine *Rossiya*, Bulgakov gained sufficient respect and popularity as an author to abandon newspaper work. Although his subsequent dramatization of the novel as *Dni Turbinykh (Days of the Turbins)* was severely criticized by orthodox communists for sympathetically portraying the officer

Courtesy of Ardis Publishers

class of the White Army, it was immediately popular with audiences and became one of Soviet Russia's best-loved plays. Joseph Stalin himself attended the production fifteen times, viewing the play as ultimately favorable to the Bolsheviks. In a letter of 1929 he wrote: "If even such people as the Turbins are compelled to lay down their arms and submit to the will of the people because they realize that their cause is definitely lost, then the Bolsheviks must be invincible and there is nothing to be done about it." From 1925 to 1928 Bulgakov worked in close association with the Moscow Art Theater as a writer, producer, and occasionally as an actor. His plays were all well received by audiences but denounced by party critics, and in 1929 his works were banned for their ideological nonconformity. For the next two years Bulgakov was unable to earn a living, and in 1930, frustrated, depressed, and penniless, he wrote to the Soviet government asking to be allowed either to work or to emigrate. Stalin personally telephoned Bulgakov three weeks later and arranged for his appointment to the Art Theater as a producer. In 1932, reportedly at Stalin's request once again, *Days of the Turbins* was returned to the stage, making it possible for Bulgakov to have other works published and peformed. He remained with the Art Theater until 1936, when he resigned in protest over what he saw as the mishandling of his drama *Kabala sviatosh (A Cabal of Hypocrites)*, at which time he became a librettist for the Bolshoi Theater.

71

Though publishing little, Bulgakov wrote steadily until his death from nephrosclerosis in 1940.

Bulgakov is believed to have written thirty-six plays, eleven of which survive. Unlike his major prose works, Bulgakov's dramas tend toward the realistic, and are often based on historical events or figures. In direct opposition to Soviet conventions, Bulgakov refused to portray his characters as either wholly positive or negative; rather, they are drawn as individuals with human strengths and frailties. The theme of adjustment to the new Soviet way of life dominates his plays of the 1920s. His best-known drama, *Days of the Turbins*, has been viewed as Moscow's most important theatrical event of the decade and served as the focus for the debate then being waged over the place of art in post-revolutionary society. The play, which deals with the life of a family of Russian intellectuals in Kiev during the Civil War, was the first Soviet play to portray the White intelligentsia as sympathetic figures, rather than the malicious characters common to socialist realist productions. Critical opposition was violent; party critics immediately accused Bulgakov of glorifying the class enemy and denounced the play as counterrevolutionary. Nevertheless, playgoers who had lost relatives in the Civil War identified with the Turbin family and flocked to performances. According to one account, "The women were hysterical; there were tears in the eyes of the men." Bulgakov's next play, *Zoikina kvartira (Zoya's Apartment)*, concerns the goings-on at a brothel disguised as a sewing shop in Moscow of the 1920s. A comic melodrama, the play satirizes communist institutions and life under Stalin's New Economic Policy. Popular with audiences, it was condemned by Soviet critics for being "pornographic" as well as for failing to convey the proper ideological viewpoint. His next play, *Bagrovyi ostrov (The Crimson Island)*, a comic attack on censorship, prompted counterattacks on Bulgakov's reputation and was taken out of the Art Theater repertory after only four performances.

Beg (Flight), the play considered by some critics to be Bulgakov's best, was not allowed to be staged in the Soviet Union until 1957. In *Flight*, Bulgakov blended comic and tragic situations in eight acts he labelled "dreams" to depict the plight of a group of defeated White generals and a few civilians who elect to emigrate rather than live under communism. Critics have praised *Flight*'s careful construction, character development, and language, as well as its masterful use of stage effects. In *A Cabal of Hypocrites*, based on the life of Molière, Bulgakov addressed the problem of the artist in a repressive society, a theme that he was to return to in later works. The play is based on one of Bulgakov's literary heroes (Bulgakov once told his wife that Molière was the first person he would go to see in the afterlife), but is as much fiction as fact, its emphasis being the creator and the creative act rather than historical accuracy. *A Cabal of Hypocrites* was accepted by the Moscow Art Theater in 1931 but was not performed until 1936, after five years of delays and disagreements between Bulgakov and the renowned founder and director of the Art Theater, Konstantin Stanislavsky, over the staging of the play. Bulgakov refused to rewrite crucial scenes and Stanislavsky attempted to make significant changes in the character of Molière over Bulgakov's protests. *A Cabal of Hypocrites* finally reached the stage after nearly three hundred rehearsals, but closed after seven performances because of hostile critical reception. *Pravda* criticized Bulgakov's "incorrect" interpretation of history and denounced his "reactionary view of artistic creativity as 'pure' art." Angry and frustrated, Bulgakov resigned from the Art Theater in protest. As his next play, *Ivan Vasil'evich*, was

officially proscribed before its premiere, *A Cabal of Hypocrites* was the last of Bulgakov's dramas to be performed in his lifetime.

In addition to his dramas, Bulgakov wrote numerous short stories and novels. His first published collection of stories, *D'iavoliada (Diaboliad, and Other Stories)*, was strongly influenced by Gogol: realism dissolves into fantasy and absurdity, and light comic satire erupts into sudden brutality. Included is his best-known story, "Rokovye iaitsa" ("The Fatal Eggs"), in which a well-meaning scientist discovers a red ray that stimulates growth. The ray is appropriated by a bureaucrat to increase the country's chicken population, but through a mix-up produces instead a crop of giant reptiles that ravage the countryside. Critics have read the story as a satirical treatment of the Russian Revolution, or, less specifically, as a commentary on progress and a rejection of revolution in favor of evolution. "The Fatal Eggs" also introduces another of Bulgakov's favorite themes: the consequences of power in the hands of the ignorant. Although written during the same period as *Diaboliad*, Bulgakov's *A Country Doctor's Notebooks* differs radically from these stories as well as from most of his longer fiction in its strict realism and exclusion of the fantastic and grotesque. Another early work, *Sobach'e serdtse (The Heart of a Dog)*, is included among Bulgakov's most important. Considered one of Soviet Russia's best satirical novellas, the work portrays a scientist's transformation of a dog into a man. The creature develops reprehensible human qualities, and the scientist changes him back into the good-natured dog he once was. The story, which has obvious thematic parallels to "The Fatal Eggs," has never been published in the Soviet Union because of its counterrevolutionary cast. Critical readings have been similar to those of "The Fatal Eggs": some critics consider it a blatant political satire, equating the operation with the Revolution, while others stress a moral and philosophical interpretation of the conflict between the intellectual scientist and the uneducated masses, and of the disastrous results of interfering with a natural process. Bulgakov's relationship with the Moscow Art Theater, in particular the clashes over the staging of *A Cabal of Hypocrites*, served as the source for his novel *Teatral'nyi roman (Black Snow: A Theatrical Novel)*. In this humorous roman à clef of Moscow's theatrical world, Bulgakov portrayed the revered Stanislavsky as a petty tyrant and the Art Theater actors as a group of feuding, scheming egomaniacs. An excellent example of Bulgakov's mature prose, *Black Snow* was unfortunately left unfinished at his death.

Bulgakov's acknowledged masterwork, *The Master and Margarita*, developed over a period of twelve years through the drafting of eight separate versions. According to biographers, Bulgakov knew that the novel would be his masterpiece and set aside all other projects during the last years of his illness in order to finish it before his death, dictating final corrections to his wife after he became blind, and adding the epilogue after the manuscript was bound. He gave copies to his wife and to a friend for safekeeping, and they remained a closely guarded secret until Bulgakov's rehabilitation during Nikita Khrushchev's cultural thaw of the late 1950s and early 1960s, a period in which the cult of Stalin was repudiated and the Soviets began to confront some of the excesses of his reign. *The Master and Margarita* was finally published in a heavily censored form in two installments in the journal *Moskva* in 1966 and 1967. It caused an immediate sensation and has received an extraordinary amount of critical attention ever since. A blend of satire, realism, and fantasy, the novel is not easily classified or reduced to a single interpretation. Most critics agree that *The*

Master and Margarita is composed of three narrative strands. The first concerns the devil (named Woland) and his associates, who visit modern Moscow and create havoc in the lives of the stupid, the scheming, and the avaricious. The second deals with a persecuted novelist (The Master) and his mistress (Margarita), who bargains with Woland for the sake of her beloved. The third level of the book is the Master's novel, a retelling of the story of Pilate and Christ which involved a tremendous amount of research into the history of Jerusalem and early Christian thought. What little negative criticism that has been written on *The Master and Margarita* has focused on the lack of cohesion among these three levels of narrative. The nature of good and evil constitutes a basic philosophical problem in the novel, and much critical attention has been devoted to the nature of Bulgakov's devil, who appears less an evil being in opposition to God than as God's counterpart, whose task it is to punish the corrupt. His relationship with the Master has been seen as a Faustian pact; indeed, references to Johann Wolfgang von Goethe's *Faust* permeate the novel. Like Bulgakov's characterization of the devil, the portrait of Jesus in *The Master and Margarita* is equally unorthodox; although his character asserts the fundamental beliefs of orthodox Christianity, he complains that everything written about him by his only disciple, Matthew, is inaccurate. With the story of the Master, Bulgakov returns to the theme of the artist in society. He writes that "manuscripts don't burn," asserting his belief that art will endure the vicissitudes of political repression because of its eternal nature, existing as it does apart from the transitory world of political power. Similarly, an important parallel theme to the conflict between the artist and society is developed in the conflict between the spiritual and material worlds, a conflict that in Bulgakov's view ultimately results in the triumph of the spiritual.

As in Bulgakov's other major works, the heroes of *The Master and Margarita* are independent spirits who exist outside their society, with Bulgakov's sharpest satire reserved for those ruled by self-interest. Two English versions of the novel exist, one by Mirra Ginsburg based on the censored edition printed in *Moskva*, which eliminates much of the anti-Soviet satire in Bulgakov's work, and one by Michael Glenny based on the complete text. While there has been some controversy regarding their relative merits as translations, both are considered valuable to an English-language reader's understanding of Bulgakov's masterpiece, which is now considered one of the greatest works of twentieth-century Russian literature.

(See also *Contemporary Authors*, Vol. 105.)

PRINCIPAL WORKS

D'iavoliada (short stories) 1925
  [*Diaboliad, and Other Stories*, 1972]
*Dni Turbinykh (drama) 1926
  [*Days of the Turbins* published in *Six Soviet Plays*, 1934; also published as *Days of the Turbins* in *An Anthology of Russian Plays*, 1963; and *The Days of the Turbins* in *The Early Plays of Mikhail Bulgakov*, 1972]
Zoikina kvartira (drama) 1926
  [*Zoya's Apartment* published in *The Early Plays of Mikhail Bulgakov*, 1972]
Belaia gvardiia: Dni Turbinykh (novel) 1927
  [*The White Guard*, 1971]
Bagrovyi ostrov (drama) 1928
  [*The Crimson Island* published in *The Early Plays of Mikhail Bulgakov*, 1972]

Mertvye dushi [adaptor; from a novel by Nikolai Gogol] (drama) 1932
Kabala sviatosh (drama) 1936
  [*A Cabal of Hypocrites (Molière)* published in *The Early Plays of Mikhail Bulgakov*, 1972]
Posledniye dni (drama) [written 1934-35] 1943
  [*The Last Days (Pushkin)* published in journal *Russian Literature Triquarterly*, 1976]
Beg (drama) [written 1928] 1957
  [*Flight*, 1970; also published as *Flight* in *The Early Plays of Mikhail Bulgakov*, 1972; and *On the Run*, 1972]
Zhizn' gospodina de Mol'era (biography) [written 1932-33] 1962
  [*The Life of Monsieur de Molière*, 1970]
**Zapiski iunogo vracha (short stories) 1963
  [*A Country Doctor's Notebooks*, 1975]
Ivan Vasil'evich [first publication] (drama) [written 1935] 1964
Teatral'nyi roman (unfinished novel) [written 1936-37] 1965; published in journal *Novyi mir*
  [*Black Snow: A Theatrical Novel*, 1967]
Blazhenstvo [first publication] (drama) [written 1930s] 1966; published in journal *Zvezdo Vostoka*
  [*Bliss* published in journal *Russian Literature Triquarterly*, 1976]
Master i Margarita [censored edition] (novel) [written 1928?-40] 1966-67; published in journal *Moskva;* also published as *Master i Margarita* [uncensored edition], 1969
  [*The Master and Margarita* (censored edition), 1967; also published as *The Master and Margarita* (uncensored edition), 1967]
Sobach'e serdtse (novel) [written 1925] 1969
  [*The Heart of a Dog*, 1968; also published as *Heart of a Dog*, 1968]
The Early Plays of Mikhail Bulgakov (dramas) 1972

*This drama is an adaptation of the novel *Belaia gvardiia: Dni Turbinykh.*

**This work is comprised of uncollected short stories published in Russian periodicals betwen 1925 and 1927.

WALTER DURANTY (essay date 1926)

[*Duranty was an English novelist and journalist. During the 1920s and 1930s he worked as Moscow correspondent for* The New York Times, *and he also wrote several books on Russia which have been praised for their insight and objectivity. In the following excerpt from a review of the Moscow Art Theater production of* The Days of the Turbins, *Duranty finds the play technically weak but very moving in its accurate portrayal of the destruction of the czarist state.*]

Enormous interest among the Moscow "Intelligentsia," both Communist and non-Communist, has been aroused by the historical play now being presented three or four times a week at the Stanislawski's Art Theatre. It was written by a "new" satirist, Bulgakof, whose first book of short stories caused a sensation here eighteen months ago because it included a daring skit on some of the weak points in Bolshevist methods. It was called **"The Fatal Eggs."**

The singing of the czarist anthem in Act I of the original production of Days of the Turbins *in 1926. Courtesy of Ardis Publishers.*

The play was first entitled **"The White Guard,"** but its name was changed on account of the censorship to **"The Days of the Turbins,"** Colonel Turbin of the old imperial army being the hero and the whole story revolving around his family.

The scene is laid at Kiev during the Summer of 1918, when the wavering power of the Ukrainian "Hetman" Skoropadski was buttressed only by German forces. Skoropadski flees with the Germans, leaving the city to the mercy of the semi-bandit leader Petlura, who by the way, was killed in Paris recently by a half-crazed relative of one of his murdered victims.

The story ends with the entry into the city of the Red Army, but the Bolsheviki otherwise play no part.

What thrills Moscow is the fact that the play gives a realistic picture of the Russian débacle without paying any attention to the Bolshevist tenet of class distinction.

The Turbin family, of the small nobility, is presented quite sympathetically and truthfully, and it may be said en passant that the play is superbly staged and acted by a younger group of the Stanislawskia company. The Czarist officers are shown as courageous, bewildered, gay, weak or riotous—in fact, as human beings instead of as brutal scoundrels.

Many declared that they knew lots of officers like Colonel Turbin—a high-minded, devoted soldier, who finally commits suicide after telling a handful of gallant young cadets that it is

impossible to resist Petlura's vastly superior forces and "anyway our Russia is doomed." . . .

Each of the half-dozen leading characters typifies the weaknesses that made the Bolshevist victory possible.

Colonel Turbin, like Hamlet, cannot decide on any action until it is too late. His brother-in-law, a Baltic Baron, puts his German blood above his loyalty to Russia. One of his brother officers is brave, but a drunkard, and another is trained by long discipline to put his trust only in his superiors instead of facing facts. At the end the latter flies to join General Denikin.

Colonel Turbin's young brother, crippled, for no purpose, by Petlura's bandits, typifies the waste of Russia's upper class and bourgeois youth.

His cousin, a young student, babbles parrot phrases while the Fatherland falls to pieces about his ears.

Technically, the play is weak in that the centre of interest is a march of events which affect individual characters without linking them to the inevitable sweep of destiny that makes the strength of the Greek tragedies.

Here and there for a moment the play rises to an epic height, but the rest is a mere series of episodes, natural, truthful, pathetic or comic but not dramatically compelling.

The real interest for the audience lies in the fact that this is the first time since the revolution that the revolutionary period has been presented, so to speak, "without prejudice" and as it really occurred....

Behind *The New York Times* correspondent last night sat a young Communist who sneered audibly during the earlier part of the play. But Turbin's last speech and death and the next scene, when his desperately wounded young brother relates the news to the family, literally made him weep.

"What's the matter. friend?" the correspondent asked him.

"I can't help it," he replied. "It is too real. I saw things like that myself."

There you have it, scarcely a person in last night's audience was not reviving similar scenes in his own memory.

Walter Duranty, "Red Intelligentsia Is Stirred by Play," in The New York Times, *Section 7, November 7, 1926, p. 20.*

CHARLES MORGAN (essay date 1934)

[*Morgan was an English novelist, dramatist, and critic. Concerned with mystical themes—particularly, in Morgan's words, "the conflict between the spirit and the flesh"—his works have been described as pretentious by some critics and profound by others. From 1926 to 1939, Morgan served as drama critic for the London* Times. *In the following excerpt from a review of a London production of* The Days of the Turbins (The White Guard), *Morgan finds that although Bulgakov's purpose may have been to satirize the incompetence of the White Guard, he actually succeeds in drawing a delightful portrait of their charm and individuality.*]

I am told that when [**"The White Guard"**] was performed in Moscow it was permitted, and indeed welcomed, by the Soviet authorities as a satire on the weakness, futility and inconstancy of the White Guard....

The portraits that Bulgakov draws are certainly not flattering. One receives an impression of hopeless infirmity of purpose and lack of vigor among the White Guard, and I suppose one is intended to conclude that it was, after all, a very good thing that they were supplanted as rulers of their country. Thus far the play may be regarded as indirect Red propaganda.

I remember that Tolstoy, in his criticism of Chekhov's story "The Darling," said that Chekhov, intending to satirize and attack the old-fashioned woman who took her color from the man she loved, unintentionally exalted her. Intending to curse, he blessed her instead. Bulgakov has perhaps done likewise in his treatment of the White Guard. He shows that they were drunken, vain, incompetent, unstable, but still the sympathy of the audience remains with them because all their defects spring from their astonishing elasticity of mind, their incurable lightness of heart.

There is in them the same element of childishness that appears in "The Cherry Orchard." By our Anglo-Saxon standards of efficiency in war, they are contemptible. They sing songs when they ought to be organizing their forces; they are blown to and fro by every emotional puff of romanticism and sentiment. Among them is a young officer who is a very peacock in his boasting, his vanity, his glib, absurd lies; another is, quite plainly, a drunkard; a third, a boy student, hurries about with earnest inconsequence, vaguely making love, vaguely reciting poetry.

But what a relief they are from the stern frown of supermen which nowadays suppresses the individuality of man through-

out Europe and Asia! How delightful it is to laugh again and to know that once there were people who lived in the sparkling moment and did not plod forever in battalions down the dreary avenue of a Five-Year Plan! Even in this play there is some solemn fighting. Shots are fired; the feet of infantry tramp in the distance; the best of the officers is killed. But the essence of the play is in its supper parties, its lovemaking, its casual songs, its innumerable absurdities. Every one fiddles while Rome burns. How antisocial, but how charming!

Charles Morgan, "East of the Narrows," in The New York Times, *Section 10, April 8, 1934, p. 2.*

M[ICHAEL] V. GLENNY (essay date 1967)

[*Glenny is an English author, critic, and translator. Among his translations from modern Russian literature are several of Bulgakov's works, including* The Heart of a Dog *and* The Master and Margarita. *In the following excerpt, he provides an overview of Bulgakov's literary career.*]

It would be meaningless to say that [Bulgakov] was a 'better' novelist than playwright—the two are different but linked func-

Montage which appeared in The New Viewer *magazine, combining photos of Konstantin Stanislavsky (the director of* Days of the Turbins*), the play's main actors, and fragments of negative reviews of the play. Courtesy of Ardis Publishers.*

tions of one talent; but the novels are inevitably accessible to a wider public than his plays, their intellectual and artistic scope is wider, in keeping with the greater breadth and elasticity of the novel form. In addition to the built-in characteristics of the novel, which Bulgakov exploits to the uttermost limits, one of his strengths as a novelist is a gift 'borrowed', as it were, from his playwriting self: his quite extraordinary power of conveying intensely real, visual effects with an unerring economy of means. The images leap instantly from the page, three-dimensional, true and alive. Such is Bulgakov's command of this rare ability that it is one of the greatest sources of pleasure to be gained from reading his novels. They are compulsively readable, because Bulgakov is one of nature's born storytellers. He does not just string together a narrative sequence, dabbing in the colour and describing states of mind; he is primarily a creator of a teeming fantasy world of people who range from the grotesque to the starkly realistic and, who, as he describes them, begin to move and act in accordance with the often strange but inescapable logic of their natures.... [A] most important element in Bulgakov's artistic make-up was one which he shared with Chekhov—he was a doctor.... He made direct literary use of his experiences as a young GP in the series of stories called *Notes of a Young Physician*.... These are enjoyable if rather slight sketches, sober and full of clinical detail, in which Bulgakov kept in check his natural bent for fantasy and elaboration—presumably because his original editors wanted fairly 'straight' pieces. They make very easy reading and convey vividly what it feels like to be flung straight from medical school into a remote country practice where the nearest town is forty horse-drawn miles away. The *Notes* also have a considerable documentary value on clinical practice of the time, and clearly show that although GPs were worked hard, the standard of medical services in 'backward' rural Russia in the year of the revolution was surprisingly high.... Yet, disappointingly, these stories do not really convey those characteristics bred by his medical career which gave an extra dimension to Bulgakov the writer—that special combination of trained observation, sensitivity to the human condition, and detachment.

To find this, and much more, one must read *The White Guard*. (pp. 5-6)

To describe a few months in the lives of a few people Bulgakov constructed a rich, finely detailed, multi-faceted, if anything slightly overladen novel. He deployed almost every literary device in a tremendous effort to record the totality of an experience that he had lived through himself: impressionistic description, terse realistic narrative, stream-of-consciousness, lyrical evocation, frequent passages of dialogue in Ukrainian (very confusing, this, for those of us who have no Ukrainian), snatches of verse and song, reflection and flashback, dream sequences, remarks addressed straight at the reader (a special Bulgakov quirk, which he uses in all his novels), and a rapid cross-cutting back and forth from sequence to sequence, always varying the pace. In fact, in technique this novel more than anything resembles a film script; it could be put on the screen more or less as it stands. When you reach the end, slightly dazed, the images of that winter are fixed on the inward screen of your mind forever; you know, with a sense of physical impact, in a way that no historian and few writers can convey, exactly what revolution and civil war meant to ordinary people. (p. 8)

Superficially, *The White Guard* is closely linked with Bulgakov's *Black Snow: A Theatrical Novel*.... Basically this is the story of the genesis of *The White Guard* and its stage variant, *The Days of the Turbins*, and of Bulgakov's introduction to Stanislavsky and the Moscow Art Theatre where he was to work for ten years. *Black Snow* as it stands is in two parts (it is unfinished, so the parts are slightly unevenly balanced). The first or 'literary' part describes the pains and tribulation suffered by the naive young aspirant author, Maksudov, in trying to write his first novel 'by moonlight' whilst working in the daytime at the hated job of newspaper reporter, and simultaneously straining to be accepted into the weird, cliquey, fake-bohemian world of literary Moscow of the early twenties. By what seems a miracle the novel is published and the 'Independent Theatre' (alias the Moscow Art Theatre) commissions Maksudov to make it into a play. Thus begins the second or 'theatrical' part of the novel, and we move into the fascinating, enclosed, arcane world of the theatre.

Here Bulgakov's quite extraordinary gifts of wit, irony, and deadpan humour are revealed as a force with scarcely an equal in twentieth-century writing. In Russian literature he can be compared only with Ilf and Petrov for humour; with Saltykov-Shchedrin for the force of his critical satire; and with Gogol for his nervous, even neurotic, relish for the grotesque. Allowing for the differences in cultural climate, Bulgakov's nearest equivalent in Anglo-American literature would be an amalgam (if such can be imagined) of Edgar Allan Poe and Evelyn Waugh. Delighted readers can now relish the spectacle of this formidable talent addressing itself to the task of lampooning that great sacred cow of theatre—Stanislavsky—and his dedicated flock, the Moscow Art Theatre.... As Bulgakov adds stroke after stroke to his bitterly comic picture of backstage life, it becomes a matter of some wonder that this menagerie of inflated egos actually managed to stage a performance every night. It is of course a caricature and not a photograph, but like all great ironists he exaggerates and distorts for a purpose.

The fact is that the main episode which *Black Snow: A Theatrical Novel* purports to describe—the dramatisation and staging of *The White Guard*—was not the exasperating farce that he implies.... Bulgakov's disillusionment with Stanislavsky, which was of that intensity peculiar to soured affection, dates from an event that took place ten years *after* the highly successful première of his first play.

In 1932 Bulgakov wrote a tragedy entitled *Molière*. It records with great poignancy the last months of Molière's life when the great actor-playwright, after a life of exhausting struggle finally crowned with success, was harried to death by a clique of jealous hypocrites surrounding Louis XIV (hence the play's alternative title—... *The Clique of Hypocrites*). The parallel with Bulgakov's own treatment by Stalin (it was written at a time when all his plays and short stories had been banned in the USSR and Bulgakov's plea to Stalin to let him emigrate had been rejected by a personal telephone call from the 'pockmarked Caligula') was intentional and evident to anybody who could read between the lines (i.e. everybody).... The Soviet press understood the play's intention only too well, and after a blistering review in *Pravda* headed '*Vneshnii blesk i falshivoe soderzhanie*' (*Glittering outside, false inside*), which was at once echoed by every other newspaper, *Molière* was taken off after a run of only seven nights. (pp. 8-10)

With its subject-matter antedated by ten years to his debut as a playwright, *Black Snow: A Theatrical Novel* is Bulgakov's revenge on Stanislavsky for the failure of *Molière*.... He knew that it would never be published in his lifetime; with grim irony he originally entitled it *Zapiski Pokoinika* (*Notes of a Dead*

Konstantin Stanislavsky. Courtesy of Ardis Publishers.

Man) and preceded the novel with a comic foreword in which he pretended that the book had been written by someone else who '. . . had no connection with playwriting or with the theatre in his life . . .'. Yet although the *effect* of the satire is deadly and much of the book was written under appalling circumstances—Bulgakov dictated the bulk of it to his wife when he was incurably ill with sclerosis of the kidneys, blind, and in constant pain—it is executed with an enchanting lightness of touch, a precision and a polished, muscular elegance of language which, compared with most Soviet prose writing with its flabby sentimentality, its windiness, and moral equivocation, is like an ice-cold draught of spring-water after a lifetime of tepid, flat lemonade. Although in conception a work of bitter catharsis based on autobiography, by its tremendous charge of imaginative voltage and its rich fantasy *Black Snow* is a work of art that far transcends its origin and genre; with its unique fusion of delicate realism, wry humour, and a nervous, disturbing sense of mystery, this novel has alerted literate Russia to the promise of one of the greatest virtuosi of Russian prose of this century.

The fulfilment of this promise is to be found in the long novel, which although published eighteen months after the *Theatrical Novel,* was finished before it. This is *The Master and Margarita.* . . . (pp. 10-11)

It differs from *The White Guard* and the *Theatrical Novel* in that, whereas these two had their origin as forms of exorcism of traumatic events in Bulgakov's life, *The Master and Mar-*

garita is a novel of ideas brought to life in the guise of fantasy. Bulgakov's chosen technique has a long and distinguished literary ancestry; the Soviet scholar A. Vulis traces its origin to the satires of Menippus, a shadowy figure of ancient Greek literature none of whose works is extant, but who is known through other authors who copied his methods, of whom the most notable was Aesop. Without going so far back, Bulgakov is known to have been influenced by Lesage's picaresque satire *Le Diable Boîteux,* whilst for English readers the most illuminating parallel to his work is perhaps *Gulliver's Travels,* where Swift employs the device of a series of exotic journeys to express his caustic views on human folly. There is much in it, too, of Gogol—the 'Ukrainian' Gogol of witches, warlocks, and devils as well as the 'Petersburg' Gogol of *The Nose* and *The Diary of a Madman.* Echoes of Dostoevsky, in particular Ivan Karamazov, are there, and the debt to Goethe's *Faust* is explicit both in the book's title and in its epigraph, which is a passage of dialogue between Faust and Mephistopheles. Over it all there broods the uneasy sense of the immanent supernatural which Bulgakov shares (of course in his case it is conscious artifice) with E.T.A. Hoffmann.

The time is the twenties and the Devil in person comes to Moscow. . . . Deploying every trick of magic and necromancy, the Devil sets about creating havoc in Moscow. . . . Some of the Devil's pranks have been sheer anarchic fun, but more often they have been chosen to bring out the worst in everybody. People are shown up in all their weakness, greed, cowardice, and gullibility. Merciless fun is poked at all the institutions that Bulgakov knew best and detested most—medicine, bureaucracy, the theatre, and the snobbish, clique-ridden literary world.

Amid this bizarre and hugely funny pantomime of slapstick and supernatural tomfoolery, two people somehow remain immune and undiminished by the Devil's malicious trickery. These two are the Master and Margarita of the title. The story of their passionate, unlucky, and illicit love-affair (Margarita is married to someone else) forms the wholly serious and very moving second level in this multilayered book. The Master is a writer, a man single-mindedly devoted to the search for truth, who has poured all the wisdom of a lifetime into a book in which he grapples with the problem of good and evil. He does so in the form of a re-interpretation of the trial, execution, and death of Christ. (pp. 11-12)

In this, the third level of his book, Bulgakov has produced an absolute *tour de force:* it is a complete novel within the novel, written in a triple-distilled prose of quite extraordinary power and totally different in style from the rip-roaring black humour of the 'Devil-in-Moscow' sequences. (p. 13)

No synopsis can possibly do justice to this remarkable book. As a philosophical disquisition in a fictional vehicle it is extraordinarily stimulating, yet it leaves a sense that there is still something missing; there is a feeling that Bulgakov just failed to place the keystone on his philosophical construct. The difficulty centres on his attitude to his Devil. Surrounded with all the traditional paraphernalia of diabolism, in the first half of the book Satan appears to play the accepted role of the Prince of Darkness—the cosmic mischief-maker and source of evil. Yet all the people that he has frightened and punished are themselves weak, cowardly, or corrupt, and in the end Satan's treatment of them looks more like a kind of divine justice. At the same time the Devil implicitly bows before the virtues of love, charity, loyalty, and faith, whilst appearing to treat the incorruptible Christ almost as a spiritual equal. To see this work as a schematised parable of the evils of Stalinism is a mistaken over-simplification. If anything, it is perhaps an attempt to construct a paradox—a humanist metaphysic, or perhaps it is a parable justifying a morality of Judaeo-Christian origin but without a God: man is at once his own God and his own Devil.

The enigma must stand for the moment. There is nothing enigmatic about the stature of *The Master and Margarita* as a work of art. Its language has all the virtues of Bulgakov's writing at the top of his bent, and by some magic the whole, despite the less than total cohesion of its parts in an intellectual sense, adds up to an aesthetic experience of the most satisfying completeness. Volumes and volumes of criticism and exegesis will be written on it in years to come. For the moment our happy duty is to enjoy what may well come to be regarded as the glory of twentieth-century Russian literature.

It is difficult to 'place' Bulgakov the novelist in any particular grouping of Soviet literature. Publicly he belonged to the theatre; his novel-writing (except for *The White Guard*) was very much a desk-drawer career. As a satirist he undoubtedly shares some common attitudes with Ilf and Petrov, though he might have denied this. His whole cast of mind seems to have been totally different from the miniaturism of Zoshchenko; nor was Bulgakov so stamped by his origins as was Babel, although he lacked Babel's fierce self-discipline as a writer: artistically Bulgakov suffers from attacks of quirky self-indulgence that may make people judge Babel the more finished writer. Temperamentally and artistically Bulgakov was perhaps closest to Zamyatin, whom he resembled in several ways: his lack of interest in realism for realism's sake; the primacy of his irrepressible fantasy, and above all his courage under the blows of fate and his faith in his own vision, which he believed—with justification, as we now know—to be stronger than 'principalities and powers'. (pp. 13-14)

M[ichael] V. Glenny, "Mikhail Bulgakov," in Survey, No. 65, October, 1967, pp. 3-14.

RAYMOND ROSENTHAL   (essay date 1967)

[*Rosenthal is an American critic and educator. In the following excerpt, he claims that, despite a certain artfulness,* The Master and Margarita *falls short of a masterpiece because of its clichéd characters, sentimental treatment of the contest between good and evil, and lack of insight into human motivation.*]

Mikhail Bulgakov's *The Master and Margarita* was written in the late '20s, when the Bolshevik Revolution—originally seen by the literati as a natural cataclysm that would sweep away the debris of the old world—had settled into a banal routine under the control of mean and petty bureaucrats. Bulgakov managed to survive the Stalin purges by retiring into silence. He is supposed to have worked on this most ambitious of his novels until his death in 1940, continuously retouching and improving the original draft. Yet the impact of the first great wave of disillusionment with the Revolution's aims and ideals among the intellectuals is the most notable aspect of the novel, despite the gaiety of its excited movement, its almost baroque invention, and its curious spiritual hierarchy.

In this hierarchy, the Devil proves to be the master of the universe. God is nowhere to be seen, although fleeting mention is made of him at the start. On his visit to Moscow, the Devil assumes the guise of a consultant in magic, his grotesque retinue resembles a vaudeville troupe, and the demonic pranks

they engage in devolve entirely upon the necessities and trivial greeds occupying the minds of the harassed Muscovites after 10 years of the revolutionary regime—suitable living quarters, fine clothes, and the foreign currency to buy them. All this is an echo of the NEP period and probably explains the recent publication in the Soviet literary magazine *Moskva* of a censored version of the original text. For Bulgakov's novel, no matter how much he revised it, is tied to that long-gone period of the '20s and most of its satire has lost its bite.

Most, but fortunately not all. Bulgakov had healthy hatreds that he brilliantly worked into his fast-moving plot. He hated editors, literary parasites, the whole machinery of bureaucracy which the triumphant Revolution placed over the artist to tempt and harass him. Bulgakov knew this world inside out, and the picture he limned is unforgettable—the villas given as plums to the most tractable, the vacations, the sumptuous meals, the ostracism and hounding that even the slightest independence aroused in the watchdogs of the fleshpots of literary expression. The milieu he evokes is strangely middle-class—theatrical entrepreneurs, janitors, barmen, literary hacks—the lower and upper reaches of that segment of the professional intelligentsia and their hangers-on and servants which somehow managed to survive the October overthrow. The majority of them are mediocrities, and the Devil has a field-day toying with their greeds, pettinesses, occupational idiocies. In Bulgakov's eyes, the Russian Revolution was the occasion for the triumph of the second-rate; it reflected the eternal meanness and shabbiness of the human condition. But he has not written a political novel, in the sense that Victor Serge's or Ignazio Silone's novels are political. (p. 18)

Pontius Pilate is the most moving and fully realized character in the novel, indeed the only real character. The Devil, beside him, seems a necessary device; the Master, who is writing a novel about Pontius Pilate, a cliché of the uprooted artist; while his mistress, Margarita, does not achieve individuality even when she becomes a witch in order to rescue her beloved Master. The second chapter, where Bulgakov recreates the meeting between Jesus and Pontius Pilate with overpowering imaginative freshness, is unfortunately the high point of the book. Nothing after that, including the working out of the Jesus story as a sort of supernatural echo to the earthly action in Moscow, ever reaches the same pitch of psychological insight.

But in this whole supernatural section of his novel, Bulgakov appears to be telling us, indirectly, glancingly, though quite explicitly, what he thinks of the Russian Revolution and the great changes it has supposedly brought about. The real drama for him took place long ago in Jerusalem, when a frightened Jesus in Herod's palace pleaded for the goodness in man, when Judas took his spy's silver and was murdered, when Pontius Pilate, driven by state and material necessity, played out his role as the emissary of power and the unwilling representative of evil. It is precisely Pilate's unwillingness that distinguishes Bulgakov's view of the struggle between good and evil. Pilate would have preferred not to execute Jesus, for in their short interview Jesus has been the first man to reveal Pilate to himself and to speak honestly. But Pilate represents the Roman power which demands that "the rebel" be crucified. He complies, out of cowardice, and spends the next 2,000 years racked with headaches and remorse. His pardon comes when the Master and the Margarita plead with Devil for his deliverance, and the Devil has a moment of charity.

So Bulgakov takes a rather sentimental view of the august contest between good and evil. The Devil has contempt for human beings, in the approved classical tradition, yet he finds that their inexplicably sudden impulses of charity are rather charming and should now and then be indulged. No other explanation can be given for the climax of the novel, and there is in fact a somewhat ludicrous contrast between the immensity of the scene—a mountaintop overlooking all of history—and the pat, consolatory ending that Bulgakov has contrived.

In the Epilogue this sentimental view is prolonged in the dreams of the clerk Ivan Nikolayevich, who is still suffering from his transformation into a pig by one of the Devil's witches. After his drug injection, Ivan Nikolayevich has pleasant dreams about Pilate and Jesus: ''A wide path of moonlight stretches from the bed to the window, a man in a white cloak with blood-red lining ascends the road and walks toward the moon. Next to him is a young man in a torn chiton, with a badly bruised face. They talk heatedly about something, debating, trying to reach an agreement.

'''Gods, gods!' says the man in the cloak, turning his haughty face to his companion. 'What a vulgar execution! But tell me, please tell me,' and his face is no longer haughty but pleading, 'it never happened! I beg you, tell me, it never happened?'

'''Of course, it never happened,' his companion answers in a hoarse voice. 'You imagined it.'''

If this is satiric playfulness on Bulgakov's part it is sadly self-defeating. The suffocating effects of a dictatorial regime on artistic expression are well-known. Less well-known are its insidious effects on a first-rate writer such as Bulgakov. The artfulness of this novel is often breath-taking—its speed, charm, and incredible inventiveness, its comic agility and brilliance. Yet **The Master and Margarita** is far from a masterpiece. The horror of its devilish detail is not matched by a correspondingly profound insight into the basest human motives. Pontius Pilate, the weary bureaucrat, typifies all too completely the weary, rather cynical attitude that Bulgakov can only mask at the end with an unpersuasive sentimentality.

The theme he has chosen to elaborate is not a new one in modern Russian literature—one can find it in the poet Alexander Blok and in philosophical thinkers such as Shestov and Rozanov. In comparison, Bulgakov's vision is as cramped and petty as the Moscow he has chosen to depict. The truth is that he is not a philosophical writer at all; he is a writer of an almost indelibly realistic turn of mind, with that valuable feeling for the opaqueness and substantiality of things, persons, ideas, which runs like iron through all of the best modern Russian writing. His fantastic vein is always, or should always be, grounded in fact. I prefer his short novel, **The Fatal Eggs,** with its unpretentious comic sweep, to the moon-dazed musings in **The Master and Margarita.** (pp. 18-19)

Raymond Rosenthal, ''Bulgakov's Sentimental Devil,'' in The New Leader, Vol. L, No. 23, November 20, 1967, pp. 18-19.

IRVING HOWE   (essay date 1968)

[*A longtime editor of the leftist magazine* Dissent *and a regular contributor to* The New Republic, *Howe is one of America's most highly respected literary critics and social historians. He has been a socialist since the 1930s, and his criticism is frequently informed by a liberal social viewpoint. Howe is widely praised for what F. R. Dulles has termed his ''knowledgeable understanding, critical acumen and forthright candor.'' Howe has written: ''My work has fallen into two fields: social history and literary criticism. I have tried to strike a balance between the social and the literary:*

to fructify one with the other; yet not to confuse one with the other. Though I believe in the social approach to literature, it seems to me peculiarly open to misuse; it requires particular delicacy and care.'' In the following excerpt, Howe analyzes the three distinct narratives in The Master and Margarita, *and finds that their interrelationship lacks apparent coherence.*]

The Master and Margarita is a very difficult book. Those reviews I have seen mostly skirt the critical problem it raises: the reviewers declare it a splendid novel and a work of spiritual force, all of which is true, but they do not offer a coherent account of plot, character, and theme. That such an account can be offered after a first reading I doubt; whether it would be possible after several readings I am not sure. Bulgakov left the book in an unfinished state and it is possible that we are dealing with a masterpiece never brought to complete focus. Or perhaps a masterpiece that, like *Ulysses*, requires some years of study before it fully reveals itself. I can only say, at this moment, that while the book yields great pleasures, it does not yet fall into shape as a coherent work of art.

The action moves along three narrative planes, each of which can be grasped independently without much trouble:

(1) *The devil comes to Moscow.* Bulgakov's devil owes something to Dostoevsky and Mann: he is a shabby, debonair scoundrel, a little world-weary yet ready for mischief, and devoted not so much to positive evil as to scoffing at the idea of positive good. Woland, as Bulgakov calls the devil, masquerades as a professor of magic, and is attended by a canting choirmaster, a red-haired vampire who parades about naked, and an enormous black cat called Behemoth who smokes cigars and is a dead shot with an automatic. This gang throws Moscow into superb confusion. A literary editor is suddenly deprived of his head; a theatrical official is spirited off to Yalta; a suit of clothes sits, minus its body, and continues the rigmarole of a bureaucrat; clothing vanishes from the backs of ladies in the streets; bank notes change into champagne labels; a sparrow does a fox-trot on a doctor's desk; and a choral society, like a broken record, must endlessly repeat ''The Volga Boatman.''

This part of the novel is sheer pleasure, an orgy of malice and revelation in which the devil strips the society to its inner corruption, as if he, Woland, were a buffoonish Dostoevskian double of the state of things under Stalinism. Woland strikes one as an inner emanation from within the society itself, revealing the reality of its disorder beneath the stiff surface of authoritarian order; he is also intent upon upsetting the stuffy atheism of official Russia by demonstrating the powers of the supernatural. As social satire, this part of the novel is remarkable: Gogol reincarnated.

(2) *The Master struggles for freedom.* The Master is a Russian novelist, an eccentric genius shut up in an insane asylum (Bulgakov here anticipated a punitive device of the post-Stalin dictatorship) because he has written a novel about Christ which the editors will not print. Together with his mistress Margarita, the Master seems to strike a bargain with Woland by which Margarita joins the devil at his annual ball, a witches' sabbath at which a dazzling cast of sinners appears, Johann Strauss conducts an oversized orchestra, and Caligula makes a bow. Then, apparently as a reward for Margarita's descent, the Master's freedom will be restored.

(3) *Pontius Pilate wrestles with his conscience.* Meanwhile the Master's novel is being unfolded within **The Master and Margarita,** a profoundly stirring narrative about a lonely Palestinian preacher named Yeshua, seemingly without disciples, whose

only word to the Roman procurator, Pontius Pilate, is that of defenseless love. Bulgakov's version of the Christ story approximates the spirit of primitive Christianity, and his Jesus is a figure Dostoevsky would have recognized and loved. The Palestinian setting is evoked with rich detail; Pontius is as credible as Dean Rusk; and, as if to provide his own apocrypha, the Master has Pontius arrange for the murder of Judas shortly after the Crucifixion.

The first and third of these narratives are self-sufficient and masterly; the second, dealing with the Master and Margarita, is for me clouded and problematic. One gains a general sense of what Bulgakov is doing here. The Master is canny, upright, beleaguered in his duel with the authorities; when Christ, in the Master's heterodox gloss, says to Pilate, "One of the greatest human sins is cowardice," we know that an oblique reference is being made to the shame and disorder of the Russia portrayed in Bulgakov's novel; and we also have some vague awareness that the Master must make a deal of sorts with Woland, or that Margarita must make it for him, in order to gain a respite in his struggle for freedom as a writer. But examined with some strictness, the relationship between the story dealing with the Master and the story dealing with Woland is far from clear. It is as if all the pieces of the puzzle were there, but the pattern had not yet become visible.

Meanwhile, however, it is a book to enjoy and ponder: a trophy salvaged from the most terrible decade of twentieth-century life. (pp. 71-2)

> *Irving Howe, "The Continuity of Russian Voices,"* in Harper's Magazine, *Vol. 236, No. 1412, January, 1968, pp. 69-75.**

ANATOLY AL'TSHULER (essay date 1968)

[*In the following excerpt, Al'tshuler offers a reading of Bulgakov's works from a Soviet perspective and finds Bulgakov's weakness to be his inability to place the welfare of the group above that of the individual, as well as his failure to recognize the necessity of renouncing the past after the Russian Revolution. For another discussion of Bulgakov's attitude toward prerevolutionary Russia, see the excerpt by Carol Avins (1983).*]

Mikhail Bulgakov came into literature with a distinctive theme, to which he remained loyal. That theme was revolution and culture, although the conjunction "and"—this is something we must say at the outset—sometimes sounded for the writer like the disjunctive "or."

Bulgakov's artistic world was paradoxical. Unrestrained fantasy and precise mundane detail; caustic ridicule and melancholy lyricism. The uniqueness of Bulgakov's vision is best identified by his own words written about Molière: "But his eyes are remarkable. I read in them a strange, ever-present, mordant smile and at the same time an eternal amazement before the world around him."

The world surrounding Bulgakov was shaken by revolution. To hear the music of the times in its thunder was particularly difficult for people who had been shaped in the bosom of the old culture, cultivated on the "world's best . . . books, redolent of mysterious, old-time chocolate," books the mother bequeathed to the heroes of *White Guard* [*Belaia gvardiia*].

The doom of the old, capitalist, "unmusical" world (as Blok put it) was not a matter of doubt. All writers of any talent at all agreed on this. The disagreements began on the fact that the old world had accumulated a culture developed through

millennia of civilization. Was it, too, condemned to destruction?

It was not only the adherents of the Proletkult who gave an affirmative answer to that question. Many major artists who were very remote from the Proletkult nihilism also considered "the collapse of culture" historically inevitable and justified by virtue of that alone.

For Bulgakov, however, it was *only* culture and the world of the intelligentsia that bring order, harmony, "comfort" into the chaos of human existence. Thinking about Russia, the writer could not conceive of it as the principal force in historical development without the intelligentsia.

This idea takes on a tragic ring in the novel *White Guard*. The attempt of the Turbin family to defend with sword in hand a way of life that had already spent its vitality was regarded by Bulgakov as quixotism. But the essence of the matter was that with their death, it seemed to the artist, everything perished.

The artistic space of the novel is divided into two parts. On the one hand there is the world of the Turbins, an organized and structured space, fundamentally delimited from chaos (we recall the famous "cream-colored blinds"). On the other hand, there is a space of elements, barbarism, and the Petliura terror, unorganized, unbounded, hostile to the town. The world of the Turbins dies, but Petliura, too, rotted away. The armored train "Proletarii" enters the town. The decisive force in history is in many respects still incomprehensible to Bulgakov, but the writer regards it as a force of organization and not of chaos and therefore looks upon it with confidence and hope.

This same problem defined the satire of the young Bulgakov, but here, unlike in the novel, it was resolved gloomily: culture was dissolved into elements—"El'pit House, No. 13, the Workers' Commune" burned down, and it proved impossible to revive the "red ray" of life after the ignorant experiment of the retired flautist Aleksandr Rokk (**"Fatal Eggs"** [**"Rokovye iaitsa"**]).

Of course the intellectual atmosphere of that period contained tendencies that fed the fears of the artist. They—these tendencies—were formulated paradoxically by Ehrenburg's Julio Jurenito: "Now is a time of beginning, that is, barbarism, indiscriminate negation, the primitive power of first steps. . . . Forgive a word of gynecology: in order for an infant to live, the umbilical cord must be cut. Then he is raised to his mother's nipples, and a double Renaissance occurs."

Bulgakov believed that it was impossible to cut the umbilical cord and that a new world could be built only on the shoulders and not the bones of the old. But the artist's intellectual drama, which predetermined the contradictoriness of Bulgakov's prose in the twenties, lay in the fact that the writer, who set down with amazing power the inevitable downfall of the old world and its culture, did not as yet see the appearance of a new culture and its bearer—a new person.

The Notes of a Young Doctor [*Zapiski iunogo vracha*] were written in an atmosphere of fierce dispute over *The Days of the Turbins* [*Dni Turbinykh*]. Behind the calm, unhurried tone in this cycle of stories we distinctly sense another, deeply polemical, plane and behind the subject, familiar to the Russian reader (if only from Veresaev), there is an idea that he had agonized out himself. I have in mind the relationships between "culture and the elements," the people and the intelligentsia. "Egyptian Darkness" [T'me egipetskoi], which appears in the title of one story, is opposed by a doctor, an intellectual who takes it on with stethoscope in hand. The entire cycle is permeated with the image of a gale, a wind—the esthetic equivalent of revolution. The same image is carried out in the title of the central tale in the series: "The Blizzard" [V'iuga].

The epigraph: "Now it howls like a beast, now cries like a child," sends us back to Pushkin and establishes the scope of what is described. Bulgakov consciously built *The Notes of a Young Doctor* on motifs of the greatest importance in Russian literature: "roads," "coachmen," "blizzards." A search is made for Russia's road, that same road which Pushkin in "The Devils" [Besy], Gogol in *Dead Souls* [Mertvye dushi], and Korolenko in *Fires* [Ogni], tried to see through the snowstorm, the tempest, the blizzard of history.

The young doctor wanders off the road. A blizzard: "all roads are drifted high; for the life of me, I cannot see a track; we are lost. What are we to do!"

Where is the road? The answer to Pushkin's question and to the principal question of his own time was given by the writer: the road is lit by the hospital lantern, science, light. The "good individual," the doctor who is prepared for self-sacrifice, is the only bearer of these principles.

The entire cycle is built on the struggle between these two leitmotifs: blizzards and the elements against the light and good. "The heavy snow fell and covered everything; the lantern shone; and my house was alone, calm, and important."

The young doctor's program is traditional: "The shroud of Egyptian darkness hung heavy . . . and in it, it is as though I . . . have in hand either a sword or a stethoscope. I . . . go on, I struggle . . . in this backwater. But I am not alone. My company marches with me: Dem'ian Lukin, Anna Nikolavna, Pelegeia Ivanna. All in white smocks, and all forward, forward. . . ." But immediately after this program comes a sharp letdown ("sleep—that is something good! . . ."), enabling one to perceive bitter irony behind the main motif of the cycle: "I go on . . . I struggle. . . ."

The platform of the "young doctor," the ideas of the Russian Enlightenment and populist democracy, were a stage already past. A different "road" was being laid out. The interrelationships between revolution and inelligentsia did not take shape in accordance with what had been written in the "chocolate" books which their mother had willed to the Turbins.

"The mother said to her children: 'Live,'" writes Bulgakov. "But they have to suffer and die."

The clash was between the people reared on the "chocolate books" and the real course of history, which overthrew all their preconceptions: it is out of this clash that the distinctive, two-layered, pathetic and ironical style of Bulgakov's prose was born.

Some critics of Bulgakov, confusing the author and his characters, accused him of writing apologetics for the white-guard movement. However, right after *White Guard,* he wrote the play *Days of the Turbins* [Dni Turbinykh] and its sequel *Flight* [Beg].

Here we have a revised view of history. In *White Guard,* despite the fogginess and illogicality of the world of the old intelligentsia, there is confidence nonetheless that outside that world all is chaos and emptiness. If it, the old intelligentsia, perishes—all perishes.

In *Days of the Turbins* and *Flight,* the death of the Turbins does not bring with it the death of a whole world but only of part of it. The tragic heroes—Turbin and Khludov—acquire parodic doubles—Lariosik and Charnota. The romantic irony of *White Guard* becomes tragicomedy.

We recall how, at the most intense and tragic moment, when Aleksei Turbin alone remains to defend the town and its culture, the watchman Maxim enters the school. He tearfully begs Turbin not to break up the desks, to protect the property, because "the Mister Principal" had left him, Maxim, and he was responsible for everything. The heroism and personal tragedy of Turbin, defending the high school *in solitude,* are reduced to parody by the farce of the speech of the *sole* watchman, prepared to save the desks at the cost of his life.

Maxim is a kind of double of the Turbins. They too have a "Mr. Principal" who disappeared into non-existence, and their lives are given just as senselessly in the cause of a historical illusion.

Here is the heart of Bulgakov's poetics. Tragedy and farce coexist, permeate each other, are reflected one in the other, and now define his understanding of the world. No one and nothing are sanctioned as indispensable: laughter and farce erode all the claims of the Turbins to historical finality for their words.

Behind the violent and often necessary dispute, Bulgakov's opponents did not notice the most complex process: the process whereby the writer overcame the "world historical confusion" of the democratic Russian intelligentsia during the Revolution. Instead of a serious debate, instead of a profound and sensitive analysis needed by a writer who had sought a road in suffering and who, despite this, was still largely at odds with the new reality, literary criticism, at the end of the twenties, was already drawing conclusions about his creative path.

Criticism was drawing conclusions while the problem of the relationship between the creative artist and reality was intruding imperiously into Bulgakov's consciousness. The writer turned to history in an attempt to find there the laws defining these interrelationships. His novel and play about Molière made their appearance, and then a play on the death of Pushkin.

During the final decade of his life, Bulgakov worked on the novel *The Master and Margarita.* The book absorbs into itself and philosophically interprets the fundamental ideas in his prose of the thirties. (pp. 61-6)

Bulgakov has a tragic concept of the interrelation between the artist and the government and always dissolves the concrete situation into the unified, undivided, extra temporal flow of History.

The concept of time in the structure of the novel is extremely significant: events occurring separately in history are presented in the novel as simultaneous. The real and the historical strata, superimposing on each other, express the basic notion of the writer. The personality of the Master and the deeds of man-the-creator stand opposed, in the novel, both to the real world of ordinary men and to the supra-personal fantastic world of Voland. He, the Master, finds support within himself and nowhere else, and is, according to Bulgakov, the sole bearer of good, without regard to any differences in social organization. Therefore good cannot triumph; the lonesome individual can only "infect" with good, but he is unable to triumph. (p. 70)

The idea of personal good stands contrasted, in the creative conception underlying *The Master and Margarita,* to all historical purposefulness. This is the origin of the weakness—philosophical and creative—of the novel's climax. An idea and conception that are out of time cannot serve as foundation for a correct evaluation of the deeds of a revolutionary epoch, its complexity and contradictions.

The insoluble antinomy between good and evil, love and hate, destruction and creation, acquires, at the hands of Bulgakov, a nuance of fatalism: history does not develop, but merely extends. It does not improve, but continues endlessly. (pp. 70-1)

The Master and Margarita was Bulgakov's final work. The novel permits us to trace and see the entire course followed by the writer from **White Guard,** built on romantic irony and on the effort to reconcile opposites in the process of history, to **The Master and Margarita,** in which the dispute and interaction of man and history are not reconciled but remain its eternal motive force.

This anti-historicism introduces a tragic coloration into Mikhail Bulgakov's perception.

The time is past for leveling reproaches against the writer, and, in any case, it is impossible to limit oneself to reproaches.

Today we have a much deeper view of the history of Soviet literature and clearly understand by what complex paths the culture of the new world was founded. We are studying the laws that defined those paths. Bulgakov's work therefore requires neither indiscriminate condemnation nor rhetorical eulogy. (p. 71)

> *Anatoly Al'tshuler, "Bulgakov as Prose Writer," in* Soviet Studies in Literature, *Vol. IV, No. 2, Spring, 1968, pp. 60-71.*

MIRRA GINSBURG   (essay date 1969)

[*Ginsburg is a Russian-born American author and translator specializing in Russian and Yiddish literature. Among her translations from modern Russian literature are several works by Bulgakov, including* Heart of a Dog *and* The Master and Margarita. *In the following excerpt from the introduction to her translation of* Flight, *Ginsburg asserts that the theme of the play—the struggle of the displaced person—is a problem central to modern society.*]

Flight, though an independent play, may, historically speaking, be regarded as a sequel to **The Days of the Turbins.** It takes up where the earlier play left off. Its characters are different, but the milieu is the same. It opens during the last hours of the Civil War and follows the defeated and escaping Whites into exile, to Constantinople and, briefly, to Paris.

An evocation of the aftermath of defeat of the Tsarist forces in Russia, the play moves swiftly, creating a vivid sense of chaos and disintegration—the tragic turning into comic, the respected and respectable into the disreputable and grotesque.

Like Zamyatin, Blok, Mandelshtam, and other significant writers and poets of the period, Bulgakov possessed an extraordinary sense of history. He was keenly aware of the present as a moment in the constant flow of change, never losing sight, if only implicitly, of the past and the possible future. Hence the prophetic and apocalyptic quality of much of his work.

Both in theme and in treatment, **Flight** is as relevant today as it was at the time of writing. It is a tragicomic picture of man violently uprooted and struggling for some sort of survival—each on his own terms—in an alien, indifferent, if not hostile world. Bulgakov comes close to one of the central problems of our time, the problem of the displaced person, repeated in the course of the past half-century in endless variations—geographic, political, cultural, moral, and philosophic.

The immediate roots of the play are in the realities of the period, and some of its characters are based on actual persons. Thus, the commander in chief is modeled after General Wrangel, who commanded the White Armies in 1919-20. Archbishop Africanus is based on Bishop Veniamin. Khludov is based on the notorious General Slashchov, commander of the Wrangel forces in the Crimea in 1920, who returned to Russia with a confession of guilt soon after the rout of the White Armies. (By one of the strange freaks of fate in a time of total upheaval, he was pardoned and reinstated in the army—the Red Army—in which he served loyally until his death.)

The nightmare image of Khludov, which dominates the play, is a portrait of a man who disintegrates as his world disintegrates, a man who is both executioner and victim. It foreshadows that dissolution of moral standards and restraints which made possible the mass extermination of human beings witnessed by the world in subsequent decades.

On the other hand, the hyperbolic image of General Charnota, hell-bent for destruction after his world is destroyed, is a masterpiece of portraiture, individual, yet superbly generalized. It is tragedy in the mask of laughter.

At the end of the play, which is divided into "dreams" rather than scenes, three go home: the crazed general who sought to stem the new by absolute terror and is returning to expiate his guilt, and the man and woman in love, who have also been corrupted and despairing in the process of flight, but who still retain enough integrity to opt for life and order. And there might well have been a sequel to **Flight.** For "home," as they knew it, is also gone. And so the ending, which might at first glance seem happily sentimental and affirmative, is in reality as ironic as the rest of the play and, indeed, as all of Bulgakov's sharp and satirical works. (pp. 8-10)

> *Mirra Ginsburg, in an introduction to* Flight: A Play in Eight Dreams & Four Acts *by Mikhail Bulgakov, translated by Mirra Ginsburg, Grove Press, Inc., 1969, pp. 5-10.*

V. S. PRITCHETT   (essay date 1971)

[*Pritchett is a highly esteemed English novelist, short story writer, and critic. A twentieth-century successor to such early nineteenth-century essayist-critics as William Hazlitt and Charles Lamb, Pritchett employs much the same critical method: his own experience, judgment, and sense of literary art are emphasized, rather than a codified critical doctrine derived from a school of psychological or philosophical speculation. His criticism is often described as fair, reliable, and insightful. In the following excerpt from a review of* The White Guard, *Pritchett praises the novel's vividness and realism.*]

Bulgakov belongs to the brilliant and unlucky group of Russian writers—Olesha, Ilf and Petrov, Zoschenko—who satirised the new Soviet society and who eventually 'disappeared' in the Thirties. (p. 184)

The case against him was the usual one: the politicians of the new State could not bear satirical or humorous criticism; his fantasies made them uneasy and they had the power to squash his dangerous thoughts.

The White Guard survived because it was turned into a popular play about Kiev on the eve of the Revolution, *The Days of the Turbins*. In the novel the Germans are preparing to leave Kiev, the situation in the Ukraine is confused particularly by the presence of Petlyura's bandit army, the city is packed with rich refugees from Moscow who are gambling on the overthrow of the Bolsheviks, but outside the city the first Bolshevik armoured train waits for its moment. The young Turbin family, living the cosy and rather touching bourgeois life, are feeling the first assaults of revolutionary confusion. The strength of the novel lies in its vivacious dramatisation of rumour and unease; and the city is so vivid to the eye that it is the real hero of the book. Bulgakov, who began writing as a journalist, was a tormented artist and poet. He knew one thing about cities: that they are places of familiar streets and short journeys, and every page has that peculiar Russian gift of giving at once a report of what happens in them and what, in any hour, everyone felt. There is the power to convey the mixture of timelessness—day and night passing like a stream through the lives of the characters—and the hour's urgency: the sense of life being a personal guessing of a path through dramas that are themselves guesses. The ability to step aside from novelists' dramatic time into the quite different, inconsequent time in which we feel that life means this or that to us, is at the heart of Bulgakov's talent. His contemporaries had this, too, before ideological time set in and introduced its predictable stodge.

Bulgakov's characters are always physically vivid, but because when they are described they are always doing something. Everyone's head, whether he is getting a bandage, running for his life, snoring on a sofa, preparing for civil defence, or buying milk from a peasant who has put the price up, is busy. A young man being chased at night by would-be assassins has no idea that he has shot and killed one of them: how perfectly that evokes the insulating sensation of terror. Bulgakov has the common gift for terse realism breaking into extravagant fantasy—carried to philosophical lengths in *The Master and Margarita*—but look at the detail in any passage and note how the fantastic is, so to say, domesticated. (pp. 184-85)

One sees the old Kiev in its mingling of charm, corruption and anxiety. The effect—despite the flashes of ugliness, pain and horror—is of a powerful reverie. What will happen to the Turbins? For a few days we are with them, we shall know the essence of their lives, and then, because they will scatter, these days will always be warm in our minds. This is a good deal due to Bulgakov's image-making, and is enhanced by the power of the final chapter of the book which triumphantly discloses the theme of the novel. It is a novel about waiting—waiting for a history or a future to declare itself; and that is evoked by the description of the troop train, with steam up, standing outside the city, and which will bring the real revolution in. If Bulgakov is more than a reporter of actualities, as Helen Muchnic says, he is interested in man as a believer rather than a doer; and if the Turbins exist for us it is because, without lecturing us and without overloaded dramatics, he conveys what they felt life was for, for good or for ill, as best they could. I have used the word 'reverie', for it conveys what must have got him into trouble with the authorities: his belief in the superiority of the artist's vision. It was probably the sheer reporting in *The White Guard* and the play he made out of it that enabled him, in this instance, to get by. (p. 185)

V. S. Pritchett, "Waiting for a Future," in New Statesman, Vol. 81, No. 2081, February 5, 1971, pp. 184-85.

ELLENDEA PROFFER AND CARL R. PROFFER (essay date 1971)

[*Carl and Ellendea Proffer are the founders of Ardis Publishers, the largest publishers of Russian literature outside the Soviet Union. This venture has been responsible for the publication of works by dissident and exiled Russian authors who otherwise would have remained unknown. In addition, both of the Proffers are recognized as important critics and translators of modern Russian literature, their translations including numerous works by Bulgakov. In the following excerpt, the Proffers examine theme and technique in the short stories of* Diaboliad.]

"Diaboliad" belongs to the tradition of Russian stories about "little men" and civil servants started by Gogol in "The Nose" and "The Overcoat" and continued less successfully by Dostoevsky in *The Double*. Character types are similar, including civil servant heroes suffering from sexual isolation and menacing superiors. The systemizing world of bureaucracy reduces people to categories, prizing sameness over individuality—and thus it produces frightening doubles. The boundaries which separate people begin to disintegrate, as does the sanity of the hero; when this happens the distinction between the "real" world and a fantastic world is not far behind. Madness and fantasy are age-old satirical devices. Gogol's Poprishchin ("Notes of a Madman") imagines noses living on the moon; Bulgakov's Korotkov sees Underwarr turning first into a phosphorescent black cat (forerunner of Behemoth in *The Master and Margarita*) and then into a white cock smelling of sulphur. Dostoevsky's Golyadkin Sr. loses his identity to an arrogant serial self and Korotkov loses his identity to a similar upstart—through documents, for as Soviet satirists have noted, without identification papers a man is not a man. In Gogol, without a nose a man is not a man.

Stylistic grotesqueries accompany thematic ones. Comic similes and realized metaphors appear on every page (Underwarr has a voice "like a copper pan"; after the first reference in the simile it is always "clanged the pan" or "rang the pan"). Ordinary verbs of saying are rare; the dialogue is marked by all kinds of "squeaks," "sings," and "mutters" rather than "he saids." Inanimate objects such as typewriters or teapots sing and talk to characters. People are turned into synecdoches (usually colors or clothing), and many minor characters remain nameless except for some dominant feature ("the blond one," "the *kuntush*").

Neither in the use of fantasy nor in stylistic grotesqueries is Bulgakov unique for the mid-twenties. The short story was the dominant genre, and there was a great deal of experimentation in the realm of verbal stylization and fantasy—much of it more radical, and ephemeral, than Bulgakov's style. . . . In all of these stories, as in Bulgakov's, characterization suffered at the expense of style—true, sometimes as an intentional reduction of the characters to the status of robots. One of the ways Bulgakov does this—and it is obviously borrowed from Gogol's "The Nose" and Dostoevsky's *The Double*—is the exaggeratedly detailed registering of Korotkov's physical gestures and changes of location.

Korotkov's mortal plunge provides a natural ending, but it is not "the bone of the bone and the blood of the blood of the beginning," as Robert Louis Stevenson has said endings of short stories must be. It is typical of Bulgakov (for example, **"The Fatal Eggs," "A Chinese Tale," "No. 13"**) that what seemed harmless fun and fairly mild topical satire should unexpectedly end in death—which is no laughing matter. Of course, the mixture of satire and death is not unusual; (indeed it has ancient roots), and this is found in works by the best Russian satirists of the twenties—in Zamyatin's *We,* for example, or Zoshchenko's *Tales of Nazar Ilich Sinebryukhov.* But as is frequently the case (recall Gogol's "The Overcoat" again) the reader is faced with the problem of sympathy. If Korotkov has been made flat and ridiculous in the beginning, can we feel his death as a real tragedy? The problem of irony which undercuts irony is one which Bulgakov faces in other stories too, including "**The Fatal Eggs.**"

"**The Fatal Eggs**" is the most famous and ambitious story of the collection. . . . In "**The Fatal Eggs,**" using the plot of H. G. Wells' *The Food of the Gods,* Bulgakov created a horrifying picture of the catastrophe that results when the state interferes in scientific endeavors. The story is brilliant in its details, but as allegory it is somewhat unclear. Although it is the leather-jacketed Feyt and the journalist Bronsky who are responsible for getting the government interested in using the ray for chicken breeding, it is some unknown person who switches the reptile and chicken eggs. This means that the *direct* cause of the reptile invasion is an accidental switching of boxes—which seems rather pointless. Bulgakov's critique of the Revolutionary handling of scientific inventions and the attempt to circumvent natural evolution is presented far more lucidly and logically in *Heart of a Dog*—written only a few months after "**The Fatal Eggs.**"

Feyt himself is at first portrayed as an extremely unpleasant man with a Mauser at his hip—but then we suddenly discover that he had been a flute player before the Revolution and that he has a nice wife and is really just a kind, simple man. We are told all of this in chapter eight, which is devoted to an idyllic (and humorous) description of the night on the Sovkhoz: Feyt is fluting, his nice wife is listening—and the next day she is crushed by a giant reptile in a scene described in horrifying naturalistic, clinical detail. This is a shock from which the reader never really recovers; although the deaths that follow are many and frightening, they are expected—except perhaps for Persikov's death at the hands of the Moscow mob.

The reptiles and ostriches, like Napoleon, are finally destroyed not by the Russians, but by an incredible frost. The frost comes at the end of August in true *deus ex machina* fashion. While interesting on first reading, the plot itself is not all-important, which one can conclude from the fact that Bulgakov's basic plot differs from Wells' only in that Persikov is killed—Wells' persecuted scientist escapes the mob and lives out his days in safe obscurity.

Bulgakov's originality consists in the way he adapts the story to the Russian environment—the Deaconess Drozdova's story, for example, is all his own invention. Also in evidence is Bulgakov's great talent for arousing readers' interest by creating an air of mystery and suspense. However, all of these abilities are as nothing when compared with Bulgakov's ability to make the fantastic seem real—as in the description of the giant reptiles ravaging the land. Scientific precision and a proclivity for naturalistic detail might explain the extraordinarily powerful effect of these descriptions of horrible events—but only partially. Perhaps it is explained by the visual nature of Bulgakov's imagination, the fact that whatever he described he had "seen," if only in a nightmare. Elena Sergeevna Bulgakova has related how when dictating Bulgakov would stand staring out a window, interrupting himself only to correct a detail which he could see but was describing imprecisely. In *Theatrical Novel* there is an obviously autobiographical de-

scription of a dramatist "merely" transcribing the pictures which of themselves appear before his eyes.

The visual side of Bulgakov's imagination is perhaps most effective in the six scenes of "**A Chinese Tale.**" This story is somehow enchanting in its description of a Chinese coolie in the Red Army. Bulgakov's repeated evocation of the coolie's childhood under the hot sun is an effective and touching contrast to the cold of Moscow and the Kremlin wall. The repetition of certain key details, details which are packed with memory and meaning for the character—the kaoliang, the keen-edged shadow, the buckets of ice-cold water—is typical of the mature Bulgakov's prose. The cocaine dream with its careful incorporation of details from the coolie's immediate past and mystical foreshadowing of the future (the Chinaman being rewarded for a decapitation) is another successful feature of the story. (The irreverent references to Lenin make the story unpublishable now.) Bulgakov later used the cocaine, the Finnish knife, and Hellish vision of a Chinese dwelling in Moscow in his play *Zoya's Apartment.*

As noted by critics at the time *Diaboliad* was published, "**A Chinese Tale**" appears to be a polemic with Vsevolod Ivanov's celebrated story "Armored Train 14-69"—which was made into a play and put on the Moscow Art Theater shortly after Bulgakov's own *Days of the Turbins,* with much less trouble politically. Ivanov also has a Chinese hero, but a *real* hero who joins the Bolsheviks and intelligently and consciously serves the cause. In the end he deliberately sacrifices his life for his comrades, throwing himself under the wheels of a train which has to be stopped. Contrast Bulgakov's coolie, who owes his original acceptance by the Red Army merely to his utterance of three words, the Russian national oath ("Fuck your mother"), and who serves and kills strictly for bread, with not a whisper of ideology.

"**The Adventures of Chichikov**" is one of Bulgakov's "Gogolisms." The title is the title which Gogol's censors insisted he use above *Dead Souls.* Basically the story uses characters and lines from *Dead Souls* (both Part I and Part II), but other works by Gogol, including *The Inspector General* and "The Nose," are also incorporated parodistically. Much of the narration is composed of bits and pieces of sentences from Gogol—such as the last sentence of the story, which from "again life went parading before me" is from the end of a Homeric simile in *Dead Souls.* Bulgakov's ironic "dream" ending mimics both Gogol's original version of "The Nose" and the denial of reality in the preface to "The Tale of How Ivan Ivanovich Quarrelled with Ivan Nikiforovich"—the narrator claims it is all fantasy, but the reader knows that it is all too real. For this reason, Bulgakov was attacked by politically minded critics who, like the critics mentioned in *Dead Souls* ("they will come scurrying from their crannies"), saw the story as unpatriotic slander. . . . Even before "**The Adventures of Chichikov,**" which is really an overgrown feuilleton, Bulgakov used Gogolian epigraphs, characters, themes, and parodies in several of his feuilletons for *The Whistle* (see especially the hilarious "**Inspector General with a Kicking Out**").

"**No. 13. The Elpit-Rabkommun Building**" (from *Rabochaja kommuna*—Workers' Commune) is also a feuilletonistic piece. Its themes (the housing shortage, problems of communal living, "ignorant" or "uneducated" people—*temnye ljundi*) recur in Bulgakov's early humorous works and then in his plays (*Zoya's Apartment, Bliss*), as well as in *The Master and Margarita.* Indeed, the number of the fatal apartment—50—is used again in *The Master and Margarita* (Berlioz's and Woland's apartment), and No. 13 was the Bulgakovs' address in Kiev. In this story the narrator's sympathies seem to lie primarily with the old order, and the ignorant people, the unwashed multitudes represented by Annushka, are to blame for tragedies of this sort. The repeated images and metaphors (the naked stone girl, the fire as beast), the secret servicemen, hints of demonism (the devil is disguised as a snowstorm), allusion to Meyerbeer's *The Huguenots,* and the sudden intrusion of electrifying death are all typical of Bulgakov's fiction.

Three of the feuilletons published in a tiny book called *A Treatise on Housing* (the title story, **"Four Portraits,"** and **"Moonshine Lake"**) are characteristic of the best of Bulgakov's early newspaper humor—which is not to say much. They are not really fiction, and are of interest now mainly for the topical humor—after all, Bulgakov was rather bold to poke fun at pictures of Lenin and Marx. They are also useful for a study of Bulgakov's narrators. Typically these early works had quotations from Worker Correspondent Reporters as epigraphs. Bulgakov would then bring the epigraph to life—a frequent device was a mix-up caused, say, by the combination of a snack bar and a library, or what would occur when the political indoctrination class, choir practice, and the movie "The Daughter of Montezuma" would all take place simultaneously. His success with feuilletons is due in large part to Bulgakov's natural abilities as a storyteller—since feuilletons are unified by the narrator rather than by plot. The narrator-storyteller was one that was natural to Bulgakov, and he employed him in most of his prose. This narrator is especially visible when a work is long and tends toward the comic. For example, the narrator is fairly unobtrusive in **"Diaboliad,"** but he makes his presence felt in **"The Fatal Eggs."**

The need for refuge in the midst of real and metaphorical storms is a theme which runs through most of Bulgakov's fiction. **"Psalm,"** however, is very unusual for him. He had written feuilletons in which dialogue dominates, and some of the impressionistic devices are used in other stories (especially **"The Raid"**), but **"Psalm"** is wistful, personal, and delicate in a way unusual for the early Bulgakov. Here we have no satire, no science fiction, none of the grotesqueries which dominate virtually all of his other early stories—only a quietly lyrical set of scenes between a lonely man and a lonely woman. It is a touching story, affecting partly because Bulgakov has his characters transform homely details, such as the buttons, into apt symbols of complicated and pathetic situations in a way which we recognize as very human.

Abram in **"The Raid"** also has a very human triumph, a minor victory of quiet inner dignity over the indignity of physical ridiculousness, the arrogance of Yak, and the torment of Revolution. In manner **"The Raid"** is close to the battle scenes in *White Guard,* and to a certain extent, some scenes in **"A Chinese Tale."** This happens when the narrator's mind merges with that of the main character and we see things, estranged, through the eyes of a wounded man—Abram recalls the warmth and unfinished watercolor as the Chinaman had the kaoliang. Stories about the Civil War were probably numerically dominant in the early twenties, and the naturalistic description of physical cruelty can also be found in the tales of Vsevolod Ivanov, Mikhail Slonimsky, and Nikolai Nikitin. The metaphorical, impressionistic description of the storm and attack also owes something to the ornamentalism typical of the twenties, although the light effects are typically Bulgakovian.

"The Crimson Island" was published in the Berlin newspaper *On the Eve* in 1924. . . . Bulgakov's story appears to be a

parody of the kind of propagandistic stories written after the Revolution, allegories in which history is simplified and characters are either heroes or villains. It is full of hyperbole, gross caricature, incongruous juxtapositions, and funny non sequiturs. It is an amusing piece, but hardly significant; one would not give it much attention if Bulgakov had never written a play called *The Crimson Island.* The play was written in 1927 and premiered at the Kamerny Theater in December 1928. While the play was very popular with the public, the critics violently denounced it as "talentless, toothless, humble" and a "pasquinade on the Revolution." The play is quite different from the story—in fact the basic story is made into a play within the play, and the main theme becomes censorship. So *The Crimson Island* served as the final piece of evidence in the trial by press of Bulgakov, and soon he was run out of Russian literature.

A complete picture of Bulgakov's early prose would also have to include such diverse genres as **"Notes on the Cuffs,"** the stories which make up *The Notes of a Young Doctor,* and *Heart of a Dog.* The first of these is a curious work—a fragmentary autobiograhical account given the appearance of a fictional feuilleton describing Bulgakov's literary life in the Caucasus (with many famous writers such as Mandelstam and Pilnyak appearing briefly) and then in Moscow's labyrinthine corridors. The six stories which form *The Notes of a Young Doctor,* told in the first person, are again closer to *White Guard,* with little grotesque satire, more in the realistic vein. There are strong echoes of Tolstoy's story "The Snowstorm," Pushkin's story with the same title, and such Chekhov stories as "The Enemies." Here one again finds a hero, common to many of Bulgakov's works at different periods, who suffers agonizing self-doubt, but survives inhuman trials because of his aristocratic sense of human dignity and humane compassion. The young doctor is an aristocrat in ability, as are the scientific heroes of **"The Fatal Eggs,"** *Adam and Eve,* and *Heart of a Dog.* All three of these works describe the confident misuse of knowledge which, while promising human good, leads only to injustice and inhumanity.

Bulgakov once referred to himself as a "mystical writer"—but he is only mystical in that he believes there is more to the world than common sense can know. There is no absorption in the otherworldly in his works—even in *The Master and Margarita* he describes Yeshua and his character, not God and His divinity. Bulgakov's world is moved by the desire for justice here and now, and his most powerful satire comes from the frustration of that desire. (pp. xi-xix)

> *Ellendea Proffer and Carl R. Proffer, in an introduction to* Diaboliad, and Other Stories *by Mikhail Bulgakov, edited by Ellendea Proffer and Carl R. Proffer, translated by Carl R. Proffer, Indiana University Press, 1972, p. vii-xx.*

D.G.B. PIPER (essay date 1971)

[*In the following excerpt, Piper finds reflections in* The Master and Margarita *of both Bulgakov's life and of the events in the Soviet Union during Stalin's purges of the 1930s.*]

Bulgakov's great fantasy, *The Master and Margarita,* was written between the years 1928 and 1940. In 1930 he burned a rough draft of the three chapters which he had written and, only in 1932, after marrying his third wife, did he begin to rewrite the novel, abandoning other work and fully aware that the novel would not be published in his lifetime. A censored version of the work appeared in the Soviet Union in the winter of 1966-67 and the censored passages have since been published in the West.

Some of the themes of Bulgakov's earlier work and some of the events in his personal life are, I think, relevant to *The Master and Margarita.* He was born in Kiev in a politically conservative household dominated by Bulgakov's father, Afanasy Ivanovich, a professor at Kiev Academy, a theological scholar and a man whose moral integrity and devotion to scholarship were much admired by his son. His father was also the cousin of the Russian philosopher and theologian, Sergei Bulgakov, with whom he disagreed when the latter flirted with Marxism. Bulgakov himself remained a Christian throughout his life, although his interpretation of the Crucifixion in *The Master and Margarita,* an interpretation based on a wide reading about the rise of Christianity, shows the unorthodox nature of his beliefs.

Belonging to an old aristocratic family, he clearly did not sympathize with the Bolsheviks in the Civil War. Hence, although in his first novel, *The White Guard,* he shows the inevitability of the Whites' political debacle, he describes their way of life and ethical values with sympathy. The Turbin family, modelled on his own, possesses a Tolstoyan humanity and sense of principle. Here exist a warm domesticity, culture and, above all, honour. In an important passage, when one of the characters is about to pack and leave for abroad, Bulgakov writes: "Never tear a shade from a lamp. Never scurry from danger like a rat into the unknown. Drowse near the shade, read by it—let the storm howl—wait for them to come to you." The small light against the threatening darkness represents in his work civilization, culture, the arts and sciences. In spite of an ambivalence and occasional hostility to these qualities, nevertheless the "comfort" (*uyut*) and "peace" (*pokoi*) of the Turbin household become almost a symbol.

The forces threatening this "peace" he associates with the dark images of Pushkin, Tyutchev and Blok—the night and the blizzard. The influence of his favourite writer, Gogol', also makes itself felt in *The White Guard.* The mass uprising becomes menacing and evil, while the writing becomes apocalyptic as Father Aleksandr associates this disorder with Satanic forces and the crazed poet Rusakov identifies Trotsky as the angel-destroyer, Abadonna. This is in fact Bulgakov's second identification of a Bolshevik leader with a supernatural force. In an early autobiographical work, describing his experiences in the Literary Section of the People's Commissariat for Education, he explains the ludicrous appointment of his incompetent boss, Kritskaya, as follows: "Rok, in fact, is responsible for it." The woman in charge of this Section was Lenin's wife, Krupskaya, while Rok, meaning Fate, is clearly Lenin.

Bulgakov too was a satirist, the object of whose satire was the Soviet *sushchestvovatel'* (an "exister"), to borrow Gogol's own term. Of one of them, a girl's father, he writes in an early work: "There will be further storms. Oh, there will be more of them. And everyone may perish. But papa, he will not die." Bulgakov's *suschestvovateli,* like Gogol's, go on and on and on existing.

Inevitably there was a campaign against him which was crowned with success in 1929 when Stalin himself passed moderate censure on his plays, all of which were then withdrawn. In March 1930, now destitute, he burned the three chapters of his novel. Simultaneously, he was under emotional stress, having in May 1929 fallen in love with a married woman who

became his mistress. Although morals were lax at this time and divorce easy, he was evidently unable to confide in anyone about his love, because "the fate of too many people were involved in this matter". He could not even "whisper" to a friend about it and "had to keep silent". On March 28th, 1930 he wrote to Stalin, expressing his "profound scepticism" about the Revolution and requesting permission to leave the Soviet Union as it was impossible for him to live and work there. On April 18th Stalin phoned Bulgakov, gave him work in the Arts Theatre, subsequently ordered the restaging of his play, *The Days of the Turbins,* which was based on *The White Guard,* and attended the play fifteen times. On each visit Stalin would enquire about Bulgakov's health and work, and praise his talent. It is known too that Bulgakov wrote a play about the young Stalin—*Batum.* It was not staged and has not been published. Bulgakov, however, worked on it with the utmost seriousness and passion. Indeed, after Bulgakov's death the telephone rang at his home: "The call was from Stalin's secretariat. 'Is it true that comrade Bulgakov has died?' 'Yes, he has.' The phone was quietly put down." The mysterious sense of kinship which exists between the Master, Margarita and Woland in the novel is probably an aesthetic interpretation of the relationship between Bulgakov, his third wife and Stalin.

Stalin's act of patronage affected his life and work. He married at the end of 1932 and simultaneously began re-writing his novel, now introducing into it the Master and Margarita and their love. Of Bulgakov and his wife a friend writes that "their home, as if to spite the hostile elements, was aglow with happiness." The lamp was again burning beneath the shade. Indeed, throughout the Terror Bulgakov and his friends would tell "anecdotes" about people "in whom our life was reflected". Meanwhile in plays about Pushkin, Molière and Don Quixote he examined the relationship between the artist and his patron, between the world of fact and that of imagination. He had earlier touched upon this problem in an essay on the work of a friend, Yury Slyozkin, referring to his novels as "brilliantly organised lying". The essence of literature is the lie, that creative imagination which persuades the reader to accept the unreal as real and creates other realities. This idea is relevant to *The Master and Margarita,* as is his other concept of the writer's role—that of a "knight" who also plays his part in the age-old battle between good and evil. Yet, save for his stage version of *Dead Souls,* only two of his plays were briefly staged in the thirties and were both withdrawn after savage attacks.

These themes—"comfort" and "peace", the *sushchestvovatel',* the patron-figure, evil itself, the writer as a knight, the relationship of the creative imagination to historical facts—comprise the essence of the novel.

Finally, the black comedy of the work was clearly prompted by contemporary history. Bulgakov began writing his novel in 1928, the year of Trotsky's expulsion to Alma Ata, and continued writing through the period of collectivisation which claimed about 3½ million lives, the famine of 1932-33 during which about 5½ million died and the Terror which added a further seven million arrests to the five millions already in camps or jails at the end of 1936. Of these, three millions had died or had been executed by December 1938. Thus, although the events of the novel take place in four days and there are many references to life in the Soviet Union over the period 1928-38, Bulgakov refers the reader to a specific year and month during the Terror Hence, references to Pushkin abound in the text. In 1937 journals, radio and theatres celebrated the centenary of Pushkin's death. The opening chapter has the heading: "Never speak to strangers." In March 1937 Stalin delivered his notorious speech about deficiencies in the Party, revealing that the country was aswarm with Trotskyists, White-Guardists and foreign agents. It was indeed dangerous to speak to a stranger. The month is May when "mass arrests and wholesale executions made the population live through the darkest hours of the Civil War." (pp. 134-37)

It is not surprising, therefore, that the motif of death and murder unites the three distinct levels on which *The Master and Margarita* is written. The first comprises the Devil's adventures in Moscow which begin with the murder of the writer, Berlioz. Annoyed by Berlioz's assertion that Satan does not exist, Woland *foretells* the exact circumstances of his death and foresees that his companion, the poet Bezdomnyi, will be sent to an asylum suffering from schizophrenia. Hereafter strange events take place in Moscow. Accompanied by his gang—an interpreter and ex-choir master, Korov'ev, the fanged demon, Azazello, a large black cat, Begemot, and the beautiful witch, Gella—Woland occupies Berlioz's flat which the deceased shared with Likhodeev, the director of a variety theatre. At this theatre Woland insists on staging an exhibition of black magic which involves the dismissal of the entire theatre-administration. Some are terrorised or flee; others are framed by the gang and ar-

Apartment building where Bulgakov lived in Moscow and which he made the site of Berlioz's apartment in The Master and Margarita. *Courtesy of Ardis Publishers.*

rested. At their performance the gang distributes free money and Western clothing. The money turns into bottle labels and the clothes disappear: the audience, like the Emperor, is left naked: there are hundreds of arrests.

The second level of the novel is concerned with another murder—that of the Master and Margarita. The Master, broken both by savage criticism of his novel about Pontius Pilate and by physical fear, burns his work and takes refuge in the asylum where the luckless Bezdomnyi is dispatched. His release, however, is secured by Margarita, whose impeccable behaviour as Queen Witch at Woland's Sabbat wins the Devil's favour and leads to the miraculous restoration of the Master's burned manuscript. After a brief period of "peace", both are poisoned by Azazello and the manuscript is again burned. Then in the company of the devils, both ride out towards the moon where the Master releases Pilate who, after two thousand years of torment, walks up a shaft of moonlight with Christ toward "light". The Master himself is rewarded with "peace". Finally, the figures of the Master and Margarita haunt the memory of Bezdomnyi, now the Master's follower, who will write a continuation of the Master's novel.

However, the most important and powerful section of the book is Bulgakov's interpretation of Christ's last day on earth and the mental agony of Pilate. Woland tells the story of Pilate's interrogation of Christ, called Ieshua in the novel: the Crucifixion itself is a dream of Bezdomnyi: the final two chapters in which Pilate orders the murder of Judas are the burned part of the Master's manuscript which Woland briefly restores to him.

Once again the theme of the ancient chapters is death and murder, while the predicament which they describe is not untypical of the year 1937. Ieshua, an innocent idealist, has been framed by Caiaphas in whose pay is Judas. The account of Ieshua's Crucifixion differs radically from the account given in any of the Gospels. He has but one disciple, Matthew the Levite. He is charged on the evidence of two *parchments*. On the basis of one of them, written by Matthew, he is accused of sedition on the grounds that he incited the mob to destroy the Temple. Ieshua replies that in fact he simply stated that a new temple of truth would replace the old and that Matthew is so wont to confuse and *lie* about his actions and words that he once advised him to burn his parchments. With sudden insight Ieshua expresses a fear that "this confusion (*putanitsa*) will last for a very long time. And all because he untruthfully notes down what I say." . . . A second parchment is then handed to Pilate alleging that Ieshua made treasonable remarks about Caesar in the presence of Judas. Although Pilate is aware that the allegation is false, the nature of the charge unnerves him. Alleged treason against the state was the reason for the Stalinist Terror. In terror of being implicated, Pilate bellows his loyalty to Caesar and confirms the death-sentence. Vainly he tries to bring political pressure on Caiaphas to release Ieshua instead of Bar-Abba. But in the personal wrath of Pilate Caiaphas sees only high politics. Ieshua's utopian ideas would have caused disorders necessitating the use of Roman power and its subsequent aggrandizement. Pilate is impotent, but enigmatically threatens Caiaphas and the Jews and then says "It is time!" (*Pora!*), even as Christ said "The hour is come". It is time to die.

The grim execution takes place. Ieshua's death is not only brutal, but meaningless: it is a premeditated murder chilling in its senseless finality. But watching on Golgotha is the Levite whose faith in the Jewish God, severely tested by Ieshua's five-hour torment in the torrid heat, at last snaps: "There were other gods and better. No other god would have let a man like Ieshua be scorched to death on a pole . . . You are an evil God! . . . A God of darkness! I curse you, God of bandits, their protector and moving spirit!'' . . . The storm breaks and the hated city of Jerusalem is plunged into darkness.

The predicament of Pilate is the heart of the novel. His head splitting with pain, the Procurator hates this city of rogues and religious fanatics. He likes Ieshua whose words strangely relieve his pain and spiritually resuscitate him. He is aware that Ieshua has been framed and that there is no real evidence against this utopian dreamer whose message that all people are good is refuted by the position in which he finds himself. Pilate's behaviour is conditioned by the limitations of his office, his experience of political lying, intrigue and violence. When he roars that he does not believe in a Kingdom of Truth, asks what is truth and questions Ieshua's premise that all people are good, he is sincere. As a powerful politician, Pilate is suspicious of every human motive and has been taught by experience to despise humanity. His attitude is not unlike Stalin's who once rounded on H. G. Wells with the comment that Wells' arguments were based on the assumption that "people are good", whereas he, Stalin, knew "many evil people". As a politician, Pilate would also have had no scruples about ordering the killing of anyone whose political activities threatened his own position. But Ieshua is simply a good man and not a political activist, although he is the victim of political intrigue. Further, a relationship based upon mutual respect has already been established and when Ieshua realises that "they want to kill me" and that "you should release me," . . . he appeals to this relationship. Now Pilate really understands the meaning of Ieshua's words that cowardice is one of the worst of human sins, for Pilate, the charge being treason, fears for his own life and sacrifices the life of a good and innocent man with whom he would converse to save his own. Pilate confirms the murder of an innocent human being and, in so doing, betrays himself and fails to discharge the obligations of his own cruel, but just office. Conscience-stricken, haunted by a sense of loss after Ieshua has gone, he orders the murder of Judas, hoping that this action will compensate his former cowardice. Then, this murder ordered, frightened by the darkness and evil he senses in the palace, he sleeps on the balcony bathed in moonlight and fulfils his wishes in a dream of ascending a shaft of moonlight in the company of Ieshua and begging to be told that the execution did not take place. On the closing pages of the book his pleas are granted. Why? Because it is the message of the novel that dreams are necessary, that myth and ideals constitute other and better realities. (pp. 138-40)

The third level of the work comprises the relationship between the Master, Margarita and the gang, the Master's death being contrasted by that of Berlioz. Just as there is something of Bulgakov in the master, so the last days of Maksim Gor'ky may have suggested the last hours of Berlioz. But whoever he may be Berlioz's head is necessary to the argument. Woland addresses it: "Everything came true, didn't it? . . . Your head was cut off by a woman . . . and I'm living in your flat. That is a fact. And a fact is the most obdurate thing in the world. . . . You always were a fervent proponent of the theory that when a man's head is cut off his life ceases, he turns into dust and the vital spark perishes. . . . However, all theories are of equal value. There is another according to which each man will receive his deserts in accordance with his beliefs. So be it. You will depart into the void and from the goblet into which

our head is turning I shall have the pleasure of drinking to eternal life.'' (pp. 152-53)

Two theories: two worlds. The here-and-now and the ever-after. Existence and immortality. Although even here Woland's speech contains a quotation from Stalin, gradually in the second half of the novel events begin to move out of the context of reality: by the final pages the devils have lost their human masks and become spiritual entities. As death approaches, their sway over the Master and Margarita diminishes. The Master ceases to resemble Bulgakov and his destiny is interwoven with other masters of Russian literature, while Margarita's role blends with that of other female saviour-figures of fact and fiction. (p. 153)

Moved by events in the Soviet Union to ponder questions of good and evil, life and death, existence and immortality, Bulgakov discovers in the example, the Deed, of Christ the sole means of combating evil. The moral qualities which he ascribes to Ieshua are an honesty and courage unto *death* which is the ultimate test of every ideal, while the ideal which alone can justify such self-sacrifice is the conviction that men are potentially good, or ultimately will be good.

Such a conviction, which initially appears to be disproved by the circumstances of Ieshua's arrest and the manner of his death, is not shared by Pilate nor by the Master. Pilate, the Master's creation, is not one who believes that men are good, while the Writer, whose role is the Word and not the Deed, has of necessity to remain alive, which in itself will involve a compromise with his conscience. There is no suggestion that the Master is a Christ-figure. Rather, he is a sublime liar whose torment ends when his work is written. Then it is time to die. He has at last peace and takes his place with other masters. Bulgakov's attitude to the Master, as it is to the ideal of *pokoi*, is ambivalent.

Yet the Deed is as crucial to the Writer as the Writer is to the Deed. In a most human way the cruel murder of the good Ieshua gives birth to a demand that reality be other than it is and that the ideals which Ieshua held should have validity. At this point . . . the "confusion" begins and reality dissolves, victim of the spirit's insistence upon the reality of other worlds and other value systems. Good and evil are inextricably interlocked and especially so in the personality of the Writer, an important knight in an age-old battle, whose role, like that of Matthew, is to assert spiritual values in the teeth of and because of an evil whose existence he knows full well. As Pilate resorts to evil to do good, so Bulgakov enjoyed the "peace" granted him by Stalin to write a novel which reduces the thirties to a black farce and asserts the Crucifixion as the ultimate reality. As Ieshua assures Pilate that the Crucifixion did not take place, so Bulgakov asks whether the thirties took place. Perhaps they were only a nightmare, for are there not other realities?

People, he argues, can and do embody spiritual forces and life is governed by moral laws with which, if one has courage, one complies. There will most certainly be danger, but cowardice is the worst of sins. The least one can do is to "drowse near the shade, read by it—let the storm howl—wait for them to come to you". They will come in their own good time, when it is time to die and, as Margarita tells Bezdomnyi, everything will be as it should be, for evil inevitably engenders in the spirit of man by way of protest aspirations for its antithesis: and this explains the quotation from Faust which opens the book: "I am part of that force which wills forever evil and creates forever good." (pp. 156-57)

D.G.B. Piper, ''An Approach to Bulgakov's 'The Master and Margarita','' in Forum for Modern Language Studies, *Vol. VII, No. 2, April, 1971, p. 134-57.*

JOAN DELANEY [GROSSMAN]   (essay date 1972)

[*In the following excerpt, Delaney examines parallels between Bulgakov's literary career and the fate of the artist in* The Master and Margarita.]

The Faust theme is used intermittently and with extreme freedom, even whimsy, in *The Master and Margarita.* At times it seems rather the Mephistopheles theme that is being emphasized. (p. 91)

Mephistopheles enters the novel on the first pages as Professor Woland (one of the names he used in Goethe's *Faust*). He has come to Moscow as a special consultant in black magic. Pretending to entertain the city, Woland and his picaresque cohort trick it into a display of greed and credulity. Some of their pranks are reminiscent of Faust and Mephistopheles at the emperor's court.

But this is still not the story of Faust. So far it reads more like a later chapter in the adventures of Mephistopheles among humans. In his previous visitation the devil had been given permission to lead astray, if he could, a certain man who stood above his fellows by reason of his questing spirit. Mephistopheles's dim view of human nature was pitted against the Lord's confidence in his servant. Faust was the devil's target, like Job of old. On this later visit Woland seems to have a slightly different mission—investigation, not temptation. Indeed, temptation is unnecessary. In a passage excluded from the *Moskva* version, Woland indicates that he has come to see if the Muscovites have changed inwardly for the better. He quickly concludes that they have not. In fact, the progress of Woland and his retinue through Moscow turns willy-nilly into a search for an honest man. Disgust with the state of affairs apparently converts even Satan to supporting good where and if he can find it. The only man in Moscow who positively benefits from Woland's visit is the Master. He, too, is the exception, the lonely searcher after truth—though in a different sense than Faust was. Perhaps a twentieth-century Faust knows that all mysteries are not unraveled through knowledge—nor does happiness lie in touching the distant star. At any rate, the Master's striving is of a different nature. He is the Artist. His search is contained in his book.

Bulgakov's novel is in a basic way a book about a book, a work about art and the artist. This is a feature that it shares with several important representatives of that growing Russian-language genre—works ''written for the drawer.'' *Doctor Zhivago* is a prime example. Siniavsky's *Makepeace Experiment* takes the form of a chronicle, which is consigned by its author to the floorboards on the last page. And of course there are Nerzhin's precious notes in *The First Circle*. It is not surprising that men writing under these circumstances would turn to such devices and themes. The efforts of the literary artist to strive for and transmit some measure of human truth, and his right to search in whatever direction his inspiration takes him—these themes are perennial in art. They flowered with Romanticism. Certainly they have been prominent in Russian literature since the time of Pushkin. Nowhere in twentieth-century Russian literature are they more central than in Bulgakov's novel.

In *The Master and Margarita* the theme of the artist's experience takes a universalized mythological form, but there seems no doubt that it has deep roots in Bulgakov's own immediate circumstances. (pp. 92-3)

[Like Bulgakov] the Master is a disappointed author, embittered by the treatment that his honest creation has received from editors, fellow artists, critics—in a word, the whole corrupt artistic-political world. (p. 94)

In the chapter suspiciously entitled ''Enter the Hero'' the Master enters the room of his neighbor in the madhouse, the poet Ivan. In answer to Ivan's innocent question, ''Are you a writer?'' he scowls, shakes his finger at Ivan, and announces, ''I am a master.'' He then produces a greasy black cap with the letter *M* embroidered in yellow silk—Margarita's handiwork. As Bulgakov tells it, ''He put the cap on and showed himself to Ivan in profile and full face to prove that he was a master.'' (pp. 95-6)

Bulgakov is a master of parody and polemic, of variation on a theme. He employs this talent in a dozen minor ways in this novel. It is no surprise to find it governing the presentation of his hero. We have seen that he uses the Faust legend to underline the element of quest. The Master too was a scholar and a searcher, but one who sought his ultimate meanings through the novel in which he reinterpreted the story of Pilate and Jesus. He did not roam the universe testing all experience. Art was the vehicle of his search, and his studio the locale. In the tradition of the Romantic dreamers of the nineteenth century, he searched in isolation, cut off from everyone but his love. True, his quest has come to a dead stop before we meet him in the novel. He has been shattered by his venture into the outside world and by the reception which that world has given his novel and its truth. The truth he has come to—both artistically and experientially—is that cowardice is one of the chief human sins. He explores it in his characterization of Pontius Pilate. He meets it in the time-serving treachery of the Moscow literary world. Then paradoxically he experiences it in himself: he becomes afraid. And with good reason.

In an elliptical and little-noted passage in chapter 13 we learn that the Master has spent some three months under arrest. He tells Ivan that the criticism of his book had risen to such heights that he had sensed a campaign. (This detail is not in the *Moskva* version.) Then, on that fatal October night after he had burned his manuscript, the knock came. The next few sentences of his account are whispered for Ivan's ears alone. But when the narrative continues, the Master describes himself standing in the yard on a *January* evening in his old overcoat but with the buttons torn off—the telltale sign of a sojourn in prison. And now, in total despair and with no place else to go, he consigns himself to the asylum of Dr. Stravinsky.

Only through Margarita and the pact with Woland is he rescued. [In an Afterword to the *Moskva* version, A. Vulis] says that Bulgakov added Margarita to his plan only in 1934. One may guess that it was at about that time that the Master also took definite shape. What is Margarita? Certainly she is the antithesis of Pilate: courage is one of her leading characteristics. She is the very embodiment of love that will stop at nothing—that will go through hell for the beloved. In this case the beloved is an artist, and in some miraculous way she is his art. She comes to him at the beginning of his task and spends with him the long days and months of creation. The novel, she tells him, is her life. The novel is destroyed just when she and the Master are forcibly separated, and its restoration coincides with their reunion. Together the novel and Margarita effect his resurrection. Thus, art—abetted by courage and love—struggles with despair for the soul of this artist, which is embodied in his truthful book. The struggle over a human soul recalls the medieval morality tale, which the Faust story indeed represents. But the roles are allotted somewhat differently. Instead of the traditional angelic and demonic powers, we have a different opposition: Margarita is allied with the devil in her battle against those who would crush the artist's soul. Bulgakov clearly suggests that the real forces of evil in the situation are the latter. Salvation comes through Margarita—no angel indeed. Margarita plucks some remnants of the Master's manuscript from the fire and Satan produces the rest. With Satan's aid, she also plucks the Master's soul from oblivion and his body from the madhouse. Thus Satan gives "virtue" its due and assists it in continuing its quest for truth, knowing full well that that goal can never be reached—at least not below.

The destiny of the two is settled through the intervention of Yeshua. Their reunion was earned through Margarita's daring, but their final reward is earned by the Master's art. Matthew, the disciple, delivers Yeshua's message to Woland: "He has read the Master's writings . . . and asks you to take the Master with you and reward him by granting him peace. Would that be hard for you to do, spirit of evil?" "Nothing is hard for me to do," Woland replies, "as you very well know." . . . The Master has not earned light, but he has earned peace— peace in which to continue his work on his reconstituted manuscript.

Manuscripts never burn, says Satan. But cities do, especially sinful ones. Near the end of the novel the Master and his consort are escorted from Moscow by Satan and his companions. The moment on Sparrow Hills when they turn to say farewell, there is the illusion that Moscow is burning. Indeed fire has preceded their departure, for Behemoth the cat and Koroviev have seen to the destruction of Griboedov House, the headquarters for the literary sycophants who wrecked the Master's hopes. And the basement flat has been left in flames. The departing cries of the Master and Margarita are exultant: "Burn away, past!" "Burn, suffering!" Now for a moment a thousand suns are reflected from the city's windows, and the city exhales smoke and haze. When Margarita looks back in flight, she sees that "not only the many-colored towers but the whole city had long since vanished from sight, swallowed by the earth, leaving only mist and smoke where it had been." . . . One recalls Lot's departure from Sodom—that city destroyed by divine wrath because of a shortage of honest men. Satan is leaving Moscow in disarray—her sins exposed if not thoroughly punished. Her artistic colony especially has suffered from exposure. In all the city Satan has found only one man honest enough to follow his artistic inspiration, even though it led him to an unpopular truth about human nature, to arrest, and finally to the asylum.

Fortunately Margarita, unlike Lot's wife, is not punished for her backward look. Yet despite her courage and his honesty, it is not salvation and ultimate answers that are granted to this couple. Nor do they expect them. Yeshua has read his novel, Woland tells the Master, and the fate he has begged for them is a peculiarly fitting one. "You are a romantic, Master!" says Woland. . . . As such he is to be given his romantic haven, where he can live, dream, and create forever with his Margarita. In their earlier interview the Master had expressed revulsion at Woland's suggestion that he return to his novel: "I hate that novel. . . . I have been through too much because of it." Yet Woland had urged him, "Believe me, your novel has some more surprises in store for you." . . . Art is inexhaustible; who knows to what further discoveries it may lead? Closing

the circle of reference, Woland addresses the Master, "O, thrice-romantic Master . . . Don't you want, like Faust, to sit over a retort in the hope of fashioning a new homunculus?" . . . The reward is not in the completion of the task but in the hope and the striving. Once, the Master says, he *had* finished a novel, and on that day his life "came to an end." . . . Now his quest will go on, but in rest and quiet and timeless delight.

Bulgakov's Master is not, after all, the scholar-adventurer Faust. He is an artist seeking artistic truth, and his happiness consists chiefly in the endless, free, peaceful pursuit of his art. This he was denied by Moscow's literary establishment. But the so-called powers of evil grant it to him. In a wonderful final moment, which reminds one of Vrubel's painting *The Flight of Faust and Mephistopheles,* "the black Woland" and his cohort plunge into the abyss. And the Master and Margarita enter their eternity.

To return to the connecting thread of interpretation, it seems eminently reasonable to explain the Master as autobiographical at base. Certain elements in *Black Snow* make this clearer, considering that the writing of this novel coincided with presumably the most important years of Bulgakov's work on *The Master and Margarita.* He had begun the latter at the end of the NEP period, when literature, along with everything else, was being drawn firmly under political control. The satirical buffoonery of its early sections is entirely in keeping with his own tone and that of other satirists of the period. As has often been noted, disillusion with the immediate results of the Revolution stimulated this genre. But a second disillusion came upon these writers and grew more intense as the decade ended: it concerned the possibility of a free art. The problem earlier had in part been one of factional fighting among literary groups. But when it became one of repression from above, the situation seemed to call for a larger genre, at least in Bulgakov's notebook. Retaining some of his earlier style and techniques, he enlarged his scenario, objectified his own plight, and universalized his experience, even finding a myth to suit. He seems to have concluded that the artist is by definition a romantic seeker, and that his salvation, if he has any, lies in being just that. Only such artists can survive as men and as artists. And he indulged a pious hope: if there is any justice in heaven or on earth, artists will be given a haven to continue unhindered their quest for beauty and truth.

Sometime in the mid-thirties Bulgakov's anger evidently overflowed. The theater, which had been for him a haven of sorts, had also betrayed him: art had betrayed art. To pacify the censors his play *Molière* had been mauled and disfigured by his colleagues in the Moscow Art Theater. When it finally reached the stage, it was removed by the censorship. Bulgakov poured his very fresh venom into *Black Snow,* where the autobiographical allusions are quite deliberately clear. If we assume the interaction between the two novels, Bulgakov worked back and forth between the universal and the specific, sometimes between fantasy and realism. Thus the interwoven pattern of the two books supports the fundamental identification of Bulgakov-Maksudov [Maksudov the protagonist of *Black Snow*] and the Master and thereby strengthens Bulgakov's statement about the artist.

Casting his Master as Faust in a hospital gown was a kind of romantic irony by which the author mocked his own helpless position. On the other hand, it opened to him the whole wealth of the Faust symbol, which he used on several levels. Aspiration toward a goal, the achievement of which eludes human grasp, marks both the strivings of Faust and the more muted desires of Bulgakov's Master. Woland, the father of lies, none-theless speaks the truth when he calls the Master a true ro-mantic. Bulgakov, too, and through him the artist as such, by analogy take on this character. It is surely not to be counted too heavily against Bulgakov's art if, in the conception of his finest novel, his reach sometimes exceeded his grasp. (pp. 96-100)

Joan Delaney [Grossman], "'The Master and Mar-garita': The Reach Exceeds the Grasp," in Slavic Review, *Vol. 31, No. 1, March, 1972, pp. 89-100.*

MICHAEL GLENNY (essay date 1975)

[*In the following excerpt, Glenny discusses Bulgakov's portrayal of isolation and his examination of the conflict between reason and the irrational in* A Country Doctor's Notebooks.]

There have been several doctor-writers, Russian and English, in recent times—Chekhov, Somerset Maugham and A. J. Cronin are perhaps three of the best known—and with [*A Country Doctor's Notebook*] Mikhail Bulgakov is revealed as another writer who gained his earliest and perhaps his deepest insights into human nature through the practice of medicine.

Born in 1891, Mikhail Bulgakov was the eldest of the six children of a professor at Kiev Theological Academy. He stud-ied at Kiev University and qualified in medicine in 1916. After eighteen strenuous months in general practice (the subject-matter of most of [*A Country Doctor's Notebook*]) he decided to specialise, and set up in Kiev as a venereologist. Another eighteen months or so later, the upheavals of the Civil War caused Bulgakov to move to the Caucasus, where he resolved to give up medicine in favour of writing. (p. 7)

Bulgakov served his medical apprenticeship near the village of Nikolskoye in the province or *guberniya* of Smolensk, one of the north-western regions of European Russia, and to judge by his description of the facilities and equipment available to him, the medical services of this *Zemstvo* ["provincial gov-ernment"] were among the best.

Even so, it is very clear from these stories that as a means of initiation into medicine, Bulgakov's assignment to this remote country practice was much like learning to swim by being thrown into the deep end of the pool. Nowadays it can only be in some of the remoter parts of the 'third world' that totally inexperienced young doctors find themselves 'thirty-two miles from the nearest electric light', entirely cut off from the outside world for long spells, or obliged to keep a pack of wolves at bay with a pistol while driving back from a night call. Perhaps most demoralising for a nervous beginner were the primitive communications: carts or sleighs the only transport, roads that were poor at the best of times and often impassable in the springtime thaw or the winter blizzards, erratic mails or none for weeks on end and above all—no telephone. The effects of this isolation and confinement on anyone of less than robust and balanced temperament is grimly illustrated in the story called '**Morphine**'.

For Bulgakov, however, the greatest underlying source of unease, amounting at times to despair, was something less tangible though very real to him, since it occurs as an ever-present refrain throughout these stories. This was the sense of being a lone soldier of reason and enlightenment pitted against the vast, dark, ocean-like mass of peasant ignorance and super-stition. Again and again Bulgakov stresses what it meant to experience in physical reality the moral anomaly which for a

century and more before the revolution had caused such agony to the liberal, educated élite of Russia: that intolerable dis-crepancy between the advanced civilisation and culture enjoyed by a small minority and the fearsome, pre-literate, mediaeval world of the peasantry. Although his patients are his contem-poraries and fellow citizens of what purports to be a modern state, Bulgakov is constantly haunted by an awareness that in dealing with them he is actually at the point of contact between two cultures which are about five hundred years apart in time. It is books like this which make one appreciate the tremendous achievements of the Soviet education programme since 1917.

It will not escape the reader's notice that much of Bulgakov's narrative dwells on night, winter, blizzards and gales. This is not just a literary device to heighten the sense of drama, urgency and danger: it expresses the author's profound feeling that in the rural Russia of his early career, a doctor was literally someone fighting an elemental force. The dominant, recurrent image in his stories is that of light and dark: the light over the gateway to his little hospital, the welcoming green-shaded lamp in his study, the single light burning in an otherwise darkened, storm-swept building. These brave pinpoints of light—the light of reason—are always contrasted with the vast, malevolent, surrounding darkness which threatens to engulf them yet never succeeds in putting them out.

Despite this background intimation of an almost mythic conflict between enlightenment and unreason, Bulgakov's writing in *A Country Doctor's Notebook* is thoroughly down-to-earth, real-istic, and far removed from the grotesque fantasy that was the distinctive style of much of his other work in the mid-twenties. This contrast is so marked that it is hard to credit 'Dr. Bul-gakov' as being also the author of such fierce, surrealistic satire as *The Heart of a Dog* and the diablerie of *The Master and Margarita*. These date from Bulgakov's richly productive pe-riod of 1924-1927, when the publication of his first novel, *The White Guard*, and the overnight success of its subsequent stage version, *The Days of the Turbins*, were making it possible for him to give up hack journalism for a living and turn to full-time writing for the theatre. Yet at the same time Bulgakov would, as it were, regularly lay aside the sardonic *persona* of the satirist and put on again the white coat he had finally doffed some five or six years earlier and would recreate, with keen, fresh observation and gentle self-deprecating humour, the agonies and triumphs of a medical novice pitched into a job of terrifying responsibility. (pp. 8-9)

Michael Glenny, in an introduction to A Country Doctor's Notebook *by Mikhail Bulgakov, translated by Michael Glenny, Collins & Harvill Press, 1975, pp. 7-10.*

DIANA L. BURGIN (essay date 1978)

[*In the following excerpt, Burgin offers a detailed analysis of* The Heart of a Dog *and notes that an interpretation of the novel as simply a political allegory ignores its narrative complexity and the complexity of its protaganist. For readings of this novel as a political allegory, see the excerpt by Peter Doyle (1978) and the Michael Glenny entry in the Additional Bibliography.*]

Because of the overwhelming critical interest in Bulgakov's magnum opus, *The Master and Margarita,* commentators have tended to overlook his other novels. This neglect is particularly unfortunate in the case of his early short novel, *Heart of a Dog (Sobač 'e serdce . . .).* Those who have discussed the book have also overemphasized the obvious satirical meaning of the text while ignoring, or at best, merely hinting at its underlying tragic significance. This black-comic tale of a great creative scientist's ill-fated laboratory experiment that turns a likeable dog into a hideous "human" creature, whose violent, sadistic nature is exploited by the Soviet state, has been read by one of its translators, Michael Glenny, as a political allegory of the Bolsheviks' disastrous attempt to force revolution on Russia prematurely. This anti-revolutionary interpretation is supported by the scientist-hero's comment to his loyal assistant, Bormental', that his experiment backfired because it was unnaturally hasty, that is, counter-evolutionary. . . . (p. 494)

To interpret *Heart of a Dog* solely as a political parable is to oversimplify the novel in two important ways. First, by emphasizing the allegorical significance of the Professor's experiment at the expense of his highly individualistic personality and creativity this interpretation reduces a complex literary character—a potentially tragic hero, in fact—to a unidimensional allegorical symbol. Such an explanation of the text overlooks Bulgakov's multi-faceted attitude toward his hero, who serves as an autobiographical spokesman for his political and social satire and as a tragic, Romantic hero in the Frankenstein tradition. To reveal the monumental, tragic proportions of his hero, Bulgakov employs three different narrators to offer a broad assessment of the great man's character and work. Glenny's interpretation overlooks entirely the most striking characteristic of the novel: its narrative complexity. Second, the political message of the novel does not depend only on the allegorical meaning of the misfired experiment (as Glenny's interpretation suggests), but is conveyed explicitly through confrontation between the individualist Professor and House-Committee Head Švonder—a self-proclaimed representative of the "revolutionary" collective way of life and, therefore, of the pervasive banality in Soviet society.

That the significance of the Professor's experiment transcends a narrow political explanation is strongly suggested by the novel's conclusion. If, having admitted and corrected his mistake, the Professor ceased experimentation in revolutionary science, the point of this political parable would have been made. Yet, for the Professor, the ending is not a resolution, but rather a frighteningly ambiguous continuation. The Professor does not cease experimenting. The last lines of the novel focus on the "stubborn, persistent, important man," driven to continue his search for a scientific method for "manufacturing Spinozas." . . . This final view of the seeking, creative hero—ironically colored at the beginning by the dog-narrator's complacent estranged perception of his "benefactor"—invites us to speculate on the "important man's" motives and begs for serious consideration of the implications of his persistent experimentation. At the very least, this final image of the hero suggests there is more to the story of *Heart of a Dog* than a uni-dimensional, politico-allegorical interpretation provides.

The play on two narrative viewpoints (the dog's and the omniscient narrator's) in the final passages of *Heart of a Dog* is typical of the shifting perspectives offered throughout the novel. Indeed, by manipulating point of view Bulgakov lends this superficially unpretentious comic novel a deeply ironic and ultimately tragic dimension. The narrative structure thus deserves detailed examination.

Heart of a Dog is narrated from three distinctive points of view: two (the dog's, Bormental''s) may be described as personal or subjective; the third (the omniscient narrator's) is impersonal, objective. Each has his own special voice, language, and mode of expression. The omniscient narrator's account provides the

outer, frame narrative into which the two personal accounts are interpolated in sequential order. The dog begins the novel with his jaunty, sardonic, "slice-of-life" anecdote detailing how he came under the Professor's "protection." Bormental''s scientific notes on the experiment take over when the dog ceases to exist; and at the very end, the dog returns to offer his "rejuvenated" perspective. Both Šarik's and Bormental''s narrations are thus framed narrations. These inner personal viewpoints are contrasted in terms of tone, but are similar in their naivete. Neither personal narrator is fully aware of the implications of his story. The irony of the dog's tale is particularly acute since he thinks of himself, and is initially presented to us, as a shrewd, albeit estranged observer of humanity, yet his initial perspicacity is drastically at odds with his ultimate complacency. Similarly, Bormental''s notes—although sincere and scientific—constitute, ironically enough, a nearly absurd point of view because his naive enthusiasm beclouds his comprehension. In his own way Bormental', like Šarik, is an eternal disciple and his judgments of his "god" must finally be corrected by the master himself. The irony in both personal viewpoints derives not so much from the perceivers' worship of the Professor (he seems to deserve it, after all) as from their naivete. This irony is clarified through the omniscient narrator's subtle, persistent reevaluation of the disciples' points of view.

Bulgakov uses this triple perspective to reveal the complexity, ambiguity, and greatness of his hero's personality and scientific quest. The hero's ambiguousness, as well as the impossibility of defining him, is indicated by the apparent difficulty of the narrators to determine his identity: he is called at different times in the novel magician, enchanter, shaman, prophet, deity, priest, doctor, creator, "daddy," Faust, higher being and benefactor of dogs, and finally, "important man." This startling array of suggested names, some comic and some serious, shows the hero's central role as a *personality* of nearly confounding magnitude and the importance of point of view in deciphering his identity. This identity, it seems, depends on whom one asks; yet the use of an omniscient narrator to qualify the various personal opinions suggests that the hero's essence is greater than the sum of all opinions offered.

The elusive identity of this hero has been discussed in the critical literature on the novel. In comparing the heroes of **"The Fatal Eggs"** and *Heart of a Dog,* Ellendea and Carl Proffer [see excerpt dated 1971] comment that these "scientific heros" illustrate ". . . the confident misuse of knowledge which, while promising human good, leads only to injustice and inhumanity." I would go further and say that the misuse of knowledge is not only confident, but supremely arrogant, and perhaps most important, ultimately tragic for the misuser. Very interesting in this respect is Glenny's comment that *Heart of a Dog* is a tale of a "modern Frankenstein." [see Additional Bibliography] . . . Yet Glenny, who sees the deeper meaning of the novel as its political allegory, fails to develop the tragic implications of the Frankenstein parallel. Like the Frankenstein story, *Heart of a Dog* pertains to creation—more specifically, to the relationship between creator and creature and the moral question of responsibility for the creative act. Its political message notwithstanding, *Heart of a Dog* is a tale of a creative personality whose essentially noble, yet arrogant creative effort ends if not in tragedy, then at least in moral ambiguity. As such, the novel represents an original contribution to Romantic "literature of the overreacher." The fact that the Professor is Bulgakov's most autobiographical hero suggests, moreover, that the tragic fate of the scientist constantly battling the unchanging banality of human nature and seeking at his own peril a way to overcome it parallels the similar fate of the creative artist in Soviet society. Such a parallel reveals a direct connection between this early novel and *The Master and Margarita,* a connection even more obvious when one realizes that Bulgakov synthesizes his tale of creation in *Heart of a Dog* from the same universal literary sources that he employs in the later, more monumental work. He draws on the Frankenstein story as well as the Christian and Faustian traditions, which is strikingly appropriate since the fundamental identity of his scientist-hero lies in his godlike (or "man-god-like") nature and the tragedy of his scientific creation resounds with Faustian overtones.

The crux of the Professor's tragedy is to be found in the Bulgakovian principle that creation necessarily implies its antithesis, anti-creation. The man who would be a god must suffer, understand, and transcend the power of the anti-creative forces that run amok in a chaotic world. Such transcendence alone is tantamount to deification. In the first half of *Heart of a Dog* (up through the creative act detailed in chapter five), Bulgakov uses his omniscient narrator to debunk the hero-worshipping attitudes of those who idolize the Professor through expediency or naivete. The hero thus seems to fall from his high status; indeed, when he is compared by the omniscient narrator to a "sated vampire" (after the operation), he appears to be more demon than deity. If the Professor is to be a true creator, or even to aspire to that title, however, his creativity must be tested, even if this necessitates his knowing hell in order to attain to heaven. The Professor's spiritual journey through the depths—which he willfully undertakes when he "raises the curtain" and attempts to transform the image of humanity—is revealed by Bulgakov through irony and reverse parody.

Our first impressions of the Professor's practice and scientific interests are filtered through the estranged perceptions of Šarik, and the effusions of his patients—a microcosm of tasteless, crass humanity, whose major concern in life seems to be "eternal youth" and sexual potency. We overhear with Šarik, one of the Professor's sexually rejuvenated, grotesque patients praising his magical powers: "I am positively enchanted. You are a magician." An aging woman, desperately desiring to recover her youth, alludes to the devilish attractiveness of her young lover: "He is so fiendishly young." These testimonies to the Professor's magical powers and greatness are unworthy of him—they amount to little more than base flattery of a man who has satisfied the most banal of human desires. Whereas the Professor is certainly aware of the vulgarity of his patients, his powers of rejuvenation are nevertheless associated early in the novel with the devil. Šarik's speculation, "What the Devil did he need me for?" strikes an ironically ominous note, particularly in retrospect. (pp. 494-98)

Bulgakov's attitude to the Faustian scientific spirit in this novel seems to be ambivalent, and this too helps to explain the ambiguity (the mixture of sympathy and irony) of his hero's image. He lauds the striver, but is aware of the chaos that such a man can unwittingly unleash upon himself. . . . Ironically, it is the Professor himself who questions the rationale of his obsessive quest for the scientific method of transforming, even transfiguring, humanity. There is deep pessimism in the Professor's implicit admission that it may just be impossible to transform mankind, to transcend the pervasive and entrenched banality of the Čugunkins and Švonders; and there is moral tragedy in the benevolent Professor being forced to commit violence to restore peace. The denouement of *Heart of a Dog* reveals the tragedy of creative self-destruction as the scientist

Bulgakov in 1928. Courtesy of Ardis Publishers.

is forced to negate, by the violent means he deplores, the unexpected, devastatingly negative result of his experimental fervor. Like *Frankenstein* the *Heart of a Dog* is a story of the tragedy of after-birth which threatens the premises of the genuinely creative act and is in fact its very antithesis. (p. 504)

The complexity of the hero of *Heart of a Dog* lends the novel a high seriousness more characteristic of *The Master and Margarita* than of Bulgakov's earlier prose works. (p. 506)

> Diana L. Burgin, "Bulgakov's Early Tragedy of the Scientist-Creator: An Interpretation of 'The Heart of a Dog'," in Slavic and East European Journal, *n.s. Vol. 22, No. 4, Winter, 1978, pp. 494-508.*

KONSTANTIN RUDNITSKY (essay date 1978)

[*Rudnitsky is a contemporary Soviet critic. In the following excerpt, he provides a discussion of theme, character, and technique in Bulgakov's plays.*]

Three of Bulgakov's works are devoted to the fall of the White Guard. When young Doctor Bulgakov, having travelled over much of Russia in the years of civil war, took up the pen, the fate of the White movement had already been decided. Anyone who addressed this theme had to take into consideration that he wrote about an event which had ended, about a movement which had ingloriously exhausted itself, about ideas which had gone out of use, about persons who had lost the game. Inarguably, Bulgakov understood this. But following the novel *White Guard* . . . he wrote the play *Days of the Turbins* . . . , and after that—the play *Flight*. . . . Such a consistent predilection for the chosen problematics is not explained by the need to share impressions, even shatteringly strong ones. We must think that Bulgakov steadfastly gazed into the fate of the White Guard for much more important and significant reasons.

In the sphere of this theme lay, for Bulgakov, the only possibility for comprehending revolution. A thinking individual could not live in post-revolutionary Russia without having defined his own relationship to the historical turn that had destroyed all the previous foundations of Russian life.

Understanding of revolution came to Bulgakov in the process of artistic investigation of those forces which revolution had brought into conflict. This "proof from the negative" was entirely natural for a man who had matured in the environment of the old Russian intelligentsia, a man who had in the years of civil war stood aside from the fighting, who had not given himself account of the social nature of the events he witnessed. Bulgakov knew the vanquished better than the victors.

From work to work, all the more manfully, all the more decisively, Bulgakov moved towards the truth. He was true to life in *White Guard,* in *Days of the Turbins* and in *Flight*. But ideas which are hinted at in *White Guard,* ideas which move in the murky, wavering outlines of the novel's hasty, breathless prose, emerge in *Days of the Turbins* into the light of refined thought, and in *Flight* acquire the form of sharp, mercilessly final decisions.

At first glance, the remarkable characteristic of *White Guard* is its humor, which would seem, in the given circumstances, so out of place. This is nervous, reckless humor, which, in principle, admits to nothing final, to nothing absolutely decided upon. The fateful minutes and days of *White Guard* described by the author lure him with their external sharpness, with their unusualness, with the rare whimsicality of a "sujet" created and complicated by life itself. Everything that Bulgakov describes is momentary, changing and unstable. In these events—stormy, headspinning, now tragic, now comic, and most often tragic and comic at once—there is no feeling of the historical magnitude of what is occurring. The pages of the novel shine with sparkling, fresh talent. The pen seems to dance with joy at being able to secure, to capture and to reproduce all this which is momentary, fleeting, chaotic and full of motion. Bulgakov's book is rare witness of rapture at the possibilities opening before an author; it is a fascinating probe of the pen, of talent, of expressive possibilities.

The events which Bulgakov witnessed struck him by their unusual, exclusive nature, and by their threatening beauty. Kiev in 1918 lived, in his words, "a strange, unnatural life which, very possibly, will not be repeated in the twentieth century." The epithets are characteristic: life is "strange, unnatural." Bulgakov almost directly says that he dares not analyze this life fully. He spins about in the whirlpool of events. The world seems to him a blizzard; everything is in snow; everything is covered with snowflakes; everything is bright, unusual; everything serves artistic expression. And how good it is that expression comes and succeeds!

In this generous expressiveness is the unwilted charm of Bulgakov's early prose. No matter what his pen touches—everything comes alive; everything breathes with the freshness and unrepeatable accuracy of comparisons. His glance falls on a bookshelf and in passing he notes, ". . . in a mighty phalanx

stood the gold and black cavalrymen: Brokhaus-Ephron." (pp. 124-26)

He sees everything; everything interests him. His descriptions are often exhalted. Elena Talberg's red hair reminds him of a "polished, theatrical crown."

Describing turbulent and threatening events, Bulgakov observes in the first pages of the novel that "in spite of all these events, in the dining room, basically, it was excellent. It was warm, comfortable, the cream-colored curtains were drawn. . . ." Oh, those cream-colored curtains! How many times have they been used to impute guilt to Bulgakov by the assurance that he hid from the revolution behind cream-colored curtains. . . . Actually, in the novel, especially in its first part, grief at fleeting comfort and peace sounds insistently. "Oh, our grandfather fir tree, glittering with snow and happiness! Mama, queen of light, where are you?" exclaims Bulgakov together with the Turbins. He willingly holds his gaze on the remaining relics of a way of life just now destroyed. "Under the shade of the hydrangea were a small plate with a blue design, several slices of sausage, butter in a clear butter dish, and a biscuit tray with a serrated knife and a long, oval loaf of white bread"—the carefully served, although poor, repast; the old clocks; the dear, old things—all of this is touching, as touching as the Turbins' cream-colored curtains.

But Bulgakov understands already that this earlier life is supported by a rotten foundation. He sees "the black, thundering sky," and "the banners of blue smoke," and the vomit of drunks, and blood, and hanged men. . . .

Compassion for the wonderful (in Bulgakov's judgement) past merges in a sickly and sharp manner with his repugnance for what arose from that very past. Bulgakov's vision is sharpened, his nerves are tense. The German armored train abandons Kiev. This is how Bulgakov describes the event:

> At one in the morning, on the fifth track, out of the darkness, which was hammered by the cemeteries of empty freight cars, gathering great, rumbling speed, blazing with the red heat of the ash-pit, the gray, like a toad; armored train left, howling wildly.

You can hear this wild, heart-rending, dying howl and rumble; you can see how the Turbins became wary, uneasily glancing at each other and falling silent.

With all its colorful diversity, the description is alarming; with all the diffusion and disorder of the picture, it breathes with inarguable veracity. And although, I repeat, by all appearances Bulgakov here, least of all, gives attention to the goal of social analysis, although he rarely tries to make sense of what he sees—still, observations drawn directly from life acquire under the pen the strength of unexpected generalizations. (p. 126)

Affirmation of the higher justice of revolution inarguably emerges as the general emotional result of the work, and not only because "all that occurs is always as it must be and only for the better," but also because "the white situation" internally rotted, because the Turbins "sentimentalized away their lives" and brought down on themselves the merciless "muzhik anger."

These thoughts, already emerging through the variegated fabric of the prose of *White Guard,* were to be expressed in full precision by Bulgakov in the drama *Day of the Turbins.*

Colonel Malyshev and Dr. Alexei Turbin, described not without condescending humor in the novel *White Guard,* are combined in the play in the single image of Colonel Alexei Turbin, a man of crystal purity and unconditional fidelity to duty. He is decisive intelligent and free. This excellent man perishes in the play as a real hero. It would seem that such a depiction of the death of a White Guardsman would necessarily serve to glorify the White Guard and the "White movement."

But in the play, Alexei Turbin passes through a tormenting disillusionment.

The reader or viewer can completely understand Alexei Turbin only if he feels the atmosphere in which this man lived, only if he sees the background on which the image is sketched. Bulgakov is a master of the symphonic drama. He creates not only a direct, exposed and sharp collision of characters, goals and human wills, but also orchestrates a nervous rhythm which is felt in the entire scenic life—the "human" dramatism of seemingly coincidental details, of seemingly trivial words, of petty and externally capricious actions. In Bulgakov's plays, everything is in motion, everything is encompassed by the burst of struggle, everything is meaningful and changing until that time when the basic idea crystallizes in this turbulence of life, until the main, decisive action is taken. In Bulgakov, every ordinary and direct sketch of life is full of action and struggle.

In other words, Bulgakov's dramatism lies not in the attempt to wrench events which contain drama from the daily flow of life, but in the attempt to fill the daily flow of life with dramatism, to introduce drama into all life's petty detail, all its nuances, all its seemingly insignificant movements, waverings, roughness and whimsicality. The dramatic nerve penetrates all the cells of the work's live tissue. (pp. 126-28)

The basic motifs of the novel *White Guard* and the play *Days of the Turbins* were subsequently developed and continued by Bulgakov in *Flight.*

Flight addresses the problem of a man's selfless, desperate service to an idea which has completely outlived itself and which is morally compromised. Bulgakov's thought is that the need for oppressors and hangmen for the defense of an idea is a sign that the idea is doomed.

Khludov's fate, perceptively grasped by Bulgakov from the smoky, moving chaos of civil war, is decisive and firm proof of the correctness of Bulgakov's judgement.

Khludov is portrayed by Bulgakov with the irresistible accuracy of consistent psychology. Every word is wrenched from the depths of his soul—and this depth, this abyss, opens. Before us, in the full sense of the word, is a human portrait done in Rembrandtian richness of chiaroscuro, with cruel and even tormenting objectivity of portrayal, with a wealth of sniperish, fine details which are impossible to ignore. The critic B. Emelianov is right when he writes of the development, in *Flight,* of the Chekhovian traditions of Realism and of Chekhovian themes—in part, the theme of despair for the loss of meaning of one's personal life. The same critic affirms that *Flight* is "a Chekhovian 'play of mood' . . ." transferred into a revolutionary situation of civil war. He adds that "in terms of genre, *Flight* is a Gogolian phantasmagoria or, if you like, a Chekhovian tragi-farce developed to its end."

In these apparently unexpected juxtapositions (either a Chekhovian play of mood or a Gogolian phantasmagoria—one of the two?) there is a certain accuracy. The biography of Bulgakov-dramatist begins with the Art Theater, the theater of Chekhov.

On the other hand, it is known that "leftist" theatrical experimentation displeased Bulgakov and that Meyerhold's *Magnanimous Cuckold* evoked sarcastic commentary from Bulgakov. Nonetheless, *Flight* shows that the experience of Meyerhold's and Vakhtangov's theatrical searchings either opened much for Bulgakov or, more likely, coincided with his personal searchings. Bulgakov's art, directly emerging from Chekhov, finds support in the far past—in Gogol, Dostoevsky, in part in Saltykov-Shchedrin—and in theater contemporary to Bulgakov—most of all, I believe, in Mikhail Chekhov's *Hamlet* and Meyerhold's *Inspector General.*

The composition of *Flight* in particular indicates these links to the past and to the present. The traditional division of a play into three or four "lifelike" acts is altered and emphatically replaced by a principle of "irrationality": "eight dreams." This principle allows Bulgakov, while retaining the inexorable persistence and perspicacity of psychology, to introduce into the play sudden shifts of genre.

Tragedy falls into farce; drama intersects vaudeville; the mood of the play really turns into phantasmagoria—and despite all these (using M. Bakhtin's expression) mesalliances of genre, human psychology preserves its stern logic of development. (pp. 137-38)

The entire play is in unsure light. The entire play gives a sense of strangeness, almost unreality, to the events that transpire. It is expressed by Golubkov as soon as the curtain rises: "Really, how strange this all is. You know, at times it begins to seem to me that I am dreaming, honest! . . . The farther I go, the less understandable it becomes. . . ."

Bulgakov continually and insistently brings the action as if to the edge of reality. He is continually in danger of falling into some kind of supernaturalism, mysticality, demonism—and nonetheless he never forgets the entirely real motivation of the events which transpire. His stage directions are wondrously precise and expressive—Bulgakov, in general, is an unsurpassed master of laconic stage directions which suddenly flare up and illuminate everything with a brief, bright light. In *Flight* this talent is brought to new heights. Monk Paisii "appears noiselessly, *dark,* frightened," and then "disappears as if he were falling through the earth." All sounds reach us softly, dully, as if through cotton: "a *soft* cannon shot" is heard; "suddenly the bell rang *softly*"; "beyond the window was heard the *toneless* command, and all grew quiet, *as if there had been* nothing." (p. 138)

[The comedy *Ivan Vasilevich*], we must assume, was for Bulgakov, when he was writing it, a merry pause. It is untroubled. There is in it none of the characeristic and excellent Bulgakovian nervousness. There are none of those incomparable phrases, which suddenly plummet down, as if into a well. And there are none of those flights of haughtily victorious rhythm—the rhythm of unexpected assuredness ready to crush everything, the rhythm of triumphant humanity, proud and unbending. Here, all is filled with carefree frivolity.

Themes, even those that are for Bulgakov very important—the scholar's mission, the relationship between history and the present—are expressed with charming lightheartedness in a tonality of playful vaudeville.

If the scholar-genius Timofeev invented a time machine, then why not with the help of this machine drag Ivan the Terrible into an ordinary Moscow communal apartment? Is it not amusing: the all-powerful Tsar of all Rus in all his magnificent vestments thrust into the disorderly, crowded, and incomprehensible, to him, Moscow life of the mid-1930s? From the other side, why not send back to the sixteenth century, for example, a Moscow thief and a Moscow house manager? Indeed, a number of amusing occurrences also come to mind at the thought of how such Muscovites would be met at the court of Ivan IV!

The idea for the play opened unlimited possibilities for comic mischief. But Bulgakov understood that this seductive temptation was dangerous, that sprawling and unbridled fantasizing brings with itself blurring and disorganization of form, that is, the destruction of the entire work. Bulgakov, the master, knew that frivolity requires precision, that a prank requires the strictest economy of comic side-effects. The strict formal organization of **Ivan Vasilevich** lends this comedy, despite all its proximity to vaudeville, a special charm and fascination. Bulgakov's literary and theatrical palette is rich and multicolored. But vulgarity is never among those means of expression which Bulgakov uses. Bulgakov is a refined writer. (p. 146)

The fate of Molière and of his works held Bulgakov's interest over a period of many years. "One could say," observed V. Kaverin, "that he was shaken by his love for Molière, as Madjnun was shaken by his love for Leili."

Bulgakov, of course, was intrigued by the complex dramatic collision that appeared openly in the struggle for permission to stage *Tartuffe.* (p. 149)

In his forty-odd years Molière had been a skillful politician, having studied to perfection the manners of the court and almost without error having discerned the slightest changes in Louis's moods. Why did Molière nonetheless decide to write the comedy *Tartuffe,* which perplexed and nonplussed the king himself? Why, finally, did Molière—after *Tartuffe* had been written, played, and forbidden, after it had evoked a storm of indignation—why then did this clever, political court comedian, who was not at all inclined to heroic deeds and who feared royal disfavor, not destroy his manuscript? Why did he not, in case of a bad outcome, hide it somewhere? Why did he instead continue to insist that the play be staged, write the King rather impertinent and cutting letters, try to enlist the support of certain influential personages, and, in general, refuse to be calmed? What is this strange flood of courage? Whence this sudden readiness to balance on the edge of danger, to risk all—the troupe, his excellent position, his own life in the end?

Here was something to think about, and Bulgakov became more and more deeply absorbed in studying the remarkable life of the royal actor. In 1932 the play about Molière was essentially finished. But Bulgakov could not stop at this point. It was as if his life split—he was simultaneously in the Moscow of the 1930s and in the Paris of the mid-seventeenth century. "I can no longer remember what year it is," he wrote at the time, ". . . I live in the spectral, fairy-tale Paris of the seventeenth century." (p. 150)

The play about Molière, I repeat, had already been finished and at the end of this play Molière dies. But Bulgakov suddenly began writing again. His novel, **The Life of M. de Molière,** opens with the episode of the birth of "an infant of male sex," and this infant is Molière. The entire biography of the comic writer—from birth to death—is presented by Bulgakov impetuously, lightly, and precisely. Of course, this precision is relative—many details, obviously, arose in Bulgakov's fan-

tasy, for where history is silent, Bulgakov had to surmise how in reality events developed. But towards this time and at this stage of his work, he had to such an extent become accustomed to, and become intimate with, Molière, to such an extent come to identify with Molière and his epoch, that Bulgakov even decided at times to rebut Molière's contemporaries. Having recounted this or that episode and cited an authoritative source, Bulgakov will suddenly categorically observe: "To my way of thinking, this is all untrue. . . ." Then he offers his own version. I must be sad that in almost every case, Bulgakov's propositions are more convincing than the testimony of the memoirists whom he bravely disputes. (p. 151)

In one of the articles addressing Bulgakov it has been justly noted that his novel about Molière "sooner resembles a theatrical scenario, a skillfully played production in the costume and staging of the eighteenth century." Yes, the novel is theatrical, and theatricality is one of its principle features. Theater is here not only a theme—it is a form of existence, the only one possible for Molière and thus essential for his biographer.

It is interesting, however, that the most dramatic moment in Molière's life—the whole tormenting and critical situation with *Tartuffe*—occupies a relatively modest place in this novel. It is given as one of a number of episodes which supplement and develop each other. It is not presented as the highest flight of Molière's genius nor as the most important struggle of Molière's entire life. The book **The Life of M. de Molière,** written *after* the play **Cabal of Hypocrites,** appears to be, as it were, a foreword to the play. The whole life of Molière is given as a long and impetuous exposition to the tragedy, in which the themes are made more dense, are concentrated, and at once start towards catastrophe.

Molière's relationship with Louis is described in the book in detail and with irony. However, if in the novel the basic dramatic collision is the relation between Molière and the king, then in the play this collision is made more complex. A third powerful force enters in—the strength of the Church. Marquis de Charron, archbishop for the city of Paris (we easily recognize in him the real archbishop Arduin, who forbade his entire congregation under threat of excommunication, to watch, hear or read *Tartuffe*) appears on stage a gloomy and alarming illumination. The Society of Holy Gifts is called in the play the Cabal of the Holy Writ. The pamphleteer Pierre Roulez appears in the form of the preacher, Father Bartholomew, who is brought to the King by Charron. With no superfluous words, this "holy fool" informs Louis, "in your country the Antichrist has appeared. An atheist, a poisonous worm, gnawing the base of your throne. His name is Jean Baptiste Molière. Burn him on the square together with his vile creation *Tartuffe.*" When the King angered by the disrespectful tone of the vagabond, casually removes this insolent pawn from the board, the archbishop himself enters the game. Louis asks him, "Archbishop, do you find this Molière dangerous?" The archbishop answers, "My Lord, he is Satan." The subtlety which Bulgakov discloses here is that Charron, throughout the entire play, struggles not so much with Molière as with the King. Only by winning and convincing the King can he destroy Molière. But Molière, knowing whence danger threatens, in his own turn—now humbly, now fiercely, by any means, for it is a matter of life and death—strives to preserve the favor and patronage of the King and to drag *Tartuffe* onto the stage.

And again arises the same central, most essential question: in the name of what? What hinders Molière?—indeed in the play he is worn out and weak, he has "aged much, his face is sickly, gray''—what hinders him from retreating and giving up *Tartuffe*? Bulgakov answers this question quite distinctly. There are situations in which the creation is stronger than the creator. Having once arisen, *Tartuffe* becomes invincible. Molière himself can do nothing, but *Tartuffe* accomplishes miracles. *Tartuffe* transforms Molière, compels this cautious and weary man to accomplish miracles of courage, impels Molière to overcome his own weakness and cowardice. Moreover, even Molière's own merits are sacrificed to his composition. The composition acquires a fateful strength and power, for it, this composition, is a work of genius.

Let the author be powerless; the words he has written are full of irresistible strength. They are stronger than the all-powerful **Cabal of Hypocrites,** stronger than the magnificent autocrat, stronger than time. All passes. All are gone—both Louis and Molière. But *Tartuffe* continues to live and will always provoke the impotent hatred of future Charrons.

In this tragic opposition of creator and creation lies the most secret, most deeply hidden theme of Bulgakov's play. This theme wholly defines the strikingly capacious and psychologically irreproachably veracious image of Molière. Bulgakov bravely and sharply moves Molière's weaknesses to the front. The strength of his spirit is disclosed gradually, emerges in details which are externally insignificant but irrefutably accurate.

Molière is great to the extent that he is a pitiful and powerless slave to his genius. He is enslaved by his own *Tartuffe* and no one has the strength to free him from this servitude—neither friend nor enemy, neither king nor archbishop.

Gorky, having read Bulgakov's play in manuscript, at once appreciated its worth. His comment was brief but eloquent. Bulgakov, Gorky wrote, ''excellently drew the portrait of Molière near the end of his days. A Molière grown weary of the disorder of his personal life and the burden of fame. Just as well, as bravely, and—I would say—beautifully drawn is the Sun-King; and in general, all the roles are good. . . . An excellent play.'' (pp. 152-53)

Molière, in Bulgakov's drama, dies on stage in a ''dressing gown and cap, in stage make-up with a caricature nose.'' He dies among monstrously funny personages, created by his imagination. His death is, as it were, surrounded by his immortality, by art unyielding to reality, art more durable and stronger than yielding, weary, human flesh.

The drama, *Pushkin (Last Days)* in principle addresses this same problem still more decisively, while the refusal to attempt the scenic portrait of a genius is announced almost declaratively. For in this play the viewers do not see Pushkin. All the time he is somewhere near, next door—it seems at times as if he is about to pay a neighborly visit—the sense of his presence is achieved with rare and virtuoso mastery. . . .

If Molière acts as the direct antagonist of Louis and the entire court clique, then the heroes of *Last Days* struggle for Pushkin or against him, but he himself is only the unseen object of struggle. (p. 164)

''Akh, what a pity,'' says Vorontsova, ''that only a few can understand the superiority of unusual individuals. . . . How wonderfully in Pushkin are joined genius and enlightenment. But, alas, there are many who envy him. He has many enemies!''

There are many; they are strong. Bulgakov shows them to us one after another—usurers, harrassing the poet; spies, sniffing every corner of his quarters; D'Anthès, posing in front of Pushkin; envious, ''empty and unnatural'' literators; the Tsar himself, flirting with the poet's wife. . . .

Today we know much more about the duel and Pushkin's death than Bulgakov knew forty years ago. Much information, which Bulgakov accepted as irrefutable, can now be subject to doubt or entirely discarded. Nonetheless, from the position of a Pushkin scholar contemporary to Bulgakov, it is impossible to deny Bulgakov's irreproachably precise understanding of the sense of the poet's tragedy, or the unusually acute perception of the whole atmosphere of persecution and intrigue that smothered Pushkin.

The peculiarity and originality of Bulgakov's perception of the conspiracy against the poet is that no one directly arranges anything with anyone. The complex intrigue develops, as it were, at the will of chance, with no mutual awareness on the side of the interested parties.

They act as if by agreement, but without having agreed or arranged matters. They understand each other at half a word, or even without words.

It seems as if the unseen hand of a secret director has organized events and juggled coincidences so as to lead the poet before the bullet of his cynical opponent.

Against such strength and such methods, those few persons to whom Pushkin is dear and who want to save him are obviously powerless. Zhukovsky is powerless, as he tries to reconcile the Tsar with the poet, and the poet with the Tsar. And entirely powerless are the manor serfs, like Nikita, who stand beyond the boundaries of the world in which the intrigue weaves itself.

The inevitability of the poet's death permeates the play and moves it. This movement is sad and elegiac. In this play about Pushkin, there is none of the passionate tension, none of the powerful temperament that mutinies in the play about Molière.

The drama of Molière is played out beneath the laughter of comics; the drama of Pushkin is accomplished in cold palace halls and officials' studies accompanied by insignificant societal banter and businesslike conversations of accurate courtiers. However, both plays converge at one point: in the same prophecy of inevitable—be it even posthumous—triumph of truth, torn by the artist from transient, mutable life and returned to life for eternity. (pp. 164-65)

> *Konstantin Rudnitsky, ''Bulgakov's Plays,'' translated by William Bowler, in* Russian Literature Triquarterly, *No. 15, Spring, 1978, pp. 123-66.*

SYDNEY SCHULTZE (essay date 1978)

[*In the following excerpt, Schultze discusses the significance of the two epigraphs which introduce the novel* The White Guard.]

Mikhail Bulgakov begins his novel **White Guard** with two epigraphs, one from Pushkin's *The Captain's Daughter*, the other from the book of Revelation. The purpose of this short essay is to examine the relevance of the two epigraphs to the novel.

The first epigraph is taken from the early pages of *The Captain's Daughter:*

> A light snow was falling, which suddenly changed to thick, heavy flakes. The wind began

to howl; it was a snowstorm. Within a moment the dark sky had merged with the ocean of snow. Everything disappeared.

"Looks bad, sir," shouted the coachman. "A blizzard."

The storm which threatens in *The Captain's Daughter* is more than a snowstorm: the warm, gentle family life portrayed in the story is threatened by the blizzard of Pugachev's uprising. *White Guard* itself opens in a frosty December in a Kiev menaced by war. As in *The Captain's Daughter,* it is the fate of the main characters, and the cosy home life and civilized values they stand for, that engage our imagination, rather than the political fortunes of the various sides. Bulgakov captures the fragility and preciousness of the home itself as a metaphor for the people and the civilization they represent. He dwells lovingly on the old clock, the stove, the lamps, the curtains: these are eternal things, which "however bad the times might be . . . [are] always there to radiate light and warmth." The world inside is "warm and cosy . . . insulated from the outside world . . . [which is] filthy, bloody, and senseless." It is "the only thing worth fighting for."

Besides recalling earlier troubled times, the epigraph from *The Captain's Daughter* gives the first hint of the central position Russian literature as a whole occupies in the story about to unfold. The walls of the Turbins' warm cocoon are lined with "books that smelled mysteriously of old chocolate with their Natasha Rostovs and their Captain's Daughters. . . ." Books also line the downstairs apartment, and they make it, too, a "world of comfort and security." The well-loved books not only represent the security of the past, they also influence the perception of the present. Elena looks like Liza in Pushkin's "Queen of Spades"; Shpolyansky resembles Eugene Onegin. Vasily Lisovich is called Vasilisa—bringing to mind not only the fairy-tale character, but also the character Vasilisa in *The Captain's Daughter.*

The people in *White Guard* are well versed in Russian literature. As the story progresses, they discuss Pushkin, Lermontov, Tolstoi. Alexei is reading *The Possessed,* and Elena "The Gentleman from San Francisco." Shpolyansky is working on an article about Gogol. Most of these authors and works, as well as other works never mentioned by name, are reflected in the novel. *War and Peace* is a particularly rich source for *White Guard.* Both books show the effects of war on families; both alternate scenes of conflict with intimate domestic scenes. The Turbins often remind us of the Rostovs with their high spirits and their devotion to one another. Like the Rostovs, the Turbins represent what is best in their culture, and like the earlier family they are called on to display their finest qualities in a time of stress. Both books show the senselessness and bloodiness of war, but both at the same time acknowledge the excitement that it generates, especially in young men.

In one scene Myshlaevsky naively praises *War and Peace* because it was written by an artilleryman; his only regret is that Tolstoi left a promising career in the army to return to his estate "where anyone might turn to novel-writing out of boredom." In this amusing scene, Bulgakov shows that much of the appeal of *War and Peace* comes from the naturalness of its story and its faithfulness to real life, even in military matters. *White Guard* appeals for the same reasons: it has an aura of naturalness and fidelity to life.

The Turbins and their friends cannot help reflecting on Borodino, the battle that looms so large in *War and Peace.* On their stove one of them has written "All Russia will recall the day of glorious Borodino!" The reflections come in a rush when they gather at the old Alexander I School. In a portrait on the walls of the School gallops a radiant Alexander. Alexei Turbin wonders if the Tsar can save the building with all the regiments of Borodino. He muses that if Alexander were to come alive and lead them down from the canvas, "they'd smash Petlyura all right." But the dead past cannot save those living in the present, and those now living may not even be able to save mementoes of the past: Myshlaevsky fears that Petlyura may take the armory, the weapons, and worst of all—the portrait of Alexander. Myshlaevsky and Alexei Turbin identify their cause with that of Alexander, so it is not surprising that Petlyura is seen as Napoleon. Petlyura is clearly connected to Napoleon early in the novel: "Petlyura was a myth. He didn't exist. It was a myth as remarkable as the older myth of the nonexistent Napoleon Bonaparte, but a great deal less colorful."

Petlyura like Napoleon is associated with the idea of the Antichrist, and we recall that the second epigraph to *White Guard* is in fact taken from the Apocalypse. In *War and Peace,* Pierre learns from a Mason how to give numerical values to the letters of L(e) Empereur Napoleon. The resultant numbers add up to 666, which the Apocalypse calls "the number of the beast." And what is the number of Petlyura's prison cell? He is imprisoned in cell 666! Later in the novel, blind singers drone on about the Last Judgment while a crowd awaits Petlyura's appearance.

The Turbins seem to sense the apocalyptic nature of their time, once again viewing it partly through literature. For example, Elena reads "The Gentleman from San Francisco," which has several motifs drawn from the Apocalypse. Apocalypticism has appeared throughout Russian history and it was a common way for writers of the period to view what was happening in their country. It is not surprising then that Bulgakov's second epigraph is drawn from Revelation 20:12.

But the full significance of the dual epigraphs has not yet been realized. *The Captain's Daughter* and the Apocalypse both deal with times of upheaval, it is true. But there is another, deeper reason why they were chosen, and clues to this deeper significance are given early in the novel. At the beginning of the novel, the dying mother of the Turbins says "Go on living . . . and be kind to one another. . . ." The characters in *The Captain's Daughter* are in *White Guard* do just that. They live through the worst kind of horrors, and yet again and again show generosity and kindness of one another. In fact, the epigraph chosen from *The Captain's Daughter* is at the beginnng of the scene where the hero meets Pugachev for the first time and give him his hareskin coat. Pugachev thanks him, saying, "May God reward you for your goodness. I shall not forget your kindness as long as I live." And, of course Pugachev does not: he later spares the young man's life. In *White Guard,* Nikolka, as an act of kindness, finds the brave Nai-Tuts's body for his family. At anguishing personal cost, Elena offers up to the Virgin her husband's return in exchange for her brother's life. Truly, the characters follow their mother's admonition.

The immediate impression of the Apocalypse is that it contains a message of destruction, but it has a second message, one of consolation, of peace in the age to come. The lines which Bulgakov has chosen for his second epigraph are "and the dead were judged out of those things which were written in the books according to their works. . . ." It is not until later in the novel that the full significance of these words comes clear. Again, the first clue comes right at the beginning of the novel, when the priest gives his own admonition: "We must never lose heart. . . . Faintness of heart is a great sin," and goes on to quote from the Apocalypse. "And the third angel poured out his vial upon the rivers and fountains of waters; and they became blood." The syphilitic Russian later quotes the same lines to Alexei Turbin, who has just been saved from death by his sister's prayer. Rusakov is a former atheist poet who sees in his ex-companion Shpolyansky the precursor of Satan, and in Trotski the Evil One himself. Rusakov feels that the only salvation lies above, but Turbin tells him he has been spending too much time reading Revelation. Later, however, as Rusakov's eyes travel over the Apocalypse once more, his sickness actually does fall away. He sees the procession of millenia to come and peace enters his soul. He reads this message from Revelation which includes and goes beyond the epigraph: "And the dead were judged out of those things which were written in the books, according to their works. . . . And God shall wipe away all tears from their eyes; and there shall be no more death, neither sorrow nor crying, neither shall there be any more pain: for the former things are passed away." After these verses in Revelation itself comes a condemnation of the cowardly, just as the priest has warned at the beginning of the novel. But the Turbins have nothing to fear: they have been kind, and they have been brave. All things pass, and these hard times shall pass too. They have followed the advice of their mother and of the priest, and have fulfilled the highest moral aspirations of their culture, their civilization.

In the early pages, it is promised that the Turbins' lot is to suffer and die and that *The Captain's Daughter* will be burned. It is true that the Turbins do suffer and that they will die, but, as Bulgakov makes us see at the end, in language reminiscent of the Apocalypse, "Everything passes away—suffering, pain, blood, hunger, and pestilence . . . but the stars will still remain. . . . There is no man who does not know that. Why, then, will we not turn our eyes toward the stars? Why?" (pp. 213-17)

Sydney Schultze, "The Epigraphs in 'White Guard'," in Russian Literature Triquarterly, *No. 15, Spring, 1978, pp. 213-18.*

EFIM ETKIND (essay date 1978)

[In the following excerpt from a paper presented at a 1978 conference on East European and Soviet literature, Etkind compares the character types in The Master and Margarita *with those in contemporary Soviet society.]*

Bulgakov's book [*The Master and Margarita*]—in the form of a tragicomic fantasy—shows the reader "the Soviet irreality" of the thirties. Satan and several of his assistants appear in Moscow, sowing panic among the populace through unexpected miracles: they destroy the laws of space and time, physiology and psychology; they are capable of foreseeing the future and even changing it. All these deeds overturn the primitive, materialistic logic, the vulgar rationalism of the Soviet intellectuals. (p. 144)

Berlioz, the first victim of Satan's interference, is the most consistent rationalist among the novel's characters. He is a dialectician, an atheist, an erudite, and, importantly, free of the least doubt in the correctness of his knowledge. But everything is not as simple as he thought. Berlioz, having self-assuredly negated that which "cannot be," would perish under the wheels of a tram; he would slip in a puddle of sunflower seed oil, spilled by Annuška. This was preordained for him, although this "could not be." In an argument with a pseudo-foreigner, that is, with the devil, Berlioz proves to be bereft of individuality. This is perhaps the most important feature of this well-educated literary *činovnik;* he speaks not in his own name, but in the name of some sort of "us": ". . . neither of us believes in God," "we're atheists," "in our country there's nothing surprising about atheism . . . ," ". . . with all respect to you as a scholar, we take a different attitude on that point." . . . Thus, by condemning Berlioz's rationalistic narrowmindedness, Bulgakov condemns the collective world view of Soviet society, of those who do not know how to think independently and, instead, accept something shared by all of "us." But one should not draw conclusions about Bulgakov's religiosity: he does not maintain any belief whatsoever; he only disaffirms the self-assurance of vulgar all-knowingness. The position that "something cannot be" is fatuous because everything, even Satan, is possible. Rationalists of the Soviet school have learned to explain everything in terms of the simplest cause-effect relationships. Thus, the investigator puts forth sensible explanations for obviously irrational occurrences: ". . . and the detective was convinced that Berlioz had thrown himself (or had fallen) beneath the car while under hypnosis." . . . It is easy to explain any incredibility in this way; but miracles still do occur: in Moscow the devils are the masters.

But even such irrational circumstances are, it would seem, real—that is to say "real devilry." It was also subjected to censorial terror for it is linked with the NKVD. This Soviet-police reality first appears, strangely enough, in the ancient Judean episode, when the procurator, having questioned Yeshua, speaks to the centurion in Latin: "This criminal calls me "good man.' Take him away for a minute and show him the proper way to address me. But do not mutilate him." . . .

Anyone who imagines the speech pattern of an NKVD investigator will recognize these phrases. And further along in the interrogation of Pontius Pilate everything is *familiar:* for example, the background questions he asks, and even the attempts to save the accused: "Listen, Ha-Notsri, the Procurator said, looking at Yeshua somehow strangely: the face of the Procurator was terrifying, but his eyes betrayed anxiety. 'Have you ever said anything about great Caesar? Answer! Did you ever say anything of the sort? Or did you not? . . .'"

Such cases, although rare, have occurred from time to time, where the investigator has tried, even partially, to aid the alleged criminal and remove from him at least the charge of slander against the leader, against "the great Caesar." The entire interrogation and even Pilate's inner monologue, thinking about himself as follows, is in this familiar vein: "the hegemon had examined the case of the vagrant philosopher Yeshua surnamed Ha-Notsri, and could not substantiate the criminal charge made against him. In particular he could not find the slightest connection between Yeshua's actions and the recent disorders in Jerusalem. The vagrant philosopher was mentally ill, as a result of which the sentence of death pronounced on Ha-Notsri by the Lesser Senhedrin would not be confirmed." . . .

If, in this text, we replace *Yeshua Ha-Notsri* and the *wandering philosopher* with Russian names, *Jerusalem* with Moscow or Kiev, *procurator* with investigator, *Lesser Senhedrin* with Special Deliberation, the text will be directly relevant to the Soviet reality of the thirties—its stylistic characteristic is apparent. (pp. 144-45)

Soviet phraseology is otherwise presented through the direct speech of the devils, who represent different variants of it. The most interesting among them is the cat Begemont, who personifies the boorish bureaucrat, the militant citizen, and the supervisor who inspires trepidation—all this in one individual. The cat is "the size of a pig, black as soot and with luxuriant cavalry officer's whiskers." . . . This is how the cat speaks: Having responded (this was already mentioned above) to Poplavskij, Berlioz' uncle from Kiev, that it was he who had given the telegram, and having added: "'. . . what else?'" the cat drily continues, 'I, it would seem, am asking in good Russian, what else?' But Poplavskij didn't give any answer. 'Passport!' bellowed the cat and stretched out a bloated paw . . . 'Which department issued the document?' the cat asked, staring at the page. There was no answer. 'Department 412,' the cat answered his own question, pointing his paw across the passport which he held up with his feet. 'Well, of course, I know that department. There they issue passports to anybody. While I, for example, wouldn't have issued one to someone like you! . . .' The cat got so mad that he threw the passport to the floor. 'Your presence at the funeral is cancelled,' continued the cat in an official voice. 'Try to go to your place of residence'."

Each intonational nuance is authentic: from the boorish-bureaucratic tone of "I, it would seem, am asking in good Russian" to the word "document," to the impersonal "is cancelled," the seemingly courteous paraphrase "try to go" and the bureaucratically lifeless "place of residence." The cat's line of speech is continued when he, playing chess with Voland, using live figures, is forced to surrender to a devil who is stronger than he: "I give up," he says, "but I give up only because I cannot play in an atmosphere of persecution on the part of envious people." . . . This episode with living chess figures is symbolic, and the cat Begemont or, rather, the cat Bureaucrat is especially funny and terrifying here. Finally, the cat fulfills his bureaucratic function when Nikolaj Ivanovič asks him for a document certifying where he spent the night: "'What for?' asked the cat sternly. 'To show my wife and *to the police*,' said Nikolai Ivanovich firmly [the italicized items were deleted by the censors, E. E.]. 'We don't usually give certificates,' replied the cat frowning, 'but since it's for you we'll make an exception.' Before Nikolai Ivanovich knew what was happening, the naked Hella was sitting beside a typewriter and the cat was dictating to her: "'This is to certify that the bearer, Nikolai Ivanovich, spent the night in question at Satan's Ball, having been enticed there in a vehicular capacity." Hella, put in brackets after that "[pig]." "Signed—Begemont."'" 'What about the date?' squeaked Nikolai Ivanovich. 'We don't mention the date, the document becomes invalid if it's dated,' replied the cat, waving the piece of paper. Then the animal produced a rubber stamp, breathed on it in the approved fashion, stamped 'Paid' on the paper and handed the document to Nikolai Ivanovich. He vanished without a trace . . ." . . .

Here, phantasmagoria is combined with the most "everyday" reality of the Soviet establishment. Bulgakov's conjuring lies in this: It would seem that the devilry should contrast with more than the usual, trivial bureaucratic life; however, the narrative is so constructed that the absurdity of this life naturally gives rise to devilry, for the absurd in and of itself is phantasmagoric. If Gogol's Nose could run a department, for Bulgakov an empty, headless suit fills the absurd functions of a bureaucrat. (pp. 146-47)

[Over] the years the irreality of Soviet reality has ever grown. In the book *Zapiski nezagovorščika* I related a story, similar to Kafka's novel, concerning the fate of a single phrase. Bulgakov apparently had not read Kafka, but his perception of Soviet everyday life exposes the absurdity which is its major characteristic. The absurdity is growing, devilry also. Mixail Bulgakov, a writer of the thirties, was born as the author of *Master i Margarita* at the end of the sixties and became one of the most popular Soviet authors in the world during the seventies. The amazing characteristic of his prophetic novel has turned out to be not the lessening but the growth of its timeliness. (pp. 148-49)

Efim Etkind, "Mixail Bulgakov, Our Contemporary," in Fiction and Drama in Eastern and Southeastern Europe: Evolution and Experiment in the Postwar Period, *edited by Henrik Birnbaum and Thomas Eekman, Slavica Publishers, Inc., 1980, pp. 137-49.*

PETER DOYLE (essay date 1978)

[*In the following excerpt, Doyle discusses the theme of progress in* "The Fatal Eggs" *and* The Heart of a Dog. *He finds that both works constitute a general ideological rejection of change through political revolution in favor of change through social evolution, and that neither work need be read as specific allegorical denunciations of the Russian Revolution of 1917. For a reading of* The Heart of a Dog *as a specific allegory of the Russian Revolution, see the Michael Glenny entry in the Additional Bibliography; for a discussion of* The Heart of a Dog *that challenges the political reading of this novel, see the excerpt by Diana L. Burgin (1978).*]

[*Rokovye iaitsa* and *Sobach'e Serdtse*] have much in common. Both stories concern a scientific experiment which goes wrong and has unforeseen consequences. Both stories warn of the dangers of science but also have a more specific political message. Both stories reveal the influence of H. G. Wells. The red ray in *Rokovye iaitsa* is a variation of Wells' "herakleophorbia" in *The Food of the Gods,* in which scientists discover a compound that causes living things to grow to six times their normal size. The surgical transformation of an animal into a human being in *Sobach'e serdtse* recalls Wells' *The Island of Doctor Moreau,* a novel in which a whole variety of animals are given human form by a fanatical vivisectionist. In addition, though the stories constitute the clearest statements of Bulgakov's view of the Bolshevik Revolution and the new Soviet society, to date they have been comparatively neglected by commentators, both Soviet (for obvious reasons) and Western (whose concern has mainly been with *Master i Margarita*). The purpose of this article, therefore, is to indicate that these early satires are worthy of a place in the mature Bulgakov canon, by examining the different ways in which each work treats the same theme—the rejection of revolution as a means for achieving human progress.

Rokovye iaitsa relates how the ignorant and politically powerful misapply knowledge in an attempt to force the pace of progress, with disastrous results. The title is a pun meaning either "The Fatal Eggs" or "Rokk's Eggs," and the main events of the story, briefly summarized, are as follows. Professor Persikov, a Moscow zoologist, discovers by chance a red ray which, when directed at living things, causes them to multiply and grow with alarming speed. With the help of his assistant, Ivanov, Persikov constructs some experimental chambers and sends abroad for a consignment of reptiles' eggs in order to pursue his research further. Meanwhile, a chicken plague strikes the Soviet Union and spreads rapidly throughout the country. A communist official named Rokk, authorized by the Soviet government, removes Persikov's experimental chambers to a state farm in order to use them to accelerate the hatching of chicken eggs, and thus to combat the chicken plague. Persikov's protests that his ray is experimental and untried are to no avail. Because of an administrative error the state farm is given the wrong eggs and the ray produces monster reptiles, which quickly spread throughout the district and begin to threaten Moscow as the Red Army fights a losing battle. Persikov is lynched by an angry mob and his laboratory is destroyed. The country is only saved by an exceptionally severe frost in August, which kills off the rampaging monsters.

What, however, is the main object of Bulgakov's satire in *Rokovye iaitsa*? As Shchedrin wrote: "If satire is to achieve its aim, the reader must be able to sense the ideal which is the writer's basis; ... he must be quite clear against what object the sting of the satire is directed." Many readers of Bulgakov's story, misled perhaps by the author's all-pervasive irony, have felt puzzled by the work and have pointed to its ambiguity as its basic defect as satire. (pp. 468-69)

To these commentators the generally anti-communist tone of the story is apparent but the detail is confusing, and the story is considered a failure.

Others have attempted to see the story as a political allegory mirroring the Bolshevik Revolution. Thus, it has been argued, the ray represents the Bolshevik cause, giving new life to the Russian lower classes, while the fact that the new ray-produced generation slaughters the older generation is suggestive of the Civil War. Another interpretation states that Bulgakov "satirized Lenin . . . allegorically in the figure of a scientist who brought out of some rare eggs the improbable monsters and reptiles of communism." The fact that the eggs in question are imported from abroad suggests, one commentator argues, the destructive political ideas imported by the Bolsheviks. For I. Nusimov, a Soviet critic of the 'twenties, "the political meaning of the fantasy is clear: the revolution has given birth to 'reptiles' from which we can be saved only by such a miracle as an eighteen-degree frost in August."

At first sight there would perhaps seem to be evidence for the view that *Rokovye iaitsa* is an allegory of the Bolshevik Revolution. In addition to the points made above, one could note that Persikov's first name is Vladimir, his initials are V.I., and we are told that in April 1928 he was exactly 58 years old, that is, he had been born in April 1870, as had Lenin. On the other hand, one might just as well argue that, as Bulgakov once made a veiled reference to Lenin as "Rok" in *Zapiski na manzhetakh*, Persikov's role is more that of Marx whose ideas are misapplied in the wrong circumstances by Rokk-Lenin! It is not surprising that those who persist in trying to wring out of the text a detailed allegory of the revolution find *Rokovye iaitsa* puzzling. For though Bulgakov is attacking some of the basic principles of the Bolshevik Revolution, he is not doing it by means of an allegory in which, for example, Persikov represents Lenin, the experiment the revolution, and the monsters communism.

Several objections can be made to such an allegorical interpretation of *Rokovye iaitsa* to show that it does fit the text. In the first place, the catastrophe is not brought about by Persikov; on the contrary, he makes his objections clear when he telephones the Kremlin: "Without my agreement or advice . . . I categorically protest. I do not sanction experiments with eggs." He also announces "I wash my hands of the business," . . .

and warns Rokk that the ray has not been sufficiently studied. As he says to Ivanov, "neither you nor I can say what kind of chickens will hatch." ... Secondly, having already produced swarms of huge, vicious frogs which had to be gassed, Persikov sees the need for caution in continuing his experiments: his precautions include protective suits, helmets, a stock of poisonous gas, and an OGPU electric revolver. Persikov is anything but a reckless experimenter. Thirdly, Persikov, the scientist whose discovery is misused against his will, is a victim of the politically powerful to whose influence he has to submit. He does not direct events and is powerless to prevent the exploitation of his discovery. His role is similarly that of a victim when he is unjustly made the scapegoat and murdered by the mob.

In his letter to Stalin of March 1930, Bulgakov expressed his respect for the intelligentsia, "the finest stratum of society in our country." He wrote, with reference to his satirical works, that they demonstrated "profound scepticism in relation to the revolutionary process taking place in my backward country, in opposition to which I put my beloved Great Process of Evolution (*Velikaia Evoliutsiia*)." In these words Bulgakov touches on the basic idea which underlies *Rokovye iaitsa* (and indeed *Sobach'e serdtse*), for his fundamental concern is with the nature of progress, with gradual evoluton as opposed to sudden revolution. Progress cannot be forced; whatever is accomplished is only achieved over a long period of time, the result of years of dedicated work by intelligent men. Those unenlightened people, whoever they may be, who attempt to compress the effort and evolution of centuries into a few weeks, are doomed to failure. They are interfering with forces which are beyond their control and which they do not understand. As O. Mikhailov points out, the catastrophe in *Rokovye iaitsa* "allows Bulgakov to remind us of the enormous complexity and uncertainty of the consequences of a hurried and mechanical invasion of the infinite and mysterious world—the world which is the basis of nature and of man." In *Rokovye iaitsa* this general principle is given a particular form and political relevance. *Rokovye iaitsa* rejects revolution as a form of progress, firstly, because the revolutionary mentality oversimplifies; secondly, because revolutions put political power into the wrong hands, those of the ignorant and stupid; and thirdly because ignorance combined with political power inevitably leads to disaster. Similarly, the hope that the great power of science can be easily exploited for bringing about enforced change is shown to be a delusion, for in the hands of the ignorant, scientific power, like political power, will be abused, with equally chaotic results. The story of Rokk and his disastrous experiment provides a specific illustration of this theme. (pp. 470-71)

By implication, *Rokovye iaitsa* is an eloquent defence of the necessity of freedom for the creative genius, scientist or writer, who works on a level of inspiration and dedication beyond the understanding of the mass of people, from whom he may consequently need protection. Persikov meets a violent end at the hand of a "short man on bandy ape-like legs" . . . who leads a mob whose indiscriminate fury knows no bounds.... (pp. 473-74)

Convincing evidence of the depth of Bulgakov's satirical insight is the prophetic quality of *Rokovye iaitsa*. Bulgakov was not looking back and writing an allegory of the revolution itself. Rather, he was looking forward and pointing to the disasters of the future. With its anachronistic description of Rokk, and set as it is in the future of 1928, *Rokovye iaitsa* seems to presage the eventual re-emergence on the Soviet political scene of the gun-toting Civil War figure, with dire consequences; in reality the violence of Stalin's 1930's was to dwarf that of the Civil War. Similarly, the exploitation and destruction of Persikov seems to presage the forced subservience and destruction of the intelligentsia: the 1930's saw the domination of Soviet life by Stalin's tough, uneducated upstarts, devoid of moral standards or intellectual qualities. Not only did such men reduce Soviet intellectual life to a dead level of conformist mediocrity, they virtually wiped out the intelligentsia and men of quality *en masse*.

With the benefit of hindsight one can appreciate the aptness of the central images of *Rokovye iaitsa:* an experiment that goes wrong, a ray in which the most ruthless and brutal thrive and slaughter, and which produces rampaging monsters that cannot be controlled. Even the nature of the experiment, a vain attempt to increase agricultural production, is fitting. Within a few years Soviet agriculture was to be suddenly and forcibly collectivized, a disastrous policy carried out by predominantly urban party activists with little or no knowledge of agricultural problems. This is not of course to suggest that the story is an allegory of Stalin's collectivization of agriculture. It is simply an illustration of Bulgakov's uncannily sharp satirical vision. On a more general level, the history of the last fifty years confirms the accuracy of Bulgakov's warnings about the dangers of the abuse of science for political ends.

The image of the experiment that goes wrong is equally apt for an allegory of the revolution itself. In *Rokovye iaitsa,* however, Bulgakov uses significant details, such as the fact that the ray is red, merely to invite the reader to infer by analogy that the revolution has been just such a doomed experimental attempt to force the pace as Rokk's efforts with the eggs. It is only in *Sobach'e serdtse* that Bulgakov uses this image in order to write a specific political allegory of the revolution itself.

As well as its rejection of revolution, *Rokovye iaitsa,* set as it is in the Soviet Union of 1928, also contains a good deal of satire on many aspects of Soviet life, familiar targets in Bulgakov's early work, but here essentially secondary. Bureaucratic incompetence, the poor quality of Soviet products, the monotony of the Soviet press, journalist hacks, Meierkhol'd's "biomechanics," Erenburg's artistic "adaptability"—all receive some measure of mocking attention. The secret police are thrice ridiculed: The Extraordinary Commission for Combating the Chicken Plague is ineffective; the OGPU men who visited Persikov are caricatured; while their colleagues who go to Rokk's farm meet a gruesome end. As with their counterparts in *Master i Margarita,* their explanation of events as a hallucination is inadequate. Bulgakov's irony spares no one: all characters, including Persikov, are sharply satired. Gor'kii was quite right to describe the story as "wittily and cunningly written," for it is an excellent satirical work, written by a master not an apprentice.

Sobach'e serdtse, on a secondary level, satirizes many of the same things as *Rokovye iaitsa,* such as the press, the poor quality of Soviet goods, the housing shortage and the harsh conditions of life for the average citizen. It also shares with *Rokovye iaitsa* the same underlying theme: that artificial attempts to compress the process of evolution into a short period cannot succeed. In the later work, however, not only is the story an allegory of the revolution itself, but the political implications of the basic theme are clearly developed. In his story Bulgakov exposes the pretentiousness of the Bolsheviks who think that by their experimental revolution they can civilize the proletarian masses and transform them into "new men" almost overnight.

Even a brief résumé of the plot indicates its similarities with that of *Rokovye iaitsa.* The appropriately named Professor Preobrazhenskii, a Moscow specialist in rejuvenation, experimentally transplants the testicles and pituitary gland of Klim Chugunkin, a recently deceased proletarian, into Sharik, a stray mongrel dog. To the professor's surprise the dog survives, gradually acquires a passably human size and form, but soon begins to make a nuisance of himself. The new man, Poligraf Poligrafovich Sharikov, as he insists on calling himself, falls under the influence of the militant communist Shvonder and eventually writes a denunciation of the professor. Angered by such misdemeanours on Sharikov's part, Preobrazhenskii and his assistant Bormental' perform another operation so that when Shvonder and several policemen arrive to investigate the disappearance of Sharikov a few days later, they are able to point to a benign, though slightly odd-looking dog.

Clearly, *Sobach'e serdtse* is closely linked to *Rokovye iaitsa.* A world-famous Moscow professor, aided by a young collaborator, is engaged in experimental work; the experiment itself has unforeseen consequences which have sinister potential; the result of the experiemnt is eventually cancelled out. In contrast to *Rokovye iaitsa,* however, it is the professor himself who expertly and responsibly carries out the experiment, and yet it still goes wrong. Here science is not abused by the politically powerful, but reveals its own deficiencies. Science cannot be relied upon to produce revolutionary change, not only because it will be abused, but also because science itself is limited and does not have the power to change everything. As the professor acknowledges, he himself must bear the responsibility for his mistake. Accordingly, he puts right the wrong by returning Sharikov to his original state.

Another difference from *Rokovye iaitsa* is that the political relevance of the allegorical events is made clear throughout by Professor Preobrazhenskii, an articulate spokesman of definite political views, whose conversations with Bormental' serve as an explanatory commentary.

The reader is introduced to the professor's ideas as early as the second chapter when, in reply to Bormental''s question as to how he had managed to lure such a nervous dog to his flat, Preobrazhenskii answers: "By kindness. The only possible method when dealing with a living creature. You'll get nowhere with an animal if you use terror, no matter what its level of development may be. . . . They are wrong when they think that terror will help them. No, no, it won't help, whatever kind of terror it is: white, red, or even brown! Terror completely paralyzes the nervous system!" According to the professor, then, nothing should ever be imposed on any living being by force. Significantly, when he acts against his own dictum, goes against nature and operates on the dog by force, against its wishes, the consequences are unforeseen and unpleasant.

Preobrazhenskii makes no secret of his political views. Accused by members of the new house committee of being a "hater of the proletariat", he frankly admits the charge. In the following chapter, he expounds at length to Bormental' on recent political changes in Russia. Basing his observations simply on facts, he points out that until March 1917 nothing untoward happened in the house but that since the arrival of the proletariat in power all the galoshes, rugs and plants have been stolen, the staircase is dirty, the front door is boarded up, and the electricity which formerly went out twice in twenty years is now cut off once a month. . . . When Bormental' jokes that he is saying counter-revolutionary things, the professor asserts the primacy of his own common sense and practical experience over meaningless slogans. As Preobrazhenskii sees it, the proletarian masses should know their proper place. Once they are elevated to positions of power by force, the result is the chaos he sees around him.

When it comes to the operation on the dog, however, Preobrazhenskii, unintentionally it is true, does precisely this in miniature. His dog is happy and content with its lot (hence the work's original title *"Sobach'e schast'e"*), pleased to be a gentleman's dog, and convinced that his former freedom was "smoke, a mirage, a fiction." . . . Sensing that the professor and his assistant are up to something, he thinks: "Well, take me if you want. But you ought to be ashamed." . . . His last thought before the anaesthetic takes effect is "Why?" Then "the whole world was turned upside down," . . . both literally and figuratively. Bulgakov thus makes it clear that the operation is imposed on a reluctant, bewildered, hitherto happy dog. The violence of the operation itself is stressed. In addition to a vivid description of the gory details, the professor is shown to be acting like a man possessed, a fanatical high-priest. He is "positively terrifying," looks round "like a beast," his face becomes that of an "inspired robber"; both he and Bormental' are "tensed up, like murderers in a hurry," and at the end Preobrazhenskii is like a "satiated vampire." . . . (pp. 474-77)

The result of this bloody operation is the emergence of Sharikov, a "new human individual," a "new organism," a "laboratory creature." . . . As the story progresses this new man Sharikov is seen to be an old-style proletarian. The friendly dog Sharik "who somehow possessed the secret of winning over people's hearts," . . . becomes the loutish and unappealing Sharikov—hardly an improvement. (pp. 477-78)

Sharikov is foul-mouthed, over-familiar, insolent; he spits and urinates on the floor; he chases cats, floods the flat, throws stones at a neighbour's window, foists his attentions on the women of the house, begins to steal money and to drink too much. In fact, the more he shakes off the character of the dog Sharik, the more his behaviour deteriorates. He also shows himself to be material ripe for exploitation at the hands of the leather-jacketed Shvonder. Thus it is at Shvonder's suggestion that Sharikov acquires a name, demands documents and his rights to living-space; it is from Shvonder that Sharikov picks up a variety of political clichés; it is at Shvonder's instigation that Sharikov reads Engels, though he does not understand what he reads.

Professor Preobrazhenskii fully realizes what is happening and he explains everything to be the more naive Bormental', who hopes he can develop Sharikov into a "mentally very highly advanced personality." . . . When Bormental' says that Sharikov is a man with the heart of a dog, the professor tells him not to insult the dog for "The whole horror lies in the fact that he no longer has a dog's, but precisely a human heart. And about the rottenest of all that exist in nature!" . . . The worst features of the new man Sharikov are derived from the ignorant proletarian Klim Chugunkin whose personality he is now acquiring. Preobrazhenskii is certain that the operation has been the biggest mistake of his career, whose apparent scientific success is illusory. As he puts it, he has spent five years reseaching "so that one fine day a nice little dog could be turned into such rubbish that it makes your hair stand on end." . . . He is clear where he went wrong: "This is what happens, Doctor, when a researcher, instead of groping along in step

with nature, forces the pace and lifts the veil." . . . To Bormental''s objection that a Spinoza rather than a Sharikov might have been produced, the professor, extolling evolutionary as opposed to revolutionary change, replies: "Why is it necessary to manufacture Spinozas artificially when any peasant women can give birth to one at any time? . . . Doctor, mankind itself takes care of that and every year, selecting them in the evolutionary order of things from among the mass of riff-raff, it stubbornly creates dozens of outstanding geniuses who embellish the world." . . . (pp. 478-79)

There is also a more sinister side to all this. Sharikov's ignorance and stupidity can be easily exploited by the forces of evil, as Bormental' appreciates when he says: "But just think, Filipp Filippovich, what he may turn into if that character Shvonder keeps on at him! By God, I'm only just beginning to realize what Sharikov may become!" . . . Not only this, but if Sharikov is put in a position of power, he will turn on those who put him there, as the professor clearly sees. . . . In fact, Sharikov quickly begins to prove his sinister potential. When he returns after being missed for two days, his appearance is rather different for "he was wearing a second-hand leather jacket, worn leather trousers and high English leather boots, laced up to the knee." . . . Now officially employed to rid Moscow of vagrant animals, he stinks of cats, for he has spent the day "strangling cat after cat." . . . He bullies his fiancée and, abusing his position of authority, threatens to get her fired; he denounces the professor and Bormental' to OGPU; and finally he draws a revolver on Bormental'.

After Preobrazhenskii's comments on the Soviet Union of the 'twenties and his explanation of the operation, the implications of Bulgakov's story for the Soviet situation are clear. Contemptuously allegorized as a bloody operation on a dog's testicles, the Bolshevik Revolution has been an experimental and violent attempt to bring about enforced evolution, whose consequences were not fully appreciated. To no lesser degree than Rokk, the pre-revolutionary Russian intelligentsia, complacently confident in their expertise, were guilty of oversimplification. They must be held responsible for the unexpected results of their actions, which have given power to the proletariat but brought no benefits to them, and only ushered in chaos. To believe that the mere fact of the revolution has transformed the proletariat into "new men" is a dangerous delusion, as is the hope that science is an omnipotent instrument for bringing about further dramatic changes. The proletariat is incapable of governing the country and putting the world to rights. (p. 479)

Both *Rokovye iaitsa* and *Sobach'e serdtse,* each in its own way and with differences of emphasis, treat the same theme: revolution is rejected in favour of evolution, for revolutions produce not progress but a moral vacuum in which values are destroyed, power is given to the ignorant and unworthy, and evil consequently predominates, violently and bloodily. For a country such as Russia, where the intellectual élite forms a small minority easily swamped by the "dark masses," the dangers of revolution are particularly acute. The specific significance of Bulgakov's message is confirmed by the events of the 'thirties in the Soviet Union. His works, however, though primarily political satires, also transcend their time and have a more universal relevance: they comment on the nature of progress; they point out the grave dangers of allowing the ignorant to control political and scientific power; they expose the presumptuousness of those who think that they can control nature; and they question the wisdom of inherently imperfect

First page of the third draft of The Master and Margarita.
Courtesy of Ardis Publishers.

men meddling with the powerful forces of modern science.
(pp. 480-81)

> Peter Doyle, ''Bulgakov's Satirical View of Revo-
> lution in 'Rokovye iaitsa' and 'Sobach'e serdtse','
> in Canadian Slavonic Papers, *Vol. XX, December,*
> *1978, pp. 467-82.*

A. COLIN WRIGHT (essay date 1978)

[*Wright is a Canadian critic and educator whose* Mikhail Bulgakov: Life and Interpretations *was the first full-length biographical and critical study of the author. Regarding his critical approach to Bulgakov's works, Wright states in the introduction to
his study: ''[In] my discussions, although I have not neglected
questions of form, I have taken an unashamedly ideological approach, hence the ''Interpretations'' of the title. It seems to me
that a reader is initially concerned with the outlook an author
has on the world and society, and that a detailed examination of
his techniques, however important, can be safely left to individual
articles or later monographs.'' In the following excerpt, Wright
provides a discussion of the characters, themes, and philosophical
background of* The Master and Margarita.]

Sometime towards the end of Bulgakov's life his neighbour
Gabrilovich had asked what he was writing. 'Oh, I'm writing
something,' he had answered, 'just a trivial little thing.' This

'little thing' had developed over twelve years and had involved
an enormous amount of research, which included the history
of ancient Rome and of early Christianity. Many of the books
which were probably familiar to Bulgakov from his childhood
in the family of a professor of theology must have been reread
and studied. Eight separate versions had been produced.

The Master and Margarita, in its final, complete version, revolves around four days when Moscow is visited by the devil,
referred to by the somewhat obscure name—found principally
in Goethe's *Faust*—of Woland. With him are his assistants,
Azazello, Koroviev (also referred to as Fagot), an enormous
tom-cat, Behemoth, and a vampire maid, Hella. Among bureaucrats, petty crooks, and those simply concerned with personal gain these 'gangsters' cause havoc. But they give aid
and protection to a persecuted writer in an asylum, the master,
and to his love, Margarita, after she has agreed to act as hostess
for Satan's Ball. A hack poet, Ivan Homeless—who introduces
us to the whole story—is brought to a deeper understanding
of life and becomes a 'disciple' of the master. Central to the
book is the Master's novel about Christ and Pontius Pilate, the
chapters of which form part of Bulgakov's text and conclude
simultaneously with the story about the Master in the final
chapter. . . . (p. 258)

The number of critical articles since the book's appearance is
staggering: for indeed *The Master and Margarita* seems to demand interpretation. Understandably, some communist criticisms have tended to tone down the religious aspects and ac-
centuate the social ones, while a number of Western articles
have taken a more religious, sometimes anti-Soviet, line. But
the sum total of these commentaries is confusing: ultimately
one is forced to return to the book itself and recognize that,
despite the intellectual exercises it can give rise to, it is not
exhausted by interpretation. *The Master and Margarita* is not
a tidy work, nor does it present a logically structured argument:
like many a great book, ultimately its greatness lies in its power
to evoke responses intuitively from the reader. It also contains
a great deal of simple entertainment, fantasy, and comedy
which has no inherent significance. But despite the, at times,
bewildering mass of detail, we may none the less distinguish
a number of essential themes and even a basic philosophy.

At the most general level *The Master and Margarita* is concerned with the conflict of the spiritual with the material world
of everyday—a theme that, in one form or another, underlies
the whole of Bulgakov. Man, in society, prefers to rely on
himself and thinks he can ignore spiritual issues. 'But what
troubles me,' Woland says to Ivan Homeless in the first, essential conversation with him and an editor Berlioz, 'is this:
if there is no God, then, you might ask, who governs the life
of men and, generally, the entire situation here on earth?' 'Man
himself governs it,' Homeless replies. . . . The whole book is
a demonstration of the fact that man does *not* govern the world—
although he usually thinks he does. The trouble is that man is
mortal, even—as Woland puts it—'suddenly mortal,' unable
to guarantee his own next day, which is demonstrated by Berlioz' dramatic death by decapitation under a tram, as Woland
has foreseen. In Moscow it is Woland, the devil, who represents the spiritual; in ancient Jerusalem Yeshua-ha-Nozri, Christ
himself: 'And keep in mind that Jesus existed,' Woland says.
Yeshua, in the Master's novel as recounted by Woland, in fact
echoes Woland's thoughts, saying—when Pilate tells him his
life hangs by a hair that he can cut—'There, too, you are
mistaken . . . You must agree that the hair can surely be cut
only by him who had hung it?' . . . (p. 261)

In the end, it is the spiritual that triumphs, of necessity, for it is eternal. In *The White Guard* Bulgakov had written: 'Everything passes away—suffering, pain, blood, hunger, and pestilence. The sword will pass away too, but the stars will still remain when the shadows of our presence and our deeds have vanished from the earth. There is no man who does not know that. Why, then, will we not turn our eyes toward the stars? Why?' The passage might almost be a description of the ending of *The Master and Margarita,* with the group of riders (the devil and his company) leaving the earth, surrounded by stars and the light of the moon, and the departure of the Master and Margarita for their eternal abode. The heroes of this novel are those who are aware of more than trivial and temporary issues. For linked with the idea of eternity is the whole question of immortality—and the kind of immortality one achieves. In this respect Pilate is an interesting hero, for he is indeed concerned with immortality: ironically his fame has come to rest not on his genuinely great deeds but on his one cowardly execution. Yet at the end he is allowed to find his fulfilment in eternity, when his desire for communion with the man he has executed is granted. The Master and Margarita too are given what they most desire: 'peace' (not 'light,' which for one reason or another they have not deserved) and sharing each other's fate. In all of this we find a fundamental optimism about the basis of the world. 'Everything will turn out right,' Woland tells Margarita. 'That's what the world is built on.' . . . (p. 262)

It will be obvious that Bulgakov's whole conception is broader than that of traditional Christianity, and indeed Yeshua-ha-Nozri is a character in his own right differing considerably from the Jesus of the gospels. . . . Various possibilities have been suggested to account for the changes in the story: the fact that it is (in part, at least) told by the devil, who traditionally lies (not very convincing, for elsewhere he does not lie when talking seriously), or that it is the story seen from Pilate's point of view. Bulgakov, however, is simply using the gospels as a source, writing anew an old story and in so doing revitalizing it, establishing all the more firmly Christ as an actual, living person. . . . (pp. 262-63)

Bulgakov presents us with facts that differ in detail but ultimately do nothing to alter the fundamental message of the gospels, which essentially is set out in the first three chapters, in the all-important conversations between Woland, Berlioz, and Homeless, and between Yeshua and Pilate. Yeshua's basic philosophy involves a belief in God, the coming of the 'kingdom of truth,' and love of man. For him, all are 'good people,' even those who act cruelly, or betray him. Pilate has no such beliefs. 'The trouble,' Yeshua says, 'is that you keep to yourself too much and have lost all faith in men . . . Your life is too barren, Hegemon'. . . . His is a philosophy, like Bulgakov's, involving the importance of the individual as opposed to the needs of the state—for which reason he is crucified. As Yeshua explains: 'every form of authority means coercion over men and . . . a time will come when there shall be neither Caesars, nor any other rulers. Man will come into the kingdom of truth and justice, where there will be no need for any authority'. . . . Pilate represents the state and, although as a man he may hate his role, in his official capacity he can recognize only expediency. Yet ultimately all temporal power is an illusion—as Woland says, its influence 'microcopic' in comparison with his own, so that those who wield it 'become quite laughable, even pathetic'. . . . This is certainly true of Pilate who, even within the limited time of his life-span, is forced by his position to do not as he wants but as the high priest

Kaiyapha has decided, and then to resort to subterfuge to take his revenge on a man he despises.

It is in the manifestations of temporal power, as seen in the novel, that we can find most similarity between ancient Jerusalem and Moscow under Stalin: where Christ's words about authority disappearing sound like a hollow parody of a communist theory. For both societies represent dictatorships of a different kind, and the parallels are clear—however much they were toned down in the censored version. . . . (pp. 263-64)

The problem is, of course, that individuals barter away their individuality to the state, through their desire for riches, comfort, or security—or through plain cowardice, which Pilate, who epitomizes it in his relationship to Yeshua, comes to understand as the most terrible of human sins. For Yeshua's 'good people' are shown to be weak, and in the Moscow episodes their all too human vices are unmercifully satirized, providing much of the comedy in the book. . . . With some of these figures, like bartender Andrey Fokich Somov, who is left with money that has turned into just strips of paper, we can even sympathize. 'But how trivial is this paper money,' we read, 'when with Fokich there is speaking eternity itself.' For one of the themes of the book is surely that Christ is the saviour of precisely such people—and that the temporal state does not provide a substitute. Thus Woland has arrived in Moscow to find out what the Moscow inhabitants are like and if they have changed inside. Watching the audience at the Variety Theatre, where he performs, he finds their only concern is for money and material goods despite the aims of communism to transform them, although they are capable at times of compassion: 'They're ordinary people, in fact they remind me very much of their predecessors, except that the housing shortage has soured them . . .' (pp. 264-65)

It is the state . . . which has tried to foster certain attitudes, which also receive their share of attention. Foreigners, such as Woland, are for that fact alone treated with suspicion. Busybodies like master-of-ceremonies Bengalsky and a theatrical official in the Variety Theatre can self-importantly make socially 'correct' comments and demand proper explanations, whether these are desired or not—but here the reader is allowed his sense of gratification as, in contrast to real life, these figures are put down. An office director goes overboard on instigating clubs of different kinds which the employees are forced to join—and is parodied by Koroviev, who founds a choral club and sets them all singing against their will, so that they cannot stop. Bureaucracy is such that an empty suit can continue to write resolutions, which are all approved by the suit's owner when he reappears. . . . (p. 265)

In all of this there are a number of allusions to actual persons or events, and elsewhere Piper (who regards the book as 'an aesthetic interpretation of the relationship beteen Bulgakov, his third wife and Stalin') tries to identify various figures: Woland—Stalin, Fagot—Molotov, Hella—his wife, Azaello—Kaganovich, Behemoth—Voroshilov, and so on [see excerpt dated 1971]. All this is somewhat fanciful, but there are none the less a few deliberate allusions at least to Stalin: Pilate's toast to Caesar, for example—'For us, for thee, Caesar, father of the Romans, most beloved and best of all men!' . . . the last half significantly deleted in the censored version—is remarkably similar to those addressed to Stalin. There are also a number of more veiled allusions to Soviet life: to the Lubyanka (the infamous prison and headquarters of the secret police), to the orgies which were rumoured to take place in Moscow in the late twenties and early thirties (compare Satan's Ball), and so on. And Baron Meigel is based on an actual spy, Baron Shteiger, whose job was to listen in to social conversations of foreign diplomats.

The target for Bulgakov's bitterest satire, however, is once again the literary and theatrical world. 'Dostoevsky is immortal!' Behemoth says . . .—but few of the writers here are concerned with immortality, for it is those who conform who enjoy the comforts and advantages. . . . The Master himself is persecuted for writing a novel on an inadmissible theme, Pilate and Christ. 'In this day and age?' Woland parodies official literary attitudes. 'Couldn't you have chosen another subject?' . . . The critics attack the Master unmercifully, even though his novel is not being published, and 'In literally every line of those articles one could detect a sense of falsity, of unease, in spite of their confident and threatening tone. I couldn't help feeling—and the conviction grew stronger the more I read— that the people writing those articles were not saying what they had really wanted to say and that *this* was the cause of their fury.' . . . Clearly, this was the same as had happened in Bulgakov's own life but here, in a perfect piece of wish-fulfilment, Margarita, as an invisible flying witch, is allowed to avenge the Master and wreak havoc on the flat of one of these critics.

For ultimately in this novel, justice triumphs, whether in Moscow or ancient Jerusalem. Ill-doers are punished, on a minor or major level according to their deserts. The greedy have their gains taken away from them. Fools and hypocrites are discomfitted. Yehuda of Kerioth and Baron Meigel are executed. Berlioz is given what he believes in—nothingness.

As opposed to all this, there stands, in Jerusalem, the eternal figure of Yeshua; in Moscow that of the Master, the eternal artist, master perhaps in the sense of a master in a masonic order, as Lakshin has suggested. Here we have the same problem that is the basis for Bulgakov's plays about Pushkin and Molière, the conflict between the artist and the apparatus of state. As the American scholar Ewa Thompson points out, the Master stands apart from the pettiness which rules other people's lives because he has no time for it, being totally involved in creativity; underlying it all is 'Bulgakov's awareness of the contest between grandeur and pettiness, the truth and the lie, strength and weakness. Because of his novel, the Master—like other sincere writers—is imprisoned, and then finds himself in an asylum. As a man he is broken, cowed by the system, without dreams or inspiration, but his novel, in which he has tried to write the truth as he understands it, exists. 'Manuscripts don't burn', . . . Woland says, probably the most famous line in the book. The novel is read, acted upon in the world beyond time. For art too is eternal, and in the same way Matthu Levi's parchment, which Yeshua wished him to burn, is saved and has become the basis for the gospels. . . . (pp. 266-68)

Much of the discussion of the book has naturally centred round the role of the devil. If one accepts that, in Moscow, he is the representative of the spiritual, is he in fact the best? How can a traditional spirit of darkness, of evil, be a power of good, except perhaps unwillingly, as indicated by the epigraph taken from Goethe? It is here perhaps that there is the greatest disagreement, between the critics who consider Woland as the traditional figure of evil (maintaining that he misleads the Master and Margarita, and that good is brought about in spite of him) and those who see him as acting essentially for the good of mankind and hence not in any way an evil spirit. Here the writer must state that he belongs decisively to those who would place the devil on the side of the angels. Elsewhere I have tried to show that Bulgakov's devil is closer to the Old Testament

concept of Satan rather than the New: the angel of God who tempts and tries man rather than the fallen angel concerned only with working evil [see Additional Bibliography]. (All early Jewish writings, in fact, point to the fundamental unity of God and the devil.) Thus Woland is not shown as opposed to God's will—indeed he carries it out by granting the Master peace as requested—but only as punishing, in most cases purely by temporary discomfiture, those who are guilty of greed, self-interest, and petty stupidity. Good and evil (light and darkness) as such are a fundamental philosophical problem in the novel. Woland indeed complains that Matthu Levi seems not to recognize the existence of shadows or evil, which are necessary to give meaning to light and good: 'What would your good be doing if there were no evil, and what would the earth look like if shadows disappeared from it?' . . . For in Bulgakov's world good and evil are seen as two sides of a single moral problem. Woland on the one hand and Yeshua on the other are similarly part of one unified spiritual view of life: their function may be different—Woland, we might note, is unable to forgive sin since 'Every department must take care of its own affairs' . . .—but the reality they represent is the same.

There are further implications in such a gnostic view of the world. After all, 'Shadows are cast by objects and people'— people who 'sin' because of their freedom gained by the 'original sin' of Adam and Eve in the Garden, when they ate of the tree of knowledge of good and evil. The more traditional view of the devil is that he too rebelled against God in much the same way, and hence becomes 'Prince of the World,' where innocence is rejected in favour of experience: at Satan's Ball Woland plays his more traditional role of master of the damned. (Thompson considers him as a devil in the romantic tradition of Lermontov.) Significantly, the most important source on which the book relies is the Faust tradition, with its obvious links to gnosticism. For Faust, of course, is the great rebel, standing for striving, rebellious man himself. Throughout the book there are constant references to Goethe's *Faust:* the names Woland and Margarita ('Gretchen'), the references to a poodle, to a homunculus, and the epigraph, to mention only a few. It is possible to equate Woland with Lucifer or Satan; Azazello with his servant Mephistopheles—with whom Margarita, usurping Faust's role, makes the pact: 'Really, I would pawn my soul to the devil to find out whether he is alive or dead'. . . . It has been suggested that Koroviev too is based on Faust, now in the service of the devil as his 'interpreter.' In the sense that the Master is a creative artist, man's closest attempt at rivalling God's powers, he too may be seen as another incarnation of Faust. And here we find the key to the whole book for, as we have seen, it is the individual non-conformists who are Bulgakov's heroes, those who rebel—whether against God or man. it is totally logical, then, that it should be the devil who aids the Master and Margarita, and at the end that they should be granted 'peace' and not 'light,' which in the traditional Christian sense they have not deserved, and probably would not desire. Healthy gnosticism, a total acceptance of good and evil as necessary for mankind, is seen as a positive force, as opposed to doctrinaire narrowmindedness; one only need have faith that 'everything will turn out right.' There can be little doubt that this reflects Bulgakov's own religious attitude, for he has no time for orthodoxy in any area of life: it is the thinking, struggling man whom he admires, and this book is ultimately an expression of his whole life. . . . (pp. 269-70)

A. Colin Wright, in his Mikhail Bulgakov: Life and Interpretations, *University of Toronto Press, 1978, 324 p.*

CAROL AVINS (essay date 1983)

[*In the following excerpt, Avins examines the way in which* The Master and Margarita *portrays Soviet society's exclusion of traditions and values that Bulgakov considered important ties to Russia's past and to Western civilization as a whole. For a Soviet critic's view of the value Bulgakov placed on prerevolutionary Russia, see the excerpt by Anatoly Al'tshuler (1968).*]

Lévi-Strauss defines a culture as "a fragment of humanity which . . . presents significant discontinuities in relation to the rest of humanity." Straightforward enough—but not as simple as it may appear. How are these demarcation lines established? A culture has natural borders, gradually worn in to the collective mind over time. Each successive political system and each successive political policy might be pictured as laying its own grid on top of it. These new lines may lie outside the culture's boundaries, thus allowing it to maintain its integrity and continue to develop; or they may cross into it, narrowing it and omitting parts of the culture that to some inhabitants, at least, are vital. (p. 184)

In *The Master and Margarita,* Soviet society appears rigidified: its boundaries are only growing narrower, eliminating more and more from the realm of the acceptable. Bulgakov is concerned with the values excluded from the system—with traditions of thought and behavior that should be at its core. Russia's natural borders are violated by the regime: it excludes principles essential to Russia's humanity. In order to demonstrate the culture's present narrowness, Bulgakov "violates" its borders in a literary sense, by thrusting two "foreign" elements into the Moscow of the 1930s. The society satirized in the novel can be schematized as a circle containing several smaller, intersecting circles: the theater world, the mental clinic, the literary establishment, and the other microcosms of Bulgakov's Moscow. Surrounding this large circle, and concentric with it, is a far larger one, which encompasses what is excluded from the system. From this "extrasystematic" realm come the devices that penetrate the closed system: the story of Pilate and Jesus, and the supernatural dimension of Woland. If the system thinks it has become insulated from judgment, exults Bulgakov's muse, it is in for a shock.

This now renowned novel, which lay unpublished for a quarter-century after the author's death, has so many riches that no brief treatment can mine them all. The scholar who said that after reading it one has the sensation of having lived through a festival put it well: one becomes engrossed in each segment, and on emerging one looks back at a brilliant whole.

The figure of Woland dominates the work; it is sometimes thought of as "that novel in which the Devil comes to Moscow." On a structural level, this punishing and redeeming Devil plays the role of a foreign specialist who brings with him the skills and insight of his foreign world. Beside him, other literary examples of the type pale in comparison. . . . As the novel unfolds, we increasingly see that Woland transcends not only borders but time and matter.

Woland is (among other things) a parody of the foreigner imported in the name of progress. He and his henchmen do not come to serve the aims of the state. One of the novel's many echoes of Goethe's *Faust* is the epigraph—Mephistopheles' self-introduction as a part of that force "which wills forever evil and works forever good." . . . "Progress," like "good" and "evil," is a relative term: one's judgment of Woland depends on where one stands. The reader who is averse to what he destroys, and who values what he saves, sees that he "wills evil" and "works good" with keen discretion.

Literary devils commonly adopt the guise of a stranger. Goethe's enters as a traveling scholar; Woland presents himself as a foreign professor (of black magic). Before he explains this, the uneasy editor and poet whom he accosts stab at clues to his identity. Each of them mentally runs through a range of possible nationalities, and the chapter contains a slew of synonyms for the word "foreigner." This visitor cannot be tucked into any of their categories. From the beginning, they have no doubt of Woland's absolute foreignness to the world of Moscow (or of his uncanny familiarity with it). Nor does the reader doubt the profound impact he will have on it. Woland loses no time in unpacking his foreign wares—his control over mere matter, his power to challenge the established order, and the story of Pontius Pilate and Jesus (called "Yeshua") that he begins at the end of chapter I.

This story, spread through the novel in four parts, seems at first as alien to Moscow as Woland himself. Its foreignness has several aspects. The most evident is spatial and temporal distance—the setting in ancient Jerusalem; it is also stylistically distinct from the Moscow chapters. This study of a ruler gripped by the insights of a daring philosopher and moved to repent for having condemned him is, however, closely connected to the novel's Moscow level. Its relevance (implied by its very inclusion in the novel) emerges gradually. It becomes apparent with each installment of the Jerusalem story that the issues it raises are hidden in Moscow. They are conspicuous by their absence. The exercise of political and moral power, the problems of conscience, of justice, of cowardice—these are important to Bulgakov's Moscow, but he develops them more explicitly in the Jerusalem setting.

What impact does this use of a separate context have? One effect is to provoke the question of how distant from the present this story actually is. The reader (who may be as stimulated after the first episode as Woland's Muscovite listeners) is induced to work out the story's significance. The issues must be pondered more deeply than might be the case if they arose only in the contemporary setting. Certainly the reworking of this fundamental episode of Christianity—with its central place in Russian culture and in Western civilization as a whole—gives the issues power and breadth. The biblical subject aside, the use of a separate context, whether one so loaded or not, has another effect. It suggests that this story could not be given a Soviet setting—that in the contemporary world of Moscow one cannot find a high official who is susceptible to a power higher than the state, who can be made to doubt his own authority, who is tormented by his conscience. Nor, we are prompted to think, can one find the belief in human goodness, the honesty, the healing presence of so penetrating a preacher. Given the system of which Bulgakov was writing, his use of external figures is a device essential to his purpose. The system allows inside itself nothing capable of successfully challenging it. "The foreign" is, therefore, needed to expose the native. First-century Jerusalem and Woland's supernatural must puncture the border of the Soviet present.

Within the Jerusalem level, foreignness . . . plays a role. Pontius Pilate and the Roman government he represents are a foreign presence in Jerusalem. It is emphasized that he detests the city in which he must serve, detests the populace crowding its streets. The cities of Jerusalem and Moscow are linked in the novel; thus one is led to find the Soviet state figuratively alien, and antipathetic to those under its control.

The Pilate-Yeshua story cannot be examined without discussing its status as a novel within the novel, and without turning to the character who is its author. The constraints on contemporary existence may be many, but this is, after all, a novel written in a Moscow basement apartment. Its creator is a Muscovite who, eschewing the now debased title of "writer," calls himself a "master." (By one of those unfortunate quirks of translation, the English word, in addition to conveying the Russian meaning of "expert artisan," adds the misleading connotations of ownership and domination.) The Master's writing is not an isolated element of the book. At the end his manuscript merges with the larger novel, and we come to see that the whole book, not just the novel within it, is the work of the Master—and that his identity is tied to Bulgakov's. Within the system, then, it *is* possible to generate an independent, heretical work of art. But to do so requires an exceptional individual and exceptional circumstances. The Master can partially transcend his environment through chance—a winning lottery ticket that allows him to work for himself—and through the loving dedication of Margarita. But while he can thrive for long enough to write the novel, the system drives him to destroy it—to burn it in a fit of despair (as Bulgakov himself did with part of *The Master and Margarita*). Not only could the manuscript not survive in that environment: its author could not either. Broken by the assault of the critics—and by his brief imprisonment, due to an informant who wants his apartment—the Master withdraws to a mental clinic. A figure fundamental to Bulgakov's system of values finds himself unable to exist within society. Recall the "cornerstone" metaphor. The individual who raises challenging issues is pressured out of society, its present cornerstone—its power structure and dominant values—rejecting what he represents.

The Master is returned to his love, and the novel restored to life, by Woland. His intervention is also needed to bring the manuscript to Bulgakov's reader. (Its first part is told by the intruder Woland; the next is dreamed by Bezdomny after meeting Woland and the Master; the rest is read by Margarita from the pages Woland has reconstituted from ashes.) When the lovers find themselves again in the beloved basement, the Master is skeptical about the forces that have brought them there. Encouraged by Margarita, he acknowledges that no earthly force could be responsible—that such "ravaged" people as they could expect salvation only from the supernatural. The word "supernatural" in Russian is *potustoronnii*; etymologically it refers to something from "the other side." Only an alien from the "outer circle" surrounding the system can overcome the system's power. But Bulgakov's supernatural crew do not substantially change the system: they simply wreak a little havoc and attack a few objectionable targets. There is no question of destroying Moscow's foundations. The system stands, and the hero and heroine survive it only by departing their earthly lives and being spirited away to the "eternal refuge" made possible by Woland and Yeshua.

By training, the Master is a historian and translator. He tells Ivan when they meet in the asylum that he knows five languages: English, French, German, Latin, Greek, and a little Italian. He is connected to the intellectual heritage Russia shares with Europe—and that heritage is obviously important to Bulgakov. The author's use of the Bible and of Goethe are indications of his tie to the cultural past and of his belief in the absence of cultural walls. The home to which Woland directs the two lovers at the end is another. In Woland's description it seems a soft-toned scene from an old book, a setting of no specific time or place. "Oh, thrice romantic master," he per-

suades, "wouldn't you like to stroll with your love under newly blossoming cherry trees in the daytime, and listen to Schubert in the evening? Won't you enjoy writing by candlelight with a goose quill? Don't you want, like Faust, to sit over a retort in the hope that you'll succeed in fashioning a new homunculus?" Margarita says of their future home as they approach it: "I know that in the evening people will come to see you, people you care for, who interest you, who will not upset you." While this wholly untroubled haven is an idyllic realm, the eternal home embodies eternal values achievable on earth: the freedom to strive in one's own way, to live in harmony among one's friends. These values are absent from the society depicted in the novel—made "discontinuous" with it, to use Lévi-Strauss's term. The system's boundaries have been falsely drawn: too much that is human is on the other side.

What is involved here is partly a loss of contact with the moral and intellectual heritage of the past. Not of the national past alone, but of the open-bordered past that holds Western civilization's experience. (Hence the Master's training in history and languages, and the fact that Ivan, his partly comprehending disciple, becomes a professor of history and philosophy.) The contemporary West is out of sight, peripheral to Bulgakov's concerns in this novel. When Moscow becomes inhospitable terrain for the Master and Margarita, their only exit point is an intangible border that lies "up," not westward. One of the issues implicit in the novel is how Russia can be native space again, a place in which individuals can thrive. Barring that, there is no satisfactory way of living—except through the sort of transcendence which Bulgakov (with evident pleasure) creates for his protagonists. (pp. 185-89)

> Carol Avins, "Violating Russia's Borders," in her Border Crossings: The West and Russian Identity in Soviet Literature, 1917-1934, *University of California Press, 1983, pp. 184-90.*

ELLENDEA PROFFER (essay date 1984)

[*Proffer's* Bulgakov: Life and Work *is the most extensive biographical and critical study of the author. In the following excerpt from that study's concluding chapter, entitled "The World According to Bulgakov," Proffer provides a comprehensive analysis of the themes, motifs, and character types appearing throughout Bulgakov's works.*]

At first glance Bulgakov's literary world appears extremely diverse, encompassing as it does Jerusalem at the time of Pilate, Louis XIV's France, and Stalin's Moscow. However the same characters and themes persist from the earliest works to the last, although they undergo various transformations. (pp. 567-68)

Bulgakov's literary world is interesting for what it lacks. There are few detailed descriptions of a given character's background, of nature, or of love; and those seeking examples of the "Russian soul" style of self-revelation would be greatly disappointed. Traditionally Russian literature is known for a certain lethargy of plot, usually more than made up for by descriptive and psychological intensity. Bulgakov, however, is by nature inclined toward action, suspense, and an economy of means, things more typical of Pushkin than any other Russian prose writer. Bulgakov's irony often leads to ambiguity and deliberate mystery—qualities not typical of Russian writing in general. Bulgakov's world is complex, but an overview of his body of work reveals many unexpected points of intersection.

In this world weather is an active plot element—commenting, destroying, changing the outcome of events. Weather extends

Gravesite of Bulgakov and his wife Elena Sergeevna Bulgakov in the cherry garden of the Novodevichy Monastery in Moscow. Courtesy of Ardis Publishers.

across time and space: the heat that torments Pilate in Jerusalem also torments Khludov in Constantinople 2000 years later. The sudden, unseasonal frost which destroys the reptiles in *The Fatal Eggs* also allows the Bolsheviks to cross the frozen river in *Flight,* thus destroying the White army. (p. 569)

Like weather, time of year is significant. *White Guard* is set around Christmas time, as are so many of the Civil War stories; many of the comedies take place in the spring, especially the month of May, which is also the time of *The Master and Margarita,* which is simultaneously set during Easter, Passover and the Ball of the Spring Full Moon. Numbers and dates are often fatidic: "apartment 50" and "the night of the third" come up with regularity. The best example, however, is the number of Petliura's cell—999, the number of the beast, the anti-Christ.

Physically, Bulgakov's world is crowded. The only major character who does not live in an apartment is Margarita, an indication of how the housing shortage influences art. The location for most of the action in Bulgakov's plays and prose is an apartment, laboratory or, less often, a theater. The characters are not especially drawn to nature, and neither is their creator—a relatively rare thing among Russian writers. Bulgakov was a lover of cities, and the evocations of Kiev, Moscow and Jerusalem are his equivalent of the typical Russian nature description. However, his descriptions are functional, and rarely reflect a simple desire to describe. (p. 571)

Bulgakov's motifs are structured musically, rather than logically. This ostinato effect is used most interestingly in *The Master and Margarita,* but it is present in the earliest works. While one may profitably trace a particular motif, such as roses, colors or poison through one novel, one may also trace the evolution of a motif through the works as a whole. An example of this sort is the mention of the cavalryman brother in "The Red Crown." In *White Guard* we find the *Brockhaus-Efron Encyclopedia* compared to a row of black and gold cavalryman, and Nai-Turs is described as a black cavalryman in a dream. In *The Life of Molière* the writer dies and sees a cavalier in black, wiping blood from his head, just like the brother in "The Red Crown." In *The Master and Margarita* we find a number of cavalrymen: there is Pilate himself, often described and with the epithet "cavalryman" (*vsadnik*), as well as Woland and his band, all of whom, significantly, ride away to the abyss. The black rider (and the word is always the same in Russian) is Bulgakov's equivalent of Chekhov's Black Monk: he is death itself. (pp. 572-73)

Violence and disease are present in his writing to a greater degree than one would expect. Hospitals and operating tables wind through many works: all the bloody details are provided in *Notes of a Young Doctor, Heart of a Dog,* and *The Master and Margarita.* The disease most often mentioned is syphilis. Rusakov is treated for it in *White Guard;* Pushkin's letter accuses his rival of having it; Molière dies playing in *Le Malade imaginaire* to lines about venereologists—lines written by Bulgakov, a former venereologist.

However, physical disease is not as important as mental disease. The narrator of "The Red Crown," Rusakov in *The White Guard,* Dymogatsky in *The Crimson Island,* Maxudov in *Theatrical Novel*—all of these characters have nervous breakdowns. In *The Master and Margarita* the illnesses multiply. The Master has a breakdown, Pilate has terrible migraines, and almost everyone else in the work ends up in Stravinsky's clinic, driven insane by the tricks of Woland's band.

Violence is also a prominent feature of this world. The most purely terrifying violence is the first scene of the giant reptiles eating the characters in *The Fatal Eggs.* In *White Guard, Flight* and the Civil War stories there are many horrible tortures and deaths, but the effect is less shocking since these are works about war. The violent moments in *The Master and Margarita,* however, are more cruel. No rhetoric softens the death of Berlioz, and the description of his body lying on *three* tables is worse than Nikolka's visit to the morgue in *White Guard,* because it is so unexpected in what at first seems to be a comic novel. The violent acts are scattered through the novel and have the effect of preventing the reader from taking the material too lightly. The use of violence here cannot be explained as merely a former doctor's inclination to naturalistic detail. It is possible to explain it as an expression of implacable anger, anger that the world is a cruel place. Woland's globe shows the dark side of existence, a mother and child burning to death. But, oddly, there are only two real moments of violent revenge in the novel, one the murder of Iuda, the other the execution of the spy, Baron Maigel. A form of execution is reserved for informers. (pp. 573-74)

Bulgakov's world is inhabited by literally thousands of minor characters, ranging from the Syrian cavalry commander who leads his men to Golgotha to the milk-maid Yavdokha of *White Guard.* These minor characters are individualized briefly, but with great skill, and are varied. When one examines the major characters, however, it becomes evident that, like most writers, Bulgakov was drawn to a limited number of basic characters, his own archetypes. Bulgakov changed the characters from work to work more than many writers did, but the archetype is still visible.

In some cases the change is a physical one which is misleading: the Figaro-like Shervinsky of *Days of the Turbins* has much in common with the cat Begemot. The Shervinsky line is a prolific one: Ametistov, Miloslavsky and Kiri-Kuki are his direct descendants, and Charnota and Koroviev have some of his traits as well. These characters share Shervinsky's exuberance and some of his linguistic habits. When Shervinsky lies, he likes to add that someone "shed tears." His rascal relations preface lies with lines such as "You're just going to sob." Begemot's vanity, as well as his lies, link him to Shervinsky; both of them are inflamed by perfectly true implications that they are lying or cheating. Bulgakov liked contrasting the vulgar with the refined—there are many such pairs: Persikov/Rokk, Preobrazhensky/Sharikov, Radamanov/Miloslavsky.

Where there is a rascal figure there is also the officious Building Manager. He is ubiquitous, and is often connected with the theme of money, which he usually takes in the form of bribes and then hoards. He is present in the early feuilletons and is featured prominently in *Zoya's Apartment, Ivan Vasilievich* and *Bliss.* His name changes, but his personality remains the same—obnoxious. The last in this line is the ill-fated Nikanor Iva-

novich in *The Master and Margarita* who gets caught for taking a bribe, just as his predecessor in *Zoya's Apartment* did. This character is always comic, but he is far from negligible. Bulgakov's letters and early feuilletons portray this figure as an unbearable combination of the spy and concierge. The building managers made it their business to monitor both the political and private lives of the inhabitants of their buildings. For Bulgakov the building manager was the start of the police state on the lowest level. A character like the building manager appears more comic and less realistic as he progresses through the works. The further away Bulgakov got in time and geography from that first "cursed apartment" in Moscow, the more comic the memory became. A far more appealing archetype is the pert maid, a line which starts with Anyuta in *White Guard* and ends with Margarita's Natasha. The maids are always repulsing unwanted advances with sarcastic comments reminiscent of Molière's characters. There is little development of these characters from work to work, although they may reveal slightly different facets. It is otherwise with the serious characters.

Grading from the comic to the serious are the characters who may be grouped under the label "naif." These characters start out as naive observers or reflectors, but they are often educated by events. The naif is funny and he engages our sympathy. His main characteristic is his youthful idealism, often accompanied by immaturity, Lariosik and Nikolka of *White Guard* and *Days of the Turbins* are good examples of this type. His next appearance is in *Flight,* in the person of Golubkov, who has many traits of the naif type, but is also related, as we shall see, to the weak intellectual line. Other main characters who share the characteristics of the naif are Dymogatsky of *The Crimson Island* and Maxudov of *Theatrical Novel,* both inexperienced beginners who are initiated into the world of the theater. Another good example of this type is Bitkov, the minor spy in *Last Days.* This line ends with the Master's disciple, Ivan Bezdomny, a naif who is thoroughly changed by his experiences. The naif changed from work to work much more than any of the purely comic figures did, probably because the comic characters are portrayed externally, while the naif is given more dimensions.

The naif is usually found admiring a man of action. Lariosik admires Myshlaevsky, just as Golubkov admires General Charnota. Other men of action are Shpolyansky of *White Guard* and Tokhonga of *The Crimson Island.* Sometimes the man of action is caught in a disastrous situation: Khludov and Pilate began as men of action, but events transform them into guilt-ridden sufferers. Charnota, however, is a more typical example. In general, the men of action are not introspective intellectuals—they are romantic figures who, if they fail, fail gallantly.

Equally gallant are the main female characters. The differences among the female characters are more subtle than those among the masculine ones. Elena of *White Guard* is the first important female figure. She is both home-maker and love object (something that often goes together in this world). She prays for a miracle to save Alexei, and her prayer is answered. Although Elena takes care of everyone, she is not a dominating woman. The feminine characters are often easily persuaded: Elena's resolve to resist Shervinsky quickly fades, as does Armande's resolve to resist Moirron in *Molière* and Natasha's to resist d'Anthès in *Last Days.* But the similarities among these women are superficial. Natasha and Armande belong to the category of beautiful women who are betrayers. Serafima of *Flight* is at first a victim, weak from her sickness, but she does summon up enough strength to castigate Khludov, and it is she, not Golubkov, who resists interrogation and breaks a window to get help. Most of Bulgakov's major women characters are strong and decisive, as opposed to the men, a typical situation for Russian literature. There is a feminine side to Bulgakov's writing, a kind of delicacy and subtlety, and there is no doubt that throughout his life his main confidantes were women rather than men. The energy of the female characters is sometimes misused; a sub-category is the adventuress, as exemplified by Zoya of *Zoya's Apartment* and Lyuska of *Flight*. They both do what must be done to survive, whether it is managing a bordello or becoming a prostitute. The men in their lives, however, show weakness when subjected to pressure. Later in Bulgakov's works these two types, the gallant good woman and the adventuress, are merged. Aurora of *Bliss* is far nicer than Zoya, but has the same sort of wild streak, and is close to the character of Margarita herself. Margarita is the ultimate combination: home-maker, mistress, and, like Zoya, a witch. Like Aurora, Margarita wants to taste danger, and her passion for anyone who does things in a "first-rate" way is one which both Aurora and Lyuska share. These two types, unlike the beautiful betrayers, often save their men, like the first woman-saviour to appear in Bulgakov's world, the mysterious Julia Reiss of *White Guard*. Finally, there is Margarita, who makes a pact with the devil to save her lover.

Men who lack the love of women are seen to lack humanity. Here the archetype is that of the brilliant scientist—Persikov, Preobrazhensky, and Efrosimov, of *The Fatal Eggs*, *Heart of a Dog* and *Adam and Eve*, respectively—who are absorbed only in their work. Interestingly, Efrosimov develops beyond his predecessors and finally falls in love, which, of course, saves him.

At first glance, one might assume that the doctors who people this world are related to the scientist archetype, but this is only true at times. The doctors are more interesting than the scientists, as well as more human. The insecure young doctor of *Notes of a Young Doctor* is an early relative of the venereologist Alexei Turbin. Preobrazhensky, a far more developed character than Persikov, shares much with *The Master and Margarita*'s Stravinsky. The doctor line is naturally intertwined with the themes of death and disease, but an interesting evolution occurs over time in these works. At first, in *Notes of a Young Doctor*, doctors are deeply respected, and their belief that death is the enemy to be conquered at all costs is shown favorably. But by the time of *The Master and Margarita* doctors are no longer such glamorous, powerful figures. Stravinsky is intelligent, but he is wrong in all of his diagnoses. As for death, it is no longer an enemy—it is a longed-for release.

One of the most important archetypes in Bulgakov's works is the weak intellectual, the character who is called a "rag" of a man (*triapka*). These characters may be essentially pitiful, like Korotkov in "Diaboliad," or intelligent, like Alexei in *White Guard;* but they are unable to deal effectively with their problems, and despise themselves for their weakness, whatever form it may take. Alexei hates Talberg, but he kisses him good-bye anyway. In *Flight,* Golubkov is completely unable to protect the woman he loves. Dymogatsky, one of many neurotic artist characters, has a breakdown when he can no longer bear the situation he is in, just as *Theatrical Novel*'s Maxudov is so weak he is driven to suicide. The aging Molière is too weak to fight any more, and despises himself for having grovelled before the king. These characers may have other, stronger

sides, but what matters is how they perceive themselves. The intellectual heroes of Bulgakov's Civil War stories are horrified by their own impotence in the face of violence, but an objective analysis shows that they could have done nothing to help anyway. This, however, does not matter to the characters: they curse themselves for having failed to live up to their own expectations. This type begins as the doctor of the early works, and is gradually transformed into an artist. The last example of this type is the Master, who combines characteristics of the early impotent intellectuals with those of the writers, especially Dymogatsky and Maxudov.

Most of Bulgakov's heroes (whether artists or the analogue of the artist, the scientist) do not triumph. In certain ways Yeshua himself fits into this category—he is an artist in that his words influence Matvei, and a doctor in that he heals Pilate. Like the Jews of the early stories, he is a victim, first beaten by the centurion, then executed; and, like the intellectuals, he shows no defiance in the face of force. After Krysoboi beats him he is very careful about how he addresses Pilate: he is afraid.

But Pilate is not the highest representative of evil in Bulgakov's world. There is a precise hierarchy. The immediate enemy of the artist or the scientist is the interfering fanatic who is doing something "for the good of the state," or is simply obsessed by an idea. The fanatics are oppressors, from Rokk (*The Fatal Eggs*) to Afrikan (*Flight*) to Charron (*Molière*) to Savvich (*Bliss*) to Kaifa. (pp. 574-78)

The despots and fanatics are helped by the betrayers, who are distinguished from the spies in that they are not professional: Moirron turns on his beloved Molière, Mogarych on his friend the Master. Interestingly, these characters are quite different from each other, and do not seem to be related to a single archetype. The spies and policemen, however, are a different matter. The betrayers report to the heads of the secret police, whose names may be Tikhi, Likki, Charron, Benckendorff or Aphranius. But there are many professional spies as well: Bitkov, Bogomazov, Baron Maigel, and Iuda.

Existing on another plane are the characters perceived as magical and mysterious by those around them: Shpolyansky, Zoya, Rudolfi, and Woland. These figures have some void at the center which makes their actions both inexplicable and fateful. Like the comic characters, these magical beings are described externally; we have no sense of their inner life.

Just as Bulgakov was attracted to a certain set of characters, he was also attracted to a certain set of situations. The clearest instance of this, as has been noted many times in this work, is the weakness of a man in the face of force, cowardice punished by madness and terrible guilt. In retrospect, Bulgakov included an important clue to his own thinking in the quote he chose from Gassendi for his biography of Molière: "commit no crimes, my children, and you shall feel neither repentance nor regret, and only these make men unhappy.' The main ethical dilemma which causes Bulgakov's heroes to suffer is one which in certain ways seems central to his century. (pp. 579-80)

The movement in Bulgakov's works as an entity is away from cruel, solitary suffering to final forgiveness. The narrator in "The Red Crown" has no hope of finding peace, nor has Alexei Turbin in *White Guard,* but Khludov suffers and begins expiation of his sins. It is only in *The Master and Margarita* that a character finally receives absolution after expiation—Pilate is finally freed from his self-torture. Bulgakov's suffering characters no longer expect happiness, they desire only peace—as Pushkin wrote, there is no happiness, but there is liberty and peace. Khludov desires nothing more than peace, nor does Efrosimov in **Adam and Eve** (who equates it with Switzerland, a region which was hardly peaceful for the imprisoned Pilate). But peace, as in the play about Pushkin, is often seen as an undesirable thing, a settling for the status quo. The Master wants only peace because he is too weak to fight for light. (pp. 580-81)

As a writer, Bulgakov was attracted to major themes: the nature of justice as administered by both the worthy and the cruel; the meaning of death; and the nature of a man's social contract with his own society. This last is very important: underneath the brightly colored, imaginative and ironic style are the observations of a social moralist. Bulgakov referred to himself as a mystical writer, but he is only mystical in that he believes there is more to the world than common sense can explain, and nowhere is this more apparent than in the nature of artistic talent. But Bulgakov does not really write as a mystic. He describes Yeshua and his character, not God and his divinity. This world is moved by the desire for justice on earth, and his most powerful writing has its source in the frustration of that desire. (p. 582)

Ellendea Proffer, in her Bulgakov: Life and Work, *Ardis, 1984, 670 p.*

ADDITIONAL BIBLIOGRAPHY

Bagby, Lewis. "Eternal Themes in Mixail Bulgakov's *The Master and Margarita*." *The International Fiction Review* 1, No. 1 (January 1974): 27-31.
　　Examines the way in which Bulgakov uses style and characterization to convey his philosophical views.

Beajour, Elizabeth Klosty. "The Use of Witches in Fedin and Bulgakov." *Slavic Review* 33, No. 4 (December 1974): 695-707.*
　　Argues that the devil in *The Master and Margarita* is a source of the energy of life, while the witch Margarita is a healing, nurturing force.

Beatie, Bruce A., and Powell, Phyllis W. "Story and Symbol: Notes Toward a Structural Analysis of Bulgakov's *The Master and Margarita*." *Russian Literature Triquarterly*, No. 15 (Spring 1978): 219-51.
　　Detailed analysis of the temporal structure and recurring verbal patterns in *The Master and Margarita*.

Belozerskaya-Bulgakova, Lyubov. *My Life with Mikhail Bulgakov*. Ann Arbor: Ardis, 1983, 136 p.
　　Personal account by Bulgakov's second wife.

Bethea, David M. "History as Hippodrome: The Apocalyptic Horse and Rider in *The Master and Margarita*." *The Russian Review* 41, No. 4 (October 1982): 373-99.
　　Apocalyptic imagery in *The Master and Margarita* as a key to the novel's themes of imagination, justice, and mystery.

Block, Anita. "Contemporary Drama of a New Social Order: Plays of Soviet Russia." In her *The Changing World in Plays and Theater*, pp. 352-411. Boston: Little, Brown and Co., 1939.*
　　Plot summary of *Days of the Turbins*, which Block calls "one of the least patterned and most literary of the Soviet plays."

Chudakova, M. "*The Master and Margarita*: The Development of a Novel." *Russian Literature Triquarterly*, No. 15 (Spring 1978): 177-209.
　　Follows Bulgakov's composition of *The Master and Margarita* over a twelve-year period.

Ericson, Edward E., Jr. "The Satanic Incarnation: Parody in Bulgakov's *The Master and Margarita*." *The Russian Review* 33, No. 1 (January 1974): 20-36.
　　Demonstrates how events and characters in *The Master and Margarita* can be seen as parodies of those in the Christian tradition.

Ginsburg, Mirra. Preface to *The Life of Monsieur de Molière*, by Mikhail Bulgakov, translated by Mirra Ginsburg, pp. vii-xii. New York: Funk & Wagnalls, 1970.
　　Biography and critical comment emphasizing Bulgakov's admiration for his subject and noting parallels between the personalities and careers of the two men.

Glenny, Michael. "About Mikhail Bulgakov, His Novel, the Moscow Art Theater, Stanislavski." In *Black Snow: A Theatrical Novel*, by Mikhail Bulgakov, translated by Michael Glenny, pp. 5-12. New York: Simon and Schuster, 1967.
　　Bulgakov's relationship with the Moscow Art Theater as the source of his novel *Black Snow*.

————. Introduction to *The Heart of a Dog*, by Mikhail Bulgakov, translated by Michael Glenny, pp. v-ix. New York: Harcourt, Brace & World, 1968.
　　Biographical and critical essay presenting *The Heart of a Dog* as a parable of the Russian Revolution.

Goscilo, Helena. "Point of View in Bulgakov's *Heart of a Dog*." *Russian Literature Triquarterly*, No. 15 (Spring 1978): 281-91.
　　Examines the four narrative viewpoints in *The Heart of a Dog* and the way shifting points of view affect the story.

Hart, Pierre R. "*The Master and Margarita* as Creative Process." *Modern Fiction Studies* 19, No. 2 (Summer 1973): 169-78.
　　Views *The Master and Margarita* as a commentary on the creative process. Hart maintains that the character of Ivan Bezdomny is necessary to the creation of the Christ-Pilate tale, and speculates that the Master himself may be a product of Ivan's imagination.

Hatfield, Henry. "The Walpurgis Night: Theme and Variations." *Journal of European Studies* 13, Nos. 49/50 (March/June 1983): 56-74.*
　　Examines Bulgakov's largely humorous treatment of Walpurgis Night, or the Witches' Sabbath, in *The Master and Margarita*.

Hoisington, Sona. "Fairy-tale Elements in Bulgakov's *The Master and Margarita*." *Slavic and East European Journal* 25, No. 2 (Summer 1981): 44-55.
　　Analyzes the fairy-tale elements in *The Master and Margarita* and concludes that Bulgakov has chosen the perfect form in which to express his belief in an absolute morality and the magic power of art.

Lakshin, Vladimir. "The Lessons of Bulgakov." *Russian Literature Triquarterly*, No. 15 (Spring 1978): 167-75.
　　Appreciation of the "freedom of spirit" in Bulgakov's life and works. Lakshin writes that "Bulgakov teaches his reader courage, human worth and sincerity; he teaches a noble attitude toward the artist's duty and a respect for one's native language."

Lowe, David. "Bulgakov and Dostoevsky: A Tale of Two Ivans." *Russian Literature Triquarterly*, No. 15 (Spring 1978): 253-62.*
　　Maintains that Bulgakov was strongly influenced by Fedor Dostoevsky's *The Brothers Karamazov* in writing *The Master and Margarita*, and demonstrates parallels between the two novels.

Mahlow, Elena N. *Bulgakov's 'The Master and Margarita': The Text as Cipher*. New York: Vantage Press, 1975, 202 p.
　　Detailed examination of *The Master and Margarita* as an allegory on the Russian Revolution and the Soviet system, equating each major and minor character with a Soviet counterpart.

McLaughlin, Sigrid. "Structure and Meaning in Bulgakov's *The Fatal Eggs*." *Russian Literature Triquarterly*, No. 15 (Spring 1978): 263-79.
　　Demonstrates the way in which Bulgakov uses narrative structure and technique to blend social satire with a moral and philosophical statement in *The Fatal Eggs*.

Milne, Lesley. *The Master and Margarita: A Comedy of Victory.* Birmingham, England: Department of Russian Langauge & Literature, University of Birmingham, 1977, 55 p.

A close examination of the use in *The Master and Margarita* of the medieval figura, a method by which certain "figures" or "types" used in a work relate the parts to one another and to the structure as a whole, creating order and unity in a work made up of several separate narratives.

Nekrasov, Victor. "Epilogue: The House of the Turbins." In *The White Guard,* by Mikhail Bulgakov, translated by Michael Glenny, pp. 301-20. New York: McGraw-Hill Book Co., 1971.

Personal recollection of the author's discovery of the house in which the (fictional) Turbin family and the (actual) Bulgakov family lived.

Proffer, Ellendea. "Bulgakov's *The Master and Margarita:* Genre and Motif." *Canadian Slavic Studies* 3, No. 4 (Winter 1969): 615-28.

Demonstrates the ways in which *The Master and Margarita* conforms to the genre of Menippean satire, and traces Bulgakov's use of repeated images—particularly the sun and the moon—to emphasize parallels between the novel's separate narratives. For Proffer's discussion of aspects of *The Master and Margarita* that are not characteristic of Menippean satire, see Additional Bibliography (1973).

————. Introduction to *The Early Plays of Mikhail Bulgakov,* by Mikhail Bulgakov, edited by Ellendea Proffer, translated by Carl R. Proffer and Ellendea Proffer, pp. xi-xxvii. Bloomington: Indiana University Press, 1972.

Biographical essay.

————. "On *The Master and Margarita.*" *Russian Literature Triquarterly,* No. 6 (Spring 1973): 533-65.

Presents aspects of *The Master and Margarita* that are not characteristic of Menippean satire, and discusses the novel's recurring motifs.

————. *An International Bibliography of Works by and about Mikhail Bulgakov.* Ann Arbor, Mich.: Ardis, 1976, 133 p.

Most comprehensive bibliography; also reproduces several photographs of Bulgakov.

————. *A Pictorial Biography of Mikhail Bulgakov.* Ann Arbor, Mich.: Ardis, 1984, 151 p.

Includes photographs of Bulgakov's contemporaries, Moscow, Kiev, and scenes from his plays, with quotes from those who knew him and selections from his works in both Russian and English.

Rydel, Christine. "Bulgakov and H. G. Wells." *Russian Literature Triquarterly,* No. 15 (Spring 1978): 293-311.*

Sketches resemblances between the works of Bulgakov and those of H. G. Wells.

Sharrat, Barbara Kenja. "*Flight:* A Symphonic Play." *Canadian Slavonic Papers* XIV, No. 1 (1972): 76-86.

Details the "symphonic" aspects of *Flight;* that is, the careful orchestration of symbols, images, language, and other narrative elements.

Stenbock-Fermor, Elisabeth. "Bulgakov's *The Master and Margarita* and Goethe's *Faust.*" *The Slavic and East European Journal* XIII, No. 3 (1969): 309-25.*

Presents a study of the allusions and parallels to Johann Wolfgang von Goethe's *Faust* in *The Master and Margarita* as a means of better understanding Bulgakov's novel.

Wright, A. C. "Satan in Moscow: An Approach to Bulgakov's *The Master and Margarita.*" *Publications of the Modern Language Association of America* 88, No. 5 (October 1973): 1162-72.*

Examines the satanic elements and the story of Pilate and Christ in *The Master and Margarita* in relation to the *Bible,* Johann Wolfgang von Goethe's *Faust,* and popular tradition.

Wright, A. Colin. "Mikhail Bulgakov's Developing World View." *Canadian American Slavic Studies* 15, Nos. 2-3 (Summer-Fall 1981): 151-66.

Follows the development of Bulgakov's personal philosophy as affected by events in his life and as reflected in his works, from his earliest writings through *The Master and Margarita.*

(Sidonie-Gabrielle) Colette

1873-1954

French novelist, short story writer, and journalist.

The following entry presents criticism of recent English translations of Colette's selected letters and collected stories. For a complete discussion of Colette's career, see *TCLC*, Volumes 1 and 5.

Colette is recognized as one of France's leading twentieth-century novelists. Critics praise her warm, subjective style, her keen observation of nature, and the lyrical beauty of her prose. The central theme in much of her work is the reconciliation of women's struggle for independence with the insistent demands of physical passion. Many of her characters yearn to abandon the conflicts of adult life to return to the protected innocence of childhood.

The vicissitudes of Colette's life are mirrored in her novels and short stories. She spent an idyllic childhood in the region of Burgundy, where her mother instilled in her a lifelong love for the countryside. At the age of twenty she married a much older man, Henry Gouthier-Villars, a hack writer who introduced her to the enervating decadence of the Paris demimonde. Under her husband's insistence she began to record her memories of her childhood and school days. The results were the "Claudine" series. The first, *Claudine à l'école (Claudine at School)*, which her husband published under his pen name, "Willy," enjoyed tremendous popular success. After divorcing Gouthier-Villars, Colette embarked on a career as a music hall dancer and mime. During her second marriage, she devoted her full energies to her literary career, firmly establishing herself in French letters. Having gained the respect of her contemporaries, she was elected to the prestigious Académie Royale Belge and Académie Goncourt.

Critics generally divide Colette's work into four phases: the "Claudine" novels; novels dealing with life in the theater; novels of love; and, written during the later part of her career, her touching and sensitive reminiscences of her youth and family. Although many critics consider the "Claudine" novels to be little better than pot-boilers, they still praise her fluid prose style and sensitive portrayal of character. Her work of this period also reveals her special affinity to nature and an almost mystic understanding of animals. After the "Claudine" novels, Colette abandoned the cheap titillation Gouthier-Villars had encouraged and wrote *La vagabonde (The Vagabond)*, a novel that skillfully evokes the seedy atmosphere of backstage life, and the spiritual torment of a young actress's search for dignity and self-reliance. All of the novels of the subsequent theatrical cycle explore the problems inherent in a woman's pursuit of self-realization.

The subject of Colette's third phase is love and its politics. Thus in *Chéri (Chéri)* and *La fin de Chéri (The Last of Chéri)*, considered the masterpieces of this period, Colette contrasts the dissolution of a pampered young gigolo, Chéri, with the growth and self-acceptance of his lover, Léa, a rich middle-aged cocotte. In *The Last of Chéri*, Cheri's inability to cope with the responsibilities of life away from Léa leads to his nihilism and suicide, while Léa's withdrawal from men and sex results in deep internal peace. As if to echo the serenity

Léa found late in life, Colette became increasingly concerned with reenacting scenes from her childhood. Many critics judge the novels of this, her last period, to be her finest achievements. In her rapturous descriptions of plants and animals in *La Maison de Claudine (My Mother's House)*, and in her loving portrait of her mother in *Sido (Sido)*, Colette idealizes childhood and nature, which to her represent primordial innocence and purity.

Although some critics regard her work as naive and sentimental, the excellence of her style, her fresh use of metaphor, and her intensity of feeling have earned Colette an esteemed place in French literature.

(See also *Contemporary Authors*, Vol. 104.)

PRINCIPAL WORKS

Claudine à l'école (novel) 1900
  [*Claudine at School*, 1930]
Claudine à Paris (novel) 1901
  [*Claudine in Paris*, 1958]
Claudine en ménage (novel) 1902
  [*The Indulgent Husband*, 1935; also published as *Claudine Married*, 1960]

Claudine s'en va (novel) 1903
  [*The Innocent Wife*, 1934; also published as *Claudine and Annie*, 1962]
L'ingénue libertine (novel) 1909
  [*The Gentle Libertine*, 1931; also published as *The Innocent Libertine*, 1961]
La vagabonde (novel) 1910
  [*The Vagabond*, 1954]
L'entrave (novel) 1913
  [*Recaptured*, 1931; also published as *The Shackle*, 1964]
Mitsou (novel) 1919
  [*Mitsou*, 1930]
Chéri (novel) 1920
  [*Chéri*, 1929]
La maison de Claudine (novel) 1922
  [*My Mother's House*, 1953]
La fin de Chéri (novel) 1926
  [*The Last of Chéri*, 1932]
La naissance du jour (novel) 1928
  [*Break of Day*, 1961]
La seconde (novel) 1929
  [*The Other One*, 1931]
Sido (novel) 1929
  [*Sido*, 1953]
La chatte (novel) 1933
  [*The Cat*, 1936]
Duo (novel) 1934
  [*Duo*, 1935; also published as *The Married Lover*, 1935]
Gigi (novel) 1944
  [*Gigi*, 1952]
Le fanal bleu (diaries) 1949
  [*The Blue Lantern*, 1963]
Earthly Paradise (autobiographical writings) 1966
Letters from Colette (letters) 1980
The Collected Stories of Colette (short stories) 1983

ROBERT PHELPS (essay date 1979)

[*Phelps is an American novelist, literary critic, and editor who has worked extensively on the writings of Colette. His editions of her work include* Earthly Paradise: Colette's Autobiography Drawn from the Writings of Her Lifetime *(1966)*, Letters from Colette *(1980), and* The Collected Stories of Colette *(1983). In the following excerpt from his introduction to her letters, he states that his intention when editing the letters was not to be definitive, but to show the vitality and diversity of Colette's activities and interests through her correspondence.*]

A quarter of a century after her death in 1954, Colette continues to emerge not only as the widely admired author of *Chéri, Gigi,* and *La Vagabonde,* and as one of the subtlest stylists ever to explore the resources of the French language, but as a savory, even fierce personality in her own right. As her autobiographical *Earthly Paradise* made clear, Colette is her own most memorable character, a sort of twentieth-century earth goddess who lived most of her life in Paris, watching the world around her so attentively that she was able to describe how a single rose petal sounds when it falls. Now, as a further gloss to her life, we are beginning to have her letters.

According to Maurice Goudeket, her third husband, she averaged half a dozen daily, all spontaneous, abundant, dashed-off, like nothing so much as an armful of field flowers, fresh, fragrant, still sparkling with dew, which Ceres, let's say, brought in from her morning walk. Unlike certain other great writers—Thomas Mann, for instance, or Yeats or Rilke—who tend to be formal, posed, and even posturing, in their correspondence, Colette is everywhere impulsive and intimate. She writes about her daily ambience, about weather and her new apartment, about moral and physical health, about how to witch a well or pet a panther, about deadlines and earning a living, about roses and truffles and Beaujolais and brie and planting tangerine trees and learning (at fifty!) to ski. There is good gossip and intelligent malice and reticent tenderness on every page: and, above all, *"pas de littérature."*

In France, as of 1980, five volumes of these bulletins have been published. The first three were devoted to single correspondents—actress Marguerite Moreno, poet Hélène Picard, and a younger writer, Renée Hamon, whom Colette nicknamed the "little pirate." The other two volumes included letters to assorted friends and associates in the theater and the arts. In addition, Maurice Goudeket has published excerpts from letters to himself in *La Douceur de vieillir (The Delights of Growing Old)*, and bits from other correspondences—to Colette's stepson, Renaud de Jouvenel, for example—have appeared in periodicals and catalogues.

But the principal collections of letters are yet to come: to Colette's daughter, notably; to her three husbands, Willy, Henry de Jouvenel, and Maurice Goudeket; and to such important friends as the Marquise de Belbeuf, with whom she lived after her first marriage. A large number to Sido, Colette's mother, were destroyed in 1914, but other hefty packets—to novelist Germaine Beaumont, to violinist Hélène Jourdan-Morhange, to assorted members of the de Jouvenel family—are all waiting—not to mention half a century's communication with publishers and editors.

So the present selection, mostly taken from the five French volumes . . . , can make no claim to being definitive. I have followed my own taste, trimming freely and trying simply to show Colette in her daily zest, meeting her deadlines, paying her bills, at play with her family and friends, at work in the theater, on the lecture platform, in her short-lived beauty salon, and at her lifelong writing desk. Letters and memoirs to come will certainly deepen the image this book makes, but it is unlikely that they will radically alter it.

Colette's life story is that of a robust country girl who comes to the big city and prevails, earning herself a place in the sun. Oddly enough, Colette always disclaimed any sense of literary vocation, insisting that she became a writer because she was paid to do so. . . . So she wrote, "slowly, submissively, patiently," without any pretention and theory, and obliging herself only to remain as faithful as possible to what she had seen and felt. In a review of *As You Like It,* she once observed that "Shakespeare wrote without knowing that he would become Shakespeare." The same might be said of Colette.

Nor can any comparable writer be said to have flourished so independently of the tastes and ideologies of the time. Except for automobiles and electric lights, Colette's world is as uncontemporary as the seventeenth century. (pp. iii-iv)

And though today, for many of her readers, Colette is the embodiment of the emancipated woman, whose social status and economy and sex life are unhectored by male hegemony, she never thought of herself as representing anything. Her only "role" amounted to creating, or becoming, the self we call Colette.

There is a line from Shakespeare's *All's Well That Ends Well* that kept humming in my mind all through the summer by the sea that I worked on this translation:

> *... simply the thing I am*
> *Shall make me live.*

In her least postcard, as well as in her novels, her gardens, her friendships, and her loves, it seems to me that Colette's lifetime, and lifework, fulfills this promise. (p. v)

> *Robert Phelps, in an editor's note to* Letters from Colette *by Colette, edited and translated by Robert Phelps, Farrar Straus and Giroux, 1980, pp. iii-v.*

DORIS GRUMBACH (essay date 1980)

[*Grumbach is an American novelist, critic, and biographer. She is best known for her novel* Chamber Music *(1979), a fictional memoir which depicts aberrant sexual relationships, such as incest, lesbianism, and homosexuality, as well as a decidedly feminist vision in elegant, archaic language. Grumbach first received wide critical attention for her controversial biography of novelist Mary McCarthy,* The Company She Kept *(1967), in which she attempted to show that McCarthy's fiction is extremely autobiographical. Grumbach is a widely respected reviewer who has been a frequent contributor to many periodicals and has been the author of a column on nonfiction for* The New York Times Book Review *since 1976. In the following excerpt she criticizes* Letters from Colette *for containing correspondence that is too freely excerpted to impart the dramatic events in Colette's life.*]

[*Letters from Colette*] are fascinating but tantalizing, like a few grapes when one is ravenous for fruit. Colette was a prolific correspondent, often writing six letters a day—hasty, charming, scrappy notes about the state of her health and that of her dog or cat or parakeet; about her loves and marriages and divorces, her pregnancy and then the infancy of her beloved daughter; about the beauty of the natural world and often, just in passing, about the books she is writing or struggling to write. On occasion she reveals her financial condition....

True, we see in these scraps of letters (many of which have been excerpted through a process Mr. Phelps describes as "trimming freely") the compassionate, energetic, gallant, strong-minded, loving writer who never "abused time," as she accused her daughter of doing. The author of more than 50 books, she struggled against the deprivations of two wars; but she managed to live well, to survive passionate amours with both men and women and to become, in spite of everything, a memorable literary figure.

But such stringent selection—and trimming—reduce a magnificent woman and a dramatic life to the dimensions of soap opera, so that we seem to witness one crisis after another in too few pages. A new book is being born every third or fourth page, another illness suffered through, a friend dying, and so on. I am not sure why Mr. Phelps and his publishers decided to offer us this hors d'oeuvre, knowing we might feel deprived of the main course. Perhaps the entree is forthcoming: If not, these tidbits in English will have to serve.

> *Doris Grumbach, in a review of "Letters from Colette," in* The New York Times Book Review, *November 16, 1980, p. 16.*

JOHN UPDIKE (essay date 1980)

[*Considered a perceptive observer of the human condition and an extraordinary stylist, Updike is one of America's most distinguished men of letters. Best known for such novels as* Rabbit Run *(1960),* Rabbit Redux *(1971), and* Rabbit Is Rich *(1981), he is a chronicler of life in Protestant, middle-class America. Against this setting and in concurrence with his interpretation of the thought of Søren Kierkegaard and of Karl Barth, Updike presents people searching for meaning in their lives while facing the painful awareness of their mortality and basic powerlessness. A contributor of literary reviews to various periodicals, he has frequently written the "Books" column in* The New Yorker *since 1955. In the following excerpt from his 1980 review of the* Letters from Colette *in* The New Yorker, *Updike states that the collection will probably most satisfy those readers who are already familiar with Colette's life and writings. He quotes freely from letters which illustrate Colette's attitudes toward writing and the resilience of womanhood.*]

In a time of biographical blockbusters and elephantine assemblages of the letters of the dead, *Letters from Colette* ... is an attractively airy, relatively skimpy production. Robert Phelps, previously the compiler of the ingenious *Earthly Paradise,* a portrait of Colette's life as drawn from her writings, and of the charming *Belles Saisons,* a scrapbook, with full captions, of photographs from that colorful life, has here, in a veritable mist of the triple dots of ellipsis, distilled a mere two hundred and twelve pages of English from the five volumes of Colette's letters already published ... in France, plus a number printed by her third husband, Maurice Goudeket, in his memoirs and a few that have appeared in periodicals and catalogues. This mass of material does not include the major correspondences that Colette energetically conducted with such important figures in her life as her three husbands and "Missy"—the Marquise de Belbeuf, her lesbian consort from 1906 to 1911. Approximately two thousand letters that Colette wrote to her mother, the beloved Sido, were destroyed by her brother Achille when Sido died, in 1912; but Colette's abundant epistles to her daughter, her editors and publishers, and a number of close friends survive and await publication. Her French editors, on principles of priority no doubt well considered, have issued, as of 1980, in separate volumes, Colette's letters to the actress Marguerite Moreno, her "greatest friend," according to Maurice Goudeket; to Hélène Picard, a poet and at one time Colette's secretary on *Le Matin,* "after which she lived in aloof retirement in an apartment decorated in blue, tending her parakeets and writing poems"; and to Renée Hamon, a traveller and journalist whom Colette nicknamed *"le petit corsaire."* These three female friends, and most of the assorted correspondents lumped in the two additional French volumes, *Lettres de la Vagabonde* and *Lettres à ses Pairs,* are more witnesses to Colette's life than actresses or actors in it, and are addressed with candor but not with passion, in blithe accents, so that our and Mr. Phelps's disposition to perceive Colette's checkered and sometimes tumultuous career as a kind of idyll meets little that will contradict it. Not only were the letters themselves, the "Editor's Note" tells us, "all spontaneous, abundant, dashed-off, like nothing so much as an armful of field flowers, fresh, fragrant, still sparkling with dew, which Ceres, let's say, brought in from her morning walk" but an idyllic carefreeness characterized the editor's labors "all through the summer by the sea that I worked on this translation," in a place he specifies as "Gayhead, Mass."—a more tripping version of the spondaic "Gay Head" one finds on maps of Martha's Vineyard.... (pp. 150-52)

The image this freely trimmed book makes will perhaps most enchant those who come to it already loving Colette. I am not sure one could begin to love her from these letters, though they are, like her fiction, swift, frank, tender, balanced, witty, and vivid, yet with something severe just beneath their deceptively accessible and limpid surfaces. . . . Somehow, though all the letters Mr. Phelps has chosen are friendly and many are loving, one never quite forgets that in the prize ring of life few of us would have lasted ten rounds with Colette. (p. 152)

She worked hard, with increasing perfectionism. "Am I working? Yes, if working means tearing up what I wrote last week and beginning over." "This *Fin de Chéri* will be my own, it torments me so. But I'm working terribly." "I've finished—or think I've finished—*Le Seuil*. But not without torment! The last page, precisely, cost me my entire first day here—and I defy you, when you read it, to suspect this. Alas, that a mere twenty lines, without fancy effects or embossing of any kind, should make such demands. It's the *proportions* that give me the greatest trouble. And I have such a horror of grandiloquent finales. . . ." "Scratching paper is such a somber battle. There are no witnesses, no one else in your corner, no passion. And all the while, waiting outside, there are your blue spring, the cries of your peacocks, and the fragrance of the air. It's very sad." She accepted and executed many drudging assignments. She scribbled off the Claudine novels for [her first husband] Willy, which he muddled with touches of lubricity and malice; she edited the literary page of *Le Matin* while she was de Jouvenel's wife; for five years she served as drama critic for *Le Journal*. In 1932, "to make a bit of money, I've agreed to write the French subtitles for a German film, 'Mädchen in Uniform.'" With her third husband, after a trip to America in 1935, she translated a Broadway play by George Kaufman and Edna Ferber, *The Royal Family*. Yet amid all this facility the artist's necessary curse of self-doubt never deserted her: "All the same, it's terrible to think, as I do every time I begin a book, that I no longer have any talent, that in fact I never had any." She disliked discussing "*la littérature*," and the exact shape of her strict inner standards must be guessed at, from such clues as the word "rhythmical" in a confession from *The Vagabond*—"I have a writer's need to express my thoughts in rhythmical language"—and her exhortations to Marguerite Moreno, who had composed some reminiscences:

> Do you realize that in all that not one *word makes me see and hear* what you're talking about? If you were telling me this in person, you would paint old Madame A. and her husband, Papa Anatole France, and the whole company in fifteen lines. You would transform your "untethered mischiefmaking" into a single line of *dialogue*, of heard conversation, and it would all come alive. No mere narration, for God's sake! Concrete details and colors! And no need of summing up!

The gods had given her a splendidly vital nature. . . . [At] the age of sixty-eight, already feeling the arthritis that was to cripple her, she bought a bicycle. Over seventy, in occupied, besieged Paris, she wrote, "This morning the sky was a ceiling of airplanes. How strange it all is, and how eager I am not to die before I have seen it all!" Bedridden and in constant pain, laden with more honors than the French republic had ever before bestowed upon a woman, she died at the age of eighty-one. One of her letters speaks of "that elasticity which is the miraculous resort of the female creature, and about which I

know something." Her own had enabled her to survive poverty, scandal, and the repeated heartbreak that an adventurous woman must suffer. From provincial maiden to Paris bohemian, from marriage to lesbianism and back again, from the demi-monde to the Académie Goncourt—Colette managed these transformations without sacrificing to her necessary elasticity a central firmness and clarity of vantage marvellous in man or woman. Throughout a life of celebrity, she kept her distinct Burgundian accent and a self-esteem rooted in her native village of Saint-Sauveur. (pp. 154-56)

Colette remains, even now, the century's best translator of feminine vigor into words, the woman who brought to her vocation of writing the most generous measure of experience and health. *The Vagabond* still reads as a remarkably just and debonair study of a female consciousness waking to the possibility of independence—a feminist novel to shame, in its subtlety, the feminists. It is not easy, to be another Colette. Her verve and discipline, her exhibitionism and classicism do not combine every day. Her younger sisters in self-revelation seem, often, merely bawdy, or caustic, or beyond or above it all, where she placed herself at the center of the wide and living world:

> You cannot imagine the pure—and purgative—joy of eating black cherries which the sun has

Cover of the first edition of Colette's collection of stories Les Vrilles de la Vigne. *Studio Martina-Latour.*

ripened on the tree. It rains, it shines, I get up
at six and am in bed by nine. I am turning the
color of a pigskin valise.

It's raining gently, and feels very good on the
face and in the eyes. The entire park is starred
with the white behinds of rabbits!

I am the friend of humidity and a west wind.

The book of life she was always composing gains, in this breezy
selection of letters, another chapter. (p. 157)

John Updike, "An Armful of Field Flowers," in his
Hugging the Shore: Essays and Criticism, *Alfred A.*
Knopf, 1983, pp. 150-57.

JACOB STOCKINGER (essay date 1981)

[*In the following excerpt, Stockinger examines the short story*
"The Patriarch" and discusses the ways in which Colette, who
he maintains is frequently and erringly viewed by critcs as an
apolitical libertine, uses its concerns with incest and male dom-
inance to express harsh social criticism.]

The better part of Colette's literary reputation rests on her
novels, where many of her most direct and even daring responses to feminist questions can be found. Yet as we have
increasingly learned, the greatness of Colette can also be seen
in her smaller works, and she must clearly rank among the
master of the short story in this century. Her short fictions
promise to be, in fact, one of the most fertile grounds of current
research into Colette.

"The Patriarch," which appears in the collection *Bella Vista* . . . ,
is a case in point. That the story has so far escaped the attention
of Colette's critics is unfortunate, for it provides in miniature
a summary introduction to our new understanding of Colette.
Moreover, the text may even supplement our insights into this
pioneering writer by bringing to light the purpose behind Colette's taste for sexual scandal and transgression and by making
manifest certain ideological implications of her work.

On the surface the text bears all the hallmarks of Colette. It is
not a short story in the strictest sense, and lacks the single
focal point and narrative economy that make the stories in *The*
Hidden Woman so exceptional. Rather it is an associative narrative, similar to the information and episodic tales in *My*
Mother's House, Sido, My Apprenticeships, and *The Blue Lan-*
tern. The story also seems typical in its reliance on autobiographical material. Sido, Achille, the scenes of country life,
the descriptions of flora and fauna, the narrative "I"—all are
familiar to the reader of Colette. And although the terms themselves are never used, the tale turns on "purity" and "impurity," those imprecise concepts that provide a constant in
Colette's ethical and esthetic visions from the early Claudine
novels to the ambitious *The Pure and the Impure* where the
ambiguities of such moralist terminology generate an entire
system of narration, characters, events, and images.

As the narrative line of **"The Patriarch"** meanders, however,
it reveals some quiet but disquieting surprises. It soon becomes
evident that this is more than just another example of vintage
Colette, that the story should compel our interest for special
reasons.

The opening of the story, like so many of Colette's expositions,
is a simple premise of recollection:

Between the ages of sixteen and twenty-five,
Achille, my half-brother by blood—but wholly
and entirely my brother by affection, choice
and likeness—was extremely handsome. Little
by little, he became less so as a result of leading
the hard life of a country doctor in the old days;
a life which lacked all comfort and repose.

Since family affections and dramas so often form the core of
Colette's writings, there appears to be nothing unexpected about
the passage. It is, at least on first reading, simply an homage
to Achille, a portrait of what seems an ideal sibling relationship.
So strong is Colette's identification with her brother that she
projects her feelings onto the natural world, describing the
harmony that exists between him and his grey mare who accompanies him on his rounds, listening to his words during
medical procedures, and recognizing the classical music he
hums to himself.

Affinity between brother and sister runs deep because of their
mutual attachment to nature and the person who sealed that
bond: "Happily, his professional curiosity never left him. Neither did that other curiosity which both of us inherited from
our mother." What makes Achille an influential role model,
and also one of the most positive male figures in Colette, is
his blending of strength and sensitivity to both the human and
natural worlds. Not only does the young Colette energetically
help him in his daily practice, she aspires to be like him: "I
was fifteen or sixteen; the age of great devotions, of vocations.
I wanted to become a woman doctor."

Of course Colette never did study medicine. But she did become a writer, and we might recall certain figures—Rabelais,
Chekhov, Joyce, Céline, William Carlos Williams—who underscore the historical links between the two disciplines. A
doctor's interest in diagnosis and pathology is comparable to
a writer's attention to detail and denomination. The observation
is particularly pertinent to Colette, for although stereotypes of
women writers credit them with an intuitive sense of natural
detail, Colette goes beyond the stereotypes by bringing into
texts such as this one the kind of technical competence and
medical exactitude—split lips, deep cuts, sutures, amputa-
tions—that the social mythology holds squeemish women to
find repulsive rather than engaging.

More than a record of Colette's adolescent aspirations, medicine turns out to be the transitional topic of the story. It provides Colette with a pretext for discussing what really interests
her: a pathology of country life where rustic myths give way
to hard rural realities. The young Achille, she notes, "was
surprised when he first came up against the peaceful immorality
of country life, of desire which is born and satisfied in the
depths of the ripe grass or between the warm flanks of sleeping
cattle. Paris and the Latin Quarter had not prepared him for so
much amorous knowledge, secrecy and variety."

It is not just the correction of Achille's preconceptions about
the country that Colette wants to record; she also wants to
revise the misconceptions of readers in an urban age which
naively entertains notions about the innocence of a country life
it no longer knows firsthand. By destroying the equations of
city = impurity and country = purity, Colette is undertaking a
demystification of the provinces in the realist and naturalist
traditions of Balzac, Flaubert, DeMaupassant, and Zola. She
wants to violate taboos, to speak about such unspeakables as
the accepted practice of rural abortion and "the women who
knew about herbs."

She does this, moreover, through the main characters of the story. The next anecdote concerns a young woman, "the Hardon girl," who is a virgin but who claims to be pregnant and insists on a gynecological examination from Achille. Having planned her moves and made her advances, her seduction is successful. (pp. 359-62)

But the brother's participation is not just a surrender, for he continues to "consult" with her in the fields. "From these almost silent encounters, a very beautiful child was born. And I admit," adds Colette, "that I should be glad to see, even now, what his face is like." Once again, Colette faces with enthusiasm the kind of events that women, according to patriarchal values, should condemn. Typically she offers no reproaches, no accusations aimed at the unwed mother, the consenting brother, or the fatherless child. Instead she summons the image of Sido, always amorally curious, who confides to her daughter her approval of the beautiful and independent-minded mother and admits her almost irresistible desire to take the child, against the proud mother's wishes, into her own home.

Viewed from the perspective of doctor-patient relations, of peer models for young women, of male standards of parenting which stigmatize bastards, the incident should be scandalous. Not for Colette, however, who remarks: "However, everything in our neighborhood was not so simple as this warm idyll, cradled on its bed of pine-needles, and these silent lovers who took no notice of the autumn mists or a little rain, for the grey mare lent them her blanket." The incident between Achille and the Hardon girl proves them to be, at least to Colette's cool eyes and empathetic allegiances, at peace with themselves and nature. Wrongdoing lies with imposed mythologies and moralities, not with these country lovers.

But lest we think that Colette is ready to sanction all forms of sexual behavior as natural, she contrasts this comparatively "pure" incident, however impure our social code might call it, with one that is for her genuinely impure: "There is another episode of which I have a vivid and less touching memory. We used to refer to it as 'The Monsieur Binard story'."

The anecdote concerns Achille who is summoned by Monsieur Binard to deliver his frail daughter of fourteen and a half of "a remarkably fine and well-made boy." Binard, the patriarch of the story's title, is a completely unsympathetic character. He is gruff with the doctor, indifferent to his daughter, and unadmiring of the child. When Achille suggests that the girl was lucky to have survived this delivery and asks if Binard knows the boy who impregnated her, it becomes obvious that Binard is the father of his daughter's son. And from his remarks, we glean that Binard, whose wife has died and who has no sons, has had incestuous relations with his three other daughters. His power and privilege as a patriarch are total.

Achille leaves the scene, where a certain normality is lent to this rural situation by the health of the in-bred baby and the celebration of the sisters, without comment. But as always, there is Sido as a reference point and observer: "Sido, my mother, did not like this story which she often turned over in her mind. Sometimes she spoke violently about Monsieur Binard, calling him bitterly 'the corrupt widower,' sometimes she let herself go off into commentaries for which afterwards she would blush."

With that introduction, Colette gives us an example. Sido begins her remarks by expressing a certain admiration tinged with fondness: "Their house is very well kept. The child of the youngest one has eyelashes as long as *that*. I saw her the other day, she was suckling her baby on the doorstep, it was enchanting."

For Sido and Colette alike, beauty is the primary appeal.

But Sido suddenly catches herself and checks her remarks: "Whatever am I saying? It was abominable, of course, when one knows the facts." Her first impulse is to accept things, and only then to judge them. Tolerance is a telling trait of this mother-daughter conversation in a tale about patriarchy. Offering a matriarchal lesson that her daughter learned well, Sido reduces condemnation to an afterthought which can only lead to silence:

> She went off into a dream, impatiently untwisting the entangled steel chain and black cord from which hung her two pairs of spectacles.
>
> 'After all,' she began again, 'the ancient patriarchs . . .'
>
> But she suddenly became aware that I was only fifteen and a half and she went no further.

It is, of course, an artificially unresolved ending. It is too late for silence to have meaning since Sido has already imparted to her daughter, who is a year older than the Binard girl, the pertinent facts and the correct priority of values.

For the reader, the ending is rich in suggestions for interpreting the story. With Sido's final and unfinished words, the inevitable question lingers: What about the modern patriarchs? And by way of answering that question we can formulate some of the features which define purity and impurity for Colette and can make sense of the seemingly unrelated anecdotes in the story.

What clearly distinguishes two forms of illegitimacy from each other, the Achille-Hardon girl affair from the Binard incest, making the first one pure and the second impure, is the loss of female equality. What patriarchy, ancient or modern, takes away from women is the power to act, to initiate and to consent; what it imposes on them is domination and subjugation. Colette, like Sido, remains ideologically reluctant and will not belabor the point, let alone develop and articulate it polemically. Though unstated, her stand is not absent; it is communicated through the structure of the story, not the words of the narrator. Contrary to traditional critical notions, Colette was not wholly apolitical simply because she did not forcefully identify herself and her work with the women's movement of her time. As this story proves, she was aware of the woman's condition and did protest its injustices—but in her own, largely literary way.

To arrive at sociopolitical conclusions, however implicit, through tales of illicit sex and incest, seems a curiously irregular route. But if we return to the opening of the story, we see the care Colette takes to prepare her narrative progress. Her closeness to Achille announces the incest motif, and her fortuitous choice of words to describe her feelings for him—"affection, choice and likeness"—pinpoints the very qualities that redeem some forms of illegitimacy and condemn others. It also stresses the features that allow women in love, familial or romantic, to remain free.

Similarly, the mother-daughter coupling of Colette and Sido is not a gratuitous remembrance but sets off the father-daughter relationship of Binard's by contrasting matriarchal nurturing with patriarchal violence, sharing with exploitation. Colette's structuring of a text is digressive only in appearance. On closer and more suggestive readings, it is almost always found to be rigorous and creative, ordered and purposeful.

This short text is, then, typical of Colette in many ways. It reveals her preoccupation with a narrative vision that is, by prescriptive social standards, amoral in its stance toward humans, animals, and plants. It also illustrates Colette's interest in all forms of desire and the idiosyncratic values that allowed her to condemn the normal and normalize the aberrant. The story is a fine example of the conscientiousness with which, as we now recognize, Colette crafted her writings beyond the purely anecdotal or confessional methods her early critics imputed to her. In addition, it emphasizes the degree to which the mother-daughter relationship constitutes an axis of Colette's entire corpus. Finally, **"The Patriarch"** helps us to discern the social critic in Colette. Though hardly a militantly feminist statement about sexual politics, it nonetheless forces us to re-think and revise the mythologies, categorizations, and moral codes we bring to bear on human affairs. In style and substance, the story is a timely and undeservedly obscure reminder of why Colette is, perhaps more than ever, a contemporary. (pp. 362-65)

Jacob Stockinger, *"Impurity and Sexual Politics in the Provinces: Colette's Anti-Idyll in 'The Patriarch',"* in Women's Studies, *Vol. 8, No. 3, 1981, pp. 359-66.*

MARI McCARTY (essay date 1981)

[McCarty is an American educator who has written extensively on Colette. In the following excerpt she examines the short story "The Tender Shoot" and discusses the contrast between the natural, unspoiled world of young female sensuality and the artificial, calculating elements of the patriarchal order which threatens to destroy it, as in the liaison portrayed in the story between the young country girl and the lecherous middle-aged man.]

All of Colette's work can be seen as an exodus from patriarchal space. Claudine's *Retreat from Love* is not a withdrawal in deference to her husband's memory, but a refusal of the androcentric community. Claudine's friend Annie leaves her husband to embark on a frightening but exhilarating voyage of discovery. *Duo*'s Alice returns to her sister's flat after Michel's death to find the *toutounier*, a refuge from the male world and a representation of the positive non-phallic values of childhood. (Colette, too, remembered her childhood as an "earthly paradise" of gynocentric space). In *Chéri*, Léa builds her mirrored spaces around men; in *The Last of Chéri*, she lives in a new space free from men. At the end of *The Other One*, Fannie and Jane have just begun their escape from male shallowness by cultivating their "inner reserves, which man had not dared to affront."

One short story, **"The Tender Shoot"** (**"Le Tendron"**), is revelatory of Colette's view of female space. While "tendron" can refer to a tender shoot of a plant, it also means a very young nubile girl who is often the object of desire by an older man. The *Petit Robert* dictionary provides an old aphorism to illustrate its common usage: "Il lui faut des tendrons" ("He must have young girls"). This story will trace the fascination of the aging Lothario Albin for young Louisette, an attraction which the aphorism seems to codify as once having been fairly accepted, if not widespread. Colette allows Albin to tell the tale in his own words, but within her own narrative framework. She herself, as narrator, introduces Albin Chaveriat to the reader.

Albin himself is unaware of the reader; he is simply recounting his story to his friend Colette. Once he begins the body of his tale, always within quotation marks (conversational dashes in the French version), Colette does not interrupt him. She does, however, react to his story with an occasional raised eyebrow or interjection which we perceive only through Albin's response to it.

Albin's fascination for a girl who has "gone beyond certain limits" takes place when he is visiting friends on an exclusive country estate whose definite boundaries are ill tended and beginning to crumble. Albin professes his sense of direction to be unerring ("I never do get off my track, you know"), but one day, when "outside the domain," he sees a dwelling shrouded in mist, surrounded by an overgrown garden. Just outside the garden he finds a modern-day Eve, Louisette, a young girl without artifice who wears a homemade necklace of berries. Later, Albin will offer her a store-bought necklace "whose beads were exactly the same bright pink as the 'square-cap' berries"—this she refuses, preferring the natural to the manufactured.

The magical garden contains a spring (*source* in French, indicating source of ever-flowing water, and perhaps source of life as well) from which Albin wishes to drink, but Louisette refuses through fear of her mother. She does, however, lead

Colette and her first husband, Willy. Pictorial Parade, Inc.

Albin down "the sheltered path at the edge of the wood, the whole length of the low, half-collapsed wall" which separates the garden from the conventional scenery around it. Although Albin would like to visit the mystical spring, he cannot do so "without crossing the barrier," so Louisette brings him a drink. Once back at the domain of his frineds, Albin finds "a definite charm in playing bridge on a shady terrace, in reading the illustrated papers with the cool six o'clock wind ruffling their pages." These "civilized" pursuits are reassuring reminders that he is in control of his male world.

As the days go on, however, and his fascination for Louisette deepens, he marvels that she responds "so naturally, so eagerly" to his kisses: "I believe that the sensuality of any grown-up woman who behaved like Louisette would have revolted me." Albin forgives a child like Louisette for "having gone beyond certain limits" of sensual propriety, but is nevertheless disgruntled and faintly scandalized that she never expresses any gratitude or devotion to him: "she treated sensual pleasure as a lawful right." From a different "domain" than Albin, Louisette is also attuned to different stimuli beyond his capacity: "She listened to me, certainly, but she was also listening to other sounds I did not hear and now and then would sign to me, sometimes rather rudely, to be quiet." He is also baffled when she continues to refuse his gifts:

> She tore the ring off her finger and brutally flung it back at me. 'I've already commanded you (she said commanded!) not to give me anything.' When I had sheepishly taken back my humble jewel, she made sure that the little cardboard box, the tissue paper and the blue tinsel ribbon were not still lying about on our chair of rocks and lichen. Odd, wasn't it?

Of course, it is not odd at all. Louisette does not want the unspoiled charm of her garden soiled by his artifical accoutrements. It is as if she senses the danger inherent in accepting something that is not of her world. A Persephone who refuses the pomegranate offered by Albin/Pluto, she will be able to remain with her mother/Demeter.

Although enjoying Albin's kisses, Louisette has thus far refused him entrance into the garden itself (and to her body), curtailing their meetings to "the spot where the garden wall overhung the path and gave it deepest shelter"—that is, the boundary zone itself. But a sudden rainstorm one night causes Louisette to take Albin by the hand and guide him into her domain: "I realized, from the denser darkness, that I had crossed a threshold, the threshold of Louisette's 'chateau.'" Once in that female space, Albin finds himself without his normal male defenses: "my spirit of aggression was severely checked by this unfamiliar haven and the total darkness." Louisette reacts quite differently, feeling "warm and relaxed" in her home space. Suddenly a light appears: "There is a great difference between electric light and any other kind. It was the flame of a lamp, beyond all possibility of doubt, that was coming toward us." Electricity, invention of a phallic industrial society, has no place in this female zone. . . . Louisette immediately screams for help: "Mamma!" Louisette's flirtation with a man from outside the walls of her female domain is immediately forgotten, and she allies herself solidly with her mother, who berates and ridicules Albin. When Louisette offers to join her mother in chasing him out of the house, Albin suddenly flees: "Any set-to between men, even war, is less alarming to us men, less alarming to our nerves, than the fury of a woman." Reaching that "narrow path that skirted the outer wall," he

forces himself to slow down until he reaches a breach in the wall. There he is suddenly inspired by belated rage "to assault the breach and the two hussies":

> No doubt they too suddenly recovered their reason and remembered that they were females, and I was a male, for, after hesitating, they fled and disappeared into the neglected garden behind some pyramid fruit trees and a feathery clump of asparagus.

Albin's posturings notwithstanding, his gesture of bravado has not sent them scurrying back to their cottage in fright. On the contrary, the women are returning to their own territory not out of fear, but from relief at again finding their space (the paradisaical garden) once more inviolate. Having gone beyond Demeter, Louisette's mother has actively prevented her daughter from being abducted by the male, and, indeed, has sent the male away forever (Albin admits to having lost his taste for young girls after that episode). It is interesting that **"Green Sealing-wax,"** the story which follows **"The Tender Shoot"** in the collection [*Le Képi*] begins with an account of Sido's journey to rescue the young Colette from a lecherous man who gazed at her "like the meditative Demon on the edge of Notre-Dame" as she played in a garden. Like Louisette's mother, Sido was successful in her mission.

The mission of these mothers is not the repressive condemnation of desire in young girls. Both mothers/mentors are intervening not to keep their daughters forever virgin, but to prevent them from becoming the victim in a sexual power relationship. Indeed, it can be argued that Louisette brought Albin into the house for the very purpose of being discovered by her mother. Louisette's motivation may have been subconscious, but she must have sensed the inherent inequality in the relationship. The "tender shoot" must be nurtured and cared for in the garden, an allegorical embodiment of female space in which diffused and abundant sexuality is a positive force. If Albin had been an appropriate (equal) partner for Louisette, the couple would have made love in the garden, in a natural setting (as do the young lovers in *The Ripening Seed*), with the mother's blessing—and with Colette's as well. But Albin is an aging roué without real love for Louisette, a patriarchal power figure who will do nothing but corrupt her native sensuality; this makes him a demon who must be exorcized.

By serving as the narrator, and a character as well, in **"The Tender Shoot,"** Colette has exercised dominion over the story much as Louisette's mother reigns over her female domain. Colette's environment is the page on which she writes, and in this story, as in many others, she has retained control of her own space. It is no accident that "Colette" appears as narrator and/or character in many of her works. In **"The Tender Shoot,"** Albin's patriarchal assumptions do not go unchallenged, for Colette's understated yet constant presence does not really leave him the last word. The ending quotation marks are visible reminders that Albin is only a guest on the page, and that Colette herself has tacitly claimed possession of its entire expanse. With Sido, and herself, as mentor, Colette has discovered her power to tap into ever-expanding, non-limiting space. (pp. 369-74)

> *Mari McCarty, "Possessing Female Space: 'The Tender Shoot',"* in Women's Studies, *Vol. 8, No. 3, 1981, pp. 367-74.*

ERICA M. EISINGER (essay date 1981)

[*Eisinger is an American educator and literary critic specializing in French language and literature. In the following excerpt, she discusses the stages of androgyny all women pass through in Colette's fiction in order to come to terms with a sense of their individual wholeness. She also examines the ways in which the androgynous work of the music hall liberates the heroine in Colette's novel* Le Vagabonde *from the frustrations of her marriage and enables her to explore her desires to work and create, activities traditionally sanctioned only for men.]*

La Vagabonde reveals Colette's persistent concern with the question of psychosexual identity. *La Vagabonde,* in the tradition of the French *roman d'analyse,* recounts a renunciation of love. From a contemporary feminist perspective which seeks to eradicate sex roles and strive toward a vision of psychic wholeness or androgyny, the theme of renunciation of love in women's writing takes on new significance. A refusal such as that of Renée Néré in *La Vagabonde* may reflect a revolt against androcentric relationships and a search for personal autonomy. Renée's project can be viewed as the struggle to establish an androgynous identity after an intense experience of sexual polarization: her choice of vagabondage becomes a specific rejection of the traditional female sphere of house and family for the androgynous world of freedom and creativity.

An androgynous interpretation of *La Vagabonde* integrates this novel with Colette's lifelong examination of sexual ambiguity. . . . Colette consistently sought the unity behind creation: "There is only *one* animal," she often said. Whatever the division—flora or fauna, male or female—Colette resisted imposed duality and embraced a vision of wholeness which has much to offer contemporary students of androgyny. Androgyny has been defined as the existence, real or ideal, of psychic unity within the sexes. Androgyny comprises the notion that an individual, regardless of sex, can aspire to the full range of human potential. Although Colette never articulated a complete philosophical position on this or any other matter (indeed she said that general ideas suited her as little as hats with feathers), one work, *Le Pur et l'impur,* is an investigation of what Colette called "true mental hermaphrodism." And her fiction is infused with a unique androgynous vision: one that is not static, but in process throughout the life stages; one that is fully sensual, embracing the widest range of sexual preferences; in short, a vision which celebrates female strength and creativity. "You understand," wrote Colette in *Le Pur et l'impur,* "a woman who remains a woman is a complete being."

It is Colette's inspiration to see androgyny not as "a static image of perfection," but as a dynamic series of life stages. The pattern of Colette's fiction can be seen as the journey of a "pure" protagonist away from the androgynous paradise of youth, through the impurity of rigid sex assignment, and back toward an ideal which unifies male and female. It is axiomatic for Colette that the closer the creature to a natural state, the more androgynous. Thus a woman will experience androgyny in phases: first in the gender-free world of childhood and adolescence, then in the liberating world of work such as the music-hall, and finally through time, in the androgynous harmony of aging.

La Vagabonde illustrates Colette's concept of androgyny as prelapsarian, as a recollection of adolescent purity, to be renewed through the dual disciplines of work and solitude. *La Vagabonde* recounts Renée Néré's search for self-definition which is discoverable through a liberating chastity. Renée's task, the restoration of her androgynous identity, is accomplished on three levels: through the recovery of contact with an earlier, natural creature, the strong, sexless adolescent Renée; through the validation of her present self, the Renée of the music-hall; and through acceptance of a future Renée, and implicitly, of advancing age.

The novel begins with Renée at thirty-three, recently divorced from a tyrannical painter husband, a disguised Willy, and earning her living on the music-hall stage as a mime and dancer. Into Renée's fragile equilibrium intrudes an aristocratic admirer, Maxime, who forces Renée into a genuine self-recognition. The novel transcribes not simply the choice between love and freedom, but Renée's growing awareness and acceptance of her unique androgynous nature and creative gifts. The cold, empty solitude of the opening chapters reflects less the absence of a man in Renée's life than Renée's isolation from her own self, from the source of her creative energy, which is her vibrant contact with the physical world first experienced in youth. The early scenes show Renée alone at her mirror, which highlight her isolation and her growing sense of panic at advancing age. Renée has after all only a limited number of years in which to earn her living as a music-hall performer. Hence the importance of make-up which masks her years, yet hides Renée from herself. (pp. 95-6)

It is the subtle memory of a cherished childhood close to nature which restores Renée to psychic wholeness. Her exile from her natural state of unity with creation is symbolized by her urban exile. It is precisely when Renée physically leaves the capital and returns to the land of her childhood in the novel's final section that her decision to refuse Max becomes inevitable. To refuse the security of love and choose the awful freedom of vagabondage, Renée must first replace the narrow optic of the mirror with the open vista of the train window. For it is through the train window, a symbol of movement and process, that Renée sees her true self in her youthful double, a young girl with eyes "ageless, almost sexless," who recalls Renée's early freedom. The restoration of her youthful persona enables the character to look forward to advancing age with equanimity, even with pleasure, as a renewal of psychic wholeness.

Renée's search for androgyny infuses the setting, characterizations, plot, and imagery of *La Vagabonde,* none of which are rigidly sex-specific, and all of which promote role reversal or role transcendence. Each element of the novel's structure contributes to strengthening Renée's acceptance of her androgynous identity; each enlarges the protagonist's and the reader's conception of androgynous possibility.

La Vagabonde is one of three novels set against the background of the music-hall. The music-hall plays a critical role in the affirmation of Renée's androgynous identity for the theatre is a lesson in role, a deliberate masquerade, where the tentative divorcée can try on parts and discard them. On the stage, all is pretense, travesty, impersonation. The music-hall for Renée is an apprenticeship in androgyny. Like the writer, the great stage performer, Colette suggests, needs to be both masculine and feminine, like Marguerite Moreno, Colette's interlocutor in *Le Pur et l'impur,* whose strong, sexless features can suggest the total human experience.

The music-hall offers a milieu where the vulnerable, wounded Renée can heal, where she can move from the exclusively female world of marriage and domesticity, into the male world of work and activity. Here Renée gains strength and confidence through earning her living, traveling, seeing the world independently, meeting her former social class on a new footing—in short, the music-hall provides an initiation into the abandoned realm of androgyny.

The music-hall even more than the theatre is a world of marginality. Yet the music-hall is invariably positive in Colette's writing; whatever is potentially degrading in the life of the *artiste* becomes heroic for Colette. On stage Renée is an object, after all. But even her semi-nudity becomes a statement of virility, a display of muscular control, of discipline, and power. Her beauty on stage, which renders her vulnerable to male affronts, is neither fragile nor ornamental: it is athletic. She turns these suggestive performances into celebrations of movement, of rhythm and beauty—all the qualities of her writing. So the music-hall becomes a literary apprenticeship as well, and reinforces the affirmation of artistic vocation which enables Renée to refuse her admirer.

The silence of the mime play further suggests a primaeval, animal-like quality which Colette associates with purity. The mime can be sex-free because no voice betrays gender. To talk is to fall into the trap of sexual polarization. Renée admires the stoic reticence of the *artistes*, their wordless camaraderie. (pp. 97-8)

The music-hall provides an opportunity for Renée to meet men freed of the humiliation of unequal sex roles. In the world of the stage, men and women experience each other as coworkers, comrades, not as lovers or enemies. The exhausting physical labor of the theatre provides a reprieve from love, like the *retraite sentimentale* of the natural world, a sublimation of sexual tension. The stage demands a commitment, Colette implies, which is superior to the demands of love.

The theatre requires both men and women to earn their livelihood by virtue of their physical attributes. Both sexes put on make-up, exhibit their bodies, receive propositions, and fear the loss of their ability to please. Stage life equalizes or neutralizes sexuality. In the camaraderie of hard work, men and women lose their modesty, and also their coquetry. Entering the world of the *artiste* from the outside, Renée Néré's admirer, and the Blue Lieutenant in *Mitsou,* are shocked at the easy acceptance of nudity and intimacy.

The music-hall performers share the fine physical development of Colette's youthful androgynes: lanky, slim-hipped creatures whose bodies betray no age or sex. They share the moral healthiness of adolescents though their work may bring sickness and even death. Colette admires the steady heroism of these *artistes*—so many with asexual names: Jadin, Mitsou, Bouty—who triumph over hardship, illness, discomfort, poverty, and exploitation.

But the freedom of the music-hall is illusory. The stage cannot function as a permanent resting place for the creative androgynous person, because its demands are finally ruinous. The stage provides a temporary respite from the battle of the sexes, the endless "pursuit" which is the title of the mime play performed by Renée and Brague. The stage experience is literally a rehearsal for freedom. . . . The experience of performing provides a bridge for Renée Néré, which spans the sexual abyss of maturity and connects the older self with the remembered world of adolescent androgyny. The music-hall renews Renée's concept of autonomy, brutalized in marriage and divorce, and permits her to restore faith in her own incomparable vision, to pursue her true vocation as a writer.

If Renée feels at home in the hermaphroditic world of the music-hall, it is because of her fundamental receptivity to sexual ambiguity, both in the domain of sex-linked attributes and sexual preference. The name Renée, so apt to incarnate renewal, also recalls Colette's friend, the Sapphic poet, Renée

Vivien, who is profiled in *Le Pur et l'impur.* Indeed it is the appearance in the novel of Amalia Barally, another character out of the pages of *Le Pur et l'impur,* which sharpens the rift between Renée and Max, for Renée views the lesbian Amalia with tolerance, and even attraction. Androgyny represents for Colette a widening of options and naturally includes homosexuality. Although Colette takes pains in *Le Pur et l'impur* to disassociate physical and psychic bisexuality, androgyny is clearly linked wtih acceptance of, and participation in, bisexual experience.

Renée can understand attraction to both men and women for she combines within herself both the stereotypical "masculine" traits of ambition and activity and the "feminine" attributes of warmth and nurturance. Like Léa in *Chéri* whom she anticipates, or like Claudine whom she recalls, Renée as an archetypal Colette hero is simultaneously virile and vulnerable. She wears man-tailored suits and loose-fitting kimonos. She has a head for figures, and a sensitivity for feelings. In her marriage, where she was a victim of sexual tyranny, she nonetheless wrote three novels. (pp. 98-9)

The supporting characters, particularly the two confidants, Hamond and Margot, reinforce the sexual ambiguity of the central figures. Hamond shares with Renée a "feminine" inclination for subjugation in love. But unlike Renée who considers this attitude ignoble, Hamond never combats his weakness. Love for him, as for Max, is his whole existence, in Byron's phrase. For Renée, love increasingly becomes "a thing apart." If Hamond works, we never seem to know at what. His sole occupation is to serve as go-between, or procurer, to promote Renée's love affair, like the female *duennas* of courtly literature.

Margot joins with Hamond to watch over Renée almost as if they were surrogate parents, but it is Hamond who talks of love, and Margot who talks of money. It is Margot, moreover, who provides Renée with the crucial monthly stipend which permits her to exist independently as few divorcées could.

Such reversals of sex role or coincidence within one individual of cross-sex characteristics suggest an identity of the sexes, a view which frees the character from the confines of gender. Colette excels in alluding to the resemblance of the sexes even at the moment of the most intense role separation, in the love relationship. Renée and Max, so different psychically, are physical equals, identical in pleasure. The are significantly the same age. Colette's plots are likewise androgynous, that is, not gender-specific: what happens is equally appropriate for either sex. (pp. 99-100)

In *La Vagabonde,* Colette manipulates the story line to provide Renée with a forum for movement and activity, while Max stays immobile and passive. At Renée's departure on tour, she is explicitly compared to a soldier leaving a sweetheart behind. The novel's structure neatly follows the curve of Renée's feelings for Max. When she is active and in motion and has work, in the first and third parts, she rejects Max. It is only in the novel's middle section, when Renée is out of work and stationary in Paris, that she allows Max to enter her life. The cycle of rejection-acceptance-rejection of the male admirer reproduces in reverse the basic cycle of androgyny which moves from adolescent acceptance to mid-life rejection to final readmission. The circularity of the pattern suggests finally a basic wholeness, or unity, the image of which is the sphere.

The initial change in Renée's feeling toward Max from indifference to attraction is directly related to her temporary as-

Colette in costume for a music-hall performance. From Belles Saisons: A Colette Scrapbook, *assembled, and with commentary, by Robert Phelps. Copyright © 1978 by Robert Phelps. Reproduced by permission of Farrar, Straus and Giroux, Inc.*

sumption of the spectator role: it is when she sits backstage and watches Jadin's performance, and Max's subsequent admiration, that she experiences jealousy, which feeds romantic passion. The male assumes an all-important role in a woman's life, Colette implies, when she is denied access to mobility, to work, to self-fulfilling occupations. The moment Renée is herself on stage, or traveling, Max recedes into unimportance. It is not the distance which separates Renée from Max in the final part of the novel that is devastating to their love, but the physical act of travel itself, which reopens the world of visual experience to Renée: locomotion brings perception.

The androgynous message of **La Vagabonde** is expressed in the novel's controlling visual imagery. For the vagabond is also a visionary; Colette here takes the Sido injunction ''Look!'' as a moral imperative. In **La Vagabonde** to see means to be in control of one's own creative powers, to possess the treasures of the natural world with one's own eyes, to live the solitary experience of the artist. Conversely, to be seen implies an appropriation of oneself, a loss of creative energy, the transformation into a sexual object.

Renée's lucid moments, in solitude, in front of mirrors or open windows, are previews of the final self-realization. The self Renée discovers behind the mask of the heavily made-up music-hall *artiste* is the writer. The two professions are alike; both

are creative and rhythmic. The small circle of light of the desk lamp under which Renée writes (Colette's own *fanal bleu*, her blue lantern) reproduces the stage spotlight, symbolic, in turn, of the artist's self-generated illumination which is represented by the sphere. (pp. 100-01)

In contrast to the glow of the creative act, love for Renée Néré imposes darkness. Max is described as somber; he casts a shadow over Renée's radiant creativity as he wishes ultimately for her to stand in his shadow. From the first, Max's contact with Renée has been visual only; for him, *voir* (to see) is synonymous with *vouloir* (to want). ''That man wants nothing good for me; he just wants me.'' Renée is astonished that one can fall in love merely by looking at someone. She is impatient when Max attaches more importance to the play of light on her hair than to her words. The crucial moment of reversal, when Renée sees Max as a spectacle, alerts her to his basic unworthiness.

Renée is perhaps one of the first career women in literature, a new creature for whom love and work are equal pulls. Passionate love exposes one to the risk of living forever on stage in front of someone's admiring gaze. In her first love, Renée served as the painter's model, literally *his* vision; with Maxime Dufferein-Chautel, she is similarly a visual object, an apparition. Both men, one kind, one cruel, seek to appropriate Renée's own light, to bathe her instead in the "banal dawn" of domesticity. Beyond his innocent air of the bourgeois paterfamilias, Renée correctly senses in Max the master, who, in giving her everything, would steal from her her most precious possession, her own "incomparable vision (*chimère*)."

Renée rejects Max, finally, in the name of her artistic vocation. In a Proustian moment of privilege, looking out of a train window by the sea at Sète, Renée awakens to the urgency of possessing the marvels of the earth through her own eyes. Renée recalls an earlier self, a queen of the earth, who belonged to no one but herself. Renée's rejection of Max is also a rejection of a limiting definition of femininity, which would subjugate a woman's whole being to a man and to her biological capacity to bear children. For Renée who knows friendship with men on terms of equality, Max is almost an indecently masculine man; he is too "virile" to suit Renée, in spite of his courtesan-like idleness. In short, he is a man, which means an enemy, not a friend.

Renée rejects Max in the name of freedom, the freedom to see. . . . Renée is free: to travel, to earn her living, to write, to be alone, but not to love. The strong androgynous persona cannot survive, Colette seems to believe, the onslaught of intense sexual passion. The fear of the loss of integrity leads Renée to choose a self-protective chastity. The solution to seek the self in solitude is often the only viable alternative for the sexually mature woman in Colette's universe. But the retreat from love is only temporary. With advancing age it is possible for the women in Colette's world to regain the full androgynous paradise, that is, peace with themselves and with men, who become no longer enemies, but as in adolescence, other selves. Acceptance of male-female love comes after the acceptance of the androgynous self; and it comes late, after the long, sleepless night of sexual embattlement, at dawn, *la naissance du jour*, which is a new beginning. (pp. 101-02)

Renée's rejection of Max is not a renunciation, but an affirmation of her unique, androgynous self. Though fragile, this self demands a more worthy partner than Max. In sacrificing Max, Renée is, in fact, losing very little, merely the comforting temptation of an adoring mediocrity. He does not read; he is not analytic; he can hardly appreciate Renée's gifts; he could not understand her reluctance to bear a child, nor her dedication to her craft; he could not accept the appeal of homosexuality as Renée does. In short, he is not an androgynous man. Renée rejects Max in part because she fears his domination, but also because she fears he is unworthy. She rejects Max, very simply, because she loves her work, and finds in that calling a superior passion.

Colette sees androgyny as an option for "certain strongly-organized beings." It is a privilege but also a burden. Often misunderstood, the androgynous creature may be condemned to solitary "vagabondage," as the search for a worthy partner proves fruitless. For the androgyne, single-sex individuals, men and women, are but half-equals. "He retains the right, even the duty, to never be happy." As Renée Néré's itinerary shows, beyond ordinary happiness lies perhaps the greater pleasure, the recognition of special creative powers made possible through the renewed contact with the androgynous paradise of the natural world.

As the very structure of *La Vagabonde* shows, the life of an exceptional woman is cyclic; stages of rebirth and productivity follow periods of sexual polarization and sterility. The periodic flowering of the rose-cactus which the wise Sido knows to

treasure above the ephemeral pleasures of human relationships, the lesson of *La Naissance du jour,* is anticipated by Renée's choice of celibacy. Creativity is firmly associated with androgynous self-sufficiency: the creative process is one of self-insemination. To attain her freedom and give expression to her artistic vision, Renée must recapture the psychic wholeness of her youth; she must shun the narrow definition of female purpose as centered on house and family. She must, in fact, choose the opposite: vagabondage, the homeless existence of the wandering androgyne. (pp. 102-03)

Erica M. Eisinger, "'The Vagabond': A Vision of Androgyny," in Colette: The Woman, the Writer, *edited by Erica Mendelson Eisinger and Mari Ward McCarty, The Pennsylvania State University Press, University Park, 1981, pp. 95-103.*

ROBERT PHELPS (essay date 1983)

[*In the following excerpt from his introduction to* The Collected Stories of Colette, *Phelps states that Colette's primary interest as a writer was the joy and pain found in the private lives of individuals. He compares her involvement as a reasoning presence in her fiction to that of Marcel Proust and maintains that it was her personal observations and perceptions of life that she strove to share with her readers.*]

[The one hundred stories in *The Collected Stories of Colette*] are taken from some dozen volumes published during and after Colette's lifetime. Dating from 1908 to 1945, they vary in length and intensity, but even the slightest is *echt* Colette, and if the one called **"The Kepi"** is probably the least sentimental love story ever told, the one called **"April,"** about a teenaged Adam and Eve, is probably the truest.

As always in Colette's world, the subject matter avoids any political or metaphysical themes and remains firmly implanted in the private life, in the joys and stresses of what Tolstoy once called "man's most tormenting tragedy—the tragedy of the bedroom." The backgrounds shift from Paris to the Mediterranean coast, from North African gardens to theater dressing rooms, from louche yet somehow wholesome bars to the fresh, sane countryside of the author's native Burgundy. The people we meet are lovers, loners, liberated women, sexual outsiders, acrobats and mimes, children and adolescents, old maids and divorcees, and to their needful lives Colette brings not only her classically trim art of storytelling but the canny, profoundly generous knowledge of all-too-human nature for which her name has become virtually a synonym.

These stories also represent Colette as an innovator, as well as a master, of the art of fiction. Most of our past century's experimentation with the novel has tried to impose omniscience on it, ignoring its primary reality as something being told by the voice whose name is on the title page (Valéry: "When all is said and done, a book is merely a selection from its author's monologue"). Like Proust, Colette declined anonymity and, in her most original work, establishes her own presence firmly in the foreground.

With closely observed action and dialogue, she mixes some of the intimacy and even irrelevancy (yet so keenly selected and arranged) of a good memoir. The result—imaginary autobiography, post-novel, whatever you want to call it—communicates that quality of truth Thoreau had in mind when he said, "I desire to speak like a man in a waking moment to men in their waking moments."

Hence any mere digest of the plots of the stories would be misleading. For even when, as in **"The Rendezvous"** or **"Bella-Vista,"** there is a surprise ending, this is the least of the matter. Even the supple and wonderfully economic narrative line, even the lean precision of the prose itself, are peripheral to, or contained in, what remains the most imposing element in Colette's art: the use of herself.

This has nothing to do with her actual private life. It has simply to do with art, the art of using her own first person, and creating on the printed page a savory and magnetic presence (imaginary for all I know) called Colette. She has created many memorable characters—Léa, Chéri, Phil and Vinca, Julie de Carneilhan, Gigi. But Colette eclipses them all: tart, moody, hardworking, she could take St. Benedict's "Laborare est orare" as her motto. Capable of reckless lyricism on behalf of what moves her, capable also of a superb contempt, she is essentially a born watcher, fierce, dedicated, with an absolute vocation to behold. (pp. xi-xii)

Essentially Colette was a lyric poet, and her basic subject matter was not the world she described so reverently but the drama of her personal relation to the world. Her injunction to those around her was always "Look!" and her own capacity to behold was acute and untiring. But when she is writing at her best, it is not what she describes so much as her own presence, the dramatic act of herself watching, say, a butterfly, which becomes so absorbing, morally exemplary, and memorable. This is no accident, for the very delicate art of using the first person without indulgence is one that Colette developed as thoroughly, and as consciously, as Joyce explored the art of eschewing it.

At first she practiced it in only her non-fiction, and whether she was writing a brochure for a perfume manufacturer, or a text to be read over Paris Mondial Radio to American students, or marginal notes for an almanac, she wove a deliberate thread of her personal life, her private myth, into the fabric. Later she began to do the same thing in her fiction. The result was a story in which the author sets aside Joyce's aloofness and brings the art of narration back to its origins, with Colette herself consciously in the foreground, intimately, unfearfully telling the reader what she has seen or heard, or maybe even imagined, and no longer pretending she is not there.

It is not, of course, a genre Colette invented. Prosper Mérimée probably suggested it to her, as much as anyone, in stories like "Carmen" and "The Venus of Ille." But it is certainly a genre which Colette perfected. In **"Bella-Vista,"** for instance, she tells us about a middle-aged couple—both women—who keep a small offbeat hotel in the South of France. As a guest, Colette studies their relationship, its frailties, vulnerableness, risks; judges and revises her judgments; and then discovers the truth: which I shall not reveal here except to say that their secret is quite other than it seems. It is a strange, even beautiful story, but the character who is telling it, reconstructing it from day to day, is its greatest center of interest. It is the progression of *her* reactions that—in the best sense—instructs us in the morality of being a neighbor. And it is the qualitative greatness of her example that makes it just and unfulsome, exact and prescient, to think of her, as Glenway Wescott once did, as "a kind of female Montaigne," who wrote stories as well as essays. (pp. xii-xiii)

Robert Phelps, in an introduction to The Collected Stories of Colette *by Colette, edited by Robert Phelps, translated by Matthew Ward & others, Farrar, Straus and Giroux, 1983, pp. xi-xiii.*

V. S. PRITCHETT (essay date 1983)

[Pritchett is a highly esteemed English novelist, short story writer, and critic. Considered one of the modern masters of the short story, he is also one of the world's most respected and well-read literary critics. Pritchett writes in the conversational tone of the familiar essay, a method by which he approaches literature from the viewpoint of a lettered but not overly scholarly reader. A twentieth-century successor to such early nineteenth-century essayist-critics as William Hazlitt and Charles Lamb, Pritchett employs much the same critical method: his own experience, judgment, and sense of literary art are emphasized, rather than a codified critical doctrine derived from a school of psychological or philosophical speculation. His criticism is often described as fair, reliable, and insightful. In the following excerpt from his review of The Collected Stories of Colette, *he discusses her role as an observer in her fiction. Pritchett also notes the sensuous detail of the descriptive passages in her stories.]*

"Look for a long time at what pleases you, and longer still at what pains you"—Colette's advice to a young writer defines her as a born watcher, not only of men, women, children, animals, and landscapes but of herself. She was very much an autobiographer, as a portrait painter, novelist, and storyteller.

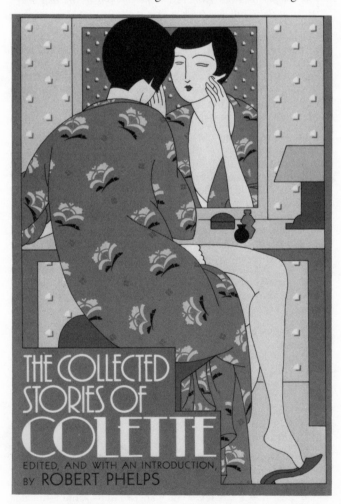

Dust jacket design from The Collected Stories of Colette, *edited, and with an introduction, by Robert Phelps. Reproduced by permission of Farrar, Straus and Giroux, Inc.*

She watched with the candor of a child and a poet, and watched herself watching. Her work has also the apparent spontaneity of one who revised continuously—sometimes to sharpen, at other times to elaborate. In elaboration and in her own presence in a story, she was Proustian, and rarely the invisible narrator. (In some of her short stories, she seems to hark back to a master like Mérimée when she openly intrudes in her tale and distributes her own personality.) The role of the privileged observer may strike us today as being old-fashioned or too easygoing, and close to the vice of explanation, but in his introduction to *The Collected Stories of Colette* . . . Robert Phelps makes an interesting defense of Colette's habit of being "there" [see excerpt dated 1983]. In a well-known story like "**Bella-Vista**," when we see her pretty well camped in the middle of it—and with one of those favorite, uncannily responsive dogs of hers, too—she is there, he says, not to explain but, like a good neighbor, to experience her changing judgments of the people. She is there as the traditional French day-to-day moralist, with more on her hands than she realizes. This has the virtue of taking out the trickery of the surprise ending, which would otherwise be a mere fooling of the reader. . . . The volume contains a hundred of her sketches, portraits, and fuller stories, a third of which have never before appeared in English translation. Among the distinguished translators are Antonia White, Herma Briffault, Anne-Marie Callimachi, and Matthew Ward. The last is not always apt with French colloquialisms—the translator's nightmare. It is jarring, for example, to find the phrase "You must be kidding" uttered in *la belle époque*.

In the early "**Chéri**" stories, Colette was not there in person. She is almost anonymous in the early tales of the run-down music-hall companies in which, as a hungry young actress, she went through the mill, but here she is imbued with the comradeship of the theatre, though she has to put up with some isolation. She is bourgeoise! What she does share with the company is a passion for attire, costume, the inborn fantasies of the actors and actresses. One says "inborn" because as a country child she saw nature not raw but arraying itself. If she is a sensual pagan realist and has a peasant's eye for the object, she is, like all French novelists, a moralist who formulates her *précisions* at once when her emotions and imagination are shamelessly aroused. She sees nature, and lives in its modes and seasons. She is at once moralist and *couturière:* in the spring landscapes the plum blossom appears, shines, and blows away, but it is she who notices that it changes color at first light, changes to pink at sunrise, and becomes pinker until, in the last hours, it flies away like snow. A cycle. So people, too, in their moods and feelings have their frills and style, their *maquillage,* their scents and fashions. She is one for the comedies, tragedies, and vanities of appearance, for the sight of the body dressed in temperament. (Young girls are dangerous in their torpor. Women are fastidious in their dress, but in rage they are not fastidious.) She is detached and exact about both. . . . In many portraits or stories, we shall see . . . "pink sparks" from some object lighting up teeth, lips, chins, skin; hear asides on the formation, even the language, of noses long, straight, or squashed. We shall see necks Roman or stringy, skin smooth or coarse or wrinkled, and scores of pairs of eyes—the blue, one must say, to the point of surfeit and idolatry, but also brown, brown turning to orange, and coffee. Some blondes have chestnut eyelashes. In nature, flowers, trees, insects, dogs, cats, birds will have the same emotive examination. The facts and fantasies of appearance belong to the paganism of *la belle époque*—Proust himself lived for them. As with the body, so with the emotions: the passion of love—whether it is by nature heterosexual, homosexual, lesbian, narcissistic, or maternal—

enlarges and remakes everyone even when it turns to agony, disillusion, and sorrow. Do not lose your sorrow too soon, a woman advises her miserable friend. In it lies the indispensable therapy; suddenly she will find herself set free, and rediscover the affections of her neglected friends, the easy norms of society, work, and living which keep us sane. (pp. 137-38)

Colette was clearly a shrewd rebel in her time. What never bored her was "ordinary" life, and earning a living. In her theatre stories, she knew all about poverty, hunger, the almost debonair human will to survive and live out one's life. She knew the dark side of the music halls, and the dressing up that gives the actors a double life and sustains their iron will. I think of Gonzalez, the actor in "**The Starveling,**" who at mealtimes did not stay to eat but left the company on the pretext that he was going to "have a look at the neighborhood." His clothes were wretched, his bilious face—especially his awful nose—was a disaster. His aim in life? Not to spend his earnings on the tour, so that he would be able to eat for the two months when he would be looking for a new job. "Once again," Colette writes, "I am confronted by real poverty. When, if ever, shall I cease to find it?" And not only poverty but cheating and exploitation—*la belle époque* not all that *belle*. Yet "**The Starveling**" is not a sob story: "The stage bell started to ring above our heads, and Gonzalez, incurably late, fluttered off to his dressing room with all the lightness of a dead leaf, with the airy macabre grace of a young skeleton, dancing."

Colette is rarely frivolous in her detachment. She is sustained by stoicism; she is compassionate but tough. Her continuing subject is illusion. Although these theatre stories are presented through the veil of reminiscence, they break out into realism, partly because of her visual flashes and her genius for real dialogue. "**The Starveling**" is a story; others are portraits of acrobats, conjurers, and knife-throwers, but the "acts" and the risks of each one are precise. The girl who plays the sinister scenes in sketches about The Hall of Poisons, Satan, The Paradise of Forbidden Pleasures, The Beheaded Woman, and Messalina has a superb neck but a meagre body; off-stage she picks up her velvet robe and cheerfully reveals that she has bowlegs. . . . The backstage scurryings, head-tossings, and shouting are excellent. In the long story "**Gribiche,**" a scream breaks out—a girl has caught her shoe in the iron staircase and falls headlong, bleeding. The other girls rush to help, and they guess at once what has happened: the girl has had a back-street abortion. She is carried off to the miserable room where her sly, frightened mother looks after her. Colette is excellent at drawing wary old women—indeed, all women when they are on the defensive. The members of the cast club together on the girl's behalf, out of their miserable pay. The scene of awkward politeness is extraordinary. The girls guess Gribiche will die. She does. The story ends with Colette rather too studiously seeking an "emblematic" phrase that will define the tragedy. In fact, the story has a far better end in an earlier paragraph, when we see the whispering of the girls, nature being the better artist:

> The next evening little Impéria came hobbling hurriedly up to us. I saw her whispering anxiously into Lise's ear. Balanced on one leg, she was clutching the foot that hurt her most with both hands. Lise listened to her, wearing her whitest, most statuesque mask and holding one hand over her mouth. She removed her hand and furtively made the sign of the cross.

These observations of body attitudes are astonishing and, I suppose, have the instinctive feminine preoccupation. (pp. 138-39)

There are a number of slight, witty sketches of husbands pursuing wives, confrontations of mistresses, the ironies of adultery and concealed jealousy. The sketches are briefly piquant, but today the genre seems faded. Also, one cannot guess the backgrounds of these smooth sinners. Where Colette is strongest is in stories into which she brings the working life. In the famous **"The Kepi,"** for example, we are in the seedy world of ghostwriters who turn out romances to order—Colette's early world. A plain, ill-dressed, aging lady in this business, one who has never had a lover, answers a lonely-hearts advertisement from a young army officer. The parties meet and are both transformed by instant sexual victory; indeed, this is one of Colette's rare overtly sexual scenes. . . . A Maupassant story: but, after that, rather spoiled by a knowing chat about the phases of love between Colette and a too ironical friend.

In a long story, **"The Rainy Moon,"** Colette makes a more sophisticated use of her role as the watcher inside the tale. She becomes elaborate, and every incident makes the mystery more intricate and edgy. She is seen delivering a manuscript to her slaving typist, who supports a sister called Délia, who is ill and will soon appear to be on the verge of insanity. Délia's husband, one Eugène, has left her, and, listening to the typist's lamentations and complaints, Colette guesses that she, too, had been in love with the missing husband and was jealous. Quite wrong: superstition and relics of popular magic and witchcraft haunt the minds of the sisters. Délia is plotting a murder: she is engaged in "convoking" spirits, by the ancient routine of unceasingly, silently pronouncing and cursing the name of the husband, hundreds of times a day, willing his death. . . . How can such a tale be made tolerable or credible? By what seems to me a stroke of genius. Colette herself, the rational narrator, catches the infection of murderous passion:

> I kept relapsing into a nightmare in which I was now my real self, now identified with Délia. Half reclining like her on *our* divan-bed, in the dark part of our room, I "convoked" with a powerful summons, with a thousand repetitions of his name, a man who was not called Eugène.

She has remembered that she, too, had someone to hate. Of course, the next day the rational Colette comes to her senses. But—second turn of the screw—months later she will see Délia outside a stall in the street eating from a bag of chips and wearing the white crêpe band of a widow. Grand Guignol, of course. But—as Henry James once showed—there is a probable third turn: a concealed neurotic history inhabits the implausible. Colette has prepared us for this, without our noticing it much, at the beginning of the story. Rereading it, one notices how much she stresses that the flat the two sisters live in was one in which she had once lived. The room that Délia slept in had been Colette's room. The impossible story is perhaps, like "The Turn of the Screw," the narrator's own fantasy. . . . Yes, a Mérimée might have contrived this imbroglio and convinced us because he, too, was in his tale. And Colette's beloved Balzac—whom she read avidly when she was a child—had taught her to pack in the furniture, even the wallpaper, when you elect to chill. It is noticeable that the two sinister things in the story are, first, "something to wear" and, second, physical allure: that band of white crêpe and Délia's "little Roman chin." (pp. 139-40)

V. S. Pritchett, "Colette," in The New Yorker, *Vol. LIX, No. 44, December 19, 1983, pp. 137-40.*

PHYLLIS ROSE (essay date 1983)

[*Rose is an American poet, educator, and literary critic. In the following excerpt, she criticizes* The Collected Stories of Colette *by noting that it contains too many short and weak pieces. She also mentions several of what she considers Colette's finest stories that have been excluded from the volume. In addition, Rose takes issue with the editor's arrangement and categorization of the stories, saying that it is fundamentally confusing and illogical.*]

Imagine yourself in full makeup and suddenly wanting to cry. What great writer could tell you how to wipe away the tears without ruining your mascara? What great writer would care? Colette comes uniquely to mind. The heroism of women is a theme that attracts her repeatedly, and she appreciates that trying to look good while suffering is a form of heroism— "The heroism of a doll, but heroism just the same." The limitations on women's lives, which in so much writing by women are sources of irritation, depression or anger, appear in the works of Colette as exhilarating challenges. [*The Collected Stories of Colette*] allows us to share her exhilaration and to sample the pleasures of her prose, even though it may not be the ideal way to encounter Colette's work or get to know it better. (p. 3)

Distinctions between novels, novellas and short stories do not apply well to Colette's work. In the three-volume French collection of her work, no novel runs over 150 pages. . . . Nor does the distinction between fiction and nonfiction work well for Colette. A character named Colette turns up often in her stories. As do Bel-Gazou [her daughter] and Colette's mother, Silo. Autobiographical sketches metamorphose into prose lyrics or firm up (like **"The Photographer's Wife"**) into traditional short stories. This is Colette's innovative and distinctive form—an indirect, changing narrative line that allows the author to move in and out of the personal. With a writer who so flagrantly transgressed boundaries in her life and in her art, what sense does it make to single out for attention her "stories," as Robert Phelps has done?

I question, too, his choice of stories. Why, for example, is **"Gigi"** left out? It is no longer than **"The Rainy Moon,"** which is included. It is cetainly not autobiographical. Mr. Phelps, who has done so much to introduce Colette to Americans, explains the principles behind his selection confusingly. He says he tried to "include all the stories that are patently fiction yet that have never before appeared in one volume," to include texts that have not been available in English and to exclude the animal dialogues, purely autobiographical sketches and reportage [see excerpt dated 1983]. But the categories "patently fiction" and "purely autobiographical" have little meaning applied to Colette. The sketches of backstage life that form a large part of this volume seem pretty patently autobiographical. **"The Seamstress," "The Watchman"** and **"The Hollow Nut"** are all pieces taken from Colette's autobiographical volume, *My Mother's House.*

Of the 100 stories in this volume, I count 25 that have not previously appeared in English. That may sound like a significant number, but all of them are short and their cumulative impact is not great. The seven **"Dialogues for One Voice"** are little caricatures—monologues by a corset-maker, a masseuse, a hat saleswoman and others. Seven other "stories" never before in English are early versions of *Chéri,* published in Le

Matin in 1911-12. In four of these early pieces, the rich young man is ugly and snuffling. His name is Clouk. Colette finds him too repulsive to continue with, so she changes him into the irresistible, beloved Chéri in three snippets that more closely resemble but are still inferior to the novel we know. You would only understand what these fragments are if you had read *Chéri,* and, if you had read *Chéri,* you would find them of historical interest only.

The rest of the book consists largely of stories that have appeared in English in the volumes *Music-Hall Sidelights,* translated by Anne-Marie Callimachi, *The Tender Shoot,* translated by Antonia White, and ''The Other Wife'' retranslated for this volume by Matthew Ward, who also translated the pieces that are new to English. All the translations are good, and if Antonia White's seem the best, perhaps it is because she had the best material to work with. The most satisfying stories—**''The Kepi,'' ''The Photographer's Wife,'' ''Bella-Vista,'' ''Green Sealing Wax,'' ''The Tender Shoot,'' ''Gribiche''**—are all from *The Tender Shoot,* which remains the best collection of Colette's short stories in English.

The present collection adds a number of pieces without substantially adding to our sense of Colette's quality. In fact, one is left with an overall impression of sketchiness. Less, in this case, might have been more. Colette at her best is a delicate writer who risks seeming elusive if not downright lightweight. Her fullest and greatest stories are fragile houses of cards—gravity-defying aggregations of portrait, reminiscence, narrative and opinion. The number of very short pieces—sketches—in this volume contributes unduly to the impression that Colette is a writer of wisps and fragments.

The volume is divided into four sections: Early Stories, Music Hall Days, Varieties of Human Nature and Love, an arrangement that is neither consistently chronological nor topical. How can one distinguish in any meaningful way between stories about love and stories about the varieties of human nature? Don't the music-hall pieces deal with love and human nature? It's as though one divided Shakespeare's oeuvre into Plays about Life, Plays about Death, Plays about Denmark and Early Plays. I suspect Mr. Phelps knows Colette's work so well that the relationship between the stories and their place in her life is clear to him. But for the rest of us a more objective arrangement would have been a help. There is neither utility nor esthetic impact in the ordering. Colette deserves better. (pp. 3, 14)

> *Phyllis Rose, ''Having the Best of Both Worlds,'' in* The New York Times Book Review, *December 25, 1983, pp. 3, 14.*

JOAN HINDE STEWART (essay date 1983)

[*Stewart is an American educator specializing in French literature. In the following excerpt, she discusses the salient features of Colette's shorter fiction, paying particular attention to the narrator's ambivalent attitude toward involvement with the characters whose stories she both relates and participates in.*]

Colette's major volumes of short pieces include *Bella-Vista* (1937), *Chambre d'hôtel* (1940), *Le Képi* (1943), and *Gigi* (1944). The beguiling stories within their pages deserve extensive study for their ambiguities of form and problematics of narration. Some are traditional third-person narrative, like **''The Sick Child,''** an almost surrealistic account of a little boy's affliction with polio. But the greater number are in the first person;

narrated by a woman called ''Colette,'' they have filiations with autobiography as well as fiction, and include some of Colette's most experimental and most original pieces. (p. 110)

The later and longer stories which concern us here are related to the Claudine novels, to *The Tendrils of the Vine, The Pure and the Impure, My Apprenticeships,* and *Break of Day*—to name only the most illustrious antecedents. But in these stories there is no obvious fictional transposition, as from Colette to Claudine; and unlike *My Apprenticeships,* most of them are not explicitly the author's own story. They have a lot in common with sections of *The Tendrils of the Vine,* where Colette describes visits from her ''friend Valentine.'' In certain of the later pieces, however, it is less a question of friends than, as the title of one proclaims, of ''chance acquaintances,'' passers-by whose dramas she witnesses. In a passage at the beginning of *My Apprenticeships,* Colette notes that, paradoxically, those features most deeply engraved in her memory ''are not of people who have played decisive parts in my life. I have it in me to keep a cherished corner for the chance acquaintance as well as for the husband or relation, for the unexpected as fondly as for the everyday.'' . . . Throughout the short stories, she gives us to understand that fleeting encounters enriched her as woman and as writer.

Structured by the play of coincidence and only partial explanation, these pieces tend more toward anecdote than rigorously articulated narratives. Deliberate, digressive, meditative, they are internally nourished and linked to each other by their settings, and by the predominance of a single voice. In spite of a variety of incidents from the trivial to the criminal, the pieces are curiously reiterative; situations, characterizations, and obsessions reflect the historical Colette's preoccupations. They illustrate—may we say they prove?—certain of her convictions about sexuality, memory, the past, men and women. The heroines are memorable, sometimes attaining what Colette labeled in *Mitsou* a ''banal heroism,'' and their vitality echoes the narrator's own vigor while it shapes the stories.

The tone is somewhere between journalistic and autobiographical, while the fabulations are subtle and difficult to delimit. They are all supposed to be ''real'' stories, accounts of true experiences in which Colette plays the double role of observer and protagonist. The ambiguous mixture of fiction and autobiography makes for a special effect, a genre I am calling ''autography,'' and of which *The Pure and the Impure* is another important example. The idea is bewitchingly simple: Colette tells stories about herself, only the stories are not quite true. She toys with the formal generic distinction which the twentieth century generally respects by fictionalizing *in her own name,* recreating a self who lives a series of imagined events. Her narrator shares the writer's history as country girl, dancer, novelist, and divorcée, and the characters this ''Colette'' encounters allude to her past, both personal and literary—to Sido and Achille, to Claudine, Minne, and Toby-Dog. But these references are principally symbols intended to sustain credibility; they are not elaborated, their meanings rarely expanded. They are less revelations of the author than part of a codified aesthetic structure. Colette seems to enjoy the prerogative of rewriting her past by setting her stories against a detailed background of actual autobiography, while being apparently as fanciful as she pleases in the creation of character and plot. The narrator Colette, who mimics and embellishes her creator's biography, emerges as quintessentially feminine and sensitive, immensely experienced and a wise interpretor of experience. It is difficult in the final analysis to assess the overlap between *her* history and the real Colette's, to determine the precise point at which imagination begins to supplement biographical data. (pp. 110-12)

Major first-person novels like *The Vagabond* and *The Shackle,* whose autobiographical inspiration is perceptible, may be assimilated to Colette's romances. But she insists that the short pieces she came to favor in the end reveal an equally crucial aspect of a "woman's life." Love blinds one to the fascinating discoveries that can be made in periods free of passion. As woman writer, Colette's task is both to address the subject of love and to set its limits; part of her mission is to redeem those "empty" periods of female experience which might be considered insignificant because they take no account of love. She fills in the blanks with stories about events in some ways more enthralling and more romantic than those of the novels.

In "Bella-Vista," the narrator has just purchased a modest vineyard in Provence. While the house is being modernized, she and her dog Pati spend a few weeks in a nearby hotel, the "Bella-Vista." Its middle-aged owners are Madame Suzanne, winsome but not very intelligent, and Madame Ruby, who has a thick American accent, thicker fingers, a heavy-set neck, and a T-shaped torso. There is one other guest, the sinister M. Daste, whom animals especially find antipathetic. One night Colette overhears a quarrel in the next room and discovers the owners' secret: Ruby is really Richard, a man in hiding for some reason and masquerading as a woman. And he has recently stepped so far out of his role as to get the maid pregnant. The apparently eccentric pair of lesbians who had charmed Colette are in fact just an old couple. That same night Daste inexplicably murders all of Suzanne's parakeets and secretly moves out. As the transvestite proprietor accompanies an exasperated Colette to the train station next morning, her predominant sentiment is annoyance. . . . (pp. 112-13)

Hotel life, Colette maintains, tends rapidly to become demoralizing. . . . Daste, Suzanne, and Ruby preoccupy her unnaturally by dint of their proximity and her own isolation from normal routine. But the sociability into which they force her foregrounds an inner tension; her neighbors simultaneously attract and repel her. Her articulated misanthropy (she reiterates her preference for the company of animals to that of humans) belies an instinctive fascination with strangers. As the days draw on, she notes, "My only idea was to get away yet, against my will, I was growing used to the place. That mysterious attraction of what we do not like is always dangerous. It is fatally easy to go on staying in a place which has no soul, provided that every morning offers us the chance to escape." . . . "Fatally easy," but fatal to whom? Certainly not to Colette herself, who acts on her "keen and slightly cowardly desire to leave Bella-Vista" the very day she learns the truth about Ruby. But very likely fatal to Richard, who comes close to being discovered by Daste; and certainly fatal to the parakeets. Perhaps the ultimate fatality resides in the inevitable inscription of the story: "If the idle looker-on in me exclaimed delightedly 'What a story!,' my honourable side warned me to keep the story to myself. I have done so for a very long time." . . . (pp. 113-14)

Colette intimates that seemingly ordinary people like Ruby and Suzanne appear quite extraordinary if the observer is willing to take time for careful study. But does every apparently anodine existence conceal a drama? At least three other stories, the lengthy *Chance Acquaintances,* "The Rainy Moon," and "The Photographer's Missus," suggest an affirmative answer. . . .

These curious affirmations appear at the beginning of *Chance Acquaintances* (*Chambre d'hôtel,* in a volume by that name, 1940). Colette illustrates her meaning with an anecdote from her music-hall days. Half prostitute, half actress, Lucette d'Orgeville would cross Colette's path every year or so. Now she would appear draped in sable and emeralds, now impoverished. They meet on one particular occasion when she is in the latter state. Lucette has retained a summer chalet in a mountain thermal resort in the Dauphiné, for herself and her favorite lover, the faithful Luigi. But financial wisdom forces her to change her plans and accept instead the proposition of a wealthier suitor; regretfully, she is off to America. She persuades Colette to enjoy the chalet in her stead. Colette goes but dislikes the dust and assembly-line construction, and takes a room in a nearby hotel instead, intending to return to Paris the next day.

She is hardly settled in the hotel when, through the offices of her cat, who strays across the balcony, she makes the acquaintance of Antoinette and Gérard Haume. (p. 114)

Like Lucette, the Haumes latch on to Colette. In spite of Antoinette's excessive familiarity, impersonal stylish looks and clichéd speech, Colette is drawn by the kindness of her neighbor and her courageous determination to triumph over the illness which brought the couple to the thermal waters of "X-les-Bains." From day to day, then week to week, Colette postpones her departure. Gérard remains for some time a mystery. Colette's initial assumption is that *he* must be the sick one, and her misprision is based on an accurate assessment of his weakness and propensity to self-indulgence. Eventually he confides (virtually all the characters in Colette's short fiction sooner or later confide in the narrator) that he is in despair over the silence of his Parisian mistress, Madame Leyrisse, who has not answered his letters for eighteen days. He persuades Colette to return briefly to Paris at his expense to check on her, for Gérard himself cannot decently leave Antoinette. Colette reports back that his mistress has moved out, leaving no forwarding address. The distraught lover attempts suicide, broods for weeks, and only perks up when Colette introduces him to Lucette. She has returned from her transatlantic expedition raped, beaten, and with a nasty untreated wound on the nape of the neck, but still nonchalant. She and Luigi have come to occupy the villa near the hotel. A new affair begins: Luigi is still her true love, but they need money, so Lucette accommodates Gérard. But not for long. One day a terse note from Luigi brings the hotel news of Lucette's death from blood poisoning.

These "nonentities" whom the narrator condemns in fact reveal themselves as both consequential and significant, since beneath their colorless exterior lurk dangerous susceptibilities, immense reserves of energy, and inclinations to high romance and despair. . . . [Gérard's] charm and vanity disguise both his moral pallor and his flair for drama. Antoinette is equally contradictory, her thoughtlessness and vulgarity of dress concealing an essential superiority, just as Madame Suzanne in "Bella-Vista" turns out to be morally superior, even though intellectually inferior, to her male companion. In the short stories, like the novels, the women—strong, generous, and self-effacing—are heroic.

The narrator's own role is the most complicated aspect of *Chance Acquaintances.* Her connivance in the story takes two forms: first, she acts (grudgingly) as Gérard's intermediary with Madame Leyrisse and (unwittingly) with Lucette d'Orgeville; and, secondly, she isolates and thereby elevates to the level of story a cycle of events which would not otherwise be identified as such. All the connections between the villa and the hotel, Luigi and Gérard, and Lucette and Madame Leyrisse, are visible from no vantage point other than Colette's. Her own situation and feelings provide, moreover, a partial and problematic explanation of her role as go-between. For Colette stresses her own attitudes: her fear of strangers, on the one hand; her loneliness, impecuniousness, uneasiness, and "vague longing to be happy," on the other. (pp. 115-16)

Chance Acquaintances crystallizes obscure tensions. Drama is the undersurface of ordinariness, the latter thereby containing something like its own denial. And Colette's very "fear of strangers" and "fear of displeasing strangers" paradoxically produce minatory friendships based on entrapment. There is, finally, the opposition between the narrator's articulated boredom and desire to distance herself from the events, and her involvement in the story she creates. Colette defines herself as the intermediary who lures chance acquaintances from the abyss of their nonentity, the initial allusion to the nether-world and its shadowy beings suggesting that these beings adumbrate a mysterious, and perhaps maleficent force in Colette herself.

Through the most apparently ordinary acquaintance imaginable, Colette discovers the sensational event she recounts in "The Rainy Moon" ("La Lune de Pluie," also in the volume *Chambre d'hôtel*). Rosita Barberet is a typist, shortsighted, and prematurely withered. She has the solicitous appearance of "a well-trained nurse or a fashionable dentist's receptionist or one of those women of uncertain age who do vague odd jobs in beauty-parlors." . . . But this inoffensive young woman inhabits a murky world where devilry and witchcraft operate. Near the beginning of her narrative, Colette offhandedly recalls the astrologers, card readers, and palmists she has often consulted, only to discount their powers. . . . (pp. 116-17)

The narrator's typist quits to get married and recommends a replacement. Colette takes her a manuscript and discovers that her Montmartre flat is one Colette herself once occupied. . . . Rosita Barberet lives there with her younger and prettier sister, Délia Essendier, a semirecluse who waits day and night for the return of the husband who abandoned her. Colette does not tell them that the flat was once hers, nor does she immediately learn much about the Barberets. But her curiosity takes her obsessively back to "the scene of [her] unhappy, fascinating past" . . . , where she searches for clues to the mystery of these sisters, and especially for traces of her own passage. She resolves to decipher what she terms the "enigma" of Délia—a young woman "pretending, out of sheer obstinacy and jealousy, to relive a moment of [Colette's] own life." . . . Rosita at last confides that Délia is planning her husband's death by witchcraft, and has secluded herself to cast a spell on poor Eugène, "convoking" him to die by endless repetitions of his name. Distaste supplants Colette's initial interest—"I am frightened of harmless lunatics, of people who deliver long monologues in the street without seeing us, of purple-faced drunks who shake their fists at empty space and walk zigzag" . . .—and she returns no more to the Barberet flat. But in spite of this effort to trivialize the event, she begins running into Délia in the street, "by pure chance," as it were. And the last time she spots her, Délia Essendier is wearing the black dress and white neck band of mourning.

Colette meets the Barberet sisters during one of those "empty" periods in her life. During just such a period she sojourned at the Bella-Vista. . . . (pp. 117-18)

Among the experiences of such periods of idleness, relaxation, and virtual sexlessness, this particular anecdote is prepotent, because it is at one and the same time the story of chance acquaintances and—if not historically, then potentially and perhaps morally—her own. The play of coincidence is more personal here than in "Bella-Vista" or *Chance Acquaintances,* because it brings her face to face with an avatar of her former self, interweaving her present state, a problematic past, and someone else's drama.

In the old building, Colette finds the familiar stairs, and in the apartment, the same window latch which spontaneously responds to her knowing grip, the same style of faded wallpaper, and the same bedroom furniture arrangement. On a daybed in one corner, Délia half reclines. Just so did an anxious Colette in lonely years past. Her penetration into the lowery flat is a return home, a descent into her past, and her fascination with those melancholy sisters an attraction toward the young woman she was. . . . The past is the writer's obsession, then, and the woman's, too, while "The Rainy Moon" is a fable about its dangerous seductions. Colette's entire opus, from *Claudine at School* to *The Blue Lantern,* testifies to the magic of the past, to her tendency to look inward and downward. The liminary piece in *Landscapes and Portraits (Paysages et portraits)*—a posthumous collection of previously unpublished essays—reads like a gloss on "The Rainy Moon." In five pages Colette lyrically describes the irresistible attraction exerted on her by her own past and, specifically, her anguished fascination each time she drives by an apartment she once inhabited. How she would love to resurrect the woman she was, to relive even a single hour among all those she has lived. She savors her past like a streaming cup exhaling memory, illusion, and regret (her metaphor).

What, in fact, is Délia's relation to Colette? Does the apartment autonomously breed unhappiness, or did Colette herself plant the seeds of Délia's drama? The last possibility emerges most clearly when Colette explains how a blister of glass in a windowpane catches a ray of sun and projects a tiny rainbow onto the wall opposite. During her residence there, she used to call the little planet with its seven colors her "rainy moon," and it charmed her solitude. But Délia, according to Rosita, dubs the refracted light her sad little sun: "she says it only shines to warn her something bad is going to happen." . . . Colette silently wonders, "Whatever can I have bequeathed to that reflection?" (pp. 118-20)

Does Délia, in her murderous design, realize a proclivity of the younger Colette? After her last visit with Rosita, Colette goes to bed early: "I kept relapsing into a nightmare in which I was now my real self, now identified with Délia. Half-reclining like her on *our* divan-bed, in the dark part of our room, I 'convoked' with a powerful summons, with a thousand repetitions of his name, a man who was not called Eugène." . . . The dream association links the end of the story to the beginning, for her very first visit to the apartment also entails a dream image. After climbing first the hill to Montmartre and then the stairs to the mezzanine apartment, Colette looks out of the window and down into the street: "Immediately, I was conscious of the faint, rather pleasant giddiness that accompanies dreams of falling and flying." . . . Is her return to this apartment a dream of revenge for past abandonment? Her first sight of Délia jolts her, and she compares the vision, which is at once numinous and fearsome, to a dream: "I had that experience only dreams dare conjure up; I saw before me, hostile, hurt, stubbornly hoping, the young self I should never be again,

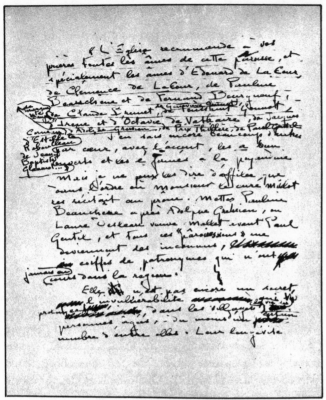

Holograph copy of one of Colette's last manuscripts, the story "Ces dames anciennes". From Belles Saisons: A Colette Scrapbook, *assembled, and with commentary, by Robert Phelps. Copyright © 1978 by Robert Phelps. Reproduced by permission of Farrar, Straus and Giroux, Inc.*

whom I never ceased disowning and regretting." . . . The movements of ascent (going up to Montmartre, walking up to the mezzanine, flying) and descent (going back to her younger days, looking down into the street, falling) parallel those of "disowning and regretting." The double movement of rejection and nostalgia in a general way describes the relation to her past which characterizes Colette's work and particularly structures this story. She harbors the extravagant dream/anecdote of these passing acquaintances not in her unconscious, but in her writer's memory. Its inscription completes its exorcism.

For her suicide, Madame Armand, "the photographer's missus," goes to bed in silk stockings and black satin shoes in order to conceal her corns and crooked third toe, takes an overdose of drugs and leaves two notes. One says, "My darling Geo, don't scold me. Forgive me for leaving you. In death, as in life, I remain your faithful Georgina." A second scrap of paper, also intended for her husband, reads: "Everything is paid except the washerwoman who had no change on Wednesday." . . . But her attempt to die fails.

The narrator's acquaintance with the unhappy woman is slim. Colette gets to know her a bit only because the studio/flat of a photographer nicknamed "Big Eyes," "Geo," or "Exo," is across the hall from that of Mademoiselle Devoidy, a pearl stringer to whom Colette goes to have her necklace rethreaded. (Madame Armand's story is, like that of another of Colette's suicidal characters, Chéri, under the sign of the pearl.) Oc-

casionally Colette notices Madame Armand encamped on the landing, with an "air of vague expectancy." . . . Mademoiselle Devoidy gives her client a scaled-down version of the attempted suicide, and a few days later Colette visits the convalescent Madame Armand and hears the story from her—a story both funny and moving in its schematic evocation of a simple female existence. Madame Armand wanted to die because her life was trivial.

Structurally, **"The Photographer's Missus"** . . . resembles **"The Rainy Moon."** Its setting is a working-class Parisian apartment house where Colette goes on business, and it involves three women and one man who, although crucial to the story, appears only once or twice. It too recounts disappointment and desperate resolution. In both, Colette meets the principal character through the mediation of a respectable tradeswoman. Like Rosita Barberet, Mademoiselle Devoidy is dry, unmarried, neither young nor old, and superlatively practices a humble trade.

Here as in **"The Rainy Moon,"** Colette transcribes her ambivalence toward the actors and events. As she inevitably becomes disenchanted with Délia and Rosita, judging them, respectively, dangerous and colorless, and their home a "desert," so the moment arrives when a harsh judgment of Madame Armand and Mademoiselle Devoidy corrects a previously favorable one: the former is merely a "stale, insipid mystery," while Mademoiselle Devoidy presents only "the attraction of the void." . . . Yet Colette writes the story, as she did the Barberets', and with the same reservations about the importance to be accorded to such passers-by:

> Do those transient figures who featured in long-past periods of my life, deserve to live again in a handful of pages as I here compel them to? They were important enough for me to keep them secret, at least during the time I was involved with them. For example, my husband, at home, did not know of the existence of Mademoiselle Devoidy.
>
> (pp. 120-22)

The concluding passage in **"The Photographer's Missus"** is interesting as part of the same problematics of "autographical" narration. When Colette relates, at the story's end, Madame Armand's own explanation of the "suicide" (the photographer's missus gives it the status of an accomplished fact), she accords the oral narrative about eight pages of almost uninterrupted direct discourse. We read pretty much exactly what Madame Armand is supposed to have said—with one important reservation:

> Beginning with the words, "I have always had a very trivial life . . ." I feel absolved from the tiresome meticulousness imposed on a writer, such as carefully noting the over-many reiterations of "in one way" and "what poor creatures we are" that rose like bubbles to the surface of Madame Armand's story. Though they helped her to tell it, it is for me to remove them. It is my duty as a writer to abridge our conversation and also to suppress my own unimportant contribution to it. . . .

The writer Colette impinges here on her own persona. Her short fiction beguiles in large measure because of the interweaving of styles—autobiographical, journalistic, novelistic. Passages like these . . . underscore the tension resulting from Colette's multiplicity of roles as participant, observer, narrator, and writer. The invocation of the writer's duty obliquely reminds us that the principal function is doubtless the last.

With simplicity, Madame Armand recites the concerns of her life as "photographer's missus": the cleaning, washing, ironing, menu-planning (she can't serve breast of veal again; they had it just last Sunday), shopping, jam-making. She insists that she never despised these tasks; but still, one day she asked herself, "Is that all? Is that the whole of my day, today, yesterday, tomorrow?" . . . She struggled against her "mania for something big," reminding herself that she had a "perfect" husband, but finally concluded that only in death would she find the desired "apotheosis" (it is her auditor, Colette, who suggests the word). So she dressed, wrote her notes, took the drug, went to bed, waited and had the "fidgets," worrying, for example, that her husband would have only a cold supper when he came in that night. Death fails her, but unlike Gérard Haume in *Chance Acquaintances,* Madame Armand does not pout. Quite the contrary, she learns an invaluable lesson: "What I am sure of is that never, never again will I commit suicide. I know now that suicide can't be the slightest use to me, I'm staying here." . . . (pp. 122-23)

In her apparent frailty, in the very triviality of her life and concerns, Madame Armand, thin and solitary on her dark landing, has the solidity and grandeur of Colette's women, and is perhaps the most heroic of them all. The moral at the end is explicit: "Whenever I think of her, I always see her shored up by those scruples she modestly called fidgets and sustained by the sheer force of humble, everyday feminine greatness; that unrecognized greatness she had misnamed 'a very trivial life'." . . . (p. 123)

Its setting seems to attach "The Kepi" . . . to an earlier period than "Bella-Vista," *Chance Acquaintances,* "The Rainy Moon," or "The Photographer's Missus." Here Colette is the young wife of Willy, and the episode takes place around 1897. Thematically, it belongs, with *Chéri, The Last of Chéri,* and *Break of Day,* to the cycle of books about renunciation, suggesting that a woman's body ages tragically faster than her emotions. Marco is a middle-aged woman who is separated from her husband and earns a meager living as a ghostwriter. All day long she pores over dusty volumes at the Bibliothèque Nationale to produce manuscripts for which she gets one sou a line from a man who gets two sous a line from a chap who gets four from a fellow who gets ten. One day Marco answers, in jest, a personal ad: "Lieutenant (regular army), garrisoned near Paris, warm-hearted, cultured, wishes to maintain correspondence with intelligent, affectionate woman" . . . , and it develops into a love affair, miraculously rejuvenating her. But after an idyll of under a year with Lieutenant Trallard, her forty-five years catch up with her. Cavorting in bed one afternoon, she plants her young lieutenant's cap on her own head in a roguish gesture which, according to Colette's superior wisdom, only a younger woman could allow herself. Colette's message is by no means reassuring. Marco forgets for an instant . . . that the aging mistress of a young man must constantly monitor her looks. Relaxing her vigilance, she acts the young woman she feels like but no longer resembles. With its visor and its flat top sloping toward the eyes, the kepi throws into fearful relief all Marco's age marks, and the indiscretion costs her the lover.

What has Colette to do with all this? Counselor and confidante, she follows from a lesser or greater distance the vagaries of Marco's romance. But for her, Marco is a "story" even before they meet. This is how "The Kepi" begins:

If I remember rightly, I have now and then mentioned Paul Masson, known as Lemice-Térieux on account of his delight—and his dangerous efficiency—in creating mysteries. As ex-President of the Law Courts of Pondichéry, he was attached to the cataloguing section of the Bibliothèque Nationale. It was through him and through the Library that I came to know the woman, the story of whose one and only romantic adventure I am about to tell.

(pp. 124-25)

In "The Kepi," she explains how Masson would visit the housebound young wife she was then, with a view to cheering her up. She appreciates his caustic wit and marvelous stories. One such story is "the lady of the Library," who writes for one sou a line, and leads a poor and chaste existence, having never had a real romance. "Her Christian name is Marco, as you might have guessed," observes Masson. "Women of a certain age, when they belong to the artistic world, have only a few names to choose from, such as Marco, Léo, Ludo, Aldo. It's a legacy from the excellent Madame Sand." . . . Intrigued to discover that the story of Marco is no mere fabulation, Colette wants to meet her. She finds her sensitive and well bred, with a "perfect voice" and "impeccable table-manners." So much so that Willy regards her as a desirable companion for his wife. Marco vacations with the Willys, and the two women become "great friends," a phrase Colette nuances to exclude serious intimacy: they talk a lot about clothes.

One day Masson proposes that he, Colette, and Marco compete at producing the best answer to an ad in the personals column. It is thus as a literary pastime that the second phase of Marco's story begins. Already a professional ghostwriter, Marco was already a part of Masson's repertory. With the sexual act, she becomes one of *Colette*'s stories, a part of *her* written text in addition to Masson's oral one. Colette narrates what she saw of the affair and what Marco told her, depending on Marco's account for the episode of the kepi. And here Colette edits and abridges Marco's words, underscoring her interference. . . . (p. 125)

Few of Colette's narratives so starkly differentiate masculine and feminine. Exquisitely symbolic, "The Kepi" is constellated with discourse, objects, and events which are generically charged. Marco, like Délia Essendier in "The Rainy Moon," is one of Colette's doubles, for Marco and Colette share not only a profession, but the same complicated status of underling. Both write books for men to sign, both are exploited economically and professionally. Colette by no means dwells here on her victimization by Willy, but there are allusions to the unhappiness and loneliness which she glosses in *My Apprenticeships.*

Many of the conversations between Colette and Marco center on traditionally feminine concerns: fashions, makeup, interior decoration. Both as narrator and as protagonist, Colette is especially preoccupied by women's fashion, and her lines on turn-of-the-century styles are fetching and precise, echoing numerous remarks in *My Apprenticeships* on the styles of 1900. She censures Marco for betraying by her preference for ruffles and frills the fact that she "naturally belonged" to an earlier period. Although only half Marco's age, Colette plays the maternal role, counsels her on frocks and fabrics, arranges her hair, shadows her eyes, and colors her cheeks. When Marco gets a windfall from her estranged husband, Colette advises her on stylish acquisitions and Marco becomes attractive enough to seduce a young officer.

Colette's secondhand account of the affair is almost clinical in its precision, a woman's analysis of the changes wrought by passion in another woman. She speaks of her friend's "belated puberty," comparing her also to a "traveller who was setting off on a dangerous voyage, with no ballast but a pair of silk stockings, some pink makeup, some fruit and a bottle of champagne." . . . Marco's calm becomes fears, fever, then blissful immolation and satiety.

The last phase does her in. Marco's original beauty is discreet, firm, and slender, masculine in a word, like her name: "She looked less like a pretty woman than like one of those chiselled, clear-cut aristocratic men who adorned the eighteenth century and were not ashamed of being handsome." . . . Like those of Camille in *The Cat*, her sexual cravings arouse other desires, and satisfied love makes her grow heavier. (p. 126)

Her changes in weight, symbol of an active sexuality, incur the mockery of Masson and Willy. "Madame Dracula" is how Willy describes her during the early stage, when she is still thin. Colette, whose own judgments are none too favorable, nonetheless feels her "blood boil" at the critical comments of two "disillusioned" men, who make fun of her friend "as if the romance that lit up Marco's Indian summer were no more than some stale bit of gossip." . . . Masson reacts with humor and disgust to Marco's new fleshy femininity, which he dubs the phase of the dray-horse: "Marco's first, most urgent duty was to remain slender, charming, elusive, a twilight creature beaded with rain-drops, not to be bursting with health and frightening people in the streets by shouting: 'I've done it! I've done it!'" When she was a dry little library mouse, Masson deemed Marco colorful, good material for his tales; when she was still a stranger to impulsiveness and indiscretion, Willy, too, found her appealing. But when Marco's sexuality is emphasized, she in some way emasculates them and their horror finds expression in cynicism. Her own severity toward the changes in Marco notwithstanding, Colette is ready to exculpate her in the face of a male onslaught.

The new and sexual Marco is *Colette*'s story—a feminine story turning on feminine words, acts, and destiny. Vestimentary concerns, traditionally female, shape Marco's fate, and an object of clothing ultimately betrays her. Not just any object of clothing but one typically masculine, military, and not subject to fashion: the kepi. Marco only confusedly perceives that the military cap is her undoing, confiding to Colette, "I can't get rid of the idea that the kepi was fatal to me. Did it bring back some unpleasant memory? I'd like to know what *you* think." . . . Colette understands instantly and replies silently:

> I saw you just as Alexis Trallard had seen you. My contemptuous eyes took in the slack breasts and the slipped shoulder-straps of the crumpled chemise. And the leathery, furrowed neck, the red patches on the skin below the ears, the chin left to its own devices and past hope. . . . And, crowning all that, the kepi! The kepi—with its stiff lining and its jaunty peak, slanted over one roguishly-winked eye. . . .

From a man's story (Masson's) of professionalism and exploitation, Marco becomes a woman's (Colette's), the thread of which is sexuality—nascent, betrayed, moribund. . . . Once the kepi has put an end to the affair, Colette quickly loses touch: it is difficult, she metaphorically remarks, to hold onto

someone who is losing weight fast. Marco ceases to be the subject of passion or the object of desire, and her desexing is symbolized by her weight loss and by her reentry into Masson's repertory. She is again simply "the lady of the Library," and Colette becomes again dependent on Masson for news. The concluding lines of the story, a conversation between the two principal storytellers, signify Marco's return from the sexual to the economic sphere:

> "So she's taken up her old life again," I said thoughtfully. "Exactly as it was before Lieutenant Trallard . . ."
>
> "Oh no," said Masson. "There's a tremendous change in her existence!"
>
> "What change? Really, one positively has to drag things out of you!"
>
> "Nowadays," said Mason, "Marco gets paid two sous a line." . . .
>
> (pp. 127-28)

As discrete tales, these stories are original, artistic, and haunting, while the persona who emerges from their accumulation is one of Colette's major accomplishments. The narrator is a clear, lyric voice which the reader comes to associate with wisdom, vigor, and femininity, and which suggests the sense of her opus.

The interest of the pieces is thematic as well as formal, and they are also marked by the predominance of strong female characters who write a new self-definition for women, one of the constitutive elements of which is an outright or implicit dissociation from men. Most of the heroines decline to derive identity exclusively from sexuality or from relations with men; they claim dominance over their destinies rather than allow their lives to be shaped by masculine criminality, sensuality, triviality, and fickleness. And even those whom sexuality rules are bound neither by convention nor habit, but forge responses which are consistently unexpected. When polite, reserved Marco in **"The Kepi"** finally has a romance, neither prudence nor decorum deters her from a total commitment to sex which can only amaze and amuse her jaded male friends. Masson, Gérard Haume, Albin Chaveriat, and Lieutenant Trallard are devastatingly predictable and easily astonished, but the women are full of surprises and hard to surprise. Their analyses of situations and determined rejection of traditional perspectives serve to redistribute normal textual emphasis and to clarify and demystify male-female relations. (p. 133)

Hotel-keepers, typists, pearl-stringers, goat-herds, the women are capable and productive, displaying a taste for survival and most effectively functioning as creative agents when they have established autonomy—whatever effort and anguish the process costs. They are independent signifiers in these stories, with clusters of meaning centering on them rather than on the male characters whom they surpass in almost every conceivable way. It is not simply that Antoinette's strength dwarfs Gérard's in **Chance Acquaintances,** as Suzanne's does Ruby/Richard's in **"Bella-Vista."** . . . Colette's women seem to usurp the traditionally male privilege of originating action and significance. And a woman, the narrating Colette, is of course the central figure in all the stories she discovers, glosses, and frames. The plot of **"The Kepi"** provides an interesting commentary on this schema, for there the young Colette's profession as writer (doubled by that of Marco as ghostwriter) contrasts with Masson's function: he inspires Colette, arousing the initial interest in "the lady of the Library," but he never makes a real (written) story of the oral anecdote. Woman-as-writer and woman-as-story thus stand in opposition to man-as-muse (or gossip), and that important paradigmatic relation traced in *My Apprenticeships* between a writing Colette and an ingenious but impotent Willy finds its echo here. (p. 134)

Joan Hinde Stewart, in her Colette, *Twayne Publishers, 1983, 158 p.*

GABRIELE ANNAN (essay date 1984)

[*In the following review of* The Collected Stories of Colette, *Annan criticizes Colette's ever-present personality in her fiction as well as her undiscriminating inclusion of subjective impressions. She also discusses several of the stories in the collection in some detail, pointing out their strengths and weaknesses.*]

[*The Collected Stories of Colette*] contains exactly a hundred stories, which is far too many. Some of them have never been translated before and are as wispy as May flies: plotless sketches two or three pages long, they might have been composed postprandially straight down the telephone into the drowsy ear of a woman's-page editor. Others, more substantial, have a whiff of women's magazines. Set among sub-beautiful people with face lifts and their pictures in the boulevard papers, stories like **"In the Flower of Age," "The Respite,"** and **"The Rivals"** exude a cheap, bitchy wisdom which, to use one of [her biographer Joanna] Richardson's favorite phrases, one might call "unworthy of Colette." The trouble is that about half of Colette's work is unworthy of her. So there is no sense in calling it names: it belongs to her as much as the lovely prose. . . .

Phelps's book is a bedside Colette for dipping into, though the irritations of finding no index or indication of where the stories come from or when they were written may give some readers sleepless nights. The decision about what is a story had to be fairly arbitrary because Colette contrived to blur still further the line between autobiography, fiction, and *causerie* which had been getting blurrier throughout the nineteenth century. To Phelps, "the most imposing element in Colette's art is the use of herself."

> This has nothing to do with her actual private life. It has simply to do with art, the art of using her own first person, and creating on the printed page a savory and magnetic presence (imaginary for all I know) called Colette. . . .
>   (p. 12)

> This is no accident, for the very delicate art of using the first person without indulgence is one that Colette developed as thoroughly, and as consciously, as Joyce explored the art of eschewing it.

Without indulgence? Reading through *The Collected Stories* (or indeed the collected works) one might come to agree not with Phelps, but with Pascal, that *"le moi est haïssable."* Yes, almost every word Colette wrote is stamped with herself, and sometimes one wishes she would go away for a moment or two.

When Maurice Goudeket was introduced to her, he thought "like a great many people when they first met her, that she was playing at being Colette. But after living with her for thirty years I came to the conclusion that she must indeed *be* Colette." He was right both the first time and thirty years later: she was

a performance artist, her personality as much a work of fiction as her writing. Still, it was she; there was no other. And this makes nonsense of the "female Montaigne" idea. Montaigne's every word is imbued with his personality, and for all one knows (though it's not what one feels) that personality may have been a fiction: but not a fiction that he performed live to a live audience every day, and even on days when he was not feeling up to it. Besides, his personality is not so self-conscious, or provocative, or *m'as-tu-vu* as Colette's. If everything is to be buttered with self, then it should be the *best* butter.

Colette herself said: "I am no thinker, I have no *pensées.*" But she went ahead and thought just the same, and the result is often vulgar and banal. The more vatic she grows, the more she uses the vocative, apostrophizing anything that happens to be around—the sea, animals, her furniture, her heart. ("There, there, heart. There, there. Softly, softly. At least you have always despised happiness. That justice we two can do ourselves.") But the ear she bends most is that of her dead mother, Sidonie.

Colette devoted a memoir—*Sido*—to Sidonie, who also crops up all over her other work. Her mother, she declared, was the person she had always loved most. She also liked to think that she inherited from her a special affinity with animals and nature in general. *Sido* is a favorite with Colette fans, but there is something phony about the central portrait, and in her doting Colette can fall into a dreadfully arch irony: "My mother thought it natural, nay, obligatory, to perform miracles." As for Sido, she seems to have used her empathy with nature to play faintly cruel games with people, particularly her loving, *unijambiste* husband:

> "You are so human," my mother would sometimes say to him, with a note of suspicion in her voice.

> And so as not to hurt him too much she would add: "Yes—I mean you hold out your hand to see if it's raining."

Sido herself, it is to be understood, knew instinctively whether it was raining or not. The false candor of "so as not to hurt him too much" only makes the put-down more crushing.

Colette herself was a great practitioner of the put-down. The character "my friend Valentine," who is the subject of eleven boring stories in Phelps's collection, exists only to be shown up (or put down) for being superficial, conventional, and a slave to fashion, while the first-person narrator demonstrates her indifference to what people think and her closeness to nature by going barefoot (Colette herself always affected sandals without stockings) and not minding wasps on her food. Valentine is a tiresome early invention and her name soon disappears from Colette's work. But not her presence: it is you, dear reader, so insensitive, hidebound, unobservant, and psychologically clumsy compared to the writer. (pp. 12, 14)

Colette was born in 1873, just as the second wave of the romantic "pathetic fallacy" was gathering momentum (the swell continued well into the Thirties). During the first wave at the turn of the eighteenth century, writers addressed themselves to rocks and streams and felt at one with nature (or desperate when they didn't). This time around there was a scramble to get into the skins of animals. Mowgli, half boy, half wolf, was halfway there by definition. Chekhov congratulated Tolstoy on his story about a horse by saying: "I think you must once have been one." Animals were no longer human beings in disguise as they had been in fables like La Fontaine's: they were beginning to take the place the noble savage had occupied a few decades earlier. They were dignified, proud, brave, aloof, undivided, and loyal. In Belgium Maeterlinck celebrated his birds and bees, in Germany there was Felix Salten's Bambi, whose aspirations to authentic deerhood have been overlaid by Disney's silly celluloid fawn. On the stage Pavlova fluttered full of insight into the souls of swans and dragonflies, while Colette herself appeared as a male faun. (p. 14)

Colette's sinuous prose is just the stuff to wrap around animals, and she writes of them with incomparable allure, particularly when she is not over-demonstrating her tactile, olfactory, and visual virtuosity. The novel *La Chatte,* not overwritten and as elegant as its feline heroine, is "an extraordinary version of the eternal triangle," Richardson says . . . , "for the third protagonist is the cat itself." The cat wins, recapturing the young husband from his bride. She is a real cat, not a person, and Colette makes us feel her misery at being displaced as though we were cats too. Her fastidiousness is contrasted with the bride's vulgarity, but the cat is also the symbol of the young man's immaturity and unfitness for marriage: that is the real subject of this harsh story. Pure animal fiction, however pathetic or charming, is a literary cul-de-sac. It cannot help being spurious because no one really knows what it is like inside an animal's skin, and false pathos and the faux naif lurk ready to pounce on the impostor.

They also lie in wait for Claudine, the adolescent heroine of Colette's first, highly biographical, and wildly successful novel *Claudine à l'école.* It was published in 1900 under the name Willy, the nom-de-plume of Colette's first husband, Henry Gauthier-Villars. She had married this middle-aged literary roué when she was twenty, dazzled by him and also, perhaps, by the prospect of getting away from the Burgundian village where she was born and for which afterward she never stopped pining, at any rate in print. No one seems agreed how much of a hand Willy had in the series of Claudine novels. . . . He has been blamed (by Colette among others) for the lubricity of these successful potboilers; but Colette herself must be responsible for their terrible cuteness, which comes precisely from the choice of a first-person narrator. Claudine/Colette presents herself as a harum-scarum charmer. By the third installment, *Claudine en ménage,* this monster of self-adulation is talking about "impulsive Claudineries." It is really too much to take.

The reading public took it all the same, and Willy and Colette were on to a good thing. Tomboys, like animals, were fashionable at the turn of the century; and Claudine, a leggy schoolgirl with a dash of wood nymph, was the sister of countless fictional nymphets of all nationalities. The difference was that Colette made her innocent but not sexually obtuse like all the rest: Claudine knows about men and women and also about lesbian attachments in girls' schools. In the second volume she marries a Willy-type figure and her sexual range increases. In the third he is encouraging her in an affair with another young married woman. It's all very unlike the home life of Louisa M. Alcott's Jo, to whom the early Claudine bore a period resemblance.

Colette herself moved on to the lesbian scene after the collapse of her marriage to Willy. . . . She also began living with the Marquise de Belboeuf, known as Missy, a member of the large circle of aristocratic or otherwise high-profile lesbians known as Paris-Lesbos. (pp. 14-15)

Colette's luscious descriptions of young girls leave no doubt that she was attracted to women, and she paid her debt of gratitude to Missy and her circle *passim* throughout her writing, and explicitly in *Le Pur et l'impur,* which appeared in 1932, the year she opened her beauty salon. She thought it was her best book, but that seems doubtful. A collection of half essays, half sketches, it is crammed with *pensées,* tremulous woolly ones, and authoritative pretentious ones. But it contains a charming account of the dandified young homosexuals who kept her company when Willy neglected her, and a hymn to the quiet joys of a long, happy, rustic marriage with the ladies of Llangollen as Philemon and Baucis.

Colette thought that Proust illuminated Sodom but got Gomorrha wrong by describing it as a gang of "inscrutable and depraved young girls . . . an entente, a collectivity, a frenzy of bad angels. . . .'' In her view,

> there is no such thing as Gomorrha. Puberty, boarding-school solitude, prisons, aberrations, snobbishness—they are all seedbeds, but too shallow to engender and sustain a vice that could attract a great number. . . . Sodom looks down from its great height upon its puny counterfeit.

Her point is that while Sodom is a world without women, the citizens of Gomorrha are only too conscious of men, looking over their shoulders at them, aping them, trying to *be* men.

In a feminist semiologist symposium, *Colette: The Woman, The Writer,* Erica Eisinger reads the autobiographical novel *La Vagabonde* . . . as an aspiration toward androgyny:

> Renée (the heroine) must recapture the psychic wholeness of her youth: she must shun the narrow definition of female purpose as centered on house and family. She must, in fact, choose the opposite: vagabondage, the homeless existence of the wandering androgyne [see excerpt dated 1981].

Déclassé by her husband's desertion as Colette was by Willy's, Renée, like Colette, earns a hard living on the music-hall stage. A rich and charming lover appears, but even though she loves him too, she turns down his proposal of marriage. Renée is a self-obsessed bore, perpetually demonstrating her strength in frailty, her supersensitivity, and her pluckiness. Her music-hall colleagues are mere sketches: effective as quick-action drawings of dancers, acrobats, and jugglers often are, but two-dimensional and frequently sentimental. The best thing about this novel is the vivid sense it gives of music-hall life: the smell of the dressing rooms, nerve-racking high-speed costume changes, chilly dawns on provincial railway stations, weary rehearsals after sleepless nights on the train. All this can also be found in the "Music Hall" section of Phelps's book, a series of sketches spun off from *La Vagabonde.* (p. 15)

It was inevitable that feminist critics should adopt Colette, and perhaps she would have been pleased with their homage: her boldness in writing about female sexuality makes her a sort of pioneer. She explored female comradeship, solidarity, and complicity more carefully and consciously than they had been explored before; and she defined the weariness with men that affects women between love affairs and in old age, and the exhilaration of learning to do without them that heals broken hearts and the pain of aging.

Aging and its *Angst,* however, were Colette's most haunting preoccupations. (Later on, when she herself had aged, she tended to preach the joys of overcoming the *Angst*.) It shows first in Claudine's husband, who is obsessed with the difference between their ages; it is the subject of the most impressive story in Phelps's collection—**"Le Képi"**; and it is the core of Colette's best-known and best novels, *Chéri* and *La Fin de Chéri*. The eponymous hero is a stunningly beautiful, spoiled, heart- and mindless boy, the son of a successful retired cocotte. He is having an affair with one of his mother's ex-colleagues, a woman in her fifties whom he loves in his fashion while she dotes on him. Elegant still and desirable, Léa knows that she is too old for Chéri and will soon be too old for love. She turns him out so that he can marry the rich, pretty daughter of yet another retired colleague.

The first novel is set in 1914; the second after the war. Chéri is now pushing thirty and his narcissist's perfectionist eye tells him that he is no longer quite as beautiful as he was at the time of his liaison with Léa. His wife has developed from a meek *jeune fille* into an efficient hospital administrator who is having an affair with the American army doctor in charge. Chéri feels disoriented and unwanted. Desolate, he runs back to Léa and finds that five years have turned this voluptuous soignée beauty into a sexless old bag with no interest in him at all. He falls into depression and finally shoots himself.

His suicide is a tour de force of writing. Only Colette could have described it entirely in terms of mechanics:

> Without getting up he experimented in finding a suitable position. Finally he stretched out supported on his bent right arm which also held the pistol. He pressed his ear to the barrel buried among the pillows. Immediately his arm began to go numb, and when his fingers started to prickle he realized that if he did not hurry they would refuse to obey him. So he hurried. Crushed beneath his body his right forearm gave him trouble. He uttered a few stifled groans with the effort of adjusting his body. Then he knew no more of life except the pressure of his index finger on a little knob of polished steel.

In its context Chéri's death (and life) is desolating. No wonder the Jansenist Mauriac pounced on the two novels as examples of

> what Pascal called the wretchedness of man without God. . . . These two wonderful books do not abase us, do not soil us; the last page does not leave us with anything like the nausea, the impoverishment we suffer when we read licentious books. With her old courtesans, her handsome, animal, miserable young man, Colette moves us to our very depths. She shows us to the point of horror the ephemeral miracle of youth, obliges us to feel the tragedy of the poor lives which stake everything upon a love as perishable, as corruptible, as its very object: the flesh. . . . This pagan, this woman of the flesh leads us irresistibly to God.

In spite of the Savonarola tone, this judgment is no exaggeration, though some critics might read the novels as a justification not of Christianity but of some other philosophy—stoicism or epicureanism, perhaps. Anyway, there can be no doubt about their tragic impression. There is no first person here, no "I" at all, but complete objectivity and economy: Both novels are also exremely funny in exactly the same way as the novella

Colette in her later years. From Belles Saisons: A Colette Scrapbook, *assembled, and with commentary, by Robert Phelps. Copyright © 1978 by Robert Phelps. Reproduced by permission of Farrar, Straus and Giroux, Inc.*

Gigi about the training of a future *poule de luxe*. In both cases the comedy springs from social observation, from Colette's discovery that the demi-monde "which seems so disorderly in fact observes a code almost as narrow as bourgeois prejudice." The conversations in Léa's circle and among Gigi's relatives firmly lay down this code and hilariously embroider it with the Bouvard and Pécuchet clichés of women who are uneducated and unsophisticated except in matters of sex, investment, and jewelry.

How could Phelps leave *Gigi* out of his collection? It is and deserves to be Colette's most famous short story and it is no longer than some of the ones he includes. Perhaps he doesn't like funny stories. There is not a single one in all his book. . . . It could be argued that her comedy is based on mimicry of speech and therefore less like her than her other writing. But that could be an advantage. (pp. 15-16)

> Gabriele Annan, "Not So Close to Colette," in The New York Review of Books, *Vol. XXXI, No. 7, April 26, 1984, pp. 12, 14-16.*

KAY DICK (essay date 1984)

[*Dick is an English novelist, scriptwriter, and editor. In the following excerpt she praises the selection and arrangement of* The Collected Stories of Colette. *She particularly cites the stories based on Colette's music hall experiences as lending valuable insight into her little-considered work ethic.*]

[*The Collected Stories of Colette*] is a rich delight. Even the shortest piece smells Colettish. [Editor Robert] Phelps offers the following categories: chroniques consisting of personal re-portage (Colette was an accomplished journalist), portraits of people, animals, flowers, theatre reviews, autobiographical sketches selected from her wonderful fiction about her mother, immortalised as Sido, meditations, and stories 'proper'.

Each group is prefaced by an aptly selected Colette quotation. Two of these are worth mentioning, since they combine the two sources that most inspired Colette to be so prolific and professional. 'The day necessity put a pen in my hand, and in return for my written pages I was given a little money, I realised that every day thereafter I would slowly, tractably, patiently have to write . . .' And then the motivating force behind the will to write: 'Love has never been a question of age. I shall never be so old as to forget what love is.'

Mr Phelps includes *Bella-Vista* which is really a short novel, yet why quibble about its inclusion when it is one of Colette's masterpieces? Printed at the end, it is a bonus, this first-person-narrated story by the writer Colette participating in the drama. Her narrators are ever a tease, so clearly based on her own personality: Renée of *La Vagabonde* and *L'Entrave,* Claudine of the much underrated early fiction which is source material to most of her work, and often just factually (as in *Bella-Vista*) Colette the writer caught up in her own plot. I could prove, had I space enough to spare, that Colette is both Lea and Chèri. Bella-Vista is a small hotel in the South of France . . . kept by a well-preserved woman (and a good cook—Colette was awfully keen about food), herself served by a mannish charmer, Miss Ruby, who in fact turns out to be a man, following Miss Ruby's seduction of a serving maid. Love and secrecy and sex and grimness prevail; all this observed by Colette, accompanied by her inevitable companion, a devoted dog, whose instinct tracks down the killer of a group of merry parakeets. A magnificent end to this splendid volume. Mr Phelps was clever to arrange this final pure Colette at her most suave and sage.

What best to select further from this cornucopia of delight? I think the music-hall stories and anecdotes, all based on Colette's own experience as a very hard-working mime and dancer, express something important in her psychology which has not sufficiently been stressed: her contempt for idleness, for those who do not work for their living. Her mime-dancer Renée in *La Vagabonde* and *L'Entrave* gives up her rich lovers not because she is sexually satiated with them, but because, as idle men, they are morally dismissible. All the characters in these music-hall stories are based on people Colette met as she toured out-of-season resorts, mostly one-night stands, her fellow co-medians. They shared a common fatality, and refused to con-template the day to come, ill fortune or old age. In love and sex they are ambivalent, bisexuality or homosexuality being as natural an expression of concern for another as heterosex-uality—despair in love belonging equally to all categories. Poverty ('being broke is like a damned illness', wrote Colette) was as bruising and natural to all of them as their insecure way of life, yet all remain instantly open to joy and the small wonders life occasionally presents them with. . . . In these sto-ries of the travelling comedians (singers, dancers, acrobats, jugglers and clowns), there is the reassuring Brague, Colette's teacher and partner, who in the other novels is called Wague. Few, if any, have written so touchingly, so rawly, so humor-ously, so acutely about these denizens of the illegitimate theatre whose art is pure *commedia dell' arte.*

Among the Sido stories here included is the significant **'Green Sealing Wax'.** Sido was the mother beloved above all others, the mother who, to translate Colette, inspired the whole of her

work, whose portrait (there is hardly a book in which Sido is not mentioned) Colette admitted she could never properly com-plete. **'Green Sealing Wax'** is based on Sido's relationship with Colette's irresponsible, idle yet enchanting father, le Capitaine, who nursed secret ambitions of being a writer. His room held a desk properly equipped for such a task: blotting paper, ebony ruler, pencils, penknife, pens with several different nibs, inkpot full, reams of cream paper (Colette wrote on hand-made blue paper), all these tidily spread out yet never used. Only after his death did Colette discover that the sole words written on these virgin pages was the name J-J Colette. And, instinctively, she grabbed her own name from it, creating her own seal.

'Distrust', she once wrote, 'anything which has a bad shape', and it can be said that this was a stylistic criterion she applied to all her work. Evidence of this is plentiful in this volume of the stories 'proper' as distinct from the anecdotal and personal fictionalised autobiography. One of these stories is a master-piece: **'The Tender Shoot',** one of the most erotic stories ever written, erotic as distinct from purely sensual. It records with intense precision an older man's passionate obsession with a younger girl, Louisette, who is, in effect, the prototype of Colette's superficially virginal seducers (of both men and women)—one recalls Luce of the Claudine novels, Annie and Mime and even Gigi. In creating Louisette, Colette wrote that she was thinking of Boucher's drawings of the 16-year-old Louise O'Morphy, a creature who had not finished growing up, and whose dimpled body (the 'dimpled' hardly conveys the fruitiness of the French *'potélé'*) proclaims an urgency as strident as if she had cried, 'Do rape me, deliver me from myself, otherwise I shall explode with frustration.' Surely there is much of Nabokov's Lolita here. Louisette of the story, half-peasant, ill-educated, socially gauche, is, in the act of love, forcibly affirmative: 'she treated sexual pleasure as a lawful right'. The middle-aged seducer becomes the seduced one.

'It is an occupation without end to be a vibrant human being,' wrote Colette, and it is this sense of infinity, of reverence almost, for the vibrant life which glitters through this book. Seldom could be found so gorgeously satisfying a collection of stories as this. (pp. 20-1)

Kay Dick, "Under the Blue Lamp," in The Spec-tator, *Vol. 253, No. 8143, August 4, 1984, pp. 20-1.*

DONNA RIFKIND (essay date 1984)

[*In the following excerpt Rifkind discusses the nature of Colette's fiction as represented in her short stories, concluding that it is a blend of memoir, journalism, and dramatic dialogue. She em-phasizes what she considers Colette's difficulty at adequately dis-tancing herself from her characters, which she feels jeopardizes the overall quality of Colette's fiction. Nevertheless, Rifkind states that Colette's work is enduring and demands to be forgiven its weaknesses.*]

"I want to tell, tell, tell everything I know, all my thoughts, all my surmises," Colette wrote in her little fable, **"The Ten-drils of the Vine."** That impulse is clear throughout this large new collection of stories; Colette is eager to present us not just with a world, but with *her* world, her voice, her experience. In each of these sketches, whether or not she appears directly as a character, Colette's presence dominates the scene; and as she narrates she expresses her intention to propel herself into the action and to own it. Although not exclusively autobio-graphical, the stories read like specifically located fragments of recollection whose author has missed no detail in the act of remembering. (p. 549)

Always impulsive, always intimate, Colette's fiction blurs the boundaries between memoir, journalism, dramatic dialogue, and standard fictional techniques in order to concentrate on what she considered more important: the workings of the female mind. Colette's women are all as engaging as their keenly observant creator, and as eager to display their sophistication in matters of fashion and gossip, beauty and sexuality. "When you've been all around the world, you'll think like me," a pantomime artist declares in **"The Circus Horse."** "Over and above that, there are nasty people everywhere, so one has to learn to keep one's distance; and one can count oneself lucky when one comes into contact, like today, with people who are good company and have class."

Every story in this collection contains a character who knows what Colette knows, who is indeed some aspect of Colette herself, delivering large and confident insights, most of which carry a similar tone and subject matter:

> There is hardly a woman who feels threatened by her age who does not know, after a period of trial and error, how first to try on, then how to give her face a characteristic look, a style which will defy the work of time for ten, fifteen years. (**"Alix's Refusal"**)

> For even if she is fond of her, a woman always judges another woman harshly. (**"The Kepi"**)

> Isn't a woman entirely in what she doesn't say? . . . for a woman forgives a man—even a reporter—everything but insight. (**"An Interview"**)

After imposing such rigid specifications for character types upon her women, Colette goes on to endow them with a rich, spontaneous variety of details. She elaborately describes brilliant costumes, showing how they disguise women who are plain or aging, "combative and desperate." Friends in the stories offer long, excessive compliments to one another, but each takes "pitying and ironic pleasure" in silently calculating the other's imperfections. With all of these details heaped on so little surface, we can begin to feel rather like the women wearing these costumes, confined and a little breathless.

Colette also uses stagecraft in her fiction, designing her stories so that each achieves an elegantly planned mood. No matter how various the situations, we always detect the mind creating them: the clairvoyant again looms larger than the vision she has summoned. Colette is quite aware of this fact and uses it to her advantage, making her characters' most thoughtless gestures seem deliberate, thereby displaying her own control over the scene. In **"The Kepi,"** which describes an older woman as "all too tiresomely like every woman in love," Colette shows us how familiar she is with this kind of woman and how monotonous her love affair seems to her now. Even vehemence is boring for Colette, who, writing about the woman's impassioned young lover, remarks that "impetuosity has its own particular ritual."

This habit of highlighting her authority over her characters comes dangerously close to ruining our pleasure in them. If we read too many of these stories at a sitting, each can become "all too tiresomely" like every other, despite the variations of setting and detail. It is of course difficult to write wearily without wearying one's readers, but, fortunately, Colette's failure to remain altogether dominant over her characters saves us from giving up in exhaustion. André Gide, noting that Colette, "despite all her superiority," seems to have been tainted by her milieu, points to this same tension in Colette between wishing to remain superior to her situation and wishing to be included as a part of it.

All the poignancy of these stories comes from this condition of feeling simultaneously outside and inside a predicament. "I belong to a country which I have left," Colette writes in **"Gray Days,"** and because she is still attached to this country (which represents both her first home in Burgundy and her abandoned state of childhood innocence), she is still vulnerable to the loss she feels in leaving it. Outside the country where Colette belongs, all desire is unrequited and is therefore certain to result in pain; yet neither she nor her characters can shake free from that desire. Love keeps leaving and returning to the people in Colette's world and is as familiar a burden as their poverty or their ennui. "I don't believe I'd know what to do with myself if I didn't have my sorrow," a young actress says in **"Gitanette."** "It keeps me company." Colette here is no longer cool or detached; she shares completely in the woman's sorrow—keeping Gitanette company.

So Colette struggles between sympathy with and detachment from her characters, and she tries to offer us an entire world despite the limitations of her strongly subjective vision. Generous in her intention if not usually in her execution, Colette wants to give us Paris in all of its fin de siècle color and variety; what we receive, however, is Colette's Paris, which is something quite different. Again, more like memoir than fiction, these stories strictly limit themselves to Colette's experience. We can never quite approach any character's mind other than the one onto which Colette projects herself; the other people she writes about are "mannequins," "dolls," figures in a dream. Here Paris is almost entirely a feminine city, where men are conspicuous by their absence, serving as mere occasions for the women's actions and preoccupations. In this Paris, almost every woman, regardless of her position, is a survivor, struggling through her day, exhibiting "le gout de durer"—the will to survive in confrontation with poverty, obligation, loss of love.

However limited this world of Colette's is, it nevertheless is as rich as a series of memoirs could hope to be. George Eliot has written that memory has as many moods as temper, and here within Colette's memory we are given every mood, every detail of gesture and impulse possible. All of the nostalgia that accompanies memoir enriches Colette's stories, making them moving but not sentimental; the characters here are aware of a better, less fractioned world, a world they have left, and the memory of that world, along with the hope for its return, keeps them going. Somehow we share this nostalgia with the characters who speak for Colette, and we share her conflicting desires to approach and retreat from the preoccupations of her characters. The tension between these impulses remains as unresolved as dreams, as sustained as music, and the moods of the stories, like dreams, stay with us even after we have forgotten their details.

By traveling the distance between cognition and recognition, between imagination and memory, Colette has placed herself in a unique position as a writer. Her insights, spread loosely throughout these brief sketches and stories, become a bit diluted, just as memory becomes experience-once-removed in the act of recollection, with details applied thickly in some places and obscured or ignored in others. Despite this weakness, Colette's work demands to be taken seriously. The mind that remembers these dreams for us and makes us nostalgic for a time we did not know is extraordinary, for it allows us to gain from the mixture of memory and fiction something akin to the rich immediacy of an intense experience. The shared longing for it to stay, and to stay whole, remains. (pp. 550, 52)

> *Donna Rifkind, "Herself," in* The American Scholar, *Vol. 53, No. 4, Autumn, 1984, pp. 549-50, 552.*

ADDITIONAL BIBLIOGRAPHY

Blake, Patricia. "Cornucopia." *Time* CXXIII, No. 2 (9 January 1984): 70, 73.
A favorable review of *The Collected Stories of Colette.*

Cottrell, Robert D. *Colette.* New York: Frederick Ungar Publishing Co., 1974, 150 p.
A biographically based discussion of Colette's major novels.

Crosland, Margaret. *Colette: The Difficulty of Loving, a Biography.* London: Peter Owen, 1973, 200 p.

Biography of Colette with chronology and bibliography.

Dranch, Sherry A. "Reading through the Veiled Text: Colette's *The Pure and the Impure.*" *Contemporary Literature* XXIV, No. 2 (Summer 1983): 176-89.
A structuralist discussion of the implications of the unwritten subtext in Colette's loosely-connected series of stories centered around the theme of homosexuality.

Duchêne, Anne. "From Sequins to *monstre sacré.*" *The Times Literary Supplement* No. 4257 (2 November 1984): 1238.
A mixed review of *The Collected Stories.*

Kapp, Isa. "Mistress of Tristess." *The New Republic* 190, No. 3620 (4 June 1984): 38-42.
A generally favorable review of *The Collected Stories* with many quotes from the text to illustrate the reviewer's arguments.

Sackett, Victoria. Review of *The Collected Stories of Colette,* by Colette. *The American Spectator* XVII, No. 6 (June 1984): 43-4.
A favorable review which praises the variety of the editor's selection.

Wescott, Glenway. "An Introduction to Colette." In his *Images of Truth,* pp. 86-141. London: Hamish Hamilton, 1963.
A detailed survey of Colette's major works.

Charlotte L(ottie) Forten (Grimké)

1837-1914

American diarist, poet, and essayist.

The Journal of Charlotte L. Forten is a record of the intellectual coming of age of a genteel black woman in the 1850s and 1860s. Forten kept the diary from the ages of 16 to 26, an exciting decade in her life and a turbulent era in American history. A revealing testimony to the psychological impact of racial hatred on a sensitive and idealistic person, *The Journal* is also an important historical document that details the progress and setbacks of the abolitionist movement and provides portraits of such notable movement figures as William Lloyd Garrison, Wendell Phillips, and John Greenleaf Whittier.

Forten was born into one of Philadelphia's most prominent and politically active black families. Her grandfather, James Forten, was a free-born man who became a wealthy sail maker and prominent abolitionist; consequently, Forten grew up in a household dominated by discussions of slavery and America's racial policies—discussions that significantly influenced her perspective on the country's social and political practices. When Forten was still a young girl her mother died, and the youngster divided her time between her father's home and that of her aunt and uncle, Harriet and Robert Purvis, who lived in suburban Byberry. Purvis, a black abolitionist who had inherited substantial wealth from his English father, owned an estate where political meetings were held, runaway slaves were offered sanctuary, and traveling agents for various antislavery associations were lodged. Forten enjoyed the excitement and sense of righteousness such activities brought to her surroundings, and also welcomed the chance to be with her cousins; previously, her exposure to other children had been limited because her father had chosen to have her privately tutored rather than send her to Philadelphia's segregated schools. However in 1854, when Forten was sixteen, she was sent to the Salem, Massachusetts, home of Charles and Amy Remond, who were to act as her foster parents while she attended the integrated Salem Grammar School.

Remond, his brother, and his sister Sarah lectured as agents of the American Anti-Slavery Society, a position to which Forten aspired. In the childless home a bond like that between mother and daughter developed between Forten and Sarah, who was twenty-three years her senior. The Remond home was congenial, and Forten welcomed the challenge offered by her new school, writing in her diary at the semester's end that "this year has been a very happy one. Happy because the field of knowledge, for the first time has seemed widely open to me; because I have studied more, and, I trust, learned more than during any other year of my life. . . . I feel an earnest desire to become very much wiser. . . ." She was further encouraged by her friendship with her teacher, a woman she admired even more when she learned of her abolitionist sympathies. However, Forten remained distant from her classmates, and was sensitive to the hypocrisy of white students who were friendly within the confines of the classroom, but who refused to acknowledge her presence in public. "These are but trifles," she wrote, "certainly, to the great, public wrongs which we as people are obliged to endure. But to those who experience them, these trifles are most wearing and dis-

couraging.'' Such behavior on the part of others gave Forten additional reason for wanting to excel; through her personal accomplishments she believed she could prove that black people deserved the respect afforded other Americans. She was considered an exemplary student, and embarked on a course of self-improvement that included teaching herself French, Latin, and German, and attending lectures on literature and politics. During a single year, her diary shows, Forten completed a reading list of over one hundred books, including those of Charles Dickens, Elizabeth Barrett Browning, and Ralph Waldo Emerson, whom she heard lecture on several occasions. Her appraisals of literature and of lecturers was based not only on literary merit or oratorical excellence, but also upon the degree to which they reflected liberal sentiments about black people and women. Nevertheless, despite her diligence in pursuing her goals, and her obvious excellence, Forten remained modest to the point of self-deprecation, even hesitating to take credit for a poem that was accepted for publication by Garrison's antislavery journal *The Liberator*.

Because of her excellent work and genteel demeanor, Forten was accepted as a student at the Salem Normal School, where she prepared for a teaching career. However, her happiness at her graduation in 1856 was marred by the illness and subsequent death of Amy Remond. Forten remained in the Remond home for over a year after Amy's death, teaching at a local grammar school, but was forced to move in with another family as Charles Remond became increasingly irritable and difficult to live with; an orator of international reputation who was considered by many to be the leading spokesman of black Americans, Remond never accepted the secondary role assigned him in the abolitionist movement after the rapid rise of Frederick Douglass. During this period Forten tired of teaching and longed for a life devoted to cultural and intellectual pursuits. In 1858 she left Salem and returned to Pennsylvania, where she remained for four years, reading, studying, and recovering her strength after recurrent attacks of tuberculosis. Although she published several poems in antislavery periodicals during these years, she decided to return to teaching, and in 1862 applied for a position on St. Helena Island, South Carolina, in an experimental project which was designed to prove that former slaves could be educated and become valuable citizens.

St. Helena, an island in Confederate territory, had been taken by the Union army; with the approach of that army, 8,000 slaves had been deserted by the land owners. The former slaves, who were isolated from the mainland, spoke Gullah (a dialect that combines various African languages), and were suspicious of the outsiders who poured onto the island. Forten found her young, undisciplined students a striking contrast to the white students she had instructed in Salem, but the unusual language, their love of music, and the challenge of helping them gave her a deep satisfaction. Forten particularly enjoyed the children's singing; a letter on their vocal abilities to Whittier, whom Forten had met along with many other celebrated persons while living with the Remonds, inspired the poet to compose a special Christmas hymn for her charges. Correspondents for several years, Forten and Whittier admired one another for their dedication to the cause of abolition, and when Forten sent him an essay about the project on St. Helena Island and the beauty of the natural surroundings, Whittier saw that it was published in *The Atlantic Monthly*.

In her diary, Forten demonstrated as much concern for the black regiment that was formed from among the Island's inhabitants as she did for her students, and so records the history of their battles with the Confederate army. On one occasion she wrote, "They say the black soldiers fought the rebels bravely;—... I can think of nothing but this reg[iment]. How proud of it I am!" Despite such feelings of pride, Forten still considered Independence Day celebrations and other forms of patriotism hypocritical in a nation that had enslaved people for centuries: "*Patriotic* young America kept up such a din in celebrating their glorious *Fourth*, that *rest* was impossible. My soul is sick of such a mockery." In May of 1864, suffering again from ill health, Forten returned to Philadelphia satisfied with the success of the experiment on St. Helena Island, and for the next decade lived a quiet life writing essays and poetry, and taking an occasional teaching position.

In addition to recording her reactions to the abolitionist movement, slavery, and the Civil War, Forten also wrote about her personal loneliness, her desire to feel completely at ease with her numerous white friends, and her belief that no man would ever love her. "Though I had *almost* resolved to forbear committing sad thoughts and gloomy feelings to my pages, dear Journal,... to-night I long for a confidant—and *thou* art my only one.... I am *lonely* to-night.... I long for the pressure of a loving hand in mine, the touch of loving lips upon my aching brow.... There is none, for me, and never will be. I

could only love one whom I could look up to, and reverence...." Forten was to find such a man in Francis Grimké, the son of a South Carolina plantation owner and his slave, and the nephew of Sarah and Angelina Grimké, famous and ardent abolitionists and feminists. After a youth of enslavement, escape, imprisonment, and liberation, Francis Grimké became the valedictorian of his graduating class at Lincoln College and went on to Princeton, earning a degree in theology. With her husband, who was thirteen years younger than she was when they married in 1878, Forten led what appears to have been a satisfying life of social work and cultural enrichment.

Forten is considered a minor creator of sentimental verse and a competent if not exceptional essayist. Her highest praise came from contemporaries who knew and admired her as a person, and therefore were influenced by her sincerity as much as by her admittedly meager talents. However, her journal, which was composed as a personal document with no intention of publication and was not published until 1953, remains an outstanding accomplishment. One of only a few such works composed by black Americans during her era that have survived, *The Journal* is an important human and historical document which Ray Allen Billington has called Forten's "bequest to humanity ... which could reveal to a later generation her underlying belief in human decency and equality."

PRINCIPAL WORKS

"To W. L. G. on Reading His 'Chosen Queen'" (poetry) 1855; published in journal *The Liberator*
"Poem" (poetry) 1856; published in journal *The Liberator*
"Glimpses of New England" (essay) 1858; published in journal *National Anti-Slavery Standard*
"The Two Voices" (poetry) 1859; published in journal *National Anti-Slavery Standard*
"The Wind among the Poplars" (poetry) 1859; published in journal *The Liberator*
"In the Country" (poetry) 1860; published in journal *National Anti-Slavery Standard*
"The Slave Girl's Prayer" (poetry) 1860; published in journal *The Liberator*
"Life on the Sea Islands" (essay) 1864; published in journal *The Atlantic Monthly*
The Journal of Charlotte L. Forten (journal) 1953

Selections of Forten's poetry have appeared in *An Anthology of American Negro Literature; The Black Man; Cavalcade; Life and Writings of the Grimké Family; Negro Poets and Their Poems;* and *The Rising Son*.

CHARLOTTE L. FORTEN (journal date 1855-60)

[*The following excerpts from* The Journal of Charlotte L. Forten *illustrate the all-encompassing influence Forten's attitudes toward racism had on her choice of friends, her desire to improve herself, and her outlook on life.*]

Wednesday, Sept. 12. [1855] To-day school commenced.— Most happy am I to return to the companionship of my studies,—ever my most valued friends. It is pleasant to meet the scholars again; most of them greeted me cordially, and were it not for the thought that *will* intrude, of the want of *entire sympathy* even of those I know and like best, I should greatly enjoy their society. There is one young girl and only one— Miss [Sarah] B[rown] who I believe thoroughly and heartily appreciates anti-slavery,—*radical* anti-slavery, and has no prejudice against color. I wonder that every colored person is not a misanthrope. Surely we have everything to make us hate mankind. I have met girls in the schoolroom [-]they have been thoroughly kind and cordial to me,—perhaps the next day met them in the street—they feared to recognize me; these I can but regard now with scorn and contempt,—once I liked them, believing them incapable of such meanness. Others give the most distant recognition possible.—I, of course, acknowledge no such recognitions, and they soon cease entirely. These are but trifles, certainly, to the great, public wrongs which we as a people are obliged to endure. But to those who experience them, these apparent trifles are most wearing and discouraging; even to the child's mind they reveal volumes of deceit and heartlessness, and early teach a lesson of suspicion and distrust. Oh! it is hard to go through life meeting contempt with contempt, hatred with hatred, fearing, with too good reason, to love and trust hardly any one whose skin is white,—however lovable, attractive and congenial in seeming. In the bitter, passionate feelings of my soul again and again there rises the questions "When, oh! when shall this cease?" "Is there no help?" "How long oh! how long must we continue to suffer— to endure?" Conscience answers it is wrong, it is ignoble to despair; let us labor earnestly and faithfully to acquire knowledge, to break down the barriers of prejudice and oppression. Let us take courage; never ceasing to work,—hoping and believing that if not for us, for another generation there is a better, brighter day in store,—when slavery and prejudice shall vanish before the glorious light of Liberty and Truth; when the rights of every colored man shall everywhere be acknowledged and respected, and he shall be treated as a *man* and a *brother*!

September This evening Miss B[rown] and I joined the Female Anti-Slavery Society. I am glad to have persuaded her to do so. She seems an earnest hearted girl, in whom I cannot help having some confidence. I can only hope and pray that she will be true, and courageous enough to meet the opposition which every friend of freedom must encounter. . . . (pp. 62-3)

Saturday, May 11. [1856] All day I have been worrying about that poem. That troublesome poem which has yet to be commenced. Oh! that I could become suddenly inspired and write as only great poets can write. Or that I might write a beautiful poem of two hundred lines in my sleep as Coleridge did. Alas! in vain are all such longings. I must depend upon *myself* alone. And what can that self produce? Nothing, nothing but *doggerel*! This evening read Plutarch's Lycurgus.—(pp. 68-9)

Tuesday, July 22. [1856] This afternoon we were examined in "School and Schoolmaster." Essays were read. Miss Pitman's D[issertation], My poor poem, and Lizzie's V[aledictory]— which is a beautiful production; charming as dear Lizzie's self. Crowds of people were there. Our diplomas were awarded. I was lucky enough to get one. This evening we had a delightful meeting at the school house,—our last. It was one of the pleasantest meetings we have had. And now I realize that my school days are indeed over. And many sad regrets I feel that it is indeed so. The days of my N[ew] England school life, though spent far from home and early friends, have still been among the happiest of my life. I have been fortunate enough to receive the instruction of the best and kindest teachers; and the few friends I have made are warm and true.—New England! I love

to tread thy soil,—trod by the few noble spirits,—Garrison, Phillips and others,—the truest and noblest in the land; to breathe the pure air of thy hills, which is breathed by them; to gaze upon thy grand old rocks, "lashed by the fury of the ocean wave," upon thy granite hills, thy noble trees, and winding, sparkling streams, to all of which a greater charm is added by the thought that *they* the good and gifted ones, have gazed upon them also. (p. 71)

Monday, Aug. 10. [1857] I scarcely know myself tonight;—a great and sudden joy has completely dazzled—overpowered me. This evening Miss R[emond] sent for me in haste saying a gentleman wished to see me. I went wondering who it *could* be, and found————Whittier! one of the few men whom I truly reverence for their great minds and greater hearts. I cannot *say* all that I *felt*—even to *thee,* my Journal! I stood like one bewildered before the noble poet, whose kindly, earnest greeting *could* not increase my love and admiration for him;—my heart was full, but I *could* not speak, though constantly tormented by the thought that *he* would think me very stupid, very foolish;—but after a few simple words from him I felt more at ease, and though I still could say but very little, and left the talking part to Miss R[emond] who can *always talk,* it was such a pleasure to listen to *him,* to have *him* before me, to watch that noble, spiritual face, those glorious eyes—there are no eyes like them—that I felt *very, very* happy.—The memory of this interview will be a life-long happiness to me.— Shall I try to tell thee, my Journal, *something* of what he said? First we spoke of my old home and my present home. He asked me if I liked N[ew] E[ngland]—it was *such* a pleasure to tell him that I loved it well,—to see the approving smile, the sudden lighting of those earnest eyes!In comparing P[ennsylvani]a and N[ew] E[ngland] he spoke of the superior richness of the soil of the former, but said that here, though there were fewer and smaller farms, larger crops were raised on the same extent of ground, because vastly more labor and pains were bestowed upon its cultivation. Then I remembered that the poet was also a *farmer.* By some strange transition we got from *agriculture* to *spiritualism.* Whittier said that he too (having read them) thought that Prof. F[elton's] views were most uncharitable. Though *he* cannot believe in it; he thinks it wrong and unjust to condemn all interested in it.—The transition from this subject to that of the "future life" was easy. I shall never forget how earnestly, how beautifully the poet expressed his *perfect faith,* that faith so evident in his writings, in his holy and consistent life.—

At his request I took him to see Miss S[hepard]. The joy and surprise were almost more than she could bear. I stayed but a little while, then left them together. The poet gave me a cordial invitation to visit him and his sister at their home. God bless him! This is a day to be marked with a white stone. . . . (pp. 93-4)

Monday, Aug. 17 [1857]—My twentieth birthday.—Very, very fast the years are passing away,—and I,—Ah! how little am I improving them. I thought so to-day after I had finished "Jane Eyre," which has so powerfully interested and excited me. The excitement was not a healthy one, I know—and reason told me I *ought* to have been better employed.—But we have so much company now that it is impossible to accomplish anything.—This afternoon was regularly bored, victimized by two dull people.—I do wish they would leave us to the enjoyment of our own family circle, which is such a pleasant one now.—Twenty years! I have lived. I shall *not* live twenty years more,—I feel it. I believe I have but few years to live.—Them I *must,* I *will* improve.—I will pray for strength to keep *this* resolution;—I have broken so many. *This* I *must* keep. . . .

Thursday, Aug 20. . . . Went to see Miss S[hepard], and had a long talk with her about our noble Whittier. He has been pleased to speak most approvingly of my poor attempts at letter writing. I thank him, with all my heart. Miss S[hepard], with her usual great kindness, has made several plans for our mutual enjoyment, during vacation. . . . (p. 94)

Friday, Sept. 4. Very hot morning. . . . I have been examining myself, to-night,—trying to fathom my own thoughts and feelings; and I find, alas! too much, too much of *selfishness!* And yet I know that, in this world of care and sorrow, however weary and sad the heart my be, true *un*selfishness must ever be a source of the purest and highest happiness. Every kindly word, every gentle and generous deed we bestow upon others,—every ray of sunshine which penetrates the darkness of another's life, through the opening which *our* hands have made, *must* give to us a truer, nobler pleasure than any self-indulgence can impart. Knowing this feeling it with my whole heart,—I ask thee, Oh! Heavenly Father! to make me truly *unselfish,* to give to me a heart-felt interest in the welfare of others;—a spirit willing to sacrifice *my own;*—to live "for the *good* that I can do!". . . (p. 95)

Tuesday, June 15. [1858] Have been under-going a thorough self-examination. The result is a mingled feeling of sorrow, shame and self-contempt. Have realized more deeply and bit-terly than ever in my life my own ignorance and folly. Not only am I without the gifts of Nature,—wit, beauty and talent; without the accomplishments which nearly every one of my age, whom I know, possesses; but I am not even *intelligent.* And for *this* there is not the *shadow* of an excuse. Have had many advantages of late years; and it is entirely owning to my own want of energy, perseverance and application, that I have not improved them. It grieves me deeply to think of this. I have read an immense quantity, and it has all amounted to nothing,—because I have been too indolent and foolish to take the trouble of *reflecting.* Have wasted more time than I dare think of, in idle day-dreams, one of which was, how much I should *know* and *do* before I was twenty-one. And here I am nearly twenty-one, and only a *wasted life* to look back upon.— Add to intellectual defects a disposition whose despondency and fretfulness have constantly led me to look on the dark side of things, and effectually prevented me from contributing to the happiness of others; whose contrariness has often induced me to "do those things which I ought *not* to have done, and to leave undone those which I *ought* to have done," and *wanted* to do,—and we have as dismal a picture as one could look upon; and yet hardly dismal enough to be faithful. Of course, I want to *try* to reform. But how to begin! Havn't the least spark of order or method in my composition, and fear I'm wholly incapable of forming any regular plan of improvement.

Charlotte Forten—seated and holding the open book—with her husband and three prominent women of the Washington, D.C. intellectual world. From The Negro History Bulletin, *Vol. X, No. 4, January, 1947. Reproduced by permission of the Association of the Study of Negro Life and History.*

Wish I had some of the superabundant energy and perseverance which some whom I know possess, just to enable me to *keep* the good resolutions which are so easily made and so very easily broken.... (p. 106)

Tuesday, Aug. 17. [1858] My birthday. Twenty-one to-day! It grieves me to think of it;—to think that I have wasted so many years. I dare not dare not dwell upon the thought! Saw to-day a book of leaves from Rome, and all the "hallowed shrines" of Italy. They were beautiful; and ah what a passionate longing—as ever—did such names as the Coliseum, The Forum, the Tomb of Juliet, Venice, St. Peter's, Florence, awake in this too restless,—eager soul of mine. Sacred, sacred spots! Scared to genius and beauty and deathless fame, ah little did I think, years ago, that twenty-one summers should pass over me without my realizing the cherished all-absorbing dream of my heart—the dream of beholding ye! And now when all hope of such happiness should have flown, the dream still lingers on. Foolish, foolish girl! When will you be strong and sensible!

I suppose I *ought* to rejoice to-day for all the city seems to be rejoicing. The Queen's message arrived safely through the wonderful submarine telegraph, the bells are pealing forth merrily. But *I cannot* rejoice that England, my beloved England should be brought so very near this wicked land. I tremble for the consequences, but I will *hope* for the best. Thank God for Hope!... (pp. 107-08)

Monday, Nov. 15. [1858] A gloomy, chilly, and, to me, most depressing day. We have our first snow. It is an earnest of Winter, which I dread more than I have words to express. I am *sick* today, sick, sick, at heart;—and though I had *almost* resolved to forbear committing sad thoughts and gloomy feelings to my pages, dear Journal, and have very rarely done so, yet, to-night I long for a confidant—and *thou* art my only one. In the twilight I sat by the fire and watched the bright, usually so cheering blaze. But it cheered me not. Thoughts of the past came thronging upon me;—thoughts of the loved faces on which I used to look so fondly;—of the loved voices which were music to my ear, and ever sent a thrill of joy to my heart—voices now silent forever. I am *lonely* to-night. I long for one earnest sympathizing soul to be in close communion with my own. I long for the pressure of a loving hand in mine, the touch of loving lips upon my aching brow. I long to lay my weary head upon an earnest heart, which beats for me,—to which *I* am dearer far than all the world beside. There is none, for me, and never will be. I could only love one whom I could look up to, and reverence, and that *one* would never think of such a poor little ignoramus as I. But what a selfish creature I am. This is a forlorn old maid's reverie, and yet I am only twenty-one. But I am weary of life, and would gladly lay me down the rest in the quiet grave. There, alone, is peace, peace!... (p. 109)

Salem, Jan. 1, 1860. Can it be possible that so many months have elapsed since my pen last touched thy pages, old friend! Carelessly enough we say "time flies." Do we, after all, realize *how* it flies? How the months, days and hours *rush* along, bearing us on—on upon their swift, unwearying wings! To me there is something deeply impressive in this strange flight of Time. Standing now upon the threshold of another year, how solemn, how strangely solemn seem the Past and the Future; the *dead* and *newly born* year;—memories, gladdening and sorrowing of the one, eager hopes, desires, resolves for the other;—how they crowd upon us now! Do they avail aught? I ask myself. Alas! too often, I fear they do not. Too often past experiences, and high resolves for the Future, are forgotten,

swallowed up in the excitement of the Present moment. Have been reading to-day Arnold's History of Rome. How it thrills one to know of those heroic deeds done "in the brave days of old." And how blessed it is that all the wealth of the ages can be ours, if we choose to grasp it! That we can live, not in this century, this corner of the world, alone, but in every century, and every age, and every clime! That we can listen to the words of orators, poets and sages; that we can enter into every conflict, share every joy, thrill with every noble deed, known since the world began. And hence are *books* to us a treasure and a blessing unspeakable. And they are doubly this when one is shut out from society as I am, and has not opportunities of studying those living, breathing, *human* books, which are, I doubt not, after all, the most profoundly interesting and useful study. From that kind of pleasure, that kind of improvement I am barred; but, thank God! none can deprive me of the other kind. And I will strive to be resigned during the little while we have to stay here.—and in that higher sphere do I not *know* the cruelty the injustice of man ceases? There do Right, and Justice and Love abide. (pp. 113-14)

> *Charlotte L. Forten, in her* The Journal of Charlotte
> L. Forten, *edited by Ray Allen Billington, The Dry-
> den Press, Publishers, 1953, 248 p.*

RAY ALLEN BILLINGTON   (essay date 1953)

[*Billington was an American historian and editor who specialized in the history of America in the nineteenth century. In the following excerpt from his introduction to* The Journal of Charlotte L. Forten, *he discusses Forten's personal aspirations and her opinions concerning race relations in America as they are revealed in her journal.*]

Charlotte L. Forten was a delicate young woman of sixteen when in 1854 she left her native Philadelphia to launch the educational and teaching career described in the . . . *Journal.* Her interests were those of other intelligent girls reared in that calm Quaker city during its antebellum days; she read widely and with a catholic taste that embraced everything from the classics to sentimental poetry, attended lectures avidly, listened rapturously to the musical recitals of wandering artists, gazed worshipfully on the steel engravings that passed for art among unsophisticated Americans, and took mild pleasure in the ailments that were the stock in trade of all well-bred females during the Victorian era. Yet one thing distinguished Charlotte Forten from other Philadelphia belles. She was a Negro, destined to endure the constant insults that were the lot of persons of color in pre-Civil-War America.

That no other influence was so strong in shaping Charlotte Forten's thoughts is amply revealed in the *Journal*. . . . When she began keeping that record, on a warm May morning in 1854, she had just arrived in Salem, Massachusetts, from Philadelphia. . . . [As] the pages of her *Journal* disclose, she was destined to long periods when "lung fever" forced her to forsake her studies and teaching. But on that May morning illness was furthest from her thoughts. Ahead lay the adventure of learning, and that was exciting enough to justify the diary she was beginning.

Miss Forten could not know, as she traced the opening words in a fine, bold hand, that she was starting a uniquely human document. Nor did her first entry reveal the unusual nature of the entries to follow: "A wish to record the passing events of my life, which, even if quite unimportant to others, naturally possess great interest to myself, and of which it will be pleasant to have some remembrance, has induced me to commence this journal.'' This, even in its stilted phrases, might have launched any one of the thousands of diaries kept by young women of that era. Yet the *Journal* that unfolded during the next decade bore no resemblance to any other. Instead it served as a moving record of the reactions of a sensitive young Negro to the white world about her.

For her race was always uppermost in Charlotte Forten's thoughts. The color of her skin determined her attitude toward her fellow humans, toward her country, and toward her God. From the accident of pigmentation stemmed even her driving ambition. She *must* excel among the students of the Salem grammar school in which she first enrolled or the normal school where she completed her education. She *must* read constantly; tucked among the pages of her manuscript *Journal* was a yellowed paper listing more than one hundred books completed in one year. She *must* master French, German, and Latin in addition to her regular school work. Every lesson learned well was a triumph not only for herself but for the oppressed Negro people of mid-century America. By excelling in all things she could help convince a hostile world that Negroes were as capable of self-improvement as whites.

That this was the source of her ambition was abundantly revealed in Miss Forten's *Journal.* ''Would that there were far more intelligent colored people!';' she wrote at one time. ''And yet we could hardly expect more of those, who have so many unsurmountable difficulties to contend with. But despite them all let our motto still be 'Excelsior' and we cannot fail to make some improvement. At times I feel it almost impossible not to despond entirely of there ever being a better, brighter day for us. None but those who experience it can know what it is— this constant, galling sense of cruel injustice and wrong. I cannot help feeling it very often,—it intrudes upon my happiest moments, and spreads a dark, deep gloom over everything.'' Miss Forten was plunged into equal despair whenever a Negro failed to excel in competition with whites. (pp. 1-2)

Every page of Charlotte Forten's *Journal* reflected her determination to excel in all things. She was vexed, on the morning she began her diary, that the sun had risen before her, even though she had awakened before five o'clock. A few months later, as she looked back over her first seventeen years on the occasion of a birthday, she asked herself: ''Have I improved them as I should have done?'' Overcritical as always, she felt that she had not. ''I feel grieved and ashamed to think how very little I know to what I should know of what is really good and useful. May this knowledge of my *want* of knowledge be to me a fresh incentive to more earnest, thoughtful action, more persevering study.'' Little wonder, in view of this attitude, that progress seemed alarmingly slow. Charlotte Forten might impress others with the catholicity of her literary tastes or with her rich knowledge of the past, but she was always more conscious of the tasks remaining than of those accomplished. (p. 3)

If ambition was one of Miss Forten's virtues, modesty was another. ''When I read of the great and gifted ones of the earth,'' she confided in her *Journal,* ''I feel more deeply my own ignorance and inefficiency.—How very little after the most diligent and persevering study can I hope to resemble them.'' Later triumphs did not decrease her humility. Thus she could not believe that her poetic efforts were worthy of the name, despite the publication of her verses in magazines and newspapers. ''How often,'' she complained, ''have I invoked in vain the 'spirit of song'; the muse is always most unyielding,

despite my assurances, that should she deign to bless me, my first offering would be upon the shrine of Liberty.'' Even her friendships were marred by the fear that her presence was distasteful to others. Once, on leaving Salem briefly, she said her good-bys to a favorite teacher who ''gently reproved me when we were parting, for not returning her embrace. I fear she thought me cold, but it was not so. I know not why it is that when I think and feel the most, I say the least. I suppose it is my nature, not to express by word or action how much I really feel.''

Charlotte Forten's conflicts—between modesty and talent, ambition and apparent lack of realization, affection and shyness— all stemmed from her constant awareness that she was a Negro. A product of generations of discrimination, she could never hope to establish bonds of perfect friendship with whites, no matter how unprejudiced those whites might be. Between the two races, in that day of slavery, was a barrier that neither could completely remove. (pp. 3-4)

This racial consciousness endows Miss Forten's *Journal* with an importance in the twentieth century that it scarcely enjoyed in the nineteenth. Enlightened individuals today have dedicated themselves to a crusade for equality and human decency. Yet how few among them—how few among the nonpersecuted, that is—can know the effect of prejudice on its victims. Miss Forten's *Journal* makes this effect terrifyingly clear. Whenever she was barred from the railroad cars or an ''ice cream saloon'' or a museum or a school because of the color of her skin she returned home, sick at heart, to pour out her resentment on the pages of her diary. No believer in the golden rule can read that record today without reawakening to the need for decency among men. (p. 4)

Try as she did to counsel patience to the oppressed, Charlotte Forten found the practice more difficult than the preaching— and little wonder. Each new insult drove her to more outspoken rebellion. In the end prejudice drove this sensitive girl, who was an ardent patriot and a zealous Christian, to the point where she could denounce her country and almost deny her God.

That she should denounce the United States for sanctioning the institution of slavery was almost inevitable. Every Fourth of July celebration allowed her to contrast, in her *Journal,* the boast of liberty made by orators with the grim reality of the slave system. ''The *patriots,* poor fools, were celebrating the anniversary of their vaunted *independence,''* she wrote on one occasion. ''Strange! that they cannot feel their *own* degradation—the weight of the chains which they have imposed upon *themselves.''*. . .

To Miss Forten life in England seemed vastly preferable to life in a land where her countrymen were held in bondage. ''Oh! England,'' she confided in her *Journal,* ''my heart yearns towards thee as to a loved and loving friend! I long to behold thee, to dwell in one of thy quiet homes, far from the scenes of my early childhood; far from the land, my native land— where I am hated and oppressed because God has given me a *dark skin.''*. . . (p. 5)

The hatred of discrimination that drove Charlotte Forten to the point where she denied her national heritage almost forced her, on one gloomy day, to renounce her God. ''Hatred of oppression,'' she confessed, ''seems to me so blended with hatred of the oppressor that I cannot separate them. I feel that no other injury could be so hard to bear, so very hard to forgive, as that inflicted by cruel oppression and prejudice. How *can* I be a Christian when so many in common with myself, for

Holograph copy of a poem by Forten.

no crime suffer so cruelly, so unjustly? It seems in vain to try, even to hope."

That the racial question should constantly intrude on Charlotte Forten's consciousness as she wrote her *Journal* was not surprising; for sixteen years she had been regularly reminded that her dark skin doomed her to an inferior social station. When she was still a child, she and her parents had been barred from stores and denied service in restaurants. They had been forced to sit in segregated sections of omnibuses and railroad cars. They had been turned away from lectures and theaters. They had heard thoughtless white men refer to them as "niggers" without even realizing the insulting sting of that word. From behind drawn curtains in her grandfather's spacious Philadelphia home on Lombard Street the youthful Charlotte had watched terror-stricken as runaway slaves were hounded by mobs or returned in shackles to their masters. The continual recurrence of these incidents was enough to convince any young women of sensitivity that nothing else in the world was so important as the battle against prejudice.

The environment in which she lived was not the only factor that led Miss Forten to dedicate her life to the cause of decency. Equally influential was her immediate background. From the time that she lisped her first words she heard talk of Negro rights about the family table; from the time she could first comprehend she listened to abolitionists as they plotted freedom for the slaves while gathered in the Forten living room. Reared in an atmosphere of crusading zeal, she was predestined to play a minor yet significant role in the contest that ended with Abraham Lincoln's Emancipation Proclamation. Most influential among those who turned her youthful mind in that direction was her grandfather, James Forten. A man of wealth, idealism, and determination, he cast his shadow over the two generations of Fortens who followed in his footsteps. (pp. 5-6)

For a generation the Fortens' Philadelphia home was a mecca for abolitionists. So warm was their hospitality and so persuasive their charm that the great poet of abolitionism, John Greenleaf Whittier, immortalized them in a poem, "To the Daughters of James Forten". . . . (p. 13)

Little wonder that when Miss Forten was ready to launch her own career she was so steeped in the cause that the plight of the slave transcended all other interests in her life. (p. 15)

Having decided on a career as a teacher, Miss Forten enrolled in the Salem Normal School, from which she was graduated, in the language of the *Salem Register*, "with decided éclat" in July, 1856. Through the intercession of the principal of the normal school, Richard Edwards, and with the hearty support of her grammar-school teachers, she immediately became a teacher in the Epes Grammar School of Salem. Despite the prejudice that existed among the less enlightened townsmen, her appointment was accepted by both school board and pupils without even a flurry of excitement, and Miss Forten soon found herself immersed in the routine of classes. lecture-going, and study that was the lot of village teachers a century ago.

The next two years were among the happiest in Charlotte Forten's life. Although she never enjoyed teaching, Salem offered plentiful opportunity for her to pursue her real interests: abolitionism and learning. (pp. 17-8)

From the time her **"Parting Hymn"** was acclaimed at [her] grammar-school graduation [Miss Forten] produced a succession of sentimental poems and essays which ranged from a hymn sung at the semiannual normal-school examination in 1856 through such poetic effusions as **"The Two Voices,"** **"The Wind Among the Poplars,"** **"The Angel's Visit,"** and **"The Slave-Girl's Prayer."** Perhaps her literary style was best portrayed in an essay, **"Glimpses of New England,"** which was published in the *National Anti-Slavery Standard*:

> The beach, which is at some distance from the town, is delightful. It was here that I first saw the sea, and stood 'entranced in silent awe,' gazing upon the waves as they marched, in one mass of the richest green, to the shore, then suddenly broke into foam, white and beautiful as the winter snow. I remember one pleasant afternoon which I spent with a friend, gathering shells and seaweed on the beach, or sitting on the rocks, listening to the wild music of the waves, and watching the clouds of spray as they sprang high up in the air, then fell again in snowy wreaths at our feet. We lingered there until the sun had sunk into his ocean bed. . . .

Perhaps wishful thinking occasioned a contemporary to remark that her writing, "for style and true poetical diction, is not surpassed by anything in the English language." (p. 18)

Charlotte Forten, bearing a letter from John Greenleaf Whittier, went before the Boston Educational Commission in August, 1862, asking to be sent to Port Royal as a teacher. . . .

Miss Forten found much to interest her when she reached her new home on St. Helena Island. She was fascinated by the tropical vegetation, the warm winter days, and the great plantation houses. She was entranced by the children who flocked to her school. She was captivated by the older Negroes and never tired of recording their quaint speech or their religious songs. But most of all she was intrigued with the social experiment that had brought her to Port Royal. She and her fellow teachers were destined to prove that Negroes were as capable of self-improvement as whites! Here was a cause worth any sacrifice, when the future of a whole race depended on the outcome. Little wonder that no other subject was treated in such detail in the pages of her *Journal.*

The experiment was just being launched when Charlotte Forten arrived at Port Royal. The teachers and officials hoped to demonstrate two things. One was the ability of the former slaves to learn; Miss Forten and her fellow workers labored mightily to instruct their charges in the three R's and exhibited unrestrained delight whenever success crowned their efforts. The other was the bravery of the Negro men; General Saxton wanted to show that they fought as fearlessly as their white-skinned brethren. Miss Forten was as interested in the Negro troops as she was in the youngsters who crowded her schoolroom. Intimately acquainted with both the soldiers and their officers, she recorded their experiences with an enthusiasm that she had formerly reserved for abolition meetings. (p. 25)

The Negro troops did not have to wait long before showing their mettle, for during the summer of 1863 the long-awaited attack on Charleston plunged them into one of the war's bloodiest battles. (p. 26)

Charlotte Forten witnesed these stirring events from the comparative safety of Port Royal. She cheered the Negro troops as they sallied out to raid the enemy coast, rejoiced when they returned triumphant, and tearfully recorded the loss of their dead. She thrilled as the fleet sailed away to attack Charleston, suffered while awaiting news of the assault, and mourned when she learned that the Fifty-Fourth Massachusetts Regiment had been cut to pieces and its brave leader, Colonel Shaw, had been killed. Yet Miss Forten never forgot the principal task before her. Even in the midst of battle she found time to care for her school, initiate former slaves into the mysteries of reading and writing, and comfort the Negro troops stationed at Port Royal. Her only reward was the knowledge that the social experiment was successful. Dispatches indicated that more and more freedmen were buying land on the Sea Islands, that two thousand children were enrolled in schools, that thousands of adults were receiving instruction in the churches before the Sunday-morning services. Charlotte Forten could return north in May, 1864, knowing that Negroes were as capable of progress as whites. (pp. 28-9)

> *Ray Allen Billington, in an introduction to* The Journal of Charlotte L. Forten, *The Dryden Press, Publishers, 1953, pp. 1-32.*

FRANCES GAITHER   (essay date 1953)

[*Gaither, an American short story writer, children's writer, biographer, and novelist, was born in Tennessee and has written extensively upon slavery in America. In the following excerpt, Gaither calls* The Journal of Charlotte L. Forten *an important "contribution to the most momentous chapter in American Negro history."*]

The 16-year-old girl who began her journal from only "a wish to record the passing events of my life—even if quite unimportant to others" was already afire with longing not to remain unimportant. She was afire to serve those others of her own race, who unlike herself, had been born to slavery. Because of her zeal and because of the epoch represented, 1854 to 1864, *The Journal of Charlotte L. Forten* is, over and above the relation of passing events in one young person's days, a valuable contribution to the most momentous chapter in American

Negro history. It well deserves, after almost a century, the honor of being made into a book. . . .

In the first entry, she might be any school girl of that epoch, breaking off a rhapsody on a beautiful May morning to do an arithmetic lesson before breakfast. But in the second her own small doings are forgotten in the "indignation and sorrow" she feels at news of the arrest of a "fugitive from bondage." She succumbs to the pathos of Little Nell and Paul Dombey, is "perfectly enchanted" by Mrs. Kemble's reading of *The Merchant of Venice.* Yet her deeper springs always are fed by Helper's *Impending Crisis,* Mr. Garrison's *The Liberator* and even more the impassioned living voices devoutly heard at every anti-slavery meeting within her reach.

For all her steady advancement as pupil and then as teacher of Salem white children, she continually deplores her "wasted life." But on her twenty-fifth birthday, Aug. 17, 1862, she is hoping for—and, thanks to wonderful Whittier, soon thereafter winning—a post in the schools newly set up under the occupying Federal forces among the freedmen in the South Carolina Sea Islands. (p. 6)

Every day is soon abrim. . . . One wonders how she can find time to describe it all. Yet she does—even to mansions silent but for the still-echoing sea beyond their margins of roses and white azaleas and magnolia trees in bud. (p. 22)

> *Frances Gaither, "The Will to Serve," in* The New York Times Book Review, *April 12, 1953, pp. 6, 22.*

THE UNITED STATES QUARTERLY BOOK REVIEW   (essay date 1953)

[*In the following excerpt, the reviewer regards* The Journal of Charlotte L. Forten *as the personal record of a sensitive individual as well as an important historical record.*]

This diary [*The Journal of Charlotte L. Forten*], concerned with the life of its author during the years 1854-64, is a remarkably revealing testament to her intellectual growth, her participation in the abolition movement, and her life among the freedmen at Port Royal, South Carolina. The full personal record of an intelligent and sensitive Negro girl, the journal is especially valuable because there are so few human documents of its kind. It shows Miss Forten's inmost thoughts about racial prejudice, her burning sense of injustice, and her never-ceasing concern for the betterment of her people. Professor Billington's discerning introduction and his meticulous editing of the manuscript greatly enhance its usefulness to historians, sociologists, and students of race relations. (p. 113)

> *A review of "The Journal of Chalotte L. Forten," in* The United States Quarterly Book Review, *Vol. 9, No. 2, June, 1953, pp. 113-14.*

RICHARD BARKSDALE AND KENETH KINNAMON   (essay date 1972)

[*Barksdale and Kinnamon are both American educators, editors, and essayists who have written widely on black American literature. In the following excerpt, they describe the entries in Forten's journal as candid and written in a "lilting" style that displays effective imagery.*]

[Charlotte Forten's *Journal* describes] her experiences during her stay on St. Helena, one of South Carolina's Sea Islands.

Masthead of William Lloyd Garrison's journal The Liberator.

During the two years that she served here as a teacher, there were many privations and many wartime aggravations, but the lines of her *Journal* pulse with happy optimism and *joie de vivre*. She also emerges as a person of considerable intellectual breadth, obviously well acquainted with poetry and philosophy and always eager for more knowledge, and possessing a gift for writing. Her style is lilting and her descriptive imagery at times quite effective. These effects, along with her candor, combine to make the *Journal* a remarkable piece of writing for a young Black girl who lived on the fringe of a slave culture. (p. 276)

> *Richard Barksdale and Keneth Kinnamon, in a headnote to "Two Black Women Serve and Observe: From 'Journal of Charlotte Forten',"* in Black Writers of America: A Comprehensive Anthology, *edited by Richard Barksdale and Keneth Kinnamon, The Macmillan Company, 1972, pp. 275-76.*

JOAN R. SHERMAN (essay date 1974)

[*In the following excerpt, Sherman discusses Forten's poetry and prose, concluding that while she was not a great writer, her mature works show sensitivity and creativity.*]

The City of Brotherly Love was "old abominable Philadelpia," a stronghold of segregation, to Charlotte Forten, who was born there on August 17, 1837, into the leading black family of the city. (p. 88)

At the age of sixteen she moved to Salem, Massachusetts, to live in [an] abolitionist haven, the home of Charles Lenox Remond. Here, in May, 1854, Miss Forten began her remarkable *Journal*. . . . (pp. 88-9)

In her *Journal* she expresses outraged despair every time a fugitive slave is brutally captured, anguish when she and her friends are barred from ice cream saloons, trains, and museums in Philadelphia or when she is snubbed by white schoolmates in Salem. Assailed by the din of July Fourth celebrations, she

denounces the mockery of freedom in a land of slaves. . . . (pp. 89-90)

In August, 1862, with a letter of recommendation from [her friend John Greenleaf] Whittier, she asked the Boston Educational Commission to send her to the Sea Islands of South Carolina as a teacher. Here the Port Royal experiment to educate and acculturate recently emancipated slaves was in progress. . . . However, from the landing at Hilton Head until May, 1864, Miss Forten, braving heat, fleas, and warfare, taught and succored contrabands of all ages, worked in their store and in the military hospital. She was among the first to appreciate and set down the hymns and shouts of the Sea Islanders, and she contributed a valuable record of the Port Royal experience in vivid letters to the *Liberator* and to Whittier, which he had published in the *Atlantic Monthly*. (p. 91)

In 1877 she met Francis James Grimké, son of the South Carolina planter Henry Grimké—a brother of abolitionists Sarah and Angelina (Mrs. Theodore Weld) Grimké—and his slave Nancy Weston. . . . When they were married on December 19, 1878, Miss Forten was forty-one, thirteen years older than her husband. (p. 92)

During these years she wrote a few more poems, many well-informed fiery letters on racial issues to newspapers, essays on art, the Philadelphia Exposition. . . , and Washington events, and her moving tributes to Frederick Douglass and Whittier. Intellectual and emotional maturity mark this late work, which reveals her fine talent for strong, succinct, and beautifully descriptive prose. . . . To perpetuate her memory, Grimké endowed a scholarship in her name at Lincoln University. But the most valuable legacy remains Mrs. Grimké's *Journal* of the turbulent years 1854-64, both a chronicle of great men and events and a categorical imperative of racial justice.

The fourteen published poems by Mrs. Grimké show a decided maturing of poetic technique and sentiment from 1855 to the 1890's. In the *Journal* she disparages her earlier efforts. When complimented on her first poem, **"To W. L. G. on Reading**

Charlotte L. Forten.

His 'Chosen Queen'" (which she had signed, "C. L. F."),
Miss Forten replied, "If I ever write doggerel again I shall be
careful not to sign my own initials." The verse is a warm and
worshipful accolade to Garrison, who battles "With truer
weapons than the blood-stained sword, / And teachest us that
greater is the might / Of *moral* warfare, noble thought and
word." Similarly schoolgirlish is **"A Parting Hymn,"** written
"for examination" in 1856 at Salem Normal School. The "onward and upward" counsel of this sentimental farewell are set
in a pleasing, naturally flowing meter. Miss Forten read another
poem of 1856, titled simply **"Poem,"** at her normal school
graduation. She was "heartily ashamed" of the "poor, miserable poem," and hoped it would not be published. "I think
this will be the last of my attempts at poetizing," she wrote.
The *Salem Register,* however, complimented the skillful writing and graceful delivery of **"Poem,"** which is but a slightly
inferior sequel to Longfellow's celebrated **"Psalm of Life":**

> No vain dreams of earthly glory
>   Urge us onward to explore
> Far-extending realms of knowledge,
>   With their rich and varied store;
> But, with hope of aiding others,
>   Gladly we perform our part;
> Nor forget, the mind, while storing,
>   We must educate the heart,—

> Teach it hatred of oppression,
>   Truest love of God and man;
> Thus our high and holy calling
>   May accomplish His great plan.

Among five poems of the years 1858-60, **"Two Voices"** (1858)
offers a choice to a "homeless outcast": voice one counsels
retributive "hate for hate and scorn for scorn" or the peace of
the grave; voice two (which wins) exalts altruistic striving and
suffering in a "holy cause" as far nobler. **"The Wind among
the Poplars"** (1859) is a monologue on a lover lost at sea, and
"A Slave Girl's Prayer," a diffuse supplication for death as
the "only hope of peace." The best of this group is **"The
Angel's Visit"** (1860?), which, said William Wells Brown,
"for style and true poetical diction, is not surpassed by anything
in the English language." His compliment is perhaps extreme,
but **"The Angel's Visit"** offers admirable variation in emotional range, a sustained narrative line, and adroit matching of
sound and sense. In easy-flowing lines Miss Forten maintains
a dreamlike mood edged with pathos for the musings of a
sensitive motherless girl. Her despair is conveyed tersely:

> For bitter thoughts had filled my breast,
>   And sad, and sick at heart,
> I longed to lay me down and rest,
>   From all the world apart.

But after her angel mother's visit in a dream, the girl's soul
knows harmony and peaceful courage. . . . Among later poems
"Charles Sumner" (1874) places this warrior among the "glorious band" of "Poet, and saint, and sage, painter and king"
depicted in paintings which decorate his home, and the poet
seeks guidance and courage from his departed spirit. **"At New-
port"** (1888), a love poem in blank verse, sustains an artistic
comparison of the sea's action to the heart's emotions. . . .
Mrs. Grimké's last dated poem, **"In Florida"** (1893), recalls
with yearning Florida's lush, fragrant flora and mild blue skies.
The color, warmth, and indolence of the scene are communicated by personified Nature.

Two poems in blank verse of later years (undated) are Mrs.
Grimké's best efforts. Richness is obtained through the use of
run-on lines and shifting of caesuras and syllabic stress. **"Charlotte Corday"** (28 lines) has a tone of quiet simplicity and
controlled tension which conveys this martyr's determined
courage before her dramatic murder of Marat:

> She leans her head against her prison bars
> How wearily! The heavy, tear-dimmed eyes
> Gaze at us, from the pale pathetic face,
> In utter mournfulness. One slender hand
> Clasps the rough bars; the other holds the pen
> With which, in words with love and courage fraught,
> She bids farewell to kindred, home, and life.

The other poem, **"Wordsworth"** (20 lines), appreciatively greets
the "Poet of the serene and thoughful lay!" In youth, Mrs.
Grimké writes, we cherish "The thrilling strains of more impassioned bards":

> But, in our riper years, when through the heat
> And burden of the day we struggle on,
> Breasting the stream upon whose shores we dreamed,
> Weary of all the turmoil and the din
> Which drowns the finer voices of the soul;
> We turn to thee, true priest of Nature's fane,
> And find the rest our fainting spirits need,—
> That calm, more ardent singers cannot give. . . .

The "mild and steadfast" quality of Wordsworth's tranquil song is nicely echoed in this tribute. Charlotte Forten Grimké was not a major poet; however, the quality of her mature verse and of her poetic prose indicates that she possessed sensitivity and creative skills beyond the ordinary. (pp. 92-96)

> *Joan R. Sherman, "Charlotte L. Forten Grimké," in her* Invisible Poets: Afro-Americans of the Nineteenth Century, *University of Illinois Press, 1974, pp. 88-96.*

ADDITIONAL BIBLIOGRAPHY

Brown, William Wells. "Charlotte L. Forten." In his *The Black Man: His Antecedents, His Genius, and His Achievements*, pp. 190-99. 1863. Reprint. New York and London: Johnson Reprint Corporation, 1968.
    Biographical sketch and poetry. Brown, a personal friend and fellow abolitionist, praises Forten's works.

Cooper, Anna Julia. *Life and Writings of the Grimké Family*. 2 Vols. Privately printed, 1951.*
    Contains selections from Forten's writings, as well as biographical information.

Dannett, Sylvia G.L. "Charlotte L. Forten." In her *Profiles of Negro Womanhood*, Vol. 1, pp. 86-93. New York and Philadelphia: M. W. Lads, 1964.
    Biographical information and excerpts from Forten's works.

The Negro History Bulletin X, No. 4 (January 1947): 75, 79, 95.
    Historical information about the Forten, Grimké, and Purvis families. The article includes the poem "To Keep the Memory of Charlotte Forten Grimké," written by her niece Angelina Grimké.

Wilson, Edmund. "Northerners in the South: Charlotte Forten and Colonel Higginson." In his *Patriotic Gore: Studies in the Literature of the American Civil War*, pp. 239-57. New York: Oxford University Press, 1962.*
    Account of the St. Helena Island experiment. Wilson briefly discusses Forten and her family background, but gives a lengthy discussion of Colonel Thomas W. Higginson, who was Forten's friend and the leader of the regiment composed of former slaves from St. Helena Island.

Henrik (Johann) Ibsen

1828-1906

(Also wrote under pseudonym of Brynjolf Bjarme) Norwegian dramatist and poet.

The following entry presents criticism of Ibsen's drama *Vildanden (The Wild Duck)*, first published in 1884 and first performed in 1885. For a complete discussion of Ibsen's career, see *TCLC*, Volumes 2 and 8.

The Wild Duck is one of the most often-performed and extensively analyzed plays by the Norwegian dramatist who is regarded as the father of modern drama. Considered a masterpiece in the genre of tragicomedy, *The Wild Duck* blends realism and symbolism to explore the role of illusion and self-deception in everyday life.

The massive body of Ibsen's work is generally divided by critics into three phases. The first consists of verse dramas influenced by the prevailing romanticism of nineteenth-century European theater. The second phase is made up of prose dramas concerned with social realism, written for the most part during his twenty-seven-year sojourn outside Norway. *The Wild Duck* is often seen by critics as a transitional work, written at the close of Ibsen's social realist period and heralding his final phase, in which he produced works that still dealt with modern, realistic themes but made increasing use of symbol and metaphor. Thus *The Wild Duck,* though on one level a play replete with naturalistic minuteness of detail, also contains complex symbolism which has been subject to a variety of interpretations.

The Wild Duck was written in 1883 and 1884, while Ibsen was living abroad, dividing his time between Rome and the Tyrolean village of Gossensass. It was widely praised from its initial appearance, marking the first time in Ibsen's career that critics and the public alike were united in acclaiming his work. Ibsen was hailed as one of Norway's—indeed, all of Scandinavia's—greatest literary figures. This unaccustomed approval encouraged Ibsen in the summer of 1885 to visit his homeland for the first time in ten years. But, annoyed by attempts on the part of various political factions to ally him with their causes, he resumed his expatriation that autumn, not returning to Norway for another six years.

The wild duck of the title is the special pet of fourteen-year-old Hedvig Ekdal, whose parents operate a photography studio. Hjalmar Ekdal, Hedvig's father, is lazy and self-indulgent; his wife Gina does most of the work. Gregers Werle, an old friend of Hjalmar, learns that Gina was once a maid in his father's house and that Hedvig may actually be the elder Werle's child. Gregers reveals this to Hjalmar, maintaining that knowledge of the complete truth will enable the Ekdals to enter into a "true marriage." Hjalmar, however, rejects his marriage as false and Hedvig as an "interloper." Gregers suggests to the uncomprehending child that she sacrifice the wild duck as a symbolic gesture to demonstrate her love for Hjalmar; instead, she kills herself.

Much critical controversy about *The Wild Duck* centers on the complicated and equivocal nature of the events that take place prior to the opening scenes of the play, and which are gradually

disclosed as the play progresses. Some sixteen years before the action of the play, Gregers's father, Haakon Werle, and Hjalmar Ekdal's father were business partners. The elder Ekdal was jailed for illegally felling timber on state-owned land, while Werle escaped any legal action. In addition, Gina admits that an affair with Haakon Werle took place before her marriage to Hjalmar, putting Hedvig's paternity into question. Critical readings of *The Wild Duck* often focus on these two major plot elements. While most commentators on the play assume that Haakon Werle was both guilty of timber-fraud and responsible for Hedvig's birth, some believe that both charges were false. Another group of critics, however, considers these issues unresolvable and maintains that Ibsen intended them to remain as such. Another aspect of the play that has garnered differing interpretations is the state of affairs in the Ekdal household as the play opens. The general critical consensus is that the Ekdals' home life is happy before Gregers Werle's intrusion. In Hermann J. Weigand's words, "The crisis that we witness in the play is the result of the wholly gratuitous meddling of an outsider." Charles A. Hallett, however, maintains that Ibsen intended the family's meager finances, Hjalmar's lack of regard for his father and for Gina, old Ekdal's dependence on alcohol, and Hedvig's lack of preparedness for her coming blindness, to show that Gregers disrupts a household on the brink of collapse from within.

Critics have ascribed to the character of Gregers Werle a myriad of reasons for his actions, ranging from a sincere desire to help his friend to a fanatical devotion to the truth at any cost. The majority of commentators on the play generally assess his character negatively, condemning him for his attempts to force his "claim of the ideal" upon others. Often a degree of psychopathology is attributed to Gregers. Some critics rather grudgingly allow that Gregers may have been a well-meaning, if misguided, idealist, but still deplore his meddling; while Hallett has adopted the view that Gregers is a tragic hero standing boldly opposed to his despicable father and wrong only in his assessment of Hjalmar Ekdal as a man capable of ennoblement through adversity.

The wild duck functions both as a real object and as a symbol throughout the play. Errol Durbach has called Ibsen's duck "perhaps the most grotesquely over-symbolized creature in dramatic literature"—and commentators on *The Wild Duck* have found that the bird symbolically represents many of the play's characters and situations. The duck is most often linked symbolically with Hedvig, whose uncertain parentage is prefigured in her own remark about the duck: that it is special because "nobody knows her and nobody knows where she came from either." Janel M. Mueller and G. Wilson Knight are among the critics who find that Hedvig ultimately kills herself to spare her pet's life, while Mary McCarthy [see *TCLC*, Volume 2] writes that Hedvig shoots herself because she confuses her own identity with that of the duck. The formerly wild bird, shot and wounded by old Werle, captured and given to Hedvig, and grown fat in captivity, is also compared by critics with the character of Hjalmar Ekdal, a man with a history of youthful "bad ways" who has settled comfortably into his domestic routine. Ibsen also has the characters in the drama use the wild duck and its fate to define metaphorically the conditions of their own lives and the lives of others. Thus Haakon Werle compares the duck's self-destructive actions when shot with old Ekdal's inability to recover from adversity; Hjalmar also says that his father is like the wounded bird, leading a pale imitation of his former life; while Gregers believes that his old friend Hjalmar is like the injured wildfowl, doomed unless a rescue is effected by some outside agency. Gregers, of course, believes that he is to be the means of Hjalmar's "rescue." He does not see, as Mueller writes, that "through the agency of Gina the rescue has already taken place." Hjalmar, who craves attention and pampering, has found in Gina the ideal mate, and even those critics who do not absolutely condemn Gregers for his interference in the Ekdals' marriage agree that Gregers, mistaken in holding a high opinion of Hjalmar's nature, is mistaken too in believing he is better able than Gina to show Hjalmar the way to lead a happy life. Some critics, such as Edmund Gosse, stress the wild nature of the duck and its significance as an untamed captive. Most, however, choose to discuss the significance of the bird's adaptation to a domestic existence and parallel it with Hjalmar's similar adaptation.

Georg Brandes has surmised that *The Wild Duck* was written largely in angry reaction to the hostile reception of *Gengangere* (*Ghosts*). Upon the appearance of *Ghosts* in 1882, Ibsen was excoriated for references in the drama to venereal disease and incest. Brandes's theory, which has received a great deal of critical support, is that in *The Wild Duck* Ibsen cast himself satirically as Gregers Werle, the destroyer of comforting illusions. Critics note that in an earlier drama, *En folkefiende* (*An Enemy of the People*), Ibsen had seemingly been a proponent of the stance taken by the character Dr. Stockmann,

who was steadfast in bringing to light an unpopular truth. Yet in *The Wild Duck* Ibsen apparently performed an about-face, recommending the socially expedient falsehood and presenting his truth-seeker in an unfavorable light. Sydney Mendel has written that Ibsen's views regarding the value of indiscriminate truth-telling had changed somewhat, and that "in *The Wild Duck* Ibsen is attacking his old self in the person of Gregers Werle." It is often argued that if Ibsen was lampooning his former beliefs in the figure of Gregers, then some other character in the play must represent his true point of view. The most frequently named candidate for this position is the cynical Dr. Relling, who fosters the delusions or "life-lies" that assuage the dull lives of the other characters in the play. Critics who see Relling as the *raisonneur* of *The Wild Duck* tend to concur with Gosse that the play's central theme lies in the following words spoken by Relling: "If you rob the average man of his illusions, you are almost certain to rob him of his happiness." Other commentators on the play, however, maintain that in this work Ibsen, for the first time in his career, did not appear to be making a statement of his own beliefs and did not identify with either Gregers or Relling. Rather, Ibsen was attempting to tell a story about individuals and not "types" of people—a tendency that became even more pronounced in subsequent dramas, perhaps most notably in *Hedda Gabler*. Weigand maintains that it is a "mistake on the reader's part to identify himself too closely with any of the characters of *The Wild Duck*. He must hold himself aloof if he is to catch the mood of the author."

Although the subject matter of *The Wild Duck* has been described as sordid, tragic, and horrific, relief from the almost overwhelming pessimism of the play comes from the serio-comic characterization of several major figures. Hjalmar Ekdal, in particular, with his dramatic posturing before his friends and family, is poised between the ludicrous and the genuinely touching. He is most often, however, merely absurd. Other elements of characterization that could have been turned to comic advantage, such as old Ekdal's doddering and Gina Ekdal's ungrammatical and malaprop-laden speech, are often found by critics to transcend their humorous application, becoming moving pieces of skillful character delineation. Ibsen's meticulous blending of tragic and comic elements puzzled some early viewers and reviewers of *The Wild Duck*, but has resulted in almost universal praise from critics ever since Bernard Shaw called Ibsen "the dramatic poet who firmly established tragicomedy as a much deeper and grimmer entertainment than tragedy." As a world masterpiece of tragicomedy, as a uniquely modern experiment in its time for its combination of realism and symbolism, and above all as an eminently actable play, *The Wild Duck* remains one of Ibsen's best-known and most noted achievements.

(See also *Contemporary Authors*, Vol. 104.)

HENRIK IBSEN (letter date 1884)

[In the following excerpt from a letter that Ibsen sent to his publisher, Frederik Hegel, with the manuscript of The Wild Duck, *he expresses his belief that the play represents a change in his dramatic method, but does not specify the nature of the change. Archibald Henderson (1926), an early commentator on the play, found that* The Wild Duck *was innovative in two ways: it was the first of Ibsen's symbolic dramas, as well as the first work in which*

the dramatist posed problems without offering solutions. Ibsen also states—correctly, as it turned out—that critics of this new play would "find several things to squabble about and several things to interpret."]

Dear Mr. Hegel—Along with this letter I send you the manuscript of my new play, *The Wild Duck.* For the last four months I have worked at it every day; and it is not without a certain feeling of regret that I part from it. Long, daily association with the persons in this play has endeared them to me, in spite of their manifold failings; and I am not without hope that they may find good and kind friends among the great reading public, and more particularly among the actor tribe—to whom they offer rôles which will well repay the trouble spent on them. The study and representation of these characters will not be an easy task. . . . (pp. 383-84)

In some ways this new play occupies a position by itself among my dramatic works; in its method it differs in several respects from my former ones. But I shall say no more on this subject at present. I hope that my critics will discover the points alluded to; they will, at any rate, find several things to squabble about and several things to interpret. I also think that *The Wild Duck* may very probably entice some of our young dramatists into new paths; and this I consider a result to be desired. (p. 384)

> *Henrik Ibsen, in a letter to Frederik Hegel on September 2, 1884, in his* Letters of Henrik Ibsen, *translated by John Nilsen Laurvik and Mary Morison, Fox, Duffield and Company, 1905, pp. 383-85.*

EDMUND GOSSE   (essay date 1889)

[*Gosse's importance as a critic is due primarily to his introduction of Ibsen's "new drama" to an English audience. He was among the chief English translators and critics of Scandinavian literature and was decorated by the Norwegian, Swedish, and Danish governments for his efforts. Among his other works are studies of John Donne, Thomas Gray, Sir Thomas Browne, and important early articles on French authors of the late nineteenth century. Although Gosse's works are varied and voluminous, his intellectual style is somewhat casual, with the consequence that his commentary lacks depth and is not considered to be in the first rank of modern critical thought. However, his broad interests and knowledge of foreign literatures lend his works much more than a documentary value. In the following excerpt, Gosse characterizes* The Wild Duck *as "a strange, melancholy, and pessimistic drama" that is "by far the most difficult of Ibsen's works for a reader to comprehend."*]

In *An Enemy of the People* the animal spirits of the poet seemed to support him on a high wave of indignant idealism. He declared the majority tame and cowardly and hypocritical, it is true, but vowed that the good man, even if quite solitary, may find his virtue his own reward, and exult like the sons of the morning. But all this physical glow of battle had faded out when he came to write *The Wild Duck,* a strange, melancholy, and pessimistic drama, almost without a ray of light from end to end. This is a very long play, by far the most extended of the series [of Ibsen's social dramas] and is, on the whole, the least interesting to read, although, like all its author's works, it possesses scenes of a thrilling vivacity. The wild duck which gives its name to the piece is an unhappy bird which is kept in captivity in a garret, and is supposed to be shot at last with a pistol by a morbid little girl. Unfortunately it is herself the little girl is found to have shot, and by no means accidentally. The hero is a most distressing Gregers Werle, a type of the new neurotic class: a weak and bloodless creature, full of half-

formed aspirations and half-delirious hopes for the future of humanity. In *The Wild Duck* cynical selfishness is absolutely dominant; it has it all its own way to the end, and, if I comprehend the undercurrent of the plot at all, the ideal spirit of goodness is the untamed bird in its close and miserable garret, captive to circumstances, and with no hope of escape. There is really not a character in the book that inspires confidence or liking. I confess a preference for the merry cynic, Dr. Relling, with his monstrous set of immoral paradoxes. The photographer, Helling [sic] Ekdal, who bullies the wild duck and drives his relatives crazy with his hateful tricks and his manners, is almost beyond what a reader can bear. . . . There can be no doubt that it is by far the most difficult of Ibsen's dramas for a reader to comprehend. I am told, however, that it is effective enough on the stage. (pp. 117-18)

> *Edmund Gosse, "Ibsen's Social Dramas," in* The Fortnightly Review, *Vol. XLV, No. CCLXV, January 1, 1889, pp. 107-21.*

HAVELOCK ELLIS   (essay date 1890)

[*Ellis was a pioneering sexual psychologist and a respected English man of letters. His most famous work is his seven-volume* The Psychology of Sex *(1897-1928), a study containing frankly stated case histories of sex-related psychological abnormalities that was greatly responsible for changing British and American attitudes toward the hitherto forbidden subject of sexuality. In addition to his psychological writings, Ellis edited the Mermaid Series of sixteenth-eighteenth century English dramatists (1887-89) and retained an active interest in literature throughout his life. As a critic, according to Desmond MacCarthy, Ellis looked for the expression of the individuality of the author under discussion. "The first question he asked himself as a critic," wrote MacCarthy, "was 'What does this writer affirm?' The next, 'How did he come to affirm precisely that?' His statement of a writer's 'message' was always trenchant and clear, his psychological analysis of the man extremely acute, and the estimate of the value of his contribution impartial. What moved him most in literature was the sincere expression of preferences and beliefs, and the energy which springs from sincerity." In the following excerpt, Ellis interprets* The Wild Duck *as a satire on the convictions earlier expressed by Ibsen in the dramas* A Doll's House *and* The Pillars of Society, *a view that recurs in the excerpts by Smith Ely Jelliffe and Louise Brink (1918), Hermann J. Weigand (1925), and Ronald Gray (1977). Ellis also maintains that the play sets forth Ibsen's own opinions regarding fairness in the matter of premarital sexual experience.*]

The Wild Duck is, as a drama, the least remarkable of Ibsen's [tragedies]. There is no central personage who absorbs our attention, and no great situation. For the first time also we detect a certain tendency to mannerism, and the dramatist's love of symbolism, here centered in the wild duck, becomes obtrusive and disturbing. Yet this play has a distinct and peculiar interest for the student of Ibsen's works. The satirist who has so keenly pursued others has never spared himself; in the lines that he has set at the end of the charming little volume in which he has collected his poems, he declares that, "to write poetry is to hold a doomsday over oneself." Or, as he has elsewhere expressed it: "All that I have written corresponds to something that I have lived through, if not actually experienced. Every new poem has served as a spiritual process of emancipation and purification." In both *Brand* and *Peer Gynt* we may detect this process. In *The Wild Duck* Ibsen has set himself on the side of his enemies, and written, as a kind of anti-mask to *The Doll's House* and *The Pillars of Society,* a play in which, from the standpoint to which the dramatist has accustomed us, everything is topsy-turvy. Gregers Werle is a young man, possessing something of the reckless will-power of Brand, who is devoted to the claims of the ideal, and who is doubtless an enthusiastic student of Ibsen's social dramas. On returning home after a long absence he learns that his father has provided for a cast-off mistress by marrying her to an unsuspecting man who is an old friend of Gregers'. He resolves at once that it is his duty at all costs to destroy the element of falsehood in this household, and to lay the foundations of a true marriage. His interference ends in disaster; the weak average human being fails to respond properly to "the claims of the ideal;" while Werle's father, the chief pillar of conventional society in the play, spontaneously forms a true marriage, founded on mutual confessions and mutual trust. If the play may be regarded, not quite unfairly, as a burlesque of possible deductions from the earlier plays, it witnesses also, like *Ghosts,* to Ibsen's profound conviction that all vital development must be spontaneous and from within, conditioned by the nature of the individual.

In *The Wild Duck* Ibsen approaches in his own manner, without, however, much insistence, the moral aspects of the equality of the sexes. Is a woman, who has had no relationships with a man before marriage, entitled to expect the same in her husband? Is a man, who has had relationships with other women before marriage, entitled to complain if his wife has also had such relationships? These are the sort of questions which the Scandinavian and Danish dramatists—Björnson, Eduard Brandes, Charlotte Edgren, Benzon—seem never tired of discussing. (pp. 159-61)

Ibsen's solution of the matter in *The Wild Duck* seems to be that there can be no true marriage without mutual knowledge and mutual confession. (p. 163)

> Havelock Ellis, "Ibsen," in his The New Spirit,
> *1890. Reprint by Boni and Liveright, 1921, pp. 128-66.*

GEORG BRANDES (essay date 1898)

[*Brandes was a Danish literary critic and biographer whose extensive writings on such authors as Ibsen, August Strindberg, and Søren Kierkegaard helped make their works better known outside of Scandinavia. He was one of the first critics to understand and encourage the innovative drama of Ibsen, and he virtually "discovered" Friedrich Nietzsche, providing the first serious critical attention that the German philosopher received. In his major critical work,* Main Currents in Nineteenth-Century Literature *(1872-90), Brandes viewed French, German, and English literary movements as a series of reactions against eighteenth-century thought. Brandes said of himself that he was more than a critic but less than a philosopher. In a letter to him, Nietzsche called Brandes a "missionary of culture." This is perhaps the best definition of Brandes's function within literature. He possessed the ability to view literary movements and the individuals who contributed to those movements within the broader context of virtually all of nineteenth-century literature. In the following excerpt from a study completed in 1898, Brandes theorizes that Ibsen's unflattering portrayal of Gregers Werle's obsessive truth-seeking was indicative of his anger at the hostile reception given his controversial drama* Ghosts *and reflects the dramatist's disgust at the average person's preference for embracing comforting falsehoods rather than facing unpleasant truths.*]

After *An Enemy of the People* came *The Wild Duck,* a masterpiece, and perhaps the most pessimistic play that Ibsen had yet written; though even a character of such a low type as Gina, who had been old Werle's mistress before she was married to the lazy and affected Hjalmar Ekdal, is drawn almost affec-

tionately. All the light of the play, however, is centred round the head of Hedvig, that pathetically lovable and noble-hearted child. In this important work also we can trace an after-effect of the maltreatment that was Ibsen's recompense for *Ghosts,* in the character, namely, of Gregers Werle, who is a caricature of the man who insists on bearing witness for the truth. After having poured out the vials of his wrath, and spoken his mind freely, in *An Enemy of the People,* Ibsen seems to have asked himself for the first time if it were really worth the trouble, if it were really his duty to proclaim the truth to average people like his readers, if it were not rather falsehood that was necessary to them in the conduct of their lives. The quietly humorous spirit of his answer to this question led to the creation of Gregers Werle, an everywhere superfluous and intrusive personage, who goes from house to house urging the claim of the ideal, and only at the end of the play learns the wise lesson that if you take away all falsehood from the average man, you take happiness away from him at the same time—a truth which is imparted to Gregers by the cynically good-natured Relling, another humorous incarnation of Ibsen himself.

The high standard of excellence attained by Ibsen in *The Wild Duck,* and the progress in his art which it denotes, is best understood by comparing this drama with *The Pillars of Society.* In the earlier play we have a melodramatic ending, the conversion of the principal character, the rescue of the ship, and even of the runaway son, all meant to smooth away what is bad and horrible; here we have the beautiful and bitter reality of life, the full austerity together with the full suavity of art. (pp. 99-100)

> Georg Brandes, in his Henrik Ibsen: A Critical Study,
> *edited by William Archer, translated by Jessie Muir,*
> *1899. Reprint by Benjamin Blom, Inc., 1964, 171 p.*

W. D. HOWELLS (essay date 1906)

[*Howells was the chief progenitor of American realism and the most influential American literary critic during the late nineteenth century. He was the author of nearly three dozen novels and stands as one of the major literary figures of the nineteenth century: he successfully weaned American literature away from the sentimental romanticism of its infancy, earning the popular sobriquet "the Dean of American Letters." Through realism, a theory central to his fiction and criticism, Howells sought to disperse "the conventional acceptations by which men live on easy terms with themselves" that they might "examine the grounds of their social and moral opinions." To accomplish this, according to Howells, the writer must strive to record impressions of everyday life in detail, endowing characters with true-to-life motives and avoiding authorial comment in the narrative.* Criticism and Fiction *(1891), a patchwork of essays from* Harper's Magazine, *is often considered Howells's manifesto of realism, although, as René Wellek has noted, the book is actually "only a skirmish in a long campaign for his doctrines." In addition to many notable studies of the works of his friends Mark Twain and Henry James, Howells perceptively reviewed three generations of international literature, urging Americans to read Émile Zola, Bernard Shaw, Ibsen, Emily Dickinson, and other important authors. In the following excerpt, Howells addresses Ibsen's seemingly ambivalent attitude toward truth, as presented in his dramas* The Pillars of Society *(1878) and* The Wild Duck. *The nature of Ibsen's conception of truth and illusion is a common concern in criticism of* The Wild Duck.]

[Ibsen] sees that the world which a wise and merciful and perfect God has created seems full of stupidity and cruelty and out of joint to utter deformity, and he shows it as he sees it. If he is apparently inconsistent, it is because the world is really inconsistent; and if we hold him to any hard and fast rule of logic, we may indeed *have* him, but his best meaning will escape us. In *Pillars of Society,* that tragedy of his which comes nearest being a satirical comedy, or for the most part is so, the misery comes because Bernick will be a hypocrite and a liar; and the inference is, that any sort of truth, or anybody's, would be better than the falsehood in which he lives. In *The Wild Duck,* the truth is brought home from the outside to a wretched creature unable to bear it, who has existed through the lie become vital to him, and who goes to pieces at the touch of the truth, and drags those around him to ruin and death in his fall; and the inference is that the truth is not for every one always, but may sometimes be a real mischief. The two plays seem to contradict each other, but they do not; they are both true to different predicaments and situations of life, and can no more be blamed for inconsistency than God's world which they faithfully mirror. (pp. 6-7)

W. D. Howells, ''Henrik Ibsen,'' in The North American Review, *Vol. CLXXXIII, No. 596, Summer, 1906, pp. 1-14.*

BERNARD SHAW   (essay date 1913)

[*Shaw is generally considered the greatest and best-known dramatist to write in the English language since Shakespeare. Following the example of Henrik Ibsen, he succeeded in revolutionizing the English stage, disposing of the romantic conventions and devices of the ''well-made play,'' and instituting the theater of ideas, grounded in realism. During the late nineteenth century, Shaw was also a prominent literary, art, and music critic. In 1895, he became the drama critic for* The Saturday Review, *and his reviews therein became known for their biting wit and brilliance. During his three years at* The Saturday Review, *Shaw determined that the theater was meant to be a ''moral institution'' and an ''elucidator of social conduct.'' The standards he applied to drama were quite simple: ''Is the play like real life? Does it convey sensible, socially progressive ideas?'' Because most of the dramas produced during the 1890s failed to approach these ideals, Shaw usually assumed a severely critical and satirical attitude toward his subjects. Although he later wrote criticism of poetry and fiction—much of it collected in* Pen Portraits and Reviews *(1932)—Shaw was out of sympathy with both of these genres. He had little use for poetry, believing it poorly suited for the expression of ideas, and in his criticism of fiction he rarely got beyond the search for ideology. As Samuel Hynes has noted, Shaw was driven by a rage to better the world. A Fabian socialist, he wrote criticism that is usually concerned with the humanitarian and political intent of the work under discussion. In the following excerpt, Shaw interprets* The Wild Duck *as a satire directed at Ibsen's own overly idealistic admirers. Shaw perceives Gregers Werle as a meddlesome busybody who fails to recognize the danger of revealing harsh truths to people who are intellectually and emotionally unprepared to accept them.*]

After *An Enemy of the People,* Ibsen . . . left the vulgar ideals for dead, and set about the exposure of those of the choicer spirits, beginning with the incorrigible idealists who had idealized his very self, and were becoming known as Ibsenites. His first move in this direction was such a tragi-comic slaughtering of sham Ibsenism that his astonished victims plaintively declared that *The Wild Duck,* as the new play was called, was a satire on his former works; whilst the pious, whom he had disappointed so severely by his interpretation of *Brand,* began to hope that he was coming back repentant to the fold. The household to which we are introduced in *The Wild Duck* is not, like Mrs. Alving's, a handsome one made miserable by superstitious illusions, but a shabby one made happy by romantic

illusions. The only member of it who sees it as it really is is the wife, a good-natured Philistine who desires nothing better. The husband, a vain, petted, spoilt dawdler, believes that he is a delicate and high-souled man, devoting his life to redeeming his old father's name from the disgrace brought on it by imprisonment for breach of the forest laws. This redemption he proposes to effect by making himself famous as a great inventor some day when he has the necessary inspiration. Their daughter, a girl in her teens, believes intensely in her father and in the promised invention. The disgraced grandfather cheers himself by drink whenever he can get it; but his chief resource is a wonderful garret full of rabbits and pigeons. The old man has procured a number of second-hand Christmas trees; and with these he has turned the garret into a sort of toy forest, in which he can play at bear hunting, which was one of the sports of his youth and prosperity. The weapons employed in the hunting expeditions are a gun which will not go off, and a pistol which occasionally brings down a rabbit or a pigeon. A crowning touch is given to the illusion by a wild duck, which, however, must not be shot, as it is the special property of the girl, who reads and dreams whilst her mother cooks, washes, sweeps and carries on the photographic work which is supposed to be the business of her husband. Mrs. Ekdal does not appreciate Hjalmar's highly strung sensitiveness of character, which is constantly suffering agonizing jars from her vulgarity; but then she does not appreciate that other fact that he is a lazy and idle impostor. Downstairs there is a disgraceful clergyman named Molvik, a hopeless drunkard; but even he respects himself and is tolerated because of a special illusion invented for him by another lodger, Dr. Relling, upon whom the lesson of the household above has not been thrown away. Molvik, says the doctor, must break out into drinking fits because he is daimonic, an imposing explanation which completely relieves the reverend gentleman from the imputation of vulgar tippling.

Into this domestic circle there comes a new lodger, an idealist of the most advanced type. He greedily swallows the daimonic theory of the clergyman's drunkenness, and enthusiastically accepts the photographer as the high-souled hero he supposes himself to be; but he is troubled because the relations of the man and his wife do not constitute an ideal marriage. He happens to know that the woman, before her marriage, was the cast-off mistress of his own father; and because she has not told her husband this, he conceives her life as founded on a lie, like that of Bernick in *Pillars of Society.* He accordingly sets himself to work out the woman's salvation for her, and establish ideally frank relations between the pair, by simply blurting out the truth, and then asking them, with fatuous self-satisfaction, whether they do not feel much the better for it. This wanton piece of mischief has more serious results than a mere domestic scene. The husband is too weak to act on his bluster about outraged honor and the impossibility of his ever living with his wife again; and the woman is merely annoyed with the idealist for telling on her; but the girl takes the matter to heart and shoots herself. The doubt cast on her parentage, with her father's theatrical repudiation of her, destroy her ideal place in the home, and make her a source of discord there; so she sacrifices herself, thereby carrying out the teaching of the idealist mischief-maker, who has talked a good deal to her about the duty and beauty of self-sacrifice, without foreseeing that he might be taken in mortal earnest. The busybody thus finds that people cannot be freed from their failings from without. They must free themselves. When Nora is strong enough to live out of the doll's house, she will go out of it of her own accord if the door stands open; but if before that period you take her by the scruff of the neck and thrust her out, she will

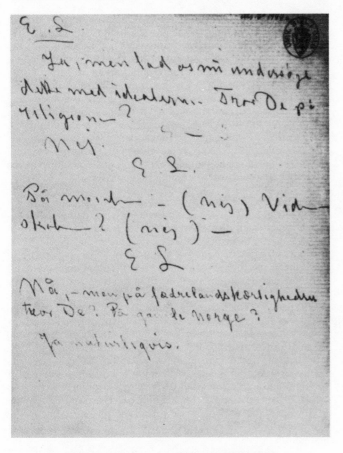

Ibsen's handwritten notes for The Wild Duck.

only take refuge in the next establishment of the kind that offers to receive her. Woman has thus two enemies to deal with: the old-fashioned one who wants to keep the door locked, and the new-fashioned one who wants to thrust her into the street before she is ready to go. In the cognate case of a hypocrite and liar like Bernick, exposing him is a mere police measure: he is none the less a liar and hypocrite when you have exposed him. If you want to make a sincere and truthful man of him, all you can wisely do is to remove what you can of the external obstacles to his exposing himself, and then wait for the operation of his internal impulse to confess. If he has no such impulse, then you must put up with him as he is. It is useless to make claims on him which he is not yet prepared to meet. Whether, like Brand, we make such claims because to refrain would be to compromise with evil, or, like Gregers Werle, because we think their moral beauty must recommend them at sight to every one, we shall alike incur Relling's impatient assurance that "life would be quite tolerable if we could only get rid of the confounded duns that keep on pestering us in our poverty with the claims of the ideal." (pp. 97-100)

Bernard Shaw, in his The Quintessence of Ibsenism: Now Completed to the Death of Ibsen, *1913. Reprint by Hill and Wang, 1957, 188 p.*

SMITH ELY JELLIFFE AND LOUISE BRINK (lecture date 1918)

[The following excerpt is taken from a paper that was originally read before the American Psychoanalytic Association in 1918 and published in the Psychoanalytic Review *the following year. Jelliffe and Brink analyze several of the characters from* The Wild Duck *in terms of contemporary psychoanalytic theory. In the actions of Gregers Werle they find a caricature of "false blundering therapy," and posit that he "whimsically represents" Ibsen's "own earlier zeal and fate as a reformer." Havelock Ellis (1890), Hermann J. Weigand (1925), and Ronald Gray (1977) similarly maintain that the character of Gregers was intended as a satirical self-portrait of the dramatist.]*

Ibsen's power and genius for touching the finer intimate realities of life close at hand, are perhaps most evident in [*The Wild Duck*]. . . . His message lies peculiarly in the circle and through the intercourse of humble almost sordid daily life. Yet critical thought almost refuses to see in the midst of ordinary life the truth of such characters as he has drawn. The world has always tried to avoid its own too intimate features, projecting them into something which it considers not of itself, or which it believes transcends or denies the pettiness and sordidness and thereby even the finer depths which lie close at hand. The dramatic message is usually looked for in the unusual or in the embodiment of the ordinary in the unusual or striking form. And so at first it is missed here. (p. 357)

[Ibsen's] characters come from the real world and he follows in them as a rule no particular line of heredity, of degeneracy or what not, under which the psychiatrist tries to subsume them. He recognizes far more varying fluctuations of sickness or health and their causes, and at the same time an equally diversified and adjustable line of therapy. He does this, we believe, not with a definite conscious purpose which would lead him to subscribe to these technical words, which may seem to impute to him a more distinct psychiatrical attitude that he ever had clearly in mind. But his very intuitive perception of these actual individual characters and situations in society and his fearless way of granting them also a place in dramatic consideration presents them nevertheless in just such possibility to his audiences.

In this he becomes especially the apostle of reality not only but of that nice adjustment to reality which life requires for success. This must be found not most effectively in conventional generalizations of thought and conduct but in individually varying adaptations. He does not find therefore the psychopathology of life only where careless and self-blinded thinking of it in the lump is likely to relegate it, in certain large groups of obvious mental abnormalities and aberrations. Far more truthful, far more delicately appreciative of the limitations within the possibilities of mankind is the hand that traces the finely wrought drama of the *Wild Duck*. It sketches into it the small tragedies and comedies which make up the greater tragedy as well as the joy of life. Deeply and firmly it incises the subtle tragedy beneath. It covers it softly with no false veil of idealism but instead allows it the glamor of illusion which daily, hourly, in greater or less degree, relieves every life of the too piercing and rending reality of self, which is thus partially hidden and rendered more tolerable. In this Ibsen is the truest of naturalistic realists, for this is life as it is lived and in this alone it is able to continue and progress. Its own naked exposure of the lines beneath, which is all the idealmonger can see of realism, would be life's own suicide and that of all its possibilities.

Ibsen knows this well and yet he also knows that life may not stagnate among its own illusions. They are there and for the sake of certain ones who are psychically weak and sick they must be tenderly handled and carefully preserved. This is not the least message of his whole dramatic activity. Yet for the larger public, in whom after all lies the hope of progress, self control and wider freedom through such knowledge, he brings also a wholesome message of self-revelation and need for improvement. He holds up the sicknesses which have not been called such in order to summon the stronger ones to leave them and come to a freer and more effective use of reality. He calls attention to the weaker ones for whom society must have a care, in a more thorough appreciation of these saving compromises, its illusions, and in order, knowing man more clearly, to grant wider opportunity for the varying abilities and disabilities of humanity to exert themselves. Then the weaker ones may realize their possibilities and through greater opportunity gradually outgrow their limitations.

The Wild Duck is therefore a drama of this duller side of existence, but so infused with a poetry of sympathy and symbolism that it is etched deep within the reality of life as it is, and is warm with a possibility of life and love, which no sordidness in the midst of living energy can quench. The drama attempts no such heights as those to which Ibsen's poetry aspires in some of his early romances built on the skaldic legends nor the stern purpose and determination of the ideal-inspired Brand. Neither does love rise to that exaltation of desire which could only end in the utter sacrifice at the mill race in *Rosmersholm*. There are no heights but there are infinite depths beneath the dull sordidness within photographer Ekdal's rooms. The wild duck can no longer fly in the sphere to which she once belonged and to this she owes her place in the symbolism and action of the play. It is the depth from which she has been rescued with trailing wing and foot, which center about her the interest and devotion of the family and give her a worth to Hedvig that includes her in the child's anxious prayers. "For I pray for the wild duck every night, and ask that it may be preserved from death and all that is evil."

She has lain in "the depths of the sea" where she had bitten herself fast and would have perished had not a stronger than herself brought her forth to a life of comfort, care and appreciation, where she "thrives as well as possible in the garret there." She typifies the wild free nature to do and dare without let and hindrance in the open air, but growing as easily content to adapt herself to a life of dependence and care as the human beings among whom her lot has fallen. Even the sacrifice to the false interference of ideals is not asked of the symbolic creature, but falls rather upon the child, the one embodiment in the home of the budding activity of the indomitably real life arising out of the mass of illusion and self-obscurity.

"A regular psychopathic conference we meet with" in this play, "a council of fools," it has been said [in Wilhelm Wegandt's *Abnorme charaktere in der dramatischen Literatur*]. Yet even in these characters are the people we meet in ordinary life and who are not far to seek. Many such fools' councils gather daily around us, in many of them we all participate. Ibsen's keen penetration subtly perceives this but his touch is far more than that of the cynic pointing out the fact to his readers or the beholders of the pictures he has traced. It has been said by various critics that his touch did not heal, that he brought man to a realization of himself but to no saving "grace" beyond himself. This play in itself alone is a poignant denial of such a pessimism, and its acknowledged effect of self-accusation and self-examination on the part of its spectators is a sincere testimony to the regenerating moral power which Ibsen the writer could never conceal. His is that masterly therapy which knows just how carefully to lift the veil of illusion, where the light of self-condemnation might wholesomely enter, or can drop it again when man is too weak to bear the harder truth but can thrive only in the fictitiously adorned garret of

his self-deceptions. He is stern and direct enough in his denunciations of a strong social group which fosters and profits to its selfish advantage upon false codes and formulations, but with the individual he is patient and protecting, while none the less true and sincere in his representations of self-deceit. But he knows how far the individual may make use of the self-revelation and where it would form but a precipitous ending to happiness and courage and even the possibility for better things. This the illusions serve to protect while it germinates. So he caricatures false blundering therapy in the stupid Gregers and thus even whimsically represents his own earlier zeal and fate as a reformer. He suggests too a gentler handling in the wiser but too easily self-contented Doctor Relling.

Ibsen preceded the more modern spirit of therapeutic research which recognizes in every disability a form and degree of illness and for each such disease trait a cause, usually far remote, in the beginning, from its final manifestation. . . . Werle has a son but a barrier of hatred divides them. It is noteworthy in the light of psychological discoveries of recent years, as well as of the later development of the play and the younger Werle's part therein, that the hatred is more manifest in him than in the father and finds greater necessity to express itself. The father has the complacence of the man who has followed his own course and been able so to bend circumstances to his external power that his sins have escaped detection and have left him still free to pursue his way. So far his own power is secure. Retribution is slowly creeping upon him in the loss of his sight and in the final and determined severance by his son of all further relationship between them. Therefore he may be somewhat summarily dismissed from the play, except for the nemesis which follows upon others largely through his indirect instigation.

The first act is, however, deeper in its fundamentally tragic revelation than a casual reader might suppose. Up there at the "Höidal works" Gregers Werle has had "plenty of leisure to think and think about things," a dangerous proceeding for a man who has added to his original childish bent toward an intense mother love a darkling suspicion of a father whom he has seen through his boyhood "at too close quarters." Moreover this brooding child was the son of a mother neurotically weak and lacking in self-control, at times in her difficulties under the influence of the false security of drugs, likely to exaggerate her real or fancied wrongs and to present an exaggerated reaction to them. We know also how Ibsen in his sincerely loyal yet utterly truthful championship of woman never falters in his representation of the weapon of selfish destructiveness which woman too often wields nor does he mitigate the responsibility which her weakness and inadequacy bear toward the man's course of action and his ultimate fate. (pp. 357-61)

The father's superiority sexually, his first claim, is overthrown in the boy's imagination when he adopts the mother's suspicions, the defense on her part against her own sense of inadequacy, and then finds occasion to magnify and support these by the actual misdemeanors of the father. There is no more complete compensation for his envy of the father and resentment toward his course than an identification with his mother in his unconscious desire to suffer through her, to make her his in common cause. He asserts his superiority and greater power over the father in his own impeccable moral attainment as well as the strength of his moral ideal, which must thrust itself up through the illusions, the lies, wholesome or otherwise, of all mankind. Thus also he defends himself from the consciousness of his own jealousy and vindictiveness, and the egoism at their core. He is, if he but knew it, equally self-deceived and unable therefore to direct his consciously honestly intended effort toward his fellow men with the same candor and directness with which Relling more judiciously measures the amount of his reform, or non-reform of that which serves a better purpose as it stands.

The cause of failure for so much apparently well-meaning effort is unrecognized because of actual inability and lack of courage to see the egoistic impulses which primarily and fundamentally actuate. This blindness produces blunder, where courage would pierce to these impulses and by utilizing them more frankly would by that very method obtain a far greater amount of emotional power for unhampered yet socially directed effort, a psychic energy value for the actual work of society and the growing welfare of its members. Ibsen subtly touches these depths in their dynamic value and cannot tolerate the formal masks behind which such true individual power has retreated, so long as they represent merely lifeless ideals. Toward such the individual cannot effectually strive and they kill rather than inspire and render possible individual effort at development. The individual, however, appearing as he does in society in any one of varying degrees of ability to cope with the realities of life, finds some form of illusion under which he dwells more secure, without which in his special weakness all security would be lost and effort be impossible. Ibsen sees in this a form of therapy which cares for the weak if it does not cure them. (p. 362)

The would-be reformer Gregers has already gone clumsily at work when in the light of his ideal he has invited his old friend Hjalmar to his father's house to the dinner celebrating Gregers' return from the Höidal works. Hjalmar is, however, an awkward and unpleasing guest. His very different circumstances of life make him so, beside his relationship of dependence upon the older Werle's bounty, of which however Gregers is still ignorant, as well as the natural shyness and inability to make successful social contacts, which belong to Hjalmar's self-centered nature. He lingers long enough after dinner to outline to Gregers his present situation and the debt he owes the father of the latter, and also to present a sorry social appearance in response to the kindly efforts of his hostess and the persiflage of the other guests. Moreover his cowardly ignoring of his father's sudden intrusion into the room forms only one more weapon of self-pity and self-indulgence in the discomforts to himself which he delights later to magnify and declaim upon.

His revelation of his circumstances together with his abrupt departure serve as occasion for Gregers' attack upon his father and the severance of all further relations with him. Gregers has full faith and admiration toward this friend of his earlier years, or at least sees in him a suitable object for his own exalted mission of proclaiming and establishing his "claim of the ideal." So he betakes himself almost at once to Hjalmar's house to begin the work of redemption he feels is sorely needed there. For from Hjalmar he has discovered a part of the truth, the crueller part of which he has later surprised from his father. Gregers learns that Hjalmar, contentedly established in the business of photography, with a practical wife, efficient in her humble sphere and faithfully devoted to him, is living under a completely falsely understood position. The favors he has received from the elder Werle were only bestowed to discharge from that gentleman's conscience a deep obligation toward Hjalmar's father, who had suffered ruin and imprisonment for

an offense against the state in the matter of the forests for which Werle had been equally guilty but in which he had been able to go free. Furthermore it had been to Werle's advantage to throw Hjalmar into the way of marrying Gina, a former housemaid with whom Werle had been on terms of intimacy, and in this indirect way to provide for her support. From such an arrangement, which had nevertheless worked out to the happiness of those most concerned, Gregers feels it his duty to tear the covering of deceit.

Meanwhile Hjalmar has returned to his humble home where the now utterly faithful wife and their daughter Hedvig await his return. The contentment in this home is of a sorry sort viewed from the exalted plane of the "ideal," that ideal which makes an equal claim upon all alike regardless of the varying degrees of ability to face practical issues and of the weaker characters who would fail utterly in the glaring light of these. This home is instead the harboring place of illusions by which life is made bearable. If life accomplishes but little here, the characters representing it would accomplish still less without these or would utterly and tragically fail. Gina is however of a more courageous, independent nature, although limited in social and intellectual acquirements. No illusions disturb or blind her, but she is able to take the reality of her own life, and philosopher that she is, the real service of the lies in which the others live, and make the best of things as they are, weaknesses, mistakes and all. She is the saving practical pragmatist, living wisely in the best she can make of the present without footless anxiety and concern for the unhappy past.

Then there is the daughter Hedvig, light-hearted though not entirely carefree. She is not deceived by the illusions of her father's or grandfather's lives, any more than by those of the garret, but from them both she extracts much of the joy and strength of life in the little things that go to make up all that is worth while. She can use these things, false in themselves, for her own pastime and profit, and much more in a watchfulness toward father and grandfather, ready for service, ready to turn everything as much as may be to their best account. . . . She represents the truth that can afford to thrive in the greater depths which underlie the passing illusions and which in the course of development must outgrow them, even if only to shelter itself for another period of time under some new form of these. This truth is won nevertheless through the bitterness of a sacrifice which arises from some hidden entanglement after all in the atmosphere of falseness, and this does not fail in Hedvig's case. Ibsen is representing the course of life as it reveals itself, developing under and through such imperfect means, while incompleteness and destructiveness take their toll from the course of progress. (pp. 363-65)

The high-sounding phrases and the grandiose schemes of Hjalmar are all the food he has to offer eager little Hedvig, who has been awaiting his return from the dinner with the goodies which his generous intention had promised her from another man's table. The intricate finesse in the weaving of the symbolism of this play gives frequent pause. The skeleton framework of the play, the elaborated relationship, though a secret one, of the Ekdal family toward the Werle family, is constantly being brought through symbolically to the surface. The family gratefully feel they owe even the duck to Werle but the dramatist's keener sense of truth represents the wild bird not as a symbol of generosity or of the advantage of proximity to the great man but rather as indicative also of the bondage of spirit in which they are placed. She had bitten herself fast in the tangle and seaweed as the result of Werle's shot, and it was only secondarily that she was rescued in her maimed condition and secured by them. Nothing but that which he has wounded, which proves worthless to him, Werle passes on to these recipients of his seeming generosity, but the two childish men rest complacently in their self-deception and in a feeble way set to work, as Gina more efficiently did, to rebuild and in their limited measure to restore, what has been broken.

The rented or borrowed coat which Hjalmar has worn to the party is laid aside, the two or three new ideas which he had ignominiously to receive through his discomfiture at the party, are discharged now as his own to his admiring family. Hjalmar settles himself to the joy of their adoration, particularly that of the more romantically devoted and idealizing little daughter and to the satisfaction of no little interspersed self-pity. Meanwhile the grandfather has preceded Hjalmar home, also provided with the cheer which particularly warms his heart. His support and his indulgence are from the same hands which have dispensed the means of livelihood to the family, and all at the price of his own freedom and self-respect as at bottom of that of each other member. Yet both men are blinded to that or have succeeded in so glossing it that it has all the value of unreality, only makes another theme for Hjalmar's ready declamation. Gina alone, practical and courageous enough to meet reality with action, needs no blinding for herself, and Hedvig is yet unspoiled by it.

Gina is placidly tolerant of the sham and boasting which surround their life, Hedvig throws herself into it with all the grace and seriousness of a growing child spirit. (pp. 365-66)

Hope probably lies here in the growing child, whose life is protected by the peace and happiness of the home, while it finds the true self-expression which is to be hers. And this even though she must develop under the physical handicaps of insufficient food that her father may be fed, the threatening blindness, her inheritance from Werle, perhaps the real father, and intellectually preyed upon by the too infantile attitude of much of the home. There are also the intellectual disadvantages which she owes to her father's self-absorption and inherent indolence. "Father has promised to read with me; but he never has had time yet." Yet these may all be but stimuli to an actually unfolding nature, full within itself of the spirit of inquiry and activity. There lurks, however, a deeper danger, which, rightfully set free, will become a source of power, but which needs the same gentle opening as the folded rosebud with its guarded store of sweetness and beauty. Rude interference destroys its promise and turns the delicate petals to a crumpled lifeless mass, the beauty desecrated and the fragrance a thing of nought.

Gregers, in his blinded moral pride, dares to lay his hand upon the child's inner treasure and tears it out to a cruel self-revelation, terror and death. It seems to him in his own exaggerated attitude toward life that the finest thing he can do will be to bring his "claim of the ideal" here and, by opening the eyes of all concerned to the darker and sterner truths which underlie their contentment, to raise them to a higher plane of satisfaction and power. His own intolerance of weaknesses and differences of adjustment toward life show him no other way for his friends as well. And who can say how much unconscious satisfaction is also his, in his bitterness of reaction, in tearing down this happier structure which his father has so carefully built up, to his own advantage to be sure, but by no means to the disadvantage of the objects of his benefactions?

Gregers blunders first and most in the appraisement of Hjalmar's character. . . . Gregers soon lays bare the truth concern-

ing Gina's early life, the source of Werle's generosity in the secret reasons for it. He is but a rude physician amid the disease and poison which he claims to discover here. One might snatch a strong well man suddenly from such an atmosphere but no careful therapist would attempt immediately so radical a cure for the weak. The result is exactly what a wiser man would have foreseen. There is a wiser man below stairs, Doctor Relling, weak and dissolute fellow as regards his own life but in an unobtrusive way trying to be of service to those he finds in need. (pp. 369-70)

He has encouraged Hjalmar in a belief in an invention to be made by him, which therefore preserves to him a faith in himself and a contentment with the present, even though this ambition constantly recedes into a future of unattainable rewards and serves largely to feed and nourish Hjalmar's self-worship and self-importance. Gina is placidly tolerant of it because it satisfies her husband and it adds one more element to Hedvig's happy humoring of her father and her half credulous pride in him. Meanwhile Hjalmar is actually engaged neither in this nor in the work of photography, in which his wife and even the almost blind daughter do the work, while he actually fritters his time in childish occupation with the more completely and openly childish old man in the garret.

In fact, so far as Hjalmar is concerned, Gregers' efforts to renovate the condition of things can amount to but little. No great good and no great harm can result. The effect upon him is only momentary, a flurry of emotionalism and a fresh exercise of the neurotic ability for self-enjoyment and self-aggrandizement through self-pity and heroic declamations. Simple, faithful Gina is more keenly hurt by the reality of the accusations made and the interference with her sincere and successful efforts to atone by a life of useful adaptation for the mistakes of the past. The old father in his isolated world of phantasy is as untouched by this as by all else that transpires among the rest. Gina however knows the way of recovery from this fresh wound and is fully ready to do whatever is her share of readjustment. That at first is largely to provide for the distraction and uncertainty and indecision into which her husband has been thrown. For he reacts with a child's easy power of being disturbed, along with the child's outcry often expressive of nothing more real than a desire to attract attention to himself. So he will make a quick recovery of his former complacence, actually too indolent and unaccustomed to taking or following any course of action, to do anything more than raise a temporary teapot storm.

But alas! there is one whom the true physician Relling has tried to guard, who suffers most from the evil genius which has come to disturb the home. In Hedvig phantasy and reality meet. In childhood's right the one is arising from the other. The wish dreams of childhood and approaching maturity are seeking to establish themselves in a grasp of realities which will know these in their unclouded worth and yet tone them and harmonize them in the phantasy life which is as truly hers. Such a task in this home is, however, no easy one. The inner wish life assumes a too ugly form in the aggressive selfishness and self-worship of the deluded father. The guidance of intellectual training and culture are also sadly meager. Moreover, there is that love and infatuation with which every daughter at some time in her life, it may be only very early, views her father and with which she dwells upon him in loving dependence or in loving motherly care. For the latter there was peculiar opportunity in the presence of so infantile a father as Hedvig's, calling forth all the response of the loving child's nature, which binds him to her by the bonds of her devoted service. This all tends toward a deep fixation of the child upon the father which is either a model and source of power in her later life, or failing its healthy transference out into the things and upon the objects of her own more contemporary world, may become a source of limitation and disaster. The fact that he is perhaps only her foster father makes him no less the real object of her love and inclination through lifelong association. (pp. 370-72)

[Gregers'] words, the suspicions he has launched into the household, particularly in regard to Hedvig's true paternal parentage, violently tear apart the petals of this folded flower. Some precipitation was inevitable but it need not have been this. Yet even now the child's path of self-destruction is a purer one and more direct than if the struggle had carried itself as with Hedda through long years of self-indulgence and self-complaint, in a dissatisfied effort to adjust the inner disturbed relations first set in motion in the early relations of child with parent. . . . Ibsen seems to have had an inner appreciation of the universality of this early determinant in the lives of his men and women, for he always gives a certain artistically suggestive allusion to this first love relationship of the child. . . . Mention has already been made of Gregers' child conflict and Ibsen has inserted a few lines from the mouth of the direct and practical Relling which give a key to Hjalmar's inner bondage. Gregers mentions the "loving care with which he [Hjalmar] was brought up." "By those two high-flown, hysterical maiden aunts, you mean? . . . I know all about those ladies; for he has ladled out no end of rhetoric on the subject of his 'two soul-mothers.'"

Relling is no less frank with Gregers himself. He assures him that he is indeed stone blind: "Yes you are—or not far from it. You are a sick man, too, you see. . . . First of all there is that plaguey integrity-fever; and then—what's worse—you are always in a delirium of hero-wroship; you must always have something to adore, outside yourself." No one but a man blind and sick, and there are many such, both men and women, in this self-deceived world, would have approached a sensitive growing child in so rude and cruel an absorption in his own hard ideals, with the infection of his "integrity-fever." Yet there is nothing more exquisite in Ibsen's delicate yet decisive character drawing than these interviews between the well-meaning but blinded bungler and the shyly guarded frankness of this loving child psyche. She dwells in a world of sordid practicality and merrily and industriously fills her place in it, yet she never loses the transforming and redeeming background of the imaginary world and the glimpses of a far-away real world different from that she knows.

She has the sea-captain's treasures stored in the garret, particularly the "one great big book called 'Harrison's History of London,'" which, by the way, we learn was Ibsen's peculiar childhood treasure. Most of all, however, the wonderful duck speaks of the open life beyond and around it the child's interests and affections largely center. Her phantasy is so wholesomely grounded in these things and so busily active with a desire to know and touch the real things of life that it is actually only the background to a growing contact with reality in the child's life. To Hedvig the fancy is all so lightly yet truly real; Gregers distorts it as he tries to press into it his "claim of the ideal" and the self-exaggerated importance in his mission to perform the part of the rescuing dog who will drag this family up from these "miasmas" into light and truth. He finds a heavy ponderous mystery which it is his duty to dredge. (pp. 372-74)

Prayer, too, the prayer that included the wild duck, is such a simple practical thing with little Hedvig. The sacrifice of the wild fowl, too, which Gregers urges upon her in his morbid confusion of ways and means and inner values in the light of a falsely conceived ideal, comes to her in a saner light. "Yesterday evening, at the moment, I thought there was something so delightful about it; but since I have slept and thought of it again, it somehow doesn't seem worth while." Yet the suffering and pain into which her rude awakening have thrown the child confuse also her view of this and she listens again to Gregers' urging. Not finding herself able to present the shooting of the wild duck convincingly to her grandfather, only learning from him how to do the shooting most effectively, she herself creeps into the garret with the old pistol in her hand to offer up the sacrifice for her father's love. While there she overhears her father's wild and selfish lamentations over her possible want of faith in him, her possible treachery and falseness to him, the blot that she is, with the almost certain suspicion of her other parentage, upon the sunlight of his whole life. She hears also Gregers' equally self-blinded assurances that Hjalmar is to have proof, in a supreme sacrifice, of Hedvig's true love for him, and her father's scornful answer out of the luxury of self-worship and self-pity in which he is indulging: "If I then asked her: Hedwig, are you willing to renounce that life for me? No thank you! You would soon hear what answer I should get." The pistol shot which ends her own life and not that of the duck is his answer.

And even this he is too blind and self-absorbed to read in its truth and for his own release at last from self-deception. Her death will only form one more illusory exercise in self-pity and self-adulation under which he may continue to live. (p. 375)

Ibsen's aim in his dramatic writing is not to present an ideal solution of problems, in which disorder and pain and destruction melt away into happy solution. That is not life and therefore cannot be the true solution of these same difficulties. Ibsen's truth and realism do not, however, leave his audience hopeless and disheartened. Strength, redemption, healing lie in the very events and struggles and problems themselves. (pp. 375-76)

It is the psychic something within which is clarified, forwarded, re-impelled not merely to continue living in patient resignation, but far rather to gird up its loins in this great task of living for something better. But this something better is only within itself, within the strife and effort to live and live out creatively through gradually clearer understanding and control of the inner psychic power with which life is lived. Thus the lessons of Ibsen's plays incise themselves into this deepest heart of failure as of success, and direct individual attention and effort to the power and life which lie alone in such living. Here is cure for the sick in entering a life where self-deception is purged away by the very business of living, which is effected truly only by an effort and a direction out toward reality, with which life has to do. It is his aim and message to enable men and women to know themselves that they may know these hindering weaknesses and whence they spring, see them in their destructiveness and turn them to better account. His mirroring of them is not for purposes of ridicule or in cynical bitterness of scorn and complaint. He would rouse each individual to himself, and he would rouse society to dispel its complacent deceits and its deadening formalities that the individual may find and live himself out in the "constant active appropriation of liberty." (p. 376)

Smith Ely Jelliffe and Louise Brink, "The Wild Duck'," in The Psychoanalytic Review, *Vol. VI, No. 4, October, 1919, pp. 357-78.*

HERMANN J. WEIGAND   (essay date 1925)

[*The following excerpt is from Weigand's* The Modern Ibsen: A Reconsideration, *which provides a close textual examination of Ibsen's later plays. Praising* The Wild Duck *as primarily a comedy, Weigand notes the skillful blend of tragedy and comedy in the play, a point that is expanded upon by Karl S. Guthke (1966) and Edvard Beyer (1978). Concurring with Havelock Ellis (1890), Smith Ely Jelliffe and Louise Brink (1918), and Ronald Gray (1977), Weigand interprets Gregers Werle—the teller of unpleasant truths—as Ibsen's caricatured self-portrait.*]

The reader of the *Wild Duck* is apt to close the book with the feeling of coming away from a madhouse. The horror of the concluding scene—the most daring thing aesthetically, that Ibsen ever penned—is likely to reduce him to a state of physical weakness bordering on nausea. The realization of the import of that shot in the garret comes upon him with staggering suddenness; the hocus-pocus of the survivors over the corpse of the child is ghastly. . . .

Revolt against the unmediated grafting of tragedy upon satire will subside as he comes to perceive that Ibsen, with a boldness from which any other man would have shrunk, here uses tragic pathos as a device to make comedy but the more poignant. (p. 134)

[It] would be a mistake on the reader's part to identify himself too closely with any of the characters of *The Wild Duck.* He must hold himself aloof, if he is to catch the mood of the author. To enter into the lives of Old Ekdal, Gina and Hedwig in a spirit of compassionate sympathy and to feel a corresponding resentment against Hjalmar, would be to spoil the unity of the tableau which Ibsen has painted. The Ekdal family does not call for any compassion; they have, if anything, a greater share of contentment and happiness than average human beings. . . . If any compassion were called for, it would be because these people are so contented with their lot, because they have no higher aspirations, not because of any aspirations that have been checked and stifled by a tragic turn of their lives. But Ibsen does not treat the theme from that angle. He contemplates the situation from above; he extracts from it the humor with which the situation abounds. Like the Comic Spirit personified, he hovers over his creation and runs through the gamut of comedy, from kindly humor to the bloodiest satire; and if we would see this creation with its author's eyes, we must ascend to his high plane, we must fill our nostrils with the rarefied air of the heights and keep a close tether on our emotions.

A man who has but one talent, that of enacting melodrama, is forced by an officious quacksalver to give himself the air of rebuilding his life on a new foundation of truth: this is essentially a comic subject. (pp. 136-38)

The melodrama is played to a finish over the corpse of the child. Not even the presence of death can force a hush. For a last time all the warped and maimed existences of this household are gathered together to act an ensemble so shockingly grotesque that the reader must be steeled with an Aristophanic sense of the comic in order not to succumb to the ghastly aspect of the performance. Hjalmar makes the house reverberate with his theatrical pathos. Relling, the cynic, affects a cold and dispassionate attitude. Old Ekdal departs for the garret with imbecile mutterings. The sodden theologian travesties the words of Christ. Of them all, only the mother deports herself with a simple dignity which adds a touch of nobility to the drab prose of her existence.

This ending shows that in the poet's mind the basic mood of comedy survives even the pathos of Hedwig's futile sacrifice. And if we join him in viewing the spectacle of her death from on high, we are reconciled in a measure to the thought of her passing. In her voluntary death the shy and backward, yet altogether winsome child achieves a beauty which continued life could not have maintained. (p. 145)

So *The Wild Duck* does not begin as a comedy and end as a tragedy. It is a comedy from start to finish. Ibsen injects tragedy into comedy, to make comedy but the more poignant. (pp. 145-46)

The Wild Duck is an instance of the most remarkable self-discipline imposed by the dramatist upon a very active part of his self. The moralist in him is for once put under lock and key, securely gagged and bound, while the intelligence of the artist contemplates from above with lingering minuteness the existence of the human animal that lives and thrives on lie, on sham, on make-believe. From above, from heights sufficiently far removed, so as to reduce the spectacle of life to the proportions of a marionette-show; from heights that leave the clarity of vision free from the beclouding vapors of hot indignation or intense sympathy.

The high perspective of comedy from which the interlaced lives of the characters in *The Wild Duck* are contemplated, involved several deviations from Ibsen's usual dramatic method. As a rule, critics have stressed the structural similarity linking *The Wild Duck* with *A Doll's House* and *Ghosts,* to the point of overlooking some very striking differences. Like that of its two forerunners, the method of *The Wild Duck* is analytic; it reveals the past of the Werle and the Ekdal families piecemeal; a considerable share of the exposition is scattered through the fourth and fifth acts. What action there is in the play turns about the bringing to light of the hidden past. The two earlier plays, however, each present a situation which has long harbored a latent germ of conflict, and the action sets in at the point where matters are heading towards a crisis—a crisis that was bound to become manifest sooner or later. This type of play has been aptly called "the drama of ripe condition." Now *The Wild Duck* is not a drama of ripe condition in that sense at all. The affairs of the Ekdal family have not been drifting toward any crisis during the fifteen years of that marriage. The longer that marriage continued, in fact, the more impossible it was that any crisis should develop to disrupt its harmony. The crisis that we witness in the play is the result of the wholly gratuitous meddling of an outsider with the affairs of the Ekdals. As a matter of fact it leaves the relation between husband and wife substantially unchanged; and but for the extension of the intruder's meddling to the adolescent child, the artificially induced crisis would pass over in a few days, leaving scarcely a trace.

And we observe another technical peculiarity of *The Wild Duck.* In *A Doll's House,* in *Ghosts,* and later in *Rosmersholm,* the dramatic spectacle is viewed essentially as a causal sequence. We are led to comprehend, link by link, the circumstances that have made the characters what they are. Ibsen's most subtle art is employed in the retrospective analysis to make us understand the significance of the crisis. In *The Wild Duck,* on the other hand, it is rather a spatial tableau than a causal chain, which is put before us. Two whole acts are filled with a detailed presentation of the daily life of the Ekdals. Our interest is so completely absorbed by their daily occupation, their manner of talking and the make-believe world they have built up around them to make existence interesting, that the question as to how

A scene from The Wild Duck. *Courtesy of Norwegian Information Service.*

they came to develop into these people with these particular habits of living is quite secondary. So the remarks about their past, profuse though they are, strike us rather as obligatory incidentals than as revelations of primary importance. The fact that Hjalmar was coddled by two maiden aunts, that he was idolized at school and at college, is an interesting side light on his development, but it opens up no new perspectives as to the man's character. Some quite important aspects of the past are purposely, perhaps, left rather hazy. For instance, the degree of blame on Old Werle's part for the souring and warping of his son's disposition is impossible to compute. (pp. 146-48)

Likewise, the poet keeps us guessing as to the true parentage of Hedwig, despite the fact that some critics positively identify her as Werle's child while others just as emphatically claim her for Hjalmar. The evidence is all circumstantial. (p. 148)

Gregers suspects Hedwig of being his half sister; Old Werle believes her to be his child; Gina does not know; Hjalmar is out of the reckoning. What conclusion is the reader expected to reach?

As I see it, no precise conclusion at all. We may think that circumstances lean strongly in the direction of establishing Werle's fatherhood; or we may read her temperament and her artistic gifts as an indication pointing to Hjalmar as her father. But who is going to separate out with a sure hand the strands of heredity, and circumscribe neatly the effects of her home environment on the child? Unless one is a lover of argument for argument's sake, one does best to let the matter rest. The

physical fact of Hedwig's parentage does not affect the development of the play one jot. What counts, and counts alone, is the psychological effect on the characters of Hedwig's dubious parentage.

In *The Wild Duck* the analysis of the past is subordinate and secondary in interest to the actual present situation. What interests us in the characters is the fixed individuality of each and their interaction. How they have come to be what they are—at this we shy a glance only in passing. No other play of Ibsen's approaches *The Wild Duck* in its detailed delineation of the *milieu* of a family.

The development of the action is correspondingly slow. Up to the interval between Acts III and IV nothing has happened. It is then that Gregers makes his disclosure to Hjalmar. Act I, so far as it is not exposition of the Werle family and its relation to the Ekdals, gives a snapshot of Old Ekdal and a time exposure of Hjalmar in an environment in which he is not at his ease. Gregers' remark at the end of the act, that at last he sees his mission in life, indicates his intention to provoke a crisis; it marks the incentive moment of the action. Act II presents a picture of the domestic ménage of the Ekdals. First we see mother and daughter in their accustomed daily environment. Then the old Grandfather makes his entrance and retires to his room to make merry by himself with his bottle of cognac. Hjalmar returns from the dinner party at the Werles', and now we see the central character of the play moving at his ease in his family circle; we note the contrast between his mood and his manners among guests and at home, and we take the man's measure. There is a knock at the door, and Gregers enters, apparently to make a friendly call, in reality to probe into Hjalmar's domestic life with the zeal of a social service worker. . . . At the end of this act the action is advanced one step by Gregers' arranging, despite Gina's reluctance, to move into the Ekdals' unoccupied room on the morrow. So far nothing has happened, we have at best a faint presentiment of Gregers' intent; but our curiosity is kept active by the realization that Gregers is entering the Ekdal household with an ulterior purpose.

In Act III the tableau is presented by daylight. Now we see by degrees how completely the life of the Ekdal family, always excepting the efficient and prosaic Gina, revolves about the garret with its furry and feathered inmates. We see the calibre of Hjalmar's work as photographer, and we come to understand that it is Gina who earns the family's living, while Hjalmar's thoughts run only to perfecting the contrivances in his make-believe game-park. Hjalmar soon disappears behind the curtain to saw away at a new contraption, after leaving Hedwig, his beloved child whose impending blindness he has been lamenting, to continue his work of retouching photographs "on her own responsibility." Gregers, who has already made a mess of his room thanks to his hobby of self-help, wanders in and engages in conversation with Hedwig; and by accident he establishes a bond of sympathy between himself and the child—a bond that is fated to have disastrous consequences. Gregers happens to use the expression "paa havsens bund" (in the depths of the sea) instead of the more prosaic every-day expression "paa havets bund" or "Havbunden" (at the bottom of the sea). It is a coincidence that the imaginative child has been in the habit of using that identical phrase in her daydreams to express the sense of mystery which she feels about the strange contents of the garret. Gregers' use of her favorite expression stirs a sympathetic chord in Hedwig, who had, up to this moment, not felt at her ease in the presence of the newcomer. This one phrase establishes a secret understanding between them and replaces shyness by confidence, so that from now on Gregers has a hold on the child and can influence her in line with his purposes. This incident, a master stroke of motivation, is utilized by Ibsen toward a second end, as will appear later.

Hjalmar reappears, and soon we see Gregers preparing in earnest to open his eyes as to the unworthy foundation of his existence. He does not get beyond symbolical generalities, however, before the summons to lunch is heard. With that two more habitués of the Ekdal household make their appearance, the cynical Doctor Relling and the "demonic" theologian Molvik whom the former carries in tow. (pp. 151-53)

Three full acts are consumed in the preparation for the revelation that was to open Hjalmar's eyes. In the two acts remaining we witness the consequences of Gregers' well-meant but stupid meddling.

The revelation of the principal characters is handled in a similar leisurely way. This applies to Gregers and Hjalmar. We observe Hjalmar closely in the first act. . . . However, it is only in the second act that the obscured lines of his character give way to full clearness. The contrast between his silence in company and the airs he gives himself at home is exceedingly droll. Once we have heard him boast of the way he gave it to the chamberlains we cannot possibly take him seriously any more. It is as if a veil had dropped suddenly from our eyes.

We size up Hjalmar correctly almost the moment he steps into his home. It takes us far longer to make up our minds in regard to Gregers. Without being forewarned, the reader would not suspect the Gregers of the first act to figure later as the butt of the poet's ridicule. His sentiments, as expressed during his first reunion with his old friend, strike us as high-minded; his manner, in dealing with his father whom he hates, shows him to be high-strung, neurotic, in fact; but we know too little about him as yet even to suspect him of being "cracked." His appearance in the second act does not materially alter that impression. We, who have seen through Hjalmar by this time, know, of course, how grotesquely Gregers is misjudging his friend, but then Gregers has not shared with us the opportunity of observing Hjalmar off his guard. (pp. 154-55)

But if our attitude up to this time has been one of rather neutral curiosity with regard to Gregers, the developments of the next act force the conviction upon us that he must be viewed from the satirical angle. Gina's account of his clumsy mishaps in putting into practice his theories of self-help evokes a lightly contemptuous smile. Then Gregers enters and engages in a long conversation with Hedwig. Apparently he is lowering himself to her mental level, as he leads her on to chat about her wild duck and her other treasures; in reality he is thinking of nothing but his fancied mission. To the initiated the scene is replete with irony, so far as Gregers' part in it is concerned. However, we have not been sufficiently forewarned to detect this irony. Hence Gregers' mysterious question to Hedwig, "Are you quite sure that it's only a garret," mystifies us as much as it startles the child. But the scene that follows is scarcely mistakable in its intent. With the spotlight of comedy fully turned on Hjalmar, his satellite catches enough of its reflection to be rendered exceedingly grotesque. We see him listening with imperturbable gravity to Hjalmar's account of the crises in his life and of the sustaining invention, and we witness his attempt to prepare the refractory ground of Hjalmar's soul for the seed of spiritual rebirth which he expects to implant by his revelation. For the reader who is skilled in detecting the overtones of Ibsen's orchestration, there is something subtly comic in Gregers' avowal: "I too have a mission in life now; I found it yesterday." Then in comes the Doctor and fires his satirical shafts point-blank at Gregers. The grotesque image of Gregers carrying the claim of the ideal in his coat-tail pocket and presenting it to every humble cottager sticks in one's mind. With that remark the signal is given for releasing our mirth. If its ebullition has been held in check up to this point by lingering doubt as to the author's intentions, it now breaks forth without restraint. Nothing can rehabilitate Gregers after that, as a character to be taken seriously. We review his earlier appearances, and now his whole personality is suffused with the hue of satire. Moreover, each of his subsequent acts compromises him further.

Hjalmar and Gregers are both comic figures, but the difference in treatment accorded them is enormous. There is personal rancor in the shafts shot at Gregers; in Hjalmar's case indignation is disarmed by the entertaining nature of his virtuosity. . . . The poet's delight is apparent in the deftness with which Hjalmar exploits his hypothetical invention for purposes of self-admiration, self-justification and self-pity. . . . Hjalmar pictures himself as expiring under the exhausting mental strain, happy in the consciousness of leaving his widow well provided for. Again the entire proceeds of the invention are requisitioned for repaying Werle to the last penny. And lastly, it was only tender love for Hedwig, the ungrateful child, which caused him to foster in himself the illusion of the invention, now recognized as vaporous. "Great heavens, what would you have me invent?" he exclaims. "Other people have invented almost everything already. It becomes more and more difficult every day." Here the humor touches upon buffoonery, just as it does in the passage where Hjalmar expatiates on the low estate to which his father has fallen, "he, who had shot nine bears, and who was descended from two lieutenant-colonels—one after the other of course"—all of which Gregers takes in with the same jaundiced serious mien. Some of the humorous exhibitions of Hjalmar, it is true, are not without a sharp sting of pathos, as when, having promised Hedwig in his thoughtless, impulsive way that he would stuff his pockets with dainties from the banquet table, he returns to regale the child with the French menu card and a description of the delicacies that had tickled his palate. . . . Given a character like Hjalmar's, the predicament in which he finds himself, thanks to Gregers' meddling, is so real, that curiosity as to how he will extricate himself from the idealist's clutches is even accompanied by a faint undercurrent of sympathy.

Not so in the case of Gregers. . . . Gregers only drew the poet's scorn, whereas he might have been made an object of pity. For he also has a hunger for melodrama, the hunger of an empty, drab life for a touch of color. In forcing himself upon the presence of husband and wife when he expects the grand moment of the reconciliation to be due, in clinging to Hjalmar's heels as a watchdog ever after, he reveals this craving. But he lacks the virtuosity of talent to appease this hunger by his own means, and being without it, he consumes himself in self-hatred.

Too much of Ibsen's own self—the self that he smarted under all his days—has gone into the making of Gregers to permit of the tolerant, good-natured elaboration accorded to Hjalmar. Gregers is Ibsen's self-projection in caricature. (pp. 155-58)

But the cruel sport of self-caricature reaches its height in Ibsen's making Gregers the spokesman of the claim of the ideal. Gregers' idealism can not be honored with the name of a mission; it is a hobby. (p. 159)

Gregers' idealism is the attempt of a superfluous man—one who feels it his destiny to be the thirteenth at table—to dignify his existence by persuading himself that he is of some use in the world. He is an empty vessel, hungering to be filled with the fermenting overflow of a personality; a man of the kind Strindberg would have ranged in his gallery of vampires. He has no personality of his own. . . .

Gregers could have been rendered pathetic; instead Ibsen chose to turn the shafts of his ridicule upon him. His blind worship of Hjalmar through the successive acts of the melodrama gives rise to mocking laughter. Even Gina, handicapped by the servant's native respect for her betters, is this gentleman's superior in knowledge of human nature. (p. 160)

The interpretation of Gregers' character is most closely bound up with the symbolism of the play. The symbolism of *The Wild Duck* has taxed the ingenuity of interpreters to the utmost. The wild duck has given the play its title; it is the topic on which a large portion of the dialogue turns; and it is an indispensable factor in the plot, as the motivation of Hedwig's suicide hinges on its presence.

Werle is the first to employ this symbolism in alluding to the fate of Old Ekdal. "There are people in the world," he tells Gregers, "who dive to the bottom the moment they get a couple of slugs in their body, and never come to the surface again."

In his mouth the figure is perfectly natural, the experience of his duck-hunt in the marshes still being fresh in his mind. . . . (p. 161)

But when Gregers, on his first visit to the Ekdal studio, sees the wounded duck exhibited and hears its strange history, all the details of its story crystallize in his mind into a pattern symbolizing the fate of Hjalmar Ekdal, in accordance with his fixed idea of Hjalmar's character: Hjalmar of the fiery temperament is Werle's wounded victim, he has dived deep down and bitten himself fast in the marsh of the garret, where he is certain to die unless a clever dog dives after him and forcibly drags him up to the light of truth. Gregers feels it his mission to be this dog; and without our being expressly told so, we are aware how keenly Gregers enjoys the irony of fate that has singled out him, the despoiler's son, for the mission of opening the eyes of his father's victim. The symbolism which he has detected gives to his mission an added dignity; and henceforth his language reflects his esoteric insight, causing the child to remark after his departure: "It seemed to me that he meant something different from what he said—all the time."

A coincidence the next morning bestows on Gregers' mission, as it were, its consecration. He had left the house the night before, his mind agitated by the parallelism between the garret and the sea-bottom to which the wild duck, i.e., Hjalmar, had dived, and he has been unable to think of another thing ever since. Now, in the course of his talk with Hedwig, he hears to his astonishment that she also associated "the whole room and everything in it" with the depths of the sea. She displays a child's natural embarrassment in confessing her secret. . . . But upon Gregers her confession must have had the effect of a sign from above. (pp. 161-62)

Up to this time Gregers had resolved the symbolism of the wild duck in his own mind. But in the course of the scene following, when Hjalmar's emotions are agitated by his account of the pistol and of his invention, and he is presumably in a receptive mood, Gregers attempts to use the symbol of the wild duck as a vehicle for conveying to him the truth about his condition. Hjalmar's quick move in self-defense, the moment he senses the danger to his comfort, frustrates the first attempt; but Gregers succeeds in cornering his victim during their walk together, when Hjalmar's caution had unwisely yielded to his curiosity. Henceforth the symbolism, no longer confined to Gregers' solo part, reappears as a duet, chanted by the two luckless men in unison. In Act IV Hjalmar proclaims himself in Relling's presence "Mr. Werle's wing-broken victim."

What is the purpose of all this symbolism? There can be no doubt that its prime function is to characterize Gregers; for all this symbolism, applied to Hjalmar, is grotesquely inept. There is nothing of the wild duck in his make-up. The more Gregers harps on their fancied likeness, the more vividly does the incongruity between Hjalmar's domestic rabbit-soul and that creature of the wilds impinge upon our consciousness. What this symbolism does is to reveal the mentality of Gregers. We perceive his penchant for wallowing in symbols—his *Geheimniskrämerei* as the Germans would say—to be one of the most conspicuous traits of his character. Symbol-mongering is his favorite way of evading the drab color of matter-of-fact reality. It is his way of achieving the illusion, the stimulating principle of life. It is to him what the garret is to Old Ekdal, his invention to Hjalmar and his demonic nature to Molvik. And we see Ibsen's eyes fixed upon the symbol-monger in grim amusement.

Yet to assert that the wild-duck symbolism was interwoven with the play solely for the purpose of satirizing Gregers would seem to me somewhat rash. It must be remembered that we catch Ibsen's satirical intent in exhibiting the symbol-monger rather late; the choicest bits of satire—among them, what I have called the consecration of Gregers' mission—are so subtle as almost to escape detection. Ibsen obviously delights in laying traps for the reader, in mystifying him as to his intentions, in making him sift the most innocent allusion as to a symbolical meaning lurking underneath. It must have amused him to find critics racking their brains to interpret the symbolism of Ekdal's fowling-piece that would no longer shoot. He was prepared for that sort of thing; he predicted it when he posted his manuscript: "My critics will, at any rate, find several things to squabble about and several things to interpret" [see excerpt dated 1884]. He knew his own, not undeserved, reputation for juggling symbols. So we will hardly go wrong in numbering the wild-duck symbolism as among those bits of "tomfoolery" which made the work of writing this play so entertaining to Ibsen. Having once caught Ibsen's sly wink, we relish this symbolism like a subtly compounded sauce imparting to the whole dish an exotic flavor of particular delight for the aesthetic gourmand.

What has been said here about the symbolism of the wild duck does not apply to the transparent symbolism immanent to the situation proper of the play. . . . Those dwellers of the garret, each cherishing his distinct illusion, reflect the need of the average man for a life-lie, an ideal, with which to paint over the grim face of reality. Rob them of their illusions, and their happiness is gone, either for good, or until their ingenuity develops some new make-believe to stay their despair. (pp. 163-65)

The cynic has the last word. Gregers sums up his point of view in the words: "If you are right and I am wrong, then life is not worth living." To which Relling makes answer: "Oh, life would be quite tolerable, after all, if only we could be rid of the confounded duns that keep on pestering us, in our poverty, with the claim of the ideal." (p. 165)

The Wild Duck examines the status of the average run of men with regard to their capacity for truth and records as its finding that, far from truth affording the foundation on which the life of the average man can thrive, life is so steeped in make-believe that the habit of fostering illusions can better afford cultivating than destroying. (p. 166)

> Hermann J. Weigand, in his The Modern Ibsen: A
> Reconsideration, 1925. Reprint by E. P. Dutton &
> Co., Inc., 1960, 416 p.

ARCHIBALD HENDERSON   (essay date 1926)

[*Henderson was a noted American mathematician, literary biographer, critic, essayist, and historian who became known as the foremost American expert on the life and works of Bernard Shaw. He and Shaw met several times and corresponded extensively. Henderson's studies and biographies of Shaw include* George Bernard Shaw: His Life and Works *(1911) and* George Bernard Shaw: Man of the Century *(1956). Henderson has also written biographical and critical studies of Mark Twain and O. Henry, as well as a massive history of North Carolina. In the following excerpt, Henderson notes the innovative nature of* The Wild Duck, *a point that Ibsen also commented on after completing the play (see excerpt dated 1884). The Wild Duck is, Henderson notes, the first of Ibsen's dramas to employ extensive symbolism, as well as the first in which Ibsen presented problems without supplying*

solutions. Although he finds that the play is most commonly interpreted as "an expression of Ibsen's dark pessimism," Henderson calls The Wild Duck *an exploration of the problem of self-realization—the search for one's mission and place in life.*]

The Wild Duck is Ibsen's first step along a new path. This is true in a double sense. Heretofore, Ibsen has been giving very positive, very defiant solutions to the questions he himself has posed. In many cases, he even goes so far as to formulate his solution of the dramatic complex in a single momentous action or even in a memorable, solitary phrase. *The Wild Duck* first fully justifies Ibsen's statement that his vocation was to question rather than to answer. No one was so sure of this as Ibsen himself; he said that, to all, this play offered "problems worth the solving." . . . [Here] for the first time, Ibsen sets his foot in the alien path of symbolism,—that symbolism so strangely interwoven in *Rosmersholm,* so mystic in *Little Eyolf,* so magically potent in *The Lady From the Sea*! The disquieting figure of the wounded wild duck, suggested to Ibsen as a dramatic symbol by Welhaven's beautiful poem *The Sea Bird,* flutters mysteriously through this disturbing play—symbolizing now the wounded soul of Werle, now the "evil genius of the house" (baldly stated in the "forework"), now the symbolic adumbration of the fateful secret of Hedwig's parentage bequeathed by the old Werle to the Ekdal family.

It is usual for critics to find in *The Wild Duck* an expression of Ibsen's dark pessimism, distrust in his mission, incipient disbelief in "the claim of the ideal." It is interpreted as a reaction against the dogmatic "All or Nothing" of *Brand,* against Stockmann's cocksureness in the virtue of his mission in *An Enemy of the People.* In *The Wild Duck,* does Ibsen merely question whether "the bitter tonic-draught of truth" is the fundamental pre-requisite for the happiness and well-being of humanity, as it now is, or even as it may be for Heaven knows how long yet to come? This seems to me to be a superficial judgment. The real problem around which Ibsen's mind continually hovered was the problem, for the individual, of discovering himself in life. In the very year in which he wrote *The Wild Duck,* Ibsen spoke, not once, but twice, in letters, of "the duty and the right, of realizing one's self." Self-realization, in its amplest sense, for Ibsen, means not only the discovery of one's mission, but also the discovery of the great meaning, the great happiness even, that life holds for the individual soul. *The Wild Duck* is a dark and ironic commentary upon the wrong-headed reformer, who would turn the world upside down in a mad and meddlesome effort to realize his own extravagant ideals. This play is as little a *reduction ad absurdum* of Ibsen's own doctrine and ideal of the efficacy of truth as *How He Lied to Her Husband* is a caricature of *Candida.* In Hjalmar Ekdal's attitude towards Gina is satirized the absolute moral demand of Svava Riis in Björnson's *A Glove.* . . . And in Gregers Werle is mordantly satirized that "untutored idealism"—of which we have recently heard so much in America.

Gregers Werle is in pursuit of illusions. He is that "sick conscience" which subsequently found such memorable incarnation in Halvard Solness. He is the inevitable product of his own environment and his own heredity. In his reaction against the Life Lie of his own father, he absorbs the *idée fixe* of a mother rendered morbid and hysterical by her own domestic tragedy. With a grotesque mania for hero-worship and a ludicrous misapprehension of the moral bankruptcy of Hjalmar Ekdal, Gregers Werle flourishes aloft the banner of the ideal and revels in bearing heedless witness to the truth. In his misguided efforts to force upon weaker vessels, made of common clay, that which they are unable to hold, he succeeds only in shattering them into fragments. His passion for communicating to others his ''fever for doing right'' leaves disaster and death in his wake. ''Oh, life would be quite tolerable, after all,'' says Relling—the real Ibsen speaking, undoubtedly *in propria persona*—''if only we could be rid of the confounded duns that keep on pestering us, in our poverty, with the claim of the ideal.''

Nowhere has Ibsen's power of minute and veracious characterization showed itself so supreme. Gregers Werle is the classic embodiment of the misguided reformer. Hjalmar Ekdal is Ibsen's most striking embodiment of the pitiable moral bankrupt, self-deceiving, self-deceived—grotesquely failing to live up to standards inconsiderately applied from without. He is the tragic figure of the average sensual man, betrayed by ideals he has not really made his own—feeding upon his illusions, those illusions by which his very peace of mind, his happiness, are conditioned. Gina Ekdal, without any ideals save the eminently materialistic, eminently prosaic desire to preserve the comfortable *status quo,* is irresistibly natural and likable—perhaps because she is so utterly of the earth earthy. The gentle Hedwig, tender, appealing, young enough to make a hero of her selfish father, too young to detect his glaring faults, is Ibsen's most poetic feminine figure. . . . *The Wild Duck* has been regarded as a perfect example of Ibsen's individual technique. But its most lamentable technical fault has been succinctly pointed out by Bernard Shaw: ''The logic by which Gregers Werle persuades Hedwig to kill the wild duck in order that she may be provided with a pistol to kill herself, strains my credulity.''

From this time forward, Ibsen's plays concern themselves less and less with society, more and more with individual problems of character and conscience. Just as *The Wild Duck* marks the transition from realism to symbolism, so *Rosmersholm* marks the transition from society to the individual. After this point, Ibsen's dramas are no longer sociological. They are psychological, and at times psychic, concern themselves with the inner life of thought and conscience, and verge ever towards symbolism, mysticism and poetry. (pp. 131-36)

In *The Wild Duck* Ibsen reaches the extreme point of his realism. Here he brings us face to face with ''cheap, earthenware souls''; he he paints, in garish colors, the unromantic hero—that ludicrous contradiction in terms. At last we have the true *bourgeois* drama, dealing with the thoughts and passions, the loves and hates, the comedies and tragedies, of people such as we brush against every day in the street. The protagonist of to-day has ''lost the last gleam from the sunset of the heroes.'' Here is the hero *manqué*, struggling in vain against the overwhelming pressure of environment, the brand of heredity, the coil of circumstance, the chains of character, the damning verdict of self-mockery, self-distrust, and self-contempt. (pp. 136-37)

> *Archibald Henderson, ''Henrik Ibsen,'' in his* European Dramatists, *D. Appleton & Co., 1926, pp. 75-198.*

BRIAN W. DOWNS (essay date 1950)

[*In the following excerpt Downs takes exception to those interpretations of* The Wild Duck *that view the duck as an essential element, terming the duck a ''detachable'' symbol that could have been omitted without significantly altering the play's meaning, though unquestionably diminishing the work as an artistic ac-*

complishment. For an opposing view of the duck's importance, see the excerpt by Janel M. Mueller (1969). Downs concludes that the basic idea underlying The Wild Duck *is that '''ideals' are a luxury and as such'' are ''inaccessible to the great mass of humanity,'' of which the play's characters are representative.*]

The pathos of Hedvig's fate has led those for whom it is the most moving and the most arresting thing in *The Wild Duck* to look upon her as the heroine of the play and, as a not unnatural corollary, to identify her in some measure with the wild duck itself: for, after all, it is not an unusual practice to name a drama after its foremost character. Hedvig may be the most admirable personage presented in the play, but that in itself does not guarantee the validity of the theory; the virtuous Kent is not the hero of *King Lear,* nor the blameless Cassandra of *Agamemnon;* neither can it rightly be maintained that the play fundamentally is 'about' Hedvig, that her fate is the constant preoccupation either of the other personages or of the spectators: she is a victim like Ophelia in *Hamlet,* and almost an accidental victim.

The same, to be sure, can be said of the wild duck, but is there really any other close parallel between them? Does the wild duck's fate mirror that of her owner and, in doing so, give it a wider significance? They who incline to such a view remark that both of them live in a world of pretences for which they are not responsible and that they are the noblest, the least corrupted denizens of that world. Both perish. But further the parallel cannot be extended, and the dissimilarities are greater than the resemblances. Nothing goes to show that Hedvig has been wounded or maimed or even that the environment of pretence in which she has been brought up is marring desirable potentialities in her. . . . Nothing indicates a distortion in her nature except her reported playing with fire, which Relling expressly puts down not to anything in her environment, but to the stage which she has reached in her natural physical development. And where are we to find the application of the wild duck's plunge to the bottom of the sea and her recovery by Haaken Werle's incredibly clever dog?

Why does Hedvig shoot herself? Accident, . . . should be ruled out. Hers is an intentional act, induced by the notion of sacrifice which Gregers has put into her head: to regain her father's love she is to offer up what she holds dearest in the world. She does not hesitate in designating as the sacrificial victim her pet, the maimed wild duck: she will get her grandfather, Old Ekdal, to shoot it dead. The construction that, on further reflection, as a conscious perseverance in Gregers's idea, Hedvig considered her own life to be even more precious than the wild duck must, I think, be rejected, even if unconsciously her act may conform to it. The act is a violent, perhaps hysterical one of self-destruction, the cause of it despair at Hjalmar's rejection of her as an interloper and the manner suggested by the mocking rhetorical question she overhears: 'Hedvig, are you willing to renounce that life for me? [*Laughs scornfully.*] No thank you! You would soon hear what answer I should get.'

Hedvig loves the wild duck partly because it has been wounded and is thriving again under her care, partly because it is the rarest, most aristocratic denizen of the attic and her very own property, partly because there are about it the romantic, fairy-tale associations of having lived its wild life a long way away and, at the time it was wounded, having 'been down in the depths of the sea'. Even if Hedvig were capable of conceiving a 'symbol'—which, of course, she is not—there is nothing to suggest that the wild duck is a symbol to her in any deeper sense any more than that a boy's passion for his rocking-horse is a symbol to him of his pride of possession or love of mastery.

The other characters' attitude towards the bird is not quite so straightforward. For old Ekdal she is part, the most authentic part, of the surrogate wild life in which he can still see himself leading the primitive sportsman's existence where he had been happiest; for Hjalmar, similarly, one of the distractions enabling him to escape from a reality that otherwise would depress him by its squalor and his own conviction of failure. But it is Gregers, with his proneness to read sermons in stones, who weaves speculative phantasies about the wild duck, not merely as one (if the most outstanding) of the elements in the make-believe wild life of the attic—which he dislikes as a sham and an obfuscation of reality—but in herself. It is not an exuberant imagination that makes him do this; significantly, the ideas are put into his head by others, first by his father, when, before the wild duck has ever been mentioned, he says *à propos* of Old Ekdal 'there are people in the world who dive to the bottom the moment they get a couple of slugs in their body, and never come to the surface again', and then by Old Ekdal himself, who, after repeating the hunters' lore that, when a wild duck is shot, it plunges to the bottom and bites itself fast to the weed and rubbish there, recalls that this particular wild duck, having done this, was retrieved by an 'amazingly clever dog' belonging to Haaken Werle, who then made a present of the bird to the Ekdal family. Gregers immediately fastens on the parallel between this story and the carefree, naïve life of Old Ekdal, which was shattered by the action of his old partner, but continued in a kind of twilight, amid filth and rubbish, barely conscious, half dead. He sees himself as the incredibly clever dog who dives down and restores submerged creatures to light and renewed utility above. (pp. 160-63)

It is clear that, to Gregers, Hedvig's wild duck is a symbol, which can possess, as the most thoroughgoing symbolists seem always to hold, an active property of its own in relation to what it is held to symbolise. For, in inducing Hedvig to kill her pet, he intends to destroy the bogus, 'lying' make-believe which poisons the atmosphere of her family.

We must, however, beware of identifying the calamity-fraught notions of Gregers Werle with Ibsen's own. Like many another author, especially when a comparatively concentrated literary form, like the dramatic, enjoins economy, Ibsen could give prominence to a single phrase or object or concept (where in real life a number of rather similar phrases or objects or concepts would more usually occur), without necessarily attaching any unique and thus mysterious significance to the one chosen as representative; and an occasional, not over-recondite, coincidence or parallel can have its uses for giving unobtrusive emphasis. Because only the orphanage is mentioned during the eighteen hours or so in which *Ghosts* plays, we are not to suppose that Fru Alving had kept her late husband's memory alive in no other ways. (p. 164)

But the pervasiveness of the wild duck, the repeated references to it and the way in which so many of the human beings round about are preoccupied with it raise a presumption that this single small object, which is not even seen, possesses an importance of a novel order. After all, the play is called *The Wild Duck.* The wild duck and its associations can scarcely be dismissed *prima facie* as 'detachable' in the sense just argued. Should not a significance be attached to it greater than the aggregate of things which it means to the various personages who mention it, something overriding all the small 'lessons' and 'morals' which those who will can derive from almost any work of art,

a significance for which the author himself can be made responsible? The same question presents itself more or less insistently with *Rosmersholm* and the 'White Horses' after which that play was originally named, with Ellida's love of bathing in *The Lady from the Sea,* with the vine-leaves in Løvborg's hair of which even so prosaic a person as Hedda Gabler makes mention, with the tower on Master Builder Solness's new house, with the great statuary group on which Rubek of *When We Dead Awaken* had founded his fame. Is any paramount importance to be attached to the fact that little Eyolf's crutch is seen floating after he is drowned or that the night on which John Gabriel Borkman dies should be a specially cold one? Has at the end of Ibsen's career the symbolism, in Mr Tennant's phrase [see Additional Bibliography], become 'organic'—something, so to speak, without which the plays would fall to pieces as artistic and intellectual constructions, be nothing but trivial and rather painful anecdotes? Mr Tennant declares:

> Ibsen gave the play the name *Vildanden* and I maintain that it was not a title chosen because of the association such a name would arouse but because the wild duck is the chief protagonist of the play.... The play is not called *Vildanden* because Hedvig's fate was like that of a wild duck, nor because the wild duck, under the censorship of morals, conventions or religion, is the distorted expression of elementary urges. It is because the wild duck by its mere presence so affects the conditions of Gregers, Hjalmar and Hedvig by the various associations it suggests that it bears the sole responsibility for the final catastrophe.

> (pp. 165-66)

Mr Tennant, I think, overstates his case. The catastrophe, Hedvig's death, is brought about by Hjalmar's unkindness to her, which Gregers's doctrinaire interference unnaturally stimulates, and a play ending similarly could have been constructed by omitting the wild duck altogether (as indeed Ibsen seems at first to have conceived it) or by, so to speak, putting its various functions in commission instead of concentrating them in a single focus. Very likely, such a play would have been less effective than *The Wild Duck* we have. But the fact that Ibsen seems to have contemplated it at first goes some considerable way to proving that the symbolism again is 'detachable'.

In general, Ibsen was disdainful of symbolic explanations. (p. 167)

If in one way (to put it at its lowest) the wild duck serves to hold together the play called after her, in another way Relling does so too. Whatever it is, his is a somewhat more limited function. For he has next to nothing to do with the sphere of which Haaken Werle forms the centre: his activities are confined to the Ekdal household. Not unlike Gregers Werle, he is a man with a mission, though he would probably have repudiated any such ascription to him other than the good physician's principle to do his best for his patients, for each according to his diathesis and complaint. In the play, he is called in to examine Hedvig after her suicide; but otherwise, his ministrations belong entirely to the psychological and moral realm; and, though he proceeds with professional empiricism, he acknowledges a therapeutic principle. It is formulated as keeping the 'life-lie alive' in his 'patients', to maintain them, in other words, in the atmosphere of illusion where they thrive. (p. 168)

Relling's only concern is the happiness of his patient—though it may be noted that that happiness nowhere involves the unhappiness of others: but concepts like the good of society or the moral efficacy of the individual are not only excluded but repudiated.

Relling accordingly stands as the poles apart to the man of principle, Gregers Werle, who is in every way antipathetic to him. He rejects ideals in themselves . . . ; and particularly because the impossible demands which they make are the direct cause of individual dissatisfaction and unhappiness. 'Life would be quite tolerable', he exclaims at the very end of the play: 'Life would be quite tolerable, after all, if only we could be rid of the confounded duns that keep on pestering us, in our poverty, with the claim of the ideal.' Pragmatically he is justified: as long as it was he who was in control of the situation in Hjalmar's house, all went well; but, from the moment he is ousted by the idealist, *malaise*, unhappiness and disaster ensue.

Relling being thus justified according to the most reliable test available, how far may we identify Ibsen's own attitude with his? 'Ideals' are seen as the hostile agent, standing in the way of human happiness. Has Ibsen finally come round to this view? If we make the identification of Relling and Ibsen, is there not a grave inconsistency between the position which the latter takes up in *The Wild Duck* and that to be inferred from the earlier plays, where truth, honesty, candour, straight-dealing, the resolute facing of facts, everything indeed repugnant to the 'life-lie', seem to be exalted? Undoubtedly there is a great difference. But we have noted before, in connection with *Brand* and *Peer Gynt* particularly, how Ibsen could make his work embody two opposing points of view, could impartially scrutinise them and show them as issuing in similar results; he realised more and more clearly that everything, even truth, was relative, that it was impossible to make universally valid demands, and he was insistent that every factor must be weighed, all circumstances of an individual case taken into account. This is in a way a consequence of self-criticism. If Ibsen felt that he had been too hard on Brand, he redressed the balance by subjecting to similar castigation one who had none of the qualities of Brand, seeing himself or part of himself in both. Similarly he could see himself, the author of *Pillars of Society, A Doll's House* and *An Enemy of the People,* going about the world with the demands of the ideal in his pocket just like Gregers Werle among the cottagers at Højdal. Could he be sure that he had produced nothing but good? Were there not, to put it at its lowest, circumstances in which a Relling would be absolutely right in rounding upon him? The Lie, against which Falk so exuberantly declared war, may sometimes have its justification.

In the circumstances that must be taken into account in any verdict upon *The Wild Duck,* there is one of particular importance which has already been glanced at. The personages in the play are by comparison with their predecessors of a diminished stature, they are much more ordinary people. Is it fair, the inference seems to be, is it proper in the last analysis, is it profitable to ask such ordinary people to raise themselves to the moral level of a Thomas Stockmann or Helene Alving, not to mention a Brand and an Agnes? In other words, may not 'ideals' be a luxury and as such inaccessible to the great mass of humanity? The pragmatical test represented by *The Wild Duck* seems to return the answer Yes.

They who scan a work of art for ideals are themselves idealists in the popular accepted meaning of the term: they attribute the best motives and await the highest in mankind. A conclusion like that to which Relling attains, in much of which Ibsen himself seems also to concur, is profoundly repugnant to them or if not repugnant, at least grieving. It is on that account, no doubt, that *The Wild Duck* has been called the most pessimistic of Ibsen's plays and that the pessimism vulgarly attributed to all tragedies is confirmed in his case. (pp. 169-71)

If Hjalmar be regarded as a diminished, even less heroic, Peer Gynt and Gregers Werle as a smaller Brand who has fostered his idealism in similarly remote and barren tracts, the tragedy of *The Wild Duck* proceeds from an impact of these two characters, and the smash-up of Hjalmar's domestic felicity, with the death of Hedvig, has a two-fold cause. The catastrophe is most obviously induced by Gregers, who, presenting the demands of the ideal, first undermines the mutual confidence on which the Ekdal household is reared, replaces its security by disquieting doubts about its past and its future, turns a collectively and individually happy family into an unhappy one, and also puts the idea of a blood sacrifice into Hedvig's head. In the second place and more particularly, however, as we have seen, Hedvig's substitution of herself for the Wild Duck as the sacrificial victim is due to Hjalmar's thoughtless cruelty towards her. Such cruelty does not seem an obvious attribute of an easy-going, comfort-loving nature like his; but in the circumstances it proceeds naturally from his complete egoism, his inability to realise the bearings of the situation in which he finds himself and from the angry *malaise* engendered by his uncertainty.

Hjalmar has been very suddenly thrust into this situation through the interference of Gregers, and the situation from which the tragedy ensues is therefore fortuitous. It is not every Peer Gynt who runs up against a Brand, and most of the Peer Gynts of this world proceed happily to their obscure graves. If the second phase of Gregers's interference—his action upon Hedvig—had not supervened upon the first, all might still have been well, especially if the practised healer Relling had remained at hand to soothe and guide. In fact we see the reintegration of Hjalmar's shattered family life taking place before our eyes at the beginning of the fifth act when he consents to sit down to lunch and to postpone his removal from the house to a more convenient season. And Relling's bitter prophecy: 'Before a year is over little Hedvig will be nothing to him but a pretty theme for declamation', from which it is impossible to dissent, indicates that in so far as he is concerned that process of reintegration will continue, though of course to a lesser completeness.

Besides the grotesque, the comic elements associated with the attic menagerie and inherent in the character of Hjalmar and his father, Ibsen thus had a double justification for describing his play as a tragi-comedy and withholding the full designation of tragedy: the fortuitous juxtaposition of Hjalmar and Gregers and the evanescent effect on the former of the catastrophe that overtakes him.

There is, however, another—at least one other—aspect from which the 'tragedy' of *The Wild Duck* may be explored. The catastrophe is undeniably the catastrophe of Gregers. He has had a great chance of the sort for which he has been waiting, the chance to have justice done to his old friend's family, which, rightly or wrongly, he believes to have been outrageously treated, and to raise at any rate some of his fellow men to that high moral level on which he thinks that all should have their being; and nothing but evil has ensued upon these selfless efforts. Cannot, therefore, *The Wild Duck* be construed as the idealist's tragedy? Undoubtedly it can (subject to the overriding consideration that it should be the idealist's, the active moralist's, constant preoccupation to take the circumstances of every case into account and that he must take full responsibility if he fails to do so). But it seems as if Ibsen wished to minimise this aspect of *The Wild Duck*—and by so doing to refrain from casting a justifying glow around those activities of his own which resemble Gregers Werle's. For one thing, he withheld from Gregers not only the greatness and nobility with which he endowed Brand, but all amiability as well: Gregers is animated by no real love for mankind in general or of Tom, Dick and Harry in particular, and no one cares for him. In the second place, important as he is in the scheme of *The Wild Duck,* he never holds the centre of the stage: he is an ominous rather than a sinister figure, standing at the side, fatally involving others in the darkness of his personality. Moreover, his final exit deprives him of the last opportunity of assuming heroic stature: he expresses no regret—beyond the apology that he always acted with the best intentions—no contrition or repentance like that of Brand or Peer Gynt. He betrays no resolve, like Nora, to think things out in the light of fresh knowledge and, in a new life, make good the ill he has committed, turn himself into a real benefactor of his kind. If he really intends to commit suicide, he slinks off as one who just sees that he has no luck on his side. Neither in Gregers nor in Hjalmar does calamity induce a purgation—yet another card in the hand of those who contend for Ibsen's pessimism. (pp. 172-74)

Brian W. Downs, *in his* A Study of Six Plays by Ibsen, *Cambridge at the University Press, 1950, 213 p.*

OTTO REINERT   (essay date 1956)

[*In the following excerpt, Reinert examines the way in which Ibsen used images of sight and blindness in* The Wild Duck *both as plot devices and as symbols. Reinert considers but rejects a comparison between the function of the sight imagery in* The Wild Duck *and in the classic tragedies* King Lear *and* Oedipus Rex, *finding that the loss of sight in* The Wild Duck, *whether actual or symbolic, is never accompanied by a corresponding realization of the truth, as happens in the two classic dramas.*]

Impressive as [Ibsen's] command of dramatic structure and symbol was, he was in addition a genuine poet. My purpose here is to call attention to a pattern of imagery in *The Wild Duck* that serves the same integrating and value-defining functions as similar patterns in Shakespeare's mature plays and in much metaphysical and modern poetry. Ostensibly representational and simply communicative, the language of the dialogue operates on an imagistic level as well, reinforcing and clarifying the meaning of the action, embodying the dramatic metaphor.

Blindness, it will be recalled, is an important plot element in *The Wild Duck.* It is when he learns about Old Werle's approaching blindness that Hjalmar Ekdal concludes that little Hedvig is not his own but Werle's child, since she too is losing her sight. And his repulsion of Hedvig precipitates the catastrophe, the girl's pathetic suicide. To readers of Ibsen there is nothing unusual in this. Once again we find him using a fact of biological heredity both as plot device and as symbol of the visitation of the past upon the present.

What has not been clearly recognized is that images of sight and blindness occur throughout the play, constituting a substratum of ironical values beneath the naturalistic surface. The images help to define the play's action: the struggle between Gregers Werle and Dr. Relling for control over Hjalmar Ekdal's destiny becomes a conflict between two views—one "idealistic," dim, and distorted; one "realistic," clear, and accurate—of modern Everyman's diminished nature. In the strict economy of Ibsen's art the validity of Relling's realistic view is stated only by negative implication. It is vindicated by the setting of Gregers' idealistic view of Hjalmar and Hjalmar's view of himself (the two are almost identical, since Hjalmar takes the cue for his concept of himself from Gregers) in a context of imagistic irony. (pp. 457-58)

What is one man's truth is another man's poison. It is this skeptical, relativistic theme that Ibsen allows ironical play in the images of sight and blindness. Hjalmar Ekdal is not the kind of man who can live comfortably with an unpleasant truth, and the ruin of the Ekdal happiness is the result of Gregers Werle's mistaken view of Hjalmar's character.

But Gregers goes through the whole play thinking of himself as a man who, if he does nothing else, at least *sees*. His self-hatred, conditioned by a neurotic mother and a miserable adolescence, is modified on this one point only: he prides himself on his ability to see the truth and on his courage to bring it out into the open. In Act I he turns down his father's offer of reconciliation with the words, "I have seen too much of you" (literally: "I have seen you from too close up"). Gregers' choice of phrase is ironic, since there *is* something myopic about his view of his father, and Werle's answer suggests, at an early point in the play, the dubious validity of his son's vision: "You have seen me with your mother's eyes. . . . But you should remember that those eyes were—clouded at times." In a play premised on heredity it is not overly ingenious to take this to mean that Gregers' sight is affected, figuratively speaking, by inheritance from both his father and his mother. To his father's offer Gregers opposes his confidence in his clearsightedness: "Now at last I see a mission to live for." The mission, we soon learn, is "to open Hjalmar Ekdal's eyes. He shall see his situation as it is; . . ." Ibsen's curtain speeches frequently carry a load of ulterior meaning, and it is Gregers who delivers the curtain speech in Act I: "Look, father; the chamberlains are playing blindman's buff with Mrs. Sørby." The speech is a cruel taunt to a man who is about to go blind, a veiled insult to his father's wife-to-be, a declaration on Gregers' part that blindman's buff is not a game *he* chooses to play—and an anticipation of the kind of game he is, in fact, about to involve the Ekdals in. On the first morning of his residence with the Ekdals he tries to light the stove in his room but succeeds only in filling the room with smoke. Before the play is over he has reduced the Ekdal home to a similar dark and messy state. But to him it is Hjalmar, not himself, who is living in darkness, like a wild duck that has dived down from the light of day. (pp. 458-59)

Hjalmar, too, thinks he sees, and his occupation would seem to support his claim. It is the business of a photographer to see straight and to record his vision objectively. But, significantly, he has not himself chosen his occupation, and it is Gina who actually carries on the daily business. Every afternoon he spends hours on the sofa with his eyes shut—i.e., fast asleep— while his family believes, and he believes himself, that he is visualizing a great photographic invention. His "badness of vision" is, like Gregers', established in the first act, when his father passes through Werle's study where his dinner guests are assembled. Ill at ease among his social superiors Hjalmar refuses to acknowledge his shabby and doddering old father, and is consequently forced—there is a kind of poetic justice in the incident, though Hjalmar is, of course, unaware of it—to pretend to less powers of observation than even "the near-sighted gentleman" who asks him if he knows Old Ekdal. In his misery Hjalmar mutters that he "didn't notice. . . ." But spiritual blindness does not prevent Hjalmar, any more than Gregers, from referring to himself as a person of superior insight, a lover of light. . . . Just prior to the climactic scene with his wife, in which he forces her to confess to the old affair with Werle, he asks in a characteristically pregnant speech: "Let me have the lamp lit!" He reproaches Gina that she never "casts a probing glance" at her past, and he silences Relling's warning that the old stories are better left buried with, "You've never had an eye for the claims of the ideal, Relling." Once Gregers has "opened his eyes" he looks back upon the years he has lived in illusion as one long blindness. Werle becomes a man who "has once blinded a trusting fellow being," but he finds comfort in the justice of Werle's own approaching blindness, and concludes sententiously: "It is useful, at times, to plunge oneself into the night side of existence." When he learns about Werle's gift letter to his father and Hedvig, he exclaims: "Oh, what vistas, what perspectives open up before me!" He thinks he has had "his eyes opened" to Hedvig's disloyalty to him. "It is Hedvig who stands in the way," he tells Gregers. "She it is who is shutting out the sun from my whole life." Blind as he is to Hedvig's love for him, he is forced to close his eyes to the ugly facts of the surface truth he *does* see. He sends her away with a "I can't stand to look at you," and is deaf to Gina's plea for the heartbroken girl: "Look at the child, Ekdal! Look at the child!" He doesn't, and the shot in the attic follows.

Gregers' use of sight imagery thus points up his blindness to Hjalmar's true character and to the true nature of the Ekdal family's modicum of happiness. Hjalmar's use of such imagery emphasizes his blindness to Gina's and Hedvig's loyal devotion. The more they think they see the more lost they are in darkness. Hjalmar's stupid cruelty to Hedvig leads to her death, and Gregers' faith in the greatness of Hjalmar's soul remains unshaken even after the catastrophe. Both are incapable of seeing beneath the surface of facts; both are blind to their own reality.

It might be tempting, once the function of this sight imagery is recognized, to extend the pattern and find it analogous to the sight-blindness ironies of *Oedipus Rex* and *King Lear*. But such analogy would not be valid. The painful discovery of truth does not, in *The Wild Duck,* coincide with any loss of physical sight; neither Hjalmar nor Gregers corresponds to an Oedipus or a Gloucester. It might even be argued that neither of them ever attains any real insight. Relling's prophecy of what the dead Hedvig will mean to Hjalmar a year hence is undoubtedly correct, and Gregers leaves the play with no more than a sense of bringing people bad luck. And there is nothing wrong with the eyesight of Dr. Relling, the most perceptive character in the play: he is not a Tiresias. Nor do the two characters who *do* go blind, Old Werle and Hedvig, discover any new truth in the course of the play. For all the reasonableness of his adjustment to life it is difficult to consider Werle a representative of spiritual enlightenment, and his relatively minor part in the play disqualifies him in any case for the part of foil to his son and Hjalmar. With her sensitivity and imagination and capacity for love Hedvig is, in a sense, a source of light, but she is, after all, a child, only dimly comprehending the strange adult doings around her. And her unwavering devotion to Hjalmar and worship of him, beautiful though her sentiments are,

are hardly the attitudes of a clearsighted girl. If anything, her physical blindness is simply a symbol of her blindness to her father's obvious moral shortcomings.

But if *The Wild Duck* is not tragedy in the great tradition transposed to a modern middle class setting, it does, like the older plays, make use of responsible images. It is a poetic achievement. It succeeds in expressing its sardonic and tender wisdom about the little souls of men in a form that combines the rich suggestiveness of metaphorical language with the insistent and solid actuality of naturalism. The sight imagery never becomes intrusive; the ironies do not call attention to themselves by breaking through the surface of commonplace idiom. But they are there, and their presence makes for moral spaciousness. Their suggestion of values more true than mere facts, truer than the idealist's misty generalities, proves that the poet in Ibsen was active even in his most sordid play. (pp. 460-62)

*Otto Reinert, "Sight Imagery in 'The Wild Duck',"
in* The Journal of English and Germanic Philology,
Vol. LV, 1956, pp. 457-62.

G. WILSON KNIGHT   (essay date 1962)

[*Knight is one of the most influential of modern Shakespearean critics, as well as a noted Shakespearean actor. He has also written studies of Lord Byron, Alexander Pope, John Masefield, John Cowper Powys, and of Ibsen. In the following excerpt, Knight notes in* The Wild Duck *"the two terms of a typical Ibsen opposition, the false surface and the revealer"—and concludes that both are shown to be ineffectual in maintaining a useful illusion on the one hand, or in enabling characters to come to grips with a particular truth on the other, thus resulting in a more profound dramatic statement.*]

[We observe] in *Ghosts* a surmounting of easy solutions, and from the peculiarly objective and at times almost comic self-diagnosis of *An Enemy of the People* we learn that too sudden a revelation of the social lie creates as many problems as it solves. The process is carried further in *The Wild Duck.* . . . It is a difficult work containing symbols that at first appear to assert themselves without the natural flowering which we normally demand.

The people are, for once, weak. Apart from the doctor, Relling, as the voice of common sense, there are no men worthy of respect. In Gina, the housewife, we have a responsible and genuine if colourless and unimaginative woman. Only Hedvig the child has a dramatic aura.

Hialmar Ekdal, our central person, is a neat study in egotism and ineffectuality developing one strand of *Peer Gynt,* though without anything of Peer's irrepressible buoyancy. Hialmar is lazy, self-centred and sentimental, living on thought of a projected invention which will never materialise. The conception is Chekhovian.

Werle is a rich industrialist who had formerly involved Hialmar's father in some illegal felling of timber on State land, with the result that old Ekdal was sent to prison while Werle himself escaped. Werle has since compounded with his conscience by helping the Ekdal family. Gregers Werle, Werle's son, is an idealist who attempts to put the Ekdal family—that is Hialmar, his old father, his wife Gina, and his daughter Hedvig—on their feet by making Hialmar face unpleasant facts. Hialmar learns that his marriage was deliberately promoted by Gregers' father because Gina had been his mistress, and he soon realises that Hedvig may not be his own daughter. By unearthing the past Gregers makes chaos of what had been a reasonably harmonious home. As Dr Relling observes . . . , the dispelling of a person's life-illusion robs him of all happiness.

Ironically, Werle, the villain of the piece, finally makes a good marriage on an honest basis, so meeting the demands of truth towards which the apparently more worthy people make ineffectual gestures. Not that we admire Werle, nor is he unpunished. He is going blind; so is Hedvig, presumably his daughter. Blindness is here emphatic. Humanity is blind.

If there were no more than this in *The Wild Duck*, there would be little to say beyond praising the subtlety of its characterisation; but there is much more, mainly symbolic. Dionysus is, in passing, honoured when Dr Relling tells us that his friend the divinity student Molvik has a "demonic" nature that must from time to time be allowed release in drink. . . . Our main symbols are more expansive. Hialmar is a photographer, and his studio is an attic opening into a loft in which the Ekdals keep hens, rabbits, pigeons, and even trees. You can see through the opening to moonlight or daylight. The sea is suggested by a curtain of sail-cloth and a fishing net. Among the lumber is an old history book containing a picture of Death with an hour-glass, and other pictures of churches and palaces, and big sea-going ships. The place was formerly owned by a sea-captain, known by the romantic name of "the Flying Dutchman," who was later drowned. . . . It is as though the whole universe were *packed into* this loft: space and time, life and death, forests and sea, animals, civilisation, and art. In it time stands still. . . . It is a kind of make-believe reflexion of all those greater categories from which our tawdry human drama is cut off. That is why Hialmar, rightly bored by his photography and supposed invention, awakes and becomes active and purposive as soon as there is an excuse for tinkering in the loft. His neurotic state is to this extent not merely understandable, but praiseworthy; he is sick from loss of contact with the greater powers.

Those most attuned to the loft are old Ekdal and Hedvig, age and childhood. Old Ekdal was once a lieutenant, and though he may not after his imprisonment wear his uniform in public, he does so, on choice occasions, at home. But his greatest pleasure is to go shooting in the loft. He had formerly been a bold bear-hunter, such as Olaf in *Pillars of Society* had wished to be, and now he acts over again his days of virility, bears replaced by rabbits. As for Hedvig, she loves the old books and pictures, and wants to learn real engraving herself, the wish establishing a vivid contrast to the family's profession of photography and the touching-up of photographs in which she and her mother assist. It is important to observe that the loft holds in it two primary Ibsen powers, nature and art.

It is, of course, mainly an escape-world, a dream-world. But it has one most vital occupant: the Wild Duck. The bird had been shot by Werle, had plunged to the muddy sea-bed, but been saved by a dog, and though winged it is now kept in a basket with some water to flounder in. The symbolism is pointed by Gregers: the Ekdals are the duck and he means to be the dog. Yet there is more to this strange creature of wild life than that. It is, says Hedvig . . . , mysterious: "Nobody knows her, and nobody knows where she came from either." The Duck is as mysterious as life itself. Besides, it has been down, in Gregers' words, to "the depths of the sea," a phrase that fascinates Hedvig, who is in the habit of applying it to the loft, and is associated by Gregers at the play's conclusion with death. . . . The wounded Duck's happiness depends on its being

kept from sight of the cosmic freedoms of sea and sky. . . . It belongs primarily to Hedvig. . . . She nurtures and mothers it; in the child-consciousness the mystery finds a home. When, after Hialmar, suspecting that she is not his child, turns against her, and Gregers suggests that she sacrifice the Duck to regain his love, she shoots herself instead. The action may appear unnatural, but in Ibsen's world suicides hold an especial place; satire is directed against both Old Ekdal and Hialmar for not having dared to shoot themselves in the past . . . ; and it is, in Ibsen's terms, right that this dramatic honour should be reserved for Hedvig. Though she disliked its gruesome portrait of death, she loved to call the loft "the depths of the sea," and it is in this magical place that she shoots herself. We must help out the conclusion with our imaginations and see Hedvig as dying rather than hurt the Wild Duck; or, more simply, as dying for it and to find union with what it symbolises.

We have here an example of what at first seems to be a technical weakness turning out to be intrinsic to the drama's meaning. In *Ghosts* veil after veil was removed till we were brought up against the simple fact of humanity's inability in our era to establish contact with the positive powers of its existence. In *The Wild Duck* we are shown the two terms of a typical Ibsen opposition, the false surface and the revealer, as both alike ineffectual and their dramatic interaction pointless. Now, though the satiric diagnosis is brilliant, it is no more than a basis for a richer statement within which these terms are transcended rather as Ibsen willed the transcending of political parties. For over against the Hialmar-Ekdal opposition stand the greater realities, crammed into the loft, of nature and virile manhood, of expanse in time and space, of art, of mysterious life and mysterious death. The real conflict lies in the impingement of these on the semi-social drama being played out before them. The two worlds are linked by (*i*) the Wild Duck, mysterious creature of sky life, now wounded, and (*ii*) the child Hedvig, going blind, successor to Oswald and other wronged children, perfect in love, aspiring to art, and embracing death like a miniature Christ. The technical discrepancy, the drama's apparent awkwardness in trying to cram the universe into a loft, drives home the difficulty of placing the greater powers within a contemporary setting and psychology. One moral to be drawn is given on a simple level by Old Ekdal's concluding remark that the forests have avenged themselves; for Hedvig, in death, there may be some deeper understanding. (pp. 54-8)

> *G. Wilson Knight, in his* Henrik Ibsen, *Grove Press, Inc., 1962, 119 p.*

KARL S. GUTHKE   (essay date 1966)

[*The following excerpt is from Guthke's* Modern Tragicomedy: An Investigation into the Nature of the Genre, *in which he defines tragicomedy as "drama which is comic and tragic at the same time throughout the duration of the action." In tracing the history of the tragicomic drama, which he finds to be a distinctly modern dramatic trend, Guthke concurs with the assessment made by Bernard Shaw in his 1921 essay "Tolstoy: Tragedian or Comedian?" that Ibsen was "the great initiator of tragicomedy in modern European literature." Guthke calls* The Wild Duck *"the consummate realization of the tragicomic mode in drama." Rather than concentrating upon the "problem" or "thesis" of* The Wild Duck, *Guthke examines Ibsen's skillful blending of tragic and comic effects, especially in the characterization of Hjalmar Ekdal. He identifies the tragicomic ambiguity of Hjalmar by noting that though the character suffers, he suffers in an exaggerated and therefore comic way. For further discussion of the tragicomic characterization in* The Wild Duck, *see the excerpts by Hermann*

J. Weigand (1925), Edvard Beyer (1978), and the essay by James Huneker in the Additional Bibliography.]

[Though ***The Wild Duck***] has frequently been called the author's masterpiece, interpretations have to date been primarily concerned with, on the one hand, the "problem" or "thesis" of the play and with its symbolism on the other rather than with the characteristic tragicomic mode in which it is couched. But neither line of investigation has yielded satisfactory results, as the practitioners of these two varieties of the craft of interpretation readily admit. It is still hard to understand why Ibsen, while generally insisting on the value of truth and truthfulness as the real pillars of society, should suddenly proclaim in ***The Wild Duck*** that the actual basis for happiness is a lasting illusion or a "lie"—especially disturbing in view of the fact that in the play preceding ***The Wild Duck, An Enemy of the People*** . . . , as well as in the one following it, ***Rosmersholm*** . . . , Ibsen is so explicit about the diametrically opposite thesis. On the other hand, critics are far from agreement on the question of the meaning and function of the symbol of the wild duck, so much so, in fact, that one writer has stated flatly that so many different and incompatible things are brought together, but not held together, by this device that it would be a futile exercise of critical ingenuity to try to pin down the meaning of the strange bird and its purpose in the drama.

Thus, Ibsen was more right than he could have anticipated when he wrote his publisher, Frederik Hegel, on September 2, 1884 that "in any case they [the critics] will find plenty to quarrel about, plenty to interpret" [see excerpt dated 1884]. It was more than author's vanity that prompted him to say this, for an unusual amount of thought and persevering energy had gone into the making of ***The Wild Duck,*** more precisely: into the refinement of the *dramatis personae* and their dialogue. (pp. 145-46)

The aspect of ***The Wild Duck*** that must be pointed out in the present context promises to be particularly rewarding. One has a hunch that one of the reasons why this play has so consistently been called Ibsen's masterpiece by critics of the most divergent persuasions is its generic quality. Not surprisingly, then, it has almost as frequently been termed the most perfectly realized tragicomedy in Western literature. (p. 146)

Ibsen achieved [an] integration of comic and tragic effects, especially in the main character, Hjalmar Ekdal, the dilettante photographer in the garret who fancies himself a genius of invention. Hjalmar, around whom all the characters and the action are rather neatly centered, is indeed the triumph of Ibsen's workmanship in this play. He has been duped into believing that all's right with his world, and from the outset the drama is concerned with the shattering of this illusion. This kind of motif is, of course, familiar in farce, but clearly Hjalmar is not the type of *dramatis persona* that farce usually requires as the butt of its derisive banter; rather, he is, in spite of all his ridiculousness, a person of human worth and substance which makes him not a comic but a tragicomic victim of the illusion and the shattering of the illusion which is imminent in four out of the five acts of the play. The final act shows the equally tragicomic re-birth of the inadequate relation to reality that had been Hjalmar's problem all along.

In the first act, which is largely and, it must be admitted, somewhat clumsily dedicated to the exposition—that is, to the revelation of the past which is then brought to bear on the present situation of the characters—we are made to anticipate the impending disaster that is to overtake Hjalmar. (p. 149)

In clever alternation with the dominant note with which the first act dismisses us, Hjalmar's *comic* features are emphasized the moment he appears in the second act. He returns home from the Werle party and immediately starts bragging to his family about the grand role he played there, which is, of course, purely imaginary. Posing as the connoisseur he will never be and as the bold social critic that he never was, he shows a good bit more amusing vanity than one would ordinarily expect from a tragic hero. . . . Also, having previously appeared as enduring his multifarious family woes with renunciation and noblesse of mind, he now seems to be given to comical egotistical petulance. . . . Whereas Gregers called Hjalmar childlike, one wonders if childish would not have been the more suitable description of his attitude, of which he gives several samples as soon as he has returned home. . . . All this, slightly theatrical as it is, has a comical effect, of course. The same may be said about Hjalmar's next melodramatic declamation: "Our rooms may be poor and humble, Gina—but they're home all the same. And I can say from the bottom of my heart: it's good to be here." . . . "Highly sentimental"—exactly like the tune he played on the flute just a moment before, and as such highly amusing. But if we recall at this point that this marital happiness, no matter how trashily expressed, is about to be destroyed, we sense that close at hand is a much severer "catastrophe" than the business scandal discussed in the first act ever was.

And, indeed, just at this moment who should appear but Gregers, whose very presence brings this threat to mind, and as if to show just how much is at stake, Ibsen carefully uses the first minutes of the ensuing conversation to portray the intimacy of this family in its joys as well as its sorrows. This is done by discussing Hjalmar's daughter, Hedvig, who—like Mr. Werle, senior—is losing her eyesight. But no sooner has the genuine togetherness of the Ekdal family been suggested than Gregers is allowed to ask more probing questions about the circumstances leading to Gina's and Hjalmar's marriage, and darker clouds gather over the proletarian idyll. "How long is it now since you were married?" . . . There is undoubtably a sense of impending doom as Gregers pursues this line of investigation. It becomes even more pointed as Gregers jumps at the opportunity to lodge with the Ekdals while Gina distinctly resents and opposes the idea. . . . Naturally, Hjalmar would be the most severely struck by the shattering of the illusion on which his marriage seems to be built. This we can foresee even at this early point, especially since Ibsen has made it clear so far that his family life means everything to Hjalmar. (pp. 153-54)

In the third act, Hjalmar's illusions are still not destroyed. The main function of this central part of the play is, rather, to increase the audience's apprehension that the disaster is about to overtake Hjalmar. (p. 155)

It is his indirect relation to reality that makes Hjalmar comic and tragic at the same time: his love of illusion reaches ridiculous proportions . . . ; it is the inadequacy of [his] attitude that we find funny, and this inadequacy is precisely what invites the impending disaster.

As if to sharpen our awareness of the extremely bitter nature of this calamity, the dramatist parallels for several minutes Gregers' attempts to open Hjalmar's eyes and Dr. Relling's endeavors to foil his design by accentuating the happiness that prevails in the Ekdal household. . . . In a way, then, it is Hjalmar's fate that is at stake in this exchange of the two outsiders. Hjalmar himself is comparatively passive while it goes on, but what glimpses we get of him show him as the tragicomic dupe of his illusions. . . . At the end of the act the shattering of Hjalmar's illusions is close at hand: Gregers finally seems to be within grasping distance of success as he leaves with Hjalmar for a walk on which he will open his friend's eyes.

This is, indeed, what happens between the acts. When Hjalmar returns home in the fourth act he echoes Gregers' talk about the claim of the ideal; and as though their roles had been exchanged, he now begins to question Gina about the circumstances preceding their marriage some fifteen years ago. The dramatic significance of this device is that, though the audience was not made a witness of the revelatory conversation between the two friends, it is not cheated out of the experience of the shattering of Hjalmar's life-long illusion that it has been anticipating all along. And a tragicomic experience it is. Admittedly, Hjalmar's expression of shock and grief is genuine to begin with. . . . One cannot doubt the unadulterated sincerity of the distress of this husband and father who suddenly sees the foundations of his happiness crumbling under him. And yet it takes Hjalmar only a few minutes to let his characteristic theatricality creep into his lamentation, and that, of course, removes him from the confines of tragedy pure and simple to that borderland between the two major dramatic genres where twilight never fades or darkens. (pp. 157-58)

Still, the worst is yet to come. Ibsen carries the disillusionment one step further by suggesting (though not definitely asserting) that not only was Werle Gina's lover but that he is also Hedvig's father. And even at this turn of the screw the dramatist contrives to show the tragic-comic ambiguity of Hjalmar's situation. (p. 159)

[When] the tragic revelation finally does come with full force toward the end of the act, that is, when Hjalmar becomes convinced that he is not Hedvig's father, the ridiculousness of the dupe is all but obscured:

> HJALMAR: Answer me! Does Hedvig belong to me—or—? Well?
>
> GINA: *(Looks at him coldly and defiantly):* I don't know.
>
> HJALMAR: *(Trembling slightly):* You don't know?
>
> GINA: No. How should I? A creature like me—?
>
> HJALMAR: *(Quietly turning away from her):* Then I have nothing more to do in this house. . . .

It would be hard to contend that this is the theatrical poseur speaking. The simplicity of the language, reënforced by the simplicity of mimetic representation, is undoubtedly meant to show us Hjalmar's tragedy and nothing but his tragic suffering in his moment of truth. But Ibsen's aesthetic detachment is such that he manages to point to the element of comedy even in the bitterest moment of tragedy. When, in reply to Gregers' quick warning to consider what he is doing, Hjalmar exclaims: "What is there to consider? For a man like me there can be no alternative," we cannot resist the urge to smile since this statement of Hjalmar's is a clear reference to Hjalmar's newly acquired sense of the "claim of the ideal," and we already know that Hjalmar is not quite the person to live up to such high expectations. Thus, if we take the two bits of dialogue together, a shade of the comic is inevitably intermixed with the tragic even at the point of its most intense expression. The two are blended perfectly in each sentence and each word immediately after this exchange when Hjalmar leaves his house and family with an expression of tragic pathos, which has just

enough sentimental exaggeration in it to suggest that while his suffering is tragic, he suffers comically: "I don't want to," he replies to Gregers' suggestion that he should take the chance to "start afresh in a spirit of forgiveness and self-sacrifice." "Never, Never! My hat! *(Takes his hat)* My home is nothing but a mass of ruins! *(Bursts into tears)* Gregers! I have no child!" . . . More drastic exaggeration of Hjalmar's theatricality would easily have been possible, but the subtle effect would have been destroyed by such extreme means; the caricature would have obscured the essential fact that we are dealing with a potentially tragic hero. Instead, Ibsen intended the tragic-comic *clair-obscure* ["blend of light and shade"], and in employing artistic restraint in order to achieve it, he once again proved himself the master of the nuance, which he has frequently been called.

In a way, this is the climax of the drama. It is hard to imagine how the tragicomic integration of effects could be carried any further and how new aspects of Hjalmar's illusion and disillusionment could be exploited for such tragicomic effects. Realizing this, Ibsen aptly introduces the last act of the play with a retrospective discussion of Hjalmar's case. To be sure, it is primarily a clinical anatomy of the advantages and disadvantages of the "Basic Lie . . . that makes life possible," in rather general terms at that, not only of Hjalmar's illusion which has just been destroyed. But as Gregers and Dr. Relling comment on Hjalmar's particular malaise and its questionable cure, Ibsen sees to it that the comic as well as the tragic is brought out. To achieve this double effect, he uses the point of view technique. That is to say, in Werle's comments, Hjalmar appears as the tragic hero who has his "spiritual crisis" and his "spiritual upheaval"; in Dr. Relling's comments as the comic fool whose ridiculousness stands revealed at last. . . . (pp. 160-61)

This would seem to be the last word on the matter: Hjalmar's dismissal papers, as it were, authoritatively stamped by Dr. Relling's professional approval and the traditionally creditable seal of the idealist. And yet, as Hjalmar himself enters the stage, the dramatist presents us with still another surprise, which, occurring in the second half of the last act, accentuates the tragicomic nature of the main character in yet another, quite novel way.

Now the tragicomic effects are no longer derived from the delusion of the protagonist and the gradual destruction of this delusion, for when Hjalmar appears in the last act, there is no longer any doubt in his mind as to the reality that he must face. He is eager and ready to honor the "claim of the ideal," with which Gregers has imbued him. Practically, this means that he is going to leave his family. And this is what he is getting ready for when he comes on stage. But it turns out that in the very preparations for life according to the ideal, Hjalmar is unable to live up to the ideal. Weak, comfort-loving, and half-hearted, he lacks the format of the traditional tragic protagonist who would have endured this crisis "heroically," living up to the dictates of his conscience, no matter how painful. Not so Hjalmar Ekdal. Instead of leaving his house, he again succumbs to its spell. To be sure, he only puts off his departure, but the audience is sure that he will never leave, and towards the end of the play, there is no more talk of his departure at all, nor will there ever be. His family life is definitely restored. What this means with regard to the theme of the drama is obvious: as soon as he has come out of his tragicomic delusion, Hjalmar plunges himself, whether intentionally or unintentionally we shall never know, into the same *self*-delusion, and this, of course, is equally tragicomic. Formerly he did not face reality because he did not know what it was; now he does not face reality because he knows it. In either case, he is duped: by reality before, by himself now. The aesthetic effect is the same. There is no need to point out the comedy of this restoration of Hjalmar's family life, of his return to his delusion by blinding himself to the facts of his life or to the attitude that he knows he should take to it. The comedy is, in fact, obvious to a fault. Yet the tragedy is nonetheless hinted at in no uncertain terms, for while Hjalmar now willingly adjusts himself to the delusion that his family life has been for him all along, he now for the first time acutely feels the mental anguish that is implied in it: Nothing is genuine for Hjalmar any more now that the myth of his family happiness has been exploded, not even the love of his daughter for him. (pp. 161-63)

The sudden crumbling of the foundations of his life have wrought havoc with Hjalmar's emotions, and surely Ibsen expects the audience to feel that kind of sympathy with him that it usually feels in great tragedy. Still, it is only one step from the tragic to the ludicrous, and under the impact of the force of Hjalmar's emotional outburst, we nearly forget that the dramatic craftsman takes that step here as he had done elsewhere in the play: Hjalmar's suspicions about the love of his daughter Hedvig are, as we well know by now, such an absurd misinterpretation of the reality that they do not fail to strike us also as slightly funny, its painfully sad implications for Hjalmar's state of mind notwithstanding. And just as throughout the drama, it is again Hjalmar's inadequate, delusive relation to reality that makes him comic and tragic at the same time.

The Wild Duck ends with a shock. A shot is heard from the attic; Hedvig has killed herself. The motivation is not entirely satisfactory although psychologists, forgetting that they are dealing with a play and not with a case history, have been eloquent in their explanations [see excerpt by Jelliffe and Brink dated 1918]. What matters is how Hjalmar reacts to the suicide of his daughter. "Oh, God! And I drove her from me like a dog! She died for love of me: she crept into the attic, filled with grief and terror, and died for love of me! *(Sobs)* Never to be able to tell her! Never to be able to atone! *(Clenches his fists and looks upwards shouting)* You, up there—! If you *are* there—! Why have you done this thing to me!'' (pp. 163-64)

At this point, during the last minutes of the drama, tragedy pure and simple seems to prevail irrevocably. Needless to say, this would mean that the characteristic tone of the play changes radically at the last moment. But it does not, in fact. Even in the face of the most gripping agony of his characters, Ibsen remained detached, cleverly suggesting the comic overtones of the tragedy. Was not Hjalmar's lamentation a trifle too declamatory and, thus, not to be taken entirely seriously, we wonder, remembering that Hjalmar is, after all, a virtuoso of self-pitying rhetoric. And indeed, the dramatist wants us to nurture precisely this suspicion, for he has Dr. Relling cast these doubts on Hjalmar's protestation of grief, doubts which, of course, make it appear a little amusing for all the suffering they express.

> Most people are noble in the presence of death. One wonders how long this nobility will last. . . . Before this year is out, little Hedvig will be no more than a theme on which to exercise his eloquence. . . . We'll talk of this again when this year's grass has withered on her grave. You'll see: He'll be spouting about "the child snatched from her father's loving arms by an untimely death"; he'll be wallowing in a sea

of self-pity and maudlin sentimentality. You wait. You'll see. . . .

(p. 164)

The dramatic intent and function of this remark is that the audience begins to "see" even now. And as the curtain falls, the spectators retain an image of Hjalmar Ekdal that is untainted by features distracting from the characteristic trait that Ibsen had been endeavoring to draw from the moment the protagonist appeared on the stage: a tragicomic dupe deceived by his world and, even more so, by himself. (p. 165)

> *Karl S. Guthke, "The Meaning and Significance of Modern Tragicomedy," in his* Modern Tragicomedy: An Investigation into the Nature of the Genre, *Random House, 1966, pp. 95-174.**

JANEL M. MUELLER (essay date 1969)

[*In the following excerpt, Mueller identifies the duck as the central element of the play* The Wild Duck, *finding that it serves both as a metaphor and as an organic part of the dramatic action. The duck is linked metaphorically with several of the major characters, but is found to have its most significant analogy with Hedvig. For a contrasting discussion which questions the symbolic importance of the duck, see the excerpt by Brian W. Downs (1950).*]

When Ibsen mailed the manuscript of *The Wild Duck* to his publisher in September 1884, he noted in his covering letter that the method of the new play gave it a place apart in his work. He would say no more, he added; the critics would find enough to squabble about and interpret [see excerpt dated 1884]. (p. 347)

Ibsen's prediction has proved abundantly correct. Although some have found novelty in its mixture of tragedy and farce, in its involved, equivocal exposition, or in its notoriously squalid setting, most have agreed that the novelty of *The Wild Duck* is in its structure. As the title alerts us to see, the play is built around the wild duck which, though it remains unglimpsed by the audience, becomes the most instrumental element in the drama. Ibsen uses it to bring out the nature and relations of the characters and to point the way to our understanding of the course of events. In fact, his choice of title is our best clue to the meaning of his teasing remarks, for *"The Wild Duck"* all but ensures recognition of the peculiar concentric arrangement of the play.

But squabbling does not end with this generally accepted reading of Ibsen's letter. Conflicting interpretations of the play take up with the title and ultimately touch on almost every aspect of style, characterization, and action. Yet in our observations we do well to take heed of the rapturous obscurity of much comment about *The Wild Duck* and try to find a direct perspective on it as a work written for a theater audience. We may begin by assuming that the title is metaphorical; if we insist on taking it literally we forego the human focus that drama has had ever since the Greeks. P.F.D. Tennant to the contrary, the wild duck is not "the chief protagonist of the play" [see Additional Bibliography]. Moreover, we note that a metaphorical title is unusual with Ibsen: *"A Doll's House"* and *"Pillars of Society"* (also, possibly, *"Ghosts"*) are the only others of the kind. Most important, however, is the fact that *The Wild Duck* is the one play where Ibsen undertakes to express his titular metaphor in the concrete terms of the physical theater. That is to say, in using an actual wild duck as one term of a metaphor (with several characters serving in turn as the other), Ibsen is dramatizing a figure of speech. It is fascinating to observe the workings of the process which in itself constitutes the main artistic achievement of the play.

Critics often imply that the possible meanings of *The Wild Duck* are infinite. As a truism about masterpieces, the implication need not concern us greatly. However, it is misleading as a special statement about the play. If the wild duck serves no other function, its stage presence and its definite role in the development of plot and theme have the effect not merely of generating but also of directing and delimiting the suprarealistic content. Indeed, Ibsen takes pains (in his dialogue, action, and lighting and set directions) to fix the attention of his characters and his audience alike upon the object, the phenomenon, the theatrical image. In *The Wild Duck* he deals pre-eminently with visual rather than envisionable implications, his realm being the stage and not the study. We ought equally to keep a stage perspective on the wild duck and inquire not what it may conceivably represent but what in dramatic terms it does.

On both sides of the proscenium, interest is aroused initially by the duck's strange divided nature—most wild when free, most tame when domesticated, as Darwin had observed. Perhaps Ibsen knew of the observation from his friend Jens Peter Jacobsen, the Danish translator of Darwin. At any rate, true to the spirit of realistic drama, the enigma of the duck is based upon scientific truth. In the play much is made of the contrast between the duck's former existence in the wild and its present habitat: a basket of straw and a bucket of water in the Ekdal's attic. Also, in introducing the duck in Act II Ibsen appears to presuppose a general familiarity (due to ''The Sea-bird,'' a much admired lyric by his countryman and contemporary, Welhaven) with the wild duck's instinct to elude capture after being shot by diving down and biting itself fast to die in the weeds at the sea bottom. The dialogue at this point in the play is more explicit about the cleverness of Old Werle's dog in retrieving the duck and the curiosity of its survival in captivity.

Through the subsequent action Ibsen establishes a specific association between the duck and the three characters—Old Ekdal, Hjalmar, and Hedvig—who care for it and frequent the attic. Other characters are as specifically dissociated from the duck: Gina by her lack of imagination (she complains of cold when the attic doors are open), Gregers by his disdain, Dr. Relling by his psychological insight. Correspondingly, they do not go into the attic. Thus, even from the outset when the wild duck seems to betoken no more than an exotic pastime for an all too ordinary family, the force of the central metaphor is controlled by its dramatic context.

Our first impression of the duck is made too simple, however, when Hjalmar's friend Gregers Werle is persuaded to look into the attic and is told the duck's story, which he then proposes to treat as a parable. Gregers' devotion to ''the claim of the ideal'' has prompted an impatience with face values and a consequent search for deeper meanings. Despite his exalted cast of mind, he is not without self-conceit; he identifies personally with the duck at first. Uninspired by this, he dallies with the notion (adumbrated by his father in Act I) that the duck represents Old Ekdal. That in turn he rejects as he rejects his father and fastens on a far more congenial interpretation. His idolized Hjalmar is the duck, ensnared in deceit and illusions; Gregers himself will be the ''really clever dog.'' Since announcing an idealistic but undefined ''mission in life'' at the end of Act I, he had been rabid for action and a mental picture to clarify his nebulous purposes. Curiously, his interpretation recommends itself at the time to no one else, not even the egotistical Hjalmar. As the action proceeds Ibsen reveals the

interpretation in a stronger negative light. The problem is that, as always, Gregers has misjudged. Whatever value there might have been in a figurative construction, it has been wrongly applied. Through the agency of Gina the rescue has already taken place. Ibsen indicates as much in his visual parallel: Hjalmar, like the duck in the attic, is growing fat.

How Hjalmar arrives at his abstract view of the wild duck is also a trenchant means of character revelation. As Dr. Relling has seen (with vision as unsentimental as that of his prototype, Dr. Borg, in Strindberg's *The Red Room*), Hjalmar is incapable of original thinking, but he can respond to figures of speech and figments of the imagination of others. Upon hearing Gregers' idea he decides, with resolute selflessness, to view his father as the wild duck. The prospect of a rescue—he would be the dog—fits beautifully with Hjalmar's fantasies about his great invention. Here again Ibsen manages matters so as to expose the inaptness of Hjalmar's analogy. The wild duck can be kept captive only if she is never allowed to see the sea and the sky again; Old Ekdal is astonished that Gregers expects him to consider seriously the offer to return him to Højdal. Moreover, his constant behavior shows that Old Ekdal is not now (has he ever been?) a spirited and proud creature. He is absolutely snug in his little world. The attic is only its heartland, for when he is not actually there he nests in overpaid copywork and stays afloat on gift bottles of brandy in his room.

In making the wild duck organic to the play Ibsen does not restrict himself to reflecting discredit upon the analogies advanced by his two most obtuse characters. He takes a much more active hand in the case of Hedvig, the third character linked through the action with the wild duck. We find yet another analogy beginning to emerge, based on resemblances between Hedvig and the duck. We also infer that it must be Ibsen's own, since it is not given to any character to point out. As this analogy takes shape subtly but systematically, Ibsen places it in distinct opposition to the tone and implication of the other two. How is this done? Drawing plausibility and intelligibility from the deep split in the nature of the actual bird, Ibsen in effect splits his central metaphor in two. More precisely, he accommodates his dramatic image to the projection of not merely different ideas but of completely disparate ones. Although this is a poetic innovation, Ibsen's objectives are those of a playwright. The resemblance between Hedvig and the wild duck must be unique in order to set the child off from the adult world about her. Her isolation prepares for the sudden final action, so seemingly senseless, yet so full of significance.

In pursuing his objectives Ibsen draws the analogy between the wild duck and Hedvig with the most affecting means he has: the child's own voice. In vivid contrast to the contrived (and invalid) parallels drawn by Gregers and Hjalmar, Hedvig is unaware of the truths she is speaking of herself when she explains the distinctiveness of the wild duck: it is a real, live, natural thing; it is all alone; and nobody knows it or where it is from. Other unconscious truths are Hjalmar's observations, made to Gregers on separate occasions, that Hedvig and the duck are perfectly healthy save for a single defect each. Led by Ibsen in this line of thinking, we may perhaps notice that the child and her pet are both donations to the Ekdal household from Old Werle and that the blindness and the drooping wing alike are unfortunate consequences of his sport. . . . What is made explicit, however, as the play nears its climax is Hedvig's strong instinctive identification with the duck. At the beginning of Act IV she reacts to her father's threats against it as if he had threatened her; at the end of the act she is still upset and unreceptive to Gregers' urging that she have her grandfather kill the duck. The urging continues of course through Act V, and when the shot finally rings out in the attic Hedvig has, quite literally, put herself in the wild duck's place.

To sharpen the opposition between the analogy involving Hedvig and those involving Old Ekdal and Hjalmar, Ibsen addresses himself to our eyes and ears. Through particulars in dialogue, setting, and action he evokes, essentially, two attics—the men's and the child's—in order to illustrate the crucial distinction in the applications of his dramatized metaphor. More simply, in Act III, the central section of the play, Ibsen first shows us Old Ekdal and Hjalmar in their attic, one kind of place, and then has Hedvig describe at length to Gregers her attic, another kind of place altogether. It is strange that the precision and coherence of these scenes often go unremarked, for they are the finest and most extended demonstration of the allusive technique of *The Wild Duck*. (pp. 347-51)

For the two men, Old Ekdal and Hjalmar, who have been in the outside world and retreated from it, the attic is one kind of substitute—a replacement. Ibsen indicates just how good a replacement it is by a brilliant yet controlled use of detail: the men's attic contains withered Christmas trees and caged rabbits, chickens, and pigeons. Old Ekdal and Hjalmar are drawn to it as an escape which itself draws about them (Ibsen shows us both peering through the fishnet of the curtain, caught in their own fantasies). And, like all means of escape, this one is always on the verge of being an inadequate shelter from reality. There is, as the opening of Act III demonstrates, endless carpentry and maintenance work to do.

For Hedvig, though, who has had virtually no outside experience (she now no longer even goes to school), the attic is an altogether different kind of substitute—a makeshift. The sense of another place is conveyed through her separate inventory of objects: a large desk full of compartments and drawers, a clock with mechanical figures that no longer works, a variety of old volumes. The one element in common is the wild duck. Hedvig has worlds to explore among the foreign books, furniture, and other keepsakes of the old sea captain who had formerly lived in the flat. In her attic she does not escape experience; rather, she acquires it in the only way she can. . . . All her special feelings are summed up in a carefully chosen poetic phrase. In the attic, she says, she is "in the depths of the sea" (*på havsens bund*), not, prosaically, "at the sea bottom (*på havets bund, havbunden*). Character revelation is given the guise of "well-made" coincidence when Gregers happens to use Hedvig's poetic phrase; his thought is chronically grandiose. But Ibsen follows up by showing up the hellishness of good intentions as Gregers first turns Hedvig's phrase into evidence for his view of Hjalmar as the wild duck and then exploits the trust that Hedvig places in him.

Why, we ask, are Hedvig's times in the attic exalting rather than degrading? The answer lies in the mind of the child, whose image the attic becomes. By nature Hedvig's thinking exhibits a perfect if precarious grasp of the distinction between fact and fantasy. After all, she says, "it's just an old attic, you know." "But is it?" asks Gregers, spreading a cloud where light had been. (pp. 351-53)

Above all, however, Ibsen reveals the simplicity of the child's nature through her singleness of vision. Like her mother, the "uncultivated" Gina, Hedvig is incapable of the double perspective—saying one thing but meaning another—that is the basis of the generalities and innuendoes used constantly by the other adults. As the play's atmosphere darkens in Acts IV and V, this double perspective becomes associated with the duplicity that Ibsen at this period—the period of *Ghosts, An Enemy of the People,* and *Rosmersholm*—saw everywhere in society. Moreover, to Gregers' discredit, in *The Wild Duck* this double perspective is bound up with the error and futility of an uncompromising philosophical dualism. By degrees the language, the morals, and the metaphysics confuse Hedvig—at last, fatally.

Her death, then, is brought about by society's encroachment on the free exercise and expression of her instinctive nature. Except for Dr. Relling who issues a pointed warning in Act IV, the adults are too involved with their concerns to recognize Hedvig's vulnerability and danger. Never able to connect Gregers' promptings to "the brave, sacrificial spirit" with her love for her father and her pet, she overhears a last taunt of Hjalmar's in another "well-made" but ill-fated coincidence. Thereupon she chooses to die with the absoluteness of her love, her spontaneity, and her innocence—all for which the wild duck in association with her had stood—still intact. (p. 353)

Hjalmar claims to suspect Hedvig of hypocrisy, the sin of coming of age in Ibsen. As the duck feeling the buckshot in its breast dove down and bit itself fast to die, the child, cut to the heart by her father's rejection, dies "in the depths of the sea." Hjalmar's scenemaking was really only a show to impress Gregers and an outlet for his resentment at his friend's intrusion. But, like the duck, Hedvig did not and could not realize that she was wounded in sport; such games childhood does not know. Thus, unattended by any Aristotelian recognition, her tragedy is fortuitous—accidental in the purest sense of the word.

Yet, as Hedvig's death is the final event, it is also the ultimate issue of *The Wild Duck*. And Ibsen's peculiar structure—his placing of the duck at the center of the action and characters—produces in the finished play the tragicomedy he wanted. As originally conceived without the dramatic metaphor, Act I does not differ much in humorous effect from its final form. But the wild duck is indispensable to the further development of the plot. It integrates Hedvig's death with the two elements of comic interest: the ludicrous insensibility of Old Ekdal (and, to a lesser extent, Hjalmar) and the futile showdown between Gregers and Dr. Relling. (It is interesting to find that Ibsen criticized the first Copenhagen production for having overdone the comedy, making the tragedy unintelligible. The balance, like that in Hedvig's thinking, is a delicate one.)

To be sure, a no less important step toward unity in *The Wild Duck* was Ibsen's decision to link the economic theme with the ethical, as exemplified in Dr. Relling's observation that Gregers will never be able to collect on his "claim of the ideal" (*den ideale fordring*) from persons of modest means. They "simply cannot pay." (p. 354)

At issue between Gregers and Dr. Relling is the nature of Hjalmar, himself a lesser Peer Gynt. By analogy with the wild duck Gregers views Hjalmar as a victim of society—a noble creature entangled in deceit and illusions. Together the analogy and the character estimate prove false, but the deceit and illusions are actual enough. Ibsen shows us that the error lies in Gregers' belief that his friend is better off with the truth. Although the scientific Relling would not resort to argument from analogy, we have seen that Ibsen puts one onstage anyway, ready to hand: Hjalmar, like the duck, thrives under notions that they are unwilling to follow where the playwright's vision has led. The critical confusion generated by Henrik Ibsen's *The Wild Duck* since it was first published in 1884 suggests that sometimes both elements are involved. (p. 419)

Highly realistic in its rendering of "ordinary" people in an "ordinary" world of social events and institutions, of domestic occupations and preoccupations, it records the details of existence with a photographic literalness. *The Wild Duck* is also naturalistic in its emphasis on the importance of heredity and environment as dominant forces in shaping men's destinies and in its emphasis on the mean and trivial facts of daily life. But above all, it is an intensely poetic, highly "romantic" play dominated by the symbolism of the wild bird and the "heavenly" attic, where it dwells with the poor and the meek and the "wounded" in the blessedness of love.

Although the action itself is relatively unified and simple, following the pattern of homecoming and holocaust set in *Ghosts* and other plays, the complexity of the antecedent action, revealed with tantalizing skill during the five acts, is also partly responsible for the varied responses to the play. (pp. 419-20)

The characters were so "completely new," Ibsen's characterizations of heroic and villainous figures were so compassionate, and his refusal to deny tragic stature to common men and women was so remarkably daring that it is small wonder that critics were and have continued to be in disagreement about the principal participants in the struggle and their significance.

Unwilling to risk approaching that "limit of knowledge" that Ibsen dared in creating his people, following their predilections, insisting that theme comes before character rather than follows from it, critics have hurled labels with wildest abandon. Perhaps the best indication of how confused matters are may be gained from the summing up by Professor Theodore Jorgenson in his recent study [see Additional Bibliography]. He says that if the need of illusions is taken as the main theme, the leading tragic character is Hjalmar Ekdal; if it is absolute idealism, Gregers Werle; if it is the belief that the finest are destroyed by the prophets of absolute idealism and the illusion-ridden masses, it is Hedvig. "Thus *The Wild Duck* may be regarded as three plays in one." . . . In addition to all those "major" possibilities for the heroic role, Dr. Relling has also been offered as candidate.

Relling's candidacy as protagonist, I think, is easiest to dismiss, for the reasons that Professor Reinert and others have pointed out: his structurally unprepared late arrival; his place among the chorus as commentator; his flawed character—as Mrs. Sorby says, he has "frittered away all that was good in him"; his questionable remedies for his patients' ills. To be sure, he has helped to protect the ego of Molvik by diagnosing him as a "demonic personality" rather than an alcoholic and that of Hjalmar by leading him to believe that his laziness is but the incubation period of a great inventor, but his nostrums are those of a quacksalver rather than a doctor.

Nor is it possible to accept seriously the notion that Hedvig is the protagonist. The delicate, shy, loving little girl is essentially where Relling insists that she must be: "outside of all this." We weep over her willingness to turn the pistol against herself rather than the wild duck; we are not participants in the anguished struggle.

Although Gregers Werle has been suggested as the leading tragic character as well as "a kind of bitter self-parody by Ibsen of his own reforming fervour" [by F. L. Lucas in his

Caricature of Ibsen. Mary Evans Picture Library.

coddling. But the play's catastrophe renders all argument absurd; the only victory, Relling's, is a theoretical one. For, as the adults mismanage and misconstrue, circumstances claim a victim, a noble creature, a hurt, baffled child who would rather be destroyed than destroy. And we are made to sense far more strongly than Hedvig that she could not have remained as she was and continued to live. How inevitable, we say, how right in a way her tragedy seems! Then we see in what company our reaction has placed us. Our easy acceptance, with Hjalmar, of Hedvig's death is perhaps the most damning and enduring exposure of society ever made by Ibsen. (pp. 354-55)

> Janel M. Mueller, "Ibsen's 'Wild Duck'," in Modern Drama, *Vol. XI, No. 4, February, 1969, pp. 347-55.*

RUTH HARMER (essay date 1970)

[*In the following excerpt, Harmer examines each of the main characters in* The Wild Duck *in order to establish one of them as the protagonist; that is, the character whose values and viewpoint were intended by Ibsen to convey the meaning of his drama. Harmer argues that the actual protagonist of the play is Gina.*]

When a play is widely acclaimed as a masterpiece by critics who disagree radically about its nature and meaning, it may be that the work possesses such richness of content, such poetic density, that critics are unable to comprehend its totality; it may be that it contains an element so alien to conventional

The Drama of Ibsen and Strindberg], he is neither a heroic nor a farcical character. Indeed, two of the characters he calls to mind are Iago in his wanton destruction of another man's happiness and (here the resemblance is closer, I think) Roger Chillingworth in the systematic manner in which he violates the sanctity of a human heart.

Gregers makes himself believe that his intentions are good, that all he desires is to free his friend from false illusions so that he can rebuild his life and marriage on the solid foundations of truth and justice. But Ibsen calls attention to what he is up to through the pointed comments of Relling. When Gregers talks about the "marsh vapors" in the house, Relling retorts sharply: "Excuse me—may it not be you yourself that have brought the taint from those mines up here?" When Gregers speaks about ideals, Relling brings him up coldly: "While I think of it, Mr. Werle, junior—don't use that foreign word: ideals. We have the excellent native word: lies." (pp. 423-24)

His love for his joyless mother has poisoned his heart and mind. Gregers acts not from love, but from hatred. His one moment of insight comes when he tells his father that: "If I am to go on living, I must try to find some cure for my sick conscience." . . . His father is correct when he replies that it will never be sound. Gregers is powerless to destroy his father, but he is successful in his assault on the Ekdals. And in his spiritual pride, he indicates his readiness to go right on playing God. Unchastened by the ruin of his friend's marriage, by the suicide of the child, he tells Relling grandly as the curtain falls that he is *glad* his destiny is what it is: "to be the thirteenth at the table" . . .—that is, to play Christ. (p. 425)

Far more likely a candidate for the role, as August Lindberg [the director of the first production of *The Wild Duck*] seems to have recognized quickly, is Hjalmar—a character shaped by Ibsen with exquisite skill. Hjalmar is a catalog of frailties. He is greedy, consuming vast quantities of butter and beer so that Gina and Hedvig have to starve themselves in order that the food bills may be paid; he is lazy, napping all afternoon, playing in the attic, dreaming about the inventions that will happen without his exertions; he is proud of his appearance, his curly locks, his still young figure; he is thoughtless, forgetting to bring home from the Werle party the gift he had promised Hedvig (he returns with a menu instead!). Hjalmar is a coward, denying his father at the party because Old Ekdal is not socially acceptable, rejecting Hedvig because of conventions; he is pretentious, posing as an authority to his simple family and trying to maintain his reputation for sophistication by discouraging Hedvig from reading. He is full of self pity and sentimentality, and he is almost utterly shallow. Briefly ennobled by the death of Hedvig, his sorrow, we feel with Dr. Relling, will quickly pass, and "before a year is over, little Hedvig will be nothing to him but a pretty theme for declamation."

But he is not totally to blame. "Ekdal's misfortune," as Dr. Relling points out, "is that in his own circle he has always been looked upon as a shining light." . . . Brought up by two "high-flown, hysterical maiden aunts" and an overly fond father:

> When our dear, sweet Hjalmar went to college, he at once passed for the great light of the future amongst his comrades too. He was handsome, the rascal—red and white—a shop-girl's dream of manly beauty; and with his superficially emotional temperament, and his sympathetic

voice, and his talent for declaiming other people's verses and other people's thoughts. . . .

(pp. 425-26)

Moreover, his failings are human failings, and they are free from malice. He is gentle; he is not suspicious—it would never have occurred to him to think ill of Old Werle or Gina or anyone else. Within the framework of his limited capacity, he is affectionate—genuinely fond of his father, his child, his wife. And his romantic dreams are directed to doing something for Hedvig, making it possible for his father to go publicly in uniform. He is the victim rather than the protagonist, the soul for possession of which Gregers is struggling against . . .

Gina. For here is the truly heroic figure in *The Wild Duck*. Striving, suffering, enduring, she has been casually dismissed by critics as simple or even "weak." Admittedly, she appears an unlikely figure to assume the tragic mantle, "shuffling quietly in and out in her felt slippers, with that see-saw walk of hers." . . . But once she had been beautiful. Old Werle's unremitting pursuit of her indicates that she had been lovely to look at; Hedvig reflects her. (p. 426)

What was once an external has become an inner glow. With nothing to begin with—no education, as her speech larded with malapropisms points out; with no one to protect her (she had fled the Werle house only to be forced into a sexual relationship with Old Werle by her mother); with only a weak and dissolute young fop for a husband—her love for Hjalmar had enabled her to create a world of happiness and contentment. As hardworking as Hjalmar is lazy, she cleans and cooks for Relling and Molvik as well as her husband, Hedvig, and Hjalmar's father. She drudges as if she were receiving a favor instead of conferring one. She manages the photography business so that Hjalmar may occupy himself peacefully with his no-invention, telling clients to come during the afternoon so that they will not interfere with his nap. She is gentle with Old Ekdal, allowing him to make her house into the wild duck's domain, not reproaching him for closeting himself with the bottle that Werle's servant had given him, gently humoring the poor old man. She endures the presence of Molvik and Relling with grace, is tender with Hedvig, and transforms Hjalmar from a young man with "bad ways" into "a moral of a husband." . . . She asks nothing for herself, although she is not wantless—dreaming of the time when she and Hedvig would "be able to let ourselves go a bit, in the way of both food and clothes." . . . Her reactions are not lethargic, but marvelously controlled, as we know from the way she waits with barely concealed anguish for the blow to fall when Hjalmar returns from his disastrous walk with Gregers:

> HJALMAR. It seems to me your voice is trembling.
>
> GINA. (*putting the lamp-shade on*). Is it?
>
> HJALMAR. And your hands are shaking, are they not? . . .

Critics are not to be blamed unduly for failing to recognize Gina's stature. Such love is not easy to comprehend. When Hjalmar rushes out of the house leaving havoc behind, her one concern is to get the child quieted; her silence about the affair with Werle was imposed by love for Hjalmar: "I'd come to care for you so much." . . . Neither is the dignity that she exhibits easy to comprehend. After Gregers has put her as well as Hjalmar through one of the bitterest moments of both their lives, she says simply: "God forgive you, Mr. Werle." . . .

She allows herself one anguished cry when Relling announces that Hedvig is dead: "Oh, my child, my child." Then she picks up again her burden as guardian of what is left of the devastated house. Directing Hjalmar to help her carry the child's body to her own room, "it mustn't lie here for a show," she comforts him: "We must help each other to bear it. For now at least she belongs to both of us." (pp. 426-27)

If Gina is accepted as the protagonist, problems of theme are resolved, and the play does not—as Professor Reinert has charged—"insist on its own meaninglessness." Two main forces are in conflict: Gregers, with his "claim of the ideal," his death-truth; Gina, with her loving kindness, her life-truth. Also involved is the compromise, equivocating force: Dr. Relling, with his escape and illusion, his life-lie. The play is designed to show us that only hers is worth struggling for, only that saves life as well as art from meaninglessness. (p. 427)

Ruth Harmer, "Character, Conflict, and Meaning in 'The Wild Duck'," in Modern Drama, *Vol. XII, No. 4, February, 1970, pp. 419-27.*

JACOB H. ADLER (essay date 1970-71)

[*In the essay from which the following excerpt is taken, Adler examines the interrelationships between William Shakespeare's* Hamlet, *Anton Chekhov's* The Sea Gull, *and* The Wild Duck. *Adler theorizes that Ibsen used* Hamlet *as a source for* The Wild Duck *and that Chekhov drew upon both earlier plays in writing* The Sea Gull. *In the following excerpt, Adler traces themes and plot elements from* Hamlet *that recur in Ibsen's play. He also notes characteristics of central figures from* Hamlet *that also appear in the dramatis personae of* The Wild Duck. *Similar events and reactions to events are also found to take place in both dramas. Sidney Mendel has also drawn comparisons between the characters Hamlet and Gregers Werle, while Ibsen biographer Halvdan Koht also traces the general influence of Shakespeare upon the works of Ibsen (see Additional Bibliography).*]

Like *Hamlet* . . . *The Wild Duck* is a play about an idealist who sees rottenness almost everywhere he looks, and who unintentionally destroys when he tries to cure. Both Hamlet and Gregers Werle are appalled at what they view as a highly immoral marriage. Gregers hates his father, as Hamlet hated his stepfather. Each had what may have been an unhealthy love for his mother; each feels that his mother's husband has been her ruination. Gregers is incapable of loving any woman but his mother. While it is certainly open to question, Hamlet may conceivably have that problem too. Hamlet—correctly—suspects his stepfather of having murdered his brother and taken over the kingdom, steeped in guilt. Gregers—correctly—suspects his father of having ruined his partner and taken over the business, steeped in guilt. [The critic adds in a footnote that "This is the point of view of most critics," and quotes G. Wilson Knight: "'Werle is a rich industrialist who formerly involved Hialmar's father in some illegal felling of timber on State land, with the result that old Ekdal went to prison while Werle himself escaped'" (see excerpt dated 1962). "On the other hand, Brian Downs . . . believes that Werle's character is capable of a more favorable interpretation than it has usually been afforded, and that he may, in fact, be innocent." Gregers' father is a man of capability, force, self-assurance, and social acumen, another false pillar of society, just as Claudius was: in both cases, a realist whose adversary is an idealist. Like Claudius, too, old Werle is a sensualist, a man who remarries, as Claudius married, rather late in life (and, like Claudius, wants the son's approval of the marriage), and a man who in

the course of the play must shift from viewing his son as an embarrassment to viewing him as a positive enemy. And like Claudius, Werle is not the figure of evil incarnate that his son considers him to be.

Hamlet is famous for his suit of solemn black, and for his thoughts of suicide. Gregers is a constant picture of gloom, and hints at suicide more than once. Hamlet flirts with insanity, and there are hints that Gregers is not in his right mind. Certainly his father and Relling consider him mentally sick; and he himself gives evidence of agreeing with them. Hamlet attempts to solve the situation with a trick, the play within the play; Gregers too attempts to solve the situation with a trick, the sacrifice of the wild duck. For each, indeed, the final solution to the problem as he sees it, is to kill something: to rescue by destroying.

But there is another Hamlet-figure in *The Wild Duck*. Hialmar Ekdal, like Gregers, is an idealist, though of a much more primitive sort. In fact, if Gregers may be viewed as a denigration of the idealistic side of Hamlet, Hialmar may be viewed as a burlesque of the Hamlet who is student and poet. Like Hamlet, Hialmar has a gift of words, rhetoric, philosophy; a gift in this case not of genuine coin, but of false sentiment and hackneyed pseudo-philosophical notions. (Of course, since Hamlet can be accused of garrulousness, and has been accused of puerile philosophy, the irony works both ways.) Like Hamlet, Hialmar has lost his birthright (perhaps by fraud) as the son of a prosperous father. As Hamlet had great difficulty taking up his responsibility, so Hialmar can scarcely take up his at all—though each feels that he must do so for the sake of his father. Each young man, as a result of disaster to his father, considered suicide. (And the sentimental, falsely rhetorical, ludicrous suicide speeches of Hialmar to Gregers easily bring to mind the contrast of Hamlet's great soliloquy.) Like Hamlet, Hialmar repudiates an innocent girl who loves him, in the cruelest language; as in *Hamlet*, the end result of his behavior is her death—and in each case the death may or may not be suicide. (pp. 233-34)

Like Hamlet, Hialmar has revealed to him a shocking secret about his family; like Hamlet, Hialmar is highly self-conscious over what he should do as a result of the revelation; and each hesitates to do what he considers right—in Hamlet's case, kill the king; in Hialmar's, leave his wife. But the parallels about the secret are again degrading parallels. The secret in *Hamlet* is of vital importance, and we are surely intended to take its revelation as beneficial. The secret in *The Wild Duck* is in the context of the play trivial, and its revelation by any sensible standard useless and needlessly dangerous. But the two secrets also resemble each other. One aspect of what the ghost reveals to Hamlet is that Hamlet's mother has married a man whom the revealer regards as a monster, and that she is therefore sexually degraded. What is revealed to Hialmar is that his wife (who is for him largely a mother-figure) has had a sexual liaison with a man whom the revealer regards as a monster, and that she is therefore sexually degraded. Hamlet in one of the most dramatic and vivid scenes in the play tries to show Gertrude her guilt. Hialmar likewise in a highly dramatic scene tries to show Gina her guilt. But once more the situation in *The Wild Duck* is at a lower level. Hamlet's emotion was genuine horror; Hialmar's is righteous, superficial, and hackneyed indignation. Gertrude is brought to feel horror too. Gina feels no guilt at all, and points out quite rightly that Hialmar's accusation when he himself feels no guilt for similar conduct is an example of the double standard. On the other hand, both Gertrude and

Gina function almost exclusively as wife and mother and are clearly Philistines in the Shavian sense; so that the Gertrude-Claudius-Hamlet triangle parallels the Gina-Werle-Hialmar (or Gregers) triangle, in that both are triangles of Philistine-realist-idealist. And much is made of the fact that each woman married startlingly soon after separation from her previous sexual partner.

Hamlet had a friend, Horatio, whose deep admiration of Hamlet is rational and just. Hialmar has a friend, Gregers, whose deep admiration of him is wrong-headed, blind, and a psychological crutch for his own unstable personality. Thus Gregers has a degraded-Horatio aspect. But Gregers and Hedvig are probably brother and sister, and Hedvig dies, her death caused in part (for Gregers has his share of blame) by the Hamlet-manqué, Hialmar, whom Gregers nevertheless continues to admire; and hence Gregers has a degraded-Laertes aspect. Like Laertes to Ophelia, Gregers gives Hedvig well-meant but inadequate advice. As Laertes is more a destroyer by nature than Hamlet, so is Gregers more so than Hialmar; and Laertes destroys Hamlet, as Gregers comes close to destroying Hialmar.

Given so many parallels, it is not too far-fetched to suppose that the attic world of livestock and dead evergreens given such importance by Ibsen may also owe something to *Hamlet*. *Hamlet* has an element of the supernatural which Ibsen could not parallel in a play primarily realistic in its premises. But the atmosphere of mystery attached to the attic throughout the play brings him about as close as he can get. The ghost in *Hamlet* comes from another world. Especially in the conversations on the subject between Gregers and Hedvig—conversations whose purpose is otherwise unclear—the attic is made to seem another world too. Similarly, old Ekdal's talk about the woods' avenging themselves suggests an element of supernatural mystery, as it also suggests the theme of revenge so prominent in *Hamlet*. (And Gregers' desire to "help" Hialmar has an element of revenge—against his father—in it also.)

Finally, the opening sections of the two plays represent an elaboration of parallels in both technique and detail. We first see Hamlet in the royal court. We first see Hialmar in the Werle mansion, which in its luxury and secret degradation bears a strong resemblance to the royal court, having in it even courtiers of a sort [The critic adds in a footnote that A. E. Zucker very briefly points out that the courtiers in *The Wild Duck* resemble those in *Hamlet* (see Additional Bibliography)] (of a trivial sort, the Chamberlains, older and more self-assured but no wiser than Rosencrantz and Guildenstern). Hamlet is most uncomfortable in a court where his place has been usurped; Hialmar is equally uncomfortable in a mansion where his father was once an equal, and where now, because of his father, he, Hialmar, suffers the embarrassment of inferiority. (And the other Hamlet-figure, Gregers, feels for other reasons equally uncomfortable and unnatural in his father's house.) Then in *Hamlet,* the ghost of Hamlet's father walks, and Hamlet is left uncertain whether to accept or repudiate it. Similarly, Hialmar's father walks through the Werle study where the guests are assembled, and he is like a ghost out of the past, and Hialmar, uncertain what to do, rejects him. Old Ekdal is as out of place in that world as the ghost of Hamlet Senior is in this; and like Hamlet Senior he has undergone punishment for his sins. Thus as Gregers has aspects of Hamlet, Horatio, Laertes, and (because he reveals the fatal secret) the ghost, so old Ekdal has aspects of Polonius and the ghost. If this seems over-complex, it may be remembered that the wild duck itself is used in every bit as complex a manner, having aspects which

connect it, at a minimum, with Hialmar, his father, Hedvig, and Gina (because, like Gina, it has "been through those hands"). (pp. 234-36)

Ibsen displays in *The Wild Duck* a degraded Hamletesque world; a world where rottenness cannot be cleansed, a world where to live almost always requires illusion, a world of Hamlet-figures but no Hamlets. (p. 236)

The Wild Duck is a play deeply concerned with the difference between illusion and reality, with the possibility that illusion can be desirable and the truth a snare, and with, therefore, the desirability of Leaving Well Enough Alone. But is not this a defensible criticism of *Hamlet*—or at any rate of Hamlet? How much is really rotten in the state of Denmark, and how much is Hamlet's psychological sickness, that common psychological sickness which sees evil everywhere? It would have been better for Gregers to stay away and leave the Ekdal marriage alone. Would it have been better if the ghost had stayed away from Hamlet? Hialmar should have ignored Gregers. Should Hamlet have ignored the ghost? (It is interesting, too, that Gregers takes Hialmar for a walk to tell him the truth, as the ghost takes Hamlet. And in each case the man's friends try to keep him from going.)

The Wild Duck says that one should not attempt to eradicate evil if the result will be a worse evil. Ibsen would certainly have agreed that evil is to be destroyed at the cost of a *lesser* evil; for example, lives should be saved (*An Enemy of the People*) at a sacrifice of money, prosperity, comfort, security. But should a king like Claudius, in many ways capable and effective (more so, very likely, than Hamlet would have been), be killed at a cost of several innocent, and several less guilty, lives, with the country saved from chaos only by the timely and coincident arrival of a sound candidate for king? In terms of a casual symbol in *The Wild Duck,* should one clean a stove if one irretrievably stains the whole room in the process? It is at least an open question, and if the answer in *The Wild Duck* is No (as it is), then Ibsen may have had in mind that a possible answer in *Hamlet* is No also.... At any rate, intentional or not, *The Wild Duck* exposes a flaw in Hamlet's idealism, and thus shows that the attack against false idealism has not merely "modern" but permanent validity.

Or it may be, of course, that the answer in *Hamlet* is still Yes, even though it is No in the Ekdal studio. It was Yes, as Ibsen doubtless knew and as it is interesting to remember, as far back as that great reformer-idealist the Antigone of Sophocles; and Ibsen certainly intends in his plays to differentiate between the true and the false idealist. Hence, once again, if Ibsen accepts *Hamlet*, then his play shows that the modern world differs from the *Hamlet*-world in lacking that nobler world's greater potential and justification for idealism.

More likely however, in view of the complexity of the subject and of Ibsen's own perceptive ambivalence toward it, the play shows both. Ibsen, that is, may be displaying a tentative attitude toward *Hamlet*. Reformers may be right (Dr. Stockmann) or wrong (Gregers). Which category Hamlet falls into—Ibsen may be saying—is open to question. *The Wild Duck* has still such relevance that it is tempting, as it is certainly proper, to believe that it is thus modern in its ambiguity. (pp. 237-38)

Jacob H. Adler, "Two 'Hamlet' Plays: 'The Wild Duck' and 'The Sea Gull'," in Journal of Modern Literature, *Vol. 1, No. 2, 1970-71, pp. 226-48.*

CHARLES A. HALLETT (essay date 1975)

[In the following excerpt Hallett provides a unique interpretation of The Wild Duck, *presenting Gregers Werle as the tragic hero of the play and denying that any character in* The Wild Duck *represents the voice of reason or the authorial point of view.]*

Ibsen is regarded as the first playwright to have made relativism a dramatic theme, and since Relling is invariably viewed as a spokesman for relativism, this character has been catapulted by critics into the role of *raisonneur*. A brief summary of what we know of him quickly disproves his right to either of these positions. The man is by profession a doctor. Years ago he had had a flourishing practice near Werle's Höidal factory, and, apparently, had once been in love with Mrs. Sörby. She rejected him, and, according to her, Relling has since "wasted all that was best in him." . . . When we meet him, he is sharing a flat in a shabby tenement with a former student of theology, who has also lost his calling. Both are devoting a major portion of their energies to discovering the benign illusions locked in alcohol. Relling's pose is to be exactly what scholars have accepted him as, the compassionate observer of humanity, the doctor of the spirit, the man who mixes universal kindness with world-weary cynicism.

Far from being the disinterested passionless observer of things as they are, Relling instead turns out to be another wild duck, another wounded spirit who has sought refuge from reality in illusion. When he asserts that "if you take away make-believe from the average man, you take away his happiness as well" . . . , he is making a passionate defense of what he wants to believe about life. Relling has an involved personal stake in every stand that he takes, including his stand against the "demand of the ideal." To view Relling as the spokesman for relativism, then, is to misunderstand both the character and his role in the play. He is a man with a mission, a fully-committed nihilist, and his nihilism is presented as the product of a weak man's encounter with disappointment. While he stands as a partial corrective to some of Gregers Werle's excesses, he no more possesses the whole truth than Gregers does.

The play, then, has no *raisonneur*. Should this initial step seem to increase the difficulties of interpretation, locating the central action of the play and its protagonist may have the opposite effect. Once one defines the single action that stitches through all the events and realizes that only one character is continuously central to this action, individual units no longer seem extraneous; the parts fall into place in an integrated whole. This central action is Gregers Werle's commitment to a mistaken ideal, his attempt to transform that ideal into reality, his reversal of fortune, and his recognition. The only character who can possibly qualify as the protagonist of this action is Gregers himself.

Aside from providing general exposition, the main function of act 1 is to introduce Gregers. One meets in these early scenes not the meddlesome do-gooder and confirmed busybody that critics have made of him, but merely a young man whose primary motive is to renew his acquaintance with an old friend. The central event in act 1, the reunion of Gregers Werle with Hjalmar Ekdal after more than sixteen years of separation, triggers the action of the entire play. . . . In the unraveling of his story, Hjalmar also reveals to Gregers something which he himself does not realize. One man has been at the root of each setback to the Ekdal family—Gregers's father. The knowledge that his own father, who is not only living in great comfort but enjoys immense power and prestige, had allowed his business partner to be jailed for an offense for which he was himself

responsible and had later tricked Hjalmar into marrying a chambermaid he had gotten pregnant—this knowledge is at the root of the confrontation between father and son which ends act 1. Ibsen, who was addicted to the strong curtain, builds the action from the point at which Gregers welcomes Hjalmar to the dinner party to the dramatic moment when he denounces his father and vows to alleviate the sufferings of the Ekdals. As always in Ibsen, the curtain falls on an event that not only rounds out the action of the preceding act but also serves as a hook into the future. Obviously it is Gregers's newly discovered purpose in life that precipitates act 2.

It is difficult to find the unhinged fanatic of whom the critics speak in act 1—unless one thinks it psychopathic for Gregers to find Haakon Werle's conduct reprehensible, or pathological for him to want to undo the damage old Werle has caused, or neurotic for him to be conscience-stricken to know that his father's position in society and consequently his own had been obtained through criminal actions for which those nearest his father were wrongfully blamed and punished. Or unless one accepts Haakon Werle's defensive accusation that Gregers is "hysterial" as fact rather than as the attempt of a guilty man to cover his embarrassment at having been exposed. (pp. 57-9)

Perhaps it is in the second act that the sinister side of Gregers Werle is supposed to reveal itself. But his actions may not seem those of a man possessed even then if, before following Gregers Werle to the Ekdal home, one understands his motives for going there. The motive most often cited is that he was driven by his fanaticism into the "misguided efforts of an idealist who believed that the truth should be told at whatever cost." But Gregers actually proceeds on an entirely different set of motives. By the end of act 1, Hjalmar has succeeded in convincing Gregers that life in the Ekdal home is a continuous torture for him; after all, that is part of his pose. Confronting his father, Gregers asks, "How could you let that family come so miserably to grief?" . . . And finally, having reached the decision to help the Ekdals back on their feet, he tells his father, "When I look back on all you have done, it is like looking at a battle-field strewn on every side with ruined lives." . . . In other words, the young man's impression of life at the Ekdal home is *not* that they are living blissfully in an illusion which he must shatter for their own good. He is distinctly operating on the impression that life is misery for the Ekdals and that his father is the central cause. Thus, Gregers is not motivated by some evangelical notion that it is far better to live unhappily with the truth than happily with a lie. He goes to the Ekdal home hoping to bring them happiness. It turns out that the results are just the opposite of what he intended; however, such irony is the stuff of drama. If the play is to be understood for what it is, one must realize that the man whose intention it is to help the Ekdals is not only sane, but fairly intelligent and compassionate, and operating on what seem at this point to be admirable motives.

In act 1 the audience and Gregers have both been treated by Hjalmar to a rather fanciful account of life in the Ekdal home. Act 2 is meant to demonstrate exactly what their home life is. Ibsen's commentators emphasize the obvious contentment of the family as though its members had made a wholesome adjustment to their situation. But Ibsen has filled the play with many details that should not be ignored, such as the habitual neglect of the photography business, the steadily decreasing income, the progressive alcoholism and madness of the grandfather, the boundless egoism of Hjalmar and his total insensitivity to the needs of his family, the approaching blindness of Hedvig and her lack of preparation for it. With these problems, the Ekdals need more than Dr. Relling's "life—lie" to save them.

Certainly this is no revelation to anyone alert to the symbolism of the play. The Ekdal home is the home of the wild duck, the bird that, when wounded, dives immediately to the "boundless deep," there to die rather than continue the struggle for survival in the hostile world. The wild duck symbolizes most of the denizens of the Ekdal house. Each of them is wounded by life; each, in a withdrawal from reality that is equivalent to spiritual death, makes a vain attempt to escape from the hostile environment.

Old Ekdal, ex-military man and big game hunter, does more than just "putter about in the garret." Haunted by the disgrace of imprisonment, he lamely tries to forget what life has made of him. He has developed two routes of escape, alcohol and "hunting." For him, the attic is not the dingy garret crammed with chickens and rabbits and second-hand Christmas trees that we glimpse through the sliding doors; it is the clean, fresh woodlands he hunted as a young man, where life was uncomplicated and comprehensible, and where he was master of his fate. And if there is any doubt that Ibsen wanted us to see the senior Ekdal as a wild duck, we need only remember that when Gregers offers him the opportunity to return to the forest he dreams of, he refuses, preferring the illusion in the garret to the reality in the world.

The second act also reveals that Hjalmar is not the tower of strength he takes such pains to picture himself as—in whose shadow his "white-haired old father" finds comfort. He was mortally wounded by the same blast that caught his father. . . . When the "catastrophe" hit, it found him vain but brittle. Guilty of nothing himself, he was also innocent of any qualities that could have sustained him in the crisis; he too dived to the boundless deep. He does not appear as pathetic as his father, largely because he has been able to maintain his pride with the illusion that he is a great inventor who will clear the Ekdal name—will, as soon as he has his breakthrough, that is. For this event, he dedicatedly prepares himself by an indulgence in the only luxuries he can afford, indolence and gluttony.

If Hjalmar has much of the wild duck in him, Hedvig seems at times almost a personification of it. Mueller argues that Ibsen makes a distinction between Hedvig's use of the attic in a healthy quest for experience of the world and her father's use of it as an escape [see excerpt dated 1969]. Yet Hedvig's experience is no less unreal. Whether she is looking at the romantic pictures of far-off places or creating her own make-believe with the wild duck or playing "house-on-fire," her whole life is spent in fantasy.

Certainly it is not Relling's encouragement of the family's escapism that keeps this household of spiritual invalids going; it is Gina, the only member of the family with a tenacious grip on reality. There is nothing sentimental about Ibsen's portrait of Gina. She, too, of course, is a victim of life. But being of peasant stock, with all the strengths and weaknesses of her class, she knows in her bones that she cannot afford the luxury of sulking and turning her back on life merely because it has treated her badly. Her people have learned to survive by being as tough and supple as life itself, and Gina meets each crisis, an eventual setback, with instinctual stolidness. It is she who photographs the customers while Hjalmar waits for the inspiration which will save the family from ruin, she who places the ads, manages the accounts, handles the complaints. It is

Gina who warns Gregers that before Hjalmar can think about secluding himself to "contemplate the truth," Hedvig must be calmed. Without Gina, the one person in the house who is not a wild duck, the others could not survive.

Such, then, is the home life of the Ekdals to which the audience and Gregers are introduced in act 2—only the two drunkard neighbors, Relling and Molvik, are missing from the tableau. . . . The Ekdals, particularly Hjalmar, have undeniably found a degree of comfort in their squalor, but Hjalmar's comfort is that of a well-fed animal. The human spark has been extinguished in him. Gregers believes that he can rekindle that spark by reintroducing reality into the home, can get Hjalmar to shoulder the burdens he has shuffled off onto Gina, and can thus bring true happiness to the Ekdals. (pp. 59-62)

John Gassner's notion of the Ekdals subsisting on benign illusion misses the dramatic point completely [see Additional Bibliography]. Obviously if someone finds the real world too harsh to live in and seeks escape from it through the creation of a fantasy world, he is going to create a world more hospitable and more to his liking than the one he is leaving behind. Yet to regard this creation as a *benign* illusion is to assume in advance that its creator is intrinsically incapable of functioning in the real world. To say that there is virtually no hope for him at this point in the play would be premature, since one of the major dramatic questions in *The Wild Duck* is whether the average man can bear to live in the real world. At this point Gregers believes he can, and Dr. Relling is equally convinced that he cannot. If the audience immediately sides with Dr. Relling, there can be no drama: Gregers is wrong, and there's an end to it. But approaching the play objectively, the audience may receive the same impression of the Ekdal home life that Gregers does—namely, that the Ekdals could use an extraordinarily clever dog to rescue them from the tangled weeds that grow at the bottom of the sea.

It is significant that in act 3, after having seen the home, Gregers continues to act in the same manner and with the same motives:

> GREG. The wrong that both I and—others have done to old Ekdal can never be undone; but I can set Hjalmar free from the falsehood and dissimulation that are dragging him down.
>
> WERLE Do you imagine you will do any good by that?
>
> GREG. I am confident of it.
>
> WERLE Do you really think Hjalmar Ekdal is the sort of man to thank you for such a service?
>
> GREG. Certainly. . . .

[It] is not that Gregers is wrong about the necessity for truth; it is that he fails to see that truth does not necessarily guarantee happiness, that, in fact, it more often precipitates a period of intense personal suffering. . . . (pp. 62-4)

Even in act 3, then, there is no mention of preaching the truth "at whatever cost." One sees at this point, however, that Gregers has missed something that both Relling and old Werle have seen. Hjalmar is not the man Gregers takes him for. For this reason, Relling's warning is ominous—not because one feels that Gregers is threatening the tranquil world of the Ekdals but because one questions Hjalmar's strength of character. When Hjalmar leaves the house with Gregers at the end of act 3 for the fateful talk, the audience fears what he will be like upon his return. The drama of *The Wild Duck* is similar to that of the lifting of a half-starved man out of the well he had stumbled into: has he the strength to hold on until they get him to the surface or will his grip fail him? Will he fall back a second time deeper, and more injured, than the first?

There still remains the question of Hedvig's suicide. This event, obviously, is essential to the unraveling of the central action, Gregers Werle's attempt to bring happiness to the Ekdals, and an understanding of its dramatic function is prerequisite to an understanding of the nature of the reversal and recognition experienced by the protagonist. But it is not the catastrophe. A catastrophe must be inevitable, and the inevitable, at this point in *The Wild Duck,* is not so much Hedvig's suicide as Gregers's discovery that what he thinks he has been doing all along—bringing happiness—is not in fact what he has been doing.

To attempt to place the blame for Hedvig's death is to miss the point. It is not reasonable to assume that Gregers could have known the effect his plan would have on Hedvig, nor is it fair to suggest, as many do, that in speaking to the child of self-sacrifice, Gregers "poisons" the innocent mind of Hedvig with "fanciful notions" which makes her suicide a certainty. Ibsen has diffused the blame too widely to allow the fixing of responsibility upon any single individual. [The critic adds in a footnote that "Undoubtedly Gregers initiates the plan that puts Hedvig in the attic with the gun, but Haakon Werle is implicated in that it was he and not Gregers who made it plain to Hjalmar that Hedvig's paternity was in question and thus caused Hjalmar's rejection of the child. And since the timing of the pistol shot indicates that Hedvig has overheard her father's plea for proof of her love, the immediate cause of the girl's suicide is actually Hjalmar himself."] If Ibsen's focus remains upon Gregers, it is for another reason. It is not toward the suicide itself but toward its effect upon Gregers Werle that the action is driving. Hedvig's death functions rather like the sudden, unexpected and unprepared for arrival of the messenger from Corinth who tells Oedipus of the death of King Polybus; it is not the catastrophe but the shocking event which triggers the catastrophe.

An approach that has proved helpful in understanding the actions of plays like *Othello* and *Volpone,* in which one of the characters manipulates the actions of the other characters, might help explain the dramatic structure of the second half of *The Wild Duck.* Iago and Mosca have frequently been regarded as characters who have been cast as dramatists; they are not merely participants in the actions of the plays in which they are found but are also the creators of those actions. So it is in *The Wild Duck.* However, Ibsen depicts not one, but two dramatists at work.

From the opening of the play it is obvious that Hjalmar is the leading actor in a drama of his own making, which he finds a good deal more interesting than life itself. The drama in which Hjalmar casts himself is strictly a play for voices, a fantasy in which any resemblances to persons living or dead is purely coincidental. In it, he is not the insignificant, self-centered failure the audience knows him to be but the long-suffering, hard-working, self-sacrificing misunderstood inventive genius. Dr. Relling calls the drama of Hjalmar his life-lie; Eugene O'Neill would have called it his pipe-dream. Whatever one calls it, it is in this role that he presented himself to Gregers in act 1 and it is in this role that Gregers continues to picture him.

From act 3 onward, Hjalmar is in competition with another playwright who is equally determined to write the drama of the Ekdal family, Gregers Werle. From what he learned in act 1 of the Ekdals' present condition, Gregers has determined that they have the making for a drama of high seriousness, one in which Hjalmar is to emulate the heroes of classic tragedy by dedicating himself to the "higher things." Gregers understands perfectly well that at the center of such a drama he must have a person of extraordinary abilities. He regards Hjalmar as such a person and chooses him for his protagonist. But Gregers is a man of his age, an age in which Shakespeare's tragedies were still being made palpable by the addition of happy endings. And so he shall have it with his own drama: to the tragic triad of do-suffer-know, Gregers would add the optimistic denouement—and be happy. Hjalmar is to be a suffering hero in a sentimental drama with a happy ending. Though this play is never completed, one learns of the effect he wished to achieve from the scenario that Gregers sketches. . . . (pp. 64-6)

On the surface, the two dramas appear similar: in each, Hjalmar Ekdal is to be the suffering hero. However, despite his sentimentalism, Gregers the dramatist has a taste for realism not shared by his fellow playwright. He would have Hjalmar experience the suffering to know the happiness. In contrast, Hjalmar, the dramatist, makes no such demand on Hjalmar, the man. Though he never systematically compartmentalized his life into its real and imaginary aspects, nevertheless, before the arrival of Gregers, he knew well enough not to try living his fantasy. Nor did anyone expect him to. At the end of act 3, Gregers demands that he act as if the man and the mask were one and the same. And unfortunately for Hjalmar, not to do so would force an admission that he is not the man he claims to be. Thus poor Hjalmar, himself a comic figure, tries in vain to be the hero of Gregers's drama of the ideal.

It is Gregers's naïve attempt to make a tragic protagonist of a man who is already playing the leading role in a soap opera that gives *The Wild Duck* its peculiar tragicomic tone and establishes a pattern of action that dominates the last two acts of the play. At the beginning of act 4, after the long offstage talk he has had with Hjalmar, Gregers is shocked to find his friend despondent. Gregers the dramatist hardly expected this from his leading man. . . . The strain of trying to be what he was content to pose as is clearly too much for Hjalmar. Yet he cannot confess that he is not what he has tried so hard to seem. . . . Like his invention, his new dedication to "higher things" will take time to develop, time which people in the Ekdal household have always allowed him. And so it goes. Each time Gregers tries to work him to the point of a tragic recognition, Hjalmar fizzles out, and what Gregers meant to be a tragic anagnorisis ends up a comic anticlimax.

One of the ironies the audience is to be aware of is that as it senses with growing conviction that things are not going to work out as anyone had supposed, it also sees that in setting events going as he does, Gregers has only the best of intentions. Yet each time Hjalmar recoils from Gregers's attempts at having him enlarge himself and tries to wind himself back into the illusions from which Gregers is twisting him free, comedy and tragedy become inseparably mingled. Hjalmar continually refuses to act out any of the climactic scenes Gregers constructs for him. And the aborted climaxes spin off into comic anticlimaxes. Yet even in the comedy there remains the tragic pathos of seeing a man, albeit a weak one, stripped of his illusions.

Another irony of *The Wild Duck* is that Gregers, who wants to construct a drama in which Hjalmar is the protagonist, himself ends up as the protagonist. Try as he may, he cannot persuade Hjalmar to assume responsibility for the dramatic action. He fails to impart to Hjalmar the motivating desire to find happiness by facing the truth. The consequence is that rather than being, as he intended, the man who merely set the action in motion and then faded into the background to watch the unfolding action reveal the truth of his theories, Gregers remains the protagonist. He cannot rid himself of the role. The action stalls unless he stands at the center. For this reason, the tearful comedy in which everything works out well at the end never materializes. This truncated drama, which continually loses its tragic momentum and drops into comedy, is the cause of the confusing ending to *The Wild Duck.*

Ibsen was well aware of the confusing nature of the play, as is evidenced by his statement to his publisher, Frederick Hegel, ''in any case [the critics] will find plenty to quarrel about, plenty to interpret'' [see excerpt dated 1884]. I think it would not be too much to say that Ibsen meant his ending to be confusing—not merely for the sake of controversy but because he saw the nature of the material he was dealing with as composed of irreconcilable factors, the serious consideration of which can only lead men into confusion.

The nature of the catastrophe is particularly confusing: Gregers would have it in one place, Ibsen in another. In constructing his play, Gregers Werle's final attempt as a dramatist to bring Hjalmar to a peripety is to have Hedvig show her love for her father through an act of self-sacrifice which would also finally free the family from their illusions—that is, she must kill the wild duck. There is nothing diabolical either in the plan to kill the duck nor in Gregers's mind when he proposes it. In fact, had Hedvig killed only the duck, the plan might—to a degree—have been successful. When Hjalmar is told that Hedvig has shot the wild duck, he is immediately repentant. . . . Obviously one is not to believe in the spiritual renewal that Gregers hoped for and that Hjalmar's speech promises. Hjalmar has made some rash threats which he is now seeking excuses to forget; he welcomes the opportunity he is to be forgiving. But for whatever reasons, the family might have been reunited and Gregers's drama would have had not only its catastrophe but also its happy ending.

But of course that is not the way it happens. Hjalmar, in another of his self-dramatizing episodes, makes some maudlin remarks which his daughter overhears, and Hedvig shoots herself rather than the duck. Again we see the two dramatists at odds. When it is learned that Hedvig has committed suicide, Gregers, recognizing Hedvig's purpose, seizes on her death as the perfect event to climax his drama. Hedvig's sacrifices will not have been in vain. Surely the suffering that Hjalmar will now undergo will release the nobility of character his unfortunate condition has kept submerged for so long. And the forgiving Hjalmar will introduce a transformation into the lives of those around him. But the dramatist in Hjalmar would not have it so. Though he relished the dramatic possibilities of the moment, he saw it more in terms of his own drama, ''the child torn prematurely from her father's loving heart'' by an untimely death. Relling is no doubt right: Hjalmar's nobility is temporary and will quickly give way to ''emotional fits of self-admiration and self-compassion.'' . . . Once again the climax is truncated and Gregers's hero proves a clown. Hedvig's suicide remains a catastrophe only in the literal (not the technical) sense.

Although Gregers saw the suicide as the climax of the play, Ibsen, like Hjalmar, never intended it as such. The play Ibsen wrote is not the one Gregers had in mind, for in Ibsen's play it is Gregers who is the tragic protagonist. Because his ideal is wrong he must suffer the reversal and undergo the recognition. Truth does not bring happiness. However, he does not learn this from Hedvig's suicide; paradoxically, it is precisely because her death fails to become a dramatic climax that his eyes are opened. It is in the anticlimax following her death, while watching Hjalmar scrambling about in a frantic effort to avoid the truth and thus turning what should have been tragedy into a grotesque comedy, that Gregers begins to receive his own illumination. Hjalmar knew intuitively that to face the truth would destroy him. Watching Hjalmar construct his defenses . . . is the climactic moment of the tragic action in which Gregers is the protagonist.

Almost in the same manner as Hjalmar attempts to evade the truth, Gregers tries desperately to avoid the recognition that presents itself to him. Though Hjalmar has only a moment before been guilty of the worst sentimentality. . . . [Gregers] maintains that ''Hedvig has not died in vain. You saw how his grief called out all the best that was in him.'' . . . But Relling's cynical insistence that Hjalmar will play his own role, not the one Gregers has constructed for him, drives home to Gregers the truth which he has been trying to escape—that Hjalmar has turned his tragedy into a farce. For Gregers, to admit that Relling's characterization of Hjalmar is accurate, is to admit, once and for all, that truth does not bring happiness, that what he thought he had been doing all along is not in fact what he had been doing at all. Hjalmar's failure to be transformed by Hedvig's death impresses upon Gregers, sharply and inescapably, the disillusioning fact that he who would bring truth to the average man is destined ''to be the thirteenth at table.'' . . . He will of necessity initiate suffering. In the final lines of the play Gregers accepts this burden.

But if Gregers is the single-minded hero at the center of a tragic action, the play as a whole does not share his single-mindedness. Nor does it follow, as Relling believes it does, that the truth should not be told. But whether it is better, when dealing with the common man, to acquiesce to spiritual death, with the life-lie, or to risk precipitating physical death, with the truth, remains a moot point. In the end, Gina, who lacks the capacity to grasp the problem at all, ironically seems best equipped to cope with the situation. Dr. Relling, Gregers and Gina are all spokesmen for different points of view. And yet none of the three speaks for Ibsen. None of them sees the complexity of the human condition. Relling is as much an absolutist as Gregers, whereas the informing intellect of *The Wild Duck* is one committed to relativism, a relativism which in this case is not so concerned with showing that absolutists of every persuasion are wrong as with showing that they are necessarily only partially correct. Life is composed of so many incompatible varibles that it is impossible to formulate any hard and fast rules. And that is equally true for the rule that man must have a life-lie as for the rule that he must face the truth.

Unlike earlier dramatists who believed life would yield a coherent meaning to the hero strong enough to pursue the tragic insight into and beyond the dark night, Ibsen's concept of the complexity of man, in *The Wild Duck* at any rate, does not imply that the contradictory aspects will merge at a higher level of integration. For Ibsen, the contradictions are real and permanent. The vision in *The Wild Duck* is therefore a vision of men doomed by life to live in a world beyond their comprehension, a world filled with shallow half-truths that refuse to be pieced together into a coherent whole, where there is no final resolution of multiplicities into unities.

In such a world, tragedy as Sophocles and Shakespeare knew it is impossible. Gregers stands at the center of a tragic action. He enters the play with convictions which, when acted upon, do not hold up to the test of reality. He has a reversal and a recognition. But the recognition puts the world together only for him. It does not permeate the rest of the community, simply because it is not necessarily true for them. Consequently, though he participates in a tragic action, the play of which he is the protagonist is not itself a tragedy, or not solely a tragedy. How could it be if what Gregers learns is only a part of what the play as a whole sees, and if the other things grasped by the vision of the play are not compatible with Gregers's insight—or even, for that matter with the tragic concept of life? By counterpointing the comic and the tragic and undercutting the tragic climaxes with comic anticlimaxes, Ibsen ends the play on a note of profound and permanent irreconcilability. (pp. 66-70)

> *Charles A. Hallett, '' 'The Wild Duck' and Critical Cliché,'' in* Papers on Language and Literature, *Vol. 11, No. 1, Winter, 1975, pp. 54-70.*

RONALD GRAY (essay date 1977)

[*The following excerpt is taken from an essay in which Gray discusses* The Wild Duck *and* An Enemy of the People *as two slightly differing explorations by Ibsen of the same theme: a consideration of when—if ever—a demand for the whole and unvarnished truth can be justified. Gray calls the duck ''an image with many meanings'' that never stands for any one thing but is linked at various times with several of the main characters. Concurring with Havelock Ellis (1890), Smith Ely Jelliffe and Louise Brink (1918), and Hermann J. Weigand (1925), Gray interprets Gregers Werle as Ibsen's caricatured self-portrait.*]

The pairing of Ibsen's plays is nowhere easier to see than in *An Enemy of the People* and *The Wild Duck,* the one about a man who seems to have a degree of justification in his demand that the truth be told, the other about the fatal consequences of a similar demand. The man who seems to sum up the main trend of *The Wild Duck* is the cynical Dr Relling, with his doctrine that no man can live without illusions, without a 'life-lie' to sustain him. The two plays are curiously like two of Goethe's, in this pairing. Goethe's *Egmont,* like his *Iphigenia in Tauris* of a few years later, is about having the confidence to reveal the whole truth, even to those who may use it against one. Egmont is executed for his presumptuous trustfulness, Iphigenia succeeds in converting her captor to tolerance. . . . Like Goethe, Ibsen divides his dramatic analysis of truth-telling into two separate plays with contrary conclusions. Also like Goethe, however, he simplifies each part so much as to inspire some scepticism, so far as any general 'message' may be intended. It may be that he had in mind, as Goethe possibly also had, a dialectical demonstration, an affirmation of both a positive and a negative—though, like all dialectical pairs, neither side would totally exclude the other. If that is so, *The Wild Duck* turns out to be little more convincing than *An Enemy of the People.* Yet there is a matter of real human concern at stake: the play could have depth in treating the tragic and comic consequences of conceit and attempts at devotion. The chief hindrance is the symbolism. But technical awkwardness occurs too.

An initial weakness shows as early as the exposition. Ibsen starts traditionally enough with the device of a conversation between two servants, one permanent, the other hired only for the evening, and therefore needing to be told who everyone is. Tennant calls this clumsy . . . , but it is acceptable, however well-worn, as a swift means of sketching in the background. It is in the scene between Gregers Werle and Hjalmar Ekdal, later in Act One, that more serious difficulties become noticeable.

There is a complex situation to be divulged: first, that fourteen years ago Werle senior has had a child, Hedvig, by his former housekeeper, Gina, and has arranged for the mother to marry Hjalmar, whom he has set up in business as a professional photographer. (pp. 99-100)

These events may pass well enough as credible at a performance, when there is no time to consider them. As on other occasions, Ibsen gains by not presenting them as staged action. Reflection shows that the story depends on some considerable degree of naivety in Hjalmar, and a willingness in old Werle to gamble on very long odds. We are asked to believe that after Werle discovered Gina's pregnancy he first dismissed her from her job as his housekeeper, then arranged matters so that Hjalmar took up lodgings in her mother's house, and finally waited until Hjalmar not only fell in love with Gina but married her before her pregnancy became obvious to him—and then failed to notice that she gave birth rather soon after their marriage. Given that Hjalmar is extraordinarily naive, or very willing to be deceived, this is not impossible. But with only four or five months for all this to happen—Hjalmar could hardly have failed to notice if Gina had given birth within three or four months of marriage—the time-scheme is rather tight.

A greater awkwardness arises from the needs of the exposition. Gregers, who describes Hjalmar as his 'best and only friend', must be brought into conversation with him in such a way that Hjalmar reveals all the facts about his engagement and marriage, and, while suspecting nothing himself, causes Gregers to see the hidden hand of his self-interested father in all the ostensibly generous benefactions intended to hush up the past. This is dramatically useful: the audience hears just what Gregers hears, and puts two and two together just as he does: its interest is actively engaged. The question arises, though, how Gregers can be so completely uninformed about the affairs of so close a friend. He has been away, it appears, for sixteen or seventeen years, working 'up at Høidal', 'slaving away like any ordinary clerk', and in the whole of that time he has never been back to town or heard any news except what his father chose to tell him in postscripts to business letters. He did learn tht Hjalmar Ekdal's father had been in prison on account of a dishonest business deal, which almost involved Werle senior also (hence the elder man's only apparently charitable care for old Ekdal), but this did not induce him to write to Hjalmar, despite his own father's involvement. . . . Ibsen has covered every conceivable objection that a critic of the Scribe school could make. As an exposition this cannot be faulted: there is an explanation for everything. But the demands of the exposition have required the characters to seem naive or unintelligent to a degree that makes them in themselves less interesting. The exposition has taken precedence over the character-drawing. (pp. 100-01)

Gregers is equally near to a caricature, though again not altogether incredible. His absence of curiosity about his old friend need not be taken as a mark of his character, rather as a distortion caused by technical considerations. The difficulty about being moved by the play comes from his unreasoning and fanatical insistence on opening Hjalmar's eyes to the truth. The need for this is never discussed. Gregers merely speaks of freeing Hjalmar from 'all the lies and deceit that are causing his ruination,' and is never challenged to say what that ruination is. So far as the play shows us, Hjalmar is comfortably off in his marriage, and it might be more to the point to ask him to show consideration for Hedvig and his wife, rather than to insist on his knowing his daughter is illegitimate. Gregers never reflects on the likely consequences of telling Hjalmar the truth about the past, but assumes the results can only be good, and this blindness in both of them is not offered so that we may understand it: it is the mainstay of the play.

As Relling says, Gregers is 'an acute case of inflamed scruples'. But he is precisely that, a 'case', not a man with whom one feels any degree of affinity. . . . [The] deep need most people feel to get at the truth is not adequately represented by Gregers' bald-headed rush at it. We suppress the truth about ourselves for reasons of which Gregers is ignorant; we have more inhibitions than his puritan zeal comprehends, and Ibsen, in showing the results of zeal of that order, is plugging away at the obvious. The place for such a grotesque is farce.

Gregers' proposal to Hedvig that she should show her love for her father by sacrificing the wild duck, her dearest possession, is a crux of the play: without it there could be no catastrophe. But this is based on no better grounds than Gregers' revelation to Hjalmar about Hedvig's parentage. In his first wild reaction to that news, Hjalmar turned on Hedvig in a fit of bad temper and said he would like to wring the duck's neck. There was no reason to take this any more seriously than other unthinking things he says throughout the play. But as though grateful to the dramatist for giving him a cue, Gregers reminds Hedvig in Act Four that her father used such language, and turns it into a pretext for sacrificing the bird for Hjalmar. At this point, when Gregers says, 'Supposing you offered to sacrfice the wild duck for *his* sake . . . Suppose you were ready to sacrifice for him the most precious thing you had in the world,' the play ceases to be about any desire for truth and becomes at best— but it is not really this—a study of a man slightly crazed. (The number of characters whose sanity one begins to doubt increases from here on.)

Gregers is surely not meant to be crazed, despite the remarks to this effect which his father makes about him. One indication of that is his similarity, on this particular point, with other Ibsen characters, so many of whom expect their relatives or friends to behave as Gregers suggests Hedvig should. [In *A Doll's House,*] Nora supposes her husband will quite certainly destroy his own reputation to preserve hers, and is astonished when he does not. [In *Rosmersholm,*] Rosmer accepts willingly Rebecca West's idea that she should drown herself to restore his faith in mankind. [In *Hedda Gabler,*] Hedda suggests suicide to Løvborg. [In *Ghosts,*] Oswald takes it for granted that Regine will end his life if he asks her to. The sacrifice Gregers proposes is nothing like so great as some of these, which are not presented as acts of madness, and in some cases seem to be seen as great, tragic necessities. . . . Besides, Gregers' case is not studied by the dramatist; it is simply the means by which the plot is furthered, and this puts an end to any serious pretensions. Gregers, again, gives no account of how he thinks his proposed course of action will help anybody. With the zeal of a leech he fastens onto the idea of self-sacrifice, as he does to the idea of truth, and is astounded by the results of his inspirations.

With two such men as Gregers and Hjalmar at the centre the play is bound to remain at a crude level; humanly speaking it does, however, also introduce a new kind of play, in which symbolism is more important than in any previous work of Ibsen's. Hitherto, symbolism had generally been only apparent here and there. Bernick's leaky ships, Nora's forgery, Oswald's disease, Stockmann's sewers all had at least a metaphoric value. But so far no play had made the symbol so predominant, or so interrelated with all the characters' lives, as the wild duck is, and on this account it is possible to discuss here the question of Ibsen's achieving a *poésie de théâtre*.

The bird is certainly an image with many potential meanings. It can expand with something like the iridescence of poetry, by virtue of its ambiguity, for it never stands for any one thing. In some places it seems to be associated with despair: it is compared implicitly with 'some people in this world that dive straight to the bottom the moment they get a couple of bullets in them, and never come up again,' and is thus linked, sometimes explicitly, with the despair of old Ekdal and Hedvig. They are the people who have, like the duck, dived to the bottom of the river or sea, and clung fast there, or so the explicit parallels suggest, though it is not clear how this can be said of Hedvig: the symbol is forced upon her, yet she is not remotely like her shattered grandfather. Gregers' self-imposed task, as he sees it, is to dive down like a well-trained dog, and save both Hjalmar and Hedvig, who to his way of thinking have gone down to die in the dark. (It really is not true; Hjalmar is too self-centred for despair, and Hedvig is spirited in her difficult situation.) Yet the bird also stands for the opposite of despair. In one sense it is the creature that tried to commit suicide when it was only slightly hurt, in another, it is, as Hedvig says, the most important thing in the room, 'because she's a *real* wild bird'. The place where it lives is also the place where the clock does not work, which leads Gregers to say, with the disclosure of symbolism characteristic of him, that 'time stands still in there . . . beside the wild duck'. We may be chary of accepting this offer of a symbol at face value— the metaphor is so pressed into service—but the suggestion is surely that there is something of eternity about the duck. Is it that total freedom Skule dreamed of, and Brand, and Julian, perhaps? But if we choose to think that, the attribution is tacked on. There is nothing more timeless or eternal about the duck than the fact that the clock in the same room has stopped; the duck has no function in the play that could be described in this particular symbolical way.

Other ambiguities include the fact that, though the bird symbolises the depths, it lives in the highest part of the building, and that, though 'wild', it lives cooped up in the attic, even though it is often said to have been saved. (This relationship between imprisonment and freedom will seem more notable still in Hedda Gabler's desire to liberate Løvborg.)

The rôle of the dog which rescues the duck is equally ambiguous. The purpose of the dog which belonged to Gregers' father was not to save the duck's life by refusing to let it bite fast to the weeds on the sea-bed, but to bring it back to the hunter, who for some reason kept it alive where he would normally have killed it. (What was old Werle doing, sending a duck with two slugs in its body and a damaged neck as a pet for Hedvig? Presumably he shot it in order to eat it). Gregers, however, when he says that he would like to be a dog, speaks as though his purpose would be to rescue the duck, or people in a similar situation. His lack of success, indeed the bungled job he makes of the whole operation, is related to this confusion in the symbols themselves. Gregers does not know what he intends by 'liberating' Hjalmar and Hedvig; he plunges in and brings Hedvig, at least, straight to her death.

These are not poetic images: the ambiguity is not enlivening but confusing, both to audience and to characters. Yet it almost seems at times as though Ibsen were aware of this, as though he were presenting in Gregers a parody of himself. That he is to a degree such a parody, so far as Ibsen was a man continually concerned with 'the claims of the ideal', is self-evident. That he is a parody of Ibsen's 'poetic' character needs more showing, and cannot be said so definitely in every case. Yet the hint is often proffered.

In *The Wild Duck,* more than in any other play, Ibsen seems to ridicule the habit of talking in a double sense, in inappropriate metaphors, as when Gregers is asked by Hjalmar what he would most like to be, if not himself. . . .

> GREGERS If I could choose, I should most of all like to be a clever dog.
>
> GINA A dog!
>
> HEDVIG *(involuntarily)* Oh, no.!
>
> GREGERS Yes, a really absurdly clever dog, the sort that goes down to the bottom after wild ducks, when they dive down and bite fast on to the seaweed and the tangle down there in the mud.
>
> HJALMAR You know, Gregers . . . I don't understand a word of what you are saying. . . .

Yet the possibility of a certain self-ridicule by Ibsen looks more remote when he at once follows this dialogue with another in which Gina's hard-headedness turns to a kind of awe, only increased by the comments of the innocent child Hedvig:

> GINA *(staring into space, her sewing on her lap)* Wasn't that funny, him saying he wanted to be a dog?
>
> HEDVIG I'll tell you what, Mother . . . I think he meant something else.
>
> GINA And what else might that be?
>
> HEDVIG Well, I don't know. But it was just as though he meant something different from what he was saying—all the time. . . .

This heavy underlining, of a symbolical sense which must already be thoroughly clear to the audience, might well be a mark of Ibsen's involvement with his symbols to the point of not realising how obvious they are. (pp. 103-07)

Yet there must surely be irony in the scene in which Hedvig's dead body is discovered, however movingly it may be staged. For Gina this is an instant when she is desolated; her response is pure motherly grief. For Hjalmar his daughter's death is something to be denied, for Relling it is an occasion to reprove Hjalmar for his sentimentality. For Gregers, it is a symbol:

> HJALMAR Well, Relling . . . why don't you say something?
>
> RELLING The bullet hit her in the breast.
>
> HJALMAR Yes, but she'll be coming round.
>
> GINA *(bursts into tears)* Oh my little one!

GREGERS *(huskily)* In the briny deep . . . .

Gregers' line is grotesque, not only because of the fact that he speaks symbolically, but because of the particular words he uses, which could hardly make the symbolism more obvious. . . . [In] Act Three Ibsen has deliberately drawn attention to the oddity of these words. When Gregers uses them for the first time, Hedvig at once asks why he uses that particular phrase. It is true that the alternatives she proposes are closer to one another in sound than 'the briny deep' is to 'the seabed': where Gregers says *på havsens bund*, which uses a slightly archaic and 'poetic' form of the genitive, she suggests as more natural *havets bund* or *havbunden*, and clearly his phrase, though only slightly different in Norwegian, sounds out of place to her. When it is repeated after Hedvig's death, the oddity must strike us, and the incongruousness of Gregers' response must be brought home to us. (On the other hand, Hedvig admits that she herself uses the archaism for the room of the wild duck, so that the repetition of it reflects on her also.)

Ibsen, then, wanted the moment of Hedvig's death to be tinged with criticism of the man whose blundering way of speaking has helped to bring it about. Gregers has implanted in Hedvig's mind the idea that she herself is the wild duck who must be sacrificed, and now he is refusing to face the consequences. But it is the symbolical mode, rather than the idealism, which is criticised through the 'poetic' words, and that same mode is the chief feature of the play Ibsen is presenting.

He had no real need of a symbol at all, in order to cope dramatically with the shattering of illusions. Gregers could simply have humiliated Hjalmar to the point where Hedvig would do anything, even kill herself to demonstrate to him that he was still loved. The device of the duck seems to give a greater scope to the play, to hint at Freedom in a more than local sense, but only serves to produce a less moving, more confusing work. The duck is a mere *fait divers,* and the play would be more telling without it.

Any resistance we may still feel to the idea that Ibsen is ironically detached from such symbolising probably comes from the awareness that for his own part, as a dramatist, he continues to use symbolism, both now and in later plays, in exactly the same way. There is comedy in the moment when Gregers asks Hedvig whether she is so certain the loft is really only a loft, as there is in his prim retort to Relling's accusation that he carries the 'claim of the ideal' around in his back-pocket: 'It is in my breast that I carry it.' Yet it is Ibsen who makes Gina say that Gregers has lit a stove and then damped it too much, and finally thrown water all over it and the floor too. Gina cannot herself mean that symbolically, but Ibsen means us to understand it so, and to see in it an epitome of all the mess that Gregers causes throughout the play. Ibsen is by now incapable of writing without some degree of symbolism, and that is precisely what prevents *The Wild Duck* from being deeply moving. Take, for instance, the actual moment of Hedvig's death, which is as artificial as anything Ibsen wrote:

> HJALMAR . . . Suppose the others [Mrs Sörby and old Werle] came along, their hands loaded with good things, and they called to the child: 'Come away from him. With us, life is awaiting you . . .'
>
> GREGERS *(quickly)* Well, what then, d'you think?
>
> HJALMAR If I then asked her: 'Hedvig, are you willing to give up life for my sake'? *(Laughs*

scornfully) Oh yes! I must say. You would soon hear the sort of answer I would get!

(A pistol shot is heard within the loft.) . . .

Such appropriate coincidences are not uncommon in Ibsen's plays. Whether Hedvig has heard what Hjalmar has said and misinterpreted it is uncertain. She may have understood 'life' to mean not life with Mrs Sörby but life of any kind, and the pistol shot may be an answer saying that she does love Hjalmar, enough to sacrifice herself, or that she is in despair at his (only recently and unexpectedly expressed) doubt about her love. The indisputable point is that the pistol-shot is, metaphorically, an answer, and that same fact is what makes the moment stagey. It is also a quality not of any particular character but of the play.

The final touch is given in the conversation between Gregers and Relling, just before the curtain falls. They have been discussing whether Hedvig's death will have any notable effect on Hjalmar, or whether he will be ennobled by it or return to wallowing deeper and deeper in self-pity. Gregers is convinced that some good will come of the sacrifice he has unwittingly caused:

> GREGERS If *you* are right and *I* am wrong, life will no longer be worth living.
>
> RELLING Oh, life wouldn't be so bad if we could only be left in peace by these blessed people who come running round to us poor folk with their claims of the ideal all the time.
>
> GREGERS *(staring into space)* In that case I am glad my destiny is what it is.
>
> RELLING If I may ask—what is your destiny?
>
> GREGERS *(turning to leave)* To be thirteenth at table.
>
> RELLING The devil it is! . . .

Gregers' portentousness still leaves some doubt about the significance of this exchange. He is still talking in a symbol, and rather an obscure one. Whether he means merely that it is unlucky to be thirteenth, or that he is the Christ-figure among the twelve others, or the Judas-figure, is disputable, and no doubt Ibsen intended ambiguity here as he did in the case of the wild duck itself: to himself Gregers is a Christ, to others a Judas. It is both good and bad that the claim of the ideal should be presented—that might well be Gregers' view. But Ibsen himself has carefully made that remark possible, and given the symbol a basis in the reality of the play's action. Gregers actually was thirteenth, or at any rate one of thirteen, at table in Act One, as was carefully brought out at the time, and this seems to lend a kind of weight to what would otherwise be a remark out of the blue. On the other hand, Relling's scepticism and his colloquial reference to the Devil (echoing the same unintentional use of the word by Regine at the beginning of **Ghosts,** and several other similar uses scattered through the plays) suggest a final negative, or at least a doubt.

There is an intriguing quality here, tempting us to unravel the puzzle. In reality, though, there is no unravelling it: it is an indeterminate ending as well as a portentous one, and that is the most serious criticism that the play has to meet, at this point. In the final moment Ibsen is not really concerned about the death of Hedvig, any more than Gregers was. He is concerned to maintain the ambiguity of his position, both main-

taining his symbolism and decrying the impulse which draws him towards it. In that comprehensiveness, he may have felt, lay the only full realisation of himself as an artist. (pp. 108-11)

Ibsen had by [the time he wrote **The Wild Duck**] become very familiar with the alternating poles of negation and affirmation, following first one course, then the other, from play to play, and occasionally attempting a synthesis, as he did in **Emperor and Galilean.** By now, he had become more conscious of his method, and had a greater wish to take up a position with relation to that, rather than to the immediate content of the plays. Thus, although **The Wild Duck** is a negative, on the whole, to the affirmative claim made by Stockmann on behalf of 'the ideal', it is also a stock-taking, a reckoning up of the advantages and disadvantages of Ibsen's own mode of playwriting. A further coil of the spiral has been entered upon, a further refinement of the eternal affirmation and negation. What **The Wild Duck** shows is not merely the folly of Gregers' idealism and use of symbols—at the same time as it seems to allow the possibility that it was not folly, but necessary and beneficial—but also the folly of all symbolism, including Ibsen's own. It is true that we have to add to this, as we do for Gregers, the possibility that the symbolism may be fruitful after all. There is no end to the spirals, the dialectic continues indefinitely. Yet such an account could explain why Ibsen seems at one and the same time to condemn Gregers, while he himself uses an identical mode of approach to things and people. This is the perennial spin of the wheel of the polar opposites, and would seem to justify even the ambiguities about Christ and Judas in Gregers' final exchange with Relling. These merely continue the ambiguities in the wild duck, in the attic, in the ideal, and even in Hedvig's sacrifice. It is true that the ambiguities usually correspond to no particular realities. It is the system itself that counts, not the human beings involved, who are manipulated in this play as they generally are in all Ibsen's work, and this is a flaw, since in theory the system, the Idea, should become the phenomena of a real world. What the Idea does in Ibsen is to become the phenomena of an artificial world, which has only a superficial resemblance to the world of human beings. It is a world of art, but of an art removed from contact with reality, spinning its own cocoon, walking along the spider's filament thrown out by its own body, a fundamentally solipsistic affair. We are never likely to be touched by any humanity in it, unless by Gina's. (pp. 112-13)

> *Ronald Gray, in his* Ibsen—A Dissenting View: A Study of the Last Twelve Plays, *Cambridge University Press, 1977, 231 p.*

EDVARD BEYER (essay date 1978)

[*In the following excerpt, Beyer characterizes* The Wild Duck *as a tragicomedy, with the elements of tragedy and comedy carefully fused. Hermann J. Weigand (1925) and Karl S. Guthke (1966) proffer similar interpretations, while James Huneker contends that the mixture of tragedy and comedy in* The Wild Duck *is incongruous and ineffective (see Additional Bibliography). Beyer disagrees with the critical contention that* The Wild Duck *stands as a corrective to the ''all or nothing'' dogmatism of the title character of* Brand *and to Dr. Stockmann's insistence upon bringing forward the truth in* An Enemy of the People, *finding instead that* The Wild Duck *represents a continuation of Ibsen's ongoing examination of the nature of such opposing forces as doubt and faith, idealism and skepticism.*]

In September 1884 Ibsen sent the manuscript of **The Wild Duck** to his publisher, and in the accompanying letter said that 'in some ways this new work occupies a place apart in my dramatic production, the method of procedure differing in several respects from my earlier one'. He also prophesied that 'the study and rendering of these people' on the stage would not be easy, and that the critics would find 'plenty to squabble about, plenty to interpret' [see excerpt dated 1884]. His prophesy came true. Contemporary critics were confused, the public likewise, and later actors, critics and scholars have interpreted the work in widely differing ways.

It was not, however, Ibsen's intention to mystify. He knew what he wanted, and he hoped to be understood. He had detailed discussions with Schrøder, the director of the Christiania Theatre, about the casting of the play, stressed that both ensemble and staging demanded 'naturalness and realism in every aspect', and placed particular emphasis on the lighting: 'it is different in every act, and designed to correspond to the basic mood which gives each of the five acts its own special character'.

This last feature is far better sustained and far more subtly worked out than in any of the earlier Ibsen dramas, even though lighting was also important in *Ghosts*. However, one can hardly say that the use of lighting is different in *The Wild Duck*. Where there is a difference is in the social setting, the use of symbols and attitude. Whereas all Ibsen's other modern plays are set in well-to-do bourgeois or academic circles, four of the five acts of this play are set in a lower middle-class milieu, in a family in difficult and economically dependent circumstances. The family is portrayed with an intimacy which is unique in Ibsen, and with a concern for the characteristic features both of the interior and in the use of language. Never has he been more realistic than here, and yet in the midst of the realism there is the central symbol. This subtle blending of scenic realism and poetic symbolism is one of the most important innovations in the play.

In *Ghosts* too the title points to the main symbol, but there despite everything it is only a metaphor. The wild duck, on the other hand, is a real bird, which for good reasons is not visible, but is nonetheless a part of the reality depicted on the stage, for we know that it lives in the strange forest of Christmas trees there in the loft. It is of significance to the plot, while at the same time both it and the loft acquire an ever richer symbolic content, with obvious, half-hidden or possible links with nearly all the characters in the work. In addition it is charged with meaning and is a vital element in the creation of mood.

All the same, the most daring feature of the play is the sustained combination of tragedy and comedy. There are comic elements in the tragedy of *Ghosts,* and we glimpse tragic possibilities in the comedy of *An Enemy of the People,* but only in *The Wild Duck* do the tragic and comic elements fuse. Comedy or farce scenes, such as the breakfast scene in Act III, can take place between profoundly serious ones, but the same scene can also contain comic and pathetic elements, and at the end even the death scene is tinged with a macabre humour. *The Wild Duck* is a tragi-comedy, as Ibsen himself described it, and it is so in the deepest sense of the word: human life and the human condition consistently seen in a double perspective.

The core of the tragedy, as of the comedy, lies in the clash between Gregers Werle's idealism, his talk of the 'claims of the ideal', and the reality to which he directs them. It was here that 'the method of procedure' was most 'different' and therefore most confusing for Ibsen's contemporaries. That the ide-

alist and proclaimer of the truth should come into conflict with his surroundings, was normal for an Ibsen play, but here it was as if everything was turned upside-down.

If one looks at the structure of the play, it becomes evident that Gregers Werle is both the main character and the one who carries the action. He sets himself a noble task, that of rescuing Hjalmar Ekdal from lies and concealment. He pursues his task, overcomes all obstacles, and reveals to Hjalmar 'the truth' about his marriage to Gina. But he is defeated in that 'the truth' does not have the intended effect, but on the contrary poisons Hjalmar's relations not only with Gina, but even more with Hedvig—and with catastrophic results. Perhaps Gregers will draw the ultimate conclusion from his mistakes and his 'destiny': 'to be the thirteenth at table'.

In this way we can trace a basically tragic element through the play, one that is linked to Gregers Werle. From one point of view, it is even possible to see him as a tragic hero, the idealist who suffers defeat against a wretched reality, and the play has been interpreted and played in this way. But from the beginning the motives behind his idealism reveal themselves to be somewhat mixed in character, and one of the strongest is the need to assuage a sick conscience, not by his own sacrifices, but by intervening in the lives of others with his excessive demands. Nor is it beyond question that in all things he represents the truth, or that he interprets the past correctly. He is so blinded by his own needs, and by what Dr Relling calls his 'fits of hero-worship', that he gravely misjudges those he wishes to help. He overestimates Hjalmar Ekdal in a way which casts a comic light on what one could otherwise call his tragic blindness, and he leads Hedvig into ways of thinking that bring about her shocking and tragic, though—if Relling is right—pointless, sacrificial death. It is she, not Gregers, who pays the price of his idealism and his fateful miscalculations.

That is how mercilessly the sick roots of the idealist's preaching are exposed, and are highlighted by their effects. Gregers' idealism is also accurately diagnosed by Dr Relling, who may be a cynic without illusions, but who nevertheless shows, particularly in what he says about Hedvig, that he understands people. The milieu into which Gregers intrudes, on the other hand, is characterized by simple human values, warmth and mutual concern, and the characters are presented with humour and tolerant understanding despite their failings. Hjalmar Ekdal, who is the most colourful and vital character in the play, is certainly wretched and laughable, weak, ridiculous, spoilt and irresponsible, full of excuses and self-dramatizing phrases, lazy and cowardly, and given to dreams which in his heart of hearts he does not believe. But he is also a charming dilettante artist, a good father and in his own egocentric way a good husband, who is happy in his simple but cosy home. Ibsen has definitely exposed him, but he felt very strongly that the comic sides should not be overplayed. . . . Old Ekdal too has his obvious faults, but a certain dignity nonetheless. Gina is down-to-earth and practical, also somewhat comical, and totally without feeling for the heroic gesture, but despite this, quietly heroic in her everyday struggle. Dr Relling too has his redeeming features and his weak spot. Above all, however, Hedvig—she is named after Ibsen's sister—is drawn with a tenderness that is rare in Ibsen's writing, with a deep understanding of the distinctive quality of her soul and her peculiar situation, her love, her dreams and her self-sacrifice. She is not idealized, but is a living poetic creation which shines all the brighter in its trivial surroundings. She possesses a tragic greatness which transcends the gloomy realities of the world in which she lives.

In the centre of this circle stands the wild duck. It is of decisive significance for the action, but at the same time it is a symbol. The basis for the symbolic value which Gregers Werle ascribes to it lies in the fact that it is not living in its natural environment, that it is wounded, and that in popular belief wounded wild ducks dive to the bottom and there hold on with their beaks. It thus becomes an image of the need wounded people have to cling to illusions. In this way Gregers associates it both with old Ekdal and with Hjalmar. It is tempting for a reader or audience to draw further parallels, with Molvik and Relling— and Gregers himself. The relationship to Hedvig is different, and this was probably the original one for the writer, for in the draft it says, '—Hedvig as wild duck—' For her the duck is primarily a living creature, strange and foreign, but she also feels a mysterious affinity with it, senses that they share a common fate, and dies the death that was intended for it. It is the same with the loft in which the duck lives. For old Ekdal it is a substitute for the open-air life he once led, for Hjalmar a refuge when everyday life becomes too difficult, and for Gregers an image of false reality, a caricature of the free life he knows from the Høydal forests. For Hedvig, however, it is something quite different. She does not seek refuge there from a greater and richer reality, instead she seeks and finds such a reality in the loft, in everything frightening and fascinating, death and life, 'churches and palaces and streets and big ships sailing on the sea'. All the strange things in there, in 'the depths of the sea', as she calls it, speaks to her childlike imagination, while at the same time she—in contrast to her father and grandfather—has the child's sharp and natural sense of reality, 'for of course it's only a loft'.

In this way the duck and the loft serve directly and indirectly to characterize the individuals and their various attitudes to life. They reflect a reality which is complex and rich in contrasts, and which the play opposes to a narrow, categorical moralism. They broaden the perspective, become a poetic, focal and ambiguous image of life as the majority of us live it in this imperfect world.

Many have seen *The Wild Duck* as an expression of a change in Ibsen's writing, as a reaction against the works immediately preceding it, a confrontation with the zeal for truth, and a resigned recognition of the necessity of illusions and the 'life lie'. But *The Wild Duck* does not invalidate Stockmann's criticism of the lies and deceit of those in power [in *An Enemy of the People*]. Here it is a matter of something else: the modest happiness of individuals wounded by life, set against alien ideals; and of their right to live their own lives, 'undisturbed by these confounded hawkers who keep banging on the doors of us poor folk with the claims of the ideal'. (pp. 136-44)

To the extent that *The Wild Duck* reflects a growing scepticism, and recognition of the mutability and relativity of truth, it continues a trend already established in Ibsen's earlier plays. The work may take a snipe at the abstract zeal for truth, but at the same time it extends the demand for truth in that it defends the claims of reality against ideals that are remote from life. Looked at in this way, *The Wild Duck* becomes part of the struggle whch realism and naturalism waged against the idealism which was a heritage from romanticism, and which in Ibsen reached a peak in *Brand*. At the same time, the profound psychological insights and the imaginative and poetic use of symbols point towards the 'neo-romanticism' and 'symbolism' of the 1890s.

Does *The Wild Duck* indicate that Ibsen has abandoned all idealism and lost all faith in people? Has he once and for all characterized all high aims, all ideal demands, as a camouflage for purely personal motivation? Is Gregers Werle the beginning of an ongoing exposure of the tragic 'hero'?

There are critics and scholars who believe this. Others maintain that even after *The Wild Duck,* Ibsen's main characters are inspired by high ideals, but that they often suffer defeat because—as so many before them—they have incurred guilt or betrayed themselves. Despite this, their downfall becomes a triumph for the ideals which they nevertheless believe in and which they affirm by their death.

A case can be made for both these points of view, but there is also a third, namely that the circumstances are more complicated, and that it changes from work to work and character to character, and is an expression of the continuous struggle and uninterrupted dialogue between opposing forces in the writer himself, those of doubt and faith, idealism and sceptical realism. (pp. 44-45)

> *Edvard Beyer, in his* Ibsen: The Man and His Work, *translated by Marie Wells, Souvenir Press (E & A) Ltd., 1978, 223 p.*

EVERT SPRINCHORN (essay date 1980)

[*In the following excerpt, Sprinchorn suggests that the character Gregers Werle gains a new dimension if a common critical premise—that in* The Wild Duck *Ibsen repudiated his earlier stand as a crusader for truth—is discarded. This interpretation of the play, Sprinchorn contends, allows Gregers to appear to the reader or audience only as Dr. Relling sees him, as an "obsessed truth-seeker."*]

It might be thought that dramatic characters when recreated by succeeding generations of actors would grow richer and more complicated, with subtle traits and telling acting points being invented by imaginative actors and passed on to others. But such is often not the case. One reason for this is that dramatic characters are rooted in their time, and when transported to another time they lose their fragrance and bouquet. Another reason is that great acting parts, with the enormous demands that they make, are constantly being reduced to the actor's and director's level of ability, intelligence, and knowledge. All too often actors do not do their homework properly. They settle for a characterisation that fits one of the stereotypes they are familiar with. (p. 119)

Both these reasons help account for the prevailing lacklustre way of acting Ibsen, especially in America. There is yet another reason, however, which applies especially to Ibsen. This has to do with the stereotype to which we have reduced Ibsen. Although we hear much about his power of characterisation, the fact is that he is usually played for his ideas. We go to see an Ibsen play because for once we want an intellectual evening in the theatre or because we wish to pay tribute to a man who helped us think the right things. Though actors and actresses may regard the big Ibsen parts as living characters, they are played as if they incarnated certain social or philosophical ideas. Nora and Hedda, for example, are nowadays usually represented essentially as women trapped in a man's world, while the other characters around them exist primarily to point up the theme or dominant idea.

This approach is certainly not wrong in itself, but to stress it, as nearly everyone does, is to distort the characters and warp the real drama of the plays. (pp. 119-20)

Gregers Werle in *The Wild Duck* is a uniquely Ibsenian creation, an idealist tormented by guilt, imposing himself where he is not wanted, and wreaking havoc where he thought he was bringing peace and harmony. Everyone knows that in writing *The Wild Duck* Ibsen was repudiating his former crusading self, and that in Gregers he wished to show the harm caused by a zealot bent on making the world live up to his idea of perfection. Even actors know this, or find it out soon enough, and inevitably they end up portraying a Gregers who fits this preconception of the part. And sure enough, everything the actor finds in the script appears to fit this preconception. Gregers is harmful: he blunders into the happy Ekdal home and destroys it. His influence is pernicious: little Hedwig commits suicide because of his mad talk. He is a fool: he idolises Hjalmar Ekdal, though it is obvious to every other adult in the play that he is a self-indulgent, lazy, pampered egotist. And to make certain that the audience recognises Gregers from the first moment as a hostile figure, Ibsen has made him repulsive in appearance, ugly of feature and physically clumsy. The portrait verges on caricature.

But suppose we were to examine Gregers without any preconceptions about Ibsen's ideas. We would see all that I have mentioned, but we would see much else besides. We would see a man who had an unhappy childhood, brought up in a house in which mother and father had nothing in common, who saw hate grow between his parents, saw his mother become a hopeless alcoholic, and, seeing his mother decline, came to hate his father. When he was an adolescent, his closest friend was Hjalmar Ekdal, a cheerful, handsome young man, coddled by the two aunts who reared him and loved by a father who shared with his boy many of the pleasures of life, taking the boy out hunting with him, for example; and those happy days in the forest are the ones father and son relive in their make-believe forest in the garret. Hjalmar had everything that Gregers dreamed of having. And then, when they were both about twenty years old, there occurred the business scandal that ruined the Ekdal family. His father's part in this affair made Gregers detest him all the more, and because of his own silence when his word might have helped the Ekdals, Gregers has ever since been weighed down with the burden of guilt. In trying to lighten that burden he became a crusader, a fanatic crying out to all and sundry, 'Ye shall know the truth and the truth shall make you free', believing that the cure his damaged soul needed must be good for all souls. Having been silent and untruthful at a crucial moment, he has since resolved to speak the truth, convinced that the momentary pain the truth may cost is as nothing compared to the years of anguish he has suffered for shirking the truth. This is the man who comes to the home of Hjalmar Ekdal and finds a god-given opportunity to redeem his own sin against the Ekdal family by telling Hjalmar, the idol of his youth, the truth about Hjalmar's wife and her involvement with old Werle. Monomaniacal and compulsive about the truth, especially about a truth that will allow him to atone for his silence years ago by exposing his father now as he should have exposed him then, Gregers never stops to consider the alternatives. He judges the situation from his own experience. The other side of the question is like the other side of the moon to him. He has never known the kind of happiness that comes when affection and fellow-feeling palliate the truth and make it bearable. His parents had no love for him. He will never be a husband or a father, and he knows it. He is not only psychically ill; he is also physically ill, suffering from some kind of nervous disease. At the end of the play, seeing that Hedwig has committed suicide, he is seized with convulsions (*'krampaktige rykninger'*).

All this may not make Gregers appealing, but it does help us to understand him, and understanding is not too far removed from sympathy. However, there is yet another quality in him that is slighted by the actors. Gregers is always presented as oblivious to the feelings of others. He is as gauche emotionally as he is physically. Yet it is Gregers who of all the people in the drama strikes the deepest chords in the child Hedwig. In the most haunting scene in the play Gregers penetrates Hedwig's secret world, speaks of the 'briny depths of the sea', and forges a bond with her that has the strength of absolute faith. She is decidedly the most sympathetic and endearing person in the play. She senses something in Gregers that the others do not. In order to make the outcome convincing what she senses in him must be sensed by the audience, too. That is why it is incumbent on the actor to elevate Gregers in this scene far beyond the usual conception of him as a crazy, demented fool, which is how Dr Relling sees him, and to make him, at least for the moment, a man of spiritual insight whose concerns are with man's highest endeavours. Dr Relling, who believes in the necessity of the life-lie, the need that people have for illusions about themselves, may understand ordinary mortals, but it is Gregers who understands extraordinary beings.

In the scene with Hedwig, Gregers is not some demon casting an evil spell on the child. The scene is infused with all the pain and anguish that Gregers has experienced in life, all his loneliness, and with all the special kind of understanding that he has gained from the unhappiness that he has known. Unless this positive aspect of Gregers is brought out by the actor, something vital to the play will be lost. The scene with Hedwig constitutes the preparation for Hedwig's drastic act at the end of the play. If Gregers is not made fascinating in the way that prophets are fascinating, the workings of Hedwig's mind will be only half comprehensible. If Gregers is seen by the audience only as Dr Relling sees him, and that is the usual way of looking at him, *The Wild Duck* dwindles into a thesis play, Relling is reduced to being the author's mouthpiece, and Gregers appears as only the husk of a living person.

Because actors and directors have failed to explore the depths of Ibsen's characters, we are seeing only a part of the plays that Ibsen wrote, and perhaps only a part of the plays that our grandparents saw. Though there has been a general improvement in acting, our actors and directors have lost some of the insight and instinctive understanding that an earlier generation may have had, since they were closer in time and spirit to the original figures. To regain that lost ground and advance beyond it, it is necessary to look at these characters freshly and to put into the stage representation of them all the apparent inconsistencies, all the convolutions of thought, all the layers of emotional life that lie in the scripts of the plays. Actors now give us the emerging feminist in Nora and the crazy idealist in Gregers. But how much more interesting these characters would be, and how much more controversial and stimulating the plays would become if the actors presented not only the feminist in Nora but also the hysterical woman who is willing to leave husband and children in order to find out whether she alone or the whole world is right; not only the obsessed truth-seeker in Gregers but also the wretchedly unhappy man who can only give meaning to his own life by vicariously living Hjalmar's. Ideas are an essential element in Ibsen's plays, but ideas are made by people and transmitted by people. 'The actor's business', said Bernard Shaw in reviewing one of Ibsen's plays, 'is not to supply an idea with a sounding board, but with a credible, simple, and natural human being to utter it when its time comes and not before. (pp. 126-29)

Evert Sprinchorn, "Ibsen and the Actors," in Ibsen and the Theatre: The Dramatist in Production, *edited by Errol Durbach, New York University Press, 1980, pp. 118-30.*

JOHN ORR   (essay date 1981)

[*The following excerpt is from Orr's* Tragic Drama and Modern Society: Studies in the Social and Literary Theory of Drama from 1870 to the Present. *In the first section of the book, which is devoted to "The Achievement of Henrik Ibsen," Orr contends that the most recent major development in the history of world drama is the transition from heroic tragedy to "the more diffuse tragic drama of modern civilisation," typified by the bourgeois or social problem plays of Ibsen. In the following excerpt, Orr interprets* The Wild Duck *not as a simple renunciation of Ibsen's earlier idealism, but rather as a presentation of the conflicts between individuals who live by different idealistic principles.*]

The heroic victims of **The Wild Duck** are less privileged, more oppressed than Mrs Alving and Oswald in **Ghosts**. But the point at which oppression ends and heroism begins is impossible to detect. Like **Ghosts**, the main dimension of conflict in the play is generational. But not only is it a conflict between generations, it is a conflict within generations. On the one hand there is the conflict between Werle and Gregers, his son, and between Ekdal and his daughter, Hedvig. On the other hand there is the perennial feud between Werle and Ekdal and the tragic confrontation of Gregers and Hedvig. One dimension is superimposed upon the other to make the whole question of victimisation and revolt immeasurably more complex than it was in **Ghosts**. Unlike Ibsen's previous work, this is not a story of one family but of two, and this disrupts the previous pattern of familial integration. (p. 15)

The drama revolves around Gregers' quest to unite his desire for independence with the emancipation of the Ekdal family from his father's clutches. This mutual liberation is not merely materially beneficial to both parties in Gregers' eyes, but also moral proof of an incorruptible courage. The play shows us how, conceived totally in the abstract, his moral crusade comes to grief. Yet this highly abstract and ideal process operates through a concrete material symbol. Gregers' 'claim of the ideal' is obsessively focused on a living being, the wounded pet of a deprived child, on the 'reality' of the wild duck. The play is not, therefore, an exercise in symbolism as some critics have suggested but an exploration of the dialectic interplay of ideal and reality. The wild duck is symbolic of a wider reality. But it is so only by virtue of being a particular kind of bird wounded by the gun of one person and lovingly cherished by another. And here Ibsen introduces in a contemporary realist vein the theme he had represented poetically and historically in **Brand**. That theme is the vast contrast and tension between wilderness and civilisation.

The wounding of the wild duck by Haakon Werle's shotgun points to the ambiguous role of pacification possessed by modern civilisation. The act of pacification is also an act of conquest, the brutal conquest of man over nature. The taking of the winged duck into captivity by the Ekdals is seemingly a more humane version of this same process—of turning the bird into a domestic pet doted on by a child. But this apparent bourgeois domesticity conceals a deeper motive. It is a nostalgic attempt to preserve something of the bird's 'wildness' even in its wounded state. The attachment is not idyllic. It is an attachment to a living being which contains something of a wild and primitive nature. The bird belongs to a natural wilderness which is al-ready being transformed irreversibly by human development. (pp. 15-16)

The loft is both the 'space' of nature and the means of imprisoning it. In theatrical terms, the loft is an extraordinary device, and quite unique. It is not merely an appendage to Ekdal's studio. It is very much like an appendage to the stage itself. It calls into question those dimensions of bounded space which Ibsen seems to have accepted in most of his work as a necessary feature of the naturalist stage. The stage directions call for it to be 'long and irregularly shaped', 'full of dark nooks and crannies'. It too is a bounded space, a room onstage. But lacking the symmetry and accessibility of Ibsen's typical rooms, it is a jumble lying in shadow. Here, bereft of contact with nature, even with the earth beneath their feet, the Ekdals cultivate their strange captivity of nature. But it is nature as artifice where old Ekdal 'hunts' rabbits and Hedvig lovingly tends to the wounded duck.

In **The Wild Duck**, the loft represents the tragic space lacking in **Ghosts**, the dramatic space of the play's tragic denouement. It is so, however, precisely by being a reflexive illustration of Ibsen's theatrical self-constraint. Since the stage could no more mirror natural wilderness in **Peer Gynt** or **Brand** than it could in **Ghosts**, the loft as a theatrical device illuminates the illusory nature of dramatic space itself. Yet within the context of that illusion, its spatial enclosure presents us with a vivid image of the fragile boundary between nature and civilisation. Wilderness lies beyond the stage but at the same time is incorporated within it. The way in which it becomes crucial to the fate of the two families, the tragic sociation to which it gives rise, has often been overlooked. The wild duck is not important as a symbol in a loft. The loft itself, and the imprisoned animals it contains, are an integral part of the processes of sociation we see on the foreground of the stage. For the hope and joy they inspire in the Ekdal family are living proof to Gregers Werle of the kind of human illusion which he regards as poisonous and wishes to destroy.

Gregers' crusade to transform the life of his father's demoralised victims has been the most controversial issue in the play. The tragic outcome of Gregers' misguided plan has been seen by Shaw as irrefutable evidence of Ibsen's dislike of idealism as such. From this viewpoint, Gregers is a fanatical zealot who, in hoping to save people's lives merely succeeds in destroying them. This is undoubtedly true, and is the key to the play. But the process by which this comes about has been misrepresented. Following Shaw, it has been the custom to attribute to Ibsen a tendentious attack on all idealism as harmful to human life in general. Relling, when he attacks Werle at the end of the play so bitterly, has been seen as the mouthpiece of the author himself: 'Oh, life would be all right if we didn't have to put up with damn creditors who keep pestering us with the demands of their ideals.' But it is much too simplistic to reduce the play to this kind of formula and Shaw unwittingly did much damage in presenting one aspect of the play as its total meaning, and by extension, as the central feature of Ibsen's drama as a whole. The nature of idealism in **The Wild Duck**, as in **Rosmersholm**, is complex and problematical. The conflict is not between idealism and commonsense, but between different forms of idealism and between conflicting views about the material necessities of life.

There is an important duality here. Gregers and his unintended victims each have their ideal view of the world, and at the same time, a view of their own material situation within that world. But in neither case is there a binding unity between the material and the ideal. Not only do these views contradict each other, they are internally contradictory. The picture is one of external conflict and internal division. In his myopic crusade, Gregers preys on the contradictions of the Ekdal family without firstly recognising his own. The desire he expresses to Hedvig of owning a dog which would plunge into the lake and rescue the wounded duck from 'the bottom of the deep' where it has taken refuge, is inherently idealistic. But as an assault on 'the bottom of the deep' which Hedvig so reveres, it is also a crusade *against* an ideal. (pp. 17-18)

The play presents us not merely with a moral crusade but with a clash of idealisms in which Gregers blatantly ignores how much the retreat of the Ekdals is due to their past humiliations and reduced material circumstances. He also overlooks the possibility that in trying to rescue Hedvig, like the dog plunging down to drag the duck to the surface, he is complementing his father's original transgression in wounding it—the transgression of civilisation against nature.

His mission to liberate Hjalmar Ekdal is again indicative of his peculiar blindness to human experience. Whimsical and tyrannical by turns, Ekdal is a pathetic defeated figure who wounds his family whenever he feels threatened. Instead of turning Ekdal's hatred towards Haakon Werle, Gregers merely succeeds in turning it inwards onto Hedvig. The idealism then becomes suspect, not based on general principles but highly personalised. He wants to liberate specific individuals and, doing so, succumbs to the temptation of wielding power over them. Hence the warning which Ibsen sounded in his notes for the play: 'Liberation consists in securing for individuals the right to free themselves.' Gregers does not offer a vision of hope. He humiliates Ekdal and Hedvig by increasing their pain. And he unwittingly changes sides in the generational conflict. Wishing to use Ekdal as a weapon against his father, he ends up encouraging his father's victim to victimise his own daughter. In hoping to avenge one form of patriarchal tyranny, he merely encourages another. The irony of this is not lost on the audience either. For during the course of the play Haakon Werle is the one person who does not experience failure or defeat. His son's idealism is never really a threat to him.

Gregers' ideals originate in self-deception and end in catastrophe. But this does not provide proof of the pernicious nature of social ideals. Rather it points to the dangers of their deformation, and ultimately of their betrayal. Gregers' action complements his father's wounding of the wild duck by prompting a psychological parallel—Ekdal's wounding of Hedvig's heart through his rejection of her. Her growing blindness which may be inherited from Werle is significant not only as a physical ailment but also as a metaphor of victimisation. (pp. 19-20)

Hedvig's fate sets the pattern for Ibsen's subsequent tragic drama—that of suicide. It is suicide as a response to unendurable social circumstance. As a victim Hedvig becomes heroic through the act of taking her own life. The equivocations of Gregers and Ekdal at the end merely enlarge rather than diminish the cathartic effect. The loss is felt to be irreparable. And it is tragic solely through Gregers' intervention. Gregers is a vital link between Oswald Alving and Eilert Loevborg, representing one form of intellectual revolt against bourgeois society. But unlike either of the others, he is the catalyst of tragedy not its victim. His revolt works only in conjunction with what it destroys, namely another form of opposition, mute and residual, which he never comes to understand. And it is the latter which creates the tragic space of the drama, a space

which the single dichotomy of intellectual and bourgeois is powerless to accomplish. (p. 21)

John Orr, "The Achievement of Henrik Ibsen," in his Tragic Drama and Modern Society: Studies in the Social and Literary Theory of Drama from 1870 to the Present, *Barnes & Noble Books, 1981, pp. 3-56.*

ERROL DURBACH   (essay date 1982)

[*In the essay from which the following excerpt is taken, Durbach examines the significance of the death of a child, which occurs in Ibsen's dramas* Brand, The Wild Duck, *and* Little Eyolf. *Durbach condemns the deaths of Brand's child in* Brand *and of Hedvig in* The Wild Duck *as meaningless sacrifices inspired by adults serving false ideals.*]

Except for John Whiting's adolescent boy in *No Why* who in an eloquent silence asserts his integrity at the cost of his life, there are few other children in drama whose death is as painful as Hedvig's. Ruskin's formula for lucrative Victorian fiction—'When at a loss, kill a child'—is impertinent, as Shaw maintained, to the shock of Ibsen's child-deaths, which, even in drawing upon a Romantic tradition, expunge all sentimentality from the genre. Hedvig dies in a world which cannot appreciate the significance of her life nor understand the implications of her suicide. But the tradition is clearly evoked: with the death of the Romantic child, innocence and integrity pass from the world, and those who remain lose forever those intimations of immortality to which they had been blind. (p. 79)

[Gregers Werle's] sense of the fallen world, of which the Ekdal household is a living paradigm, expresses itself in the by-now familiar imagery of nausea, disgust and dirt—a distortion of reality into perverse symbolic meanings. Old Werle speaks in metaphors of those human failures who 'plunge into the depths' and never rise to rehabilitate themselves; and Old Ekdal later elaborates on the literal phenomena from which the metaphor derives: the instinct of wild ducks, when wounded, to plunge into the depths of the sea, entangle themselves in weeds and 'fandenskap'—the devil's own mess—and so perish. Gregers, typically, ignores distinctions between metaphor and fact, extrapolates from the literal meaning of 'sea-depths' to envision an image of the abyss in which man is mired in devilry, and then adds his own offensive tropes to an already grotesquely inappropriate analogue of the Ekdal household: 'en forgiftet sump', 'en snikende sott' 'sumpluft' and 'stank' . . . a poisoned swamp, an insidious plague and a stinking bog. He smells corruption everywhere. . . . Ironically, however, it is Gregers who always seems to generate those very conditions which nauseate him. *His* room stinks, filled with the smoke and muck of an ineptly doused fire. Gina, with some justification, calls him a pig; and Relling identifies him as the carrier of a plague which will eventually infect the whole household far more insidiously than the corruption of their fallen natures.

Gregers must save mankind from its condition—that is his mission, already begun (with no success) among the labourers at Höidal. Whether his claim of the ideal originated in a social conscience, or as a personal compulsion, remains obscure. His redemption of the Ekdals, however, assumes the most dangerous aspects of an obsession, a form of self-administered therapy to assuage his guilty conscience, to save Hjalmar from the evil manipulative control of Old Werle, and transform the fallen world of lies and illusion into an effulgence of truth and reality. In a gesture of moral reparation he will make good the sins of his father and restore innocence and purity to life. He puts the worst possible light on his father's charitable treatment of the Ekdals—infected, as Old Werle suspects, with his dead mother's exaggerated sense of betrayal and her hysterical suspicions of infidelity. 'Jeg er ikke overspent' . . . 'I am not neurotic', he snaps at his father in the very process of incriminating him in the foulness he sees enveloping the life of his friend; and he gives vent to the same vehemently denied condition in a perverse interpretation of some extremely ambiguous facts. Like so many of the inhabitants of this dark and obscure world, Gregers is blind. He sees, as Ibsen implies, only with the clouded and impaired vision of his mother. And this psychic deficiency is enough to disqualify him as the light-bearer and redeemer to a benighted and fallen humanity.

In no other Ibsen play does the delicate fabric of life, the reality upon which the transcendentalist operates, recede so far into the nebulous and the equivocal. In searching for truth, Gregers exhumes the past with a relentlessness typical of Ibsen's conventional plot-structures—but all he reveals is ambiguity, a world devoid of absolutes, which angels might well fear to interpret. The tone of the play is immediately established by the subdued lighting of the opening scene and the small-talk of the servants, where each attempt to elicit information is deflected into qualified conjecture or non-committal possibility: 'Fan' vet', 'Kanskje det' . . .—'The devil only knows'. 'Well, maybe.' That is as far as it goes. To take it any further is to tread on thin ice. Old Werle may (or may not) have ruined his partner, may (or may not) have betrayed his wife while she lived, may (or may not) have foisted a discarded mistress onto a gullible young man. Evidence points with equal conviction to opposing points of view, and proof becomes both impertinent and hazardous to substantiate. . . . [A] view of life as a complex of possibilities, where reality and truth have no absolute value apart from the context in which they function, and where men make reality work by accepting all value, all conventions and all relationships as creative illusions—this, it seems to me, is what Ibsen meant by the 'life-lie' or, more aptly, 'det stimulerende prinsipp' . . .—the principle of inspiration and stimulation in life. With his crass appropriation of narrow truths and his reduction of all evidence to a preconceived notion of evil, Gregers smashes through the delicate webs of accommodation and the thin-spun skeins of life only to reveal—with appalling consequences—the 'lie' that holds the whole fabric together. It is, of course, the child, life itself in all its mystery, who finally stands exposed to the smashing and the paring away of protective illusion. At the heart of the equivocal universe there is only Hedvig, conferring the illusion of 'family' upon a union which may (or may not) conform to a legitimate definition of the family unit. Like the mysterious woman in Pirandello's *Right You Are If You Think So,* her identity in the Ekdal household may (or may not) be ambiguous; but, in so far as they believe her to be their child, she sustains the illusion of a happy marriage more creatively and vitally than the various other 'lies' which fantasticate reality out of all existence.

Perhaps Hedvig was born in wedlock, perhaps not. Old Werle's complicity in arranging Hjalmar's marriage for dubious reasons may be mere neurotic surmise. The devil only knows, for both Old Werle and Hjalmar, on equally feasible grounds, may be Hedvig's blood-father. Her incipient blindness is inconclusive evidence either way: there is blindness in the medical histories of both families. And Gina is bound to admit, with alarming candour, when pressed to name the father of her child: 'I don't know.' What does it matter, after all? What is the relevance of *proof* to the reality of their lives? To search it out, in the

name of some ideal, is madness. Hedvig retains, to the end, her mystery as one of literature's 'unknowable' children, one who—like Euripides's Ion—sustains a marriage through creative illusion. (pp. 87-9)

Brutally indifferent to the subtleties of experience and fatally incapable of judging people, Gregers hastens to indict his father as evil incarnate—thus ascribing to himself the role of man's redeemer from the foulness and deceit of Old Werle's creating. Convinced that Hjalmar's home is built upon a pernicious lie, and mistaking Hjalmar himself as an innocent eligible for the kingdom of the ideal, he imagines that by reconstituting Paradise he will enable the Ekdals to exist in an epiphany of revealed truth. He bursts into the domestic idyll of their home—by no means an 'ideal' marriage, but one invested with much tenderness and underscored by the harmonies of Hjalmar's flute—and the consequences of his intrusion are the destruction of the family in the name of redemption, and the death of the child on the pretext of sacrifice. With a grotesque application of an allegorical idea, he enacts the function of the hunting-dog who rescues the wild duck from its entanglement in corruption (failing, typically, to realise the danger implicit in the allegory: the amazingly clever dog cripples the bird for life). He dedicates his life to this mission of redemption; and his language, accordingly, modulates from execration against the fall to visions of transcendent sublimity in which the consequences of the fall are reversed through revelation, confrontation and self-analysis. A crude version of psychiatry is here invested with a series of pseudo-religious imperatives. After infecting Hjalmar with the cant phrases of idealism and the image of his marriage as a swamp of deceit, the truth-telling analyst merely devastates where he hopes to cure. His view of reality utterly fails to transform his subject's bitter experience into sublimity. . . . The end of Gregers's great redemptive mission is, as he puts it, 'grunnlegger et sant ekteskap' . . .—to lay the foundations of a 'true' marriage. But he is blind to the irony, which Hjalmar draws to his attention, that the exemplar and paradigm of such a union is the match between his father and Mrs. Sørby. In fact, Gregers's strenuous attempt to create the conditions for a Paradisal marriage for the Ekdals is rendered ridiculous by the potential for just such a marriage in the 'fallen' world of Old Werle—one based upon compassion, complete honesty, mutual confidence and trust. And, in trying to enforce these values—unnecessarily—on Hjalmar, Gregers undermines the very structure he seeks to fortify. Not only is Hjalmar poor material for Gregers's therapy, but the 'lies' and the 'corruption' which the gullible Hjalmar accepts as gospel truth must inevitably lead to a radical questioning of Hedvig's legitimacy, if Gregers's insinuations are pushed to their final conclusion. The events of Act IV lead relentlessly to that moment when Hjalmar will leap to his outrageous assumption about the child's *right* to live under *his* roof.

It is a simple step from Hjalmar's rejection of the over-symbolised duck as the evil Old Werle has imposed upon his life to the rejection of Hedvig as Werle's bastard child; and the consequences of accepting Gregers's crude analogies follow with catastrophic inevitability. The purblind eyes, the deed of gift, the dark suggestion of Gina's relationship with Werle, which she later corroborates—all the equivocal evidence, distorted by the literal application to life of an inept symbol system, provokes the histrionic self-pitying cry of the self-styled cuckold: 'Jeg har ikke noe barn!' . . . , 'I have no child'—as if illegitimacy had the power to eliminate the quality of a deeply affectionate relationship, as if fourteen years of father-daughter bonding could be obviated by a biological nicety. He thrusts the grief-stricken child away from him as the fraud that makes his house uninhabitable, the lie that has brought his home down in ruins, and he stalks out of the room even as Hedvig clings to him. 'Se på barnet, Ekdal! Se på barnet!' . . . , Gina cries after him—'Look at the child, look at the child.' But no one in Ibsen ever looks at the *child,* at the living, suffering reality. They see only symbols and emblems and analogies. Or, like Gregers, they see child redeemers who, in some obscure ritual of sacrifice, can effect the hoped-for transfiguration of fallen mankind. The master-stroke of Gregers's pseudo-religion is to impose upon the child's despair a solution to the family's dilemma, an absurd Kierkegaardian proof requiring a violation of the child's humanity to save the ruined household. She must now kill what most she loves.

The wild duck. It would be tempting to say nothing at all about this most discussed of creatures and so recognise it for what it is—an object lesson gratuitous symbolising and the most outstanding instance in Ibsen of the counter-Romantic error: the failure to correlate literal and referential concepts with their abstract and non-referential analogues. The wild duck, as Hedvig insists, is not more than that: 'a *real* wild bird', . . . a child's pet defined in careful ornithological detail. Ibsen, at the height of his power as a symbolist, assigns no portentous symbolic value whatever to the duck. He merely presents it as the vehicle for the ridiculous duck-symbolism of Gregers, for whom all surface reality is a system of transcendental referents. Language, symbolism and the ambiguity of images are the very elements of tragedy in this play, as they are in *Othello,* where to assign a symbolic value to a domestic object (such as a handkerchief) and then pursue a course of action on the assumption that the symbolic and the real are identical is to destroy the world. Semantic confusion, the terrible gulf between two versions of the same image, occurs whenever Hedvig and Gregers speak to each other—as when they both refer to the attic in sea metaphors with radically different implications. And so it is with the duck. There exists between Hedvig and her pet a delicate, sympathetic affinity—as a child might project onto her doll her own most intimate sense of her condition. The loneliness, the isolation, the essentially 'unknowable' and secret identity of the child are the qualities she sees in her pet. But to Gregers, the duck symbolises the Ekdals' maimed condition and their state of servile compromise to the illusions which deprive them of light and truth. That the reality does not sustain the abstract value imposed upon it is irrelevant to Gregers, and he begins gradually to infect the child's perception of her world. (pp. 90-3)

It is difficult to infer, with any degree of certainty, exactly what Gregers means by 'sacrifice' or how he imagines that Hedvig's gesture will set the world to rights. Perhaps, in his folly, he imagines that shooting the duck will annihilate the spirit of failure and corruption of which it is the symbolic analogue. But, more to the point, there is some ill-defined conviction that a myth of salvation may be set in operation by the sacrifice of a cherished being to some obscure *telos.* In rebuking Hedvig for thinking better of killing the duck, his language reverts to the transcendentalism of Kierkegaardian theology: 'Jeg kan se på Dem at det ikke er fullbrakt' . . .— 'I can see on your face that it has not been accomplished.' As both Ansten Anstensen and John Northam point out, the phrase 'det er fullbrakt' is a direct quotation from John 19:30, a translation into Norwegian of Christ's *consummatum est.* Gregers's intentions become somewhat less obscure if no less preposterous; and with fanatical insistence he tries to break down Hedvig's reluctance to enact his scenario of redemption, over-

whelming her with pseudo-religious imperatives to manifest 'det sanne, glade, modige offersinn' . . .—the true, joyful, courageous spirit of sacrifice. And, when the shot eventually rings out, Gregers, in ecstatic anticipation of the redeeming miracle, instructs the Ekdals in the significance of the ritual. Gina weeps, and Hjalmar responds to the notion of the child's sacrifice in strains of sentimental forgiveness and visions of a new life—which all seem to affirm the efficacy of Gregers's sacrificial myth: 'Jeg viste det,' he says, 'gjennem barnet ville opprettelsen skje' . . .—'I knew it; it is through the child that redemption will come to pass.' He might be speaking of the Christ-child or the Isaac of the Kierkegaardian parable. The *real* child lies dead in the attic, rejected again and again by her father, until finally driven to her sacrificial death-in-love to restore his affection and the harmony of the family. For her, as for the other deluded Romantics in Ibsen's world, there are no longer boundaries between the literal and the metaphorical, between the real and the symbolic. Hedvig performs in *fact* what for Gregers has been a *parable.* But the myth of Isaac has been tragically inverted. It is the child who now assumes the place of the sacrificial animal, while the Abraham for whom this propitiatory offering is made strikes a series of declamatory poses which makes nonsense of the child's gesture.

The final moments of the play are given over entirely to absurdity—not the positive Kierkegaardian absurdity which Gregers claims to have achieved, but its anti-type: *galskap.* Old Ekdal makes his appearance in full military regalia, a comic-pathetic actor of his alcoholic life-lie, whose illusions are impervious to all attempts at symbolic therapy. Tragi-comic pandemonium breaks loose when the child is discovered; and then there follows the farce of her obsequies presided over by a drunken priest and his congregants, all seeking refuge from the implications of this grotesque mistake in the clichés of maudlin religiosity. The most desperate defence against *galskap,* however, is Gregers's insistence on the child's death as a sacrament, against all evidence to the contrary: 'Hedvig has not died in vain', he proclaims, mistaking Hjalmar's sentimental remorse for the recovery of a noble dignity. . . . The genius of *The Wild Duck,* it seems to me, is that it clarifies more articulately than almost any other play of the period one of the central impulses of European Romanticism—the attempt to introduce value into the world by saving it in the name of some ideal authority. More than this, it compels a wonderful sense of the frailty and beauty of life and its vulnerability to the dangers of the redemptive impulse. And it implies a solution to the Romantic dilemma of rediscovering value which, with modern hindsight, anticipates the basic premises of existential thought. (pp. 94-6)

There can be no ideal solutions to the human predicament in the world of *The Wild Duck,* no teleological absolutes to sanction the suspension of man's ethical nature. The individual self, each according to his need, must find the 'stimulating principle' which restores value to the world and affirms the nature of that selfhood. In the final analysis, and despite the stringent counter-Romanticism of the play's tone and vision, Ibsen asserts in *The Wild Duck* the ultimate conviction of Romanticism: 'that a metaphysic with its derived value-system cannot be absolute, that the only absolute, at best, is the *drive* to a metaphysic, the *drive* to order and value, never to a particular order or a particular set of values.' Peckham's description of the Romantic position might also serve to define, at its most stimulating and creative, Ibsen's idea of the 'life-lie'— that antidote to cosmic meaninglessness and futility which we recognise, in the twentieth century, as the existential hero's response to absurdity. (pp. 96-7)

> *Errol Durbach, in his* "Ibsen the Romantic:" *Analogues of Paradise in the Later Plays,* The Macmillan Press Ltd., *1982, 213 p.*

ADDITIONAL BIBLIOGRAPHY

Bradbrook, M. C. *Ibsen the Norwegian: A Revaluation.* London: Chatto & Windus, 1948, 150 p.*
  Places Ibsen in relation to contemporary European dramatists. The critic also traces early literary influences on Ibsen.

Brandes, Georg. "Henrik Ibsen." In his *Eminent Authors of the Nineteenth Century: Literary Portraits,* translated by Rasmus B. Anderson, pp. 405-60. New York: Thomas Y. Crowell, 1886.
  Early biographical and critical study of Ibsen by a major Danish critic. Brandes was one of the earliest literary commentators to understand and promulgate Ibsen's drama.

Chamberlin, John S. "Ibsen's 'Vildanden' in Relation to Georg Brandes's 'Gustave Flaubert' and Flaubert's 'Un Coeur Simple'." *Scandinavica* 14, No. 1 (May 1975): 37-43.*
  Theorizes that Brandes's "Gustave Flaubert" and Flaubert's "Un Coeur Simple" were literary sources for *The Wild Duck.*

Crompton, Louis. "The 'Demonic' in Ibsen's *The Wild Duck.*" *The Tulane Drama Review* 4, No. 1 (September 1959): 96-103.
  Contends that the function of the 'demonic' character, a traditional Norwegian literary figure, is to underscore the irony in *The Wild Duck,* since the characters are victimized by self-delusion rather than demonic influence.

Ditsky, John. "Ibsen's Myopic Calvary: *The Wild Duck.*" In his *The Onstage Christ: Studies in the Persistence of a Theme,* pp. 9-21. New York: Barnes & Noble, 1980.
  Calls the character of Hedvig a symbolic Christ-figure, and interprets the characters of Hjalmar Ekdal and Gregers Werle as false or anti-Christs.

Downs, Brian W. *Ibsen: The Intellectual Background.* Cambridge: Cambridge University Press, 1946, 187 p.
  An account of the artistic conventions and historic events that influenced Ibsen's dramas.

Franc, Miriam Alice. *Ibsen in England.* Boston: Four Seas Co., 1919, 195 p.
  Study of the popular and critical reactions to Ibsen's plays as they first appeared in England.

Gassner, John. "Ibsen, the Viking of the Drama." In his *Masters of the Drama,* pp. 354-85. New York: Dover Publications, 1945.
  Biographical and critical examination of Ibsen's life and work. Gassner calls *The Wild Duck* less an anti-idealist tract than a tragedy of human frailty, maintaining that the depiction of Gregers Werle as a psychopathological idealist diminishes the play's anti-idealist elements.

Gosse, Edmund W. *Henrik Ibsen.* New York: Charles Scribner's Sons, 1908, 244 p.
  Biography of Ibsen, with plot outlines and character descriptions from the plays.

Grain, Frances. "The Interpersonal Psychology of Some of Ibsen's Later Plays." *Ibsenaarbok* (1974): 127-47.
  Study of the interrelationships of the characters in *The Wild Duck,* focusing upon the way in which each interprets his own and others' roles.

Holtan, Orley I. "*The Wild Duck* and *Rosmersholm:* The Re-Entry of the Mythic." In his *Mythic Patterns in Ibsen's Last Plays,* pp. 35-63. Minneapolis: University of Minnesota Press, 1970.

Examines the "mythic impact" of such elements as the loft, the wild duck, and the "ironic sacrifice-redemption" pattern in the plot of *The Wild Duck.*

Huneker, James. "Henrik Ibsen." In his *Iconoclasts: A Book of Dramatists,* pp. 1-138. New York: Charles Scribner's Sons, 1905.
  Biographical and critical overview of Ibsen's life and career. The critic examines *An Enemy of the People, The Wild Duck,* and *Rosmersholm* as a trilogy linked by common themes involving the role of the ideal in everyday life. Huneker criticizes the blend of tragedy and comedy in *The Wild Duck,* finding that each element appears in an inappropriate place.

Ibsen, Bergliot. *The Three Ibsens: Memories of Henrik Ibsen, Suzannah Ibsen and Sigurd Ibsen.* London: Hutchinson & Co., 1951, 184 p.
  Reminiscences of the Ibsen family by Ibsen's daughter-in-law.

Jaeger, Henrik. *Henrik Ibsen: A Critical Biography.* Translated by William Morton Payne. Rev. ed. 1901. Reprint. New York: Hasken House Publishers, 1972, 320 p.
  Early biography recounting critical reaction to Ibsen's plays.

Jameson, Storm. "Ibsen." In her *Modern Drama in Europe,* pp. 70-109. New York: Harcourt, Brace & Howe, 1920.
  Characterizes *The Wild Duck* as "the greatest tragi-comedy in the drama of modernity" and finds that the play's tragic ending accentuates the pervasive humor of the work.

Jorgenson, Theodore. "Illusions of a Wounded Humanity." In his *Henrik Ibsen: A Study in Art and Personality,* pp. 373-91. Northfield, Minn.: St. Olaf College Press, 1945.
  Critical examination of the characters, actions, and symbols in *The Wild Duck.*

Koht, Halvdan. *The Life of Ibsen.* Translated by Ruth Lima McMahon and Hanna Astrup Larsen. 2 vols. New York: W. W. Norton & Co., 1931.
  Noncritical biography.

——. "Shakespeare and Ibsen." *Journal of English and German Philology* 44, No. 1 (January 1945): 79-86.*
  Traces the influence of Shakespeare's plays on Ibsen's career.

Lucas, F. L. *The Drama of Ibsen and Strindberg.* New York: Macmillan Co., 1962, 484 p.*
  Contains a biographical sketch of Ibsen and an analysis of his character. This study also includes plot synopses and analyses of the major plays, and draws correlations between the action of the dramas and events in Ibsen's life.

Mendel, Sydney. "Revolt Against the Father: The Adolescent Hero in *Hamlet* and *The Wild Duck.*" *Essays in Criticism* XIV, No. 2 (April 1964): 171-78.*
  Comparison of the character of Gregers Werle from *The Wild Duck* with that of Hamlet. Both are seen as archetypes of the adolescent hero in revolt against the omnipotent father.

Meyer, Michael. *Ibsen: A Biography.* New York: Doubleday & Co., 1971, 865 p.
  Biography designed to supply information about Ibsen's years as a theater director and about his old age, periods Meyer believes were neglected in Halvdan Koht's earlier biography.

Môri, Mitsuya. "Ibsen's Dramatic Irony." *Ibsenaarboken* 11 (1970-71): 118-39.
  Interprets the wild duck not as a symbol, but rather as "a sort of mirror in which we see the reverse image of every character."

Northam, John Richard. "*The Wild Duck.*" In his *Ibsen's Dramatic Method,* pp. 86-107. London: Faber and Faber, 1953.
  Close comparison of two existing early drafts of *The Wild Duck,* together with various other extant notes, with the final draft of the play.

——. "*The Wild Duck.*" In his *Ibsen: A Critical Study,* pp. 113-46. Cambridge: Cambridge University Press, 1973.

Lengthy chronological plot description, an assessment of characterization, and examination of the symbolism in *The Wild Duck*.

Scandinavian Studies: Henrik Ibsen Issue 51, No. 4 (Autumn 1979): 343-519.
Contains articles by Einer Haugen, Evert Sprinchorn, and Yvonne L. Sandstroem, among others.

Shaw, Bernard. "Ibsen Triumphant." In his *Our Theatres in the Nineties, Vol. III*, pp. 136-44. London: Constable and Co., 1932.*
High praise for *The Wild Duck* in particular and Ibsen's career in general—in an article originally published in 1897 in *The Saturday Review*.

Symons, Arthur. "Henrik Ibsen." In his *Figures of Several Centuries*, pp. 222-67. London: Constable and Co., 1916.
Study of Ibsen's character as revealed in the published volumes of his letters, along with a brief summary of his work.

Tennant, P.F.D. "A Critical Study of the Composition of Ibsen's *Vildanden*." EDDA XXXIV (1934): 327-54.
Finds that the wild duck is an organic symbol "used as a dramatic catalyst" responsible for the emotional conflicts within the play. Brian W. Downs (see excerpt dated 1950) maintains that the duck is a "detachable" symbol not necessary to the structure of the play, while Tennant finds that "the wild duck is the chief protagonist of the play."

Trilling, Lionel. "The Wild Duck: Henrik Ibsen, 1828-1906." In his *Prefaces to the Experience of Literature*, pp. 22-7. New York: Harcourt Brace Jovanovich, 1967.
Interprets the "message" of *The Wild Duck* to be "that it is wicked for one person to seek to impose upon another a greater amount of reality than can comfortably be borne."

Watts, C. T. "The Uncommon Catastrophe in Ibsen's *Vildanden*." *Scandinavica* 12, No. 2 (November 1973): 137-41.
Theorizes that the final action of the play *The Wild Duck* is the unseen, offstage suicide of Haakon Ekdal.

Wellek, René. "Masterpieces of Realism and Naturalism: Ibsen, *The Wild Duck*." In *The Continental Edition of World Masterpieces*, edited by Maynard Mack, pp. 1439-43. New York: W. W. Norton, 1956.
Offers a straightforward reading of *The Wild Duck* as Ibsen's repudiation of his role as reformer and truth-seeker, identifying Dr. Relling as Ibsen's *raisonneur* in the play.

Zucker, A. E. "The Courtiers in *Hamlet* and *The Wild Duck*." *Modern Language Notes* LIV, No. 3 (March 1939): 196-98.*
Compares the characters of Rosencrantz and Guildenstern from *Hamlet* with the "similarly fawning" chamberlains in the first act of *The Wild Duck*, theorizing that the similarities between the two sets of characters may have been suggested by Ibsen's reading of Goethe's *Wilhelm Meisters Lehrjahre*.

James (Augustine Aloysius) Joyce

1882-1941

Irish novelist, short story writer, poet, essayist, and dramatist.

The following entry presents criticism of Joyce's novel *A Portrait of the Artist as a Young Man*. For a complete discussion of Joyce's career, see *TCLC*, Volumes 3 and 8.

Joyce's "spiritual autobiography," *A Portrait of the Artist as a Young Man* is considered one of the most enigmatic and brilliant works in modern literature. Although it is often read as a straightforward, naturalistic account of the bitter youthful experiences and final artistic and spiritual liberation of Stephen Dedalus—Joyce's alter-ego in the novel—the *Portrait* is a far more complex and subtle book than such a reading suggests. In it, Joyce not only combined Imagist and Impressionist techniques with symbols borrowed from Greek mythology, Western literature, and the Roman Catholic liturgy, he also introduced narrative innovations that permanently altered the course of the English novel. These devices are responsible for the undercurrents of irony and ambiguity in the *Portrait* that have prompted some critics to question whether Joyce really intended it to be read as autobiography. Thus, although Joyce's novel is part of the same tradition of autobiographical fiction as Andre Gide's *L'immoraliste*, Marcel Proust's *À la recherche du temps perdu*, and D. H. Lawrence's *Sons and Lovers*, it is in many ways a revolutionary work with a wide range of meanings that can only be disclosed through careful analysis of its imagery and structure.

"A Portrait of the Artist" was originally the title of a four page essay that Joyce submitted to the Dublin literary magazine *Dana* in 1904. This impressionistic and obscure fragment of autobiography was rejected by the magazine's editors on the grounds that they would not publish what they could not understand. Shortly thereafter, Joyce began his first novel, *Stephen Hero*, in which he intended to expand on the theme that had inspired his "Portrait" essay: his renunciation, as an artist, of the constrained and stifling Dublin environment. Joyce conceived *Stephen Hero* as a monumental work, possibly approaching a million words in length. However, when his manuscript had grown to over a thousand pages, Joyce discarded *Stephen Hero*, destroying large portions of it and reworking others into what survives today as chapters one through three of *A Portrait of the Artist as a Young Man*. Joyce completed these chapters by 1908, then set the work aside. Critics now believe that chapters four and five of the current text were probably not written until 1914 when, after numerous rejections by publishers, the *Portrait* was finally accepted by the journal *The Egoist* for publication in serial form. For this Joyce was indebted to Ezra Pound, who had interceded with the publishers of *The Egoist* on his behalf. The *Portrait* ran serially in *The Egoist* from February 2, 1914, Joyce's thirty-second birthday, to September 1, 1915, and did not appear in book form until 1916. At that time an edition was published in the United States, for printers in England had refused to set the plates in protest over the book's "immorality." Plates from the American edition were then sent to England, and a small edition was prepared from them in 1917. In 1938, a quarter of the text of *Stephen Hero* was discovered among the papers of Sylvia Beach acquired that year by Harvard College. This fragment

Culver Pictures, Inc.

was published for the first time in 1944. Joyce's original "Portrait" essay remained unpublished, however, until 1960 when it finally appeared in *The Yale Review*.

Stephen Dedalus's life, as described in *A Portrait of the Artist as a Young Man*, closely parallels Joyce's own personal history. As Elizabeth Drew has observed: "The materials of the *Portrait* are probably all true to the spirit of Joyce's development"—if not necessarily to the facts. Like Stephen, Joyce was the son of an intemperate father whose idleness and prodigality reduced his family from a comfortable middle-class existence to poverty. Also like Stephen, Joyce attended Clongowes Wood College and other Jesuit institutions, including University College Dublin, where his classmen Vincent Cosgrave, George Clancy, and John Francis Byrne served as the respective prototypes for Lynch, Davin, and Cranly in the *Portrait*. Joyce also felt the need to flee Ireland for the sake of his survival as an artist, just as Stephen does at the conclusion of the *Portrait*. In spite of the many obvious parallels between biographical fact and fiction, however, Joyce's precise relationship to Stephen Dedalus has been a subject of frequent controversy among critics. While many accept the novel as a study of Joyce's early life, others maintain that Joyce's attitude toward Stephen was entirely detached and ironic. The reasons for these broad differences of opinion are inherent in the structure and the style of Joyce's novel. In revising *Stephen Hero*, Joyce omitted all of the explanatory material and bridge passages in an effort to achieve an impersonal tone. As William York Tindall has pointed out, Joyce was greatly influenced by the novels of Gustave Flaubert, and like Flaubert he believed that "the artist must be in his work like God in creation, present everywhere and visible nowhere." Stephen himself voices this artistic principle when, in a discussion of his aesthetic theory, he compares the artist to a god who completes the work of creation and then sits back "paring his nails."

Joyce further complicated the question of his relationship to Stephen Dedalus through his use of the then-revolutionary stream of consciousness technique. The use of stream of consciousness narration in the *Portrait* enabled Joyce to portray time as "a fluid succession of present moments," an effect that he believed complemented the novel's theme of personal identity as the product of one's past experiences. Moreover, by employing this device Joyce was also able to make Stephen's emotional and intellectual development key elements in the *Portrait*'s structure. However, the technique was not without its drawbacks. Stream of consciousness narration often conveys the impression that an author identifies with his protagonist, shares his feelings, and agrees with his observations. Joyce therefore had to maintain his authorial distance from Stephen, while following the stream of his thoughts through the use of a third person point of view. Careful reading reveals that Joyce, the mature author, never overtly approves or condemns the adolescent Stephen. However, the irony that results from the juxtaposition of Joyce's impartial presentation of the events of Stephen's life with Stephen's often humorless self-deceptions is occasionally damning, and this is the basis of most of the critical controversy over the *Portrait*. While critics such as Harry Levin read the *Portrait* as a story of artistic and spiritual liberation, in spite of its occasionally ironic tone, there are others who place great emphasis on the ironic aspects of Joyce's portrayal of Stephen. Hugh Kenner, for example, argues that the *Portrait* is not an autobiographical work, but rather, is the story of an ineffectual Dublin aesthete who is destined to failure, much like the characters in Joyce's short story collection *Dubliners*. The most common critical opinion, represented in the following entry by Wayne C. Booth and Robert Scholes, is somewhere between these two extremes. This interpretation recognizes the ironic elements in the novel but does not entirely dissociate Joyce from Stephen, maintaining that the novel's irony stops short of mocking Stephen's artistic aspirations. The publication of the surviving fragment of *Stephen Hero* in 1944 further complicated this question. The undisguised, often heavyhanded irony evident in this fragment convinced some critics that Joyce had also conceived of the *Portrait* as a purely ironic work. However, as Robert Scholes has pointed out, it is the text of the novel itself that should ultimately provide the basis for any exegesis.

Understanding the manner in which Joyce used symbols is of central importance to the understanding of his style, his thought, and his work. When *A Portrait of the Artist as a Young Man* first appeared, it was assumed by most critics that it was a naturalistic or a realistic work; that is, one in which the details of everyday existence are faithfully reproduced in order to present a picture of life as it actually was lived. However, although the *Portrait* is still often read in this way by those unfamiliar with the subtlety of Joyce's method, to read it in this manner is to miss much of its richness, and to fail to comprehend Joyce's peculiar genius. Joyce's style in the *Portrait* both encompasses and transcends realism. Tindall has pointed out that in *Stephen Hero* Joyce explicitly stated his

belief that the artist must reject the mere realistic portrayal of externals in favor of a process whereby, as Stephen declares in the *Portrait*, "the details of observed reality are transmuted into radiant images." This transmutation is effected through the removal of the image "from its mesh of confining circumstances" and its reembodiment "in artistic circumstances chosen as the most exact for it in its new office." Joyce's ability to select these "details" in such a manner that, although charged with symbolic significance, they never awkwardly obtrude or disrupt the flow of his narrative, is, according to Tindall, what has sometimes led critics to confuse Joyce with the Naturalists.

In the past several decades critics have devoted a great deal of attention to the complicated mythic and symbolic patterns that Joyce adroitly wove into the text of the *Portrait*. One of these is the Greek myth of Daedalus, the master craftsman, and his son Icarus. As critics have pointed out, Stephen, through his name and his aspirations, is associated with both the artistfather and with the ambition and destruction of the son. Another pattern is the symbolic use of the fall of Charles Stewart Parnell, leader of the Irish Home Rule Party. Parnell was a formidable politician who was guiding Ireland to independence from Britain when he was named as a correspondent in a divorce case. The Catholic church in Ireland demanded his resignation, and the resulting political conflicts destroyed his leadership and his party. Stephen identifies the course of his life with the "betrayal" of an innovative leader by self-righteous and hypocritical countrymen, likening Parnell's fate to his own alienation from Ireland and, symbolically, to the betrayal of Christ. The use of religious symbolism is perhaps the most important symbolic pattern. Through symbol and imagery, Joyce links Stephen, in his role as an artist, with the priesthood and with both Lucifer and Christ. This connection is conveyed through sometimes minute narrative details, and is at once subtle enough to be completely overlooked, and pervasive enough that one may reasonably argue, as C. G. Anderson does, that the entire final chapter of the *Portrait* evokes, in an almost allegorical fashion, the events of Holy Thursday as recorded in the Roman Catholic Holy Week liturgy. According to Anderson, the weak tea and crusts of bread that Stephen consumes at breakfast become associated, in the artistic context of the novel, with the eucharist and the miracle of transubstantiation that Christ performed for the first time at the Last Supper. This use of symbolism supports the novel's theme of the artist as a "priest of the imagination," and is in keeping with Joyce's theory of artistic "epiphany"—that is, the "transubstantiation" by the artist of the details of sordid reality into the "radiant images" of art.

Other images and symbols also recur in the manner of musical leitmotifs throughout the *Portrait*. So brilliantly is the book organized and constructed that most of these recurring images are introduced within the first few pages of the novel. Critics consider birds, blindness, water, roses, bats, and the colors red, green, blue, and white the most important of these motifs, and have traced the pattern of their recurrences in Joyce's narrative. Much study has been devoted to uncovering the meaning of these symbolic elements, and to examining the manner in which their meanings evolve each time that they are repeated in a new context. Utilizing techniques drawn from such diverse sources as Richard Wagner, Sigmund Freud, the French Symbolists, and impressionist painting, Joyce was able to incorporate all of these symbols into his text in a way that imparted both artistic unity and universality of meaning to Stephen's story. Joyce thus not only raised the *Portrait* above the level of the traditional *bildungsroman,* he also succeeded in setting new standards of artistic excellence for the novel.

By the time that Joyce finished the *Portrait,* he had already decided upon the epic theme and title for his next novel. This work, entitled *Ulysses,* is today regarded as Joyce's masterpiece, and many consider it one of the greatest novels in all of world literature. However, it is also one of literature's most controversial works, both in terms of themes and style. *A Portrait of the Artist as a Young Man,* therefore, marked a turning point in Joyce's career. After completing the *Portrait,* Joyce became more daring in his technical experiments and ceased to conceal his iconoclastic approach to novelistic form behind the appearance of conventionality. Where the *Portrait* is subtly innovative, *Ulysses* boldly defies every literary convention. However, for all the differences between them, these two works have many features in common both with each other and with Joyce's other fiction. Throughout Joyce's career, his writing unfailingly reflected his obsession with Ireland, and the unique character of the city of Dublin. Irish life and Irish politics, as well as his own autobiography were always Joyce's principal sources of inspiration, and these concerns are plainly evident in the *Portrait,* just as they are in *Ulysses,* and in Joyce's earlier works *Dubliners* and *Chamber Music.*

The extensive amount of criticism devoted to the *Portrait* indicates the continuing interest and popularity of Joyce's novel. Apart from its merits as a work of literature, the *Portrait* is important because it is an early and relatively accessible work by one of the twentieth century's most complex writers, and as such it has been studied avidly for clues to both Joyce's early experiences and the roots of his aesthetic thought. The beauty of its imagery, its intriguing irony, and its subdued emotional intensity have also made it popular outside the academic community, so much so that, in 1967, portions of *A Portait of the Artist as a Young Man* and *Stephen Hero* were successfully adapted for the stage as the play *Stephen D.* Overall, the importance of the *Portrait* and of Joyce's role in contemporary literature was well summarized by the critic William Schutte, who observed that "Joyce had one asset denied to all but the very greatest artists: the ability to move forward in each of his works without repeating himself and to make each advance both an inimitable performance and a landmark in the history of his art."

(See also *Contemporary Authors,* Vol. 104; *Dictionary of Literary Biography,* Vol. 10: *Modern British Dramatists, 1910-1945;* Vol. 19: *British Poets, 1880-1914;* and Vol. 36: *British Novelists, 1890-1929: Modernists.*)

EDWARD GARNETT   (letter date 1916)

[*Garnett was a prominent editor for several London publishing houses, and discovered or greatly influenced the work of many important English writers, including Joseph Conrad, John Galsworthy, and D. H. Lawrence. The following excerpt is taken from the rejection notice that the Duckworth Publishing Company sent to Joyce's literary agent, James B. Pinker. This notice was composed from the notes that Garnett, the firm's literary advisor, took while reading* A Portrait of the Artist as a Young Man. *While there is some question as to whether or not Garnett himself actually wrote the rejection letter reproduced below, the opinions expressed in it are elaborations of ideas that Garnett recorded in his notes, and the notice was signed with his name.*]

James Joyce's **'Portrait of the Artist as a Young Man'** wants going through carefully from start to finish. There are many 'longueurs.' Passages which, though the publisher's reader may find them entertaining, will be tedious to the ordinary man among the reading public. That public will call the book, as it stands at present, realistic, unprepossessing, unattractive. We call it ably written. The picture is 'curious,' it arouses interest and attention. But the author must revise it and let us see it again. It is too discursive, formless, unrestrained, and ugly things, ugly words, are too prominent; indeed at times they seem to be shoved in one's face, on purpose, unnecessarily. The point of view will be voted 'a little sordid.' The picture of life is good; the period well brought to the reader's eye, and the types and characters are well drawn, but it is too 'unconventional.' This would stand against it in normal times. At the present [war] time, though the old conventions are in the background, we can only see a chance for it if it is pulled into shape and made more definite.

In the earlier portion of the MS. as submitted to us, a good deal of pruning can be done. Unless the author will use restraint and proportion he will not gain readers. His pen and his thoughts seem to have run away with him sometimes.

And at the end of the book there is a complete falling to bits; the pieces of writing and the thoughts are all in pieces and they fall like damp, ineffective rockets.

The author shows us he has art, strength and originality, but this MS. wants time and trouble spent on it, to make it a more finished piece of work, to shape it more carefully as the product of the craftsmanship, mind and imagination of an artist.

> *Edward Garnett, in a letter to James B. Pinker on June 26, 1916, in* A Portrait of the Artist as a Young Man *by James Joyce, edited by Chester G. Anderson, The Viking Press, 1968, p. 320.*

EZRA POUND   (essay date 1917)

[*Pound, an American poet and critic, is regarded as one of the most innovative and influential figures in twentieth-century Anglo-American poetry. He was instrumental in editorially and financially aiding T. S. Eliot, Wyndham Lewis, James Joyce, and William Carlos Williams, among other poets. His own* Cantos *is one of the most ambitious poetic cycles of the century, and his series of satirical poems* Hugh Selwyn Mauberley *(1920) is ranked with Eliot's* The Waste Land *(1922) as a significant attack upon the decadence of modern culture. Because Pound considered the United States a cultural wasteland, he spent most of his life in Europe. In the following excerpt from a review of* A Portrait of the Artist as a Young Man, *Pound praises Joyce's novel for its honesty and the unsentimental quality of its prose. The bitter tenor of Pound's remarks betrays his frustration with the censorious English editors and printers who had, for many years, successfully delayed the publication of Joyce's novel.*]

It is unlikely that I shall say anything new about Mr. Joyce's novel, *A Portrait of the Artist as a Young Man.* I have already stated that it is a book worth reading and that it is written in good prose. In using these terms I do not employ the looseness of the half-crown reviewer.

I am very glad that it is now possible for a few hundred people to read Mr. Joyce comfortably from a bound book, instead of from a much-handled file of *Egoists* or from a slippery bundle of type-script. (p. 21)

Since Landor's *Imaginary Conversations* were bandied from pillar to post, I doubt if any manuscript has met with so much opposition, and no manuscript has been more worth supporting.

Landor is still an unpopular author. He is still a terror to fools. He is still concealed from the young (not for any alleged indecency, but simply because he did not acquiesce in certain popular follies). He, Landor, still plays an inconspicuous rôle in university courses. The amount of light which he would shed on the undergraduate mind would make students inconvenient to the average run of professors. But Landor is permanent.

Members of the "Fly-Fishers" and "Royal Automobile" clubs, and of the "Isthmian," may not read him. They will not read Mr. Joyce. *E pur si muove.* Despite the printers and publishers the British Government has recognized Mr. Joyce's literary merit. That is a definite gain for the party of intelligence. A number of qualified judges have acquiesced in my statement of two years ago, that Mr. Joyce was an excellent and important writer of prose.

The last few years have seen the gradual shaping of a party of intelligence, a party not bound by any central doctrine or theory. We cannot accurately define new writers by applying to them tag-names from old authors, but as there is no adequate means of conveying the general impression of their characteristics one may at times employ such terminology, carefully stating that the terms are nothing more than approximation.

With that qualification, I would say that James Joyce produces the nearest thing to Flaubertian prose that we have now in English, just as Wyndham Lewis has written a novel which is more like, and more fitly compared with, Dostoievsky than is the work of any of his contemporaries. In like manner Mr. T. S. Eliot comes nearer to filling the place of Jules La Forgue in our generation. (Doing the "nearest thing" need not imply an approach to a standard, from a position inferior.)

Two of these writers have met with all sorts of opposition. If Mr. Eliot probably has not yet encountered very much opposition, it is only because his work is not yet very widely known.

My own income was considerably docked because I dared to say that Gaudier-Brzeska was a good sculptor and that Wyndham Lewis was a great master of design. It has, however, reached an almost irreducible minimum, and I am, perhaps, fairly safe in reasserting Joyce's ability as a writer. It will cost me no more than a few violent attacks from several sheltered, and therefore courageous, anonymities. When you tell the Irish that they are slow in recognizing their own men of genius they reply with street riots and politics.

Now, despite the jobbing of bigots and of their sectarian publishing houses, and despite the "Fly-Fishers" and the types which they represent, and despite the unwillingness of the print-packers (a word derived from pork-packers) and the initial objections of the Dublin publishers and the later unwillingness of the English publishers, Mr. Joyce's novel appears in book form, and intelligent readers gathering few by few will read it, and it will remain a permanent part of English literature—written by an Irishman in Trieste and first published in New York City. I doubt if a comparison of Mr. Joyce to other English writers or Irish writers would much help to define him. One can only say that he is rather unlike them. *The Portrait* is very different from *L'Education Sentimentale*, but it would be easier to compare it with that novel of Flaubert's than with anything else. Flaubert pointed out that if France had studied his work they might have been saved a good deal in 1870. If

more people had read *The Portrait* and certain stories in Mr. Joyce's *Dubliners* there might have been less recent trouble in Ireland. A clear diagnosis is never without its value.

Apart from Mr. Joyce's realism—the school-life, the life in the University, the family dinner with the discussion of Parnell depicted in his novel—apart from, or of a piece with, all this is the style, the actual writing: hard, clear-cut, with no waste of words, no bundling up of useless phrases, no filling in with pages of slosh. (pp. 21-2)

The terror of clarity is not confined to any one people. The obstructionist and the provincial are everywhere, and in them alone is the permanent danger to civilization. Clear, hard prose is the safeguard and should be valued as such. The mind accustomed to it will not be cheated or stampeded by national phrases and public emotionalities.

These facts are true, even for the detesters of literature. For those who love good writing there is no need of argument. In the present instance it is enough to say to those who will believe one that Mr. Joyce's book is now procurable. (p. 22)

> *Ezra Pound, "James Joyce: At Last the Novel Appears," in* The Egoist, *Vol. IV, No. 2, February, 1917, pp. 21-2.*

F[RANCIS] H[ACKETT]   (essay date 1917)

[*Hackett was a respected Irish-American biographer, novelist, and literary critic during the first half of the twentieth century. His reviews appeared in* The New Republic, The Saturday Review of Literature, *and other prominent American periodicals. In this early favorable review of* A Portrait of the Artist as a Young Man, *Hackett praises Joyce for his emotional intensity and candor, for his portrayal of the emotional malaise of youth, and for dispelling the popular stereotype of the Irishman. Hackett's review also indicates that he foresaw many of the censorship problems that would plague Joyce for the rest of his life.*]

There is a laconic unreasonableness about the ways of creators. It is quite true that the Irish literary revival was beginning to be recognized at precisely the period of Mr. Joyce's novel [*A Portrait of the Artist as a Young Man*] and it is also true that his protagonist is a student in Dublin at the hour of the so-called renaissance, a writer and poet and dreamer of dreams. So perverse is life, however, there is scarcely one glimmer in this landscape of the flame which is supposed to have illuminated Dublin between 1890 and 1900. If Stephen Dedalus, the young man portrayed in this novel, had belonged to the Irish revival, it would be much easier for outsiders to "place" him. The essential fact is, he belonged to a more characteristic group which this novel alone has incarnated. One almost despairs of conveying it to the person who has conventionalized his idea of Ireland and modern Irish literature, yet there is a poignant Irish reality to be found in few existing plays and no pre-existent novel, presented here with extraordinary candor and beauty and power.

It is a pleasant assumption of national mythology that the southern Irish are a bright and witty people, effervescent on the sunny side and pugnacious on the other, but quick to act in any event, and frequently charming and carefree and irresponsible. It may be that the Irish exhibit this surface to outsiders and afford a case of street angel and house devil on a national scale, or it may be that the English landlord has chosen to see the Irishman as funny in the way the Southern gentleman chooses to see the Negro as funny, but, however the assumption got started it has been fortified by generations of story-tellers and has provided a fair number of popular writers with a living. It is only when a person with the invincible honesty of James Joyce comes to write of Dubliners as they are, a person who is said to be mordant largely because he isn't mushy, that the discrepancy between the people and the myth is apparent. When one says Dubliners "as they are," one of course is pronouncing a preference. One is simply insisting that the Irishmen of James Joyce are more nearly like one's own estimate of them than the Irishmen of an amiable fabulist like George Birmingham. But there is the whole of the exquisite *Portrait of the Artist as a Young Man* to substantiate the assertion that a proud, cold, critical, suspicious, meticulous human being is infinitely more to be expected among educated Catholic Irishmen than the sort of squireen whom Lever once glorified. If this is a new type in Ireland, come into existence with the recent higher education of Catholics, one can only say that it is now by far the most important type to recognize. . . .

Mr. Joyce's power is not shown in any special inventiveness. A reader of novels will see at once that he has never even thought of "plot" in the ordinary sense, or considered the advantage or importance of consulting the preferences of his reader. The thing he writes about is the thing he knows best, himself, himself at boarding school and university, and any radical variation on the actual terms of that piercing knowledge he has declined to attempt. He has sought above everything to reveal those circumstances of his life which had poignancy, and the firmest claim on him to being written was not that a thing should be amenable to his intentions as a sophisticated novelist, but that a thing should have complete personal validity. It did not weigh with him at any moment that certain phrases or certain incidents would be intensely repugnant to some readers. Was the phrase interwoven with experience? Was the incident part of the fabric of life? He asked this searchingly, and asked no more. It is not even likely that he made inquiry why, out of all that he could write, he selected particularly to reveal details that seldom find expression. Had he made the inquiry he might well have answered that the mere consciousness of silence is an incitement to expression, that expression is the only vengeance a mortal can take on the restrictions to which he finds himself subject. If others submit to those restrictions it is their own affair. To have the truth one must have a man's revelation of that which was really significant to himself.

Considering that this portrait is concluded before its subject leaves college one may gather that the really significant relations are familiar and religious, and that the adjustment is between a critical spirit and its environment. What gives its intensity to the portrait is the art Mr. Joyce has mastered of communicating the incidents of Stephen's career through the emotions they excited in him. We do not perceive Stephen's father and mother by description. We get them by the ebb and flood of Stephen's feeling, and while there are many passages of singularly lifelike conversation—such, for example, as the wrangle about Parnell that ruined the Christmas dinner or the stale banter that enunciated the father's return to Cork—the viridity is in Stephen's soul. (p. 138)

It is his mortal sin of masturbation that preys most terribly on this youth, and he suffers all the blasting isolation which is created by the sense of sin in connection with it. Eventually he makes a "retreat"—he is being educated by the Jesuits—and goes to confession and for a time knows religious happiness. The explicitness of this experience is more telling than

the veiled account of sexual stupidity in Samuel Butler's "Way of All Flesh," and Mr. Joyce is more successful than Samuel Butler in making religious belief seem real. The efforts of a Jesuit father to suggest a religious vocation to Stephen are the beginning of the end of his religion. In "lucid, supple, periodic prose" Mr. Joyce describes the transition from devotional life and a private specializing in mortification to the acceptance of nature and the earth. "His soul had arisen from the grave of boyhood, spurning her graveclothes. Yes! Yes! Yes! He would create proudly out of the freedom and power of his soul, as the great artificer whose name he bore, a living thing, new and soaring and beautiful, impalpable, imperishable." The "Yes! Yes! Yes!" gives that touch of intense youthfulness which haunts the entire book, even though Mr. Joyce can be so superb in flaunting Aristotle and Aquinas.

The last chapter of the portrait gives one the *esprit* of the Catholic nationalist students in University College. It is a marvelous version of scurrilous, supercilious, callow youth. Mr. Joyce's subject is not in sympathy with the buzzing internationalist any more than with the arcane Irishman whom he compares to Ireland, "a batlike soul waking to the consciousness of itself in darkness and secrecy and loneliness." Stephen walks by himself, disdainful and bitter, in love and not in love, a poet at dawn and a sneerer at sunset, cold exile of "this stinking dunghill of a world."

A novel in which a sensitive, critical young man is completely expressed as he is can scarcely be expected to be pleasant. *A Portrait of the Artist as a Young Man* is not entirely pleasant. But it has such beauty, such love of beauty, such intensity of feeling, such pathos, and candor, it goes beyond anything in English that reveals the inevitable malaise of serious youth. Mr. Joyce has a peculiar narrative method, and he would have made things clearer if he had adopted H. G. Wells's scheme of giving a paragraphed section to each episode. As the book is now arranged, it requires some imagination on the part of the reader. The Catholic "retreat" also demands attentiveness, it is reported with such acrimonious zeal. But no one who has any conception of the Russian-like frustrations and pessimisms of the thin-skinned and fine-grained Irishman, from early boarding school onward, can miss the tenacious fidelity of James Joyce. He has made a rare effort to transcend every literary convention as to his race and creed, and he has had high success. Many people will furiously resent his candor, whether about religion or nationalism or sex. But candor is a nobility in this instance. (pp. 138-39)

F[rancis] H[ackett], "Green Sickness," in The New Republic, Vol. X, No. 122, March 3, 1917, pp. 138-39.

HERBERT GORMAN   (essay date 1928)

[*Gorman was an American novelist and the author of several literary biographies. As the author of Joyce's "authorized" biography, he had worked with Joyce and knew him well. In the following excerpt, Gorman discusses Joyce's use of the stream of consciousness technique, and the importance of the unconscious in modern fiction.*]

When James Joyce's *A Portrait of the Artist as a Young Man* first appeared in the columns of "The Egoist" (February, 1914—September, 1915), it is doubtful if more than a handful of readers realized exactly what had come into English letters. There had been stories before, plenty of them, about the childhood and school and college life of sensitive young men but never one of quite this kidney. The unusual aspects of this

Joyce in 1904, the year he began A Portrait of the Artist as a Young Man. *Pictorial Parade, Inc.*

To this effort Mr. Joyce brought an astonishing and awe-inspiring array of talents. He brought independence and arrogance, psychological acumen and dialectical skill, vividness of conception and treatment, moral freedom and human passion, sensitivity and intuition, and, above all, a literary courage that was undisputed. It was no secret that it was himself, his own youth, that he was recreating. He realized, rightly enough, that in no better way could he develop this new form of fictional treatment, a treatment akin to pathology and infused with an uncompromising psychology, than in applying it to himself for in himself he possessed a rare subject for such an endeavor. The Stephen Dedalus of *A Portrait of the Artist as a Young Man,* delicately constituted, innately intellectual, afforded Mr. Joyce an opportunity for psychological revelation that was boundless in depth. Here was a youth, naturally fastidious in his conceptions and stirred by an obscure inward urge toward creativeness—in other words, the artist-type, set down in the midst of an antagonistic environment. He is surrounded by poverty and bickering. He is ultra-nervous as a boy. His eyesight is impaired. He passes through the phases of ridicule from his schoolmates, unjust discipline from his Jesuit-teachers, the quaking delirium of religion, the questioning arrogance of an awakening intellectualism, the broken sorrow of first love, and, at the last, he is left a proud exile about to set forth on that pilgrimage which every artist must travel. . . . Such a theme could not have been handled in an old-fashioned objective manner for too much of it was inextricably bound up in the subjective processes of the mind of Stephen Dedalus. It is the mind of a youth that is the hero of this book, and its proper treatment demanded an intensive mapping of the fluctuations and progressions of that mind. Here thought is action as well as those objective movements and surface passions that bring personalities into violent or subtle reactions. It was, then, Mr. Joyce's function as author to discover the best media for transmitting this theme to an audience. He found them in the mingled methods of objective and subjective treatment and brought to the fore in English fiction (for the first time prominently, anyway) the stream of consciousness system of character delineation. This method was to be carried to its eventual goal in *Ulysses.*

Perhaps no method has been more discussed in the last decade than this so-called stream of consciousness technique. There are enough practitioners of it now to fashion it into a well-recognized mode of fictional treatment. . . . But it is futile to enumerate names or attempt to place one's finger on the very first person who applied this method to fiction. Wyndham Lewis, for instance, appears to believe that Charles Dickens adumbrated the method in his character of Alfred Jingle. All this is unimportant. As a matter of fact, the stream of consciousness method is an evolution, the answer to a crying need of the novel which was discovering itself to be stifled within arbitrary limitations and which found a new outlet through the psychological discoveries and experimentations of the day. Mr. Joyce was certainly one of the first, if not the first, to handle this method on a large scale and with supreme and convincing ability. When he reached the immense panorama of *Ulysses* he had the mastership of his method well in hand. It was his willing slave and it performed miracles for him. But it had already manifested itself in *A Portrait of the Artist as a Young Man,* particularly in such intense scenes as close the book, and because of this that volume assumes rightly enough an extremely important place in the development of the novel-form today. It was the gateway leading directly to *Ulysses* and it opened upon a huge and unexplored terrain that has yet to be completely traveled by following novelists.

book, this impressive prelude to the then unsuspected *Ulysses,* were implicit less in the situations than in the method of handling and the suggestive innuendoes rising from apparently trivial notations. In other words the author was exploiting a new form in the novel, a form not then fully ascertained but to be carried to its logical determination in the behemoth of books that was to follow it. To understand this form it was necessary to understand the limitations of fiction. It was necessary to comprehend that the novel had (within the boundaries more or less arbitrarily set for it) fully flowered and blossomed, that in Gustave Flaubert, and, after him, Henry James, the ultimate possibilities of characterization and mental and spiritual exploration and revelation had been exhausted. There was nothing to be done but to push the apparently set boundaries of the novel back still farther, to make possible the elaboration of that new factor in life,—the subconscious. So much has come into this problem of living, so many misty awarenesses of inexplicable inhibitions, so many half-formed impulses, atavistic urges, semi-conscious cerebrations, mysterious enchantments of the heart, and involved mental gestures, that a steadily widening gap was splitting literature and life apart. It was the purpose of Mr. Joyce to fill this gap, to make possible a profounder exploration of reality in the novel-form. *A Portrait of the Artist as a Young Man,* then, was (and is) important as a pioneer effort in this direction.

Now just what is the stream of consciousness method? The solitary thoughts of characters in novels have been overheard before by god-like authors and yet we do not apply the phrase 'stream of consciousness' to these mappings of thought. The difference is in the word 'stream.' This new method is an attempt through the application of the author's psychological astuteness and intuition and profound knowledge of his character's mind, its depths, its subconscious impulses, inhibitions, and buried urges, to set down the undisturbed flow of thought—not always conscious, perhaps, to the thinker—that pours through the restless mind, a stream that is diverted constantly by a thousand and one extraneous objects, word-connotations, stifled emotions, from the consistent and built-up delineations of thought-processes to be found in the older novelists. Two objections have been brought against this style of literary treatment, that is, two paramount objections, for there are a hundred lesser ones. One of them is that the reader must take the author's word for it that his character's thought-processes are logical, that there is no proof that they are scientifically accurate. This is true enough, but, after all, the author's character is his own and to employ this form he must begin farther down to build his character up. He must lay the foundations of a subconscious person and rear on this the objective man. If he does this successfully there is no reason why his character's planned thought-processes as revealed through the stream of consciousness method may not be accurate and logical. True enough, it calls for a new type of novelist, a novelist who is psychologist and pathologist as well as a fictional creator. But that, obviously enough, is the road that the novel today is taking. The second objection is that the inclusion of haphazard musings, fragmentary cogitations, odd bits of thought, apparently irrelevant streams of brooding, changes the scheme of the novel and destroys that time-honored unity and selectiveness that so pleased our fathers. So it does. It calls for a new form in the novel, the observation and recognition of character from another plane. Instead of movement thought becomes action. This is what Mr. Joyce adumbrated in *A Portrait of the Artist as a Young Man*. At least, three quarters of this book is absorbing because of the vivid transcript of thought in it. It is the mind of Stephen Dedalus that enchants and absorbs us and it is our consciousness of the authenticity of this figure that makes us so reluctant to lay the book down. Because of this we can reread *A Portrait of the Artist as a Young Man* many times for each reading is the renewal of an intimate acquaintanceship. We know Stephen Dedalus as well as we know our closest friends although, because of that mysterious artistic divinity in the arrogant young man, his essential self is somewhat beyond our fullest comprehension.

If the subjective tone of *A Portrait of the Artist as a Young Man* is convincing and distinguished, what may be said about its objective tone? After all, there is a surface to the book, movement, description, the presentation of character. Indeed, it was this surface that first drew readers (always excepting the lucky handful who knew from the beginning the potentialities it suggested for the future novel) to its engrossing pages. Scene after scene may be plucked from the book as representative of its clear realism and power of representing life. The agonies of Stephen Dedalus as he passes through the religious hysteria brought upon him by his days in attendance at the Roman Catholic retreat, for instance, is one although that has certain permeating subjective features to it. But what could be clearer of the subjective and yet more convincing and tragically humorous than the famous Christmas dinner at Stephen's home where his aunt Dante loses her temper at the malicious proddings of the two Parnellites. The history of Ireland in little is

circumscribed in this section of a chapter where religious differences shatter to bits what promised to be a feast of love. There is irony here but it is a cold detached irony, an irony that could place this scene at a dinner ostensibly in honor of Jesus Christ but yet dominated by the rancorousness of fierce church differences. If, at times, this irony is bitter we must remember that these figures are more than fictions and that the painful autobiography of a sensitive soul, lonely and proud, is imbedded in these pages. There is humor here but it is the cold humor of a man who has detached himself deliberately from those things which first made him, things that his mind and soaring destiny refuse. The reader must never forget the symbolism in the name Dedalus. That name may be found in any primer of mythology.

The philosophical implications of the book pass the bounds of a short essay for one can do no more than indicate that Sephen progresses by a steadily maturing process of ratiocination toward his goal of reality. If, at the conclusion of the volume, he has not found himself as yet he is well on the road toward it and he has made several great steps in its direction, not the least of them being his painful self-liberation from the Church which educated him and whose tenets and scholastic reasoning still permeate his mind. He has also liberated himself from the compromises of love and reached that grave conviction that he must travel alone, an exile to time and country and faith and friends, if he is to achieve the ultimate core of reality. Michael Robartes remembered forgotten beauty and when his arms wrapped his love he held all the faded loveliness of the world; Stephen desires to press in his arms the loveliness which has not yet come into the world. So he goes, with the thought of the old Greek Dedalos and his osier-bound wings in his mind: "Old father, old artificer, stand me now and ever in good stead." So profound and beautiful and convincing a book is part of the lasting literature of our age and if it is overshadowed by the huger proportion and profundities of *Ulysses* we must still remember that out of it that vaster tome evolved and that in it is the promise of that new literature, new both in form and content, that will be the classics of tomorrow. (pp. v-xii)

> *Herbert Gorman, in an introduction to* A Portrait of the Artist as a Young Man *by James Joyce, The Modern Library, 1928, pp. v-xii.*

JAMES T. FARRELL (essay date 1944)

[*Farrell was an American novelist, short story writer, and critic who is best known for his grim Studs Lonigan trilogy, a series of novels that examine the life of a lower middle-class man in Chicago. Influenced primarily by the author's own Irish-Catholic upbringing in Chicago's rough South Side, and by the writings of Theodore Dreiser, Marcel Proust, and James Joyce, Farrell's fiction is a Naturalistic, angry portrait of urban life. His literature explores—from a compassionate, moralistic viewpoint—the problems spawned of poverty, circumstance, and spiritual sterility. Farrell has written: "I am concerned in my fiction with the patterns of American destinies and with presenting the manner in which they unfold in our times. My approach to my material can be suggested by a motto of Spinoza which I have quoted on more than one occasion: 'Not to weep or laugh, but to understand.'" In the following excerpt, Farrell discusses the historical conflicts of Ireland and the social conditions that prevailed at the turn of the century, explaining how and why these forces could have produced a character as deeply alienated from his native culture as Joyce's Stephen Dedalus.*]

"This race and this country and this life produced me," declares Stephen Dedalus—artistic image of James Joyce himself—in *A Portrait of the Artist as a Young Man. A Portrait* is the story of how Stephen was produced, how he rejected that which produced him, how he discovered that his destiny was to become a lonely one of artistic creation. It is well to look into the life out of which Stephen came, to discuss the social and national background of this novel. In Ireland a major premise of any discussion of her culture and of her literature is an understanding of Irish nationalism. And it is at least arguable that Joyce was a kind of inverted nationalist—that the nationalism which he rejects runs through him like a central thread.

Ireland, when James Joyce was a boy, suffered from a profound political defeat, the fall of Parnell. In that, once again, she was set back in her long struggle to attain nationhood. The aftermath was marked by a deeply felt and pervasive bitterness, often expressed in feelings of personal betrayal. And *A Portrait,* reflects such moods. The brilliantly written scene, early in this novel, of the Dedalus family pitilessly quarreling at the Christmas dinner table is a highly concentrated artistic representation of the magnitude of Parnell's fall in Ireland, of how it cut through families with a knifelike sharpness. The family argument is personal and its passionate anger seems to be in inverse proportion to the political impotence of those who are hurling insults at one another.

Whenever Stephen, as a youth, discusses politics he expresses himself with singular resentment. He identifies himself with the courageous men who have striven and been martyred in the cause of Ireland, feeling that they have been let down by their own followers, by those whom they were trying to free. Stephen's reaction is not a singular one for the Ireland of his time. (In fact, it is even paralleled in this period, for just as Stephen blames the Irish people for Ireland's defeats, so do many contemporary radical intellectuals blame the workers for the defeats of socialism.) The Irish people have betrayed the future of Stephen Dedalus, genius son of a declassed family. This is the real sense of his bitterness. Even the monuments and memorials to the honorable heroes of Ireland, Tone and Emmet, are tawdry, part of a tawdry Dublin present which he resents.

Ireland's national aspirations generalized real, deep-seated needs. These had been choked up in the nineteenth century by a whole series of defeats from the time of Emmet and Tone to that of Parnell. When these wide needs are thus thwarted, frustrated, they are revealed in a molecular way, a sense of multiple personal betrayal, despair and disgust with politics. When this social phenomenon is expressed in art, it is usually in terms of how it is immediately felt rather than in those of its social rationale. This is how Stephen felt about the Irish political defeats, directly with painful immediacy.

The post-Parnell period was one of groping for new orientation. Irish nationalism found this politically in Sinn Fein and culturally in the so-called Irish Literary Renaissance, the Gaelic-language movement and the Gaelic-sports movement. . . .

There is a note of foreignness, of alienness, in the first stage of the Irish literary renaissance. Nationalists often call it an Anglicized culture; what I think they really mean is that it did not adequately express Irish needs of the time. The progenitors of this movement were very talented people, and one of them, Yeats, was destined to become probably the greatest poet of his age writing in the English language. But they went to Irish materials as if from without. Sensitive to a disorientation which was pervasively felt at the time, needing sources of inspiration fresher than those of English literature and of the *fin de siecle*

when Victorian culture fell apart, they more or less discovered Ireland.

But what did they discover? This stage of the so-called renaissance produced the poetic drama. It found thematic material in the legends of Ireland's free and pre-Saxonized past. A fresh and poetic language was sought in the speech of the poorest, the most backward section of the Irish peasantry. Standish O'Grady, frequently referred to as the father of this movement, attempted to re-establish the old legends on a Homeric level. It seems as if all these writers were seeking to create images of great figures of their past in order to compensate (though perhaps not consciously) for their lack of leaders in the present; so that with Parnell gone, they could still derive some cultural subsistence, some sense of pride and inspiration, from the image of Fergus and other heroes of the legends.

Thwarted on the historical plane, Ireland set up as a counter to England an idea of her own culture. Through culture, she would show that she was a nation. (p. 6)

The emphasis of this stage of the movement was on the past. Where could Joyce fit into it? What could it teach him, a young genius who was so acutely sensitive to all of the life of the moment?

In *A Portrait,* the world presses on Stephen. His own thoughts are melancholy. His proud spirit cannot tolerate the painful burden of reality. He must rise above it. All of this burden is not directly represented in the novel; some of it is reflected in memory and in conversation. No clear and full picture of Stephen's relationship with his mother is described. Through conversation, we learn that he has had a distressing quarrel with her, in which he tells her that he has lost his faith. Additionally, Stephen loses his respect for his father; he begins to develop that feeling of being fatherless which is so important a part of his character in *Ulysses.* But here Joyce does not develop these relationships in directly written scenes. Much is not touched upon; what of the relationship between Stephen's father and mother?

The Portrait contains only a most highly concentrated sense of home, school, streets and city which press so sharply upon Stephen's spirit. In fact, Joyce introduced the city and urban life realistically into modern Irish literature. He is acutely sensitive to all that happens around him: he breathes in something of every wind which blows in Ireland. Joyce at this time felt more, saw more, brooded more than he allows Stephen to reveal to us. Stephen, as boy and youth, tramps the streets of Dublin. Sometimes in his walks he trembles with fears of damnation. Again, his mind is filled with lurid visions of sin, written of in purple passages suggestive of Pater's prose; but very often he searches, looks, listens. In these walks how much of Dublin must have attracted him, how much must have repelled him!

How much didn't the streets of Dublin tell him of life, of men, of himself? How much of Ireland's real, historic past was not poured through his senses, into the pulsing life of the present? Why is Stephen so melancholy? Obviously because he carries within him such a burden of impressions, such a burden of the life of his country, his city, his race, his own family. He feels that he, himself, is an alien in his homeland, and that he is even forced to speak a language that is not his own. He sees the results of Ireland's bitter history in the quality of the life, of the culture, even of humanity in Dublin. This quality of humanity is vividly revealed in his feelings about his own father. Unless he breaks with all that this represents, he, himself, will have no future. At one point, defending himself after he has rejected all that produced him, he says: "I am not responsible for the past." But he has seen the consequences of that past all about him in the present.

Such being the case, Joyce is not going to find literary inspiration where the leading literary men of the time have found it. He does not have to discover Ireland. He carries too much of it already in his own being.

Moreover, Joyce was born and educated a Catholic. He was trained by Jesuits at the university which Cardinal Newman helped to found. He admired Newman and was influenced by his writings. Behind the lucid prose Joyce saw revealed a man who had arrived at his conviction through spiritual agonies. Stephen is shedding convictions which Newman came to accept, but he, too, is going through spiritual agony in so doing.

From his considerable reading in the literature of the church the boy gained not only a sense of the past but also a sense of an ordered inner world and of a systematized *other* world. Eternity has filled his imagination. Still in his teens he has been shriveled by fierce fires as he sat in the chapel listening to the Jesuit retreat master describe with rigid logic the physical and spiritual agonies awaiting the damned in hell. (This is one of the most magnificently written passages in all of Joyce's work.)

After hearing such sermons Stephen becomes almost physically ill. In fact this is the period when he suffers most intensely. And his greatest sufferings are not imposed by the Dublin reality which disturbs him so much but by images of an inferno as terrifying as that of Dante. He quivers and cowers before the vision of an other world which must make that of the Irish legends seem the most pale of mists. His spiritual struggle is one involving acceptance or rejection of this ordered other world.

He comes to reject it. But his struggle leaves Stephen with a deepened sense of melancholy. He has gained a penetrating sense of the depths of experience. In *Ulysses* Joyce will say that all history is a nightmare. Stephen has known what walking nightmares can be like. He is forging such a temperament that he will never be able to find interest, inspiration, scarcely even curiosity in the ghosts which Yeats sought in castles or in those spirits with whom AE tried to converse. His whole life, his education, his conception of an inner life, all this must lead him to find literary materials different from those which could be shaped by his immediate predecessors.

Inasmuch as he is to be a writer, the literary world should presumably be the one aspect of Dublin life where Joyce might find communion of spirit. But this analysis should show how he was gravitating toward a break with it as with the rest. The young artist who develops before our eyes is one who will be able to feel creatively free only if he directs his eyes toward the future and if he seeks a loveliness that has not been born rather than one that was born centuries ago in Celtic Ireland.

Stephen, then, is the homeless genius. He needs to expand, to feel free. He needs an arena adequate for his talents. He sees no future for himself unless he rebels, ejects. And beyond this Dublin, with its misery, its poverty, its Georgian houses, its sleek patricians and its English rulers are the cities of the world. Beyond this Ireland, poor and culturally deprived, is the culture of the world. He has felt himself from early boyhood to be different and marked for a special destiny. He cannot and will not participate in politics; he cannot follow the literary men who are making a stir in Dublin.

Where can he find a career open for his talents? His feeling of need for expansion and freedom is acute. Are not feelings such as these the kind which were generalized in Ireland's national aspirations? The problems which he faces, the needs which he feels with the vision of genius—others have felt these, and they have fled. Before him Ireland has had millions of her wild geese sons and daughters. Stephen knows all this. He knows how some have died of starvation; he knows how Tone and Emmet died; and he knows how many have died in their souls.

In terms of all these conditions Stephen's soul is being born. Wherever he turns he sees "nets flung at it to hold it back from flight." But he will be free. The homeless Irishman in Ireland, the homeless genius in the world, he will fly off like Icarus, onward and upward. Proudly rebellious, he has proclaimed: "I will not serve." Instead of the vocation he could not find as a priest he will find it in service as "a priest of the eternal imagination." Creating without fetters, he will "forge in the smithy of my soul the uncreated conscience of my race." One of Ireland's most brilliant wild geese has found the wings with which he may fly away. (pp. 6, 16)

James T. Farrell, "Joyce and His First Self-Portrait," in The New York Times Book Review, *December 31, 1944, pp. 6, 16.*

MARK SCHORER   (lecture date 1947)

[*Schorer is an American critic and the author of the definitive biography of Sinclair Lewis. In his often anthologized essay "Technique as Discovery" (1948), Schorer put forth the argument that fiction deserves the same close attention to diction and metaphor that the New Critics had been lavishing on poetry. He*

Joyce in 1915, a year after the publication of A Portrait of the Artist as a Young Man. *The Granger Collection, New York.*

determined that fiction viewed only with respect to content was not art at all, but experience. For Schorer, only when individuals examine "achieved content," or form, do they speak of art, and consequently, speak as critics. Schorer also argued that the difference between content and art is technique and that the study of technique demonstrates how fictional form discovers and evaluates meaning, meaning that is often not intended by the author. Schorer has edited several collections of essays on Joyce's work; in the following excerpt from a lecture originally delivered in 1947, he examines the style of A Portrait of the Artist as a Young Man *for clues as to how Joyce evaluated Stephen Dedalus's experience. Schorer contends that the three styles utilized in the work reflect Stephen's growing alienation, and that the austere final section contains an implicit comment on Stephen's tragic separation from the human community. Schorer's reading of the novel is thus similar to that of such critics as Hugh Kenner (1965) and Robert M. Adams (1966), both of whom question the reality of Stephen's "artistic liberation" in the final pages of the novel.*

A Portrait of the Artist as a Young Man . . . analyzes its [autobiographical] material rigorously, and it defines the value and the quality of its experience not by appended comment or moral epithet, but by the texture of the style. The theme of *A Portrait,* a young artist's alienation from his environment, is explored and evaluated through three different styles and methods as Stephen Dedalus moves from childhood through boyhood into maturity. The opening pages are written in something like the Ulyssesean stream of consciousness, as the environment impinges directly on the consciousness of the infant and the child, a strange, opening world which the mind does not yet subject to questioning, selection, or judgment. But this style changes very soon, as the boy begins to explore his surroundings; and as his sensuous experience of the world is enlarged, it takes on heavier and heavier rhythms and a fuller and fuller body of sensuous detail, until it reaches a crescendo of romantic opulence in the emotional climaxes which mark Stephen's rejection of domestic and religious values. Then gradually the style subsides into the austere intellectuality of the final sections, as he defines to himself the outlines of the artistic task which is to usurp his maturity.

A highly self-conscious use of style and method defines the quality of experience in each of these sections, and, it is worth pointing out in connection with the third and concluding section, the style and method evaluate the experience. What has happened to Stephen is, of course, a progressive alienation from the life around him as he progressed in his initiation into it, and by the end of the novel, the alienation is complete. The final portion of the novel, fascinating as it may be for the developing esthetic creed of Stephen-Joyce, is peculiarly bare. The life experience was not bare, as we know from *Stephen Hero;* but Joyce is forcing technique to comment. In essence, Stephen's alienation is a denial of the human environment; it is a loss; and the austere discourse of the final section, abstract and almost wholly without sensuous detail or strong rhythm, tells us of that loss. It is a loss so great that the texture of the notation-like prose here suggests that the end is really all an illusion, that when Stephen tells us and himself that he is going forth to forge in the smithy of his soul the uncreated conscience of his race, we are to infer from the very quality of the icy, abstract void he now inhabits, the implausibility of his aim. For *Ulysses* does not create the conscience of the race; it creates our consciousness.

In the very last two or three paragraphs of the novel, the style changes once more, reverts from the bare, notative kind to the romantic prose of Stephen's adolescence. "Away! Away! The spell of arms and voices: the white arms of roads, their promise of close embraces and the black arms of tall ships that stand against the moon, their tale of distant nations. They are held out to say: We are alone—come." Might one not say that the austere ambition is founded on adolescent longing? That the excessive intellectual severity of one style is the counterpart of the excessive lyric relaxation of the other? And that the final passage of *A Portrait* punctuates the illusory nature of the whole ambition? (pp. 14-16)

> *Mark Schorer, "Technique as Discovery," from his* The World We Imagine, *Farrar, Straus and Giroux, 1968, pp. 3-23.**

C. G. ANDERSON   (essay date 1952)

[In the following excerpt, Anderson explicates the complex liturgical symbolism in chapter five of A Portrait of the Artist as a Young Man. *Anderson's careful tracing of the symbols from the Maundy Thursday liturgy that are scattered throughout Joyce's text for this chapter not only illuminates the Stephen-as-Christ-betrayed and artist-as-priest motifs in the novel, it demonstrates the minute attention to detail that Joyce invested in developing his imagery.]*

Between the writing of *Stephen Hero* and the conception of *A Portrait of the Artist as a Young Man* James Joyce epiphanized his esthetic. The *Stephen Hero* fragment contains most of the matter of Chapter V of the *Portrait,* and it contains most of the esthetic theory of the *Portrait* as a whole; what it lacks is the technique of arranging non-discursive symbols in such a way that they evoke directly feelings which cannot be expressed discursively. It is by means of this technique that Joyce presents the life of the young artist as a complete, harmonious, radiant image— as ". . . that thing which it is and no other thing." . . .

As we know from *Ulysses* and *Finnegans Wake* Joyce was fond of subtly explaining his own methods to the reader. In the *Portrait* he gives the key to the technique by pointing out that Cranly is John the Baptist: "The exhausted loins are those of Elizabeth and Zachary. Then he is the precursor. Item: he eats chiefly belly bacon and dried figs. Read locusts and wild honey." . . . (p. 3)

But, as will be shown, it is clear from Joyce's handling of Cranly, who is not only John the Baptist but also Judas and Satan, that he did not intend to produce an allegory. In everything he wrote after *Stephen Hero* he treated his subject symbolically. The distinction is, as Yeats says in *Ideas of Good and Evil,* that while "a symbol is indeed the only possible expression of some invisible essence . . . allegory is one of many possible representations of an embodied thing, or familiar principle, and belongs to fancy and not to imagination: the one is a revelation, the other an amusement." Nevertheless, on the reader's part some allegorizing is necessary if he is to understand how a symbolic work achieves its effect.

Chapter V of the *Portrait* is controlled by three principal symbols: the Daedalus myth; the poet as God—creator, redeemer, and priest; and the betrayal-crucifixion. In addition to subsuming many lesser symbols, these three are themselves related. While Icarus in the Daedalus story is an analogue for the flight of the artist from home, nation, and church into exile, "old father, old artificer" Daedalus corresponds to God the Father and Creator. God the Father is united with Christ the Son, who as the Word joins in creation and as the first priest becomes a creator in Joyce's special sense. Christ, the Creator as a young man, is betrayed and crucified in a way which corresponds to the betrayal of the artist as a young man by his family, his national society, and his church. Since the Daedalus element has been, in general, clear from the beginning, this article will examine only the second and third of these principal symbols.

Stephen's exposition of his esthetic to Lynch in Chapter V is the intellectual climax of the novel. Stephen is here an ordained priest of art proclaiming the gospel of art. As he says of himself, he is ''. . . a priest of eternal imagination, transmuting the daily bread of experience into the radiant body of everliving life.'' . . . But to understand his priesthood, we must understand his conversion and baptism.

When, in Chapter IV, the director of University College suggests that Stephen consider becoming a Jesuit, Stephen decides that he will ''. . . never swing the thurible before the altar as priest.'' . . . But later, as he walks along the beach, he hears ''. . . the call of life to his soul not the dull gross voice of the world of duties and despair, not the inhuman voice that had called him to the pale service of the altar.'' . . . He is born again, and his soul arises from the ''. . . grave of boyhood, spurning her graveclothes.'' . . . He feels that his calling and election are sure, and he immediately accepts his vocation: ''Yes! Yes! Yes! He would create proudly out of the freedom and power of his soul . . . a living thing, new and soaring and beautiful, impalpable, imperishable.'' . . . (pp. 3-5)

Stephen is baptized by wading in the sea, and he feels the regenerative power of the sacrament. He feels ''. . . a new wild life . . . singing in his veins'' and wonders, ''Where was his boyhood now? Where was the soul that had hung back from her destiny to brood alone upon the shame of her wounds . . .?'' . . . (p. 5)

At the opening of Chapter V Stephen already has passed from baptism through ordination, and is saying mass. Contrasting with the Shelleyan swoon of the baptism and its ecstatic aftermath in the final pages of Chapter IV, the first sentence of Chapter V is a rhetorical change of pace:

> He drained his third cup of watery tea to the dregs and set to chewing the crusts of fried bread that were scattered near him, staring into the dark pool of the jar. . . .

Important as this deflation is to the stylistic structure of the novel, however, the sentence is at least as important because it introduces the symbol of the eucharist—specifically, as we shall see, of the eucharist in the Maundy Thursday Mass. The tea and bread are paralleled by the cocoa which Stephen drinks with Bloom in the cabmen's shelter and at 7 Eccles Street in the Eumaeus and Ithaca episodes of *Ulysses*. After Stephen has consumed his breakfast of bread and tea (read bread and wine), he takes up ''. . . idly one after another the blue and white dockets. . . .'' . . . of his pawn brokers. These represent the communion wafers. After he has fingered them, he puts them aside and gazes ''. . . thoughtfully at the lid of the box [i.e., the tabernacle] speckled with louse marks.'' . . . Then his sister Maggie, representing the acolyte of the mass, prepares the water for the purification of his fingers, a ceremony which follows directly after the second ablution in the mass.

As is usual with Joyce, things are not so simple as they appear at second glance. Stephen's mother washes his neck. Because the reader already knows that Stephen has abhorred water since childhood and has lice . . . , he realizes at once that this is a rather singular endeavor; it is not an ordinary Ordinary of the mass, but one which no doubt has its Proper of the Season. What this Proper is, however, and what symbolic meaning it

has, is discovered more gradually. Although Joyce knows very well what day it is, Stephen and the reader do not learn that it is Thursday until Stephen reads a news-agent's placard as he walks to school. . . . Thursday is the day which Stephen in his earlier Catholic fervor had dedicated to the Most Blessed Sacrament. . . . And later, when Stephen refers to St. Thomas, *Pange lingua gloriosi,* he mentions to Lynch, who knows the fact as well as he does, that it is ''a hymn for Maundy Thursday.''. . . The Maundy Thursday Communion Verse, which follows the Purification in the order of the mass liturgy, says that ''. . . the Lord Jesus, after He had supped with His disciples, washed their feet.'' Stephen ''. . . allowed his mother to scrub his neck and root into the folds of his ears and into the interstices at the wings of his nose,'' . . . and we are reminded that Peer, in the Maundy Thursday Gospel, when he consents to Christ's washing him at all, says, ''Lord, not my feet, but my hands also, and my head.''

After Stephen as priest has purified his fingers, his mother as server thrusts ''. . . a damp overall into his hands, saying:— Dry yourself and hurry out for the love of goodness.'' . . . The overall, which represents the priest's napkin, is damp at the Purification because it has already been used in the Washing-of-the-Hands ceremony during the Offertory of the mass. The hurry and the return of Stephen's sister ''. . .making signs to him to be quick and go out quietly by the back'' . . . suggests the hustle of the final portion of the mass. Stephen gives the Benediction by ''. . . smiling and kissing the tips of his fingers in adieu.'' . . . But at least two other meanings are compressed into this single ironic action. It is the priest wiping his lips and the priest kissing the altar before he pronounces the Benediction.

As Stephen leaves the house he hears the mad nun in the nearby asylum screech, ''Jesus! Jesus! Jesus!'' . . . Her exclamation is in the correct mouth and in the correct ritualistic context to signify the thanksgiving of an individual madwoman for the mad sacrament of a mad service. But it also identifies Stephen with Christ, the first priest. That this identification is what Joyce is actually saying is borne out later in the chapter when the Maundy Thursday symbol is made more explicit by the consideration which Stephen and Lynch give to St. Thomas' *Pange lingua gloriosi* and to the *Vexilla Regis* of Venantius Fortunatus. (pp. 5-7)

The two hymns are of primary importance in understanding Joyce's method of using liturgy as symbol. The first hymn is merely named and called the ''highest glory of the hymnal.'' . . . But, Stephen says, ''. . . there is no hymn that can be put beside that mournful and majestic processional song, the *Vexilla Regis.* . . .'' . . . Lynch then sings a stanza of the second hymn from memory. In the liturgy the *Pange lingua gloriosi* is sung after the mass on Maundy Thursday, when the second Host, which has been consecrated to be reserved for the Good Friday Mass in which no consecration takes place, is carried in procession to the chapel or some other place. When the procession arrives at this place, the chalice containing the Host is incensed and placed in an urn or tabernacle. The procession then returns, and Vespers are sung in the choir. The *Vexilla Regis* is the hymn for Vespers during Passiontide.

The discussion of the hymns interrupts Stephen's expounding of the mysteries of art to Lynch, and they are by no means used merely to complete a parody or to give relief from what might have become an esthetically tedious exposition of an esthetic. The line *Pange lingua gloriosi* is translated in the missal as ''Now, my tongue the mystery telling''; and Lynch does not sing the first stanza of the *Vexilla Regis,* which begins in translation with "Behold the royal ensigns fly," but the second stanza, beginning "The mystery we now unfold." The hymns as symbol, therefore—and this is true of all Joyce's symbols—are not used as mere decoration, nor as extraneous allegorical signs; the meanings they add to the narrative are intimately important to the narrative, giving it depth of texture and expansiveness. It is important that we know that Stephen is expounding mysteries, but it is also important that we know he is expounding them in his symbolic office as Stephen-Christ, the first priest of art.

When Lynch has finished singing, he and Stephen turn into Lower Mount Street. As we shall see this may be connected with Golgotha, for when they stop the crucifixion is re-enacted; but one of its other connections is the prophecy which Stephen made when he accepted the call to the religion of art in Chapter IV: ". . . dawn . . . [would] show him strange fields and hills and faces." . . . Here is the hill, and Donovan's bloated face appears.

Stephen and Lynch halt their procession; and although it is still Thursday on the narrative level, the conversation with Donovan symbolically treats the Last Supper in retrospect. This is important because of the re-enactment of the crucifixion which is to take place shortly. Telling of a group of students (read disciples) who have passed their examinations successfully, Donovan says, "The Irish fellows in Clark's gave them a feed last night. They all ate curry." . . . These students are apostles ready to go forth to all nations: "Halpin and O'Flynn are through the home civil. Moonan got fifth place in the Indian." (pp. 7-8)

Food continues to be the controlling image in their conversation. Stephen asks Donovan twice to bring him "a few turnips and onions" the next time he goes on a botany field trip so that he can "make a stew;" . . . Donovan mentions that his sister is to make pancakes for supper; and Lynch expresses disgust that pancakeeating Donovan can get a good job while he has to smoke cheap cigarettes.

Stephen ends the delineation of his esthetic with the now famous statement, "The artist, like the God of creation, remains within or behind or beyond or above his handiwork, invisible, refined out of existence, indifferent, paring his fingernails." . . . The artist is God; God is Jesus; Stephen is Jesus. As Jesus left the companionship of his disciples on Maundy Thursday for the exile of the cross and the grave, Stephen is leaving Lynch, his pope, and Emma, his Blessed Virgin, as well as his family, nation, and church for the exile of the artist and for Paris.

But the symbols examined above are from only a very small portion of the chapter. What happens symbolically between the tea and fried bread of Stephen's breakfast and the curry eaten at Clark's? Thousands of things. And after the curry other thousands. Some of these are clearly symbolic, and their symbolic content can be allegorized for purposes of analysis.

In the narrative Stephen walks to school. As he walks he thinks of himself as a doubting monk . . . , meets a consumptive man . . . , thinks of Cranly as a guilty priest . . . , reflects on his interest in words . . . , recalls the temptation of Davin by a country wife . . . , is buttonholed by a woman selling flowers . . . , thinks with something like compassion of Dublin . . . , and thinks of Burnchapel Whaley, Buck Egan, and Buck Whaley. . . . (pp. 8-9)

After witnessing Stephen's function as priest, it is clear to the reader why he should think of himself as a doubting monk. But it may not be immediately apparent that the consumptive man is a type of Christ; and in him, as in the dwarf whom he, Cranly, and Dixon meet in the library . . . , Stephen (as Christ) sees himself as he will be on Good Friday: ". . . an ugly little man who has taken into his body the sins of the world . . . a crooked ugly body for which neither God nor man have pity." Joyce had attended the Tenebrae services of Holy Week and had taken notes on them. . . . He may have got the idea of the disfigured Christ from the Responsory of the second Nocturne of the Office of Holy Thursday: "Behold we have seen him disfigured and without beauty: his aspect is gone for him: he has borne our sins and suffered for us." To put it in a variety of theological language, the consumptive man and the dwarf are "types" of Christ (Stephen) as a scapegoat just as Noah or Jonah in the Bible are types of Christ.

The time on the dairy clock is wrong because time is out of joint in the symbolic sequence of the chapter, and also because the dairy, which fuses as symbol with the temptation of Davin by the country wife, is connected with eternity before time— at least before that aspect of time called death. Davin is Adam, who is tempted by this Irish Eve with a mug of milk for an apple. He is the person in the *Portrait* most closely related to "the broken lights of Irish myth," . . . and he is associated in Stephen's mind with primeval incest. . . . Joyce links the country wife to the woman selling flowers . . . and to temptresses in general . . . , including Emma . . . and the Blessed Virgin . . . , who is one of the lures of the fallen seraphim. . . . (pp. 9-10)

Cranly is thought of as a "guilty priest" . . . because he is, in one of his symbolic aspects, Judas. He betrays Stephen by stealing his best girl. . . . In Stephen's own interpretation of Cranly as John the Baptist he was puzzled by St. John at the Latin Gate and sees him as the "precursor trying to pick the lock." . . . He writes in his diary, "Is he the shining light now? Well, I discovered him. I protest I did." . . . (pp. 10-11)

The reader is as puzzled as Stephen unless he knows or takes the trouble to find out who St. John at the Latin Gate is. The feast of St. John before the Latin Gate, celebrated in the Church on May 6, marks the anniversary of the dedication of the Basilica of St. John Lateran outside the Gate of St. John in Rome during the time of Pope Adrian. The original church was dedicated to the Savior, but later, because it was served by a Benedictine monastery dedicated to St. John the Baptist and St. John the Evangelist, the church was dedicated to the two St. Johns as well. This later dedication has now superseded the original one in popular usage; or, in the framework of Joyce's symbolism, Christ has again been betrayed. Since the station for Maundy Thursday Mass is at St. John Lateran, Joyce's irony is apparent.

Stephen ponders "The soul of the gallant venal city" . . . of Dublin, which had ". . . shrunk with time to a faint mortal odour rising from the earth. . . ." . . . as Christ thinks of Jerusalem:

> Jerusalem! Jerusalem! thou that killest the prophets, and stoneth them that are sent unto thee, how often would I have gathered together thy children, as the hen doth gather her chickens under her wings, and thou wouldest not.

Several Irish prophets who have been killed by Irish men are mentioned in Chapter V, and all of these are connected with

Holograph copy of the first page of the manuscript of A Portrait of the Artist as a Young Man. *Courtesy of Sean O'Mordha.*

Stephen's own crucifixion. Yeats at the opening of the National Theatre is one of these: ". . . the catcalls and hisses and mocking cries ran in rude gusts around the hall." . . . And Stephen says to Davin: "No honorable and sincere man . . . has given up his life and his youth and his affection from the days of Tone to those of Parnell but you have sold him to the enemy or failed him in need or reviled him and left him for another." . . . (p. 11)

The Bucks Egan and Whaley and Burnchapel Whaley were infamous for many reasons. They performed, according to rumor, black masses while living in what was to become the University College building. Burnchapel also burns chapels, but it is Buck, his son, who is important for his connection with Cranly. Buck's second alias was "Jerusalem" Whaley because he won a bet, estimated to be between 10,000 and 15,000 pounds, for walking to Jerusalem and playing ball against the walls. This is the key to the mysterious grey handball which Cranly carries. . . . He and Davin play handball with it, "Cranly insisting his ball should be used," and in answer to its thud, he exclaims, "Your soul!" . . . In Stephen's ironic theology this supports the demonic character of Cranly as the betrayer, and it is made doubly ironic by Cranly's being the most "Roman" of Stephen's Catholic male friends.

The thoughts of the Bucks bring the narrative to Stephen's arrival at University College, where he enters the physics classroom to find the dean of studies lighting a fire in the fireplace. Stephen sees his actions as religious ritual. . . . But the position of this scene in relation to Buck Whaley, and the thoughts which Stephen has concerning the priest indicate that it is the ritual of the Catholic priest which is defective rather than the ritual of the priest of art. The dean's ". . . very soul had waxed old in that service without growing towards light and beauty," . . . ". . . in his eyes burned no spark of Ignatius' enthusiasm," . . . and ". . . it seemed as if he loved not at all the master." . . . (pp. 11-12)

During the physics class Stephen considers offering himself as a "subject for electrocution." . . . And afterwards, as Stephen goes into the crowd of students in the entrance hall, "Cranly's dark eyes were watching him." . . . The crowd has gathered to watch his trial. He is tried by Mac Cann as Pilate for not submitting to Caesar in the form of the Tsar. Mac Cann, who is "ready to shed the last drop" . . . for the "universal peace" of the Tsar (or Augustus) even pronounces Pilate's *Ecce homo!* while clearing his throat, "Hom!" . . .

Stephen and Cranly cross the "weedy garden" . . . of Gethsemane together and find Lynch, the disciple to whom Stephen will confide the innermost mysteries of the religion of art, asleep; and the parallel with *Matthew* 26:40 and the Responsory to the eighth Lesson of the third Nocturne of the Holy Thursday Tenebrae is complete: "Could ye not watch one hour with me?"

Stephen and Lynch then set out on their peripatetic discussion of Stephen's esthetic, and Stephen symbolically reassures Lynch that he is not only God but "also an animal!" This may encourage the reader to recall Stephen's doubly ironic question of a few pages earlier, "Do you fancy I am going to pay in my own life and person for debts they made?" . . . And later, in the passage dealing with Stephen's lineage, the question "Did an angel speak?" . . . carries not only narrative and obscene levels but also refers directly to the means of conception between the Holy Ghost and the Blessed Virgin.

Although the crucifixion of Stephen is represented fully only by the book as a whole, it is symbolically re-enacted on the steps of the National Library at the end of Stephen's and Lynch's walk. As they approach the library, the sky is appropriately "veiled" and it begins to rain. Emma stands silently among her companions (the "other Marys" of the gospels) and Stephen watches her with "conscious bitterness," . . . thinking of her as a lure for him and Father Moran. She is specifically identified with the Virgin by the medical students' otherwise pointless talk of obstetrics, which the dying Stephen hears ". . . as if from a distance in interrupted pulsations." . . . As she prepares to go away with her companions, Stephen considers forgiving her.

The church year is continued in the burlesque Easter Mass which Stephen celebrates in the Circe episode of *Ulysses,* but the resurrection is foreshadowed in the *Portrait* by the sleep and waking which immediately follow Stephen's symbolic crucifixion:

> A spirit filled him, pure as the purest water. . . .
> But how faintly it was inbreathed . . . as if the
> seraphim themselves were breathing upon
> him! . . .

The night had been enchanted. In a dream or
vision he had known the ecstasy of seraphic
life. . . .

(pp. 12-13)

This explication does not exhaust the meanings of even these
few strands of symbols in a single chapter of the *Portrait*, a
book which is a rich, closely woven fabric of symbol and
narrative. But since all of the elements treated as symbols in
the *Portrait* were either omitted or treated on a simple narrative
level in *Stephen Hero*, the tracing of the few strands through
a small part of the whole cloth may add to our understanding
of the growth of Joyce as an artist. (p. 13)

C. G. Anderson, "The Sacrificial Butter," in Accent, *Vol. XII, No. 1, Winter, 1952, pp. 3-13.*

WILLIAM YORK TINDALL   (essay date 1955)

[*Tindall is a noted American scholar and literary critic who has
written widely on twentieth-century literature. He is most famous
for his extensive writings on James Joyce, particularly his* Reader's Guide to James Joyce *(1959), a concise but thorough introduction to Joyce's works, and* The Joyce Country *(1960; rev. ed.
1972), a collection of photographs of Dublin locations mentioned
in Joyce's works. In the following excerpt he takes issue with
those critics who refer to Joyce as a Naturalist. Tindall argues
that Joyce is not a Naturalist, but an Imagist who is seldom
recognized as such because of the subtle way in which he embodied
images in the realistic details of his narratives. Tindall illustrates
this point by tracing the pattern of certain images such as roads,
water, flowers, and birds throughout* A Portrait of the Artist as
a Young Man. *For a contrasting discussion of the imagery of* A
Portrait of the Artist, *see the excerpt by John V. Kelleher (1958),
who finds that the work can be read on the surface as a naturalistic
novel, but that such a reading ignores the symbolic depth of
Joyce's art; for an example of the complexity and subtle application of Joyce's imagery and symbolism, see the excerpt by C. G.
Anderson (1952).*]

Joyce, who wrote the stories of *Dubliners* shortly after the
appearance of Conrad's great symbolist work [*Lord Jim*], . . .
knew pages of Flaubert by heart. What he learned from him
is expressed in *Stephen Hero* where Stephen, after rejecting
naturalistic "portrayal of externals," says that the artist must
free "the image from its mesh of defining circumstances . . .
and re-embody it in artistic circumstances chosen as the most
exact for it in its new office." In that office the details of
observed reality, so precise that they have caused critics to
confuse Joyce with the naturalists, are "transmuted," as he
puts it in *A Portrait of the Artist,* into radiant images. Not only
Flaubert, to be sure, but symbolist poets and the Hermetic
tradition led Joyce to his method; and it is fitting that *Chamber
Music,* the sketch from which his poetic novel developed, is
verse; but that Flaubert remained central in Joyce's mind is
suggested not only by his concern with the observed image but
with the *mot juste* and expressive rhythm. Many passages in
Flaubert's letters, with which Joyce must have been familiar,
anticipate and maybe helped to shape the aesthetics of Stephen
Dedalus. Speaking as Stephen was to speak of the need for
impersonality, Flaubert says in one of his letters that the artist
must "be in his work like God in creation, present everywhere
and visible nowhere. Since art is a second world, its creator
must act by analogous methods."

A Portrait of the Artist, at once the residence and the creation
of Stephen's nail-paring God, differs from most other novels
of adolescence in detachment and method. At first glance,

however, Joyce's improvement upon the *Bildungsroman* seems
simple enough because the main burden is carried, as in ordinary novels of this sort, by character and action. We have
plainly before us the story of a sensitive, gifted boy who is
disappointed in his hope of communion with parents, country,
and religion. Refusing the actual world at last, as in the role
of the Count of Monte Cristo he refuses the muscatel grapes
that Mercedes proffers, he constructs a better world to replace
it. "If you have form'd a circle to go into," says cynical Blake,
"go into it yourself, and see how you would do."

The theme of *A Portrait of the Artist* is normal enough. Joyce
differs from most of his predecessors, as Flaubert from his, in
greater dependence upon image, rhythm, juxtaposition, and
tone to supplement the narrative and in giving attitudes and
feelings body to support them. What Joyce in his notes for
Exiles called "attendant images" could be omitted without
destroying the outline of his book, but some of its quality and
depth must be attributed to this accompaniment. At times,
moreover, forgetting their capacity of attendants, images and
other devices become essential and assume the principal burden
as they were to do in *Ulysses.* Yielding place to other things
at such times, the narrative grows "obscure," a word which
means that narrative has given way to suggestion and discourse
to nondiscursive elements having more effect on feeling than
on mind. While still attendant, however, images may be too
familiar or obvious to attract notice. Even Tolstoi used them.

When Vronsky in *Anna Karenina* rides his mare to death at
the races, breaking her back by his awkwardness or zeal, his
action, unnecessary to the plot and far from realistic, embodies
his relationship with Anna. But Tolstoi's image of the mare is so
narrowly assigned and painfully deliberate that it does little
more than discourse could. Joyce's images, though partly assigned, however deliberate, are suggestive, indefinite, and not
altogether explicable. Ambivalent, they reveal not only the
quality of experience but its complexity. Without attendant or
essential images, *A Portrait of the Artist* would be so much less
immediate and less moving that few would pick it up again.

Images play other parts in the great design. Embodying Stephen's experience before he is entirely aware of it, and doing
the same service for us, they prepare for moments of realization, which could not occur without them. Operating below
conscious notice, the images, rhythms, and other forms project
an unconscious process that comes to light at last. This function
is no more important, however, than that of relating part to
part and, composing a structure which, with the dominant narrative it supplements and complicates, creates what Stephen
calls radiance or the meaning of the composite form.

The first two pages of *A Portrait of the Artist* present the images
that, when elaborated, are to compose the supplementary structure and take their place in the form. We are confronted here
with a moocow coming down the road, with a rose (maybe
green), with wetting the bed, with a girl, and with an eagle
that plucks out eyes—not to mention a number of other things
such as dancing to another's tune. Without much context as
yet, these images, acquiring fresh meanings from recurrence
and relationship with others, carry aspects of Stephen and his
trouble. Never was opening so dense as this or more important.

Take that road, long, narrow, and strictly bounded, along which
comes a moocow to meet the passive boy. Diction, rhythm,
and the opening phrase (the traditional beginning of an Irish
"story") suggest the condition of childhood and its helplessness. Confined to the road, the child cannot escape encounter

with a creature traditionally associated with Irish legend and with everything maternal. Later, Stephen delights to accompany the milkman in his round of neighboring roads, although a little discouraged by the foul green puddles of the cowyard. Cows, which have seemed so beautiful in the country on sunny days, now revolt him and he can look no longer at their milk. Yet as he pursues "the Rock Road," he thinks a milkman's life pleasant enough, and looks forward with equanimity to adopting it as his own. Innumerable connotations of word and phrase make it almost plain at last that the road suggests tradition, that the cow suggests church, country, and all maternal things, and that the milkman suggests the priest. The little episode, far from being a sign of these meanings, is no more than the embodiment of possibilities. What it implies awaits corroboration from later episodes, Stephen's rejection of the priesthood, for example, or his aethetic query about the man hacking a cow by accident from a block of wood. It is certain that none of these connected images is casual. As for the road itself, it develops into the circular track round which Mike Flynn, the old trainer, makes Stephen run; into the track at Clongowes where Stephen, breaking his glasses, is almost blinded; into the dark road alongside which Davin meets his peasant woman; and, after many reappearances, all of which confirm and enlarge the initial idea and feeling of tradition, into its opposite, the road that promises freedom on the final page.

The images of rose, water, girl, and bird are so intricately involved with one another that it seems all but impossible to separate them for analysis. Take the rose, however, a symbol which, carrying traditional significance, becomes, after much recurrence, Stephen's image of woman and creativity. Lacking sufficient context at its first appearance to have certain meaning, the rose, made green by Stephen, is not altogether without possibilities. Green is the color of Ireland, of immaturity, and of vegetable creation; yet a green rose is unnatural. Art is unnatural too. Could the green rose anticipate Stephen's immature desire for Irish art? We cannot tell for sure. At school Stephen is champion of the white rose that loses to the red in an academic war of roses; and during his period of "resolute piety" his prayers ascend to heaven "like perfume streaming upwards from a heart of white rose." It is the red rose, however, that attends his creative ecstasies near the Bull Wall, after he resolves to follow mortal beauty, and in bed, after composing a poem. His soul, "swooning into some new world," shares Dante's penultimate vision: "A world, a glimmer, or a flower? Glimmering and trembling, trembling and unfolding, a breaking light, an opening flower, it spread in endless succession to itself, breaking in full crimson and unfolding and fading to palest rose, leaf by leaf and wave of light by wave of light, flooding all the heavens with its soft flushes, every flush deeper than other." This heavenly vision, which follows the hell of the sermons and the purgatory of his repentance, anticipates his ultimate vision of Mrs. Bloom, the heavenly yet earthly rose of *Ulysses.*

Woman, associated with rose, embodies Stephen's aspiration and, increasingly, his creative power. Eileen, the girl who appears at the beginning of the book, unattainable because Protestant, is soon identified with sex and the Tower of Ivory, symbol of the Blessed Virgin. Mercedes, a dream who inhabits a garden of roses along the milkman's road, suggests the Virgin by her name while adding overtones of remoteness, exile, and revenge. At Cork, however, Stephen's "monstrous" adolescent thoughts injure her purity by desire. When Emma, a teaser, replaces Mercedes as object of desire and becomes in addition

an image of his mother country and his church, Stephen transfers his devotion to the Virgin herself, over whose sodality he presides, and whose "office" becomes his formula. The wading girl near the Bull Wall, who embodies mortal beauty, unites all previous suggestions. Associating her with Emma, the Virgin, the rose, and the womb of the imagination, whose priest he becomes, he finds her an image of his own capacity: "Heavenly God!" his soul exclaims, its eye no doubt upon himself. His repeated "Yes" anticipates Mrs. Bloom's as the girl, stirring the waters "hither and thither," anticipates the hither and thithering waters of Anna Livia Plurabelle: "He would create."

Other women take their place in the great design. There is the common girl, persisting in memory, who stops Stephen on the street to offer flowers for which he cannot pay. Connected in his mind with a kitchen girl who sings Irish songs over the dishes, she develops near the end into the servant maid, who, singing "Rosie O'Grady" in her kitchen, proffers the suggestion at least of Irish flowers, green roses perhaps. Cranly's *"Mulier cantat"* unites her in Stephen's mind with "the figure of woman as she appears in the liturgy of the Church" and with all his symbolic women. Unprepared as yet to receive what she proffers in her song or unable to pay the price of acceptance, Stephen says, "I want to see Rosie first."

That Rosie, another anticipation of Mrs. Bloom, sings in a kitchen is not unimportant. After each of his ecstasies, Stephen comes back to the kitchen, which serves not only as an ironic device for deflating him but as an image of the reality to which, if he is to be an artist, he must return. It is notable that his acceptance of Mr. Bloom and the communion with mankind that precedes the vision of Mrs. Bloom takes place in a kitchen. Rosie in her kitchen, the last great image of woman in *A Portrait of the Artist,* unites the ideal with the actual. Neither the wading girl nor Mercedes, both ethereal, can present to Stephen the idea and feeling of a union which someday he will understand. Far from seeing Rosie first, he sees her last, but by her aid, of which he is not fully aware as yet, he comes nearer his vision of above and below, of heavenly roses to be sure but of roses in kitchens.

Woman is not only rose but bird and sometimes bat. The bird, which makes its first appearance as the eagle who is to punish Stephen's guilt by making him blind as a bat, makes its next appearance as Heron, who, looking and acting like a bird of prey, tries to make Stephen conform. Bad at first, birds become good as Stephen approaches mortal beauty at the beach. He thinks of Daedalus, "a hawklike man flying sunward," and wants to utter cries of hawk or eagle, images no longer of oppression but, retaining authority, of creation. The wading girl is "a strange and beautiful seabird." "Her bosom was a bird's, soft and slight, slight and soft as the breast of some dark-plumaged dove." As Stephen observes their flight, birds also become what he calls a "symbol of departure or loneliness." When, becoming birdlike Daedalus, he takes flight across the sea to exile, he unites all these meanings and confirms their association with water. Bats are anticipated by images of blinding, not only those of the eye-plucking eagle, of glasses broken on the track, and of dull red blinds that keep light from boys of Belvedere during their retreat but that of the woman into whose eye Mr. Casey spits: "'Phth! says I to her.' 'O Jesus, Mary and Joseph!' says she . . . 'I'm blinded and drownded . . . I'm blinded entirely.'" When they appear at last, bats gather up these anticipatory associations with woman, custom, and country. Davin's peasant woman at her door along the dark lonely road seems to Stephen "a type of her race and of his own, a batlike soul waking to the consciousness of itself in darkness and secrecy and loneliness." Seeming almost a bird for a moment, Emma, revisited, becomes another bat, but its darkness, secrecy, and loneliness connect it with himself as artist about to try silence, exile, and cunning. Blind to reality as yet, he may improve. Like the images of bird and flower, the bat is ambivalent, not only bad but good. If bat suggests things as they are, and bird things as they ought to be, it is the artist's job to reconcile them. If all these women are aspects of woman, and if woman is an aspect of himself, the creative part, he too is presented by images of bird, bat, and, besides these, water.

Ambivalent from the first, water is either warm or cold, agreeable or frightening. The making of water at the beginning of the *Portrait* seems an image of creation that includes the artist's two realities. At school Stephen is shouldered into the "square ditch," square not because of shape but because it receives the flow of the urinal or "square." Plainly maternal by context, this image warns Stephen of the perils of regression, to which like one of those rats who enjoy the ditch, he is tempted by the discomforts of external reality. The "warm turf-coloured bogwater" of the bath adds something peculiarly Irish to his complex. Dirty water down the drain at the Wicklow Hotel and the watery sound of cricket bats (connected in his mind with pandybats and bats) confirm his fears. The concluding image of the first chapter, assigned only by previous associations, embodies his infantile career: "Pick, pack, pock, puck," go the cricket bats, "like drops of water in a fountain filling softly in the brimming bowl." If Stephen himself is suggested by this bowl and his development by an ablaut series, water is not altogether bad. This possibility is established toward the middle of the book, where, changing character, water becomes good on the whole and unmistakably a symbol of creation. On his way to the beach, Stephen still finds the sea cold and "infra-human." The bathing boys repel him, but the sight of the wading girl gives water another aspect. Rolling up his trousers like J. Alfred Prufrock, he himself goes wading. From that moment of baptism and rebirth inaudible music and the sound of waters attend his creative ecstasies. It is true that, relapsing a little, Stephen fears water again in *Ulysses,* but Mr. Bloom, with whom he finally unites, is a water lover, and Anna Livia Plurabelle is the river Liffey.

These families of developing images that, supplementing the narrative, give it texture, immediacy, and more body are not the only symbolic devices Joyce commands. As we have noticed, large parallels, rhythms, shifts of tone, juxtaposition, and all else that Flaubert commended complicate the "significant form." . . . [But] some of the relatively unassigned and unattached images . . . concentrate feeling at important points.

Consider, for example, the opening of the second chapter. Uncle Charles, who is addicted to black twist, is deported to the outhouse, whence rising smoke and the brim of his tall hat appear as he sings old songs in tranquillity. Position gives this image an importance that import cannot justify. Hints of exile, creation, and piety, all relevant to the theme, may divert our understanding without satisfying it entirely. Few of Joyce's images are so mysterious as this and, while occupying our feelings, so resistant to discourse. The scenery at Cork appeals more readily to the understanding. While in that town with his father, Stephen finds in the word "Foetus," carved in the wood of a desk, what Eliot would call an objective correlative of the "den of monstrous images" within him. After this corroboration of inner disorder, he emerges from schoolroom into the

sunny street where he sees cricketers and a maid watering plants; hears a German band and scale after scale from a girl's piano. In another book this urban noise and scenery might serve as setting alone. Here, more functional than that, it presents a vision of the normal, the orderly, and the quotidian from which the discovery of his monstrous interior has separated him.

Characters are no less symbolic. The two dwarfish eccentrics that Stephen encounters, one on the street and the other in the library, seem caricatures of Stephen's possible future and of the soul of Ireland, but aside from that, they evade significance. By action, speech, and context, on the other hand, the figure of Cranly becomes more nearly definite. That last interview which drives Stephen to exile concentrates in Cranly the forces of admission, submission, confession, and retreat, and he becomes the embodiment of all that has plagued the imperfect hero. Cranly's preoccupation with a book called *Diseases of the Ox* adds to the picture. Since Stephen as "Bous Stephanoumenos" has been identified with the ox, Cranly's devotion to his book reveals him as Stephen's most reactionary critic, not, as we had supposed, his friend.

When Stephen turns seaward toward his great experience with the wading girl, an image which might escape casual notice not only suggests the finality of his action but adds to our understanding of his complexity: he crosses the bridge from Dollymount to the Bull. Readers of *Dubliners* may recall that crossing bridges in that work is as portentous as Caesar's crossing of the Rubicon; in *Ulysses* Stephen, a frustrated exile back from Paris, is "a disappointed bridge." In the *Portrait,* on the bridge which marks his passage from old custom to freedom and the waters of life, he meets a squad of uncouth, tall-hatted Christian Brothers, marching two by two, going the other way. Their direction, their appearance, and their regimentation are important, but what reveals Stephen's character is the contempt with which he regards those who are socially and intellectually inferior to Jesuits. The episode, therefore, includes both his escape from one tyranny and his submission to another, the greater tyranny of pride, which, until he understands the Blooms, will keep him from uniting the regions of reality by art. Stephen may think of charity or Joyce talk of pride, but this revealing episode contributes more than all that talk or thought to the portrait of an artist. (pp. 76-86)

> *William York Tindall, "Supreme Fictions," in his* The Literary Symbol, *Columbia University Press, 1955, pp. 68-101.**

THOMAS E. CONNOLLY (essay date 1956)

[*In the following excerpt, Connolly examines the transmutations that Stephen Dedalus's aesthetic theory undergoes from the time of its first appearance in* Stephen Hero *to its final presentation in the last chapter of* A Portrait of the Artist as a Young Man.]

[The aesthetic theory advanced by Stephen Dedalus in *A Portrait of the Artist as a Young Man*] . . . is unfortunately incomplete: it makes no direct mention of the subject matter of art, and it is sketchy with respect to the "epiphany,"the one element of the aesthetic theory which has most stimulated critical attention. For a synthesis of Joyce's theory it is necessary to examine and compare three texts: *A Portrait of the Artist, Stephen Hero* (the incomplete first draft of the *Portrait*), and [Herbert] Gorman's biography of Joyce. The theory, it will be found, divides itself into four general parts: the good and the

Joyce's class at Clongowes Wood College, 1888-89, with its class master Father William Power (Father Arnall in A Portrait*). Joyce is seated by himself on the ground in front. In the back row, Rody Kickham is sixth from the left, Christopher ("Nasty") Roche fifth from the right. In the front row, Wells is second from the right and Francis Pigott fourth from the right.*

beautiful, the subject matter of art, the static principle of art, and the method of apprehending the beautiful.

Stephen first begins to discuss the good and the beautiful in the scene in *A Portrait of the Artist* in which he talks with the dean of studies while he is lighting the fire. It is interesting to notice that in the corresponding scenes with Father Butt in *Stephen Hero* no mention of the good and the beautiful is made at all; they speak briefly of the two levels of meaning for words, and only one sentence is devoted to the distinction between the useful arts and the liberal arts. In *A Portrait* Stephen sets forth the two principles from Aquinas upon which his theory is based: *Pulcra sunt quae visa placent:* those things are beautiful the perception of which pleases. (Stephen, of course, properly interprets *visa* not in the restricted sense of "sight," but in the wider sense of "esthetic intellection," or apprehension.) *Bonum est in quod tendit appetitus:* the good is that toward which the appetite tends. After merely stating these principles with no attempt to apply them to anything beyond the fire before them, Stephen receives the approval of the dean for his understanding of St. Thomas, and the conversation gets off on a discussion of the levels of usage of words. It is upon these two principles, however, that Stephen's entire theory rests. All that follows evolves from his conviction that the creative artist is concerned only with the creation of the beautiful, whereas the productive artist (or the artisan) is concerned with the production of the good.

For the next aspect of Stephen's theory it is necessary to depend entirely upon *Stephen Hero,* for it will be found in no other place. In the argument with the president of the university Stephen says: "Even admitting the corruption you speak of I see nothing unlawful in an examination of corruption." The president uses stronger language than Stephen in describing the subject matter of the writers whom Stephen praises in his lecture; he calls it "the garbage of modern society." During this debate Stephen is simply defending the subject matter which the naturalistic school has chosen as appropriate for art.

He rejects the attempt to limit the subject matter of art to the sublime. . . . The subject matter of art . . . for Stephen is anything that pleases the aesthetic sensitivity. (pp. 47-8)

In the *Portrait,* the discussion of the aesthetic theory with Lynch divides itself into two parts. The problem of the proper subject matter of art is not, as I have said, discussed. It is assumed. Stephen begins by talking of the static effect of art upon the beholder, and then introduces his theory of the beautiful, and finally his theory of the way the beautiful is apprehended by the mind. Three of the four aspects of his aesthetic theory are contained in this one dialogue.

The first half of the conversation is merely the dramatic presentation of a rather lengthy notebook entry, dated 13 February 1903, which is reproduced by Gorman. Stephen explains to Lynch that art must produce a stasis in the observer. This is merely an application of Stephen's first principle: the creative artist is concerned with the beautiful, not with the good. Good art, therefore, cannot produce a desire or a loathing in the beholder, cannot be kinetic. Rather, it must produce an emotion which in itself satisfies the aesthetic sense alone. Beyond this art cannot go; if it attempts to excite either desire or loathing (for either the good or the bad), it ceases to be creative art, since it then assumes the aim of a useful art, such as rhetoric. It is in this sense that Stephen speaks of kinetic art as "improper" art.

At this point in the *Portrait* Stephen has established two aspects of his aesthetic theory and has taken for granted the third. . . . In the second half of the conversation with Lynch (after the interruption by Donovan) Stephen goes on to present the fourth aspect of his theory, the method by which the intellect apprehends the beautiful.

Ad pulcritudinem tria requiruntur, Stephen quotes Aquinas, *integritas, consonantia, claritas.* Three things are required for the perception of beauty: wholeness or integrity, harmony or proportion, and clarity or radiance.

Before any object can be apprehended as beautiful it must be seen to be *one* thing; that is, it must be seen as a unified whole, distinguished, for example, from a totality. By using the notebook entries reproduced by Gorman . . . we are able to expand the theory at this point. Since the act of simple perception gives pleasure (his basic assumption from Aquinas and Aristotle), it is possible at this level—recognition of the *integriatas* of a thing—to say that all objects, even hideous objects, which can be simply perceived are, to the extent of the pleasure derived from the act of perception, beautiful. But in a larger sense a thing cannot be said to be beautiful simply because we have apprehended it as *one* thing, as a whole composed of parts.

The next step in the apprehension of the beauty of an object is the apprehension of the proportion or balance of its parts, both with respect to each other and with respect to the whole which they compose. This is to apprehend the *consonantia.* "You feel," as Stephen explains it, "the rhythm of its structure." Again at this level, beauty, to a degree, may be predicated of the object, because, once again, a pleasure has been derived from the simple perception of the proportion and order of the parts. Still, the beauty of the object, in the final sense, cannot yet be said to be apprehended, for the third step in the process has not yet been taken.

Finally, to *integritas* and *consonantia* must be added *claritas* to make possible the full apprehension of the beauty of any object. What Aquinas meant by *claritas* puzzled Stephen at first, but as he eventually explains it to Lynch it is the realization or the understanding of the *quidditas* of the object, the *whatness* of it. Stephen explains it very clearly:

> The instant wherein that supreme quality of beauty, the clear radiance of the esthetic image, is apprehended luminously by the mind which has been arrested by its wholeness and fascinated by its harmony is the luminous silent stasis of esthetic pleasure, a spiritual state very like . . . the enchantment of the heart.

Here is the essence of the epiphany which Spencer laments as having been "left out of the *Portrait* entirely." It is true that in *Stephen Hero,* in his conversation with Cranly, which is a rough parallel of the second half of the conversation with Lynch in the *Portrait,* Stephen definitely identifies the moment of the apprehension of the *claritas* of a thing as the epiphany: "This is the moment which I call epiphany." When these three acts of perception have been accomplished by the mind, when the object has been finally epiphanized, its full beauty is apprehended.

With this aspect of his theory, Stephen has completed the formal construction of it. He then quickly applies it to literature in general, and he is able to make a triple division of the various forms of literature. This division is based upon the relationship existing between the artist and the image represented. In the lyrical form the "center of emotional gravity" is in immediate relationship to the artist. The epic form is no longer purely personal. The "center of emotional gravity is equidistant from the artist and from others." In the dramatic form the artist is "refined out of existence." Like the creator of the universe, the dramatic artist stands apart from his work and the dramatic form exists in and for itself in a static condition. The synthesis of Stephen's aesthetic theory is complete with this pronouncement. The rain conveniently begins to fall, and Stephen, who has no more theory to advance, seeks shelter with Lynch on the library porch.

The aesthetic theory as it is presented in the *Portrait* is an admirable approach to the climax of the book, the scene in which he announces to Cranly that he has left the Church and is about to leave Ireland. When the ties with family, church, and country are cut, Stephen has as his sole possession his completely developed aesthetic theory, the theory which forced him to cut the ties. And it is the height of the novel's irony that the theory of aesthetics which drove him from the Church is derived from Aquinas. (pp. 47-50)

> *Thomas E. Connolly, "Joyce's Aesthetic Theory,"* in The University of Kansas City Review, *Vol. XXIII, No. 1, October, 1956, pp. 47-50.*

JOHN V. KELLEHER   (essay date 1958)

[*In the following excerpt, Kelleher discusses the surface naturalism and symbolic depth of* A Portrait of the Artist as a Young Man. *Kelleher makes the point that, although the* Portrait *contains many levels of meaning, it may be, and often is, read simply as a naturalistic novel. Kelleher believes that this occurs because of the subtlety of the symbolism, and because irony in the* Portrait *inheres more in its structure than in its tone or its specific incidents. Kelleher concludes that such involutions account for much of the confusion among readers regarding Joyce's intentions in the novel. For a contrasting discussion, see the excerpt by William York Tindall (1955), who decries those who consider the work a Naturalistic novel and explains the novel as an example of Imagism.*]

If the day should come that I walk into the classroom, unfurl my opening lecture on Joyce, and find at the end of the hour that I had as well been talking about Alfred Lord Tennyson, I shall not be unduly surprised. No writer's original fame lasts forever with the young. Joyce has already had an unusually long run with them; and though their interest shows no present signs of weakening, when it does fail it will likely fail suddenly. Everything in literature has its term, and, if worthy, its renewal. That the rediscovery of Joyce will occur, with full fanfare, within a generation after his rejection, may be taken as certain. However, that will be no affair of mine.

Meanwhile, I predict with confidence that when the rest of Joyce's books pass into temporary disfavor *A Portrait of the Artist as a Young Man* will go on being read, possibly as much as ever, by youths from eighteen to twenty-two. They will read it and recommend it to one another just as lads their age do now, and for the same reasons. That is, they will read it primarily as useful and reassuring revelation—not as literature, for they will be blind to its irony and its wonderful engineering, the qualities Joyce most labored to give it. They will use it as a magic mirror: as boys of thirteen use *Huckleberry Finn* and as sixteen-going-on-seventeen looks into the *Rubáiyát of Omar Khayyám* for graceful corroboration of its own grim apprehension of The Meaning of Life. I should think it doubtful that Joyce had these readers in mind when he wrote the book, any more than FitzGerald foresaw for his nearly original poem its permanent audience of callow fatalists; but, like it or not, this is part of his achievement.

Joyce did complain that readers tended to forget the last four words of the title. He could have remarked, too, that the book was not the *Self-Portrait of the Artist as a Young Man.* All too often it is read as if it were so named. Then the author himself is belabored for the sins and the more than occasional priggishness of his hero, or, conversely, is credited with having possessed in youth the same astonishing clarity of purpose and action.

Either assumption is unjust to Joyce. True, Stephen Dedalus is endowed with a personal history quite similar to his creator's; his experiences are modeled on those Joyce himself suffered or enjoyed at that age; and as Joyce, writing the book, is the mature artist, so Stephen is a representation of the artist-by-nature as he discovers his vocation, defines his creed, and sets forth to practice it. There, I think, close resemblance ends. Joyce's life happened to him as everyone's life happens—at all hours and seasons, any old way, with chronic inconvenience. Stephen's existence, though presented in rich detail, is at once the product and the illustration of deliberate composition in terms of a consciously created aesthetic.

I remember that when I first encountered Stephen Dedalus I was twenty and I wondered how Joyce could have known so much about me. That is what I mean by the sort of reading the book will continue to get, whatever literary fashion may decree. Perhaps about the third reading it dawned on me that Stephen was, after all, a bit of a prig; and to that extent I no longer identified myself with him. (How could I?) Quite a while later I perceived that Joyce knew that Stephen was a prig; that, indeed, he looked on Stephen with quite an ironic eye. So than I understood. At least I did until I had to observe that the author's glance was not one of unmixed irony. There was compassion in it too, as well as a sort of tender, humorous pride. By this time I was lecturing on Joyce, and I was having a terrible time with the book. I could not coordinate what I had to say about it; and the students, as their papers showed, were mostly wondering how Joyce could have known so much about them—which was fortunate, for the lectures made very little sense, and it as well that the victims had their own discoveries to distract them.

The trouble was, I was trying to examine separate parts of the book separately. There aren't any separate parts. One might as well attempt to study a man's gestures by pulling off his arm and dissecting it. The book is all of a piece, one organic whole. It is, as it were, written backwards and forwards and sideways and in depth, all at once. A score of premises is laid down in the first twenty-odd pages. From these, with deliberate and unobtrusive engineering, everything else is developed in the most natural-looking way possible. The same words or the same basic images in which the premise was expressed are used over and over again, development usually being measured by the variations of context in which they occur or by new combinations of these identifying words and images.

Described that way, the technique sounds dry as dust. Just some more damned symbolism. Unfortunately I can only suggest the vitality of Joyce's method by illustrating it, and . . . I can get an illustration only by dissecting it from its text. A curiously uncooperative man he always was.

One early premise is the conjunction of red and green. Stephen, as a baby, has a song:

> *O, the wild rose blossoms*
> *On the little green place.*

He sang that song. That was his song.

> *O, the green wothe botheth.*

The song is an old sentimental favorite, *Lily Dale*. The second line ought to be "On the little green grave," but this is a song taught to a very small child and so for *grave* is substituted the neutral *place*. What counts, however, is that as he sings it he confuses red and green into one image, the green rose.

On the next page the colors are still in proximity but are now separate.

> Dante [his grandaunt] had two brushes in her press. The brush with the maroon velvet back was for Michael Davitt and the brush with the green velvet back was for Parnell.

A little later in the chapter the child, now at boarding school, is coming down with a fever and finds it hard to study. He looks at his geography where there is a picture of the earth amid clouds, which another boy, not he, had colored with crayons.

> He . . . looked wearily at the green round earth in the middle of the maroon clouds. He wondered which was right, to be for the green or for the maroon, because Dante had ripped the green velvet back off the brush that was for Parnell one day with her scissors and had told him that Parnell was a bad man. . . .

He remembers the song, too. "But you could not have a green rose. But perhaps someplace in the world you could."

At night, sick and very lonely, he dreams of going home for Christmas; and home is all in terms of a conjunction of green and red.

> There were lanterns in the hall of his father's house and ropes of green branches. There were holly and ivy round the pierglass and holly and ivy, green and red, twined round the chandeliers. There were red holly and green ivy round the old portraits on the walls. Holly and ivy for him and for Christmas.

This simple union of red and green—say, of emotion and vitality, though that hardly expresses the whole meaning—is realized once more, for the last time, at the beginning of the famous Christmas dinner episode.

> A great fire, banked high and red, flamed in the grate and under the ivy twined branches of the chandelier the Christmas table was spread.

But from there out, only the red of passion and the black of grief. The argument over Parnell and the bishops cannot be avoided or hushed. Dante, aflame with outraged pietism and heartburn, and the dark-faced Mr. Casey have it out uncontrollably. When Dante stamps from the room shouting, "Devil out of hell! We won! We crushed him to death! Fiend!", the household, like Ireland itself, is split asunder, the soldierly Casey is weeping for his "dead king," all color is crushed out of the scene—and, though the reader, caught up by the wild emotionality, is not likely to remember, confidence in custom has been broken too. Before the argument, Stephen had been thinking how

> when dinner was ended the big plum pudding would be carried in, studded with peeled almonds and sprigs of holly, with bluish fire running around it and a little green flag flying from the top.

The pudding is never brought in. Stephen will never see Ireland happily on top of its own world.

Till the book reaches its climax, red and green remain apart. The dominant combination is red, black, and white: a false one for Stephen whether betokened by a red-faced priest with his white collar and black garb or by the dark hair and rosy complexion and white dress of E.C., the wrong girl for him. Meanwhile, half a dozen other themes are being developed through color, the most important being the white, gold, blue, and ivory of the Blessed Virgin to whom Stephen offers a dry and profitless devotion. The same four colors, though never all at once, indicate the image of beauty he must find among mortal women.

The book has five chapters. The first four chronicle Stephen's search for his true identity. As the very first sentence informs us, he is not truly of the family into which he was born—there he is "baby tuckoo," the cuckoo's fledgling in the cowbird's nest. He tries to find himself through obedience, through disobedience, through the family, through dream, through precocious sexuality, and finally and most earnestly through rigorous piety. Each attempt fails. He only learns in recurrent weariness and despair that he is not this, not that. Then suddenly, a little after he has refused to be trapped by vanity into falsely admitting a vocation for the priesthood, freedom possesses him. Freedom and expectation. He wanders out onto the strand at the north side of the river mouth where presentiment had long since warned him he would meet his love. Bond after bond falls away from him. Weariness is banished. Joyfully he feels his final separation from all that does not truly and wholly pertain to himself. He knows with absolute certainty that he is approaching his destiny in the "wild heart of life." Suddenly, too, color—all significant color—is around him, every hue transformed, red to russet and green to emerald. Almost on that instant he meets his Muse.

> A girl stood before him in midstream: alone and still, gazing out to sea. She seemed like one whom magic had changed into the likeness of a strange and beautiful seabird. Her long slender bare legs were delicate as a crane's and pure save where an emerald trail of seaweed had fashioned itself as a sign upon the flesh. Her thighs, fuller and softhued as ivory, were bared almost to the hips where the white fringes of her drawers were like feathering of soft white down. Her slate-blue skirts were kilted boldly about her waist and dovetailed behind her. Her bosom was as a bird's, soft and slight, slight and soft as the breast of some dark-plumaged dove. But her long fair hair was girlish: and girlish, and touched with the wonder of mortal beauty, her face.

They look at each other without speaking. Then the girl withdraws her glance and begins to stir the water with her foot

> hither and thither, hither and thither: and a faint flame trembled on her cheek.

> Heavenly God! cried Stephen's soul, in an outburst of profane joy.

Here, then, the Virgin's colors and green and red, the strand of seaweed and the flame upon the cheek, are fused with the bird imagery that continues throughout the book from "baby tuckoo" on the first page to Dedalus, the winged artificer, who is evoked in the final sentence. The whole thus created is greater than the sum of its parts and has a new and greater meaning. Stephen's joy when he recognizes that meaning must be profane. The identity, the vocation, and the destiny here revealed to him are those of the artist. They demand a dedication as absolute as that of the priest—directed, however, not to the

sacred and infinite, but to that sensual reality which is the artist's sole material. Now all that remains for Stephen to do is to free himself in actuality, work out the theology of his devotion, and after that, well, everything—with no flinching or excuses. It will be lucky for him that he has had at least this one moment of undiminished exultation.

I chose color for my illustration because, though it is much more elaborate than I have managed to indicate, it is the simplest continuing imagery in the book and because it is resolved. Other images convey more and are harder to follow, especially those based on abstract concepts like sphericity, extension, or systole and diastole (whether as the ebb and flow of tides, or the lengthening and shortening of lines in the solution of an algebraic problem, or a reaching out to infinity and a swift instinctive recurrence to self). Nearly as difficult are pair-words like "difference" and "indifference," or the notion of the "bounding line," or what seems mere natural description like the falling of rain or light, or the smell of turf smoke, or mist and vapors rising, or, in every instance, the moon. The very aesthetic that Stephen outlines to his sounding board, Lynch of the withered soul, employs a vocabulary already saturated with meaning from repeated use. When he says

> The artist, like the God of the creation, remains within or behind or beyond or above his handiwork, invisible, refined out of existence, indifferent, paring his fingernails.

we may note that fingernails have been pared before—and will be again, as in *Ulysses* where Bloom looks out of the funeral coach, sees his wife's seducer, and looks at his own nails to see if they are pared, which they are.

This way of writing—I suppose we shall have to call it symbolism, though the word has been beaten shapeless—is, I believe, Joyce's natural and most central method. It antedates the *Portrait*. There are hints of it in the first story in *Dubliners;* and in the last, "The Dead," where the ubiquitous Mr. Brown is Death himself, it has already become systematic. At the same time, symbolism is never Joyce's sole method; it is always employed in conjunction with means which, though they receive reinforcement from it, are themselves self-sustaining.

Thus the *Portrait* functions well enough simply as a naturalistic novel. It was meant to. The book has several levels, each with workable meaning of its own; and yet, since the containing form is the same for all levels, each meaning necessarily relates to the one overall statement. The irony that we remarked before depends on this. In the final chapter we have Stephen theorizing a little too positively about what he has not yet actually tried. This is his priggishness which, if honesty is to be complete, is inescapably part of the statement too. Proudly Stephen declares what qualities—fortitude, discipline, detachment—characterize the true, and the very rare, artist. The novel, telling his story so intricately and simply, is the proof of those qualities. And the proof itself is a measure of how far Stephen has yet to travel, through how much discouragement and pain, before he can practice what he so confidently preaches. Again let us remember that this is not Stephen's self-portrait. When the book is written Stephen no longer exists.

Still, does even this achievement justify so much complexity? Or as the question is more usually put, has Joyce the right to demand so much of the reader? The answer, I think, is that he demands no more than the serious artist normally expects is due his work. All that he wrote can be validly appreciated as what it outwardly appears to be, because it is what it outwardly appears, as well as much else. His short stories, his play, his novels are all true specimens. As a matter of fact, he was aggrieved that readers, probing worriedly for deeper significances, should so consistently miss what lay on the surface. He pointed out in exasperation that *Ulysses* was, after all, a funny book. It is indeed. And if the reader gets the symbolic meanings but misses the fun, he has missed a good third of what the author was at pains to provide. Again, if the reader exploits the symbolism only for its meaning and fails to grasp its structural function, he has missed the deepest pleasure of all, the apprehension of pure form purely realized. (pp. 82-8)

*John V. Kelleher, "The Perceptions of James Joyce,"
in* The Atlantic Monthly, *Vol. 201, No. 3, March,
1958, pp. 82, 84, 86, 88, 90.*

HARRY LEVIN (essay date 1960)

[*Levin is an American educator and critic whose works reveal
his wide range of interests and expertise, from Renaissance culture to the contemporary novel. He has long been an influential
advocate of comparative literature studies, and he has written
seminal works on the literature of several nations, including* The
Power of Blackness: Hawthorne, Poe, Melville *(1958),* The Gates
of Horn: A Study of Five French Realists *(1962), and* James Joyce:
A Critical Introduction *(1941; rev. ed. 1960). The latter work
was in part inspired by Joyce's comment that Levin had written
the best review of* Finnegans Wake. *Levin has noted that his "focal
points have been the connection between literature and society"
and that his "ultimate hope is for a kind of criticism which, while
analyzing the formal and esthetic qualities of a work of art, will
fit them into the cultural and social pattern to which it belongs."
In the following excerpt from his pioneering study of Joyce, Levin
traces Stephen's development in* A Portrait of the Artist as a Young
Man, *arguing that Joyce intended the novel to be read as his
autobiography, and that Stephen's attitudes are reflections of
Joyce's own.*]

Except for the thin incognito of its characters, the *Portrait of
the Artist* is based on a literal transcript of the first twenty years
of Joyce's life. If anything, it is more candid than other autobiographies. It is distinguished from them by its emphasis
on the emotional and intellectual adventures of its protagonist. . . . As the hero of a pedagogical novel, Stephen is significantly baptized. Saint Stephen Protomartyr was patron of
the green on which University College was located, and therefore of the magazine with which Joyce had had his earliest
literary misadventures.

Stephen is ever susceptible to the magic of names—particularly
of his own last name. Names and words, copybook phrases
and schoolboy slang, echoes and jingles, speeches and sermons
float through his mind and enrich the restricted realism of the
context. His own name is the wedge by which symbolism enters
the book. One day he penetrates its secret. Brooding on the
prefect of studies, who made him repeat the unfamiliar syllables
of "Dedalus," he tells himself that it is a better name than
Dolan. He hears it shouted across the surf by some friends in
swimming, and the strangeness of the sound is for him a prophecy: "Now, at the name of the fabulous artificer, he seemed
to hear the noise of dim waves and to see a winged form flying
above the waves and slowly climbing the air. What did it mean?
Was it a quaint device opening a page of some medieval book
of prophecies and symbols, a hawklike man flying sunward
above the sea, a prophecy of the end he had been born to serve
and had been following through the mists of childhood and
boyhood, a symbol of the artist forging anew in his workshop

out of the sluggish matter of the earth a new soaring impalpable
imperishable being?" (pp. 45-6)

The richness of [Stephen's] inner experience is continually
played off against the grim reality of his external surroundings.
He is trying "to build a breakwater of order and elegance
against the sordid tale of life without him." He is marked by
the aureole of the romantic hero, like Thomas Mann's outsiders, pressing their noses against the window panes of a
bourgeois society from which they feel excluded. "To merge
his life in the common tide of other lives was harder for him
than any fasting or prayer, and it was his constant failure to
do this to his own satisfaction which caused in his soul at last
a sensation of spiritual dryness together with a growth of doubts
and scruples." At school he takes an equivocal position, "a
free boy, a leader afraid of his own authority, proud and sensitive and suspicious, battling against the squalor of his life
and against the riot of his mind." At home he feels "his own
futile isolation." He feels that he is scarcely of the same blood
as his mother and brother and sister, but stands to them "rather
in the mystical kinship of fosterage, foster child and foster
brother."

Joyce's prose is the register of this intellectual and emotional
cleavage. It preserves the contrast between his rather lush verse
and his rather dry criticism, between the pathetic children and
the ironic politicians of *Dubliners.* All his sensibility is reserved
for himself; his attitude toward others is consistently caustic.
The claims to objectivity of a subjective novel, however, must
be based on its rendering of intimate experience. If Joyce's
treatment of Stephen is true to himself, we have no right to
interpose any other criteria. Mr. Eliot has made the plausible
suggestion that Joyce's two masters in prose were Newman and
Pater. Their alternating influence would account for the
oscillations of style in the *Portrait of the Artist.* The sustaining
tone, which it adopts toward the outside world, is that of precise
and mordant description. Interpolated, at strategic points in
Stephen's development, are a number of purple passages that
have faded considerably.

Joyce's own contribution to English prose is to provide a more
fluid medium for refracting sensations and impressions through
the author's mind—to facilitate the transition from photographic realism to esthetic impressionism. In the introductory
pages of the *Portrait of the Artist,* the reader is faced with
nothing less than the primary impact of life itself, presentational
continuum of the tastes and smells and sights and sounds of
earliest infancy. Emotion is integrated, from first to last, by
words. Feelings, as they filter through Stephen's sensory apparatus, become associated with phrases. His conditioned re-
flexes are literary. In one of the later dialogues of the book,
he is comparing his theory to a trimmed lamp. The dean of
studies, taking up the metaphor, mentions the lamp of Epic-
tetus, and Stephen's reply is a further allusion to the stoic
doctrine that the soul is like a bucketful of water. In his mind
this far-fetched chain of literary associations becomes attached
to the sense impressions of the moment: "A smell of molten
tallow came up from the dean's candle butts and fused itself
in Stephen's consciousness with the jingle of the words, bucket
and lamp and lamp and bucket."

This is the state of mind that confers upon language a magical
potency. It exalts the habit of verbal association into a principle
for the arrangement of experience. You gain power over a
thing by naming it; you become master of a situation by putting
it into words. It is psychological need, and not hyperfastidious

The main building and chapel of Clongowes Wood College. From The Joyce Country, *by William York Tindall. The Pennsylvania State University Press, University Park, PA, 1960. Reproduced by permission of the publisher.*

taste, that goads the writer on to search for the *mot juste,* to loot the thesaurus. (pp. 48-51)

The strength and weakness of his style, by Joyce's own diagnosis, are those of his mind and body. A few pages later he offers a cogent illustration, when Stephen dips self-consciously into his word-hoard for suitable epithets to describe a girl who is wading along the beach. We are given a paragraph of word-painting which is not easy to visualize. "Her bosom was as a bird's, soft and slight, slight and soft as the breast of some dark-plumaged dove," it concludes. "But her long fair hair was girlish: and girlish, and touched with the wonder of mortal beauty, her face." This is incantation, and not description. Joyce is thinking in rhythms rather than metaphors. Specification of the bird appeals to the sense of touch rather than to the sense of sight. What is said about the air and face is intended to produce an effect without presenting a picture. The most striking effects in Joyce's imagery are those of coldness, whiteness, and dampness, like the bodies of the bathers who shout Stephen's name.

The most vital element in Joyce's writing, in the *Portrait of the Artist* as in *Dubliners,* is his use of conversation. As a reporter of Irish life, for all his reservations, Joyce is a faithful and appreciative listener. It is a tribute to Stephen's ear that, in spite of the antagonism between father and son, Simon

Dedalus is such a ripe and congenial character. Like Sean O'Casey's *Paycock,* with all his amiable failings, he is Ireland itself. Though he takes pride in showing Cork to Stephen, and in showing off his son to his own native city, he is really the embodiment of Dublin: "A medical student, an oarsman, a tenor, an amateur actor, a shouting politician, a small landlord, a small investor, a drinker, a good fellow, a storyteller, somebody's secretary, something in a distillery, a tax-gatherer, a bankrupt and at present a praiser of his own past." The improvident worldliness of John Stanislaus Joyce had made him, in the unforgiving eyes of his son, a foster-parent. (pp. 51-2)

This disorder, "the misrule and confusion of his father's house," comes to stand in Stephen's mind for the plight of Ireland. Like [John] Synge's *Playboy,* he must go through the motions of parricide to make good his revolt. Religion and politics, to his adult perception, are among the intimations of early childhood: harsh words and bitter arguments that spoil the taste of the Christmas turkey. (p. 52)

The *Portrait of the Artist,* as Joyce's remembrance finally shaped it, is a volume of three hundred pages, symmetrically constructed around three undramatic climaxes, intimate crises of Stephen's youth. The first hundred pages, in two chapters, trace the awakening of religious doubts and sexual instincts, leading up to Stephen's carnal sin at the age of sixteen. The central portion, in two more chapters, continues the cycle of sin and repentance to the moment of Stephen's private apocalypse. The external setting for the education of the artist is, in the first chapter, Clongowes Wood College; in the second, third, and fourth, Belvedere College, Dublin. The fifth and final chapter, which is twice as long as the others, develops the theories and projects of Stephen's student days in University College, and brings him to the verge of exile. As the book advances, it becomes less sensitive to outside impressions, and more intent upon speculations of its own. Friends figure mainly as interlocutors to draw Stephen out upon various themes. Each epiphany—awakening of the body, literary vocation, farewell to Ireland—leaves him lonelier than the last.

A trivial episode at Clongowes Wood seems fraught for Joyce with a profoundly personal meaning. Young Stephen has been unable to get his lessons, because his glasses were broken on the playing-field. Father Dolan, the prefect of studies, is unwilling to accept this excuse, and disciplines Stephen with the boys who have shirked their books. Smarting with pain and a sense of palpable injustice, Stephen finally carries his case to the rector, who shows a humane understanding of the situation. (pp. 53-4)

The physical handicap, the public humiliation, the brooding sensibility, the sense of grievance, the contempt for convention, the desire for self-justification, and the appeal to higher authority—these are all elements of Joyce's attitude toward society and toward himself. He had begun his education by questioning the Jesuit discipline; he would finish by repudiating the Catholic faith. Having responded to the urgent prompting of his senses, he would be treated as a sinner; he would refer the ensuing conflict, over the head of religious authority, to the new light of his scientific and naturalistic studies; he would seek, in the end, to create his own authority by the light of his senses. In turning away from Ireland toward the world at large, he would appeal from the parochial Daly to the enlightened [rector] Conmee. That miserable day at Clongowes Wood, like that long evening at Combray when M. Swann's visit kept Marcel's mother downstairs, had unforeseen consequences.

Adolescence complicates the second chapter. Stephen is beginning to appreciate beauty, but as something illicit and mysterious, something apart from the common walks of life. Literature has begun to color his experience, and to stimulate his mind and his senses. His untimely enthusiasm for Lord Byron—"a heretic and immoral too"—provokes a beating at the hands of his classmates. Now in jest and again in earnest, he is forced to repeat the *confiteor*. One of his essays had been rewarded with the taunt of heresy from his English master, and he takes rueful consolation in the self-conscious part of the Byronic hero. He will not agree that Lord Tennyson is a poet, though he gives tacit consent to the assertion that Newman has the best prose style. But it is his other master, Pater, whose influence is felt at the climax of the chapter. Stephen's sexual initiation is presented in empurpled prose, as an esthetic ritual for which his literary heresies have been preparing him. In trying to find a cadence for his cry, he harks back to the lyricism of *Chamber Music* and the anguish of the small boy in *Dubliners:*

> He stretched out his arms in the street to hold fast the frail swooning form that eluded him and incited him: and the cry that he had strangled for so long in his throat issued from his lips. It broke from him like a wail of despair from a hell of sufferers and died in a wail of

furious entreaty, a cry for an iniquitous abandonment, a cry which was but the echo of an obscene scrawl which he had read on the oozing wall of a urinal.

The unromantic reader is prone to feel that a scrawl would have been more adequate to the occasion. The incidence of the word "swoon" is a humorless symptom of the Pateresque influence on Joyce's early writing. There is many "A swoon of shame" in *Chamber Music,* and "a slowly swooning soul" in the last paragraph of *Dubliners.* "His soul was swooning" at the end of the fourth chapter of the *Portrait of the Artist,* having been darkened by "the swoon of sin" at the end of the second chapter. Though the scene is clouded with decadent incense, it is clear that Stephen is still a child, and that the woman plays the part of a mother. Joyce's heroes are sons and lovers at the same time; his heroines are always maternal. It is like him to lavish his romantic sensibility on an encounter with a prostitute and to reserve his acrid satire for the domain of the church. In Stephen's mind a symbolic association between art and sex is established, and that precocious revelation helps him to decide his later conflict between art and religion.

Meanwhile, the third chapter is devoted to his remorse. It embodies at formidable length a sermon on hell, suffered by Stephen and his classmates during a retreat. The eloquent Jesuit preacher takes as his object-lesson the sin of Lucifer, pride of the intellect, his great refusal and his terrible fall. Stephen's repentant imagination is harrowed by the torments of the damned. This powerful discourse provides an ethical core for the book, as Father Mapple's sermon on Jonah does for *Moby-Dick,* or Ivan's legend of the Grand Inquisitor for *The Brothers Karamazov.* Joyce is orthodox enough to go on believing in hell, and—as Professor Curtius recognized—to set up his own *Inferno* in *Ulysses.* Like another tormented apostate, Christopher Marlowe, he lives in a world where there is still suffering, but no longer the prospect of salvation. Like Blake's Milton, he is a true poet, and of the devil's party. Stephen's ultimate text is the defiance of the fallen archangel: *"Non serviam!"*

Temporarily, there is confession and absolution. When Stephen sees the eggs and sausages laid out for the communion breakfast, life seems simple and beautiful after all. For a time his restlessness seems to be tranquilized by church and satisfied by school. Seeking to order his existence, he contemplates the possibilities of the Jesuit order itself: the Reverend Stephen Dedalus, S.J. After a conference with a member of that order, he is fascinated and terrified by the awful assumption of powers which ordination involve. In the fourth chapter the call comes unexpectedly—the call to another kind of priesthood. Stephen dedicates himself to art, and enters upon his peculiar novitiate. The church would have meant order, but it would also have meant a denial of the life of the senses. A walk along the strand brings him his real vocation—an outburst of profane joy at the bird-like beauty of a girl, a realization of the fabulous artificer whose name he bears, a consciousness of the power of words to confer an order and life of their own. Like the birds that circle between the sea and the sky, his soul soars in "an ecstasy of flight," in a metaphor of sexual fulfilment and artistic creation. "To live, to err, to fall, to triumph, to recreate life out of life!"

The fifth chapter is the discursive chronicle of Stephen's rebellion. He moves among his fellow-students, an aloof and pharasaic figure, unwilling to share their indignation at the first performance of the *Countess Catholeen,* or their confidence in a petition to ensure world peace. His own struggle comes when his mother requests him to make his Easter duty and his diabolic pride of intellect asserts itself. Cranly, with the sharpest instruments of casuistry, tries to probe his stubborn refusal. It is less a question of faith than of observance. Stephen will not, to please his mother, do false homage to the symbols of authority, yet he is not quite unbeliever enough to take part in a sacrilegious communion. If he cannot accept the eucharist, he must be anathema; he respects the forms by refusing to observe them. "I will not serve that in which I no longer believe, whether it call itself my home, my fatherland or my church: and I will try to express myself in some mode of life or art as freely as I can and as wholly as I can, using for my defence the only arms I allow myself to use, silence, exile and cunning."

With this peremptory gesture, emancipating himself from his petty-bourgeois family, and from Ireland and Catholicism at the same time, Stephen stands ready to take his solitary way wherever the creative life engages him. In a previous argument with other friends, he abandoned the possibility of fighting these issues out at home. "Ireland is the old sow that eats her farrow." Davin, the nationalist, is willing to admit that Stephen's position is thoroughly Irish, all too typical of their gifted countrymen. "In your heart you are an Irishman but your pride is too powerful." Stephen is unwilling to compromise: "When the soul of a man is born in this country there are nets flung at it to hold it back from flight. You talk to me of nationality, language, religion. I shall try to fly by those nets." In exile, silence, and cunning he trusts to find substitutes for those three forms of subjection.

On his way to and from Belvedere College, his soul was "disquieted and cast down by the dull phenomenon of Dublin." With his realization of the end he was soon to serve, a new vista of "the slowflowing Liffey" became visible "across the timeless air." Nomadic clouds, dappled and seaborne, voyaging westward from Europe, suggested strange tongues and marshalled races. "He heard a confused music within him as of memories and names . . ." At University College, the time-worn texts of Ovid and Horace have filled him with awe for the past and contempt of the present: ". . . it wounded him to think that he would never be but a shy guest at the feast of the world's culture and that the monkish learning, in terms of which he was striving to forge out an esthetic philosophy, was held no higher by the age he lived in than the subtle and curious jargons of heraldry and falconry."

English is as strange a tongue as Latin. "His language, so familiar and so foreign, will always be for me an acquired speech," Stephen reflects, while conversing with the dean of studies, an English convert to Catholicism. "I have not made or accepted its words. My voice holds them at bay. My soul frets in the shadow of his language." The last pages are fragments from Stephen's notebook, duly recording his final interviews with teachers and friends, with his family and "her." Spring finds him setting down "vague words for a vague emotion," his farewell to Dublin, and to sounds of the city which will never stop echoing in his ears. . . . (pp. 55-60)

> *Harry Levin, in his* James Joyce: A Critical Introduction, *revised edition, New Directions, 1960, 256 p.*

WAYNE C. BOOTH (essay date 1961)

[*Booth is an American critic associated with a group of neo-Aristotelean critics that includes R. S. Crane and Elder Olson. Basing their critical thought on the* Poetics *of Aristotle, these critics conceive literature as a representation of human experience, believing that as such it demands a plurality of aesthetic, social, and moral viewpoints for truly valid interpretation. Booth's critical doctrine views literary works as symbolic constructs that contribute to a "communal building of selves" in human society: thoughts and experiences are exchanged from mind to mind, leading toward an affirmative and more fully human approach to existence. In the following excerpt, Booth contends that although the* Portrait *is a brilliant work, it is almost impossible for the reader to judge whether Joyce intended Stephen as an heroic or an ironic figure. Booth maintains that, because Joyce's own attitude toward his protagonist was highly complex, it was difficult for him to sustain a consistent tone and an unchanging aesthetic distance from the character of Stephen Dedalus. For further discussion of these points, see the essays by: Robert Scholes (1964), who contends that Joyce's intention was not ironic; Hugh Kenner (1965) who disagrees with biographical interpretations of Stephen and contends that Joyce retained a neutral, objective attitude toward his character; and Robert M. Adams (1966), who discusses the evidence for both sympathetic and ironic interpretations of Stephen.*]

Everyone seems by now agreed that [*A Portrait of the Artist as a Young Man*] is a masterpiece in the modern mode. Perhaps we can accept it as that—indeed accept it as unquestionably great work from any viewpoint—and still feel free to ask a few irreverent questions.

The structure of this "authorless" work is based on the growth of a sensitive boy to young manhood. The steps in his growth are obviously constructed with great care. Each of the first four sections ends a period of Stephen's life with what Joyce, in an earlier draft, calls an epiphany: a peculiar revelation of the inner reality of an experience, accompanied with great elation,

Date	NAME	Punishment	Offence	
	G. Gill	6	Talking in class	A. Mac Ath
	F. Coffey	6	Constantly talking &c	"
14th March	F. McGlade	2		"
"	G. Scally		Going out of bounds	"
"	Jos Gill	·		"
"	J. Colgan	12	Bath without leave	"
"	D. Downing	10	Talking in square	"
"	C. Earsley	18	"	"
"	C. Wells	6	Romping	"
"	E. Joyce	4	Vulgar language	"
"	C. Roche	10	Constantly talking to others	"
"	A. O'Kelly	4	Out of bounds	"
19th	C. Roche	6	Rudeness	"
"	J. Colgan	9	Opening another boy's desk	Jeffcoat
"	E. Costello	9	Lessons	Gwynne
20th	J. Colgan	8	Lessons	McCormack
"	H. George	6	Lessons not known	Jeffcoat
"	Lynch	9	Not knowing Virgil	Gleeson
"	Wm Hannin	6	Idling	Macartie

The punishment book of Clongowes Wood College. This entry for 18 March 1889 notes that young James Joyce was pandied for vulgar language.

as in a mystical religious experience. Each is followed by the opening of a new chapter on a very prosaic, even depressed level. Now here is clearly a careful structural preparation—for what? For a transformation or for a merely cyclical return? Is the final exaltation a release from the depressing features of Irish life which have tainted the earlier experiences? Or is the fifth turn in an endless cycle? And in either case, is Stephen always to be viewed with the same deadly seriousness with which he views himself? Is it to artistic maturity that he grows? As the young man goes into exile from Ireland, goes "to encounter for the millionth time the reality of experience and to forge in the smithy" of his soul "the uncreated conscience" of his race, are we to take this, with Harry Levin, as a fully serious portrait of the artist Dedalus, praying to his namesake Daedalus, to stand him "now and ever in good stead"? [See the excerpt dated 1960.] Or is the inflated style, as Mark Schorer tells us, Joyce's clue that the young Icarus is flying too close to the sun, with the "excessive lyric relaxation" of Stephen's final style punctuating "the illusory nature of the whole ambition"? [See excerpt dated 1947.] The young man takes himself and his flight with deadly solemnity. Should we?

To see the difficulties clearly, let us consider three crucial episodes, all from the final section: his rejection of the priesthood, his exposition of what he takes to be Thomistic aesthetics, and his composition of a poem.

Is his rejection of the priesthood a triumph, a tragedy, or merely a comedy of errors? Most readers, even those who follow the new trend of reading Stephen ironically, seem to have read it as a triumph: the artist has rid himself of one of the chains that bound him. To Caroline Gordon, this is a serious misreading. "I suspect that Joyce's *Portrait* has been misread by a whole generation." She sees the rejection as "the picture of a soul that is being damned for time and eternity caught in the act of foreseeing and foreknowing its damnation," and she cites in evidence the fall of Icarus and Stephen's own statement to Cranly that he is not afraid to make a mistake, "even a great mistake, a lifelong mistake and perhaps for eternity, too." Well, which *Portrait* do we choose, that of the artistic soul battling through successfully to his necessary freedom, or that of the child of God, choosing, like Lucifer, his own damnation? No two books could be further from each other than the two we envision here. There may be a sufficient core of what is simply interesting to salvage the book as a great work of the sensibility, but unless we are willing to retreat into babbling and incommunicable relativism, we cannot believe that it is *both* a portrait of the prisoner freed *and* a portrait of the soul placing itself in chains.

Critics have had even more difficulty with Stephen's aesthetic theory, ostensibly developed from Aquinas. Is the book itself, as Grant Redford tells us, an "objectification of an artistic proposition and a method announced by the central character," achieving for Joyce the "wholeness, harmony, and radiance" that Stephen celebrates in his theory? Or is it, as Father Noon says, an ironic portrait of Stephen's immature aesthetics? Joyce wanted to qualify Stephen's utterances, Father Noon tells us, "by inviting attention to his own more sophisticated literary concerns," and he stands apart from the Thomist aesthetics, watching Stephen miss the clue in his drive for an impersonal, dramatic narration. "The comparison of the artist with the God of the creation, taken "straight" by many critics, is for Father Noon "the climax of Joyce's ironic development of the Dedalus aesthetic."

Finally, what of the precious villanelle? Does Joyce intend it to be taken as a serious sign of Stephen's artistry, as a sign of his genuine but amusingly pretentious precocity, or as something else entirely? (pp. 326-28)

Hardly anyone has committed himself in public about the quality of this poem. Are we to smile at Stephen or pity him in his tortured longing? Are we to marvel at his artistry, or scoff at his conceit? Or are we merely to say, "How remarkable an insight into the kind of poem that would be written by an adolescent in love, if he were artistically inclined?" The poem, we are told, "enfolded him like a shining cloud, enfolded him like water with a liquid life: and like a cloud of vapour or like waters circumfluent in space the liquid letters of speech, symbols of the element of mystery, flowed forth over his brain." As we recall Jean Paul's formula for "romantic irony," "hot baths of sentiment followed by cold showers or irony," we can only ask here which tap has been turned on. Are we to swoon—or laugh?

Some critics will no doubt answer that all these questions are irrelevant. The villanelle is not to be judged but simply experienced; the aesthetic theory is, within the art work, neither true nor false but simply "true" to the art work—that is, true to Stephen's character at this point. To read modern literature properly we must refuse to ask irrelevant questions about it; we must accept the "portrait" and no more ask whether the character portrayed is good or bad, right or wrong than we ask whether a woman painted by Picasso is moral or immoral. "All facts of any kind," as Gilbert puts it, "mental or material, sublime or ludicrous, have an equivalence of value for the artist."

This answer, which can be liberating at one stage of our development in appreciating not only modern but all art, becomes less and less satisfactory the longer we look at it. It certainly does not seem to have been Joyce's basic attitude, though he was often misleading about it. The creation and the enjoyment of art can never be a completely neutral activity. Though different works of art require different kinds of judgment for their enjoyment, the position taken in chapters three through five must stand: no work, not even the shortest lyric, can be written in complete moral, intellectual and aesthetic neutrality. We may judge falsely, we may judge unconsciously, but we cannot even bring the book to mind without judging its elements, seeing them as shaped into a given kind of thing. Even if we denied that the sequence of events has meaning in the sense of being truly sequential, that denial would itself be a judgment on the rightness of Stephen's actions and opinions at each stage: to decide that he is not growing is as much a judgment on his actions as to decide that he is becoming more and more mature. Actually everyone reads the book as some kind of progressive sequence, and to do so we judge succeeding actions and opinions to be more or less moral, sensitive, intellectually mature, than those they follow. If we felt that the question of Joyce's precise attitude toward Stephen's vocation, his aesthetics, and his villanelle were irrelevant, we would hardly dispute with each other about them. Yet I count in a recent check list at least fifteen articles and one full book disputing Joyce's attitude about the aesthetics alone.

Like most modern critics, I would prefer to settle such disputes by using internal rather than external evidence. But the experts themselves give me little hope of finding answers to my three problems by re-reading *Portrait* one more time. They all clutch happily at any wisp of comment or fragmentary document that might illuminate Joyce's intentions. And who can blame them?

The truth seems to be that Joyce was always a bit uncertain about his attitude toward Stephen. Anyone who reads Ellmann's masterful biography with this problem in mind cannot help being struck by the many shifts and turns Joyce took as he worked through the various versions. There is nothing especially strange in that, of course. Most "autobiographical" novelists probably encounter difficulty in trying to decide just how heroic their heroes are to be. But Joyce's explorations came just at a time when the traditional devices for control of distance were being repudiated, when doctrines of objectivity were in the air, and when people were taking seriously the idea that to evoke "reality" was a sufficient aim in art; the artist need not concern himself with judging or with specifying whether the reader should approve or disapprove, laugh or cry.

Now the traditional forms *had* specified in their very conceptions a certain degree of clarity about distance. If an author chose to write comedy, for example, he knew that his characters must at least to some degree be "placed" at a distance from the spectator's norms. This predetermination did not, of course, settle all of his problems. To balance sympathy and antipathy, admiration and contempt, was still a fundamental challenge, but it was a challenge for which there was considerable guidance in the practice of previous writers of comedy. If, on the other hand, he chose to write tragedy, or satire, or elegy, or celebration odes, or whatever, he could rely to some extent on conventions to guide him and his audience to a common attitude toward his characters.

The young Joyce had none of this to rely on, but he seems never to have sensed the full danger of his position. When, in his earliest years, he recorded his brief epiphanies—those bits of dialogue or description that were supposed to reveal the inner reality of things—there was always an implied identification of the recorder's norms and the reader's; both were spectators at the revealing moment, both shared in the vision of one moment of truth. Though some of the epiphanies are funny, some sad, and some mixed, the basic effect is always the same: an overwhelming sense—when they succeed—of what Jocye liked to call the "incarnation": Artistic Meaning has come to live in the world's body. The Poet has done his work.

Even in these early epiphanies there is difficulty with distance; the author inevitably expects the reader to share in his own preconceptions and interests sufficiently to catch, from each word or gesture, the precise mood or tone that they evoke for the author himself. But since complete identification with the author is a silent precondition for the success of such moments, the basic problem of distance is never a serious one. Even if the author and reader should differ in interpretation, they can share the sense of evoked reality.

It is only when Joyce places at the center of a long work a figure who experiences epiphanies, an epiphany-producing device, as it were, who is himself used by the real author as an object ambiguously distant from the norms of the work, that the complications of distance become incalculable. If he treats the author-figure satirically, as he does in much of *Stephen Hero,* that earlier, windier version of *Portrait,* then what happens to the quality of the epiphanies that *he* describes? Are they still genuine epiphanies or only what the misguided, callow youth *thinks* are epiphanies? If, as Joyce's brother Stanislaus has revealed, the word "hero" is satiric, can we take seriously that anti-hero's vision? Yet if the satirical mode is dropped, if the hero is made into a real hero, and if the reader is made to see things entirely as he sees them, what then

happens to objectivity? The portrait is no longer an objective rendering of reality, looked at from a respectable aesthetic distance, but rather a mere subjective indulgence.

Joyce can be seen, in Ellmann's account, wrestling with this problem throughout the revisions. Unlike writers before Flaubert, he had no guidance from convention or tradition or fellow artists. Neither Flaubert nor James had established any sure ground to stand on. Both of them had, in fact, stumbled on the same hurdles, and though each had on occasion surmounted the difficulties, Joyce was in no frame of mind to look behind their claims as realists to the actual problems and lessons that lay beneath their evocative surfaces. A supreme egoist struggling to deal artistically with his own ego, a humorist who could not escape the comic consequences of his portrait of that inflated ego, he faced, in the completed *Stephen Hero,* what he had to recognize as a hodge-podge of irreconcilables. Is Stephen a pompous ass or not? Is his name deliberately ridiculous, as Stanislaus, who invented it, says? Or is it a serious act of symbolism? The way out seems inevitable, but it seems a retreat nonetheless: simply present the "reality" and let the reader judge. Cut all of the author's judgments, cut all of the adjectives, produce one long, ambiguous epiphany.

Purged of the author's explicit judgment, the resulting work was so brilliant and compelling, its hero's vision so scintillating, that almost all readers overlooked the satiric and ironic content—except, of course, as the satire operated against *other* characters. So far as I know no one said anything about irony against Stephen until after *Ulysses* was published in 1922, with its opening in which Icarus-Stephen is shown with his wings clipped. Ironic readings did not become popular, in fact, until after the fragment of *Stephen Hero* was published in 1944. Readers of that work found, it is true, many authoritative confirmations of their exaltation of Stephen—for the most part in a form that might confirm anyone's prejudice against commentary. ". . . When he [Stephen] wrote it was always a mature and reasoned emotion which urged him" . . . . "This mood of indignation which was not guiltless of a certain superficiality was undoubtedly due to the excitement of release. . . . He acknowledged to himself in honest egoism that he could not take to heart the distress of a nation, the soul of which was antipathetic to his own, so bitterly as the indignity of a bad line of verse. . . ." But readers were also faced with a good many denigrations of the hero. We can agree that *Portrait* is a better work because the immature author has been effaced; Joyce may indeed have found that effacing the commentary was the only way he could obtain an air of maturity. But the fact remains that it is primarily to this immature commentary that we must go for evidence in deciphering the ironies of the later, purer work.

What we find in *Stephen Hero* is not a simple confirmation of any reading that we might have achieved on the basis of *Portrait* alone. Rather we find an extremely complicated view, combining irony and admiration in unpredictable mixtures. Thus the Thomist aesthetics "was in the main applied Aquinas and he set it forth plainly with a naif air of discovering novelties. This he did partly to satisfy his own taste for enigmatic roles and partly from a genuine predisposition in favour of all but the premises of scholasticism". . . . No one ever inferred, before this passage was available, anything like this precise and complex judgment on Stephen. The combination of blame and approval, we may be sure, is different in the finished *Portrait;* the implied author no doubt often repudiates the explicit judgments of the younger narrator who intrudes into *Ste-*

phen Hero. But we can also be sure that his judgment has not become less complex. Where do we find, in any criticism of *Portrait* based entirely on internal evidence, the following kind of juxtaposition of Stephen's views with the author's superior insight? "Having by this *simple process* established the literary form of art as the most excellent he *proceeded to examine it in favour of his theory,* or, *as he rendered it,* to establish the relations which must subsist between the literary image, the work of art itself, and that energy which had imagined and fashioned it, that center of conscious, re-acting, particular life, the artist" (. . . italics mine). Can we infer, from *Portrait,* that Joyce sees Stephen as simply rationalizing in favor of his theory? Did we guess that Joyce could refer to him mockingly as a "fiery-hearted revolutionary" and a "heaven-ascending essayist"?

In *Stephen Hero,* the author's final evaluation of the aesthetics is favorable but qualified: "Except for the eloquent and arrogant peroration Stephen's essay was a careful exposition of a carefully meditated theory of esthetic." . . . Though it might be argued that in the finished book he has cut out some of the negative elements, such as the "eloquent and arrogant peroration," and has presented the pure theory in conversational form, it is clear that Joyce himself judged his hero's theory in greater detail than we could possibly infer from the final version alone.

Similar clarifications can be found in *Stephen Hero* of our other two crucial problems, his rejection of the priesthood and his poetic ability. For example, "He had swept the moment into his memory . . . and . . . had brought forth some pages of sorry verse." . . . Can the hero of *Portrait,* be thought of as writing "sorry verse"? One would not think so, to read much of the commentary by Joyce's critics.

But who is to blame them? Whatever intelligence Joyce postulates in his reader—let us assume the unlikely case of its being comparable to his own—will not be sufficient for precise inference of a pattern of judgments which is, after all, private to Joyce. And this will be true regardless of how much distance from his own hero we believe him to have achieved by the time he concluded his final version. We simply cannot avoid the conclusion that to some extent the book itself is at fault, regardless of its great virtues. Unless we make the absurd assumption that Joyce had in reality purged himself of all judgment by the time he completed his final draft, unless we see him as having really come to look upon all of Stephen's actions as equally wise or equally foolish, equally sensitive or equally meaningless, we must conclude that many of the refinements he intended in his finished *Portrait* are, for most of us, permanently lost. Even if we were now to do our homework like dutiful students, even if we were to study all of Joyce's work, even if we were to spend the lifetime that Joyce playfully said his novels demand, presumably we should never come to as rich, as refined, and as varied a conception of the quality of Stephen's last days in Ireland as Joyce had in mind. For some of us the air of detachment and objectivity may still be worth the price, but we must never pretend that a price was not paid. (pp. 329-36)

Wayne C. Booth, "The Price of Impersonal Narration, I: Confusion of Distance," in his The Rhetoric of Fiction, *The University of California Press, 1961, pp. 311-38.**

ROBERT SCHOLES (essay date 1964)

[*Scholes is an American scholar and critic who has written widely on modern post-realistic fiction. He has also written two of the finest introductions and analyses of contemporary critical thought in* Structuralism and Literature *(1974) and* Semiotics and Interpretation *(1982). In the following excerpt, Scholes enters into the critical debate regarding Joyce's attitude toward Stephen Dedalus. In answer to Wayne C. Booth's charge that critics will not venture an opinion on the quality of Stephen's poetry (see excerpt dated 1961), Scholes explicates "The Villanelle of the Temptress," reveals its origin as one of Joyce's own early poems, and argues that Joyce intended no irony in his description of Stephen's creative efforts. For another discussion of* A Portrait *that finds no irony in the portrayal of Stephen, see the excerpt by Hugh Kenner (1965); for further discussion of Joyce's attitude toward his central character, see the excerpt by Robert M. Adams (1966).*]

The problem of Stephen Dedalus is one of the most curious and interesting in modern letters. One aspect of the problem has been brought to our attention recently in a very impressive book by Wayne C. Booth [see excerpt dated 1961]. . . . Mr. Booth notes that *A Portrait of the Artist as a Young Man* was not, by its first readers, thought to be an ironic work. It was after the publication of *Ulysses,* with its presentation of Stephen as the fallen Icarus, that the reassessment of Stephen's character began; and it was the publication of the *Stephen Hero* fragment in 1944 which really accelerated the movement toward a view of the novel as mainly ironic, with Stephen seen as a posturing esthete rather than an actual or even a potential artist. The most extreme version of this ironic view of Stephen has been proposed by Hugh Kenner, in his *Dublin's Joyce* (1955) [for a later explanation of Kenner's position, see the excerpt by Kenner dated 1965].

Joyce's Flaubertian refusal to provide authoritative commentary on his characters within his works seems to open the way to any possible interpretation, making a definitive or even a consensus interpretation extremely difficult. And, however much our new-critical yearnings make us want to consider *A Portrait* as a work in itself, we are led by Joyce's own writings in ever-widening circles. If the Stephen in *Ulysses* is the same person as the Stephen in *A Portrait*—and there seems to be no question about this—then we must consider *Ulysses* in interpreting *Portrait.* By a similar chain of reasoning we find ourselves led to *Stephen Hero,* with its theory of the epiphany, thence to Joyce's own Epiphanies—those little prose pieces which he wrote from his own observation and then often used as fictional incidents or descriptions in *Stephen Hero* and *A Portrait*—until finally we reluctantly discover that everything about Joyce is relevant in some way to our interpretation of *A Portrait,* and we either devote a large chunk of our lives to the problem of Joyce or give up the problem in despair. How much simpler the problem would be if we had only to consider Stephen as he appears in those works which Joyce meant for publication, in *A Portrait* and *Ulysses;* but the publication of *Stephen Hero* is equivalent for us to the opening of Pandora's box. It is too late now to go back. We can never recover our lost innocence.

I mean to suggest that since we cannot go back we must go on. Since we cannot rely on our innocence to preserve us from the dangers of misinterpretation, we must gain the maximum of experience. In a fallen critical world we must commit all the fallacies, including the intentional, in order to work out our own salvation. It is in this spirit that I wish to turn to one specific aspect of the problem of Stephen Dedalus, in the hope that it may illuminate the problem as a whole. The question is raised by Mr. Booth in his discussion of "The Problem of Distance in *A Portrait of the Artist*". . . . He focusses our attention on the poem which Stephen writes in the last chapter of the book: "Finally, what of the precious villanelle? Does Joyce intend it to be taken as a serious sign of Stephen's artistry,

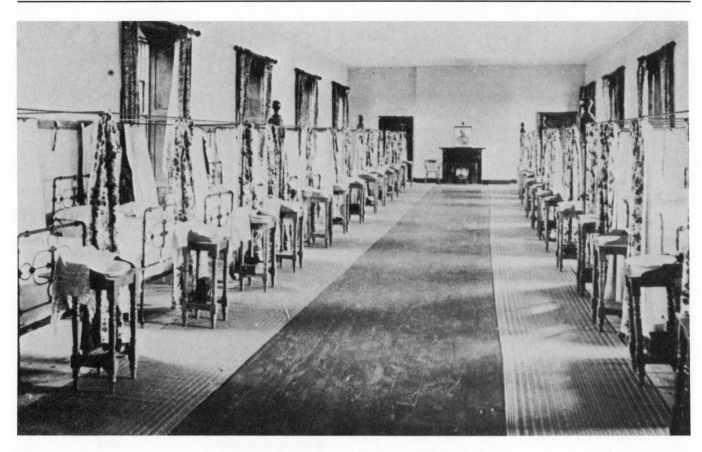

The small boys' dormitory of Clongowes Wood College, circa 1890.

as a sign of his genuine but amusingly pretentious precocity, or as something else entirely. . . . Hardly anyone has committed himself in public about the quality of this poem. Are we to smile at Stephen or pity him in his tortured longing? Are we to marvel at his artistry, or scoff at his conceit?''

I think we can answer some of those qustions, now, with considerable assurance—at least insofar as Joyce's intentions in the matter are concerned. And I hope to provide a generally satisfactory interpretation of the episode of the poem. We must begin by reviewing the composition of the poem in its narrative context. It follows directly the long episode of the esthetic discussion with Lynch, which closes with a rain-shower. Stephen and Lynch take refuge from the rain under the library arcade. There, after the shower, Stephen sees the girl who has most interested him in his youth. He has come to feel as alienated from her as from those aspects of Ireland he associates with her—the Gaelic League, the priests, and the comfortable hypocrisy of the Philistine citizens of Dublin, who are preoccupied with piety but are neither spiritual nor religious. As he sees her going off demurely with some other girls after the shower, he wonders if he has judged her too harshly. At this point the episode closes. In the next sentence we are with Stephen as he wakes the following morning, after an enchanting dream in which he has ''known the ecstasy of seraphic life''. . . . (p. 484)

As he wakes, Stephen finds that he has an idea for a poem, which he begins at once to compose. The composition of the poem is presented to us in detail during the next few pages of narration, along with Stephen's thoughts, which center on the

girl, on other women who have called out to him in the street, and on the mysterious country woman who had invited the gentle Davin into her cottage; all of whom merge into a composite symbol of Irish womanhood—batlike souls waking to consciousness in darkness and secrecy. Between them and him lies the shadow of the Irish priesthood. To the priest, the girl (E.C.) ''would unveil her soul's shy nakedness, to one who was but schooled in the discharging of a formal rite rather than to him, a priest of the eternal imagination, transmuting the daily bread of experience into the radiant body of everlasting life.'' Despite his bitterness Stephen comes, through the composition of the poem, to an understanding of her innocence, an equilibrium, a stasis, in which his new understanding and pity balance his old desire and bitterness. He turns, finally, from thoughts of the girl to a vision of the temptress of his villanelle, a personification of a feminine ideal, something like the white goddess-muse of Robert Graves's mythology. Stephen's spiritual copulation with her is a symbolic equivalent for that moment of inspiration when ''in the virgin womb of the imagination the word was made flesh''. . . . (pp. 484-85)

The temptress of his dream suggests his service to art, just as at the end of the previous chapter the girl on the beach, the ''envoy from the fair courts of life,'' symbolizes the freedom of life as opposed to the cloistered virtue offered Stephen in the priesthood: ''To live, to err, to fall, to triumph, to recreate life out of life!''. . . . The creation of life out of life is the privilege of both the lover and the artist. The physical copulation of the human animal and the spiritual copulation of the artist in which the word is made flesh are valid and complementary manifestations of the same human impulse toward creation. There is no hint of mockery in Joyce's reverent attitude toward the creative process.

In order to fulfill the term of Stephen's esthetic gestation, it was necessary for Joyce to present us with a created thing, with a literary work which was the product of his inspiration. He chose for this purpose the Villanelle of the Temptress. Why? And what, as Mr. Booth asks, are we to make of it? Here we must turn to biographical information and manuscript material for help. The poem itself (or a version of it) was actually written by Joyce long before *A Portrait.* It dates from one of his early collections of verse, probably the lost "Shine and Dark" of 1900 or 1901. . . . It is a distinctly better poem than most of the surviving fragments of that collection. . . . That Joyce thought it superior is attested to by his keeping it for 15 years though he destroyed nearly every other sample of his pre-*Chamber Music* verse, leaving us only the tattered fragments which his brother saved. But Joyce's over-riding reason for using this particular poem must have been its subject. It was the perfect poem, and it had been written by himself when he was only slightly younger than Stephen. The poem thus satisfied both the naturalistic urge and the symbolic urge in Joyce. As fact and symbolic artifact it was indisputably the right thing. (His continuing interest in this subject and the poetic materials of the Villanelle is evidenced by his re-use of them in the poem "Nightpiece" of *Pomes Penyeach,* which is very close to Stephen's poem in theme and imagery, though very different in prosody.)

How perfectly its subject matter suited Joyce's purposes can be seen only when the poem is understood. To this reader it seems obvious that the failure of critics to understand the function of the villanelle stems from their failure to understand what the poem is about. It is ironic that in this one instance, in which Joyce himself has provided a commentary on his own work, such problems in understanding should have arisen; for the poem comes to us, in *A Portrait,* imbedded not only in the circumstances of its creation but in an elaborate explication as well. But even with Joyce's explicatory narrative the poem is a difficult one. The difficulty stems from its complexity of thought. It is a far richer poem than the ninety-ish verses which it appears to resemble. (p. 485)

The first question which must be resolved is the nature of the person [that the poem addresses]. She is, as I have suggested above, a composite figure, but I want now to elaborate on her composition, taking my cues from the explication provided. In describing the moment of inspiration as that instant when "In the virgin womb of the imagination the word was made flesh," the narrator has established a parallel between artistic creation and the divine begetting of the Son of God. The next sentences gloss this parallel and provide an interpretation of the first tercet:

> Gabriel the seraph had come to the virgin's chamber. An afterglow deepened within his spirit, whence the white flame had passed, deepening into a rose and ardent light. That rose and ardent light was her strange wilful heart, strange that no man had known or would know, wilful from before the beginning of the world: and lured by that ardent roselike glow the choirs of the seraphim were falling from heaven. . . .

In this violently compressed fusion of myth and theology the ardent heart of the virgin mother of the Redeemer is seen as

the cause of the fall of the rebellious angels. This is a variation on the *felix culpa* notion that Adam's fall was fortunate because its result was the birth of the redeemer. Joyce's version upsets chronology and causality as well as theology by making one of the results of Satan's fall function as the prime cause of that fall. Mary is the "Lure of the fallen seraphim." The poem is addressed, initially at any rate, to her.

The second tercet is explicated similarly: "The roselike glow sent forth its rays of rhyme: ways, days, blaze, praise, raise. Its rays burned up the world, consumed the hearts of men and angels: the rays from the rose that was her wilful heart." . . . Here the ardent glow is seen to perform two functions. In Stephen's mind it inspires rays of rhyme for his artistic creation. In its more general manifestation it has consumed the hearts of men and angels.

In the third tercet the smoke from the burning heart of man rises as "incense ascending from the altar of the world." At this point Stephen's thoughts turn from the earth as a "ball of incense" to the phrase "an ellipsoidal ball," which is an echo of vulgar student scatology coming into Stephen's mind by association and breaking the spell of inspiration. His thoughts wander through all the various female associations mentioned above until his image of himself as "a priest of the eternal imagination transmuting the daily bread of experience into the radiant body of everlasting life" returns his mind to the altar and incense of the villanelle and he composes the fourth and fifth tercets around the image of the eucharist. The "smoke of praise" and the rimmed ocean suggest the thurible and the chalice—images which Stephen handles in the poem, though he will "never swing the thurible before the tabernacle" in actuality. After his mind has wandered back again to E.C. and his youthful romantic feelings for her, his thoughts dissolve in [a] moment of spiritual copulation. . . . Here he finds his image for the "languorous look and lavish limb" of the conclusion.

The paradox of the Virgin as Temptress has given the whole poem a peculiar tone, which, if we did not consider carefully, we might be tempted to write off as merely blasphemous. But the poem is not *merely* anything. It is a commonplace of Biblical exegesis that Eve, in the Old Testament, is a type of Mary in the New Testament, just as Adam is a type of Jesus. Joyce's awareness of this derives from his reading of St. Augustine and other Church Fathers. . . . (p. 486)

Beyond the parallel between Eve and Mary, Joyce seems to have in mind a similar and even more paradoxical parallel between Satan and Gabriel. Satan literally fell from heaven, but Gabriel was lured "to the virgin's chamber" so that the word could be made flesh. And Stephen himself has known in the arms of his dream temptress "the ecstasy of *seraphic* life" [my italics]. Thus the term "fallen seraphim" of the first tercet applies not only to Satan but to Gabriel as well, and finally, by his own imaginative extension, to Stephen himself and the male principle in general—what may be said to be represented by that rising-fallen phoenix culprit HCE in *Finnegans Wake.* And, by a similar mental process the temptress can be Eve in relation to Satan, Mary to Gabriel, E.C. to Stephen, and the female principle in general—the Anna Livia Plurabelle of *Finnegans Wake.*

The medievalness of Joyce's mind can hardly be overemphasized. Not only is he capable of a medieval kind of religious parody without blasphemy (comparable to the *Second Shepherds' Play* and other Biblical romps) but he thinks in types and tropes constantly. The whole "metempsychosis" motif in

Ulysses is allegorical in its operation, and the various multi-characters of *Finnegans Wake* are conceived in that medieval spirit which could not consider Hercules, even, without seeing Christ superimposed on him. The kind of mental process which culminates in *Finnegans Wake* seems to be operating in Joyce's handling of the villanelle in *A Portrait*. His original conception of the poem may even have been trivial. In *Stephen Hero* we are told that the insipid epiphany of the Young Lady and the Young Gentleman ... set Stephen composing "some ardent verses which he entitled "'Vilanelle [sic] of the Temptress'.'" But by the time he re-wrote the last part of *A Portrait* for publication he had seen larger possibilities in the poem, which he exploited by connecting its inspiration to Stephen's glimpse of E.C. at the library (instead of the Young Lady and Gentleman) and providing the poem with the narrative commentary which we now have. We can not be sure, of course, that we are dealing with the same poem. Joyce's drastic revision of "Tily" for *Pomes Penyeach,* in which he completely reversed the mood and meaning of the poem from a sentimental idyll to a bitter cry of anguish, is warning enough to make us proceed with caution here.... But Joyce certainly reinterpreted the poem, possibly revising it in accordance with his new view, making it unmistakably clear from the context that the "you" addressed in the opening line is, initially at least, the Virgin Mary.

Eve is our first mother and Mary is our second, a "second Eve" as Augustine saith (according to Stephen in the "Oxen of the Sun"). But in the Bible Eve figures as first temptress as well as first mother. And this feminine principle—irrational, sensual, seductive—becomes in Joyce's inversion of traditional typology equally the property of Mary and Eve. The ardent heart of the Virgin lured Gabriel the seraph to her chamber and precipitated, in advance of her own birth, the fall of Satan and his seraphim; who, through Eve, caused the fall of man. Not only are Eve and Mary fused in the image of the Temptress (and that other temptress, Lilith, perhaps) but such other figures as E.C. herself, girls who have laughed at Stephen or called out to him in the street, and the mysterious woman who invited Davin into her cottage. The last woman is of especial significance. She brings the Celtic Twilight into Joyce's narrative. Davin rejected her offer partly through his innate goodness and innocence, and partly through a vague fear that she was not all she seemed to be. The Irish fairies, the Shee, hover over Davin's story. And one in particular hovers over Stephen's poem. "The Leanhaun Shee (fairy mistress)" [Yeats wrote in his collection of *Fairy and Folk Tales of the Irish Peasantry,* 1888],

> seeks the love of mortals. If they refuse, she must be their slave; if they consent, they are hers, and can only escape by finding another to take their place. The fairy lives on their life, and they waste away. Death is no escape from her. She is the Gaelic muse, for she gives inspiration to those she persecutes. The Gaelic poets die young, for she is restless and will not let them remain long on earth—this malignant phantom ...

> She is of the dreadful solitary fairies. To her have belonged the greatest of the Irish poets, from Oisin down to the last century....

Though Oliver Gogarty addressed him as the Wandering Aengus (letters in MS at Cornell), Joyce had specifically repudiated the "Gaelic League" approach to literature. Stephen's poem

is more Catholic than Celtic. Its literary models are the poems of the nineties: the villanelles of Ernest Dowson and such "mother" poems as Swinburne's "Mater Triumphalis", ... and Francis Thompson's "The After Woman." And its ancestors are such romantic treatments of this theme as Blake's "The Mental Traveller" and Keats's "La Belle Dame Sans Merci." Thus, Stephen's villanelle must be read partly as an effort in this recognizable sub-genre, where its compressed coolness compares quite favorably with the feverish looseness of Swinburne and Co. But the Leanhaun Shee, nevertheless, haunts Stephen's poem because it is a muse-poem. Joyce has unerringly selected for Stephen's single poetic effort in *A Portrait* a great poetical archetype—what Robert Graves has called the "single poetic theme."

Joyce, steeped in Catholic theology more strongly than in Celtic mythology, nevertheless knew his Yeats as well as anyone and knew most of the nineteenth-century Irish poets as well—as his essays on Mangan indicate. He might even have known a muse-poem such as Thomas Boyd's "To the Leanán Sidhe." In the "Villanelle of the Temptress" Stephen is writing a poem to his muse, who is a traditionally feminine and mythic figure, though the imagery through which she is presented is drawn almost exclusively from Catholic ritual and ceremony. He sees himself a priest of the imagination celebrating a eucharistic ritual of transubstantiation—the daily bread of experience becoming the radiant body of everlasting life—and a ritual of incarnation as well—in the virgin womb of the imagination the word is made flesh. And to render these qualities in his vision artistically he presents them in a rigidly prescribed esthetic form, the villanelle, in which the temptress-muse is worshiped in a eucharistic ritual. From the heart set ablaze by the langorous look of the temptress rises incense of praise. For the virgin who lured the seraphim from heaven a flowing chalice is raised in celebration.

The strange woman who tempted Davin has been recognized by Stephen, while writing the poem, as a "figure of the womanhood of her country." And so is Stephen's temptress such a figure. Like the Leanan Shee herself, Ireland is a female figure who destroys those who serve her. They call her Kathleen ni Houlihan or Dark Rosaleen or the Shan Van Vocht or the old sow that eats her farrow. Stephen's particular problem is to help the bat-like soul of this female to awake, to serve her without being destroyed by her; to forge in the smithy of his own soul the uncreated conscience of *her* race. He wants, among other things, to turn her from the enchanted Celtic Twilight to the daylight of his own time. The villanelle is half his self-dedication to a hopeless task and half a prayer for release from the pitiless muse and country whose service is his accepted destiny. The appearance of the milk woman in the opening scene of *Ulysses* starts Stephen's mind working along these same lines.... (pp. 487-88)

That Joyce intended the poem to be the product of genuine inspiration can be readily demonstrated by an examination of the manuscripts. In Trieste, during the years 1907 to 1914, Joyce kept a notebook in which he jotted down many thoughts and descriptions later used in *A Portrait* and *Ulysses*. Whole sentences and large parts of paragraphs on Cranly, Lynch, Buck Mulligan, and Stephen's parents come from his notebook, which Joyce began after he had abandoned the *Stephen Hero* version of *A Portrait*. The section of this notebook labelled "Esthetic" is directly relevant to Stephen's composition of the villanelle. Here are several entries from this section of the notebook:

> An enchantment of the heart.

The instant of inspiration is a spark so brief as to be invisible. The reflection of it on many sides at once from a multitude of cloudy circumstances with no one of which it is united save by the bond of merest possibility veils its afterglow in an instant in a first confusion of form. This is the instant in which the word is made flesh.

There is a morning inspiration as there is a morning knowledge about the windless hour when the moth escapes from the chrysalis, and certain plants bloom and the feverfit of madness comes on the insane.

(Unpublished MS, the Cornell Joyce Collection, item 25)

All three of these entries are intended as statements of Joyce's esthetic theory. The first phrase, "an enchantment of the heart," finds its way into Stephen's discourse to describe the moment when the esthetic image is first conceived in the imagination. . . . The other two esthetic entries quoted here were employed by Joyce in the episode of the villanelle, and the first phrase was repeated there, making a bridge between esthetic theory and practice. Stephen woke early:

It was that windless hour of dawn when madness wakes and strange plants open to the light and the moth flies forth silently.

An enchantment of the heart! The night had been enchanted. In a dream of vision he had known the ecstasy of seraphic life. Was it an instant of enchantment only or long hours and years and ages?

The instant of inspiration seemed now to be reflected from all sides at once from a multitude of cloudy circumstances of what happened or what might have happened. The instant flashed forth like a point of light and now from cloud on cloud of vague circumstance confused form was veiling softly its afterglow. O! In the virgin womb of the imagination the word was made flesh. . . .

The words and images are drawn directly from the esthetic jottings in the notebook, but they have been transformed from exposition to narration. Joyce has deliberately set out in his description of Stephen's inspiration to fulfill the theoretical requirements he had himself set up for such inspiration. The inspiration and the poem are both intended to be genuine. And the poem, after all, is a poem about inspiration. The emotions and sensations felt by Stephen in his spiritual copulation with the temptress-muse provide him with some of the vocabulary he employs in the poem. In his esthetic discourse with Lynch, Stephen remarked, "When we come to the phenomena of artistic conception, artistic gestation and artistic reproduction, I require a new terminology and a new personal experience". . . . The episode of the villanelle provides him with both experience and terminology, locked in such a tight embrace that they produce not a theory but a poem. It is at this point that Stephen ceases to be an esthete and becomes a poet. (pp. 488-89)

Robert Scholes, "Stephen Dedalus, Poet or Esthete?" in PMLA, *79, Vol. LXXIX, No. 4, September, 1964, pp. 484-89.*

HUGH KENNER (essay date 1965)

[*Kenner is the foremost American critic and chronicler of literary Modernism. He is best known for* The Pound Era *(1971), a massive study of the Modernist movement, and for his influential works on T. S. Eliot, James Joyce, Samuel Beckett, and Wyndham Lewis. In addition to his reputation as an important scholar, Kenner is noted for his often eccentric judgments and a critical style that relies on surprising juxtapositions and wit. Kenner's well-known essay "The Portrait in Perspective" (1948) helped to ignite the debate among Joyce critics regarding Joyce's attitude toward Stephen Dedalus in* A Portrait of the Artist as a Young Man. *In "The Portrait in Perspective," Kenner insisted that, in spite of the many autobiographical elements in* A Portrait, *there were strong indications that Joyce saw Stephen Dedalus not as his alter-ego, but as just another paralyzed victim of the Dublin environment. The following excerpt is Kenner's retrospective reconsideration of this argument. In it, Kenner restates and explains the reasoning behind "The Portrait in Perspective," and clarifies some frequently misunderstood aspects of his thought. For further discussion of the controversy surrounding Joyce's attitude toward Stephen, see the excerpts by Wayne C. Booth (1961), Robert Scholes (1964), and Robert M. Adams (1966).*]

What you are about to read is a summary of conclusions, without a great deal of evidence. I assume that by now the evidence is pretty familiar. The Joyce canon is not very large, and certainly *A Portrait of the Artist as a Young Man* has been read by everyone not hopelessly given over to the supposition that the novel ceased with Bulwer-Lytton.

I am coming back to it, as I do from time to time, because, fifteen years after I first wrote an essay about it, I still think it is the key to the entire Joyce operation, though I hope I know more about it by now than I did when I wrote my essay. I am not going to deal in local explanations. . . . I am simply going to try to describe, as fully and carefully as I can, what the *Portrait* seems to be.

It has been supposed from the beginning that about this at least there is no mystery; for does not the title tell us that it is the portrait of the artist as a young man? To which I think it relevant to answer, that if we are to take this title at its face value, then it is unique among Joyce titles; and since it is too long a title to be printed conveniently upon the spine of a shortish novel—the sort of detail to which Joyce could always be relied on to pay attention—he must have wanted all those words for a purpose, and we had better look at them pretty carefully.

The first thing to be noticed, I think, is that the title imposes a pictorial and spatial analogy, an expectation of static repose, on a book in which nothing except the spiritual life of Dublin stands still: a book of fluid transitions in which the central figure is growing older by the page. The book is a becoming, which the title tells us to apprehend as a being. I shall have more to say about this in a moment; let me first draw attention to two more things we may notice in the title. One of them is this, that it has the same grammatical form as "A Portrait of the Merchant as a Young man" or "A Portrait of the Blacksmith as a Young Man". It succeeds in not wholly avowing that the Artist in question is the same being who painted the portrait; it permits us to suppose that he may be the generic artist, the artistic type, the sort of person who sets up as an artist, or acts the artist, or is even described by irreverent friends as The Artist. I do not press this scheme, though I shall later extract a consequence or two from it. The third thing the title says is that we have before us a Portrait of the Artist *as a Young Man*. Now there is a clear analogy here, and the analogy is with Rembrandt, who painted self-portraits nearly every year of his

The square ditch at Clongowes Wood College that Stephen Dedalus was pushed into. Courtesy of Sean O'Mordha.

life beginning in his early twenties. Like most Joycean analogies, however, it is an analogy with a difference, because the painter of self-portraits looks in a mirror, but the writer of such a novel as we have before us must look in the mirror of memory. A Rembrandt portrait of the artist at twenty-two shows the flesh of twenty-two and the features of twenty-two as portrayed by the hand of twenty-two and interpreted by the wisdom of twenty-two. Outlook and insight, subject and perception, feed one another in a little oscillating node of objectified introspection, all locked into an eternalized present moment. What that face knows, that painter knows, and no more. The canvas holds the mirror up to a mirror, and it is not surprising that this situation should have caught the attention of an Irish genius, since the mirror facing a mirror, the book that contains a book, the book (like *A Tale of a Tub*) which is about a book which is itself, or the book (like *Malone Dies*) which is a history of the writing both of itself and of another book like itself, or the poem (like "The Phases of the Moon") which is about people who are debating whether to tell the poet things he put into their heads when he created them, and are debating this, moreover, while he is in the very act of writing the poem about their debate: this theme, "mirror on mirror mirroring all the show," has been since at least Swift's time the inescapable mode of the Irish literary imagination, which is happiest when it can subsume ethical notions into an epistemological comedy. So far so good; but Joyce, as usual, has brooded on the theme a great deal longer than is customary, and has not been arrested, like Swift or Samuel Beckett or even Yeats, by the surface neatness of a logical antinomy. For it inheres in his highly individual application of Rembrandt's theme, that the Portrait of the Artist as a Young Man can only be painted by an older man, if older only by the time it takes to write the book. Joyce was careful to inform us at the bottom of the last page of this

book that it took ten years. We have a Portrait, then, the subject of which ages from birth to twenty years within the picture space, while the artist has lived through ten more years in the course of painting it.

There follows a conclusion of capital importance: that we shall look in vain for analogies to the two principal conventions of a normal portrait, the static subject and the static viewpoint, those data from which all Renaissance theories of painting derive. . . . The laws of perspective place painter and subject in an exact geometrical relation to one another, in space and by analogy in time; but here they are both of them moving, one twice as fast as the other. The *Portrait* may well be the first piece of cubism in the history of art.

I have already hinted that a few of the topics on which we have come already will require further development; so I am not really through with the title yet. But let us open the book and see what we discover. We discover, behind and around the central figure, what Wyndham Lewis described as a swept and tidied naturalism, and nowhere more completely than in the places, the accessory figures, the sights and sounds, the speeches and the names. Joyce is famous for his meticulous care with fact; "he is a bold man," he once wrote, "who will venture to alter what he has seen and heard." He used, in *Dubliners* and *Ulysses,* the names of real people, so often that their concerted determination to sue him the minute he should step off the boat became, I think, an implacable efficient cause for his long exile from Ireland, which commenced virtually on the eve of the publication of *Dubliners*. . . . It is clear that for Joyce authenticity of detail was of overriding moment. If actual names were artistically correct, he used them at whatever risk. If they were not, he supplied better ones, but always plausible ones. So far so good. And what stares us in the face wherever we open the first sustained narrative of this ferocious and uncompromisng realist? Why, a name like a huge smudged fingerprint: the most implausible name that could conceivably be devised for an inhabitant of lower class Catholic Dublin: a name that no accident of immigration, no freak of etymology, no canon of naturalism however stretched, can justify: the name of Stephen Dedalus.

It seems to me very odd that we accept this name without protest; it is given to no eccentric accessory figure, but to the central character himself, the subject of the Portrait. But I cannot see that it has ever had the sort of effect Joyce must have intended: he must have meant it to arrest speculation at the outset, detaching the central figure at once from the conventions of quiet naturalism. What has happened instead is instructive: for Joyce is the best case available of the principle, that the history of the reception of a writer's works is one of the basic data of criticism. Joyce himself, as the Satanic antinomian, attracted attention as soon as the book did, and far more strongly; it was at once assumed that the book was nothing more than a thinly veiled autobiography. It was a natural assumption from this premise, that the author treated his early self with considerable indulgence, especially since the Stephen of the Portrait seemed cleary destined to turn into the man Joyce was supposed to be. So it seemed clear that the name of Stephen Dedalus should be scrutinized for a piece of indulgent symbolism: and indeed it yields this symbolism quite readily, the strange name a figure of prophecy, prophecy of light and escape, and fabulous artifice.

Now it is true that Joyce exploits the symbolism of the name, in the latter part of the book; but if we could somehow get Joyce himself out of our minds for a moment, and consider the early part of the book on the terms it seems to impose, we should see a central figure with a name so odd its seems a pseudonym. And indeed it seems to have been modelled on a pseudonym. It combines a Christian martyr with a fabulous artificer. I think it very likely that it was based on another name constructed in the same way, a name adopted by a famous Irishman which also combines a Christian martyr with a fabulous wanderer. The model, I think, is the name Sebastian Melmoth, which was adopted during the brief time of his continental exile by the most lurid Dubliner of them all, Oscar Wilde.

Wilde built his pseudonym of exile deliberately. Sebastian— Saint Sebastian—may be described as the fashionable martyr of 19th century aestheticism. Melmoth—*Melmoth the Wanderer*—was the hero of a novel written 80 years before by yet another Irish romancer, Charles Maturin. The two names joined the Christian and the pagan, the sufferer and the exile; in combination they vibrate with a heavy mysterious exoticism, linking Wilde with the creed of beleaguered beauty and with the land of his ancestors, affirming at the same time something richer and stranger about this shuffling Irish scapegoat than would seem possible, in Wilde's view, to a countryman of people with names like Casey, Sullivan, and Moonan. It is a haunting homeless name, crying for exegesis, deliberately assumed by a haunted, homeless man. He was a man, furthermore, in whom Joyce did not fail to see enacted one of his own preoccupations, the artist as scapegoat for middle-class rectitude. And in modelling, as I believe he did, the name of the hero of his novel on the pseudonym of the fallen Wilde, Joyce was, I believe, deliberately invoking the Wildean parallel.

To give this remark a context, let me now say as plainly as possible what I think the *Portrait* is. The *Portrait* is a sort of Euclidean demonstration, in five parts, of how a provincial capital—for instance Dublin, though Toronto or Melbourne would do—goes about converting unusual talent into formlessly clever bohemanism. This demonstration is completed in *Ulysses,* when the bourgeois misfit *par excellence* turns out to be the bohemian's spiritual father. (The principle, by the way, that underlies the spiritual paternity of Bloom and Stephen is the simple and excellent scholastic maxim that opposites belong to the same species.) Now Dublin, by the time Joyce came to look back on the process to which he had barely escaped falling victim, had already extruded the arch-bohemian of a generation, Oscar Wilde, and Wilde had completed the Icarian myth by falling forever. If we are going to be consistent about the symbolism of names, it should be clear that Stephen is the son of Dedalus, and what the son of Dedalus did was fall. It seems clear that Joyce sees Stephen as a figure who is going to fall, not as a figure who is going to turn into the author himself. It is in *Ulysses,* of course, that we last see Stephen, aged twenty-two; and I think it significant that Joyce remarked one day, to Frank Budgen, while he was engaged on the figure of Leopold Bloom in *Ulysses,* that Stephen no longer interested him as Bloom did; for Stephen, he said, "has a shape that can't be changed." This seems decisive; but let us go back to Wilde a moment. It is, to put it plainly, possible if not sufficient to regard the *Portrait* as a lower-class Catholic parallel to Wilde's upper-class Protestant career.

This idea, for all the attention that has been devoted to Joyce's work, remains absurdly unfamiliar. Let me expand it. I am not arguing that Joyce hated Stephen, or could not bear Stephen, or was satirizing Stephen. I am merely pointing out that Joyce, though he used everything usable from his own experience, was creating all the time a character not himself, so little resemblng himself that he may well have been suggested by the notoriety of a famous compatriot who had died only a few years before the first version of the book was begun. One of the incidents for which even the careful researches of Mr. Kevin Sullivan have turned up no prototype whatever, the caning of Stephen by schoolfellows because he refuses to "admit that Byron was no good," may even have been contrived as an Irish parallel to the famous indignities Wilde suffered at Oxford.

I have said that Joyce used everything usable from his own experience to create a character not himself. Now the evidence multiplies, as biographical trivia come to light, that Joyce did this with all his characters; but the party line of Joyce exegesis is wonderfully accommodating. When we learn, as I learned recently from an eye-witness of the Paris years, that he liked grilled kidneys for breakfast, we at once remember the familiar opening lines of the second section of *Ulysses:* "Mr. Leopold Bloom ate with relish the inner organs of beasts and fowls. . . . Most of all he liked grilled mutton kidneys, which gave to his palate a fine tang of faintly scented urine." This would seem to be a clear example of Joyce's way of using any detail that was handy, including, or especially, the most intimate trivia of his own existence, in the process of building from the inside a fictional creation. But this is not what we are normally told. When such details come to light the analogy of Stephen is trotted out. Stephen shares many experiences and attitudes with his author, because Stephen is Joyce. Now here is Bloom sharing characteristics with his author, therefore Bloom is Joyce. Mr. Ellmann [see the excerpt by Richard Ellmann dated 1982] actually commits himself . . . to the judgment that Bloom is

Joyce's mature persona, and avers . . . that the movement of *Ulysses* ''is to bring Stephen, the young Joyce, into *rapport* with Bloom, the mature Joyce.''

It is surely wiser to work the analogy of Stephen the other way. If Bloom shares characteristics with Joyce and is plainly not Joyce, then Stephen, merely because he shares characteristics with Joyce, is not necessarily Joyce either.

I sketch this argument because it seems to be called for, not because I think it especially enlightening. If we want to know what Joyce is doing with the character called Stephen, we shall arrive at nothing conclusive by checking our impressions against the evidence of what he does with Leopold Bloom, simply because Leopold Bloom is—like Stephen himself, for that matter—a special case. He is a special case because he is so greatly elaborated; one would expect a good number of the author's own characteristics to find their way into the portrait of Bloom simply because so many small characteristics are needed for the presentation of a character on such a scale. The people who turn up in the sort stories provide a much better control group. Can we find in *Dubliners* any useful prototypes of Stephen Dedalus, useful because formed in a similar way, but so controlled by the smaller scale and the unchanging viewpoint that we may have less trouble deciding what they are meant to signify? The answer is that we can find a great many.

There is Mr. James Duffy, for instance, in **"A Painful Case"**. Mr. Duffy has been endowed with the author's Christian name, and a surname with just as many letters in it as there are in Joyce. (This is a tiny point, to be sure, but Joyce was a great counter of letters.) He has moved out of Dublin, though it is true that he has not moved far, only as far as suburban Chapelizod. He elected Chapelizod because he found all the other suburbs of Dublin ''mean, modern and pretentious''. He is a man obsessed with ideas of order, with pattern, symmetry, classification: he expresses these impulses by, among other things, the care with which he arranges his books. Like his creator, who kept a notebook headed **"Epiphanies"**, he keeps on his desk a sheaf of papers headed ''Bile Beans,'' held together by a brass pin, and in these papers he inscribes from time to time a sorrowful or sardonic epigram. The woman with whom he attempts to strike up a relationship is named Mrs. Sinoco, which was the name of a singing teacher Joyce frequented in Trieste. He has even translated *Michael Kramer,* as Joyce had done in the summer of 1901. The manuscript of his translation is exceptionally tidy: the stage directions are written in purple ink. And he listens, as did the author of *Exiles* and of the final pages of *Finnegans Wake,* to ''the strange impersonal voice which he recognized as his own, insisting on the soul's incurable loneliness. We cannot give ourselves, it said: we are our own.'' ''Ourselves, oursouls, alone,'' echoes Anna Livia across thirty years. Mr. Duffy, in short, is A Portrait of the Artist as Dublin Bank-clerk.

Or consider Jimmy Doyle, in **"After the Race,"** whose name is Jimmy Joyce's with only two letters altered. . . . Or consider finally Gabriel Conroy, in **"The Dead"**.

Gabriel Conroy, who is sick of his own country and has ''visited not a few places abroad,'' who writes book reviews, as did Joyce, for the *Daily Express,* teaches language, as did Joyce, parts his hair in the middle, as did Joyce, wears rimmed glasses, as did Joyce, clings to petty respectabilities, as did Joyce, has taken a wife from the savage bogs of the west counties, as did Joyce, snubs people unexpectedly, as did Joyce, and is eternally preoccupied, as was Joyce, with the notion

that his wife has had earlier lovers: Gabriel Conroy, attending a festivity in a house that belonged to Joyce's great-aunts, and restive in his patent-leather cosmopolitanism among the provincials of the capital by the Liffey, is pretty clearly modelled on his author by rather the same sort of process that was later to produce Stephen Dedalus.

There is nothing original in these observations, and we have not by any means exhausted the list of Joycean shadow-selves who turn up in these strangely intimate stories. But when we find them in the stories, instead of in an equivocally autobiographical novel, we can see more clearly what they are. They are not the author, they are potentialities contained within the author. They are what he has not become.

The sharpest exegetical instrument to bring to the work of Joyce is Aristotle's great conception of potency and act. Joyce's awareness of it, his concern with it, is what distinguishes him from every other writer who has used the conventions of naturalism. Naturalist fiction as it was developed in France was based on scientific positivism, its conviction that realities are bounded by phenomena, persons by behaviour, that what seems is, and that what *is* must be. But Joyce is always concerned with multiple possibilities. For a Zola, a Maupassant, a Flaubert, it is simply meaningless to consider what might have been; for since it was not, it is meaningless to *say* that it might have been. In the mind of Joyce, however, there hung a radiant field of potentialities: ways in which a man may go, and correspondingly selves he may become, bounding himself in one form or another while remaining the same person in the eyes of God. The events of history, Stephen considers in *Ulysses,* are branded by time and hung fettered ''in the room of the infinite possibilities they have ousted''. Pathos, the dominant or sub-dominant Joycean emotion, inheres in the inspection of such limits: men longing to become what they can never be, though it lies in them to be it, simply because they have become something else.

All potentiality is bounded by alien and circumstantial limits. The people in *Dubliners* are thwarted, all of them, by the limitation of potentiality the city imposes. They sense this, all of them, and yearn to remove themselves, but in their yearning they are subjected to another scholastic axiom, that we cannot desire what we do not know. If they have notions of what it would be like to live another way, in another place, they confect these notions out of what Dublin makes available. (pp. 1-10)

I hope no one thinks that I am forgetting Stephen Dedalus all this time. I am supplying a context for all those people in *Dubliners* who resemble the author, so as to supply in turn a context for the ways in which Stephen Dedalus resembles the author. At every moment of his life, the author, like anyone else in Dublin or anywhere else, was confronted with decisions and choices, courses of conduct elected or not elected; and each of these in turn, branches, if he elects it, into a whole branching family of further courses, or if he does not elect it, branches into a whole different family of branching courses. If the nose on Cleopatra's face had been shorter, the destiny of the world would have altered; if the swan had not come to Leda, Troy would not have fallen, nor Homer educated Greece, nor Greece Rome, and we should none of us perhaps exist. So there lies before a man an indefinitely large potentiality of events he may set in motion, ways he may go, and selves he may become. But each way, each self, each branching upon a branch, is supplied by Dublin; so the field, however large, is closed. In Dublin one can only become a Dubliner; a Dubliner in exile, since the exile was elected from within Dublin and is situated along one of the many paths leading out of Dublin and so connected to Dublin, is a Dubliner still. Even refusing Dublin is a Dublin stratagem.

He contains, then, within him, multitudes. All the people in *Dubliners* are people he might have been, all imprisoned in devious ways by the city, all come to terms of some sort with it, all meeting or refusing shadow-selves who taunt them with the spectre of yet another course once possible but possible now no longer. *Dubliners* is a portrait of the artist as many men. . . . And none of the men becomes James Joyce, nor none of the women Norah Joyce, but they might: they contain those potentialities. It is only by a fantastic series of accidents that anyone becomes what he does become, and though he can be only what he is, he can look back along the way he has come, testing it for branching-points now obsolete.

So the subject of *Dubliners* is a single subject, metamorphosing along many lines of potentiality as the circle of light directed by the story-teller moves through time, picking out, successively, a small boy of the time when he was himself a small boy, or adolescents of the time when he was an adolescent. Each story obeys, or seems to obey, the pictorial convention of a fixed perspective, subject and viewer set in place until the work of portrayal is finished. The book, however, is a succession of such pictures; or better, it is the trace of a moving subject, seen from a moving viewpoint which is always very close to him.

And if we apply this account to *A Portrait of the Artist as a Young Man* we shall find that it applies exactly: the moving point of view, product not only of a book ten years in the writing but of a standpoint which remains close to the subject as he moves; the moving subject, passing from infancy forward for twenty years; and the subject himself a potentiality drawn from within the author, the most fully developed of the alternative selves he projected over a long life with such careful labor. If the differences between Stephen and Joyce seem small, all differences are small, and it is always small differences that are decisive. One has only to accept or refuse a causal opportunity, and the curve of one's life commences a long slow bending away from what it otherwise would have been. This line of argument is not only Aristotelian but wholly familiar to a man brought up, like Joyce, in a climate of clerical exhortation. From the time he could first remember hearing human words, he must have listened to hundreds of homilies, ruminations, admonitions, developing the principle that it is the little sins that prepare the habit great sins will later gratify, or that the destiny of the soul is prepared in early youth, so that there is nothing that does not matter.

So Stephen is a perfectly normal Joyce character, not the intimate image of what Joyce in fact was, but a figure generated according to a way of working that came naturally to him in a hundred ways. Stephen, unlike a character in *Dubliners,* is followed with unflagging attention for twenty years instead of being exhibited as he was during the course of a few hours. But like the characters in *Dubliners,* who also do many things Joyce did, he also leaves undone many other things Joyce did, and does many things Joyce did not. And these, if you accept my account of Joyce's way of thinking on human destiny, are not trivial divergences, but precisely the many small points of decision that make him Stephen and not Joyce.

And, to recapitulate further, Joyce was fascinated by the way Dublin contrives to maintain its life-long hold on its denizens. He himself made no pretence of having escaped the city, except in body; he remained so thoroughly a Dubliner that he kept in repair to the last his knowledge of the shops and streets, pressing visitors from the distant town for news of civic alterations, or carefully making note of the fact that such-and-such a place of business had changed hands. Stephen's talk of flying by nets of language, nationality, religion, remains—Stephen's talk. One does not fly by Dublin's nets, though the illusion that one may fly by them may be one of Dublin's sorts of birdlime.

Once we are in possession of the formula for Stephen, his many little points of divergence from his creator cease to point toward mysterious formal requirements. Stephen is a young man rather like Joyce, who imagines that he is going to put the city behind him; he is going to fly, like Shelley's skylark; and he is going to fall into cold water, like Icarus, or like Oscar Wilde. Given this formula, Joyce used everything he could find or remember that was relevant, all the time fabricating liberally in order to simplify and heighten a being whose entire emotional life is in fact an act of ruthless simplification. (pp. 11-13)

I have a last observation to make, which concerns Joyce's tone. I am always a little surprised to find myself cited, from time to time, as the bellwether of the Stephen-hating school of critics. It is clear that Stephen is not hateful, though he is irritating when he is being put forth by the massed proprietors of the Joyce Legend as an authentic genius. Considered as a genius, he is a tedious cliché, weary, disdainful, sterile; he writes an exceedingly conventional poem in the idiom of the empurpled nineties, indeed a poem Wilde might well have admired, one which seems unlikely to pass beyond the nineties. He has, as Joyce said, a shape that can't be changed.

Or has by the end of the book. But when we were first considering the title of the book, we noticed that the title imposes a look of pictorial repose on a subject constantly changing. We noticed, too, the author's announcement, on the last line of the last page, that he has spent fully ten years revolving the subject and revising and re-revising the writing. As we observed that we had a Portrait with a difference, neither subject nor artist united in a normal geometrical relationship. This is the last thing I want to stress. What we normally call "tone" is the product of a fixed relationship between writer and ma-

The senior school building at Belvedere, referred to as 'the school house' in A Portrait.

terial. It is the exact analogy of perspective in painting. Its two familiar modes are utter sympathy and sustained irony. Irony says, "I see very well what is going on here, and I know how to value it." But Joyce's view of Stephen is not ironic; it is not determined by a standpoint of immovable superiority. Sympathy says "Withhold your judgment; if you undervalue this man you will offend *me*." Joyce's view of Stephen is not sympathetic either, by which I mean that it is not defensive, or self-defensive. Like a Chinese painter, or a mediaeval painter, Joyce expects our viewpoint to move as the subject moves. We are detached from Stephen, we comprehend his motions and emotions, we are not to reject him nor defend him, nor feel a kind of embarrassment on the writer's behalf. We have not "irony," we have simply the truth. This is so until the end. At the end, when Stephen's development ceases, when he passes into, or has very nearly passed into, the shape that can't be changed, then he is troubling; and we sense, I think, a little, Joyce deliberately withholding judgment.

It is a terrible, a shaking story; and it brings Stephen where so many other potential Joyces have been brought, into a fixed rôle, into nothing; into paralysis, frustration, or a sorry, endlessly painful, coming to terms: for the best of them, a meditating on restful symbols, as Gabriel Conroy, stretched out in living death beside his wife, turns to the snow, or as Leopold Bloom, in the room of his cuckolding, thinks on the intellectual pleasures of water. For all the potential selves we can imagine stop short of what we are, and this is true however little we may be satisfied with what we are. Dubliner after Dubliner suffers panic, thinks to escape, and accepts paralysis. It is the premise of the most sensitive of them, as it is for Stephen Dedalus, that the indispensable thing is to escape. It was Joyce's fortune that having carried through Stephen's resolve and having escaped, he saw the exile he accepted as the means of being more thoroughly a Dubliner, a citizen of the city that cannot be escaped but need not be obliterated from the mind. He celebrated it all his life, and projected the moods through which he had passed, and for which he retained an active sympathy, into fictional characters for each of whom the drab city by the Liffey, whatever else it is, is nothing at all to celebrate. (pp. 14-15)

Hugh Kenner, "Joyce's Portrait—A Reconsideration," in The University of Windsor Review, Vol. I, No. 1, Spring, 1965, pp. 1-15.

ROBERT M. ADAMS (essay date 1966)

[*Adams is a professor of English and the author of important critical works on Milton, Stendhal, and the Symbolist movement. In the following excerpt, he discusses the character of Stephen Dedalus in the* Portrait, *and presents evidence that Stephen can be interpreted as both a sympathetic and ironic figure. Adams also examines the novel's structure and its relationship to the development of Stephen's consciousness and his interpretations of life around him. For further discussion of the controversy surrounding Joyce's attitude toward Stephen, see the excerpts by Wayne C. Booth (1961), Robert Scholes (1964), and Hugh Kenner (1965).*]

How much sympathy is the reader [of James Joyce's *A Portrait of the Aritst as a Young Man*] supposed to accord Stephen Dedalus in his struggles with the political, social, religious, and artistic mores of his native land? The range of possible answers is very wide indeed. Some critics hold that Stephen is derided as a spoiled and petulant brat. Others maintain that he is a martyr, a mythical figure, and type of the Christ. It is

hard to suppose that all these judgments are right. But of course our question is actually four different questions, and it is not difficult to see that answers to them may vary considerably from passage to passage within the book. These answers also vary in considerable measure according to the age at which one reads the book and the attitudes one brings to it. The *Portrait,* as it decribes the rebellion and self-assertion of a young man at odds with his elders, is bound to be read with special feeling by young people at odds with their elders—and by elders at odds with their young people. It is a more liberating book, I think, for the young than for the old, but it speaks to both conditions. This may well be because it was composed at two different periods of Joyce's life, and often includes the basis for two quite different attitudes toward the same sequence of events or set of values.

Let us begin with some prosaic details. The *Portrait,* as we now have it, is an arranged and selective account of the growth of a consciousness. That it is literally the consciousness of James Joyce which is described at every point is too much to say, but that the broad outlines and many of the specific details of the story are taken from Joyce's actual experience is quite apparent. From beginning to end, the book covers, we may estimate, a chronological "distance" of a little less than twenty years. It begins in 1885 or 1886, when Stephen Dedalus is three or four, and ends in 1902, with his departure for the Continent at the age of 22. Public events, such as the fall of Parnell and the production of *The Countess Cathleen,* are mentioned within the book, providing a sketchy, yet consistent basis for dating it. But though we may easily estimate the total "coverage" of the book, its handling of time, as a matter of interior economy, is very uneven and irregular. (pp. 92-3)

[If] the scenes of the novel are as discontinuous as loose beads, what strings them together? Primarily, of course, the development of Stephen Dedalus. On the stage of the novel, he always stands front and center. The portrait is of him, and the other characters are all ancillary; for example, only one of his siblings has so much as a name, that name is used only once, and as for the other young Dedaloi, we do not know even so much as their precise number. . . . Stephen's central position is not automatic evidence that we are to take a favorable view of him; Sir Willoughby Patterne occupies an equally central position in *The Egoist.* It does mean, however, that the word "hero" remains appropriate to him, and that the virtues or faults we impute to him cannot very well be mediocre ones. We see things through his eyes, we see very often only his reaction to things and not the things themselves, and this sort of focus, this continuous, detailed interest in the processes of his brain, renders it most unlikely that he will prove to be such a flabby, floundering pseudo-artist as Frederic Moreau, the protagonist of Flaubert's *Sentimental Education* or the puppy who is represented in George Moore's *Confessions of a Young Man.*

For example, a major theme in Joyce's description of his literary artist's development is his growing command of words and sensitivity to them. Even as a very young man indeed, Stephen is conscious of a story and a poem; and a momentary rhyme catches and fixes in his mind a connection of far-reaching importance for the novel. The little boy who crouches under the kitchen table reciting

Pull out his eyes,
Apologize,
Apologize,
Pull out his eyes.

is memorizing a connection between guilt, submission, and weak eyesight, which, however irrational, could sink deep into the mind of a sensitive child. The power of words to hypnotize and fascinate is the least of the things demonstrated in this abbreviated scene, which looks forward to a whole series of demands for "submission," somehow connected with weak eyesight and a bird which brings punishment from on high. (Cf. Father Dolan's descent on blinded Stephen . . . ; the demand of Heron that he "admit" . . . ; his bitter sense that sin comes through the eyes. . . .) (pp. 94-5)

At Clongowes too Stephen is shown to be permeated by words and names. His own name is peculiar, and he does not know "what kind of a name" it is . . . ; the word "belt" has a funny double meaning . . . ; and the word "suck" has ugly, fascinating connotations. . . . Before long the suggestive power of words is leading Stephen to compose, within his imagination, little romantic dramas in which he sees himself dying, the bell tolling, farewell being said, a melancholy poem being recited; and by a peculiar sort of confirmation, the vision of his own funeral . . . is repeated in the outside world by the funeral of Parnell. . . . This pattern seems, perhaps, over-ingenious and arbitrary, but we know from outside sources how strong was Joyce's identification with Parnell, and within the novel this pattern recurs often enough and pointedly enough to have a serious claim on our attention. Words, for Stephen Dedalus, have a way of creating things; he thinks of the word, the symbol, first, then finds a confirmation of its existence, its meaning, in the outside world, or at least in an experience. Note how, though without the intervention of words, the green-maroon dichotomy of Dante's hairbrushes . . . is confirmed in Fleming's coloring the earth green and the clouds maroon: "he had not told Fleming to colour them those colours. Fleming had done it himself". . . . The tolling over and over of the words "dark," "cold," "pale," and "strange" produces a vision of Clongowes ghosts, specifically that Marshal Browne who had died at Prague in 1757. . . . Or again the little song Stephen learned as a child:

> O, the wild rose blossoms
> On the little green place.

turns, in the presence of Father Arnall's division of the class into Yorkists (white roses) and Lancastrians (red roses) into a distortion, a vision of a new world.

> Lavender and cream and pink roses were beautiful to think of. Perhaps a wild rose might be like those colours and he remembered the song about the wild rose blossoms on the little green place. But you could not have a green rose. But perhaps somewhere in the world you could. . . .

The sequence of thought here is deliberately indirect. Stephen's mind distorts the "natural" song into a pattern of words without referents, and finds in this world of imagery a sudden refuge from practical reality. Words, we will find if we look a little further ahead in the book, are not simply passive or imitative devices for the artist; they are active tools with which he controls, modifies, and selects the raw materials of his life—and sometimes creating them.

A curious episode, involving another use of words, takes place while Stephen is in the infirmary at Clongowes. . . . A boy named Athy points out to the slightly delirious Stephen that his name—Athy—is the name of a town, and then asks a riddle with a foolish answer: "Why is the county of Kildare like the

leg of a fellow's breeches? . . . Because there is a thigh [Athy] in it." Then he tells Stephen you can ask the same riddle in another way. Stephen wants, mildly, to know what it is, but Athy won't tell, and he never does tell. Later, when there is trouble in the school because some of the older boys have run away, Athy again has something to say; he has the inside story, and he tells it, bit by bit, always holding something back. They were caught—in the square— with Simon Moonan and Tusker Boyle—smugging. . . . The point is not that his final word is a piece of insuperably recondite dialect, though plainly it is esoteric to young Stephen; it is the mysterious way in which language can be used to conceal as well as reveal (and the immense dimensions of a verbal mystery) which fascinates the embryo artist. And perhaps he is made aware, as well, that there are topics which society will not let us talk about distinctly—crevasses of conduct as well as of language, which open under our feet.

A special development of these early pages is Stephen's habit of cradling a traumatic experience in verbal swathings. The hypnotic use of adjectives in the account of Father Dolan's pandying is a small case in point; "hot," "burning," "stinging," "tingling," "crumpled," "flaming," "livid," "scalded," "maimed," "quivering," "fierce," "maddening," all occur in less than half a page. . . . (pp. 95-7)

These little details look trifling, but out of them a number of the traits and attitudes of the fledgling artist are shown to emerge. Stephen is a fondler, a collector of words, with which he controls and in effect creates his own universe. . . . He is acutely conscious of names and their emblematic or symbolic import, he is an avid reader of emblems and omens, through which he endeavors to penetrate the veil of circumstance. He tends to find these meanings, or at least to search for them, in moments of fading consciousness, in dreams, trances, and visions; his meditations are not ordered and controlled, as by the *Spiritual Exercises,* they are always tinged with personal emotion, and the truth after which they reach is generally dim and fragmentary.

It is useful to see Stephen developing, on an almost pre-conscious level, the attitudes, not simply of an artist, but of a symbolist poet, because his actual artistic production, in the course of the book, is so scanty and dubious that some critics have thought him the butt of bitter ironic mockery. Indeed, he does very little artistic creating. It is a very literal-minded criticism, though, which insists on being introduced within the artist's workshop so that the authentic pangs of authentic genius can be duly studied and appreciated. We get this sort of thing from the purveyors of popular fiction about tormented titans. Joyce had too much sense and too much good taste to attempt such a display; so, for the most part, he limited his study to the development of those preliminary attitudes and affinities which go into the making of the artist. The creative act itself he left where it belongs—largely out of the picture; this is one more evidence of his basic respect for the artist.

A second major theme in the book, which interweaves with the theme of verbal manipulation and invention, is that of religion. From the beginning, the consciousness of Stephen Dedalus is dominated by the presence of the Church and its priests. Priests are kind and cruel, they comfort and they hurt, they bring the conscience to a shuddering state of dread, and they reward it with an ecstatic sense of purity. These are some of the first lessons which Stephen Dedalus learns about the Church, and behind all of them there is an immense sense of ecclesiastical power. Even when they are not physically present, priests dominate the scene, as at the Christmas dinner; they decide one's future, they have influence . . . ; though very much of this world and at ease with its human foibles . . . , they have immense power in another world which they use to rack, control, and order the human conscience. Above all, the Roman Church is for Stephen Dedalus a church of order and discipline; its images are all of control, coherence, perhaps limitation; he sets them against the disorder, misrule, and confusion of his father's house, of Ireland. As for the stages by which he grows into the Church and then out of it, they are not in fact very distinct. The retreat quickens into an overpowering sense of guilt a faith which had been, previously, routine and unquestioning; but the process of loss of faith is more vaguely represented. The devotions described at the beginning of Chapter IV are presented with more than a touch of malice as the manipulation of a gigantic spiritual cash register . . . , and seven pages of remote description suffice to bring Stephen through his access of religiosity, to the point where he finds it relatively easy to decline an offer to study for the priesthood. This refusal is made, we note, for peculiarly imagistic and impalpable reasons. The director making the offer, though he speaks gently and thoughtfully, stands against a brown crossblind, in a light that outlines his skull but leaves his face in shadow, and thus makes him seem sinister. At the moment of decision or something like it . . . , Stephen has a vision of a lean, embittered priest, "sourfavoured and devout, shot with pink tinges of suffocated anger"—one known sometimes as Lantern Jaws and sometimes as Foxy Campbell. These are scarcely theological arguments, but they are dramatic portents of considerable import to Stephen's intimate dialectic. Not that the theological arguments disappear wholly from view, but they are muffled. Stephen declines to take communion, as Cranly tells him, because he fears "that the host, too, may be the body and blood of the son of God and not a wafer of bread". . . . This seems more like a reason *for* taking the communion than for *not* doing so; Pascal would have interpreted it so. Evidently there is a good deal of rather willful confusion here. Stephen is fond of the "vesture of a doubting monk" . . . , the appearance both of a heretic and an ascetic . . . , and he cultivates in the austerity of his style, the dry assurance of his judgments, the manners of the order whose central faith he has left behind.

This interplay of shadow and substance is particularly difficult to pin down in the *Portrait* because the book itself is impressionistic in its technique. *Stephen Hero* is less inhibited in dealing with specific ideas, and more enlightening. Within its pages, Stephen loses his faith in the traditional manner of adolescence, with the aid of specific infidel arguments from Voltaire, Shelley, and Robert Ingersoll; he dwells at some length on the familiar *topoi* of the village atheist. But in its final form the book smoothed over these developments. Partly, no doubt, Joyce intended to make Stephen a more remote and fascinating figure by permitting him merely to enunciate conclusions instead of going through arguments; he is rendered thereby more distinguished and impenetrable. But partly also, it seems, Joyce did not want to dwell too long on purely negative arguments against the Church. For in this book, which seems so full of rejections (of Church, family, nation, friends), nothing is ever really rejected for good. Thus the Catholic Church, rejected as a vocation for Stephen, is yet retained as the exemplar of a new and private religion of which Stephen will be both founder and priest. He will not be a priest before the altar of the Christian god, but a priest of the imagination; his ways not those of order and discipline but those of "error and glory"; the emblem of his faith not the Virgin Mary who

is like the morning star, "bright and musical," but the bird-girl of mortal beauty and profane joy. His transition from one affirmation to another is made through an intermediate negation, but the continuity is there, to be sensed. . . . [A] recurrent pattern of the book is alternate expansion and contraction, unfolding and withdrawing. (pp. 98-102)

When we look at the inner structure of the *Portrait*, in fact, we find it controlled less by developing metaphors than by a number of deliberate repetitions and an overall pattern of alternating expansion and contraction. The repetitions are not, necessarily, incremental; if one takes as an example the scene of Stephen's tramway farewell to E.C. . . . , one finds several sentences of it and many scattered smaller phrases repeated . . . ; here Stephen is simply reliving an experience, or recreating it through incantation. (One of its side-effects is to suggest that the original experience was itself largely verbal, as the "day of dappled seaborne clouds" . . . is largely a verbal, rather than a climatological, experience.) Elsewhere, phrases about the "batlike soul" of Irish womanhood, which Stephen first conceives at the end of Davin's story . . . are repeated with reference to E.C. . . . , and this not only generalizes her role, but makes us aware that formulas learned in one situation serve Stephen as windows to open upon the truth of another. Still more interesting is the series of variations played on Stephen's experience of celestial music, which he hears in various circumstances, to various effects. . . . Sometimes the music is the vehicle of a message, sometimes the prelude of one; it comes from another world, beyond the world, and also from within himself. All this apart from the way in which a vague premonition of failure connected with Mike Flynn . . . recurs in connection with his father's social and business failures . . . ; or the fact that when he is with that always-interesting E.C., he hears what her eyes say to him and knows "that in some dim past whether in life or revery, he had heard their tale before". . . . The multiplicity of these repetitions and verbal parallels gives to existence as represented in the *Portrait* the quality of a palimpsest; every experience is written over some other experience, and colors as it is colored by it.

As for the expansion-contraction movement of the book, it has something to do with Joyce's prose style and something also to do with the motion of Stephen's mind. Here as elsewhere Joyce's style varies from a florid, adjectival lyricism to a hard, detailed, unrhythmic prose of deliberate meanness. On the whole, the former rhetoric has not worn as well as the latter, and there is something downright embarrassing about some of Stephen's ecstatics. Some critics have tried to redeem the weak passages by discovering irony behind them. But one can be too kind to Joyce; he does not need this sort of special pleading. There are flaws of taste in the *Portrait*, and one of them, I think, is an occasional over-lushness. But the more basic alternation of the book is dramatic—it lies in the ebb and flow of Stephen's mind, which he himself compares, in an interesting simile, to the spreading and unspreading of an equation, the folding and contraction of a peacock's tail. His soul, he thinks, goes forth to experience, "unfolding itself sin by sin, spreading abroad the balefire of its burning stars and folding back upon itself, fading slowly, quenching its own lights and fires. They were quenched: and the cold darkness filled chaos." . . . The passage is built, by the sort of repetitive expansion noted above, on an earlier one in which Stephen identifies his soul with the cold and lonely cycles of Shelley's moon. . . . There is no problem in applying this passage to Stephen Dedalus' various sentimental ventures—to his successive enthusiasms and disillusions for father, Parnell, Ireland, mother, God, Mercedes, E.C., and the ideal of good fellowship. He is a young man of great enthusiasms and bitter disillusions; and no reader will have trouble tracing the alternation of these moods through the *Portrait.* (We note in passing how this alternation fulfills the image set up by the train passing through tunnels and across open spaces, alternately, in the very first pages of the book.) But for Stephen at least his moods are not just moods. They are part of a process by which the mind journeys to the outermost stars and back, and into the worst corruptions of human nature—both forms of self-testing and self-exploration, variations of perspective which extinguish themselves in ''a cold indifferent knowledge of himself.'' . . . The cyclical motion of his mind is imitated both in the repetitions and the variations of the book—in its spreading out and drawing back and turning upon itself. Always the terminus is that cold indifferent knowledge of self. And under this aspect it is permissible to see not only Stephen's plunges into sin, but his ventures into religion and art—and, of course, *a fortiori* the *Portrait* itself—as attempts at self-confrontation. Narcissus presides over almost all phases of Stephen's career, and under this aspect it is certainly open to more than one ironic glance. (One recalls particularly the way Stephen's first effort at poetic creation, the Byronic verses to E.C., ends with a long gaze into the mirror in his mother's bedroom. . . .) So seen, the *Portrait* does not end on a note of triumphant flight at all. Stephen, as he departs for the Continent, all high resolve and abnegation, is more in bondage than ever to his own personality. He is swinging in wider and wider arcs of speculation and self-dissection, alternating like the moon between ''sad human ineffectualness'' and ''vast inhuman cycles of activity''. . . . (pp. 112-15)

It is particularly useful to see the *Portrait* as ending in this way—if one can do so without casting ultimate doubts on the authenticity of the young man's calling—because it prepares us to see, in *Ulysses,* a Stephen Dedalus still very much in bondage. To what extent *Ulysses* is an escape from the dilemma of Stephen's character and a solution to the problem of self-knowledge, to what extent simply a magnification of it, is a question to which the reader will no doubt address himself. . . . (p. 115)

> *Robert M. Adams, in his* James Joyce: Common Sense and Beyond, *Random House, 1966, 232 p.*

WILLIAM T. NOON, S.J.   (essay date 1966)

[*In the following excerpt Noon outlines the dominant themes of the* Portrait, *explains the role played by Catholicism and the Jesuit system of education in shaping Joyce's unique point of view, and identifies several important literary and philosophical sources from which Joyce drew material for his novel.*]

[In] 1966 the big questions that one needs to ask about Joyce's *A Portrait of the Artist as a Young Man* are: Does this story still come through? Is it an important novel of spiritual growth? Of artistic and intellectual rebellion? Or is it a period piece? Has it been overread, overstudied? Is it outdated in its exotic concerns? Readers sometimes admire that which they do not like.

No one claims for *A Portrait* the same quality of classic, enduring excellence that belongs unassailably to *Ulysses.* Nor might the usual reader who admires *A Portrait* and who has backed away from *Finnegans Wake* claim that Joyce's first novel has the even-now daring importance of his last major work. Is *A Portrait,* indeed, worth the close attention that most readers gladly give to Joyce's earlier *Dubliners* short stories?

I judge from my own experience with young readers, women and men, seminarians some, that for most *A Portrait* still speaks to them and is a story that most of them both admire and like. *A Portrait* shows movement, inside and outside the mind. It is not grounded as is the *Stephen Hero* fragment. Although Stephen in both versions follows a solitary path to his art, there is a note of artistic inevitability sounded in *A Portrait* that is not heard in the fragment. In both versions Stephen makes choices. But in the fragment one feels that although Stephen's life in Ireland was so lackluster he could have acted differently, whereas in *A Portrait* one feels that since his life in Ireland was this way Stephen had no other choice.

Most readers of *A Portrait* conclude that Stephen Dedalus is egocentric. At times he comes through as a kind of over-intellectualized pedant, at times he appears to be immature, a too easily wounded young man, like Richard Rowan in Joyce's play, *Exiles.* Richard, one feels, tries too hard to break all bonds, divine and human, including those of love. So one senses that his weary isolation at the end is owing to his own limitations. His ''deep, deep wound of doubt'' tires spectators just as much as it tires Richard.

Stephen Dedalus is also an intelligently sensitive young man. He is supremely dedicated to his art. Only at the end of the story does he feel obligated to withdraw from his society. He concludes at the start, however, that it is a too much settled, sick society. He concludes at the end that it can only paralyze all his artistic energies by those pressures that others have since come to call mass-cult and mass-mediocrity. His is a story of the loss of faith; it is also a story of the search for faith. And how might any story both of the loss of faith and the search for faith grow irrelevant in the twentieth century?

Stephen is searching for the good life: he wants to be whole. He hopes to be just. He is determined to be himself. *A Portrait* is certainly more than just a diatribe against turn-of-the-century Dublin society. As the title itself phrases it, this is the story of an *artist as a young man.* It is more than just a planned program of aesthetic rebellion and reform. Stephen is mixed-up, sometimes too readily injured or hurt. At the end, and in spite of his rhetoric, he realizes that he cannot replace God through the creative processes of literature, much as he might like to. Such, anyway, is Joyce's more mature point in this novel. At the end of *A Portrait,* Stephen pledges himself ''to forge in the smithy of my soul the uncreated conscience of my race.'' . . . Even in this moment of withdrawal from Dublin, he is not forever renouncing all links. He has resolved to be more than just an Outsider, even as he goes away. He badly wants always to love the city that he is leaving behind. He remembers and recalls his mother's words to him as she packed his ''new secondhand clothes'' for his journey: ''She prays now, she says, that I may learn in my own life and away from home and friends what the heart is and what it feels. Amen. So be it.'' . . . (pp. 66-8)

The story of *A Portrait* unfolds symmetrically in five stages of Stephen Dedalus' spiritual development. The inner chapters, II, III, and IV, are mostly about his days in Belvedere College, a Jesuit high school for boys in the heart of Dublin. The first chapter is mostly about Stephen's experiences as a child, his first days in school at the then rather exclusive Jesuit boarding-school for boys, Clongowes Wood College, in County Kildare, not far from Dublin. The last chapter, V, the longest, is mostly about Stephen's college days at University College, also in Dublin, and at that time also conducted by the Jesuits. There are brief interludes elsewhere. In the first chapter there is one

The bridge to the Bull, where Stephen encounters the Christian Brothers. From The Joyce Country, *by William York Tindall. The Pennsylvania State University Press, University Park, P.A., 1960. Reproduced by permission of the publisher.*

interlude that describes Stephen's troubled visit home to Dublin for Christmas; it presents the sad-glad Christmas dinner where sharp controversy about the fall of Charles Stewart Parnell bewilders young Stephen and extinguishes everyone's Christmas spirits. In the second chapter there are interludes that describe Stephen's holiday visits to Blackrock on the sea, and to Cork. These are both places where Joyce briefly lived with his family when he himself was a boy.

For each of these five chapters there is a more-or-less dominant image (or symbol), a rather pervasive emotion recollected, and at the end a rather marked pause, a stasis in the action of the story. As each chapter concludes, there is for Stephen a special, new kind of going away.

In Chapter I, the dominant image is Father Dolan's pandybat; the dominant emotion, a fear of grown-ups; and the pause of recollection, a sense of grateful relief at Father Arnall's taking his part. So it is as Stephen leaves childhood. In Chapter II, "a breakwater of order and elegance against the sordid tide of life without him" . . . variously serves as image; the guilt of the model schoolboy is the pervasive emotion (for already Stephen begins to doubt his religious faith); and "the swoon of sin" . . . in the brothel is the moment of stasis at the end. So he forsakes innocence and the life of sanctifying grace. In Chapter III, shortest of the chapters, Father Arnall's terrifying retreat-sermons on the punishment of the damned in hell—

"fetid carcasses," "pain of intensity" . . .—provide an image that is truly dominant; Stephen's emotion here is one of supernatural fright; the pause of recollection at the end describes Stephen's receiving the Holy Eucharist after he has made his retreat-confession. For the time being, at least, he goes away from a life of sin. In Chapter IV, there occurs what is probably the dominant image of the whole book, Stephen's vision (part sight, part imagination) of the young wading girl in the stream; the dominant emotion is that of profane joy for the "hawklike man" in his recognition of his true vocation, to be not a priest at the altar but a priest of the eternal imagination . . . , here the stasis at the end describes Stephen's walk in the moonlight beside the sea. He knows that he has said "no" to his priestly calling: "On and on and on and on!". . . . In the concluding Chapter V, the dominant image is that of swallows (wild geese) in flight; the pervasive emotion, loneliness; the final stasis is Stephen's silent moment of poise just before flight. As absolutely as he may, he is about to go away from home.

A Portrait has, of course, literary antecedents. There is much uncertainty here, because Joyce was too much his own man for a commentator to state categorically just what these archetypes of the author might have been. The novel of spiritual development and of adolescent revolt is one that goes back at least as far as Samuel Butler's *The Way of All Flesh* (not published until 1903) and the various confessions of George

Moore. It has roots in the French symbolists, and also in John Addington Symonds' many French-oriented volumes on the artists of the Renaissance and of Romanticism. In Germany, it has even earlier forbears in Goethe's *Werther* (1774, 1787) and *Dichtung und Wahrheit* (1831). This tradition includes, of course, and for Joyce especially, Newman's *Apologia* (1864) and, to be sure, Saint Augustine's *Confessions* (c. 400). There is already evidence available that Joyce had read all these books, or at least looked into them. How well in scholarly detail he might have known them is arguable. He probably read them hurriedly, as most artists are wont to read others' books. But he knew what was in the air! He had his own story to tell, and he ended up telling it in his own way. He had sense enough (in his mind, maybe not in his heart) to know that no artist's new way of telling a story ever catches on with others at once. There is always a time-lag. Modern minds are not nearly so modern as non-artists often imagine. With *A Portrait,* Joyce took his own risks.

As one looks back now on this story, it appears to be as much an elegy for a lost cause as it does a manifesto for the cause that its young man, an artist, proclaimed he would bring into being. *Forge* as a writer might by fabricating or counterfeiting, no artist *creates* consciences, certainly not for his entire race. God alone creates *ex nihilo sui et subjecti.* Men at their best can only hope to transform or modify. No young man can create a brand new world to suit his own tastes and specifications. God himself respects other persons' individual freedom of choice. Ireland (or Dublin) is now much different from what it was fifty years ago. Now, for example, it is proud to boast of James Joyce as a Dubliner, but its conscience is far from being the one that Stephen Dedalus promised to forge. By the time, indeed, that Joyce drew his final *Portrait* of Stephen Dedalus, he himself abroad had come to accept the situation in Dublin and all the human beings caught up in it with a wryly amused compassion. After all, 1916 was the year of the Easter Uprising, a Dublin happening that "transformed utterly" the comedy of life for all Dubliners, not just for W. B. Yeats. Francis Sheehey-Skeffington, Joyce's old friend of the University College days, was shot on the second day of that insurrection. In this story *A Portrait,* already written before the Rising, Stephen may no longer think of himself as hero, but he still likes to play the role of pure and passive martyr: Stephen martyr, *Bous Stephanoumenos, Bous Stephaneferos. . . .* He likes to think of himself as the sacrificial ox, the scapegoat, who bears his people's guilt but who also bears the poet's crown. Simon Dedalus is not the only one who is weeping for Parnell, his "uncrowned king," when the famous Christmas dinner scene in the first chapter of this novel comes to a close. So is Stephen! So are most readers. So, one supposes, was Joyce when he composed the scene. One also supposes that he smiled. *Lacrimae rerum:* the tears of things, and their absurdity too.

Joyce did not need in 1916 to look back so far through the haze at Stephen as we need to. Stephen is not altogether admirable, nor are any of these other Dubliners. With infinite pains Joyce tells their story well. It is mostly a tale of adolescent disillusionment. It is about the artistic aspiration of a young man to be self-possessed, self-achieving, self-aware. Stephen would like to be accepted by the world to which he belongs. This is usual enough. It is the kind of story that will probably never go out of date.

In reading *A Portrait,* the question of point-of-view needs to be answered. Although this novel is nowhere nearly so highly stylized a stream-of-consciousness as is *Ulysses* . . . , everything that happens in it comes to us filtered through the sensibility of Stephen Dedalus himself. Already Stephen's voice here begins to fade into the interior, withdrawn, at times barely audible monologue of a deeply introspective young man. How clear and fair a "reflector," or "center of consciousness" (to borrow Jamesian terms), are Stephen's imagination and mind? H. G. Wells is quoted on the back cover of the old 1956 Compass Book Edition of *A Portrait* as saying (much earlier, in 1917), "it is by far the most living and convincing picture that exists of an Irish Catholic upbringing." Thomas Merton, a Catholic priest and a Trappist monk, in his *Secular Journal* (1959), spoke differently, in an entry under the date of February 18, 1940, when he was a young man: "It is too bad that he [Joyce] made the same mistake that the people who hate him have always made: that of making no distinction whatever between the culture of the Irish middle-class and the sacramental life of the Church." Father Merton, I take it, assumes that James Joyce's "mistake" here is the same as Stephen's.

Any commentator on Joyce needs, to be sure, to know Catholicism if he wants to find out and talk about just what might be going on inside and outside the world of Stephen Dedalus' mind. Such knowledge for the commentator need not be from inside Catholicism, but it should be profound and careful. In **Stephen Hero,** Stephen reflects that "the entire theory, in accordance with which his entire artistic life was shaped, arose most conveniently for his purpose out of the mass of Catholic theology." . . . From inside or from outside Catholicism, it is a mistake to talk about Joyce as an "inverted mystic" and to chart the artistic development of Stephen in *A Portrait* as though it proceeded (receded?) by way of a five-fold or even three-fold inversion of the mystic's way at prayer. Father Merton does not attempt to do this, but there are others now who do. Father Merton himself too well knows from actual practice the ways of both poetry and mysticism to take the one way for the other, even in reverse. Irish Catholicism as it works out in practice is not just a checkerboard of symbols that the Joycean commentator can play with according to an improvised game of ideas. The confessions of the artists turn on pivots different from those of the saints; spiritual conversion or elections to the religion of art are not the same as what most men understand by conversions to a life of grace. The missions of the artists are of a different order from those of priests. There are likenesses and analogues between the service of God and man at the altar and the service of man and God through art, but there are also major differences that Joyce himself appreciated. Joyce did not renounce the religion of Catholicism so as to take on the uneasy practice and burden of a culture-religion. Without clear Catholic insights into some of these major differences, a commentator on Joyce may sound much like a tone-deaf analyst of Mozart or a color-blind interpreter of Van Gogh.

From the early notebooks of James Joyce and other family papers (most of them until lately unedited) at Cornell University and elsewhere, it is clear that, save for slight variations in key, Stephen Dedalus speaks as an alter ego or early voice of Joyce himself when he was a young man. These same papers as well as many already published raw materials manifest also how mistaken the reader would be to conclude from *A Portrait* that everything that happens here to Stephen in this fiction actually happened in this same way, or at all, to Joyce in real life. The artist is an imaginer, not just a chronicler. A former Dubliner who shared schooldays in Dublin with James and Stanislaus Joyce has written to me, April 14, 1958: "If James Joyce did any reading in Philosophy [at University College], it was extracurricular and just some of the desultory reading that all of us did in the National Library.'' This same correspondent speaks of the annual retreat at Belvedere College in a different vein from Stephen's version of such a retreat in Chapter III of *A Portrait:* ''At Belvedere there was an Annual Retreat lasting three days. . . . Invariably, *one* of the discourses was on Hell, or the punishment due to sin. It was only one of the discourses, and certainly at the end of the Retreat, the impression left as a climax was that the Mercy of God was boundless, and that you had but to love Him here on earth and you would enjoy His love forever in Heaven.'' But, then, *this* correspondent went on himself to Canada to be a successful engineer, not East to the Continent to be a world-famous artist. Still, there are other consciences besides the artist's and other integrities than just the artistic.

This variation in reappraisal, through the haze of time, of a Belvedere College retreat is a fair example of the difference between the truths of fiction and of fact. Both are true! Both are not the same! Whether or not the retreat discourses by Father Arnall of *A Portrait* are ones that were actually preached to Joyce while he was still at Belvedere . . . is for literature unimportant. Somebody preached this kind of retreat, to judge from Joyce's report of Stephen Dedalus' traumatic recollections in *A Portrait.* The effect of it was in the fiction to turn Stephen for a time from a life of sin to an aesthetic life untarnished. ''He saw. . . . he wept for the innocence he had lost,'' . . . ''How simple and beautiful was life after all.'' . . . (pp. 68-75)

For the sake of his fiction, Joyce shows this change of heart in Stephen as a conversion to the life beautiful. Stephen's subsequent trial by scruples shows how much the effort cost Stephen to treat this conversion as though it were to a life of supernatural grace. How understandable at the end is Stephen's refusal, ''I will not serve.'' . . .

We know by now that the particular sermons that Stephen in *A Portrait* recollects are in fact closely modeled on Father Giovanni Pinamonti's *Hell Opened to Christians.* Father Pinamonti was a seventeenth-century Italian Jesuit. These discourses of his were easily available in translation and in pamphlet form to Joyce in Dublin, and were probably used by the retreat masters who went to Belvedere College. Joyce might have read them in Dublin near the time when he started writing *Stephen Hero.* (p. 75)

So when one says that an artist needs to write from his personal experience, one needs also to add that the life of the books that an artist reads is part of that personal experience, *his* life of the mind. Joyce is a great borrower. For example, one poetical phrase from *A Portrait* that is usually assumed to be Joyce's own has been shown lately to be another of many borrowings: ''A day of dappled seaborne clouds.'' . . . James S. Atherton, in his Notes to his (Heinemann) edition of *A Portrait,* points out that this phrase is a quotation from Hugh Miller's *The Testimony of the Rocks.* . . . Atherton notes also the many pervasive echoes of Newman that are orchestrated into Joyce's *Portrait* text. Stephen once tells a friend that he considers Newman to be ''the greatest writer'' of them all. . . . Often he borrows phrases from Newman's sermon ''The Glories of Mary,'' but he also often borrows from Newman's other works. (pp. 75-6)

''But you could not have a green rose'':—so, when he was a little boy, Stephen thought to himself one day in class at the Clongowes Wood school of *A Portrait.* . . . Joyce's imagination here is searching to find a way to make ''the green rose''

blossom for Stephen and for himself, ''O, the wild rose blossoms,'' as he says here on his first page. So at the very start of this remembrance, a phrase from the song ''Lilly Dale'' announces the dominant theme of the composition as a whole. Even Stephen longs often to escape from ''the cold silence of intellectual revolt.'' . . . ''I'm a ballocks,'' not ''Ireland's hope. . . . I am and I know I am,''—so even Stephen, now a young man, once tells his friends. ''And I admit that I am.'' . . . That is one of Stephen's finest moments, and shows that Stephen does not take himself quite so seriously as some of Joyce's exegetes take him.

At the risk of appearing, oneself, to take Stephen's story too seriously, one might here, for the sake of completion, mention a possible submerged theme in this story, one to which almost no attention, so far as I know, has yet been paid. I refer to its homosexual undertone. Joyce is not explicit, Stephen appears to be unconscious that he is taking this tone, but I surmise that Joyce himself was conscious of the submerged homosexual material of *A Portrait.* He had used this kind of material already in his second *Dubliners* story, **''An Encounter.''** In that short story, significantly, Joyce shows us a young boy, Mahony, an extrovert, not at all artistic, who has a prompt and healthy reaction to perversion; and Joyce shows another young boy, the boy-narrator, the artist, who is baffled by the mystery of perversion and who needs in panic at the end to call out to his extrovert friend for rescue: ''And I was penitent; for in my heart I had always despised him a little.'' About the same time that he published *A Portrait,* Joyce used this kind of observation explicitly in his now published Notes, in his play *Exiles.* . . . (pp. 76-7)

Stephen Dedalus' voice speaking of his relations with girls (even in his ''swoon of sin'' with the prostitute . . .) conveys a strange tone, now of vagueness, now of hostility. It seems as though he does not know girls well or like them. His comments on men sound at times disturbed and disturbing, Stephen's recollections of his childhood friends, especially of Wells and of Simon Moonan, even of Mr. Gleeson (who, I suppose, is a Jesuit Scholastic), come through as though in Stephen's fantasy they were on the homosexual side. His relations with his parents, as they are here recollected, especially his many acts of sensitiveness, his hostilities to his mother and about her, appear almost at times as though they were written in a Freudian code. Freud's scientific analyses of human behavior were not Joyce's cup of tea. But Freud was much in the air in the early 1900's, his preconscious was being much talked about, and Joyce had access to all these Freudian theories in German itself, or, if he wished by 1916, in English translation. Freud was being discussed all over Europe by 1916. As an artist, Joyce did not need to commit himself to Freudianism—any more so than he needed to commit himself to Thomism. He committed himself to neither, but where it pleased him he used both as literary materials, the moralism of Saint Thomas (more so than Saint Thomas's slight, incidental aesthetics) and the psychoanalytic theories of Freud.

In Stephen's more cerebral moods a repressed aggressiveness appears, which might account for his adolescent disenchantment with ''Mother'' Church, or, for that matter, with a Father Church, or with any Church at all. Dogmatic, or doctrinal, impossibilities for those who cannot accept them, that is, longer abide by them, are more often than not rooted in moral difficulties. Cranly once tells Stephen, ''your mind is supersaturated with the religion in which you say you disbelieve.'' . . . A little later Stephen answers Cranly, ''I said that I had lost the faith, . . . but not that I had lost selfrespect.'' . . . Stephen goes away from Catholicism without visible hysteria, but Joyce here shows a mind much troubled: ''And I am not afraid to make a mistake, even a great mistake, a life-long mistake and perhaps as long as eternity too.'' . . . And Stephen goes away from Ireland alone. *He* does not take a radiant Nora with him.

So far as a homosexual syndrome is here imagined, Joyce's materials in *A Portrait* are veiled. Such a syndrome is not, to be sure, the whole story but it sounds in *A Portrait* like part of it. Stephen's homosexual memories are presented as fantasies, a war within more than without. Joyce does not represent them, it is true, as metaphysical abstractions of cosmic worth. A reader, nevertheless, is sometimes led to wonder about the odd emphases given by Joyce to some of Stephen's graphic details: ''Such was a queer word,'' . . . the much whispered-about homosexual scandal that involves Simon Moonan while Stephen is still a small boy at Clongowes Wood. . . . At Belvedere College, Stephen once notices ''a stout old lady'' kneeling at the altar ''in a dark corner of the chapel at the gospel side,'' and beside her is her son, Bertie Tallon, who is dressed in pink and ''wearing a curly golden wig.'' . . . The ''original'' for this ''pink dressed figure'' was a boy at Belvedere named Bertie Sheridan, who performed a solo dance, ''The sunbonnet dance,'' in a play, *Vice Versa,* in which Joyce himself actually performed. There actually were rough and ready boys then at Belvedere who were named Tallon; here Joyce transfers the family name of this rough, tough lot of boys to the effeminate figure. At University College, Stephen has odd impressions of Cranly at times, mysterious, dark, here inexplicable: ''a guilty priest,'' . . . ''Cranly's dark eyes were watching him.'' . . . (pp. 77-9)

Homosexual fantasies are not abnormal in childhood; at least, they are not uncommon. Nor are they uncommon even in adolescent friendships. Stephen's later kind of heterosexual bravado, even ruthlessness, is also not an uncommon later kind of reaction. Such a young man often discovers in himself a quality that he does not like. Whether this is a neurosis or a simple physical inclination, he may try with vengeance to eradicate it or reverse it. So, anyway, Joyce here arranges his verbal score. He orchestrates the dissonance; he does not, as some might today, play it as a dominant leitmotif. Stephen's adolescent fantasies are here much refined by Joyce's older, more experienced mind.

The presence of so many priests, most of them Jesuits, Stephen's educators, [also Joyce's] obliges readers of *A Portrait* to decide whether their being here is good or bad. Kevin Sullivan, in *Joyce among the Jesuits,* has gone into this question more thoroughly than has anyone else, and his report is mixed. Stephen's own report in *A Portrait* is on the whole benign: for example, ''Whatever he had heard or read of the craft of jesuits he had put aside frankly as not borne out by his own experience. His masters, even when they had not attracted him, had seemed to him always intelligent and serious priests.'' . . . Stephen recalls his traumatic experience with the cruel prefect of studies at Clongowes, Father Dolan, but he also recalls afterwards the kindness to him of his own teacher, Father Arnall: ''His voice was very gentle and soft. . . . And Father Arnall had said that he need not study till the new glasses came.'' . . . (pp. 79-80)

In some ways, certainly, these Irish Jesuits at the turn of the century failed Stephen, and their ''originals,'' it seems, failed Joyce in his aspirations to be an artist. It appears that they were not so intelligent as they should have been. Not all of them were so gentle and holy as the ideals of their priestly vocations obliged. It is not difficult to understand why such an earnest young artist as Stephen (or, for that matter, Joyce) should be unhinged by some kinds of example and counsel that were given. These Jesuits might, it seems, have opened their own minds and hearts more generously to what was going on in this young artist's creative heart and mind: so at least *A Portrait* shows.

The reader of *A Portrait* notices, as Joyce wants him imaginatively to notice, some of the awful stupidities and silences of these former priest-mentors of Stephen. Joyce also assumes, expects his readers to assume, that genius, religious or artistic, is almost never properly understood and rightly dealt with by the genius's own living mentors and peers. Being misunderstood and mishandled are included in the usual cost that any artist pays for his art. Sometimes too a built-in flaw in personality is also included in the high price that an artist needs to pay in personal cost for excellence. Achievement seldom comes cheap.

Some of Joyce's commentators tend to blur the distinction between his achievement in art and the success-failure of his religious life of supernatural faith. Joyce for himself saw the difference. Faith in art is grounded on the grace of art; no one just manufactures serious art. Religious faith is grounded on another kind of grace. Joyce's close friend Jacques Mercanton has told us, ''Although a connoisseur of blasphemies, he remained always within the most orthodox frame of reference, his mind curiously closed to every form of heresy, in the moral as in the religious order.'' When Mercanton goes on to call *Finnegans Wake* ''a work of reconciliation,'' he adds, ''not in the sense of a return to the Church, still less in a kind of spiritual substitution, a function that might conceivably be assigned to poetry. One cannot replace the Christian faith, and there is no mask for the face of Christ. Besides nothing could be more alien to Joyce's spirit.'' (pp. 80-1)

''I was telling the things I couldn't frame in words. I was singing the story of my misery and confusion, of the misunderstandings in my life I wouldn't straighten out, the story of the wrongs and outrages done to me by people I had loved and trusted. Your imagination can carry you just so far. Only those who have been hurt deeply can understand what pain is, or humiliation. Only those who are being burned know what fire is like.''

This last quotation of mine is not from *A Portrait* of Joyce, but from the autobiography (probably ghost-written) of another superb artist. It is Ethel Waters telling us how she felt as she interpreted her song ''Stormy Weather'' on the Cotton Club floor. Joyce at the end, in *Finnegans Wake,* calls the literary artist a ''shemshamsshowman.'' . . . The earlier quasi-autobiography, *A Portrait,* is a stormy story, sad-glad and troubled and defiant, as the stories of a young people who are artists almost always are. Joyce's imagination is vitally at work as he tries to frame his own story in words. As he says in his epigraph from Ovid at the start of this story, ''he devoted his mind to unknown arts.'' But, then: ''Your imagination can carry you just so far.'' (pp. 81-2)

William T. Noon, S.J., '' 'A Portrait of the Artist as a Young Man': After Fifty Years,'' in James Joyce Today: Essays on the Major Works, *edited by Thomas F. Staley, Indiana University Press, 1966, pp. 54-82.*

KENNETH GROSE (essay date 1975)

[*In the following excerpt, Grose discusses how each of the principal episodes in* A Portrait of the Artist as a Young Man *was*

The beach where Stephen encountered the wading girl. From The Joyce Country, *by William York Tindall. The Pennsylvania State University Press, University Park, PA, 1960. Reproduced by permission of the publisher.*

designed by Joyce to illustrate Stephen's emotional development as well as the themes of the novel.]

[*A Portrait of the Artist as a Young Man*] is the story, told in episodic form, of Stephen Dedalus's early life. Its title suggests that it is concerned with the development of Stephen as an artist, or rather as poet and novelist; and theories of aesthetics are discussed at some length in Chapter 5. But the main interest to many readers is the gradual emergence of Stephen's conviction that in order to survive as an artist he must shake himself loose from the fetters of Church, Country and Family, and seek exile in order to be free to 'forge in the smithy of my soul the uncreated conscience of my race', as he declares on the last page.

So the forging of the fetters, and their nature, occupy the earlier pages. Chapter I is mainly concerned with his first school, the Jesuit academy for well-to-do boys at Clongowes. The first two pages present vivid sensual impressions of babyhood, couched in the sort of language fond parents use when talking to infants . . . ; their significance as an introduction is that certain key themes are touched on: his love of words and music; his family and friends—his father's rather pretentious monocle, his great-uncle Charles, and Dante . . . ; and the political situation in Ireland epitomised in the two brushes, one greenbacked and one maroon-backed, that Dante kept in her wardrobe. . . . (pp. 25-6)

Three episodes follow. The first . . . deals with his early days at Clongowes, his fears of the dormitory light going out before he had finished his prayers at his chily bedside, his bewilderment among the bigger and rougher fellows, and his semi-delirious dream of the death of Parnell. . . . The second episode is a brilliant evocation of a family Christmas dinner which begins as a sumptuous feast, but ends in political argument and violent recriminations. The gradual build-up of emotion, fed with alcohol on the side of the Irish nationalist Mr. Casey and outraged religious bigotry on the part of Dante, is enthralling; this is possibly the most vivid scene in the book, with its careful control of detail and symbol. The bone of contention is the betrayal of Parnell, the Irish national leader at Westminster, by the hierarchy of the Catholic Church, who rejected him when his adulterous affair with Kitty O'Shea became public. . . . For Joyce, the conflict expressed the unreasoning antipathy of Church and State, both of which were demonstrably unable to provide a settled base for a seeker after truth.

In the last section of Chapter I Stephen and his schoolfellows discuss the harsh punishments at that time meted out to naughty boys. During the ensuing lesson Stephen is unjustly caned by the prefect of studies—*anglice* the headmaster—whose terror-striking, bullying behaviour reeks to a modern mind of sexual repression. Stephen, greatly daring, complains to the rector. . . . His complaint is upheld, but later the Jesuit priests had a good laugh together over the incident . . .—though some of Simon Dedalus's anticlerical bias and love of a good story must be discounted before the masters can be accused of callousness. No doubt the draconian Father Dolan devoured fewer defenceless schoolboys in consequence, at any rate for a time.

The heroic innocence of Stephen does not live long; in Chapter II, with the family's move from the idyllic Blackrock suburb into Dublin, forced on them by his father's fecklessness, he attains adolescence and is soon eating of the tree of carnal knowledge. This chapter has six episodes, in most of which Stephen's growing sexuality is balanced against the descent of the family. Stephen at Blackrock . . . is painted as a boy who enjoys his own solitary yearnings, though he has friends to play with and plenty of activity to engage in including helping the milkman on his round, as little Archie does in *Exiles*. In the second episode . . . come several disconnected flashes of his new, more sordid, life, ending in his first innocent encounters with a girl, Emma Cleary, who might have been revealed as the ideally beautiful Mercedes he imagined as he read Dumas. His experiences in his new Jesuit academy—Belvedere—where he has been awarded a free place, are not exactly congenial. The fourth episode . . . is ostensibly concerned with the School play; but Stephen is on the one hand bantered by the arrogant boy-about-town Heron, and on the other is tormented by the presence of Emma with his parents in the audience. He is also accused of heresy by a bigoted master, and is roughed up by a gang of his new schoolfellows for declaring that the heretic Byron was the greatest poet, not the milk-and-water Tennyson later mockingly described as 'Lawn Tennyson' in *Ulysses*. It is fitting that Stephen should champion an exiled poet, an immoral Cain-like figure, and suffer for it.

A visit to Cork with his father, who was selling the last remains of his inheritance, leads on to the painful final section . . . in which the extreme fecklessness of the family is amply demonstrated. What sort of a father allows—encourages even—his son to spend the money he has won in examinations on taking them all out to dinner, on delicacies from the most expensive city grocery stores, and on expeditions to the theatre, in a 'swift season of merrymaking'? To point the extravagance of his conduct, he 'wrote out resolutions', put his books in order and began to paint his bedroom with pink enamel paint—until, neat symbol, the pot of paint ran out. . . . He fell into what Catholics call 'mortal sin', and as he wanders the maze of narrow dirty streets . . . he is seduced by a prostitute.

Chapter III begins as Chapter II ends, in the sordid streets; his soul is 'going forth to experience, unfolding itself sin by sin'. . . . Now comes the climax of his religious life; at school he is a leading figure in the sodality of the Blessed Virgin Mary, but on his lips as he softly murmurs her liturgical names in the holy office lingers 'the savour itself of a lewd kiss'. . . . Clearly the turmoil of his soul cannot continue, and the three terrifying sermons preached by Father Arnall (the sympathetic understanding schoolmaster-priest from Clongowes, . . .) force Stephen into confession of his sins. The chapter ends . . . in a blaze of pure whiteness: an invisible grace 'makes light' his limbs, his soul is 'made fair', the kitchen lamp casts a 'tender shade', white pudding and eggs are the shelf, he walks to communion 'in the quiet morning', the flowers are fragrant and white on the altar, and the pale flames of the candles are 'clear and silent as his own soul'.

Now follows a period of extravagantly scrupulous holiness, in which his senses—all of them—are mortified, and his natural animal pleasure in them thwarted, in an attempt to conquer the

flesh. The first section of Chapter IV . . . describes with acute perception the self-tortures of the over-religious mind.

> A restless feeling of guilt would always be present with him . . . Perhaps that first hasty confession wrung from him by the fear of hell had not been good?

His devotion is now so obvious to all that he is, quite properly and scrupulously, asked by the director of the college to consider whether he has a vocation for the religious life. He is naturally proud at being explicitly singled out, and in his imagination the life of a priest—the Reverend Stephen Dedalus, Society of Jesus—is idealised . . . ; he is almost flattered into acceptance. But after the interview as he says goodbye at the priest's door he hears music coming from

> a quartet of young men . . . striding along with linked arms, swaying their heads and stepping to the agile melody of their leader's concertina . . . Smiling at the trivial air he raised his eyes to the priest's face and . . . detached his hand slowly which had acquiesced faintly in the companionship.

The moment is crucial, the action symbolic. Stephen makes his decision. . . . And the world obtrudes itself as soon as he gets home to his family, its squalid tea-table and the news of yet another impending removal to even deeper squalor. But the children sing together; their music, telling of human joys and sorrows, is the music of earth, of people who need companionship in their weariness and pain. . . . He cannot be satisfied with 'the pale service of the altar'; it is a few days later that the cries of his bantering schoolfellows: 'Stephanos Dedalos! Bous Stephanoumenos! Bous Stephaneforos! (Crown-bearing ox!)' announce his destiny to him. Not only is he the 'hawk-like man flying sunward above the sea', but also the sacrificial ox who wears a crown or garland as sign of his dedication to the gods. Stephen realises . . . what his life so far had been leading him towards. He may soar above the clouds but his material must be 'the sluggish matter of the earth'. It is at that moment that he sees the wading girl, whom he does not know and to whom he does not speak; but her image as of a mortal angel, rather than of the Virgin Mary, calls to him to enter the fair courts of life, with the certainty of human error but also the hope of glory. . . . (pp. 26-30)

It is in this chapter, too, that his interest in words as objects with a life of their own becomes apparent to him. Right from the start of his life he has been a manipulator of words. Now he knows that if he is ever to express both the glowing sensible world and the inner world of individual emotions, it must be with words. . . . (p. 30)

By the end of Chapter IV, then, Stephen has made one crucial decision: he has substituted art for religion, or rather he has made art his religion. An ordinary man's rejection of a call to the priesthood would in no way entail a rejection of the Church and of the orthodox Christian way of life; but Joyce was a passionate man who did nothing by halves. He was to devote his life, his present and his future family, his friends and his career, to the long and bitter labour of writing. Such devotion is rarely seen in religious people; it is the mark of the saint. It was inculcated into him, no doubt, by the discipline and example of the Jesuits who formed his mind and whom he never ceased to respect. James Joyce is more closely integrated into Stephen Dedalus in Chapter V than anywhere else in this book or in the later *Ulysses*, where a certain detachment can be observed; as Wordsworth saw a waterfall 'frozen by distance'. A good deal of this chapter is concerned, like the preceding four, with the external circumstances of Stephen's existence: the feckless family sinking further into squalor . . . ; his friendship with fellow-students such as Davin, the Irish peasant patriot . . . ; his visit to the National Theatre . . . ; student chaff and protests . . . ; the cracking of a louse . . . ; the very funny account of a physics lecture from the point of view of unruly students, who existed even in those days . . . ; and so on. These episodes (now run together in long sections, not separated as in the earlier chapters) are necessary to provide a living background to Stephen's mental and spiritual development, which is laid bare in three specially significant encounters.

The first is with the dean of studies. . . . The leading dons at University College were, of course, Jesuits like the brothers at Clongowes and Belvedere, and the dean is following in the tradition of Newman and Hopkins, both English converts and both more than nominally alien in Ireland. The foreignness of the dean is brought to Stephen's notice by his use of the simple word 'funnel' for what Stephen called a 'tundish', a utensil for pouring liquid into narrow-necked receptacles. Stephen's dissatisfaction with an Ireland dominated by the Enlgish does not seek action in the political nationalism of Davin and the Sinn Fein, or in the literary nationalism of the new theatrical venture that became the Abbey Theatre; he did not reject the English language but, as Shakespeare did, took it and bent it to his own purpose. To do this he had to leave the land where the struggle was motivated by provincial rather than universal considerations. An art such as Stephen's could not flourish in the shallow soil of nationalism; paradoxically, his love of his country could only be freely expressed in an exile which allowed him to escape also from those who did not know what a tundish was, as well as from those who were ignorant of funnels. His dislike of the condescending dean, a mere convert, later blossoms into outright hatred of the invading folklore-hunter Haines, the Englishman in the early chapters of *Ulysses*.

In a second long conversation . . . , Stephen walks with his irreverent friend Lynch as he expounds his own aesthetic theory, an individual version of the doctrine of St. Thomas Aquinas, the great 13th-century Catholic philosopher, who reconciled Aristotle's precepts with those of Christianity. Stephen's main purpose is to work towards a definition of the 'aesthetic emotion'—what happens to you when you feel pleasure at the contemplation of a work of art. A string of statements embodied his conclusions. . . . (pp. 30-2)

[He] ends his exposition with a remarkable paragraph in which he declares that the artist must, like the God of creation, remain behind his work and not be personally recognisable in its surface. The novelist or dramatist creates personages from the material of his experience of life; but his personages are not himself. In other words, Shakespeare is neither Iago nor Othello.

This passage is often taken to mean that Joyce remained impersonally in the background of both *A Portrait* and *Ulysses*, as he obviously does in most of the stories in *Dubliners*. True, he looks on his younger self with a cold clinical eye; the Stephen of both books is not indulgently treated. 'Dedalus, you're an antisocial being, wrapped up in yourself', says McCann. . . . 'An impossible person', says Buck Mulligan. . . . But stand aside he cannot. Stephen Dedalus's mind is the mind of James Joyce; and similarly Leopold Bloom's thoughts are

the thoughts of his creator, his *alter ego*. This is the paradox of dramatic creation: Shakespeare is both Iago and Othello.

The reader is not asked to swallow all this philosophical speculation in one indigestible lump. By having the irreverent interlocutor Lynch inject scurrilous quips and ask for cigarettes, by outlining the course of the walk through the streets, by letting another student friend, Donovan, interrupt the conversation . . . , Joyce not only lightens the texture but makes indirect comments which prove to be apposite—such as Donovan's remarks about the Laocoön, to which Stephen was to allude three pages later. (The German critic Lessing called his exposition of aesthetics after the famous group of statuary figures depicting the death of Laocoön and his sons, as described in Virgil's *Aeneid*.) It is of course necessary, when making a portrait of an artist, to discuss and establish the principles of the artist's work; Stephen, in rejecting the Church, embraces Art: he requires, he says, 'a new terminology and a new personal experience'. . . . (pp. 32-3)

In the second long section of this chapter his sensibilities are shown at work; his search for self-expression through the medium of words is pursued. Stephen thinks of the girl who has rejected or ignored him, links her with the Church that is too closely tied up with narrow nationalism, and allows his imagination to take flight in words, as did his namesake Daedalus with self-made wings. . . . If the poem he writes is pale and precious, it is of the same kind as all Joyce's lyrical poems, and we can only be thankful that the Poet's cloak is merely the Artist's fictional disguise. The Artist that Joyce developed into was to be a novelist, not a lyrical poet, though parts of his mature work, especially *Finnegans Wake,* are poetry rather than fiction. . . .

Stephen has his third decisive encounter: Cranly, a subtle disputant, tries to reconcile him to his home, his country and his religious vows. But Stephen declares, as Satan did, 'I will not serve' . . . [and] the final decision, to go into exile, is announced. . . . (p. 33)

One might expect the book to end here: the portrait is complete—even down to the lice on his unwashed neck. . . . Yet there are still . . . pages of extracts from Stephen's journal, containing many trivialities and unexplained references. . . . Many readers are . . . puzzled. It certainly seems a flat ending.

It does, however, enable Joyce to tie up some loose ends in an economical way, to bring together some of the themes and symbols that have been formative influences on Stephen's mind— such as the unnamed girl's rejection of him, the dean's tundish, his monocled father's proprietorial hopes for his future, and his mother's practical concern for his welfare. It is also a move towards the new technique, interior monologue, or stream of consciousness, that is to be developed to its most elaborately expressive form in *Ulysses*. And finally, it culminates in a somewhat grandiose aspiration, in which some critics have found that Joyce is making implied strictures on the callow young man by making him appear pretentious and absurd:

> Welcome, O life! I go to encounter for the
> millionth time the reality of experience and to
> forge in the smithy of my soul the uncreated
> conscience of my race.
>
> Old father, old artificer, stand me now and ever
> in good stead. . . .

To my mind, this is not a send-up. Stephen, with all his arrogance and pride, is a dedicated priest of the imagination. So was Joyce; his whole life was devoted to his art, and he took himself as seriously as any genius must. There is no room for doubt in the devouring passion of creative activity. By the time Joyce had finished his ten-year labour on the book, he had grown old enough to see that the 'impossible', solipsistic Stephen needed (as his mother prays that he will, in the sentence immediately preceding the apostrophe to life, quoted above) to learn 'what the heart is and what it feels'. This is the subject-matter of *Ulysses,* and to achieve a more humane revelation of it he has to create Bloom and Molly; in them, rather than in the intellectual Stephen Dedalus, is the word made flesh. But the artist who stands behind his creation must partake of the nature of godhead, and gods are not modest. (pp. 34-5)

> *Kenneth Grose, in his* James Joyce, *Evans Brothers Limited, 1975, 150 p.*

RICHARD ELLMANN (essay date 1982)

[*Ellmann is an American critic and the author of the definitive biography of James Joyce. He has also written widely on early twentieth-century Irish literature, most notably on William Butler Yeats and Oscar Wilde. In the following excerpt, Ellmann argues that the structure of Joyce's* Portrait *corresponds to the paradigm of the birth process. Ellmann thus interprets the novel as a description of the birth of the artist's soul, and supports this reading by citing the abundance of birth imagery (darkness, wetness, claustrophobic enclosure, etc.) to be found in the novel.*]

To write *A Portrait of the Artist as a Young Man* Joyce plunged back into his own past, mainly to justify, but also to expose it. The book's pattern, as he explained to Stanislaus, is that we are what we were; our maturity is an extension of our childhood, and the courageous boy is father of the arrogant young man. But in searching for a way to convert the episodic *Stephen Hero* into *A Portrait of the Artist,* Joyce hit upon a principle of structure which reflected his habits of mind as extremely as he could wish. The work of art, like a mother's love, must be achieved over the greatest obstacles, and Joyce, who had been dissatisfied with his earlier work as too easily done, now found the obstacles in the form of a most complicated pattern.

This is hinted at in his image of the creative process. As far back as his paper on Mangan, Joyce said that the poet takes into the vital center of his life 'the life that surrounds it, flinging it abroad again amid planetary music.' He repeated this image in *Stephen Hero,* then in *A Portrait of the Artist* developed it more fully. Stephen refers to the making of literature as 'the phenomenon of artistic conception, artistic gestation and artistic reproduction,' and then describes the progression from lyrical to epical and to dramatic art:

> The simplest epical form is seen emerging out of lyrical literature when the artist prolongs and broods upon himself as the centre of an epical event and this form progresses till the centre of emotional gravity is equidistant from the artist himself and from others. The narrative is no longer purely personal. The personality of the artist passes into the narration itself, flowing round and round the persons and the action like a vital sea. . . . The dramatic form is reached when the vitality which has flowed and eddied round each person fills every person with such vital force that he or she assumes a proper and intangible esthetic life. . . . The mystery of es-

thetic like that of material creation is accomplished.

This creator is not only male but female; Joyce goes on to borrow an image of Flaubert by calling him a 'god,' but he is also a goddess. Within his womb creatures come to life. Gabriel the seraph comes to the Virgin's chamber and, as Stephen says, 'In the virgin womb of the imagination the word is made flesh.'

Joyce did not take up such metaphors lightly. His brother records that in the first draft of *A Portrait,* Joyce thought of a man's character as developing 'from an embryo' with constant traits. (pp. 295-96)

A Portrait of the Artist as a Young Man is in fact the gestation of a soul, and in the metaphor Joyce found his new principle of order. The book begins with Stephen's father and, just before the ending, it depicts the hero's severance from his mother. From the start the soul is surrounded by liquids, urine, slime, seawater, amniotic tides, 'drops of water' (as Joyce says at the end of the first chapter) 'falling softly in the brimming bowl.' The atmosphere of biological struggle is necessarily dark and melancholy until the light of life is glimpsed. In the first chapter the foetal soul is for a few pages only slightly individualized, the organism responds only to the most primitive sensory impressions, then the heart forms and musters its affections, the being struggles towards some unspecified, uncomprehended culmination, it is flooded in ways it cannot understand or control, it gropes wordlessly toward sexual differentiation. In the third chapter shame floods Stephen's whole body as conscience develops; the lower bestial nature is put by. Then at the end of the fourth chapter the soul discovers the goal towards which it has been mysteriously proceeding—the goal of life. It must swim no more but emerge into air, the new metaphor being flight. The final chapter shows the soul, already fully developed, fattening itself for its journey until at last it is ready to leave. In the last few pages of the book, Stephen's diary, the soul is released from its confinement, its individuality is complete, and the style shifts with savage abruptness.

The sense of the soul's development as like that of an embryo not only helped Joyce to the book's imagery, but also encouraged him to work and rework the original elements in the process of gestation. Stephen's growth proceeds in waves, in accretions of flesh, in particularization of needs and desires, around and around but always ultimately forward. The episodic framework of *Stephen Hero* was renounced in favor of a group of scenes radiating backwards and forwards. In the new first chapter Joyce had three clusters of sensations: his earliest memories of infancy, his sickness at Clongowes (probably indebted like the ending of **'The Dead'** to rheumatic fever in Trieste), and his pandying at Father Daly's hands. Under these he subsumed chains of related moments, with the effect of three fleshings in time rather than of a linear succession of events. The sequence became primarily one of layers rather than of years.

In this process other human beings are not allowed much existence except as influences upon the soul's development or features of it. The same figures appear and reappear, the schoolboy Heron for example, each time in an altered way to suggest growth in the soul's view of them. E— C—, a partner in childhood games, becomes the object of Stephen's adolescent love poems; the master at Clongowes reappears as the preacher of the sermons at Belvedere. The same words, 'Apologise,' 'admit,' 'maroon,' 'green,' 'cold,' 'warm,' 'wet,' and the like, keep recurring with new implications. The book moves from rudimentary meanings to more complex ones, as in the conceptions of the call and the fall. Stephen, in the first chapter fascinated by unformed images, is next summoned by the flesh and then by the church, the second chapter ending with a prostitute's lingual kiss, the third with his reception of the Host upon his tongue. The soul that has been enraptured by body in the second chapter and by spirit in the third (both depicted in sensory images) then hears the call of art and life, which encompass both without bowing before either, in the fourth chapter; the process is virtually complete. Similarly the fall into sin, at first a terror, gradually becomes an essential part of the discovery of self and life.

Now Stephen, his character still recomposing the same elements, leaves the Catholic priesthood behind him to become 'a priest of eternal imagination, transmuting the daily bread of experience into the radiant body of everlasting life.' Having listened to sermons on ugliness in the third chapter, he makes his own sermons on beauty in the last. The Virgin is transformed into the girl wading on the strand, symbolizing a more tangible reality. In the last two chapters, to suit his new structure, Joyce minimizes Stephen's physical life to show the dominance of his mind, which has accepted but subordinated physical things. The soul is ready now, it throws off its sense of imprisonment, its melancholy, its no longer tolerable conditions of lower existence, to be born.

Joyce was obviously well-pleased with the paradox into which his method had put him, that he was, as the artist framing his own development in a constructed matrix, his own mother. The complications of this state are implied in Stephen's thought of himself as not his parents' true son, but a foster-son. (pp. 296-98)

Richard Ellmann, in his James Joyce, *new and revised edition, Oxford University Press, 1982, 887 p.*

ADDITIONAL BIBLIOGRAPHY

Beckson, Karl. "Symons's 'A Prelude to Life', Joyce's *A Portrait*, and the Religion of Art." *James Joyce Quarterly* 15, No. 3 (Spring 1978): 222-28.*
    Comparative study. Beckson, a noted Symons scholar, explores the possibility that Joyce was indebted to Symons's work *Spiritual Adventures* for his use of religious symbolism in *A Portrait of the Artist as a Young Man.*

Beebe, Maurice. "The *Portrait* as Portrait: Joyce and Impressionism." *Irish Renaissance Annual* I, No. 1 (1980): 13-31.
    Discussion of the Impressionistic aspects of Joyce's style. Beebe examines the work of such painters as Edouard Manet, Claude Monet, and Paul Cézanne, and draws correlations between their techniques and Joyce's literary style.

Brivic, Sheldon. "Part One: Stephen Oedipus." In his *Joyce Between Freud and Jung*, pp. 17-74. Port Washington, N.Y.: National University Publications/Kennikat Press, 1980.
    Examines the Oedipal imagery in *A Portrait of the Artist as a Young Man.*

Ellmann, Richard. *James Joyce*. Rev. ed. New York: Oxford University Press, 1982, 887 p.
    The standard biography. Upon its initial publication, Ellmann's widely praised work set a new standard for thoroughness in the examination of writers' lives.

Epstein, Edmund L. *The Ordeal of Stephen Dedalus: The Conflict of Generations in James Joyce's ''A Portrait of the Artist as a Young Man.''* Carbondale: Southern Illinois University Press, 219 p.

Traces the theme of father-son conflict throughout Joyce's works. References to *A Portrait of the Artist* are interspersed with references to *Ulysses* and *Finnegan's Wake.*

Feehan, Joseph, ed. *Dedalus on Crete: Essays on the Implications of Joyce's ''Portrait.''* Los Angeles: Saint Thomas More Guild of Immaculate Heart College, 1956, 88 p.
    Essays on the theme of the alienation of the artist in society as reflected in Joyce's *Portrait.*

Fleishman, Avrom. "*A Portrait of the Artist:* The Conventions Convened." In his *Figures of Autobiography: The Language of Self-Writing in Victorian and Modern England*, pp. 411-27. Berkeley: University of California Press, 1983.
    Discusses *A Portrait of the Artist as a Young Man* in terms of the Bildungsroman and Kunstleroman traditions. Fleishman attempts to show how Joyce's work both resembles and differs from the other classics of these genres.

Gifford, Don. "Notes for *A Portrait of the Artist as a Young Man* (1916)." In his *Joyce Annotated: Notes for ''Dubliners'' and ''A Portrait of the Artist as a Young Man,''* pp. 127-288. Berkeley: University of California Press, 1982.
    Provides extensive notes useful in enhancing one's appreciation of the *Portrait.* Gifford's book clarifies many subtleties in Joyce's text by explaining obscure Dublin details, literary references, and numerous vague references to the events of Irish history.

Goldberg, S. L. "Portals of Discovery: *A Portrait of the Artist as a Young Man* and *Exiles.*" In his *Joyce*, pp. 47-69. Edinburgh: Oliver and Boyd, 1962.
    Discusses the technical problems Joyce encountered in portraying Stephen's various emotional states and his changing level of maturity in *A Portrait of the Artist as a Young Man.*

Gorman, Herbert. *James Joyce*. New York: Farrar and Rinehart, 1939, 358 p.
    The authorized biography. In spite of Joyce's participation in the preparation of Gorman's book, critics agree that this is not the best Joyce biography available, due largely to Joyce's failure to cooperate fully with his chosen biographer.

Grayson, Janet. "Do You Kiss Your Mother?: Stephen Dedalus and the Sovereignty of Ireland." *James Joyce Quarterly* 19, No. 2 (Winter 1982): 119-26.
    On the symbolism of kisses given and refused in *A Portrait of the Artist as a Young Man.* Grayson links Joyce's use of the symbolic kiss to the Irish folk and fairy tradition.

Gross, John. *James Joyce*. Edited by Frank Kermode. New York: Viking Press, 1970, 102 p.
    Discusses the development of Joyce as a poet, dramatist, and novelist within a chronological study of his works.

Halper, Nathan. "James Joyce and His Fingernails." In his *Studies in Joyce*, pp. 109-16. Ann Arbor: University of Michigan Press, 1983.
    Discussion of the aesthetic theory advanced by Stephen Dedalus in *A Portrait of the Artist as a Young Man.* Halper maintains that, although Joyce's overt statements in the novel seem to support Stephen's theory, various structural devices that he used subtly undermine it.

Harris, John F. "Review of *A Portrait of the Artist as a Young Man.*" *To-day* III, No. 15, (May 1918): 88-92.
    Early favorable review of Joyce's *Portrait.*

Hayman, David. "Daedalean Imagery in *A Portrait of the Artist as a Young Man.*" In *Hereditas: Seven Essays on the Modern Experience of the Classical*, edited by Frederic Will, pp. 33-54. Austin: University of Texas Press, 1964.
    Examines the manner in which the Daedalus symbol functions in the *Portrait* and *Ulysses* and leads to Stephen's understanding of the labyrinthine nature of life.

Henke, Suzette. "Stephen Dedalus and Women: A Portrait of the Artist as a Young Misogynist." In *Women in Joyce*, edited by Suzette Henke and Elaine Unkeless, pp. 82-107. Urbana: University of Illinois Press, 1982.

Argues that Stephen Dedalus is portrayed by Joyce as fearing women because in his mind they are associated with such corporeal realities as sex, procreation, and death.

Hochman, Baruch. "The Joycean Project: *Portrait* as Portrait." In his *The Test of Character from the Victorian Novel to the Modern*, pp. 177-94. East Brunswick, N.J.: Associated Presses, 1983.

Discussion of the *Portrait*'s place in the novel tradition. Hochman also examines the psychological meaning of the symbols that Joyce used in the *Portrait*.

Kenner, Hugh. "The Portrait in Perspective." In his *Dublin's Joyce*, pp. 109-33. London: Chatto and Windus, 1955.

Critical study. In this well-known and often-quoted essay, Kenner links the *Portrait* to Joyce's other works through an examination of similarities in theme, structure, controlling images, and the role played by women. For further discussion of this essay, see the excerpt by Hugh Kenner dated 1965.

Lemon, Lee T. "*A Portrait of the Artist as a Young Man:* Motif as Motivation and Structure." *Modern Fiction Studies* XII, No. 4 (Winter 1966-67): 439-50.

Argues that "*A Portrait* is the first novel in which motifs per se are of primary importance—the first novel in which both theme and structure depend on such minor elements."

Mencken, H. L. "Criticism of Criticism of Criticism." *The Smart Set* LII, No. 4 (August 1917): 138-44.*

Early review in which the celebrated American critic Mencken praises both the structure and the style of the *Portrait*.

Scholes, Robert and Kain, Richard M., eds. *The Workshop of Dedalus: James Joyce and the Raw Materials for "A Portrait of the Artist as a Young Man"*. Evanston, Ill.: Northwestern University Press, 287 p.

Selections from Joyce's early writings such as *Epiphanies, Paris Notebook* and the notes for *Stephen Hero*. Scholes and Kain use these materials to illustrate the evolution of the final text of *A Portrait of the Artist as a Young Man*. This excellent book also devotes a chapter to the historical background of the *Portrait*, and

includes many personal reminiscences of the youthful Joyce written by such notable Dubliners as AE, William Butler Yeats, and Oliver St. John Gogarty.

Sharpless, F. Parvin. "Irony in Joyce's *Portrait:* The Stasis of Pity." *James Joyce Quarterly* 4, No. 4 (Summer 1967): 320-30.

Examination of Joyce's enigmatic attitude toward Stephen Dedalus in *A Portrait of the Artist as a Young Man*. Sharpless utilizes elements of the aesthetic theory advanced by Stephen Dedalus in the *Portrait* in framing his conclusions.

Sucksmith, Harvey Peter. *James Joyce: "A Portrait of the Artist as a Young Man."* Edited by David Daiches. London: Edward Arnold, 64 p.

General introduction. Sucksmith's study briefly examines such aspects of Joyce's novel as the subject, themes, structure, characterizations, and the use of myth and symbol.

Sullivan, Kevin. *Joyce Among the Jesuits*. New York: Columbia University Press, 1957, 259 p.

Biography covering Joyce's school years. Sullivan identifies the real-life prototypes of many characters and incidents in the *Portrait*.

"Wild Youth." *The Times Literary Supplement*, No. 789 (1 March 1917): 103-04.

Early favorable review of *A Portrait*. The critic praises Joyce's intensity and discusses the inertia that afflicts his characters.

Van Ghent, Dorothy. "On *A Portrait of the Artist as a Young Man*." In her *The English Novel: Form and Function*, pp. 263-76. New York: Holt, Rinehart and Winston, 1953.

Discusses *A Portrait* and the phenomenon of autobiographical fiction. Van Ghent contends that such works as *A Portrait, Sons and Lovers*, and *À la recherche du temps perdu* were products of an era of social instability when traditional values were no longer of much use in interpreting the meaning of daily events. Van Ghent maintains that Joyce wrote the *Portrait* in an effort to reconstruct and discover the meaning of his youthful experiences and to impose order on the chaos of his age.

Andrew Lang

1844-1912

Scottish folklorist, editor, journalist, critic, poet, historian, essayist, nonfiction writer, translator, and novelist.

Lang was one of Great Britain's preeminent men of letters during the closing decades of the nineteenth century, and is remembered today as the editor of the "color fairy book" series. This twelve-volume series of fairy tales, which was introduced with *The Blue Fairy Book* in 1889 and ended with *The Lilac Fairy Book* in 1910, has been recognized for renewing interest in this form of children's literature in Britain. The selections, representing stories from various world cultures, are an outgrowth of Lang's meticulous research into early languages and literature—research which called attention to cultural affinities in the folktales, myths, and legends of otherwise disparate societies. Lang elaborated on these correlations in *Myth, Ritual, and Religion,* which inspired a reevaluation and ultimate alteration of the course of anthropology. However, a romantic vision of the past imbued Lang's writings, coloring his work as a translator, poet, and revisionist historian. Among the chief proponents of Romanticism in a critical battle that pitted late nineteenth-century revivalist Romanticists against the defenders of Naturalism and Realism, Lang espoused in his literary criticism a strong preference for the romantic adventure novels of such authors as H. Rider Haggard and Rudyard Kipling, finding little to recommend among the works of such writers as Henry James and Émile Zola.

Lang, the oldest of seven children, was born in Selkirk County, Scotland, and raised in a permissive, middle-class Victorian household. The expansive grounds surrounding his rural home provided Lang and his siblings with an ideal setting for imaginary adventures, and fostered in Lang a lifelong appreciation of nature. His parents encouraged academic and artistic pursuits, and Lang, a precocious child who taught himself to read at age four, was reading such works as Shakespeare's *A Midsummer Night's Dream* in addition to children's books and fairy tales by the time he was six. Four years later he was enrolled at Edinburgh Academy, where he excelled in Greek, Latin, and the classics. Living with an aged relative during his first two years at Edinburgh, Lang filled his hours away from study by reading the works of Alexandre Dumas, William Makepeace Thackeray, and Charles Dickens—an author whom Lang would later defend when the critical tide turned against him. Although novels had been forbidden reading for Lang, with the single exception of those by Sir Walter Scott, they now became an obsession; he neglected his studies, completing only enough of his required material to avoid being beaten by his instructors. Ironically, retribution for this negligence came through reading—from the tales of Edgar Allan Poe; the horrors he read of haunted Lang day and night, and no doubt contributed to what he later referred to as his "abhorrence" for any fiction he considered unpleasant or sordid.

After graduation from Edinburgh, Lang matriculated at the University of St. Andrews, where he found students whose appreciation of the classics and literature was similar to his own. As one of twelve residents in the newly established, experimental St. Leonard's residence hall, Lang was admired for his easy and polished prose style, and his aid in "ghosting"

essays for other students was often in demand. He was named editor of *St. Leonard's Magazine,* a twelve-page weekly which featured articles about the arts and literature, and was the sole writer and illustrator of several issues. Lang loved both the physical and academic atmosphere at St. Andrews, but in his third year transferred to the University of Glasgow in preparation to compete for a scholarship to Oxford. He won the scholarship and was admitted to Oxford's Balliol College, where he majored in languages. He met the strict requirements of his program, mastering weekly essay assignments in Latin and English with ease. However, he preferred first-hand research to the authority of professors, and failed to attend the noncompulsory afternoon lectures in favor of fishing, playing cricket, or indulging himself in private reading. Despite this seeming nonchalance, Lang received firsts—highest standing—in two subjects, and in 1868 began work on his Master's degree as an Oxford Merton Fellow. Lang did not take his degree until 1875 because a lung ailment made it necessary for him to winter on the French Riviera in 1872 and 1873. It was there that he met Robert Louis Stevenson, whose flamboyant dress and emotional effusiveness Lang found embarassingly vulgar; Stevenson, in turn, found Lang's affectedly conservative dress and unemotional manner equally repellent. As the two discovered their kindred literary tastes, however, these surface differences diminished in importance and they formed a friendship based on respect and trust that endured until Stevenson's death.

In 1875 Lang married Leonora Alleyne, also a writer, and left Merton College to settle in Kensington and pursue a career as a London journalist. During this era, English periodicals were the forum in which contemporary disagreements of a scholarly nature were publically aired, and opinions about art and literature were discussed. Lang's success in this arena was immediate and overwhelming. In addition to leaders written for the *Daily News,* he wrote art and literature criticism which appeared in such periodicals as *The Athenaeum* and *The Spectator* in England and *Harper's* and *The Nation* in America. By the 1890's, Lang had published in over twenty-eight periodicals internationally. Some of his most popular articles were written for his column "At the Sign of the Ship," which ran in *Longman's Magazine* from the magazine's inception in 1882 until its demise in 1905. Expounding on subjects from Homer and Scottish history to golf and the supernatural, he wrote with scholarly confidence in simple prose, endearing himself to general readers without alienating fellow scholars or damaging his reputation as a serious man of letters. Some critics argue that Lang abused the convention of contributing unsigned reviews by penning his anonymous criticism of any given work for several journals, thereby receiving pay for each review and extending the influence of his critical opinion. One of the chief proponents of the rebellion against Realism and Naturalism, Lang contributed to the revival of Romantic fiction, as exemplified by the primitive and often other worldly settings in the works of Stevenson and Haggard. Zola, James, Joseph Conrad, Fedor Dostoevski, and other modern authors whose works probe the psychology of characters or examine the unpleasant aspects of life, were considered by Lang to be "a generation devoted to ... microscopic porings over human baseness." Elsewhere he stated, "We still long for a margin undiscovered, where hope and romance may dwell ... a misty domain where fancy may find a rest." He took advantage of his close ties with publishers and editors, wielding such substantial influence that he was able to have some works he considered objectionable barred from serialization in *Longman's Magazine* and *The Cornhill Magazine.* However, unlike many critics of his era, Lang never advocated the banning of books from stores or libraries.

The desire to avoid the "unpleasantness" of social and psychological realism in literature was consistent with Lang's romantic outlook on life, and influenced his choices of subject matter as an author. His earliest published poetical works, for example, are regarded by many critics as distant and concerned with "light fare." Eleanor Langstaff has called his touch in the ballade form "too tentative, one is tempted to say coy." In the collection *Ballads and Lyrics of Old France, and Other Poems,* the translations of such French forms as the rondeau and the triolet—the ballade form introduced to England by Dante Gabriel Rossetti and Algernon Charles Swinburne in the 1860s—were regarded as emotionally insignificant works that sacrificed originality in favor of nostalgic recreations of romantic ideals. Along with Edmund Gosse and Austin Dobson, Lang and other revivalists of the French forms took pride in their ability to master the difficult restraints of rhyme and meter these forms demanded. Among the exceptions to the charge of emotional detachment and too close attention to form is the poem "The Twilight on the Tweed," which is praised by modern critics for its evocation of natural Scotish environs and its lament over a lost friend or lover, themes repeated in many of Lang's serious poetic works. *Helen of Troy,* the much-anticipated six-volume work that was to fulfill Lang's poetic promise, was a disappointment to critics, who found that his interpretation of the legend censored its sensual aspects, that

his choice of the epic form was unfashionable, and that his execution, though scholarly, made for uninteresting reading. Lang continued to write poetry, but never attempted another monumental work, turning instead to social commentary, humorous light verse, and parody. Some modern critics regard him as a master of form, but also as a writer whose works lack emotional depth. Others find his light and lyrical verse delightful and consider him the most brilliant of the minor poets of his era.

Lang's expertise in the fields of foreign languages and literatures, and his scholastic preference for investigating original materials rather than depending on established reference materials for his studies, led him to discover that the folk tales, myths, and legends of primitive societies were not only quite similar from culture to culture, but that this similarity could not always be explained as the result of direct transmission of one culture's traits to another—the prevailing explanation of this phenomenon in the 1880s. Specifically, Lang regarded as unsupportable the simplistic theory of Max Müller, an Oxford professor and the leading authority in the anthropological branch of philology, who held that myths developed among later civilizations, and were a consequence of linguistic misunderstandings between the transmitter of the information and the receiver. By examining the folktales, myths, and legends of early developing cultures, as well as their customs and artifacts, Lang illustrated that myths were prevalent in all cultures, providing explanations for natural phenomena and such human phenomena as folk rituals. The battle between Lang and Müller, instigated and sustained by Lang in several books and in English journals, raged for years. Müller was supported by an academic community that had no reason to question his theories, and Lang brought his own credibility into question by employing humor in *Custom and Myth* and *Myth, Ritual, and Religion,* a practice he applied in many of his works of serious scholarship, making his revolutionary theories seem even more far-fetched. Eventually, however, critics and scientists were swayed by Lang's careful scholarship and abundant data, and Müller's reputation was toppled along with the now-outmoded bases for anthropological study.

As a further result of his studies in folklore and myth, Lang, who had loved fairy tales since early childhood, collected many such stories from around the world, preferring those emanating from an oral tradition to those conceived as literary tales, although he rendered them in literary style in the color fairy book editions. From the appearance of *The Blue Fairy Book* the collections were a success, which was remarkable because fairy tales at that time were being replaced in England by stories for children written about children. Lang was attracted to the stories primarily because he felt they suspended the imagination and also appealed to a child's natural sense of justice, theories which were later questioned in an essay on Lang by J. R. R. Tolkien, who regarded children's enjoyment of literature as no different than that of adults, based solely on the ability of the story to move the reader emotionally. Even in the most fantastic stories of the fairy books, a concern for human suffering and triumph and the transmission of a moral lesson remain central. Lang's fairy books, packaged in elaborate editions to appeal to the book collector as well as to the reader, remain among the classics in the genre today.

During his lifetime Lang was regarded as a controversial scholar who wrote on many subjects at a time when versatile men of letters were giving way to literary experts who cultivated one field of interest. Henry James, for example, was not alone among Lang's contemporaries in believing that Lang had scattered his talents and had wasted his brilliance on frivolous subjects in order to make a lucrative living as a celebrated journalist. Others, however, believed that Lang's wide-ranging interests and light-hearted style were an interesting contrast to writers of the age who took themselves too seriously; G. K. Chesterton, Lang's friend and fellow journalist, attributed much of the criticism aimed at Lang to a frustrated desire to categorize him, stating, "Andrew Lang suffered from three great disadvantages . . . : he was universal, he was amusing, and he was lucid."

(See also *Something about the Author*, Vol. 16.)

PRINCIPAL WORKS

Ballads and Lyrics of Old France, and Other Poems
 [translator]   (poetry)   1872
Helen of Troy. 6 vols.   (poetry)   1882
Custom and Myth. 2 vols.   (nonfiction)   1884
The Princess Nobody   (fairy tale)   1884
Letters to Dead Authors   (essays)   1886
The Mark of Cain   (novel)   1886
Myth, Ritual, and Religion. 2 vols.   (nonfiction)   1887
The Gold of Fairnilee   (fairy tale)   1888
The Blue Fairy Book [editor]   (fairy tales)   1889
Letters on Literature   (essays)   1889
Prince Prigio   (fairy tale)   1889
The Red Fairy Book [editor]   (fairy tales)   1890
The World's Desire [with H. Rider Haggard]   (novel)
 1890
The Green Fairy Book [editor]   (fairy tales)   1892
*Prince Ricardo of Pantouflia: Being the Adventures of
 Prince Prigio's Son*   (fairy tale)   1893
The Life and Letters of John Gibson Lockhart   (biography)
 1897
Modern Mythology: A Reply to Max Müller   (nonfiction)
 1897
Pickle the Spy; or, The Incognito of Prince Charles
 (history)   1897
The Pink Fairy Book [editor]   (fairy tales)   1897
Companions of Pickle   (history)   1898
The Grey Fairy Book [editor]   (fairy tales)   1900
History of Scotland from the Roman Occupation. 4 vols.
 (history)   1900-1907
The Mystery of Mary Stuart   (history)   1901
The Violet Fairy Book [editor]   (fairy tales)   1901
The Crimson Fairy Book [editor]   (fairy tales)   1903
The Brown Fairy Book [editor]   (fairy tales)   1904
Historical Mysteries   (history)   1904
Adventures among Books   (memoir)   1905
John Knox and the Reformation   (biography)   1905
The Orange Fairy Book [editor]   (fairy tales)   1906
The Olive Fairy Book [editor]   (fairy tales)   1907
The Maid of France   (history)   1908
The Lilac Fairy Book [editor]   (fairy tales)   1910
History of English Literature   (nonfiction)   1912
Poetical Works. 4 vols.   (poetry)   1923

E. D. A. MORSHEAD   (essay date 1882)

[*Morshead was an English educator and scholar of Greek literature who was best known for his translations of the works of Aeschylus and Sophocles. In the following excerpt he praises Lang's poetic ability, but finds that the long poem* Helen of Troy *compares unfavorably to the version of the legend in Homer's* The Illiad.]

Mr. Lang is a poetical craftsman of such merit that it is almost superfluous to say of any work by him that it is marked by a delicate sense of metre, and by classical scholarship widened and fortified by comprehensive knowledge of other literature. The present writer must frankly avow himself disappointed with **Helen of Troy;** yet he does so with a full sense that there may well be in the poem what he has failed to find there—fire as well as grace, and originality as well as technical skill. And to have expected overmuch is apt, no doubt, to make one discontented even with so fair a gift as **Helen of Troy**.

The poem consists of six books, containing the history of the Trojan War, from the first arrival of Paris as a wandering guest at the Court of Lacedaemon to the return of the Greeks after the sack of Troy, the peaceful re-establishment of Helen as Menelaus' Queen, and their final translation to the Fortunate Islands—the realm of "Rhadamanthus of the golden hair." The poem thus challenges reference not only to Homer and Virgil, but to Landor, Mr. Tennyson, and Mr. Morris. All these poets have been laid under contribution, as far as matter is concerned: the manner, I am constrained to say, is almost exclusively that of Mr. Morris. . . . The resemblance is palpable, independently of the pleasant confession lately published by Mr. Lang in the *Contemporary Review*, of his abiding preference for the "Earthly Paradise" and "Jason" as opposed to "Sigurd."

But Homer and Mr. Morris—both rhapsodists—are rhapsodists "with a difference." One may feel nothing but admiration for the latter, and yet think that Homer's subjects lose by being treated in the Morrisian manner. It is, I own, with some surprise, as recognising more of

> The surge and thunder of the Odyssey

in the prose version of Mr. Lang and his coadjutor than in any other that has ever been written, that I find so little of the Homeric directness, and so little of what Mr. Arnold taught us to call "the grand style," in Mr. Lang's verse. Here and there a touch of it may be found, as in Oenone's last words over the pyre of Corythus, and in the description of the arrival of the Grecian armament. . . . But scarcely anywhere else in the poem is the directness and rapidity of the Homeric narrative preserved. It may be replied that this is to force a comparison not challenged by the writer. But, in truth, no one can disconnect the name of Mr. Lang from Homeric scholarship; and Homeric in the sense of abounding in Homeric ideas and phrases, **Helen of Troy** assuredly is. All the more is it to be regretted that the influence of a modern singer has been so potent with Mr. Lang in the matter of style that his book reads like the completion of a small epic, of which Mr. Morris' "Death of Paris" formed one book. That would be high praise; and yet, with his power and his materials, I cannot but think Mr. Lang might have aimed higher still. His models would have been, no doubt, of a more unreached excellence; but, from this very fact, his own performance would have attained what it lacks— a measure of sublimity and fire. The grace of wistful pathos, indeed, it exhibits in many passages. . . . But, amid [the] delicate *explanation* of sadness, one sighs for something like, or even faintly recalling, the wail of Thetis in anticipation of Achilles' doom. . . .

Mr. Lang, in the article mentioned above, has set the example of recalling the effect of contemporary tentative productions upon the mind of undergraduate Oxford. He will, perhaps, permit me to say that the perusal of *Helen of Troy* has quickened in me a regret I have always felt that "The Shade of Helen," added to the "Ballads and Lyrics of Old France," should remain a fragment only. The dreamy myth, in which the real Helen sojourned in Egypt, while Greek and Trojan fought at Troy for a shadow and a phantom of her, seems to me now, as it did then, one admirably suited to the tone of Mr. Lang's fancy. Nothing in *Helen of Troy* has quite the picturesqueness of "The Shade of Helen". . . .

However, it is idle to complain of any writer that he has given over, or as yet withholds fom us, a design of which the early sketch pleased us well. We must "know to wait." *Helen of Troy* is more calculated to please those who wish to know Greek legends in a modern form than those who wish to be reminded of the originals.

The long "Note" on the character and history of Helen as conceived by the Greek mind at different periods, which closes the volume, is extremely lucid and pleasant reading.

> *E. D. A. Morshead, in a review of "Helen of Troy,"*
> *in* The Academy, *n.s. Vol. XXII, No. 544, October*
> *7, 1882, p. 251.*

[W. E. HENLEY]   (essay date 1890)

[*Henley was an important figure in the counter-decadent movement of the 1890s and the leader of an imperialistic group of young British writers—including Rudyard Kipling, H. Rider Haggard, and Robert Louis Stevenson—who stressed action, virility, and inner strength over alienation, effeminacy, and despair: characteristics they attributed to the decadents. As editor of* The National Observer *and* The New Review, *Henley was an invigorating force in English literature, publishing and defending the early works of such writers as H. G. Wells, Thomas Hardy, and Bernard Shaw. As a poet, he was a pioneer in the use of free verse, though he also wrote many poems that combine realistic social observation and description with traditional forms. His most famous poem, "Invictus," demonstrates his optimistic spirit and his braggadocio, two qualities apparent in much of his work. In the following excerpt, Henley sarcastically reviews* The World's Desire, *a novel coauthored by Lang and Haggard, attacking it as a work that signals the "artistic suicide" of its authors.*]

Mr. Lang we know and Mr. Haggard we know: but of whom (or what) is this 'tortuous and ungodly' jumble of anarchy and culture [*The World's Desire*]? Premising only that Mr. Lang is a distinguished writer and a mythologist, and that Mr. Haggard is an excellent maker and teller of strong and simple and affecting stories—for answer let the tale be told.

The Wanderer, *alias* Odysseus, *alias* Ulysses, returns to Ithaca after his second fit of wandering. . . . [There he finds] the Bow of Eurytus, 'the dreadful bow that no mortal man but the Wanderer could bend.' Now this was a bow of bows, for it was also a musical box wound up for ever and ever and going off on the slightest provocation or on none into all manner of martial and sentimental strains. . . . [Nothing] daunted by the absence of a 'pitch' the Wanderer had an interview with Aphrodite. Being of a jealous habit, she 'chaffed' him about a number of ladies, but at last discovered to his eyes the person of the World's Desire. It was a fine figure of a woman but no better than she should be; and he knew her forthwith for Helen—erstwhile of Troy, but now of Egypt, where she was known as the Strange Hathor. Thither he sailed in a ship of

Sidon, the irrepressible Bow going off with every roll of her; and, there arriving, he found the Ten Plagues sadly 'on,' and an Unauthorised Version of *Exodus* in mid career. He made friends with Rei the chief priest, and was introduced to Meriamun, queen to Pharoh, who instantly fell in love with him. Now Meriamun was what men technical in heart and mind do clepe a Madam. A little before the Wanderer's appearance she poisoned a rival; ere the body was embalmed she went forth to it at dead of night; around that clay-cold form she drew all sorts of magic circles; she raised the Ka, which was no good as a 'spook,' and she raised the Bai, which was as little, and then she raised the Khow, which told her future, whereupon she hied her home again. . . . Meantime the Wanderer went to see the Hathor. He found her singing on the roof of her abode; and a number of infuriated males were watching her; and they all sought to get at her; but lo, they were slain, and none knew how, and few knew why, and still fewer be they that care. Now the Wanderer was not slain, but got in all right; and when the Hathor looked upon him, behold it seemed to her that he was a son of Priam—even the co-respondent in the well-known case of *Menelaus v. Helen and Paris;* but at last she knew him for Odysseus, for whom she had cherished a secret passion all along. And they twain made tryst at the gate for next evening, with a view to arranging an elopement. Now, Meriamun was come aware of it all by art-magic; so she took upon herself the face and figure of the Hathor; and thus was the Wanderer deluded; and the marriage ceremony being 'held as said' . . . ! But in the morning the Bow dropped into poetry, and at the sound of the noise thereof the Wanderer turned him to consult his watch and ask the meaning of that infernal row. That is to say, 'he yawned, he stretched out his mighty arms, he opened his eyes':—and there beside him was She-Who-Must-Be-Obeyed! Unhappily he knew not his Haggard; wherefore he hesitated not to tell the lady she had made a mistake. So she went forth into the Palace of Pharaoh, and cried unto all men's hearing a version (carefully brought down to date) of the story of Joseph and the wife of Potiphar. Now, the guards were simple men, and nothing they recked of chestnuts; and in those days, of fire-escapes there was none in all the land of Egypt. So they went for the Wanderer; and his musical-box was damaged in the struggle; and they tied him fast, and, hero as he was, behold they ran him in. But Pharaoh returned alone, the Red Sea having made an end of his host (for so it is told in the Unauthorised Version); and Meriamun poisoned him after a game of chess; and the Wanderer was taken out of prison and was sent to the wars; and there, by the contrivances of Rei, he was presently joined by the Hathor; and a big fight befell them, and the Wanderer was slain; and thereafter they cremated him in state, and Meriamun consumed herself likewise; and thereupon the Hathor let fall her veil, and 'wandered forth into the desert and the night, singing as she paused.'

Last of all, the story died also; and this critic was moved to curse his literary gods and die at thought of the most complete artistic suicide it has ever been his lot to chronicle. (pp. 99-100)

> [*W. E. Henley*], "*Culture and Anarchy," in* The
> National Observer, *n.s. Vol. V, No. 108, December*
> *13, 1890, pp. 99-100.*

[MARGARET OLIPHANT]   (essay date 1897)

[*Oliphant was a nineteenth-century Scottish novelist whose most distinguished works depict provincial English and Scottish society of the last century. The author of nearly one hundred novels, she contributed fiction and literary criticism to* Blackwood's Edin-

THE

BROWN FAIRY BOOK

EDITED BY

ANDREW LANG

*WITH EIGHT COLOURED PLATES
AND NUMEROUS ILLUSTRATIONS BY H. J. FORD*

LONGMANS, GREEN, AND CO.
39 PATERNOSTER ROW, LONDON
NEW YORK AND BOMBAY
1904

Title page of The Brown Fairy Book.

burgh Magazine *throughout her long career. In the following excerpt, she offers a favorable review of Lang's book of Scottish history* Pickle, the Spy.]

Mr Andrew Lang a few years ago was chiefly known as an admirable writer, without anything very definite to say: we do not know what action of circumstances or impulse of grace has turned him into a historical student, as learned and industrious as he was once light-minded and elegant; but it is a good thing for us all that he has retained the graces of the earlier epoch to add charm to the researches of the new. His present subject is not so purely romantic, so inspiring and noble, as that study of Joan of Arc and her times which produced the **'Monk of Fife.'** It is indeed a terrible chapter of history which he unfolds in the revelation of [**'Pickle, the Spy'**], a story of human baseness and dishonour, of the downfall of high hopes and character, the worsening of everything and everybody concerned in what was at first, whatever its consequences and even motives might be, a high chivalrous enterprise, which wounds the sympathetic spectator, however little of a Jacobite he may be. Some critics have indeed attributed to Mr Lang a deliberate intention to break the charm of Jacobitism altogether by showing how poor a thing it was, much as Messrs Henley and Henderson are afraid they have done with Burns. And we doubt that a good many old-fashioned people in Scotland may object to Mr Lang's exposure of Pickle the Spy. Were we a Macdonald we should resent it warmly, especially as the evidence Mr Lang

gives, though very plausible, contains no element of certainty, and is purely circumstantial, not enough to hang a man upon, we think, therefore scarcely enough to shatter his character. In all probability Mr Lang is right; but had we any special interest in the question we think we should claim, at least, a verdict of Not Proven, which, by the bye, for all practical purposes, is worse than guilty.

Pickle, a wretch of literary tendencies, since he took his nickname from Smollett's 'Peregrine Pickle,' was a Jacobite conspirator for James III. and his son, in the days when there was still some hope for the Stuarts, in his true name: and a servile spy reporting all their conspiracies to George II. under the other. (p. 474)

It is not the Spy but the unfortunate figure of the Young Chevalier [Charles Edward], the noble youth, the broken man, victim of his birth, of his circumstances, of all that went before him, which is the chief and most interesting thing in this book. The picture is at once spirited and pathetic. The curious episode of his life so often passed over, between the great romance of the '45 and the squalid tragedy of the end; his wanderings on the Continent, seen here and there in alarmed glimpses by his friends, pursued blindly everywhere by his enemies of the English and other Governments, struggling against the inhospitality of one country after another which refused to receive him, and preferring to lead the most precarious roving life rather than be driven to the dull and spy-haunted refuge at Rome,—is put before us with great vividness and originality, no one, we think, having done it before. Mr Lang has but little of the natural foible of a Scotsman for poor Prince Charlie, and is not a partial witness, feeling no doubt that even the vagaries of a man so doomed can but increase the tragic interest of his story. (p. 476)

> [*Margaret Oliphant*], *in a review of* "Pickle, the Spy," *in* Blackwood's Edinburgh Magazine, *Vol. CLXI, No. DCCCCLXXVIII, April, 1897, pp. 474-76.*

A. T. QUILLER-COUCH   (essay date 1897)

[*Quiller-Couch was an English man of letters who is especially noted as the editor of* The Oxford Book of English Verse *(1900) and of several other distinguished anthologies. The author of many novels and short stories, his most famous work was* The Golden Spur *(1889), a novel which, like much of his fiction, is set in his native Cornwall. A contributor to various English periodicals, Quiller-Couch published many of his magazine essays under the pseudonym* "Q." *In the following excerpt from his regular column in* The Pall Mall Magazine, *he contends that Lang possesses the best English prose style of his era. Quiller-Couch's judgment drew a scornful reaction from Max Beerbohm (1897).*]

I may now declare the result of the competition announced in the March number of *Pall Mall Magazine* as follows;—''The magnificent prize of one guinea will be awarded to the reader who divines the name of the man (or woman) who is (or has been during the past ten years) master (or mistress) of the best style in English Prose.''

The result, you may remember, was not to depend on popular suffrage. I had already enclosed the great writer's name, with the guinea, in an envelope which I committed to the Editor, with a request that he would break the seal on the 1st of April or thereabouts. (p. 424)

The name in the envelope was—

MR. ANDREW LANG.

(p. 427)

There is no more futile pursuit in this wide world than dog-matising about style, or rather about one's preferences in style. It depends so closely upon temperament that, after certain qualities have been claimed and allowed, and certain patent faults discounted, a man might as well try to justify his choice of friends by the use of the syllogism as to argue upon his sensitiveness to A's writing and his comparative indifference to B's. When an author violates grammar (which is the logic of speech); when he ties up loose thought in ill-constructed sentences; when he narrates or reasons inconsequently or obscurely; when he employs ill-fitting epithets or runs riot in mere verbiage; when he cannot express himself without recourse to *anacolutha* and contortions of the mother-tongue; in sum, when he ignores or relaxes the ancient bond between thought and language, then you may safely say that his is a vicious style. But beyond this you must tread cautiously. You have to consider, among other things, whether you love a plain coat or a laced coat, and to allow for your neighbour's preference if it be not yours. For my part I prefer the plain coat with just a trifle of lace: simplicity with the touch which makes it Attic simplicity and not Doric. (pp. 427-28)

And now I suppose I must justify my choice of Mr. Lang's style against the 155 unsuccessful competitors. I have dared to call it Attic, and maintain that he has more of the Attic quality than any living writer of English. With a few reservations I think we may apply to him (merely, of course, as a master of style) what Mr. Henley has written of Thackeray:—

> His manner is the perfection of conversational writing. Graceful yet vigorous; adorably artificial yet incomparably sound; touched with modishness yet informed with distinction; easily and happily rhythmical yet full of colour and quick with malice and with meaning; instinct with urbanity and instinct with charm,— it is a type of high-bred English, a climax of literary art. . . . Setting aside Cardinal Newman's, the style he wrote is certainly less open to criticism than that of any modern Englishman. He was neither super-eloquent like Mr. Ruskin, nor a Germanised Jeremy like Carlyle; he was not marmoreally emphatic as Landor was, nor was he slovenly and inexpressive as was the great Sir Walter; he neither dallied with antithesis like Macaulay nor rioted in verbal vulgarisms with Dickens; he abstained from technology and what may be called Lord Burleighism as carefully as George Eliot indulged in them, and he avoided conceits as sedulously as Mr. George Meredith goes out of his way to hunt for them. . . .

Keeping carefully in mind the difference in their *matter*, I think we may transfer this praise of Thackeray to Mr. Andrew Lang with one or two reservations. He is less vigorous than Thackeray. Earnestness (*arrovoatórns*) seems to me the one primary quality of style in which his is lacking, the one quality needed to make it very great. (pp. 428-29)

On the other hand, his *urbanity* is more constant than Thackeray's. That Thackeray is often urbane no fair critic can deny; but I imagine it just as hard to deny that there were occasions when he forgot to be urbane. (p. 429)

[Mr. Lang's] style is accurate, lucid, simple in the best sense; happy in illustration and allusion; familiar without a trace of vulgarity, for while not disdaining the full vocabulary and even the colloquialisms of its own age, it exercises its freedom on a basis of scholarship and within limits of good taste derived from scholarship. Thus it is at once modern (even modish at times), and pure—a difficult combination; for, as Minto said, "generally speaking, when a style is such as to win the praise of being classical English, there is something stiff and old-fashioned about it." I neither know nor care whether Mr. Lang's prose would be called "classical" to-day; but as soon as he applies it to worthy subjects, it·has the qualities which will make it "classical" to-morrow. Nor, while it remains so easy to read, do I care whether he writes it with ease or no. We may pass the question of greatness. Carlyle had a theory that no great writer was ever understood without difficulty. If true, this would go some way towards proving that no great writer could possess a good style. And it is of style that we are talking just now. But I fancy we may take it that while constructing this theory Carlyle had his eye upon Carlyle rather (let us say) than on Plato. We have no one in these days to compare with Plato. Xenophon will do for Mr. Lang. "If," said Professor Gilbert Murray, the other day, in his little book on *Ancient Greek Literature*, "Xenophon became in Roman times a model of 'Atticism,' it is due to his ancient simplicity and ease, his *inaffectata jucunditas*. He is Attic in the sense that he has no bombast, and that *he can speak interestingly on many subjects 'without raising his voice.'*" Add a touch of lace to the coat, qualify the simplicity with scholarship, and the *jucunditas* with the sophisticated modishness of modern humour, and you have a description that will serve for Mr. Lang. (pp. 429-30)

> A. T. Quiller-Couch, "From a Cornish Window," *in* The Pall Mall Magazine, *Vol. XII, No. 51, July, 1897, pp. 424-32.**

MAX BEERBOHM (essay date 1897)

[*Though he lived until 1956, Beerbohm is chiefly associated with the fin de siècle period in English literature, more specifically with its lighter phases of witty sophistication and mannered elegance. His temperament was urbane and satirical, and he excelled in both literary and artistic caricatures of his contemporaries. "Entertaining" in the most complimentary sense of the word, Beerbohm's criticism for* The Saturday Review—*where he was a long-time drama critic—everywhere indicates his scrupulously developed taste and unpretentious, fair-minded response to literature. In the following excerpt, Beerbohm sarcastically rebuts A. T. Quiller-Couch's assessment of Lang as the best English prose stylist of his era (see excerpt dated 1897), contending that while Lang may be a master of stylistic mimicry, the writings composed in his own narrative voice display an unexceptional style.*]

In that House Beautiful, the "Pall Mall Magazine," are many mansions, and I can well imagine that a mere literary man must find their splendour rather too much for him. Like a skylark in a cage, Mr. A. T. Quiller-Couch seems to have suffered terribly in the glossy saloon allotted to him. Dazzled by the riches of the Hon. W. W. Astor and by the titles of Lord Frederick Hamilton and Sir Douglas Straight, he has leant his fevered brow against the panes of his Cornish Window and cast a wistful eye over the Democracy of Letters. Anything more pathetic than his *plébiscite* about Style can hardly be conceived. . . . Mr. Quiller-Couch gives the go-by to Pater, Froude, and Newman (who, with the Rev. Stopford Brooke and others, has received one vote), to Hardy, Ruskin, Stevenson and Arnold, and awards the palm to—Mr. Andrew Lang! . . .

I am convinced that he was in deadly earnest about Mr. Lang, and I can but condole with him on his aberration. As an admirer of his work, I can but regret that he has made himself ridiculous. If it be any comfort for him to know that he has made Mr. Lang ridiculous also, I assure him gladly that he has done so. Mr. Lang is very well in his way, a most accomplished gentleman, who disfigures none of the many things he touches, adorning some of them. His *ballades* and other conventional verses are nearly, though not quite, as good as such things can be. The parodies which he called **"Letters to Dead Authors"** are pieces of deft and delightful workmanship. His translations of the "Iliad" and the "Odyssey," made with Dr. Butcher, are really fine achievements in taste and scholarship. He is a master of the higher mimicry; the further from himself (as it seems to me) the better, invariably, is his work. To have called him "master of the best *styles* in English Prose" would have been a quite appropriate criticism, but surely the substitution of *"style"* makes that criticism merely foolish. Style, as one knows, is the direct outcome of personality, and it is for his style, as most clearly manifested in his essays, that Mr. Quiller-Couch heaps praises on Mr. Lang. But "there is no more futile pursuit in this wide world," says Mr. Quiller-Couch cautiously, "than dogmatizing about style, or rather about one's preferences in style. It depends so closely upon temperament that, after certain qualities have been claimed and allowed, and certain patent faults discounted, a man might as well try to justify his choice of friends by the use of the syllogism as to argue upon his sensitiveness to A's writing and his comparative indifference to B's" [see excerpt dated 1897]. Have you noticed that every critic, when he wishes to pass false coin, invariably engages poor, overworked A and B as his accomplices? This particular coin of Mr. Quiller-Couch's has a sly veneer of genuine metal. Mr. Quiller-Couch delights in Mr. Lang's style. I do not. Mr. George Moore does not. Few people, indeed, do. We agree that Mr. Lang has a nice little style, but we find it too spinsterly to be at all inspiriting, and even his slang, though it enraptures Mr. Quiller-Couch, seems to us rather like an after-spark of Girton's chaste conviviality. By the flushed disciple urbanity and charm and distinction are found in Mr. Lang's essays, which seem to us nothing but meagre, peevish and anaemic trails of little sentences. "A matter of taste!" cries Mr. Quiller-Couch. "True," I answer, "to a certain extent!" If Mr. Quiller-Couch had asserted that of the *small* styles Mr. Lang's pleased him the best, I should have been content to enumerate the small styles which please me better than Mr. Lang's. As it is, Mr. Quiller-Couch has made a vast mistake in perspective, and I must become academic. . . . In the last ten years, even if you exclude Arnold and Newman from that period, there have been great stylists, and I trust that, since returning from his cheap excursion, Mr. Quiller-Couch has realized that in comparing, in presuming for one moment to compare, Mr. Lang with these stylists, he has been guilty of a solecism which would be more painful if it were less absurd. Heaven knows I am not naturally academic! I should not be academic, but merely temperamental, in a comparison between (say) Pater's prose and Ruskin's. One lion in the Zoological Gardens may seem to me more superb than another. Of two kittens, playing on the hearthrug, one may seem to me the prettier. But I do not compare either lion with either kitten. To that extent, I am academic. (p. 109)

Max Beerbohm, "A Cheap Excursion in Criticism," in The Saturday Review, *London, Vol. LXXXIV, No. 2179, July 31, 1897, pp. 109-10.**

ÉMILE FAGUET   (essay date 1908)

[*Faguet was a prominent critic in France in the 1890s and the early decades of the twentieth century. In the following excerpt, he discusses* Historical Mysteries, *praising Lang for presenting interesting solutions to historical questions and resisting the invention of solutions when none present themselves.*]

Mr. Andrew Lang has contributed to the English magazines a dozen articles on certain obscure points of modern history; and these articles have been extremely popular. . . .

These historical mysteries [collected in *Historical Mysteries*] are as follows: The **"Iron Mask"** (you were probably expecting that), **"Kaspar Hauser," "Jacques de la Cloche," "The Count of Saint Germain," "The Conspiracies of the Gowries," "The Assassination of Escovedo,"** etc. (p. 458)

In general, in the treatment of his historical mysteries, Mr. Andrew Lang inclines toward the solution which is farthest removed from the legend. He believes that it is safer to assume the minimum of romanticism in history.

Thus, Kaspar Hauser has been considered as the son of a duke, the son of a margrave or the son of Napoleon First. According to Mr. Andrew Lang—and he proves it very well—Kaspar Hauser is merely an hysterical imposter who said not a word of truth during his three years' residence in Nuremberg; who made out of whole cloth the most effective romance possible, a romance, that is, which is neither systematic nor consecutive, but is constructed simply of vague hints that each hearer binds together to suit himself; flatly self-contradictory, moreover, from one sentence to the next. (pp. 458-59)

As for his strange death, Mr. Andrew Lang is persuaded that he committed suicide. He shows that Kaspar Hauser had more than once before inflicted injury on himself to attract attention and sympathy. The last time he probably struck a little too hard and a little too truly. On this last point Mr. Lang's argument is less convincing and his proofs less abundant. He leaves me in doubt, and I believe he is not quite sure himself.

As for the **"Iron Mask,"** the principal thought of Mr. Lang is still the same. It has been conjectured that the Iron Mask was a brother of Louis XIV, a minister of Louis XIV, a prominent political character, or Molière; a more modest guess has named him an insignificant Italian diplomat, Mattioli. This sounds more reasonable, being less romantic.

But suppose we become less romantic still? Suppose we assume that the Iron Mask was a mere servant? That would seem still more likely to be true, being still more commonplace. "The humble truth," said Maupassant. It seems that the truth can never be humble enough to satisfy Mr. Lang.

And in fact he proves to us convincingly enough that though Mattioli may have had a mask of iron—or of velvet—he died in 1694 (which seems extremely likely) and that the Iron Mask—that is, the velvet mask—followed by the restless eyes of history till 1703 and dying at Paris, in the Bastille, during that year, must be another.

And what other? A certain Martin, merely. Only a valet of Roux de Marsilly, named Martin, and the possessor, after the death of his master the only possessor, of certain important secrets.

And I must admit that the thesis is well maintained and presented with a great air of plausibility. This valet of tragedy is very interesting, in any case, and if he was what Mr. Lang believes him to have been, his vanity must have been amply satisfied. (pp. 459-60)

This Iron Mask, in the last analysis, is for Mr. Lang a character represented by two persons: Mattioli and Martin each played his part. "The fortunes of the two men have been combined in a single myth." Very well! we have another double character, this one really of noble birth. He was Jacques de la Cloche. This Jacques de la Cloche was almost certainly a natural son of the King of England, Charles II. But here is the question: Did he die obscurely, under a Jesuit robe; or, having been a Jesuit earlier, did he throw himself into a career of adventure, checkered with imprisonments and drubbings, and die an unbeliever?

Some think that the Jesuit and the adventurer were one, others that the adventurer is only a false Smerdis, a false Dmitri, a false de la Cloche in short, who assumed the role of the son of Charles II, posed as the Pretender, and lived the short and violent life I have mentioned.

The question remains extremely doubtful. (p. 460)

There are cases, however, when Mr. Lang scorns to doubt; when he expresses his convictions most decidedly. He has the levelest head a man could well boast. He is not determined to find a solution, and where there is no solution he does not insist that there is one; but when his opinion is settled, he does not, on the other hand, affect an elegant scepticism. (p. 461)

The book is amusing in a remarkable degree. It proves the hackneyed saying: "Would you have extraordinary stories, in the manner of Edgar Allan Poe and Hoffmann? They are not hard to find. Look over the pages of history. The true surpasses all the inventions of men's brains." (p. 465)

> *Émile Faguet, "Andrew Lang's 'The Mysteries of History'," translated by R. T. House, in* The Sewanee Review, *Vol. XVI, No. 4, Autumn, 1908, pp. 458-65.*

EDMUND GOSSE (essay date 1912)

[*Gosse's importance as a critic is due primarily to his introduction of Henrik Ibsen's "new drama" to an English audience. He was among the chief English translators and critics of Scandinavian literature and was decorated by the Norwegian, Swedish, and Danish governments for his efforts. Among his other works are studies of John Donne, Thomas Gray, and Sir Thomas Browne, and important early articles on French authors of the late nineteenth century. Although Gosse's works are varied and voluminous, his critical style is somewhat casual, with the consequence that his commentary lacks depth and is not considered to be in the first rank of modern critical thought. However, his broad interests and knowledge of foreign literatures lend his works much more than a documentary value. Along with Lang, Gosse was considered among the leading minor poets of his time. He envied Lang's wit and facility at improvising light verse, although he sometimes found Lang's parodies of the works of contemporaries and revered predecessors too stinging after his initial amusement had subsided. In a letter written to Henry James after Lang's death, Gosse stated that "Sometimes his memory irritates me." In the following excerpt Gosse discusses Lang's career, but unlike most critics, who regard Lang as a versatile writer, he finds Lang's interests narrow and almost solely confined to the realm of romance and illusion. He contends that it is because Lang was able to find romance in many areas of interest that he is mistakenly perceived as versatile.*]

[When Andrew Lang] died, all the newspapers were loud in proclaiming his "versatility." But I am not sure that he was

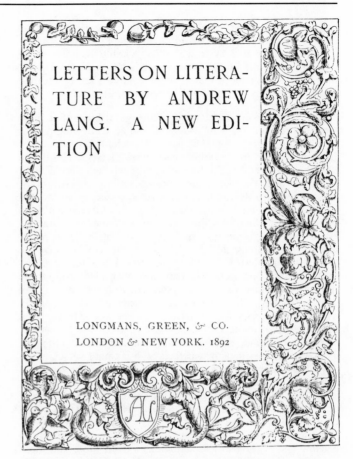

Title page of Lang's Letters on Literature.

not the very opposite of versatile. I take "versatile" to mean changeable, fickle, constantly ready to alter direction with the weather-cock. The great instance of versatility in literature is Ruskin, who adopted diametrically different views of the same subject at different times of his life, and defended them with equal ardour. To be versatile seems to be unsteady, variable. But Lang was through his long career singularly unaltered; he never changed his point of view; what he liked and admired as a youth he liked and admired as an elderly man. It is true that his interests and knowledge were vividly drawn along a surprisingly large number of channels, but while there was abundance there does not seem to me to have been versatility. If a huge body of water boils up from a crater, it may pour down a dozen paths, but these will always be the same; unless there is an earthquake, new cascades will not form nor old rivulets run dry. In some authors earthquakes do take place— as in Tolstoy, for instance, and in S. T. Coleridge—but nothing of this kind was ever manifest in Lang, who was extraordinarily multiform, yet in his varieties strictly consistent from Oxford to the grave. (p. 200)

The structure which his own individuality . . . began to build on the basis supplied by the learning of Oxford, and in particular by the study of the Greeks, and "dressed'" by courses of Matthew Arnold, was from the first eclectic. Lang eschewed as completely what was not sympathetic to him as he assimilated what was attractive to him. Those who speak of his "versatility" should recollect what large tracts of the literature of the world, and even of England, existed outside the dimmest apprehension of Andrew Lang. It is, however, more useful to consider what he did apprehend; and there were two English books, published in his Oxford days, which permanently impressed him: one of these was "The Earthly Paradise," the other D. G. Rossetti's "Poems." In after years he tried to divest himself of the traces of these volumes, but he had fed upon their honey-dew and it had permeated his veins.

Not less important an element in the garnishing of a mind already prepared for it by academic and aesthetic studies was the absorption of the romantic part of French literature. Andrew Lang in this, as in everything else, was selective. He dipped into the wonderful lucky-bag of France wherever he saw the glitter of romance. Hence his approach, in the early seventies, was threefold: towards the mediaeval *lais* and *chansons*, towards the sixteenth-century Pléiade, and towards the school of which Victor Hugo was the leader in the nineteenth century. For a long time Ronsard was Lang's poet of intensest predilection; and I think that his definite ambition was to be the Ronsard of modern England, introducing a new poetical dexterity founded on a revival of pure humanism. He had in those days what he lost, or at least dispersed, in the weariness and growing melancholia of later years—a splendid belief in poetry as a part of the renown of England, as a heritage to be received in reverence from our fathers, and to be passed on, if possible, in a brighter flame. This honest and beautiful ambition to shine as one of the permanent benefactors to national verse, in the attitude so nobly sustained four hundred years ago by Du Belly and Ronsard, was unquestionably felt by Andrew Lang through his bright intellectual April, and supported him from Oxford times until 1882, when he published **"Helen of Troy."** The cool reception of that epic by the principal judges of poetry caused him acute disappointment, and from that time forth he became less eager and less serious as a poet, more and more petulantly expending his wonderful technical gift on fugitive subjects. And here again, when one comes to think of it, the whole history repeated itself, since in **"Helen of Troy"** Lang simply suffered as Ronsard had done in the "Franciade." But the fact that 1882 was his year of crisis, and the tomb of his brightest ambition, must be recognised by every one who closely followed his fortunes at that time.

Lang's habit of picking out of literature and of life the plums of romance, and these alone, comes to be, to the dazzled observer of his extraordinarily vivid intellectual career, the principal guiding line. This determination to dwell, to the exclusion of all other sides of any question, on its romantic side is alone enough to rebut the charge of versatility. Lang was in a sense encyclopaedic; but the vast dictionary of his knowledge had blank pages, or pages pasted down, on which he would not, or could not, read what experience had printed. Absurd as it sounds, there was always something maidenly about his mind, and he glossed over ugly matters, sordid and dull conditions, so that they made no impression whatever upon him. He had a trick, which often exasperated his acquaintances, of declaring that he had "never heard" of things that everybody else was very well aware of. He had "never heard the name" of people he disliked, of books that he thought tiresome, of events that bored him; but, more than this, he used the formula for things and persons whom he did not wish to discuss. (pp. 202-05)

It must not be forgotten that we have lived to see him, always wonderful indeed, and always passionately devoted to perfection and purity, but worn, tired, harassed by the unceasing struggle, the life-long slinging of sentences from that inexhaustible ink-pot. In one of the most perfect of his poems,

"Natural Theology," Lang speaks of Cagn, the great hunter, who once was kind and good, but who was spoiled by fighting many things. Lang was never "spoiled," but he was injured; the surface of the radiant coin was rubbed by the vast and interminable handling of journalism. He was jaded by the toil of writing many things. Hence it is not possible but that those who knew him intimately in his later youth and early middle-age should prefer to look back at those years when he was the freshest, the most exhilarating figure in living literature, when a star seemed to dance upon the crest of his already silvering hair. . . . As long as he had confidence in beauty he was safe and strong; and much that, with all affection and all respect, we must admit was rasping and disappointing in his attituide to literature in his later years, seems to have been due to a decreasing sense of confidence in the intellectual sources of beauty. It is dangerous, in the end it must be fatal, to sustain the entire structure of life and thought on the illusions of romance. But that was what Lang did—he built his house upon the rainbow. (pp. 205-06)

If, as seems possible, it is as an essayist that he will ultimately take his place in English literature, this element will continue to delight fresh generations of enchanted readers. I cannot imagine that the preface to his translation of "Theocritus," **"Letters to Dead Authors," "In the Wrong Paradise," "Old Friends,"** and **"Essays in Little"** will ever lose their charm; but future admirers will have to pick their way to them through a tangle of history and anthropology and mythology, where there may be left no perfume and no sweetness. I am impatient to see this vast mass of writing reduced to the limits of its author's delicate, true, but somewhat evasive and ephemeral genius. However, as far as the circumstances of his temperament permitted, Andrew Lang has left with us the memory of one of our most surprising contemporaries, a man of letters who laboured without cesation from boyhood to the grave, who pursued his ideal with indomitable activity and perseverance, and who was never betrayed except by the loftiness of his own endeavour. Lang's only misfortune was not to be completely in contact with life, and his work will survive exactly where he was most faithful to his innermost illusions. (pp. 210-11)

Edmund Gosse, "Andrew Lang," in his Portraits and Sketches, *Charles Scribner's Sons, 1912, pp. 199-211.*

G. K. CHESTERTON (essay date 1912)

[*Regarded as one of England's premier men of letters during the first half of the twentieth century, Chesterton is best known today as a colorful bon vivant, a witty essayist, and the creator of the Father Brown mysteries and the fantasy* The Man Who Was Thursday. *Much of Chesterton's work reveals his childlike joie de vivre and reflects his pronounced Anglican and, later, Roman Catholic beliefs. His essays are characterized by their humor, frequent use of paradox, and chatty, rambling structure. In the following excerpt from an article written shortly after Lang's death, Chesterton praises his former colleague's eclecticism in the field of letters and defends him against critical attacks, which Chesterton attributes to a general mistrust of versatility in an era of specialists, and to the inability of many critics to appreciate Lang's humor.*]

Ours is an epoch of solemn and insane trifling: such atmospheres generally underrate the cheerful and well-balanced trifler—especially when he isn't really a trifler. Andrew Lang suffered from three great disadvantages in the disputes of today: he was universal, he was amusing, and he was lucid. For the first point, the universality, it certainly confused the minds of his critics and gave them an impression of being played with. That a man should write about Homer and blue crockery, about cricket and Joan of Arc, about spirit-rapping and the Stuarts, about folk-lore and about fishing, this was distracting to anyone anxious to define his achievement as one "places" an ordinary authority on Greek or golf; especially as he did not touch these things as we all do, as mere topics of conversation, but always at least with some little accumulation of special information or training. Such men were understood in the Elizabethan age. There is now not enough concern about the universe as a whole to permit people to see the connection. . . . For a man really living, the hardest task of life is not to be interested in everything in it. Nor is the judgment really impaired by such errant investigations; not, at least, so much as it is by the blinking concentration of specialists. A man may find many things in Papuan mythology that may prevent his going mad about Scotch history. It is in the small subjects that a man loses himself; not in the large ones.

The second qualification (or disqualification)—that is, being amusing—connects itself with the third, which is lucidity. There are many portentous and pretentious experts to-day in whom the only proof of wisdom is the absence of wit. . . . Certain material things cannot bear being handled heavily or roughly. But of weak intellectual things it is truer to say that they will not bear being handled lightly. The old proverbs always use the most low and farcical images, merely because they are the frankest and the most clear. . . . Browning, great as he really was, owes something to the reluctance of his readers to admit that they have taken so much trouble for nothing. Carlyle, great as he really is, owes something to his smoke as well as his flame. In comparison with such burning obscurities, the light Greek candour of such critics as Lang lends itself to the charge of mere levity. But the charge is quite false. Andrew Lang, like Carlyle, was a Scotchman. Like Carlyle, he was a controversial, an obstinate, and often an aggravating Scotchman. Like Carlyle, he had strong convictions; so strong that it was not difficult to call them prejudices. But, like Carlyle, he applied all his central and important convictions to central and important subjects; the questions on which his controversies turned were in almost all cases questions of enormous modern importance. They were concerned with real European instincts and traditions which were really in danger in his day. And if he seemed to deal with them humorously, that was because of all those instincts, humour is in the greatest danger of all.

There were at least three points on which he was consistent and controversial; and they were very important points. First, to take the thing nearest to his type and temper, he represented a fact very important and not sufficiently noticed—the revival of the romance of Scotland. In substance this meant the denial that Scotland consisted of grocers going to the kirk; and the readiness to admit, in preference, that it consisted of rebels going to the gallows, or warlocks going to the devil. In form it generally meant, from Walter Scott to Stevenson, some revival of the Jacobite legend. . . . But Andrew Lang carried his Jacobitism beyond mere emotions of regret and reaction. He carried it into concrete history, and expounded all the three centuries after the Reformation so as to maintain that the party of the kirk had been a curse to Scotland, and the party of the Stuarts comparatively quite a blessing. He had no difficulty in proving that most of the Reformers of the Scotch, as of the English, Reformation were either too dull or a very great deal too sharp—that has long been admitted by historians of all religious sympathies. What he insisted on successfully was not that the best Scotchmen were against Calvinism, but that the

most Scotch Scotchmen were against it. Scotch Calvinism was really English Calvinism, which among the fickle English passed like a fashion, but which among the fanatical Scots remained like a disease. The old Calvinist creed is now only taught at Thrums; but it was drawn up at Westminster.

The two other things Lang attacked, and attacked rightly, were the German craze for tearing up Homer and such great unities into texts and passages; and the distant and frigid study of savage beliefs. In the first case he found what many another man has found—that in dealing with the modern Northern professor he was only dealing with a boastful barbarian. In the second case he really kept real agnosticism alive. His open and accessible temper in dealing with tales of gods or spirits was all the more valuable because he never himself seems to have reached any final belief. If he could not believe in gods, he would at least believe in men: and this concession revolutionised anthropology.

> G. K. Chesterton, "Our Notebook," in The Illustrated London News, Vol. CXLI, No. 3823, July 27, 1912, p. 130.

HENRY JAMES (essay date 1912)

[*James is an American novelist whose fiction is valued for its psychological acuity and its author's complex sense of artistic form. Throughout his career, James also wrote literary criticism in which he developed his artistic ideals and applied them to the works of others. Among the numerous conceptualizations he formed to clarify the nature of fiction, he defined the novel as "a direct impression of life." The quality of this impression—the degree of moral and intellectual development—and the author's ability to communicate this impression in an effective and artistic manner were the two principal criteria by which James estimated the worth of a literary work. James admired the self-consciously formalistic methods of contemporary French writers, particularly Gustave Flaubert, whose approach contrasted with the loose, less formulated standards of English novelists. On the other hand, he favored the moral concerns of English writing over the often amoral and cynical vision that characterized much of French literature in the second half of the nineteenth century. His literary aim was to combine the qualities of each country's literature that most appealed to his temperament. After considering various fictional strategies, James arrived at what he thought the most desirable form for the novel to take. Basically objective in presentation—that is, without the intrusion of an authorial voice—the novel should be a well-integrated formal scheme of dialogue, description, and narrative action, all of which should be received from the viewpoint of a single consciousness, or "receptor." In James's novels this receptor is usually a principal character who is more an observer than a participant in the plot. Equal in importance to the artistic plan of a novel is the type of receptor a novelist chooses to use. The type demanded by James's theory possesses a consciousness that will convey a high moral vision, a humanistic worldview, and a generally uplifting sense of life. James's criteria were accepted as standards by a generation of novelists that included Ford Madox Ford, Joseph Conrad, and Virginia Woolf. In the following excerpt from a letter to Edmund Gosse, James comments on Gosse's study of Lang in his Portraits and Sketches (1912). He acknowledges the difficulties of accurately appraising the talent of a writer of such diverse interests as Lang, but posits that Lang's works are marred by their uneven quality, indicative of the "mixture of endowments and vacant holes" in his ability.*]

My dear Gosse,

I received longer ago than I quite like to give you chapter and verse for your so-vividly interesting volume of literary "Portraits".... (p. 274)

I won't deny to you that it was to your 'Andrew Lang' I turned most immediately and with most suspense—and with most of an effect of drawing a long breath when it was over. It is very prettily and artfully brought off—but you would of course have invited me to feel with you how little you felt you were doing it as we should, so to speak, have "really liked." Of course there were the difficulties, and of course you had to defer in a manner to some of them; but your paper is of value just in proportion as you more or less overrode them. His recent extinction, the facts of long acquaintance and camaraderie, let alone the wonder of several of his gifts and the mass of his achievement, couldn't, and still can't, in his case, not be complicating, clogging and qualifying circumstances; but what a pity, with them all, that a figure so lending itself to a certain amount of interesting *real* truth-telling, should, honestly speaking, enjoy such impunity, as regards some of its idiosyncrasies, should get off so scot-free ("Scot"-free is exactly the word!) on all the ground of its greatest hollowness, so much of its most "successful" puerility and perversity. Where I can't but feel that he *should* be brought to justice is in the matter of his whole "give-away" of the value of the wonderful chances he so continually enjoyed (enjoyed thanks to certain of his very gifts, I admit!)—give-away, I mean, by his *cultivation*, absolutely, of the puerile imagination and the fourth-rate opinion, the coming round to that of the old apple-woman at the corner as after all the good and the right as to any of the mysteries of mind or of art. His mixture of endowments and vacant holes, and "the making of the part" of each, would by themselves be matter for a really edifying critical study—for which, however, I quite recognise that the day and the occasion have already hurried heedlessly away. And I perhaps throw a disproportionate weight on the whole question—merely by reason of a late accident or two; such as my having recently read his (in two or three respects so able) Joan of Arc, or **"Maid of France,"** and turned over his just-published (I think posthumous) compendium of **"English Literature,"** which lies on my table downstairs. The extraordinary inexpensiveness and childishness and impertinence of this latter gave to my sense the measure of a whole side of Lang, and yet which was one of the sides of his greatest flourishing. His extraordinary *voulu* Scotch provincialism crowns it and rounds it off really making one at moments ask with what kind of an innermost intelligence such inanities and follies were compatible. The Joan of Arc is another matter, of course; but even there, with all the accomplishment, all the possession of detail, the sense of reality, the vision of the truths and processes of life, the light of experience and the finer sense of history, seem to me so wanting, that in spite of the thing's being written so intensely *at* Anatole France, and in spite of some of A. F.'s own (and so different!) perversities, one "kind of" feels and believes Andrew again and again bristlingly yet *bêtement* wrong, and Anatole sinuously, yet oh so wisely, right! (pp. 275-77)

> *Henry James, in a letter to Edmund Gosse on November 19, 1912, in his* The Letters of Henry James, *Vol. II, edited by Percy Lubbock, Charles Scribner's Sons, 1920, pp. 274-78.*

AFFABLE HAWK [PSEUDONYM OF DESMOND MacCARTHY] (essay date 1923)

[*MacCarthy was one of the foremost English literary and drama critics of the twentieth century. He served for many years on the staff of the* New Statesman *and edited* Life and Letters. *Among his many essay collections,* The Court Theatre 1904-1907: A Commentary and a Criticism (1907), *which is a detailed account of a season when the Court Theatre was dominated by Harley Granville-Barker and Bernard Shaw, is especially valued. According to other critics, MacCarthy brought to his work a wide range of reading, serious and sensitive judgment, an interest in the works of new writers, and high critical standards. In the following excerpt from a review of* Poetical Works, *MacCarthy attributes Lang's position as a minor poet to a lack of passion and curiosity which led Lang to reject the modern and to dwell upon classical forms.*]

"My mind is gay but my soul is melancholy." So Andrew Lang once said of himself; and it is the union—or the clashing—of the gaiety and the melancholy, his wife adds, that gave him his personality. He objected, for some reason, to being called "versatile"; indeed, it is a tiresome label, though one which could hardly fail to be attached to him. What was, however, even more remarkable than his versatility was his unfailing grace. Grace is not perhaps a quality for which poets long most to be praised. But if it is the least pretentious, it is not the least delightful quality which verse can possess. He was, of course, a master of social verse. "Do you suppose it is as easy to write a song as to write an epic?" said Béranger to Lucius Bonaparte. "Nor would it be as easy for a most magnanimous mouse of a Calibanic poeticule," in the opinion of Swinburne, "to write a ballad, a roundel, or a virelai, after the noble fashion of Chaucer, as to gabble at any length like a thing most brutish in the blank and blatant jargon of epic or idyllic stultiloquence." There is not much resemblance between Chaucer and Andrew Lang; but the latter does link on to the old French forms on the one hand and to the gay, tuneful, engaging wits of Queen Anne on the other. He has ingenuity, pathos and a playful pedantry. He is adept at both jibes and compliments, and he can modulate exquisitely into grave sentiment. How foolish then—and boorish, to despise this gentle verse....

I think it true of Andrew Lang that he was, as a poet, limited by being so exquisite a literary scholar. He only felt free in the humbler exercise of sentiment and wit. When he wrote poetry in the more serious sense, he could not bring himself to write verse which was not, in effect, an indirect homage to the old masters of simplicity and finality whom he loved—to the Classics, to Ronsard. His aesthetic sense was submissive. He had little curiosity, little passion. He only dared believe in beauty which had been expressed before; and admiring what was grand, simple and aloof in style , and only sedately ornate or obviously musical, he preferred himself to risk being insipid, rather than to strive after self-expression or effect. With a haughtiness and modesty sympathetic to me, he confined the expression of himself to the wistful or the whimsical mood. **Helen of Troy,** his longest poem, runs on with lucid ease through six books. It is like an unending strip of tapestry, with only here and there a stanza that, even gently, arrests one.... Here he achieves that graceful sobriety he loved in the Classics; though not their gravity, but a more tremulous tenderness inspires the verse.

We do not wonder at his love of Gérard de Nerval when we have read [his **Poetical Works**]. Andrew Lang, too, was a poet-platonist of the frailer, feminine sort, who loved regrets and lips that never could be kissed; one homesick for he knew not what, though thinking often that he found it in "Romance." From far below that longing for Romance which he defended all his life with such witty acrimony there bubbles up, now and again, a loyalty to something which, had he yielded to it utterly, would have swept him far past singing delightful songs about cricket, fishing and Bonnie Prince Charlie. . . . Andrew Lang was so many things that we are in danger of forgetting that he was also a true, though a little, poet.

Affable Hawk [pseudonym of Desmond MacCarthy], in a review of "Poetical Works," in New Statesman, *Vol. XXL, No. 540, August 18, 1923, p. 547.*

BERNARD SHAW   (essay date 1924)

[*Shaw is generally considered the greatest and best-known dramatist to write in the English language since Shakespeare. Following the example of Henrik Ibsen, he succeeded in revolutionizing the English stage, disposing of the romantic conventions and devices of the "well-made play," and instituting the theater of ideas, grounded in realism. During the late nineteenth century, Shaw was also a prominent literary, art, and music critic. In 1895 he became the drama critic for* The Saturday Review, *and his reviews therein became known for their biting wit and brilliance. During his three years at* The Saturday Reveiw, *Shaw determined that the theater was meant to be a "moral institution" and an "elucidator of social conduct." The standards he applied to drama were quite simple: "Is the play like real life? Does it convey sensible, socially progressive ideas?" Because most of the drama produced during the 1890s failed to approach these ideals, Shaw usually assumed a severely critical and satirical attitude toward his subjects. Although he later wrote criticism of poetry and fiction—much of it collected in* Pen Portraits and Reviews *(1932)—Shaw was out of sympathy with both of these genres. He had little use for poetry, believing it poorly suited for the expression of ideas, and in his criticism of fiction he rarely got beyond the search for ideology. As Samuel Hynes has noted, Shaw was driven by a rage to better the world. A Fabian socialist, he wrote criticism that is often concerned with the humanitarian and political intent of the work under discussion. In the following excerpt from the preface to his* Saint Joan: A Chronicle Play in Six Scenes and an Epilogue, *Shaw compares Lang's treatment of Joan of Arc in* The Maid of France *to that of Mark Twain, which Shaw regards as "downright worship." Shaw notes that Lang's work, a reply to Anatole France's characterization of Joan as the dupe of the military and clerics, has a romantic bent that misinterprets the fundamental role of the Catholic faith in the development of European civilization.*]

Typical products of [the interest in Joan of Arc] in America and England are the histories of Joan by Mark Twain and Andrew Lang. Mark Twain was converted to downright worship of Joan directly by Quicherat. Later on, another man of Genius, Anatole France, reacted against the Quicheratic wave of enthusiasm, and wrote a Life of Joan in which he attributed Joan's ideas to clerical prompting and her military success to an adroit use of her by Dunois as a *mascotte;* in short, he denied that she had any serious military or political ability. At this Andrew saw red, and went for Anatole's scalp in a rival Life of her [*The Maid of France*] which should be read as a corrective to the other. Lang had no difficulty in shewing that Joan's ability was not an unnatural fiction to be explained away as an illusion manufactured by priests and soldiers, but a straightforward fact.

It has been lightly pleaded in explanation that Anatole France is a Parisian of the art world, into whose scheme of things the able, hardheaded, hardhanded female, though she dominates provincial France and business Paris, does not enter; whereas Lang was a Scot, and every Scot knows that the grey mare is as likely as not to be the better horse. But this explanation does not convince me. I cannot believe that Anatole France does

not know what everybody knows. I wish everybody knew all that he knows. One feels antipathies at work in his book. He is not anti-Joan; but he is anti-clerical, anti-mystic, and fundamentally unable to believe that there ever was any such person as the real Joan. (pp. xxxviii-xxxix)

Andrew Lang and Mark Twain are equally determined to make Joan a beautiful and most ladylike Victorian; but both of them recognize and insist on her capacity for leadership, though the Scots scholar is less romantic about it than the Mississippi pilot. But then Lang was, by lifelong professional habit, a critic of biographies rather than a biographer, whereas Mark Twain writes his biography frankly in the form of a romance. (p. xl)

Andrew Lang was better read; but, like Walter Scott, he enjoyed medieval history as a string of border romances rather than as the record of a high European civilization based on a catholic faith. Both of them were baptized as Protestants, and impressed by all their schooling and most of their reading with the belief that Catholic bishops who burnt heretics were persecutors capable of any villainy; that all heretics were Albigensians or Husites or Jews or Protestants of the highest character; and that the Inquisition was a Chamber of Horrors invented expressly and exclusively for such burnings. Accordingly we find them representing Peter Cauchon, Bishop of Beauvais, the judge who sent Joan to the stake, as an unconscionable scoundrel, and all the questions put to her as "traps" to ensnare and destroy her. And they assume unhesitatingly that the two or three score of canons and doctors of law and divinity who sat with Cauchon as assessors, were exact reproductions of him on slightly less elevated chairs and with a different headdress. (pp. xli-xlii)

Mark and Andrew would have shared her innocence and her fate had they been dealt with by the Inquisition: that is why their accounts of the trial are as absurd as hers might have been could she have written one. (p. xlvii)

Bernard Shaw, in a preface to his Saint Joan: A Chronicle Play in Six Scenes and an Epilogue, *1924. Reprint by Brentano's, 1926, pp. v-lxxxiv.**

GEORGE SAINTSBURY   (essay date 1929)

[*Saintsbury has been called the most influential English literary historian and critic of the late nineteenth and early twentieth centuries. His studies of French literature, particularly his* History of the French Novel *(1917-19), have established him as a leading authority on such writers as Guy de Maupassant and Honoré de Balzac. Saintsbury adhered to two distinct sets of critical standards: one for the novel and the other for poetry and drama. As a critic of novels, he maintained that "the novel has nothing to do with any beliefs, with any convictions, with any thoughts in the strict sense, except as mere garnishings. Its substance must always be life not thought, conduct not belief, the passions not the intellect, manners and morals not creeds and theories. . . . The novel is . . . mainly and firstly a criticism of life." As a critic of poetry and drama, Saintsbury was a radical formalist who frequently asserted that subject is of little importance and that "the so-called 'formal' part is of the essence." René Wellek has praised Saintsbury's critical qualities: his "enormous reading, the almost universal scope of his subject matter, the zest and zeal of his exposition" and "the audacity with which he handles the most ambitious and unattempted arguments." In the following excerpt, Saintsbury, Lang's friend and colleague, praises Lang's journalistic skill.*]

[No] editor who had the very slightest fitness for his business could hesitate about annexing anything of Lang's that was offered to him and promptly demanding more. I have had myself no short or small experience of editing or assisting to edit; a very large experience in contributing; and, until quite recently, what it is not, I think, extravagant to call an immense experience in reading this division of literature. I do not hesitate to say that, allowing for his not taking service in the political, the religious and some technical departments, Lang was quite the king of all the contributors to 'the papers' that I have known. His vessel did not carry—thanks to the limitations just mentioned it did not require—such heavy metal as H. D. Traill's; I fancy that it may itself have been of slightly too heavy a draught in respect of knowledge on the part of the reader to be able to skim the waves of universal popularity as did, especially latterly, the craft of our common friend Sir Edmund Gosse. But for a compound of scholarship and lighthandedness, of multilegence and complete freedom from pedantry, of what may be called literary good manners, infinite wit and a peculiar humour he had, I think, in his own generation no equal—certainly no superior. (pp. 83-4)

You could not, after you had seen a little of his writing, mistake it for any one else's or any one else's for his. Nor did this individuality depend upon any tricks of style in the lower sense like the snipsnap of Macaulay; the chaotic riches of Carlyle; the repetitions and word-groupings of Arnold; the infused blank verse (in their so different kinds) of Ruskin and Dickens; the elaborate rhythm and colouring of Pater. It was most commonly said to be like Thackeray's, and no doubt there was a strong resemblance of spirit; but I really doubt whether the greatest similarity between their manners was not the fact that neither had *any* manner easy to analyse or capable of being pinned out and down. Only great incompetence or great prejudice—for choice perhaps a skilful combination of the two—could fail to recognise this idiosyncrasy. . . . [Lang] copied nobody and . . . nobody had ever succeeded in copying him. I have indeed been told that some wicked men in clubs have ticketed others as 'Sham Langs,' but the resemblance was merely caricatural in personal ways and simply non-existent in literary form. (pp. 84-5)

[The] quality of his literariness itself was, if not as unique as his delivery of it, very unusual. It was pervasive but not obtrusive; varied but not superficial; facile to a wonderful degree, but never trivial or trumpery. It may be that in one way it did not concentrate itself enough—did not leave two or three big books instead of thirty or forty little ones; and in another concentrated itself too much by writing not very small books on subjects which might have been adequately treated in not very long essays. So also in his behaviour there may sometimes have been a little too much abstraction, and too much indifference to the existence of those agreeable folk who always put the worst construction on everything. . . . Meanwhile if Lang is (more's the pity!) gone, and some of his work gone with him or recoverable only with infinite labour and pains, there is a great body of it accessible, and the old 'Take it and Read it' may be said with unusual confidence to anybody hesitating about the matter. 'Selections', of course, suggest themselves and have been suggested. It is possible to conceive not merely one but more than one which would supply reading of the most refreshing kind. But it would be an extraordinarily difficult job; and while selections often fail to satisfy their readers, this selection would be so unlikely to satisfy the selector that he would probably never get it finished. So the *Tolle, lege,* had better be completed with the most elegant

Latin available for whatever of Lang's you come across. It is ten to one you will not go wrong. (pp. 95-6)

George Saintsbury, "Andrew Lang in the 'Seventies—And After," in The Eighteen-Seventies: Essays by Fellows of the Royal Society of Literature, *edited by Harley Granville-Barker, The Macmillan Company, 1929, pp. 81-96.*

MALCOLM ELWIN (essay date 1939)

[*Elwin was an English author, critic, and editor who specialized in nineteenth-century literature. In the following excerpt from his* Old Gods Falling, *Elwin discusses Lang's influence as a literary critic and the underlying reasons for his popular appeal among "highbrows" as well as the masses.*]

Lang occupied an unique position in the literary world of his day, wielding a dominant influence beyond that of any individual critic before or since. Relating how an obscure shilling book on dining-out in London was made popular into a big success by a notice of Lang's in the *Daily News,* Mr. Grant Richards remarked in his *Memories of a Misspent Youth* that, excepting Arnold Bennett's *Evening Standard* articles in the last years of his life, "no man alive, no newspaper, has all that power." Lang contributed largely to the making of Stevenson's reputation; he contributed equally to the making of Rider Haggard's; he started the sensational success of Anthony Hope's *Prisoner of Zenda,* the vogue of Stanley Weyman, and the selling of S. R. Crockett's novels. The secret of his power is far to seek in the constitution of a curious individuality. He commanded the respect of all classes by the profundity of his scholarship, the extent and variety of his reading; the barbs of his wit and sarcasm opponents were chary of challenging; he possessed an easy grace of style which won the envy of highbrows, and charmed the masses by its unprententiousness, its familiarity, its lack of conscious superiority and condescension; he was not himself a popular writer, but he was a voluminous author in so many fields, with no much distinction, that he created the impression that he might do anything if he chose, and was therefore admirably qualified to assess the achievements of others. (p. 183)

His facility was equalled only by his versatility; to him alone of his generation descended from the famous Scotch reviewers—from Jeffrey, Lockhart, Maginn, and Christopher North—the faculty of writing knowledgeably on anything. On only two subjects he never touched in journalism—politics and religion. In his boyhood reading of Macaulay's *Lays of Ancient Rome,* his sympathies were with the exiled kings, and finding beside the slaying of Valerius by the youngest Tarquin the boyish marginal note, "Well done, the Jacobites," he remarked long afterwards, "Perhaps my politics have never gone much beyond this sentiment." (p.188)

[Contempt] for illusion characterised Lang's attitude, not only to politics, but to religion and the whole business of life. His studies in folk-lore and comparative mythology—which found expression in his books on [*Custom and Myth; Myth, Ritual, and Religion;* and *The Making of Religion*] . . . , and which Edward Clodd considered his work of most abiding value—taught him that all the religions of the world have a common origin in the practical needs of human ignorance, each religion having been formulated by an imaginative leader, whether Mohammed, Christ, or Buddha, as a code for the regulation of a community's conduct—to supply, in fact, general principles of guidance for the vast majority in every community lacking the intelligence and imagination to evolve an independent philosophy. To Lang, as to any other intelligent student of history, the petty bigotry and squabbles of religious faction presented the futility, without the dignity, of political idealism. When Papal authority caused his **Myth, Ritual, and Religion** to be listed on the *Index Expurgatorius,* he requested an episcopal explanation, which was naturally not forthcoming, since bishops are educated only for the pulpit of declamation and not for the arena of logical debate; when the biologist St. George Mivart was excommunicated by Cardinal Vaughan, Lang was moved to irreverent levity; he supported Rider Haggard's opinion that the Christian missionaries ruined the Zulu race, by converting to monogamy a people whose high standards of morality depended upon the more natural condition of polygamy. He was a sceptic, conscious of the agnosticism which is the logical realisation of the intelligent scholar.

Meredith said of Lang that he "had no heart, otherwise he might have been a good poet." This Clodd, who knew him better than Meredith, denied, citing the verses in memory of his sister-in-law in **Rhymes à la Mode** as evidence of Lang's depth of feeling. But Meredith was right in thinking that Lang lacked the passion to write inspired poetry. Passion flourishes only in the soil of unreason; it cannot flower without illusion. Lang had the cynical serenity of wide and varied knowledge; he was too acutely conscious of his own littleness, and the littleness of the contemporary world by comparison with the colossal scheme of eternity, to excite himself with idealist emotions. The "superciliousness" of manner, detected by the writer of his obituary notice in the *Times,* was the impression upon the undiscerning of this serenity, giving a sense of aloofness, and the sardonic humour with which he habitually looked on life. He despised the age in which he lived, with its humbug and hypocrisy, its graft, and its unnatural respectability, but he did not seek to alter it, like the reformers, nor score off its deficiencies, like George Moore—he merely accepted it for what it was, the age in which he was born to live his life. (pp. 189-90)

Perhaps he would have preferred to live in the days of Bolingbroke and Congreve; at least he preferred to read about the best and brightest of the eighteenth century in Dumas and Stanley Weyman, rather than the worst and saddest of his own day in Hardy and Gissing. The clear critical discernment of his culture fairly measured the artistic achievement of Hardy and Gissing, but he felt discomfort at the reproach of their preoccupation with life's sordidness. Why should art be wasted on ugliness, with so much beauty in the world? And what was artistic achievement anyhow if more pleasure was procurable from a plain-spun yarn of improbable adventure in lands remote from Fleet Street? "More claymores, less psychology, suit a simple taste," he wrote of *Catriona,* which may be taken as his slogan as a critic, and earned him the execration of serious novelists. "Lang," wrote Henry James to Stevenson, "in the D.N. *(Daily News)* every morning, and I believe in a hundred other places, uses his beautiful thin facility to write everything down to the lowest level of Philistine twaddle—the view of the old lady round the corner or the clever person at the dinner party."

James's accusation was hardly exaggerated, even to the "hundred other places." . . . [Lang] shamelessly used the cloak of anonymity to reiterate the same view of the same book in half-a-dozen different papers. . . . Another still prevalent abuse, that of the reader-critic, was shamelessly practised by Lang; he was literary adviser to Longmans, and rarely failed to boost a Longmans book as a reviewer. (pp. 190-91)

His tendency to write what he disliked "down to the lowest level of Philistine twaddle" sprang from a cultivated practice in his critical art; he was a master of ridicule. His guying of Tolstoy's *Kreutzer Sonata* is a masterpiece of destructive satire. He found the book in Sutherland Edwards's translation "very much like other shilling novels, not only in price, but in absence of humour," but mockingly reproached admiring critics who supposed that Tolstoy himself "held the ideas of his murderous hero, Pozdnisheff, about love, marriage, and those fair beings whom Guy Heavistone dismissed as 'poor little beasts.'" (p. 191)

Not till Frank Harris engaged Bernard Shaw on the *Saturday Review,* was there another critic who ventured on such impudent *badinerie,* much less one of the skill and prestige to get away with it. (p. 192)

Lang liked to be entertained, and probably the only dolorous contemporary novels he ever praised were George Douglas's *House With Green Shutters* and W. E. Tirebuck's *Dorrie.* He describes Gissing as a realist—that is, "one of the 'idealists' who select and present the more disagreeable facts of life"— and frequently disparaged "that woebegone work *The Story of an African Farm,* a farm on which people were always tackling religious problems, or falling in love on new and heterodox lines, instead of shooting deer, and finding diamonds, or hunting up the archaeological remains of the Transvaal." He deplored the tendency of the modern novelist to "gummidge", and when highbrow critics mocked "modern novels of hard blows as a recrudescence of barbarism," he retorted that polyandry was likewise "a recrudescence of savagery in its worst and least human form," and though "nothing could be much more disagreeable, in practice, than either antique diversion," he preferred "to read about fighting rather than about free love."

He never flinched before attack, and deprecating violence in criticism, held an enormous advantage over his adversaries, apart from his armoury of wit and the superior scope of his reading, in never allowing his urbanity to be ruffled. When Hardy inserted a preface to the fifth edition of *Tess of the D'Urbervilles,* taunting Lang with "gentility" for objecting to the novel's offences against respectability, he replied with a marshalled array of his objections to *Tess,* supporting them with the strictures on *Two on a Tower,* which he found equally "forbidding in conception," and concluded by coolly intimating that he did not intend "to speak again about any work of Mr. Hardy's." He likewise avoided reviewing the novels of Henry James and W. D. Howells, but he kept up continual warfare with Howells in his critical capacity as literary commentator of *Harper's Magazine.* (pp.192-93)

It was unjust to accuse Lang, as Gosse and Saintsbury could be fairly accused, of praising only that which had stood the test of time, for no reviewer of his day read more contemporary fiction. Apart from being among the first to recognise Stevenson, Kipling, Bridges, and Barrie, he virtually made the reputations of Rider Haggard, Stanley Weyman, and S. R. Crockett, and *The House With the Green Shutters* and Anthony Hope's *Mr. Witt's Widow* were not the only novels by little-known writers to which he drew timely attention—he praised *Love and Mr. Lewisham,* though he had not liked "Mr. Wells's apocalyptic and extranatural romances about Mars and the future." . . . (pp. 194-95)

None can deny that Lang was instinctively conservative in taste, or that he obstinately insisted on limiting the scope of the novelist's function. When the *Athenaeum* for 30th July,

1892, complained that English literature was "gagged", and novelists "must work under painfully soul-killing restrictions," Lang argued that "a novel is not a treatise," and if "an author is a Malthusian, or a Free Lover, or has a just and natural desire to reform the world," he should state his theories "simply, directly, with all authorities and evidence," and "they ought not to be mixed up with flirtations, love affairs, and fanciful episodes."

> *Nana*, for example, may contain what we should know, and circumstances which we should endeavour to rectify. But a reform of morals would not be aided by letting *Nana* circulate among the readers of Miss Yonge.

Why the principles of Malthus, the practice of promiscuity, or the career of a prostitute should not enter the province of the novelist as freely as the animal fashion of Victorian procreation, the vicissitudes of matrimony, or the misdeeds of thieves and murderers, Lang never deigned to explain. Nor did he apparently recognise that the reformer reached a wider public with a novel than a treatise, and that Dickens with *Oliver Twist* and Reade with *Hard Cash* achieved more towards the correction of abuses respectively in workhouses and lunatic asylums than many treatises and commissioners' reports. And his trite remarks about *Nana* echo the hackneyed argument of the intellectual ostrich, indicted by Reade as the "prurient prude", who has flourished in every age from Jeremy Collier to the censors of *Ulysses*, *Lady Chatterley's Lover*, and *The Well of Loneliness*, though he was doubtless right in thinking that the reactions of Miss Yonge's readers to *Nana* would be unproductive of moral amelioration, even if the conclusion reflects unfortunately upon the achievements of education in an enlightened democracy.

Lang allowed his personal preference for romance and tales of adventure to force him into a position of prejudice so unjustifiable that he merited the disgust expressed by Henry James, and shared by most serious students of the novel's artistic development. He declined to review Olive Schreiner's *Trooper Peter Halket* "because you cannot argue fairly on a political topic in a romance," and though he was interested in Israel Zangwill's *Children of the Ghetto* as a study of the "polyglot cosmopolitan modern Israelite," finding the book "more full of words needing a glossary than the early Anglo-Indian tales of Mr. Kipling," he asked "why did he write a treatise when he might have done it so well?" It did not occur to him that many of his admired historical romances argued politics of past ages, and that some of the volumes in the "Standard Edition" of the "recrudescence of barbarism and Jingo reaction," Lang forgot his usual candid argument for pure entertainment, and attempted to attribute its revival to "the revival of historical studies." He admitted that Besant and "the authors of *The Splendid Spur* and *Micah Clarke* . . . would probably have written whether history was being more closely and widely studied or not," but mentioning Stevenson's *Kidnapped* and Haggard's *Cleopatra* as instances where "the history is not 'got up' for the novel, the novel comes out of the knowledge of history." . . . (pp. 195-97)

Though he wished to make novelists only purveyors of entertainment for athletic undergraduates, and refused to allow that contemporary Humbug "gagged" expression, Lang shared no fellow-feeling with the gaitered moralist, who advertised having put *Jude the Obscure* on the fire with the tongs. Though he never missed a chance go gibe at Zola, he felt uncomfortable when Zola was banned. His sense of sportsmanship revolted

from the mediaeval bigotry of forcibly silencing a man because he did not agree with the majority, and his intellectual independence resented authority's dictation about what was good for him. So, while repeating his remarks on the inadvisability of turning Zola loose on Miss Yonge's readers, he approved the morality of Zola's intentions, and asserted that "grown-up readers are much more likely to be disgusted than to be depraved" by Zola. And, with a burst of spleen against Humbug, he added sarcastically, "when one considered what is published daily by the press, there seems a want of complete consistency in forbidding the publication of any literary work."

Probably it tickled his taste in irony tht he should earn his living from a source for which he never concealed his contempt. His mockery of Zola, of the Russian novelists, of Howells and the intellectual critics, always rang whimsically flippant and ironic, but his tone assumed the intensity of loathing when he tilted at another favourite butt, the sensationalism of newspapers. He went out of his way to praise Richard Whiteing's *The Island*, a novel outside his usual taste, for the pleasure of quoting its attack on the "cool devilry of mocking headlines, as though all the woe and all the folly of the world were but one stupendous joke." To Lang newspapers reflected the worst vice of contemporary society: "we all sit in the Ear of Dionysius," he wrote, "in the whispering gallery of the world, and hear the reverberations of every mad word and deed, of every sorrow and disgrace."

Though his instincts were unlighted by even the faintest flicker of the reformer's fire, and in literature, as in life, he accepted existing conditions with lazy cynicism, he was unafraid to utter startlingly unconventional comments, which came the more forcibly from one who was not given to explosiveness. When Churton Collins lamented the state of literary decadence in 1901, Lang, though always finding some new book to praise, not only admitted the fact of the decadence, but coolly added the discomforting truth that "our literary decadence is partly the result of education." He rarely attacked a book or scored off an author, because he avoided reviewing books he did not like. He believed an editor should "request his reviewer to leave the bad books alone, except when some Robert Montgomery needs exposure." Usually he only attacked books and authors when he thought they were being generally praised beyond their merits, as when he guyed Tolstoy, or when, everybody in the late 'nineties being ready to acclaim everything by Kipling as the work of inspired genius, he remarked that the heroes of *Stalky and Co.* "are not normal schoolboys," and preferred the characters in Eden Phillpotts's *The Human Boy*. In his experience, "most reviewers are like cat-doctors—they do not know much." He believed that "a critic ought to be able to correct an author where his author is wrong, and to add, if only a little, to the information." But he found that few editors liked a review "full of condensed knowledge" which might be "even harder reading than the book itself"; many preferred that their reviewer should "only give a summary of the book's contents and say whether it interests him, by style and manner, or not," which though "it is not criticism," forms "the not useless function of the 'newsman of the Republic of Letters.'" But too often Lang found that editors lacked the knowledge and conscience to secure even so much as this, and were content to print "the vapid jottings of a weary, uninterested, ignorant hack, who dare not venture on an original remark for fear of 'putting his foot in it.'" (pp. 197-99)

[Lang] was not a great critic; except Stevenson, he did little to assist recognition of any man of outstanding genius—Conrad, Bennett, Galsworthy, Shaw, all failed to impress him, and he disliked Meredith only less than Henry James and Hardy. But he assumed a dominance over public taste by reason of the alliance between obvious limitations and gifts curiously inappropriate in a popular journalist. His power lay in his avowed preference for light literature coming from one of the most accomplished scholars of the day, who was admitted even by his bitterest opponents to be incapable of writing otherwise than with grace and charm. The new middle-classes, eager to acquire a veneer of culture, were delighted to find a pundit whose reputation for scholarship commanded universal reverence, who astonishingly encouraged their improvement with books of entertainment—he appealed alike to their snobbery and inclination. (p. 200)

> Malcolm Elwin, "Andrew Lang and Other Critics," in his Old Gods Falling, *The Macmillan Company, 1939, pp. 182-217.*

ROGER LANCELYN GREEN (essay date 1946)

[*Green, an English poet, novelist, critic, biographer, and editor, is a prolific writer and the author of works on the lives and careers of Andrew Lang, Lewis Carroll, J. M. Barrie, and C. S. Lewis. In the following excerpt from* Andrew Lang: A Critical Biography, *the first book-length biography of Lang, Green discusses Lang's role as the primary revivalist of traditional fairy tales in England, and finds that his selections reflect a concern for the lessons to be learned from human joy and suffering. For further discussion of Lang's work as a collector and editor of fairy tales, see the excerpts by J. R. R. Tolkien (1947) and Roger Sale (1981).*]

Folk-lore and ballad literature were . . . the deepest and most potent influences on Lang as a boy, and their influence was increased and broadened into an intellectual as well as a sentimental interest as he became more and more engrossed in the study of anthropology.

Thus it was as an anthropologist that Lang came first to the serious consideration of fairy stories, and the result was that for long he felt almost a distaste for the more literary tales. "The folklorist is not unnaturally jealous," he wrote, "of what, in some degree, looks like folk-lore. He apprehends that purely literary stories may win their way, pruned of their excrescences, to the fabulous, and may confuse the speculations of later mythologists . . . There was a time when I regarded all *contes*, except *contes populaires*, as frivolous and vexatious."

But even by the time that his first collection of traditional fairy-tales, *The Blue Fairy Book* . . . appeared, Lang had fallen away from his earlier and rather fanatical intolerance, and had already written three literary fairy stories of his own.

The "Fairy Book Series," however, contained little besides traditional tales, although these were adapted and re-written so as to make them suitable for children. It is actually only the first of the series that contains much besides folk-tales—and Lang departs further than he ever does in later volumes from any settled scheme. Thus, besides five stories from Madame d'Aulnoy, one from Madame Le Prince de Beaumont and one adaption from Madame de Villeneuve, there are two from *The Arabian Nights*, and—strangest choice of all—a condensed version of the first part of *Gulliver's Travels* made by May Kendall. How Lang came to allow this last to be included is inexplicable, for it is quite alien to anything in any of the fairy books, which never again depart from the traditional tales fur-

ther than Madame d'Aulnoy, Hans Andersen and "The Three Bears."

But the book was an experiment, and of a kind that must have caused a certain amount of anxiety to Longman, the publisher, even with the great "draw" of Lang's name. For at that time the fairy-tale had almost ceased to be read in British nurseries, and the novel of child life, the stories of Mrs. Ewing, Mrs. Molesworth, and L. T. Meade, were the only fare. Writing early in 1889 in her history of children's books, Mrs. E. M. Field says: "At the present moment the fairy-tale seems to have given way entirely in popularity to the child's story of real life, the novel of childhood, in which no effort is spared to make children appear as they are." But just before the publication of the book early in 1891, she added a note: "Since the above was written eighteen months ago, the tide of popularity seems to have set strongly in the direction of the old fairy stories."

It would probably be no exaggeration to say that Lang was entirely responsible for this change in the public taste; for *The Blue Fairy Book* . . . and *The Red Fairy Book* . . . , were both enormously popular from the very start, and the later volumes in the series were sure always of a wide and appreciative welcome. (pp. 80-2)

[His] own share in any of the fairy books is limited almost exclusively to the Preface—and, of course, the actual selection and choice of the stories included. These are drawn from nearly every race and nation of the ancient or modern world, and are the finest and most enduring monument to Andrew Lang the folklorist.

The tales themselves were retold, translated or adapted mainly by Mrs. Lang, though in the earlier volumes she had the assistance of many people, including May Kendall, Florence Sellar and Sir W. A. Craigie. The *True Story Book* and its

Illustration from "Hansel and Gretel," in The Blue Fairy Book.

sequel boast a greater variety of authors, including Rider Haggard, Florence Sellar and Lang himself, who told the story of Joan of Arc at some length.

Only in the first two fairy books proper does Lang re-tell any of the stories, and there his work is of considerable interest. In *The Blue Fairy Book* he takes the story of Perseus, drawing his material from Pindar, Simonides and Apollodoros, but he recasts it in the form of an ordinary folk-tale by the suppression of all personal and local names; Perseus is simply "The Prince," while even the Herperides appear as "The Western Fairies." . . . (p. 82)

The absence of names is not, of course, essential to the ordinary folk-tale; but in the case of such a story as this, it is only by such a suppression that it can be regarded with any ease as a fairy-tale of the type best exemplified in the Grimm collection, and not merely as a fragment of the grand legendary history of Homeric Greece.

In *The Red Fairy Book* . . . , Lang re-tells "The Story of Sigurd" from Morris's version of the Volsunga saga, and treats it rather as he had done "The Terrible Head," though without suppressing the names. This gives us the impression that Lang considered a northern setting still to be suitable for a fairy-tale, but that the Greek scene, by literary association, was no longer sufficiently simple and wild. (p. 83)

However this may be, Lang's aim is obvious, and in none of the other fairy books does he include any but savage or folk-tales, the *French Cabinet des Fées* and Hans Andersen being the only sophisticated stories admitted. And he does not again attempt to adapt any stories from the "higher mythology" of Greece, Egypt or Scandinavia, though, of course, the northern folk-tales are included.

When, later, he came to re-tell the Greek myths for children, he presented his *Tales of Troy and Greece* . . . in the tradition of Kingsley's *Heroes;* and we feel that it is Lang the classical scholar rather than Lang the folklorist who is telling of "Odysseus the Sacker of Cities" or "The Story of the Golden Fleece." (pp. 83-4)

[It] was out of his profound knowledge of folk-tales and his intimate acquaintance with all the formulae of the traditional stories that Lang drew the inspiration for his own original tales. Only in *The Gold of Fairnilee* does he stay away from what had become the recognized method of writing a modern fairy-tale; but in the Pantouflia stories, and also in the little *Princess Nobody,* he is following in the steps of a respectable literary tradition, taking Thackeray as his most immediate model. (p. 84)

Lang, before he came to write his more serious fairy-stories, and before *The Blue Fairy Book* had made him king undisputed of the nursery shelf, had tossed off, in the midst of his anthropological labours, a little *jeu d'esprit* that is now quite forgotten, *The Princess Nobody, A Tale of Fairyland.* . . . (p. 86)

The story itself is very slight, and consists mainly of a re-grouping of certain elements traditional in many nursery tales and folk-legends, both savage and civilized. (p. 87)

In 1888 Lang turned aside from the high road of the literary fairy story to seek his inspiration for *The Gold of Fairnilee* among the dark shadows of the genuine old fairy beliefs. But a year later he returned to the Fairy Court tradition, and wrote *Prince Prigio,* the first of his *Chronicles of Pantouflia.*

In this series, even more than in *The Princess Nobody,* Lang employs the methods which he assigns to the old folk-tales;

"a certain number of incidents are shaken into many varying combinations, like the fragments of coloured glass in the kaleidoscope." "Nobody can write a *new* fairy-tale; you can only mix up and dress up the old, old stories, and put the characters into new dresses." (pp. 88-9)

It is story-land rather than fairyland in which Lang's tales are set, and in *Prince Prigio* he acknowledges his "several obligations to the Learned," which include Allan Quatermain, Cyrano de Bergerac and M. Paul Sébillot (an anthropologist); while in *Prince Ricardo* his most obvious debts are to Madame d'Aulnoy, Cornelius Agrippa, Ariosto, *The Arabian Nights,* and the history of Scotland.

But the guiding spirit is Thackeray's: King Grognio is own cousin to Valoroso, and Captain McDougal, who "maintained a stern military reserve" when the whole court was in tears, is nearly allied to Captain Kuttazoff Hedzoff. Indeed, Grognio claims descent, in the story, from Cinderella and Prince Giglio—by which means Lang "places" his stories in the history of Märchenland.

In the collected edition (*My Own Fairy Book* . . .) of his fairy tales, Lang groups *Prigio* and *Ricardo* together as *Chronicles of Pantouflia* (under which title they were later reprinted as a separate volume) and he gives, in a Preface, a delightful account of the founding of the royal family of this "central European" kingdom, which was descended, he tells us, from the "Hypnotidoe" of Greece, and whose crest "is a dormouse, dormant, proper, on a field vert, and the motto, when translated out of the original Greek, means *Anything for a Quiet Life.*" (p. 89)

Prince Ricardo is not altogether as successful as *Prince Prigio,* largely on account of its lack of plot, and the episodic nature of its incidents, which occasionally seem a trifle forced and unwieldy—while *Prigio* goes all with a swing and an inevitability that is irresistible.

The adventure with Prince Charlie bears no relation to the plot of the book, and is so alien as to seem a disfigurement, nor is the Giant quite as satisfactory a monster as either Fire-drake in *Prigio,* or even the Yellow Dwarf in *Ricardo.* This is the more to be regretted, as there are scenes in the book of exquisite humour, and touches also of poetic feeling that is absent from *Prigio.* The adventure on the Moon is one of these scenes, and the chapter describing how Princess Jacqueline "Drank the Moon" to learn King Prigio's secret is an even more charming example, and contains a very attractive magic spell. . . . *Prince Ricardo* differs from its predecessor in being assigned to a definite period in history, for a reference to Beatrix Esmond, and the introduction of Prince Charlie at the age of fifteen would date it as 1735; from which we would assume that the events described in the main portion of *Prince Prigio* happened in 1718; but the cheque which King Grognio makes out to Prigio is dated 1768—a sad slip in chronology on the part of that monarch—or of the meticulous historian Andrew Lang!

Actually, *Prince Prigio* has no very definite period, and Gordon Browne's illustrations suggest the late middle ages or the early sixteenth century. But in *Ricardo* he observes the eighteenth century setting with care; as does A. A. Dixon, also, in *Tales of a Fairy Court,* even though in other respects he does not seem to have read his original with much attention.

As regards this, the last work in the series, very little need be said. It was published in 1907, and is very much an attempt to recapture the atmosphere of the earlier volumes. It is more a collection of short stories than a complete whole, and is built, not very carefully, round *Prince Prigio,* much of which has in consequence to be retold in a shortened form which departs from the original in a number of ways.... (pp. 94-5)

Tales of a Fairy Court is the most scrappy of the fairy stories, and the book as a whole is inferior to *Prince Ricardo.* Here, again, the introduction of an adventure in a Scottish historical setting detracts greatly from the verisimilitude. But in other respects the use of the traditional fairy machinery is as clever and as amusingly worked out as in the earlier books; though here, too, the lack of plot makes itself felt again and again.

This was the last of Lang's adventures into the realm of Fairy-land, and is itself isolated from the earlier period when he was exploring that dim region in so many directions. (pp. 95-6)

As a writer of original fairy stories, Andrew Lang was very much the literary man at play, and was usually content to let his light and Puckish fancy dance gaily among the scenes and situations of a generally accepted and somewhat artificial Fairy-land.

But on one occasion he seems to have thrown off his habitual "cloak of indifference and light banter," and, seeking for a new and deeper well of magical and romantic inspiration, to have found it in the legends and memories of his much-loved Border home.

"For us," he writes, "the true poetry is the poetry that wakes again the true self; the wistful soul slumbering undisturbed in the tumult of the world, and only aroused, like the Sleeping Princess in the Scottish fairy-tale, by the magic song". And in his case the magic song was the music of the Tweed and of the waters of the north wandering among the hills where dwelt yet the echoes of old story and old belief. (p. 97)

"The spirit of Faery," he said, "is a Northern spirit", and it was this spirit that he invoked when he wrote *The Gold of Fairnilee* in 1888.

In deserting all the literary traditions of Fairyland and going for his inspiration to the Border ballads and to the ancient folk beliefs and superstitions, Lang was not acting unreasonably or from any spirit of forced innovation: for the fairies of the north are indeed the true fairies, and they were the products of the popular and literary creed of many centuries. (pp. 97-8)

The valley of the Tweed and the lands about Fairnilee were of all the Border country the parts most loved by Lang, and it is this which gives to *The Gold of Fairnilee* its sincerity and its depth of feeling. (p. 102)

With all this of memory and ballad lore behind him, Lang produced in *The Gold of Fairnilee,* perhaps the best prose work of his whole career. The spirit and manner of this tale differ utterly from those of all his other fairy stories, and from nearly all else that he wrote save in the most heartfelt of his poems. One can glimpse him from time to time in *The World's Desire* and *A Monk of Fife;* he is plainly apparent in the short story **"The Romance of the First Radical,"** in *Aucassin and Nicolete,* we feel the same spirit at work; but Andrew Lang, the poet with the wistful, melancholy soul, can nowhere be seen more clearly than in this simple little tale.

The cold, clear magic of the north, austere as the hills of Ettrick and of Yarrow, is breathed over the whole piece. But the austerity is the quiet simplicity of the truest affection, and the coldness is the gentle calm of the love that is beyond passion.

The Gold of Fairnilee is quite spontaneous, quite sincere: Lang was by nature a romantic, permeated by northern fairy-lore and the deep, clear feelings of the north; and when the depths of these feelings overcame his habitual reserve—when the melancholy soul looked forth without the vizor of the gay mind— it was in the poignant simplicity of the northern romance that he found his natural and truest expression. This explains, too, his dislike of Morris's prose romances, which at first sight would have seemed in Lang's own vein. The medium, perhaps, is too near for either to have been able fully to appreciate the other's working in it: it was Morris's method that jarred on Lang, the Gothic decoration, the wealth of words, the warmth and bright colouring—the pre-Raphaelite technique applied to literature.... His own simplicity in romantic writing was increased and clarified by the classics; and the unpublished prologue and the early chapters of *The World's Desire,* although in a Greek and not a northern setting, come very near to *The Gold of Fairnilee*—thus illustrating Lang's assertion that the true fairy spirit dwelt only in Greece and the north. Morris, on the other hand, although influenced also by the classics, and later by the sagas, came to them indirectly, and saw them to a great extent as reflections in a rich medieval mirror. Nowhere is the difference in technique and temperament more easily apparent than in their translations of the *Odyssey.* Lang condemned Morris's version often and repeatedly, and parodied it on more than one occasion. What Morris thought of the "Butcher and Lang" version can only be surmised from the fact that when Lang, with whom he was slightly acquainted, sent him a copy, he ignored it completely. (pp. 102-03)

The Gold of Fairnilee is probably the fullest example that we possess of Lang's true voice as a romantic; apart from this, the voice is heard clearly only in some of the poems, and, besides the more finite instances already mentioned, in some stray passages scattered up and down the vast concourse of his writings. Otherwise, the gay mind hides the melancholy soul almost completely; the one is seldom altogether lacking; we feel again and again that it is there, but the other is the visible, tangible part—the iron mask hiding we know not what Prince of Fairyland. "There was a touch of the elf about him," says J. M. Barrie. "Touch seems hardly the right word, because one could never touch him; he was too elusive for that."

It was perhaps part of this very elusiveness that led Lang away from the depth and wistfulness of his Border fairy-tale to the light, humorous, gently burlesque court of Pantouflia.

The mildly satirical fairy-story of the Thackeray tradition is a far easier form of literature to write than anything approaching the old folk-tales and legendary romances; and it was also a type of writing that came most easily to Lang of the gay mind, who confessed once that he was possessed by "the literary *follét* who delights in mild mischief." Yet in its essentials *Prince Prigio* goes contrary to Lang's own ideals, for it is a burlesque, however kindly, of the old tales. Of course, he was inventing no new *genre* when he wrote the Chronicles of Pantouflia, but merely carrying the methods of F. E. Paget, Thackeray and Tom Hood one step further, even as they had elaborated the methods of Madame d'Aulnoy and her followers. *The Gold Fairnilee* should not be compared with *Prince Prigio,* any more than *Alice* with Grimm's tales. It is dangerous to make any very definite attempt to put fairy stories into precise categories, for most of them lie somewhere between the extremes of "primitive" (to which we would assign *Alice Learmont* and *The Gold of Fairnilee*) and "sophisticated" (to which *The Rose and the Ring* and *Prince Prigio* belong), and are best left scattered indeterminately between these extremes.

Thus, although it would be unfair to criticize one of Lang's tales by the standards of the other, we can go so far as to say that the Pantouflia stories belong to a lower and commoner form of art than *The Gold of Fairnilee*. And yet, considered solely as books for children, one would be forced reluctantly to set *Prince Prigio* first. For lightness, humour, gay adventure have ever been the most popular with the majority of young readers. (pp. 105-06)

In its own field, *Prince Prigio* is only surpassed by *The Rose and the Ring*, but the two are sufficiently dissimilar for there to be ample room for both. Thackeray is a second Fielding—more gentle, more refined, more whimsical—but still the bold dash and the breadth of outline are there. He is the novelist at play, creating strongly-defined characters, however much burlesqued: "Angelica is a child's Blanche Amory, Betsinda is a child's Laura Bell, Bulbo is the Foker of the nursery", as Lang himself observed. His scenes and characters stand out in hard outline like an illustration by Walter Crane, while Lang's recall the fine strokes and delicate drawing of Leslie Brooke. Lang has none of Fielding's violence, nor his loud-voiced hilarity; as ever, he is gentle, almost dreamy, almost apologetic. To the adult reader Lang is far more acceptable than Thackeray, for his story still amuses in its quiet, unpretentious way, while the slap-stick and the loud burlesque of *The Rose and the Ring* fail to hold the attention quite as it used to do. The child of today, if we may take the fare spread for him as symptomatic of his own tastes, delights in bright colours heavily and ruthlessly laid on, in awkward and uncouth figures from which refinement has been drained away with sentiment, and beauty with the subtler shades of the imagination. And so *Prince Prigio*, though still read and still enjoyed, hangs still on the border-line between the few real nursery classics and the oblivion that has swallowed up so much that well deserves to live.

It is the undercurrent of that power and vision which produced *The Gold of Fairnilee* that gives to *Prince Prigio*, and to much of *Prince Ricardo* also, the intangible something—one might almost call it the soul—which makes of them living works of literature that will not easily die. Although they must be regarded to some extent as burlesque, yet the sense of reality in a serious and living world is seldom lost: the characters are never overdrawn as Thackeray's tend to be, nor are they reduced to the cruel level of the everyday world as are Mrs. Gaskell's in her tale "Curious if True." Prigio's adventures are all very serious matters to him, his love for Lady Rosalind is a romantic and not a courtly passion; Ricardo and Jacqueline are more like children than grown-up people, yet they are sincere and simple in their affections, and there is no hint of the lush sentimentality over young love that defiles S. R. Crockett's otherwise excellent children's stories. It is this underlying texture of romance that serves to bring *Prigio* and even *Ricardo* near to *The Gold of Fairnilee*, for it gives something more than humour and charm, though so indefinitely that hardly any particular passage can be pointed out as possessing the magic touch. The simple love-making of Prigio and Rosalind—"So the two went into the garden together and talked about a number of things"—or Prigio's meeting with the Ladies of the Moon: all very slight touches, yet never out of place as they would be in *The Rose and the Ring*.

In whatever setting he placed his stories, Lang never failed to profit by his unequalled knowledge of the old folk-tales, and their seriousness of purpose is never absent, even at the Court of Pantouflia. "In the old stories," he says, "despite the impossibility of the incidents, the interest is always real and human. The princes and princesses fall in love and marry—nothing could be more human than that. Their lives and loves are crossed by human sorrows . . . The hero and heroine are persecuted or separated by cruel step-mothers or enchanters; they have wandering and sorrows to suffer; they have adventures to achieve and difficulties to overcome. They must display courage, loyalty and address, courtesy, gentleness and gratitude. Thus they are living in a real human world, though it wears a mythical face, though there are giants and lions in the way. The old fairy-tales which a silly sort of people disparage . . . are really 'full of matter,' and unobtrusively teach the true lessons of our wayfaring in a world of perplexities and obstructions."

All this is present in Pantouflia, however much hidden by the humour and apparent flippancy. It is more surely there in *The Gold of Fairnilee*, for that, as I have suggested, is the clearer, more sincere revelation of the true mind of its maker, and greater book, even if not so successful in its appeal to its professed audience, or so much a book for constant and delighted reading as *Prince Prigio*. (pp. 106-07)

> *Roger Lancelyn Green, in his* Andrew Lang: A Critical Biography, *Edmund Ward, 1946, 265 p.*

J. R. R. TOLKIEN (essay date 1947)

[*Tolkien is famous as the author of the mythopoeic* Lord of the Rings *trilogy (1954-56) and of its much simpler prequel,* The Hobbit *(1938). With his friend C. S. Lewis and with Charles Williams, Tolkien was also a central member of the Oxford Christians, or "Inklings," a group of like-minded writers and friends who met weekly to discuss literature and read works-in-progress to each other. A longtime professor of medieval English literature and philology at Merton College, Oxford, Tolkien was of quite conservative literary tastes; for years he campaigned to keep "modern" (nineteenth- and twentieth-century) English literature off the curriculum at Merton. Like Lewis, he disliked nearly all the formal developments in twentieth-century writing, and his reading tended toward the traditional and the epic, his favorite literature being the ancient Norse sagas. In the following excerpt, Tolkien discusses Lang's theories about the function of the fairy tale, and disagrees with his belief that the fairy tale should be tailored specifically to an audience of children. For further discussion of Lang's work as a collector and editor of fairy tales, see the excerpts by Roger Lancelyn Green (1946) and Roger Sale (1981).*]

[In] recent times fairy-stories have usually been written or 'adapted' for children. But so may music be, or verse, or novels, or history, or scientific manuals. It is a dangerous process, even when it is necessary. It is indeed only saved from disaster by the fact that the arts and sciences are not as a whole relegated to the nursery; the nursery and schoolroom are merely given such tastes and glimpses of the adult thing as seem fit for them in adult opinion (often much mistaken). Any one of these things would, if left altogether in the nursery, become gravely impaired. . . . Fairy-stories banished in this way, cut off from a full adult art, would in the end be ruined; indeed in so far as they have been so banished, they have been ruined. All children's books are on a strict judgement poor books. Books written entirely for children are poor even as children's books.

The value of fairy-stories is thus not, in my opinion, to be found by considering children in particular. Collections of fairy-stories are, in fact, by nature attics and lumber-rooms, only by temporary and local custom play-rooms. Their contents are disordered, and often battered, a jumble of different dates, purposes, and tastes; but among them may occasionally be found a thing of permanent virtue: an old work of art, not too much damaged, that only stupidity would ever have stuffed away.

Andrew Lang's **Fairy Books** are not, perhaps, lumber-rooms. They are more like stalls in a rummage-sale. Someone with a duster and a fair eye for things that retain some value has been round the attics and box-rooms. His collections are largely a by-product of his adult study of mythology and folk-lore; but they were made into and presented as books for children. Some of the reasons that Lang gave are worth considering.

The introduction to the first of the series speaks of 'children to whom and for whom they are told'. 'They represent', he says, 'the young age of man true to his early loves, and have his unblunted edge of belief, a fresh appetite for marvels.' ''Is it true?'' he says, 'is the great question children ask.' (pp. 59-60)

It seems fairly clear that Lang was using belief in its ordinary sense: belief that a thing exists or can happen in the real (primary) world. If so, then I fear that Lang's words, stripped of sentiment, can only imply that the teller of marvellous tales to children must, or may, or at any rate does trade on their *credulity*, on the lack of experience which makes it less easy for children to distinguish fact from fiction in particular cases, though the distinction in itself is fundamental to the sane human mind, and to fairy-stories.

Children are capable, of course, of *literary belief*, when the story-maker's art is good enough to produce it. That state of mind has been called 'willing suspension of disbelief'. But this does not seem to me a good description of what happens. What really happens is that the story-maker proves a successful 'sub-creator'. He makes a Secondary World which your mind can enter. Inside it, what he relates is 'true': it accords with the laws of that world. You therefore believe it, while you are, as it were, inside. The moment disbelief arises, the spell is broken; the magic, or rather art, has failed. You are then out in the Primary World again, looking at the little abortive Secondary World from outside. (p. 60)

Now I was one of the children whom Andrew Lang was addressing—I was born at about the same time as the **Green Fairy Book**—the children for whom he seemed to think that fairy-stories were the equivalent of the adult novel, and of whom he said: 'Their taste remains like the taste of their naked ancestors thousands of years ago; and they seem to like fairy-tales better than history, poetry, geography, or arithmetic.' But do we really know much about those 'naked ancestors', except that they certainly were not naked? Our fairy-stories, however old certain elements in them may be, are certainly not the same as theirs. Yet if it is assumed that we have fairy-stories because they did, then probably we have history, geography, poetry, and arithmetic because they liked these things too, as far as they could get them, and in so far as they had yet separated the many branches of their general interest in everything. (pp. 61-2)

I had no special childish 'wish to believe'. I wanted to know. Belief depended on the way in which stories were presented to me, by older people, or by the authors, or on the inherent tone and quality of the tale. But at no time can I remember that the enjoyment of a story was dependent on belief that such things could happen, or had happened, in 'real life'. Fairy-stories saw plainly not primarily concerned with possibility,

Illustration from ''Beauty and the Beast,'' in The Blue Fairy Book.

but with desirability. If they awakened *desire*, satisfying it while often whetting it unbearably, they succeeded. (p. 62)

[In] my opinion fairy-stories should not be *specially* associated with children. They are associated with them: naturally, because children are human and fairy-stories are a natural human taste (though not necessarily a universal one); accidentally, because fairy-stories are a large part of the literary lumber that in latter-day Europe has been stuffed away in attics; unnaturally, because of erroneous sentiment about children, a sentiment that seems to increase with the decline in children.

It is true that the age of childhood-sentiment has produced some delightful books (especially charming, however, to adults) of the fairy kind or near to it; but it has also produced a dreadful undergrowth of stories written or adapted to what was or is conceived to be the measure of children's minds and needs. The old stories are mollified or bowdlerized, instead of being reserved; the imitations are often merely silly, Pigwiggenry without even the intrigue; or patronizing; or (deadliest of all) covertly sniggering, with an eye on the other grown-ups present. I will not accuse Andrew Lang of sniggering, but certainly he smiled to himself, and certainly too often he had an eye on the faces of other clever people over the heads of his child-audience—to the very grave detriment of the **Chronicles of Pantouflia**. (p. 64)

I do not deny that there is a truth in Andrew Lang's words (sentimental though they may sound): 'He who would enter into the Kingdom of Faërie should have the heart of a little child.' For that possession is necessary to all high adventure, into kingdoms both less and far greater than Faërie. But humility and innocence—these things 'the heart of a child' must mean in such a context—do not necessarily imply an uncritical wonder, nor indeed an uncritical tenderness. Chesterton once remarked that the children in whose company he saw Maeterlinck's *Blue Bird* were dissatisfied 'because it did not end with a Day of Judgement, and it was not revealed to the hero and the heroine that the Dog had been faithful and the Cat faithless'. 'For children', he says, 'are innocent and love justice; while most of us are wicked and naturally prefer mercy.'

Andrew Lang was confused on this point. He was at pains to defend the slaying of the Yellow Dwarf by Prince Ricardo in one of his own fairy-stories. 'I hate cruelty', he said, '. . . but that was in fair fight, sword in hand, and the dwarf, peace to his ashes! died in harness.' Yet it is not clear that 'fair fight' is less cruel than 'fair judgement'; or that piercing a dwarf with a sword is more just than the execution of wicked kings and evil stepmothers—which Lang abjures: he sends the criminals (as he boasts) to retirement on ample pensions. That is mercy untempered by justice. It is true that this plea was not addressed to children but to parents and guardians, to whom Lang was recommending his own *Prince Prigio* and *Prince Ricardo* as suitable for their charges. It is parents and guardians who have classified fairy-stories as *Juvenilia*. (pp. 64-5)

It is the mark of a good fairy-story, of the higher or more complete kind, that however wild its events, however fantastic or terrible the adventures, it can give to child or man that hears it, when the 'turn' comes, a catch of the breath, a beat and lifting of the heart, near to (or indeed accompanied by) tears, as keen as that given by any form of literary art, and having a peculiar quality.

Even modern fairy-stories can produce this effect sometimes. It is not an easy thing to do; it depends on the whole story which is the setting of the turn, and yet it reflects a glory backwards. A tale that in any measure succeeds in this point has not wholly failed, whatever flaws it may possess, and whatever mixture or confusion of purpose. It happens even in Andrew Lang's own fairy-story, *Prince Prigio,* unsatisfactory in many ways as that is. When 'each knight came alive and lifted his sword and shouted "long live Prince Prigio"', the joy has a little of that strange mythical fairy-story quality, greater than the event described. It would have none in Lang's tale, if the event described were not a piece of more serious fairy-story 'fantasy' than the main bulk of the story, which is in general more frivolous, having the half-mocking smile of the courtly, sophisticated *Conte*. (pp. 81-2)

> J. R. R. Tolkien, *"On Fairy-Stories,"* in Essays Presented to Charles Williams *by Dorothy Sayers & others, Oxford University Press, 1947, pp. 38-89.*

GARDNER B. TAPLIN   (essay date 1965)

[*In the following excerpt, Taplin examines Lang's theories on the relationship between ballads, folk poetry, and nursery stories, their origins, and their importance in anthropological study.*]

Perhaps no figure in the late-Victorian literary scene was more versatile, original, and productive than Andrew Lang, whose published works testify to an extraordinary range and depth of interests and talents. . . . This extraordinary breadth of literary activity, however, did not prevent him from becoming one of the most brilliant students of the ballad in his time. . . . His interest in the subject was not a short-lived fancy, nor did he hesitate to express his own views, which were often controversial; in the introduction to a collection of ballads which he edited, he wrote that he did not "merely plough with Professor Child's heifer," but that he had "made a study of ballads from his boyhood.

In Lang's first writing on balladry, his article in *The Encyclopaedia Britannica* of 1875, he definitely placed himself among the "communalists," a position which he held throughout his life, although he greatly modified his views in later years. Further research led him to believe that this early article had been based upon insufficient evidence, but it is significant as one of the early important expressions—indeed the first from a British writer—that folk poetry is the product of the people as a whole rather than of individual poets. In this article Lang wrote that after adducing examples of the identity of features in European balladry, he would attempt to prove that all ballads take their origin from the primitive dance and improvised song, which were still to be found in Greece and other countries with a warm climate. Basing his argument upon *a priori* considerations, he then inferred that since many ballads in Scotland had characteristics similar to those in Greece and Italy, the Scottish ballads must also have been derived from the institution of the dance. In contrast to epic literature written for an aristocracy and treating of individual passions and feelings, folk songs, as well as nursery tales, or *Märchen*, are popular in origin and impersonal in their subject matter. Folk songs, or ballads, according to Lang's article, are composed by the people and for the enjoyment of the people and are handed down among the people by oral tradition. They "date from times, and are composed by peoples who find, in a natural improvisation, a natural utterance of modulated and rhythmic speech, the appropriate relief of their emotions, in moments of high-wrought feeling or on solemn occasions.'"

The vagueness of this theory exposed Lang to attack from Thomas F. Henderson, who objected especially to Lang's wide and inflexible application of his hypothesis. . . . A particular weakness in Lang's thesis of absolute communal authorship, Henderson pointed out, was that Lang was not referring in general terms to the beginnings of poetry in primitive times, but to the authorship of ballads which were actually in existence.

This criticism of Lang's work was a salutary influence, in that it prompted him to clarify his position in an article on Scottish and English ballads in *Chambers's Cyclopaedia of English Literature*, which was published in 1901. He acknowledged Henderson's unfavorable judgments of his earlier views and then qualified his theory of ballad origins by hypothesizing that although originally there must have been an author of each ballad, his name and date are lost forever and that the ballads which are extant are popular patchworks from many different authors and altered into scores of variants. Their "communistic" source is to be understood in the sense that they were made "by the people, for the people." . . . To Lang's qualification of his "communistic" thesis, Henderson answered that Lang was not justified in attributing any kind of verse which has a connection with "the heart of the people" to the collective poetic effort of the people and in classing all such verse, regardless of its form, with ballads.

Lang's most considered judgment on the question of ballad origins appeared in 1903 in *Folk-Lore,* where he stated his position with a caution which placed him beyond any possible imputation of indiscretion. Ballads, he wrote, are of communal origin only in the sense that popular poetry is improvised collaboratively, with each individual contributing his quota. In the process of oral tradition, the reciters often filled in gaps of memory with fragments from other ballads and occasionally invented new verses according to their own taste. Although the recurring formula is public property, at one time it must have been invented by an individual. As for ballads with many existing variants, such as "Mary Hamilton," Lang maintained that it would be impossible to trace the authorship of the whole of any one extant version. The large number of variants shows the extent of popular collaboration, but the exact nature of the first version of the ballad cannot be ascertained. Lang humorously suggested that when he had written in 1875 that the origin of the ballad from the heart of the people might be contrasted with the origin of epic literature for an aristocracy, he had not supposed that "the 'people' simultaneously and automatically bellowed out this or that new ballad." The distinction which he made here, as Francis B. Gummere did several years later, was between origins of balladry and the traditional narrative ballads in their present form. Possibly none of the extant ballads derives its origin from improvisation in a primitive dance. In concluding the article, Lang declared that some ballads are degraded romances, while some literary romances and popular ballads on the same theme come down in oral tradition side by side. He was skeptical that any formula could explain all folk song and realized that the history of each ballad had to be considered separately.

The last utterance by Lang on the subject of ballad origins was his article in *The Encyclopaedia Britannica* of 1910, which, except for some corrections and additions, was largely based on his study of 1875. In the article which he contributed to the edition of 1910 he wrote that only the "earlier *genre* of ballads with refrain" sprang from the primitive custom of dance and song. To the account of ballad origins he added the following qualification of his earlier statement: "Their present form, of course, is relatively recent; in centuries of oral recitation the language altered automatically, but the stock situations and ideas of many *romantic* ballads are of dateless age and worldwide diffusion." (pp. 57-60)

[Lang] brought to his studies of the subject the scholarly qualities of patient investigation, close reasoning, and accuracy in his use of source materials, as well as a poetic insight and imagination which enabled him intuitively to grasp the significance of the data which he unearthed. Since he was a writer of ballads himself, he had an ability to judge of the authenticity of a ballad which was never granted to scholars of the school of "Higher Criticism." And perhaps not the least mark of Lang's stature as a student of the ballad is that, more than any of his colleagues, such as Henderson or Elliot, he showed in many expressions of gratitude and respect in his letters and published writings that he recognized the greatness of Francis James Child, the master of all ballad scholars. (p. 73)

> *Gardner B. Taplin, "Andrew Lang as a Student of the Traditional Narrative Ballad," in* TSE: Tulane Studies in English, *Vol. XIV, 1965, pp. 57-73.*

ELEANOR DE SELMS LANGSTAFF (essay date 1978)

[*Langstaff is an educator, biographer, and editor whose work as a foreign service officer and journalist has taken her to Zaire and Nigeria. In the following excerpt from her* Andrew Lang, *Langstaff examines Lang's success as a revisionist historian concerned with legends about the Stuart family and other controversial historical figures.*]

Whatever you do, don't write the history of people who want *not* to know the facts and regard History as the process of conserving their illusions," Lang wrote to R. S. Rait, historian at the University of Glasgow. Lang spoke from experience, for he was deeply enough involved in the study of myths and

myth-making by the time he started writing Scottish history to appreciate the need mankind has to make and treasure its myths. But the howl of indignation that went up when Lang started debunking the great Jacobite heroes was real and may have surprised him; for the substance of myths should be basic truths, however much disguised, not deliberate falsehoods. It must have been painful to be accused of being disloyal to Scotland; Lang was the son of a long line of loyal Scots accustomed to public service rendered without heroics.

In 1897, both *Pickle the Spy* and Lang's edition of Dicken's works (the Gadshill edition) appeared and the Letters to the Editor columns bristled with condemnations of his work: not Scottish enough with his history; too Scottish to appreciate Dickens. The Dickensian critics were so incensed they ridiculed Lang's supposed Scots accent, an ethnic attack to which no response was possible.

Pickle the Spy was an important book, an important contribution to history. It concerned the incognito of Prince Charles during an eighteen-month period following the 1745 attempt to free Scotland from English rule and return the throne to the House of Stuart. As a byway of history this tale is interesting in itself. But the work had another aim: it identified one of the important Jacobite leaders (Alistair Ruadh Macdonnell, son of the Laird of Glengary) as a double agent with the unlikely cover name of Pickle. Lang then proceeded to show how this double agent thwarted a second major attempt to free Scotland and how he continually undermined the Scots cause by passing to the English information about Jacobite plans and by furthering small misunderstandings among the Jacobite leaders so that concerted action became difficult if not impossible.

How did Lang, an ardent Scot and known romantic, fall into the role of revisionist historian? Lang gave us the answer: "Always go to the MSS." Fresh examination of the documents in their earliest forms became the keystone of Lang's historical technique after painfully learning his lesson from his university history, *St. Andrews*. . . . In writing of the institution so well loved by him, Lang wrote from secondary sources and failed to verify them. The result was a work riddled with embarrassing inaccuracies which could not be glossed over by readers far too familiar with the subject.

Lang's technique in handling textual evidence had been sharpened by his work in the classics. His ability to read the French of all centuries, Scottish Gaelic, and Latin added considerably to his contribution. Further, he had the imagination to guess where documents might be located and the charm and scholarly standing to gain access to them. No French scholar, for instance, had thought to examine the Scottish records concerning the Scots regiment that fought for the Dauphin during the time of Joan of Arc.

The material for *Pickle* was gathered not for the purpose of history, but to provide factual background for an historical novel by Robert Louis Stevenson. After Stevenson's death, the notes were returned to Lang, who put them together as *Pickle the Spy*. Pickle had been used by Sir Walter Scott in *Redgauntlet*, written in 1832, and Pickle's period covered 1750-1763, scarcely two generations earlier, and documents were not readily available for general use; Scott perforce took the traditional view as to Pickle's identity. Lang considered that Pickle was like Thackeray's Barry Lyndon in character, but much more wicked (somewhat akin to Stevenson's Master of Ballantrae). "The cool, good-humored, smiling, unscrupulous villain of high rank and noble lineage; the scoundrel happily unconscious of his own unspeakable infamy, proud and sensitive upon the point of honour; the picturesque hypocrite in religion, is a being we do not meet in Sir Walter's romances.'' But such was the character of the historical Pickle. (pp. 73-5)

Lang followed *Pickle* with *The Companions of Pickle* . . . , in which he developed in greater detail the characters of some of the people surrounding Pickle. . . . Modern historians specializing in the Stuarts consider *Pickle the Spy* and related studies ''conclusive'' for the period of Prince Charles's life. (p. 76)

Lang wrote several books about the House of Stuart, including the *Mystery of Mary Stuart, Prince Charles Edward Stuart,* and *Portraits and Jewels of Mary Stuart.* His interest in the House of Stuart was, on at least one occasion, carried to extremes when he introduced an article on Queen Victoria's sixtieth jubilee by pointing out that the Old Pretender had been king longer than she had been queen. Reaction to this statement was irate and intense.

The pathos of the Stuart cause was never far from Lang's thought. Rait thought that the biography of Prince Charles Edward was Lang's best-developed historical work—balanced in content, judicious in tone, making a graceful and witty statement about an historical figure. In **''The Three Portraits,''** it is clear that Lang would have preferred a more heroic end for Charles:

> Ah, My Prince, it were well,
> To have fallen where Keppoch fell,
> With the war-pipe loud in thine ear!
> To have died with never a stain
> On the fair White Rose of Renown,
> To have fallen, fighting in vain
> For thy father, thy faith and thy crown!

(pp.77-8)

Today, Lang would have been known as the Scottish revisionist historian. Although he agreed that true glory and romance existed in history, he insisted that significant men of the time should not be shorn of their total personality in order to make them fit some ideal mold. In 1900, the first volume of his *History of Scotland from the Roman Occupation* appeared to generally favorable reviews. The *New York Times* critic saw its audience as the students of history and predicted that if the rest of the volumes maintained the quality of the first, the work would rank as the most succinct, thorough, and accurate history of Scotland. Strong criticism was reserved for the third volume which covered the period from Charles I through 1688—a tumultuous time for theology and politics and a period of great appeal to historians, who wrote copiously about it. T. D. Wanlis's *Scotland and Presbyterianism Vindicated*—published at John Knox's House, Edinburgh—is a biting example of this criticism. Wanlis was far too angry to verify his references and quite mangled the sentences he quoted from Lang's *History.* His real complaint was that Lang had betrayed Scotland, but he also accused him of an hysterical style. ''Feeling that his jerky but plodding analistic style of writing history was not likely to attract attention, he may have been induced to take a hint from the tactics of 'the shrieking sisterhood,' and to pen his wild sentences such as 'ravens not yet gorged with gore,' 'this is the theology of Anahuac and Ashanti'; 'the stupidest of superstitions'; 'these wolves'; 'the infamy of the fanatic preachers,' in order to attract attention to his views.'' The epithets quoted by Wanlis were used by Lang in deprecating the violence employed by both sides in the religious strife, the issue of which was so important to England and to Scotland.

No one was or could be indifferent to the outcome: which was to be the Established Church of Scotland—Presbyterian or Anglican?

Lang abhorred violence, as being both immoral and distasteful. His adventure stories were pretense, and though he might criticize Charles Edward for not dying as befitted a prince beneath the sword, he could not condone fighting to the death for a religious principle (or, what is more appropriate here, two otherwise homogeneous groups fighting for opposing sets of religious principles), especially when death included a majority of those who accepted the current religion as they accepted the current government. Death for a political principle was more seemly to Lang, as instanced in his sonnet on Colonel Burnaby, who died defending the Afghan frontier—but not death inflicted by Christians on other Christians.

Martyrs are important in instilling loyalty within a group. Lang considered the tactics of both sides in the sixteenth-century Presbyterian-Anglican upheaval equally unscrupulous. Such an opinion could not be acceptable to the Presbyterians of Lang's generation. The unwelcome reminder that one's own side may also have used reprehensible techniques of persuasion (or dissuasion) may receive a dispassionate hearing if enough time has elapsed. In Lang's case, there had not been sufficient lapse of time. His comparative technique—utilizing knowledge of other cultures, other religions; his obvious championing the cause of the Independents; his graphic detail of torture; his citing of Gardiner's *Puritan Revolution*—these make the history readable if the reader is not too partisan. The extremely detailed nature of the four-volume *History of Scotland* does limit readership to the student of history, especially since the student has modern histories available from which to choose.

For less stalwart souls, Lang published a one-volume *Short History of Scotland* in 1911. It is not merely an abridgement of his four-volume *History;* it also incorporates other research Lang had since been doing in Scotland. In the last years of his life, Lang had been spending more and more time in Scotland, using the library of Saint Andrews University as well as other sources. The *Short History* stops at 1752, after some three hundred pages. . . . (pp. 79-80)

In style, the *Short History* is fluid, clear, and bright. There is no attempt to cover all aspects of history—social, economic, and political. It treats of the politics revolving around the monarchy with little exploration of economic or social factors. Ongoing references to current and standard works on the subject, as well as triumphant refutation of error, make this small book a typical late Lang work.

The educated English reader of Lang's day knew John Knox (1512?-1572) via Thomas Carlyle; the young ones knew about him through hero stories. . . . [Knox] left behind him a *History of the Reformation* in which he showed himself as the *sine qua non* of the Scottish Reformation, an assessment accepted at face value throughout the seventeenth to nineteenth centuries.

Lang, who referred to himself jocularly as a ''dissenting Historian,'' determined to correct history's picture of Knox, so essentially a self-portrait, in *John Knox and the Reformation.* . . . He did so in the context of the period described in his *History of Scotland.* Concern over whether there should be candlesticks on the altar of a church or even an altar at all, a concern that had men and women willing to die rather than kneel, could not but seem hysterical to the relatively rational and broadminded late nineteenth century. Lang, however frequently he may have ridiculed certain events of the period of the Reformation, realized their inner significance. As he wrote to Rait: "... Knox treated Mary of Guise [Mary Queen of Scots' mother] in the spirit of a thoroughly damnable Society journalist. ... He had the right end of the stick, he gave a shove in the right direction, so blindly, so clumsily, so hypocritically, so unchristianly, so to speak—and probably a Christian could not have done the job."

Central to debunking of Knox was the question as to why Knox did not revise his written record of events—not published during his lifetime, but intended for ultimate publication. He had ample time and opportunity, but he did not. Instead he left behind him what was called a *History* but was in fact a work of propaganda. William Dickinson, half a century later, gently points out that Knox's *History* was *designed* to be propaganda but was not published when it was written because the immediate need had passed. This had been a standard argument during Lang's time; Lang countered that Knox had had years not to modify or destroy, but merely to annotate his statement. Knox's failure to do so, Lang suggested, stemmed from vanity. Reviews at the time exhibited strong disparity in points of reference. Catholics rejoiced that their side had a hearing: others registered horror at an attempt to discredit the great Reformer. A. F. Pollard, writing in the *English Historical Review* (1906), gives the most balanced assessment: "The book is rather a criticism of other biographies than a biography itself, and herein lie at once its value and its limitations. Yet the book has many merits, though it is not free from casual errors. It should always be read with the ordinary lives of Knox, and should not be read without one or other of them." (pp. 81-2)

Lang did not write history in a vacuum; other writers were working on the same or similar subjects. When Lang undertook to write a biography of Joan of Arc, however, there were no adequate works in English on her life. ... There was no real reason for the English to modify Shakespeare's negative description of the Maid, for then the record of her exploits could only show the English to be dastardly. But Lang was not English; the Scots had nothing to be ashamed about; they had been allies of the Dauphin and hence of Joan. ... How typical of Lang to emphasize the blamelessness of the Scots and the incident of the miniature portrait shown her by a Scottish archer. He found in Jeanne d'Arc unalloyed romance: she was a heroine, a beautiful unblemished ideal, unlike Helen of Troy, whose only too evident faults had to be explained away.

In writing *The Maid of France,* Lang determined to establish an historical figure in her proper place. The scientific difficulties offered by Jeannne d'Arc's Voices, her lack of any kind of education (including politics and military science), the array of available documentation—all posed tantalizing challenges. Lang had the methodology and skills developed by his anthropological, historical, classical, and, most recently, his psychological studies. He also had in Jeanne d'Arc a personage who had become a modern mythological-historical figure, as Charlemagne had become centuries earlier. Lang's intent was to remove the myth (although not to discount it) and establish the history. To do so he had to familiarize the reader with the complex historical, military, and political epoch. (pp. 83-4)

The lack of nationalism, petty intrigues, the uncharismatic Dauphin are all vividly described. The folklore of Domremy also is charmingly limned. Lang's anthropological background prevented the cheap attitude that Anatole France indulged in his own biography of Joan (1904). Instead Lang shows the reader Domremy's near mingling of myth and miracle, the lore not quite believed, but always passed down to the younger

generation, if not from grandparent to grandchild, or parent to child, then from older children to younger ones.

Lang gives the documents in the case his usual painstaking scrutiny: both the original trial documents and those belonging to her trial of rehabilitation. This last was held to review and, finally, to reverse the conviction of Jeanne d'Arc as a heretic and witch. Many of the rehabilitation witnesses had taken part in battles led by her; their testimony had a mixed value, since those testifying sought to make up for their participation in the kangaroo court that condemned Jeanne to death.

A good deal of important information is contained in Lang's appendixes which might better have been incorporated into the body of the work. The busy author often found himself unable to balance natural drama with evidence, and in this work, he evidently did not wish to interfere with the presentation of his heroic main character. (p. 85)

The Maid of France displays the weakness inherent in "a book about a book." The writing of it was triggered by Anatole France's *La Vie de Jeanne d'Arc* (1904) and its thrust is more a refutation of France's remarks than a statement standing on its own. Indeed the narrative is often interrupted to summarize France's arguments and refute them. France, who was agnostic and anticlerical, saw in Joan's life an instance of an innocent girl duped into being an unconscious tool in the hands of the Church. The chief value of the France book is its insights into the credulous mentality of the fifteenth century, but its thesis has no historical foundation. It created an immense stir in France, and not only among the Catholics; Joan was a national symbol, a symbol of patriotism, long before her beatification by the Catholic Church in 1908.

Critics and reviewers frequently commented on Lang's enthusiasm for Jeanne d'Arc. His lyric verse about her showed more admiration than the carefully measured tribute he paid her in the preface to the *Maid of France*. He evidently saw an audience for her story that must be moved past the surface drama of the story, an audience not necessarily impressed because the Catholic Church seemed to have a sudden interest in Joan. He was emphatic over the care he took with his sources. He provided a survey of the more recent studies and discussed to some extent the primary documents available. A recurring criticism of Anatole France's works was that his citations are untraceable: Lang verified his references three times so not to be vulnerable for the same reason. (pp. 85-6)

The French translation of *The Maid of France* was rushed into print in Paris, but parts of it were separately published earlier as *La "Jeanne d'Arc" de M. Anatole France.* Lang's works on Jeanne were used by the Church in France in its battle against the skepticism of the age and against the influence of Anatole France. Concerning such use, Lang wrote to a friend that the "French Jesuits have only ploughed with my heifer,"—sardonic humor of Lang at its best. He was intellectually and romantically annoyed that the Catholic Church was unable to use its own weapons to fight its battles; thus he chose the most apposite Biblical allusion to express it.

The most sensitive point in Jeanne's life for the rationalists were her Voices. A rationalist who accepted Jeanne's contribution to French history as valid had no way to deal with features that went beyond observable fact. Miracles were outside the subject area of physicists and chemists, though accessible for analysis through the social sciences. Lang examined Jeanne's Voices in the light of what was then known about extrasensory perception, employing the technique used by the

Caricature of Lang by David Levine. Copyright © 1967 Nyrev, Inc. Reprinted with permission from The New York Review of Books.

Society for Psychical Research (of which Lang was a founder member), which was to collect case histories as authoritative as possible and to examine them for clues. . . . From them he found that to scientists Jeanne's Voices were auditory hallucination. But, that whereas to the layman the term hallucination invariably refers to hysterically induced phenomena, the scientist recognized another type, whose cause was not clearly understood, possibly coming from either the unconscious or some kind of extrasensory experience. Although Lang himself had experienced ESP phenomena, he was not quite willing to state that Jeanne's Voices fell into that category; there was not enough evidence. Instead he opted . . . for some sort of activity of Jeanne's unconscious.

Who shall have the last word on Lang and the Maid? George Bernard Shaw, in his long preface to *Saint Joan,* tackles Twain and Lang together and concludes that the sheer romanticism of Twain's book makes for a better work [see excerpt dated 1924]. Lang was hampered not only by the fact that he was writing nonfiction, but even more by his need to document conclusions so thoroughly that they could never be doubted. Green saw *The Maid of France* as epitomizing Lang's romance of history: here was history as it should be lived; here was a person who had that quality so eminently lacking in Prince Charles—Jeanne had the heroism to die for a cause; she was the larger-than-life mythological person that the Jacobites wanted Charles to be. History here provides the catharsis usually known only in tragic literature. (pp. 86-8)

> *Eleanor De Selms Langstaff, in her* Andrew Lang, *Twayne Publishers, 1978, 176 p.*

ROGER SALE (essay date 1981)

[*In the following excerpt, Sale offers a general discussion of Lang's fairy-tale anthologies, noting his seeming indiscriminate selection of both distinguished and undistinguished stories for inclusion in the collections. For further discussion of Lang's work as a collector and editor of fairy tales, see the excerpts by Roger Lancelyn Green (1946) and J. R. R. Tolkien (1947).*]

Andrew Lang wrote over a hundred books, poems and prose romances, criticism, anthropology, Scottish history. He made what was for a few generations the standard translations of Homer, and what is still the standard translation of the French romance *Aucassin and Nicolete.* For almost two decades he wrote frequent columns for London papers, often written about as fast as an editorial board could decide their subject, and good enough that Shaw could say that a day started with a Lang piece was a day well begun. Given this, it is ironic that he is now best known for the color fairy books, which he only edited, and much of the work for which was done by his wife and a team of not-quite anonymous translators, all women. (p. 7)

Throughout the years he published these books, Lang had to keep repeating that these were not his tales (though between the *Green* and the *Yellow* he did publish *My Own Fairy Book,* but no one really wanted Lang to be an author of fairy tales). By some alchemy of editorial genius and public taste, Lang's collections became the classics, and everything else he did was sooner or later forgotten. Furthermore, later fairy tale collections, even some very good ones, have failed to last. When I have used the *Blue Fairy Book* to teach fairy tales, the only students who protest are those who prefer a different Lang book.

The one obvious characteristic of Lang's collecting is its lack of characteristics. Having read *all* of *them,* Lang responded to the profusion and variety of fairy tales, and neither in his choice of stories nor in his use of translations did Lang seek to impose a style. Looking at these first four books [the *Blue Fairy Book, Red Fairy Book, Green Fairy Book,* and *Yellow Fairy Book*], one would be hard pressed to know that Thackeray's *The Rose and the Ring,* the last readable descendant of the *contes des fées,* was Lang's favorite. Long and intricate tales are placed next to short, little-known German maerchen. . . . One tours the world, constantly discovering its samenesses as well as its piquant differences. (p. 9)

> *Roger Sale, "A Victorian's Collection of Colorful Tales," in* Book World—The Washington Post, *January 11, 1981, pp. 7, 9.**

ADDITIONAL BIBLIOGRAPHY

Beerbohm, Max. "Two Glimpses of Andrew Lang." *Life and Letters* I, No. 1 (June 1928): 1-11.
    Unflattering, sarcastic recollections of social encounters with Lang.

Brown, Robert, Jr. "Mr. Lang's Latest Attack upon Professor Müller." In his *Semitic Influence in Hellenic Mythology,* pp. 23-79. London: Williams and Norgate, 1898.
    Discussion of the anthropological theories of Lang and Max Müller. Brown considers Lang's attack upon the opinions of Müller, an acknowledged scholar of linguistics and mythology, unnecessarily disputatious and inconclusive.

Chesterton, G. K. "Mr. Andrew Lang." *Literature,* No. 214 (23 November 1901): 484-86.

A general essay on Lang's accomplishments, focusing on the wide diversity of his interests.

Dickinson, William Croft. *Andrew Lang, John Knox, and Scottish Presbyterianism*. Edinburgh: Thomas Nelson and Sons, 1952, 32 p.*
From a University of St. Andrews "Andrew Lang Lecture." Dickinson considers the critical analysis of John Knox's *History of the Reform of Religion within the Realm of Scotland* in Lang's works "Knox in the Hands of Philistines" and *John Knox and the Reformation* to be naive; while Lang regarded Knox as a man of good intentions who wrote a propagandistic history, Dickinson notes that history is necessarily propaganda. Despite this reservation, Dickinson regards much of Lang's criticism as "brilliant".

Dorson, Richard M. "Andrew Lang's Folklore Interests as Revealed in 'At the Sign of the Ship'." *Western Folklore* XI, No. 1 (January 1952): 1-19.
Examines Lang's use of his newspaper column to popularize legends and folklore. Dorson notes that in his diversified column "At the Sign of the Ship" in *Longman's Magazine*, Lang encouraged readers to send him information about local legends, folklore, and spiritual anecdotes, thus lending his scholarly reputation to a field long considered frivolous.

Falconer, Charles. *The Writings of Andrew Lang*. 1894. Reprint. Folcroft, Pa: Folcroft Library Editions, 1974, 24 p.
Early annotated bibliography of Lang's poetry, books, and newspaper and periodical articles.

Green, Roger Lancelyn. "The Mystery of Andrew Lang." *Blackwood's Magazine* 306, No. 1850 (December 1969): 522-38.
From a University of St. Andrews "Andrew Lang Lecture." Green discusses Lang's career, noting that despite the influence he wielded through his newspaper columns, essays, and books, Lang himself did not write a "great" or "big" work that does justice to his memory and his literary accomplishments.

Grierson, H. J. C. *Lang, Lockhart, and Biography*. London: Oxford University Press, 1934, 65 p.*
From a University of St. Andrews "Andrew Lang Lecture." Grierson discusses Lang's approach to writing biography, noting his penchant for challenging accepted historical facts. Grierson regards Lang's *The Life and Letters of John Gibson Lockhart* as an *apologia* that unintentionally over-sympathizes with Lockhart, with whom Lang shared personality traits, literary interests, and an admiration for Sir Walter Scott.

Gross, John. "The Bookmen." In his *The Rise and Fall of the Man of Letters*, pp. 131-66. New York: Macmillan, 1969.*

Places Lang among the influential journalists of the era. Calling Lang a "don lost to journalism," Gross charges that he wasted his talent.

Matthews, Brander. "Andrew Lang." *The Century Magazine* XLVII, No. 3 (January 1894): 375-81.
Discussion of Lang as a man of letters. Matthews compares Lang to past and contemporary poets, critics, and fiction writers, praising his versatility in an age that encouraged literary specialists.

Murray, Gilbert. In his *Andrew Lang the Poet*. London: Oxford University Press, 1948, 27 p.
From a University of St. Andrews "Andrew Lang Lecture." Murray contends that Lang never reached his full poetic potential because his intellect was drawn to many subjects and because his romantic escapism led him to believe that his deepest emotions had already been best expressed in the classical poetry of Scotland, Greece, and France.

Oliphant, Margaret. "John Gibson Lockhart." *Blackwood's Magazine* CLX, No. DCCCCLXXIII (November 1896): 607-25.
Discussion of Lang's *The Life and Letters of John Gibson Lockhart*. Oliphant contends that Lang takes an unnecessarily apologetic stance in writing the biography and at times draws strange, unsupported conclusions; nevertheless, she concludes that Lang renders the latter years of Lockhart's life with convincing pity and emotion.

Ormerod, James. *The Poetry of Andrew Lang*. Derby, England: Harpur & Sons, 1943, 12 p.
Laudatory appraisal of Lang's poetry.

Parker, W. M. "The Literary Side of Andrew Lang." In his *Modern Scottish Writers*, pp. 3-24. 1917. Reprint. Freeport, New York: Books for Libraries Press, 1968.
Discussion of Lang as a writer of first-rate light poetry.

Salmond, J. B. *Andrew Lang and Journalism*. Edinburgh: Thomas Nelson and Sons, 1951, 35 p.
University of St. Andrews "Andrew Lang Lecture." Salmond praises Lang for inspiring a generation of writers. He notes that Lang's romantic bent colored his criticism, particularly of contemporary fiction.

Weintraub, Joseph. "Andrew Lang: Critic of Romance." *English Literature in Transition* 18, No. 1 (1975): 5-15.
Places Lang in the forefront of the romantic revival of the 1880s. Weintraub traces Lang's appreciation of Homer and H. Rider Haggard to his romantic love of "ancestral barbarianism," which Lang believed would be durable after other literary forms had passed from fashion.

D(avid) H(erbert) Lawrence

1885-1930

(Also wrote under pseudonym of Lawrence H. Davison) English novelist, novella and short story writer, poet, essayist, translator, and dramatist.

The following entry presents criticism of Lawrence's novel *Sons and Lovers*. For a complete discussion of Lawrence's career, see *TCLC*, Volumes 2 and 9.

The first major novel of Lawrence's career, *Sons and Lovers* is considered one of the most important and innovative novels of the twentieth century. Regarded as revolutionary for its subject matter rather than its style, *Sons and Lovers* was modeled after the traditional nineteenth-century English bildungs-roman best exemplified by Charles Dickens's *Great Expectations* and Samuel Butler's *The Way of All Flesh*. Unlike other experimental novelists of the early twentieth century such as James Joyce and Virginia Woolf, Lawrence was not concerned with radical prose techniques. Instead, the innovative nature of his novel lies in the way it traces the psychological development of the young protagonist, Paul Morel, as he attempts to understand and resolve the powerful ambivalence he feels toward his mother and the other women in his life and become an independent individual. Because Lawrence introduced many themes in *Sons and Lovers* which were developed in his later works, it is of crucial importance to any reader desiring a full appreciation of the development of Lawrence's art.

Lawrence closely modeled Paul Morel's life after his own youth. Like Morel, Lawrence was born to a Nottingham coal miner and his wife, a woman who had fallen below her middle-class background and who attempted to overcome her frustrations through the aspirations she had for her son. Convinced of her son's genius, Lydia Lawrence urged him to pursue his education and develop his talents so that he might escape a life in the mines. Unfortunately for Lawrence, as for Paul Morel, well-intended maternal praise and encouragement evolved into a harmful symbiotic bond with his mother which, accordingto biographers, severely distorted his perception of women in that he saw all as inferior to his mother—in virtue and in their ability to know and love him. In addition to his mother, Lawrence was encouraged in his ambitions by Jessie Chambers, a long-time companion on whom he based the character of Miriam Leivers. However, though *Sons and Lovers* in many ways reflects the events of Lawrence's youth, the dangers of an autobiographical interpretation of the novel are demonstrated by John Middleton Murry's critical biography of Lawrence, *D. H. Lawrence: Son of Woman,* in which Murry discusses Lawrence and Paul Morel as if they are psychologically interchangeable. Murry, once Lawrence's closest friend, was aware of Lawrence's obsessive relationship with his mother and the difficulty it caused him in his association with women; he therefore treated Paul Morel's similar dilemma as if it were Lawrence's own. Many critics, including Aldous Huxley and F. R. Leavis, denounced Murry's appraisal on the grounds that it was too strongly influenced by his personal relationship with Lawrence and that it ignored Lawrence's role as an artist who transformed autobiographical material into fiction. In a later edition of *Son of Woman,* Murry somewhat modified his ar-

gument by deemphasizing the correlation between Lawrence and his fictional creation.

Lawrence began *Sons and Lovers,* originally entitled *Paul Morel,* in 1910. He showed the early draft to Chambers, who actually wrote some passages for the novel and made extensive suggestions for its revision. Chambers stated in her memoir of Lawrence that, although she could see Lawrence's genius in the work, she considered the early version tense, awkward, and "storybookish," and that she encouraged Lawrence to keep the story as close to reality as possible. Chambers also wrote that she hoped that by writing about his parents' marriage and his obsessive relationship with his mother, Lawrence would be freed from the emotional torment his bond with her had caused him. When Chambers saw the final version of the novel she was devastated by what she considered Lawrence's unfair treatment of Miriam, who is cruelly rejected by Paul, and his handing the "laurels of victory" to Paul's mother. Most biographical and critical sources which discuss Chambers involvement with Lawrence indicate that their relationship abruptly and bitterly ended when *Sons and Lovers* was near completion. It was at this time that Lawrence eloped with Frieda von Richthofen Weekly, the wife of one of his college professors. Like Chambers, Frieda helped Lawrence write several passages of the novel, giving him greater insight into the psychology of Clara Dawes, a married woman with whom Paul Morel has an affair. While many critics praise Lawrence's understanding and portrayal of women, feminist commentators on *Sons and Lovers* frequently attack the novel on the grounds that Lawrence, like Paul Morel, exploited the intelligence of the women who loved him.

When the novel was completed, Lawrence offered it to William Heinemann, the publisher of his first two novels, but Heinemann rejected *Sons and Lovers* on the grounds that it was "one of the dirtiest books he had ever read." The novel was published by Duckworth in 1913, only after Lawrence satisfied their demand that he tone down its sexual content. Lawrence had already attracted considerable attention from critics and reviewers for his early poetry and his first two novels, *The White Peacock* and *The Trespasser,* but with the publication of *Sons and Lovers* he was heralded as one of the most important novelists of his day. Although most of the early reviews of the novel were favorable and Lawrence himself was pleased with them, R. P. Draper states that few of the early reviewers demonstrated any real understanding of the novel's theme. For example, some critics excessively praised the character of the "heroic little mother" and completely overlooked the destructive effect Mrs. Morel had on her sons, while others ignored the power of Lawrence's psychological study and attacked the book on the grounds that it was too sexually explicit. Draper maintains that many critics have been deceived by the novel's traditional and seemingly straightforward narrative style and contends that the work is far more complex than any single critical interpretation can satisfactorily address.

Because *Sons and Lovers* is such a detailed psychological portrait of Paul Morel and his family, it is not surprising that the most prominent critical method used to examine the novel is a psychoanalytic approach. In an early and influential Freudian interpretation of the novel, Alfred Kuttner discussed the destructive nature of Mrs. Morel's maternal love and the way she restricts Paul's ability to become emotionally involved with other women. Kuttner found that in *Sons and Lovers* Lawrence portrayed "the struggle of a man to emancipate himself from his maternal allegiance and to transfer his affection to a woman who stands outside of his family circle." Many critics consider this the central issue of the novel and have discussed at length the psychological turmoil resulting from Mrs. Morel's excessive devotion to Paul. One popular reading contends that Paul Morel suffers from an emotional and physical "split" which renders him incapable of having an emotional as well as physical bond with the same woman. With women such as his mother and Miriam he has an emotional and intellectual affinity, while with Clara Dawes he is involved in a purely physical relationship. Because of demands implicit in his mother's possessive form of love, Paul perceives all women as beings that want to destroy his autonomy and consume him. In order to preserve his fragile sense of self, Paul is able to give only a portion of himself to each and must ultimately flee in order to find the freedom necessary to develop as a man and artist. Psychoanalytic readings of the novel also frequently discuss Paul Morel's behavior in terms of the classic Oedipal complex, because the intimate nature of his relationship with his mother is so complete that he finds the quality of love he can give to and receive from other women deficient and unsatisfying by comparison. For this reason there are widely divergent readings of the novel's conclusion, with some believing that Paul is at last moving toward an autonomous adult existence, and others contending that he is an emotional derelict drifting toward death out of a desire to remain with his dead mother.

While nearly all critics acknowledge the strong emphasis on individual psychology in *Sons and Lovers,* some choose to examine it in terms of larger social issues that emerge in the story. Some consider the conflicting values of the working class and the middle class, as represented in the marriage of Walter and Gertrude Morel, as being of central importance in Paul's development. Scott Sanders maintains that "the conflict between mother and father, which is clearly grounded in class differences, is too readily translated into a personal, psychological struggle" in many discussions of the novel. Sanders contends that Paul's conflict stems from his alienation from the male working-class world around him because the inordinately strong bond with his mother has caused him to adapt to her bourgeois values and aspirations. Thus, Paul's relationships with Miriam and Clara fail not because of his Oedipal attachment to his mother, but because those women lack the middle-class attributes Paul has been programmed to seek in a prospective mate. According to Sanders, Lawrence himself "underrates the importance of Mrs. Morel's ambition that Paul marry a 'lady'—a category which Miriam [and Clara do] not fit."

Despite the fact that *Sons and Lovers* has inspired a tremendous amount of criticism that focuses on its content rather than its aesthetic qualities, there are a substantial number of critics who have concentrated on the structure of the novel. Although most of these critics conclude that it was a much more accomplished work than Lawrence's two previous novels, they also agree that it exhibits certain weaknesses. Many are of the opinion that Lawrence was unable to adequately distance himself from the autobiographical material and that he failed to maintain the necessary objectivity needed to artistically transform his personal experience into a work of fiction endowed with clarity and an independent vision. Mark Schorer asserts that Lawrence failed to thoroughly examine the psychological conflicts he sets up in the novel, that he is "merely repeating his emotions, and . . . avoids an austerer technical scrutiny of his material because it would compel him to master them." Several critics have cited the treatment of Paul's father and Miriam as particularly confusing and problematic, because while they are generally portrayed sympathetically, many passages in the narration deliver strong, authoritative arguments concerning their character defects and the necessity of Paul's rejection of them.

That *Sons and Lovers* has inspired such a wide range of critical interpretation since its publication testifies to its enduring status as a masterpiece of twentieth-century literature. Frank Kermode has noted that the novel's flexibility and ability to challenge a reader liberates it "from the burden of finality and completeness placed on it by [Lawrence's] enemies . . . who, in his opinion, mistook it for life, and novelistic custom for natural law." Although many critics consider the two novels which followed, *The Rainbow* and *Women in Love,* Lawrence's finest, and even though his last novel, *Lady Chatterley's Lover,* received a great deal of attention because of the censorship measures taken against it, *Sons and Lovers* remains Lawrence's most widely read and popular work.

(See also *Dictionary of Literary Biography,* Vol. 10: *Modern British Dramatists, 1900-1945; Vol. 19: British Poets, 1880-1914;* and Vol. 36: *British Novelists, 1890-1929: Modernists.*)

D. H. LAWRENCE   (letter date 1912)

[*In the following excerpt, Lawrence discusses the themes of* Sons and Lovers.]

Dear Garnett: Your letter has just come. I hasten to tell you I sent the MS. of the *Paul Morel* novel to Duckworth registered, yesterday. And I want to defend it, quick. I wrote it again, pruning it and shaping it and filling it in. I tell you it has got form—*form:* haven't I made it patiently, out of sweat as well as blood. It follows this idea: a woman of character and refinement goes into the lower class, and has no satisfaction in her own life. She has had a passion for her husband, so the children are born of passion, and have heaps of vitality. But as her sons grow up she selects them as lovers—first the eldest, then the second. These sons are *urged* into life by their reciprocal love of their mother—urged on and on. But when they come to manhood, they can't love, because their mother is the strongest power in their lives, and holds them. . . . As soon as the young men come into contact with women, there's a split. William gives his sex to a fribble, and his mother holds his soul. But the split kills him, because he doesn't know where he is. The next son gets a woman who fights for his soul—fights his mother. The son loves the mother—all the sons hate and are jealous of the father. The battle goes on between the mother and the girl, with the son as object. The mother gradually proves stronger, because of the tie of blood. The son decides to leave his soul in his mother's hands, and, like his elder brother go for passion. He gets passion. Then the split begins to tell again. But, almost unconsciously, the mother realises what is the matter, and begins to die. The son casts off his mistress, attends to his mother dying. He is left in the end naked of everything, with the drift towards death.

It is a great tragedy, and I tell you I have written a great book. It's the tragedy of thousands of young men in England. . . . I think it was Ruskin's, and men like him.—Now tell me if I haven't worked out my theme, like life, but always my theme. Read my novel. It's a great novel. If *you* can't see the development—which is slow, like growth—I can. (pp. 160-61)

I should like to dedicate the *Paul Morel* to you—may I? But not unless you think it's really a good work. 'To Edward Garnett, in Gratitude.' But you can put it better. (p. 161)

> *D. H. Lawrence, in a letter to Edward Garnett on November 14, 1912, in his* The Collected Letters of D. H. Lawrence, Vol. 1, *edited by Harry T. Moore, The Viking Press, 1962, pp. 160-62.*

HAROLD MASSINGHAM (essay date 1913)

[*In the following excerpt, originally a review of* Sons and Lovers *in the* Daily Chronicle *of 17 June 1913, Massingham notes Lawrence's indebtedness to Arnold Bennett's techniques of detailed portraiture and praises the complexity of Lawrence's character analysis.*]

Mr. Lawrence's *Sons and Lovers* [is] far and away the best book he has yet written.

It has little or no pretensions to plot-architecture, its incident is not external, and in the crisis of psychological evolution it bothers hardly at all about continuity, balance or arrangement. It possesses surprisingly few of the more obvious attractions of the novel. It is simply an objective record of a collier's family in the Midlands, over a period of twenty to thirty years, conveyed without extenuation, without partiality, and with a ruthless fidelity to things as they were in that family which leaves no loophole for special pleading on behalf of the immaculate heroine and the hero without fear or reproach.

Mr. Arnold Bennett, as all the world knows, is the modern specialist in accurate and minute portraiture, using not the scalpel like Zola and Flaubert, but the microscope; pursuing the mental and spiritual motions of his creatures with a scientific detachment. . . . And it is plain that Mr. Lawrence, though less of an artist, is in some measure indebted to Mr. Bennett's method. Curiously enough, they employ a similar background, and are vivified by the same genius of locality.

But where Mr. Bennett observes, Mr. Lawrence analyses. Indeed, unity and sharpness of outline are often obscured upon his canvas by a passion for probing the motives and processes of his characters, not as beings, but as thinkers. This introspective fever is peculiarly prominent in his treatment of Paul, the second son of the Morels. We are, of course, on conjectural ground here, but we suspect that Paul is a projection of the writer's own personality. We see him, moreover, never in relation to himself, but to the three women he loved, his mother, the shrinking, mystical Miriam, and the material, defiant Clara Dawes. Within these three he revolves and they determine his destiny. And we feel that Paul can never get far enough away from his creator to solidify into a self-sufficient person.

All this portion of the narrative is more fanciful, more impressionist, and more coloured than the first part, and quite definitely parts company from the Bennett type. It is infinitely more curious and more intense. The 'ego' of the author is, we imagine, more involved. But the earlier pictures of Mrs. Morel and her husband, of her eldest son, William, and his betrothed, Lily Western, are unerringly painted in, without any tragic infusion of the personal element. The irony is in themselves and their circumstances, not in the author's interpretation of them.

But the real triumph of *Sons and Lovers* is William and his fiancée. They are wedged into the smallest possible compass, but the quintessence of their fatal communion is thereby the more poignantly realized. The horror of his entanglement with her has a far more tragic purport than Paul's with Miriam. The one is life, the other an aspect of psychology. We wish we could have seen more of Annie, the only daughter of the household. Her effacement leaves a gap in the structure of the family, and impairs the finish of the perspective.

It is obvious that Mr. Lawrence's latest book is also his most ambitious. Not only are his figures numerous and radically diverse, but in style and treatment he plays upon a many-stringed instrument. It is perhaps its intricate nature that gives to portions of it an abrupt and feverish air. It is at times painfully crowded and intense, and at times a little careless in minor deficiencies. . . . But as a whole his work is, in the most vital sense, suggestive and imaginative. (pp. 62-4)

> *Harold Massingham, in an extract from* D. H. Lawrence, the Critical Heritage, *edited by R. P. Draper, Barnes & Noble, Inc., 1970, pp. 62-4.*

THE SATURDAY REVIEW, LONDON (essay date 1913)

[*In the following excerpt the reviewer praises the emotional power of Lawrence's prose in* Sons and Lovers, *but also points to Lawrence's occasional inability to distance himself from the passions of his characters. For an extensive discussion of this aspect of* Sons and Lovers, *see the excerpt by Eliseo Vivas (1960).*]

When were there written novels so strange as these of Mr. Lawrence? Now that he has given us three of them we should be able to make some estimate of his position among writers, yet there is about him something wilful which eludes judgment. Passages in *Sons and Lovers* tempt us to place him in a high class; and it is indeed a good book, even though it has pages where the author's vision is revealed only behind a dense cloud. As a story it is the record of the lives of a miner and his family in the middle counties of England, and from *The White Peacock* we knew how well the Derbyshire and Nottinghamshire country would be pictured. It can now be added that the scenes from the towns are little less good. The ruling idea in the book is the pitiful wastage of the best in men and women, and it is first shown in the persons of Morel and his wife. The former is physically a grand specimen of a race which puts its strength into manual labor, but he is ruined by drink, for his will is always weak. Mrs. Morel is a good housewife and a decent woman. Her superior ways mark her to her husband as a lady; yet she shirks none of the duties which his mate should perform for him, the children, and the home. Unhappily there is in her something of the shrew, and the association between the pair serves only to bring out their unpleasant sides. The young family grows up zealous for the mother; but with the touch of skill Mr. Lawrence can show the father as the good fellow whom these others never knew. ''He'', we read, ''always sang when he mended boots because of the jolly sound of hammering''; and in that single sentence is revealed the human creature who should have had pure joy of life and an author whose inspiration leaves behind the common artifices of the novelist. There are many other places where the writer quite surprises us by his power to make the narrative pass from fiction into glowing reality. (p. 780)

Paul Morel, the miner's second son, is the chief person in the book, and his tragedy is his devotion to his mother, for she absorbs almost everything in him but his passions. Miriam . . . does battle for him. Despite her fierce purity she gives herself to his desire, but cannot hold him even by her sacrifice, and he drifts into a passionate friendship with a second woman. The idea of waste still rules the story. The mother, who has dreaded the influence of Miriam on his affections, almost welcomes the intrigue with Clara, because the latter is less exacting in her demands. Puritan as she is, Mrs. Morel condones the affair with a married woman in order to keep the greater part of her son for herself. The strife between the generations is admirably suggested, and we know of no active English novelist—to-day—who has Mr. Lawrence's power to put in words the rise and fall of passion. The death of the mother and Paul's derelict state are the ends to which the story naturally leads, for the author is too good an artist to allow a conclusion which could stultify the force of all that he has built on the characters of his people. What is wrong in the book is the frequent intrusion of the writer. The men and women use words which are his and not their own; their reading is in the literature for which he cares; often they express thoughts which belong to him and not to them. Mr. Lawrence's inability to efface himself is now his most serious weakness, for the faulty construction of his earlier work is in no way evident in *Sons and Lovers*. After reading most of the more ''important'' novels of the present year, we can say that we have seen none to excel it in interest and power; the sum of its defects is astonishingly large, but we only note it when they are weighed against the sum of its own qualities. (p. 781)

A review of ''Sons and Lovers,'' in The Saturday Review, *London, Vol. 115, No. 3008, June 21, 1913, pp. 780-81.*

ALFRED BOOTH KUTTNER (essay date 1916)

[*In the following excerpt, Kuttner applies Freud's psycho-sexual theory of the Oedipal complex to Paul Morel's development in* Sons and Lovers. *Kuttner notes that Paul's relationship with his mother keeps him from maturing and from developing love for other women. He concludes that Paul's psychologically confining relationship with his mother stems from the absence of a positive male role model in the Morel home as well as from Mrs. Morel's excessive emotional attachment to her sons. For a contrasting interpretation that denigrates psychoanalytic readings of the novel, see the excerpt by John Macy (1922).*]

Sons and Lovers has the great distinction of being very solidly based upon a veritable commonplace of our emotional life; it deals with a son who loved his mother too dearly, and with a mother who lavished all her affection upon her son.

Neither this distinction nor its undeniable freshness and often amazing style would of itself entitle Mr. D. H. Lawrence's novel to anything beyond an appreciative book review. But it sometimes happens that a piece of literature acquires an added significance by virtue of the support it gives to the scientific study of human motives. Literary records have the advantage of being the fixed and classic expression of human emotions which in the living individual are usually too fluid and elusive for deliberate study. . . . Literature thus becomes an invaluable accessory to the psychologist, who usually does well to regard with suspicion any new generalization from his researches for which the whole range of literary expression yields no corroboration. But if he can succeed in finding support there his position is immensely strengthened. For a new truth about ourselves, which may seem altogether grotesque and impossible when presented to us as an arid theory, often gains unexpected confirmation when presented to us in a powerful work of literature as an authentic piece of life. When at last we recognize ourselves we like the thrill of having made a discovery.

Sons and Lovers possesses this double quality to a high degree. It ranks high, very high as a piece of literature and at the same time it embodies a theory which it illustrates and exemplifies with a completeness that is nothing less than astonishing. Fortunately there can be no doubt as to the authenticity of the author's inspiration. For it would be fatal if the novel had been written with the express purpose of illustrating a theory: it would, by that very admission, be worthless as a proof of that theory. But it happens that Mr. Lawrence has already produced notable work, mainly some early and evidently autobiographical poems, which show his preoccupation with the identical theme. *Sons and Lovers* is thus truly creative, in that it is built up internally—as any masterpiece must be—out of the psychic conflicts of the author, and any testimony which it may bear to the truth of the theory involved will therefore be first hand.

The theory to which I have been referring is Professor Sigmund Freud's theory of the psychological evolution of the emotion of love as finally expressed by a man or a woman towards a member of the other sex, and the problem which Mr. Lawrence voices is the struggle of a man to emancipate himself from his maternal allegiance and to transfer his affections to a woman who stands outside of his family circle. What the poet has seen as a personal problem the scientist has formulated as a theory. I shall outline the problem first and then relate it to the theory. If the theory can succeed in generalizing the truth which Mr. Lawrence's novel presents the reader will realize with fresh force that fiction, to be great art, must be based upon human verities.

First we shall see how it happened that the mother in this story came to lavish all her affections upon her son. In the opening chapter Mrs. Morel, the wife of a Derbyshire coal miner, is expecting her third child, the boy Paul, who is to become the central figure of the story. Her life with her husband has already turned out to be a complete fiasco. He is a drunkard and a bully, a man with whom she shares neither intellectual, moral or religious sympathies. What strikes her most about Morel is that he presents a striking contrast to her father, who was to her *"the type of all men."* ... At the time of the birth of her third child the breach is already irreparable. Mrs. Morel dreads the coming of another child, conceived unwillingly out of a loveless relation, and at the sight of it a sense of guilt steals over her. She will atone:

> With all her force, with all her soul she would make up to it for having brought it into the world unloved. She would love it all the more now it was hers; carry it in her love.

Towards Paul she feels, as to none of the other children, that she must make up to him for an injury or a sin committed by her and that he must recompense her for all that she has missed in her shattered love for her husband.

All the early formative influences in Paul's life radiate from his mother. Physically he is more delicate than the other children so that his illnesses tend to further her concentration upon him still more. Paul is a "pale, quiet child" who seems "old for his years" and "very conscious of what other people felt, particularly his mother. When she fretted he understood, and could have no peace. His soul seemed always attentive to her." His mother and for a time his sister Annie are his only real companions. His brother William is too old to be his playmate and other children play no role in his early childhood. One vicious bond of sympathy unites all the Morel children: their common hate and contempt for their father.... The strain is greatest upon Paul.... Already at an early age these hostile feelings take definite shape. He often prays: "Lord, let my father die." And then, with a kind of guilty conscience: "Let him not be killed at pit." ... Indelible among his earliest impressions must have been that gross and terrifying figure, threatening his life and that of his mother, whose convulsive movements to protect him must have aroused an answering quiver in the child.

The early relations between mother and child are full of a delicate and poetic charm. Paul's admiration for his mother knows no bounds; her presence is always absorbing. Often, at the sight of her, "his heart contracts with love." Everything he does is for her, the flowers he picks as well as the prizes he wins at school. His mother is his intimate and his confidant, he has no other chums. When Morel is confined to the hospital through an accident in the mine, Paul joyfully plays the husband, "I'm the man in the house now." He is happiest when alone with her. By this time the interaction between mother and son is complete; she lives in him and he in her. In fact his whole attitude towards her is but the answer which she gradually evokes from him as her whole life finds expression in her son.

> In the end she shared everything with him without knowing.... She waited for his coming home in the evening, and then she unburdened herself of all she had pondered, or of all that had occurred to her during the day. He sat and

listened with his earnestness. The two shared lives. . . .

Mother and son are one; the husband is completely effaced and the father exists merely as a rival.

But now Paul is to strike out for himself. He takes up an occupation and finds himself attracted to women. His mother's whole emphasis has always been towards making Paul interested in some other occupation than his father's dirty digging, as a protest against the sordidness of the life that she herself has been compelled to lead with him. She therefore encourages the boy's liking for pretty things, for flowers and sunsets and fancy stuffs, and is delighted when his slender artistic endowment begins to express itself in pencil and paint. Her emotional revolt against her husband here takes an esthetic turn, as people are often driven to beauty by their loathing of the ugly, and it is interesting to note that Mrs. Morel's tendencies to estheticize Paul and to effeminate him go hand in hand, as if the two sprang from a common root. Paul never becomes a real artist. He uses his painting to please his mother and to court his women, but in the crises of his life his art means nothing to him either as a consolation or as a satisfying expression.... He himself has no ambition. All that he wants is

> quietly to earn his thirty or thirty-five shillings a week somewhere near home, and then, when his father died, have a cottage with his mother, paint and go out as he liked, and live happy ever after.

Not, like any normal boy, to strike out for himself, to adventure, to emulate and surpass his father, but to go on living with his mother forever! That is the real seed of Paul's undoing. We shall now trace the various attempts on his part to emancipate himself from his mother by centering his affections upon some other woman.

The first woman to attract Paul is Miriam Leivers, a shy, exalted and romantic girl who leads a rather lonely life with her parents and brothers on a neighboring farm. Paul's approach is characteristically indirect; he begins by avoiding the girl and cultivating her mother. Meanwhile Miriam, piqued by the neglect of this well-mannered boy, who seems so gentle and superior, has fallen in love with him. Paul is fascinated but uneasy and fights shy of personal intimacy with her. The intensity of her emotions frightens him and impresses him as unwholesome. He finds her growing absorption in him strangely discomfitting: "Always something in his breast shrank from these close, intimate, dazzled looks of hers." His feminine attitude towards her tends to reverse the usual method of courtship; it is Miriam who has to seek him out, to call for him and make sure of his coming again. Paul tries to approach her in two ways; through his art and as her teacher. Both methods are really self-defensive, they are barriers that he erects against Miriam to prevent anything too personal from arising between them to keep his real self, as it were, inviolate. (pp. 295-300)

Paul resists every intimation that he is falling in love with Miriam. He indignantly repudiates his mother's insinuation that he is courting and hastens to assure Miriam: "We aren't lovers, we are friends." And Miriam, who has already gone so far, tries to fortify herself with a prayer. "O Lord, let me not love Paul Morel. Keep me from loving him, if I ought not to love him." But her love breaks through again and her healthier instincts triumph. Henceforth Paul can do with her as he will. But he can do nothing with her love because he cannot return it. Love seems to him like a "very terrible thing." The honest and more impersonal passion that he feels for her frightens him. "He was afraid of her. The fact that he might want her as a man wants a woman had in him been suppressed into a shame." He cannot even kiss her. And he hates her again because she makes him despise himself. They gradually move to the edge of a quarrel.

And now Mrs. Morel makes her appeal. Almost from the first she has mistrusted Miriam. She fears that Miriam will absorb him and take him away from her. "She is one of those who will want to suck a man's soul out till he has none of his own left." Her jealousy revels in the exaggerated simile of the vampire. "She exults—she exults as she carries him off from me. . . . She's not like an ordinary woman . . . she wants to absorb him . . . she will suck him up." So she throws down the gauntlet to her rival. She makes Paul feel wretched, as only a mother can make a son feel, whenever he has been with Miriam. Her comments grow spiteful and satiric; she no longer takes the trouble to hide her jealousy and plagues him like a cast woman. . . . But Mrs. Morel does not stop there. She makes the final, ruthless, cowardly appeal.

> "And I've never—you know, Paul—I've never had a husband—not—really—"
>
> He stroked his mother's hair, and his mouth was on her throat.
>
> "Well, I don't love her, mother," he murmured, bowing his head and hiding his eyes on her shoulder in misery. His mother kissed him, a long, fervent kiss.
>
> "My boy!" she said, in a voice trembling with passionate love.
>
> Without knowing, he gently stroked her face.

Thus she wins him back. He will continue to console her for her husband. There follows the scene where Paul almost thrashes his drunken father and implores his mother not to share the same bed with him. It is a crisis in his life:

> . . . he was at peace because he still loved his mother best. It was the bitter peace of resignation.

But there is some resistance in him still. For a time he stands divided between his two loves. "And he felt dreary and hopeless between the two." In church, sitting between them, he feels at peace: "uniting his two loves under the spell of the place of worship." But most of the time he is torn between the two women. He does not understand his feelings. "And why did he hate Miriam and feel so cruel towards her at the thought of his mother?" His emotions towards Miriam are constantly changing. Sometimes his passion tries to break through. But it cannot free itself. "I'm so damned spiritual with *you* always!" He blames her for the humiliating sense of impotence which he feels. It is all her fault. He transfers all his inhibitions to her and consciously echoes his mother's accusations. "You absorb, absorb, as if you must fill yourself up with love, because you've got a shortage somewhere." . . . But at last he tells her that he does not love her, that he cannot love her physically. "I can only give friendship—it's all I'm capable of—it's a flaw in my make-up. . . . Let us have done." And finally he writes:

> "In all our relations no body enters. I do not talk to you through the senses—rather through

the spirit. That is why we cannot love in common sense. Ours is not an everyday affection."

Thus he tries to spiritualize their relations out of existence. He would persuade himself of his own impotence.

Paul's whole experience with Miriam has thrown him back upon his mother; he gets away from Miriam by returning to her. . . . "She loved him first; he loved her first." He is her child again and for a time he feels content. They go off on a charming excursion to Lincoln Cathedral. He behaves like a lover out with his girl, buying her flowers and treating her. Suddenly there surges up in him a childhood memory of the time when his mother was young and fair, before life wrung her dry and withered her. If only he had been her eldest son so that his memory of her could still be more youthful!

> "What are you old for!" he said, mad with his own impotence. "Why can't you walk, why can't you come with me to places?"

He does not like to have such an old sweetheart.

At the same time his whole outlook upon life also grows childish again. When his sister Annie marries he tries to console his mother. "But I shan't marry, mother. I shall live with you, and we'll have a servant." . . . His plans for the future have not changed. He thinks at twenty-two as he thought at fourteen, like a child that goes on living a fairy-tale. But it is a false contentment and he pays the penalty for it. In resigning the natural impulse to love he also resigns the impulse to live. Life cannot expand in him, it is turned back upon itself and becomes the impulse to die. . . . Mrs. Morel sees the danger and divines the remedy.

> At this rate she knew he would not live. . . . She wished she knew some nice woman—she did not know what she wished, but left it vague.

But now she knows that she can no longer hold her son to her exclusively.

At this point Paul begins to turn to another woman, Clara Dawes, a friend of Miriam. She is married, but lives separated from her husband. Paul has known her for some time before becoming intimate with her. She exerts a frankly sensual attraction upon him without having any of that mystical unattainableness about her which he felt so strongly with Miriam. Her presence has had the effect of gradually seducing him away from Miriam without his knowing it. There would be less difficulty with her. She is a married woman and is unhappy with her husband, like his mother. To love her would not be so momentous a thing, he would be less unfaithful to his mother if he had an affair with a woman who already belonged to someone else. Their relations threaten to become typical of the young man and the woman of thirty. . . . Clara's first service to him is to talk to him like a woman of the world and thus correct his self-delusion about Miriam: ". . . she doesn't want any of your soul communion. That's your own imagination. She wants you." He objects. "'You've never tried,' she answered." Thus she gives him courage to do what he never could have done of his own accord.

The force which drives him back to Miriam is nothing but the sheer, pent-up sexual desire that has alternately been provoked and repressed in him. Now indeed it is a completely detached thing which does not belong to any woman. He has almost entirely succeeded in de-personalizing it. That is why he feels that he can let it run its course. But not in any personal way.

He did no feel that he wanted marriage with Miriam. He wished he did. He would have given his head to have felt a joyous desire to marry her and have her. Then why couldn't he bring it off? There was some obstacle; and what was the obstacle? It lay in the physical bondage. He shrank from the physical contact. But why? With her he felt bound up inside himself. He could not go out to her. Something struggled in him, but he could not get to her. Why?

And Miriam does not insist upon marriage, she is willing to try out their feelings for each other. Theirs is a pitiful love-making. He cannot bear the blaze of love in her eyes; it is as if he must first draw a veil over her face and forget her. . . . He turns back to his men friends and to Clara's company and the old quarrel between him and Miriam breaks out afresh. He decides to break off his relations with her. But at last he is to hear the truth about himself from Miriam. "'Always—it has been so!' she cried. 'It has been one long battle between us— you fighting away from me.'" He tries to tell her that they have had some perfect hours. But she knows that these do not make up the healthy continuity of life. "Always, from the very beginning—always the same!" She has called him a child of four. It is the truth, and it goes to the heart of his vanity. She has treated him as a mother treats a perverse child. He cannot stand it.

> He hated her. All these years she had treated him as if he were a hero, and thought of him secretly as an infant, a foolish child. Then why had she left the foolish child to his folly? His heart was hard against her.

The full flood of his passion, freed of some of its incubus through his experience with Miriam, now turns to Clara. He tries to wear it out on her in the same impersonal way, and for a time lives in sheer physical ecstasy. With her at least he has had some solace, some relief. His mother has not stood so much between them. But it is only temporary, he cannot give himself to Clara any more than he could give himself to Miriam. Clara loves him or would love him if he could only rise above the mere passion that threw them together.

> "I feel," she continued slowly, "as if I hadn't got you, as if all of you weren't there, and as if it weren't *me* you were taking—" "Who then?" "Something just for yourself. It has been fine, so that I daren't think of it. But is it me you want, or is it *It*?" . . . He again felt guilty. Did he leave Clara out of count and take simply woman? But he thought that was splitting a hair.

They begin to drift apart. He rehearses his old difficulties with his mother. "I feel sometimes as if I wronged my women, mother." But he doesn't know why.

> "I even love Clara, and I did Miriam; but to give myself to them in marriage I couldn't. I couldn't belong to them. They seem to want *me,* and I can't even give it them."
>
> "You haven't met the right woman."
>
> "And I shall never meet the right woman while you live."

His relations with Clara have brought about a marked change in Paul's attitude towards his mother. It is as if he realized at last that she is destroying his life's happiness. . . . But his realization, as far as it goes, brings no new initiative. He is twenty-four years old now but he still sums up his ambition as before: "Go somewhere in a pretty house near London with my mother."

The book now rounds out with the death of Paul's mother. Mrs. Morel gradually wastes away with a slow and changeful illness; it is an incurable tumor, with great pain. Paul takes charge and never leaves his mother until the end. Their intimacy is occasionally disturbed by the clumsy intrusion of Morel, whose presence merely serves to irritate his wife. Paul and she commune with the old tenderness. . . . Their reserve drops before the imminence of death, it seems as if they would be frank at last. But there is also the old constraint. "They were both afraid of the veils that were ripping between them." He suffers intensely. "He felt as if his life were being destroyed, piece by piece, within him." But mingled with his love and his anguish at her suffering there now enters a new feeling: the wish that she should die. Something in him wants her to die; seeing that she cannot live he would free both her and himself by hastening her death. So he gradually cuts down her nourishment and increases the deadliness of her medicine. Here again he approaches close to the source of his trouble; he dimly realizes that he has never lived outside of his mother and therefore has never really lived. The feeling that he cannot live without her and the feeling that he cannot live a life of his own as long as she is alive, here run side by side. But when the death which he himself has hastened overtakes her, he cries with a lover's anguish:

> "My love—my love—oh, my love!" he whispered again and again. "My love—oh, my love!"

But death has not freed Paul from his mother. It has completed his allegiance to her. For death has merely removed the last earthly obstacle to their ideal union; now he can love her as Dante loved his Beatrice. He avows his faithfulness to her by breaking off with the only two other women who have meant anything to him. He is completely resigned, life and death are no longer distinguished in his thinking. Life for him is only where his mother is and she is dead. So why live? He cannot answer, life has become contradictory.

> There seemed no reason why people should go along the street, and houses pile up in the daylight. There seemed no reason why these things should occupy space, instead of leaving it empty. . . . He wanted everything to stand still, so that he could be with her again.

But life in him is just a hair stronger than death.

> He would not say it. He would not admit that he wanted to die, to have done. He would not own that life had beaten him, or that death had beaten him.

The last chapter of the book is called "Derelict." The title emphasizes Mr. Lawrence's already unmistakable meaning. Paul is adrift now; with the death of his mother he has lost his only mooring in life. There is no need to follow him further; when he is through despairing he will hope again and when he has compared one woman to his mother and found her wanting, he will go on to another, in endless repetition. (pp. 300-06)

Such is the condensed account of Paul's love-life. Textual testimony could hardly go further to show that Paul loved his mother too dearly. And shall we now say that it was *because* Mrs. Morel lavished all her affection upon her son? But then, most mothers lavish a good deal of affection upon their sons and it is only natural for sons to love their mothers dearly. Why should an excess of these sacred sentiments produce such devastating results? For it is undoubtedly the intention of the author to show us Paul as a wreck and a ruin, a man damned out of all happiness at the age of twenty-five, who has barely the strength left to will not to die. And why should we accept as a type this man who seems to bear so many ear-marks of degeneracy and abnormal impulse, who is alternately a ruthless egotist and a vicious weakling in his dealings with women, and who in the end stoops to shorten the life of his own mother? Surely the thing is deeper and due to profounder causes. But of these the author gives us no indication. Let us therefore assume for the moment that Paul is by no means a degenerate, but merely an exaggeration of the normal, unhealthily nursed into morbid manifestations by an abnormal environment. If that can be established it may very well be that the story of Paul's love-life simply throws into high relief an intimate and constant relation between parent and child the significance of which has hitherto escaped general observation. Perhaps all men have something of Paul in them. In that case their instinctive recognition of their kinship with the hero of the book would go a great way towards explaining the potency of *Sons and Lovers*. We are fond of saying something like that about Hamlet. (pp. 306-07)

We can now return to *Sons and Lovers* with a new understanding. Why has the attitude of the son to his mother here had such a devastating effect upon his whole life? Why could he not overcome this obstacle like other children and ultimately attain some measure of manhood? Why, in short, was the surrender so complete? In Paul's case the abnormal fixation upon the mother is most obviously conditioned by the father, whose unnatural position in the family is responsible for the distortion of the normal attitude of the child towards its parents. The father ideal simply does not exist for Paul; where there should have been an attractive standard of masculinity to imitate, he can only fear and despise. The child's normal dependence upon the mother is perpetuated because there is no counter-influence to detach it from her. But there is another distortion, equally obvious, which fatally influences the natural development. Paul's early fixation upon his mother is met and enhanced by Mrs. Morel's abnormally concentrated affection for her son. Her unappeased love, which can no longer go out towards her husband, turns to Paul for consolation; she *makes* him love her too well. Her love becomes a veritable Pandora's box of evil. For Paul is now hemmed in on all sides by too much love and too much hate.

If now we compare Paul's boyhood and adolescence with, let us say, the reader's own, we find that the difference is, to a great extent, one of consciousness and unconsciousness. All those psychic processes which are usually unconscious or at least heavily veiled in the normal psycho-sexual development lie close to consciousness in Paul and break through into his waking thoughts at every favorable opportunity. Everything is raw and exposed in him and remains so, kept quick to the touch by the pressure of an abnormal environment which instead of moulding, misshapes him. The normal hostility towards the father which is conditioned in every boy by a natural jealousy of the mother's affection, is nursed in him to a conscious hate through Morel's actual brutality and his mother's undisguised bitterness and contempt. And the normal love for the mother which ordinarily serves as a model for the man's love for other women is in him perverted into abnormal expression almost at his mother's breast, so that he is always conscious of his infatuation with his mother and can never free his love-making from that paralyzing influence. These powerful determinants of the love-life which we acquire from our parents would be too overwhelming in every case were it not for the process of submersion or repression already referred to. This repression usually sets in at an early stage of childhood and acts biologically as a protective mechanism by allowing us to develop a slowly expanding sense of selfhood through which we gradually differentiate ourselves from our parents. In this way the fateful dominance of the parents is broken, though their influence remains in the unconscious as a formative and directing impulse.

In Paul this salutary process never takes place because he cannot free himself from the incubus of his parents long enough to come to some sense of himself. He remains enslaved by his parent complex instead of being moulded and guided by it.

Paul cannot expand towards the universe in normal activity and form an independent sex interest because for him his mother

---

SONS AND LOVERS

BY

D. H. LAWRENCE

AUTHOR OF
"LOVE POEMS," "THE WHITE PEACOCK," "THE TRESPASSER"

LONDON : DUCKWORTH & CO.
HENRIETTA STREET, COVENT GARDEN
1913

Title page of the first edition of Sons and Lovers.

has become the universe; she stands between him and life and the other woman. There is a kind of bottomless childishness about him; life in a pretty house with his mother—the iteration sounds like a childish prattle. Miriam feels it when she calls him a child of four which she can no longer nurse. Nor can Clara help him by becoming a wanton substitute for his mother. Only the one impossible ideal holds him, and that means the constant turning in upon himself which is death. Paul goes to pieces because he can never make the mature sexual decision away from his mother, he can never accomplish the physical and emotional transfer.

If now this striking book, taken as it stands, bears such unexpected witness to the truth of Freud's remarkable psychosexual theory, it is at least presumable that the author himself and the rest of his work also stand in some very definite relation to this theory. The feeling that *Sons and Lovers* must be autobiographical is considerably strengthened by the somewhat meager personal detail which Mr. Edwin Björkman supplies in an introduction to Mr. Lawrence's first play. Mr. Lawrence was himself the son of a collier in the Derbyshire coal-mining district and his mother seems to have occupied an exceptional position in the family, showing herself to be a woman of great fortitude and initiative, who evidently dominated the household. Mr. Björkman is silent concerning the father, but gives us the interesting information that *Sons and Lovers* was written not long after the mother's death. This information is not sufficient, however, to warrant our inquiry going beyond the author's writings, a step for which, in any case, it would be necessary to have both his permission and his coöperation. We must therefore limit ourselves to the testimony of Mr. Lawrence's work. This consists of two additional novels, a volume of poems, and a play. What is truly astonishing is that all of these, in various disguises and transparent elaborations, hark back to the same problem: the direct and indirect effects of an excessive maternal allegiance and the attempt to become emancipated from it. (pp. 311-14)

In the story of Paul the author has reached the final expression of a problem which haunts his every effort. The creative labor of self-realization which makes *Sons and Lovers* such a priceless commentary on the love-life of to-day, accomplished itself but slowly in Mr. Lawrence, waiting, no doubt, for his artistic maturity and the final clarity which the death of his mother must have brought. And if, as I have tried to show, he has been able, though unknowingly, to attest the truth of what is perhaps the most far-reaching psychological theory ever propounded, he has also given us an illuminating insight into the mystery of artistic creation. For Mr. Lawrence has escaped the destructive fate that dogs the hapless Paul by the grace of expression: out of the dark struggles of his own soul he has emerged as a triumphant artist. In every epoch the soul of the artist is sick with the problems of his generation. He cures himself by expression in his art. And by producing a catharsis in the spectator through the enjoyment of his art he also heals his fellow beings. His artistic stature is measured by the universality of the problem which his art has transfigured. (pp. 316-17)

Alfred Booth Kuttner, "'Sons and Lovers': A Freudian Appreciation," in The Psychoanalytic Review, *Vol. III, No. 3, July, 1916, pp. 295-317.*

JOHN MACY (essay date 1922)

[*Macy was an American literary critic and an editor of the* Boston Herald *and* The Nation. *His most important work was* The Spirit

of American Literature *(1913), which denounced the genteel tradition and called for realism and the use of native materials in American literature. In the following excerpt Macy praises* Sons and Lovers, *claiming that it demonstrates the full range of Lawrence's art: his gifts of presenting the realistic, the lyric, and the tragic. He compares Lawrence's talent as a novelist to that of Thomas Hardy and George Meredith. In an aside, Macy denigrates those who would read the novel as a demonstration of any psychoanalytic theory. For one example of such a reading, see the excerpt by Alfred Booth Kuttner (1916).*]

[*Sons and Lovers* is]—a masterpiece in which every sentence counts, a book crammed with significant thought and beautiful, arresting phrases, the work of a singular genius whose gifts are more richly various than those of any other young English novelist.

To appreciate the rich variety of Mr. Lawrence we must read his later novels and his volumes of poetry. But *Sons and Lovers* reveals the range of his power. Here are combined and fused the hardest sort of "realism" and almost lyric imagery and rhythm. The speech of the people is that of daily life and the things that happen to them are normal adventures and accidents; they fall in love, marry, work, fail, succeed, die. But of their deeper emotions and of the relations of these little human beings to the earth and to the stars Mr. Lawrence makes something as near to poetry as prose dare be without violating its proper "other harmony."

Take the marvellous paragraph on next to the last page (Mr. Lawrence depends so little on plot in the ordinary sense of the word that it is perfectly fair to read the end of his book first):

> Where was he? One tiny upright speck of flesh, less than an ear of wheat lost in the field. He could not bear it. On every side the immense dark silence seemed pressing him, so tiny a spark, into extinction, and yet, almost nothing, he could not be extinct. Night, in which everything was lost, went reaching out, beyond stars and sun, stars and sun, a few bright grains, went spinning round for terror, and holding each other in embrace, there in the darkness that outpassed them all, and left them tiny and daunted. So much, and himself, infinitesimal, at the core a nothingness, and yet not nothing.

Such glorious writing (and this lovely passage is matched by many others) lifts the book far above a novel which is merely a story. I beg the reader to attend to every line of it and not to miss a single one of the many sentences that haunt, startle, and waylay. Some are rhapsodical and cosmic, like the foregoing; others are shrewd, "realistic" observations of things and people. In one of his books Mr. Lawrence makes a character say, or think, that life is "mixed." That indicates his philosophy and his method. He blends the accurately literal and trivial with the immensely poetic.

To find a similar blending of minute diurnal detail and wide imaginative vision we must go back to two older novelists, Hardy and Meredith. I do not mean that Mr. Lawrence derives immediately from them or, indeed, that he is clearly the disciple of any master. I do feel simply that he is of the elder stature of Hardy and Meredith, and I know of no other young novelist who is quite worthy of their company. (pp. v-vi)

Mr. Lawrence possesses supremely in his way a sense which Meredith and Hardy possess supremely in theirs, a sense of the earth, of nature, of the soil in which human nature is rooted.

His landscapes are not painted cloth; they are the living land and sky, inseparable from the characters of the people who move upon the land, are pathetically adrift under the splendid inscrutable heavens. The beauty of the scene, for all its splendour, is usually sad; nature is baffling and tragic in its loveliness. Young people in love make ecstatic flights to the clouds and meet with Icarian disasters. From luminous moments they plunge into what Mr. Lawrence calls "the bitterness of ecstasy." Their pain outweighs their joy many times over, as in Hardy, and as in the more genial Meredith, whose rapturous digression played on a penny whistle in *Richard Feverel* is a heart-breaking preparation for the agonies that ensue.

Does not the phrase, "bitterness of ecstasy," sound, with all honour to Mr. Lawrence, as if Hardy might have made it? And would you be surprised if you found in Hardy the following sentence . . .? "Annie's candle flickered, and she whimpered as the first men appeared, and the limbs and bowed heads of six men struggled to climb into the room bearing the coffin that rode like sorrow on their living flesh."

Mr. Lawrence's tragic sense and the prevalent indifference to magnificent writing probably account for the fact that this fine novel did not instantly win a large audience. . . . The weak and the ignorant are quite safe from this austere artist, for they will not read a third of the way through any of his novels.

Though with this book Mr. Lawrence took his place at once among the established veterans, nevertheless he belongs to our time, to this century, not to the age of Victoria. He is solid and mature, but he shows his youth in an inquisitive restlessness, and he betrays his modernity, if in no other way, by his interest in psychoanalysis. He has made amateurish excursions into that subject, which may or may not be a fruitful subject for a novelist to study. What he has brought back in the form of exposition interests me very little, but there is no doubt that his investigations have influenced his fiction, even this book which was written before everybody went a-freuding. . . . Mr. Lawrence is too fine an artist to import into his art the dubious lingo of psychoanalysis. I doubt, however, if without that muddled pseudo-science (muddled because the facts are muddled) Mr. Lawrence's later fiction would be just what it is. And the main theme of *Sons and Lovers* is the relation of Paul to his mother. No, it is not an Œdipus-Jocasta "complex" nor a Hamlet-Gertrude "complex," though you may assimilate this touching story to those complexes if you enjoy translating human life in such terms. The important thing is that Mr. Lawrence has created a new version of the old son-mother story which is more ancient than Sophocles and which shall be a modern instance as long as there are poets and novelists. In its lowest form it is the sentimental home-and-mother theme so dear, and rightly dear, to the hearts of the people. In its highest form it is tragic poetry. And only a little below that poetry is the tremendous pathos of Paul's last whimper in this book.

Let whoever cares to try analyse or psychoanalyse. I doubt if Mr. Lawrence himself could make clear work of explaining his book. It is not necessary. It is enough that he has made his characters understandable through and through, even their perplexities understandable as perplexities. That is all the artist, the interpreter of life in fiction, can do or ought to do. And to do it with clearness and fidelity and with magical command of words, the mysterious thing called "style," is to be a great artist. (pp. vi-viii)

John Macy, in an introduction to Sons and Lovers *by D. H. Lawrence, 1922. Reprint by The Modern Library, 1923, pp. v-viii.*

JOHN MIDDLETON MURRY   (essay date 1931)

[*Murry was a noted magazine editor and influential literary critic during the first half of the twentieth century. A longtime contributor of literary criticism to* The Times Literary Supplement, *he was the last editor of the distinguished review* The Atheneaum *before its absorption by* The Nation, *and founding editor of* The Adelphi. *Murry is perhaps best known as the husband of short-story writer Katherine Mansfield, whose letters and journals he published after her death. Considered a perceptive and romantic critic whose work reveals his "honesty to the point of masochism," he has contributed important studies on the works of Mansfield, John Keats, Fedor Dostoevski, William Blake, and his intimate friend, D. H. Lawrence. In the following excerpt from* Son of Woman: The Story of D. H. Lawrence, *Murry claims that* Sons and Lovers *was Lawrence's attempt to free himself from his past, and so examines the novel's close correspondence to Lawrence's life, treating Lawrence and his character Paul Morel interchangeably. For a reading of the novel critical of Murry's interpretation, see the excerpt by R. P. Draper (1958).*]

"The first part of *Sons and Lovers*," Lawrence wrote in an account of himself not many months before he died, "is all autobiography." The direct assurance was hardly necessary. We have only to compare *The White Peacock*, which preceded it, with *Sons and Lovers* to be instantly aware of a new element of immediate veracity. *The White Peacock* is a story, *Sons and Lovers* is the life of a man. (p. 6)

It is a magnificent book: for those who do not care to follow Lawrence in the passionate exploration of life which subsequently engrossed him, it will probably remain his greatest book. If Lawrence is to be judged as the "pure artist," then it is true that he never surpassed, and barely equalled, this rich and moving record of a life. But Lawrence is not to be judged as a "pure artist"; if ever a writer had "an axe to grind" it was he. Set in the perspective—the only relevant perspective—of his own revealed intentions, *Sons and Lovers* appears as the gesture of man who makes the heroic effort to liberate himself from the matrix of his own past. With it he tries to put his youth firmly behind him, and to stand stripped to run his own race. He is the brilliant, jewel-brown horse-chestnut, of his favourite image, newly issued from the burr. He breaks forth from the husk of his youth, from the husk which had been one flesh with him till this emergence, and takes the past into consciousness and cognizance. That knowing is as much a severance, as an acknowledgment. Lawrence therefore tried to make it extraordinarily complete.

Sons and Lovers has a double richness: as the intimate life-history of the youth of a genius, and as a significant act. The significance of the act of writing the book will only be fully apparent when we have considered the life-history which it records. (pp. 7-8)

Sons and Lovers is the story of Paul Morel's desperate attempts to break away from the tie that was strangling him. All unconsciously, his mother had roused in him the stirrings of sexual desire; she had, by the sheer intensity of her diverted affection made him a man before his time. He felt for his mother what he should have felt for the girl of his choice. . . . Lawrence was not, so far as we can tell, sexually precocious; he was spiritually precocious. We are told that Paul Morel remained virgin till twenty-three. But his spiritual love for his mother was fully developed long before. What could be more poignant, or in implication more fearful, than the story he tells of the illness which fell upon him at sixteen? . . .

> Paul was very ill. His mother lay in bed at nights with him; they could not afford a nurse. He grew worse, and the crisis approached. One night he tossed into consciousness in the ghastly, sickly feeling of dissolution, when all the cells in the body seem in intense irritability to be breaking down, and consciousness makes a last flare of struggle, like madness.
>
> "I s'll die, mother!" he cried, heaving for breath on the pillow.
>
> She lifted him up, crying in a small voice:
>
> "Oh, my son—my son!"
>
> That brought him to. He realized her. His whole will rose up and arrested him. He put his head on her breast, and took ease of her for love.

It is terribly poignant, and terribly wrong. Almost better that a boy should die than have such an effort forced upon him by such means. He is called upon to feel in full consciousness for his mother all that a full-grown man might feel for the wife of his bosom.

In this same year, when Lawrence was sixteen, he met the girl Miriam, whose destiny was to be linked with his own for the next ten years, until his mother's death. He also met the farm and the family of which Miriam was the daughter. It became a second home to him. Beautifully situated in a valley about three miles away from the miner's cottage in Eastwood, the small decaying farm, with its pastures nibbled by rabbits to the quick, gave him the full freedom of that natural life which was always washing to the edge of the mining village. There he found the richness of life without which he wilted. He became as one of the family, and the Leivers' kitchen more dear to him than his own. (pp. 13-14)

Miriam was about the same age as himself, perhaps a year younger, when Lawrence met her. She encouraged, stimulated, and appreciated his gifts; she saw in him the wonderful being that he was, and she had fallen in love with him long before he with her. She was free to fall in love; he was not. So that when we say that Lawrence fell in love with Miriam, we mean that had he been free, and not bound, and ever more deliberately and tightly bound, he might have fallen in love with her, as she undoubtedly did with him. He fell in love with her only so far as he was capable of falling in love.

The history is painful. In *Sons and Lovers,* Lawrence tells it as though Miriam failed him; and he tried, even at the end of his life in *Lady Chatterley's Lover,* to tell the story thus.

> I held forth with rapture to her, positively with rapture. I simply went up in smoke. And she adored me. The serpent in the grass was sex. She somehow didn't have any, at least not where it's supposed to be. I got thinner and crazier. Then I said we'd got to be lovers. I talked her into it. So she let me. I was excited, and she never wanted it. She adored me, and loved me to talk to her and kiss her; in that way she had a passion for me. But the other she just didn't want. And there are lots of women like her.

And it was just the other that I *did* want. So there we split. I was cruel and left her.

Lawrence at all times needed desperately to convince himself in this matter of Miriam, and to the end he did not succeed. He does not tell the truth in *Sons and Lovers,* still less in *Lady Chatterley:* he comes closest to the truth in the *Fantasia.* Actually, while his mother still lived, he was incapable of giving to another woman the love without which sexual possession must be a kind of violence done: done not to the woman only, but also and equally to the man: above all to a man like Lawrence. All his life long Lawrence laboured to convince himself, and other people, that sexual desire carried with it its own validity: that the spiritual and the sexual were distinct. In fact, he never could believe it. What he did believe was something quite different, and quite true, namely that, in a man and woman who are whole, as he never was whole, the spiritual and the sexual might be one. This he declared in *Fantasia,* and yet again with his latest breath, in *The Escaped Cock.* He believed in a harmony which it was impossible for him personally to achieve, without a physical resurrection.

So saying, we anticipate: but it is essential to grasp as clearly as we can the subtle human tragedy of the affair with Miriam. It was the tragedy of Lawrence's entry into sexual life, and it haunted him all his days. In *Sons and Lovers* he conceals the truth. He cannot endure really to face it in consciousness. The story told there is subtly inconsistent with itself. At one moment comes a gleam of full recognition, as when he says of his mother: "She bore him, loved him, kept him, and his love turned back into her, so that he could not be free to go forward with his own life, really love another woman." But as he tells the story of the passion itself, he represents that it is not himself, but Miriam who is at fault. She is frigid, she shrinks from sexual passion; and this may be true in part. But the truth was only partial. When later Lawrence came to a woman who was not frigid, the failure, though long drawn out, was more painful still. In representing that the fault was Miriam's, Lawrence wronged her. But we have to remember that *Sons and Lovers* was written after the death of his mother at a moment when Lawrence believed that he had attained sexual fulfilment. If he had not attained it with Miriam, he had some faint excuse for thinking that the fault was hers. He felt that it was not his own fault, and he had good reason for that. Nevertheless, it was his duty in *Sons and Lovers* to put the blame where it lay—if on a person at all, then upon his mother, who had taken from him that to which she had no right, and had used the full weight of her tremendous influence to prevent her son from giving to a woman the love which she so jealously guarded for herself. The fight was between his mother and Miriam, and it was an utterly unequal battle, between a strong and jealous woman and a diffident and unawakened girl.

In the story, Miriam is sacrificed, because Lawrence cannot tell the truth. Probably he could not tell it even to himself. The physical relation with Miriam was impossible. "You will not easily get a man to believe," he wrote in *Fantasia,* "that his carnal love for the woman he has made his wife is as high a love as that he felt for his mother." If Lawrence could write that when he had found his wife, and when his mother had been dead ten years, what did he feel while his mother was still alive, and he was engaged in talking Miriam into being his lover? He might talk and talk, but how could he convince her of what he did not himself believe—namely, that it was good that she should yield herself to him. He was a divided man. His love and his passion were separated. And because his passion was separated from his love, his passion was not true passion; it had but half the man behind, and to his own thinking, the worse half. This was the poisoned sting. He was, in his own eyes, degrading her, and degrading himself by his demand upon her.

What there was between Miriam and himself was an intense spiritual communion, and mutual stimulation of the mind. Whether it would ever, or could ever, have ripened into love on his side, who can say? Whatever it might have been was cankered in the bud. But I do not believe it ever could have ripened: Lawrence's subsequent history makes that plain to me. Happiness in love was not in Lawrence's destiny.

The appeal he made to Miriam was to her charity. He needed the comfort of her body, and she yielded herself to the sacrifice. (pp. 15-18)

Paul did not want her, but, as Mellors says in **Lady Chatterley's Lover,** "he wanted *it.*" Miriam did not want him, but she wanted to give him *it,* because he wanted it. The indulgence of their "passion" was disastrous, because it was not passion at all. On both sides it was deliberate, and not passionate. Miriam's charity was passionate, but she had no sexual desire for Paul; Paul's need for the release and rest of sexual communion was passionate, but not his desire for Miriam. Each was a divided and tortured being. Miriam strove to subdue her body to her spirit, Paul strove to subdue his spirit to his body. They hurt themselves, and they hurt each other. Consider Lawrence's own words in **Sons and Lovers**. . . . (p. 18)

Yet Paul did the hurt, the injustice, to Miriam, and still more to himself in the process. And the hurt he does her and himself is more delicate than he can acknowledge here. He does not and cannot feel towards her what by his own standards he must feel in order to justify his demand of her. He sacrifices her, or allows her to sacrifice herself, and in so doing, he violates himself. And the consequence is disaster; for their "passion" brings not the release from the torment of inward division which he seeks, but an exasperation of the torment.

From the new torment, new release is sought: and the appeal is always to the woman's charity. Clara Dawes is a married woman, where Miriam was virgin. It is easier for her to give, and easier for Paul to take. But the desire is not for the woman, but for release through the woman; and the woman gives not from desire but from pity. (p. 19)

At the crucial moment, we cannot distinguish between Clara and Miriam. One is married, one is virgin; but their attitude towards him is the same, the appeal he makes to them the same.

One's instinct shrinks from it all. It is all wrong, humanly wrong. This man, we feel, has no business with sex at all. He is born to be a saint: then let him be one, and become a eunuch for the sake of the Kingdom of Heaven. For him, we prophesy, sex must be one long laceration, one long and tortured striving for the unattainable. This feverish effort to become a man turns fatally upon itself; it makes him more a child than before. He struggles frenziedly to escape being child-man to his mother, and he becomes only child-man again to other women, and the first great bond is not broken. If the woman is virgin like Miriam, he breaks her, by communicating to her the agony of his own division; if the woman is married like Clara, she breaks him, by abasing him in his own eyes.

To love a woman, in the simplest and most universal sense of the word, was impossible to Lawrence while his mother lived.

Whether it was possible afterwards, the event will show. It will need almost a miracle, if he is to find his sexual salvation; for the fearful phrase of his own later invention fits him. It should fit him. He made it for himself. He is a man who is "crucified into sex," and he will carry the stigmata all his life.

Is it, we ask in pity and wonder, just a destiny? Is it simply that the sin of the father is visited through the mother upon the child? Was no escape possible? There is no answer to these questions; yet they return again and again to the mind. Surely, we say to ourselves, he could have broken that fearful bond that bound him to his mother. Was there not some ultimate weakness in the man that held him back? We may say that it was the terror of inflicting pain upon her. But there is a point at which the rarest and most tender virtue becomes a vice and a weakness; and perhaps to decide where that point lies is not so hard as it seems. When we begin to resent the compulsion of our virtues, they have become vices. Then the necessity of a choice and a decision is upon us: we must either cease to resent, or cease to obey, our virtues. Integrity lies either way. But to continue to obey, and to continue to resent—this means a cleavage which, once past a certain point, can never be healed again. Perhaps the final tragedy of Lawrence—and his life was finally a bitter tragedy—was that he could never make the choice on which his own integrity depended. To the end he resented his virtues, yet in act obeyed them, and in imagination blasphemed them.

Certainly, while his mother lived, until he himself was twenty-six, he resented the compulsion of his fear of paining her more and more deeply, yet he obeyed it. She was determined, consciously or unconsciously, that no woman save herself should have her son's love; and he obeyed her. What genuine and unhesitating passion there was in Lawrence's life before his mother's death went to a man, not a woman.

Miriam's eldest brother, the farmer's eldest son, Edgar Leivers of **Sons and Lovers,** George Saxton of **The White Peacock,** called forth in Lawrence something far more near to what most of us understand by passionate love than either Miriam or Clara. Contact with Miriam made him glow with a kind of spiritual incandescence; they throbbed together in a tense vibration of soul, which Paul strove vainly to convert into a passion of the body. His passion for Clara was from the beginning a physical need. But for the original of George and Edgar he must have felt something for which the best name is the simple one of love. In **Sons and Lovers** this friendship is but lightly touched; in **The White Peacock** the tremor of authenticity is not to be mistaken. . . . The record of this "friendship at its mystical best" culminates in the chapter, "A Poem of Friendship," and in the description of the two young men bathing together in the lake. They bathed in the morning cool of the hay-harvest, evidently the same hay-harvest which Paul and Edgar worked through together in **Sons and Lovers.**

> We stood and looked at each other as we rubbed ourselves dry. . . . He knew how I admired the noble, white fruitfulness of his form. As I watched him, he stood in white relief against the mass of green. He polished his arm, holding it out straight and solid; he rubbed his hair into curls, while I watched the deep muscles of his shoulders, and the bands stand out in his neck as he held it firm. . . .
>
> He saw I had forgotten to continue my rubbing, and laughing he took hold of me and began to

rub me briskly, as if I were a child, or rather, a woman he loved and did not fear. I left myself quite limply in his hands, and, to get a better grip of me, he put his arm round me and pressed me against him, and the sweetness of the touch of our naked bodies against each other was superb. It satisfied in some measure the vague, indecipherable yearning of my soul, and it was the same with him. When he had rubbed me all warm, he let me go, and we looked at each other with eyes of still laughter, and our love was perfect for a moment, more perfect than any love I have known since, either for man or woman.

(pp. 19-22)

John Middleton Murry, in his Son of Woman: The Story of D. H. Lawrence, *Jonathan Cape & Harrison Smith, 1931, 367 p.*

FRIEDA LAWRENCE   (essay date 1934)

[*Frieda Lawrence was the wife of D. H. Lawrence. In the following excerpt from her memoir,* Not I, but the Wind . . . , *she mentions her contribution to* Sons and Lovers *as well as the ways that Lawrence's perception of the novel altered through the years.*]

[**"Sons and Lovers"** was] the first book he wrote with me, and I lived and suffered that book, and wrote bits of it when he would ask me: "What do you think my mother felt like then?" I had to go deeply into the character of Miriam and all the others; when he wrote his mother's death he was ill and his grief made me ill too, and he said: "If my mother had lived I could never have loved you, she wouldn't have let me go." But I think he got over it; only, this fierce and overpowerful love had harmed the boy who was not strong enough to bear it. In after years he said: "I would write a different **'Sons and Lovers'** now; my mother was wrong, and I thought she was absolutely right."

I think a man is born twice: first his mother bears him, then he has to be reborn from the woman he loves. Once, sitting on the little steamer on the lake he said: "Look, that little woman is like my mother." His mother, though dead, seemed so alive and *there* still to him. (p. 56)

Frieda Lawrence, in her Not I, but the Wind. . .", *1934. Reprint by Scholarly Press, Inc., 1972, 297 p.*

JESSIE CHAMBERS   (essay date 1935)

[*Jessie Chambers was a close personal friend of Lawrence on whom he modeled the character of Miriam Leivers in* Sons and Lovers. *In the following excerpt from her memoir,* D. H. Lawrence: A Personal Record *(1935), Chambers discusses her relationship with Lawrence during the writing of* Sons and Lovers, *her influence on the novel, and her feelings of disappointment and betrayal over the portrayal of the conflict between Miriam and Mrs. Morel.*]

Lawrence began to write his autobiographical novel [*Sons and Lovers*] during 1911, which was perhaps the most arid year of his life. He did not tell me that he was at work upon this theme. . . . He had been working on it for the greater part of the year, and it was some time after our brief meeting in October that he sent the entire manuscript to me, and asked me to tell him what I thought of it.

He had written about two-thirds of the story, and seemed to have come to a standstill. The whole thing was somehow tied up. The characters were locked together in a frustrating bondage, and there seemed no way out. The writing oppressed me with a sense of strain. It was extremely tired writing. I was sure that Lawrence had had to force himself to do it. The spontaneity that I had come to regard as the distinguishing feature of his writing was quite lacking. He was telling the story of his mother's married life, but the telling seemed to be at second hand, and lacked the living touch. I could not help feeling that his treatment of the theme was far behind the reality in vividness and dramatic strength. Now and again he seemed to strike a curious, half-apologetic note, bordering on the sentimental. . . . It was story-bookish. The elder brother Ernest, whose short career had always seemed to me most moving and dramatic, was not there at all. I was amazed to find there was no mention of him. The character Lawrence called Miriam was in the story, but placed in a bourgeois setting, in the same family from which he later took the Alvina of *The Lost Girl*. He had placed Miriam in this household as a sort of foundling, and it was there that Paul Morel made her acquaintance.

The theme developed into the mother's opposition to Paul's love for Miriam. In this connection several remarks in this first draft impressed me particularly. Lawrence had written: 'What was it he (Paul Morel) wanted of her (Miriam)? Did he want her to break his mother down in him? Was that what he wanted?'

And again: 'Mrs. Morel saw that if Miriam could only win her son's sex sympathy there would be nothing left for her.'

In another place he said: 'Miriam looked upon Paul as a young man tied to his mother's apron-strings.' Finally, referring to the people around Miriam, he said: 'How should they understand her—petty tradespeople!' But the issue was left quite unresolved. Lawrence had carried the situation to the point of deadlock and stopped there.

As I read through the manuscript I had before me all the time the vivid picture of the reality. I felt again the tenseness of the conflict, and the impending spiritual clash. So in my reply I told him I was very surprised that he had kept so far from reality in his story; that I thought what had really happened was much more poignant and interesting than the situations he had invented. In particular I was surprised that he had omitted the story of Ernest, which seemed to me vital enough to be worth telling as it actually happened. Finally I suggested that he should write the whole story again, and keep it true to life.

Two considerations prompted me to make these suggestions. First of all I felt that the theme, if treated adequately, had in it the stuff of a magnificent story. It only wanted setting down, and Lawrence possessed the miraculous power of translating the raw material of life into significant form. That was my first reaction to the problem. My deeper thought was that in the doing of it Lawrence might free himself from his strange obsession with his mother. I thought he might be able to work out the theme in the realm of spiritual reality, where alone it could be worked out, and so resolve the conflict in himself. Since he had elected to deal with the big and difficult subject of his family, and the interactions of the various relationships, I felt he ought to do it faithfully—'with both hands earnestly', as he was fond of quoting. It seemed to me that if he was able to treat the theme with strict integrity he would thereby walk into freedom, and cast off the trammelling past like an old skin.

The particular issue he might give to the story never entered my head. That was of no consequence. The great thing was that I thought I could see a liberated Lawrence coming out of it. Towards Lawrence's mother I had no bitter feeling, and could have none, because she was his mother. But I felt that he was being strangled in a bond that was even more powerful since her death, and that until he was freed from it he was held in check and unable to develop.

In all this I acted from pure intuition, arising out of my deep knowledge of his situation. I said no word of this to him because I thought it must inevitably work itself out in the novel, provided he treated the subject with integrity. And I had a profound faith in Lawrence's fundamental integrity.

He fell in absolutely with my suggestion and asked me to write what I could remember of our early days, because, as he truthfully said, my recollection of those days was so much clearer than his. (pp. 190-93)

Lawrence passed the manuscript on to me as he wrote it, a few sheets at a time, just as he had done with *The White Peacock,* only that this story was written with incomparably greater speed and intensity.

The early pages delighted me. Here was all that spontaneous flow, the seemingly effortless translation of life that filled me with admiration. His descriptions of family life were so vivid, so exact, and so concerned with everyday things we had never

Jessie Chambers, the model for Miriam in Sons and Lovers.

even noticed before. There was Mrs. Morel ready for ironing, lightly spitting on the iron to test its heat, invested with a reality and significance hitherto unsuspected. It was his power to transmute the common experiences into significance that I always felt to be Lawrence's greatest gift. He did not distinguish between small and great happenings; the common round was full of mystery, awaiting interpretation. Born and bred of working people, he had the rare gift of seeing them from within, and revealing them on their own plane. An incident that particularly pleased me was where Morel was recovering from an accident at the pit, and his friend Jerry came to see him. The conversation of the two men and their tenderness to one another were a revelation to me. I felt that Lawrence was coming into his true kingdom as a creative artist, and an interpreter of the people to whom he belonged.

I saw him fairly frequently during the first weeks of the writing of *Sons and Lovers.* He went quite often also to my married sister's cottage, where he talked about himself with his customary frankness. (pp. 197-98)

But then he was not the same.... The sunny disposition that used to create such a happy atmosphere was seldom in evidence. He was spasmodic and restless, resentful of the need to be careful of his health, and not well adapted to fit into the rather grim midlands life now that he had no mother to make a home for him. In company he would maintain his jaunty exterior, but below the surface was a hopelessness hardly to be distinguished from despair. He seemed like a man with a broken mainspring. With all his gifts, he was somehow cut off, unable to attain that complete participation in life that he craved for. (p. 199)

We talked about his writing and he upbraided me for not making an effort to do something myself. He was so sure I could write if I would try. 'If you had only two books out, I shouldn't care,' he said. I knew he was reproaching himself for having occupied my time with his own work. Presently he said in a halting way, as if struggling to find the exact words:

> 'When we are not together, since I have been
> away from you, I don't think the same, feel
> the same; I'm not the same man. *I* can't write
> poetry.'

The words went to my heart, for his tone was the extreme of sincerity and of despair. We were together again, and outwardly there was nothing to keep us apart, but his mother's ban was more powerful now than in her lifetime. I began to realize that whatever approach Lawrence made to me inevitably involved him in a sense of disloyalty to his mother. Some bond, some understanding, most likely unformulated and all the stronger for that, seemed to exist between them. It was a bond that definitely excluded me from the only position in which I could be of vital help to him. We were back in the old dilemma, but it was a thousand times more cruel because of the altered circumstances. He seemed to be fixed in the centre of the tension, helpless, waiting for one pull to triumph over the other.

The novel was written in this state of spirit, at a white heat of concentration. The writing of it was fundamentally a terrific fight for a bursting of the tension. The break came in the treatment of Miriam. As the sheets of manuscript came rapidly to me I was bewildered and dismayed at that treatment. I began to perceive that I had set Lawrence a task far beyond his strength. In my confidence I had not doubted that he would work out the problem with integrity. But he burked the real issue. It was his old inability to face his problem squarely. His mother had to be supreme, and for the sake of that supremacy every disloyalty was permissible.

The realization of this slowly dawned on me as I read the manuscript. He asked for my opinion, but comment seemed futile—not merely futile, but impossible. I could not appeal to Lawrence for justice as between his treatment of Mrs. Morel and Miriam. He left off coming to see me and sent the manuscript by post. His avoidance of me was significant. I felt it was useless to attempt to argue the matter out with him. Either he was aware of what he was doing and persisted, or he did not know, and in that case no amount of telling would enlighten him. It was one of the things he had to find out for himself. The baffling truth, of course, lay between the two. He was aware, but he was under the spell of the domination that had ruled his life hitherto, and he refused to know. So instead of a release and a deliverance from bondage, the bondage was glorified and made absolute. His mother conquered indeed, but the vanquished one was her son. In *Sons and Lovers* Lawrence handed his mother the laurels of victory.

The Clara of the second half of the story was a clever adaptation of elements from three people, and her creation arose as a complement to Lawrence's mood of failure and defeat. The events related had no foundation in fact, whatever their psychological significance. Having utterly failed to come to grips with his problem in real life, he created the imaginary Clara as a compensation. Even in the novel the compensation is unreal and illusory, for at the end Paul Morel calmly hands her back to her husband, and remains suspended over the abyss of his despair. Many of the incidents struck me as cheap and commonplace, in spite of the hard brilliance of the narration. I realized that I had naively credited Lawrence with superhuman powers of detachment.

The shock of *Sons and Lovers* gave the death-blow to our friendship. If I had told Lawrence that I had died before, I certainly died again. I had a strange feeling of separation from the body. The daily life was sheer illusion. The only reality was the betrayal of *Sons and Lovers*. I felt it was a betrayal in an inner sense, for I had always believed that there was a bond between us, if it was no more that the bond of a common suffering. But the brutality of his treatment seemed to deny any bond. That I understood so well what made him do it only deepened my despair. He had to present a distorted picture of our association so that the martyr's halo might sit becomingly on his mother's brow. But to give a recognizable picture of our friendship which yet completely left out the years of devotion to the development of his genius—devotion that had been pure joy—seemed to me like presenting *Hamlet* without the Prince of Denmark. What else but the devotion to a common end had held us together against his mother's repeated assaults? Neither could I feel that he had represented in any degree faithfully the nature and quality of our desperate search for a right relationship. I was hurt beyond all expression. I didn't know how to bear it.

Lawrence had said that he never took sides; but his attitude placed him tacitly on the side of those who had mocked at love—except mother-love. He seemed to have identified himself with the prevailing atmosphere of ridicule and innuendo. It was a fatal alignment, for it made me see him as a philistine of the philistines, and not, as I had always believed, inwardly honouring an unspoken bond, and suffering himself from the strange hostility to love. He had sometimes argued—in an effort to convince himself—that morality and art have nothing to do with one another. However that might be, I could not help feeling that integrity and art have a great deal to do with one another. The best I could think of him was that he had run with the hare and hunted with the hounds. . . His significance withered and his dimensions shrank. He ceased to matter supremely.

I tried hard to remind myself that after all *Sons and Lovers* was only a novel. It was not the truth, although it must inevitably stand for truth.

And as I sat and looked at the subtle distortion of what had been the deepest values of my life, the one gleam of light was the realization that Lawrence had overstated his case; that some day his epic of maternal love and filial devotion would be viewed from another angle, that of his own final despair. (pp. 200-04)

Jessie Chambers, in her D. H. Lawrence: A Personal Record, *edited by J. D. Chambers, second edition, Frank Cass & Co. Ltd., 1965, 242 p.*

MARK SCHORER (essay date 1948)

[*Schorer is an American critic and biographer who wrote the definitive life of Sinclair Lewis. In his often anthologized essay "Technique as Discovery" (1948), Schorer put forth the argument that fiction deserves the same close attention to diction and metaphor that the New Critics had been lavishing on poetry. He determined that fiction viewed only with respect to content was not art at all, but experience. For Schorer, only when individuals examine "achieved content," or form, do they speak of art, and consequently, speak as critics. Schorer also argued that the difference between content and art is "technique," and that the study of technique demonstrates how fictional form discovers and evaluates meaning, meaning that is often not intended by the author. In the following excerpt from "Technique as Discovery," he discusses the conflict which exists between the two dominant themes in* Sons and Lovers, *the stifling effect of excessive maternal love, and the division between spiritual and physical love in Paul Morel's two romantic relationships. In Lawrence's failure to fully examine the implications of these themes, Schorer finds the central failure of his career.*]

To say what one means in art is never easy, and the more intimately one is implicated in one's material, the more difficult it is. If, besides, one commits fiction to a therapeutic function which is to be operative not on the audience but on the author, declaring, as D. H. Lawrence did, that "One sheds one's sicknesses in books, repeats and presents again one's emotions to be master of them," the difficulty is vast. It is an acceptable theory only with the qualification that technique, which objectifies, is under no other circumstances so imperative. For merely to repeat one's emotions, merely to look into one's heart and write, is also merely to repeat the round of emotional bondage. If our books are to be exercises in self-analysis, then technique must—and alone can—take the place of the absent analyst.

Lawrence, in the relatively late Introduction to his *Collected Poems*, made that distinction of the amateur between his "real" poems and his "composed" poems, between the poems which expressed his demon directly and created their own form "willy-nilly," and the poems which, through the hocus pocus of technique, he spuriously put together and could, if necessary, revise. His belief in a "poetry of the immediate present," poetry in which nothing is fixed, static, or final, where all is shimmeriness and impermanence and vitalistic essense, arose from this mistaken notion of technique. And from this notion, an unsympathetic critic like D. S. Savage can construct a case which shows Lawrence driven "concurrently to the dissolution of personality and the dissolution of art." The argument suggests that Lawrence's early, crucial novel, *Sons and Lovers,* is another example of meanings confused by an impatience with technical resources.

The novel has two themes: the crippling effects of a mother's love on the emotional development of her son; and the "split" between kinds of love, physical and spiritual, which the son develops, the kinds represented by two young women, Clara and Miriam. The two themes should, of course, work together, the second being, actually, the result of the first: this "split" is the "crippling." So one would expect to see the novel developed, and so Lawrence, in his famous letter to Edward Garnett, where he says that Paul is left at the end with the "drift towards death," apparently thought he had developed it [see excerpt dated 1912]. Yet in the last few sentences of the novel, Paul rejects his desire for extinction and turns towards "the faintly humming, glowing town," to life—as nothing in his previous history persuades us that he could unfalteringly do.

The discrepancy suggests that the book may reveal certain confusions between intention and performance.

The first of these is the contradiction between Lawrence's explicit characterizations of the mother and father and his tonal evaluations of them. It is a problem not only of style (of the contradiction between expressed moral epithets and the more general texture of the prose which applies to them) but of point of view. Morel and Lawrence are never separated, which is a way of saying that Lawrence maintains for himself in this book the confused attitude of his character. The mother is a "proud, *honorable* soul,' but the father has a "small, *mean* head." This is the sustained contrast: the epithets are characteristic of the whole; and they represent half of Lawrence's feelings. But what is the other half? Which of these characters is given his real sympathy—the hard, self-righteous, aggressive, demanding mother who comes through to us, or the simple, direct, gentle, downright, fumbling, ruined father? There are two attitudes here. Lawrence (and Morel) loves his mother, but he also hates her for compelling his love; and he hates his father with the true Freudian jealousy, but he also loves him for what he is in himself, and he sympathizes more deeply with him because his wholeness has been destroyed by the mother's domination, just as his, Lawrence-Morel's, has been.

This is a psychological tension which disrupts the form of the novel and obscures its meaning, because neither the contradiction in style nor the confusion in point of view is made to right itself. Lawrence is merely repeating his emotions, and he avoids an austerer technical scrutiny of his material because it would compel him to master them. He would not let the artist be stronger than the man.

The result is that, at the same time that the book condemns the mother, it justifies her; at the same time that it shows Paul's failure, it offers rationalizations which place the failure elsewhere. The handling of the girl, Miriam, if viewed closely, is pathetic in what it signifies for Lawrence, both as man and artist. For Miriam is made the mother's scape-goat, and in a different way from the way that she was in life. The central section of the novel is shot through with alternate statements as to the source of the difficulty: Paul is unable to love Miriam wholly, and Miriam can love only his spirit. The contradictions appear sometimes within single paragraphs, and the point of view is never adequately objectified and sustained to tell us which is true. The material is never seen as material; the writer is caught in it exactly as firmly as he was caught in his experience of it. "That's how women are with me," said Paul. "They want me like mad, but they don't want to belong to me." So he might have said, and believed it; but at the end of the novel, Lawrence is still saying that, and himself believing it.

For the full history of this technical failure, one must read *Sons and Lovers* carefully and then learn the history of the manuscript from the book called *D. H. Lawrence: A Personal Record,* by one E. T. [Jessie Chambers; see excerpt dated 1935], who was Miriam in life. The basic situation is clear enough. The first theme—the crippling effects of the mother's love—is developed right through to the end; and then suddenly, in the last few sentences, turns on itself, and Paul gives himself to life, not death. But all the way through, the insidious rationalizations of the second theme have crept in to destroy the artistic coherence of the work. A "split" would occur in Paul; but as the split is treated, it is superimposed upon rather than developed in support of the first theme. It is a rationalization made from it. If Miriam is made to insist on spiritual love, the meaning and the power of theme one are reduced; yet Paul's weakness is disguised. Lawrence could not separate the investigating analyst, who must be objective, from Lawrence, the subject of the book; and the sickness was not healed, the emotion not mastered, the novel not perfected. All this, and the character of a whole career, would have been altered if Lawrence had allowed his technique to discover the fullest meaning of his subject. (pp. 75-8)

> Mark Schorer, "Technique as Discovery," *in* The Hudson Review, *Vol. 1, No. 1, Spring, 1948, pp. 67-87.* *

MARK SPILKA   (essay date 1955)

[*Spilka is an American educator and scholar specializing in twentieth-century English fiction. In the following excerpt from his book* The Love Ethic of D. H. Lawrence, *he examines the three destructive forms of love from which Paul Morel struggles to free himself in* Sons and Lovers: *Oedipal love, spiritual love, and unbalanced-possessive love, which respectively define his relationships with his mother, Miriam, and Clara. Spilka asserts that by rejecting each of these inadequate and unhealthy forms of love, Paul chooses life, independence, and his own individuality.*]

Sons and Lovers is interpreted, much too often, in terms of the "split" theory which Lawrence once outlined in a letter to Edward Garnett. According to that letter, William and Paul Morel are unable to love normally when they come to manhood, because their dominant mother holds them back, so that a split occurs between body and soul—their sweethearts getting the former; their mother, the latter; while the boys themselves are shattered, inwardly, in the course of the struggle.

Admittedly, this theory accounts for much of the surface tension of the novel; but as Mark Schorer has pointed out, it seems to conflict with a second and wholly different scheme of motivation [see excerpt dated 1948]. Unless I am badly mistaken, this second scheme is more important than the first. For there seem to be *two* psychologies at work in **Sons and Lovers,** one imposed upon the other, though without destroying its effectiveness. We know, for example, that Lawrence had heard about Freud before he wrote the final draft of the novel. We also know that the Garnett letter refers to the final draft, and that previous versions of the book had followed somewhat different lines. So Lawrence may well have written the book, at first, in accord with his own developing psychology, and then rewritten it in garbled accord with Freud's: hence the confusion, and the effect of superimposition, which bothers Mr. Schorer and many other readers. But if this is so, then the novel takes its strength from Lawrence's psychology and its weakness (inadvertently) from Freud's. The "split" theory, for example, is more Freudian than Laurentian; it involves a kind of Freudian triangle—mother-son-sweetheart—while the conflict in all future novels centers upon a single man and woman, a specific couple, whose relationship is judged or resolved in terms of its own vitality. We have already seen such conflicts, incidentally, in the floral scenes in *Sons and Lovers,* where vitality, or the full glow of the life-flame, is the chief criterion in Paul's specific relations with his mother, and with Miriam and Clara—where each affair is judged, in other words, in terms of its effect upon the life-flow, or the "livingness," of the man and woman involved. And as a matter of fact, each of Paul's three loves is actually significant in itself, since each contributes something vital to his development, yet finally proves destructive and inadequate. So all three loves—spiritual, oedipal, and possessive—resemble the counterfeit loves of later stories, and this in spite of the obvious Freudian twist which Lawrence seems to give them in his final draft.

Romantic Miriam Leivers, for example, with her love of intellect, her heavy dumb will, and her attempt to abstract the soul right out of Paul's body, has something in common with Hermione Roddice, that harsh creature of will and intellect in *Women in Love.* There is common ground, too, between what Clara Dawes wants out of Paul—possession, imprisoning personal love—and the princess-slave relationship in later stories like **"The Captain's Doll."** In the same vein, Mrs. Morel resembles the later and less appealing mothers in Lawrence's short stories (say, Pauline Attenborough in **"The Lovely Lady,"** or Rachel Bodoin in **"Mother and Daughter"**) who sap the life from their children, regardless of outside competition, because oedipal love is sterile in itself. The truth is, then, that *Sons and Lovers* is mainly an exploration of destructive or counterfeit loves—with a garbled Freudian "split" imposed upon it. At least this helps to explain the unique emotional tenor of the book: for in spite of all confusion there is a strange new reading experience here, a unique event in the realm of fiction, and in the realm of morality as well. Indeed, if *Sons and Lovers* is (as Harry Moore tells us) "the last novel of the nineteenth century," it is also one of the first novels of the twentieth. The book is only outwardly conventional; it draws its greatest strength from Lawrence's radical new insight, moral as well as psychological, into the complex nature of emotional conflict.

Jessie Chambers cites a number of significant lines which appeared in the first draft of *Sons and Lovers,* but which were eliminated in the final version:

> 'What was it he (Paul Morel) wanted of her (Miriam)? Did he want her to break his mother down in him? Was that what he wanted?'

> And again: 'Mrs. Morel saw that if Miriam could only win her son's sex sympathy there would be nothing left for her.'

In the final draft of the book, and in Lawrence's letter to Garnett, this conflict is *stated* somewhat differently: if Miriam should win Paul's *soul,* then there would be nothing left for Mrs. Morel; as for his sex sympathy, the mother wants her to win that, if she will only leave his soul in her possession. Yet Lawrence makes it perfectly clear, through dramatic portions of the book, that Miriam's failure to attract Paul, physically, has led to her defeat in the spiritual conflict, and we see at once that the excised lines hold true to the actual situation. The girl's sexual failure is deeply rooted, for example, in her own emotional make-up. As Lawrence amply demonstrates, she is unable to lose herself in any simple pleasurable occasion, her body is tense and lifeless, her abnormal spiritual intensity is coupled with a genuine fear of things physical. . . . (pp. 60-4)

Yet both Paul and Miriam are prudes in their early courtship. She recoils from "the continual business of birth and begetting" on the farm, and he takes his cue from her. Their own friendship is always pitched, moreover, at an intensely spiritual and intellectual level, so that even the simplest contact seems repellent: "His consciousness seemed to split. The place where she was touching him ran hot with friction. He was one internecine battle, and he became cruel to her because of it." Again, when the two chaste lovers are out for a walk one night, Paul suddenly stands transfixed at the sight of an enormous orange moon; his blood concentrates "like a flame in his chest," but this time Miriam shrinks away from actual contact: "it was as if she could scarcely stand the shock of physical love, even a passionate kiss, and then he was too shrinking and sensitive to give it."

Thus the chief "split" between Paul and Miriam comes from the abstract nature of their love, and not from the mother's hold upon the young man's soul. And the final responsibility for this split belongs with Miriam. When the friendship between the young couple wanes, for example, Paul resigns himself to the old love for his mother. But in the spring of his twenty-third year, he returns to the girl for another try at sensual love. This time, he seeks "the great hunger and impersonality of passion" with her, and though she agrees to this, she decides to submit herself religiously, as if to a sacrifice. Even as their love-making becomes more frequent, she continues to clench herself for the "sacrifice," as she had clenched herself on the swing in earlier days. So the lovers part once more, with this final confirmation that Miriam's frigidity is rooted in her own nature, and not in mere ignorance of sex. Her purity is nullity rather than innocence; she lacks real warmth, and Paul, in his youthful inexperience, is unable to rouse it in her. Although they meet again, after his mother's death, they are still divided by her incompleteness. Paul is shattered and adrift toward death himself; he wants her to respond to him out of warmth, out of womanly instinct. But she merely offers the old familiar sacrifice, and Paul rejects it: "he did not hope to give life to her by denying his own."

Yet if Miriam lacks warmth, she has strength of will to spare. She endures Paul's insults, his cruel probings, his wrongheaded arguments; she lets him go, time and again, out of the conviction that she holds the ultimate key to his soul. And she does have the ability to stimulate him in his work, to arouse his own spiritual nature to fever pitch, and to serve as the necessary "threshing floor" for his ideas. Because of this ability, she believes "he cannot do without her"; but her belief results in a significant lapse—a kind of self-betrayal—when Paul decides to break away: "Always—it has always been so," she cries out. "It has been one long battle between us—you fighting away from me." The statement shocks Paul profoundly; he reasons that if she had known this all along, and had said nothing, then their love "had been monstrous." (pp. 65-7)

The exposure of this duplicity (contempt disguised by reverence) shows Miriam in her truest colors. Quite plainly she resembles the willful Hermione Roddice of **Women in Love,** though she is never so poised, skillful, and predatory as Hermione. But the heavy dumb will is undeniably there, and this, coupled with her fierce desire to be a man, to succeed through intellectual knowledge, makes her a decided forerunner of those feminine creatures of intellect and will whom Lawrence would later deplore as spiritual vampires. Thus Miriam is a nun, in Paul's eyes, who would reduce the world to a nunnery garden: on the one hand, her excessive spirituality smothers his spirit; on the other, it destroys her own capacity to respond, sympathetically, to his newly-awakened need for sensual love. And so she defeats herself in the struggle for Paul's heart, by thwarting his deep male instinct to be loved, impersonally, as a man, rather than as a mind or soul or personality. And she loses to Paul's mother by default, but she is not really defeated, at the deepest level of the conflict, by Mrs. Morel.

Nor is Clara Dawes defeated by Paul's mother, though she fits in better with the older woman's plans: she takes care of Paul's sexual needs, that is, and leaves plenty of him over for Mrs. Morel. So the mother is "not hostile to the idea of Clara"; in fact, she finds the relationship rather wholesome, after the soul-sucking affair with Miriam. She even likes Clara, but judges her as somehow not large enough to hold her son. Paul reaches a similar verdict about his mistress, independently, when he gives her back to her husband. But since Clara brings him a potentially fuller love than either Miriam or his mother, we must examine her role in the book with special care. She is, after all, the first imperfect version of the Laurentian woman, the "lost girl" in search of true womanhood.

Paul is 23 when he meets Clara, and she is about 30. He responds at once to her slumbering warmth, and senses that her aloofness is just a defensive pose. For her part, Clara admires his animal quickness: he brings her the promise of renewed vitality, and they draw close together and make love, once Paul has broken away from Miriam. Thus Paul receives the impersonal love he needs, "the real, real flame of feeling through another person," and Clara comes to full awakening as a woman. (pp. 68-9)

When he embraces her, she feels glad, erect, and proud again: "It was her restoration and her recognition." She falls passionately in love with him, and he with her ("as far as passion went"), till their love becomes an actual immersion in the "fourth dimension." One night, for instance, they take each other in an open field:

> It was all so much bigger than themselves that he was hushed. They had met, and included in their meeting the thrust of the manifold grass-stems, the cry of the peewit, the wheel of the stars. . . .
>
> And after such an evening, they were both very still, having known the immensity of passion. . . . To know their own nothingness, to know the tremendous living flood which carried them always, gave them rest within themselves. If so great a magnificent power could overwhelm them, identify them altogether with itself, so that they knew they were only grains in the tremendous heave that lifted every grass-

> blade its little height, and every tree, and every living thing, then why fret about themselves? They could let themselves be carried by life, and they felt a sort of peace each in the other. There was a verification which they had had together. Nothing could nullify it, nothing could take it away; it was almost their belief in life. . . .

Later on, Lawrence drops the "almost" out of that final phrase, and develops his belief in life from sexual love, or from the connection with the life-force which sexual love implies. But in **Sons and Lovers,** his belief has barely taken shape, and the conflict between Paul and Clara is never well-defined. Nevertheless, the lines of definition are there, and Lawrence makes good use of them. Thus Clara is soon dissatisfied with impersonal love; like Miriam, she wants to grasp hold of Paul and to possess him personally. So she begins to crowd her love into the daytime hours at Jordan's factory. She presses Paul for little personal intimacies, but he shrinks away from this: "The night is free to you," he says. "In the daytime I want to be by myself. . . . Love-making stifles me in the daytime." But Paul is even more disturbed about another failing: he believes that Clara is unable to "keep his soul steady," that he is simply beyond her, in his creative and intellectual self, and in the breadth and depth of his emotional entanglement—which anticipates a later belief: that men and women must be in balance with each other, as individuals with distinct "life-flows" of their own, before genuine love can flourish. In **Sons and Lovers,** Clara falls short on this count: her "balance" with Paul is scarcely stable, and the growing uneasiness in their affair can be traced, for the most part, to her own inadequacy as an independent being. But even their common bond in passion begins to weaken, under this double burden of "imbalance" and possessive love. . . . (pp. 71-2)

This disintegration in love is soon followed by an unexpected but climactic incident. Paul meets Clara's husband one night in a lonely field; Dawes has been waiting for him there and a wild battle follows, in which both opponents are badly damaged. Afterwards, the affair with Clara continues, but only on a mechanical plane: for Dawes has fought with the desperate strength of a man who wants his woman back, and Paul, for all his blind resistance, does not want the woman badly. And so he sheds his dying love in the battle, and a bit later on, he makes his restitution: he finds Dawes in the hospital at Sheffield, befriends him, and gradually brings husband and wife together again. Since Clara really needs her stable, personal, daytime lover, she agrees to the reunion. However that may be, she fails with Paul because of her own shortcomings, for (along with her possessiveness) she lacks the capacity, the breadth of being, to take on the full burden of his troubled soul. But if both Miriam and Clara defeat themselves, this tells us something important about Mrs. Morel: it is not her interference which destroys her sons, but the strength and peculiar nature of her love. . . . [She is] easily the most vital woman in the novel. She is warm and lively, for example, with those she loves, for the early months with her husband were months of passionate fulfillment. Though intellectual herself, she was first attracted to Morel by "the dusky, golden softness of his sensuous flame of life"—and this passion for manly, sensual men continues throughout the book. She approves, for example, of "the feel of *men* on things," and she takes immediately to the good-looking Mr. Leivers. (pp. 73-4)

She also likes the quiet, compact miner, Mr. Barker, who takes good care of his pregnant wife, buys the week's groceries and meats on Friday nights, and keeps a level head. "Barker's little," she tells her husband, "but he's ten times the man you are." And the remark, however vindictive, holds true, for Morel has lost his manhood, and Lawrence gives us ample evidence of this throughout the novel. Unable to live up to his wife's high ideals, afraid of her mind, her will, and above all, her status as "that thing of mystery and fascination, a lady," Morel quarrels with her about money, he takes to drink, begins to mistreat her, and eventually, rather than face the problem in his own home, he retreats from the battle and breaks his own manhood. To be sure, there is a dual responsibility here, since Mrs. Morel has actually driven him to destroy himself. But the fact remains that Lawrence holds his men accountable, in the end, for their own integrity of being, and this will prove an important theme in future novels. (p. 75)

At this point in *Sons and Lovers,* Mrs. Morel turns to her children for fulfillment. And here we run into one of the curious strengths of the book, for the companionship between mother and sons is described, at first, in completely wholesome terms. The destructive potential is there, of course, and Lawrence marks it out as he goes along; but on the whole this is a healthy relationship, and it remains so until the boys come of age. (pp. 75-6)

[The] tenor begins to change once William, the eldest son, dies in London of pneumonia and erysipelas. The death comes as a terrible blow to Mrs. Morel, who loved him passionately, and thought of him almost as "her knight who wore *her* favour in the battle." Now she loses all interest in life, and remains shut off from the family. But a few months later, Paul comes down with pneumonia too. "I should have watched the living, not the dead," she tells herself, and rouses her strength to save him. . . . (pp. 77-8)

Paul is saved—saved, paradoxically, to be almost destroyed by the oedipal love which follows this event. For the beauty and richness of the scene is this: Lawrence has marshalled all the forces of destruction at precisely the same point at which he has just affirmed, dramatically, all that previous liveliness and love between Paul and his mother: William, the first son-lover, has been destroyed; now Paul will take his place in his mother's heart; he will *become* her second lover, he will in turn be sapped of his vitality, but at the moment he has just become her most beloved son.

In the years that follow, the relations between Paul and his mother are sometimes rich in satisfaction. He wins prizes for her with his artwork, and she looks upon them as part of her fulfillment. Paul sees it this way too: "All his work was hers." But there are quarrels over his love affairs, and Paul becomes increasingly unhappy. Then, late in the book, he finds "the quick of his trouble": he has loved both Miriam and Clara, but he can belong to neither of them while his mother lives; so long as she holds him, he can never "really love another woman." Thus Lawrence invokes the "split" theory, the pull between mother and sweethearts, to explain his hero's debilitation. But as we have already seen, this theory fails to account for the actual nature of Paul's affairs. We must look elsewhere, then, for the "quick" of his troubles; more specifically, we must look ahead to *Psychoanalysis and the Unconscious* . . . , where Lawrence was finally able to straighten out his views on oedipal love.

In this frontal attack on Freudian psychology, Lawrence decided that the incest-craving is never the normal outcome of the parent-child relationship, but always the result of impres-

sions planted in the child's unconscious mind by an unsatisfied parent. But therefore oedipal love is mechanistic, and if mechanistic, then destructive and abnormal in itself. In one of the late stories, for example, an avaricious mother sends an unspoken whisper through her household—*There must be more money!*—and her young boy destroys himself in his attempts to get it. Now significantly enough, this pattern is already at work in *Sons and Lovers,* though here the whisper runs—*There must be fulfillment!*—as when Paul lies on the sofa, recovering from an early bout with bronchitis:

> He, in his semi-conscious sleep, was vaguely aware of the clatter of the iron on the ironstand, of the faint thud, thud on the ironing-board. Once roused, he opened his eyes to see his mother standing on the hearthrug with the hot iron near her cheek, listening, as it were, to the heat. Her still face, with the mouth closed tight from suffering and disillusion and self-denial, and her nose the smallest bit on one side, and her blue eyes so young, quick, and warm, made his heart contract with love. When she was quiet, so, she looked brave and rich with life, but as if she had been done out of her rights. It hurt the boy keenly, this feeling about her that she had never had her life's fulfilment: and his own incapability to make [it?] up to her hurt him with a sense of impotence, yet made him patiently dogged inside. It was his childish aim. . . .

Here, then, is the planting of the incest germ, the unwitting imposition of the idea of fulfillment in the young boy's mind. Later on, when Paul becomes the actual agent of his mother's fulfillment, this idea leads inevitably to the incest-craving . . . , and from thence to the disintegration of his essential being. For the proof of this theory, take the constant wrangling with his mother; his fury at her old age; the almost violent quarrel with his father; his own mad restlessness; his obvious "will to die"; and, after the fight with Dawes, the complete blankness of his life. He is closer to his mother now than at any stage in the book, and the only thing which saves him from destruction is her own impending death. For Mrs. Morel falls ill with cancer now, and Paul cares for her, handling all the details with the doctors, as if he were the father. He is dazed and isolated from those around him; his grief stays with him like a mechanical thing which can't be shut off; he wants his mother to die, but she holds on to life, as always, with her powerful will; finally, he gives her an overdose of morphia, and this kills her. He has openly played the lover in these last days, and his mother, though reduced to a strange, shrivelled-up little girl, is almost the young wife. But the very desperation of the situation gives it dignity: this is their special, private, intimate grief over an impossible dream, and the magnificence of the woman, and the devotional quality of Paul's love, render the deathbed scenes poignant and innocent.

Paul gives Clara back to her husband after this; he rejects Miriam, and is himself on the deathward drift, following his mother's spirit. And it is here, in the final pages, that his debilitation is most clearly the result, not of any split between mother and sweethearts, but of his powerful, sterile, obsessive and mechanistic love for his mother.

Thus, it is not the "split" theory which gives *Sons and Lovers* its marvelous power, but the successful dramatization of three destructive forms of love—oedipal, spiritual, and "unbalanced-possessive." It seems almost as if Paul were caught, at various times, within the swirling waters of three terrible whirlpools, each of which drags him down toward a form of death-in-life; and it is not so much the violent shifts from one pool to the next which harm him, but the damage he sustains within each separate pool: and the most deathward swirl of them all is with his mother.

These three disintegrative loves, when viewed separately, help to account for the emotional depth of the book. But there is still Paul's "death" as a son to account for, and his subsequent rebirth as a man, which Lawrence dimly hints at in the final lines. Paul is alone at night in the fields outside Nottingham, and wants only to follow his mother toward the grave—

> But no, he would not give in. Turning sharply, he walked towards the city's gold phosphorescence. His fists were shut, his mouth set fast. He would not take that direction, to the darkness, to follow her. He walked towards the faintly humming, glowing town, quickly.

As Harry Moore points out, Paul's return to life hinges upon the final word, "quickly," which means *livingly* rather than *rapidly:* "The last word in *Sons and Lovers* is an adverb attesting not only to the hero's desire to live but also to his deep ability to do so." And it is this quickness, this vitality, which has enabled Paul to turn away, first from Miriam, then Clara, and now, finally, from his mother. For if Paul has failed in his three loves, he has also drawn from them the necessary strength to live. We know, for example, that Paul is a promising young artist, and Lawrence also tells us something significant about his art: "From his mother he drew the life-warmth, the strength to produce; Miriam urged this warmth into intensity like a white light." Now Clara must be considered, for she adds to this life-warmth and creative vision the gift of manhood, the "baptism of fire in passion" which will enable Paul "to go on and mature." Indeed, *nothing* can nullify this verification which he and Clara have had together—"it was almost their belief in life". . . . (pp. 79-84)

[At] the end of *Sons and Lovers,* we know, we have experienced the fact that Paul Morel has achieved a kind of half-realized, or jigsaw success, consisting of mixed elements of life-warmth, creative vision, incipient manhood, and most important of all, a belief (almost) in life itself: and this is the nutritive force which enables him, at the end, to become a man, and to turn quickly toward the glowing city, away from his mother. (p. 85)

> *Mark Spilka, in his* The Love Ethic of D. H. Lawrence, *Indiana University Press, 1955, 244 p.*

R. P. DRAPER (essay date 1958)

[*Draper is an English educator, scholar, and editor specializing in British fiction from the sixteenth century to the present. In the following excerpt, he examines the distorted nature of maternal love in* Sons and Lovers. *According to Draper, Mrs. Morel forces Paul, as a young child, to respond to her demands for adult love by becoming "wife-submissive" to him while rejecting her husband. Draper states that such a relationship blocks all outlets for the young boy's growing need for sexual expression, thereby causing considerable sexual confusion and anxiety, and ultimately inhibiting his ability to have normal relationships with women.*]

In *Fantasia of the Unconscious* Lawrence describes the disastrous effect of excessive mother-love, and, as is well known, Middleton Murry uses this as the basis of his treatment of Lawrence's life in *Son of Woman* [see excerpt dated 1931]. 'That is Lawrence's history of his own life. It is the history of *Sons and Lovers* told again, eight years later, with the added insight and detachment that comes of maturity.' From this results a distortion of Lawrence's life and work which has heaped upon Middleton Murry a mountain of blame which in the 1954 Introduction to *Son of Woman* he admits to be partly deserved. But my purpose is not to revive the Middleton Murry controversy. Present-day criticism has learnt to see the importance of the conclusion to *Sons and Lovers,* with its deliberate refusal to sink into nihilism, expressed in Paul's determination to face the amorphous industrial growth of Nottingham, and to give Frieda Lawrence her due as a woman courageous and devoted enough, without being servile, to help Lawrence to throw off the domination of his mother's image. What I wish to do is to question Murry's assertion that in *Fantasia* the history of *Sons and Lovers* is retold with 'added insight and detachment'—in particular, to show the difference between Lawrence's description of mother-love in *Fantasia* and his novelist's presentment of it in *Sons and Lovers.*

The passage quoted by Murry is from Chapter X of *Fantasia of the Unconscious,* 'Parent Love':

> If you want to see the real desirable wife-spirit, look at a mother with her boy of eighteen. How she serves him, how she stimulates him, how her true female self is his, is wife-submissive to him as never, never it could be to a husband. This is the quiescent, flowering love of a mature woman. It is the very flower of a woman's love: sexually asking nothing, asking nothing of the beloved, save that he shall be himself, and that for his living he shall accept the gift of her love. This is the perfect flower of married love, which a husband should put in his cap as he goes forward into the future in his supreme activity. For the husband, it is a great pledge, and a blossom. For the son also it seems wonderful. The woman now feels for the first time as a true wife might feel. And her feeling is towards her son.

On a first reading this has the accent of truth. The mother who has poured her love into her son instead of giving it to her husband does seem, in Lawrence's own cherished meaning of the phrase, 'wife-submissive'. But at the same time that phrase is a give-away. It sounds an old familiar note. Here is the mother being wife-submissive to her son, says the exasperated voice of Lawrence, when she ought to be precisely that to her husband—a simple case of misdirected energy. In the exasperation we are made to overlook that something has happened to the woman's love when it has been transferred from the husband to the son. It has not been simply misdirected, but distorted as well. . . . Sexual frustration inevitably follows, and this is excellently diagnosed in *Fantasia.* Over-stimulation of the son's 'upper centres' leads to stimulation of the lower as well and to the establishment between parent and child of 'the bond of adult love'. But, short of direct incest, which the Lawrentian Non-conformist background makes even more impossible than usual, there is no sexual outlet for the son. Even more important than this, however, is the fact that the mother's love, on closer examination, proves to be only superficially 'wife-submissive'; in reality it is a form of domination, subtly disguised as submission. The mother exploits her son, making him subserve her own need and refusing him the right to an independent life of his own.

All this is amply demonstrated in *Sons and Lovers*. In that novel Paul Morel is struggling for independence—not merely for the right to choose his own sweetheart, but for the very independence of his soul. (pp. 285-86)

When her eldest son, William, dies, Mrs. Morel concentrates all her frustrated longing on Paul. Without being seriously interested in his intellectual pursuits . . . , she gives them emotional support because they are a means by which she can achieve her end of making her son a successful figure, an image of herself that she can project on to the society around her. Her opposition to Miriam is intense, while she scarcely feels Clara as a competitor, because she regards Miriam as a rival for just this kind of direction of her son's life as a whole. There is considerable irony (too often ignored) in the novel in connection with this. Miriam's love also has a strong motherly-possessive element in it—witness her excessive demand for response from Hubert: '"Yes, you love me, don't you?" she murmured deep in her throat . . . "You love me, don't you?"' . . . but it is ironical that Mrs. Morel should perceive this and express it in words that exactly describe her own domination of Paul:

> '"She is one of those who will want to suck a man's soul out till he has none of his own left," she said to herself; "and he is just such a gaby as to let himself be absorbed. She will never let him become a man; she never will."'

Paul's vacillation between Clara and Miriam is, of course, an expression of his struggle towards wholeness of being. He feels the intense, spiritual-'ideal' stimulation of Miriam, who also provides the serious interest in his art that his mother does not, but he is dissatisfied with the absence of a real sensual foundation to his relationship with her and turns to Clara for this, instead. But this is only a branch of the parent theme of the novel, which is Paul's struggle to stand on his own in the midst of a tragically ironical struggle between two mother-tyrants, each of whom perceives the disastrous influence of the other whilst remaining blind to her own possessiveness.

The end of the novel confirms all this. Paul's freedom can only come through the death of his mother, and we find him, like Princess Maria in *War and Peace*, self-torturingly willing the parent's death; in fact, as Lawrence arranges it in *Sons and Lovers*, actually giving an overdose of morphia. The extent of his mother's influence is testified in the almost overwhelming death-wish that overtakes Paul afterwards. . . . Eventually he struggles towards recovery, but it is significant that his recovery does not involve a renewal of the relationship with Miriam. The final episode with her seems to have been put in for a definingly negative purpose. His recovery is towards self-reliance; to turn to Miriam would be to turn to another mother-tyrant.

In *Sons and Lovers*, then, Lawrence shows that mother-wife-submissiveness is far from being 'the quiescent, flowering love of a mature woman', but a deadly form of domination. In *Fantasia*, of course, Lawrence is also denouncing the mother-wife's destruction of her son-husband, and, as he declares in the Foreword, he is there making his inferences *from* the 'pure passionate experience' of the novels, *Sons and Lovers* in particular. The difference is that the theorist is obsessed with a certain *idée fixe* about the right relationship between husband and wife which he imports into the novelist's acute perception of the wrong relationship between mother and son. Lawrence, the propagandist for male hegemony on marriage, hysterically demands that woman must submit to the man, and so, when looking back at the picture drawn by Lawrence, the novelist, of a superficially beautiful relationship between mother and son, he is more taken in by it than ever the novelist had been.

All this is perhaps only a way of saying that the novelist is superior to the propagandist—with which few, presumably, would disagree—but it is worth while showing in a concrete instance precisely *how* that superiority manifests itself. We see that it is not merely an 'artistic' superiority, a gift for writing more pleasingly in fiction, but a superiority of moral accuracy and vision. Lawrence was right in saying that 'Men live and see according to some gradually developing and gradually withering vision', but, surely, wrong when he went on to add, 'This vision exists also as a dynamic idea of metaphysics—exists first as such.' His own practice gives this the lie. The dynamism is there in *Sons and Lovers*, but it scarcely amounts to an 'idea' or a 'metaphysics', and when one comes to the philosophising of it in *Fantasia of the Unconscious*, the informing vision seems already to have begun the process of gradual withering. (pp. 287-89)

> R. P. Draper, "D. H. Lawrence on Mother-Love," in Essays in Criticism, Vol. VIII, No. 3, July, 1958, pp. 285-89.

ELISEO VIVAS (essay date 1960)

[*Vivas is a Colombian-born educator and literary critic who, in the 1930s, contributed to the critical school known as New Criticism, an influential movement in American criticism which also included Allen Tate, Cleanth Brooks, R. P. Blackmur, and Robert Penn Warren, and which paralleled a critical movement in England led by I. A. Richards, T. S. Eliot, and William Empson. Although the various New Critics did not subscribe to a single set of principles, all believed that a work of literature had to be examined as an object in itself through a process of close analysis of symbol, image, and metaphor. For the New Critics, a literary work was not a manifestation of ethics, sociology, or psychology, and could not be evaluated in the general terms of any nonliterary discipline. For Vivas, art is a process of both creation and discovery and must be judged as such. The literary creation does not imitate life but is a "constitutive symbol" through which we learn about our world. Vivas has been a prolific critic, and some of his most important essays are included in the collection* Vivas as Critic: Essays in Poetics and Criticism *(1981). Vivas also wrote the widely discussed study* D. H. Lawrence: The Failure and Triumph of Art *(1960), in which he minimizes the importance of biographical elements in Lawrence's work on the basis of his belief that all writers create from their own experience and that what is important to literature is the quality of the transformation of that experience through the creative process. In general, Vivas contends that Lawrence fails as an artist when he leaves matter untransformed—that is, when he adheres too closely to the facts of his life without the distance and control of artistic craftsmanship. While many reviewers of this book have disagreed with Vivas's approach and conclusion, they agree that it is an extremely important contribution to Lawrence criticism. In the following excerpt from that work, Vivas claims that* Sons and Lovers *is the first great novel of Lawrence's career, but also discusses one aspect of the book which he considers a significant weakness: Lawrence's tendency to render ugly emotional scenes too graphically. Vivas furthermore contends that, in his depiction of Paul Morel and his mother, Lawrence unwittingly created two people incapable of love in any healthy or mature sense.*]

It is generally agreed that *Sons and Lovers* is one of Lawrence's best novels. I take it to be one of his best three and perhaps one of the best novels written in the English language in the first half of our century. . . . The work has faults, of course.

But after these are taken into account even a most exacting reader will probably be hard put to disagree with Lawrence's own estimate of it in a letter to Edward Garnett: "I tell you I have written a great book. . . . Read my novel, it is a great novel." If we remember the relaxed manner in which we paste the label "great" on any achievement that is distinctly above the mediocre, there can be no serious objection to Lawrence's estimate of his own achievement.

Because *Sons and Lovers* is one of Lawrence's best novels, a study of his art may be expected to include a thorough and perhaps even an extended examination of it. And indeed critical works on Lawrence usually devote to it the attention which its quality deserves. But I am going to treat it from a restricted point of view. I have two reasons for my decision, either of which, by itself, justifies it in my opinion. The first is that, frankly, I have little to say about it that has not already been said. The second is that while, along with everybody else, I recognize its superior quality, it does not properly belong, in my estimation, with Lawrence's mature work. I do not mean it is immature; it is not like his first two novels, the work of a talented, promising apprentice. I mean that it is not Lawrence at his fullest and ripest. It does not embody the substance of his vision, as we find it, whether successfully or unsuccessfully, embodied in later works. And for that reason it cannot be put in the class with *The Rainbow* and *Women in Love*. (pp. 173-74)

It is well known that *Sons and Lovers* is an autobiographical novel, and Lawrence himself so considered it. It is known that the Miriam of the story is Jessie Chambers Wood and that a good many scenes are direct transcripts from Lawrence's own life. . . . But it is too often forgotten that a literary work is not a picture taken by a photographic camera and that to the degree that the artist is creative, what he has taken from experience is thrown into the furnace of his mind, where often, at depths far beyond the reach of consciousness, it loses its identity and gains new form, new significance, and a capacity for resonance that is altogether lacking before the act of composition. *Sons and Lovers* is a novel that should serve as a good test of this claim.

Sons and Lovers is not a mere transcription of events in Lawrence's life up to the death of his mother. From his remembered experience Lawrence had first to make a selection. He did not attempt to put into the book everything that he remembered as happening to him or his family and friends. Some episodes he discarded. But even the notion of "selecting" episodes is not adequate to describe what Lawrence did. No doubt, in a rough way, Lawrence performed such a selection. As he was thinking of his novel, he decided to give accounts of quarrels between his mother and his father, he also decided to include the incident of his giving Jessie a ride in the swing on his sweetheart's farm, the account of his life in the factory, probably including the occasion on which a girl gave him a present on his birthday. He also decided that one theme he had to explore in full was his gradual realization that the sweetheart of his childhood could offer him only the spiritual love of a nun and not the kind of passion for which he, as he grew older, came more and more clearly and insistently to crave. It may be assumed for our purposes that these and many other remembered experiences he "selected" from his actual life. But the material thus selected was subjected, for various reasons, to the creative process. (pp. 175-76)

What Lawrence was trying to do in *Sons and Lovers*—besides writing a book that would give him the rewards of authorship and other purely external ends—was to achieve a grasp of his experience in its context. This called for his producing a coherent picture of his life and of the life of his family in terms of those factors that he took to have been important in their development. Central to the picture there had to be an account of two conflicts: the first, that between his father on the one hand and his mother and the children on the other; the second, the triangular conflict between his mother, his sweetheart, and himself. There also had to be an account of the discovery of his talent and its growth. The selected episodes had, finally, to be fitted into a harmonious whole. (p. 176)

It is well known that *Sons and Lovers* attempts to elucidate the triangular relationship between Paul, his mother, and Miriam. If Paul's interest in literature and in painting comes into the picture, it is not because Lawrence, like Joyce, is centrally interested in giving us the portrait of the development of an artist. And if the relationship between the parents is accented, it is in order to give us the background out of which the triangular relationship grew. Lawrence wants to show how Paul and his mother were forced to come together because Gertrude's husband, the uncouth, drinking, bullying miner, was no husband to her nor was he, properly speaking, a father to his children.

Lawrence's gift as a writer, the living quality of his scenes, enable him almost to get away with his intention and to write off the father and the sweetheart. But he did not altogether succeed in doing so. And the novel shows the novelist to be not only a dribbling liar but in some respects, and in spite of his magnificent capacity to see, almost altogether blind. In *Sons and Lovers* Lawrence's intention and the intention of the novel are disparate. But I should add that in this case, the disparity does not constitute an artistic defect: it merely gives the novel qualities that Lawrence did not see were there, and that, within my knowledge, have not been generally noticed.

For Lawrence wants us to believe that both Paul's father and his sweetheart were at fault, and that his mother, Gertrude Morel, was a superior person, who rose above her miserable world by virtue of superiority of class and personal endowment, a loving mother and a wife made unhappy by an uncouth, drinking, irresponsible husband. But in terms of the evidence to be found in the novel, was this actually the case? There is no question that Morel was not the right man for Gertrude, but was Gertrude the right wife for the miner?

Take the early scene in which Mrs. Morel comes downstairs to find William shorn of "the twining wisp of hair clustering around his head." Mrs. Morel is furious and with gripped, lifted fists, comes forward. Morel shrinks back. "I could kill you, I could!" she says. She cries and later tells her husband she has been silly. But we are told that "she knew, and Morel knew, that the act had caused something momentous to take place in her soul. She remembered the scene all her life, as one in which she had suffered the most intensely." And Lawrence goes on in the next paragraph: "The act of masculine clumsiness was the spear through the side of her love for Morel. Before, while she had striven against him bitterly, she had fretted after him, as if he had gone astray from her. Now she ceased to fret for his love: he was an outsider to her." . . . But before he cut his son's curls Morel was already an outsider. And because without asking her the man had clipped her boy's curls, she would remember the scene all her life. All one can say, confronted with the writer's statement, is that whether he knew it or not, he was giving us a vivid and living picture of a woman who had an unusual capacity to nurse a slight injury and had a powerful capacity for resentment. But does the writer know what he is presenting us with? Since the novel gives the writer the lie, the answer must be that he does and he does not. And we are here faced, not with a contradiction, but with a psychological conflict.

In any case, Paul's mother-sweetheart is a hard woman, a willful, unbending woman, and Paul is a myopic, love-blinded boy and young man. She would reform the miner she married, she would bring him up to her level of manners and gentility, and when it becomes clear to her that her husband cannot be reformed and when the physical attraction that brought them together subsides, she begins a relentless, ruthless war against him, setting the children against their father. The reason for her attitude is that he bullied them and drank. . . . But Mrs. Morel was more than a willful, unbending woman. Paul, in the entanglement of an Oedipal relationship, could not see it, and Lawrence gives no indication that he sees it, but Mrs. Morel was not a good mother to Paul and while Lawrence did in fact try to hand Paul's mother "the laurels of victory," as Jessie Chambers points out, and while Miriam was indeed defeated and cast off, the price was high. We do not know what happens to Paul when he reaches the city towards which he turns at the end of the book. But we know that the struggle has turned him already into a cruel man and has damaged his capacity for normal sexual relations.

With cruelty goes pathos. For the reader who reads it with care the book is instinct with desolating pathos, when he considers the illusions in which Mrs. Morel and her children live. The belief in the mother's superiority because she comes from a class just a notch higher than her husband, the belief that theirs is a home superior to their neighbors' because, living in a corner house, they pay a few more pennies for it than their neighbors do, the belief that they have better taste and superior education (which they do have, but which makes them pitiful snobs)— the hollowness of their values is pathetic. And Lawrence does not see their pathos. Neither through irony nor by any other means does he give us an indication that he sees through Gertrude Morel and her children. He is utterly lucid about the miner's faults. But about Paul's and his mother's false values he is blind.

How do we know about Paul's cruelty? We know from his treatment of his sweetheart. It is true that there is an important extenuating circumstance. The love between Paul and Miriam developed so slowly and so unconsciously, that by the time Paul realized clearly that Miriam could not satisfy his sexual needs, the involvement between them could only be severed by brutal surgery; there was no other way. When Miriam was twenty-one, Paul wrote to her that she was a nun and reproached her because in all their relations the body did not enter. After this letter was sent we are told that Paul, then twenty-three, was still a virgin, and that this was the end of the first phase of Paul's love-affair with Miriam. One can hardly blame Paul for discovering that what he needed was, in Miriam's words, "a sort of baptism of fire in passion." . . . But while it is not necessary to take the attitude of a judge, and while in any case passing moral judgments on characters in books is an act of supererogation which interferes with the revelation the artist seeks to make, we cannot overlook the fact that Paul was cruel and that he knew it. Lawrence tells us that Paul "fought against his mother almost as he fought against Miriam." . . . But this statement we may disregard, for the evidence of the novel gives it the lie. He did not fight against his mother; he grew in bondage and until her death in bondage he remained. And while

his mother did not fear Clara and did not interfere with his affair with her, she resented Miriam bitterly and she did not interfere when her son-lover was unspeakably cruel towards his sweetheart. His cruelty was part of the fruits of her victory.

We know that the struggle damaged Paul's capacity for normal sexual relations from the account of Paul's affair with Clara Dawes. For a brief moment the affair appeared to be satisfactory. On one occasion at least it led to an experience the depth and amplitude of which was what Paul had yearned for and Miriam had not been able to provide. But the affair soon peters out and Paul ends up by virtually making Clara return to her husband. What is wrong between Paul and Clara? The book does not reveal the cause and therefore we cannot answer the question. But the fact that the book does not reveal it is itself significant. . . . Surely this is a question in which we are legitimately interested and to which we need an answer. The failure to give an answer leaves us in the dark about the relationship between Clara and Paul. What went wrong between them? For a man who has had a sexual experience with a woman as complete and deep as that which Paul had with Clara, and who had wanted just that kind of experience, would not give the woman up as easily as Paul did. But the point I wish to make is not that Paul handed Clara back to her husband, but that the action is not grounded in anything that happens to them. We are left here with an unanswered question that the story itself gives rise to, not one we introduced from the outside.

This is not the only piece of evidence we have of Paul's incapacity for the complete sexual experience for which he craves. There is something else in the account of the affair between Paul and Clara that we must examine. [On at least one occasion] we are told that the experience constituted for both a complete and deep consummation. But why then did the experience fail to be the first cause of the ripening of the bond between them? The universe was involved in their affair the evening the pee-wits were screaming in the field. This is as it should be: they are part of the earth, and at the moment of love-death, the earth and the stars are part of their experience. After the evening Paul and Clara are still, having known "the immensity of passion." But the experience does not lead to tenderness between them. The fierceness, the wildness, the naked hunger are appeased and we are told that "in the morning Paul had considerable peace and was happy in himself." This sentence suggests a kind of emotional solipsism which neither Paul nor Clara broke out of during their liaison. Even at the time he was most completely satisfied by her, Paul's mode of being is that of aloneness. . . . The morning after the evening when the peewits screamed in the field, we are told that "the intensity of passion began to burn him again," and of Clara we are told that she "was mad with desire of him." . . . But each seems to be, for the other, a mere means to an end, and when the end is achieved, it is enjoyed in isolation. (pp. 180-85)

There is a sense, one which has been generally acknowledged, in which **Sons and Lovers** constitutes indisputably a great triumph of Lawrence's art. But there can be no serious harm in bringing it forth again.

Lawrence will keep a place in the history of English literature because he was first and last and all the time *a writer*. When I speak of Lawrence *the writer*, I mean the term in the sense in which Allen Tate means it when he applies it to Flaubert. In his brilliant essay, "Techniques of Fiction," Mr. Tate reminds us of Henry James's constant admonition, "'Don't state,' says James, time and again—'render! Don't tell us what is happening, let it happen.'" This is what Flaubert does in a small scene quoted by Mr. Tate from *Madame Bovary*. This Jamesian "rendering" is what I call "a presentation," something the artist is capable of achieving, and something which, when achieved, is the evidence we need in order to know a writer is back of it. And this is a power of which Lawrence gave evidence in almost everything he wrote. By the time he wrote *Sons and Lovers* his power as writer was fully developed. The earlier novels are over-written. From *Sons and Lovers* on Lawrence demonstrated fully and constantly that he was a great writer. (p. 188)

There are times, however, when Lawrence's mastery over language, as evinced in his power of immediacy, betrays him. At such times Lawrence is *obscene*, in the primitive sense of the word: for he brings into the scene things that should be left out, and that should be left out for a very good reason. Shakespeare is obscene in *Lear*—oh, the pity that such a grave fault is found in such a great play!—when he brings onto the stage the eye-plucking episode. Obscenities of this sort arouse the spectator of the scene, breaking the delicate poise, pushing him into the scene itself, and forcing him to engage as partisan in the action. Paradoxically, then, it is Lawrence's power of language that betrays him. He gets carried away by the description and the excessive immediacy pole-vaults us into the thick of the action. He forces us to respond to the emotions of the scene or to resist them, in any case forcing us to lose the poise by which an act of aesthesis is possible. If the purpose of reading Lawrence—or any author who claims the stature of artist— were to indulge in an emotional binge, these scenes, flawed with excess of immediacy, would be the highest peak of his achievement. But I cannot believe that this is the purpose of reading poetry. And if it were, it would not give art the status it has because outside itself there is no substitute for art. Emotional binges we can indulge in by many other means.

These abstract statements will probably not carry the force that a concrete illustration can carry. In *Sons and Lovers* there is an account of a quarrel between Walter Morel and his wife which is done with great force, indeed with an excess of emotion that embarrasses the reader. It's an ugly scene, in which Lawrence does Walter Morel in, obviously in the attempt to show that Paul's mother was the victim of the miner and his faults. Walter Morel left The Nelson in a jolly mood but before he arrived home he grew irritable. As a result, a quarrel follows. The scene is short, not over a page and a half in length, and it is pure drama, pure presentation. This is superb mastery of language, the result is pure immediacy. But there is another result: the reader cannot help entering into the quarrel and the complex emotions aroused by the quarrel leave him embarrassed and confused. However, the reader is not so utterly confused that he overlooks the fact that Lawrence himself is on the side of the young wife against the drunken husband and this injects the suspicion in him that Lawrence here is not merely presenting a quarrel but is doing more, he is probably justifying a private grudge of his own. (pp. 191-92)

But what is the point of dragging the reader into the quarrel? The point is the need to prove that the hatred that the wife finally developed for her husband and that she transferred to her children is fully justified. But why should the reader be made a partisan in this quarrel? He did not pick up the novel in order to exercise his gifts as judge, and particularly as judge of a quarrel between a man and his wife. He need not be wise in order to know that the right is very seldom, if ever, altogether on the side of one and the wrong altogether on the side of the other.

The Lawrence family: from left to right, top row: Emily, George, and Ernest. Bottom row: Ada, Mrs. Lawrence, David Herbert, and Mr. Lawrence.

In point of fact, this is the case in *Sons and Lovers*. The novel gives the lie to the dribbling liar who is the novelist and gives us evidence that Mrs. Morel, having married below her precious and ever so superior social level, soon had to face the fact that she had made a horrible mistake. The matter is not quite as simple, of course, for two reasons: it is obvious that for a time the sexual flame that was kindled in Mrs. Morel by her miner husband kept her from facing the truth, and it is also clear that at the very beginning, at any rate, Morel had tried to live up to the factitious standards which his wife set for him—he took the pledge and in general tried to raise himself from the level on which he had always lived. But I shan't pursue this question. For the point that must be made is, I hope, already adequately made, namely that the experience of being dragged into the quarrel is anything but pleasant and it induces in the reader ugly and frustrated emotions which he could very well do without. (pp. 193-94)

This is not the only scene in *Sons and Lovers* open to the criticism of obscenity because of excessive immediacy. The brutal fight between Clara's husband, Baxter Dawes, and Paul, is another in which the excess of hatred embarrasses and roils the reader's emotion. . . . The objection to the account of this fight may be put from a shifted point of view, in different terms: It is as if Lawrence were, as he wrote, living over an experience he had actually undergone, and living it over as he underwent it, without the benefit of aesthetic transformation; living it over, rather than recollecting it in tranquillity. The description of the fight with Dawes takes less than a thousand words; but they are not words one is reading but an action one is participating in and the experience is exhausting and extremely unpleasant. (pp. 194-95)

Another feature of the description of Paul's fight with Dawes adds to the reader's embarrassment, although it is not related to the problem of excess of immediacy. The reader cannot help feeling that the writer is distinctly on the side of Paul Morel and is justifying his defeat and is trying to picture him as a formidable antagonist. But the fact is that Paul is not a formidable antagonist and Lawrence has not altogether been able to conceal that Paul is afraid of Baxter Dawes. Indeed no hero of Lawrence drawn from autobiographical matter gives one convincing evidence of physical courage. On the contrary one gets the impression, a very definite if elusive impression, that they are all cowards. Whether Lawrence was a physical coward or not is not here in question. That he was a physical bully, we know. The story Knud Merrild tells about the beating Lawrence gave the dog is enough evidence. But whatever the case, his heroes are not "men" in the sense in which a marine sergeant or a Spanish-American would use the term. (p. 195)

And yet, when all these factors are taken into account, as they must be by the critic, the fact remains that Lawrence was a great writer and that **Sons and Lovers,** the first of his three great novels, is a superbly written book. He was a great *artist*, but he was also a great *writer*, which is to say, a master of language. As an artist he frequently fails, as I have attempted to show. . . . He does not compose with care, he pads, he often lacks inventiveness, he copies himself, he dramatizes concepts, and under the very poor excuse of bringing health where unhealthy prudishness reigns, he is obscene. Even as a writer, he fails occasionally. He is often extremely careless. At such times his prose loses its power of immediacy. . . . Lawrence has been criticized for the monotony of his prose; others have objected to its repetitiousness. Some of these animadversions are unimportant and some irrelevant. The repetitiousness is there, but to consider it a fault is to fail to notice what he achieves by means of it. He has also been criticized for attempting the impossible by seeking to give us the felt quality of an experience by direct presentation in words. The truth is that when he makes such attempts he sometimes falls into incoherence, straining the language and piling metaphor on image, with disastrous results. But at his best, the quality of experience as felt is conveyed by Lawrence successfully. . . . So that when the worst is said against him, it must be acknowledged that Lawrence was a superb artist and writer. He had his faults. But his triumphs more than make up for them. (pp. 198-99)

Eliseo Vivas, in his D. H. Lawrence: The Failure and the Triumph of Art, *1960. Reprint by George Allen & Unwin Ltd., 1961, 302 p.*

ALFRED KAZIN   (essay date 1962)

[*A highly respected American literary critic, Kazin is best known for his essay collections* The Inmost Leaf *(1955) and* Contemporaries *(1962), and particularly for* On Native Grounds *(1942), a study of American prose writing since the era of William Dean Howells. Having studied the works of "the critics who were the best writers—from Sainte-Beuve and Matthew Arnold to Edmund Wilson and Van Wyck Brooks" as an aid to his own critical understanding, Kazin has found that "criticism focussed many— if by no means all—of my own urges as a writer: to show literature as a deed in human history, and to find in each writer the unique-*

ness of the gift, of the essential vision, through which I hoped to penetrate into the mystery and sacredness of the individual soul." In the following excerpt, he discusses Lawrence's sense of his own authority and artistic power as revealed in the characterization of Paul Morel. Kazin also maintains that Lawrence's primary interest as a novelist was his exploration of the energy generated in the relationships between human beings.]

Sons and Lovers . . . seems easy to imitate. One reason, apart from the relationships involved, is the very directness and surface conventionality of its technique. James Joyce's *A Portrait of the Artist As a Young Man,* published only three years after **Sons and Lovers,** takes us immediately into the "new" novel of the twentieth century. It opens on a bewildering series of images faithful to the unconsciousness of childhood. Proust, who brought out the first volume of his great novel, *A la recherche du temps perdu,* in the same year that Lawrence published **Sons and Lovers,** imposed so highly stylized a unity of mood on the "Ouverture" to *Du côté de chez Swann,* that these impressions of childhood read as if they had been reconstructed to make a dream. But **Sons and Lovers** opens as a nineteenth-century novel with a matter-of-fact description of the setting—the mine, the landscape of "Bestwood," the neighboring streets and houses. This opening could have been written by Arnold Bennett, or any other of the excellent "realists" of the period whose work does not summon up, fifty years later, the ecstasy of imagination that Lawrence's work, along with that of Joyce and Proust, does provide to us. Lawrence is writing close to the actual facts. In his old-fashioned way he is even writing *about* the actual facts. No wonder that a young novelist with nothing but *his* own experiences to start him off may feel that Lawrence's example represents the triumph of experience. Literature has no rites in **Sons and Lovers;** everything follows as if from memory alone. When the struggle begins that makes the novel—the universal modern story of a "refined" and discontented woman who pours out on her sons love she refuses the husband too "common" for her—the equally universal young novelist to whom all this has happened, the novelist who in our times is likely to have been all too mothered and fatherless, cannot help saying to himself—"Why can't I write this good a novel out of myself? Haven't I suffered as much as D. H. Lawrence and am I not just as sensitive? And isn't this a highly selective age in which 'sensitive' writers count?"

But the most striking thing about Lawrence—as it is about Paul Morel in this novel—is his sense of his own authority. . . . You can easily dislike Lawrence for this air of authority, just as many people dislike him for the influence that he exerted during his lifetime and that has grown steadily since his death in 1930. There is already an unmistakeable priggish conceit about Paul Morel in this novel. Here is a miner's son who is asked by his mother if his is a "divine discontent" and replies in this style: "Yes. I don't care about its divinity. But damn your happiness! So long as life's full, it doesn't matter whether it's happy or not. I'm afraid your happiness would bore me." But even this contains Lawrence's sense of his own authority. He saw his talent as a sacred possession—he was almost too proud to think of his career as a *literary* one. This sense of having a power that makes for righteousness—this was so strong in Lawrence, and so intimately associated with his mother's influence, that the struggle he describes in **Sons and Lovers,** the struggle to love another woman as he had loved his mother, must be seen as the connection he made between his magic "demon," his gift, and his relationship to his mother. (pp. vii-ix)

Lawrence, who was so full of his own gift, so fully engaged in working it out that he would not acknowledge his gifted contemporaries, certainly did feel that the "essential soul" of him as he would have said, his special demon, his particular gift of vision, his particular claim on immortality, was bound up with his mother. Not "love" in the psychological sense of conscious consideration, but love in the mythological sense of a sacred connection, was what Lawrence associated with his mother and Paul with Mrs. Morel. Lawrence's power over others is directly traceable to his own sense of the sacredness still possible to life, arising from the powers hidden in ordinary human relationships. . . . Lawrence's "authority" which made him seem unbearably full of himself to those who disliked him, was certainly of a very singular kind. He had an implicit confidence in his views on many questions—on politics as on sex and love; he was able to pontificate in later life about the Etruscans, of whom he knew nothing, as well as to talk dangerous nonsense about "knowing through the blood" and the leader priniciple. Yet it is Lawrence's struggle to retain all the moral authority that he identified with his mother's love that explains the intensity of *Sons and Lovers,* as it does the particular intensity of Lawrence's style in this book, which he later criticized as too violent. Yet behind this style lies Lawrence's lifelong belief in what he called "quickness," his need to see the "shimmer," the life force in everything, as opposed to the "dead crust" of its external form. Destiny for Lawrence meant his privileged and constant sense of the holiness implicit in this recognition of the life force. Destiny also meant his recognition, as a delicate boy who had already seen his older brother Ernest (the "William" of *Sons and Lovers*) sicken and die of the struggle to attach himself to another woman, that his survival was somehow bound up with fidelity to his mother. Lawrence had absolute faith in his gift, but it was bound up with his physical existence, which was always on trial. He felt that it was in his mother's hands. (p. x)

With so much at stake, Lawrence put into ultimate terms, life or death, the struggle between Paul Morel's need to hold onto his mother and his desire to love Miriam Leivers as well. The struggle in *Sons and Lovers* is not between love of the mother and love of a young woman; it is the hero's struggle to *keep* the mother as his special strength, never to lose her, not to offend or even to vex her by showing too much partiality to other women. This is why the original of "Miriam Leivers," Jessie Chambers, says in her touching memoir . . . that she had to break with Lawrence after she had seen the final draft of the book, that "the shock of *Sons and Lovers* gave the death-blow to our friendship," for in that book "Lawrence handed his mother the laurels of victory" [see excerpt dated 1935].

That is indeed what Lawrence did; it would not have occurred to him to do anything else. And Jessie Chambers also honestly felt that she minded this for Lawrence's sake, not her own, since by this time there was no longer any question of marriage between them. Jessie, who certainly loved Lawrence for his genius even after she had relinquished all personal claim on him, had launched Lawrence's career by sending out his poems. When Lawrence, after his mother's death, wrote a first draft of *Sons and Lovers,* he was still unable to work out his situation in a novel. Jessie encouraged him to drop this unsatisfactory version of the later novel and to portray the emotional struggle directly. At his request, she even wrote out narrative sections which Lawrence revised and incorporated into his novel. (Lawrence often had women write out passages for his novels when he wanted to know how a woman would react to a particular situation; Frieda Lawrence was to contribute to his characterization of Mrs. Morel.) Lawrence sent Jessie parts of the manuscript for her comments and further notes. After so much help and even collaboration, Jessie felt betrayed by the book. Lawrence had failed to show, she said, how important a role the girl had played in the development of the young man as an artist. "It was his old inability to face his problem squarely. His mother had to be supreme, and for the sake of that supremacy every disloyalty was permissible." (p. xi)

Jessie Chambers herself became an embittered woman. She tried to find her salvation in politics, where the fierce hopes of her generation before 1914 for a new England were certainly not fulfilled. But Lawrence, taking the new draft of *Sons and Lovers* with him to finish in Germany after he had run off with Frieda, was able, if not to "liberate" himself from his mother in his novel, to write a great novel out of his earliest life and struggles.

That is the triumph Jessie Chambers would not acknowledge in *Sons and Lovers,* that she could not see—the Lawrence "unable to face his problem squarely" made a great novel out of the "problem," out of his mother, father, brother, the miners, the village, the youthful sweetheart. . . . Lawrence felt his "problem" not as something to be solved, but as a subject to be represented. All these early experiences weighed on him with a pressure that he was able to communicate—later he called it "that hard violent style full of sensation and presentation." Jessie Chambers herself described Lawrence's accomplishment when she said, speaking of the new draft of *Sons and Lovers* that she drove Lawrence to write, "It was his power to transmute the common experiences into significance that I always felt to be Lawrence's greatest gift. He did not distinguish between small and great happenings. The common round was full of mystery, awaiting interpretation." . . . (p. xii)

Lawrence's particular gift was this ability to represent as valuable anything that came his way. He had the essential religious attribute of *valuing* life, of seeing the most trivial things as a kind of consecration. In part, at least, one can trace this to the poverty, austerity and simplicity of his upbringing. . . . Delight in simple things is one of the recurring features of the working-class existence described in *Sons and Lovers*. We can understand better the special value that Lawrence identified with his mother's laboriousness and self-denial in the scene where Mrs. Morel, wickedly extravagant, comes home clutching the pot that cost her fivepence and the bunch of pansies and daisies that cost her fourpence. The rapture of the commonest enjoyments and simplest possessions is represented in the mother and father as well as in the young artist Paul, the future D. H. Lawrence. This autobiographical novel rooted in the writer's early struggles is charged with feeling for his class, his region, his people. Lawrence was not a workingman himself, despite the brief experience in the surgical appliances factory that in the novel becomes Paul Morel's continued job. Chekhov said that the working-class writer purchases with his youth that which a more genteel writer is born with. But Lawrence gained everything, as a writer, from being brought up in the working class, and lost nothing by it. In *Sons and Lovers* he portrays the miners without idealizing them, as a socialist would; he relishes their human qualities (perhaps even a little jealously) and works them up as a subject for his art. He does not identify himself with them; his mother, too, we can be sure from the portrait of Mrs. Morel, tended to be somewhat aloof among the miners' wives. But Lawrence knows *as a writer* that he is related to working people, that he is bound up with them in the same order of physical and intimate existence, that it is workers' lives he has always looked on. Some of the most affecting passages in this novel are based on the force and directness of working-class speech. "'E's niver gone, child?" Morel says to his son when William dies. Paul answers in "educated" and even prissy English, but the voice of the mines, the fields and the kitchens is rendered straight and unashamed. Lawrence, who knew how much he had lost as a man by siding with his mother in the conflict, describes the miner Morel getting his own breakfast, sitting "down to an hour of joy," with an irresistible appreciation of the physical and human picture involved: "He toasted his bacon on a fork and caught the drops of fat on his bread; then he put the rasher on his thick slice of bread, and cut off chunks with a clasp-knife, poured his tea into his saucer, and was happy."

The writer alone in Lawrence redeemed the weaknesses of being too much his mother's son. We see the common round of life among the miners' families very much as the young Lawrence must have seen it, with the same peculiar directness. His mental world was startlingly without superfluities and wasted motions. What he wrote, he wrote. The striking sense of authority, of inner conviction, that he associated with his mother's love gave him a cutting briskness with things he disapproved. But this same immediacy of response, when it touched what he loved, could reach the greatest emotional depths. The description of William Morel's coffin being carried into the house is a particular example of this. "The coffin swayed, the men began to mount the three steps with their load. Annie's candle flickered, and she whimpered as the first men appeared, and the limbs and bowed heads of six men struggled to climb into the room, bearing the coffin that rode like sorrow on their living flesh." Lawrence's power to move the reader lies in this ability to summon up all the physical attributes associated with an object; he puts you into direct contact with all its properties *as* an object. Rarely has the realistic novelist's need to *present*, to present vividly, continually, and at the highest pitch of pictorial concentration—the gift which has made the novel the supreme literary form of modern times—rarely has this reached such intense clarity of representation as it does in *Sons and Lovers.* (pp. xiii-xiv)

Lawrence does not describe, he would not attempt to describe, the object as in *itself* it really is. The effect of his prose is always to heighten our consciousness of something, to relate it to ourselves. He is a romantic—and in this book is concerned with the most romantic possible subject for a novelist, the growth of the writer's own consciousness. Yet he succeeded as a novelist, he succeeded brilliantly, because he was convinced that the novel is the great literary form, for no other could reproduce so much of the actual motion or "shimmer" of life, especially as expressed in the relationships between people. Since for Lawrence the great subject of literature was not the writer's own consciousness but consciousness between people, the living felt relationship between them, it was his very concern to represent the "shimmer" of life, the "wholeness"—these could have been mere romantic slogans—that made possible his brilliance as a novelist. . . . It was relationship that was sacred to him, as it was the relationship with his mother, her continuing presence in his mind and life, that gave him that sense of authority on which all his power rested. And as a novelist in *Sons and Lovers* he was able to rise above every conventional pitfall in an autobiographical novel by centering his whole vision on character as the focus of a relationship, not as an absolute.

After *Sons and Lovers,* which was his attempt to close up the past, Lawrence was to move on to novels like *The Rainbow* . . .

and *Women in Love* . . . , where the "non-human in humanity" was to be more important to him than "the old-fashioned human element." The First World War was to make impossible for Lawrence his belief in the old "stable ego" of character. Relationships, as the continuing interest of life, became in these more "problematical," less "conventional" novels, a version of man's general relationship, as an unknown to himself, to his unexplained universe. But the emphasis on growth and change in *Sons and Lovers,* the great book that closes Lawrence's first period, is from the known to the unknown; as Frank O'Connor has said, the book begins as a nineteenth-century novel and turns into a twentieth-century one [see Additional Bibliography]. Where autobiographical novels with a "sensitive" artist or novelist as hero tend to emphasize the hero's growth to self-knowledge, the history of his "development," the striking thing about *Sons and Lovers,* and an instance of the creative mind behind it, is that it does not hand the "laurels of victory" to the hero. It does not allow him any self-sufficient victory over his circumstances. With the greatest possible vividness it shows Paul Morel engulfed in relationships—with the mother he loves all too sufficiently, with the "spiritual" Miriam and Clara, neither of whom he can love whole-heartedly—relationships that are difficult and painful, and that Lawrence leaves arrested in their pain and conflict. . . . Lawrence's primary interest and concern as a novelist, his sense of the continuing *flow* of relationship between people, no matter how unclear and painful, no matter how far away it was from the "solution" that the people themselves may have longed for, is what makes this whole last section of the novel so telling.

But of course it is the opening half of *Sons and Lovers* that makes the book great. The struggle between husband and wife is described with a direct, unflinching power. Lawrence does not try to bring anything to a psychological conclusion. The marriage is a struggle, a continuing friction, a relationship where the wife's old desire for her husband can still flash up through her resentment of his "lowness." That is why everything in the "common round" can be described with such tenderness, for the relationship of husband and wife sweeps into its unconscious passion everything that the young Lawrence loved, and was attached to. Living in a mining village on the edge of old Sherwood Forest, always close to the country, Lawrence was as intimate with nature as any country poet could have been, but he was lucky to see rural England and the industrial Midlands in relation to each other; the country soothed his senses, but a job all day long in a Nottingham factory making out orders for surgical appliances did not encourage nature worship. . . . Lawrence is a great novelist *of* landscape, for he is concerned with the relationships of people living on farms, or walking out into the country after the week's work in the city. He does not romanticize nature, he describes it in its minute vibrations. In *Sons and Lovers* the emotional effect of the "lyrical" passages depends on Lawrence's extraordinary ability to convey movement and meaning even in nonhuman things. But in this book nature never provides evasion of human conflict and is not even a projection of human feelings; it is the physical world that Lawrence grew up in, and includes the pit down which a miner must go every day. Paul in convalescence, sitting up in bed, would "see the fluffy horses feeding at the troughs in the field, scattering their hay on the trodden yellow snow; watch the miners troop home—small, black figures trailing slowly in gangs across the white field."

This miniature, exquisite as a Japanese watercolor, is typical of the book—in *Sons and Lovers* the country lives and seethes, but it has no mystical value. It is the landscape of Nottinghamshire and Derbyshire, and in the book is still what it was to Lawrence growing up in it, an oasis of refreshment in an industrial world. The countryside arouses young lovers to their buried feelings and it supplies images for the "quickness," the vital current of relationship, that Lawrence valued most in life. It is never sacred in itself. When you consider that this novel came out in 1913, at the height of the "Georgian" period, when so many young poets of Lawrence's generation were mooning over nature, it is striking that *his* chief interest is always the irreducible ambiguity of human relationships. Lawrence's language, in certain key scenes, certainly recalls the emotional inflation of fiction in the "romantic" heyday preceding World War I. But the style is actually exalted rather than literary. There is an unmistakably scriptural quality to Lawrence's communication of extreme human feeling. Mr. Morel secretly cuts young William's hair, and Mrs. Morel feels that "this act of masculine clumsiness was the spear through the side of her love." The Lawrences were Congregationalist, like American Puritans. They felt close to the Lord. The strong sense of himself that Lawrence was always to have, the conviction that what he felt was always terribly important just in the way he felt it, is imparted to Mrs. Morel herself in the great scene in which the insulted husband, dizzy with drink, locks her out of the house. The description of Mrs. Morel's feelings is charged with a kind of frenzy of concern for her; the language sweeps from pole to pole of feeling. Mrs. Morel is pregnant, and her sense of her moral aloneness at this moment is overwhelming. "Mrs. Morel, seared with passion, shivered to find herself out there in a great white light, that fell cold on her, and gave a shock to her inflamed soul." Later we read that "After a time the child, too, melted with her in the mixing-pot of moonlight, and she rested with the hills and lilies and houses, all swum together in a kind of swoon."

In this key scene of the mother's "trouble" (which must have been based on things that Lawrence later heard from his mother), the sense we get of Mrs. Morel, humiliated and enraged but in her innermost being haughtily inviolate, gives us a sense of all the power that Lawrence connected with his mother and of the power in the relationship that flowed between them. In this book he was able to re-create, for all time, the moment when the sympathetic bond between them reached its greatest intensity—and the moment when her death broke it. Ever after, Lawrence was to try to re-create this living bond, this magic sympathy, between himself and life.... Unlike Henry James, James Joyce, Marcel Proust, T. S. Eliot, Lawrence always makes you feel that not art but the quality of the lived experience is his greatest concern. That is why it is impossible to pick up anything by him without feeling revivified. Never were a writer's works more truly an allegory of his life, and no other writer with his imaginative standing has in our time written books that are so open to life. (pp. xiv-xviii)

> *Alfred Kazin, in an introduction to* Sons and Lovers *by D. H. Lawrence, The Modern Library, 1962, pp. vii-xix.*

JULIAN MOYNAHAN (essay date 1963)

[*Moynahan is an American novelist, critic, and educator who has written extensively on D. H. Lawrence. In the following excerpt from his book* The Deed of Life: The Novels and Shorter Fiction of D. H. Lawrence, *Moynahan examines the organization of* Sons and Lovers *and discusses what he considers to be points of confusion in the novel's structure.*]

Despite its popular appeal, which appears to be quite legitimate, *Sons and Lovers* has sometimes been charged with formlessness and with confusion of form. These two charges are usually presented as one. The first appears quite false, and so far as I know has never been substantiated. The second claim, that the novel is confused, appears more legitimate but can hardly be considered until the first has been disallowed. That is what I propose to do: to discuss how the novel is organized, and where and how a certain confusion disturbs its essential composure.

Actually, *Sons and Lovers* has three formal orders or matrices, which inhabit the same serial order of narrated words. To a degree, they blend with each other, and enrich one another. The first matrix is autobiographical narrative; the second a scheme taken over from psychoanalytic theory; the third is difficult to name because Lawrence was the first novelist to use it as a context, as opposed to a quality, of human experience, but it might be called the matrix of "life."

Each matrix has its own kind of logical articulation. The autobiographical narrative is articulated in terms of historical sequence (Mrs. Morel gave William his tea *and then* he went to the "Wakes"), and ordinary causality (Paul stopped school at the age of fourteen and went to work at Jordan's Surgical Appliance Co. *because* his family needed the money). The logic of the psychoanalytic scheme depends on a particular explanation of behavior provided by a psychological system that assumes and explains such mechanisms as unconscious motivation and projection. When the narrator says at one point about Paul's attitude toward Miriam, "He wanted now to give her passion and tenderness, and could not," it is a straightforward statement of fact according to the first matrix. But in terms of the psychological scheme it is a diagnostic description of a neurotic symptom belonging to a syndrome precisely defined by Sigmund Freud in a paper first published in 1912.

The logic of the third matrix may be termed, following Lawrence's own usage, "vital" or "passional." It is easier to show in operation than to define a priori. For example: after Mrs. Morel dies of cancer and is laid out in her bedroom, her husband Walter Morel is peculiarly reluctant to enter the room to pay his last respects. When he finally summons courage he stays only long enough to see that the body is there in the darkened room under a sheet. He does not look directly at her and see her, and in fact has not looked directly at her since the beginning of her illness.... It is still ordinary and typical according to the second matrix: the death of a close relative may precipitate an anxiety state in a survivor, and so forth. The same sequence in the vital context, where it actually takes place, leads to a severe judgment on Morel:

> And that was how he tried to dismiss her. He never thought of her personally. Everything deep in him he denied. Paul hated his father for sitting sentimentalising over her. He knew he would do it in the public-houses. For the real tragedy went on in Morel in spite of himself....

Passional or vital logic dictates this judgment. The larger indictment against the father in the novel is that he denies the life within him. Here the denial is expressed through his refusal to "see" his dead wife, and his willingness to tell sentimental lies about their relation. In the other contexts these are his experiences. In the vital context the experience violates sanctions that may be mysterious but are also specific and real. The violation is a form of self-violation and is a tragedy, according to the firm, though compassionate, view of the narration.

The three formal orders of *Sons and Lovers* can perhaps best be illustrated by following the hero Paul Morel through the series. As the hero of an autobiographical novel Paul is a youth who grew up in a colliery village, loved and left two women, became a successful commercial artist specializing in designs for textiles, with outlets for his work in such great London stores as Liberty's, and lost a beloved mother in his mid-twenties. According to the psychological scheme, he is a classic instance of oedipal fixation. In the context of what Lawrence was soon to call in his *Study of Thomas Hardy* ''the vast unexplored morality of life itself,'' Paul is a passionate pilgrim whose every action and impulse is a decision for or against life and accumulates to a body of fate that quite literally spells life or death for him.

The expressive means through which each of these forms is represented can be partially differentiated. The first is represented through a painstaking, richly detailed rendering of the naturalistic surface of ordinary life in both expository and dramatic terms. The psychoanalytic scheme is occasionally pointed up through explicit interpretative commentary, but is largely implicit in the autobiographical narrative as an underlying pattern. The vital context informs the naturalistic narrative, is sometimes pointed up through specific narrative comment (''For the real tragedy went on in Morel in spite of himself''), and is also expressed direct in isolable dramatic scenes of a peculiar kind and in passages of extended description that carry an intensely poetic charge. These scenes and expository passages, in which characters act out their vital destinies, sometimes mislead critics on the prowl for symbolism into supposing they were planted in the narration as ''keys'' to hidden meaning. But in the sense that symbols always point beyond themselves to something buried, there is little symbolism in *Sons and Lovers.* (pp. 13-16)

Not every character functions in all three matrices, although all the major characters do. Paul's younger brother Arthur, for example, has no part in the oedipal pattern, and his vitality, while evident enough, is never at issue. The elder brother William who dies at the end of Part I because he cannot resolve the conflict between his attachments to his mother and to his fiancée belongs mainly to the second matrix, as the first of Mrs. Morel's two fixated son-lovers. Miss Limb, the lonely farm woman in love with the stallion, who appears briefly in Chapter IX: ''The Defeat of Miriam,'' belongs mainly to the third context. Lawrence is interested, not in her psychology or her personal history, but solely in her rapport with the animal as that rapport affects Paul, Miriam, and Clara. Their reactions to her define qualities of being each possesses and clarify the continually modified emotional currents passing among the three young people, constituting their relation at that particular time.

Now that the form of *Sons and Lovers* has been defined, it becomes possible to deal with the charge of formal confusion. Confusion arises owing to a final inescapable conflict between the psychoanalytic and the vital contexts. Each approaches experience from a somewhat different angle, interprets it differently, and posits a different sort of hero. Paul is finally caught in a dual focus. As a case study of neurosis he is trapped in a pattern of ''repetition compulsion'' from which there is no escape this side of the analyst's couch. (pp. 17-18)

The conflict, with its attendant ambiguities which confuse the presentation of Miriam and Clara as well as Paul, is real but

ought not to be exaggerated, as it has been by critics whose notions of formal coherence are narrowly based. Psychoanalysis and Lawrence's kind of vitalism have many points in common as readings of experience. There is a sense in which the ''drift toward death'' means as much in passional as in neurotic terms. But the two systems of interpretation finally do not coincide. The Freudian system is weighted toward determinism. Paul, given his conditioning and the axiom that unconscious processes cannot become conscious and therefore modifiable without a therapist's aid, is doomed. The vital context is a fluid system that is fully indeterminate. Short of death there is no occasion in experience when the individual cannot make the correct, life-enhancing choice. Even an old wreck like Morel *could* at last look at his dead wife—the possibility is implied by the very strictness with which his refusal to do so is judged. The issues of life and death are fully worked into the very texture of events, and the road to salvation runs along the edge of the abyss where Paul stands after his mother's death and his double rejection of Clara and Miriam.

Although both novels draw upon the same set of remembered facts, *Sons and Lovers* is infinitely superior to *The White Peacock* as an autobiographical narrative. . . . Cyril, who is quite obviously an early study for Paul Morel, is also quite obviously in love with his mother. That is really why he is so half-hearted in his spasmodic search for adult love and relatedness. But except for a few brief indications, this crucial relationship is missing from the book. In Cyril, we get the burden of sick feeling without its referent—a devouring maternal possessiveness which destroys a son's capacity to move on from childhood attachments into adulthood.

Sons and Lovers not only confronts the mother-son relation directly but places it at the center of a real world built up through an astonishingly detailed recreation of a complex human environment. In the early chapters the mother's shift of her affections from her husband to her sons is sketched against a background that includes the social and economic history of the Nottinghamshire-Derbyshire border region going back nearly two centuries. . . . When Paul begins to visit the Leivers' farm the exposition broadens to include full descriptions of the countryside, which contrasts so finally and suggestively with the grimy village, and of Miriam's entire family, how they came to the farm and how they work it. When he takes a job in Nottingham the exposition broadens again. We come to understand the exact routines of a small Victorian factory, and its human environment as well. And we learn of the surrounding city, with its great grey castle, swift river, hurtling trams, and enormous mills.

This background is deeply relevant to the central conflicts of the book. It conditions the struggle of some of the characters to realize themselves and helps explain the baffled compromise that other characters make with the circumstances into which they were born. I know of no other English novel, with the possible exception of George Eliot's *Middlemarch*, where people are so rooted in concrete social history, and in a region so concretely rendered. It becomes possible to measure the precise degree of freedom or unfreedom enjoyed by each major character in relation to the full human environment.

It is worth spelling some of this out. Gertrude Morel's incompatibility with her husband is conditioned by particular social facts. Her father had been a Nottingham lace manufacturer ruined by an industrial slump. . . . When she comes to the village of Bestwood to live with Morel she leaves a large city in touch with the great world for a narrow, spiritually and economically impoverished mining community dominated by traditional codes affecting all areas of life from child care to the manner in which a collier divides his time, and money, between the pub and the home. She tries to adapt herself, but is soon put off by the uncouth slackness of her husband. Yet his qualities are also conditioned by social facts. His fecklessness is in tune with the community as a whole. . . . The warm physical nature which had attracted Gertrude to him is soon ruined by hard work, by serious accidents occurring in the pit at regular intervals, and by drink. The rupture between husband and wife, although inevitable, is never total. In the midst of her contempt she respects what he once was; and Morel's drunken tirades hide an inarticulate admiration for her real refinement and intellectual superiority.

Still, it is equally inevitable that she should turn to her sons as they mature toward manhood. They become the channels into which she pours her long dammed up spiritual energy, and she cannot help using them destructively to break a way through the walls separating her from a larger world. The older son is taken over completely. He wears himself out in ambitious pursuits reflecting an intensity of frustration that is more his mother's than his own. Denied its legitimate satisfactions, Mrs. Morel's will has become inhuman. Paul, with some of the traditional slipperiness of the artist type, evades the full force of the mother's will, but is severely injured by the erotic concomitants of her drive for self-realization through a son's life. At the same time, both sons' choices are closely circumscribed by social facts. They can follow the father into the pit—while fully idiomatic, the expression has a peculiar ring in the context of Bestwood's chapel-going religiosity—or side with their mother in favor of culture, education, and money. (pp. 18-21)

The same sort of conditioning operates on characters other than the Morels. Miriam's frigid attitude toward sex and her masochistic, compensatory version of Christian belief comes to her from her mother, a town woman of rather low physical vigor forced to live on a small tenant farm where all must work to the point of exhaustion if the rent is to be cleared each year. Exhausted by her work and childbearing, repelled by the spectacle of farm animals in heat or giving birth, Mrs. Leivers recoils from the sex relation and solaces herself with chapel religion. Clara Dawes's poignant blend of hauteur and humility, as well as her bitter quarrel with Baxter, reflects the conflict between her aspirations and her circumstances. She wants freedom to become someone, but is only free to choose between the factory and a damaged marriage to an ordinary workman. As a suffragette she blames her troubles on the unfranchised status of women, yet the novel makes clear that her lot is the same as her husband's and like poor people's generally. (pp. 21-2)

Paul Morel is the proper hero of *Sons and Lovers* because he holds and uses this freedom in a greater measure than any other character. He imposes himself. In calling the book an autobiographical narrative I do not mean that it is a faithful reproduction of Lawrence's career up to the time his mother died. Recollected material has been reorganized and new material has been added to make a dramatic pattern emphasizing Paul's dominating character. Paul's vitality is stronger, his awareness of vital issues is finer than Lawrence's. The paradox is only apparent and can easily be sustained. In life Lawrence was baffled by Jessie Chambers, whose indignant assertion that they never became lovers compels belief. Lawrence was initiated into sex by a Mrs. Dax. She took him upstairs one afternoon because she thought he needed it. As a boy he worked for a surgical appliance company like Jordan's but left after only a

few weeks because the factory girls jeered at him and one day removed his trousers in a dark corner of one of the storerooms.

In *Sons and Lovers* Paul forces his agonized relation with Miriam to the final issue of sexual union and then leaves her only when he is satisfied that they are too much at emotional cross-purposes to marry. He is entirely dominant in the affair with Clara, even to the point of forcing a reconciliation between Baxter and Clara before withdrawing into a *nuit blanche* of grief over his mother's death. He enjoys his work in the factory, develops affectionate ties with the girls who work there, and after several years has so thoroughly shaped the routines of his job to his own needs that he manages to spend only the mornings as a spiral clerk, using his afternoons to paint in a spare room. Finally, he copes with his mother during her illness. After speaking the ghastly sentence, "It is the living I want, not the dead," Mrs. Morel has fixed her will on survival even though she has a metastasized cancer and is in monstrous pain. Paul's decision to perform a mercy killing is simultaneously an act of the purest love, and a victory over the maternal will which guarantees that at the end he will find a way to escape the "drift toward death" which follows her death. It is also a free decision to take a constructive line of action against the destructiveness implicit in Mrs. Morel's will to survive after any real life has left her. (pp. 23-4)

Certainly Paul is bigger and freer than the young Lawrence, but he is not freer and bigger than Lawrence's vision of what life can be. Nevertheless it is mainly because Paul is a hero rather than a victim in the context of autobiographical narrative that Lawrence's employment of the psychoanalytic scheme works at cross purposes with the other matrices.

It will be useful here to summarize Lawrence's relation to Freud with particular reference to the period in which he was composing *Sons and Lovers.* We do not know whether Lawrence had read Freud before he wrote the final draft of *Sons and Lovers,* but it is definitely known that Frieda had read Freud and discussed psychoanalytic ideas with Lawrence on numerous occasions while he worked on the final draft of the novel. . . . In Lawrence's later writings he frequently took issue with the Freudians on two points: on the primacy of the sexual impulse in the individual's psychological development; on the value of bringing neurotics to a conscious awareness of repressed instincts and drives. Since one of the principal stresses in his entire career was his attack on the modern tendency to over-conceptualize experience, it was inevitable that he should come to take issue with the Freudian school.

It remains to determine the accuracy of Lawrence's representation of the Oedipus complex from the Freudian standpoint. Without claiming expertness in these matters I should say that Lawrence's construction of a sort of neurotic case history for Paul is both accurate and comprehensive. *Sons and Lovers* presents the mother fixation, the abnormal jealousy of the father, and shows both these tendencies persisting as a disturbing influence in Paul's dealings with men and women outside the family circle; for instance, the affair with Clara, which is broken off as the result of a savage fight between Paul and the jealous husband, represents on one level an acting out of an oedipal fantasy wherein Clara and Baxter Dawes, the estranged and quarrelsome married couple, replace Gertrude and Walter Morel, the hero's own mother and father. Furthermore, the novel dramatizes the conflict in the hero between normal desires and unconscious fixations. It presents his ambivalence—his oscillations between love and hate in the affair with Miriam—and it dramatizes the mechanism of projection whereby Paul transfers his internal conflicts to the outside world.

One further point. The psychological theme of the "split" which Lawrence develops both within the novel and also in the letter to Edward Garnett . . . is actually the same as that developed by Sigmund Freud in his essay, "The Most Prevalent Form of Degradation in Erotic Life." Here is described a widespread condition of psychical impotence in modern, cultivated men in which individuals, because of an unresolved incestuous attachment for their mothers, combined with an unusually repressed childhood and adolescence, find it impossible to fuse tender and sensual feelings into a wholesome love for a woman of their own age and station in life. These men are sexually attracted by women who are in some way inferior to them, while the tenderness they feel for their feminine social equals lacks a sensual quality. They give their souls to women who play the role of mother figures and their bodies to women who for one reason or another can never aspire to represent the overidealized mother.

Thus as Lawrence wrote to Garnett, William Morel "gives his sex to a fribble, and his mother holds his soul." Paul seems to do better by consummating his love for the companionable Miriam. But his constant complaints that she is too soulful and that she is frigid, alike with the death urges he frequently experiences after intercourse with her, show that he cannot heal the split in his affective life through Miriam. Later on he divides his love between the idealized mother and the passionate, shamed, compromised Clara Dawes. In classical neurotic fashion he re-creates again and again the very conditions of unhealth from which he is attempting to escape.

Paul's vitality, his extraordinary capacity to make boldly sensuous responses to his environment, suggest that he is somehow free. The above summary of the facts of his "case" show that he is not. This difference cannot be compromised. It represents a collision between opposed ways of looking at a character, opposed definitions of human instinct and of human life. One summer evening, after Paul has been sleeping with Miriam for an entire year, he steps suddenly out of doors:

> The beauty of the night made him want to shout. A half-moon, dusky gold, was sinking behind the black sycamore at the end of the garden, making the sky dull purple with its glow. Nearer, a dim white fence of lilies went across the garden, and the air all round seemed to stir with scent, as if it were alive. He went across the bed of pinks, whose keen perfume came sharply across the rocking, heavy scent of the lilies, and stood alongside the white barrier of flowers. They flagged all loose, as if they were panting. The scent made him drunk. He went down to the field to watch the moon sink under.

> A corncrake in the hay-close called insistently. The moon slid quite quickly downwards, growing more flushed. Behind him the great flowers leaned as if they were calling. And then, like a shock, he caught another perfume, something raw and coarse. Hunting round, he found the purple iris, touched their fleshy throats and their dark, grasping hands. At any rate, he had found something. They stood stiff in the darkness. Their scent was brutal. The moon was melting

down upon the crest of the hill. It was gone; all was dark. The corncrake called still.

> Breaking off a pink, he suddenly went indoors.

> "Come, my boy," said his mother. "I'm sure it's time you went to bed."

> He stood with the pink against his lips.

> "I shall break off with Miriam, mother," he answered calmly. . . .

After noting that the raw coarse scent of the iris evokes Clara, as the pinks whose petals he soon spits into the fire evoke Miriam; after noting the presence of the mother and her characteristically domineering mode of address, one must still insist that the decision springs to life out of Paul's fully concrete experience of the night, the garden and the flowers in their nearly overpowering physical actuality. We may find the hero's relation to these a mystery and his decision brutal, but we have to admit that the experience is *sui generis,* not simply another instance of Paul's enslavement to what Freud called, rather abstractedly, an *imago.* Scenes of this type suggest that beneath the layer of disordered instinctual trends constituting Paul's neurosis lie other vital impulses which remain intact and occasionally break through, with a consequent shock of recognition for both the reader and the character. Paul is tied but carries his freedom somewhere inside him, whence it might issue, given the appropriate challenge from the life teeming around him, here represented by a beautiful summer night, to dissolve his bonds and transform his existence. (pp. 24-8)

The ending of *Sons and Lovers* shows that Paul Morel's nature does contain an intact core of vitality which is his freedom, that while his responses to his family and mistresses have been "overdetermined" by neuroticism, his fate remains indeterminate *au fond.* When Mrs. Morel is dead, the hero cries out, "My love—my love—oh, my love!" echoing the cry of the mother—"My son, oh my son"—over the body of William. But for Paul there is no one to turn to, no one to build a new life upon, and he turns away into his white night of spiritual and emotional numbness. He puts his affairs in order by reconciling Clara with Baxter and goes alone to encounter his self-annihilating vision of the voidness of a world which no longer contains his mother. Darkness washes over him in a great flood. It pours from the infinite reaches of space, and wells up from inside, "from his breast, from his mouth." It is a flood of dissolution:

> When he turned away he felt the last hold for him had gone. The town, as he sat upon the car, stretched away over the bay of railway, a level fume of lights. Beyond the town the country, little smouldering spots for more towns—the sea—the night—on and on! And he had no place in it! Whatever spot he stood on, there he stood alone. . . . He got off the car. In the country all was dead still. Little stars shone high up; little stars spread far away in the floodwaters, a firmament below. Everywhere the vastness and terror of the immense night which is roused and stirred for a brief while by the day, but which returns, and will remain at last eternal, holding everything in its silence and its living gloom. There was no Time, only Space. Who could say his mother had lived and did not live? She had been in one place, and was

in another; that was all. And his soul could not leave her, wherever she was. Now she was gone abroad into the night, and he was with her still. They were together. But yet there was his body, his chest, that leaned against the stile, his hands on the wooden bar. They seemed something. Where was he?—one tiny upright speck of flesh, less than an ear of wheat lost in the field. He could not bear it. On every side the immense dark silence seemed pressing him, so tiny a spark, into extinction, and yet, almost nothing, he could not be extinct. Night, in which everything was lost, went reaching out, beyond stars and sun. Stars and sun, a few bright grains, went spinning round for terror, and holding each other in embrace, there in a darkness that outpassed them all, and left them tiny and daunted. So much, and himself, infinitesimal, at the core a nothingness, and yet not nothing. . . .

"After such knowledge what forgiveness?" The hero stands on the brink of disintegration, a nothingness, "and yet not nothing." It is clear from the passage that if he is somehow to be saved he has only the stubborn physical fact of his own body and its mysterious life with which to resist the night. The pressure of his body leaning against the stile effectively prevents him from moving toward death and the mother. And in the comparison of the body to an "ear of wheat" there is the faintest suggestion of a germinating potential out of which may spring forth the opportunity of renewal. There is not the slightest indication that escape from self-disintegration will be easy or assured. The movement toward the city's "gold phosphorescence" does not contradict, as some critics have thought, the drift toward death of which Lawrence's thematic summary speaks. (pp. 29-30)

Paul Morel at the end is of necessity and by virtue of his own free act released from the maternal bondage which, if long continued, would have destroyed him. But this freedom involves alienation and isolation from the world. As he moves toward the urban settlement which Lawrence describes in his **Study of Thomas Hardy** as "the little fold of law and order, the little walled city within which man has to defend himself against the waste enormity of nature," it is possible to see the hero embarking on a quest after health and relatedness. For the dramatization of such a quest, the reader must turn to the later novels.

Here it is enough to attempt some definition of the stance of the vital hero, vis-à-vis the world, since Paul is assuredly the first hero of Lawrence's fiction who can be so called. He faces life with the knowledge that no theological sanctions exist to make its burdens tolerable; that life itself represents the faintest glimmer of warmth within the cold, infinite reaches of dead space; that human life in its various social, economic, and personal orders is filled with destructive forces; that his own integrity is blighted by the conditioning to which he has been exposed. In the face of this knowledge he accepts freely his responsibility for action in conformity with an instinctive morality of life which is largely inscrutable yet by which he will be mercilessly judged. The stance may be considered quixotic, but not unheroic, especially when compared with the postures of neo-orthodoxy, metaphysical rebellion, or bland indifference which have been assumed by various sorts of gifted people in this century. (p. 31)

Julian Moynahan, in his The Deed of Life: The Novels and Tales of D. H. Lawrence, *Princeton University Press, 1963, 229 p.*

KATE MILLETT　(essay date 1970)

[*Millett is an American novelist and radical feminist critic. In the following excerpt from her book* Sexual Politics, *Millett examines Paul Morel's relationships with women, concluding that he uses them to bolster his confidence and ambition and then discards them when they are no longer able to assist him. Millett regards the women as being virtually powerless in the novel, trapped by the early twentieth-century social structure which denies them an outlet for their own creativity and ambitions but permits them to experience vicarious satisfaction through the achievements of the man they love. For a reading that discusses how bildungsroman characters such as Paul use many people, not just women, see the excerpt by Richard D. Beards (1974).*]

Sons and Lovers is a great novel because it has the ring of something written from deeply felt experience. The past remembered, it conveys more of Lawrence's own knowledge of life than anything else he wrote. His other novels appear somehow artificial beside it.

Paul Morel is of course Lawrence himself, treated with a self-regarding irony which is often adulation: "He was solitary and strong and his eyes had a beautiful light"; "She saw him, slender and firm, as if the setting sun had given him to her. A deep pain took hold of her, and she knew she must love him"—and so forth. In the précis, Lawrence (and his critics after him) have placed all the emphasis in this tale of the artist as an ambitious young man, upon the spectral role his mother plays in rendering him incapable of complete relations with women his own age—his sexual or emotional frigidity. That the book is a great tribute to his mother and a moving record of the strongest and most formative love of the author's life, is, of course, indisputable. For all their potential morbidity, the idyllic scenes of the son and mother's walking in the fields, their excited purchases of a flower or a plate and their visit to Lincoln cathedral, are splendid and moving, as only **Sons and Lovers,** among the whole of Lawrence's work, has the power to move a reader. But critics have also come to see Mrs. Morel as a devouring maternal vampire as well, smothering her son with affection past the years of his need of it, and Lawrence himself has encouraged this with the self-pitying defeatism of phrases such as "naked of everything," "with the drift toward death," and the final chapter heading "Derelict."

The précis itself is so determinedly Freudian, after the fact as it were, that it neglects the two other levels at which the novel operates—both the superb naturalism of its descriptive power, which make it probably still the greatest novel of proletarian life in English, but also the vitalist level beneath the Freudian diagram. And at this level Paul is never in any danger whatsoever. He is the perfection of self-sustaining ego. The women in the book exist in Paul's orbit and to cater to his needs: Clara to awaken him sexually, Miriam to worship his talent in the role of disciple and Mrs. Morel to provide always that enormous and expansive support, that dynamic motivation which can inspire the son of a coal miner to rise above the circumstances of his birth and become a great artist. The curious shift in sympathy between the presentation of Mrs. Morel from the early sections of the novel where she is a woman tied by poverty to a man she despises, "done out of her rights" as a human being, compelled, despite her education and earlier aspirations, to accept the tedium of poverty and childbearing in cohabitation with a man for whom she no longer feels any sympathy and whose alcoholic brutality repells and enslaves her, to the possessive matron guarding her beloved son from maturity—is but the shift of Paul's self-centered understanding. While a boy, Paul hates his father and identifies with his mother; both are emotionally crushed and physically afraid before the paternal tyrant. (pp. 246-47)

The book even provides us with glimpses of the Oedipal situation at its most erotic: "'I've never had a husband—not really'... His mother gave him a long fervent kiss." (p. 247)

But the Oedipus complex is rather less a matter of the son's passion for the mother than his passion for attaining the level of power to which adult male status is supposed to entitle him. Sexual possession of adult woman may be the first, but is hardly the most impressive manifestation of that rank. Mrs. Morel (in only one short passage of the novel is she ever referred to by her own name—Gertrude Coppard) has had no independent existence and is utterly deprived of any avenue of achievement. Her method of continuing to seek some existence through a vicarious role in the success she urges on her sons, is, however regrettable, fairly understandable. The son, because of his class and its poverty, has perceived that the means to the power he seeks is not in following his father down to the pits, but in following his mother's behest and going to school, then to an office, and finally into art. The way out of his dilemma lies then in becoming, at first, like his mother rather than his father. (pp. 247-48)

When Paul's ambition inspires his escape from [the circumstances of his parents' marriage] it will be upon the necks of the women whom he has used, who have constituted his steppingstones up into the middle class. For Paul kills or discards the women who have been of use to him. Freud, another Oedipal son, and a specialist in such affairs, predicted that "he who is a favorite of the mother becomes a 'conqueror.'" Paul is to be just that. By adolescence, he has grown pompous enough under the influence of maternal encouragement to proclaim himself full of a "divine discontent" superior to any experience Mrs. Morel might understand. And when his mother has ceased to be of service, he quietly murders her. When she takes an unseasonably long time to die of cancer, he dilutes the milk she has been prescribed to drink: "'I don't want her to eat... I wish she'd die'... And he would put some water with it so that it would not nourish her." By a nice irony the son is murdering her who gave him life, so that he may have a bit more for himself: he who once was fed upon her milk now waters what he gives her to be rid of her. Motherhood, of the all-absorbing variety, is a dangerous vocation. When his first plan doesn't work, he tries morphine poisoning: "That evening he got all the morphia pills there were, and took them downstairs. Carefully, he crushed them to powder." This too goes into the milk, and when it doesn't take hold at once, he considers stifling her with the bedclothes.

A young man who takes such liberties must be sustained by a powerful faith. Paul is upheld by several—the Nietzschean creed that the artist is beyond morality; another which he shares with his mother that he is an anointed child (at his birth she has the dream of Joseph and all the sheaves in the field bow to her paragon); and a faith in male supremacy which he has imbibed from his father and enlarged upon himself. Grown to man's estate, Paul is fervid in this piety, but Paul the child is very ambivalent. Despite the ritual observances of this cult which Paul witnessed on pay night and in his father's feckless irresponsibility toward family obligations, he was as yet too

young to see much in them beyond the injustices of those who hold rank over him as they did over his mother. Seeing that his father's drinking takes bread from his young mouth, he identifies with women and children and is at first unenthusiastic about masculine prerogative. (pp. 248-49)

Lawrence later became convinced that the miner's life and the curse of industrialism had reduced this sacred male authority to the oafishness of drinking and wife- and child-beating. Young Paul has been on the unpleasant end of this sort of power, and is acute enough to see that the real control lies in the bosses, the moneyed men at the top. Under industrialism, the male supremacy he yearns after is, in his eyes, vitiated by poverty and brutality, and it grants a noisy power over all too little. This is part of the unfortunately more ignoble side of Lawrence's lifelong hatred for industrialism. In his middle period he was to concentrate his envy upon the capitalist middle classes, and in his last years he championed primitive societies, where he was reassured male supremacy was not merely a social phenomenon all too often attenuated by class differences, but a religious and total way of life.

The place of the female in such schemes is fairly clear, but in Lawrence's own time it was already becoming a great deal less so. As in *The Rainbow*, this novel's real contrasts are between the older women like his mother, who know their place, and the newer breed, like his mistresses, who fail to discern it. Mrs. Morel has her traditional vicarious joys: "Now she had two sons in the world. She could think of two places, great centers of industry, and feel she had put a man into each of them, that these men would work out what she wanted: they were derived from her, they were of her, and their works would also be hers."... She irons his collars with the rapture of a saint: "It was a joy to her to have him proud of his collars. There was no laundry. So she used to rub away at them with her little convex iron, to polish them till they shone from the sheer pressure of her arm." Miriam's mother, Mrs. Leivers, also goes a way toward making a god of the young egoist: "She did him that great kindness of treating him almost with reverence." Lawrence describes with aplomb how Miriam idolizes Paul; even stealing a thrush's nest, he is so superior that she catches her breath: "He was concentrated on the act. Seeing him so, she loved him; he seemed so simple and sufficient to himself. And she could not get to him." Here we are treated not only to idealized self-portraiture but to a preview of the later godlike and indifferent Lawrentian male.

Paul is indeed enviable in his rocklike self-sufficiency, basking in the reverence of the bevy of women who surround him, all eager to serve and stroke—all disposable when their time comes. Meredith's *Egoist* is comic exposure; Lawrence's is heroic romance. When Paul first ventures forth into the larger male world, it is again the women who prepare the way for his victories. In a few days he is a favorite of all the "girls" at Jordan's Surgical Appliances.... We are told that "they all liked him and he adored them." But as Paul makes his way at the factory the adoration is plainly all on their side. They give him inordinately expensive oil colors for his birthday and he comes more and more to represent the boss, ordering silence, insisting on speed and, although in the time-honored manner of sexual capitalism, he is sleeping with one of his underlings, he insists on a rigid division between sex and business.

The novel's center of conflict is said to lie in Paul's divided loyalty to mother and mistresses. In *Fantasia of the Unconscious,* one of two amateur essays in psychoanalysis in which

Lawrence disputes with Freud, he is very explicit about the effect of doting motherhood:. . .

> What is he actually to do with his sensual, sexual self? Bury it? Or make an effort with a stranger? For he is taught, even by his mother, that his manhood must not forego sex. Yet he is linked up in ideal love already, the best he will ever know . . . You will not easily get a man to believe that his carnal love for the woman he has made his wife is as high a love as that he felt for his mother or sister.

What such a skeptic will do instead is outlined fairly succinctly in Freud's, "The Most Prevalent Form of Degradation in Erotic Life," he will make a rigid separation of sex from sensibility, body from soul; he will also develop a rationale to help him through this trying schizophrenic experience. The Victorians employed the lily-rose dichotomy; Lawrence appeared to have invented something new in blaming it on his mother. But the lily/rose division, which Lawrence is so harsh in excoriating in Hardy, is also a prominent feature of *Sons and Lovers*. Miriam is Paul's spiritual mistress, Clara his sexual one—the whole arrangement is carefully planned so that neither is strong enough to offset his mother's ultimate control. Yet the mother too is finally dispensable, not so that Paul may be free to find a complete relationship with either young woman, but simply because he wishes to be rid of the whole pack of his female supporters so that he may venture forth and inherit the great masculine world which awaits him. Therefore the last words of the book are directed, not at the self-sorrowing of Paul's "nuit blanche," his "dereliction" and "drift towards death," but at the lights of the city, the brave new world which awaits the conqueror.

When Paul wonders incoherently aloud—"I think there's something the matter with me that I can't . . . to give myself to them in marriage, I couldn't, . . . something in me shrinks from her like hell"—just as when Miriam reproaches him, "It has always been you fighting me off," the reader is expected to follow the précis and the critics and understand that this is all part of the young man's unfortunate Oedipal plight. Lawrence himself attempts to provide a better clue to Paul's type of fixation:

> . . . the nicest men he knew . . . were so sensitive to their women that they would go without them forever rather than do them a hurt. Being the sons of women whose husbands had blundered rather brutally through their feminine sanctities, they themselves were too diffident and shy. They could easier deny themselves then incur any reproach from a woman; for a woman was like their mother, and they were full of the sense of their mother. . . .

Yet all this well-intentioned puritanism dissolves before the reader's observation of the callowness with which Paul treats both Miriam and Clara. The first girl is, like Paul himself, a bright youngster restless within the narrow limitations of her class and anxious to escape it through the learning which has freed Paul. Less privileged than he, enjoying no support in a home where she is bullied by her brothers and taught the most lethal variety of Christian resignation by her mother, she retains some rebellious hope despite her far more discouraging circumstances. Having no one else to turn to, she asks Paul, whom she has worshiped as her senior and superior, to help her eke

out an education. The scenes of his condescension are some of the most remarkable instances of sexual sadism disguised as masculine pedagogy which literature affords until Ionesco's memorable *Lesson*.

Paul has grandly offered to teach her French and mathematics. We are told the Miriam's "eyes dilated. She mistrusted him as a teacher." Well she might, in view of what follows. Paul is explaining simple equations to her:

> "Do you see?" she looked up at him, her eyes wide with the half-laugh that comes of fear. "Don't you?" he cried . . . It made his blood boil to see her there, as it were, at his mercy, her mouth open, her eyes dilated with laughter that was afraid, apologetic, ashamed. Then Edgar came along with two buckets of milk.
>
> "Hello!" he said. "What are you doing?"
>
> "Algebra," replied Paul.
>
> "Algebra!" repeated Edgar curiously. Then he passed on with a laugh.

Paul is roused by the mixture of tears and beauty; Miriam is beautiful to him when she suffers and cringes: "She was ruddy and beautiful. Yet her soul seemed to be intensely supplicating. The algebra-book she closed, shrinking, knowing he was angered."

As she is self-conscious and without confidence (Miriam's sense of inferiority is the key to her character), she cannot learn well: "Things came slowly to her. And she held herself in a grip, seemed so utterly humble before the lesson, it made his blood rouse." Blood roused is, of course, the Lawrentian formula for sexual excitement and an erection; the algebra lesson is something of a symbol for the couple's entire relationship. The sight of Miriam suffering or humiliated (she later gives Paul her virginity in a delirium of both emotions) is the very essence of her attractiveness to him, but his response is never without an element of hostility and sadism. His reaction here is typical: "In spite of himself, his blood began to boil with her. It was strange that no one else made him in such a fury. He flared against her. Once he threw the pencil in her face. There was a silence. She turned her face slightly aside." Of course, Miriam is not angry, for one does not get angry at God. . . . The reader is made uncomfortably aware that "pencil" is etymologically, and perhaps even in the author's conscious mind as well, related to "penis" and both are instruments which have here become equated with literacy and punishment.

Miriam's aspirations are not respected; her failures are understood to be due to inferiority of talent. There are also a great many explanations provided the reader that she is frigid, and everything in her situation would seem to confirm this. Her mother's literal Victorian repugnance toward sexuality is the most plausible explanation, even without our knowledge of Miriam's debilitating insecurity. When she thinks of giving herself to Paul, she foresees beforehand that "he would be disappointed, he would find no satisfaction, and then he would go away." The chapter where Paul finally brings her to bed is entitled, "The Test on Miriam." Needless to say, she does not measure up, cannot pass his demanding examination. So her prediction comes true and Paul throws her away and takes up Clara. Yet the situation is somehow not this simple; even within the muddled explanations of Lawrence's text, it is several times made clear that Paul withholds himself quite as much as does Miriam. (pp. 249-54)

While the first half of **Sons and Lovers** is perfectly realized, the second part is deeply flawed by Lawrence's overparticipation in Paul's endless scheming to disentangle himself from the persons who have helped him most. Lawrence is so ambivalent here that he is far from being clear, or perhaps even honest, and he offers us two contrary reasons for Paul's rejection of Miriam. One is that she will "put him in her pocket." And the other, totally contradictory, is the puzzling excuse that in their last interview, she failed him by not seizing upon him and claiming him as her mate and property.

It would seem that for reasons of his own, Lawrence has chosen to confuse the sensitive and intelligent young woman who was Jessie Chambers with the tired old lily of another age's literary convention. The same discrepancy is noticeable in his portrait of Clara, who is really two people, the rebellious feminist and political activist whom Paul accuses of penis envy and even man-hating, and who tempts him the more for being a harder conquest, and, at a later stage, the sensuous rose, who by the end of the novel is changed once again—now beyond recognition—into a "loose woman" whom Paul nonchalantly disposes of when he has exhausted her sexual utility. Returning her to her husband, Paul even finds it convenient to enter into one of Lawrence's Blutbruderschaft bonds with Baxter Dawes, arranging an assignation in the country where Clara, meek as a sheep, is delivered over to the man she hated and left years before. The text makes it clear that Dawes had beat and deceived his wife. Yet, with a consummate emotional manipulation, Paul manages to impose his own version of her marriage on Clara, finally bringing her to say that its failure was her fault. Paul, formerly her pupil in sexuality, now imagines he has relieved Clara of what he smugly describes as the "femme incomprise" quality which had driven her to the errors of feminism. We are given to understand that through the sexual instruction of this novice, Clara was granted feminine "fulfillment." Paul is now pleased to make a gift of Clara to her former owner fancying, that as the latter has degenerated through illness and poverty (Paul has had Dawes fired) he ought to be glad of salvaging such a brotherly castoff. (pp. 254-55)

The sexual therapy Clara affords to Paul is meant to be a balm to his virulent Oedipal syndrome, but is even more obviously a salve to his ego. Only in the fleeting moments of the orgasm can the egoist escape his egotism, but Lawrence's account fails to confirm this:

> She knew how stark and alone he was, and she felt it was great that he came to her, and she took him simply because his need was bigger than either her or him, and her soul was still within her. She did this for him in his need, even if he left her, for she loved him

This is a dazzling example of how men think women ought to think, but the book is full of them. By relieving his "needs" with a woman he rigidly confines to a "stranger in the dark" category, Paul has touched the great Lawrentian sexual mystery and discovered "the cry of the peewit" and the "wheel of the stars."

Having achieved this transcendence through Clara's offices, he finds it convenient to dismiss her. (p. 255)

It is Paul's habit to lecture his mistresses that, as women, they are incapable of the sort of wholehearted attention to task or

achievement that is the province of the male and the cause of his superiority.

> "I suppose work can be everything to a man . . . . But a woman only works with a part of herself. The real and vital part is covered up."

The idea seems to be that the female's lower nature, here gently phrased as her "true nature," is incapable of objective activity and finds its only satisfactions in human relationship where she may be of service to men and to children. Men in later Lawrence novels, men such as Aaron, constantly ridicule trivial female efforts at art or ideas.

Given such views, it is not very surprising that Paul should make such excellent use of women, Clara included, and when they have outlived their usefulness to him, discard them. As Clara is a creature of the double standard of morality, the woman as rose or sensuality, he invokes the double standard to get rid of her, declaring sententiously that "after all, she was a married woman, and she had no right even to what he gave her." He finally betakes himself to a fustian view of the indissolubility of marriage, decrees that she is completely Dawes's property, and with a sense of righteousness, returns her, no worse, indeed much the better, for wear.

Having rid himself of the two young women, time-consuming sex objects, who may have posed some other threat as well, possibly one of intellectual competition, Paul is free to make moan over his mother's corpse, give Miriam a final brushoff, and turn his face to the city. The elaborate descriptions of his suicidal state, however much they may spring from a deep, though much earlier, sorrow over the loss of his mother, appear rather tacked on in the book itself, as do certain of the Freudian explanations of his coldness as being due to his mother's baneful influence. Paul is actually in brilliant condition when the novel ends, having extracted every conceivable service from his women, now neatly disposed of, so that he may go on to grander adventures. Even here, the force of his mother, the endless spring of Lawrence's sacred font, will support him: "She was the only thing that held him up, himself amid all this. And she was gone, intermingled herself." But Paul has managed to devour all of mother that he needs; the meal will last a lifetime. And the great adventure of his success will henceforward be his own. "Turning sharply, he walked toward the city's gold phosphorescence. His fists were shut, his mouth set fast." Paul may now dismiss his mother's shade with confidence; all she had to offer is with him still. (pp. 256-57)

Kate Millett, "D. H. Lawrence," in her Sexual Politics, *Doubleday & Company, Inc., 1970, pp. 237-93.*

FRANK KERMODE (essay date 1973)

[Kermode is an English critic whose career combines modern critical methods with expert traditional scholarship, particularly in his work on Shakespeare. In his critical discussions of modern literature, Kermode has embraced many of the conceptions of structuralism and phenomenology. Kermode characterizes all human knowledge as poetic, or fictive: constructed by humans and affected by the perceptual and emotional limitations of human consciousness. Because perceptions of life and the world change, so does human knowledge and the meaning attached to things and events. Thus, there is no single fixed reality over time. Similarly, for Kermode, a work of art has no single fixed meaning, but a multiplicity of possible interpretations. In fact, the best of modern writing is constructed so that it invites a variety of interpretations, all of which depend upon the sensibility of the reader. Kermode believes his critical writings exist to stimulate thought, to offer

possible interpretations, but not to fix a single meaning to a work of art. True or "classic" literature, to Kermode, is thus a constantly reinterpreted living text, "complex and indeterminate enough to allow us our necessary pluralities." In the following excerpt from his study of Lawrence, he discusses the multiple critical interpretations Sons and Lovers *has attracted since its publication and states that its flexibility and openness to all interpretations, yet its resistance to any single definition, determine its greatness as a work of literature.*]

Sons and Lovers, the masterpiece of Lawrence's first phase, was begun in October 1910. In November he ended his engagement to Jessie Chambers ("Miriam"), and on December 3 began one with Louie Burrows. His mother died on December 10. He restarted the novel, then called *Paul Morel,* early in 1911 but set it aside to write **The Trespasser.** Resuming the *Bildungsroman,* he finished it in May 1912, and rewrote it that autumn. Much of importance occurred between these versions. In January 1912 illness forced him to give up teaching; he returned to the Nottingham area and met Frieda Weekley, the German wife of a professor at Nottingham University College. The composition of his autobiographical novel therefore coincided with a period of multiple crises in his life. It was begun before the death of his mother, which is its climax; it was rewritten at the behest of an early lover, Miriam, and then it was rewritten again under the eye of Frieda, after their elopement. It would be difficult to think of any other writer who wrote his life into successive texts of his fiction as Lawrence did; he habitually confronted his tale with new experience, and new interpretations of the past. There is in consequence an abundance, even a confusion, of life; one cannot feel that the published version is the last possible rehandling of the tale; and this openness is not the consequence of inefficiency. Flexibility, the power of a story to challenge a reader (including himself), is one of the marks of the novel as Lawrence wanted it to be, liberated from the burden of finality and completeness placed on it by his enemies, the novelists who, in his opinion, mistook structure for life, and novelistic custom for natural law.

Sons and Lovers is probably still the best known of the novels, and it would be wrong to cavil at this, for it is certainly a great achievement. In the first part the brief inset of the courtship of Paul's parents, the father's gaiety, his "sensuous flame of life" melting the mother's puritanism, has that single-minded veracity of impression which was consistent, in Lawrence, with more abstract intentions. Morel, in his caressing dialect, speaks, as Dorothy Van Ghent notes, Lawrence's language of physical tenderness [see excerpt dated 1953]. . . . This is the dark dancing miner whom marriage will reduce, both physically and morally; whose son will be lost to a mother who makes refinement the instrument of her conquest. The placing of the parents and children, as of the ravaged landscape and its colliers, is done with extraordinary narrative tact and energy. Morel, obscurely fighting for a manhood sapped at the root by the absorbing care of the mother, cuts off the one-year-old William's curls and causes his wife the most intense suffering of her life. . . . Mrs. Morel is locked out by an angry husband; under a great moon she buries her face in a lily, and returns to the house smeared with pollen. This scene is so intensely realized—night scents and sounds, gray-white light, fear and cold—that the mind is satisfied without further interpretation, though interpretation, if offered, will be absorbed. Does the lily, a flower which Lawrence admired for its sexual blossoms and mired roots, daub Mrs. Morel satirically, or is there sympathy between them? Miriam is later taken to task for trying to identify with or possess the flowers she is admiring. But

Mrs. Morel is for once identified with the night; when her normal prudence returns she makes her husband let her in, and his punishment for the misdeed is to be further reduced. There are other scenes in which narrative is transcended, caught up into some symbolic mode, without damage to the relation of acts and persons; for example, the moment when the blood of the mother, struck by the husband, drops into the baby Paul's hair. This boy sleeps with his mother, and lovingly cleans the mire off her fine shoes; episodes of everyday life will tell their own story better when the entire narrative context is capable of assuming, at any moment, large symbolic meanings. An understanding of how this worked is what chiefly distinguishes Lawrence as a critic of fiction, especially in his studies of American literature. Thus it is not enough to say that the perversely close relationship of Paul with his mother precludes the possibility, at least during her life, of his satisfactorily choosing a sexual partner; Miriam is not merely a rival but also, in some ways a double; the rejection of her for the mother is also a rejection of the mother.

So too with Morel, the detested father; his defeat is not simply Oedipal; it is also the defeat of the dark virility of the pit, of unashamed and easy male grace and strength, beauty with its roots in muck. And all these meanings are in the complexity of the text, its power to suggest meanings other than that vouched for by a narrator apparently half-committed to Paul's own preference for the mother.

It has been argued that the narrative method alters in Part II; that objective omniscience gives way to a subtler mode, in which we can no longer trust the narrator: "the point of view adopted is that of Paul; but since confusion, self-deception, and desperate self-justification are essential to that point of view, we can never tell . . . where the real truth lies" except "by seeking out the portrait of Miriam that lies beneath the over-painted commentary of the Paul-narrator." This nonce-technique Louis L. Martz regards as having served on one occasion only; but Lawrence is the great overpainter, his habitual method is to confront the text again and again, to rehandle it in precisely this style. The product grows progressively more complex in relation to the intention; that is why he insists that we do not isolate an intention and trust it. Trust the tale. If there is more than one Miriam under its surface paint, then so be it. Any novel, by virtue of its length, the intermittency of such controls as "point of view," and the indeterminate nature of narrative, permits a great many such doublings and, consequently, an indefinite range of interpretation. . . . So there is nothing unusual about [Lawrence's] employment of the method in **Sons and Lovers,** though Martz is right to find it there, and his demonstration of its effect on the representation of Miriam is finely achieved.

Jessie Chambers did not like the Miriam she saw—unwilling to let go, subtly wrong in her attitude to the non-human or the animal, too much, in the end, the woman who buttons up or reduces men. She saw how much the confusions of Paul had colored her image, how unfair his condemnation and rejection of her for a failure in which he shared at least equally. Yet all this is in the book; it is he who, possessed, resents her possessiveness, he whose "sex desire was a sort of detached thing that did not belong to a woman" (X). The only woman who might really please him would be one he did not know (compare the story **"Love among the Haystacks,"** probably written in 1911). And it is he who forces the girl to accept him sexually: "He said that possession was a great moment in life" (XI). This is what Lawrence later came to call sex in the head. When

Miriam makes her sacrifice he identifies the initiatory experience with death. Miriam has two faces, the vital and sensitive, often snubbed by Paul; and the timid, restrained, and possessive, both of which somewhat resemble Mrs. Morel. Both are visible, simultaneously.

So with Clara: the success with which Lawrence renders the pleasures of this sexual relationship is not always recognized. It is true that she is a licensed mother substitute; the first thing Paul does after making love to her is to clean her boots. But the very completeness of his sexual satisfaction sets it apart from life; she is for night, not day. Dawes, so often called a reflection of Morel, is Clara's true husband; Paul ritually fights him and comes to terms with the married couple, as he might with his reconciled parents, but the death that inhabits his sex manifests itself in the same chapter as the fight, when his mother confesses her cancer.

Such are the complexities which life, and reflection upon it, brought into the overpainting of *Sons and Lovers*. The cutting of all the knots is the death of the mother, in the chapter called "Release." Paul says goodby to her, and to Clara; he oscillates between death and a mechanical kind of life, swings back briefly and for the last time to Miriam, and then departs for the future, "a nothingness and yet not nothing" (XV), walking toward light not darkness. The novel originates in an intense and prolonged personal crisis; it is remarkable that it should be so unselfish, so unsentimental. One could hardly ask for further proof of the seriousness with which Lawrence believed that "the novel, properly handled, can reveal the most secret places of life," as no other discourse can, and do so beyond the intention, and despite the defenses, of its author.

Much has been said of the relation of *Sons and Lovers* to Freud; its theme is Oedipal, and in the later stages of composition Lawrence had learned something about Freud from Frieda—his first contact with a thinker whom he was repeatedly to attack. The degree to which the personal relationships in the novel comply with Freud's account of mother fixation is surely a tribute to the accuracy of Freud's generalization rather than a proof of Lawrence's indebtedness. Freud observed and generalized, Lawrence observed, but believed that the text of a novel was more than an occasion for drawing abstract conclusions. Freud was, as it happens, the kind of scientist Lawrence believed to be incapacitated, by the very nature of his interests and methods, from giving a truthful version of reality. It is nevertheless true . . . that there are interesting common elements in *Sons and Lovers* and Freud's important, and almost contemporaneous paper, "The Most Prevalent Form of Degradation in Erotic Life" (1912). This is the disorder Freud calls "psychical impotence"—impotence which has no physical cause, and is manifested only in relation to some women. There is a conflict between affection and sex, traceable to an incestuous fixation on mother or sister. It may not take the extreme form of impotence, and indeed in most people it does not; but Freud is clear that "very few people of culture" can achieve an ideal fusion of tenderness and sensuality, and this manifests itself in a lack of sexual desire for women who inspire affection, and is remedied "in the presence of a lower type of sexual object." The consequence is an inability to get on with one's well-brought-up wife. . . . The sexual difficulties of the age, Freud was sure, stemmed from the basic Oedipal situation, assisted by another unchangeable condition, the proximity of the genital and excrementatory organs in an animal which, since it learned to walk upright, has tried culturally to sever the associations between them. It cannot be done; the genitals

remain animal, and so does love, which perhaps will never "be reconciled with the demands of culture."

This diagnosis is certainly directed toward a situation of which Lawrence was aware, though for him "the demands of culture" originated in and were insisted upon by woman. Paul is almost aware (as is Morel) that his relationship with his mother is not entirely a matter of sexless "affection"—he is at times a phantom husband. And he knows, however obscurely, that one reason why Miriam will not do is that he attributes to her a denial of animal nature which he associates with superior women—with Clara he has much better sex because she is, in a measure, inferior. The story makes it plain enough that an explanation similar to Freud's is also lurking in it.

Lawrence's own reaction to the sex-culture dilemma proposed by Freud would certainly have been, "To hell with culture." And this meant, partly, to hell with women, its agents. Later he was explicitly to reject the Oedipal hypothesis, though he defended with increasing ferocity the position that women inhibited the full expression of a man's inmost self, defiled his angel. His reflections on the genital-excrementatory syndrome persisted through many years, and in practice his answer was to teach a woman better by enforcing it on her in its animal reality. Yet it is clear enough that Freud and Lawrence, however different their instruments and diagnoses, were in a sense talking about the same thing, an epochal sickness with deep roots in the past, and, as to its symptoms as well as its causes, a malfunction of sexual relationships within the culture. . . . Their intellectual traditions were very different, and Lawrence's opinions, mystical and rational, have their origin in English radical thought, not in the clinics of Vienna; but their concurrence, as far as it goes, is testimony that, as Europe moved into the Great War, to speak well of obvious ills of civilization one had to reflect deeply on sons and what they love.

Lawrence was soon to feel a need to give systematic form to such reflections; the war developed them and made them urgent, but they are implicit in *Sons and Lovers* and in the poems of *Look! We Have Come Through*! which celebrate recovery and marriage. *Sons and Lovers* is the only major work of Lawrence which had no doctrinal double, in which there is no possible dissension between life and what he called "metaphysic." Henceforth all is different. (pp. 11-19)

Frank Kermode, in his D. H. Lawrence, *The Viking Press, 1973, 174 p.*

SCOTT SANDERS   (essay date 1973)

[*Sanders is an American educator, literary critic, and fiction writer. In the following excerpt from his study of Lawrence's five major novels, Sanders maintains that Lawrence largely ignored the social and historic influences operating in England during the years that the action of* Sons and Lovers *takes place. He proceeds to examine how those factors helped shape the values and motivations of the characters in the novel.*]

We view the world of *Sons and Lovers* with a double vision: through the eyes of the boy who has experienced this life on his own senses, and through those of the alienated artist who is striving to account for his social isolation, and to derive some message from his past. The artist faithfully records the boy's memories of historic people, providing us with the raw data for interpreting their feelings and actions in terms of their social situation. But the narrator makes little use of this data. Although it is easy to describe the underlying social matrix which binds together the people and places of the novel's world, Lawrence generally ignored the social existence of his characters, as if some astigmatism had blinded him to the historical forces at work in their lives. The conflict between the father and mother, for example, which is clearly grounded in class differences, is translated into moral terms, as a struggle between bad and good, and then into psychological terms, as the conflict between unconscious and conscious, and finally into an opposition between body and mind. Similarly the discontent of womenfolk in *Sons and Lovers,* which is clearly part of the contemporary ferment for women's emancipation, is reduced to purely physical terms, so that social grievances are interpreted as sexual frustration. Strife between men and women is not linked to the difference in their status, but to a clash between their a-historical "natures," which becomes formalized in the course of Lawrence's thought as the opposition between the female principle and the male. In each case social categories are transformed into psychological categories, which harden into a metaphysic. (pp. 23-4)

Except for William, the eldest son who has gone away to work in London, the Morel children remain at home, and with their mother they share the long evening wait for their father to come back from the mine:

> In the winter nights, when it was cold, and grew dark early, Mrs Morel would put a brass candlestick on the table, light a tallow candle to save the gas. The children finished their bread-and-butter, or dripping, and were ready to go out to play. But if Morel had not come they faltered. The sense of his sitting in his pit-dirt, drinking, after a long day's work, not coming home and eating and washing, but sitting, getting drunk, on an empty stomach, made Mrs Moral unable to bear herself. From her the feeling was transmitted to the other children. She never suffered alone any more: the children suffered with her.
>
> Paul went out to play with the rest. Down in the great trough of twilight, tiny clusters of lights burned where the pits were. A few last colliers struggled up the dim field-path. The lamplighter came along. No more colliers came. Darkness shut down over the valley; work was gone. It was night.
>
> Then Paul ran anxiously into the kitchen. The one candle still burned on the table, the big fire glowed red. Mrs Morel sat alone. On the hob the saucepan steamed; the dinner-plate lay waiting on the table. All the room was full of the sense of waiting, waiting for the man who was sitting in his pit-dirt, dinner-less, some mile away from home, across the darkness, drinking himself drunk. Paul stood in the doorway.
>
> 'Has my dad come?' he asked.
>
> 'You can see he hasn't,' said Mrs Morel, cross with the futility of the question.
>
> Then the boy dawdled about near his mother. They shared the same anxiety. Presently Mrs Morel went out and strained the potatoes.
>
> 'They're ruined and black,' she said; 'but what do I care?'

> Not many words were spoken. Paul almost hated his mother for suffering because his father did not come home from work.
>
> 'What do you bother yourself for?' he said. 'If he wants to stop and get drunk, why don't you let him?'
>
> (pp. 24-5)

Paul is bewildered by his mother's suffering, which he shares with the other children, for he does not yet understand why, in terms of Mrs Morel's values, it is such a grave affair for a husband and father to linger at the pub. Although he sides with her against his father, Paul has not yet fully internalized the values on which her judgment is based. In this episode we see him learning, along with his brothers and sisters, to view the world as his mother views it—a learing process that covers the first half of the novel.

Mrs Morel's feelings dominate the scene. They cause a hitch in the children's play, they imbue the kitchen with a sense of tension, of waiting. . . . That the candle in this scene is tallow rather than wax, that it is used to save the gas, and that there is only one—all this is meant and is felt to contrast with Morel's self-indulgence. (pp. 25-6)

The home atmosphere of revulsion mixed with fear—revulsion towards Morel's character and fear that he might fail to support his family—obviously infects the children, as the bitterness and anxiety of elders work upon young people in Ibsen or Dickens. For Paul, dominated by his mother's feelings, the very night seems agitated. Consider the second paragraph: the paratactic syntax breaks the night up into a sequence of disconnected, fragmentary impressions; nothing hangs together; the world reflects Mrs Morel's disturbed feelings, the causes of which Paul does not yet comprehend. The encounter between mother and son emerges as a specific instance of what happens on those long winter nights when Morel is late in coming home, a specific instance that sums up a crucial phase in Paul's development, as he drifts away from his father and clings ever more closely to his mother. No time is indicated other than an evening in winter. Even the portion of Paul's childhood in which such a scene might have occurred can only be judged approximately. It epitomizes the "waiting evenings," a category of experience rather than a specific event. Hence the scene is less important as a biographical detail than as a concentrated image of a general condition. This is typical of Lawrence's practice throughout *Sons and Lovers,* which like all his other novels has little of what is conventionally called plot: Paul grows up, goes to work in Nottingham, has two love affairs, loses him mother and one brother to death. Rather than complexity of action, we are presented with an account of Paul's *formation,* of the living conditions, parental attitudes, work and friendships which shape his character. In scenes such as this one, general trends—in this case the progressive estrangement between husband and wife, together with the effects of that estrangement on their children—are distilled in the form of brief but intense human encounters.

Throughout the novel, as in the scene before us, dialogue is presented with an almost Biblical economy. Mrs Morel says really very little about what she feels or why ("Not many words were spoken."). Most of what she communicates to her son is nonverbal. Gesture, facial expression, posture, tone of voice, nervous activity, arrangement of objects, narrative commentary of all sorts—these are the principal means by which the most powerful feelings are communicated. Characters in

The row houses of Victoria Street in Eastwood, where D. H. Lawrence was born. Reproduced by permission of University of Nottingham Library.

the novel rarely speak more than three sentences at a time, generally only one, and that one usually quite simple. Yet Lawrence manages to create, by means of narrative devices, the impression of a powerful if inarticulate interplay of emotions between his figures, who seem to be groping for language. . . . Dialogue in *Sons and Lovers* really exposes less about fixed personalities than about relationships, and about identity in the process of formation. But these are always intensely personal, one-to-one relationships, and because they are inarticulate they encompass little beyond the immediate issue of personal feelings. Hence the concentration of dialogue on feeling, spoken as it is by characters who are largely unconscious of their relation to the larger forces and conditions of their environment, tends to mask the broader social context within which individual relationships revolve. The gulf between language and experience, particularly between the impersonal terms of social discourse and the extremes of personal experience, remains visible in all of the novels, but is especially prominent in *The Rainbow* and *Lady Chatterley's Lover.*

Few words need be exchanged between mother and son: because so much is understood, so much can be left unspoken. Already the two have drawn very close together in feeling and outlook: "When she fretted he understood, and could have no peace. His soul seemed always attentive to her." Paul's emotions come by reflection from his mother, from her suffering and anxiety, her brooding and impatience. . . . Mrs Morel's response to people, her ideas, her categories of judgment, even

her metaphors creep into Paul's speech, and they permeate the narrative description of his thought. Thus he argues her views on political questions, lacking opinions of his own; he echoes her verdict on Morel, the drunken wreck; and he parrots her assessment of Miriam. It is she who forces Paul to view his own father's work as bestial, and therefore to despise the man himself, treating the miner's fate within the industrial system as proof of his personal weakness.

Morel is necessarily excluded from the linguistic domain shared by mother and son. Unable to speak as they do, he cannot conceive reality as they do. (pp. 26-8)

Mrs Morel speaks the language of the narrator, Morel speaks the language of Bestwood streets. Her refined speech—for thus it sounds in the ears of Bestwood—fascinates the young Morel, who thinks it foreign and ladylike, and it distinguishes her from the working-class neighbors with whom she is never at ease. The husband's Derbyshire dialect has the contrary effect of identifying him with the community. Following the mother in all things, the children have learned her speech, which Paul in particular feels to be the medium of educated discourse. Bound within the regional dialect, Morel is equally bound by the local assumption that the son should accompany his father into the mine. A stranger to that dialect, Mrs Morel is free to envision another role for her sons: they are to be gentlemen. (p. 29)

Although Paul takes over much of his mother's language, he quickly outstrips her in learning, ideas and expressiveness. She does not care about Schopenhauer, she does not understand his art, she reads no Baudelaire. Eventually he surpasses her range of speech, as he has surpassed Morel's. For talk about ideas he must go to Miriam, who is also finally not articulate enough to satisfy him, driving him to complain of her wordless and cloying emotion. However much he extolls silence, however halting his speech, Paul is continually pressing toward an articulation of all those feelings—about love, God, nature, death, the blood, sex—which Lawrence argued could not be translated without distortion into language. And this paradox lies at the heart of all Lawrence's work: he could only use verbal means to explore those dimensions of experience which, he maintained, were incompatible with language. For Paul the achievement of integral personality, the process of individuation in Jung's sense, is intimately bound up with self-expression. According to the linguistic norms established for the voices of Mrs Morel, Paul and the narrator, Walter Morel appears to be a limited character, with only a vague sense of his condition or his identity, because his capacity for self-expression is so limited. In this case the linguistic limits to self-realization reflect social, economic, educational and occupational limits: the circumscription of language is only one symptom of a general circumscription of life. (p. 30)

The growth of [Paul's] expressiveness, together with the increasing complexity of thought and feeling attributed to him, which gradually converge toward (without actually matching) the linguistic standards set by the narrator, record the development of a totally alien sensibility within the Bestwood ethos. The mother's influence turns Paul against his father, then education and life in the city wean him away from his mother. So long as she lives, Mrs Morel remains the source of Paul's ambitions, she prompts him to that struggle into consciousness which eventually carries him not simply beyond his father's class, but beyond her own, indeed beyond all human groups whatsoever. His utter despair after her death is only partially explained, in Freudian terms, as the anguish of Oedipus over the dead Jocasta. It is also the despair of the isolated intellectual, the more isolated because he started out as the son of a miner rather than the son of a bourgeois. . . . The declassed artist, he belongs nowhere. True, at the end Paul turns toward the town, a gesture which commentators have interpreted as negative or positive according to their temperaments. By either interpretation, the group with which Paul can identify remains to be discovered, beyond the confines of the novel. That is largely the subject of *The Rainbow,* where the quest for social involvement fails. By *Women in Love* that quest has been abandoned, the sensitive and isolated man having accepted his estrangement from society.

The hero of *Sons and Lovers,* like Stephen Dedalus in *A Portrait of the Artist as a Young Man* or like Julien Sorel in *Le Rouge et le Noir,* extricates himself from a limiting social background. But not to move into any new community—and this is symptomatic of Lawrence's dilemma as an isolated intellectual. Although the hostility between individual and society is not as marked here as it becomes in later novels, Lawrence's fundamentally individualistic perspective, shying away from social commitment, focusing on personal growth in opposition to the growth of community, is already dominant. What is problematic in *Sons and Lovers* is individual character and personal relationships, rather than community, the larger society within which character and relationships develop. The highly personal nature of the material, so close to him in time and feeling, doubtless hindered him from recognizing the broader social and historical coordinates of individual lives in *Sons and*

Lovers. At the same time, because this material is given, because it is for the most part autobiographical, features of contemporary society force themselves into the novel willy-nilly. (pp. 30-2)

The first half of *Sons and Lovers* is built of scenes . . . focusing on a moment of conflict within the family, each one adding an increment to the distance which separates Gertrude and Walter Morel. (p. 32)

We have seen that the difference in speech between Walter and Gertrude Morel, marking as it does their differences in class background and education, corresponds to an underlying conflict in outlook and aspiration. Mrs Morel comes from solid bourgeois stock, stout Congregationalists all. In the memory of her grandfather, a failed lace manufacturer, she possesses an image of lost social eminence that might be regained. From her father, an engineer whose chief concern seems to have been the size of his salary, and who was well-educated and stern-minded, she formed her ideal of manhood. As a young woman she had all but married one John Field, "the son of a well-to-do tradesman," also an educated man who aspired to the ministry and settled upon merchandising. She is well-educated herself, having taught school for some time. This side of her character emerges in chats with the vicar over starched tablecloths, in her activities with the Women's Guild, and in her promotion of the Morel children's education. Through her sons, for whom she wants middle-class jobs, comfortable homes and "ladies" to wive, she attempts to regain some of the status which she has lost through marriage to Morel.

Morel on the other hand, who left school at age ten to work in the mine, is barely literate, spelling painfully through the headlines and seeing no value whatsoever in the reading of books. He has no use for Mrs Morel's religion, preferring the pub to chapel, and fails to understand either her highfalutin ideas or Paul's art. Unlike his wife, he does not feel specially pinched by poverty, never dreams of clawing his way into the middle-class, nor does he envision a very different future for his children. Little beyond Bestwood attracts him, and little within Bestwood repels him.

Morel clearly does not live up to Mrs Morel's ideal of manhood, and she communicates her judgment to the children. In scenes other than those we have already considered the children learn from her to mock their father's manners, to belittle his work at the mine, to sneer at his lack of formal education and in general to degrade his manhood. Even though specific grievances often emerge during money squabbles, it is evident that something more basic than customary domestic wrangles over shillings and pence—vital as shillings and pence are—has motivated this total assault upon Morel as father and husband. Of course he scants her budget, but so do the other miners when times are bad. It is far more significant that he does not share her education, religion, social aspirations, aesthetic training, economic motivations, manners, language, moral views or political interests. Their marriage is wrecked by differences that are primarily social rather than personal. (pp. 32-4)

Her disenchantment with the marriage dates from this experience: "She said very little to her husband, but her manner had changed towards him. Something in her proud, honourable soul had crystallized out hard as rock." Because she remains aloof from the other miners' wives, who beard her for having put a stop to Morel's career as dancing master, and by implication for having fettered his free spirit with her puritan scruples, she feels increasingly isolated, "miles away from her own people." Her own people, of course, are the ministers engineers, teachers and the like whom she knew as a girl. We are told that this marks the beginning of their marital battle, a beginning which Lawrence depicts with perfect clarity in social terms. But then what conclusion does he draw?

> She fought to make him undertake his own responsibilities, to make him fulfil his obligations. But he was too different from her. His nature was purely sensuous, and she strove to make him moral, religious. She tried to force him to face things. He could not endure it—it drove him out of his mind.

The narrator has translated social differences into moral and psychological terms: the wife is responsible, aware of obligations, bearing the reformer's burden; the husband is irresponsible, blind to obligations, the crude soil which she is to cultivate; he is sensuous, the body; she is religious, the spirit. . . . Their differences in expectation are translated into valued "opposites": she has a high moral instinct, he by implication has a low; he sins and she redeems; he is content with mediocrity while she aspires to noble heights; she strives to shape him, he remains the passive clay; although he is destroyed, she, miraculously, loses "none of her worth." . . . Thus concrete differences between particular human beings, differences which are comprehensible in social terms, serve as the basis for constructing a metaphysic which opposes the body to the mind. (pp. 34-5)

The narrator consistently views the father through the mother's eyes:

> As he bent over, lacing his boots, there was a certain vulgar gusto in his movement that divided him from the reserved, watchful rest of the family. He always ran away from the battle with himself.

Lawrence was later to use the contrast between reserve and gusto as a means of distinguishing the neurotically repressed middle-classes from the instinctive and sensuous common people. But here the miner appears "vulgar;" elsewhere we have found him described as a "knave", "poltroon," "nasty" and "brutal". When he returns home sweaty and exhausted from the mines, to find the Congregational minister sipping tea over a table-cloth in the kitchen, and when he is treated as a crude beast by his wife, Morel understandably grows furious. The minister is one of Mrs Morel's "own people," he is an educated man, a spiritual man, possessed of proper manners. He is a reincarnation of John Field, a middle-class substitute for her husband. Enough has passed before to persuade us that Morel appreciates the significance of the minister's presence and of his wife's behavior; certainly the reader does. Yet the narrator endorses Mrs Morel's opinion that, by fussing and complaining, the miner is just showing off. . . . We are told that as Morel ages he acts in increasingly "dirty and disgusting ways," but all we learn of this behavior is that "His manners in the house were the same as he used among the colliers down pit." Yet what was the determining reality for this miner, cut off from the rest of his family, if it was not that gathering of colliers down pit? His ways were disgusting from Mrs Morel's point of view, according to her middle-class upbringing, and it is this point of view which Lawrence employs throughout the novel, in matters great and small.

Even Morel's lack of education is turned against him. In one important scene Paul reluctantly tells his father of winning a prize in a writing competition for a child's paper:

Morel turned round to him.

'Have you, my boy? What sort of a competition?'

'Oh, nothing—about famous women.'

'And how much is the prize, then, as you've got?'

'It's a book.'

'Oh, indeed!'

'About birds.'

'Hm—hm!'

And that was all. Conversation was impossible between the father and any other member of the family. He was an outsider. He had denied the God in him.

[This] demonstration of Morel's educational backwardness (previous scenes have demonstrated his drunkenness, his brutality, his ignorance of bourgeois manners and his indifference to bourgeois culture, his refusal to stand up for his own rights and his inability to "get on" at work) is made occasion for the judgment that he is *personally* guilty of failing to become a whole human being: "He had denied the God in him." Although it is difficult to see how any but an exceptional man could have overcome his disadvantages—poverty, inadequate education and limited class expectations, work that is physically exhausting while mentally undemanding, cramped housing and political impotence—nevertheless Mrs Morel condemns him for failing to achieve precisely this miraculous escape. Paul accepts her class-bound judgment. Lawrence, having himself freshly escaped at the time he wrote the novel, accepted it as well.

In making that judgment Mrs Morel applied what can best be called a 'bourgeois' perspective, wholly consistent with her Protestant ethics, a perspective which treats the individual as the unit of success or failure, without regard to the conditions which shape him, without regard to the collective social reality within which he dwells. Like St Paul, whom her father admired more than any other man, and like the great Reformation theologians who looked to St Paul for their authority, Mrs Morel held the individual responsible for his salvation or damnation. Her individualist perspective dominates the book, as her feelings dominate Paul, as her values dominate the Morel household. (pp. 36-8)

For Lawrence, writing *Sons and Lovers* between 1910 and 1913, before experiencing the mass insanity of the War, before really understanding his characters' problems as problems of contemporary society, this individualist perspective was convincing. After all, had he not scrambled out of the working class, had he not escaped the industrial system, had he not wooed a lady? Individual autonomy, at least for those who were willing to give a tug at their own bootstraps, seemed to him a proven fact. Enjoying an exile's comparative social independence, he exaggerated man's freedom, since anyone estranged from the conditions and institutions of his society, whether physically exiled like Rousseau, or emotionally like Blake, is prone to stress man's freedom rather than his bondage. Of course the exile is at once the most and the least free of men; his very isolation from all social groups prevents him from effectively acting upon his ideas. Such isolation commonly leads . . . to frustration and disgust, equally with oneself and one's society. Like Swift and Orwell, two other emotional exiles, Lawrence was by spells the aloof yet penetrating observer, and the misanthrope, manifesting by turns the profoundest concern for his countrymen and the most consummate disgust, each alike the fruit of social isolation.

Lawrence's exaggerated sense of individual autonomy led him to distort his representation of reality—especially in *Sons and Lovers,* but to a varying degree in all his novels—by isolating personal existence partly or wholly from social existence. Although *Sons and Lovers* abounds in references to social conditions and historical movements, these are not used to account for the quality, the changes and crises, of individual lives. That is to say, Lawrence explains the problems of his characters psychologically rather than historically, in terms of a personal rather than a collective past. When in a later essay he wrote that "I feel it is the change inside the individual which is my real concern. The great social change interests me and troubles me, but it is not my field," he posited a dichotomy between individual psychology and social existence which would have seemed alien to George Eliot, Dickens or Austen, and to all of the great Continental realists such as Stendhal, Balzac or Tolstoy. Of course he was entitled to occupy himself primarily with subjectivity, and did so, but when he set himself the task of *explaining* subjectivity, or of passing judgment on individuals, he often failed, as in the case of Morel, to take the social dimension into account.

Morel's failure should be grounds for criticizing the industrial and economic system which has maimed him, rather than for criticizing the man. Mrs Morel's bitter repudiation of her married state expresses more than class prejudice. Her outrage and Morel's ruin were to be translated by Lawrence into a basic critique of the social order which had produced this humanly degraded way of life. This woman is determined not only to help her children escape the financial straits in which she finds herself, but also to liberate them from the brutal working conditions and from the domestic squalor which the industrial order has imposed upon generations of Morels. To her son she transmits both outrage and frustration, and she teaches him to defend precisely those values which the industrial system—with its associated politics, economics, housing and schools—denies. The son of Mrs Lawrence was to protest—in plays and essays and novels—the evil which had been committed against the human spirit in Eastwood's mines and streets. (pp. 39-40)

As in the case of Morel, so with the principal women of the novel, the account which Lawrence gives of individuals and of personal relationships often ignores or even contradicts the interpretation which is suggested by the objective social existence of the characters involved. There are no satisfied women in *Sons and Lovers,* and the most important four—Mrs Morel, Mrs Leivers, Miriam and Clara—are downright frustrated. All of them squirm in the cramped circumstances which they have been allotted by marriage or birth. All of them seek to escape the narrow bounds of their existence, either through education, religion, political activity or through men. Lawrence never acknowledges these connections among his womenfolk, because he treats their problems as personal and therefore explicable in terms of their separate pasts or their unique personalities, which appear isolated from each other and from their social context.

But the frustration of these four women certainly has a common source: during the latter decades of the nineteenth century and the first decades of the twentieth, women's education expanded faster than the social opportunities which were available to them; their political awareness increased while they remained politically impotent; their rising self-estimate conflicted with their low status in society. These contradictions in the social condition of women issued, during the decade before the war, in a militant and violent feminist movement. . . . It is against this historical background of feminist unrest and dissent that his four frustrated women must be viewed.

Mrs Morel's case has already been discussed. Her husband having failed to live up to her bourgeois ideal, she seeks to realize her social aspirations through her sons. William is broken by the strain, and Paul very nearly so. The elder son's exhausting study, his passion to advance in his work, his hectic rise through the social circles of Bestwood, Nottingham and London, even his destructive hunger to marry that tawdry "lady," derive from Mrs Morel's ambitions. The same ambitions motivate Paul, if not with William's intensity. The two sons are forced by their mother and by their own education to repudiate their father's values and way of life. . . . The result is a crippling interdependence between sons and mother, which has usually been explained in Freudian terms. But such a psychological account ignores the social causes of Mrs Morel's frustration and of Morel's inadequacy as a father figure. This frustration is never more evident than in her descent towards death. What is tragic in Mrs Morel's dying is not the torture, nor death itself, but rather the fact that she has failed while living to realize the freer existence which she has imagined for Paul, and that she dies just at the moment when her son shows promise of fulfilling at least some of her expectations.

About Mrs Leivers we are told little, except that she finds housewifing on the farm a bitter chore, and that she charges every aspect of life with religious significance. . . . It is precisely this religiosity which makes her farm life bearable, by giving meaning to menial work, and dignity to an existence which she considers brutal, for she is exhausted by the labor and repelled by the crudeness of her menfolk. Mrs Leivers transmits to Miriam her distaste for this life, together with her compensating religion. Marx and Nietzsche were agreed in criticizing this tendency of Christianity to rationalize a painful social existence or to compensate for poverty of life. . . . Paul never recognizes this compensatory function which religion serves for the Leivers women, nor is it fully acknowledged by Lawrence, who treats this intense religiosity as an accidental trait of the mother, which is bequeathed with damaging consequences to the daughter.

Such is the background for Miriam's frustration, which is whetted by her education and by her contact with the larger world of Nottingham through Paul. . . . Paul, who has no intention of sinking into the colliery life of his father, resents the fact that Miriam cannot let herself merge happily and unconsciously into life on the farm. Lawrence translates her distaste for the farm into psychological terms as an aversion to the physical. She cannot bear to hear that the mare is in foal, we are told, because she is unable to accept her own sexuality; whereas she is clearly rejecting a whole way of life, in which mares are forever in foal, brothers are cruel and brutal, muddied floors wait to be scrubbed, meals to be cooked, errands to be run. She is an educated Cinderella who resents serving as drudge to her farming menfolk; like Paul she yearns to escape by the one means available to her—her mind. Thus when Lawrence criticizes her for being too spiritual, too hungry for knowledge, too earnest, too restless, he is condemning in her precisely those impulses which alienated him from his own social origins. The opposition between body and mind which he invokes as explanation is a metaphysical cloak dragged in after the fact. Neither Paul within the novel nor Lawrence without respects Miriam's social aspirations, but must reduce them to sexual frustrations. (pp. 43-5)

Miriam's isolation and the influence of her mother adequately explain that sexual timidity which angers Paul—who also holds the girl responsible for his own timidity, which in fact derives from his attachment to *his* mother. The sexual attitudes of both the boy and girl, their fears and expectations, are largely shaped by their mothers, for both of whom marriage has been a painful ordeal. But Lawrence ignores the effects of the frustration which was common to the two wives. He also underrates the importance of Mrs Morel's ambition that Paul marry a "lady"—a category which Miriam does not fit. The mother "frankly *wanted* him to climb into the middle class, a thing not very difficult, she knew. And she wanted him in the end to marry a lady." She has implanted the same desire in William, who ruins himself for the stupid, careless and vain Miss Western, because she is genteel, she is a lady. By claiming that Paul acquires his sexual inhibitions from Miriam, Lawrence underestimates the impact upon the son of Morel's failure to satisfy Gertrude, for Paul fears the same kind of inadequacy. . . . Preferring a metaphysical or psychological explanation to a sociological one, Lawrence is reluctant to explore the basis in social existence for the factors which he does stress: Paul's love for his mother, Miriam's religiosity, and the sexual immaturity which they share. Each of these traits stems in part from class conflicts, as we have seen, or from the contemporary predicament of women. Even Miriam's possessiveness could be explained in terms of the girl's desire to escape into a freer life through Paul, seeing him, as his mother sees him, to be a way out. In terms of psychological differences alone, therefore, the conflict between Paul and Miriam is not comprehensible.

The fourth frustrated woman is Clara Dawes. Like Mrs Morel, she is unhappily married to a man whom industrial work and scanty education have brutalized. Like Miriam, she has sought to escape her position through education, with the result that she finds factory labor more confining and demeaning than before. Unlike the other two women, however, she is a militant feminist, seeking to achieve the collective advancement of women and to regain a sense of her own dignity through the feminist movement. . . . Yet Lawrence treats Clara's association with the feminist movement as a casual or amusing fact about her, even though that feminism is a direct expression of the historical situation which binds together all of the frustrated women in the novel. Once again his individualist perspective suppresses the actual social connections between characters and events.

Perceiving Clara, in the light of his own needs, as a sensual object, Paul is unable to allow due weight to her social aspirations. Instead he interprets her social frustrations as sexual frustrations, her desire for education, meaningful work and a dignified place in the community as a mask for sexual yearning. Accordingly he returns her at the end to Baxter Dawes, his own amorous attentions having "healed" her, although her social situation is more cramped then ever. Lawrence clearly reveals the narrowness of Paul's perspective, without however suggesting any alternative view, when the young man brushes off his mother's concern for Clara's reputation by arguing that people "know she's a suffragette, and so on"—"and so on" meaning that because Clara "lives separate from her husband, and talks on platforms" she "hasn't much to lose," "her life's nothing to her." Paul has in fact *used* Clara, without regard

to her needs or desires as a person, and without respecting the broader movement for women's emancipation in which she is involved; for one of the goals of that movement, as Clara herself proclaims, is to abolish those attitudes which justify the exploitation of women. Although she satisfies Paul's animal needs, Clara is no more a lady than Miriam is, and so she cannot satisfy his social ambition. Lawrence's own position at the time he was writing *Sons and Lovers* made it difficult for him to present without distortion the humbler, less articulate social aspirations of a Miriam or a Clara. His success as scholar, teacher, writer and, most recently, lover, doubtless made the persistent frustration of such women more puzzling. The woman he loved of course, was Frieda Weekley, with whom he was living abroad while completing the novel, a woman who by virtue of family estates and pedigree was aristocrat enough to satisfy the notion of "lady" entertained by the son of a Nottingham miner. (pp. 45-7)

I point to the general condition underlying these four cases of frustration, not to suggest that Lawrence should have written a sociological study of feminism, nor to deny the individuality of his women characters, but rather to indicate that he suppressed the connections which were *there*, implicit in his material, in the structure of the society on which *Sons and Lovers* is based. I am of course bringing Lawrence to bear witness against himself. His brilliant portraits of the simmering Mrs Morel, the resigned Mrs Leivers, the yearning Miriam, the sullenly frustrated Clara, provide us with rich social evidence that contradicts his explicit judgements. Once again, as in the portrayal of the conflict between Mr and Mrs Morel, narrative description which is grounded in concrete social experience undercuts the individualist perspective which governs the novel as a whole. (p. 48)

The sentimental education of a working-class boy, the lives of a mining family, a farming family and a suffragette: these appear to be the chief subjects of *Sons and Lovers*. We are presented with the drama of "an organic disturbance in the relationships of men and women," to use Dorothy Van Ghent's phrase, and with the Oedipal dilemma of a miner's son. But these materials have an historical content which Lawrence, on account of his psychological focus, did not fully acknowledge. That is to say, the true underlying subject of the novel is a larger historical reality, the movements and qualities of which are concretely focused in the lives of individual characters, who are "typical" in the sense defined by Lukács. The psychology of these characters can be interpreted as a response to social conditions; their motives and behavior are comprehensible in terms of their social existence. Whether we examine Mrs Morel's frustrated bourgeois aspirations, Morel's brutalization, Mrs Leivers' bitterness, Miriam's compensating religiosity, Clara's feminism, Dawes's demoralization, or the middle class values and emotional lameness of Paul, we find evidence of crucial trends in contemporary society: the deprivations of working class life; the increasing mechanization of society which was to result in the horrors of the 1914-1918 War; the conflict between bourgeois and proletarian ideologies which would lead to revolutions after the war; the proliferating sense of *anomie;* and the movement of women for emancipation. To claim this is not to deny the richness of the novel's world, but on the contrary to indicate the ground of its coherence, to reveal the matrix of social trends which gives it unity. Indeed the novel derives its significance as much from this larger historical reality as from the individual lives through which history is concretely grasped. Although Lawrence focuses on personal relations and subjectivity, it is a subjectivity permeated by social forces, which registers the stress of growing up within a working community that was being transformed by industry, the schools, and the awakening of social consciousness.

Furthermore, Lawrence's own psychology, like that of his characters, is rooted in the social and moral conditions which govern the world of *Sons and Lovers*. Like them, his values and thought developed within the bounds of a specific social existence. His ideas and his art, whatever enduring interest they may possess, represent first and foremost a coherent response to a concrete historical situation. (pp. 58-9)

I have suggested that Lawrence was relatively unaware, at this point in his development, of the larger social implications of his characters' problems, that he was for the most part unconscious of the image and critique of society which is implicit in *Sons and Lovers*—a limitation of vision due to the immediacy, intimacy and subjectivity of the material from which the novel is built, and due also to his acceptance of his mother's Puritan and bourgeois perspective. In *The Rainbow* he sought to overcome this isolation of personal experience, not however by integrating the individual into society, but by immersing him in nature. Whereas in *Sons and Lovers* he was largely unconscious of the impact of society on the individual, in *The Rainbow* he was to become acutely conscious, and was to regard the social world as the enemy of private life. (p. 59)

> Scott Sanders, in his D. H. Lawrence: The World of the Five Major Novels, *1973. Reprint by The Viking Press, 1974, 224 p.*

RICHARD D. BEARDS   (essay date 1974)

[*In the following excerpt, Beards examines* Sons and Lovers *against the pattern of the traditional bildungsroman, a novel in which a youthful protagonist receives initiation into life that will enhance his or her sense of self. Beards discusses the values formed by Paul Morel in relation to four crucial areas of concern in the bildungsroman: vocation, mating, religion, and identity.*]

There are two traditional approaches to *Sons and Lovers*, one of which treats the novel as a psychological study, emphasizing particularly Paul's Oedipal complex; the second of which focuses on the autobiographical, exploring the many passages where Lawrence seems to be retelling his own experience fictionally.... While the first approach risks reducing the novel to a case history, the second has the danger of undermining *Sons and Lovers*' effectiveness as fictional vision, turning it instead into a confessional autobiography, and vitiating Lawrence's achievement with plot, symbol, dramatic scene, and invented character. Moreover, these two approaches often join forces, so that autobiography is used to support the claims of psychological analysis, psychological generalizations cited to strengthen the autobiographical critique—especially where there are gaps in what we know of Lawrence's life. (p. 204)

It is my contention in this essay that seeing *Sons and Lovers* against the pattern of the traditional *Bildungsroman* illuminates many of the literary aspects of the novel about which neither the psychological nor the autobiographical approach cares and that this view does justice to one of Lawrence's best artistic achievements. In addition, because the *Bildungsroman* emerges in the nineteenth century and continues into our own, its focus on the conflict between an alienated individual and the cultural forces (family, neighborhood, class, religious and ethical milieu) against which this individual seeks to establish himself relates directly to the lives of our students. Moreover, the kind of conflict I have outlined comprises the real plot of *Sons and Lovers*, expressed jointly in Paul's struggle to free his soul from his mother and to become an artist where economic necessity all but rules out such a possibility. Paul's movement toward self-realization is expressed symbolically in his rejection of adjustment to the everyday (an adjustment made by his brother Arthur and sister, Annie) in favor of the starry night in which he finds hope at the novel's end; in his attraction to cities (first Nottingham, then London, and ultimately perhaps even Paris) instead of "The Bottom" or, later, the houses on Scargill Street; and in his refusal to make life for himself in terms of provincial possibilities. But before an examination of the specific details of *Sons and Lovers*, it would be wise to review some of the general characteristics of the *Bildungsroman*.

The *Bildungsroman* ("novel of self-development" or "apprenticeship novel" are the best English equivalents) features a protagonist, an apprentice to life, whose goal is to master it so that he can achieve an ideal or ambition, fulfillment of which will heighten his sense of self. A look at related types of fiction may serve to clarify the *Bildungsroman* itself. Close to the confession and the autobiography, the *Bildungsroman* is often a first or second novel which fictionalizes its author's growing up. It is also similar to the picaresque novel, though in the *Bildungsroman* the journey through life has been internalized; adventures are important principally for their effect on the protagonist's psychological development and sense of self. The *Bildungsroman* protagonist is usually more passive, reflective, intellectual and artistic than his picaresque counterpart, probably because the author, himself introverted and creative. has fashioned his character out of himself. Still another type of related fiction is the initiation story or novel, though here the focus is a single moment of vision where the protagonist accepts either the code of his elders or the hard facts of life itself, or both (e.g. Faulkner's "The Bear," James' "The Lesson of the Master," Crane's "The Red Badge of Courage"). Compared to the initiation novel, the *Bildungsroman* compounds the choices which the central character is called upon to make, forcing him to define separately but in a continuous process his values in regard to four crucial concerns: vocation, mating, religion, and identity.

All of these decisions must be made without the aid of formal education, for whenever schooling is depicted in novels of self-development it is shown to be sterile and hopelessly anachronistic, if not downright farcical (e.g. *Pendennis, Great Expectations, The Ordeal of Richard Feverel*).... While the college teacher understandably will feel a bit defensive pointing out the *Bildungsroman's* typical assessment of formal education—*Sons and Lovers* doesn't even bother to mention Paul's schooling—it should be noted that this decision results from wider forces than mere pedagogical incompetence. It is no accident that the *Bildungsroman* emerges strongest in the nineteenth century, for it is during this epoch that the traditional class society and its heavily class-weighted institutions and values, in effect since the Renaissance, undergo pressure and serious erosion. It is in this century too that for the first time a young man who was not born a gentleman could choose to ignore the social status and even the particular work of his father without necessarily facing near-suicidal odds (see, for example, Robinson Crusoe's regrets and guilt over ignoring his father's advice). While large numbers of the more intelligent and energetic members of the lower and middle classes sought to rise above their inherited stations in life, the educational system continued to reflect an outmoded society where class determined the content and quality of one's education....

In *Sons and Lovers* Paul Morel's education is casual rather than institutional; he is tutored in French and German by the local minister, Mr. Heaton; coached in composition by his brother William; encouraged in his art by his mother; and self-taught when it comes to literature, Miriam serving in both of the last two instances to inspire Paul to his best.

The same independence which characterizes Paul's education helps to prevent his capitulation to the economic and social outlook of his elders and peers, though his mother's distaste for her husband and the way of life he stands for certainly stiffens her son's resistance. Like many of his nineteenth-century predecessors, Paul shows considerable pluck, resilience and idealism in pushing his way toward an artist's future, though the usual stress laid by critics on his Oedipal conflict undermines our sense of Paul's consistency and force of character. Persistent belief in his future as an artist accounts for Paul's refusal to accept provincial goals and expectations. Surprisingly, economics plays a much larger role in *Sons and Lovers* than is often recognized, partly because it bears little if any relationship to Paul's psychological emergence, nor much more to Lawrence's own personal experience (though his letters reveal considerable concern over his finances, Lawrence never allowed making a living to interfere with his writing). (pp. 204-06)

A second characteristic of all *Bildungsromane* is that their protagonists must always decide on a suitable mate or at least define the ideal who waits in the near-distant future; the central figures in self-development novels are thus, among other things, apprentice lovers. This aspect of *Sons and Lovers* has received close attention from critics of all persuasions; if the plot of mother-son love itself is not enough, Lawrence's treatment of Gertrude, Miriam, and Clara, and their respective relationships to Paul have aroused heated debate, charge and counter-charge. The way in which the novel appears to blame Gertrude for dominating and almost destroying Paul and to indict Miriam for her near-frigidity and squeamishness has given rise to a great deal of angry discussion almost from the day the novel appeared. In our own time by far the most provocative attack on this aspect of *Sons and Lovers* has been Kate Millett's in *Sexual Politics* [see excerpt dated 1970]. Writing from a Marxist-feminist perspective, Millett accuses Paul (and by implication, Lawrence) of using the three women in his life, then discarding them when they no longer serve his self-centered interests. Millett describes Paul as the "perfection of self-sustaining ego" and states, "the women in the book exist in Paul's orbit and cater to his needs: Clara to awaken him sexually, Miriam to worship his talent in the role of disciple and Mrs. Morel to provide always that enormous and expansive support." . . . Despite the bluntness and even crudeness of her critique, and the fact that in regard to Gertrude, Millett seems to contradict herself (elsewhere in her discussion she calls the novel "a great tribute to his mother and a moving record of the strongest and most formative love of the author's life," . . .— one must admit some truth to the charge.

Students today are especially sensitive to the treatment of female characters in fiction, particularly where, as in *Sons and Lovers,* there is sufficient development to assess a life pattern or an unachieved potential in these lives. Undeniably, Gertrude's life is laid before us; we know enough of her history to see the sources of her aspirations, first for herself, then for herself and her husband, finally for her successive sons. Her sense of entrapment in a dead-end marriage to Morel, her envy of Mrs. Leiver's life, her vicarious participation in life through

her children—these and other details allow us to know her predicament. And when, in her final illness, Paul administers a fatal dose of morphine, her victimization—by unavoidable pregnancies which bind her tighter to her despised mate and which sap her strength and by a culture which discourages women from working in the world—is made final by her son. Likewise, Clara and Miriam, opposite as they are in character, seem purposeless and incomplete unless they can join in a vitalizing relationship with a male. Clara—listless, cynical and cold (several scenes show her kneeling before a fire, presumably trying to imbibe its warmth)—drifts until she consummates her relationship to Paul, who, when he realizes their relationship is merely physical, brings Clara and her estranged husband Baxter back together again. Miriam's faith that Paul will ultimately return to her, that his spiritual and idealistic side will triumph over his need for sex, seems pathetic finally, in view of her sacrificial sexual surrender to him, her compulsive chapel going when Paul is involved with Clara, and his final dismissal of her: "'Will you have me, to marry me?' he said very low . . . 'Do you want it?' she asked very gravely. 'Not much,' he replied, with pain.'' . . . (pp. 207-08)

The tradition of the *Bildungsroman* itself provides an explanation for this apparent male bias, for fiction with a developmental focus always slights characters not of the protagonist's sex, and for that matter, *all* the other characters. One of the distinguishing traits of the apprenticeship novel is the strong central figure for whose experience and development the lesser figures exist, and from whose process of self-realization the novel receives one of its principal unifying elements. Furthermore, the novel of self-development generally is written from a narrowly omniscient point of view, the author standing beside his character, as it were, and most often interpreting experience through his character's mind, senses and emotions. Thus the *Bildungsroman's* customary point of view adds to a sense of the protagonist's egoism and lends emphasis to his seeming exploitation of the novel's other figures.

Because mating plays such a significant part in maturation—and thus in apprenticeship fiction—protagonists, whether male or female, will inevitably use and exploit at least several members of the opposite sex. Thackeray's Pendennis, for example, eponymous hero of the novel sometimes called the first *Bildungsroman* in English (1849-1850), is involved several times (with Fotheringay, an Irish actress; with Fanny Bolton, a "poor but honest" girl from the lower classes; and with Blanche Amory, a continental adventuress in the manner of George Sand and her heroines) before succumbing in marriage to his mother's ward, companion and protege, Laura, whom he has all but ignored through most of the novel. . . . Thus Millett's account of Paul's position at the conclusion of *Sons and Lovers* ("Having rid himself of the two young women, . . . Paul is free to make moan over his mother's corpse, give Miriam a final brushoff, and turn his face to the city") [see excerpt dated 1969] is hardly very convincing when one has in mind fictional tradition, in particular, the *Bildungsroman's* tendency to adopt the protagonist's point of view, to maximize for the reader the central figure's sense of self-concern, to give other characters instrumental rather than independent functions.

Ursula Brangwen's goal in *The Rainbow,* "to be oneself . . . a oneness with the infinite," realized in botany lab as she peers down a microscope after her professor had denied any mystical dimension in life, brings us to both of the remaining concerns of the *Bildungsroman* protagonist: his quest for identity and for the right relationship to the transcendent and non-human in the universe. Admittedly, some apprenticeship novels . . . , in their intensive treatment of social reality, largely ignore supernatural and intangible realities. Yet from Carlyle's *Sartor Resartus* (1833-1834) on, the religious crisis and the more general search for the transcendent meanings of life have typified novels of self-development. For Paul Morel as for Ursula, religious sense and identity are deeply intertwined; this interrelationship has become, of course, a hallmark of Lawrence's mature fictions, where a knowledge of oneness is brought about by an interfusion of the individual and the natural world via sex or a "lapsing out" of consciousness. It is quite easy to misread symbolic scenes in *Sons and Lovers*—and I think Millett and others are guilty of this—through failing to take into account Lawrence's idea of one's relationship to the infinite. It is possible for instance to interpret Paul's vision of Clara bathing—he sees her as "not much more than a clot of foam being blown and rolled over the sand . . . just a concentrated speck blown along, a tiny white foam-bubble, almost nothing among the morning" . . .—as his belittling of her, preparatory to his terminating their relationship. . . . Other critics have judged Paul lost and despondent in the final paragraphs of the novel because he feels like "so tiny a spark" being pressed into extinction. Both assessments are wrong, for they ignore the implicit paradox in Lawrence's definition of self, where real being requires this feeling of tininess, of being infinitesimal. (pp. 209-10)

Still another recent critic, Calvin Bedient, has effectively argued that for Lawrence the fusion of soul which the author himself felt with his mother transcended the Oedipal, giving Lawrence—and therefore his fictional projection Paul—the sense of a mystical oneness next to which other relationships to women seem ordinary, flat, and merely personal. Only at the peak of physical or sexual exhilaration does Paul experience the infinite; such moments occur when he is swinging in the Leiver's barn, riding his bicycle recklessly home after a strained evening at the farm, making love with Clara on a steep clay river bank or with Miriam in a pine grove. As Paul expresses it after the latter experience, "the highest of all was to melt out into the darkness and sway there, identified with the great Being." . . . Bedient is convincing when he suggests that although Lawrence wasn't aware of it in *Sons and Lovers,* the work conveys rather fully its author's vision of the highest state of being and how that state can be obtained.

In counterbalance to those scenes where Paul lapses out of consciousness, often outdoors and frequently at night, *Sons and Lovers* furnishes occasional comments on its protagonist's changing relationship to traditional religious life and practice; Paul's fall from orthodoxy coincides with the growth of his mystic awareness and his ability to summon it, while, on the literal level, it evidences his growth away from the Morel family's habitual and easy chapel going. At twenty-one, we are told, "he was beginning to question the orthodox creed," . . . the following spring "he was setting now full sail towards Agnosticism, but such a religious Agnosticism that Miriam did not suffer badly." . . . The term "religious Agnosticism" indicates, I think, the growth in Paul of the mystical sense I have been describing, "agnostic" both because Lawrence speaks of God only metaphorically and because Paul's "religion" has nothing to do with any institutional faith. (pp. 210-11)

What *Sons and Lovers* depicts in the way of identity for the protagonist, then, is two-fold; there is the Paul who is second son to the Morel family, a Bestwood provincial aiming for the artist's life, the one whose personal history and day-by-day

development the novel charts, and there is the Paul who is increasingly opened up to manifestations of a living natural universe, a speck of which he is and in whose dark precincts his mother exists "intermingled." . . . It is this mystical level of identity that Lawrence illuminates so effectively, for the first time in *Sons and Lovers,* it is indeed hard to think of another novelist who conveys this dimension so convincingly. Thus Lawrence is able to contribute to the *Bildungsroman* and to English fiction generally a deeper interpenetration of the human and the vital natural world than had been previously envisioned—or than has been created fictionally since. (pp. 211-12)

The concluding pages of *Sons and Lovers* present several difficult but ultimately answerable questions as to Paul's probable future which the apprenticeship novel can help clarify. In an interesting article entitled "Autobiograph in the English *Bildungsroman,*" Jerome Buckley argues that because the novel of self-development is highly subjective, commonly fictionalizing the author's own experience, "the novel has frequently an inconclusive or contrived ending," its creator being too close to the experience being retold "to achieve an adequate perspective on (it)." *Sons and Lovers,*" he adds, "scarcely persuades us that Paul Morel at last finds the release from his fixation that Lawrence apparently won, perhaps in the very act of writing the novel." . . . Commenting on the final paragraph of *Sons and Lovers,* Buckley asserts that "nothing has prepared us for so positive a resolution. If Paul is at last free and whole, his victory is not inherent in his story; it is imposed upon it from without." . . . Even with the added weight of Lawrence's own judgment on the ending ("Paul is left in the end naked of everything, with the drift toward death") I would maintain that Paul's triumph *is* "inherent in his story" and that a knowledge of the *Bildungsroman,* precisely in those characteristics I have been discussing, helps us to see the rightness of the final affirmation.

Paul's trajectory all through *Sons and Lovers,* like that of many other *Bildungsroman* protagonists (Ursula Brangwen. Wihelm Meister, and Augie March among them) has been away from pressure to conform—whether social, familial or economic—and toward the accomplishment of his own ideal. Paul's brothers, first William, then Arthur, are foils to his aspiration; William prostitutes his attractive personality for social and business success; Arthur, initially rebellious and impulsive, capitulates to provincial expectations: "He buckled to work, undertook his responsibilities, acknowledged that he belonged to his wife and child." . . . William's life, presented in far more detail than Arthur's, forms a compressed *Bildungsroman* in itself, wherein his mercurial rise to social and financial success, his quick movement from the provinces to London, and his absurd romance with Gypsy Western come close to forming a grim parody of apprenticeship fiction. William's rapid and thoughtless climb contrasts dramatically with Paul's slow, painful, self-conscious struggle toward freedom and self-realization. The dramatic contrast between the two brothers serves to support the promising view of Paul's future suggested by the final paragraph of *Sons and Lovers;* Paul's values are nothing like his older brother's, and Paul consciously rejects a business career and the social approval and circumstances William is so desperate to gain. Lawrence reflects this difference symbolically when Paul goes to Nottingham to receive first prize for his painting. Dressed in William's altered evening suit, Paul "did not look particularly a gentleman." . . . Moreover, Paul argues vigorously against his mother's advice that he ought "in the end to marry a lady." . . . Having refused to follow

William's ambitions, condemned by Lawrence's tone and treatment as well as by the obvious pattern of self-destruction and folly implicit in the older brother's choices, Paul is freed from William's fate. (pp. 213-14)

Paul's movement in the final sentences of the novel toward the "city's gold phosphorescence . . . the faintly humming, glowing town" . . . fits perfectly the province-to-city pattern of most *Bildungsromane.* All through the nineteenth century and into our own time, the city has been the place where the ambitious have sought their challenge, have striven to define themselves. Jude, Pip, Augie March, Eugene Gant, Julien Sorel, Martha Quest, Ernest Pontifex—all seek out the city in search of their imagined and idealized selves. The glow that Lawrence here ascribes to Nottingham symbolizes its hopefulness, for throughout the novel gold and flames have stood for the vital impulse of life. In the opening pages of *Sons and Lovers,* to cite an early example, we learn of Paul's mother's attraction to Arthur Morel, epitomized by "the dusky, golden softness of this man's sensuous flame of life, that flowed off his flesh like the flame of a candle." . . . (pp. 214-15)

It is undeniably true that Paul's life is still in process when *Sons and Lovers* concludes, yet all the signs of ultimate success and of a promising independence are there; Lawrence's next novel, also a novel of self-development, ends with its heroine Ursula, having lived through a traumatic love affair, a pregnancy and a miscarriage, understanding the rainbow to promise, like the sign of the covenant, new life in a recreated world. Like her, Paul Morel, whose trauma is his mother's death, perceives a vision of unity between the night and the stars, his mother's spirit and his own, which sends him back into the fight—fist clenched—after his temporary depression and withdrawal. Even Kate Millett, openly hostile to Lawrence's art, recognizes Paul's movement toward the world of men, evidenced by her description of him as wishing "to be rid of the whole pack of his female supporters so that he may venture forth and inherit the masculine world that awaits him." . . . Paul is, she asserts, "in brilliant shape when the novel ends." . . .

More importantly, when we consider, as I have tried to do here, the four distinct trials which the *Bildungsroman* protagonist must traditionally master—vocation, mating, religion and identity—Paul's future, though Lawrence's tone is typically equivocal, seems assured. He knows what he wants to do in life; has realized the dimensions of sexual relationship, even if he hasn't found his ideal mate; has forged a new religious sense; and knows, largely because he's defined these other questions, who he is, and, equally important, what "selves" he has left behind. (p. 215)

Richard D. Beards, "'Sons and Lovers' as 'Bildungsroman'," in College Literature, *Vol. I, No. 3, Fall, 1974, pp. 204-17.*

GEORGE J. BECKER (essay date 1980)

[*Becker is an American educator, literary critic, and translator. In the following excerpt, he examines the three aspects of Lawrence's fiction technique as demonstrated in* Sons and Lovers: *the shifting viewpoint of the narrator, the nonlogical order of presenting action in the novel, and the use of nature imagery as a metaphorical evaluation of the relationship each character has to life and his or her own being.*]

Three observations about technique need to be made in respect to [*Sons and Lovers*]. There is, first of all, a noticeable variation in the point of view of the narrator. This in a not unlikely penalty of writing an autobiographical novel. There can be a blurring of emotional tone and judgment when the subject of the life takes over from the impersonal, objective narrator. Sometimes this is a matter of distance merely. A scene or incident is so painfully and indelibly inscribed in memory that it is given primacy out of harmony with the predominant tone of the work. The critic Eliseo Vivas, for example, finds some of the scenes of family conflict unacceptable because of their intensity [see excerpt dated 1961]. It seems to me that there is no harm, even possibly some gain, in this, though it is true that the novel becomes uneven in texture, some incidents standing out with more immediacy than others. This is particularly true after invention predominates and the later scenes lack the sharpness of earlier ones.

Another problem arising from this uncertain position of the narrator is that characters may not be consistent. This is most notable in the case of Walter Morel. In the beginning he is oaf and ogre. Even the children are against him. But at critical points in the narrative he emerges quite different, a sympathetic and warm human being, for example, when he learns of Paul's prizes for his painting. Psychologically I find this duality of view not only acceptable but advantageous. The mind as it works its way reflectively through past experience does come to have second thoughts, to vacillate in the face of contradictory evidence, to perceive some white beneath the black. In other words, such ambivalence is part of the basic psychological process of the narrative and actually increases its validity. (pp. 38-9)

The second observation about technique is that Lawrence does not plot his novels in the logical, analytical way of his great nineteenth-century predecessors. There is no neatly geometrical pattern with parallel actions, balancing scenes, and a demonstrably climactic point. Rather the technique is one of assembling pieces of a mosaic in a pattern that, while not random, nonetheless gives the impression of casualness. A better way of putting it is to say that the narrating intelligence, possessed of a comprehensive memory of the events related, assembles them through the nonlogical process of recollection. There is some order in the process, since it is deliberate, but it also entails repetition and violations of temporal and logical order. The problem set is to follow Paul, whose origins are a set of givens, to the point at which the novel leaves him. The solution is to summon up relevant memory, with the meanderings and omissions that memory makes. The result is a density and verisimilitude not often achieved by more formal patterning. (Edith Wharton, a master of the traditional novel, was appalled by *Sons and Lovers,* which a friend had recommended to her attention, calling it "a botched and bungled piece of work."

The most distinctive technical device is the third. The reader cannot escape observing the frequency and intensity of the passages describing nature, specifically flowers and flowering things. There is an awareness of nature in its inspiriting and nurturing function which constitutes an implicit statement that for a human being to be whole he must have a proper rapport with nature. This wholeness, or an aspiration to it, is present in Paul from early on. It is because of his intuitive sense of a proper relation that we can accept his opting for life over death at the end of the novel. His innate nature, in other words, is stronger than imposed psychological patterns.

The passages stressing nature imagery give an important guide to evaluation of the principal characters. The most memorable episodes are the ones where this device is used. On that oc-

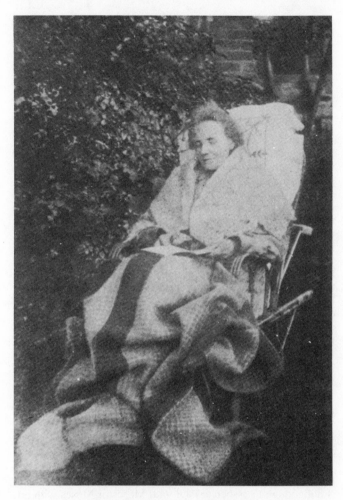

Lawrence's mother shortly before her death in 1911.

casion early in the novel when Morel shuts his wife out of the house, her anger at her husband is qualified by her response to the tall white lilies "reeling in the moonlight," the air "charged with their perfume, as with a presence." She puts her hands on the flowers, then shivers. She inhales their scent, which makes her dizzy. She is, in other words, both attracted and repelled by the intensity of sex in nature. The incident concludes with the words: "In the mysterious out-of-doors she felt forlorn."

However, in general Mrs. Morel's response to nature is sounder than Miriam's. . . . Miriam tends to spiritualize nature, thus destroying the natural, spontaneous relationship that is good, as exemplified by Mrs. Morel's response to the scyllas that turn up unexpectedly in her garden. Miriam, we are told, hates spring, even though she is drawn to the "blood heat" of the thrush eggs. On his first walk with Clara, Paul learns that she doesn't like to pick flowers; she doesn't want their corpses around her. Miriam decides in her characteristic way that it's all right "if you treat them with reverence." Paul takes a matter-of-fact position: "You get 'em because you want 'em, and that's all."

The prelude to Paul's and Miriam's first sexual embrace is a detailed nature vignette. He is high in a cherry tree gathering the ripe fruit. She is on the ground, where the skeletons of four dead marauding birds are laid out. In the tree Paul sees

stems consisting only of cherry pits that have been picked clean like skeletons. He pelts Miriam with cherries and she hangs a pair of them over each ear. This double image is very effective. For a moment she is one with nature in natural and spontaneous response. But underneath is fear and denial, an equating of nature with death—death of the spirit, no doubt—as suggested by the previous image. This is the attitude that accompanies her yielding to Paul a few minutes later in a setting dominated by dead leaves.

The most impressive instance of all occurs on the evening when Paul decides to break with Miriam. He is drawn out of doors by the scent of the madonna lilies into the night glowing with the light of a half moon. The scent of the flowers intoxicates him pleasantly until "like a shock he caught another perfume, something raw and coarse." It is the purple iris with fleshy throats that "stood stiff in the darkness" and whose "scent was brutal." This underside of nature, this phallic aspect, which is just as important, just as much a part of life as moonglow and madonna lilies, is what his relationship with Miriam lacks, and will continue to lack.

The attentive reader will early become aware of this super-addition of nature imagery at critical points in the narrative. Like all image patterns it is to a degree unnatural, but the test is rather the degree to which it appears spontaneous and naturally emergent from narrative incident. As I have suggested, with Lawrence it works both as an overall statement of the importance of a right relationship with nature and as a commentary on persons and events within the novel. It is both a constant and a variable. It is not strident, though ultimately by repetition it does become insistent. It heightens the novel's meaning without diminishing its credibility as everyday experience.

When *Sons and Lovers* was published in 1913, there was no novelist in England or America equal to Lawrence in his power to make readers live in the world of his fiction. The author never again received so spontaneous an acclamation, in spite of the fact that William Heinemann, his previous publisher, thought *Sons and Lovers* "one of the dirtiest books he had ever read" and turned it down. Perhaps that refusal should have forewarned Lawrence. Never again did his novels gain so wholeheartedly favorable a reception. (pp. 39-42)

> *George J. Becker, in his* D. H. Lawrence, *Frederick Ungar Publishing Co., 1980, 165 p.*

AVROM FLEISHMAN (essay date 1983)

[*In the following excerpt, Fleishman examines biblical themes in* Sons and Lovers *and traces the development of Paul Morel as a prophet figure.*]

Sons and Lovers . . . is so much an autobiographical novel that our knowledge of its roots in the author's life threatens to overwhelm our critical appreciation of the book. So powerful are these links between life and art that its composition was influenced by Lawrence's (and others') concern for its autobiographical accuracy so that, for example, the girl who provided the model for Miriam in the novel could read an early draft and suggest changes in characterization (including her own) to make it more true to life—a rare instance of an aesthetic object debating about itself with its creator. There has been a commendable effort in recent criticism to get away from assessing the novel on the sole ground of its psychological penetration and to grasp its vision of love and growth in symbolic terms.

Sons and Lovers has been seen as structured by a symbolic pattern that runs throughout Lawrence's work: the simultaneous attraction and repulsion between a fair, sexually repressed girl and a dark, sexually virile man—often recalling the seduction and divided conquest of Persephone by Pluto in the classical myth. Lawrence is by now recognized not only as a student of mythologies from a wide variety of cultures but also as a mythmaker in his own right, and it is no longer surprising that he portrayed the members of his own family and the ordinary folk of Midlands England in his own versions of well-known psychological types or archetypes.

It is also widely acknowledged that Lawrence was a student of the Bible from his youth to his last days and owes a greater debt to scriptural style and figuration than any major artist in England since Blake. The presence of patriarchal and prophetic figures from the Bible is less obvious but no less significant in ***Sons and Lovers*** than it is in ***The Rainbow*** or ***The Man Who Died***. There is no surprise in the idea that the self-writing of a mighty individualist and iconoclast may have an elaborate religious background, for Lawrence's preoccupation with the cycle of the generations, sibling rivalries, and parental preferences for younger and older sons finds a seedbed in the stories with which Genesis, especially, is filled. (pp. 396-97)

From birth, Paul Morel, Lawrence's surrogate in the novel, is conceived as a biblical hero of continuing fascination: Joseph. Mrs. Morel establishes the younger son as her favorite in the struggle against her husband, and we are invited to see the family romance as a modern instance of the succession of younger sons, like Jacob and Isaac, who are preferred to the elder. Mrs. Morel herself is conscious of the tradition as she walks in the fields with the newly born Paul: "A few shocks of corn in a corner of the fallow stood up as if alive; she imagined them bowing; perhaps her son would be a Joseph"*. . . .* The preference for the younger in the novel takes the form not of conflict between the brothers but rather of alliance between the mother and the favorite son: "She felt as if the navel string that had connected its frail little body with hers had not been broken. . . . She thrust the infant forward to the crimson, throbbing sun, almost with relief. She saw him lift his little fist. Then she put him to her bosom again, ashamed almost of her impulse to give him back again whence he came"*. . . .* The child is established as a specially favored, perhaps a divinely endowed one, and in his gesture of raising his fist toward the sun one can sense that he is born for struggle and competitive success—as Freud noted about intensely mother-loved sons.

The figure of Joseph with its burden of favored standing, high intellectual aptitude, and power to control large forces—rulers and brothers, father if not mother—is not allowed to stand alone as the type for Lawrence's protagonist and self-image. He was inordinately self-aware and honest in acknowledging the strong repressive and life-denying impulses in himself and etched these into his portrait by allusions to the hero's namesake, Paul. Mrs. Morel names him for her father's favorite apostle; just as her father is for her "the type of all men," so George Coppard "drew near in sympathy only to one man, the Apostle Paul; who was harsh in government, and in familiarity ironic; who ignored all sensuous pleasure". . . . It is this aspect of the Pauline heritage that seems at work in Mrs. Morel when she names her child; it involves the "impulse to

give him back again whence he came," the shame at such an impulse, and the anxiety generated by conflicting feelings:

> "If he lives," she thought to herself, "what will become of him—what will he be?"
>
> Her heart was anxious.
>
> "I will call him Paul," she said suddenly; she knew not why.

(pp. 397-99)

If the figurative composition of the protagonist were restricted to his Joseph and Paul components, his Old Testament competence and his New Testament restraints, he could be understood by reduction to the dual principles represented by his parents. But Paul is not merely the sum of the Pauline, puritan mother and the "sensuous flame of life"—emerging from the dark Plutonian or Dionysian figure that is, or originally was, his father. He is also, in a sum that is greater than its parts, an artist, and this is an essential, though largely potential, aspect of Paul—neglected in most criticism probably because the work does not announce itself as a *Künstler-roman*. The budding painter has been somewhat slighted in most readings of the novel, and the figure adapted for that role is even more easily overlooked as it is, on its face, an unlikely one. Yet there it stands:

> Another day [Miriam] sat at sunset whilst he was painting some pine-trees which caught the red glare from the west. He had been quiet.
>
> "There you are!" he said suddenly. "I wanted that. Now, look at them and tell me, are they pine trunks or are they red coals, standing-up pieces of fire in that darkness? There's God's burning bush for you, that burned not away." . . .

By itself, this allusion—even with its precise verbal citation—is not enough to associate Paul with Moses or Moses with art, but the seed has been planted for a sustained identification. (pp. 399-400)

The typological dimensions of Lawrence's Mosaic image of himself are enforced by his relationship with Miriam. The figure of Miriam in Numbers 12, who as Moses's sister is both an adjunct and a competitor to him in his prophetic role—and who is partially protected from divine displeasure by the magnanimous hero—informs Lawrence's conception of Paul's sisterly lover. But he does not allow her female hero stature to outweigh her symbolic value as a figure of repression and life denial. She is presented mainly in terms of virginal heroines: St. Catherine, Mary at the annunciation, and cloistered nuns in general. But in contact with Paul she plays a role in another Mosaic scene, a revelation of the virile force in nature as focused in a wild rose bush: "In bosses of ivory and in large splashed stars the roses gleamed on the darkness of foliage and stems and grass. Paul and Miriam stood close together, silent, and watched. Point after point the steady roses shone out to them, seeming to kindle something in their souls. The dusk came like smoke around and still did not put out the roses." . . . Their responses to this burning bush are indicative of their differing spiritual energies. Miriam wants "communion" with Paul in a shared emotional relationship whereas Paul is absorbed less by tender emotions and more by the manifestation of power. . . . In contrast to Paul's burning bush, Miriam has her own moment of epiphany, expressed in another figure of biblical manifestation: "She always regarded that sudden coming upon him in the lane as a revelation. And this conversation remained graven in her mind as one of the letters of the law.'' . . . Although the Moses figure does not achieve as much prominence in *Sons and Lovers* as it does later in *Aaron's Rod*, there is enough linguistic heightening in these scenes to afford the hero the stature of an isolated but energetic prophet in touch with the mysteries of the universe.

Lawrence superimposes these three biblical figures to blend the most salient aspects of his created self-image: Joseph for his masterly and combative streak, Paul for his underlying Puritanism and pull toward negation, Moses for his power to communicate with the sources of being and to make them manifest in art. But, conscious novelist as he was, Lawrence still faced the task of narrative, just as—self-writer and not merely self-portraitist as he was—he had to seek out a plot in the matter of his early life. The most available plot forms are those implied by the novel's title: the successions of sons—favored status passing from the elder William to Paul—and the series of lovers, from mother to mother surrogate to mature sexual mate (although the latter is not the final term in the series). To accomplish the imperatives of plotting, a writer of Lawrence's breeding would readily fall in with autobiographical tradition in appropriating biblical stories to shape his personal experience. But the special features of Lawrence's childhood, together with the relentlessly individualist cast of his mind, ensured that *Sons and Lovers* would make significant revisions in the sequence and content of the traditional stages of life.

The novel begins in hell: '' 'The Bottoms' succeeded to 'Hell Row'.'' . . . Indeed, the Morels' working-class housing is not merely linguistically abased and socioeconomically low, but it is fallen from a prior condition that the opening pages lightly but unmistakably sketch in. . . . The symbols of the lost English past, dear to the mythology of Tory conservatism and Morrisite socialism alike, are here deployed without indignation or hope of resurgence.

Indeed, the Edenic time is not only mythologically remote but its decadence continues, though in modern forms. There is a place below Hell Row, the Bottoms. . . . Here, Mrs. Morel steadily declines: ''She descended to it from Bestwood''; ''She came down in the July, and in the September expected her third baby.'' . . . Thus is Paul Morel brought into a world not only long fallen but much resembling hell in its family relationships as well as in its domestic arrangements.

In the absence of the conventional setting for a natural childhood, country pleasures are still available close by, and Lawrence can play on surviving elements of the traditional idyll of origins. In place of the garden and its associated theme of expulsion, there is a bitter parody of the figure when Morel puts his wife out during an argument: ''I should laugh, laugh, my lord, if I could get away from you,'' Mrs. Morel says to her husband, satanic in his rage and drunkenness. (pp. 401-03)

The expulsion motifs quickly give way to the language of annunciation; under the light of a moon laden with a White Goddess aura, Mrs. Morel smears her face with the golden pollen of tall white lilies and experiences an ecstatic moment not only for herself but for her unborn child. . . . (p. 403)

[We] may surmise that this is the true point of insemination and irradiation of the hero's life. It is the moment in which his mother takes into herself the maternal powers of the moon and the vital forces of vegetative reproduction—fusing herself with the external scene and merging into her nascent life. Despite the harried events that lead to this postlapsarian scene

and the ''forlorn'' feeling the mother experiences in their wake, the language underscores the dual life of mother and son, one which is to become as much a fatal curse as a vital source in his career. (p. 404)

From these both promising and unpromising beginnings, Paul's lot is cast in a state of bondage to his mother—the equivalent in modern psychological terms of the exiled fate of the fallen or the wilderness condition of the outcast or prodigal. Much of Part I of *Sons and Lovers* is taken up with the exemplary growth, marriage, and death of the elder brother, William. The talons of the motherly embrace are not far to seek in his poor choice of a mate although they are less patently responsible for William's poor health and early demise. Mrs. Morel's response to the loss confirms her in her vocation and seals Paul's fate: ''I should have watched the living, not the dead.'' . . . When Paul comes down with pneumonia, the language waxes eschatological:

> She lifted him up, crying in a small voice; ''Oh, my son—my son!''
>
> That brought him to. He realised her. His whole will rose up and arrested him. He put his head on her breast, and took ease of her for love.
>
> ''For some things,'' said his aunt, ''it was a good thing Paul was ill that Christmas. I believe it saved his mother.''. . .

The salvific effect on Paul is less clear as ''the two knitted together in perfect intimacy. Mrs. Morel's life now rooted itself in Paul.'' . . . (pp. 404-05)

Under the constraints of this first lover, Paul's youthful friendship with his second love stands condemned to failure. Much can be—and has been—said on either side for the partners in this long process of falling out of love, but it is clear to Miriam, if not to Paul, that his mother is the bar. In a passage framed from Miriam's point of view: ''He had come back to his mother. Hers was the strongest tie in his life. . . . And nobody else mattered. There was one place in the world that stood solid and did not melt into unreality: the place where his mother was.'' . . . (p. 405)

What Miriam and Paul are less aware of is the degree to which she is cast in the same mold as Mrs. Morel. Yet Paul's decisive letter to her bears out his general awareness of the resemblance: ''You see, I can give you a spirit love. I have given it you this long, long time; but not embodied passion. See, you are a nun. I have given you what I would give a holy nun—as a mystic monk to a mystic nun. Surely you esteem it best.'' . . . Miriam chafes under the imputation of her nun's estate; but she tends to see the mother as the impediment rather than her own similarity to Mrs. Morel's Puritanism, which affects Paul in the same life-negating way. She therefore mythologizes the maternal intruder in an overly simple figure: ''But there was a serpent in her Eden.'' . . . The serpent in Miriam's Eden is, of course, her own repressed and converted sexuality, and the mythos developed in *Sons and Lovers* transvaluates biblical values and sees her aversion to natural sexuality as original sin.

In place of her fastidiousness, Clara Dawes provides the full response of mature womanhood: ''And after such an evening they both were very still, having known the immensity of passion. They felt small, half-afraid, childish and wondering, like Adam and Eve when they lost their innocence and realised the magnificence of the power which drove them out of Paradise and across the great night and the great day of humanity. It was for each of them an initiation and a satisfaction.'' . . . So the loss of sexual innocence is depicted in Lawrencian mythology as the dawn of full humanity; and the unblushing sexuality of Clara-Eve makes a new Adam of Paul.

Yet Paul still lies in bondage, in the exile of the maternal embrace. For one thing, he cannot join this side of his life with the new vitality flowing from Clara: "Paul would have died rather than his mother should get to know of this affair. He suffered tortures of humiliation and self-consciousness. . . . He had a life apart from her—his sexual life. The rest she still kept.'' . . . For another, there is at work in him the same tendency toward extinction of consciousness in which he participated in the prenatal state and which parallels his mother's strong death wish: "To him now, life seemed a shadow, day a white shadow; night, and death, and stillness, and inaction, this seemed like *being*. To be alive, to be urgent and insistent—that was *not-to-be*. The highest of all was to melt out into the darkness and sway there, identified with the great Being.'' . . . It is such an impulse—which Lawrence never lost and which crops up frequently in the entire *oeuvre*—that underlies the winding down of his affair with Clara, the sympathy-cum-blood rivalry he develops with her derelict husband, Baxter Dawes, and his general drift out of life in the final third of the novel.

Yet Paul's emulation of his mother is not perfect, for she makes a strong claim on life, which comes to seem unwarranted if not ghoulish. As she succumbs to cancer, her hold on Paul only intensifies: "It's the living I want, not the dead,'' she declares in an echo of her determination to fasten on Paul after William's death. . . . In this depraved condition, Paul is sucked into the ghastly business of euthanasia to relieve her from agony. . . . (pp. 405-07)

This is the crisis not only in the mother's illness but in the son's hold on life. She succumbs, and he very nearly does: "Paul felt crumpled up and lonely. His mother had really supported his life. He had loved her; they two had, in fact, faced the world together. Now she was gone, and for ever behind him was the gap in life, the tear in the veil, through which his life seemed to drift slowly, as if he were drawn towards death.'' . . . At this lowest point in his career, a sudden turn is given. It is not clear from where, inside or outside Paul, the epiphany comes, but it is undoubtedly delivered in the language of religious revelation:

> In the country all was dead still. Little stars shone high up; little stars spread far away in the flood-waters, a firmament below. Everywhere the vastness and terror of the immense night which is roused and stirred for a brief while by the day, but which returns, and will remain at last eternal, holding everything in its silence and its living gloom. There was no Time, only Space. . . . Where was he?—one tiny upright speck of flesh, less than an ear of wheat lost in the field. He could not bear it. On every side the immense dark silence seemed pressing him, so tiny a spark, into extinction, and yet, almost nothing, he could not be extinct. . . .
>
> So much, and himself, infinitesimal, at the core of nothingness, and yet not nothing. . . . But no, he would not give in. Turning sharply, he walked towards the city's gold phosphorescence. His fists were shut, his mouth set fast.

He would not take that direction, to the darkness, to follow her. He walked towards the faintly humming, glowing town, quickly.

In the course of *Sons and Lovers,* and especially in its final scene, we are shown a process of self-creation in which the individual emerges distinct from the forces that go into his making. At the close, Lawrence's hero stands like a prophet on a hill, ready to come down and lead his people.

This sublime finale provides some justification for the indeterminacy in which the hero's future is left. He finds no parabolic formula, no clear explanation, nor even a firm grasp of his identity in this spectacle, but he does derive an intuition of the universe's life that carries the seeds of personal religion. It is apparent that the epiphany involves a new hold on life, amounting to a rebirth, but it is less evident that this renewal involves a return to origins or first things. Lawrence shifts the implications of Paul's turning toward his city to suggest not a future domesticity but a protracted journey. That Paul Morel derives from this epiphany the impetus to live and work suggests that he can become a culture bearer for a Lawrencian gospel—although his artistic vocation is not specified here. That this apostolic imitation may well begin a career of missionary travels, haranguing the established culture with doctrines of sexual liberation, neopagan vitalism, and tragic apocalypticism, completes the picture of a Paul displaced and transvalued for modern times. (pp. 408-10)

> *Avrom Fleishman, "'Sons and Lovers': A Prophet in the Making," in his* Figures of Autobiography: The Language of Self-Writing in Victorian and Modern England, *University of California Press, 1983, pp. 395-410.*

ADDITIONAL BIBLIOGRAPHY

Balbert, Peter H. "Forging and Feminism: *Sons and Lovers* and the Phallic Imagination.'' *The D.H. Lawrence Review* II, No. 2 (Summer 1978): 93-113.
    Discusses the reasons why the love given to Paul Morel by each of the women with whom he is involved is unsatisfactory and incapable of meeting his needs as a Lawrentian artist figure who requires transcendent sexual experience in order to fully reach his creative potential.

Burwell, Rose Marie. "Schopenhauer, Hardy and Lawrence: Toward a New Understanding of *Sons and Lovers*.'' *Western Humanities Review* XXVIII, No. 2 (Spring 1974): 105-17.*
    Discusses the influence of Schopenhauer's theory of tragedy on the development of *Sons and Lovers*.

Daleski, H.M. "The Release: The First Period.'' In his *The Forked Flame: A Study of D.H. Lawrence*, pp. 42-73. Evanston: Northwestern University Press, 1965.
    Views *Sons and Lovers* as a cathartic work that liberated Lawrence from the confusion of his youth and enabled him to develop as a man and writer.

Gomme, A.H. "Jessie Chambers and Miriam Leivers—An Essay on *Sons and Lovers*.'' In *D.H. Lawrence: A Critical Study of the Major Novels and Other Writings*, edited by A.H. Gomme, pp. 30-52. Sussex: Harvester Press, 1978.
    Discusses Jessie Chambers's (Lawrence's model for Miriam Leivers) embittered reaction to *Sons and Lovers* as well as the reasons why Lawrence failed to convincingly depict Mrs. Morel, who was

modelled after his own mother, as the triumphant force in Paul Morel's life.

Gose, Elliott B., Jr. "An Expense of Spirit." *New Mexico Quarterly* XXV, No. 4 (Winter 1955-56): 358-63.
Examines the contradictions found in the use of nature imagery in the second half of *Sons and Lovers*.

Littlewood, J.C.F. "Son and Lover." *The Cambridge Quarterly* IV, No. 1 (Winter 1968-69): 323-61.
Discusses Lawrence's early life as it relates to *Sons and Lovers*.

Marks W.S. "D.H. Lawrence and his Rabbit Adolph: Three Symbolic Perceptions." *Criticism* X (Summer 1968): 200-16.
Examines how Paul Morel's contact with farm animals provided him with exposure to the "life-force," which ultimately enabled him to conquer the stifling aspects of his relationships with women in *Sons and Lovers*.

Martz, Louis J. "Portrait of Miriam: A Study in the Design of *Sons and Lovers*." In *Imagined Worlds: Essays on Some English Novels and Novelists in Honour of John Butt*, edited by Maynard Mack and Ian Gregor, pp. 343-70. London: Methuen & Co., 1968.*
Examines the character Miriam Leivers and dismisses popular critical evaluations of her personality as possessive, frigid, and unhealthy. Martz demonstrates with texual evidence that Miriam exhibits a full and natural potential for life that is not recognized by Paul Morel because of his absorption of his mother's impressions of the girl.

Moore, Harry T. "The Genesis of *Sons and Lovers* as Revealed in the Miriam Papers." In his *D.H. Lawrence: His Life and Works*, pp. 285-305. New York: Twayne Publishers, 1964.
Discusses the evolution of the final version of *Sons and Lovers* by examining the manuscript sections of the novel written by Lawrence's friend and model for Miriam Leivers, Jessie Chambers, and by comparing her contributions and commentary to the same passages as edited and revised by Lawrence.

———. *The Priest of Love: A Life of D.H. Lawrence*. New York: Farrar, Straus and Giroux, 1973, 550 p.
An extensively revised and augmented edition of Moore's critical biography *The Intelligent Heart* (1954).

Nahal, Chaman. "Love and Marriage: *Sons and Lovers*." In his *D.H. Lawrence: An Eastern View*, pp. 129-36. South Brunswick and New York: A.S. Barnes and Co., 1970.
Discusses the failure of Paul Morel's sexual relationships with Miriam Leivers and Clara Dawes.

New, William H. "Character of Symbol: Annie's Role in *Sons and Lovers*." *The D.H. Lawrence Review* I, No. 1 (Spring 1968): 31-43.
Examines the ways in which Paul's relationship with his sister Annie helps him sever childhood fixations and seek independence and manhood.

Niven, Alastair. "*Sons and Lovers*." In his *D. H. Lawrence: The Novels*, pp. 37-58. Cambridge: Cambridge University Press, 1978.
Discusses the ways in which Lawrence's investigation of Paul's new experiences (first job, first love, first encounter with death) creates the central intensity in *Sons and Lovers*.

O'Connor, Frank. "D.H. Lawrence: *Sons and Lovers*." In his *The Mirror in the Roadway: A Study of the Modern Novel*, pp. 270-79. New York: Alfred A. Knopf, 1956.
Examines the ways in which *Sons and Lovers* signified Lawrence's break with his English Midland roots and considers this aspect of the novel its triumph. O'Connor also discusses what he considers to be the novel's primary weakness: the artificiality of Paul Morel's love affairs with Miriam Leivers and Clara Dawes. He asserts that Paul's main latent attraction was to Clara's husband, Baxter Dawes, who fulfilled Paul's desire for homoerotic contact as well as his need to enact his Oedipal fantasy.

Panken, Shirley. "Some Psychodynamics in *Sons and Lovers*: A New Look at the Oedipal Theme." *The Psychoanalytic Review* LXI, No. 4 (Winter 1974-75): 571-89.

Examines the Oedipal theme in *Sons and Lovers* paying particular attention to the importance of Paul Morel's surrogate mother and father figures.

Potter, Stephen. "Autobiography: The Failure of Love." In his *D.H. Lawrence: A First Study*, pp. 37-49. London: Jonathan Cape, 1930.
A close comparison of Lawrence's autobiographical writing and the text of *Sons and Lovers*.

Pullin, Faith. "Lawrence's Treatment of Women in *Sons and Lovers*." In *Lawrence and Women*, edited by Anne Smith, pp. 49-74. London: Vision Press, 1978.
Examines the novel from a feminist perspective. Pullin especially discusses the ways in which Lawrence reduces his female characters to stereotypes and props which illuminate and assist the development of his male hero.

Reddick, Bryan. "*Sons and Lovers*: The Omniscient Narrator." *Explicator* XL, No. 4 (Summer 1982): 68-75.
Examines the ways in which the commentary of the narrator contributes to a sense of ambiguity in *Sons and Lovers*.

Rossman, Charles. "The Gospel According to D.H. Lawrence: Religion in *Sons and Lovers*." *The D.H. Lawrence Review* III, No. 1 (Spring 1970): 31-41.
Discussion of religious allusions in the novel.

Sagar, Keith. "The Bases of the Normal (1910-1913)." In his *The Art of D.H. Lawrence*, pp. 19-40. Cambridge: Cambridge University Press, 1966.
Discussion of the ways in which the writing of *Sons and Lovers* largely enabled Lawrence to analyze and exorcise the conflicts of his youth, particularly in terms of his attitudes toward his mother and other women.

Sale, Roger. "D.H. Lawrence: 1910-1916." In his *Modern Heroism: Essays on D.H. Lawrence, William Empson, & J.R.R. Tolkien*, pp. 16-106. Berkeley and Los Angeles: University of California Press, 1973.*
A close biographical examination of Lawrence's career between 1910 and 1916, the period in which he completed *Sons and Lovers*, *The Rainbow*, and *Women in Love*.

Schwartz, Daniel R. "Speaking of Paul Morel: Voice, Unity, and Meaning in *Sons and Lovers*." *Studies in the Novel* VIII, No. 3 (Fall 1976): 255-77.
Presents the view that the complex and fluctuating relationship between the narrator and the characters in *Sons and Lovers* is essential in drawing the reader into the novel's aesthetic process.

Seligmann, Herbert J. *D.H. Lawrence: An American Interpretation*. New York: Thomas Seltzer, 1924, 77 p.
Sees Paul Morel as a male figure of central importance to the development of male characterization throughout the rest of Lawrence's fiction.

Stoll, John E. *D.H. Lawrence's "Sons and Lovers": Self-Encounter and the Unknown Self*. Muncie, Ind.: Ball State University, 1968, 48 p.
Examines the ways in which the underlying theory of consciousness shapes *Sons and Lovers* with significant attention paid to the importance of the family unit and social environment.

Swigg, Richard. "Tragedy and the Unconscious: *Sons and Lovers*." In his *Lawrence, Hardy, and American Literature*, pp. 44-57. London: Oxford University Press, 1972.*
Discusses how Paul Morel's determination and self-assertion differ from the defeatist visions of the protagonists of Lawrence's earlier novels.

Taylor, John A. "The Greatness in *Sons and Lovers*." *Modern Philology* LXXI, No. 4 (May 1974): 380-87.
Examines the development of Paul Morel as a heroic figure.

Weiss, Daniel A. "The Mother in the Mind." In his *Oedipus in*

Nottingham: D.H. Lawrence, pp. 39-68. Seattle: University of Washington Press, 1962.

Examines *Sons and Lovers* in terms of the classical Freudian concept of the Oedipal complex and traces the ways in which Paul Morel emerges from his role as a guilt-ridden son and lover to embrace the masculine values of the world represented by his father.

Woolf, Virginia. "Notes on D.H. Lawrence." In *Twentieth Century Interpretations of "Sons and Lovers": A Collection of Critical Essays,* edited by Judith Farr, pp. 24-7. Englewood Cliffs, N.J.: Prentice-Hall, 1970.

Praises the clarity and precision of Lawrence's prose as well as his unaffected ease of narration in *Sons and Lovers.* Woolf also criticizes Lawrence's inability to satisfy the reader because of what she views as a tone of transience and restlessness in his fiction, which she traces to his being ungrounded in a class or tradition.

John Middleton Murry

1889-1957

English critic, editor, essayist, biographer, autobiographer, translator, poet, playwright, and novelist.

Murry is recognized as one of the most significant English critics and editors of the twentieth century. Anticipating later scholarly opinion, he championed the writings of Marcel Proust, James Joyce, Paul Valéry, D. H. Lawrence, and the poetry of Thomas Hardy through his positions as the editor of *The Athenaeum* and as a long time contributor to *The Times Literary Supplement* and other periodicals. As with his magazine essays, Murry's book-length critical works are noted for their unusually impassioned tone and startling discoveries; such biographically centered critical studies as *Keats and Shakespeare: A Study of Keats' Poetic Life from 1816-1820* and *Son of Woman: The Story of D. H. Lawrence* contain esoteric, controversial conclusions that have angered scholars who favor more traditional approaches. Nevertheless, Murry is cited for his perspicuity, clarity, and supportive argumentation. His early exposition on literary appreciation, *The Problem of Style,* has become a widely read and often-referred-to work, while his extensive command of and deep interest in his subjects has earned him prominence as a profoundly conscientious—if controversial—thinker.

Born into a civil servant's family in Peckham, London, Murry gained early recognition as a particularly brilliant student and, upon winning a scholarship, entered Christ's Hospital School in 1901, advancing to Brasenose College, Oxford, seven years later. There he launched an avant-garde magazine called *Rhythm,* which later became *The Blue Review.* Shortly after the magazine was founded, Murry met Katherine Mansfield, whose story ''The Woman at the Store'' he had admired and published in his journal, and the artistic and personal attachment that developed between the two led to marriage. In later years, the nature of their relationship received nearly as much attention as their literary careers: following Mansfield's death from tuberculosis in 1923, Murry's publication of her stories, letters,and journals, and his coauthored biography of her, sparked charges, to some extent substantiated, that Murry created a ''cult of Katherine'' and benefitted financially from the process. What cannot be argued, however, is the fact that during her life, Mansfield exerted tremendous influence on Murry's professional and artistic growth. Another figure who helped shape Murry intellectually was D. H. Lawrence, whom Mansfield and Murry met in 1913. Lawrence was among the first to direct Murry toward a career as a critic, believing this, rather than fiction or verse, to be the area wherein his friend's greatest talents lay. Lawrence's advice was borne out by the fact that Murry's novels, poetry, and verse dramas brought few favorable reviews. On the other hand, his early criticism and journalistic efforts—as editor of *Rhythm,* art critic for *The Westminster Gazette,* contributor to *The Nation* and *The Times Literary Supplement,* and author of the critical study *Fyodor Dostoevsky* —were generally well received. Murry, Mansfield, and Lawrence shared in the editor-authorship of a short-lived periodical entitled *The Signature,* begun in 1915. During World War I they, together with Lawrence's wife, Frieda, formed a close friendship that soon disintegrated due to highly sensitized personal issues and professional differences. The relationship be-

tween the four was later symbolically depicted in Lawrence's 1920 novel *Women in Love.*

With his appointment as editor of *The Athenaeum* in 1919, and his subsequent outspoken, perceptive writing for that journal after its absorption by *The Nation* in 1921, Murry attained considerable prestige as an original, influential man of letters. In 1922 he published *The Problem of Style,* a collection of lectures he had delivered at Oxford. These lectures are not so much textbook treatments of the complexities encountered when defining the literary term ''style'' as they are blueprints for critics to employ when discussing various manifestations of the creative process. A chief criterion that Murry offered the critic when forming evaluative judgments was the writer's mastery of ''crystallization''—the essential component of a writer's style that enables him to present his innermost impressions and convictions in precise, emotive language to the reader. This concept, which informs all of Murry's later critical writings, gained fuller force following his lapse into severe depression over Mansfield's tragic death from tuberculosis at the age of thirty-four. After weeks of grieving Murry experienced an instantaneous, overwhelming sense of enlightenment and renewal, which he describes in part in *God: An Introduction to the Science of Metabiology.* ''I became aware of myself as a had reached a pinnacle of personal being. I was I, as I had never been before—and never should be again. . . . But a moment came when the darkness of that ocean changed to light, the cold to warmth; when it swept in one great wave over the shores and frontiers of my self; when it bathed me and I was renewed; when the room was filled with a presence, and I knew I was not alone—that I never could be alone any more." Many, including Murry, recognize this event as a pivotal point from which all his subsequent works, in some way, stem.

In 1923, with a sense of renewed purpose and an avowed intent to promote Lawrence as England's literary prophet, Murry founded *The Adelphi*. The magazine was based on a liberal, utilitarian platform, merging an exploration of literature with commentary on contemporary religious and political life and directing these viewpoints outside traditional upper-class readerships. This anti-elitist approach, coupled with Lawrence's declaration in his *Adelphi*-serialized *Fantasia of the Unconscious* that "Jesus was a failure," alienated Murry from a largely conservative reading public and severed alliances formed earlier with members of the Bloomsbury Group, including Virginia and Leonard Woolf. Yet he maintained a long association with the journal, eventually conferring its editorship on his colleagues Max Plowman and Richard Rees. During the 1930s and 1940s Murry spoke out on various global topics through *The Adelphi* as well as through such books as *The Necessity of Communism* and *The Defence of Democracy*. For a time he converted to pacifism, joining the Peace Pledge Union, editing the paper *Peace News*, and devoting himself to related causes. At one point he seriously considered joining the Anglican priesthood. Although Murry's frequent fusion of his personal and professional lives gives a distinct flavor to his criticism of this period, his numerous concerns have caused many critics to question his philosophic integrity, since the viewpoints stated in his studies often contradict one another.

In the spring of 1942 Murry acquired Lodge Farm in Thelnetham, Norfolk, and launched a small agrarian community, the life of which he records in *Community Farm*. During his remaining years he adopted the role of gentleman-farmer, though he continued to pursue his initial vocation. Among his canon, one of his last works, *Jonathan Swift: A Critical Biography*, remains unique—for here Murry purposely studied a figure to whom he had no special allegiance, attempting to present an unbiased, unmistakably scholarly example of his critical abilities. Murry died of a heart attack at the age of fifty-seven in Bury St. Edmonds, Suffolk.

Murry's fictional and poetic efforts received little critical acclaim. His three novels occasionally display fine descriptive prose, but critics agree that he was unable to fully develop his characters or themes. Ernest G. Griffin has posited that "one might say that there is [in Murry's fiction] perplexity without solution. He was not enough of an artist to supply an aesthetic resolution to a thoughtful and troubled mind. He was better when he studied and interpreted the profundity of artists who had achieved a form of resolution." Murry's first study of this sort, *Fyodor Dostoevsky*, though less refined and less important than his works on Keats and Shakespeare, for example, was in many respects typical of all his later critical studies. In it Murry traced the evolution of the author's soul, as perceived through his works, to a final consummation of artistic vision, in Dostoevsky's case *Brat'ya Karamazovy* (*The Brothers Karamazov*). As in his later works, Murry frequently bolstered his interpretations through selective textual analysis, showcasing those passages of his subject's work that helped best disclose

the progression towards that mature artistic vision with which he was predominantly concerned. Ultimately, Murry's conclusions were optimistic and humanistic; he tended to endorse those qualities, inclinations, or motifs in a writer's work that represented a unified, essentially compassionate understanding of the human condition. Consequently, he denied primacy to the works of such contemporaries as W. B. Yeats and T. S. Eliot, perceiving them as empty or overly dismal expressions of reality. William Shakespeare and John Keats, who Murry's critics and biographers regard as the two subjects of his greatest devotion, represented for Murry archetypal, soul-searching poets who arrived at a realization and perfect aesthetic representation of variegated humanity in absolute agreement with his own mystic affirmation of life. Hence his critical method was romantic in nature, and opposed to that of his friendly rival Eliot, who adhered to a rigid foundation of classicism. Murry's imperfections—occasionally imprecise prose, a disregard for scholastic objectivity, and a zealous, questionable progression of ideas—have not prevented his studies from commanding the respect of important scholars for their many original and insightful, though sometimes controversial, conclusions.

Keats and Shakespeare, written as a means of approaching Shakespeare through his disciple John Keats, is recognized for its illuminating discussions of Keats's poetic temperament. Murry's intimate identification with his subject enabled him to construct interpretations that others with more detached viewpoints had overlooked. The book has been criticized for its idealistic, emotionally charged outlook and especially for its thesis that in Keats's soul-journey he struggled between the creative influences of John Milton and Shakespeare and finally chose the latter as his spiritual guide. Critics note that while Murry presents an intimate, sympathetic understanding of Keats, his treatment of Milton shows a considerably less judicious view. Nevertheless, the study was seminal in establishing Keats as a major figure in English poetry. Likewise, Murry's *Shakespeare* has been accorded high importance for its remarkably informed analysis of the playwright's thematic concerns. Because Murry chose to write a comprehensive study of Shakespeare, some works are given only brief treatment, contrasting sharply with Murry's other, more detailed discussions. Yet several scholars consider *Shakespeare* the author's finest achievement.

Less highly regarded than these works are his *Son of Woman*, a study of D. H. Lawrence, and *William Blake*, though neither are considered to be without value. Critics of *Son of Woman* discover Murry's own persona lingering near the surface too often; although some agree that Murry was capable of probing Lawrence and his works more deeply than anyone else, his excessively passionate interpretation and objectionable characterization of his antithetical, hero-friend has led to sharp reaction against the work. The most prevalent criticism of *William Blake* is that Murry, when confronted with Blake's enigmatic, highly symbolic poetry, gives even further license to his penchant for fervid, inventive interpretation. *Jonathan Swift* invites criticism for opposite reasons, the consensus being that while the work may display admirable objectivity and scholarship, it lacks vividness and enthusiasm. Some critics believe that aside from his studies of Keats and Shakespeare, Murry evidenced his best qualities when exploring respected minor literary figures, such as the poets John Clare and Lady Winchelsea, and his own discovery, novelist Henry Williamson. Of all his critical works, his essay collection *Heaven—And Earth* is regarded by many as the author's greatest achievement. The study, which includes essays on twelve important literary little island against whose slender shores a cold, dark boundless ocean lapped devouring. Somehow, in that moment, I knew I and political figures in European history, is often discussed as the most complete expression of Murry's thought. However, some have considered this the greatest weakness of the work, noting that the continual presence of Murry's spiritual convictions impedes the force of his discussions of the works of others.

Deriving his critical principles from the philosophers Aristotle, Plato, Ludwig Wittgenstein, George Santayana, and especially Matthew Arnold, Murry espoused a belief in literature's integral relationship with religious faith and practice, and a conviction that the true critic must consistently reveal that which is not only beautiful in construction but essentially moral in inspiration. As he wrote in his "The Function of Criticism": "The great artist's work is in all its parts a revelation of the ideal as a principle of activity in human life." Further, he considered the critic's primary duty to be the methodic separation of the true or great artists from the false, and a hierarchical delineation of those worthy of extended study. A prolific and often profound writer, Murry has had considerable impact on twentieth-century literature and thought and continues to be remembered for his many original, illuminating studies.

PRINCIPAL WORKS

Fyodor Dostoevsky: A Critical Study (criticism) 1916
The Critic in Judgment; or, Belshazzar of Barons Court
    (criticism) 1919
Aspects of Literature (criticism) 1920
Cinnamon and Angelica (drama) 1920
The Problem of Style (criticism) 1922
The Things We Are (novel) 1922
Keats and Shakespeare: A Study of Keats' Poetic Life From
    1816 to 1820 (criticism) 1925
The Life of Jesus (biography) 1926; also published as
    Jesus, Man of Genius, 1926
God: An Introduction to the Science of Metabiology (essay)
    1929
Countries of the Mind (criticism) 1931
Son of Woman: The Story of D. H. Lawrence (criticism)
    1931
The Necessity of Communism (essay) 1932
William Blake (criticism) 1933
Between Two Worlds (autobiography) 1935
Shakespeare (criticism) 1936
Heaven—And Earth (criticism) 1938; also published as
    Heroes of Thought, 1938
The Defence of Democracy (essay) 1939
The Price of Leadership (essay) 1939
The Betrayal of Christ by the Churches (essay) 1940
Community Farm (essay) 1952
Jonathan Swift (biography and criticism) 1954
Unprofessional Essays (criticism) 1956
Love, Freedom, and Society (essay) 1957
Katherine Mansfield, and Other Literary Studies (criticism)
    1959
Selected Criticism: 1916-1957 (criticism) 1960
The Letters of John Middleton Murry to Katherine Mansfield
    (letters) 1983

THE TIMES LITERARY SUPPLEMENT (essay date 1916)

[*In the following excerpt from a review of* Fyodor Dostoevsky, *the critic disagrees with several of Murry's interpretations and conclusions, but nevertheless recommends the book for its provocative ideas.*]

The interest of [*Fyodor Dostoevsky*], which is great, lies in the manner in which Mr. Murry has experienced Dostoevsky. To him Dostoevsky is not an artist, he is not one great writer among many to be compared with other great writers; he is, for the moment, the whole of life; and what he says about Dostoevsky is really what he has to say about life itself, about the whole relation of mankind to the universe. Dostoevsky is to him a complete and concentrated example of this relation. What he says about Dostoevsky is to him true about all men, except that it is more true about Dostoevsky, because morally, intellectually, and aesthetically he experienced life more intensely than other men.

To Mr. Murry at the moment, and in his own present state of development, there is neither harmony nor the promise of harmony in man's relation to the universe; and so to him Dostoevsky is an expression of this tragic conflict which seems to him the essence of the life of man, a conflict which has in it no prophecy of a reconciliation, but which is both terrible and beautiful in itself, because it is conflict. So, to us, he seems to misunderstand Dostoevsky; but the very misunderstanding is interesting, as being the expression of a sincere if transient state of mind. We have, when we read Dostoevsky, an incessant sense of pain; and to Mr. Murry this pain is the essence of Dostoevsky. It is what he has to tell us about life; it is his truth, and his beauty, and his conscience. Dostoevsky has struck him like an actual experience, and he writes under the shock of that experience, he himself feels the pain which Dostoevsky felt and expressed with such enormous force. . . .

But to Mr. Murry this pain in the art of Dostoevsky is a pain in the nature of the universe—it is something which Dostoevsky has discovered in life itself, not an accident of his own mind or body; and he believes that to Dostoevsky himself it was the essence of life; that to Dostoevsky, not merely as an epileptic but also as a philosopher, life was something frightening, like a bad dream. Here, we think, he is utterly mistaken. Dostoevsky put all the pain into his version of life that he felt himself because he was a great artist. He could not pretend to have found a harmony where he had not yet found it; but he wrote always with faith in such a harmony, and it is that faith which gives beauty to his work. . . .

Mr. Murry thinks that in his last work, "The Brothers Karamazov," Dostoevsky conquered despair, but Alyosha is to him "the man who is the promise of all humanity, for whom the old problems are solved by his very being and are not." "The Brothers Karamazov" is unfinished, and we do not know what would have been the end of Alyosha; but we do not see that there are more signs of triumph in it than in "The Idiot," although it is less tragic so far as it goes. Mr. Murry says that each of Dostoevsky's great final works was "a desperate battleground, wherein his spirit fought all night long against despair." But we do not believe that he took despair seriously in "The Idiot," any more than in "The Brothers Karamazov." . . .

Mr. Murry is particularly interesting in what he says about Dostoevsky's relation to Christianity. It is, he says,

> easy to claim Dostoevsky for a Christian if you
> do not care to understand his conception of

Christ. He loved Christ, indeed, as few men have loved him; but such a love of Christ will work havoc with Christianity. Dostoevsky never faltered in this love, but the love could never satisfy his hunger for belief. Those two things are sundered by an abyss. It may even be that they cannot in great hearts be reconciled. A Dostoevsky would not purchase the security of faith in Christ's divinity at the price of His mortal agonies. His soul was tortured with the desire for that security, yet would he have refused it had it been offered to him; so devouring was his love for Christ.

But what he says there of Dostoevsky is true of every Christian, of every man who is possessed by religion. Religion is not security, but the passionate refusal of it; and Christianity, above all religion, is the refusal of all comfort for faith, hope and charity. . . .

To the mind of Dostoevsky, says Mr. Murry, "there are two ways by which mortal man can contend with the world, in which good and evil are for ever intertwined. The one is to act, the other to suffer. These things are to the outward eye of opposite complexion, only they are the same. In each the individual will is pitted against the unknown power." No; they are not the same to Dostoevsky, or according to the Christian doctrine. Rather, man is in his nature a being that experiences rather than one that acts. Action is the result of the manner in which he experiences, and his will should be applied to his own manner of experiencing. If it is applied only to action, it will be impotent. That is why Dostoevsky tells us about the manner in which his characters experience things more than about what they do. . . . Mr. Murry says that there is in Dostoevsky's novels the absence of a sense of time. This, we think, is due to his conception of reality as experience not as action. For we have far less sense of time when we think of what happens to us than when we think of what we do. When life is an intense experience, as when we listen to music, we almost pass into eternity and lose our sense of duration. So it was with all life as Dostoevsky experienced it, even in his pain; and so he gives us this sense of eternity in his books.

At nearly every point we have seemed to disagree with Mr. Murry; yet we would advise every one to read his book. For the more you differ from him the more you are provoked to thought.

"A Study of Dostoevsky," in The Times Literary Supplement, *No. 762, August 24, 1916, p. 403.*

GEORGE MIDDLETON   (essay date 1916)

[*In the following excerpt, Middleton offers an ambivalent view of Fyodor Dostoevsky, finding it to be at once an extremely profound study of Dostoevsky's works and an interpretation that is weakened by Murry's obsessive interest in the spiritual aspects of Dostoevsky's life and fiction.*]

[In his **Fyodor Dostoevsky**, Mr. Murry] has approached Dostoevsky with an air of reverance. Disdaining only the slightest biographical reference, he has penetrated into the spiritual aspects of the author of *Crime and Punishment* with the result that his study is in many ways the most profound which the great Russian has inspired. While it lacks the charm of Mr. Paul's analysis, partly due to the rigidity with which it clings to its critical premise, it is a volume which will appeal to the

more diligent of Dostoevsky's admirers. Its very profundity may tend to warn prospective readers away from the Russian, since at times one feels Mr. Murry has read into Dostoevsky more than the author himself intended. But this is ever the fault of such a study where each fact is bent to build a thesis.

There is nothing comparative in Mr. Murry's method nor is little attention paid to a purely literary criticism. It is not in form but in thought and spirit that Dostoevsky is an influence, and as the author pointed out himself, it is only through a close reading of his works that his thought can be comprehended. Dostoevsky is fundamentally the dramatiser of abstract thought in terms of fiction. His works alone explain his life since his real life was one of imagination. Therefore Mr. Murry is little concerned with external facts as Dostoevsky existed more "truly as an idea than as a man." Upon this premise, that he was "more a brooding mind than a human being," this study is essentially concerned with his spiritual evolution as expressed in his successive creations. It is a bit startling to learn that Dostoevsky was not a novelist since his books—beginning with *Crime and Punishment*—cannot be regarded as human histories, for though his symbolic figures "are real and human, their reality and humanity no more belong to the active world." Without analysing, in this brief notice, all the subtle distinctions which Mr. Murry advances to prove his contention, one may point to this as a general comment on the extreme heresy of most of his opinions. (pp. 299-300)

To those who have followed the translations of Mrs. Garnett as they have appeared, Dostoevsky offers many more attractions than this purely spiritual side which Mr. Murry presents with such minute persistency. That it is possible to write so profound a book about him is only another evidence of the Russian's many sidedness which has given him his place among the greatest of writers. (p. 300)

George Middleton, in a review of "Fyodor Dostoevsky," in The Bookman, *New York, Vol. XLIV, No. 3, November, 1916, pp. 299-300.*

[VIRGINIA WOOLF]   (essay date 1919)

[*Woolf is considered one of the most prominent figures of twentieth-century English literature. Like her contemporary James Joyce, with whom she is often compared, Woolf is remembered as one of the most innovative of the stream-of-consciousness novelists. Concerned primarily with depicting the life of the mind, she revolted against traditional narrative techniques and developed her own highly individualized style. Woolf's works, noted for their subjective explorations of characters' inner lives and their delicate poetic quality, have had a lasting effect on the art of the novel. A discerning and influential critic and essayist as well as a novelist, Woolf began writing reviews for* The Times Literary Supplement *at an early age. Her critical essays, which cover almost the entire range of English literature, contain some of her finest prose and are praised for their insight. Along with Lytton Strachey, Roger Fry, Clive Bell, and several others, Woolf and her husband Leonard formed the literary coterie known as the "Bloomsbury Group." In the following excerpt from a review of the verse drama* The Critic in Judgment—*a work published by the Woolfs' Hogarth Press—Woolf questions the authenticity of Murry's poetic sensibility.*]

[We] have to recognize in our own mind as little serenity and certainty as is compatible with what we have done our best to make a thorough understanding of [**"The Critic in Judgment"**]. As a first step towards understanding, rub out as many years as divide you from the youth which, stark, stiff, severe, terribly sanguine, has not yet been absorbed into the main activities of the world. Never again is one so serious, so uncompromising and so clear-sighted. That is Mr. Murry's position. He stands upright, surveys the prospect, in which as yet he plays no part, and asks himself, What is the aim of life? What can one believe? . . .

One after another the forms of Ulysses, Helen, and Plato rise before him and give him their versions of the faith upon which the poet makes his comment—but we will not tread out the steps of the argument. At our age we are inclined to say that the argument does not matter, since most certainly nothing can be proved. Yet as we read the strong, egotistical, sunless poem, such is the force of youth that the argument once more seems to matter. Honesty matters, courage matters,—devil take them! one may add, seeing what a springless jolt over the cobbles they are apt to lead one. But does Mr. Murry make the journey worth while? Is he, that is to say, what, for convenience sake, we call a poet? Does he give us what after all matters so much more than the end of any journey or the truth of any argument? This, indeed, is what we find it difficult to decide. A healthy glow pervades anyone who takes hard exercise, but that you can get to perfection by mastering an Act of Parliament. Poetry—this of course is an individual experience—suddenly bestows its beauty without solicitation; you possess it before you know what it contains. But in **"The Critic in Judgment"** one feels that one has earned every word that one is given; and the payment is exact; there is no suspicion of gratuity. And yet, how is it that without these graces and bounties the poem makes us read it? In part, of course, the subtle English logic carries us along. Beyond that, however, there are passages and phrases where the glow and heat that we require appear, giving us, not the easy beauty that we are used to call inspiration, but a more difficult variety born of friction which, from the effort that it exacts, makes us ask in the midst of our exaltation, ''Is this poetry?''

> [*Virginia Woolf*], *''Is This Poetry?''* in The Athenaeum, *No. 4651, June 20, 1919, p. 491.*

T.S.E. [T. S. ELIOT]   (essay date 1920)

[*Perhaps the most influential poet and critic of the first half of the twentieth century, Eliot is closely identified with many of the qualities denoted by the term Modernism: experimentation, formal complexity, artistic and intellectual eclecticism, and a classicist view of the artist working at an emotional distance from his or her creation. He introduced a number of terms and concepts that strongly affected critical thought in his lifetime, among them the idea that poets must be conscious of the living tradition of literature in order for their work to have artistic and spiritual validity. In general, Eliot upheld values of traditionalism and discipline, and in 1928 he annexed Christian theology to his overall conservative world view. Of his criticism, he stated: "It is a by-product of my private poetry-workshop: or a prolongation of the thinking that went into the formation of my verse." Early in his career, Eliot was asked by Murry to serve as his assistant editor at* The Athenaeum *on the strength of his first book,* Prufrock, and Other Observations. *Eliot hesitantly declined, though he did contribute many reviews published in* The Athenaeum *during Murry's editorship. Over the years, as Murry's and Eliot's literary theories became more sharply defined, the two men drifted apart in outlook, occasionally entering into critical debate in the pages of their respective magazines,* The Adelphi *and* The Criterion. *In the following excerpt from an early review, Eliot affirms Murry's high potential for composing superior poetic drama—an artistic form which he regards as extremely difficult to master in contem-*

porary times—but exposes Murry's ultimate failure to do so in Cinnamon and Angelica.]

The impotence of contemporary drama is a commonplace riddle of cultured pessimism. A convocation of dramatic enthusiasts recently revealed, that on the one hand there are plenty of writers who could compose good plays if anyone would stage them, and that on the other hand there are a dozen producers ready to snap up a good play if they could find one. Poetic dramas are not infrequently printed; we have abandoned the speculation of why they are so dull. But Mr. Murry is an interesting case—interesting enough to revive once more the whole discussion; for he is a writer who might be, or might in a happier age have been (according to our hopeful or pessimistic humours), a poetic dramatist. He has virtues which are his own, and vices which are general. It is therefore a real pleasure, an exceptional pleasure, to have a patient like Mr. Murry extended on the operating table; we need our sharpest instruments, and steadiest nerves, if we are to do him justice.

Two possibilities we may exclude at once. A poetic drama may be simply bad, in which case the cause of its failure will not be worth further examination. Or it may be poetry which should have been cast in some form which is not dramatic. Plays of this sort are written at times when drama is decaying, but when no other form is at hand. . . . The poet who now applies himself to the drama (I exclude, of course, those who are competent for nothing) will be one with a strong and (we may even say) philosophic conviction in favour of this form. He will be a very conscious poet, with an historical imagination; it is the consciousness, the construction of the possible meaning, the possible value in feeling which a triumphant poetic drama might have for the sensibilities of the most sensitive contemporary, that has moved him. This poet will be a complex person: he is impelled both by a desire to give form to something in his mind, and by a desire that a certain desirable emotional state should be produced. He is troubled and hampered by the complexity of conscious motives which lay claim to his attention. Such, we believe, is Mr. Murry.

The composition of a poetic drama is in fact the most difficult, the most exhausting task that a poet can set himself, and—this is the heart of the matter—it is infinitely more difficult for a poet of to-day than it was for a poet of no greater talent three hundred years ago. . . .

The difficulty is very baldly stated, as it has been stated so many times before, by saying that there is no audience. It will not do, of course, to leave the matter there. There is, ''waiting'' for poetry on the stage, a quite sufficient number of persons to fill a playhouse; there are even a few willing to subsidize the performance of any play of the mildest promise; there is enough effort on the part of both writers and the possible patrons and audiences. But what is needed is not sympathy or encouragement or appreciation—we need not assume that the best of the Athenian or the Elizabethan drama was ''appreciated'' by its audiences, relatively to the second-best—but a kind of unconscious co-operation. The ideal condition is that under which everything, except what only the individual genius can supply, is provided for the poet. A *framework* is provided. We do not mean ''plot''; a poet may incorporate, adapt, or invent as he prefers or as occasion suggests. But a dramatic poet needs to have some *kind* of dramatic form given to him as the condition of his time, a form which in itself is neither good nor bad but which permits an artist to fashion it into a work of art. And by a ''kind of dramatic form'' one means almost the temper of the age (not the temper of a few intellectuals); a preparedness, a habit, on the part of the public, to respond in a predictable way, however crudely, to certain stimuli. (p. 635)

Consider now the position of Mr. Murry, a position which we may seriously call Promethean. He has to supply his own framework, his own myth, he must do without the commonplaces which so stoutly supported even Æschylus and Shakespeare. He must stand quite alone: which means that he must, if he can, write poetry (not merely good blank verse) *at every moment*. The strain of such an enterprise is probably responsible for inelegancies which occasionally disfigure the more relaxed passages of the play ["**Cinnamon and Angelica**"]

> . . . new-fangled tin artillery . . .
> Garlic tried *to load*
> *The patent off on me*. . . .

may be appropriate speech for the rough soldier, but it is not appropriate that the same person should a few lines later remark of himself that

> to myself I seem a *wanton* child . . .

This is not a blemish due to haste or carelessness. It is due to a concentration on the central interest, the focal moment of the piece, which has distracted the author's attention. There is enough evidence that Mr. Murry has studied blank verse with great care, and where he is excited he is also attentive to detail. But he is not held down by the necessity of *entertaining* an audience cruder than himself; the emotional structure is the only structure. In a dramatic structure the minor emotions, or the emotions of the minor characters, are related to the major emotions through the actions. "**Cinnamon and Angelica**" is deficient in dramatic structure—although the emotions (the major emotions) are dramatic.

The labour and danger do not end here. . . . Mr. Murry cannot escape an audience—comparatively small and comparatively cultivated—which has no dramatic habits, but desires to share, to destroy his solitude. We may suspect that Mr. Murry is aware of this audience, and that he instinctively protects himself from its intrusion by the titles which he gives his characters:

> I thought I heard the spinning of the wheel
> Of Destiny, and this is what she span:
> Such close-knit intertexture of two hearts . . .
> That even the hungry Fates must hold their shears
> From so divine a pattern.

The adjective "hungry" may be questioned as irrelevant to the figure; but it is a fine passage. And I quote it to ask why the author should place such language in the mouths of personages to whom he gives names like Cinnamon, Angelica, Caraway, and Vanilla Bean. The key of the music is a lovers' melancholy with many under-and over-tones; the third act is pitched at that intensity at which language strives to become silence, and the end is definitely tragic. Why these grocery names? It is a movement of protection against the cultivated audience. Whoever is acutely sensitive of the pressure of this intruder will have his own grimace or buffoonery, to avoid sentiment or to decorate sentiment so that it will no longer appear personal, but at most—safely fashionable. This concealment is a "give-away"; but we cannot say that Mr. Murry has given himself away either, for his "close-knit intertexture" is a maze of such subtilized and elusive feelings as will hardly be threaded by any but those whom he would be willing to admit. (pp. 635-36)

> *T.S.E.* [*T. S. Eliot*], *"The Poetic Drama," in* The Athenaeum, *No. 4698, May 14, 1920, pp. 635-36.*

Murry with Frieda and D. H. Lawrence, on the Lawrences' wedding day (1914).

KATHERINE MANSFIELD   (letter date 1920)

[*From their first meeting in 1911, Mansfield and Murry constantly shared with each other their literary views and works-in-progress. Over the years the two were often separated, as Mansfield sought treatment for her tubercular condition outside England while Murry remained in London, working as a critic. This situation led to a voluminous exchange of letters in which the two often critiqued each other's writings in addition to addressing more personal matters. In the following excerpt from one of Mansfield's letters, she first praises* Aspects of Literature *and then, objectifying her comments, delineates the study's faults.*]

About your Book

My dear Bogey,

I have now read your book [*Aspects of Literature*], and though we can't really discuss it until you come, I should feel ungracious were I not to write you quelques mots.

Well, Bogey, I'm your admirer. Accept my admiration. It's from my heart and head! There is real achievement in that book. While I read you on Tchekhov, Butler, the first essay, Shakespeare criticism, I liked to pretend you were a stranger. I imagined what I'd feel like if this book had fallen out of the sky—and that really gave me your measure. (There's a female standard!) At your best no one can touch you. You simply are first chop. For the first time *je me trouve* underlining your sentences—putting marks in the margin—as one so *very* seldom does, Boge. You re-create—no less—Tchekhov, for instance. I want to make you feel what a great little fellow you are for this book! And how it makes me believe in you—stand by you in my thoughts and respect you. There! Shake hands with me. And of course I want 'to criticise'—to tell you all I feel. But not before you realize how firm and unyielding are the foundations of my praise. Here goes.

Your Hardy doesn't quite come off to my thinking. You seem to be hinting at a special understanding between yourself and the author. That's not fair: it puts me off. You (in the name of your age, true, but not quite, not wholly) intrude your age, your experience of suffering. . . . This destroys the balance.

Your Keats is performance, right enough, but it's more promise. Makes me feel you ought to write a book on Keats. It's deeply interesting. The last paragraph is a pity—when you praise Sir Sidney [Colvin]. Here again I seem to catch a faint breath of *pride*.

I think Edward Thomas is seen out of proportion. It's not in his poems; he's not *all that*. Your emotions are too apparent. I feel one ought to replace Thomas with another and say it all about *him*. There was the beginning of all that in Thomas but you've filled it out yourself—to suit what you wanted him to be. It's not wholly sincere, either, for that reason.

Let me make my meaning clearer. Take your Tchekhov. Now you make Tchekhov greater than one sees him but NOT greater than he was. This is an *important dangerous* distinction. A critic must see a man as great as his potentialities but NOT greater. Falsity creeps in immediately then.

You ought to guard against this. Its another 'aspect' of your special pleading danger—as in your essay on Hardy. In your tremendously just desire to prove him a major poet, you mustn't make yourself Counsel for the Prisoner! I mean that in all its implications.

You might have borne this trick of yours in mind when you are so down on S[amuel] T[aylor] C[oleridge] for his idolatry. Remember how Shakespeare *was* regarded at that time—the extraordinary ignorance, stupidity and meanness of the point of view. I don't think you take that into account enough. It's too easy to talk of laudanum and soft braindedness. The reason for his *überfluss* is more psychological. (I don't defend S.T.C. but I think he and you are both wrong in 'considering' far too specially a 'special' audience). On the other hand you are splendidly just to his amazing *Venus and Adonis* criticism. (I must say that chapter on *V. and A.* is a gem of the first water).

Ronsard is interesting because you have conveyed the chap's quality so well, tho' I deeply disagree with one of the 'charming' quotations—the complexion one is perfect.

Now, I'll be franker still. There are still traces of what I call your sham personality in this book and they mar it—the personality that expressed itself in the opening paragraphs of your Santayana review in *The Nation*. Can't you see what a *farce* it makes of you preaching the good life? The good life indeed,—rowing about in your little boat with the worm-eaten ship and chaos! Look here! How *can* you! How can you lay up your sweat in a phial for future generations! I don't ask for false courage from anyone but I do think that even if you are shivering it is your duty as an artist and a man *not* to shiver. The devil and the angel in you both fight in that review. I must speak out plainly because your friends flatter you. They are not really taken in by your 'sham personality', but they are too uncertain of themselves not to pretend that they are, and you are deceived by their pretence because you want to be. It is this which mars you and it is for this reason you will not

be popular. It's the BAD in you people can't stomach—not the good. But tho' they don't understand it, they sense it as treachery—as something that *is not done*. Don't be proud of your unpopularity, Bogey. It is right you should be unpopular for this.

Now let me point to your remark in the preface that you can 'do no less than afford your readers . . . a similar enjoyment in your case'. My dear Bogey! How could a person say such a thing. It's so naive as to be silly, or so arrogant as to be fantastique. Suppose I wrote: 'I have dated my stories as I venture to hope my readers may enjoy tracing my development—the ripening of my powers. . . .' What *would* you think! You'd faint! It is indecent, no less, to say such things. And one doesn't think them!

It always seems to me you let yourself go in *The Nation* especially; you count on Massingham's weakness. The worst of it is that whenever one is less than true to oneself in work, even what is true becomes tainted. I feel whenever I *am* true my good angel wipes out one bad mark—doesn't give me a good one—but, at any rate, next time, there is one bad mark the less to get over. Now you only get half-marks, and they are no marks at all, because you cannot resist this awful insidious temptation to show your wounds. Until you do, you are a great writer marred. Lynd called it 'highbrowism'. It's much more subtle. (pp. 617-20)

Katherine Mansfield, in a letter to John Middleton Murry in December, 1920, in her Katherine Mansfield's Letters to John Middleton Murry: 1913-1922, *revised edition, edited by John Middleton Murry, Alfred A. Knopf, 1951, pp. 617-20.*

REBECCA WEST   (essay date 1922)

[*West is considered one of the foremost English novelists and critics to write during the twentieth century. Born Cecily Isabel Fairfield, she began her career as an actress—taking the name Rebecca West from the emancipated heroine of Henrik Ibsen's drama* Rosmersholm—*and as a book reviewer for* The Freewoman. *Her early criticism was noted for its militantly feminist stance and its reflection of West's Fabian socialist concerns. Her first novel,* The Return of the Soldier (1918), *evidences a concern that entered into much of her later work: the psychology of the individual. West's greatest works include* The Meaning of Treason (1947), *which analyzes the motives of Britain's wartime traitors—notably, William Joyce ("Lord Haw-Haw")—and* Black Lamb and Grey Falcon (1942), *a record of the author's 1937 journey through Yugoslavia. West's literary criticism is noted for its wit, its aversion to cant, and its perceptiveness. Of her own work, West has commented: "I have always written in order to discover the truth for my own use, on the one hand, and on the other hand to earn money for myself and my family, and in this department of my work I hope I have honoured the truth I had already discovered. I have like most women written only a quarter of what I might have written, owing to my family responsibilities. I dislike heartily the literary philosophy and practice of my time, which I think has lagged behind in the past and has little relevance to the present, and it distresses me that so much contemporary work is dominated by the ideas (particularly the political and religious ideas) of the late eighteenth or nineteenth century, and those misunderstood." In the following excerpt from a review, West contrasts Murry's critical and novelistic skills. She regards* The Things We Are *as a predominantly amorphous and bland novel which compares unfavorably to his lucid, competent criticism.*]

It is always interesting to read the purely creative work of an author whom one has known previously in the debatably creative sphere of criticism, and usually it is disconcerting. We saw an example of that a year or two ago when Mr. James Agate produced his novel *Responsibility*. We all knew Mr. Agate as a dramatic critic; a Falstaffian sort of fellow, with a great gusto for poetic phrases that tasted rich in the mouth, and absorbedly infatuated with that trim and limited art-form, even to the extent of being tolerant towards that specially limited type of play, almost universally despised in these days, which is designed as a frame for a great actor's personality. But Mr. Agate the novelist was quite a different person. He had fewer chins and more of a waist. In intellectually subtle rather than sensuous English he took the fullest advantage of the freedom that the novel, most elastic of art-forms, has won for itself. He was, in fact, the antithesis of Mr. Agate the dramatic critic.

Now here is another book by a critic—Mr. Middleton Murry's *The Things We Are*—which presents just the same puzzle. Mr. Middleton Murry is one of the most distinguished of our younger critics, and he will be always remembered as having been an inspired editor. He is fastidious, and an ardent legitimist in the cause of beauty. Experiment, if it set something other than beauty on the throne, was intensely distasteful to him, but he also had the legitimist's taste for pedigree-hunting and delighted to do honour to the blood royal in its remotest descendant in authors forgotten or disesteemed. Occasionally he was also a most lucid critic. He could condense a deal of hard thinking and hard reading into something clear and globed like a raindrop. Now, this is not true of *The Things We Are*. About Mr. Middleton Murry one could come to very definite conclusions. It is very hard to bring anything definite at all from a reading of *The Things We Are,* except perhaps a desire to congratulate Mr. Murry for having found a title for his book that would suit almost every novel that ever was written. It has an interesting theme with some moments of beauty. Boston is a man of thirty whose soul has turned in upon itself because of his inability to struggle out of the absorbing grief caused by his mother's death ten years before, and the novel treats of the efforts made to bring him back to life by his nice friend, Bettington, common, timid, stupid, golden-spirited; by Felicia, who loves him, whom he would love if he could win to normal serenity and courage; and by a delicious pair, invented out of a deep poetical delight in rural England and its people, an innkeeper and his wife, into whose inn near St. Albans he strays when he is on a hag-ridden flight from London. It has its quality, its occasional (as in the account of the card-game the innkeeper and his wife play to distract Boston's mind) triumphs of observation and feeling and humour. But the substance of the book is without resemblance to the substance of Mr. Murry's criticisms. It is certainly not lucid. As a creator Mr. Murry seems to feel that a work of art may as well look like a choppy sea as anything else. The letters by which Boston tries to dissuade Bettington and Felicia from their mission to his ailing mind are presented curiously, without any of the clarifying process which one expects of art. They tease, just as such neurotic symptoms would tease if one encountered them in real life. And when Mr. Murry becomes befogged by his own lack of lucidity he falls back, with a complete lack of that fastidiousness one expects from him, on what we can call fashionable writing. When Boston goes to see the gipsy-like woman, Mrs. Kennington, the church worker who has left the Church because of her rage with God, who let her son be killed in the war, Mr. Murry flounders into wasting the intensity of his emotional realisation of her by resorting to the well-known Russian formula of inarticulate ecstasy. When he has to fill in a blank scene, which he needs for the purpose of creating suspense, and Bettington shamefacedly goes to take Felicia the

letter in which their sick, ungracious friend tries to get them to leave him alone in his sickness, full of phrases that must wound Felicia's pride, he uses a wholly uncharacteristic guy of Garden Suburb people talking about psycho-analysis which might have been written by Mr. Aldous Huxley in his cheap moods. That is indeed the salient characteristic of *The Things We Are*. It is uncharacteristic. That is not at all to its disadvantage. The tenderness in the account of the drive that the kind old innkeeper takes Boston, heartening him up with frequent tankards of ale and talk with ruddy landlords at inn-doors, is the pleasantest possible revelation of Mr. Murry's quality. But it is unexpected.

Rebecca West, in a review of "The Things We Are," in New Statesman, *Vol. XIX, No. 480, June 24, 1922, p. 326.*

BONAMY DOBRÉE (essay date 1925)

[*Dobrée was an English historian and critic and one of the leading authorities on Restoration drama. He was also among a select group of biographers who attempted to establish biography as a new art form and a legitimate department of creative literature. In the following excerpt from a review of* Keats and Shakespeare, *Dobrée notes Murry's excessive adulation of Keats, but remarks that "there is no book on Keats I would rather possess and keep by me on my shelves."*]

Though the phrase is liable to be misused, and thus subsequently to be hounded out of court, it it certain that no good thing is written without "high seriousness," that is, a complete loyalty of the whole personality to the matter in hand. Keats himself would have called it "intensity." But when throughout a book the notion is continually forced upon your attention, the thing itself is apt to disappear. Something else extrudes, and hides the subject from you. This is what happens in Mr. Murry's . . . [*Keats and Shakespeare*], and often, instead of having our minds turned upon Keats, we suddenly find we are being scolded. We are being told we are not highly serious, and therefore will probably not be able to understand either Keats or Mr. Murry. But to whom is Mr. Murry speaking? For surely anyone who is prepared to tackle so large a book as this, which from the beginning warns him that he will have to employ all his faculties, considers poetry of the highest value to life. As a result we begin to feel that it is Mr. Murry who is not highly serious, that he is afraid of something, for he seems all the time to be making war upon imaginary enemies, phantoms, perhaps, of his past thought. We ask whether there is not some element somewhere in Keats or in himself that he dare not face; we suspect him vaguely, and probably unjustifiably, of the worst of literary crimes: a lack of faith in his subject.

This is not mere idle girding at Mr. Murry. To clear up this point is essential to our attitude towards his book. In it he has tried, by tracing "the movement of Keats's soul" through the four relevant years of his poetic life, to establish what exactly is the pure poetic nature; and unless we can be quite certain of his absolute integrity we must be on our guard lest he is just a little distorting Keats to fit into his ideal picture. It is not so much that he ignores the influence of Dryden, nor even that he omits to face the question as to whether Keats contracted syphilis, as that his *exaggerated* hero worship is disturbing. What is admirable in Mr. Murry is his passionate love for Keats, his whole-hearted reverence, and his desire that we should share them, but his "hands off John Keats" position suggests fear. The true mystic can jest with God, and about him; Blake could call him Old Nobodaddy; it is only the fragile and tarnishable things we need to put in glass cases. Gods and heroes, if they are really such, are solid, ever-fixed marks. . . .

[Throughout] the book Mr. Murry keeps his main argument in view, the correspondence of Keats with Shakespeare, the inspiration for *life* that he drew from him, at the end so consciously that he literally felt himself guided, even possessed by Shakespeare. It is an illuminating, deeply pondered study, and, whatever its faults may be, there is no book on Keats I would rather possess and keep by me on my shelves.

Mr. Murry has finally destroyed the romantic view of Keats as a lovely dreamer, an O'Shaughnessy poet, and with great discrimination traces his growth to the iron hardness of a great poet, to a Keats who, like his own Moneta, had pallor and immortal sickness in his face, but eyes shining with benignant light. "Beauty is truth, truth beauty," that is not a sloppy, evasive, non-adult utterance. It is of the same kind as "l'amor che move il sole e l'altre stelle," and the position is not easily achieved, only indeed through hell and purgatory. Keats had been through them, "following in the print of the beloved feet," not of Virgil, but of Shakespeare; but alas! it was not Beatrice who greeted him in his elusive paradise. Harsh, implacable thought, the thought of the body and of the heart as well as of the mind, had gone with him on his journey to the classical goal, but it is just here that Mr. Murry causes us to doubt, for at the very end he insists that Keats was a romantic, a "true romantic," so rigid is his refusal to abandon his own position. And it is not a mere matter of nomenclature. . . .

But to begin to take up the gauntlets Mr. Murry throws down so often would be to occupy a whole issue of this paper; it is that which helps to make the book so stimulating, for you cannot ignore them. Nevertheless, challenges apart, the book in its main lines is a sound and penetrative piece of work, even if it might be less redundant. For Mr. Murry has shown, without the shadow of a doubt, that in spirit and in act Keats is indeed not only with Shakespeare, but like him.

> Bonamy Dobrée, "Mr. Murry's Keats," in The Nation and the Athenaeum, *Vol. XXXVII, No. 26, September 26, 1925, p. 766.*

H. L. MENCKEN   (essay date 1930)

[*From the era of World War I until the early years of the Great Depression, Mencken was one of the most influential figures in American letters. His strongly individualistic, irreverent outlook on life and his vigorous, invective-charged writing style helped establish the iconoclastic spirit of the Jazz Age and significantly shaped the direction of American literature. As a social and literary critic—the roles for which he is best known—Mencken was the scourge of evangelical Christianity, public service organizations, literary censorship, boosterism, provincialism, democracy, all advocates of personal or social improvement, and every other facet of American life that he perceived as humbug. In his literary criticism, Mencken encouraged American writers to shun the anglophilic, moralistic bent of the nineteenth century and to practice realism, an artistic call-to-arms that is most fully developed in his essay "Puritanism as a Literary Force," one of the seminal essays in modern literary criticism. A man who was widely renowned or feared during his lifetime as a would-be destroyer of established American values, Mencken once wrote: "All of my work, barring a few obvious burlesques, is based upon three fundamental ideas. 1. That knowledge is better than ignorance; 2. That it is better to tell the truth than to lie; and 3. That it is better to be free than to be a slave." In the following excerpt from a review of* God: An Introduction to the Science of Meta-*

biology, Mencken rejects Murry's metaphysics, but finds his study, on the whole, to be an interesting and fresh reformulation of the belief that ideas represent a form of objective reality.*]

Mr. Murry will be recalled as the husband of the late Katherine Mansfield. Though he has since married again, her death seems to have been a staggering blow to him, and in this curious book he describes some of its consequences. For months, living alone in a remote Sussex cottage, he inhabited a world of shadows, seeing no one and lying under great depression of spirits. He thought of himself as completely solitary and forsaken; he found it quite impossible to relate himself to the lives of other people. Sitting one day before his fire, he became conscious of the feeling that he was "a little island against whose slender shores a cold, dark, boundless ocean lapped devouring." And then, of a sudden, came deliverance.

> The darkness of that ocean changed to light, the cold to warmth; it swept in one great wave over the shores and frontiers of myself, it bathed me and I was renewed; the room was filled with a presence, and I knew I was not alone— that I never could be alone any more, that the universe beyond held no menace, for I was part of it, that in some way for which I had sought in vain for so many years, I *belonged,* and because I belonged I was no longer I, but something different, which could never be afraid in the old ways or cowardly with the old cowardice. . . .

[Though Mr. Murry] seems to believe that he is an agnostic it is plain that he is really a mystic, and so he seeks an answer [to this experience] in the domain of metaphysics. In so far as I can make it out, it appears to be that ideas have a sort of objective reality—that what a man hopes for and dreams of is as real as what he is.

This, of course, is not new. Many men, in ancient and modern times, have argued for it, and most of us go through life on the assumption that it is true. But Mr. Murry, being more eloquent than most, gives it a certain air of newness [in **"God: An Introduction to the Science of Metabiology"**], and thus produces an interesting if somewhat chaotic book. His trouble, I suspect, is as I have hinted: he is religious without knowing it. Holy Church, if he could induce himself to yield to her embrace, could do a lot for him; as it is, his groping for light and leading leaves him palpably unhappy. But all the same his book is worth reading, for there is great frankness in it, and persons who are interested in the mental processes of Oxford intellectuals will find it very instructive.

> H. L. Mencken, "Confessional," in American Mercury, *Vol. XIX, No. 74, February, 1930, p. 255.*

G. K. CHESTERTON   (essay date 1933)

[*Regarded as one of England's premier men of letters during the first half of the twentieth century, Chesterton is best known today as a colorful bon vivant, a witty essayist, and creator of the Father Brown mysteries and the fantasy* The Man Who Was Thursday. *Much of Chesterton's work reveals his childlike joie de vivre and reflects his pronounced Anglican and, later, Roman Catholic beliefs. His essays are characterized by their humor, frequent use of paradox, and chatty, rambling structure. In the following excerpt from a favorable review of* William Blake, *Chesterton offers a succinct summary of Murry's most salient fault as a critic: "He yields too much to his beautiful gift of faith and religious devotion."*]

You will all be depressed to hear that I am going to talk about Mysticism. Mysticism is a mystery—it is a mystery to sceptics, because they do not understand it; it is a mystery to mystics, because they do. . . . [A recent] book curiously combines the two mysteries of the sceptic and the mystic—Mr. Middleton Murry's very valuable and stimulating *William Blake*. . . . Mr. Middleton Murry is himself both a sceptic and a mystic and in a rather peculiar way of his own. In this book he describes what we commonly call religion as idolatry. Oddly enough I myself feel, especially in his case, that it is the absence of religion that produces idolatry. Now if I say that he idolatrises William Blake I do not in the least mean that he admires William Blake too much. Nobody could admire William Blake too much—one does not admire Dante or Michelangelo too much, but only conceivably for the wrong reasons. I mean by idolatry something more dogmatic; I mean that Mr. Murry is so passionately pious—I might say so abjectly devotional—he has such an elemental appetite for religion, that he worships what he admires; that is, he worships it as an absolute and even as an origin. He says here that Blake was a good Communist, and it reminds me a little of the Communist view of Karl Marx. We know that cry from Moscow like the Muslim cry ringing through the world—the cry from Moscow: 'There is no God, and Marx is His prophet'. That is how he takes Blake in this book—not as the last prophet, not even as the best prophet, but as the first prophet, as if he had no background and no beginnings.

The book opens with some pages of very singular beauty and power about the direct effect of imagination and its real reality; how it clarifies all objects under a new light; and illustrates it by one of Blake's most perfect lyrics. It is a lyric about children, and perhaps it is right to begin with the very soul of childhood. But he says nothing at all about the childhood of Blake; for that matter he says nothing about the manhood of Blake save for an interesting theory about his marriage. In this book Blake starts out as a full-grown prophet like those great grey-bearded figures that Blake drew, each of them looking like the Ancient of Days. Blake is from the beginning; he is a primitive thing like Adam or even God. Now I may have a weakness for idolatry, but this is idolatry. What strikes me about Blake is that he was a mystic, and that he had the huge disadvantage of being a modern mystic—that is, he was a mystic ignorant of mysticism, or at least of the history of mysticism. Nobody, of course, could expect Mr. Murry to give the history of mysticism when he has not even room for the history of Blake. But there was a history of Blake, and, much more important, there was a place of Blake in history.

Mr. Murry hits the right nail on the head splendidly on one historical point. He insists on Blake's hatred of the Deists and the new scientific rationalists. He insists, of course, that Blake hated equally both the old theologies and the mere logic of the new rationalists. Logically, as two points marked on the blank map of Urizen, this is doubtless true; but historically, as of a human being, the things were very different. Blake knew all about the Age of Reason; he was a friend of pain, he lived in it, he loathed it. Blake knew nothing about the Ages of Faith—he might have loathed them, but, in many ways, he would have loved them. Both ages would probably have discouraged him from walking about naked in his garden and saying he was Adam, but in the Middle Ages he would really have found out that he was not the first man or the first mystic. And I

Portrait of Murry by William Rothenstein. The Tate Gallery, London.

think he would have been happier if he had lived with other mystics, for, with all respect to this great genius and essentially noble spirit, it seems to me obvious that Blake floundered through all the first fallacies and false simplifications to which generous youth is always tempted. We have the regular symptom of the young thinker saying 'There is no evil'; which invariably ends in his screaming aloud that the whole world is evil because it will not believe that there is no evil. . . .

So the passing and patronising allusions of Mr. Murry to orthodox religion make me laugh a little, for I can see for myself that Blake was blundering like a blind giant in a jungle for want of that very guidance which the old orthodox mystics could have given him. He did not know the old controversy about the Gnostics and the Manichees, and all kinds of things which I know, that Blake did not know, and which I rather suspect Mr. Middleton Murry does not know. To mention one point. I know not what moral theology ever stated what he incessantly repeats—Woman's love is sin. I think it was an effect of the stale and stuffy modern world in which Blake, and Middleton Murry, and myself, and everybody else, have to live. Anyhow, I am sure that Mr. Murry is wrong in beginning all philosophy with Blake, and all politics with Marx. He yields too much to his beautiful gift of faith and religious devotion.

G. K. Chesterton, "Prophets and Poets," in The
Listener, Vol. X, No. 249, October 18, 1933, p. 600.*

RAYNER HEPPENSTALL (essay date 1934)

[*Heppenstall was an English novelist, critic, and autobiographer who wrote extensively of his experiences with such literary figures as George Orwell and Dylan Thomas. As a literary theorist, Heppenstall is closely allied with the philosophy of the nouveau roman (New Novel or Anti-Novel), an antirealistic novel form developed in France during the 1950s. The New Novelists wanted the forms of their works to express their existential vision of a world without order or ultimate purpose, a world in which nothing can be fully known or understood. For this reason they broke up narrative sequence, avoided statements of moral purpose, treated material objects with the same meticulous attention given to characters by previous novelists, and gave characters no past or future because they held that a person can be known only as he or she exists in an isolated moment of time. Heppenstall's later novels demonstrate his allegiance to this school, and he has written perceptively on the New Novelists Alain Robbe-Grillet, Michel Butor, and Nathalie Sarraute. Heppenstall has been widely praised for the philosophical and theoretical complexity of his literary criticism. Heppenstall, who knew Murry during the 1930s through their mutual devotion to pacifist causes, wrote the first extended study of Murry's thought. In an unexcerpted portion of this study he offers the equation (Jesus + Shakespeare + Blake + Marx) × Murry = Good Modernity. In the following excerpt Heppenstall affirms Murry's development into a profoundly conscientious thinker and regards* The Necessity of Communism *as his most complete intellectual accomplishment.*]

I consider Murry not to have been ineluctably fated to literary practice. He has not, it seems to me, one of those unfortunate though often highly valuable minds which are forced into one or another of the arts by a process of exclusion of possibilities. It is my belief that, like another man, he might quite as successfully have practised law, divinity, statesmanship or naval command, though he might have found it difficult to live up to the ideals of dishonesty and servility which appear to obtain at present in these professions. In psychological terms, he shows, like the mere ordinary man, an extravert mind—one, that is, which flows outward into activity in the field which is prepared before him rather than feed on its own entrails. (pp. 19-20)

The strongly extraverted mind is rare in literature, especially at the present day. And, particularly in critical work, where introspective analysis of reactions plays so considerable a *rôle*, it will manifest certain clearly marked tendencies which seem alien to the craft and will in consequence be distrusted, but which, as they work out in Murry, are a warrant of that very integrity which they have on occasion been held to deny. To make this clearer I can quote and comment on a very serious criticism of Murry made—in a private letter, unfortunately—by one who knew him well and who is, and justly so, widely esteemed.

> The trouble with Murry is that he doesn't know what he doesn't know. The integrated man is completely confident about what he knows, but has an equally delicate realization of his ignorance. Murry literally doesn't sense, in his own being, the difference between certainty [a whole-man sensation] and belief [a mental persuasion subject to change].

This was a comment upon the term 'integrity', which I had used about Murry, and intends to prove it inapplicable. Ac-

tually, I not only accept the statement as being broadly true but maintain that it vindicates the term.

For, because of the constant check which introverted thought places on activity, the introvert can tolerate a temporary disintegrity, can cope patiently, that is, with the partial dislocation that comes of introducing into the configuration of his beliefs and certainties a new belief. . . . But the extraverted mind, in which thought is a function of activity and stubborn against unnecessary self-analytics, must respond with the whole man or not at all. A mind like Murry's will be slower to entertain new beliefs than an almost wholly introverted mind like Mr. T. S. Eliot's, but once entertained the new belief will secure such total response that it will indeed, as our text declares, be subjectively indistinguishable from certainty. Instead of a new attitude being accepted at the end of a long process of trial adjustments by the intellect, acceptance will come first, out of the whole man, will impose the new integration as it were convulsively, and the intellect will make its own adjustments subsequently. (pp. 20-2)

Horrid indiscretion as it may be to announce them thus, two unargued characteristics in Murry seem to me to follow from the above. One is the frequent inadequacy of his prose. The other is an occasional appearance of intellectual naivety. In reality these are a single characteristic. The best of Murry's prose attains increasingly to a lucidity in the management of difficult concepts which it would not be easy to match. But a certain absence of sustained self-consciousness permits sometimes the overworking of a set of phrases which, admirable at first and retaining their force doubtless for their author, come eventually to be a mere cumulative mechanism for the reader. Examples of this are the words 'jejune' and 'nugatory', which become at last mere terms of gentle reproach, and those two favourite syntactical forms, 'If . . . then . . .' and the equation of infinitives. And an uncritical assumption that the detail of a reader's experience in a given matter will be approximately the same as his own determines a frequent lack of concreteness in Murry's writing and allows him to proceed too quickly to generalization, in what sometimes seem on that account, by the omission of their actual solid basis of concrete detail, to be mere emotive gestures.

Hence also a certain lack of humour. I do not think that Murry is congenitally without a sense of humour. In fact I am sure he is not. But there is a certain evident distrust of wit and humour as critical instruments—a distrust which a great deal of current intellectual acrobatics more than justifies. In any case, Murry has recognized the characteristic, and the fundamentally humourless man hardly does that. (pp. 23-4)

These general criticisms of Murry are external to the purpose of this essay. I come to praise Murry, not to bury him. But since I do hold a far higher estimate of his work than is considered proper in my generation, since in fact I am going to be accused of uncritical adulation, I want to discount some reactions by indicating, to begin with, that my view is not due entirely to bad eyesight. I am, I must insist, aware of all that has been urged in condemnation of Murry's work, having spent more hours than I care to reckon in arguing to extinction or to a due placing one accusation after another—some of them made initially by myself. . . . The mainly significant fact, for me at least, is that Murry's thought represents the only contemporary intellectual atmosphere in which I find it possible to breathe at all deeply. This, and the feeling that, if I do any hard thinking myself during the next few years, Murry's is the thought with which I would most like my own to seem continuous.

Murry, in short, is one immeasurably antiseptic in his age. (pp. 24-5)

Man in society—man with his straight neck and his eyes turned outwards on the splendid turbulence of an indefeasible reality. Man who joined with his fellows to serve common ends and involved himself thus in increasing complexities of relationship. This is the thesis [once it was the synthesis]. Man in a realm of the intellect—man whose frustrated acts bend his neck and turn inward his eyes to make manageable patterns of what they have perceived in frustration. Man who segregates himself, finding illumination and joy within, proud with his new instrument of command, but finally disabling himself, in its intensive cultivation, for other uses. This is the antithesis. To reach a synthesis, man must negate the antithesis, which negates the thesis, by fulfilling both. And to envisage a synthesis, the individual man will endure the negation to its extreme and in that very process attain the point of supersession both of the negation and of what it negated. The intellectual sub-process will be a pressing to intolerable conclusiveness of the operations of the intellect and the perception therein of intellect's final impotence—that is, of the point at which dissolution is necessarily resolved into unity. This, I am maintaining, is essentially the pattern of Murry's work.

It is a movement outwards from the utmost inwrenching. Out from the individual tripes, it is a turning outward of eyes. And then out from the individual to the ideal mankind, from the ideal mankind to the function, from the function to the society, from the society to real mankind and the phenomenal world. And there alone can the individual breathe altogether other than intestinal airs. . . . His work never had to make the first outward movement, from the isolated individual to the ideal mankind. He starts there. But he had to perform, and has performed, the acts of extraversion which shift major concern, progressively—not in arithmetic, geometric, or harmonic but in organic progression—to function, society, real mankind, the phenomenal world. And certainly his truly significant work dates from

> A pressing to intolerable conclusiveness of the operations of the intellect and the perception therein of intellect's final impotence.

To leave and relieve this general plane of talk, call up two characteristic statements—separated in utterance by ten years.

> Art is autonomous, and to be pursued for its own sake, precisely because it comprehends the whole of human life. . . .

Excellent in many ways, and it is the only belief in which any art can be practised with an undivided loyalty. But it is equivocal and may—conveniently, perhaps, according to nothing more substantial than mood—imply simply a constriction of 'the whole of human life'. Later there is none of this ambiguity. Art is related to 'the whole of human life' organically, and the attitude shows greater concern with the detail of objective situations.

> The necessary condition of great art is that the artist should be able to take elemental things for granted . . . The artist to-day finds no spiritual authority which he instinctively acknowledges. If he acknowledges any it is the authority of Art itself, which is mere wordy nonsense. Art is not an authority, it is the means by which authority may be revealed and expressed. . . .

Contradiction? Not at all. A dialectical growth perhaps, but these are one assertion rendered in different modes. The first statement is from *Aspects of Literature,* the second from *Son of Woman.* Between the making of these two books Murry has gone through the whole strenuous movement outwards—indeed, and upward—from the ideal to the real. And this movement, together with its precondition, before *Aspects of Literature,* and its perfection, after *Son of Woman,* makes the pattern of work which is claimed here as essentially Murry's.

For the most inwrenched of all accepted activities is literary criticism. It is the characteristic activity of our time—even our 'creative' work being predominantly critical, of itself commonly. And Murry's first intellectual act was to exhaust the validities of literary criticism—or to exhaust himself temporarily in looking for them, which means the same. It is impossible to understand the constancy of this effort—of the great movement outwards—without reading consecutively *The Adelphi's* editorials. And I can only insist here on my own recurrently confirmed sense of it. (pp. 123-28)

[It is obvious], surely, not only that Murry had to become a Marxist but also what precisely his approach to Marx must be and furthermore how people afflicted according to the terms of our preliminary diagnosis must react thereto. The book *God* contains the whole of Marxism in solution. It must be fairly evident too that [*William Blake*] . . . had to be written—that the acceptance of Marxian thought and Marxian practice, preconditioned as it was in Murry, had to be completed by a full incorporation and giving out of the present revolutionary significance of that man who was both the purest poet and the most skilful metabiologist, the completest focus of traditional values and the least equivocal revolutionary, in all our history. [*The Necessity of Communism*] will have to be also a final testimony on valuable living, a final personal testimony altogether—and Murry will not go beyond it, whatever subsequently he writes: he can only elaborate and refine. (pp. 141-42)

> *Rayner Heppenstall, in his* Middleton Murry: A Study in Excellent Normality, *Jonathan Cape, 1934, 175 p.*

V. S. PRITCHETT   (essay date 1935)

[*Pritchett is a highly esteemed English novelist, short story writer, and critic. Considered one of the modern masters of the short story, he is also considered one of the world's most respected and well-read literary critics. Pritchett writes in the conversational tone of the familiar essay, a method by which he approaches literature from the viewpoint of a lettered but not overly scholarly reader. A twentieth-century successor to such early nineteenth-century essayist-critics as William Hazlitt and Charles Lamb, Pritchett employs much the same critical method: his own experience, judgment, and sense of literary art are emphasized, rather than a codified critical doctrine derived from a school of psychological or philosophical speculation. His criticism is often described as fair, reliable, and insightful. In the following excerpt, Pritchett offers an ambivalent review of Murry's autobiography,* Between Two Worlds. *Condemning the book's often romantic, histrionic tone, Pritchett nevertheless cites passages of fine descriptive or narrative quality.*]

["**Betweeen Two Worlds**"] will not be everybody's book and Mr. Murry is not everybody's man. One imagines the more devout disciples scrupulously treading from word to word "as by stepping stones of their dead selves" to the "higher things" indicated by Mr. Murry; and one pictures those who love literary scandals, skipping the agonies and apologia inevitable to unrestrained subjective biography, in search of further "low-down" on the Lawrences, Katherine Mansfield and all that group whose worried religion of personal relationships led them to live their private lives in public.

This extreme romanticism became a spiritual sensationalism—see the strange Dostoevsky phase in the early twenties—and, finally, sound and fury signifying nothing. In Lawrence the gold is mixed with an hysterical dross; in Mr. Murry a useful, critical talent has been stained with the histrionic and pretentious. Only Katherine Mansfield, cherishing her small, biting talent, seems to have had a suspicion that she was out of her depth.

But putting these controversies aside there is an aspect of **"Between Two Worlds"** which is worth thinking about. Although Mr. Murry has always tended to run about crying, "I have been saved," he is one of those critics who are good weathercocks for current tendency. Intensely self-centered, isolated and instinctively preserving his isolation by acting a part, he is an exaggeration of a new English type and the embodiment of a new social dilemma. Like hundreds of thousands of Englishmen who have sprung from the lower middle class which found its way to power after the Education Act of the nineteenth century, he is, in Matthew Arnold's words:

> Wandering between two worlds, one dead,
> The other powerless to be born. . . .

Mr. Murry's life story is an interesting psychological illustration of this theme and the earlier part of the book is very good indeed. He has, of course, the habit of escaping into dubious absolutes—"She was Life to me"—which give a feeling of unconscious insincerity even at the time of most mortifying confession. It is no doubt impossible for the intensely self-aware man to be completely sincere. But where Mr. Murry is objective, and particularly in the account of his childhood and his school days, he is stimulating and often delightful. His picture of a simple farming family in the Cotswolds, where he had gone from Oxford to read for a crucial examination, is excellent. He forgets his oppressive soul in an unselfed observation of other people. This, the least explanatory part of his book, is the most profound. . . . It required courage to write this book, but a great deal of the actor has gone into it, too.

> *V. S. Pritchett, "Mr. Murry Explains Himself," in*
> The Christian Science Monitor Weekly Magazine
> Section, *March 20, 1935, p. 12.*

CHARLES I. GLICKSBERG   (essay date 1939)

[*Glicksberg is a Polish-born American scholar who has written extensively on the interrelationship of literature with modern philosophy and contemporary social movements. In the following excerpt Glicksberg examines Murry's personality in relation to his work.*]

In his recently published autobiography [*Between Two Worlds*], Mr. Murry probes with painstaking honesty into the history of his past. Like Rousseau, he is determined to tell the truth about himself, even if the truth reveals him in a pitiful light. He is bent on a curious and fascinating quest: to glimpse the essential reality of an elusive, phantasmal, chameleon-like creature—himself. That quest, he realizes, is the task of every artist, whether he portray himself in fiction or verse, in drama or straightforward personal confession. Mr. Murry's unsparing candor of self-analysis, however, has been misunderstood and cruelly maligned. The weaknesses, the vices, the quirks and crotchets that all men possess in varying degrees, but which

few have the courage openly to betray—these have been hilariously satirized. What makes matters worse is Mr. Murry's brooding habit of introspection which magnifies every failing, however venial, into an absolute sin.

He is a dreamer and a thinker, but he is neither the one nor the other with any measure of completeness. Could he yield himself without conscious interference to the flow of fantasy, bathe like Keats in the warm, sun-glinting stream of sensations, he would develop into a fine poet. But his mind will give him no rest. It will pulse and dissect and hunt for the meaning of the unintelligible mystery. Consciousness is at war with intuition, the critic is at odds with the potential poet. From this conflict springs his obsession with intellectual mysticism, his distrust of logic, psychology, and the truths of science. A sensitive, highly trained intelligence is burdened with irrational beliefs and intuitive convictions that cannot stand the test of reason or empirical evidence.

Perhaps it is only those akin in some respects to Mr. Murry in temperament and outlook who can appreciate the peculiar character of the man. What the psychologists tell us about the defence-mechanism of the mind, its power of sublimating unendurable tensions and frustrations, can be applied to his case. His weaknesses have given him strength. (pp. 82-3)

His suggestibility, the plasticity of his character and mind, these are the traits that determined to a large extent the quality of his critical contribution. He was extraordinarily sensitive, faithful to the call of Beauty, his intelligence as receptive as a sponge. . . . [Even] in his theory of aesthetics, as in all of his writings, his personal perplexities come conspicuously to the surface. He is the most subjective of critics. Intellectual mysticism is his besetting sin; it lifts him to towering heights of ecstasy; it fills his homeless, disembodied soul with a renewed sense of cosmic identity. He calls it a kind of private drug-taking, and that describes it accurately. "I was," he confesses, "and am, the kind of fool who always has to believe in somebody or something." An extreme introvert, he exploits criticism as a form of emotional self-realization. Though he wrote some creditable poetry, though he was smitten with the ambition to become a novelist and actually wrote and published three novels, he soon felt, in the stress of creative experience, that he was not born to be either a novelist or a poet. It was Lawrence who, at the start of their passionate but ill-starred friendship, told him the truth about himself: "You must stick to criticism." He has followed that advice.

The history of a sensitive and inquiring mind is also the history of a generation. Even its aberrations, its mystical excesses, are significant. Like symptoms that point to the presence of disease, they indicate the existence of strain, the degree of emotional pressure. In one respect, the nonconformist is, by sheer force of contrast, more revealing than his more "normal" contemporaries. The rebel attracts attention to himself by virtue of his negations. His protests testify to the existence of real or imaginary abuses. He holds up a mirror—it may, of course, be cracked—to the face of nature in his time. He moves us by dint of his opposition to many issues and beliefs which have been complacently accepted as final and beyond question. Such opposition can be sustained consistently only by a profound singleness of faith, by a temperament, mystical, clairvoyant, and consecrated, such as Mr. Murry possesses. It takes rare courage to stand, solitary and steadfast, against a concerted majority.

Mr. Murry is a tangle of unresolved contradictions. He is and is not, of this age. He is a realist and a mystic, a mind too self-conscious to write spontaneously; a mind too intuitive and spirit-haunted to write dispassionate criticism. He objects, for instance, to the Sexual Mysticism of D. H. Lawrence; he himself imports a brand that is far more lunar and abstract. Despite his fondness for luminous abstractions like Eternity and the Divine Vision and the annihilation of Self, it is evident that he has not won the serene certitude of faith. He is doomed by his own nature to suffer the torments of ceaseless doubt. In the midst of his most poignant utterance of belief, the devil will tempt him. He is the doubting Thomas of contemporary English criticism—a doubting Thomas with a messianic, Christ-complex. He doubts his doubts, he questions the validity of his visions. He humbles himself before God, and then, after denying Him, asserts that the denial, the resistance to God, is part of Man's painful and necessary climb to human Godhood.

Thus Mr. Murry's progress has been a littered trail of extinctions and revivals, of destruction and renewal, of death and the resurrection, of blindness transformed to dazzling vision. He has passed from one crisis to another: from the pure and exclusive worship of sensuous Beauty to that search of God which is the annihilation of Self, and from there to the reconciliation of his spiritual creed with messianic Marxism. He has made a cult of doubt and pain, of love and self-annihilation. (pp. 83-5)

Mr. Murry's work affords a vigorous refutation of the theory that criticism is a parasitic and obsolescent occupation. For in literature he finds not books but men who communicate a deeper insight into life. He looks for essences, for that which is enduringly significant. It is a testimony to the vitality of his criticism that the essays he contributed to various periodicals and reprinted in *Aspects of Literature,* have worn so well. (p. 86)

Mr. Murry presents an enigmatic and somewhat hysterical personality because he takes his mysticism with such deadly seriousness. The critical vagaries induced by extreme personal suffering or great inner need he treats as authentic revelations, oracular intuitions of the inscrutable mystery inherent in the universe. This would be ridiculous if it were altogether naïve, but it is rendered plausible and interesting by virtue of his gift of dramatizing his inner conflicts. When he looks back in calm retrospection at the strange spiritual experiences he has undergone, he is able to temper them with a touch of skepticism, keep them within bounds by applying the brake of reason and common sense, though he at no time repudiates them. Yet it is obvious that he is hopelessly committed to mysticism. It is in his blood. At heart he is a Christian turned transcendentalist, a religious mystic whose Church is Beauty and whose Bible is a kind of aesthetic humanism. Unable to employ the figurative language of the established Church—though he frequently falls back upon the Bible for quotations—he plays variations on terms like Beauty, Humanity, the higher consciousness, superior truth, organic unity, depersonalization, disinterestedness.

And his criticism is a mystical act of affirmation, the testimony of the Holy Ghost. His work is all of a piece—a brilliant intellectual autobiography, but it is intellectual autobiography with emotional emphases and subjective impulsions of a peculiar quality. He does not hold himself back. At all time he is the prophet, the seeker, the spiritual crusader. The Absolute or nothing—that might very well be the motto emblazoned on the shield of this St. George. He is prone to passionate enthusiasms, paroxysms of faith, intense emotional upheavals. But it is the malady of intensity that it can live only in the moment; like life's candle it burns brightly but briefly. The next moment

it is extinguished. So Mr. Murry sways from heights of ecstasy to the pits of despair, from spiritual intoxication to moods of self-disgust, from puissant strength to virtual exhaustion. The seeker after the Absolute periodically suffers a decline into blank disillusionment; then his heady visions seem the snares of Satan, a product of hallucination. When this happens, he is driven to seek a new source of intoxication, a new faith. To preserve his ideal inviolate, he must like Mr. Murry cast out the devils of logic and science. Even the elementary canons of consistency must be sacrificed. He strives to be honest on higher grounds; he calls in the aid of Intuition. So that if Mr. Murry's critical ideas and ideals—his passions and obsessions—are held in judgment and found to be false, what is left but a quivering sensitivity, an earnest mind—the copious recording of an eager and gifted impressionist? (pp. 98-9)

Charles I. Glicksberg, "John Middleton Murry: Christ among the Critics," in South Atlantic Quarterly, *Vol. XXXVIII, No. 1, January, 1939, pp. 82-99.*

CHARLES WILLIAMS   (essay date 1941)

[Williams was a writer of supernatural fiction, a poet whose best works treat the legends of Logres (Arthurian Britain), and one of the central figures among the literary group known as the Oxford Christians, or "Inklings." The religious, the magical, and the mythical are recurrent concerns in his works, reflecting his devout Anglicanism and lifelong interest in all aspects of the preternatural. Although his works are not today as well known as those of his fellow-Inklings C. S. Lewis and J. R. R. Tolkien, Williams was an important source of encouragement and influence among the group. In the following excerpt from a review of The Betrayal of Christ by the Churches, *Williams, though admitting disagreement with some of Murry's thought, emphasizes his importance as a reformer of the Christian Church.]*

Mr. Middleton Murry belongs to the age-long school of the great reformers, those who rebuke the Christian bodies for their weakness and denounce them for their worldliness. They are found in all ages, and in all places, from the gutter to the Holy See; they are an absolute necessity to the Church, and it is perhaps only by their virtue that the gates of hell shall not prevail. They are always right, but they are at the same time frequently in error.

So, I think, with Mr. Murry. What he says [in *The Betrayal of Christ by the Churches*] is so important to our souls that we ought to listen, and profoundly as I at times disagree with him, it is necessary that the passionate recurrence in him of the ancient call to repentance should be properly heard. Much of what he says in detail is accurate, and practically all that he says about the tendency of the influential members of the Christian Church to ally themselves with secular force and secular fashion. (pp. 127-28)

Mr. Murry is not only one of the reformers, he is one of the spirituals. He holds that the "desire for the experience of inward assurance of the divine grace, as distinct from the acceptance of the assurance given by the supernatural authority of the Church . . . marked an advance from magical towards spiritual religion". But why is it more "spiritual" to desire personal assurance than to receive that assurance through others? To desire that God shall communicate directly rather than indirectly? Men were one; they learnt from each other; they lived from each other: why is that web of souls less spiritual than one soul?

A similar repudiation marks Mr. Murry's writing on the Resurrection. He will not have a "physical resurrection"—not for us and not, it seems, for our Lord. But this is to deny that matter can be redeemed. It is no more easy to believe in this than Mr. Murry finds it to believe "all the time" in a spiritual body. But that the great harmonious flesh shall be part of our celestial joy is surely rooted in the Nature of Our Lord. Our sufferings in the flesh are united with His, in the holy and glorious flesh which the perverted soul has dragged down with it. "The means of grace and the hope of glory" are in our bodies also, and the name of them is love.

It is perhaps unfair to demur to such proposals in a book whose main energy is evangelical. I think Mr. Murry too much limits the Christian idea. But I agree wholly that without repentance and passion we shall (humanly speaking) lose the Christian idea. (pp. 128-29)

> *Charles Williams, in a review of "The Betrayal of Christ by the Churches," in* Dublin Review, *Vol. 208, No. 416, first quarter, 1941, pp. 127-29.*

T. S. ELIOT   (essay date 1959)

[*In the following excerpt from his foreword to Murry's* Katherine Mansfield, and Other Literary Studies, *Eliot discusses Murry's unique, introspective form of criticism.*]

I am not in every respect the person best qualified to introduce [**Katherine Mansfield, and Other Literary Studies**]. The three essays here posthumously published are studies of three writers of prose fiction. With the exception of one article and two prefaces, and a very few pieces of literary journalism which remain uncollected, I have never attempted criticism of prose fiction: it follows that I have no special competence to criticise criticism of prose fiction. It is, therefore, of Middleton Murry as a literary critic in general that I shall speak; and I shall try to indicate the kind of literary criticism that he practised, and to indicate his eminence—I might say solitary eminence—in this kind of criticism in my generation.

There are several kinds of literary critic: I think that the most important distinction is between the writer whose criticism is a by-product of his creative activity, and the writer whose criticism is itself his creative act. . . . [Middleton Murry] was a literary critic first and foremost. He had published poems, a verse play and several novels; and had achieved no great success in any of these forms. His originality—and he had indeed an original mind—went into his criticism, a kind of criticism which, in exploring the mind and soul of some creative writer, explored his own mind and soul also. His compositions in verse and in prose fiction may I think be ignored, except for the curious light they throw here and there upon the author; and his other writings, those concerned directly with theological, social or political matter, should be considered as by-products of a mind of which the primary activity was literary criticism. (pp. vii-viii)

[Murry] proved from the start of the new *Athenaeum* to be a first-rate editor: and it seems to me that the period when we had both *The Times Literary Supplement* under Richmond and *The Athenaeum* under Murry (we had also for a time *Art and Letters* and *The Calendar*) was the high summer of literary journalism in London in my lifetime. To be a good editor requires a certain humility and tolerance as well as a positive personality: for the editor himself must give his paper its coherence and its purpose, while allowing the greatest possible freedom, within the limits of sanity and good taste, to his chosen contributors. And it is more difficult still to be a good editor when a man has, as Murry had, the vocation to be a literary critic himself.

A similar combination of contrasted qualities made Murry the kind of critic that he was. He could immerse himself in the work of one or another author the study of whose writings responded to his own need, and in so doing reveal his own mind. (pp. ix-x)

Readers unfamiliar with the scope of his criticism may associate Murry as a critic with his studies of Dostoievsky or of Keats, and, among contemporaries, with D. H. Lawrence and Katherine Mansfield, and may think of his mind as parasitic upon the minds of certain authors whose work he would have liked to emulate. Such a judgment, apart from its misunderstanding of the critical mind in general, would ignore the diversity of subject matter which Murry could appreciate and of authors whose merits he could recognise. (pp. x-xi)

[Critics] of literature of the kind to which Middleton Murry belonged are among the rarest. The three writers [Mansfield, George Gissing, and Henry Williamson], essays on whom compose this book, have all their own importance: but they are also important to us because they were important to Murry, and because we are interested in what happened to Murry's mind and sensibility when they came in contact with literature that he found important. (pp. xi-xii)

> *T. S. Eliot, in a foreword to* Katherine Mansfield, and Other Literary Studies *by J. Middleton Murry, edited by Mary Middleton Murry, Constable, 1959, pp. vii-xii.*

F. A. LEA   (essay date 1959)

[*Lea wrote the first comprehensive biographical study of Murry. In the following excerpt from that study, Lea examines* Heaven—And Earth, *calling it Murry's greatest work.*]

Of the twelve studies composing **Heaven—And Earth,** only those of Chaucer, Milton and Wordsworth were entirely new. Earlier versions of '**Goethe**' and '**Morris**' had appeared in 1932, of '**Montaigne**' in 1933, '**Rousseau**', '**Godwin**', '**Shelley**' and '**Marx**' in 1934, '**Shakespeare**' in 1936. Originally, in fact, it was conceived as a sequel to *Countries of the Mind*—and individually these studies are at least as penetrating as any in the earlier volumes. But, by selecting only such figures as had been more or less consciously involved in the social changes of their day, Murry was able to achieve something more than a series of individual portraits. His purpose, in drastically re-handling the earlier material, was not merely to throw fresh light on the men by setting them in their historical context, but to throw fresh light on the context by showing how it had been actually experienced by men of prophetic insight.

The result was a work that gave the utmost scope to his distinctive gift—a work which, whether classified as biography or history, is as impressive as it is original. For no one but he could have made so intimately his own the contrasting viewpoints of Marx and Godwin, Morris and Goethe; and only a mind thereby 'habituated to work simultaneously on many different levels—on three, certainly—on the economic, on the political and on the moral; and I am impelled to add a fourth— namely the religious' could have acquired so comprehensive a vision of the period.

What is implicit, moreover, is as usual explicit. For instance, 'There is more than one revelation of the truth,' he writes: 'My own conviction is that we need, above all to-day, the imagination to see how and where the different revelations correct, complete and fructify one another.' And the emergence of such an imagination—contemplative in Shakespeare, 'the prophetic soul of the wide world dreaming on things to come'; militant in Cromwell, the soldier of toleration, speculative in Rousseau, the philosopher of democracy—is the actual theme of the book. This, and its steady endeavour to embody itself in a society, constituted, in Murry's eyes, the 'meaning' of the past four centuries, of Renaissance, Reformation and Revolution.

Heaven—And Earth challenges comparison with *Heroes and Hero-Worship*. It is not merely that several of Murry's heroes—Shakespeare, Goethe, Cromwell, Rousseau—happen to be the same as Carlyle's. Like Carlyle, he is keenly conscious of what has been lost, as well as gained, in these centuries: the sense of collective responsibility fostered by the village commune, the personal relationship between men, the communion of a common faith—all sacrificed to individualism, economic, political and religious. Like Carlyle, he foretells the nemesis of individualism; and, like him, he looks forward to a new ecumenical society combining freedom of conscience with social responsibility. Yet, of the two books, *Heaven—And Earth* is the richer. More lines of thought are gathered together, more vistas opened up by it. And what it lacks in literary genius it makes up for in political insight, since, unlike Carlyle, Murry really understood Rousseau, and understanding him, could see in democracy itself the germ of the new society.

He himself thought the study of Rousseau the best in the book. Certainly one has only to set it beside the essay in *Aspects of Literature* to realize how greatly his political preoccupation had deepened his understanding. (pp. 252-53)

In Rousseau he recognized the creative counterpart to Marx. As Marx had shown what disaster must overtake a society whose economic activity was abandoned to the play of self-interest, Rousseau had shown what was needed if that disaster was to be forestalled: namely, a voluntary acceptance, by every citizen, of such restraints as were necessary to promote the well-being of each—in other words, a conscious endeavour to convert the secular collective into a 'religious' brotherhood. This being Murry's own central idea, the persistent theme of his life, it is not surprising that he bit straight to the core of the *Contrat Social,* as few political philosophers have done. His 'Rousseau' may be regarded as the germ of both his succeeding books, *The Price of Leadership* and *The Defence of Democracy.*

These, like *Heaven—And Earth,* incorporated earlier material: lectures and articles (including **'The Purgation of Christianity'**) in the one case, the critique of Marxism in the other. But both grew under his hands into expositions of this 'Idea' of democracy as 'a Christian political society'. *The Price of Leadership* is Murry's *Emile,* its point of departure being a consideration of the role of education in such a society. Like other Socialists, he was opposed to the dual educational system, more rigid then than now, which resulted in a ruling-class recruited on a basis of wealth and inherently biassed against any Left Wing legislation. Where he differed from many others was in clearly acknowledging the necessity of a functional ruling-class, and of its being reared in an ethos of responsibility to society as a whole. Product as he himself was alike of Rolles Road and Christ's Hospital, he whole-heartedly approved of the precedence accorded in the English public schools to 'char-

acter', rather than learning. The failure of Socialists to reaffirm this was a long-standing grievance of his. What was new was his insistence on the need for an explicitly Christian ethos and on the vocation of the Church to provide it.

In both books, the 'Idea' is developed with a wealth of historical illustration and practical proposals (some of which have since been adopted); in both, of course, he dwells lovingly on the opportunities confronting the country parson as 'the instructed guardian of a system of social relations which are concrete and personal instead of abstract and impersonal'. Essential to his standpoint was the view that the secular institution of the Church and the religious institution of democracy, to the extent that they realized their common aim of constitution fraternal societies, were destined to converge and finally amalgamate. If 'many lines of real creative thinking—the thinking, not of the mere intelligence, but of the total being, which is the prerogative of creative and prophetic genius—converged to bring *The Social Contract* to birth', hardly less can be said of *The Defence of Democracy.* Indeed, re-reading these books after an interval of twenty years, one finds it hard to believe that, even at that date, there were still pundits who thought of Murry, if they thought of him at all, as a literary critic who had missed his way. Give a dog a *good* name and hang it. Even so, it may be admitted that the best parts of *The Price of Leadership* itself are those devoted to the elucidation of Coleridge and Arnold—Murry's two earliest heroes, with whom, by virtue of a genuine affinity, he had now linked hands again. However much we may regret that other literary critics do not miss their way to the same good purpose as these three, there is no doubt that it was as an interpreter that his talent approximated to genius. Neither *The Price of Leadership* nor *The Defence of Democracy* is as fine or fertile a work as *Heaven—And Earth.* This is Murry's greatest work, and intrinsically it is great. If he had written nothing else but this, he would still have deserved well of the Commonwealth. (pp. 253-55)

F. A. Lea, in his The Life of John Middleton Murry, *Methuen & Co. Ltd., 1959, 378 p.*

R. J. KAUFMANN   (essay date 1960)

[*In the following excerpt, Kaufmann explores Murry's merits and deficiencies as a critic, concluding that Murry's obsessive nature is an asset to his work.*]

John Middleton Murry, three years dead to the flesh he wore so equivocally, had in his critical reputation died long before to all but a loyal remnant of his once enthusiastic following. His books continued to sell, but not evidently to literary people. Yet he is a gifted critic of literature and a wide-ranging and prolific one. It will be sad if the uninhibited journalistic excursions in favor of human survival, love, community and other commendable but critically unfruitful topics which obsessed his later life are permitted to bury this capable critic. It will be even sadder if we fail to see that the very human qualities which led him into salvational postures and to a very superior brand of apocalyptic rhetoric are what empower his criticism as well. Only the proportions are different. The unfashionable ardor for imaginative power, for energy, which he displays from his earliest work, his willingness to "have trusted experience even when it led me to strange conclusions" *(Evolution of an Intellectual)* probably deserve the label he himself applied to his last collection of literary work, *Unprofessional Essays. . . .* But, I take it, this "unprofessionalism" is neither a badge of defiant honor nor of shame; it is a way of differentiating work done *con amore,* responsively, and in the interest of a cause other than that of literature as an academic discipline from that which sees literature as an ultimate category.

From his first major book, ***Dostoevsky*** . . . , through his work on Lawrence, Keats, Shakespeare, Blake, Swift and Schweitzer (among a small army of others), Murry has projected a vision both humane and special. It takes some tactful analysis to read the prescription of his somewhat astigmatic critical lens. We imitate his striking description of Stendhal as a "dessicated Shakespeare" and call him a "mild and verbose El Greco." In each case the description is meant to put the man in the right company without over-valuing him. In making a case for Murry as a critic it is crucial not to assert too much; he lacks both the conviction and the fact of greatness, but he is a *good* critic of writers concerned to find some place for valid moral assertion in the equation of human life. It is because of this prejudice for the moral that his criticism has been suspect to us modern critics with our formalistic allegiance. Alongside our priestly exactitude, he seems amateur.

Yet it is hard to draw a clean line between the amateur and the professional in literary criticism unless one is willing to fall back upon crass dogmatizing. How is it that a man who spends his life reading good books critically and writing daily about them is an amateur while his counterpart in the academy who spends his holidays and summers writing about books is a professional? It takes a Boileau to uphold the claims of the latter, and surely in the limitless professionalism of a Wimsatt or a Wellek few can have missed the amateurish uncertainty about the effect being created. One often feels that professionalism in modern criticism has a dangerous alliance not with vital learning, nor even with that perspicuous humility before excellence we call responsive intelligence, but with the willingness *"ériger en lois ses impressions personnelles"* in a way that puts all the emphasis on the maintenance of the grand edifice of erected laws while erasing as thoroughly as possible the humble origins of all this grandeur in the sensitive and hopeful self. It seems that the act of contrition which authenticates professionalism is a denial of these *necessary* personal impressions, a sly wiggling out of the egocentric predicament of the responsible critic. (pp. 4-5)

[The] peculiar nature of John Middleton Murry's critical program . . . may be succinctly described as romantic literalism or definitive romantic orthodoxy. Because Murry lived his life in the interests of intensely personal realizations in such an utterly public, not to say doctrinaire, way we are liable to lose him as a critic of rare sensitivity and style. It is too easy to score him off with a knowing phrase as a "great lovable, pointless booby" (Hilary Corke), or as "a good literary critic who went wrong" (Murry himself), and hence excuse ourselves from being critical. Perhaps there is something in the routine constitution of the academic literary critic which makes enthusiasm, self-indulgence and a belief in the moral consequences of art intrinsically repellent? Fortunately, we needn't answer this question. However, we may be sure that Murry has been largely rejected in our timid, formalistic time for exercising an Arnoldian option, asserting that criticism "should openly accept the fact that its deepest judgments are moral" *(Countries of the Mind),* and that "art is the consciousness of life" *(Aspects of Literature).* Furthermore, it is hard not to believe that T. S. Eliot had Murry in mind when he said in the famous introduction to *The Sacred Wood* in 1920, "The temptation, to any man who is interested in ideas and primarily

in literature, to put literature into the corner until he cleaned up the whole country first, is almost irresistible." The special quality of Murry is explicated by this statement. He did in a sense succumb to this temptation, but literature was his instrument, the broom he wielded against the disorder of his time. (pp. 5-6)

There are clearly two equally strong currents of literary response to the repeated traumata of our time: one shows artists sticking to their lasts with Yeatsian tragic gaiety or Joycean dedication; the other shows Stendhalian openness to cultural stimuli, and characteristically it blurs traditional genre lines in pursuit of means to encompass imaginatively the fullest possible quotient of new experience. In practical terms this means: a man of great gifts for the novel descended to a cultural essayist (Forster); a religious essayist become a novelist (Aldous Huxley); a writer of private and sonnet-length lyric insight writing everything but poetry (Virginia Woolf); and book after book of serious public commentary approaching the autobiography as a limit. Murry has perhaps been truer to the Rousseau tradition to which he belongs than he admits, for with these—with the Bunyans, the Blakes, the Carlyles, the William Morrises—literature is fervently cherished beyond duty, but her lovers must use her. Indeed, they do love her, because through her they can deal with life; their loving attentions to art are jealously ulterior. One could say only half facetiously that Middleton Murry was a man of Boswellian fluidity and dependency ("I really was something infinitely plastic and suggestible with no determined character"; ***Between Two Worlds***) with the spiritual preferences of a Blake who yet thought he was like Keats. Not so strangely, this brought him (after Dostoevsky, Lawrence and Stendhal) right to Shakespeare in his vain attempt to grasp the tragic despite a personality irreducibly allergic to tragic convictions. Murry's point of view is (depending on our temporary angle of vision) too naive, too religious, or too optimistic to find the tragic vision acceptable.

Much of Murry's best writing arises from the productive strife between the well-observed suffering of his generation conjoined to his own extended subjection to radical loss, and his own almost embarrassingly positive, on-going temperament. One sees clearly in him the difference between the experience of suffering as a thing undergone and as a thing retained in the memory. Too ready a talent for survival, too remarkable a spiritual resilience arouses suspicions of selfishness and spiritual frivolity. I think clearly Murry worried about this tendency to the point of moral hypochondria. . . . Murry *is* naive (as Joan of Arc is naive), he *is* a hero worshipper, he *is* too much an enthusiast to create art unaided, so he strikes up a kind of critical marriage with classic authors in which he, quite self-consciously, plays the *anima* role to their *animus.*

The limit on the value of his criticism is that he brought a far more positive set of attitudes to this relationship than he supposed. His own predispositions, which the critic "ought to be aware of and alert to prevent from running away with him" *(Countries of the Mind),* are transparent and ignored. Just at those points where his criticism must otherwise be taken most seriously, Murry's resurgent optimism obscures that quality which Yeats named most crucial in Dante and Villon when he said, "had they lacked their Vision of Evil, had they cherished any species of optimism, they could but have found a false beauty . . . and suffered no change at all." *(The Trembling of the Veil)*

It is most probable then that Murry went finally to Shakespeare for moral ballast; with Shakespeare he could dare to imagine the things his intellect demanded the world include but which his ''characterless'' being seemed incapable of holding. One of the most profound of all Murry's statements helps us fuse this need for Shakespeare with our other key perceptions of Murry's nature. The remark stands as a kind of thesis for his last important book, *Love, Freedom, and Society* . . . : ''too many things which were once and are still incredible have been real. In order to live, we dare not imagine.'' This is not a remark an artist finally can assent to. Murry saw this in himself: ''Never, I believe, was there a man less avid of new experience than I . . . my one desire is to be left undisturbed.'' *(Between Two Worlds)* Yet there was in him as well an extra-artistic desire to know definitive and ideal truths along with the intellectual realization that to get to those truths one must be ''consumed by the fire.'' Murry's ulterior employment of Shakespeare is thus schematically displayed: Shakespeare can be for him, as *Lear* was for Keats, the place where one earns his Phoenix wings to fly at his desire.

Perhaps Murry's reading of Shakespeare is simply more honest, not more amateur, than that of most of his equally or less gifted contemporaries. It is no accident that in his journal, *The New Adelphi*, Murry gave G. Wilson Knight his start as the most original of all modern Shakespeare critics, exerting upon him a critical influence of a force and extent yet undetermined. . . . [Yet] Murry was, in Santayana's phrase, a ''transcendental reader,'' for he read ''to find out what he was thinking himself.'' Hence as a Shakespearean critic, his interest in the material and his command of it is uneven.

His misreading of *Othello* could have been predicted because Murry's romanticism simply cannot credit the possibility that a man's will could even momentarily concur in the murder of one he truly loves. Hence the play seems to him an uncomprehended victimization of Othello. Surely there are few stranger sentences in Shakespeare criticism than his ''The love of Othello and Desdemona is in itself unclouded.'' *(Countries of the Mind)* This is a strange platonizing remark and out of touch with tragedy which, do what he would, seemed a finally unreal aberration to Murry's temperament.

But if *Othello* is thus reduced, Murry's rejection of the preeminence of *Lear* among Shakespeare's tragedies and his early and subtle appreciation of *Coriolanus* are yet to be answered adequately in the first instance and appreciated in the second. His book on Shakespeare is genuinely a total response. I know of few works confidently unprofessional enough to have managed this. Finally (and this is a most reluctant admission on my part), the advantage of an unprofessional critic (notice we've abandoned ''amateur'' as contaminated) over the professional is that Murry at his best doesn't deal in answers, and he can rest comfortably before the fact of a mystery at the heart of tragic discourse—something professionals always wish to account for.

In the context of modern critical discourse and without being religious oneself, it seems strange to say that Murry gained peace from Shakespeare and that such a result is a valid consequence of critical application. Reading Shakespeare, he could see a possible and persuasive relationship ''between spiritual experiences and natural realities'' of which he admitted ''to have no clear conception'' and which he had never been ''convinced anybody else has either.'' *(Love, Freedom, and Society)* It is this sense of inclusive relationship in Shakespeare which provides for Murry the final affirmative sense that ''Mysteriously, the failure of the good is not the waste of the good.'' *(Love, Freedom, and Society)* Metaphysically this insight is

merely a beneficent illusion but still it has the human necessity recognized by Nietzsche's great dictum: ''We have art in order not to die of the truth.'' Watching Murry use literature humanely and morally, it is hard not to believe in the critical utility of a few unprofessional obsessions. (pp. 6-8)

> R. J. Kaufmann, ''On Using an Obsessed Critic: John Middleton Murry,'' in The Graduate Student of English, *Vol. III, No. 2, Winter, 1960, pp. 4-8.*

J. B. BEER (essay date 1961)

[*An English scholar, Beer has written widely on the English Romantic poets, with a particular interest in recent years in the examination by nineteenth-century writers of the concept of the unconscious. In the following excerpt, Beer measures Murry's stature as a critic by comparing Murry with other literary figures of his time: T. S. Eliot, D. H. Lawrence, and I. A. Richards.*]

'The trouble with these people in the Thirties is that they all took themselves so *seriously!*'

It is perhaps the commonest criticism. After Belsen, after Hiroshima, we take ourselves off, cannily and pennywisely, to our little burrows by the riverside, hoping that the tidal wave will not come *this* year. After what we have seen, we distrust people who take themselves too seriously.

No wonder then that we find difficulty in coming to terms with John Middleton Murry. For if Murry held one belief strongly, it was the belief that his own life and experience mattered tremendously—so much so that he was willing to expose the most intimate and trivial details in print and even go on recounting particular experiences in successive books if they seemed important enough to him.

Thus exposed, the man invited the love and hatred which he received—very often in the form of love followed by hatred when his undoubted charm was found to mask a curious inflexibility of inward character. Yet the attacks on him were usually clumsy. Huxley's Burlap, the most damaging so far as the general reader is concerned, was amusing but inaccurate. Lawrence's 'Jimmy and the Desperate Woman' was made harsh by personal pique. As for Hugh Gordon Porteous's phrase 'a sanctimonious humbug'—which he repeated proudly only the other day—that catches at a mannerism of style only to miss everything that was unsanctimonious and sincere in the man. (p. 59)

Murry, like Lawrence, was desperately in earnest, yet he also represented many of the things that Lawrence had turned away from. It is this fact that makes the relationship between the men, living and debating in close proximity during the First World War, an important moment in the development of literary thought, reminiscent of the equally seminal discussions between Wordsworth and Coleridge during an earlier European conflict. Murry himself later decided that there had been more to be said for Lawrence's views than he had acknowledged at the time, and felt that each had underestimated the strength of the other's position. He characterized the differences between them as those between a 'pre-mental' and a 'post-mental' personality. The accuracy of his diagnosis may be acknowledged. Lawrence, moving away from the dominance of his mother and now appalled by the clash of two inflexible European wills in war, had revolted against both will and sensibility, reverting to a trust in animal instinct and animal spontaneity. Murry, on the other hand, his highly-developed sensibility strained both by the slaughter of his generation and by his intense relationship with Katherine Mansfield, lapsed forward into a despairing state in which it seemed to him that the highest developed form of the personal was the impersonal. (In later life he acknowledged that, as with Lawrence, his upbringing might have had to do with some aspects of his character.)

But the difference between the two men can be placed in more common terms—it was the difference between the wild and the over-civilized. Lawrence himself put the issue perfectly when he wrote, concerning the Murrys' dislike of northern Cornwall. 'They should have a soft valley, with leaves and the ring-dove cooing. And this is a hillside of rocks and magpies and foxes.' (pp. 59-60)

If one were looking for the true and unyielding opponent to Lawrence, one would find him in T. S. Eliot. Here, as with Murry, the highly-trained sensibility lapses towards despair— the despair of *The Waste Land.* (pp. 60-1)

In order to try and seize [Murry's] distinction as a critic, we may employ a loose parallel. In much the same way that Eliot and Lawrence embody the polarity of literary attitudes in the early part of this century, Blake and Wordsworth embodied that polarity at the turn of the nineteenth century. Drawn by both Lawrence and Eliot, yet lacking the singleness of either, Murry reminds one of the later Coleridge. Coleridge revered the single-mindedness of Wordsworth, yet it was on the rare occasions when he met Blake that he talked like an angel. The parallel may be pressed. Each writer was possessed of an extraordinarily highly-developed sensibility, which made him excel in the sort of criticism that relies upon sympathy with the writer under discussion. And with Murry, as with the later Coleridge, passive sensibility was cultivated to a point where it imprisoned him and throttled his active development, leaving only a galaxy of related but unintegrated insights. The difference is that Murry came in at the end of the cult of sensibility, whereas Coleridge and Keats came in on the full tide. Small wonder that he regarded Keats as the last English poet, the poet who shows why poetry cannot any longer be written. (pp. 61-2)

Murry did not achieve greatness. His style was always uneasy. It lacked the urgent vitality of Lawrence's writing: it lacked also the cool polish of Eliot's. Sometimes he would make his sentences creak with 'nays' and 'verilys'; sometimes he would stoop to the inurbane paradoxes and journalistic mannerisms of Chesterton. His egotism could be tiresome, as when, in *The Adelphi,* he followed a poem which he was praising by a discussion beginning, 'Well, well . . .' At times, too, in spite of his negative capability, a personal opinion would lead to a restricted grasp of his subject. He suggested, for example, that Wordsworth and Coleridge were progenitors of the Oxford Movement, without, apparently, seeing that the aesthetic appeal of the past was only a secondary and later impulse in that movement. Actually, its intellectual basis was a reaction against the sort of liberalism that Coleridge preached—Newman even said so explicitly. But Murry was perhaps too near Coleridge's position to see this. Similarly, he could perceive the revolutionary change which came over Blake's work in the year 1788 and infer some extraordinary experience as the cause: yet his own personal circumstances at the time of writing led him to assume that the experience must have been connected with Blake's married life and to ignore completely the death of Blake's brother Robert in 1787. Since the experience of nursing, night and day, a brother dying of consumption was one which Blake shared with Keats, it was all the more surprising that Murry should have overlooked it.

Apart from such omissions, however, one traces through his writings, particularly the ones collected in [*Selected Criticism: 1916-1957*] . . . , the workings of a fine discriminating mind, a mind which is not prepared to take over judgments without a hard look at what is actually there in the original documents. One is also impressed by his seriousness. This is a critic who believes that literature matters—who studies books not because of some dilettante interest but from a recognition that the writer is dealing with questions with which he too is concerned. And if he sometimes went a very long way with his theory that literature was a mode of revelation, one cannot deny that there is a psychological basis for what he was saying. Without it the reading of literature would lose a good deal of its excitement, particularly for the young. Because he grasped this fact, Murry was able to write a convincing reply to I. A. Richards, which forms one of the best essays in the volume. Against Richard's assertion that the experience of joy in reading high tragedy is 'an indication that all is right here and now with the nervous system', he places a poem by Keats, voicing his determination to 'burn through' *King Lear* once again. One takes his point. Valuable as Richards's method may be, the tyro of practical criticism may well be so busy bringing his adolescent 'experience' to bear upon a great poem that he will miss the expansion of mind which might have rewarded a humbler approach.

Indeed, the two critics complement each other remarkably well. While Richards, the Cambridge Aristotelian, is showing us how a passage, removed from its context, can be judged on its own merits. Murry, the Oxford Platonist, is also looking at key passages, but with an eye firmly on the author. And his concern gives his work a significance which is independent of the value of his current arguments. As one reads the passages from Shakespeare or Keats which he quotes, their effect is heightened precisely because they have been removed from their normal setting. Viewed without their contextual colouring of Elizabethan exuberance or Regency good taste, we are made to see them as displays of naked thought.

Murry maintained to the end of his life that the primary duty of the critic was to enter into sympathy with his author. One might disagree with him, in the sense that sympathy is something which we expect of the scholar rather than the critic, whose primary task is to evaluate a work from the point of view of his own age and its standards. Yet the disagreement falls flat in this case, for Murry, with his concern for integrity and truth, was a child of his time—so that his choice of writers who share his own concerns turns out to fulfil, in a roundabout fashion, the general critical ideal.

Nevertheless, his stress on the value of sympathy points us back to his shortcomings and achievements as a critic. He lacked the positive assertions, the individual position which we look for in a great critic, but not the wise passiveness of a fine one. In the end therefore we can do honour to the man, not least for the things that he has shown us. (pp. 64-6)

> *J. B. Beer, ''John Middleton Murry,'' in* Critical Quarterly, *Vol. 3, No. 1, Spring, 1961, pp. 59-66.*

G. WILSON KNIGHT   (essay date 1964)

[*One of the most influential of modern Shakespearean critics, Knight helped shape the twentieth-century reaction against the biographical and character studies that prevailed in the criticism of Shakespeare's dramas during the nineteenth century. Knight's analytic approach stresses what he calls in his study* The Wheel of Fire *(1930) the "spatial" aspects of imagery, atmosphere, theme, and symbol in the plays. Knight is also known as a playwright and actor who has directed and starred in several Shakespearean productions. In the following excerpt, Knight credits Murry's* Adelphi *magazine for having a catalytic effect upon his own literary thought and stresses the centrality of Murry's mystical experience to all that he wrote after the death of Katherine Mansfield.]*

When after leaving Oxford I was groping for a way to express what I had to say about Shakespeare, Middleton Murry's articles in the monthly *Adelphi* magazine acted on me like an avatar; and to his writings of this period my debt remains. Here was someone who without reservations was proclaiming the religious importance of literature in a voice of authority. (p. 149)

He was a man of brilliant critical intellect who had had, and tried frantically to remain true to, a mystical experience; and the interaction of mysticism and intellect produced many apparent contradictions and seeming insincerities. He had, however, few of the characteristics usually associated with literary genius in the Renaissance era. Of these, I here emphasize two: the first, involvement, as though by instinct, with the Faustian and spiritualistic fields, and, second, sexual abnormality, sometimes pushed, perhaps with humour, to obscenity. Murry reacted against both: all his prophetic writing remained well within the conventions of twentieth-century respectability. (pp. 160-61)

In my review of [his ***Jonathan Swift***] for the *Yorkshire Post* on May 26th, 1954, high praise was countered by a reservation:

> While honestly trying to face the challenge of genius, he has always been reluctant to depart too far from traditional valuations in either religion or the psychology of sex, and that is not so easy.

Murry recognized Swift's genius but was antagonized by his neurotic disgusts. My answer, referring to men of genius, was

> Had these men been sexually normal, would they have composed their greatest works? And should we still be writing books about them? What, then, is the secret of their enduring appeal?—of this strange *malaise* which proves more vital than health?

After praising the book highly I concluded my review with the suggestion that 'it will be for others, should they choose, to delve deeper'.

I sent Murry the review. I had written to him only twice since 1929 and had on each occasion received kind replies. I now received, in his old exquisitely neat handwriting, this answer, dated May 31st, 1954, from Thelnetham:

Dear Wilson Knight,

Thank you very much for sending me the *Y.P.* review. I had seen it, and *had* wondered what you meant by yr. last sentence.

I have lately been reading some of your Shakespeare books which had escaped me—nearly 12 years farming puts one well behind; but now, being practically retired, I have begun to pick up the threads again. I was particularly concerned with yr. *Crown of Life,* because of its argument for the entire authenticity of *Henry VIII,* in which I have never been able to believe.

I am afraid you did not convince me. But you must put that down to the excessive 'normality' of my mind. Though I had not realized that my mind was a very normal one, I think it is

probably true. I am abnormally normal, so to speak: at least that seems a fair description of a man whose literary criticism ends up by putting him in charge of a co-operative farm. (I mean this literally: my farming is the direct consequence of my effort in literary criticism.)

Or, to put it differently, my mysticism is a mysticism of descent. Yours isn't. And I get lost in your high speculations as applied to Shakespeare. I was acutely conscious of this divergence as long ago as *Myth and Miracle,* though it came out at a time when I was distracted with domestic anxiety and was unable to set out the reasons of my disagreement with the fullness that initial essay of yours deserved.

However, I am in a very small minority—not perhaps a minority of one as I used to think, but very near it. My normality is therefore (as I said) peculiar.

On the particular question of Swift, you may well be right in thinking that the appalling power of Gulliver IV derives from Swift's 'unhealthy and unreasoned disgust'. But that does not justify you in generalising that supreme literary power is, in general, derivative from sexual abnormality. Indeed, I should say that the specific literary genius is utterly independent of sexual constitution, though that will certainly play an important part in the particular *manifestation* of literary genius. And, again, literary genius at the highest is not exempt from moral judgment;—though the moral judgment to which it is amenable is not the facile judgment of moral convention, but one based on the deepest philosophy (or religion) of which the critic is capable.

> Yours sincerely,
> J. Middleton Murry

That is a fair statement, though I would lay no personal claim to 'mysticism'; and what there is in my writing is, surely, 'a mysticism of descent', in that I have preferred the multi-coloured qualities of literature to the one soul-centre on which Murry concentrated. I have been more drawn to Shakespeare, Pope and Byron than to Donne and Blake.

More important is it to note Murry's conclusion. At the limit he writes not as an interpreter of genius but as a critic; the final court of appeal is his own judgment. But, it may be said, so is everyone's; and it would then be merely a question as to where to draw the line. Should not I myself be antagonized by a work deliberately counselling sadistic cruelties? My reply would be this: in so far as the imagination has ratified a work of literature, the critical intellect must be silenced. Sadistic horrors, if extreme and approved, would not have been ratified by the imagination, within which certain moral valuations appear to be contained. But the imagination has, in myself and others, already ratified the life-work of Swift. We sense in him a supreme importance: and therefore the approach must be interpretative. However far we may be, in normal life, from approving it all, there yet may be *something which our normal thinking has left out of account.* That is why an imaginative interpretation may be needed.

Murry's life-work may be defined as a continuous attempt to remain true to his one great experience. This experience he tried desperately to align with his love of literature and for a while, and within limits, succeeded magnificently. When a divergence was forced he followed the law of his own greater 'self', or 'soul', going his own wandering way. The choice was honourable. (pp. 161-63)

G. Wilson Knight, "J. Middleton Murry," in Of Books and Humankind: Essays and Poems Presented to Bonamy Dobrée, *edited by John Butt with J. M. Cameron, D. W. Jefferson, and Robin Skelton, Routledge and Kegan Paul, 1964, pp. 149-63.*

JOHN CASEY   (essay date 1966)

[*In the following excerpt, Casey discusses the shortcomings of* The Problem of Style.]

How widespread is the Romantic tendency to appeal to feeling as a means of *explanation* in literature is shown by an examination of Middleton Murry's **The Problem of Style**. This little book is almost contemporary with *Tradition and the Individual Talent* and is highly Eliotean both in doctrine and phraseology. Murry has his own doctrine of the 'objective correlative', believes that poets produce not thought but its emotional equivalent, and sets out a theory of style which centres around a particular view of the place of emotion in literature.

Early in the book Murry writes:

> By accepting the view that the source of style is to be found in a strong and decisive original emotion, we can get a closer grasp of the intention that lies under the use of the word as meaning a writer's personal idiosyncrasy. An individual way of feeling and seeing will compel an individual way of using language.

Later Murry draws a contrast between what he considers to be the unhealthy artificiality in the later work of both Meredith and James, and the artificiality of Milton which is "the natural language of an original and unfamiliar mode of feeling". With Meredith and James there is

> (an) artificiality which supervenes when the desire for accomplishment is present without any distinctive mode of feeling, or when the capacity for feeling has withered, leaving what was once a natural and healthy method of expression to run riot in a factitious existence of its own.

One thing that Murry strikingly does not do in **The Problem of Style** is to offer a catalogue of 'styles'. The last thing we can see the book as is a handbook of rhetoric in the traditional sense. This may seem too obvious a point to remark, but I shall show that it is important. What we are offered instead is an account of the *essence* of style, and this is said to be the expression of 'an individual way of feeling and seeing'. Now Murry's remark that an individual way of feeling and seeing will compel an individual way of using language certainly seems to mark an advance on Eliot, for according to Eliot . . . there is no intrinsic connection between the feeling and the language used to express it. Yet Murry's formulation betrays a fundamental uncertainty, and is brought out with a certain air of paradox. The uncertainty resides in the use of 'compel'— "will compel an individual way of using language". What sort of compulsion is this? If we say that Shakespeare could not have 'expressed' his way of seeing and feeling in the language of Milton, are we saying that his way of seeing and feeling *caused* him to use language in the way he did? It would be a very odd sort of causality since the entity which is supposed to be doing the causing can very often only be described in terms of its effects. (pp. 105-06)

Murry's insistence on the intimate connection between style and feeling is a valiant attempt to bridge the gap between the subjective and the objective, a gap which . . . is such a characteristic feature of Romantic criticism. But unfortunately Murry soon slips back into the very dualism he is trying to avoid: in a later passage he says:

> The test of a true idiosyncrasy of style is that we should feel it to be necessary and inevitable: in it we should be able to catch an immediate reference back to a whole mode of feeling that is consistent with itself. If this reference is perceptible to us, it will be accompanied by a conviction that the peculiarity of style was inevitable, and that the original emotion of which we were made sensible demanded this method of expression and this alone.

The trouble here is that if we could in this way compare the 'original emotion' with the language in which it is expressed we should have no right to say that the emotion 'demanded this method of expression and this alone'. Where there is any genuine comparison we cannot say that. We may, for instance, say that a Reynolds portrait is a very good rendering of the subject (meaning by 'subject' the actual person whose portrait Reynolds painted), but we could hardly say that the subject demanded this rendering and this alone. And when we cannot make such a comparison then we have no way of knowing whether or not the original emotion demanded this method of expression and this alone. Emotions are not inner events which language succeeds in pointing to or naming, or standing in a relation of logical analogy to. (p. 108)

When Murry asserts that the test of true idiosyncrasy of style is that the reader becomes convinced that the feeling could only be expressed in the way it *was* expressed, he is attacking the sort of separation of form and content that we find in, for instance, Eliot and . . . Yvor Winters. But Murry's own view of the connection between the inward state and its outward expression—a view more or less in the main empiricist tradition—most naturally goes with just the sort of separation which he is attacking. (p. 109)

Murry's incapacity to achieve the sort of connection which his instincts tell him should exist between the expression and the way of seeing or feeling expressed, arises from a confusion of material and intentional objects. (p. 114)

If one is doing philosophy one should avoid trying to give, as Murry does, an account of the 'essence' of style. One can no more do this than one can give the 'essence' of propositions (the 'general form' of propositions). One *can* set out in some detail the relations between different 'language-games' (one can elucidate the various types of 'speech-act', to use the Austinian phrase). One cannot appeal to 'feelings' as a means of by-passing this enquiry ('long long ago' feelings, feelings of intention and so on) any more than one can look to different material or metaphysical or mental entities to correspond to the different forms of discourse. But equally, if one is doing criticism, one has to set out in some detail the relation between different plays and poems, or, if a more general approach is preferred, one can write a text-book on Rhetoric, listing 'styles' and cataloguing them. (Philosophers influenced by Wittgenstein and Austin have investigated the various ways in which language is used almost in the spirit of grammarians; but the cataloguing of 'styles' is quite out of fashion among critics—Kenneth Burke being a notable exception.)

Another important conclusion is that Murry's tendency to remove emotions from the realm of rationality is clearly mistaken. He says: ". . . to communicate an emotion means, in fact, to impose an emotion. To do this, I have to find some symbol which will evoke . . . an emotional reaction as nearly as possible identical with the emotion I am feeling." Elsewhere he suggests that the image the writer chooses to objectify his emotion ". . . would exercise a kind of compulsion upon the mind of the reader, so that given an ordinary sensibility, he must share the emotion or the experience that the writer intended him to share." (p. 116)

Murry's **The Problem of Style** is, then, something of a *locus classicus*. It brings to the surface and attempts to resolve the central paradoxes of romantic expressionism, and at the same time shows how deeply embedded in romantic expressionism are certain philosophical assumptions which have to be discarded. This, in itself, is no mean achievement. (p. 118)

> *John Casey, "Style and Feeling: Middleton Murry,"*
> *in his* The Language of Criticism, *Methuen & Co.,*
> *Ltd., 1966, pp. 105-19.*

RICHARD REES   (essay date 1969)

[*Rees, a close friend and highly respected colleague of Murry, was entrusted with the editorship of* The Adelphi *from 1930 to 1936 after serving as Murry's assistant during the journal's formative years. When Rees took control of* The Adelphi, *he introduced a more politically consistent and leftist editorial position than that offered by Murry. In the following excerpt, Rees discusses Murry's politics and one of his most widely known political tracts,* The Necessity of Communism, *concluding that the work's most salient weakness is its supposition that the reader will readily accept the mystic outlook held by Murry.*]

[**The Necessity of Communism**] is in reality a short tract, or long sermon, of 130 pages, and to re-read it today is to be surprised at how much truth he was able to combine even in his worst writing with extravagant and intemperate fantasy. For the book does exhibit him almost at his worst; which makes it all the more remarkable that such an experienced member of the British Labour Party as Professor R. H. Tawney was able to write him an appreciative letter about it. Not that it is at all difficult to recognise the book as the product of a highly sophisticated and cultured intelligence. Among literary intellectuals in the first half of this century there were only a very few, such as Valéry, Santayana, and Thomas Mann, for example, who were Murry's equals in sophistication. But unlike them, Murry was inclined to erupt into spheres of activity for which he was temperamentally unsuited. Practical politics was one of them. It is true that his practical politics consisted, in practice, mainly in the preaching of a moral crusade, but by attaching himself to the unfortunate Independent Labour Party and contributing to its disruption, he gave himself a lot of unnecessary and wasted trouble, and he misled and disappointed a number of working class and bourgeois socialists. (p. 24)

The kindest explanation of Murry's brief phase of what he called "communism"—and one to which any reader of Mr. Lea's admirable biography of him will certainly incline—is that during a good part of the 1930's he hardly knew what he was doing. His frantic summons in **The Necessity of Communism** to "self-annihilation" and to "this destiny of nakedness" undoubtedly owes some of its violence and emotionalism to the personal predicament of the author, whose domestic life for the past fifteen years had been one long crescendo of di-

sasters, including the death of Katherine Mansfield and also of his second wife, from consumption.

If, instead of writing an impassioned sermon, he had been able to control himself and write a calm statement of his views, the book might have been of great value. Murry had acquired a remarkable grasp of Marxist theory, he had a clear understanding of the world situation, and his philosophical foundations were incomparably more solid than is usual in political writing. But before examining Murry's use of the word *communism*, let us look at the context in which he uses it. He points out that the 1914-1918 war had intensified in two contradictory ways the crisis for which "communism" is the only solution. On the one hand, by increasing the industrial interdependence between different parts of the world, the war had speeded the growth of a world economic organism: ". . . as a direct consequence of the war-demands the technique of industry was immeasurably improved and thus the coherence of the national and international economic organisms immeasurably intensified." On the other hand, the war also gave "an equal and opposite impetus to the process of national exclusiveness [and] it increased the number of independent sectarian states determined to flourish at the expense of their neighbours." In these circumstances the persistence of capitalism, the economics of self-interest, in nations and individuals alike, can only lead to disaster.

In the main, all this seems to be as relevant today as it was when Murry wrote it in 1932. And he is equally sound on what he calls the "parasitism of Labour." One of the most distinguished Labour leaders had written in 1931 that "if capitalism

Cartoon by Thomas Derrick in The Bookman, *April 1932.*

could stand all the social expenditure which ideally we desire, capitalism would be a good system.'' To this Murry retorts that it is a policy of bread and circuses. It is to offer the workers ''an eternity of parasitism''—which, again, is still a relevant comment in the 1960's. It is a fairly accurate description of the policy of every government in the world today. And what is Murry's alternative? His practical programme is summarised in three pages at the end of the book. Labour must demand the *''immediate''* establishment of ''a guaranteed decent minimum wage for every man, whether in or out of employment,'' and this must be financed and the budget must be balanced by direct taxation ''so drastic that all incomes will be reduced to a maximum of, say, Ł1000 a year.'' This will solve Britain's unemployment problem (which was chronic between the two wars) because ''with the enormous transfer of purchasing power from the richer to the poorer classes, the wheels of industry will begin to move.'' More credit will then at once be made available, based on the increased supply of real goods. Once this initial step has been taken, Murry says, educational equality and the virtual abolition of inheritance will be found to flow necessarily from it, and the way will be clear for the whole programme of the Communist Manifesto of 1848.

If all this sounds both trite and optimistic, it is the very essence of sanity and responsibility compared to what the British Russophile intellectuals were advocating in those days. Murry's book is addressed primarily to the bourgeois, who is exhorted to adopt the economics of disinterestedness and to identify himself with the demands of the working class as formulated by Murry. So the crux of the problem is, of course, disinterestedness, and Murry is aware that his policy will require sacrifices not only from the bourgeois but also from the majority of workers, who will have to forego the social benefits which might be extorted by a successful policy of ''parasitism'' upon the capitalist system. The only class for whom Murry's policy would mean a certain and immediate gain would be the unemployed.

Murry's appeal to the bourgeois to adopt the economics of disinterestedness is based upon a theory of mysticism. To introduce mysticism into a political tract is by no means inherently ridiculous; and the less so when, as in this case, the author's knowledge of the subject is profound and extensive and is confirmed, or so he believes, by personal experience. (pp. 24-6)

The book begins with a thumb-nail sketch of the confrontation between Marxism and Christianity and with the demand that Christianity should become disinterested by giving up the expectation of reward and the fear of punishment in the hereafter. Christianity, in fact, is to ''will its own annihilation. But not quite. The heresy of disinterestedness, the heresy of Jesus, will emerge unscathed.'' Marx himself was disinterested and may be regarded as a Christian prophet. His communism is the economics of disinterestedness.

So far so good; but what makes the book absurd from then on is the apparent assumption that a few pages of impassioned pep talk will suffice to turn the reader into a selfless mystic, that the contagion will rapidly spread, and that it will lead to a reform of Labour Party morality, followed by a political victory. And this blind infatuation is all the more regrettable because Murry has much of interest to say about Marxism, about England, and about the futility of trying to impose Russian Marxism upon a country with a different history and tradition.

But on page after page he lets himself down with passages like the following:

> The bourgeois is doubtful, bewildered, afraid; obscurely, yet vitally, he is aware that he does not *believe* even in his own position of privilege. As for religious belief, he has none. And those two central unfaiths of the modern bourgeois are implicit in one another. He does not believe in himself, therefore he cannot believe in God. ''Why should he believe in God?'' comes the snigger of the futile intelligentsia. Simply because to carry the life of the world through crisis, a man must believe in God. ''But the Communist himself does not believe in God!'' Oh, you *fools!* What difference is there between believing in God and believing in Man—in life, in the future, in the unknown.

Well, there was one literary man, not a member of the futile intelligentsia, who saw a difference, and that was T. S. Eliot, who when so many were becoming Communists, became an Anglo-Catholic. (pp. 27-8)

The Necessity of Communism was criticised by the Left intelligentsia, not for its fantastic political unrealism (their own programme disqualified them anyway as judges of realism) nor even for its note of hysteria, but precisely for its humanity and for the few shreds of objectivity which the author had retained. Murry's perfectly correct conviction that the British people shared his own aversion to class hatred and bloody civil war was considered to be a watering-down of the pure Marxist faith.

In reality, the book's one fatal weakness is the facile emotional language about accepting a destiny of nakedness, disentangling the impersonal Self from the personal, giving one's all, submitting to revolution within one's self and then making a holocaust of it, and so on *ad nauseam*. One could almost suppose that Murry himself had achieved all this with one hand tied behind his back, before breakfast, and that he counted upon his readers to have acquired the knack by tea-time at latest. (p. 29)

It was, of course, Murry's great virtue that he was always concerned to link theory with practice and that he understood literature and criticism as activities with an immediate bearing upon, and ultimately a religious significance for, every-day life. In this he resembled Lawrence. Both of them, however, had highly complex characters, which, for purposes of comparison, can be simplified as split personalities. In this way, the conflict in Lawrence can be seen as the conflict between a poet and a preacher, while in Murry the conflict is between a critic and a preacher. But in Lawrence the conflict was fruitful and productive, and although it was the cause of some blemishes in his works, it was chiefly a source of vitality and a potent factor in his genius. In Murry, on the other hand, the two parts of his character were ill-assorted. They affected one another frustratingly and negatively. The work of the sensitive intellectual critic and acute thinker was frequently confused and sidetracked by the enthusiast with a mission, and the force and sincerity of the enthusiast were seldom effectively harmonised with the subtleties and refinements of the intellectual.

If the untimely success of the early *Adelphi* had not given Murry the impression that large numbers of people were able and willing to understand the enthusiast's message, he might have learned to curb the enthusiasm and to prepare more soberly for the laborious campaign and the long lonely pilgrimage that awaited him. (p. 31)

Richard Rees, "Politics of a Mystic," in The D. H. Lawrence Review, *Vol. 2, No. 1, Spring, 1969, pp. 24-31.*

ERNEST G. GRIFFIN (essay date 1969)

[*In the following excerpt, Griffin discusses the unifying theme of Murry's diverse critical and expository writings: that society should place its faith in moral tradition and conscientious leaders rather than machines or other material harbingers of progress.*]

For Murry . . . criticism could not stay within narrow limits. That he was a genuine critic can surely not be doubted, although it is difficult to classify his criticism except by some vague term such as "creative criticism." It is not fair to dismiss it as "fictional," as "autobiographic," or as "poetic" criticism, as has been done; or it might be truer to say that Murry did write "fictional" criticism if this is understood to be, not untrue criticism, but criticism which employs the insight of the novelist. Murry could not invent as a true novelist—as Lawrence early pointed out and as his own attempts at the novel proved. But he could work creatively with the facts of history, especially literary history. (pp. 77-8)

For Murry, Shakespeare was the ideal and Keats was the way. Such a brief summary sounds suspect, yet there is truth in its very simplicity. Murry accepted Shakespeare simply and without qualification as supreme; it was natural for him to state at the end of an illuminating analytic study of Shakespeare's plays that "Shakespeare's dream is God's and Shakespeare God's dream." (p. 80)

[It] is easy to understand why *Keats and Shakespeare* . . . has been the most popular of his books of criticism. In some ways, it is the ideal introduction to a poet, as many undergraduates can testify; it is not an abstract of the "main points" of a poet's literary career, as introductions tend to be, but the spirited presentation of a genius who, as man and artist, is a warm and living reality for the critic writing about him.

At the same time, it must be admitted that a popular and enthusiastic presentation does not necessarily make the book sound literary criticism. In fact, the mature scholar is apt to resent the attitude of total revelation, one in which the author throws the reader a challenge but implies that it would be in bad taste to pick up the glove. (p. 81)

Probably, on first approach, it is best to accept the book as it is, without trying to classify it. Then, if the reader wishes to abstract from it a "purer" form of literary criticism—as modern critics are now doing—he will not go unrewarded. . . .

In his *Study of Keats' Poetic Life,* as he subtitles the book, Murry follows the basic pattern he had developed in his earlier book on Dostoevsky, so that, although the book has the progress of a personal biography, its landmarks are the works of the artist. One might say that Murry reads the poems into the life rather than the life into the poems. His book has the interest of a narrative, but just as the chronological events are the poems, so the conflicts are less with other people than with other poetic attitudes, such as those represented by Wordsworth and Milton. Keats endures the trials of the "Vale of Soul-Making" until, at the end of the astonishing four years of his poetic career, he "is with Shakespeare." Keats's "most intimate history," Murry observes, "could be written in terms

of his rejection first of Wordsworth, then of Milton in favour of a deeper and unchanging loyalty to Shakespeare." (p. 82)

Keats has reached a spiritual state which he terms "Negative Capability," which was to be an important—perhaps the most important—phrase in Murry's life. It becomes extended into a religious ideal, the state which Christ attained: "it is more than tolerance, it is forgiveness." Murry uses the word "acceptance," that is, "a forgiveness which forgives not only men but life itself, not only the pains which men inflict, but the pains which are knit up in the very nature of existence." Later, in an essay on "Keats and Milton," Murry goes so far as to say: "The Negative Capability of the poet achieves its natural consummation in the humility of the Christian before the Cross." One sees why Murry was just as ready to write a book on Christ as on Keats, and on God as on Shakespeare. He tried to achieve the state of "Negative Capability," in criticism and in life, to be receptively open to all that was most important to man, to partake of a sort of mystical all-roundedness. For him, "True philosophy is precisely that Negative Capability that was so supremely manifested in Shakespeare. It proceeds from a natural submission of the self to all experience."

This philosophy of being wide-open to all experience which Murry developed, helped to make him a good critic and editor, but it was less certain as a guide to conduct. He tried to explain and take over what he understood as Keats's idea of knowledge—a knowledge which is "essentially self-engendered; it is the self's creation of itself out of experience." How successful Murry was in developing for his own purposes the philosophy of a young lyrical poet is an interesting question. Perhaps the basic tension in Murry sprang from this desire for full and open experience on the one hand, and, on the other, from a strong urge to find a permanent order (evident, for example, in his constant attempts to define the true society).

It may be because of such a basic tension that Murry is particularly concerned with Keats's power to transcend contradictions. Thus in 1818, Keats, as he endured the dying of his beloved brother Tom, was learning that life was a bitter contradiction—"on the one hand its beauty, on the other its pain." When he yearns to transcend this by maturing to the state of "High reason, and the love of good and ill," he discovers this ideal in reading *King Lear*—"that example of the intensity of contemplation which 'makes all disagreeables evaporate from their being in close relationship with Beauty and Truth.'" Keats, Murry says, was developing to a point "beyond all rebellion." "I have," Keats said, "loved the principle of beauty in all things," which Murry concludes, with considerable evidence, should be read not as "I have loved the principle of beauty—in all things" but as "I have loved the principle—of beauty in all things." Unfortunately, Keats did not live long enough to put that love into full effect—to realize, as Murry is sure he would have done, the dramatic power of his genius "to reveal to men that good and ill are to be loved; not only the faculty to see that the sum of things is supremely beautiful, but the faculty to show to other men that it is supremely beautiful."

Murry insists upon a complete acceptance of the towering greatness of Keats before any attempt is made to analyze him. Thus he is "amazed, then indignant" when he reads in a *Life of Keats* that "there was a great spiritual flaw in his nature." By what measurement can one say that, he demands; and he accuses the biographer of "the old trick of average humanity when it is confronted with genius; it takes from it what it can comfortably accommodate, and throws the rest away as nothing worth." At the other extreme, however, Murry does not altogether avoid the excesses of hagiography. How far, for example, can any poet be "greater than his actual achievement"? (pp. 83-5)

The person who is determined to leave himself open to a wealth of experience and sensation often has as strong an urge to organize his experiences into a purposeful system. To the person himself this systemizing will probably seem a progress toward unity, a harmonious integration of a chaos of thoughts and feelings; but an outsider is equally apt to consider the "system" as an articulation of what was there to begin with. By an extraordinary path, the experiencer reaches the ordinary; he suffers the abnormal painfully, until he achieves his "norm."

Murry's goal was—if it may be so described without any note of deprecation—to be a "normal Englishman." With the help of Keats, Blake, Lawrence, and Christ, he eventually found his way to the normal. (p. 99)

Murry had to explore Christian humanist culture in which "Englishness" was rooted, and he had to say more about the man who was for him the perfect Englishman—Shakespeare. He undertakes these tasks in *Heaven—And Earth* and in *Shakespeare.* (p. 100)

Though *Shakespeare* was published two years before *Heaven—And Earth,* it was Shakespeare, like Keats, who was the lifelong study.

Murry could not write about Shakespeare without somehow "knowing him" personally, even intimately. He admits in his *Shakespeare* that he does not have much historical evidence to support him, but he feels obliged to put in order what clues he has: "It is on such twigs as these that I suppose to spin my theory of Shakespeare's career up to the writing of *Hamlet.* That it is no more than a theory, I am as conscious as anybody. But that it is necessary to have a theory I know by experience.

From the scholarly point of view, Murry's is a dangerous approach, of which the following may serve as an example. Murry refers to the "image-sensation" which developed from Shakespeare's apparent association of fawning flattery with spaniels receiving sweetmeats from nobles, in the complex images involving "spaniel-fawning" and "the candied tongue [licking] absurd pomp" which appear in *Julius Caesar, Hamlet,* and *Antony and Cleopatra.* Obviously the basic image of hounds under the table eating tidbits thrown to them by Elizabethan diners corresponds with something vivid and disgusting in Shakespeare's mind. Murry traces this disgust to a decisive moment in the young Shakespeare's life, his being called before Sir Thomas Lucy for stealing deer in Lucy's park.

"I am persuaded," says Murry, "that I can enter into the actual 'sensation' which Shakespeare experienced when he stood before Sir Thomas Lucy in Charlecote Hall." The occasion made "an indelible impression on his unconscious mind" as Shakespeare "was standing before the table in an Elizabethan hall, watching the hounds wagging their tails, licking the hands of a pompous company, gobbling up the rich and sticky sweetmeats thrown to them—and this experience so deeply nauseated Shakespeare that it went on working unconsciously within him, and became a self-creating image of servility and flattery." It is an appealingly dramatic picture, but it called forth the following admonition [from Edward A. Armstrong in his *Shakespeare's Imagination*]:

> Quite apart from the fact that the tale about Shakespeare's deer-stealing in Lucy's park is a

manifest fiction—Sir Thomas Lucy had no deer-park at Charlecote when Shakespeare was a boy—this kind of speculative reconstruction, by which a set of linked images is assumed without any evidence to have originated in a specific incident, is illegitimate. The device is as seductive to the imaginative writer as it is attractive to a public agog to know what Shakespeare chose not to tell. Cluster [image-cluster] criticism provides a means whereby we may in some measure draw aside the veil shrouding Shakespeare's personality, but if associative linkages are to become the subject of unthrifty inference the truth which they reveal will be submerged in a sea of specious error.

Sometimes Murry's intuitive insights had a luckier fate, one being his deduction from an elaborate simile of housebuilding in *Henry IV, Part II* that Shakespeare was, about 1598, engaged in building or renovating a house for himself, a fact which has been historically confirmed in his purchase in 1597 of the New Place, which stood in great need of repair. Murry's insights, too, lead to important themes, such as the character which develops from the Bastard in *King John,* on which E. M. W. Tillyard has remarked: "Middleton Murry has written so well of the Bastard's character and of the new vein of creation that went to his making that I need treat of him only as embodying Shakespeare's political opinions."

Murry was aware of the "hit or miss" nature of his approach, but he persevered. His reward is that he achieves, and communicates, an organic fullness in his appreciation of Shakespeare, so that, whether or not we have to check the factual truth of some of his conclusions, we can hardly fail—as several critics have pointed out—to finish the book without an enlarged understanding of Shakespeare. (pp. 108-10)

Some of his very best work on Shakespeare is in illustrative criticism, consisting of the examples he uses to demonstrate his arguments. In *The Problem of Style* he follows the structure of simile and metaphor through the death scene of Cleopatra. He examines the precise language which Shakespeare uses to express an infinite complexity; he reveals the subtle variations of a basic metaphor in "He tells her something / That makes her blood look out"; in "tonight I'll force / The wine peep through their scars"; and in other passages. In "Metaphor," on of his most instructive essays, he uses examples to show "the self-creative progress" of Shakespeare's imagery; for instance, he examines closely the imagistic structure which Shakespeare built on the account of Cleopatra about Cydnus as given in North's *Plutarch,* and the means by which North's "inconsequential panorama" is given "an organic unity." As one reads such examples one has to admire Murry's sensitive "taste"—much as Murry himself, like Wordsworth, distrusted the word.

That Murry was not always correct in some of his individual criticisms of Shakespeare's work made no difference to his fundamental attitude. Shakespeare was the fount of English culture—the great teacher-artist for Englishmen that Homer had been for the Greeks at one stage of history. If the language Murry uses about Shakespeare sounds "religious," as some critics have observed, it is because, in a sense, it *is.* Murry cannot avoid using the language of the trinity, for example, in explaining that Shakespeare "apprehended as realities a truth, a harmony, and a love—apprehended them as one and not as three"—an apprehension, incidentally, which in Murry's view, reached its apex in "The Phoenix and the Turtle," a "symbolic vision of perfect and celestial love," and "the most perfect short poem in any language."

It is notable that he also, in the superlatives he applies to this poem, says it is "platonic and mystical"; it is, in fact, a perfect synthesis of the two strains in Murry, his platonic Hellenism and mystical Christianity. In the light of this synthesis, which Murry was always seeking, we must view his seemingly extravagant statements. Thus, he shrewdly comments on *Antony and Cleopatra* as a play of loyalty—Enobarbus, Eros, Antony, Cleopatra, Charmian, Iris, "one after another make the sacrifice" for the sake of fidelity. Yet there is a sense of serenity, "a profundity of calm." How can one account for this? Murry must turn to Christ for the answer: "'Greater love hath no *man* than this that he lay down his life for a friend.' And Christ's own crucifixion is the archetype of all Shakespeare's tragedy."

Giving a reason for speaking almost entirely on Shakespeare in the lecture announced as "The Nature of Poetry," Murry maintained that the title necessarily meant "the nature of Shakespeare's poetry". Moreover, he observed in somewhat lighter vein: "I feel that if I had offered to lecture on Keats, or Reparations, or the Fascist movement, it would have turned out to be the same old thing. Shakespeare would have been the burden of my song." For Murry, whatever he said would somehow have sprung from the supreme knowledge possessed by "William Shakespeare of Stratford-upon-Avon, Gentleman." (pp. 119-20)

> *Ernest G. Griffin, in his* John Middleton Murry, *Twayne Publishers, Inc., 1969, 182 p.*

JEFFREY MEYERS (essay date 1979)

[Meyers is an American critic who has written extensively on T. E. Lawrence, George Orwell, and Katherine Mansfield, as well as on the interrelationships of various social issues with modern literature. In the following excerpt, Meyers charges that Murry lacked both critical integrity and objectivity when publishing and commenting upon Katherine Mansfield's works.]

Middleton Murry's creation of the cult of Katherine Mansfield is unique in modern literature. In a repetitive torrent of forty books, articles, introductions, poems, and letters to the press, published between 1923 and 1959, Murry expressed his anguished self-consciousness, deliberately constructed his myth of Katherine, and established a posthumous reputation far greater than she had enjoyed in her lifetime. The motives for Murry's literary crusade were closely connected to his own character and his relationship to Katherine, and were determined more by emotional and financial needs than by intellectual convictions. (p. 15)

Murry's guilt about his selfish and irresponsible treatment of Katherine, which hastened her death, led directly to the egoistic enshrinement of his wife. As high priest of Katherine's cult, Murry wrote an *apologia pro sua vita;* glorified his own role, image, and importance; exploited her tragic death at the age of thirty-four; created a sentimental and idealized portrait which obscured her literary qualities; and made a good deal of money by publishing her posthumous works. Only three of Katherine's books appeared during her lifetime; eleven others were edited by Murry after her death. (pp. 16-17)

Though Murry's biographer F. A. Lea believes, "The greatest [of his virtues] and the least conventional, was his honesty," Katherine was far more perceptive when she wrote, "His very

frankness is a falsity. In fact it seems falser than his insincerity," for she understood that his frankness was a *persona,* a pose from which to project a false image of himself. Aldous Huxley, who was Murry's editorial assistant on the *Athenaeum* in 1919, exaggerated this aspect of Murry whom he characterized as Burlap in *Point Counter Point* (1928). . . . Huxley quite accurately perceives not only the falseness of the cult and Murry's pitiful exploitation of his grief, but also the emotional immaturity and childish role-playing of both Katherine and Murry, and he describes the destructive aspect of Murry's "mystical" love in the metaphor of sexual perversion.

D. H. Lawrence's story, "Smile" (1926), is also based on Murry's response to Katherine's death, and portrays the selfish reaction of a man who sees his wife's body in a convent and feels an ambiguous mixture of guilt, self-pity, indifference, and lust for a young nun. . . . Lawrence, who knew Murry well, emphasizes his passivity and confusion.

Murry's **"In Memory of Katherine Mansfield,"** an atrociously sentimental poem in archaic diction and (like Shelley's "Adonais") in Spenserian stanza, published on the first anniversary of her death, is a fine example of the insincerity and idealization of Katherine portrayed by Huxley and Lawrence:

> For she was lonely; was she not a child
> By royalty and wisdom, captive made
> Among unlovely men, beating her wild
> Impetuous wings in anguish, and dismayed. . . .
> A child of other worlds, a perfect thing
> Vouchsafed to justify this world's imagining? . . .
> A princess manifest, a child withouten stain.

Lea points out that these lines on Katherine's death "were eight-year-old verses, re-conditioned for the occasion." The third and fourth lines idealize Katherine by alluding to Arnold's (inaccurate) description of Shelley as "A beautiful and ineffectual angel, beating in the void his luminous wings in vain." There are significant analogies between the legends of Shelley and Katherine, for as Richard Holmes writes, "where events reveal Shelley in an unpleasant light, the original texts and commentaries have attracted suppressions, distortions and questions of doubtful authenticity, originating from Victorian apologists." Though Murry knew about Katherine's bitter and destructive sexual experiences, her lesbianism, abortion, and drug addiction—Virginia Woolf thought she "dressed like a tart and behaved like a bitch"—he stressed her perfect purity and called her "a child withouten stain."

Murry had opposed Katherine's submission to the mystical rigors of [The Gurdjieff Institute] and insisted in 1951 that his "prejudice against occultism was great; and it is as deep-rooted now as it was then." But he emphasized Katherine's "spiritual" qualities one month after her death when he described [in an article for *The Adelphi* titled **"A Month After"**] a mystical experience in that confessional mode which exasperated critics and embarrassed friends. . . . (pp. 17-19)

Only Murry could write a book called **God,** and only he could begin the book with a very long first chapter about himself—as if to place the deity in proper perspective. In this introductory chapter Murry, who claimed a deep-rooted prejudice against occultism, once again describes the "mystical" experience of February 1923:

> When I say that "the room was filled with a presence," the "presence" was definitely connected with the person of Katherine Mans-

field. . . . The "presence" of Katherine Mansfield was of the same order as the "presence" which filled the room and me. In so far as the "presence" was connected with her it had a moral quality, or a moral effect: I was immediately and deeply convinced that "all was well with her."

This awkward and meaningless passage merely proves that Murry could easily convince himself of anything he wanted to believe. (p. 20)

Murry's final attempt to exorcise the guilt-ridden memory of Katherine occurred—rather oddly—in his introduction to Ruth Mantz's bibliography of Katherine's works (1931), when he described his dream of her rising, like a Gothic heroine, from the flowers of her coffin: "As I watched, Katherine Mansfield raised herself wearily out of the shallow turfy grave. With her fingertips she took back the hair from her still-closed eyes. She opened them at last, and looked at the garden and the house, and smiled. Then, as though weary, she sank back to sleep again. It was peace; it was good; and what she had seen was also good." Once again, after his *second* wife had died of tuberculosis, Murry has the dead Katherine absolve his guilt in the language of the God of Genesis, who divided the light from the darkness and "saw that it was good."

But Murry's virtuous and high-minded statements about Katherine were constantly undermined by his own selfish behavior and unscrupulous falsification of their relationship. . . . Though Murry told Ottoline Morrell, "the only thing that matters to me is that [Katherine] should have her rightful place as the most wonderful writer and the most beautiful spirit of our time," he always confused the "writer" with the "spirit," emphasized her "purity" at the expense of her genuine qualities, bathed the reality of her life in pathos and pain, distorted her actual achievement, and inflated her reputation. (pp. 20-1)

Murry is an indispensable but thoroughly unreliable guide to Katherine, for he could not disentangle himself from her legend, could not distinguish between the woman and the artist, and could never form an objective and consistent view of her work. The emotional confusion of his literary criticism also characterized his social, political, and religious ideas, which he expounded at the same time. (p. 24)

Murry's creation of the cult of Katherine can be traced through his evaluation of her work, posthumous publication of her stories, reprinting of *In a German Pension*, discussion of her relation to Chekhov, misrepresentation of her critical reception and literary career, and editing of her journals. Murry's seventeen-hundred-word essay on Katherine, published in the Literary Review of the *New York Evening Post* five weeks after her death, is a paradigm of all his repetitive criticism about her. He laid the foundation of his thought in 1923 and rarely deviated from it during the next thirty-four years. Murry's essay, the first critical work on Katherine to appear in America, contains hyperbolic praise, unwarranted comparisons with far greater writers, factual errors, and deliberate misinterpretations of her work; it exaggerates the fragile, exquisite, delicate, childlike, pure, and spiritual aspects of her life and art, and totally ignores the reckless and ruthless, the earthy and ribald, the witty and bitter side of her character. (pp. 24-5)

Murry consistently uses emotionally-charged adjectives and speaks of Katherine's "sensitiveness and courage" and the "magical" quality of her "absolutely original" stories whose "brilliant clarity is almost intolerable" and "vivid beauty unique

and incomparable." Though Katherine and Murry were contemporaries of Virginia Woolf, Joyce, Lawrence, Pound, and Eliot, he calls her [in *Between Two Worlds*] "the most perfect and accomplished literary artist of the generation to which I belong." (p. 25)

Murry created a holy trinity of Christ, Keats, and Katherine (he wrote books on all of them), was fond of reflecting on the singular likeness of Keats and Katherine, and frequently compared her to Romantic poets. As he wrote in 1933, "Katherine Mansfield did not achieve the conscious wisdom of Blake. But she was going the same path; as Keats, when he died, was going the same path." And he also asked (and answered) with complete seriousness, "What has Jesus to do with Blake, with Keats, with Katherine Mansfield? He has everything to do with them."

Although Katherine had a unique temperament and an original vision of the world, she clearly did not belong with the far greater genius of Blake and Keats; and it is a salutary experience to set Katherine's ruthless self-criticism against Murry's excessive adoration in order to place her in a clearer perspective. Katherine felt "my talent as a writer isn't a great one—I'll have to be careful of it." . . . Murry's public dishonesty about the merit of her work was related to his well-intentioned but harmful habit of privately praising Katherine's stories in order to cheer her up and express his devotion to her art. But Katherine, who needed lucid criticism, was too shrewd to accept Murry's hypocritical encouragement, though she loyally praised his intolerably precious "poetic drama," *Cinnamon and Angelica.* . . . (pp. 32-3)

Murry's desire to protect Katherine's personal image rather than tell the truth about her provides a strong contrast to the current biographical method, which presents—and accepts—the irregular and even abnormal aspects of a writer's life. Although Murry established Katherine's reputation and created her cult by acting as her literary man-midwife, making a religion of her art and substituting the delicate and sensitive for the cynical and amoral side of her character, his hagiography offended her friends and admirers and perverted critical values and judgment. By writing far more about Katherine than any other literary critic and maintaining exclusive control of her manuscripts until his death in 1957, he created a false legend which eased his guilt and filled his pockets. Since Murry's apparently authoritative account of Katherine is based on lies, distortions, evasions, and contradictions, current biographers and critics must reject his conclusions and construct a new and accurate view of her personality and her art. When Murry's critical debris is cleared away, the Katherine that emerges from the ruins is a darker and more earthly, a crueller and more capable figure than in the legend. A systematic examination of Murry's voluminous writings about Katherine, which are subjective "appreciations" rather than objective analyses and have very little value today, seriously undermines his stature as a literary critic, and it is both significant and appropriate that his reputation has declined at the same time that Katherine's has increased. (p. 38)

Jeffrey Meyers, "Murry's Cult of Mansfield," in Journal of Modern Literature, *Vol. 7, No. 1, February, 1979, pp. 15-38.*

SHARRON GREER CASSAVANT   (essay date 1982)

[*In the following excerpt Cassavant surveys Murry's career, concluding that he is an important twentieth-century critic whose "best criticism is among the best of this, or any, time."*]

Murry and Katherine Mansfield (1913). The Society of Authors on behalf of the Estates of Katherine Mansfield and John Middleton Murry.

In 1916 Murry published his first two full-length books. The first, *Dostoevsky: A Critical Study,* was a provocative introduction of Russian "spiritual biography" to English criticism; the second, *Still Life,* a novel, exposed the paucity of his creative gift. (p. 33)

Murry later accurately described the writing of *Still Life* as "analyzing my own inward life to immobility." It is a very dull novel whose dreariness is aggravated by Murry's insistence that we take the plight of his characters as seriously as he does. Their long, quasi-philosophical dialogues are never lightened by a hint of recognizing absurdity. (pp. 33-4)

[His *Poems: 1917-1918*] are uniformly marred by archaic rhetoric and arch sentimentalities. Murry's children are always "little children," whispers are always "soft." Lacking a natural ear and without aptitude for compressing meaning, Murry veers between prosiness and melodramatic exaggeration. [In *Poems: 1916-1920*] he occasionally ventures into a more modern idiom which bears the palpable imprint of his reading of T. S. Eliot. One poem, **"Sublunary,"** reads like an unfortunate parody of "The Love Song of J. Alfred Prufrock." (pp. 34-5)

Murry quickly abandoned this mode of imitation, but he never found a natural poetic voice. Even in 1921, after his brilliant editorship of the *Athenaeum,* he wrote and published poems he would never have praised in another poet. Unusually discerning as a critic of poetry, a champion of young talents, Murry was bizarrely unselfaware.

The Critic in Judgment, a discursive dramatic poem, was one of the first publications of the Woolfs' Hogarth Press, although not one on which they rested much hope. Both form and subject were better attuned to Murry's talent than the lyrics, and though *The Critic* is a negligible work, it is not embarrassing. The poem takes its inspiration from the Platonic theory of the ultimate spiritual unity of all things. The critic engages in a series of dialogues with personified ideas and ends his affirmation of a vision which comprehends "all philosophies . . . , all beauties, all desires." Hardly a helpful manual for critics, *The Critic in Judgment* was Murry's self-justification of the eclectic breadth of his literary enthusiasms and a tentative statement of what later became a fundamental tenet of his critical creed—the belief that the critic's task is to judge literature hierarchically, according to the wholeness of a life vision. Murry's intellectual ecstasy in *The Critic* pivots around his doctrine of the unity of body and sense, matter and spirit. Plato is the penultimate figure in the dialogue series because he represents the critic's most potent temptation, to judge by reason without reference to the sensual world.

Cinammon and Angelica . . . , an antiwar verse drama in the commedia dell'arte tradition, suffers, like the poems of the same period, from Murry's propensity for archness, whimsy, and artifical imagery. The tone of the piece is defined by Murry's decision to give the characters the name of spices, in a vain effort to lend the play an air of faerie. Even if Murry's blank verse were less execrable, it would be difficult to find pathos in the fatal love of King Cinammon of Peppercorn for Princess Angelica of Cloves. The antiwar theme is overridden by Murry's sentimentality about despairing romantic love, and the piece is a catalog of clichés about separated lovers. (pp. 35-6)

The critical silence met by *Cinammon and Angelica* finally discouraged Murry, and he turned back to the novel. . . . Murry's second novel is undoubtedly the best creative piece he did, and it earned a variety of mildly flattering reviews. The novel has the virtue of being nonautobiographical, hence created at a greater emotional remove than *Still Life* or the poems. Murry's most embarrassing lapses were connected with sentimental self-disclosure; his taste was always surer from a distance. The hero of *The Things We Are,* Boston, does embody many Murrian traits, including the habit of using New Testament tags such as "one must lose one's life to save it" with annoying repetition, but this tale of a mild London clerk who makes an upheaval of his life by suddenly quitting his job and retreating to a country inn has moments of realistic vigor. (p. 36)

Murry's last novel, *The Voyage* . . . , was a dismal finale to his novelistic career. A depressing, gray-mooded book, it suffers, like its predecessors, from a cargo of emotional significance heaped upon lifeless characters. (p. 37)

Reprinted more frequently than anything else Murry wrote, *The Problem of Style* has become a standard work. It is the book people refer to when they praise the early Murry and lament the religiousness or the romanticism of the later Murry. *The Problem of Style* gives evidence of being much more carefully written than any other item of the bibliography, and the gentlemanly, Erasmian tone of the book invites comparison with Forster's *Aspects of the Novel* in its deceptively easy mastery of a familiar style, its wide-ranging allusiveness, its effort to talk simply about big literary ideas. (p. 46)

The principle argument of *The Problem of Style* revolves around Murry's definition of "absolute style" manifested in crystallization and organic metaphor, but Murry also introduced ideas which became increasingly important to his practice of criticism. For Murry, the primary originating emotion of the writer lies at the center. He is critical both of the displacement of emotion by discursive reasoning and of writers in whom technique assumes a "life of its own," leading to stylistic idiosyncrasies that are not necessary and inevitable. His argument that romanticism and realism are both integral to great art anticipates the central tenet of **"Towards a Synthesis,"** the last major statement in his romanticism-realism controversy with Eliot, while the statement that the critic functions as a miniature artist is the primary locus for his critical stance. (p. 48)

Murry's "professional" criticism was written while he was editing the *Athenaeum.* The essays in *Aspects of Literature* and *Countries of the Mind,* along with those in *The Problem of Style,* contain his most widely respected writing, that which requires his most dedicated detractors to admit that Murry was a significant, original literary critic. (pp. 50-1)

Keats and Shakespeare that brilliant, idiosyncratic, pivotal book which defined the depth of Murry's romanticism, appeared in 1925. In it Keats is portrayed as the greatest poetic successor to Shakespeare and as a prototypal spiritual model. The title reflects Murry's theory of Keats's poetic growth as a discipleship to Shakespeare, as man and as poet, and Murry's conviction of their "similar completeness of humanity." Exploring Keats's soul history as he had Dostoevsky's, Murry treats the poetry as evidence of moral achievement, reflecting Keats's

life experiences, and disowns the traditional role of literary critic. . . . (p. 55)

The vitality of the work is the direct consequence of Murry's steeping himself in Keats, becoming, as it were, an alter ego of the poet. That intimacy empowers his understanding and enables him to savor nuances others had missed, to depict Keats's poetic growth more comprehensively than any previous critic could. He conveys Keats's poetic mode of thought— imagination working upon sensation—with great immediacy and so teaches a great deal about the creative process itself. *Keats and Shakespeare* is a substantial achievement for that reason alone. (p. 56)

[*William Blake*], like *Keats and Shakespeare,* is a mixture of good scholarly work, reflected in Murry's feat of tracing the symbolic system of Blake's prophetic poems (a task not undertaken so zealously before) and of emotionally charged revealings of prophetic truths suspiciously similar to Murry's own. It contains an element of forced admiration which makes the extravagent rhetoric less palatable than that of *Keats and Shakespeare.* Murry had poured light on those aspects of Keats with which he was most sympathetic, but his Keats was genuine, recognizable; we suspect his Blake of being partly fictive. (p. 63)

Murry found Blake "a great communist" who anticipated Marx's discovery that "the inevitable outcome of economic individualism within the nation was economic individualism between the nations."

The political bias of *William Blake* elicits this pronouncement, which is accompanied by a stress on Blake's anarchism and his apocalyptic expectations of a new world order arising from the French Revolution, both elements manifestly present in Blake, if less emphasized by other commentators. The Marxist influence is finally less bothersome than Murry's interpretation of Blake's religion and his doctrine of sexuality. Murry makes Blake a far less orthodox Christian than more recent commentators have. He interprets Blake's mysticism as a mysticism of descent, which rejects all supernaturalism and makes Jesus only man—man in a state of fully realized being. When Blake's poetry supports these ideas, which approximate Murry's arguments in *Jesus: Man of Genius* and *God: An Introduction to the Science of Metabiology,* Murry applauds; when Blake voices a less compatible theology, Murry is disposed to label him "mistaken." Blake's spiritual exploration he reads as a search for resolution of the elemental struggle of man and woman in the marriage relationship, a conflict between female jealousy and literal-mindedness and masculine spiritual endeavour. There is, of course, considerable textual support for these interpretations, but the exclusiveness of the critic's interest narrows the poet's range and distorts the tone. Murry gives little sense of Blake's lyricism and joyousness. When the matter leads away from discussion of his favorite topics, Murry does clarify Blake, but his remarks are never particularly acute. We can say of *William Blake,* as we could not of Murry's other major criticism, that its most valuable insights could have come from any competent critic. (pp. 64-5)

In *Shakespeare* Murry was trying to establish the poet's absolute ascendency in the English poetic tradition and to reassert Shakespeare as a cultural force in the twentieth century. (p. 72)

The most compelling reason for criticizing Murry's reconstruction of Shakespeare's odyssey is that the approach obligates him to deal with every phase of the poet's career. The task he imposed upon himself was enormous, and intermittent chapters of *Shakespeare* betray haste and a sense of obligation to glance at all sections of the canon without evincing real interest in them. (p. 76)

The most interesting chapters of *Shakespeare*, which give Murry his real standing as a Shakespeare critic, are those which deal with single plays. . . . (p. 77)

In my judgment, the essay on *Antony and Cleopatra* represents a unique pinnacle of achievement for Murry, a moment when he used apostrophic language in precisely the right way, to the right end. What might so easily be gush, what verges on hyperbole, issues as sustained eloquence. Murry's own language catches fire in the reflected radiance of the poetry of this play. (p. 79)

Before concluding, I may as well say that the epilogue is a blot which Murry ought to have had the taste to excise. This imaginary conversation between Murry and Shakespeare about the economics of being a legend and Shakespeare's consorting in a poet's paradise with Keats and Chatterton is dubious in conception; in execution it seems frankly silly, particularly in the closing passage, which grates upon us, as some of Murry's *Adelphi* essays did, by its excessive sentimentality and hints of secret significances truly understood by Murry alone. (p. 80)

Shakespeare is Murry's most successful treatment of a major poet. At its best, and that I view as the treatments of *Hamlet*, *Macbeth*, and *Antony and Cleopatra*, *Shakespeare* shows the range and sensitivity of Murry's critical intelligence and suggests the kind of reputation he would have built had he not been tempted into other endeavors. It is the last full-length critical work that Murry was compelled to write by his own quest for values. His study of Swift was undertaken late in his career in an altogether different spirit and was never invested with the moral seriousness Murry brought to his spiritual heroes. (p. 81)

Murry's writing about Lawrence was powerfully influenced by his complicated personal involvement, and he swerved between ardent praise and excoriation in synchrony with the private interaction. The inconstancy of his reactions means that his commentary is never wholly trustworthy although always interesting. Describing Lawrence in superlatives as "the starry genius of our time," "a major soul," and "a symbolic and prophetic man" even while he denounced his false doctrine, Murry took Lawrence absolutely seriously, and the intensity of his response made Lawrence important to others. (p. 87)

[*Son of Woman*] is neither biography nor literary criticism but an effort to place Lawrence's prophecy, and to explain him genetically, by tracing the path of his thought formation.

Murry's thesis is that Lawrence was a spiritual-mental being who vainly strove for sensuality, falsifying his doctrine by exalting an animality he didn't feel. (p. 93)

There is, of course, more to *Son of Woman* than a spiteful denigration of Lawrence's sexual nature. Even when he is bolstering a wrongheaded verdict about a novel, Murry is perspicacious about specifics, and of course the essentials of Murry's analysis of Lawrence's psychology have stood. It is an important book about Lawrence but by no means a wise or balanced one. Murry was far too enmeshed with him to bring any objectivity to bear. (pp. 93-4)

One of Murry's significant contributions to English letters is his restoration of interest in such minor romantic poets as Anne of Winchelsea and John Clare. In editing and introducing the

poems of Lady Winchelsea, Murry directed attention to her "exquisite sense of nuance" and "simple felicity" of expression and established a small place among the precursors of the romantics for a talent that had been admired by Wordsworth and Hunt but had fallen into obscurity. The three essays on John Clare, a contemporary of Keats, do more than simply build a sympathetic case for Clare's inclusion in the canon on the basis of his unique powers of song and "sheer natural vision." Murry locates a special individuality in Clare's naivete, his remarkably childlike response to nature, but acknowledges that he is indisputably a minor poet, without the center of "disciplined experience" found in Keats and Wordsworth. . . . It is regrettable that none of the John Clare essays were included in the *Selected Essays,* where they would be more accessible, for, as [Ernest G.] Griffin says, "all that was best in the amateur quality of Murry's criticism comes out in them."

When we scrutinize the set of companion essays on Keats and Shelley and Coleridge and Wordsworth contained in *Katherine Mansfield, and Other Literary Portraits,* we can see more clearly the sources of the marked unevenness of Murry's criticism. When Murry assumes a prophetic voice, he loses his poise. Judiciousness is lost to the imperatives of truthtelling. The argument of "Keats and Shelley," in which Murry asserts his preference for Keatsian life involvement and receptivity to experience over Shelleyian Platonism and mental ideality, is solid enough. Murry as the man of letters is suggesting what he responds to and what he doesn't. Shelley fails to satisfy him, he says, because he seldom offers the concentrated aesthetic/intellectual vision of Keats. He connects his dissatisfaction with real confusion in Shelley's absolutes (the intermixing of the concepts of eternity and the immortality of fame, for instance) and with his dividedness toward life. "At one moment he accepts and glorifies Existence, at another he rejects and denigrates it. At one moment Life is the utterance of Love, at another it is the dull, dense Matter that clogs the feet of Spirit." Keats represents the opposite relation with experience, a "capacity to absorb everything that Life may bring."

In many respects the essay is perfectly satisfactory. The quotations Murry uses to demonstrate the two poets' contrasting sensibilities are apt, his thesis that Shelley is abstract where Keats is concrete is fully validated, and nowhere else, I think, does Murry use self-confession quite so attractively and modestly. "I fear that if I had written poetry it would have been poetry of the Shelley kind: abstract, intellectual, metaphysical. But my heart demands something different." . . . What goes wrong in this essay, and often goes wrong with Murry, is a distortion of the original purpose by an anxiety that we won't agree with him. At one moment he is the genial man of letters, inviting our participation in his discovery of some private truths through some familiar poetry. In the next he is the man with a mission, requiring our ratification of his discovery that Keats is the bearer of supreme truth. This discontinuity between appreciation and prophecy unbalances both argument and rhetoric, breeding archaic syntax ("Let not the lover of these beautiful lines condemn me for sacrilege because I seek to understand them" . . .) and irrelevant nonsense. (pp. 114-15)

Heaven—And Earth . . . is an unusually far-reaching study which moves beyond appreciation and soul reading to strenuous juxtaposition of ideas. It contains the fullest, most satisfying statement of Murry's theory of modern civilization presented by studies of twelve key figures representing different epochs of English/European thought. . . . More than one person thinks it Murry's best book, a judgment with which I concur if one considers the whole, although individual chapters of *Shakespeare,* for instance, surpass individual chapters of *Heaven—And Earth.* (p. 119)

At the end of his life Murry deliberately moved outside the circle of ideas associated with the English romantic tradition and undertook a more conventional criticism. . . .

The product of this definition of his career was the decision to write some standard criticism. A few months later he was writing Henry Williamson that he intended his biography of Jonathan Swift to be "the *nec plus ultra* of objectivity." (p. 122)

Approaching this study as a critical exercise rather than as a mind- and soul-absorbing quest, Murry wrote with academic decorum, without the gushy rhetoric and moral exhortation which had often meant that Murry on Keats, Blake, or Shakespeare was not taken very seriously. The restrained tone owes something to the moderation of age but set *Jonathan Swift* against its successor, *Love, Freedom and Society,* and it is clear that Murry was cultivating dispassion, as he claimed. (p. 123)

The long essay on George Gissing published posthumously in *Katherine Mansfield, and Other Literary Studies* is a better example of "objective criticism" than *Jonathan Swift.* Here Murry's distinctive critical virtues—his responsiveness to the author behind the work, his sympathy with the themes—work inventively to produce new perspectives and fresh grounds for appreciation. (p. 128)

Murry's literary taste was sure. Nowhere in the long stream of literary comment do we find his judgment absolutely wrong, as we find [his colleague F. R.] Leavis wrong, for instance, in his applause of quite negligible writers. Of course, Murry was not as aggressive a critic as Leavis. His primary impulse was to praise artists who embodied positive values for him rather than to disparage those he disapproved of. His concentration on great figures of the past and his incompatibility with the main currents of twentieth-century literature do result in

an evasion of certain issues which Leavis confronted. The absence of sustained, forceful comment on his contemporaries (always excepting Lawrence) limited Murry's influence and is one of the reasons for his relative obscurity now. Since he primarily wrote about literature that appealed to him empathetically, he never evaluated the literature of his own age in a way that stimulated his fellow critics or gave a new direction to young artists.

When we survey the prolific body of criticism that spans the years 1912 to 1957, it is clear that Murry stands among the important twentieth-century critics. His best criticism is among the best of this, or any, time. (pp. 133-34)

> *Sharron Greer Cassavant, in her* John Middleton Murry: The Critic As Moralist, *The University of Alabama Press, 1982, 162 p.*

JOHN STEWART COLLIS   (essay date 1983)

[*In the following excerpt, Collis presents personal impressions of Murry and professional judgments on several of his works while discussing the recently issued* Letters of John Middleton Murry to Katherine Mansfield, *a collection which Collis holds in low esteem because of its excessive sentimentality.*]

Middleton Murry was the man who put Katherine Mansfield on the map. She would have arrived there in any case, but he made her reputation immediate by his swift mediation, and subsequently mythologised her by the publication of her *Letters,* her *Journals,* and her *Scrapbook.* This focus upon her life and personality has served as a considerable aid to the recognition of her genius. . . .

Katherine Mansfield, on account of her health, was obliged to live in France, Switzerland and Italy for much of the time. If Murry had joined her there it would have been necessary for him to sacrifice the journalistic career which was opening up before him, while it would also have been economically impossible. Yet he has been cast in the role of a cold, cruel, egotistical and uncaring husband.

Holograph copy of Murry's notes for his study Jonathan Swift. *From* The Life of John Middleton Murry, *by F. A. Lea. Methuen & Company Ltd., 1960.*

A lot of husbands have been unkind to a lot of wives. It is ironical that the man who did most for his wife's fame, and was completely devoted to her, should have been attacked in this way. The publication of Katherine's *Journals*, etc, contain references to Murry sometimes showing him in a bad light— cold, wayward, or indifferent at important moments. He did not attempt to censor such passages: I think he enjoyed them— for conceit can take curious forms. [*The Letters of John Middleton Murry to Katherine Mansfield*], edited by Dr Hankin, a truly remarkable literary archaeologist in the modern mode (though terribly confusing at the very moments when we really need explanation), contains over 360 pages of his letters to her during periods of separation between January 1912 and January 1923, when she died.

This volume, according to the publishers (and much of the press) 'restores the balance.' Well, you could have fooled me! True, his devotion and unceasing care for her are abundantly made manifest, though (believe it?) there were some sharp exchanges about money, and, (imagine such a thing?) he sometimes cast his eyes in the direction of another woman. The balance is certainly restored and the cold, uncaring myth reversed.

But at what a price! For the letters are really unendurable. In 1912 he was 22. He wrote to her in his twenties like a very emotional schoolboy in his 'teens—from which I do not propose to quote a single word. Later he became so high-flown in his expressions of adoration as to suggest a frantic *will to love* at all times and in all places. There are moments when he sees the two of them in such a cosmic light as to elevate them above all other mortals—passages of frightening spiritual pride. Furthermore, when he becomes increasingly well known as literary critic and editor of *The Athenaeum* and is invited by Sir Walter Raleigh to give six lectures at Oxford on **'The Problem of Style'**, his vanity goes unchecked. 'I'm afraid the truth is', he writes to Katherine, 'that you and I have carried our thoughts in literature ever so much farther than any of our contemporaries. It's not to be wondered at that I'm not particularly intelligible, I suppose. At any rate the lectures will be a succès d'estime'. (p. 21)

What is the present volume worth then, after Dr Hankin's herculean efforts? If it could have included her answers to his letters, it would have been a document of rare interest, to say the least. As it is, we do not care enough. We cannot enter into these endless ardours and protestations. We cannot mourn with these griefs. We cannot compete with the Player in *Hamlet*: what's Hecuba to us that we should weep? (p. 22)

> John Stewart Collis, *"What's Hecuba to Us?"* in The Spectator, *Vol. 250, No. 8092, August 13, 1983, pp. 21-2.*

ADDITIONAL BIBLIOGRAPHY

A. E. [pseudonym of George William Russell]. "Middleton Murry and Religion." In his *The Living Torch,* edited by Monk Gibbon, pp. 295-97. New York: Macmillan Co., 1938.
    Reprints a review in which Russell contends that Murry was spiritually and intellectually unqualified to write such a study as *The Life of Jesus.*

Benet, Mary Kathleen. "The Two Tigers" and "Murry Post Mortem." In her *Writers in Love,* pp. 40-75, 76-88. New York: Macmillan Publishing Co., 1977.
    Details Mansfield and Murry's life together and approaches their works from a psycho-biographical point of view. Benet contends that: "Katherine Mansfield was the most extraordinary event in the life of John Middleton Murry."

The D. H. Lawrence Review 2, No. 1 (Spring 1969): 1-92.
    A special issue devoted to Murry which includes, in addition to the essays excerpted in the preceding entry, articles entitled "Murry and Marriage," "John Middleton Murry on Keats," "Middleton Murry on Swift: 'The Nec Plus Ultra of Objectivity'," "The Problem of Style," and "The Circular and the Linear: The Middleton Murry—D. H. Lawrence Affair."

Eliot, T. S. Review of *The Life of Jesus,* by John Middleton Murry. *The Criterion* V, No. 11 (May 1927): 253-59.*
    A lukewarm review of Murry's biography. Eliot holds that Murry must first make clear his understanding of God before *The Life of Jesus* can attain clarity.

————. Review of *God: Being an Introduction to the Science of Metabiology,* by John Middleton Murry. *The Criterion* IX, No. 35 (January 1930): 333-36.
    Ranks *God* above *The Life of Jesus* as a clearer, more relevant philosophic essay for modern times.

————. Review of *Son of Woman: The Story of D. H. Lawrence,* by John Middleton Murry. *The Criterion* X, No. 41 (July 1931): 768-74.
    Hails *Son of Woman* as "the best piece of sustained writing that Mr. Murry has done," though he regrets the characterization of Lawrence as a tragic Christ-figure.

————. Review of *Shakespeare,* by John Middleton Murry. *The Criterion* XV, No. 61 (July 1936): 708-10.
    A generally favorable review of Murry's study. Eliot notes Murry's command of Shakespeare's work and his overall depth of understanding when studying poetry. Crediting Murry with the discovery of the Shakespearean man and several other forceful interpretations of the plays, Eliot wishes the study were not so compressed, for that caused some topics to be short-changed.

————. Review of *The Free Society,* by John Middleton Murry. *The Adelphi* XXIV, No. 4 (July/September 1948): 245-47.
    Regards *The Free Society* as a disorganized, often opaque exposition of Murry's views on Christianity, communism, and the course the free world should take, but concludes that it is nevertheless interesting for the emotive power it possesses.

————. "The Function of Criticism." In his *Selected Essays,* pp. 12-22. New York: Harcourt, Brace & World, 1950.*
    Outlines Eliot's classicist mode of criticism while addressing the deficiencies inherent in Murry's romanticism.

Fuller, Henry B. Review of *The Problem of Style,* by John Middleton Murry. *The New Republic* XXVI, No. 398 (19 July 1922): 221-22.
    Regards Murry's collection of lectures as an entertaining inquiry into matters of style. Fuller finds Murry's blurring of the boundary between prose and poetry of particular interest.

Heath, William W. "The Literary Criticism of John Middleton Murry." *PMLA* LXX, No. 1 (March 1955): 47-57.
    Studies Murry's early critical thought, particularly that expounded in *The Problem of Style.* Heath believes Murry has been unjustly denied credibility as a significant, twentieth-century critic.

Krutch, Joseph Wood. "The Most Difficult Man." *The Nation* 182, No. 2 (14 January 1956): 34-5.
    Regards Swift as a particularly complex subject for study and delineates some of the problems inherent in Murry's study of the Irish satirist.

Lawrence, D. H. *The Collected Letters of D. H. Lawrence,* Vols. I & II, edited by Harry T. Moore, pp. xlviiiff. New York: Viking Press, 1962.*
    Contains several letters to Murry in which Lawrence, after recommending that his friend concentrate on literary criticism, reproaches him for his sometimes obsequious, sometimes overzealous authorial voice. The collection commences with an

introduction by Moore, who states that "Lawrence ultimately treated Murry with some injustice, and undervalued his contribution as a creative critic," and concludes with Aldous Huxley's 1932 introduction to Lawrence's letters. Huxley, once assistant editor to Murry on *The Athenaeum*, labels Murry's *Son of Woman* a "*Hamlet* without the Prince of Denmark—for all its metaphysical subtleties and its Freudian ingenuities, very largely irrelevant."

Leavis, F. R. "Keats." *Scrutiny* IV, No. 4 (March 1936): 376-400.*
An unfavorable assessment of Murry's Keats criticism. Leavis, a noted critic and Keatsian scholar, finds many of Murry's interpretations unwarranted and, in general, believes his emotive approach damaging to Keats's reputation.

Lilley, George P. *A Bibliography of John Middleton Murry 1889-1957.* Kent, England: Wm. Dawson & Sons, 1974, 226 p.
Comprehensive bibliography of Murry's writings.

Mansfield, Katherine. *Journal of Katherine Mansfield.* Rev. ed. Edited by J. Middleton Murry. London: Constable and Co., 1954, 701 p.*
Contains numerous references to Murry. Mansfield's *Journal* covers the years 1904-22.

Margolis, John D. "The Early *Criterion*." In his *T. S. Eliot's Intellectual Development: 1922-1939*, pp. 33-70. Chicago: University of Chicago Press, 1972.*
Devotes several pages to a study of the romanticism-classicism controversy between Murry and Eliot.

Murry, Colin Middleton. *One Hand Clapping: A Memoir of Childhood.* London: Victor Gollancz, 1975, 208 p.*
Reminiscences of Murry by his son.

Murry, Mary Middleton. *To Keep Faith.* London: Constable, 1959, 190 p.*
Personal memoir by Murry's fourth wife which includes previously unpublished entries from Murry's diaries.

Philip, Jim. "John Middleton Murry and *Adelphi* Socialism, 1932-1938." *Practices of Literature and Politics*, edited by Francis Barker, Jay Bernstein, and others, pp. 218-31. Colchester, England: University of Essex, 1979.
A biographical approach to Murry's shifting political views during the 1930s.

Pritchett, V. S. Review of *Jonathan Swift*, by J. M. Murry. *The New Statesman and Nation* XLVII, No. 1209 (8 May 1954): 601-02.
Favorable review of Murry's critical study on Swift.

Rees, Richard. *A Theory of My Time: An Essay in Didactic Reminiscence*, pp. 20ff. London: Secker & Warburg, 1963.*

Contains accounts and impressions of such literary figures and thinkers as D. H. Lawrence, T. S. Eliot, Simone Weil, George Orwell, and Murry. Rees examines several of Murry's works, including *The Free Society*, which he discusses in relation to Orwell's *1984*.

Richards, I. A. "Between Truth and Truth." In his *Complementarities: Uncollected Essays*, edited by John Paul Russo, pp. 37-48. Cambridge: Harvard University Press, 1976.*
Replies to Murry's criticism of Richards's thought and discusses Murry's approach to poetry, in particular, to that of John Keats.

Seaver, George. *Albert Schweitzer: A Vindication.* Boston: Beacon Press, 1951, 120 p.*
A defense of Schweitzer's philosophy, written in response to Murry's *The Challenge of Schweitzer.*

Stanford, Derek. "Middleton Murry As Literary Critic." *The South Atlantic Quarterly* LVIII, No. 2 (Spring 1959): 196-205.
General essay on Murry's critical approach and intellectual background. Stanford points to philosophers Plato, Ludwig Wittgenstein, and George Santayana as the key forces who shaped Murry's early writings.

Tillyard, E.M.W. "Milton and Keats." In his *The Miltonic Setting: Past & Present*, pp. 29-42. London: Chatto & Windus, 1949.*
Holds that *Keats and Shakespeare* is "at once the best and worst book on Keats." In explanation, Tillyard notes that Murry, when concentrating on Keats's works alone, writes competently and compellingly but, when theorizing on the poet's "soul-journey"—Keats's struggle between the aesthetic visions of John Milton and William Shakespeare—loses authority with "fantastic" suggestions. Tillyard particularly indicts Murry for his erroneous assumptions concerning Milton.

Watson, J. H. "A Good Workman and his Friends: Recollections of John Middleton Murry." *The London Magazine* 6, No. 5 (May 1959): 51-5.
Reminiscences of the "*Adelphi* years" from one of Murry's acquaintances, who emphasizes Murry's loyalty to and concern for the common man.

Woolf, Leonard. " 'Look up There, with Me!' " In his *Essays on Literature, History, Politics, Etc.*, pp. 240-44. New York: Harcourt, Brace and Co., 1927.*
A review of *To the Unknown God*. Woolf demonstrates his disdain for Murry's vague, romantic language by quoting passages from Murry's study and from Mr. Pecksniff's speeches in Charles Dickens's *Martin Chuzzlewit*, challenging the reader to differentiate between them.

José María de Pereda

1833-1906

Spanish novelist, short story writer, essayist, poet, and dramatist.

Considered one of the most important figures behind the development of the nineteenth-century Spanish novel, Pereda wrote extensively of the rustic life of his home province of Santander in northern Spain. Portraying predominantly rural settings and characters in a realistic manner and from a religiously conservative perspective, Pereda distanced himself from both the idealism of the Romantic movement and the scientific materialism of the Naturalist movement. Many of his novels are imbued with a strong didacticism promoting conservative traditions and values while ridiculing modernization—a process Pereda viewed as threatening to the stable Catholic society in which he was raised.

Pereda was born in the village of Polanco to parents descended from nobility. His early years were spent amidst the *Montaña*, the rugged highland region surrounding his birthplace, which he recurrently portrayed in his novels, particularly *Peñas arriba*. In 1840 he and his family moved to the provincial capital of Santander, where Pereda completed his elementary and secondary education. Upon reaching the age of nineteen, Pereda left for Madrid to study advanced mathematics as preparation for artillery school. After pursuing a military career in nearby Segovia for some time, Pereda realized that his interests lay elsewhere. Attracted to the cultural-artistic milieu of Madrid, especially the theater, he sought to test his own creative abilities and composed what is believed to have been a short prose work, now lost. But, feeling more compelled to engage in political activities, Pereda postponed his literary development. Eventually he became disillusioned by city life, the unpopular reception of his Carlist or Traditionalist political leanings and, particularly, the outbreak of the July Revolution in 1854, and so he returned to Santander. Evidence of rapid social and economic change in his homeland further depressed Pereda, andafter the death of his mother in 1855 he displayed signs of an imminent nervous breakdown. The poor condition of his health was aggravated when he contracted cholera near the end of the year, necessitating a lengthy period of convalescence in the South. Returning to Santander in 1857, Pereda began contributing articles to a local literary journal, *La abeja montañesa*, and the following year helped found the journal *El tío Cayetano*. Although the magazine folded after only thirteen issues, it remains significant for publishing some of Pereda's first *cuadros de costumbres*. These local-color sketches appeared in the collection *Escenas montañesas*, which received little critical notice upon its appearance in 1864. While this neglect was damaging to Pereda's confidence, public criticism was even more so, for what Pereda believed to be realistic depictions of Santander life were received by his countrymen as unflattering portrayals of themselves and their environment.

Depressed by the failure of *Escenas montañesas*, Pereda left for Paris early the next year. However, finding the city considerably more fast-paced and corrupt than Madrid, he abruptly ended his stay there. Following his return to Spain, Pereda occupied himself primarily with politics. In 1869, intending to voice his support for Carlist causes, he revived the journal *El*

tío Cayetano, contributing numerous essays outlining his conservative ideology, which later appeared as themes in his novels. After briefly serving in Madrid as a deputy to the parliament until its break-up, Pereda withdrew from political life. During this time his second collection, *Tipos y paisajes*, appeared. Although not completely successful from the critics' standpoint, the work did receive the approval of noted poet and playwright Gaspar Núñez de Arce and the preeminent leader of the realist school in Spain, Benito Pérez Galdós. Despite antithetical philosophical positions, the relationship between the liberal Galdós and the conservative Pereda was amiable and marked by mutual respect. During this period Pereda also formed a friendship with another important writer, Marcelino Menéndez Pelayo, now recognized as the foremost scholar of nineteenth-century Spanish literature. Pereda joined with Pelayo and others in 1876 to launch the magazine *La tertulia*. In the same year Pereda published three novellas under the collective title *Bocetos al temple*. This collection, controversial for its forceful satirization of contemporary politics, received insightful commentary by Pelayo and became Pereda's first literary success.

Following the publication of *Bocetos al temple* Pereda, encouraged by Pelayo, formulated plans for a full-length novel delineating the positive aspects of pious, rural life in order to reprove in a less caustic manner the forces of secularization and modernism. The result was *El buey suelto*, a thesis novel which didactically defended marriage against bachelorhood and which was intended as a refutation of French writer Honoré de Balzac's satiric essay *Les petites misères de la vie conjugale*. Despite prevailing criticism that the novel presented a one-dimensional world view, Pereda took a similar approach in his next work, *Don Gonzalo González de la Gonzalera*. An attack upon ineffective liberal government, the novel, while somewhat antagonistic to prevailing critical and intellectual beliefs, nevertheless earned the respect of critics for its persuasive arguments. Pereda's reputation as an important, penetrating writer was firmly established when Galdós, whose progressive views were popular with readers of the time, wrote a prologue to a later novel, *El sabor de la tierruca*, respectfully recognizing Pereda's position as a conscientious traditionalist and calling him the main force behind the realistic movement in Spain—a striking statement considering Galdós's own dominance of the field. Attempting to establish himself outside the domain of regional fiction, Pereda published *Pedro Sánchez*, his only work completely based in an urban setting. Although critical approval of this novel was considerable, it was surpassed in 1885 by the overwhelmingly enthusiastic reception given *Sotileza*, Pereda's leisurely-paced *costumbrismo* ("local-color") masterpiece set in Santander's impoverished coastal region. Again seeking to display his versatility, Pereda wrote *La Montálvez*, documenting decadent Madrid life in the relentless style of the Naturalist movement then prevalent in Spain. While liberal critics predictably castigated him for his unfavorable characterizations of the aristocracy, now even his established supporters harshly criticized him for his apparent abandonment of a religious, anti-Naturalistic viewpoint.

In his last years Pereda suffered a general decline in his artistic power, although it was during this same period that he produced his most popular work, *Peñas arriba*, which is considered to rival *Sotileza* as his most outstanding composition. Of the few other distinctive events for Pereda in these last years, perhaps the most important was his election to the Royal Academy, the premier organization of the Spanish literary establishment, in 1897. In his *Discurso* addressed to the Academy, he delivered a memorable exposition on the regionalist novel, which he helped evolve. After a steady deterioration in health, Pereda died in Santander in 1906.

The most salient characteristic of Pereda's *costumbrismo* fiction is its favorable presentation of a conservative, patriarchal world order and concurrent rejection of modernizing trends, specifically the movement toward a socially integrated but morally directionless society. Pereda firmly believed that the ideal social system for Spain would be one in which a close-knit group of villagers was benevolently governed by the Spanish nobility and morally guided by the Roman Catholic Church. Hence, one of the most important figures in his novels is the village priest. Critics agree that Friar Apolinar of *Sotileza* is Pereda's finest depiction of this typically wise, resourceful, and generous figure; some consider him one of the few immortal characters in Spanish literature. In the first section of the novel his formative influence on the orphaned girl Sotileza is immense. Largely through Apolinar's guidance, Sotileza perseveres amidst her indigent surroundings and grows to maturity, retaining the Catholic values that he has instilled in her. Pereda also presents other scenarios of children educated and nurtured by Friar Apolinar; Muergo, like Sotileza an orphan, develops into a *bête humain*, a morally reprehensible character, and underscores Pereda's thematic intent of disproving Natu-

ralist Émile Zola's principle that backward environments necessarily breed base persons. Although Muergo seemingly succumbs to Zola's deterministic formula, he does so, Pereda makes clear, through his own free will. Likewise, Pereda shows that Sotileza achieved an upright state through her own determination, by choosing to adhere to Apolinar's moral guidance. More openly critical of modernization is *Peñas arriba*, which documents an urban man's step-by-step conversion to the simple orderly existence of the *Montaña*. With the novel's conclusion, protagonist Marcelo, formerly a self-centered city dweller, fully accepts the natural charm of the hilly countryside and its peoples, assumes a position of village leadership, and intends to live out his life in service to his adopted kinsman. Thus Pereda affirms not only the efficacy but the simple appeal of a traditional, rural environment in contrast to the flux and immorality indigenous to the city.

Critics note that both *Sotileza* and *Peñas arriba* expertly blend depictions of landscape with character and theme. At the same time, critics remark that in all his novels Pereda allowed an excess of descriptive detail to impede the progression of his stories. Consequently, Pereda's novels are often viewed as patchwork collections of sketches conspicuously lacking a cohesive plot. Another common criticism is that Pereda portrayed women as subservient, second-class citizens. But this view is mitigated by evidence presented by José Sánchez that Pereda, in his depiction of younger women, created strong-willed characters who upon reaching a marriageable age choose to follow their own hearts rather than the social strictures of community or family. Perhaps the harshest criticism dealt Pereda is Donald Shaw's reproach that, obsessed as Pereda was with sympathetically portraying Santander village life, he failed to address the dominant social tragedy of the region—poverty—and consequently cannot be considered a completely successful realist. Nonetheless, Pereda's novels, especially *Sotileza*, continue to be recognized for their remarkably perceptive portrayals of the lower classes.

While acknowledging that, compared to those of his contemporaries, Pereda's works were technically inferior due to overt didacticism, weak plots, and excessive verbiage, literary historian Aubrey Bell, writing in 1938, nevertheless labelled him "the greatest Spanish novelist of modern times" for his vivid local-color portraiture. This same quality led critics Hannah Lynch and Marcelino Pelayo to declare *Escenas montañesas* and *El sabor de la tierruca*, works devoid of the socio-political themes found in the more popular masterpieces *Sotileza* and *Peñas arriba*, as the author's finest achievements. Yet, regardless of such differences of opinion, nearly all critics agree that Pereda deserves his reputation, along with Galdós, as the preeminent master of realism in nineteenth-century Spanish literature.

PRINCIPAL WORKS

Escenas montañesas (essays and sketches) 1864
Tipos y paisajes (short stories and sketches) 1871
*Bocetos al temple (novellas) 1876
Tipos trashumantes (short stories and sketches) 1877
El buey suelto (novel) 1878
Don Gonzalo González de la Gonzalera (novel) 1879
   [*Don Gonzalo* (partial translation) published in *The World's Best Literature*, 1942]
De tal palo, tal astilla (novel) 1880
Esbozos y rasguños (sketches) 1881
El sabor de la tierruca (novel) 1882

Pedro Sánchez (novel) 1883
Obras completas. 17 vols. (novels, short stories, sketches, essays, poetry, and dramas) 1884-1906
Sotileza (novel) 1885
  [*Sotileza,* 1959]
La Montálvez (novel) 1888
La puchera (novel) 1889
Al primer vuelo (novel) 1891
Nubes de estío (novel) 1891
Peñas arriba (novel) 1895
Pachín González (novel) 1896
Discurso (lecture) 1897
The Last of the Breed, and Other Stories (short stories) 1914
Epistolario de Pereda y Menéndez Pelayo (letters) 1953
Memòries literàries (letters) 1962
Cartas a Galdós (letters) 1964

*This work contains *La mujer de César, Los hombres de pro,* and *Oros son triunfos.* A partial translation of *Los hombres de pro* appears in *The World's Best Literature,* 1942.

HANNAH LYNCH (essay date 1896)

[*In the following excerpt, Lynch emphasizes Pereda's virtuosity as a realist through a discussion of his sympathetic yet nonsentimental approach to his native people in a number of his works. Unlike several later critics, who consider* Sotileza *or* Peñas arriba *Pereda's crowning achievements, Lynch regards the earlier works* Escenas montañesas *and* El sabor de la tierruca *as the author's best for their unadulterated depiction of Spanish landscape and manners, a quality which she believes Pereda lost when he allowed political and philosophical views to intrude in his works.*]

José Maria de Pereda is at once the most provincial, and for that reason perhaps, because of sheer intensity of vision and a fixed compression of interest, the broadest of modern Spanish writers. That, in the matter of style, he is the greatest may be accepted from the judicial pronouncement of the eminent critic Señor Menéndez Pelayo, a critic no less equipped than Brunetière himself for the exercise of his profession. He accords Pereda direct descent from Cervantes by his style, which never loses its purity and finish however eloquent and impassioned the prompting mood; by a dialogue dense and palpitating as the flow of speech from living lips; by a vigour of clear conception of character, and the pervasion of sanity sweetened by wit. As the complete and classical expression of a race, he places this living writer between the immortal biographer of the ingenious Hidalgo and Velasquez. His realism is theirs, with the touch of melancholy that gives tenderness to irony, the witty sensibility that guards from mere sentimentality, the kindliness that blunts the edge of harsh truth.

Pereda is a realist in the highest meaning of the term, not of the document school, with its wearisome and inadequate system of classification, and its monstrous error of scientific analysis of the insignificant. Like George Eliot, he is content to ennoble the vulgar, and penetrate to the heart of commonplace existence with the fine and delicate understanding of sympathetic genius. He writes of what he knows and intimately apprehends, and because knowledge has taught him to love his subject. Bret Harte has no surer understanding of the California miner than he has of the fisher-folk of Santander, and no deeper sense of his unconscious heroism. But he is no novelist in the dramatic

signification, still less in the Tolstoian. He creates no brilliant social scenes; eschews all poignant situations except those that may be suggested by a glimpse, through a rifted cloud, of the inarticulate soul; turning instinctively from the great moments of life, from the complexities of sex, and the deep movements of passion. Where woman is concerned his pen is as cold and reticent as Stevenson's. While she is young, she is useful as an implied ornament, and perfumes the romantic atmosphere. But he deftly rounds the mystery, having no understanding of it, and by temperament being averse from study of it. He accepts the soft, nebulous condition of young and innocent love as a pretty enchantment which it behoves a middle-aged gentleman to indicate with a smile and pass on without recording its warm nonsense, its eloquent silences, without revealing the palpitating heart of youth. Love of any other sort he simply declines to recognise. Sex plays as small a part in this Spaniard's realistic studies of life as it does in Stevenson's captivating records of romance. Yet there is no lack of scoundrels and sinners in his books; but he founds their villainy on social and political humbug, on dishonour, greed, on all the vices that sin against *hidalguia* ["nobility"]. As a keen humorist, he finds matter here enough for effective exposure; and the women, upon whom he is somewhat hard, generally sin by vulgarity, by silly pretension, pride and extravagance. His claim upon the century is, however, no mean one. As a faithful painter of customs and manners of one little corner of Spain of which he is the artistic voice, he may be said to be without a rival at home, with no master abroad.

The books of this careful and finished artist, with his rare reticence and his whole power of analysis and observation directed upon a chosen society of blurred and inarticulate humanity, are cut off from the highways of civilisation as the Cantabrian coast is cut off from the rest of the Peninsula by a rigid mountain range. If it is a mountain sketch like his quaint **"Sabor de la Tierruca,"** you breathe the clear air of the Sierras through every page. If it is a fisher novel, like **"Sotileza,"** his masterpiece, the pages taste salt like the air of the coast. You may not see the ocean, for Pereda is generally scant on mere description, but you feel it round and about you. Sordid walls and a squalid street may withhold sight of the blue, but ocean's roar is ever about your ears, insistent, imperious, incessant. So blow the mountain breezes, though the persons of the tale may be saturated with alcohol. For he is no landscape painter, nor yet a describer of life upon the deep. He rarely follows his fisher-folk and sailors beyond the harbour-bar, though **"Sotileza"** contains one fine passage relating a threatened shipwreck in a few thrilling pages. It is the brutal blunders of shore existence, the waiting of the women, the momentous hour of farewell and the brightness of greeting after each voyage, the strifes, the drunkenness, the wooings, the many sorrows and the few joys, the comfortless homes, the sullen resignation and the heavy sense of fatality that weighs ever on that varied form of child and heroic animal, the sailor—this is what he paints in strokes that have the breadth, the vitality, the colour and meaning of life itself. So thoroughly has he mastered his subject that every fibre, every variety of the sailor's common thread of experience he follows, and touches with scientific certainty. (pp. 218-20)

It is this deep, unsentimental sympathy with the poor, with harbour rascals and hillside clods, the side-lights cast upon the man's character by his wholesome interpretation of nature, and the imperturbable geniality of his temper that give Pereda's writings their intrinsic value. He wisely declines to idealise life, too profoundly convinced of its need of improvement; but it is not at the bidding of pessimism that he sometimes drops his humorous pen into gall to lash the moral squalor of politics and social deceptions. He distrusts cities, and is apt to credit them with an excess of duplicity. When he enters them he exchanges the broad Cervantesque smile for an embittered sneer, except in his first novel, **"Los Hombres de Pro"** (**"Men of Worth"**), a record of his one political campaign. Here he remains the humorist, witty, suggestive, brief. The experiences and feelings of Simon C. de los Peñascales as candidate and deputy, and his wife's social pretensions constitute the highest and most delicate comedy, a bit of Daudet in "Tartarin," toned and pruned by more austere and reticent taste. Though some of his books are much too long, he cannot be charged with labouring over his characters, and he combines brevity with depth in his analysis. (pp. 220-21)

The world at large regards those two powerful novels **"Sotileza"** and **"La Puchera"** as Pereda's masterpieces, he himself agreeing that they are those which best present him. I conceived that it must be my foreign judgment that was amiss in my preference for the two lighter works **"Escenas Montañesas"** and **"Sabor de la Tierruca"**; but I have recently been set at ease by learning that Menéndez Pelayo gives his vote of preference to these same books. He admits, as I do, the superlative claims of the great and original novels, but winds up an erudite definition with a natural revulsion to personal taste:

> "It is all quite true, but every one to his special mania, and I return to the *Mountain Scenes* and the *Savour of Natal Soil*." He adds: "For me it is the Pereda of my youth I must ever love—Pereda, without transcendentalism, philosophy, or politics; the unapproachable painter of the woven mists of our coast, of storm bursting over the mountain side, of the exhilarating freshness of the meadows after rain,"

and then traces him through all the phases of common suffering and everyday joys of the delightful **"Escenas Montañesas."** It is the preference that we give "Scenes of a Clerical Life," "Silas Marner," and "The Mill on the Floss" over George Eliot's greater novels; the preference we give "La Mare au Diable" and "La Petite Fadette" over "Lélia" and George Sand's more splendid books. It is the love most of us have for the simple, the fresh, the unaffectedly pathetic, the unconsciously joyous, that such sketches as these stir profoundly.

These "mountain-scenes" contain two sketches of supreme beauty—one distinctively tragic, the other excellently witty, with that dry quaint humour which is Pereda's charm. It is not to be confounded with American humour. It is too influenced by classical tradition, for Pereda is a man of letters in the severest academical form. He has the innate worship of style that belongs by right of heritage to every gifted writer of Latin race. He writes clearly, has the art of finding the appropriate word without apparent effort, never seeks his humorous effects in anything outside the ordinary, and presents them with the smiling simplicity of Goldsmith—Goldsmith himself would have relished **"Suum cuique,"** the wittiest story Pereda has written. It is contained in a hundred pages, and is droll from first to last. The central figures are two, Don Silvestre Seturus, a middle-aged serious hidalgo, contesting a legal dispute of three generations, a country chimney-lover, with no knowledge of life beyond the mountains; and his schoolfellow, a potent Minister down at Madrid, a man of the world, who has his hours of fatigue of the dust of society, and dreams of pastoral joys and all the simpler virtues. The fun, brilliantly sustained

without a halt in an even flow of genial spirits, runs through a polished gamut of experience. (pp. 221-22)

Writing of **"La Leva"** (**"Weighing Anchor"**), Menéndez Pelayo does not scruple to assert that there is nothing in all ancient and modern Castilian literature so deep, so moving, nothing that leaves an impression so ineffaceable as the last pages of this tragic sketch. And yet it is the sordid misery of a sailor leaving his children to the care of a drunken, thriftless wife ashore. But what a figure of grim magnanimity, of taciturn sacrifice, of squalid heroism is Uncle Tremontorio, a fine fellow, who has sailed in warships and visited many strange lands, and remains ashore to comfort the womenfolk and look after his friend's drunken wife and neglected children. Here is realism, abject, miserable realism, but interpreted with tenderness and melancholy. The realism of fisher-life painted with a strong and reticent pen, not with Pierre Loti's instrument of melody and vague charm. Here and elsewhere, Pereda recalls two familiar names—though neither can have inspired him, supposing him to be acquainted with our latter-day literature, since **"La Leva"** was written in 1834—Bret Harte and Stevenson. The pages of **"La Leva"** are steeped in brine, and all the naked perils and sufferings and shamelessness of the little harbour colony are bare to an indulgent eye. It is the silent heroism and humility that he insists on rather than on the odious degradation. Beneath the filthy rags even of the drunken Sardinera he detects the human heart beating, detects the vague ineffectual manifestations of the spirit even in the mire. The difficulty of translating such a tale as **"La Leva"** lies not only in the insuperable barrier of style and colour, which can never be properly transposed from one tongue to another, but in the rough and picturesque dialect of the coast. You may find an equivalent for polished prose, but where are you to seek for an equivalent of the powerful and vivid speech of Uncle Tremontorio, with its salt flavour and unconscious poetry? (p. 223)

I have indicated Pereda's qualities of wit and pathos, and his profound knowledge of one characteristic corner of the world. I will now endeavour to give the English reader some glimpse of the features of his charming book, **"Sabor de la Tierruca."** This is not a story, but a series of connected pictures, one more enchanting than another. It is the book of an idler, a woodsman, who can write a unique and exquisite chapter about an oak-tree, who is at home upon the hillside, and finds his paradise among the pine-woods of Cumbrales. I know nothing more quaint, more odd, nothing that reaches perfection and charm by such apparent indolence of method as this slight sketch-book; and though it is pre-eminently the book of the woods and the mountains, it is never for one moment "dehumanised" by excess of description. Life is too vivid here, the characters you greet are too real, and the dialogue too piquant and delightful for the reader to be permitted to sink the personages in the scenery. It is the writer's fancy to keep you always in the open; but the characters come and go with life's own medley of profile and suggestion. It is the perfection of an unanalysable wit. The author indicates so little, and the reader understands so much, recognises so vividly a face merely glanced at, not described. In our cheerful stroll with our guide through wood and village street, recognition is as instantaneous as in actual experiences; speculation as lazy and as unexciting. We are rid of passion, with its fret and fever, of tragedy, with its bitter taste of regret, and are delighted with the every-day unfolding of existence. . . . Art is so concealed, so masterly is the reserve of this apparently discursive writer, that the pages might have been pencilled on the forest leaves as they dropped about him, without a thought of publication. And yet what breadth, what solidity, what vital freshness, what suggestion of the impeccable craftsman beneath this air of nonchalance! He makes us feel the fierce sun rays that whiten the air in the intervals of storm and rushing showers, and cast pools of throbbing gold among the thick shadows of the woods, and we are content that the story should be an unobtrusive melody, recurrent, interrupted, oozing out through pleasant philosophy and gossip at all sorts of odd corners: now in a church porch, again under a dripping umbrella, or a glorious oak, along the hilly road, or down the sunny street. (pp. 224-26)

The two novels, by reason of which Pereda takes rank by general vote as the "Master" in modern Spanish literature, are **"Sotileza"** and **"La Puchera."** It would be difficult to find a just comparison with either of these great books in our own literature. Like Balzac's studies of provincial life, like George Eliot's, they are universal by the very quality of concentrated local interest. They also have something of the vastness of nature, and ocean's thunder is their appropriate Titan-chorus. But while their realism has all the ennobling flavour, the sincerity of George Eliot's—and **"La Puchera,"** at least, contains one character who has a natural place beside the creations of Balzac—the pages have a colour, a melody of their own.

Hitherto Pereda was known as the writer of lovely short tales, full of exquisite art and deep significance, a writer of pathos and power, with every precious quality of style. Outside his provincial mission of singer of the wave and mountain-side, he had an incontestable reputation as a novelist, having written a few striking but imperfect novels, with here and there scenes and characters of the first order. At his worst, eminently the superior of Valera and Pérez Galdòs, regarded as balanced somewhere between Balzac and Dickens, not so mighty and searching as the one, more subdued and classical than the other, with a narrower vision and canvas. At his best, he made a leap back over the top of the century to stand prominently below Cervantes. . . . "Don Quixote" has come literally in two separate books, and these have already their accepted place on the bookshelves of Castilian classics as the greatest novels of the century. Far enough away both from "Don Quixote," of course, but sufficiently characteristic in the mass of more or less notable work—for literature beyond the Pyrenees has never reached so high a level since its revival in the first quarter of the century—to justify in part the excessive homage of such conjunction. I refer to it here chiefly to explain the relative importance of these powerful books—their accepted value in the eyes of Pereda's contemporaries, and their recognised position as the crown of a brilliant career.

There was still the song of ocean and its tempests after that of flowers and springtide, Menéndez Pelayo had reminded him, "Remember that you have written **'El Raquero,' 'La Leva,'** and **'El Fin de una Raza,'** and we are still waiting for the monument to your name and your people—the maritime epopee of your native town. Only you can bring into Castilian literature all its intense melancholy and rude affections."

Pereda responded to this call with **"Sotileza."** It is, indeed, the bible of sea-folk. The sufferings, the perils, the every-day heroism of sailor and fisherman, the vices and virtues of their women-folk, the play of children, and the opening heart of boyhood so diversely revealed in his three fisher lads, the lovers of Sotileza, all these forms of varied life make breathing pictures upon a vast canvas, drawn in the large free strokes of a master, filled in with such minute details as are absolutely necessary. (pp. 226-27)

"La Puchera," as a whole, takes rank below **"Sotileza,"** but it contains one character as great as any created by Balzac. The "Père Grandet" is not a more wonderful study than *el Berrugo*, but the figures are not to be confounded. The salient features of race make a sharp division, and Pereda's study of a miser and domestic tyrant, if less profound, is more humorous. It touches us less, of course, for there is only one Balzac, and he knew how to give the necessary relief to his subject by enframing it in domestic suffering of the highest quality. The Berrugo's wife we only hear of as having sunk into death a silent martyr, and his daughter is a vague ineffective creature, who inspires us with no interest either before or after her conversion to civilisation. I have already said, it is with inarticulate humanity and odd village gossips that Pereda reaches his supreme note of genius. Juan Pedro, the loquacious fisherman, and Pedro Juan, his timid silent son, with his abortive efforts to propose to the girl he loves in a dismayed, wondering fashion, are the central figures, along with the hungry doctor, who keeps himself and his poor family alive on good-humoured gossip and extravagant concern for his neighbours. These characters and the unfolding of their daily lives are excellently conceived and executed.

The dialogue is vigorous, vivid, and breezy. It is life seized on the wing, and presented to you palpitating, without being ostensibly submitted to any refining process. I say "ostensibly," because Pereda is too polished an artist not to exercise choice and discretion, and too admirable a craftsman not to be able to conceal both. "Il faut être profond dans l'art ou dans la science pour en bien posséder les éléments," said that amazing scamp, Rameau's nephew. There can be no doubt of Pereda's complete possession of the elements of his art; he has penetrated to its very depth. (p. 230)

Hannah Lynch, "Pereda, the Spanish Novelist," in Contemporary Review, *Vol. LXIX, February, 1896, pp. 218-32.*

JOAKIM REINHARD   (essay date 1900)

[*In the following excerpt, Reinhard praises the originality and lack of sentimentality in Pereda's works, but notes that Pereda occasionally presents an excess of detail. Nevertheless, Reinhard views Pereda as an instrumental force behind the development of modern Spanish fiction and the creator of one of the few immortal characters in Spanish literature—Friar Apolinar in* Sotileza.]

[Although José María de Pereda is] the contemporary of the leaders of the French naturalistic movement, he is also in a sense one of its forerunners. He began by describing country life with absolutely no purpose beyond the satisfaction of his own artistic cravings. These early writings—most of which are now gathered in the volumes **"Mountain Scenes"** and **"Sketches and Outlines"**—have more kindred with Turgenev's "Sportsman's Diary" than anything else, in that they are absolutely faithful reproductions of the author's personal observations, with no desire to make black blacker or pink pinker, or any endeavor to enhance the interest by grouping the observations round a plot. Both authors prove themselves artists solely by their skill in selecting and stating facts. The main difference between the Spaniard and the Russian would seem to be that the former had no such reformatory object with his veracious account as the latter had with his. This might be ascribed to the fact that the Russian peasants were serfs, the Spanish not, but the admission must also be made that at the start Pereda did not betray that love for the poor which was always vivid in Turgenev. It sprang up in him later to the benefit of his production, which it sweetened and mellowed without in the least impairing its truthfulness.

Pereda's aims and methods place him apart not only from those who make uneducated people serve as exemplars to their polished but unregenerate fellow-beings, but also the writers to whom as a land Spain remains ever the land of toreadors and castanets—a group whose most eminent representative was Mérimée. While Mérimée invariably selects the exceptional trait, Pereda is bent on bringing out the typical one. He paints in gray tints, shunning, even in moments of emotion approaching pathos, the loud note, the cry. His coast population is one of coarse habits: for arguments they use ugly words, heavy blows, and vicious kicks. And not a few of both men and women drink to excess. Yet such extreme cases of brutishness and vice as other modern novelists have used with telling effect find no place in Pereda's canvas. And so it is with the virtues of these people—for virtues they have in as large a measure as those socially high above them. Industrious women and honest, hard-working men are numerous among them: kindness and charity to sufferers are far from unknown. But Pereda insists as little on this as on the opposite set of qualities. He is absolutely free from sentimentality: from his entire production I recall not a single occurrence of that deliberate call for handkerchiefs which was the besetting vice of Dickens, and in which hardly a novelist of the nineteenth century has not indulged on some occasion or other.

Pereda has a way of making good and bad happen so closely intermingled as to make it often very hard to put one's finger precisely on one spot, saying, "This is all good!" and on another, "This is all bad!" Is it not generally so in life? May not this be the explanation why it is possible to relate one and the same series of events—the life of some famous person, for instance, or the history of a great catastrophe, such as the French Revolution—twice over, repeating both times the same facts, but each time interpreting them differently, making them at the first telling seem almost wholly evil, at the second almost wholly praiseworthy. I believe it is the thorough realization of this truth by Pereda, and his unique knack of embodying it in his stories, that constitute the potent and subtle charm for which it has puzzled many readers to account.

From this view of life Pereda's entire production gets its complexion. His humor, which probably more than one of his admirers would at once single out as his most remarkable quality, is remarkable above all on account of its sobriety and restraint. Undeniably in some of his earliest novels, as "**Worthy Men**" ("**Los Hombres de Pró**") and "**Don Gonzalo González de la Gonzalera**," the political satire becomes in spots so ferocious as to glide into burlesque, but these books hold no very high rank in Pereda's production, although "**Don Gonzalo**" contains a number of striking Spanish types. It is in several of the shorter sketches, in novels like "**The Soup Pot**" ("**La Puchera**"), and, above all, "**Sotileza**," that Pereda's genius has in every respect touched its high-water mark. But the peculiar nature of Pereda's genius makes it impossible to quote samples. Everybody may perceive at a glance the ludicrousness of "Sairey Gamp's" behavior at her patient's beside. But the inexhaustible fun of a character like "Macabeo" in "**A Chip of the Old Block**" crops out only gradually and through the light reflected upon it from other characters, never crystallizing into grotesque attitudes that might be appreciated if torn from their setting.

Pereda's productions derive particular interest from the circumstance that here we are evidently in the presence of that rare bird, a self-taught writer. In a period in which nine-tenths of the most popular novelists wear the cast-off clothes of either Zola or the elder Dumas or William Dean Howells, it is refreshing to come across a man dressed in homespun. Pereda has now and then been likened to Zola, but, in the first place, the resemblance is but scant, and moreover those sketches of Pereda's that were published long before anybody knew of Zola's existence reveal unmistakably the author's naturalistic bent. Moreover, naturalistic tendencies were far from unknown in older Spanish literature. "Don Quixote" and "Lazarillo of Tormes" would form all the background needed for Pereda. He himself owns indebtedness to Caballero and Trueba, and it is natural that these writers should have suggested to him the use of modern national subjects. But both of them, the man even more than the woman, remained ever far from the fearless simplicity of Pereda. And from abroad but a few, if any, suggestions appear to have reached him. Even Balzac might never have written a line, as far as this Spaniard is concerned.

He possesses not only the virtues of a self-made man, but also a share of his stubbornness and self-assertiveness. He knows not always where to stop; his instinct of selection, at times so wonderfully keen, appears here and there to be dormant, and then every detail that has caught his eye must needs be transcribed in full, regardless of its greater or lesser import. His descriptive passages, unsurpassed for convincing straightforwardness when at their best, are apt to run into mere enumeration of facts. His dialogue, which often renders so admirably the rhythm and flow of everyday conversation, with the underlying emotions discreetly but unmistakably suggested, time after time loses itself in a soulless chatter, as a once limpid stream may become lost in sand and mire. His style, bare and clean as a warrior's tent, does not always escape dreariness.

There is, furthermore, in his literary make-up a trait of clannishness: not a few of his sketches, and even some of the novels, seem written for an exclusive circle of north of Spain people, studded as they are with hints and references intelligible only to readers born and reared on the spot. On the other hand, one of the few tales of his which treat of city life ("**Pedro Sánchez**") has a long section of inestimable value to students of Spanish literature, but of no interest to anybody else.

Such pen pictures as "**The Good Glory**" and "**The Levy**" (in "**Mountain Scenes**") make one understand why enthusiastic countrymen have compared him with Velásquez. But the former—the tale of a funeral, with perfunctory piety, spontaneous brandy, and all-round fighting galore—consists of two sections wholly flawless, and a third made up of quotations from some old play on the same subject, quite stale and witless. "**The Levy**" is excellent up to the last two or three pages, where the author begins to quote from a poem of a friend of his, who, he informs us, is "the inspired singer of our national glories."

The frequent apostrophizing of the "patient reader" is another of Pereda's slightly provoking habits. I also wish he had not assured us, in a note to "**The End of a Race**," of the "strictly historical" character of that capital discussion between two shipwrecked sailors as to whether the Blessed Virgin would be likely to resent it if one of them were to drop his trousers. To be sure, they prevent him from saving himself by swimming, but at the same time they contain in one of their pockets the Virgin's scapular. A story like this needs no crutches.

Generally speaking, Pereda's novels suffer from looseness of grasp, and Spanish criticism has not allowed this failing to go unnoticed. But I am not aware that its true cause has as yet been laid bare.

Without a doubt Pereda might have constructed stories along the conventional lines, with fortunes lost and recovered, hidden crimes in the end befittingly punished, and the like—constructed them as deftly as most other people in the business; but from his very first start in literature he set himself a very different aim. The traditional "good plot" probably appeared to him a thing of a kind with the absolutely straight line or the perfect circle—interesting in its way, but with no counterpart in nature. He must have dreamed of transcribing with pen and ink part of the undulating course, the teeming multiplicity of human existence, reproducing on paper some section at least of this life of ours that revolves to-day round one center, to-morrow round a very different one, and may get from one point to another in a hundred ways, but never by the shortest. He tried over and over again, never failing ignominiously, and never conquering gloriously, until in "**Sotileza**" he brought forth a work that, although not absolutely without blemish, was superior to all his previous ones, and which none of the later ones has ever eclipsed. (pp. 161-66)

However loath one may be to use strong language, candor demands the statement that wide roamings through European and American fiction will fail to bring the reader across another book which affects his mind precisely in the manner of "**Sotileza**." Others have written stories of wasted affection, flames of passion lighted in vain, tender yearnings made the plaything of sneering calculation. But the pathos is almost always heavy, the irony strained—no-where is there anything quite equal to the sobriety and discretion of Pereda's touch.

Probably other readers besides me expected "**Sotileza**" to end tragically, and were at first disappointed at the placid conclusion. But I take it that on second thought everybody will feel that Pereda is right, and that the call for a tragical climax was not in anything that he had written, but merely an echo lingering in the reader's mind from a thousand machine-made novels and dramas. There are indeed conflicts properly to be solved only with the scythe of the Grim Reaper, and nothing but obloquy is due the author that from cowardice or sentimentality refrains from summoning such awe-inspiring assistance. But the problem in "**Sotileza**" demands no such severity. That Sotileza does not love Andrés is certain; it appears, in fact, questionable whether this hardy girl, who has spent most of her days in the open air of the beach with the boys, is at all capable of anything stronger than a feeling of good comradeship for whomsoever it might be. That ugly imp, Muergo, seems more than any one else to call forth her particular sympathy— a phenomenon due probably to a mixture of womanly kindness and a touch of coquetry. Other girls have been known to single out the apparently least attractive of their admirers for passing attention.

As for Andrés, amiable and upright boy though he be, there is not enough steel in his make-up for him to brave long and successfully the will of his parents, the prejudices of society. He has dwelt among the people of the beach as a bird of passage on a foreign shore, to return in due time to his native latitude. All of which is made clear, not by means of psychological analysis, but through a succession of lifelike pictures. Although the subject would easily lend itself to an ironical treatment, nothing of the kind is attempted. If, indeed, there be at all any smile hovering about Pereda's lips it must be one of kindly toleration. But nobody knows: he keeps himself so well hidden. To be sure, it is not romantic, nor in the conventional sense

grandiose or pathetic, what here passes before our eyes. But somehow it has the color of life and the ring of truth. It holds us while present, haunts us still when past. It is like the music of some foreign, far-away race: melody there seems to be little or none, the rhythm is almost bewildering in its oddness. But when it is all over, something in us craves its repetition.

And why not betray the secret? Pereda has practiced a very clever trick on his readers. Knowing that the deeper charm of the book would forever remain hidden from the multitude, he placed right at the entrance a figure that could not fail to lure all passers-by, be they ever so naïve or ever so fastidious— the friar Apolinar. He is the second immortal friar in Spanish literature, and I am not sure but that he is of still more imperishable stuff than Father Isla's celebrated Fray Gerundio. He is certainly very different and far more sympathetic. It is safe to say that whoever has been in the company of this man of God through two or three pages will miss not a single one of those that remain. (pp. 167-68)

"**Sotileza**" presents other sturdy men and women besides Apolinar; but, were they ever so frail and feeble, this marvelous friar could gather the whole company into the folds of his cowl and carry them unhurt down through the ages. *He* is sure to remain above ground; centuries will never kill him.

With Pereda might fitly close a review of prose fiction as evolved from the formulas laid down by Goethe, Scott, and

SOTILEZA

POR

D. JOSÉ MARIA DE PEREDA

C. DE LA REAL ACADZMIA ESPAÑOLA

F de Vial

MADRID
IMPRENTA Y FUNDICION DE M. TELLO
IMPRESOR DE CÁMARA DE S. M.
Isabel la Católica, 23
1885

Title page of Sotileza.

Balzac. At the time of Pereda's appearance in literature these formulas seemed worn out. The fault was with the novelists more than with the formulas, but it is evident that a new impetus, a bugle call, was needed to save fiction from stagnation. More than one impetus came, more than one bugle call was sounded. Vivifying currents issued almost simultaneously from France, Russia, and the northern countries, met and merged, for a while at least. When the movement reached Spain, the country's brightest minds recognized with just pride that what was most valuable in it had to no small extent been anticipated by one of their countrymen—him with whom Spanish fiction grew into manhood. (p. 169)

> Joakim Reinhard, "Spanish Fiction from Caballero to Pereda," in The Sewanee Review, Vol. VIII, No. 2, Spring, 1900, pp. 156-69.*

JAMES FITZMAURICE-KELLY   (essay date 1907)

[*In the following excerpt, Fitzmaurice-Kelly notes Pereda's artistic rendering of turn-of-the-century village life in Spain, and regards Pereda as the foremost chronicler of a traditional way of life that is rapidly disappearing in the wake of twentieth-century modernization.*]

[Pereda] was a born aristocrat, with no enthusiasm for novelties in abstract speculation, no liking for political and social theories which involved a rupture with the past; but his mind was not irreceptive, and, if his outlook is circumscribed, what he does see is conveyed with a pitiless lucidity. This power of imparting a concentrated impression is noticeable in the *Escenas montañesas* which appeared in 1864 with an introductory notice by Trueba, then in the flush of success. It is an amusing spectacle, this of the lamb standing as sponsor to the lion; and, with a timorous bleat, the lamb disengages its responsibility as far as decency allows. The book was praised by Mesonero Romanos—to whom Pereda subsequently dedicated *Don Gonzalo González de la Gonzalera;* but with few exceptions outside Santander, where local partiality rather than aesthetic taste led to a more favourable judgment, all Spain agreed with Trueba's implied view that Pereda's temperate realism was a morose caricature. The hastiest commonplaces of criticism are the most readily accepted, and Pereda was henceforth provided with a reputation which it took him about a dozen years to live down. He lived it down, but not by compromising with his censors. He remained unchanged in all but the mastery of his art which gradually increased till *Bocetos al temple* was recognised as a work of something like genius.

It is a striking volume, but the distinguishing traits of *Bocetos al temple* are precisely those which characterise *Escenas montañesas.* Pereda has developed in the sense that his touch is more confident, but his point of view is the same as before. Take, for example, "**La Mujer del César,**" the first story in the book: the moral simply is that it is not enough to be beyond reproach, but that one must also seem to be so. You may call this trite or old-fashioned in its simplicity, but it is not 'provincial.' What is true is that the atmosphere of *Bocetos al temple* is 'regional.' The writer is not so childish as to suppose that Madrid is peopled with demons, and the country hill-side with angels. Pereda had no larger an acquaintance with angels than you or I have, and his personages are pleasingly human in their blended strength and weakness; but he had convinced himself that the constant virtues of the antique world are hard to cultivate in overgrown centres of population, and that the best of men is likely to suffer from the contagion of city life. To this

thesis he returned again and again: in *Pedro Sánchez*, in *El Sabor de la Tierruca*, in *Peñas arriba*, he argues his point with the pertinacity of conviction. There is nothing provincial in the thesis, and it is good for those of us who are condemned to live in fussy cities to know that we, too, seem as narrow-minded as any fisherman or agricultural labourer. (pp. 237-39)

[Pereda] is not one of those who look forward to a new heaven and a new earth next week. If you expect to find in him the qualities which you find in Rousseau, or in any other wonderchild of the earthquake and the tempest, you will assuredly be disappointed. But, if we take him for what he is—a satirical observer of character, an artist whose instantaneous presentation of character and of the visible world has a singular relief and saliency—we shall be compelled to assign him a very high place among the realists of Spain. No one who has once met with the frivolous and vindictive Marquesa de Azulejo, with the foppish Vizconde del Cierzo, with the futile Condesa de la Rocaverde, or with Lucas Gómez, the purveyor of patchouli literature, can ever forget them. In this particular of making his secondary figures memorable, Pereda somewhat resembles Dickens, and both use—perhaps abuse—caricature as a weapon. But the element of caricature is more riotous in Dickens than in Pereda, and the acumen in Pereda is more contemptuous than in Dickens. Pereda is in Spanish literature what Narváez was in Spanish politics: he 'uses the stick, and hits hard.' Cervantes sees through and through you, notes every silly foible, and yet loves you as though you were the most perfect of mortals, and he the dullest fellow in the world. Pereda has something of Cervantes's seriousness without his constant amenity. He is nearer to Quevedo's intolerant spirit. Exasperated by absurdity and pretence, he reverses the apostolic precept: so far from suffering fools gladly, he gladly makes fools suffer. The collection entitled *Tipos trashumantes* contains admirable examples of his dexterity in malicious portraiture—the political quack in "**El Excelentísimo Señor**" who, like the rest of us Spaniards (says Pereda dryly), is able to do anything and everything; the scrofulous barber in "**Un Artista,**" whose father was killed in the *opéra-comique* revolution of '54, who condescends to visit Santander professionally in the summer, and familiarly refers to Pérez Galdós by his Christian name; the hopeless booby in "**Un Sabio,**" who has addled his poor brain by drinking German philosophy badly corked by Sanz del Río, and who abandons the belief in which he was brought up for spiritualistic antics which enable him to commune with the departed souls of Confucius and Sancho Panza. These performances are models of cruel irony.

Bocetos al temple was the first of Pereda's books to attract the public, and it may be recommended to any one who wishes to judge the writer's talent in its first phase. Pereda did greater things afterwards, but nothing more characteristic. It was always a source of weakness to his art that he had a didactic intention—an itch to prove that he is right, and that his opponents are wrong, often criminally wrong—and this tendency became more pronounced in some of his later books. Such novels as *El Buey suelto,* and the still more admirable *De tal palo, tal astilla,* have an individual interest of their own, but we are never allowed the privilege of forgetting that the one is a refutation of Balzac's *Petites misères de la vie conjugale,* and the other a refutation of Pérez Galdós's *Doña Perfecta.* (pp. 239-41)

Something of this polemical strain runs through all his romances, and, after the fall of the republic and the restoration of the Bourbons, his conservatism may have contributed to make him popular in the late seventies and the early eighties. But we are twenty or thirty years removed from the passions of that period, and Pereda's work stands the crucial test of time. He is not specially skilful in construction, and digresses into irrelevant episodes; but he can usually tell his tale forcibly, and, when he warms to it, with grim conciseness; he is seldom declamatory, is a master of diction untainted by gallicisms, and records with caustic humour every relevant detail in whatever passes before his eyes. He is the chronicler of a Spain, reactionary and picturesque, which is fast disappearing, and will soon have vanished altogether. If the generations of the future feel any curiosity as to a social system which has passed away, they will turn to Pereda for a description of it just before its dissolution. (pp. 241-42)

> James Fitzmaurice-Kelly, "Modern Spanish Novelists," in his Chapters on Spanish Literature, 1908. Reprint by Kraus Reprint Corporation, 1967, pp. 231-51.*

JOHN VAN HORNE (essay date 1919)

[In the following excerpt, Horne examines social and political conservatism in Pereda's writings. While he acknowledges Pereda's skillful depiction of traditional Spanish village life, Horne finds that Pereda's satire of the modernization of existing social structures occasionally transforms his novels into polemical tracts. For a more detailed study of this topic, in which Pereda's conservative views are examined in light of four established social institutions, see the excerpt by Maurine Mays (1926). Also see the excerpt by Sherman H. Eoff (1961), in which the paternalistic world views of Charles Dickens and Pereda are compared.]

Pereda always objected to being called a realist, because he feared that the term identified him with a school and, what is more, with a foreign school. On the other hand, he was proud to be considered a chronicler of his fellow-countrymen. He must have enjoyed the tributes paid to him by such authorities as Pérez Galdós, Menéndez y Pelayo, and Emilia Pardo Bazán when they called him virtually the interpreter to the outside world of his native province.

Pereda's literary creed is contained in his speech on the occasion of his admission to the Spanish Academy on February 21st, 1897. At that time he had reached the age of sixty-three years, and his active career was virtually at an end. His speech is a defense of what he calls the *novela regional,* or the novel that deals with the district familiar to an author through constant association with it from childhood. He defines the *novela regional,* in general, as one "whose substance is developed in a district or place that has special and distinctive life, characters, and colors, that enter the work as a principal part of it." Then he maintains that such a novel could not deal with any city that conforms with modern ideas or with modern cultivation; that it is especially appropriate in Spain; that it does not interfere with love of country by a substitution of love of a province; that it is healthy, lofty, and patriotic; that the love of a *región* can be understood only by one who has lived in it; that the inhabitants of a city can satisfy themselves with other cities, while a resident of a small district will never be contented in any other place; that the so-called *alta novela* with its politics, philosophy, problems, and conflicts is really indicative only of what is ephemeral, while the *novela regional* takes account of the eternal truths of nature and humanity; that particularly in Spain the conventional novel is an intruder; that genuine Spanish realism, dealing with the people, can trace its history back to *Don Quijote, Guzmán de Alfarache,* and other glorious products of the Golden Age; that it is therefore the purest Spanish product. (pp. 77-8)

Conservatism was the keynote of Pereda's political and social creed. Natural inclination turned him to literature as a form of expression. It was inevitable, therefore, that his writings should be influenced and even dominated by his most deep-rooted beliefs. When an author has strong convictions he may express them in two ways: by censure of what is distasteful to him, and by praise of what is dear. Thus it is with Pereda. He glorifies his beloved *Montaña,* and he protests against innovations. There is little tendency toward compromise in the man's nature. So sacred and so vital are his ideals that he cannot contemplate with patience anything at variance with them. He is unwilling to abate a jot of his lifelong convictions.

Thus, the artistic productions of Pereda are an index to his unswerving beliefs. He uses every weapon at his disposal to attack ideas and persons repellent to him. Good-natured fun gives way to irony and bitterness, and these in turn make place for straightforward abuse and argument. Irony is prominent in the *Tipos trashumantes, Los Hombres de pro, El Buey suelto,* and *Don Gonzalo González de la Gonzalera.* In these works Pereda caricatures his chosen enemies; he exposes them mercilessly to the most brilliant light, where all the ridiculous details of their unfortunate characters are readily perceived. Savage satire condemns the summer visitor in Santander, the pushing political adventurer, the selfish bachelor, the hypocritical man of importance, the ignorant *parvenu,* the purveyor of revolutionary ideas. Yet irony and satire are legitimate arms for a novelist. Pereda employs them with deadly skill. Although occasionally good-humored in his strictures, he often goes to extreme lengths to pillory the objects of his detestation. So far does he proceed that the reader recognizes at last lack of balance and bigotry.

There is a great difference between artistic (even if excessive) use of irony and employment of direct argument. The controversial tendency was probably always present in Pereda's mind. It is to be observed in some of his earliest *cuadros de costumbres.* But a short sketch may justifiably be polemical and nothing else. It is a more serious matter when irrelevant abuse is inserted into novels that more clearly aim to be works of art. Some might detect too much personal animus and unnecessary vituperation in *De tal palo, tal astilla* and in *Pedro Sánchez.* In the former work, however, the theme is frankly contentious, and nothing seems out of place or dictated by mere prejudice, if the main purpose of the author is understood; neither is the half-ironical, half-abusive style of *Pedro Sánchez* displeasing unless one is annoyed by a strong and consistent presentation of the conservative point of view, which amounts to a lost cause as far as many modern readers are concerned. Other books might well be accused of exhibiting traces of narrowness. In fact, minute search would bring to light something of a polemical nature in all of Pereda's works, except a few of the *cuadros de costumbres.*

In *La Montálvez,* however, there is no softening of the polemical attitude. It is possible to admire this book and yet to find in it page after page marked by the greatest unfairness. If we were to judge by it alone, we should be forced to regard the high society of Madrid as entirely corrupt and vicious. It is virtually a savage attack upon a world with which Pereda was not too well acquainted and against which he was moved by the most bitter prejudices. If the result is even passably good, the credit is due to the genius of Pereda and not to his judgment or sense of fairness. (pp. 79-81)

Even *Peñas arriba* is not exempt from the intrusion of the writer's opinions in a manner not justified by the plot. It is true that the lofty tone, the intense seriousness, and the exalted fervor of this masterpiece make us forget minor blemishes in admiration for the whole. It remains undeniable that conservative propaganda finds its place in several conversations wherein the artificial life of the cities is placed at a disadvantage. Perhaps Pereda could scarcely have refrained from speaking out; he was over sixty years old when he finished *Peñas arriba*, and his feelings had doubtless been growing constantly stronger as his age increased. (p. 81)

Pereda is a product of Santander, of Old Castile, and of Spain. We can easily imagine him as one of his own heroes, devoted to the soil, interested in the welfare of dependents, and intensely conscious and proud of his position. If his conservative tendencies made him unfair to modernism, they yet imparted to his artistic impulse the material for his life work, and brought within possibility of realization through his own writings the wish expressed with regard to the *novela regional* in general in the final portion of the speech before the Spanish Academy— that a record of the picturesque customs of bygone days might serve as a relaxation and consolation to the unfortunate victim of the leveling processes of civilization. (pp. 87-8)

> *John Van Horne, "The Influence of Conservatism on the Art of Pereda," in PMLA, 27, n.s. Vol. XXVII, No. 1, March, 1919, pp. 70-88.*

MAURINE MAYS (essay date 1926)

[*In the following excerpt, Mays explores Pereda's conservative beliefs as they relate to religion, family, social caste, and politics. For another discussion of Pereda's conservative views, see the excerpt by John Van Horne (1919); also see the excerpt by Sherman H. Eoff (1961), in which the patriarchal world views of Charles Dickens and Pereda are compared. For a contrasting discussion of Pereda's hostility toward mixed-class marriages, see the excerpt by José Sánchez (1941).*]

Religion is the main support of social institutions. It does not originate human institutions or human association, but through the supernatural sanction it accords them it secures their permanency and stability. In the same way the decay of religious ideas and beliefs frequently proves to be the important element working for social change.

In his religious views Pereda was a representative of the Spain of the sixteenth and seventeenth centuries. He was intense in his faith in the old Catholic religion. He believed it a faultless religion sufficient to meet every need of society, and he protested against any change in it. (p. 101)

De Tal Palo Tal Astilla is the novel which deals mainly with the religious problem. In it Pereda sets forth his firm religious convictions; his abhorrence of all that tends to irreligion; his indifference to theology and theological controversy; his hostility to any inquiry or doubt springing from a scientific view of religion. It is the story of the tragedy of love between Agueda, distinguished for her piety and devotion to the church, and Fernando, son of a scientist noted for his irreligion. Agueda returns the love of Fernando until she learns of his liberalism in matters of religion. Atheism is an insurmountable barrier and she gives him up, thus sacrificing herself for her faith. Fernando tries to accept her faith, realizes he can never believe in a religion founded on such blind ignorance in the face of scientific knowledge he has gained, loses courage in a hopeless task, and kills himself. (p. 102)

It is plainly perceived that Pereda himself saw no reconciliation between science and religion. He believed that the Catholic religion was to be accepted without question and that science was to be shunned.

Further still does he show his contempt for a science that is nothing definite and that never reaches a point of certainty. When Fernando went to the priest in an attempt to learn and accept the Catholic faith, the priest asked him about what points he had any doubt. "Doubt," exclaimed Fernando, "It is not that I doubt. It is that I believe in nothing. If I doubted, if the conflict in which I find myself consisted in more or less faith, if my reason wavered between Catholic dogmas and the principles of science, the battle would be won. But, señor curate, in my mind there is no conception or idea of God."

Pereda believed that a society which accepted scientific theories would be a society in which individuals had no principles of conduct. To him, the scientist was unrestrained. Religion was the force of social control; it was the force that restrained actions and desires; it was the force that required all individuals to live harmoniously; it produced a social mind and a standard of action for all individuals of the group. Persons with scientific leanings were not harmonious in the group. To the villagers, with their unquestioning faith, the ideas proffered by scientists were preposterous. Those who supported such preposterous ideas were ostracized from association with the other members of the group. (pp. 105-06)

Pereda's ideal village is one in which all life centers about the Church and in which all the people possess a simple, devout, unquestioning faith. The mass is everywhere mentioned as a daily religious custom. Every morning and every evening all the people of the village came together at the church to pray. The picture is very attractive in its beauty and simplicity: a beautiful setting in Nature, quiet, peaceful, content; over the stillness comes the sound of the church bell; the people lay aside their tasks to go to pray; there is peace and harmony in that group. Upon the plate, for the cause of religion, the poorest citizen would lay his last coin. He would go hungry in order to give to the church. Religion being the supreme force in their lives, religious ceremonies were as much a part of every day as their work. (pp. 111-12)

In agreement with orthodox thought even today, Pereda believed the family to be the center or nucleus of all social life. He recognized it as the institution for the propagation and perpetuation of the race. Some sociologists teach that the family is the whole social world in miniature, the most complete and the most perfectly organized group of society. It is an essential part of social life. They claim that in family life occur all the elements of the larger social life and in it, therefore, is afforded a means of training for social order. Self-restraint, obedience, service, relations to others, religion, mortality, and general culture are first experienced and taught in the family. (p. 113)

El Buey Suelto is a didactic sociological novel, furnishing a refutation of a satire against marriage. It is a lesson in behalf of marriage and a warning against the selfishness that evades the obligation of marriage. The title is a part of the old Spanish adage "el buey suelto bien se lame" (the unyoked steer licks himself with ease). It expresses the idea of complete freedom from restraint, here particularly, restraint from matrimonial bonds. The story is of a celibate who, because of selfishness engendered by a life of pampered ease, shrinks from the bonds of marriage. In this work Pereda voices his conviction of the importance of the family and shows that a celibate is of no value to society and is an ill-fitting element in it. He demonstrates that a life so badly used can end only in unhappy old age, remorse, and tragedy.

"El buey suelto," known in the world as Don Gedeón, was born into a life of wealth and ease where his every wish was satisfied and where he enjoyed indulgence and luxuries. Realizing it would mean giving up part of the luxurious living, the personal liberty, and the privileges he possessed, he opposed marriage. Gedeón had three friends who held the same opinions of matrimony. One day when the four were together Gedeón caused an explosion of wrath and of horror by asking this simple question: "Let us suppose I should marry tomorrow, what would happen to me?" Horrified they answered, one after the other, "Your ruin, your death, your annihilation." Gedeón asked for the details of this "picturesque resumé of vulgarities commonly accepted as marriage." So in detail they gave him a picture of conjugal life. (pp. 113-14)

An evil result of celibacy which Pereda points out is the immorality of these who selfishly do not take upon themselves the marriage obligations. Though each of these four celibates denied the laws of nature and each was unwilling to assume the responsibilities of family life each one secretly maintained a mistress. In keeping these mistresses and bringing illegitimate children into the world they created an element in the social group that was not in harmony with the group nor conducive to social order. Such factors struck at the foundation of society. These men were not, however, to go unpunished for their immorality. Solita, the mistress of Gedeón, destroyed his peace of mind. He tried to get rid of her but he could never succeed. She harassed him and worried him all his life. On his deathbed he was forced to marry her and make their two children his heirs. Thus he had suffered the ties and troubles of married life without ever having received any of the joys to come from a home.

To Pereda immorality was a result of the conditions of modern society. It was the outcome of luxurious self indulgence and riches. Wealth and self-interest were the causes of Gedeón's misused life. Simplicity even in matters of love and the home was the criterion of Pereda. Rare indeed are his allusions to glowing passion. He understands love only as innocent and simple. (p. 118)

In this one novel is readily discovered Pereda's idea of the value of the family to society and his conception of it as an institution of inestimable worth. However, it was not a fancy of his that lasted during the writing of *El Buey Suelto,* for there are other instances in which he expresses this belief in the family as the foundation of a good society. [Mays cites in a footnote examples from *La Montálvez* and *Pedro Sánchez.*]

As does religion, so do marriage and family ties serve as forces of social control. Pereda suggests that marriage, with its ensuing responsibilities, is a means of keeping a man within the bonds of propriety, due any position he holds. To marry demands the respect of one's fellows; it demands restraint upon personal actions; it demands wisdom and unselfishness, for "marriage in which the husband does not know how to protect his place is bad business," and it is the duty of the man to safeguard the home, because "he is lord and king of his house, not only because he is stronger but because he understands better that which surrounds him." Even in marriage Pereda favored the older system of society in which man was master of the home. (pp. 120-21)

Caste unites those who may have diverse ideas and aspirations but who are brought together by a trade. Caste isolates one group from another; it gives to an individual born within the group already molded standards of conduct, mores, and social institutions. *Sotileza* is the novel in which Pereda treats most extensively of caste. Santander was a town in which caste lines were very distinct. In one section of the town lived the fisher folk. A person born into this group, by birth became a fisherman in occupation. In the other section of the town lived the higher class, the sea captains, merchants, and such.

In the midst of the fisher folk, designated by the title of "callealteros," was the orphan girl, Silva, who, because of her qualities of meekness and neatness, was nicknamed Sotileza. Sotileza differed in ideas, aspirations, tastes, and personal qualities from the members of the caste into which she was born. Although it was not impossible for a person to rise from his caste to a higher caste, it was rarely achieved. Marriages between members of different castes were possible, but convention and public opinion rendered them rare.

Before the story develops far one finds the author's convictions against misalliances. He makes the statement, "Know you that marriages between people of different castes is not the normal thing and cannot come to any good end. A man must take a wife that is his equal and thus conform to the law of God which demands that everything stay in its proper place." He cites an example of a fisherman who married a young girl from the caste above. She lost the respect of her friends and in time she lost her self-respect and gave herself up to drinking and laziness. The husband died loaded down with griefs and miseries, leaving her a widow with a small son. She became a woman of the lowest type, and her son grew up to be the dirty, stupid, vile, half-wild, half-animal, Muergo of the story. Pereda impresses one with the fact that this is the typical occurrence when the lines of caste are disregarded. Such an alliance brings only depravation, never happiness.

Sotileza loved Andres, a youth of the upper caste. He, too, loved her. But this love so opposed custom and convention that they never dared let it be known. Andres had some good friends among the fisher folk and he frequented their section of the town because he found much enjoyable companionship there. For this friendliness with members of an inferior caste he was criticized by his friends and scolded by his parents.

Sotileza herself realized the unbreakable bonds that separated her and Andres. With the boys of her social strata there was free and easy companionship but with Andres she was always restrained and careful that there should be no intimacies. (pp. 123-24)

At last the bonds of caste were stronger than love or desire, for Sotileza married Cleto, and Andres, rather than oppose convention and fly in the face of public opinion, married a girl of his caste. It is evident that the author sanctioned such an arrangement; that he believed it proper for Sotileza to marry Cleto, and Andres, Luisa; that an alliance between Sotileza and Andres was contrary to all standards of society and nature and would inevitably result in tragedy and misery.

Sociologists say that education is the means of overcoming caste systems. But there is no such remedy in the scheme of things as far as Pereda is concerned, for education is rarely mentioned. The children of the fisher folk were not educated at all and the children of the upper class were educated only for a profession. But to Pereda there was no need of remedy. It was his firm conviction that society was rightly divided by caste lines. As he believed there were people born to rule, making a political caste, so he believed that people were born into other social castes. (pp. 125-26)

In politics Pereda was a Carlist, that is, an adherent of absolutism. The evils resulting from popular government in Spain explain, if they do not fully justify, his belief that the old type of monarchy was the best government for Spain.

In three of his works Pereda treats at length of politics and especially of the political deceptions practiced on society. These three are: ***Pedro Sánchez, Los Hombres de Pro,*** and ***Don Gonzalo González de la Gonzalera.*** In these he satirizes society's political machine. All his satire and abuse of popular suffrage resulted first, from the evils of popular suffrage as he saw it, and secondly, because popular suffrage was a characteristic of modernism. Seeing the disorganization, the panic, and the disintegration that were following in the wake of popular government he believed such a condition would always be true of democracy. (p. 128)

The political demagogs of the age realized that to gain their ends they must arouse the people to great emotional stress so they would act impulsively and without deliberation. The agitators chose as their scheme of action the tavern, where in the garrulity that accompanies drinking, they could make the people swallow their ideas. There in that emotional atmosphere they could keep alive the fire of conspiracy; there could most easily be planted the seeds of riot and revolt.

According to Pereda not only does popular rule mean an unwise rule, but it brings with it a chain of evils. Farmers leave off working, and their families must go without food, and other necessities of life. They are too excited over politics to consider the welfare of their homes and families. Nothing can overcome the spell of mixing up in politics. The farmers frequent the saloons; there is an unusual amount of drunkenness and lawlessness. One of the worst evils is the loss of the prestige of the church which was formerly the greatest influence for good in their lives. (pp. 132-33)

From the unfortunate conditions of evils Pereda took his dislike for popular government, basing his dislike upon temporary conditions which he considered permanent confusion arising out of inherent defects in the new institution.

José María de Pereda was an exponent of seventeenth century Spain. He was reactionary in his views regarding social movements and was opposed to all social evolution and progress. The dominant note in all his works is a protest against what he thought to be the corrupting moral tendencies that follow in the wake of progress. Toward the boasted achievements of modern times, which he so frankly distrusted, he was extremely hostile. (p. 135)

Pereda's philosophy was not a spontaneous product. As is universally the case, it was conditioned by his experience. He lived in a frantic age, an age of conflict between the old and the new. He could not get away from the conflict in the social world, he was forced to make a stand. Therefore his philosophy was a defense; it was apologetic and rationalistic. (p. 136)

Maurine Mays, "A Sociological Interpretation of the Works of José María de Pereda (Section II)," *in* The Culver-Stockton Quarterly, *Vol. II, No. 4, October, 1926, pp. 101-37.*

JOSÉ SÁNCHEZ   (essay date 1941)

[*In the following excerpt, Sánchez mitigates the frequent charge that Pereda portrayed women as one-dimensional, inferior characters. Through a study of interclass marriages in several of Pereda's works, Sánchez demonstrates the author's three-dimensional conception of young women torn between the acceptance of romantic love and responsibility to tradition and family. While Sánchez acknowledges Pereda's generally traditional, conservative outlook, he finds Pereda's advocacy of freedom of choice in marriage peculiarly modern. For a contrasting discussion of this topic, see the excerpt by Maurine Mays (1926).*]

Much has been written on the female characters of Pereda. Most critics agree that his treatment of women is the weakest part of his literary creation. Although this statement needs ample qualification, it may be explained if we bear in mind that the author of ***Sotileza*** deliberately relegated his women characters to what he considered their proper role—that of excellent housewives and exemplary mothers who should meekly obey and follow their husbands.

In contrast to this conservative and "old-fashioned" theory concerning the position of woman in society, we find that Pereda, the so-called apostle of traditionalism, is at the same time one of the most ardent champions of woman's rights when it is a question of choosing a husband. He endows each of his feminine characters with a will of her own, and always fights to uphold the girl's freedom of choice in marriage. This fundamental principle of freedom of choice, overlooked by the critics of Pereda, constitutes a basic tenet around which his plots revolve. Whenever parental authority overcomes the girl's will, the marriage is depicted as a failure, and the severest condemnation is meted out by the author to those responsible for the unhappy unions. Pereda presents not a single case of a successful marriage arranged by parents. He is a firm believer that, although parents may advise, they should allow a girl to have absolute freedom in the choice of a husband.

This doctrine of the freedom of choice in marriage, so constantly in the mind of our author, is another point in common with Cervantes, to whom he has been likened more than once. Pereda was an ardent admirer of Cervantes, and was also an omnivorous reader of the *Siglo de Oro* [Golden Age] literature. We may safely assume that he was very conscious of the neo-platonic doctrine found expressed so frequently in the works of Cervantes.

The most usual type of marriage found in the works of Pereda is one in which the girl succeeds in carrying out her will in spite of parental objections. It is here that Pereda delights in building up his case in favor of the girl.

Julieta in ***Los hombres de pro*** elopes with a pseudo diplomat, Arturo, disregarding more pretentious suitors considered eligible by her mother, who claims that the young man belongs to an inferior social class. But Arturo happens to be Julieta's choice. . . . Julieta is determined to keep her man, in spite of her parents' disapproval. . . . So successful is the match that Arturo saves the business firm of his father-in-law from certain bankruptcy. Julieta's mother, however, is not left free to rejoice in her daughter's happiness, but has a paralytic stroke which leaves her an invalid. (pp. 321-22)

In a short story told in ***El buey suelto*** ("Ultima jornada," chapter viii), young Ruperto is happily married to a girl of his own choice, although according to his parents "*casó con una joven de su elección particular, aunque no de su linaje, ni, en verdad hablando, de nuestro gusto*" ["he married a girl of his

Dedication written by Pereda in a copy of his novel Sotileza.

own choice, although not one of his social class, nor, to tell the truth, one to our liking'']. Equally successful in her choice is Narda of **Agosto,** who escapes with Ceto the moment her father attempts to separate them. Before Osmunda marries Don Gonzalo González de la Gonzalera she makes it plain that she is *"dueña de [su] voluntad"* [''mistress of her own will''], when it comes to choosing her man. For the same reason Don Atanasio's daughter in **Los buenos muchachos** (**Esbozos y rasguños**) rebels against her father's chosen suitor and two hours before the wedding she declares, *"No me caso ya"* [''I'm not getting married yet''], and so she does not. Teresa in the humorous play **¡Palos en seco!** succeeds in marrying the man she loves, against the wishes of her presumptuous mother who wants to force her to accept the hand of the uncultured Pascual. (p. 324)

Even when parents bring together young people with the secretly avowed purpose of making a match, the outcome is contrary to their expectation. The pedantic lawyer, Justino, in *Misseno,* a novel discussed in **La puchera** (chapter xviii), is introduced to Amparo with the hope that they will fall in love with each other and get married, but the young lady instead falls for a picaresque character whom she is not allowed to marry. (p. 325)

In Pereda's play **Terrones y pergaminos,** two families also arrange a marriage, but the interested parties oppose such a plan. Each one is in love with someone else of his or her choice.

In the second type of Pereda marriage the young lady is forced against her will, usually by her mother, into an undesirable and discordant match. In all such cases the marriage is represented as a lamentable failure and the responsible party is deservedly punished. The girl is usually in love with someone else of her own choice, but for social or financial reasons she has to accept the dictates of her parents.

The most obvious of these cases is Nica's (Verónica's) marriage to the banker, Don Mauricio, in **La Montálvez.** Besides being old enough to be her father he possesses all imaginable defects. . . . Not long after the marriage Don Mauricio is forced to flee from Spain because of his banking irregularities, and Pereda has him killed in the United States to pay for this offense and especially to atone for his treacherous intentions of laying his hands on the supposedly large inheritance of Nica. (pp. 325-26)

In the sketch **Las visitas (Esbozos y rasguños)** Mercedes is also sacrificed to an ugly, elderly, rich man at a time when she is much in love with César.

It is quite possible that at this early stage of Pereda's writing (1871) the theory of freedom of choice had not yet been fully and clearly developed in his mind. This is partly verified by the alteration of plot he makes in the play **Tanto tienes, tanto vales** (1869), which serves as basis for his **Oros son triunfos** (1876). In the play the man chosen by the mother renounces the girl's hand and goes unpunished. Her freedom of choice is thus preserved. In the reworked story **Oros son triunfos,** however, the girl is forced to marry the undesirable rich *indiano.* The mother, who is solely responsible for the unfortunate match, is rightly punished. ***Terrones y pergaminos*** (1869) was also reworked into ***Blasones y talegas*** (1876) with the girl being forced to marry against her will in the latter. Regardless of the interpretation, the important deduction to be derived from these alterations is that Pereda was thinking seriously of the solution in each case in terms of the girl's happiness and in terms of the punishment inflicted upon those responsible for her unhappiness.

There is a third type of marriage in the works of Pereda which ends happily owing to a reconsideration on the part of some member concerned.

Don Robustiano in ***Blasones y talegas (Tipos y paisajes)*** at first strenuously objects to the marriage of his daughter Verónica, but he later realizes his error and becomes one of the happiest of grandfathers. Strangely enough, this marriage of the son of a wine merchant and the daughter of a vainglorious and over-bearing *hidalgo* [nobleman] is one of the only two successful unions of persons belonging to different social classes that Pereda presents throughout his works. The explanation is that Verónica is much more humble and poor than her impoverished and pretentious father would want us to believe, as he himself acknowledges later, and the girl is therefore very much on the same level as the well-off scion of the wine dealer. The repentant *hidalgo* in the end also allows his daughter to have the final say in her choice of a husband. . . . (pp. 326-27)

Thus according to Pereda, parents may advise, but they are in no way to interfere with the girl's freedom of choice in marriage. Pereda, who saw woman's role as a minor one which must be played in a restricted field, constantly advocated freedom of choice. In three different types of marriages he shows that, when this freedom was violated, not only was the marriage a failure, but also that the persons responsible for the marriage were severely punished. Compared with some of his conservative ideas this principle is unusually modern. (pp. 328-29)

> José Sánchez, *"Freedom of Choice in Marriage in Pereda,"* in Hispania, *Vol. XXIV, No. 3, October, 1941, pp. 321-29.*

SHERMAN EOFF (essay date 1946)

[*In the following excerpt, Eoff explores the rejection of Romanticism and Naturalism in Pereda's works. Eoff finds Pereda, for his adoption of an objective, realistic point-of-view, to be a writer in consonance with the prevailing public tastes of the time.*]

The revival of the Spanish novel in the nineteenth century coincides with the growth and acceptance of realism in Spain. Pereda was a leader in the realistic movement, and his writing is exemplary of Spanish realists in general. An understanding of his conception of realism affords an important view of a prominent Spanish novelist, and it reflects at the same time the collective Spanish interpretation of the realistic trend as manifest both in theory and practice.

In several important respects Pereda may be considered a middle-of-the-road realist who steered his course between the extremes of two literary modes which enjoyed popularity within the space of his career. One was the immoderate idealization which was characteristic of the mid-nineteenth century in Spain, and the other was French Naturalism, which trickled into Spanish literature in the 1880s and evoked a considerable reaction among critics.

Aside from a few satirical sketches, Pereda's early writings were plainly a reaction against the heavy atmosphere of romantic idealism which prevaded Spanish prose fiction and literary criticism in the 1860s. (p. 281)

There is no mistaking the strong "anti-idealistic" temper of Pereda's early productions. This is seen in three principal aspects: a countermove to over-idealization of country life, an attention to materialistic and physical things, and a restraint of sentiment. . . . Essentially the same attitude toward the country persists throughout Pereda's career. The picture of coarse, rough peasants, with some view of their cruelty, their ignorance, their envious and malicious dispositions, their vulgarity, their animal instincts, is seen in the [***Escenas montañesas*** in ***Tipos y paisajes, Los hombres de pro, Don Gonzalo González de la Gonzalera, La puchera,*** and even in ***Peñas arriba***]. . . . It has been said that Pereda at first disliked the country and only gradually came to be sympathetic with peasant life. The natural development of warmth in treating his subject is noticeable in Pereda as he matures, but this observation should not be applied exclusively to his treatment of peasant life. It would be more accurate to say that he was at first intent upon counteracting the usual one-sided picture of the country, and that as the need for this gradually became less, he relaxed in his overt opposition to excessive idealization. Certainly from the outset there was no lack of sympathy for the peasants. ***La robla*** . . . strikes a happy idyllic note in its humorous, colorful presentation of a campestrian scene. In ***El espíritu moderno*** . . . the author defends country life in an imaginary conversation with a lady from Santander, and ***Al amor de los tizones*** . . . shows real warmth of sympathy for a peasant circle as opposed to the *soirées* of the city. The fact is that Pereda saw much crudeness and materialism in the particulars of rural life. He was attentive to lusty physical phenomena: food, drink, skinned beeves, robust maids, rough diction; but he saw the whole in an idealistic perspective. His favorite ideological theme—the simple peace and happiness of a patriarchal society, which finds its culmination in ***Peñas arriba***—is evident from 1864 on. Thus in ***Arroz y gallo muerto*** . . . , the peasants individually appear as coarse and mean, but collectively, under the guidance of a benevolent patriarch of the *hidalgo* class, their fundamental goodness appears, and the over-all picture is pleasant. The same perspective is evident in ***Los hombres de pro*** and again in ***Don Gonzalo***. . . . (pp. 288-89)

With the same independence that he showed in his stand against extreme idealism, Pereda pursued a course which ran counter to extreme realism. This was the result of an innate sense of balance which is evident in his works from the first to the last. In following this middle-of-the-road objective, he found himself in harmony with critical opinion in Spain after realism had become an approved form of writing, and he showed that he accepted the popular verdict as to the meaning of Naturalism. (p. 292)

How Pereda establishes a middle ground between two extremes is an important consideration in the analysis of his writings and becomes a separate study in itself [see Eoff's "Pereda's Realism: His Style" in Additional Bibliography]. But it is common knowledge that he conscientiously adheres in practice to the principle of discreetness. He avoids major plots involving adultery, prostitution, depraved humanity, refuses to give a close-up view of sex, and stops short of extremes in his depiction of rough material scenes and the physical attributes of people.

Aside from his aversion to grossness in the novel, Pereda shows his dislike for a display of scientific knowledge, a characteristic of realism as well as of Naturalism, but more commonly associated with the latter. In several places he familiarly tells the reader that he is not interested in supplying scientific information. For example, his ridicule of a precise presentation of geographical setting, utilizing chemistry and experimental physics; his refusal to bore his readers with details of medicine; his rejection of an historical, geological exposition of the setting in favor of his own supposition as to the origin of a *ría* [estuary]; satire of the worshipers of laws of natural sciences, materialistic dogmas, and the like. (pp. 297-98)

Related to Pereda's antipathy to science is his opposition to physiological analysis. In this he is once more in conformity with current opinion, which objected to extreme "anatomical" detail in emotions, passions, and vice. Despite his liking for character analysis, he ridicules a physiological technique which undertakes to explain action by an intensive examination of the inner mechanism of human beings, physical and psychological. (p. 298)

In his refusal to follow the modern trend toward the utilization of scientific data and in his occasional reproof of the users of physiological detail he showed both his own indifference to certain phases of new methods of writing and his reflection of critical opinion. That is, Pereda was aware of the accusations commonly directed at Nationalism and endorsed these criticisms by his own writings. By the time that he voices these objections, certain characteristics of realism which he himself champions (the portrayal of particular, local people in surroundings peculiar to them, abundant detail on material phenomena, commentarial pursuit of the thoughts of his characters) are generally accepted and he has no occasion to express himself on these points. Hence his reaction is limited to the more active topics of contemporary literary discussion. Of the more fundamental principles of Naturalism (environmental determinism and sociological objectives) he showed no concern, whether because, since these traits were most remote from his own manner of writing, he felt no necessity of clarifying his position on the subject, or because he had only a superficial understanding of Naturalism.

Pereda was obviously not a Naturalist, and yet he was not entirely immune to its influence. The similarities in some of his writing to the Naturalistic manner, however, have been given undue weight. Some of Pereda's contemporaries called him Naturalistic in procedure, though not in philosophy. Thus attention was directed to "Naturalistic" description in the portrait of Judas (*El buey suelto*), the portrait of Patricio Rigüelta and the tavern scene (*Don Gonzalo* . . .), the bacchanale scene in *De tal palo tal astilla,* and the depiction of adultery in *Pedro Sánchez.* Even the "excessive" detail of *Sotileza* is likened by Clarín to Zola's technique, and a shadow of determinism is read into *Pedro Sánchez.* (p. 299)

All of this criticism shows the popular tendency to identify Naturalism with the choice of crude subject matter, without proper attention to the manner of treatment. For, whereas Zola would have described such material as the bacchanale scenes in *Don Gonzalo* . . . and *De tal palo tal astilla* with grim and sober detachment, Pereda becomes impassioned, motivated by moral indignation rather than by critical judgment, and swings into hyperbolical language—burlesque and occasionally grotesque—a far cry from the impassive, factual mood of Zola. (p. 300)

The tendency to excessive detail is a common trait of nineteenth-century realists, though when this becomes a purely sober, factual enumeration without artistic effort to lift the subject above a material level, it is said to be Naturalistic. Zola felt that a great accumulation of detail was basic in science. Hence his use of it in the novel. Because of his purpose, he was often persistent and inexorable in description, losing sight at times of what was significant. Pereda, on the other hand, following both a convention and a personal liking for description rather than a scientific objective, relaxes and omits detail, frequently saying "etc., etc." The market scene in *El sabor de la tierruca* (ch. XVIII) is a long enumeration of wares for sale—somewhat longer than his usual enumeration. But Pereda's main objective is as usual to give a good view of a village custom for benefit of the "lector de ultrapuertos" ["foreign reader"], and his descriptive account is far from being an impassive concentration upon material things. (pp. 300-01)

Pereda, then, regardless of his lack of interest in literary theory and the debates on idealism, realism and Naturalism, shows that he visualized realism and his own part in the movement from essentially the same plane as that of the average public opinion of his epoch. From the time of his anti-romantic reaction to the end of his career, he was dominated by the criterion of vigorous portraiture of the physical world, within the limits of artistic decorum. A combination of "lo real" and "lo ideal" is common to all artists in varying degree, but Pereda's deliberate orientation between two extremes which seriously occupied the literary thought of his day makes an analysis of the balance between the objective and the subjective world a most important consideration in the study of his realism, particularly as pertains to one of the major realistic traits—the frank revelation of facts. This balance, especially noticeable in his style, is perhaps the literary attribute of which Pereda was most conscious. Other general realistic traits—a prominent view of the world of material things, multiplicity and variety in experiences, happenings, and character traits, exaltation of the local and particular in people and scenes, identity of personages with their surroundings, prominence of the average and commonplace—are clearly seen in Pereda's structural technique and his characterization. They conform not only to his natural inclination but also to the long tradition of realism which enjoyed an accentuated resurgence in the nineteenth century. In certain specific respects, such as lengthy description and exposition, and the commentarial reporting of his characters' thoughts, Pereda was doubtless following a convention of nineteenth-century realism. His emphasis on the external or visual realities is also characteristic of the long procession of earlier pictorial realists, with whom he must be classified.

In all these respects Pereda was abreast of his times and in fact a leader among Spanish writers. The one important trait of modern realism which he failed to share and which places him behind and out of step with modern novelists was his intellectual attitude toward contemporary conditions. The foremost realists of the nineteenth century confronted the immediate state of social and human relations critically and studiously. Pereda was alert to actualities in so far as their external appearances were concerned but he was not studious of social conditions and was only mildly so of individual character. When critically confronting his subject, he was a simple polemic on social problems and a satirist of types and customs much after the manner of the seventeenth-century picaresque novelists.

In this respect Pereda was once again representative of the average thought of his day, and indeed, typically Spanish. (pp. 301-02)

Sherman Eoff, "Pereda's Conception of Realism as
Related to His Epoch," in Hispanic Review, Vol.
XIV, No. 4, October, 1946, pp. 281-303.

SHERMAN H. EOFF (essay date 1961)

[*In the following excerpt, Eoff examines similarities between the
paternalistic world orders of Charles Dickens's* David Copperfield *(1850) and Pereda's* Sotileza. *He perceives in both novels
a harmonious, orderly universe which recalls that envisioned by
eighteenth-century thinkers who believed that the basic tenets
underlying the sciences complemented a belief in a fatherly Creator. For other studies of Pereda's traditionalist stance in his
novels, see the excerpts by John Van Horne (1919) and Maurine
Mays (1926).*]

Devotees of Spanish literature esteem Pereda above all as a
regional artist, whose vivid pictures of customs and types in
and around Santander are superlative examples of genre painting. Possibly because of this strong local focus they have overlooked the affinity that exists between the Spaniard and Dickens, while frequently naming the latter in speaking of Pérez
Galdós, Pereda's contemporary. There is, of course, a sound
basis for associating the names of Dickens and Galdós, especially in connection with their attitudes of sympathetic
amusement toward a wide variety of human specimens; and
there is no question that Galdós greatly admired Dickens, as
have many other Spanish novelists. But in a fundamental intellectual sense these two writers belong to radically different
worlds. Galdós was very alert to developments in science and
philosophy . . . and in his own independent way left a substantial novelistic interpretation of the most advanced thinking
of his day. Pereda, on the other hand, would have liked to turn
the clock back and recapture the rhythm of living that preceded
the appearance of railroads and all the noisy progress of an
industrial age. Like Dickens, though not specifically from the
same motives, he resurrected his childhood days and reconstructed a world that contrasts sharply with the modern world
of questioning search into the uncertain meanings of life.
(pp. 38-9)

The desire to revive the past is more noticeable in his novels
than in those of Dickens, who was historically in closer intellectual proximity to the world vista that he presents. Yet at his
best Pereda provides a thoroughly contemporaneous view within
the range of an old perspective. It would be difficult to find
anywhere in literature stronger support for Newton's contention
that the universe proclaims the greatness and wisdom of an
omniscient Creator than Pereda's descriptions of sea and mountains. Nor could one find anywhere a portrayal of personal
relationships more suggestive of a "fatherly" arrangement in
the world order.

Upon the broad basis of this traditional outlook the comparison
of Pereda and Dickens should be made. At the same time it
must not be assumed that the two novelists have a close affinity
in all respects. There is, indeed, a certain curious interest attached to the fact that two personalities very unlike in several
ways present fundamentally the same philosophical outlook
and do so apparently without the least intention of being philosophical. Pereda was a person of aristocratic bearing from the
well-to-do middle class, a retiring person content to live apart
from society, an orthodox Catholic, and a believer in an authoritarian social structure. Dickens, though by no means af-
filiated with the proletariat, was more a man of the people,
socially an extrovert, and in religion an anti-Catholic and rather
indifferent to the formalities of worship of any kind. He was,

also, much more personally involved in questions of social
welfare than the Spaniard, although the latter often engaged in
caustic satire of social flaws. But when the two novelists rise
above the level of controversy and attack they occupy positions
close to each other in so far as their vision of the world order
is concerned; and in their spirited and picturesque record of
this vision rests their major claim to recognition. Surely Dickens' survival value derives not so much from his social indignation as from the warmth and colorfulness with which he
portrays the human species, especially as seen in the neighborly
relationships of friends and families. The same can be said of
Pereda, whose regional sketches and novels combine with a
vivid local color a sympathetic delineation of people in broad
and simple strokes.

Pereda is at his best in *Sotileza,* probably because it is the novel
in which he becomes most enthusiastically involved. Like *David
Copperfield,* it is a personal composition; for it recalls the days
when the author was a boy in Santander, associating with the
children of the fisherfolk and taking great delight in all activities
relating to the sea. Like *David Copperfield,* also, *Sotileza* leaves
us with the impression of having been on an excursion. The
English novel, however, . . . is the record of a youth's journey
over a large area of the human community; while the Spanish
novel is more aptly described as a visit to a chosen place of
recreation, since it localizes its record of youthful experiences
within the confines of a single city. In a very real sense it can
be called a novel of customs, for Pereda clearly shows that in
so far as narrative technique is concerned his main inspiration
is the *costumbrismo* or depiction of customs in which Spanish
writers have always displayed special talent and which enjoyed
great popularity in Spain in the first half of the nineteenth
century. At times the author gives himself wholeheartedly to
the delineation of scenes, seemingly more interested in what
can be seen at any given moment than in what the action or
the situation may lead to. Consequently, the narrative progression, in the early part of the novel at least, appears to be
merely a chronological succession of episodes.

The narrative structure of the Spanish novel thus is even looser
than that of *David Copperfield.* The explanation is that in the
beginning of his story Dickens concentrates pretty much on
one person. The old way of life that he evokes gradually assumes broad dimensions as his hero, once his security is established, is drawn into a large group relationship, the picaresque aspects having to do with an orphan boy's hardships
meanwhile fading into the background. Pereda, on the other
hand, as he explains in his foreword to the reader and in the
conclusion of the first chapter of *Sotileza,* proposes to re-create
scenes, people, and customs of the fishing town of Santander
that he had known as a boy. He therefore sets about his task
of reviewing "the good old days" by visualizing a collective
picture at the outset and centering his attention on a group of
children. (pp. 39-41)

In a novel of this kind the question of plot may seem unimportant as compared to the general panoramic view of the locale
and the collective view of a humble but heroic people. Yet a
novel cannot be considered simply as a picture of something,
even though the scenic material may be its most enjoyable part.
It inevitably tells a story, and the story in turn inevitably gives
meaning to the scenes recorded. Realizing this, Pereda accepts
his narrative responsibility and in fact becomes intrigued by
the possibilities surrounding the dramatic episode that he in-
vents. As a result, he leads us into a potentially tense study of
character and situation and almost forgets his major objective

in favor of a psychological handling of the Sotileza-Andrés relationship. The major objective, however, which is to revive imaginatively a way of life by way of a group experience, reasserts itself decisively in the conclusion and gives finality to the narrative movement. This can now be defined as an account of the rather usual experiences, including the complications of youthful love, of a group of children who grow up in the Santander of the author's boyhood days. When viewed in its completeness, the novel thus becomes a colorful and sympathetic presentation of the ageless story of childhood blossoming into maturity, stumbling and bruising its collective nose, but emerging at last on an even keel in accord with the traditions of old and the lessons of experience handed down from generation to generation.

In subject and comprehensive narrative development, therefore, *Sotileza* bears a marked resemblance to *David Copperfield*, even when we grant that the latter reaches beyond the problems of young people to a larger extent than the Spanish novel. The similarity in the basic narrative concept is found in the fact that each story is something of a conducted tour over youthful pathways marked with mishaps, amusing incidents, and picturesque people, and terminating in a peaceful synchronization with the even rhythm of life. . . . Pereda has, in effect, selected and elaborated upon one portion of an extensive tour, such as that conducted by Dickens, and has done so with a kindred spirit of gaiety appropriate to a sight-seeing trip. Both writers find it difficult to pass up an opportunity to create a kind of circus entertainment by enlarging upon a promising incident. Both writers, also, have an eye for the poetry of little things and both indulge in humorous extravagance, seemingly able to lose themselves in the art of narration and the art of description without worrying about grave questions relating to human destiny. Compare Dickens' comment on Ham Peggotty's hat, "and you couldn't so properly have said he wore a hat, as that he was covered in a top, like an old building, with something pitchy," with the following from Pereda: "A Catalan cap placed in just any manner on top of his tangled hair, like a dirty rag spread out on a thatched fence." The novelists' pleasure in description is even more vividly evident in their sketching of scenes. Recording the incident when the waiter at an inn eats Davy's meal, Dickens makes a game of his narration:

> So he took a chop by the bone in one hand, and a potato in the other, and ate away with a very good appetite, to my extreme satisfaction. He afterward took another chop, and another potato . . . He entreated me more than once to come in and win, but what with his table-spoon to my tea-spoon, his despatch to my despatch, and his appetite to my appetite, I was left far behind at the first mouthful, and had no chance with him.

Pereda, lustier in his manner and more intent on physical detail, indulges in a similar exercise of playful extravagance while describing the rough Mocejón family eating a meal:

> Each spoonful was maneuvered by Mocejón like a cartload of hay. Only his wife surpassed him, not so much in the loading as in the unloading into her mouth, which came out to the encounter with lips spread back over the angular and half-open jaws . . . and then . . . then it was all over, because Silda, observant as she was, could never determine whether it was the

mouth that sprang upon its prey, or whether it was the prey that jumped, from midway in its journey, into the mouth.

Both novelists, in short, survey the human species with the amusement of sympathetic observers and with a sense of responsibility for leaving descriptive and classificatory records. The records which they leave, moreover, are characteristic of a preevolutionary outlook upon the world. In Pereda, as in Dickens, the total collection of personages is a balanced assortment representing in separate categories the variations in nature. . . . Pereda is less abstract than Dickens in his method of characterization, for his portraiture relies heavily on details of local surroundings. His characters are nonetheless typical and fixed quantities that represent general patterns of behavior. The personal motivations, social and moral, reveal the virtues and weaknesses that make up a cross section of human traits applicable to all people from time immemorial.

Even in his handling of Andrés and Sotileza, whose portraits are freer than most of the others from the limitations of type depiction, Pereda is interested primarily in generic traits. The characterization of Andrés comes near being a psychological study, but the youth is still a typical son of a middle-class family, who behaves in a typical manner as he listens to the temptations of the devil, gets into troublesome complications, is reprimanded by his elders, displays a momentary rebelliousness, repents, and quietly follows the path that he is expected to follow. In portraying Sotileza, the author deliberately tries to envelop her in an air of mystery, pointing to her lofty detachment, her obsession with cleanliness amidst sordid surroundings, and her seeming fascination for the brutish Muergo. In general Pereda professed little interest in the why of personality traits and was openly hostile to the newfangled school of realists who indulged in psychological analysis and emphasized the importance of environmental influence on character. . . . The author is less interested in her as an individual personality than he is in the group activity for which she is responsible. Hence, despite the nominal position of heroine, she is scarcely more than a representative local element in a corporate body of mutually independent parts, on equal terms with all the other elements.

We have in Pereda, therefore, a picture of neighborly separateness similar to what we find in Dickens, as regards both the relationship between one personality and another and the relationship between personality and environment. In the Spanish novel the characters seem to be on no better than an equal footing with their material background, since they are enveloped in a world of things almost as prominent and interesting to look at as they. In this respect, however, they are somewhat like children playing in the dirt—attached to it but independent of it. The reader is interested in what happens to each person, but there is no reason for any particular interest in what happens to each personality. Consequently, the narrative effect in its wholeness leaves us thinking about the disposition of an assemblage of parts that must find their allotted places in an ordered system. Operating within the limits of a freedom granted by a Supreme Father, the persons move about in friendly independence of each other, accepting the regulations of the universal order, like children who trust and obey their elders, and adopting the viewpoint that the most important questions are already settled or will be settled without the necessity of anxious searching for new interpretations. "Niños grandes" (big children), Pereda affectionately calls a group of friends who visit Andrés' father on one occasion, and he himself would hardly aspire to a philosophical outlook more complex than theirs.

Sotileza, then, is a serene composition, seemingly untouched by the provocative questions raised by modern science. Pereda was very conscious of contemporary religious skepticism, and his orientation to the past may in part be a consequent reaction. But, as in the case of Dickens, his loyalty to the old is a spontaneous manifestation of intellectual equanimity whose explanation is found not simply in religious faith but in its harmony with rational and scientific interpretation. The stand taken by both novelists is, fundamentally, the extension of an eighteenth-century outlook in which science, philosophy, and religion agree in their conception of a stabilized, mechanistic universe, whose earthly compartment is for the most part a robust and healthy order that operates smoothly in conformity with the rules of its separate Creator. (pp. 45-9)

The tranquil, compartmentalized view of the world found in *David Copperfield* and *Sotileza* contrasts sharply with the uneasiness that surges in the naturalistic novels of the nineteenth century as a result of the scientific and philosophical insistence on the identification of man (and God) with nature. In these twentieth-century days, when the gloomy preoccupation with man's position in the universe is even more intense, the novels of Dickens and Pereda may seem far removed from actuality. It is natural to look on them as friendly companions of childhood, to be recalled occasionally for a moment's innocent pastime but not to be taken seriously as subjects of philosophical contemplation. Yet they stand as reminders of more than the simple faith and simple tastes of long ago. For in their interpretation

PEÑAS

ARRIBA

POR

D. JOSÉ MARÍA DE PEREDA

C. DE LA REAL ACADEMIA ESPAÑOLA

—✳✦✧✦✳—

F de Vial

MADRID
EST. TIP. VIUDA É HIJOS DE M. TELLO
IMPRESOR DE CÁMARA DE S. M.
C. de San Francisco, 4
1895

Title page of Peñas Arriba.

of harmony between science, religion, and philosophy they illustrate in the history of thought the attainment of a goal that man seems to prize above all else. The desperate striving on the part of other modern novelists, within radically different intellectual perspectives, bears testimony to the significance of an intellectual orientation in which both science and religion allow for the ideal of a divine personality. (p. 50)

> *Sherman H. Eoff, "A Fatherly World According to Design," in his* The Modern Spanish Novel: Comparative Essays Examining the Philosophical Impact of Science on Fiction, *New York University Press, 1961, pp. 21-50.**

DONALD L. SHAW (essay date 1972)

[*In the following excerpt, Shaw provides a general discussion of Pereda's works and concludes that he was never able to fully detach himself from the political and moral themes which imbue his novels. Thus Shaw regards Pereda as a failed realist who is only of marginal influence to the movement of literary realism in Spain.*]

In [Pereda's] works can be found all the major beliefs, fears, and prejudices of the rural provincial gentry. Angry at the resurgence of power by the radical-minded urban middle class, jealous of its commercial and administrative predominance, shocked by its irreligion, and threatened by the unrest in the countryside which followed the [Spanish Revolution of 1868], Pereda and his class clung blindly to belief in a closed paternalistic pattern of rural society which provided them with a social role, and to the traditional outlook, with religion in the foreground, which maintained its stability. (p. 116)

Each of these four novels deals with a facet of social stability: [*El buey suelto* and *De tal palo, tal astilla*] . . . with the basic nucleus of that stability—marriages; *Los hombres de pro* and *Don Gonzalo González de la Gonzalera* . . . with its political dimension. *El buey suelto,* as Montesinos has shown, stands in an intermediate position between the satirical description of a 'type' (in this case 'the bachelor'), characteristic of *costumbrismo* ["depiction of customs"], and a novel proper. It labours to prove that any marriage (except the kind dealt with in *De tal palo, tal astilla*!) is better than none, and that bachelorhood means squalid discomfort, furtive sexuality, expense, and misery. Everyday observation disproves both propositions. *De tal palo, tal astilla,* a reply to [Benito Pérez] Galdós's *Gloria,* deals from the ultra-Catholic point of view with the specific case of marriages where one party is an infidel. Again Pereda's extreme outlook plays him false. Instead of exploring a painful conflict of love and religious allegiance, he presents a head-on collision of ideologies complicated by a melodramatic subplot with a religious hypocrite as the villain. Both elements are intended to throw into relief the fortitude of Águeda, the heroine, but in fact only succeed in underlining her inhuman inflexibility, at the expense of the hero, who is driven to suicide.

Los hombres de pro and *Don Gonzalo González de la Gonzalera* caricature the newly enriched provincial bourgeoisie of plebeian origin and its entry, disastrous in Pereda's view, on to the political stage. But the message of both books is in the end negative and confused. The first unwisely attempts to combine satire of Simón Cerrojo, alias Don Simón de los Peñascales, and his career in politics, with an exposure of Spanish parliamentary institutions. The result is self-contradictory. If the overt *moraleja* [moral maxim] is that of its final sentence: 'La desgracia de España, la del mundo actual, consiste en que quieran ser ministros todos los taberneros y en que haya dado in llamarse verdadera *cultura* a la de una sociedad en que *dan el tono* los *caldistas* como yo' ['The disgrace of Spain, of today's world, lies in that every barkeep wants to be a minister, and that the name of true *culture* may be given to a society in which the standards are set by *inferiors* like myself']; there is nothing in the body of the novel to suggest that the system of cynical corruption and spoils distribution of which he is a victim is in any way his creation or that the old directing class, left to themselves by the Simón Cerrojos, would dismantle it. ***Don Gonzalo González de la Gonzalera*** examines the rural end of the situation. The *status quo* of a tiny village is overturned by the wealthy *parvenu* and a trio of 'Liberal' henchmen only marginally less nasty than their confrère in Alarcón's *El niño de la bola,* published the following year. How insecure the *status quo* was, is demonstrated by the speed of Don Gonzalo's triumph over the local squire and priest. The violence of oppression which Pereda attributes to the 'Liberal' upstart does not distract us from his inability to suggest a more convincing alternative than oligarchic paternalism resting on ignorance.

The main technical feature of this early group of doctrinal novels is the excessive influence of theme on plot-structure and characterisation. Instead of appearing to be an exploration of a human or social situation, they give the impression that the reality with which they deal has been forced to conform to a ready-made framework of ideas. (pp. 117-18)

El sabor de la tierruca . . . , in contrast, is of major importance both technically and because of the shift in Pereda's attitude towards rural society which emerges in it. Though written quite rapidly in the summer of 1881, following Pereda's usual habit of composition, it is carefully put together and complex in narrative structure. The episodes, though inevitably dictated by and developed in accordance with the theme, which is once more that of the defence of a rural community against political contamination, are faultlessly patterned. Four strands of narrative (two love-affairs illustrating Pereda's insistence on closed vertical class-structure, plus two chains of political events illustrating his benevolent conservatism, but for once doing some justice to Liberal idealism) are skilfully woven together so as to take full advantage of parallelism and contrast. They reach a narrative climax in Chapter 20. After this the novel, though changing course slightly like its predecessor ***Don Gonzalo,*** rises to a dramatic climax in the bloodless battle-scene between the two rival villages. Along with its improved craftsmanship we notice in the novel the emergence of that idyllic presentation of country life, which was to reach its peak in ***Peñas arriba,*** contrasting not only with the more convincing vision of Pardo Bazán, but even with Pereda's own earlier work.

At this point reference may usefully be made to the question of Pereda's realism. Nothing more aptly illustrates the negative aspect of the legacy of *costumbrismo* to public taste than the expectation, the demand even, that reality be suitably prettified before being presented to the average reader. . . . The fact is that no satisfactory definition of realism which involves the work of Pereda can be evolved. Baudelaire's well-known statement that the aim of the realist is to present reality as it would be if he were not there, touches the essence of the movement. However unattainable objectivity is in actual fact, the realist author must convey the impression of writing objectively. This means not only presenting his material with apparent detachment, but also selecting it without undue prejudice. On both these counts Pereda fails, not only in his early sectarian novels,

but even in his later masterpieces ***Sotileza*** and ***Peñas arriba.*** Whether his theme is political or moral, or merely drawn from the life of his *patria chica* ['little homeland'], Pereda is always too close to it, too emotionally involved with it, too prone to relate it to his personal ideology. Secondly, Pereda's reality is always seen from the same viewpoint, that of the middle class. Only the squirearchy and bourgeois characters are seen from their own level. Pereda's 'interesantes patanes' ['interesting bumpkins'], as Galdós described them, are seen patronisingly from above. What finally cuts Pereda off from realism is that none of his novels, full of problems as they are, studies the real problem of the region, which is poverty, from the inside, as Galdós does with regard to his 'region'—Madrid. In that respect ***La puchera*** is a disappointment.

By the middle 1880s, Pereda was tired of 'problems' in any case and, like Galdós after the 'novelas de primera época' ['novels of the first period'], reached out towards a new phase in his work. Pereda defines his intention in writing ***Sotileza*** at the end of Chapter I as being that of offering to the consideration of later generations 'algo de pintoresco, sin dejar de ser castizo, en esta raza pejina que va desvaneciéndose entre la abigarrada e insulsa confusión de las costumbres modernas' ['something picturesque, without avoiding realism, in this low-class race that has slipped away into the motley, tasteless moral confusion of modern custom']. The sentence contains three of the classic elements of *costumbrismo*: *pintoresquismo* [picturesqueness], *casticismo* [love of purity], and rescue from oblivion of *lo periclitado* [that which is endangered]. Only moralism is lacking, and that is present in the prologue.

Two of Pereda's major mature novels [***Sotileza*** and ***Peñas arriba,*** follow this pattern, with ***La puchera***] . . . not quite at the same creative level. In contrast, [***Pedro Sánchez*** and ***La Montálvez***] . . . develop Pereda's criticisms of the bourgeois society of Madrid, from which Marcelo in ***Peñas arriba*** is gradually detached by the pleasures and responsibilities of life in the highlands of Cantabria. ***La Montálvez*** need not detain us. It is the exact opposite of a novel of observation, and shows Pereda sadly out of his depth. ***Pedro Sánchez,*** on the other hand, is the outstanding novel of Pereda's middle period. Its theme is one of the classic themes of the nineteenth-century novel: that of the young provincial who sets out to conquer the great metropolis, only to lose his soul in the process. Montesinos compares the novel with the *Episodios nacionales* [national episodes] of Galdós. But its real filiation is surely with Balzac. Told in the form of memoirs of a left-wing journalist turned revolutionary leader, the novel is set in the Madrid of the early 1850s with its dramatic climax in the Revolution of 1854. It follows a logical tripartite arrangement charting successfully Pedro's rapid rise to fame, his brief period of power and success, followed by his retirement and disillusion. Meanwhile his public career is gradually overshadowed by his erroneous marriage, and both collapse together. Wisely, Pereda devotes 70 per cent of the narrative to Pedro's early struggles against a background based on his own experiences in the capital from 1852 until 1855. The evocation of mid-century Madrid, and especially of its literary and cultural life in Chapters 11 to 16, is for those who are impatient of his earnest regionalism incomparably the best thing Pereda ever wrote.

With ***Sotileza*** and ***Peñas arriba,*** by many regarded as his masterpieces, Pereda, encouraged by Menéndez Pelayo, returned to describing the manners and customs of his native province. What both novels have in common is a markedly less well-developed plot—never Pereda's strong point—and a consequent tendency to resolve themselves into a string of episodes held together by the presence of the central characters. In *Sotileza* the story concerns the youth and mutual attraction of two young people, Sotileza herself and Andrés Solindres, in the old city of Santander, whose conversion into a modern commercial centre and resort Pereda so much regretted. Blinkered by the class-prejudices of his age as Pereda was, he was necessarily obliged to bring the affair to nothing, given the difference in social status between the two young people. Nevertheless, it is the only love-affair he ever described in his novels which holds the reader's interest, because of its very unconventionality. But the storyline, with its problems arbitrarily resolved by the storm at sea, involving Andrés—a characteristic piece of Peredan dramatic description—is a mere pretext for nostalgic description of the life and customs of the fisherfolk of Santander. They are described with a wealth of observed detail and scrupulously accurate technical language (which one suspects Pereda mistook for realism), but, as ever, from the outside. The same, however, cannot be said of *Peñas arriba.* Here Pereda, inverting the theme of *Pedro Sánchez,* depicts the unwilling conversion of a young idle *madrileño* man-about-town into a useful, industrious, and philanthropic rural squire. Set in Pereda's own *terruño* [native soil] and written with all the force of his own total conviction, the novel centres on the patriarchal figure of Don Celso. Succeeding where Don Román of *Don Gonzalo González* failed, Celso is the model rural proprietor: in him and his friends Neluco and el señor de Provedaño, Pereda synthesises the ideals, narrowly and defensively conservative, but not without nobility and sincerity, which he had consistently defended. We cannot accept them; but in *Peñas arriba,* for perhaps the only time in Pereda's work, we can respect them, because of the attractive human context in which they operate. There is, characteristically, no force in the book which seriously conflicts with them.

Pereda's other works, [*Nubes del estío, Al primer vuelo,* and *Pachín González*] . . . , are of minor interest.

In retrospect Pereda's work appears as a last strenuous attempt to resist the forces of change which were sweeping over Spanish society and, after 1868, were increasingly reflected in the novel, altering both its content and its narrative-techniques. Although Pereda contributed something, probably unconsciously and chiefly via his use of dialogue, to the development of realism, his work is really an end-product without significant influence later. (pp. 118-21)

> Donald L. Shaw, "Pereda, Valera, and Palacio Valdés," in his A Literary History of Spain: The Nineteenth Century, *Barnes & Noble Inc., 1972, pp. 115-30.**

LAWRENCE H. KLIBBE   (essay date 1975)

[*Klibbe has written the most extensive biographical and critical study of Pereda in English. In the following excerpt from that study, Klibbe surveys Pereda's career. Throughout his study Klibbe presents Pereda as a writer either unable or unwilling to achieve a balanced mixture of character, plot, theme, and narration in his novels. Yet Klibbe believes that Pereda, for his descriptive style and masterful documentation of the simple life of the Montaña, commands an important position in European literary history.*]

Pereda's early literary activities in the journals of Santander, dating between 1858 and 1879, have more than mere historical significance as part of his complete writings, because the prom-

ise of the future novelist and the defects of his vision are equally visible in the *Escritos de juventud (Youthful Writings).* The bedrock of Pereda's outlook appears throughout the articles in the rejection of the present age and in the defense of tradition. (p. 49)

There are a few glimpses of his positive traits as a writer in these early writings: the creation of types, or rudimentary character studies, as in **"Cosas de don Paco"** (**"Things of Don Paco"**); the love of Santander, in particular in **"Fragmento de una carta"** (**"Fragment of a Letter"**); the employment of dialect, in **"Correspondencia"** (**"Correspondence"**); and the humorous, warm depiction of local customs, in **"Cruzadas"** (**"Crusades"**). None of the pieces, however, is outstanding in the total canon of Pereda's writings, and all the articles are obviously intended to please the local audiences in Santander. (p. 50)

Pereda mentioned only good in the life and ways of Santander and only evil in the nineteenth century throughout his early journalistic efforts; and he is uncompromising in his entire output for the press, with stress on political rather than literary purposes. Suddenly, then, Pereda's audience received a different and radically opposed negative picture of their province, presented as an equally truthful observation in a very natural language. . . .

The eighteen stories and essays in *Escenas montañesas* [*(Mountain Scenes)*] vary greatly in style, subjects, and themes so that the only unifying factor is the setting in the province of Santander. The critical consensus has been that Pereda collected his material without any preconceived aesthetic plan; and the author, in a later note to the book in 1885, excused his work thus:

> No matter how distracted the reader may be, he will have probably observed that, between the beginning and the end of this book, the author's manner of seeing and sensing country life changes somewhat. The excuse for this inconsistency is that the *Scenes* were not written with a set plan nor at one sitting, nor are they the work of the mature reflection of the philosopher but are the fruit of an impressionable boy's leisure. . . .
>
> (p. 51)

The various dates of publication for the *Escenas montañesas* and Pereda's arrangement of the articles as a book confirm the haphazard attitude indicated in the 1885 note. The irony lies in the importance accorded *Escenas montañesas* by critics as a *costumbrista* ["local color," "regionalist"] watershed, an early naturalistic appearance, and a superior endeavor by Pereda. Another ironic feature of this first book is the effect caused on Pereda by the accidental success and scandal of these eighteen scenes from the Montaña.

The best story is usually cited as **"La leva"** (**"The Levy"**), a short narrative foreshadowing several traits of Pereda's aesthetics in the two major novels, *Sotileza* [*(Fine Spun)*] and *Peñas arriba* [*(The Upper Peaks)*]. (pp. 51-2)

The background is authentically depicted with the wharves, the houses, the common folk, and the dialect of Santander. Of course, the tale is a sad history of unfortunate people of the lower classes, cursed by bad luck; but the "unconscious naturalism" of Pereda is the result of memory and observation. The characterization can be readily acceptable, although all the actors are types representing certain values or vices, according to Pereda's moral code. The author intrudes repeatedly in this short story to insist that he is a "poor painter of customs" and not endowed with "the fresh imagination of a poet." (p. 52)

[Other] contributions to *Escenas montañesas* also anticipate Pereda's later novelistic methodology by his emphasis on the use of detailed descriptions for even minor characters, the whole picture providing the study of a type, as in **"El raquero"** (**"The Beachcomber"**), **"La costurera"** (**"The Seamstress"**), and **"Un marino"** (**"A Mariner"**). These three types represent the poorer classes of Santander, displaced and disoriented by *el espíritu moderno* ("the modern spirit"), the title of Pereda's last article in *Escenas montañesas,* in which he foresees that "within a few years industry will have completely invaded these peaceful lands, and then there will no longer be types." . . . Although Pereda's main purpose is to portray the seamen of Santander and the representatives of other sectors of Santander's humble side, chosen for their picturesque reflection of the province as well as their symbolic challenge to the new age, he also utilized the proud, aristocratic heir to the traditions of the *Montaña* ["mountainous region of northern Spain"], as in the initial story, **"Santander,"** with its revealing subtitle, **"Antaño y hogaño (Of Old and Nowadays)"**. (p. 53)

The singular exception to Pereda's general defense of regional life is **"Suum cuique"** (**"To Each His Own"**), the longest contribution in the series. If counted as a short novel, it is the forerunner to the three novelettes in *Bocetos al temple*. **"Suum cuique"** has also won recognition as the sole major expression of Pereda's antibucolic attitude that soon led to "the conception of a new bucolic spirit." Although some characters and situations in the other stories, coupled with the innovative use of the rough dialect of the humble Santander people, irked Pereda's audience, no one story is so devastating an attack upon provincial life as is **"Suum cuique."** (p. 54)

Few or no favorable aspects of the *Montaña* way of life are mentioned or advocated in **"Suum cuique"**; and, ironically, this story is one of the most effective in *Escenas montañesas,* providing needed variety and contrast with the most recognized contribution, **"La leva."** (p. 55)

The twelve stories in Pereda's second book [*Tipos y paisajes (Types and Landscapes)*], categorized as a second *Escenas montañesas,* repeat many innovative ideas of the first work and thus lack some historical as well as aesthetic merits of the initial collection. However, certain changes can be detected in *Tipos y paisajes,* although the local-color and stylistic traits— Pereda's positive contributions—remain constant. There appears to emerge a nebulous endeavor to wed the *costumbrista* sketch to the narrative inspiration. But the attempt is largely unsuccessful, with the separation between description and story too apparent. The lack of action is unfortunately compounded by the descriptions, frequent and detailed, with only a limited reader interest because of Pereda's failure to blend all the elements into a compelling, original formula. (p. 57)

With *Bocetos al temple (Sketches in Distemper)* Pereda definitively entered the arena of the novel, but the three novelettes do not form a trilogy and, in fact, share no common idea or unifying theme. Of course, common strands of Pereda's emerging ideology appear throughout *Bocetos al temple,* and the longer narrative form had characterized some of the previous sketches and stories. In short, the three novelettes are really not so different from the pioneering *Escenas montañesas* and its sequel *Tipos y paisajes*. The effort, however, is revealing and signif-

icant for the attempt to unite description, narration, and types (as Pereda understood characterization) in the decade of the 1870s, when the realistic novel began to come into prominence and perfection. (p. 59)

One more return to a collection of short stories and sketches remained for Pereda to publish in 1877 before he launched his first long novel. In *Tipos trashumantes (Nomadic Types)* Pereda offers caricatures of summer tourists and city dwellers swarming to the sea and mountains during vacations. These "nomadic types" are consistently portrayed in a satirical, scornful fashion; and possibly the author's neighbors felt that he had made amends for the sketches in *Escenas montañesas*. The articles are very ineffective, however, both as literary creations and as a faithful record of visitors to Santander: the exaggerated types are so distorted that the author's intention is too evident, too burlesque. There is no variety in this one-sided attack on middle-class and aristocratic vacationers coming to the North of Spain, and a monotonous repetition permeates this entire "summer physiognomy of Santander," making the reader doubt Pereda's conclusion about making "sketches" and not "autopsies," only "copying" the public as "the public has forged itself." . . . (p. 62)

The very productive period from 1878 until 1884, when in that latter year Pereda began the publication of his *Obras completas,* brought the author recognition based on five novels written in rapid succession. Unlike the generally ignored reception of the preceding books, these five works brought Pereda into the public and critical limelight, establishing him as a competent novelist with the artistic stamina to complete long, serious novels. If hypothetically Pereda had written no novels after this first edition of the complete works (often the sign not only of the acceptance of a writer to literary immortality but also, sadly, the apogee of his creative trajectory), the inclusion of his name within literary histories would have been still assured. His merits would have been recognized as those of a fervent polemicist, bolstered by keen observation of details and types and possessing a very effective style to serve his causes. (p. 66)

[Pereda's first novel, *El buey suelto,*] has been often criticized and classified as not a novel at all, properly speaking, because Pereda has sacrificed so many qualities of the novelistic art to serve his didactic and moralizing aims. The intention to answer Balzac's *Petites misères de la vie conjugale (Minor Miseries of Married Life)* and, less directly, the same author's *Physiologie du mariage (Physiology of Marriage)* led Pereda to produce this bold, strong, but artistically defective book. With constant sermons and moral asides he recounts the "edifying pictures of the life of a bachelor," as Pereda sarcastically subtitled *El buey suelto (The Bachelor);* and he further qualified this book, in the dedication to Menéndez Pelayo, as "this poor essay of celibate physiology," calling attention also to the work's style. It is primarily a rebuttal of Balzacian ideas, and also to liberal ideas of his age, rather than an imaginative effort as a novel. (pp. 66-7)

The artistic crisis caused by the dismal reception of *El buey suelto* resulted in a second thesis novel, so different and so greatly improved in comparison with the first *novela de tesis* [thesis novel], that Pereda must have made a complete reappraisal of his intentions. At least, he complained about the composition in letters to Menéndez Pelayo and Galdós. Indeed, a comparison and contrast of *El buey suelto* and *Don Gonzalo González de la Gonzalera,* written within a very short time of each other, show important differences, although the basis of Pereda's ideology is consistent at the heart of both endeavors.

One explanation for Pereda's success in *Don Gonzalo* and a clue to the subsequent triumphs of *Sotileza* and *Peñas arriba,* is the use of his home territory, the *Montaña,* setting of *Escenas montañesas,* which he could describe with more firsthand knowledge and with a loving concentration not associated with any writings about the city, especially the capital. Another explanation is the time, "the beginning of the memorable year, 1868," as the author states immediately. That catastrophic decade, especially for traditionalists like Pereda, remains engraved as a climax of nineteenth-century Spanish history, a political stimulus for a novelistic interpretation. The first chapters, slow in establishing the conflict, nevertheless serve to create the mood of the rural idyll, the placid, happy, unambitious mood of the Highlands, where the *romerías,* (the festive gatherings on a saint's day) and the familial histories, pleasant and not so pleasant, occupy the inhabitants' lives and conversations. The dialogues are frequently the daily gossip, with no immediate reference to the plot but with a pattern of psychological realism about the minor types. The setting, the speech, and the actors are, for the first successful time in the Peredian novels, a fusion of realism and regionalism, at the service of a political purpose. (pp. 68-9)

In *Don Gonzalo,* Pereda had defended the heritage of the *hidalgos* against the democracy of popular rule; and in *De tal palo, tal astilla (A Chip off the Old Block),* he undertook a challenge to the ideal of tolerance, at heart a concomitant part of the whole liberal process. (p. 76)

De tal palo has been more familiarly interpreted as Pereda's literary answer to the two Galdosian novels, *Gloria (Gloria)* in 1877 and *La familia de León Roch (The Family of León Roch)* in 1879. . . .

Actually, there are no structural and thematic similarities between the two novels of Galdós and *A Chip off the Old Block,* so that the basis for comparing the works involves the novelists' respective approaches to the role of religion, specifically Catholicism, in Spanish life, and for the individual person, in the present age; but the problem is also faced as to the possible irrelevancy of adherence to any formal doctrines and the sect, with the hypothesis carried to the point that orthodoxy may be indeed destructive of human happiness. Galdós, of course, touches upon this latter issue in *Gloria* and *La familia;* and Pereda concentrates upon the former questions of Catholic beliefs and practices. It is pertinent to keep in mind that Pereda, unlike Galdós, narrows his sights to Catholicism and not to the broader area of Christianity, in general, a topic that became increasingly vital to Galdosian thought and literary expression. (p. 77)

All in all, this novel represents the nadir of Pereda's career as a novelist and as a respected spokesman for a certain point of view. . . .

Most of the theological positions espoused by Pereda, although in strict alignment with nineteenth-century orthodoxy, have been swept aside by more mature literary treatments in the novels of Graham Greene and François Mauriac. Another irony of this twentieth-century progressive spirit is that the modern Catholic novelists oppose precisely the self-assured, middle-class stance (found respectively in the same examples, Greene and Mauriac) of Plácido and Agueda. Both Galdós and Pereda floundered in the quicksand of the religious issues of their age, especially in *Gloria, La familia,* and *A Chip off the Old Block;* but the Peredian reply to his friend's efforts is the more di-

sastrous because, at least, the Galdosian struggle merits contemporary respect, despite the weighted arguments. (p. 83)

[Following *A Chip off the Old Block*], Pereda published *El sabor de la tierruca (Redolent of the Soil),* considered by some critics as the best novel of his five books of this period; at very least, the work is conceded to be a meritorious effort by Pereda. (p. 86)

The characters in *El sabor de la tierruca* show realistic and naturalistic qualities; the lower classes are portrayed in a less exemplary manner than representatives of the upper stratum, the *hidalgos,* a feature not surprising by now in Pereda. . . . Unfortunately, Pereda has sketched horizontally instead of vertically in his characterizations, a decision necessarily affecting the plot. There are too many characters with too many subplots, and this unsatisfactory technique is compounded by the lack of any unity in the form of a main thread of action or a thesis. Pereda has omitted forceful, possibly controversial themes as a reaction to the negative reception of *The Bachelor, Don Gonzalo,* and *A Chip off the Old Block.* He has again made a complete about-face, too abruptly and too extremely, by now a recognized literary and psychological trait of the writer. (p. 89)

The fifth and final novel of this group, *Pedro Sánchez,* surprised the critics of Pereda without exception by the sharp turn from the thesis novel and from the idyll of the *Montaña.* (p. 93)

The form of *Pedro Sánchez,* with the narrator at the center of all the action, happenings, and interpretations has led to several attempts at classification by critics, showing thereby the richness of this creation. In the absence of any indication from the author of his intentions, all the possible definitions would seem to have value in understanding Pereda's superior piece of prose fiction; and the various generic categories help to illustrate that Pereda has certainly more potential literary talent and techniques than a mere follower of the *costumbristas,* realists, and regionalists. (pp. 95-6)

The brilliance of this Peredian creation, a fusion of the very personal, and the historical with literary authenticity, and including something of the picaresque genre, is never disturbed by artistic imbalance. The three components complement each other to impressive advantage for Pereda's literary reputation in the chapters detailing Pedro's experiences before and after the Revolution of 1854. (pp. 99-100)

Pereda's chronological development as a writer is marked by an erratic forward and backward movement, with no predictable and consistent pattern emerging as a guide from letters, prologues, or the works themselves. His two masterpieces arrived late in life, with almost a decade intervening between the very different novels, *Sotileza* and *Peñas arriba.* (p. 153)

Although Pereda can stake no claim to being a complex, evolving, or very profound thinker (a statement he would have welcomed as a surety of his successful communication of his fearless, unyielding, and sound beliefs), an outlook and attitude appear in *Peñas arriba* that, for the first time, proceed beyond a negative glance at the past and an unhappy reaction to the present. *Sotileza* is a prose epic of the sea and of a vanishing Santander with no betterment, only decline, to replace the noble traditions and stalwart race; *Peñas arriba* is an idyll of the mountains, of a province where the old is yielding to the new with an uncertain direction yet with the hope, possibility, and plan not only to maintain good ways from the past but to improve life for the challenges of the twentieth century, civilization, industrialization, and political outcries. The latter work becomes an idyllic vision of human existence with spiritual revelations and lyrical paeans of nature. *Peñas arriba* offers a more poetical style with a richer, more cultured language and vocabulary, less employment of regional expressions and speech patterns, and many very long passages of geographical description, especially. Again, this later novel shows taut construction and rigid outlines; but the dynamic component, reader interest, and a paced plot (as a minimum requirement for such a lengthy, descriptive novel) fail to win today, as earlier in the twentieth century, audiences ready to devote themselves to an appreciation of Pereda's artistry. *Sotileza*, for present readers, retains a more convenient attraction and ease of endeavor; *Peñas arriba* can be a surprisingly rewarding venture in ideas popular at this moment, but the interest in this novel has demonstrated no increase in recent times. Both novels win first-rate attention on aesthetic bases, as works of notable merit by themselves and within the framework of the European novelistic productions of this century; and the two books gained for Pereda his lasting place in literary history.

Pereda's novels before *Sotileza,* in addition to some of his stories and sketches of *Escenas montañesas*, require extensive consideration as the key to the writer's thought and techniques in his masterpieces. For better or for worse, the prejudices, religious and social, dogmatism, and the political mythology emerge forcefully and repeatedly in novels, such as *Don Gonzalo, A Chip off the Old Block,* and *Redolent of the Soil. A Chip off the Old Block,* perhaps the Peredian novel of most unbending and, essentially, most unchristian orientation and conclusion, provides an important source for many of Pereda's other, often admittedly weak, writings. *Don Gonzalo* is a seminal novel for the Peredian political credo, found in more successful books such as *Redolent of the Soil* and *Pedro Sánchez;* and the literary characteristics of the mature Pereda are perceptible in his initial novels.

Of course, the imitative romantic procedures and creaky structures of the plots and characters cannot be ignored in the first publications by Pereda as a novelist. *Pedro Sánchez,* a unique enterprise by Pereda, has been recognized consistently as a fortunate contribution to the rich picaresque inheritance from Spain, one of the author's most significant, revealing stories. These first novels, the initial phase of Pereda's devotion to this genre, are nonetheless limited in importance, historically rather than aesthetically, within the trajectory of nineteenth-century Spanish literature and their creator's own development.

Too much emphasis has been dedicated at times to Pereda's contributions between *Sotileza* and *Peñas arriba* in the hope of encountering traces of naturalism, then in vogue, and of literary mastery of other nascent themes and ideas at the end of the century. No originality and no outstanding performance characterize the Peredian writings outside the two durable novels after 1885, with a possible exception of the interesting *Pachín González*. Pereda, after *Sotileza,* was an anachronistic (and antagonistic) figure for the defenders of naturalism and the young men soon to emerge more fully as the Generation of 1898; and the acceptance of his masterpiece, in some small part, was due to the mutual affinities between several naturalists and this novel. *Peñas arriba*, of course, supplied in 1895 a rallying call for the declining values of the nineteenth century, under sharper attack; and the book marked an apogee of the century's movements in literature and thought as well as a model of polished, poetical Castilian style. (pp. 154-55)

Attention . . . in the domain of criticism has increased slowly but qualitatively, not always favorably, and with a keener eye to Pereda's strong point and durable value, style, in order to determine a more appreciative reaction to this author's best writings. Likewise, the place of this novelist in the twentieth century, historically and aesthetically, and his more equitable stature within his own times have been the concerns and questions of critics since 1945. Some interest, but no great enthusiasm and certainly no reversal in noticeable or striking measure of Pereda's role and importance, seem to be the verdicts of these contemporary judges. Nor has Pereda fared any better with popular audiences, the readers whom he wanted to interest and whose decisions affected him always, causing changes (good and bad) in his plans for the next book. Nevertheless, the novelist of the *Montaña* has evoked a sincere love of the land, a sympathy for the poor toilers of his native province, and a rejection of the excesses of twentieth-century progress, materialism, and change. Pereda is urging the defense and maintenance of a simple life, of the beauties of nature, of an unwritten moral code inherent in mutual respect and charity, and of a strong religious faith—a universal program illustrated in the little world of the *Montaña* and expressed unfailingly and as an absolute requisite in exemplary, impeccable form and style. (pp. 156-57)

> *Lawrence H. Klibbe, in his* José María de Pereda, *Twayne Publishers, 1975, 185 p.*

MARIO FORD BACIGALUPO (essay date 1981)

[*In the following excerpt, Bacigalupo traces the conversion of Marcelo, protagonist of* Peñas arriba, *from a starkly modernistic youth to a morally traditional community leader—a process which Bacigalupo believes provides the central unifying structure of the novel.*]

In Pereda's *Peñas arriba* the decision of the narrator-protagonist, Marcelo, to visit Tablanca results in what may be called his "conversion." Although it might appear at first glance that his "conversion" relates only to his change of opinion concerning his previous urban and fashionable way of life in Madrid and his dislike for the rural and isolated existence in the *Montaña*, a closer perusal of the novel shows that underneath the surface of a simple change in his likes and dislikes there is the deeper experience and awareness of regeneration. On one occasion, at least, Marcelo himself employs the term conversion to define his change in convictions. . . .

How is Marcelo's "conversion" presented in the novel, and of what does it consist? In order to answer these questions it would be appropriate to note some aspects of what is generally meant by conversion. The simplest definition of the term is that of the return of the lost soul to God: the passage of the soul from a state of sin to a state of grace. In such a spiritual metamorphosis, Catholic dogma stresses the initial relative passivity of man. The initiative is God's in so far as divine intervention is not consequent to human effort. At the beginning of the crisis there is a tacit cooperation between God, who enlightens and moves the soul, and man, who may either accept or resist divine initiative. (p. 23)

The psychology of conversion presents many and various stimuli or experiences which make possible man's spiritual change, such as moral depression, aesthetic stimulation, social and political propaganda, sorrow, misfortunes, wars, revolutions. Indeed, these experiences bring about a "state of anxiety of the intelligence and the soul" which is often translated in a need for a doctrinal system, moral direction, and love; a feeling that the world is a delusion, a craving for an outlet of activity, or disgust at physical pleasures are further examples of such a state of anxiety. Man in the midst of his anxieties begins, therefore, a more or less conscious search for Truth wherein the intellectual aspect predominates: this is the first stage, and it leads to "an affirmation after a series of negations", that is, to the intellectual comprehension of Truth. Conversion itself, if it were to happen, would be the second stage wherein the emotive aspect would predominate with the end result being a sense of equilibrium, peace, and joy.

From a psychological as well as a theological point of view, conversion is a process since it involves a duration of time, whether rapid or slow, during which the various experiences and stages take place. Even in the so-called fulminant or lightning conversions "the consciousness of the subject [experiences], prior to the crisis, the beginnings of mutation." The process, however, is not devoid of either doubts or temptations. Time and again the future convert may resist or temporarily reject a complete surrender to what intellectually he understands is the Truth. St. Augustine's conversion with all its doubts, searching, and resistence is the classic example of such a progressive and anxious pattern. Conversion is then "a progress in a continuous line; it is like a chemical process in which the addition of a catalytic agent produces a reaction for which all the elements were already present."

In *Peñas arriba* Marcelo introduces himself as a young man of thirty-two who lives comfortably in Madrid whenever he is not traveling throughout Europe. Yet Marcelo, in his own words, is a dispassionate, indifferent man to whom "muy pocas cosas [le] han llegado al alma" ["very little has touched his soul"]. . . . Although professionally trained as a lawyer, he does not occupy himself as such and instead lives from his father's somewhat substantial inheritance. . . . His life in and out of Spain revolves around fashionable social, artistic, and political circles; nevertheless, his interest in them is quite superficial and even self-serving. To be sure, Marcelo is not a great sinner in so far as he neither commits awesome crimes nor indulges wholeheartedly in evil. Yet it is his profound indifference which defines his error. The terms used to describe this victim of the *mal du siècle* ["malady of the (nineteenth) century"] are "inapetencia moral" ["spiritual indifference"] and "languidez de espíritu" ["a languorous spirit"]. . . . (pp. 24-5)

Such is the man who in response to his critically ill Uncle Celso's letter reluctantly decides to visit Tablanca. As don Celso's letter makes clear, Tablanca is radically antithetical to whatever Marcelo has known and lived in before. It is a small village located in one of the most inaccessible spots of the Cantabrian Mountains, isolated and remote from modern civilization. The fact that Tablanca is such an out-of-the-way place perched high and distant from the world of decisive historical events is neither fortuitous nor is it caused by a mere regionalistic sentiment on Pereda's part. The *Montaña* is, of course, Pereda's native region, but it is also a quite appropriate example of a more or less isolated society fortified by its geography against the inroads of the modern world. There are no highways or railroads which penetrate into valleys like Tablanca's; there are only natural mountain and river passes by which the traveler may enter. Such a fortress-like community presents to the author a most helpful literary and geographical device by which he is able to contrast opposite social, political, and moral values. Regionalism, as a literary theme or classification, may well be in *Peñas arriba* not the cause but the effect of Pereda's endeavor. (p. 25)

Marcelo's first impression of the *Montaña* is far from sympathetic. As he rides in late October across the mountain passes toward Tablanca, he reminds himself of the pleasures offered by the open valleys and towns of the lowlands which he leaves behind. (p. 26)

Despite a distaste for his surroundings, the impressive view of the mountains, precipices, and deep valleys remind him of the historical and archeological anecdotes his father used to tell. . . . Thus, even in his first encounter with Nature in the *Montaña*, notwithstanding his negative feelings, Marcelo is moved to both a begrudging and conditional expression of admiration for that rugged land and its people. . . . (pp. 26-7)

Marcelo's arrival in Tablanca and his first twenty-four hours in the old family house—the *casona*—do not ameliorate his depression. The *casona* itself is a gloomy, uncomfortable, drafty place. In his uncle's *tertulia* ["club"], which is frequented by the gargantuan Don Pedro Nolasco and the apparently uninspiring village priest, Don Sabas, the conversation reduces itself to disputes and jokes between Don Celso and Don Pedro with occasional Latin phrases interspersed by Don Sabas. The valley in which Tablanca is located is . . . tightly enclosed by mountains. . . . [The] misery of his first day in Tablanca is aggravated by bad weather. It is, in fact, at this point when what seemed to be an impossible situation begins to acquire a new dimension.

In chapters VI and VII, a development takes place which makes Marcelo's stay in Tablanca more bearable, if not an immediately happy one. In the first place, there is a certain providential lessening of tension. . . . Better weather permits Marcelo to spend the next few days exploring the surrounding mountains and to acquaint himself with some of the events and gossip of the village. In some of these explorations, during which Marcelo and two young villagers hunt rabbits, foxes, and wildcats, they are joined by Don Sabas. The presence of the priest in these outings serves as a contrast to what had been Marcelo's initial negative impression of both Don Sabas and Nature. . . . The "new" Don Sabas who Marcelo begins to discover is a fountain of information and knowledge about ways of Nature. . . . Although Don Sabas' company does not yet transform Marcelo's view of the natural geography of the *Montaña*, it has had a profound effect. . . . (pp. 27-8)

Another development which further contributes to Marcelo's change is his acquaintance with Tablanca's physician, Neluco Celis, and the conversation which the two men have concerning Art, Nature, and Society. For Neluco, Art is inferior to Nature inasmuch as the former can be no more than a mere reflection of all created things. A work of art, moreover, will not ultimately satisfy either its creator or its recipient, if only because human intelligence cannot fully recreate Nature. It is this essential impotence of the human mind to surpass Nature's harmony that negates the possibility of a better order than that which is present in the Creation. That Neluco's views would take a cosmological dimension to include all aspects of human endeavor is consistent with Pereda's own ideas on the subject. Hence, the relationship between Nature, Art, and Man—a relationship in which all three elements are both linked together yet not completely fused together—implies a rather static and precisely ordered society.

Neluco's exposition of what he believes is the monotonous characteristic of the lowlands and the cities parallels Don Celso's feeling of claustrophobia even in provincial and relatively small towns like Santander, and is in contrast, of course, with

Marcelo's asphyxia in the *Montaña*. Neluco, however, goes one step further than Don Celso in their shared dislike of urban life: Tablanca's physician projects an unequivocal social commentary upon what may in part be a mere emotional feeling. Whereas Don Celso sees "las casas en ringlera" ["uniform ranks of houses"] . . . , Neluco sees the same coupled to "la ocupación del negocio, la ocupación del café, la ocupación del paseo, la ocupación de la calle, la ocupación del casino, o del teatro, o de la Bolsa" ["the business of trade, the business of the coffee house, the business of the avenue, the business of the street, the business of the casino, or of the theater, or of the stock exchange"]. . . . It is not only the physical aspect of the modern city that repels Neluco; he is deeply critical of the very activities which are at the heart of industrial or commercial urban civilization. (p. 28)

The evils of history being equal, in Neluco's opinion, the contemporary world is neither more nor less corrupt than that of the past. The current illness consists, however, in a spiritual malaise caused by modern man's rejection of limits to his intellectual curiosity and sensory appetites. . . . [As] in the case with Don Sabas' aesthetic insights during the mountain hikes, Neluco's exposition on the virtues of the human and natural geography of the *Montaña* does not fall on deaf ears. During Marcelo's outings with the priest, those virtues—more particularly those of Nature—were extolled in a subjective and inspired manner; Neluco's statements serve as a more objective and deliberate commentary, as well as an elaboration of Don Sabas' insights. Furthermore, these two developments function as a cutting edge in Marcelo's spiritual malaise. . . . (p. 29)

The first important step in that direction takes place in chapter IX. In their previous outings, Marcelo and the priest had explored only the lower elevations. Now, in response to Don Sabas' invitation, they climb one of the higher peaks. As they ascend, and the first light of dawn begins to show through the mountain crests, Don Sabas becomes progressively more inspired and translates his emotions to Marcelo in prayers and hymns of praise. . . . As the rays of the sun illuminate and lift the fog from the valleys, [Marcelo] is able to view a vast expanse of the region and the Cantabrian Sea. . . . What Marcelo is now able to read in "the great book of Nature" is the idea that the beauty of Nature coincides with divine omnipotence and goodness. . . . (pp. 29-30)

The view from the summit and Don Sabas' guidance had put Marcelo in partial communion with the *Montaña* through an understanding of its physical beauty. Nevertheless, the aesthetic experience alone does not suffice to eliminate all of Marcelo's doubts or his desire to return to Madrid. In chapter XII, soon after his experience at the mountain peak, he is suddenly overtaken by a strong desire to escape from the *Montaña* during an unaccompanied visit to the village of Robacío. In order to resist future temptations, Marcelo proposes to himself not to make excursions out of Tablanca alone.

In effect, Marcelo is accompanied in his next outing by Neluco. Their first visit is to Promisiones, a village which used to be the home of a collateral branch of Marcelo's family. The history of these relations, the Gómez de Pomars, is instructive inasmuch as it describes the evils which can befall a patriarchal family when it no longer lives according to its traditions. (pp. 30-1)

If the saga of the Gómez de Pomars instructs Marcelo in the consequences of patriarchal irresponsibility, his visit to Pro-

vedaño and acquaintance with its resident-*hidalgo* reveal to him the character and duties of an exemplary patriarch. (p. 31)

Life in the village no longer seems unpleasant or stagnant and the people are no longer ignorant rustics with nothing to offer. His uncle's *tertulia* no longer appears dull and boorish. Marcelo now appreciates the ways and customs of the villagers and even begins to give personal advice to some of them. Indeed, Marcelo begins to put into effect Neluco's and the *hidalgo* of Provedaño's idea that it is the man of culture who should interact and deal with men of lesser formal education and advantages on their own level. (p. 33)

Among the relatively few critics who have dealt with **Peñas arriba** some have concluded that Marcelo's decision to spend his life in Tablanca is motivated by his love for Lita. . . . Undoubtedly, Marcelo's love for Lita and their subsequent marriage contribute to his fulfillment in Tablanca, but they are far from being the only or even the most important reasons for his decision to remain in the village. The relevancy of Lita and the love motif must be placed within the novel's general perspective, that is to say, within the context of Marcelo's progression from an "old" to a "new" self. (p. 36)

Far from rushing head-on into a "great passion", Marcelo chooses Lita not only because of his fondness for her but also because of Tablanca; his marriage to Lita is not motivated only by his love for her, since it is also prompted by a socio-political consideration, namely the patriarchal order of the village. (p. 38)

Marcelo's love for Lita is . . . the last experience in a series of experiences which leads Marcelo to his "conversion" to the ideals of a society such as Tablanca. Lita is, in this sense, one more bond in a series of bonds which weds Marcelo to those ideals.

In summation, Marcelo's metamorphosis follows the general theological and psychological pattern of conversion. It presents a process in time with stages which lead to the final state of regeneration. (p. 39)

[In] accordance with the general pattern of conversion is Marcelo's initial resistance toward Tablanca's physical and human geography, in so far as this attitude is reflected in his original dislike of the *Montaña* and its rustic way of life. Furthermore, Marcelo is apparently passive in the initial phase of his "conversion," since he does not consciously seek or desire to remain in that region. He is also appropriately subjected to doubts and temptations. Nor should it be forgotten that as a child and adolescent Marcelo had been exposed to the ideas and cause he was later to embrace by his father's reminiscences and stories of the *Montaña;* his previous knowledge, however imperfect and half forgotten, must be seen as a contributing factor to the nature of his general experience in Tablanca. In **Peñas arriba,** therefore, the change which the narrator-protagonist undergoes is presented in the manner of a religious conversion, and the process or progress of that "conversion" is the central theme which defines both the unity of the plot and the organization of the novel. (pp. 39-40)

Mario Ford Bacigalupo, "The Process of Conversion in Pereda's 'Peñas Arriba'," in Hispanofila, *Vol. 24, No. 71, January, 1981, pp. 23-40.*

ADDITIONAL BIBLIOGRAPHY

Bell, Aubrey F. G. "The Regionalist Novel: Pereda." In his *Contemporary Spanish Literature*, pp. 39-44. New York: Alfred A. Knopf, 1925.

A general evaluation of Pereda, whom Bell regards as "the real founder and champion of the modern Spanish school of realism, the traditional realism of Cervantes."

Eddy, Nelson W. "Pardo Bazan, Menendez y Pelayo, and Pereda Criticism." *The Romanic Review* XXXVII, No. 4 (December 1946): 336-45.*

Contrasts the critical reactions of Pereda's contemporaries Pardo Bazán and Menéndez y Pelayo to his works. Through an analysis of commentaries by each author on several different novels, Eddy demonstrates the inferiority of Bazán as a Peredian critic for her derivation of ideas from Pelayo.

Eoff, Sherman. "Pereda's Realism: His Style." In *Studies in Honor of W. Shipley.* Washington University Studies in Language and Literature, No. 14, pp. 131-57. St. Louis: Washington University Press, 1942.

Comprehensive examination of Pereda's literary traits as a realist. Eoff argues that Pereda's "extravagance"—his fusion of humor, picturesque description, and rhetorical expression—is the stylistic quality that best reveals the less-than-serious nature of Pereda's realism in comparison to the majority of nineteenth-century realists, who were fervently devoted to precipitating social reform.

————. "A Phase of Pereda's Writings in Imitation of Balzac." *Modern Language Notes* LIX, No. 7 (November 1944): 460-66.*

Examines stylistic similarities between Pereda's analytical treatises and Honoré de Balzac's *physiologies,* or satirical essays, and emphasizes the fundamentally different views and purposes each writer possessed. Eoff includes *El buey suelto,* itself a refutation of Balzac's anti-marital *Les petites misères de la vie conjugale,* in his discussion.

Ford, J.D.M. "The Novel." In his *Main Currents of Spanish Literature,* pp. 208-41. New York: Biblio and Tannen, 1968.*

Favorable general consideration of Pereda's literary career.

Giles, Mary E. "Descriptive Conventions in Pereda, Pardo Bazán, and Palacio Valdés." *Hispania* L, No. 2 (May 1967): 285-91.

Discusses Pereda as a representative writer of Spanish *costumbrista* literature, noting his adoption of common typecasting and descriptive methods in order to panoramically depict nineteenth-century Spanish life.

Mérimée, Ernest. "Contemporary Period: The Novel." In his *A History of Spanish Literature,* translated by S. Griswold Morley, pp. 541-69. New York: Henry Holt and Co., 1931.*

Brief sketch of Pereda as a "rare *costumbrista* and portrait-painter" who, "had he possessed a few secondary qualities and perhaps a trifle more *savoir-faire* and talent for self-advertisement, might have risen to the very front rank in European literature."

Qualia, Charles B. "Pereda's Naturalism in *Sotileza.*" *Hispania* XXXVII, No. 4, (December 1954): 409-13.

Studies Pereda's utilization and ultimate refutation of Naturalistic themes in *Sotileza.*

Savaiano, Eugene. "Pereda's Portrayal of Nineteenth Century Clergymen." *The Modern Language Journal* XXXVI, No. 5 (May 1952): 223-29.

Analyzes Pereda's novels to reconstruct the typical Peredian priest—a morally exemplary man of beneficent influence who assumes a role of central importance in Spanish village life.

Swain, James O. "Reactionism in Pereda's *Tío Cayetano.*" *Hispania* XVII, No. 1 (February 1934): 83-96.

Studies Pereda's conservative, elitist views on religion, politics, and society as put forth in his contributions to the periodical *El tío cayetano.*

Isaac Leib Peretz

1852(?)-1915

(Also transliterated Yitzhok and Yitskhok; also Leibush, Leybush, Laybush, Leon, and Loeb; also Perez) Polish-born Yiddish short story writer, poet, dramatist, essayist, nonfiction writer, and critic.

Known as the father of modern Yiddish literature, Peretz is best remembered for his short stories based on Hasidic folklore. By applying to traditional Jewish lore the techniques he had derived from his study of Western literature, he overcame limitations in artistic expression that had long been associated with Yiddish literature. Many of Peretz's stories, notably "Bontzye Schweig" ("Bontshe the Silent"), pose thought-provoking questions designed to challenge the Jews of the diaspora to reexamine their place in the modern world. In such stories as "Zwishen Zwei Berg" ("Between Two Mountains"), the religious fervor of traditional Hasidism is exalted, while arcane rituals and legalistic piety are attacked for placing a disproportionate emphasis on attaining heaven rather than actively addressing the problems of life on earth. Through his domination of Jewish letters and thought at the turn of the century, Peretz inspired a generation of disciples and, along with Sholem Aleichem and Mendele Mocher Sforim, created worldwide interest in Yiddish literature.

Peretz was born in Zamoszca, Poland, to a prosperous Jewish merchant and his wife, and at age three began a traditional Jewish education. His father, recognizing the boy's learning ability, allowed Peretz to augment his studies of Hebrew folklore, the Talmud, and the Bible with private lessons in German, Russian, and other subjects outside traditional Hasidic curricula. The turning point of his education, however, came during his adolescence, when he obtained the key to a loft containing 3000 volumes from a private library. Approaching the material unsystematically, Peretz read the works of such writers as William Shakespeare, Alexandre Dumas, Lord Byron, and Charles Dickens, as well as texts on physics, philosophy, and law. This sudden exposure to new and diverse philosophies caused Peretz to question the authority and validity of his traditional training, and also made him aware of the gulf that existed between the Polish Jews' cloistered ghetto life and the larger modern world. From this time on he remained skeptical of authority, seeking to modernize Judaism without sacrificing Jewish culture to assimilation. Later, this skepticism would surface in his fiction as experimentation with style and theme, and also lead to fleeting infatuations with various political movements. Peretz planned to seek higher education away from home, but his plans were thwarted when his parents arranged a marriage for him with the daughter of a local businessman. However, his father-in-law's enlightened approach to Judaism proved to be another significant influence on his thought. The two wrote poetry in collaboration, eventually publishing a book of verse. This association ended when domestic problems between Peretz and his wife led to divorce. Following a restless period of indecision, he remarried in the mid-1870s, passed the examinations necessary to obtain a law license, and settled into a comfortable legal practice.

Peretz continued to write poetry, and in 1888 submitted the long narrative poem "Monish" to Sholem Aleichem's influ-

ential Yiddish journal *Yidishe Folkbibliotek*. Aleichem, himself considered one of the founders of modern Yiddish literature, took great liberties when he edited Peretz's poem. Although the poem received critical praise and recognition, Peretz objected to Aleichem's alterations and refused to submit other works to the journal, exercising the independence that would mark his later career. The following year his life changed abruptly when an informant notified Czarist authorities, who at that time ruled the section of Poland known as Russian Poland, of Peretz's involvement in radical Jewish political activities. His law license was revoked and he was forced to move to Warsaw with his family to seek work. For a time he collected sociological statistics about the way of life of rural Polish Jews for a Jewish philanthropist. Firsthand observations of poverty and ignorance among these *shtetl* (village) Jews made Peretz conscious of the pressing need for social services and education in rural areas. His *Bilder fun a provintz raize,* published in 1894, presents compelling portraits of individuals he interviewed during this period, paying special attention to the idiosyncratic speech patterns, manners, and customs of his subjects and revealing his insights about the villagers as well as their perceptions of him as a cosmopolitan outsider. Several months after the survey was completed, he returned to Warsaw and, with the help of friends, secured a position with the Jewish Community Services Organization. Initially assigned to issue death certificates, he took on increasing responsibilities during the twenty-five years he held this job, devoting many hours to social-service needs and educational reform. Peretz continued to write after he settled in Warsaw, publishing poetry, essays, criticism, and fiction in various Yiddish journals. In his polemical writings he attacked ineffective religious leaders who stressed the study of religious doctrines at the expense of the basic physical and emotional necessities of daily life, and spoke critically of the Jewish woman's complete subjugation in education and in the home. His desire to educate the people was complementary to his involvement with Yiddish literature, which had traditionally been instructive. Reinforcing the religious teachings of Judaism, Yiddish literature had conveyed the message that salvation from earthly misery could be attained only through dedicated preparation for an afterlife. In contrast, Peretz believed that both the religious and the literary traditions needed to address the problems of human life realistically and to avoid imposing moral dictates. Consequently, his fiction was crafted to encourage Jewish readers to discover for themselves new ways of viewing their lives within the context of traditional Jewish beliefs. His stimulating and provocative arguments endeared him to Jewish students.

In the 1880s and 1890s Peretz and other Jewish intellectuals in Warsaw began to focus their attention on Yiddish language and lore. Peretz, who wrote in Hebrew, Yiddish, Russian, and Polish, agreed with intellectuals who considered Yiddish a commonplace "jargon" that lacked the potential for full poetic expression. When he reluctantly yielded to the side of those who sought to elevate the stature of Yiddish to that of a language, it was because he recognized that the Yiddish-speaking masses stood to gain from exposure to new ideas from other cultures. Peretz and others proposed a nationalistic cultural movement among East-European Jews—a movement that did not recommend a Jewish homeland but, rather, called for cultural unity among existing Jewish communities with the Yiddish language as the primary unifying element. At the Czernowitz Yiddish Conference in Rumania in 1908, Peretz argued for the validity of this language of the masses as a reasonable compromise between radical Zionism and assimilationism. The strong influence he wielded at the conference typified his persuasive powers over groups as well as individuals, resulting in a greater respect for Yiddish among intellectuals. His home became the center of Jewish intellectual thought in Poland, and his aristocratic and captivating manner attracted young writers from around the country who sought his moral and financial support, professional advice, and the camaraderie of other writers. Among Peretz's disciples were such writers as Sholem Asch, Shmuel Niger, and J. J. Trunk. Peretz's commitment to numerous causes led him into tireless social work; he eventually suffered a fatal heart attack brought on by exhaustion.

After writing poetry during his youth and early career, Peretz turned serious attention to the short story form during his middle age. Many of his early short stories were based on talmudical lore and legend because the material was already familiar to the audience Peretz wanted to reach. Despite their faithfulness to the original texts and their surface realism, many of the stories have a mystical quality. Leo Wiener, noting this elusive aspect of the largely allegorical stories, considers Peretz's symbolism, satire, and psychological insight beyond the intellectual range of a mass audience, but agrees with other critics that the stories' external realism can be easily grasped. Primarily concerned with the poor, the stories do not record minute details of gloom and squalor, but instead focus on the ability of people to act nobly under the worst circumstances.

Peretz's main intention was to incite his Jewish readers to self-examination so that they could accept their rich and unique heritage, considering themselves neither chosen saints nor doomed sinners.

Many of Peretz's stories are highly critical of the orthodox religious customs that separated Jews from the rest of the modern world. One of the most representative stories of this type, "The Fur Cap," is satirical in tone, but serious in its warning against showing respect for this traditional religious symbol without regard for the leadership qualities of the rabbi who wears it. Peretz's style breaks dramatically with the standard for modern Yiddish literary expression established by Aleichem and Sforim: their slow-paced, detailed works provide a tapestry of life among *shtetl* Jews focusing upon the elements common to the villagers as a group; Peretz, however, used few descriptive details in presenting concentrated psychological portraits of individuals. S. Niger has called such characters "typical types," falling midway between archetypes and true individuals. Peretz's examinations of ordinary individuals in common situations directly reflects his understanding of modern Western literary trends toward realism and a concern with the psychology of the individual. "Meshulah" ("The Messenger"), for example, one of Peretz's best stories, develops the background and psychology of an impoverished octogenarian in the space of a few pages. Intent on delivering a packet of money as assigned, the old messenger slowly freezes to death when blizzard winds penetrate his insufficient clothing. In the delirium that precedes his death he reviews his life without bitterness or regret. While the narrative voice of the story reveals sympathetic admiration for the messenger's strong sense of selfless duty, it also hints subtly that there is irony in a system that conditions the poor to expect less and less, and then denies them even that minimum. Peretz's most controversial story is the satirical "Bontshe the Silent," which describes the life of a poor, humble man. The final sentences tell of Bontshe being admitted into heaven, where he is offered his choice of its glories as a reward for his endurance on earth. Bontshe requests only a daily roll with butter. "Bontshe the Silent" has incited a critical debate about the author's perspective: is Peretz praising Bontshe's humility and silence, or condemning his passive acceptance of his station in life? The ironic surprise ending of the story, once considered a final comment upon the protagonist's humble demeanor, has been interpreted by many modern critics as an attack on passive submission.

In addition to writing original stories, Peretz was fascinated by the Hasidic folktale, but he wanted to secularize it by stripping away the artifice and stressing the musical soul of the Hasidic tradition; he was deeply affected by Hasidic music, which he considered a pure expression of religious joy and praise long after he had rejected the laws of the Talmud. His delicate manipulation of the material was essential because contemporary Jews accepted the tales as serious records of actual experience that were in no wise mere legends. Aware that the doubt and restlessness that permeated Western literature reflected a rapidly changing world, Peretz sought to create a continuum between fundamental Jewish traditions and their application for contemporary Jews. By retelling the folktales in a modern literary style and grafting irony onto them with narrative notes or addenda, Peretz avoided alienating his audience and forced his readers to think more freely. "Dray matones" ("The Three Gifts") is the faithful retelling of a traditional story in which a man must discover three earthly treasures as an act of penance if he is to enter heaven. After several years he collects three examples of selfless acts of martyrdom by others, only to be told that despite their rarity and beauty they are of no practical use. Another story, "Between Two Mountains," is cited by many critics as Peretz's most skillful and revealing short work. Rationalism and emotionalism are contrasted through the voices of a rigid traditional rabbi who takes Jewish law literally, and a young Hasidic rabbi who believes that celebration and song are the best ways to praise God. Despite Peretz's attempted objectivity, the character traits assigned to each rabbi reveal the author's preference for the more exuberant mode of expression. "Oib Nisht Noch Hecher" ("And Even Higher") honors the rabbi who uses religious training to help the poor and helpless. While Peretz again retells the Hasidic story faithfully, he demystifies the ending without destroying the effect; Peretz shows how the village rabbi converts a nonbeliever who discovers that, contrary to the villagers' popular belief, the rabbi does not disappear into heaven during his daily afternoon absences, but rather disguises himself and goes about the town performing godly acts of charity.

In addition to his popular short stories, Peretz wrote three mystical dramas. These plays differ from the short stories in their close examination of the negative aspects of poverty. In the comedy *Amoi is Gwen a Meliech (Once There Was a King)*, Peretz satirizes a group of naive factory workers who strike against an employer who is as poor as they are. *Die Golden Keit (The Golden Chain)*, Peretz's most famous drama, examines the struggle between romantic and realistic thought, when the spiritual chain linking several generations of a pious family weakens and finally breaks as the ancestral home gradually becomes a symbol for repression of free thought. *Nacht Olfen Alten Mark (At Night in the Market)*, a drama in rhymed verse that has been compared to a Faustian vision of a descent into hell, has been praised by some critics as one of the great Yiddish dramas. Other critics contend that despite the work's concision and ability to evoke strong emotional responses, the purpose of the philosophical fantasy remains unclear and overburdened by symbolism.

The reverence and acclaim Peretz had received as a public figure amplified his reputation as a man and as a fiction writer. Modern critics agree that his experimentation with the Yiddish language and the fusion of cosmopolitan and traditional views in his works marked a radical break with traditional Yiddish literary style and are almost solely responsible for the modernization of Yiddish literature. Irving Howe and Eliezer Greenberg, commenting upon the late nineteenth-century struggles between secularist and traditionalist factions, have stated that "Peretz stood at the very center, buffered by the opposing tendencies and expressing opinions more ambivalent, certainly more complex, than could easily be grasped by ideologies on either side." Critics who agree that Peretz was a master of subtle irony complain that while English translations of his stories capture much of his purpose, they often embellish the simple style to present a style and tone more familiar to modern readers. Some critics further note that many of the Yiddish words are untranslatable, because they are subtle composites rooted in cultural history. Despite these problems, the noted Jewish author Elie Wiesel has found value in the translated works, and has written that "to read Peretz is to plunge into an ancient dream and the fervor it calls forth. You will emerge the richer for having done so."

(See also *Contemporary Authors*, Vol. 109.)

PRINCIPAL WORKS

"Monish" (poetry) 1888; published in journal *Yidishe Folkbibliotek*

Bekannte Bilder (short stories) 1890
Poezie (poetry) 1892
Bilder fun a provintz raize (essays and short stories) 1894
Dos shtreimel (short stories) 1896
Stories and Pictures (short stories) 1906
Ale verk. 18 vols. (short stories, poetry, and essays) 1910-1913
Dramen (dramas) 1910
Mayne Zikhroynes (memoirs) 1914
   [*My Memoirs*, 1964]
Bontshe the Silent, and Other Stories (short stories) 1927
"Tale of Heaven and Hell" (short story) 1937; published in journal *Menorah Journal*
Peretz (short stories) 1947
   [*Stories from Peretz*, 1964]
Three Gifts, and Other Stories (short stories) 1947
The Three Canopies (short story) 1948
As Once We Were: Selections from the Works of Peretz (short stories) 1951
In This World and the Next: Selected Writings (short stories) 1958
The Book of Fire (short stories) 1960
Selected Stories (short stories) 1974

LEO WIENER (essay date 1899)

[*An American scholar and professor of Slavic languages, Wiener has written on the history, culture, and literature of several nations and continents, including Russia, Africa, Germany, and Mexico, and has contributed to periodicals throughout the world. In the following excerpt from his* The History of Yiddish Literature in the Nineteenth Century, *the first work of its kind in English, Wiener discusses Peretz's early works, including the short story collections* Well-Known Pictures *and* Pictures of a Provincial Journey, *which are about rural Jewish life. Wiener regards the short stories as among Peretz's best, noting the author's knowledge of and feeling for his subject. Wiener attributes many of the obscurities in the works to the threat of censorship under which Peretz worked and to intentional artistic devices—which the critic delineates.*]

The year 1888 is momentous in the history of Judeo-German literature: it gave birth to two annuals, *Die jüdische Volksbibliothēk* and *Der Hausfreund*, around which were fathered all the best forces that could be found among the Jewish writers. . . . In the *Volksbibliothēk* appeared the firstling from the pen of Leon Perez, the poet and novelist, who must be counted among the greatest writers not only of Judeo-German literature, but of literature in general at the end of the nineteenth century. If he had written nothing else but **'The Sewing of the Wedding Gown,'** his name would live as long as there could be found people to interpret the language in which he sings. But he has produced several large volumes of admirable works in prose and in verse. (pp. 110-11)

He has treated masterfully the Talmudical legend, has composed in the style of the Romancero, and has carried allegory to the highest degree of perfection. (p. 111)

Although he started with the avowed purpose of aiding his race to a better recognition of itself, yet his talents are of too high an order, where language, feelings, and thoughts soar far above the understanding of the masses. He can hardly be properly appreciated even by those who enjoy the advantages of a fair school education, not to speak of those who are merely lettered. It is only an unfortunate accident, the persecutions of the Jews, that has thrown him into so unpromising a field as that of Judeo-German letters, where to be great is to be unknown to the world at large and to be subjected to the jealous attacks of less gifted writers. He could easily gain a reputation in any other language, should he choose to try for it, but, like many of his predecessors, he is pursued by the merciless allurements of the Jewish Muse. (pp. 111-12)

'Monisch' is the name of the ballad with which Perez made his debut ten years ago. It is the old story of Satan's recovery of power over the saint by tempting him with an earthly love. But the setting of the story is all new and original. The fourth chapter . . . is the best of all. He describes there the difficulty of singing of love in a dialect that has no words for 'love' and 'sweetheart'; nevertheless he acquits himself well of his task to tell of Monisch's infatuation, for which, of course, a saint and a Jew can only become Satan's prey. Perez has written a number of stories in verse. Some of them are mosaics of gems, in which the unity of the whole is frequently marred by a mystic cloud which it is hard to penetrate. Such, for example, is his **'He and She,'** a story of the Spanish inquisition, and **'Reb Jossel,'** the temptation of a teacher of children by his hostess, the wife of a shoemaker. The latter poem is very hard to grasp at one reading, but the details, such as the description of the teacher, his pale and ailing pupil with his endless school superstitions, the jolly shoemaker, are drawn very well. Much more comprehensible are his **'The Driver'** and **'Jossel Bers and Jossel Schmaies.'** (pp. 112-13)

The shorter poems are either translations from the Russian poet Nadson, or imitations of Heine. They are well done, though some suffer somewhat by their veiled allegory, at least at a superficial reading. The best of these are those that deal with social questions, or describe the laborer's sufferings. Preëminent among them is **'The Sewing of the Wedding Gown.'** If Thomas Hood's 'Song of the Shirt' is to be compared to a fine instrument, then this poem is a whole orchestra, from the sounds of which the walls of Jericho would fall. (p. 114)

Among his voluminous works there is not one that is mediocre, not one that would lose anything of its comprehensibleness by being translated into another language. Although they at times deal with situations taken from Jewish life, it is their universal human import that interests him, not their specifically racial characteristics. It is mere inertia and the desire to serve his people that keep him in the ranks of Judeo-German writers. He does not belong there by any criterions that we [can apply] to his confreres, who themselves complain that his symbolism is inaccessible to the masses for whom he pretends to write. While this accusation is certainly just in the case of some of his works, it cannot be brought up in many other cases, where, in spite of the allegory, mysticism, or symbolism underlying his tale, there is a sufficient real residue of intelligible story for the humblest of his readers. He, too, aims at the education of his people, but in a vastly different sense from his predecessors. It is not the material information of mere facts that he strives for, nor even the broader culture of the schools that he would substitute for the Jewish lore and religious training, nor is he satisfied, with Spektor, to rouse the dormant national consciousness. His sympathies are with humanity at large, and the Jews are but one of the units that are to be redeemed from the social slavery under which the wretched of the world groan. . . . [Perez] offers gladly all he has, his genius, in the service of the lowly. Literature, according to him, is not to be

a flimsy pastime of the otiose, but a consolation to those who have no other consolation, a safe and pleasurable retreat for those who are buffeted about on the stormy sea of life. For these reasons he writes in Judeo-German and not in any other language with which he is conversant, and for these same reasons he prefers to dwell with the downtrodden and the submerged.

To these people he devotes his best energies, and he uses the same care in filing and finishing his works that he would use if he were writing for a public trained in the best thoughts of the world and used to the highest type of literature. His first prose work, though not the first to be printed, was a small volume entitled *Well-known Pictures,* containing three stories: **'The Messenger,' 'What Is a Soul?'** and **'The Crazy Beggar-Student.'** (pp. 202-04)

With such a book Perez made his entrance into the field of letters. To say that his future works show a riper talent would be to place too low an estimate on his first book, which, in spite of the many excellent things he has written, still remains among the very best. (pp. 206-07)

Of his scientific articles particular mention must be made of his long essay **'On Trades,'** which is a popularization of political economy, brought down to the level of the humblest reader. The admirable, entertaining style, the aptness of the illustrations, and the absence of doctrinarianism makes it one of the most remarkable productions in popular science. Still more literary and perfect in form are his *Pictures of a Provincial Journey.* It seems that Perez had been sent into the province for the sake of collecting statistical data on the condition of the Jews resident there. This essay is apparently a diary of his experiences on that trip. We do not remember of having read in any literature any journal approaching this one in literary value. What makes it particularly interesting is that it is written so that it will interest those very humble people about whom he is writing. The picture of misery which he unrolls before us, however saddening and distressing, is made so attractive by the manner of its telling that one cannot lay aside the book until one has read the whole seventy quarto pages.

Perez has written more than fifty sketches, all of them of the same sterling value as the three described above. Every new one is an additional gem in the crown he is making for himself. They are all characterized by the same tender pathos, the same excellence of style, the same delicacy of feeling. He generally prefers the tragic moments in life as fit objects for his sympathetic pen, but he has also treated in a masterly manner the gentle sentiment of love. But it is an entirely different kind from the romantic love, that he deems worthy of attention. It is the marital affection of the humblest families, which is developed under difficulties, strengthened by adversity, checkered by misfortune; it is the saintliest of all loves that he tells about as no one before him has ever told. In the same manner he likes to dwell on all the virtues which are brought out by suffering, which are evolved through misery and oppression, which are more gentle, more unselfish, more divine, the lower we descend in the scale of humanity. Nor need one suppose that in order to show his characters from that most advantageous side, the author has to resort to disguises of idealization. They are no better and no worse than one meets every day and all around us; but they are such as only he knows who is not deterred by the shabbiness of their dress and the squalor of their homes from making their intimate acquaintance. They do not carry their virtues for show, they do not give monetary contributions for charities, they do not join societies for the promotion of philanthropic institutions, they do not preach on duties to God and on the future life, they are not even given to the expression of moral indignation at the sight of sin. But they are none the less possessed of the finer sentiments which come to the surface only in the narrower circle of their families, in their relations to their fellow-sufferers. Not even the eloquent advocate of the people generally cares to enter that unfamiliar sphere as Perez has done. His affection for the meanest of his race is not merely platonic. He not only knows whereof he speaks: he feels it; and thus we get the saddest, the tenderest, the sweetest stories from the life of the lowliest of the Jews that have ever been written.

In 1894 Perez published a collective volume, *Literature and Life*, which contains, like his periodical, mostly productions of his own. . . . ['**Bontsie Silent'**] belongs to the same category of sketches as his '**The Messenger.**' It presents, probably better than any other, the author's conception of the character of the virtues of the long-suffering masses. Who can read it without being moved to the depth of his heart? There is no exaggeration in it, no melodrama, nothing but the bitter reality. It expresses, in a more direct way than anything else he has written, his faith that the Kingdom of Heaven belongs to the lowly.

The sketch named '**The Fur-Cap**' is one of the very few that he has written as an attack on the Khassidic Rabbi. There is here, however, a vast difference in the manner of Perez and of Linetzki. While the latter goes at it in a direct way, with club in hand, and bluntly lets it fall on the head of the fanatic, Perez has above all in mind the literary form in which he clothes his attack, and we get from him an artistic story which must please even if the thrusts be not relished. The Rabbi never appears in public without his enormous fur-cap, which is really the insignia of his office. . . . It is the cap, not the man, and his wisdom, that sanctions and legalizes his various acts. Were it not for the cap, it would not be possible to tell right from wrong. This fine bit of sarcasm is not a mere attack at the sect of the Khassidim; it is also meant as an accusation of our whole social system, with its conventional lies. Perez does not show by his writings to what particular party he belongs, but he is certainly not with the conservatives. He is with those who advocate progress in its most advanced form. He is opposed to everything that means the enslavement of any class of people. . . . The stories of the Judeo-German authors . . . cannot be free of 'tendencies' whenever the writers have in mind the treatment of subjects which would be dealt with severely by the censor. Much of the alleged obscurity of Perez's writings is just due to the desire of avoiding the censor's blue pencil, and the more dangerous a more direct approach becomes, the more delicate must be the allegory. The best of that class of literature is contained in this volume in a series entitled '**Little Stories for Big Men.**'

The first of these is called '**The Stagnant Pool.**' We are introduced here to the world of worms who live in the pool, who regard the green scum as their heaven, and pieces of eggshells that have fallen into it as the stars and the moon upon it. A number of cows stepping into the pool tear their heaven and kill all who are not hidden away in the slime. Only one worm survives to tell the story of the catastrophe, and he suggests to his fellows that that was not the heaven that was destroyed, that there is another heaven which exists eternally. For this the narrator was thought to be insane and was sent to an insane asylum. . . . There are altogether ten such excellent allegories, or fables, in the collection, all of the same value. The last of Perez's articles in the book is a popular discussion of what

constitutes property; it is written in the same style as his scientific works spoken of before. (pp. 208-13)

> Leo Wiener, "Poetry since the Eighties in Russia" and "Prose Writers since 1881: Rabinowitsch, Perez," in his The History of Yiddish Literature in the Nineteenth Century, *Charles Scribner's Sons, 1899, pp. 105-17, 194-215.**

AMY C. RICH (essay date 1906)

[*In the following excerpt from a review of* Stories and Pictures, *Rich notes the surface realism and psychological depth that characterize Peretz's stories about life among poor Jews.*]

[*Stories and Pictures*] is the first translation into English of the stories of Peretz, the gifted Russian Jew, who through the medium of the Yiddish language has given the world some of the most faithful and telling pictures of Jewish life that have appeared.

Inevitably, perhaps, dealing as they do with the lives of the poor and the down-trodden, all these sketches are depressing, and some of them are tragic to the point of grimness. The author, however, possesses the master-power which enables him to impart to commonplace and even sordid happenings that deep human interest which lifts his work above the plane of mediocrity to that of genius. The stories give realistic pictures of Jewish life and customs in the Old World, but at the same time the reader is made to feel and understand the obscure psychological influences at work among these persecuted and devoted adherents of the orthodox Jewish faith.

Among the more notable tales in these *Stories and Pictures* are "**The Seven Candles of Blessing,**" "**What Is the Soul?**" "**In the Dead Town,**" and "**The Messenger.**"

> Amy C. Rich, in a review of "Stories and Pictures," in The Arena, *Boston, Vol. XXXVI, No. CCV, December, 1906, p. 684.*

A. A. ROBACK (essay date 1940)

[*Roback was a prominent American psychologist and a scholar of folk literature. The author and editor of both scientific and literary works, he founded and organized the Harvard University Library's collection of Yiddish literature. In the following excerpt from his* The Story of Yiddish Literature, *Roback reexamines Peretz's career twenty-five years after the author's death, concluding that his forceful personality, revealed in the total body of his work, must be taken into account when assessing Peretz's greatness.*]

To many of our own generation, Peretz has become a legend. There are still those who knew him, ready to puncture this legend. His shortcomings and weaknesses have not been spared. His coevals have gone to the extent of exaggerating his foibles, yet the halo still surrounds him; and in the course of the century, unless Jewish culture declines, it is likely to take on a more luminous character as the folk-mind will continue to draw on its imaginative resources.

A quarter of a century is a long time to reconsider values. We can now begin to speak in the name of posterity. Has Peretz actually deserved the encomium showered upon him by Jewish leaders throughout the world? (p. 130)

Peretz had never even so much as attempted a full-length novel, and compressed nearly all his talent into the short story, frequently spending himself in fragments, sparks, so to speak. As to poetry, besides *Monish,* with which he made his literary début, and a few shorter specimens of good verse, he turned out very little that could take its place beside masters like Rosenfeld, Yehoash and Bialik, unless we include in this field the dramatic poems (*Sewing of the Bridal Gown*) and the versified dramas. It is, indeed, problematic whether Peretz could have reached the top rung in our own poetically fruitful decade. It is likewise with drama. So little did he accomplish in this sphere, that Pinski, with his dozens of plays, is easily his peer as a playwright. . . . Peretz's main excellence lies in the short story, but even there he has competitors who have written not only a larger number of tales in Yiddish, but who had a greater instinct for the purely narrative pattern.

It will not be necessary to extend this miniature survey. We shall grant that, just as a very attractive woman, when we begin taking her features apart, so Peretz is at a disadvantage when we start to analyze his specific contributions. *He can receive his proper evaluation only when we scan his literary physiognomy as a whole.* (pp. 132-33)

Peretz's personality decidedly overshadowed his works. Indeed, his works will be understood only in the light of his temperament and cultural sweep.

Everyone who had come in contact with him was fascinated by his dynamic and buoyant qualities. (pp. 135-36)

It must not be supposed, however, that I am diverting attention from indifferent literary achievement to a striking personality. All that is postulated here is that Peretz's personality is so interwoven with his work that we cannot understand the one without the other. We shall have occasion to see that in spite of a relatively meagre output, his personal equation means so much more when added to the content—which brings us to the positive features of his literary configuration, clearly distinguishing him from other Yiddish and perhaps, too, Jewish writers in general.

In the first instance, he was a pathfinder, what the Germans call a *Bahnbrecher.* It is curious that his very name, *Peretz . . . ,* symbolically signifies just this. Even his compeers, Mendele and Sholem Aleikhem, keen as they were in their detailed *perceptions,* browsed in a ghetto. Peretz broke the barriers between East and West, between Jew and Gentile, thus Europeanizing the literature which hitherto seemed impervious to the influences from without, and supplied a lofty *conception* to the whole framework.

Critics said he was under the sway of this Russian or that Polish writer, just as other cavillers spoke of Sholem Aleikhem as an imitator of Chekhov, but it mattered not. Peretz demonstrated that Yiddish could be set on a cultural plane alongside French, German, Russian or Polish, although he did complain of the dearth of poetic expressions, thus betraying his inadequacy in this domain. He never had cause to deplore the poverty of Yiddish diction in writing his deeply moving folk tales and sparkling feuilletons. (pp. 136-37)

Peretz not only blazed the trail by introducing new themes and a fresh style. He exploited his subjects in an original manner, discarding the elementary teacher's pointer (*teitle*) and requiring his readers to think, indicating the cue by a series of dots which were laughed out of court by his older colleagues. They said it was a pose, affecting originality, but that in reality, he himself would be hard put to tell exactly what was in his mind. Perhaps they were right in a certain degree; for Peretz did not

pretend to give us ready-made conclusions. He was original in setting the problems, in disclosing relations, without explaining their *quale.* That did not detract from his individuality, since much of what was then vague and inarticulate began to take on a definite shape and hue as the years went by, just as Beethoven's symphonies mean much more to us today than they did to the privileged first auditors.

There can be no question about Peretz being a creative mind, even if many of his products were not finished. Schubert's *Unfinished Symphony* is great music in spite of its incompleteness. Together with Schiller he would rather be in constant quest of objectives than actually attain them. And herein lies another fundamental trait of Peretz's literary personality. *He was the perpetual seeker*—of new forms, new ideas, new outlets of expression. His mercurial nature was an obstruction and at the same time a release—an obstruction to his literary reputation, and a release to the urges of his inner self.

Many of his opponents placed him in the category of a chameleon, but he did not assume the coloring of the environment. Rather did he *take the initiative in transforming it.* That is one reason why he could not be a realist or naturalist. It would be necessary for him to remain on one plane; it would spell stagnation for him. He must *transform* the mere sense-data into an ideological entity, trying out various approaches. (pp. 137-38)

Peretz was of course a romanticist, but this was only a stage in his cultural wandering. He became in turn an impressionist, a symbolist and, *in natu,* even an expressionist. Surrealism might have occupied his attention had he lived another few years. The experimentalism in modern literary movements was manifest in his unceasing search for a better understanding of situations (since the characters are only phases of a psychological situation). He thus becomes the divining rod of new forms for at least a whole generation of writers; and forsooth, if we investigate the most recent innovations in Yiddish productions, we shall discover that Peretz had already shown the way. (p. 139)

In many other writers, the passage from one story to another, from one play or novel to another, is accompanied by or mediated through the change of interest and mentality. Each of Peretz's writings, however, is merely a chip off the old block. It is Peretz objectified into a tale, poem, or feuilleton. The true literary picture of the artist can be envisaged only after all these items, fragments, and even aphorisms are welded into an integrated whole; and we must not lose sight of his great versatility in this connection: correspondence, memoirs, epigrams, publicism, allegories, poetry, drama, essays, travel pictures, criticism, popular science—all capped by his insinuating folk-tales and Khassidic stories. (p. 140)

It would seem futile to condense into a paragraph of ordinary prose a poetic gem, the setting of which is by far more important than the plot or the moral. In other words, in order to enjoy Peretz one must read him. (p. 141)

To my mind, the eerie drama *Beinakht oifn Altn Mark* is his great masterpiece. It is a Jewish conception of *Faust* with a *Walpurgisnacht* originally conceived on a ghetto scale, narrow but deep. In rhymed verse, it shows us the Peretz we might have had, were he working under propitious circumstances. That, indeed, is what we always have in the back of our mind when we pay homage to the man who had so many facets, each of which shone as if it were of a different water. We honor him for his potentialities as well as for his actualities; for we feel, as did his sworn foe, that the man was greater than his production. "Handsome is that handsome does" is not applicable to him.

Peretz not only was the foremost writer in Yiddish. He was a pillar in Hebrew literature too. His poetry, in contrast with the didactic and moralistic trends of the day, introduced an erotic note and appealed to the aesthetic sense. His sketches and playlets in Hebrew are, in part, variants of some of his Yiddish writings, sometimes preceding them. A series of fantastic pictures of *The Eighth Compartment of the Inferno* is his most ambitious contribution to Hebrew literature. Its translation into Yiddish, by the late A. Frumkin, pleased the author sufficiently to praise the rendering.

Withal, there was nothing crude or shoddy about his work. Even his **"Shtreiml,"** which is a veiled attack on traditional formality and which, because of its sophistication, has caused an acrimonious controversy in the Yiddish press of some forty years ago is, in reality, more romantic than cynical. (pp. 142-43)

> *A. A. Roback, "Yitzkhok Leibush Peretz," in his The Story of Yiddish Literature, Yiddish Scientific Institute, 1940, pp. 125-47.*

JACOB GLATSTEIN (essay date 1947)

[*A Polish-American critic and Yiddish poet, Glatstein was founder and coeditor of* In-zikh, *a journal of Yiddish poetry which inspired innovations in Yiddish literary style and subject matter and which influenced the American Yiddish poetry of the 1920s. Glatstein later returned to promoting and practicing more traditional forms of Yiddish poetic expression, and in 1938 called for a "back to the Ghetto" movement as a repudiation of the European culture that had permitted the rise of nazism. In the following excerpt, originally published in Yiddish in 1947, Glatstein credits Peretz with defining the national aspirations of an entire generation through reworked Hasidic folktales that are remarkable both in their Jewishness and their universality.*]

Among our principal writers Peretz is the most conscious stylist. . . .

I do not know whether Peretz is our greatest artist, but he is certainly our most durable artist, one who will live as long as Yiddish literature lives. His work will not require close reading and explication, nor will it need a mass of footnotes explaining a different way of life. Peretz's name will be immortal because he grasped Jewish life in its unchanging fundamentals. (p. 51)

Peretz came forth not merely as a creative artist, but as creator of a world that had not existed before his arrival. *From the outset, his task was that of creating single-handed a Jewish nineteenth century.* (p. 53)

Peretz brought us into the marching ranks of the world as conscious Jews. He joined us to the great ebb and flow of the world at large. Creating a whole Jewish century, he wove it into the cultural history of the world.

By the close of the nineteenth century Peretz had begun to write his Hasidic folklorist tales. These were the dome and the cornices of the enormous structure he erected in the course of a few years. Peretz brought consolation to a lost generation, a generation that did not by itself have the strength to transform itself in the terms of the century that stormed and thundered around it. He, the father of modern Yiddish literature, was able to take hold of that generation in the midst of its lonely wanderings and give it national aspirations. This defining of national aspirations was a subtle process, making its appearance only gradually. But the strength of Peretz's commanding personality enabled him to impose that process of definition upon his generation, which now could suddenly find the outer world reflected within itself.

In evaluating Peretz's work for its place not only in Yiddish literature but in Jewish life, one cannot help but use grandiose terms. *He placed the inner nature of the Jewish spirit upon the world-calendar of the nineteenth century, he unearthed the finest Jewish treasures and illuminated them with the first electric light.* He was also one of the first Yiddish writers to win the confidence of the Jewish student youth, who obtained from Peretz a key to the understanding of themselves, and thereby began to perceive that a thirst for education did not necessarily mean a flight from oneself but could rather be a means of entry into the world through one's self and back to one's self. Peretz was thus the first Yiddish writer to deliver a powerful blow against assimilation and make it stand with bowed head before the Jewish past. (pp. 54-5)

Peretz cast about in search of an audience for a long time, until he finally came to the conclusion that his ideal reader was someone so close to himself that he could not write any books for him until he had first tried them out on himself. . . . His reader, in the last analysis he himself, was no longer able to live by the bread of humor and satire alone. His reader, he himself, had become too perturbed to be satisfied merely with reading books. He sought, instead, a new orientation for Jewish life because he could not view that life with utter resignation.

He saw what was coming with great acuteness. Himself a Jew who had broken away from traditional Judaism, he sought within himself a solution to the problem of a great rupture in Jewish continuity. And as the prototype of all his readers, he strove to make a minimal Judaism into a maximum Judaism; this was what led him directly to Hasidism, which is, in its very essence, a minimal Judaism elevated to the most passionate faith. (p. 56)

Not for nothing did Peretz dwell so much upon melody in his Hasidic tales. In **"Between Two Mountains"** the Bialer Rebbe's Hasidim toss at him "a beginning of a melody. They burst into song and continue on their way singing." In **"The Teaching of Hasidism"** the Nemirover Rebbe's son-in-law discusses Torah, but his lesson is about the enthusiasm of the Rebbe's singing and dancing. In **"Cabbalists"** the yeshiva student dies after a voiceless spiritual melody begins singing within him; he is called aloft to the court of the heavenly host "because a singer is missing there." In **"A Conversation"** between two Hasidim the secret of why the Haggada is intoned with a tragic melody is brought out. Peretz sought the melody of Judaism in its very essence, a melody that not only needed no words, no spoken Torah, but could dispense with song itself.

There is a tragic quality in these Hasidic tales, with their superhuman effort to provide a lost generation with something more than literature—something like a new guide for the perplexed. But at least Peretz's companions in perplexity still stood near the basic sources of Judaism; for them, Peretz's marvelous tales were winged variants of an old greatness. The time is soon coming, however, when people will have to study these tales solely as literature, and not as the guide for the perplexed that they were to Peretz's generation; and when one thinks of them exclusively as literature, it is only then that one can perceive the intensity with which they were written and feel the breath of a great artist. (pp. 57-8)

Every one of Peretz's Hasidic tales is a poem, written in a dramatic rhythm. Physical descriptions are at a minimum, for they would take away from the spiritualized atmosphere that gives life to the stories. The Torah, singing out from every story, is truly the melody of Judaism. All will be well at the advent of the day when people will really be able to live with the melody itself. The moral of each tale, which raises it to a height of universality, is always a deeply Jewish one. It is never a candy-coated message; it always calls for effort—for straightforward Jewish endeavor.

In Peretz's Hasidic tales we sense the common bond between individuals who in an alien world have become a people by virtue of their acts. (p. 58)

In his **"Bridal Portion,"** Peretz not only lifted a pauper out of the rubbish heap, he even made him into a lord and a commander. Into the midst of the wealth, comfort, and privileged doubting of Reb Uzzer Hoffenstand enters Poverty in the form of a bent old Jew "with a white, wind-blown beard that was tangled up in the threads of his worn-out old gaberdine, and with a pale face under a shabby cap."

Poverty himself has entered, Peretz tells us in an aside.

And how does Jewish-Hasidic Poverty make his entrance before Reb Uzzer Hoffenstand?

"Shalom Aleichem, Mendel," the millionaire says to him. "Aleichem Shalom, Uzzer," answers Mendel-Poverty.

The truth is, that Uzzer wraps his hand in a napkin before extending it in greeting to Poverty, but Poverty is not at all taken aback at this bent for hygiene on the part of a fastidious rich man. He is not embarrassed in the slightest; rather, he goes right on to request—to demand even—a drop of brandy and a bite to eat. The two classes have met, and the poor is not at all fazed by the rich. (pp. 59-60)

Poor Mendel is called a pauper, but he is thoroughly familiar with the rules of Jewish charity; he may stand far below the heights of glory, but the crown of humanity has not been taken from him. He enters like a king demanding what is his rightful due. He even takes over Uzzer's house—and Uzzer's couch; he washes his hands of him and he washes himself for dinner, then he sleeps a peaceful sleep. But Uzzer does not lose his patience and throw Mendel out—on the contrary, he does feel indebted to him because he feels that he himself has had abundance showered upon him by God, and that he has been given many things only in trust.

Two Jews have encountered one another as equals, and what is this equal to? The new proletarian implications of Hasidism. And who is it that perceived this and gave the situation artistic embellishment? The father of modern Yiddish literature, the man who gave dramatic form to the whole body of Jewish folk tales and found Jewish wisdom in every Hasidic tale.

With all the strength of his artistic personality, Peretz sought the ideal of artistic anonymity in his folkloric tales. He wanted, as it were, to give these tales back to the people, but in the process of giving them back the words took on wings. Stripping the text to what seemed a primitive simplicity, he raised it up from the mere two-dimensionality of the folk-voice and imparted to it an additional dimension of mind. Every tale gained something in the process. The color and flavor of a modern story-teller was added to their biblical clarity, and they became neo-biblical moral fables of a newer form of Judaism—Hasidism. This great renderer of thought into imagery infused rationality into the latter-day folk-Torah of Hasidism. In the story **"Between Two Mountains"** one can see what it was that

Peretz sought artistically in Hasidism. Into the mouths of the Rebbe of Brisk and the Bialer Rebbe he placed a dialogue representing their two worlds, and in the process clearly demonstrated which of these worlds, or which of the "two mountains," he would have preferred to climb. . . . (pp. 60-1)

In Judaism of the Hasidic type, Peretz found what Christianity often claims for itself: pity for the lowest classes, for the silent and the abject—the spirit of Dostoevsky and Tolstoy. He did not need to read anything into Judaism, for he read it *out*, from the depths of our own moral treasury. To the darkness of the Jewish towns and villages that he visited in the course of a statistical expedition initiated by a Jewish apostate, he brought the artistic flame of Hasidism. (p. 61)

Jacob Glatstein, "Peretz and the Jewish Nineteenth Century," translated by Ronald Sanders, in Voices from the Yiddish: Essays, Memoirs, Diaries, *edited by Irving Howe and Eliezer Greenberg, The University of Michigan Press, 1972, pp. 51-63.*

MAURICE SAMUEL (essay date 1948)

[*Samuel was a Rumanian-American essayist, novelist, critic, and lecturer. Prolific in many areas, Samuel used his work to explain the unfamiliar Jewish world to the Western world, recreating crucial periods in Jewish history in such novels as* The Web of Lucifer *(1947) and* The Second Crucifixion *(1960). In* Prince of the Ghetto, *Samuel examines Peretz's stories to determine and illustrate his beliefs and intent. In the following excerpt from that work, Samuel discusses Peretz's stories that reveal self-contempt, and those which, uncharacteristically, reject the happy ending.*]

Peretz even in his capacity as folklorist—that is, quite apart from his Europeanized self—occasionally displayed an ambivalent attitude toward Jewish life.

In this, however, he was specifically Jewish. The self-critical spirit of the Jews is one of the strangest phenomena in history. . . . [It] is enough to say, I think, that we cannot find an instance of another people which, having been driven from its soil by peoples at least as bad as (actually much worse than) itself, should wander about the world saying: "It served us right. We lost our homeland because of our sins." (p. 121)

In the Yiddish-speaking segment of modern Jewry the self-criticism took the form of irony. A deep belief in the fundamental ethos of Judaism was accompanied by a subtle disrespect for Jews in high places. Modern Jews did not take seriously the view that God had arranged a two-thousand-year chastisement for His people. But they did feel that somewhere, somehow, something was wrong with the Jews. . . .

Occasionally the ironical attitude passed over into the savage and tormented. If one sometimes looks upon Jewry as the saint among peoples, one must sometimes hate it as well as love it. We react with a confused love and loathing toward the saint, who is as sensitive as a genius and as patient as a spittoon. Peretz was tied to the Jewish people with all the fibers of his heart. In certain moods (as in **"Devotion unto Death"** and in **"All for a Pinch of Snuff"**) his love was whole and untroubled. In other moods (that of **"Thou Shalt Not Covet,"** for instance) the note of sardonic self-deprecation is audible. And in more extreme moods it drowns out everything else. (p. 122)

The folk and Chassidic tales were his dominant and enduring mood; but in recurring fits of self-contempt he resented the idealizations that those tales embody. When the two moods overlapped, he wrote such things as **"Thou Shalt Not Covet."** (p. 124)

Peretz was a master of the story with the God-given happy ending, and he sometimes disliked himself for it. Now and again he wrote a short story in which goodness did not get its reward on this earth. He even has a sketch that shows a saintly soul refusing the offer of heaven with the remark: "I would rather go to hell, where I can be of some use." Predominantly, however, the good triumphs in his tales, and he knew that from one point of view this is not true to life. For that matter, he knew also that the function of good is not to be rewarded; it is, simply, to be good. He knew that the innocent must suffer with the guilty, if only by definition; for if they did not, they would not be innocent, they would be merely shrewd. (p. 125)

There was another source of self-repudiation in Peretz, and it was also part of his "honesty." I use quotation marks because intellectual honesty is not a simple business. "Know thyself" and "to thine own self be true" are superficial directives. One of Peretz's intellectual honesties led him away from his Jewish association. He even protested once against the limitations of the Yiddish language. In any case, he had spasms of desire to get away from the stifling disciplines of a people out of touch with the contemporaneous European world, away from the taboos and superstitions, the mumbo-jumbo, and the insularity. That side of his honesty is expressed in the sketch ["**Stories**"]. . . . (p. 126)

It deals with a Jewish unbeliever, or *the* Jewish unbeliever, who differs from other unbelievers. . . .

For the unbeliever generally, for him who rebels against his early faith, the issue seldom remains settled. Having said no, does the no remain forever? . . .

[When] one is shaken by a fit of belief, then (perversity of human thought!) the intellectual dishonesty consists in being afraid to admit our condition. What? Can those impossible people whom we have repudiated have been in the right after all?

Complete intellectual honesty consists in admitting that intellectual honesty is not everything. (p. 127)

["**Stories**" is] Peretz's sketch of the young Jewish intellectual who has renounced, in the name of honesty, participation in and even sympathy with the forms and rituals and beliefs of his people. It is written in the third person—but there is much of Peretz himself in it. (p. 132)

Maurice Samuel, "The Divided Man," in his *Prince of the Ghetto, Alfred A. Knopf, 1948, pp. 121-32.*

LESLIE A. FIEDLER   (essay date 1948)

[*Fiedler is a controversial and provocative American critic. While he has also written novels and short stories, his personal philosophy and insights are thought to be most effectively expressed in his literary criticism. Emphasizing the psychological, sociological, and ethical context of works, Fiedler often views literature as the mirror of a society's consciousness. Similarly, he believes that the conventions and values of a society are powerful determinants of the direction taken by its authors' works. The most notable instance of Fiedler's critical stance is his reading of American literature, and therefore American society, as an infantile flight from "adult heterosexual love." This idea is developed in his most important work,* Love and Death in the American Novel *(1960), along with the theory that American literature is essentially an extension of the Gothic novel. Although Fiedler has*

been criticized for what are considered eccentric pronouncements on literature, he is also highly valued for his adventuresome and eclectic approach, which complements the predominantly academic tenor of contemporary criticism. In the following excerpt from a review of Maurice Samuel's biography of Peretz, Prince of the Ghetto, *published in 1948, Fiedler discusses the many seemingly conflicting aspects of Peretz's life and work. He then examines Peretz's transmutation of traditional Jewish folk tales into modern literature and his utilization of an absurdist vision in that process.*]

It is an irony of communal memory that the bitterest critic of a way of life should be identified in recollection with the world he attacks, and yet it is a constant irony: an enlightened Aeschylus is confused with the bloody world of Agamemnon; a liberal Hawthorne blurs into the rigid Puritan commonwealth of Hester Prynne, an emancipated Peretz fades back into the ghetto from which in pain he escaped. This irony Maurice Samuel chooses to perpetuate in the title of his book, *Prince of the Ghetto.* Prince of the ghetto indeed—that believer in statistics, popular science, socialism, that "free" intellectual in a short coat who would not go home on Seder night: enemy of the ghetto, scourge of the ghetto, destroyer of the ghetto— Prince only in the sense that a revolutionist of '89 was Prince of the Bastille. And yet—

And yet there is possible another Peretz, a quite "real" Peretz, though one the living author would, I suspect, have had to deny: the *folk* Peretz—not, as Samuel misleadingly asserts, a writer of folk stories, but himself a myth of the folk, re-created by the Jewish people out of what was least conscious, most instinctive in his work. It is characteristic of greatness in writing, or of a certain kind of greatness at least, that it is amenable to precisely such mythic appropriation. There is a type of writer who permits himself to be transmuted, reinvented in response to the shifting needs of his audience; and eternally transformed, he yet integrally survives. It is Shakespeare, of course, who most spectacularly exemplifies this infinite lack of resistance to adaptation. Peretz, on his level, is almost equally responsive.

There are many possible Peretzes to be extracted from his whole work: the socialist, the enemy of orthodoxy, the exponent of Jewish self-hatred, the Yiddish Hans Christian Andersen, the rhapsodist of Romantic Love; and for some reader each of these must be especially valid, especially useful. It is always a question of *use*—and for Samuel's fictive Prince there is a clear and urgent use: to act as a mediator between the American non-Yiddish-speaking Jew (particularly the intellectual) and what is valuable in his Yiddish past—that is to say, the East European, the ghetto past as opposed to the Hebrew past. It is true, for better or worse, that for such a Jew the ethos of his recent ancestors is most easily available as "literature," at a level where not belief but the suspension of disbelief is exacted. (pp. 93-4)

Peretz was never sure of his language or his audience; he experimented with Polish and Hebrew, turned to Yiddish as a *pis aller* and not without regrets. On the one hand, he was tempted outward toward Europe as an audience, and on the other, he felt drawn inward as a teller of tales to his own people; but he could contemplate neither possibility without irony at his own expense. In a piece called **"Stories,"** Peretz satirizes his European orientation in a portrait of the Jewish writer spinning yarns to a stupid, anti-Semitic *shiksa* in hope of charming her into forgetting his ugly Jewish mug and giving him a kiss (surely, at some level he was ironically recalling *the* Kiss, the Kiss of the Shechina, the ultimate hope of the mystic Jew); and in one sketch he reports no less bitterly the attitude of an ordinary Polish Jew to his work: "What is the good of it? I don't mean to *you*. God forbid! A Jew must earn a living if he has to suck it out of a wall. But what do *they*, your readers, get out of it?"

In the end, Peretz seems to have spoken to the Europeanized Jew (a prospect rather than a fact), the cosmopolitan, rationalist, socialist Jew made in his own image; in lectures and by tracts, he tried himself to create his own ideal audience, though his total success would have meant the death of his work. After all, Yiddish is the ghetto language, and with the complete Europeanization of the Jew that Peretz dreamed, it would have disappeared as a living tongue, along with the caftan and the *sheitel*. Part of the tragic impact of Peretz' work arises from its being in intent an act of *suicide*, art's immolation of itself for the secularization of Jewish morality, and the Jew's subsumption into a common humanity. (p. 95)

As a European writer, Peretz comes toward the end of a long tradition (which begins with Percy's *Reliques* and Ossian and includes the work of such men as Novalis and Hans Christian Andersen, Goethe and George MacDonald) of appropriating to high literature folk material, and of creating a pseudo-folk literature. It is a chapter in the long history of the writer's effort to domesticate to his task what was once called the *merveilleux* and is now fashionably called the Absurd.

The problem of the nineteenth-century Jewish writer in this regard was markedly different in two main respects from that of the Gentile manipulators of the fairy tale: first, the Jewish folk tale had not sunk in social prestige to something told by old women to children; the haggadic tradition had made it possible to keep the *maase* unseparated from the main body of Jewish belief and ritual; and the Hasidic movement had instituted the Tale as one of the centers of religious life. The Jewish folk story was in the lifetime of Peretz not an old wife's tale, a degraded myth, but Myth in full flower; and the writer's problem was to secularize rather than to redeem the Absurd. Second, for Jewish literature, whose development takes place in an incredibly short time, Enlightenment and Romanticism are telescoped, so that the ideological bias of Peretz is not the anti-rationalism of, say, Andersen, but a mixture of rationalism, sentimentalism and philosophical optimism that reminds the English reader, quite improbably, of Alexander Pope.

The myth becomes literature in Peretz, therefore, by a double process: by the sentimentalizing of the Absurd and the rationalizing of the Absurd. Let us take a single example, the story called **"And Even Beyond,"** in which the "absurd" contention that the Rabbi of Nemirov spends the mornings of the Penitential Days in Heaven is challenged by a skeptical Litvak. In the end, the Litvak is content to grant the claim, after discovering that the Rabbi, disguised as a peasant, actually spends the holy mornings chopping wood for the old and the sick. For the Hasid's daring ambiguity of "Heaven," the Litvak and Peretz have substituted the rationalist (What else could Heaven mean to us moderns?), sentimental (to split kindling for a widow—what could be more Heavenly?) concept, "aiding the poor." What survives in the story, despite Peretz' conscious attempt to eliminate legend and magic, is the irreducible absurdity present as soon as the term "Heaven" is evoked, though the sentimentality endemic to Jewish emotional life nearly smothers it. Sometimes, as in **"Silent Bontche,"** one of Peretz' best-known stories, a third and saving element enters: the joke, the Jewish Joke which secularizes the Absurd as the absurd; granted the pick of Heaven's abundance, the holy simpleton asks for "every morning a hot roll with butter, please!" But

jokes are not frequent in Peretz, and he is ordinarily left to fend without the protection of wit against the shallow rationalization, the easy emotional response; so that most often, his reworkings of folk material are reductions, unintentional parodies of myth. More typical of Peretz' sensibility, though rare in its noncommittal tone, is such a study of Hasidic madness and devotion as **"The Kiss of Moses"**—in which, for once, Peretz succeeds in maintaining toward the Absurd a quizzical detachment, suspended between irony and sympathy, that makes *everything* seem possible: even the rightness of superstition and folly, even the Kiss of God. (pp. 97-8)

> *Leslie A. Fiedler, "Three Jews," in his* No! In Thunder: Essays on Myth and Literature, *Beacon Press, 1960, pp. 93-110.**

ISAIAH RABINOVICH (essay date 1968)

[*Rabinovich, a Ukrainian-Canadian educator, has a special interest in Jewish education, history, and literature. In the following excerpt, he surveys Peretz's career. An important element of his discussion is his characterization of* The Golden Chain *as a disturbing work with an inconsistent conclusion that contradicts what Peretz sought to achieve in the superior* The Voice of the People. *For a contrasting opinion of* The Golden Chain, *see the excerpt by Charles A. Madison (1968).*]

Even today in certain literary circles Peretz is spoken of as the greatest innovator of Yiddish and Hebrew, the father of *modern* Jewish literature. There is some truth in the statement, provided it is restricted to Yiddish literature and even then qualified with certain reservations.... Peretz understood the needs of Polish Jewry very well, as he showed in his survey of the Jewish townships (which appears in a special book written after a tour of Jewish settlements undertaken on behalf of the Warsaw community), and in his enlightening articles discussing educational and cultural problems as well as those connected with the political ideologies that were then engaging the attention of Jewish intellectuals. Sometimes he even devoted fictional writings quite openly to contemporary themes, as he did in **There Once Was a King,** a play in which Jewish workers raise the banner of revolution against an oppressive government and are put down by the Cossacks. Here he stresses the ideological element. But outside the realm of this ideological interest, deep within his own personality, he frequently succumbed to irrational, aesthetic impulses—a secret longing to be borne away by the sounds of some infinite harmony flowing into his soul from the outer universe and carried to a mighty ocean beyond the horizons of human imagination. He was responding to the neo-romanticism inherent in the Impressionism and Symbolism of Polish and European literature. He hoped that the younger men about him, his literary disciples, would one day create a modern Jewish literature similar to that of Poland, Russia, France, and Germany. The complaint that constantly recurred in his conversations with these younger writers was that Jewish literature "always missed the boat," that it always lagged behind contemporary trends.

In saying this, Peretz had no intention of diverting the Jewish writer from the common people, from their past, their future, their problems and visions. For Polish literature had seldom turned its back on the common people.... Yet, at that time Polish literature was wide open to the influence of the individualistic impressionism and mystic symbolism that had spilled over from French poetry in the 1880's and conquered the Slavic literatures of Russia and Poland. In these trends Peretz saw a sure heritage for himself and for the younger generation of

Jewish writers nurtured in the cultural centers of Warsaw and Odessa. He introduced these elements first into his own writings and then passed them on to the young writers to whom his home was always open. He thus encouraged them to turn in the same direction, filling them with secret longings for that splendid beauty shimmering on horizons far removed from the world of the Jewish ideologies.

The modernistic element in Peretz's writings is obvious, throughout the various periods of his work, to any sensitive reader. His style tends to be allusive and subtle, with broken phrases ending in a row of dots. The pauses are so carefully modulated that one is almost steeped in profound silences. There is no outside disturbance, no sound from the market place to disturb the reader as he listens to the character's dialogue with himself. Were we to try to illustrate this from each of the various types of Peretz's writings, there would be no end. It will suffice to quote a few lines from **"By a Dying Man's Pillow,"** whose rhythms and style are typical of the majority of his prose work.

> Toward evening, the caretaker of the Garden of Eden—an angel crowned like the others with light emanating from the Almighty—approached one of the windows of heaven and, leaning out, sorrowfully asked the setting sun:
>
> —Sun, do you know what has happened to our Leibel? . . .
>
> The sun said nothing—nothing; for he did not know. . . . The angel silently withdrew his head, closed the window, and sat down in his place even sadder than before.

The artistic purpose of this extract from one of the stories in *The Voice of the People* is quite clear. Peretz is attempting to break up the more direct, concrete style of writing, which seems to him to have exhausted itself, so that his words can convey more effectively the subtlety of variegated emotions. The hushed style of his writing, the musical pause at the close of phrases and sentences—a pause that seems to be listening to itself as it slows down the spoken dialogue between the angel seeking Leibel and the setting sun which knows nothing of his whereabouts—both suggest to the reader some divine inspiration hovering above and detaching itself from the question, "Where is Leibel?" It recalls the reader to himself; he hears it, wonders for a moment, and then succumbs to emotions that have no questions and no answers in the silence of the twilight. This impressionistic tendency pervades nearly all of Peretz's work, but it is most striking in this folktale, which begins as a legend merely retold by the author but gradually acquires a musicality over and above its folkloristic source and transcends realism.

In fact, Peretz is here entering the world of symbolism, which had conquered Russian and Polish literature at the beginning of the twentieth century, and he does this even more noticeably in the Yiddish version of his play *The Golden Chain*. Yet even in some of the stories in *The Voice of the People* this symbolism is dominant, particularly in **"Hear O Israel."** It is the tale of a poor young man who came to Tomashov and kept himself secluded from all his fellow creatures except when hunger drove him to beg for a crust of bread. Outwardly he gave the appearance of being an idiot. He could not carry even the simplest message. (pp. 25-7)

"Hear O Israel" . . . is typical of Peretz's technique not only in *The Voice of the People*, but in those other collections in which he clothes the "pure" aesthetic form in the garb of Jewish folklore. The theme of the story is not exclusively Jewish, but contains elements from world literature too. An almost primitive character, unable to think clearly, unable to express his thoughts, and driven by his inner confusion to find expression through a primitive musical instrument he finds, frequently appears in world folklore. In folklore, this primitive creature is always inferior to his cultural environment, while in **"Hear O Israel"** Peretz endows his character with a sublimity that dims his surroundings even though they are culturally superior to him. Moreover, fairy tales relate the magical expression to the magic instrument itself, the player undergoing no recognizable change, while Peretz does the contrary. From the beginning of the story, the author supplies his character with a vivid imagination that, for better or for worse, must find its outlet. The musical instrument is an ordinary double bass with nothing intrinsically remarkable about it other than its deep tone, which on the one hand emphasizes the awkwardness of its player and on the other the heavy weight of personal problems that have accumulated within him. But above all, there is the emotional catharsis itself. Under our very eyes, as it were, the author removes his hero from the category of a creature of flesh and blood in the concrete world of the wedding at Tomashov and magically transforms him into a mysterious figure transcending the world of actuality, transcending the world of lucid thought and expression, transcending even the inner struggles of the hero himself.

The story thus attempts to break away from its original realism to achieve the sense of mysterious beauty that pervades its close. It departs from a normal narrative style aimed at presenting one or two episodes with logic and clarity. Though Peretz does in fact provide us with a detailed account of the course of events, he makes every effort to desert formal realism, giving his prose the conversational tone of an older man reminiscing with friends of his own age. The carefully modulated tone, the rhythmic pauses suggestive of a person listening both to the story and his own soul, the overt and subtle allusions—all these combine the hasidic folklore with a modernistic symbolism similar to that of Maeterlinck, and show how near Peretz was approaching his literary aim. Yet that is the trouble; for this submission to an instinctual, aesthetic sense, devoid of any outwardly realistic goal and ignoring the day-to-day ideological problems of his people and his society, is disturbed by the general course of the story, for it almost always responds to the dictates of an external and rational "morality." In **"By a Dying Man's Pillow,"** . . . the mystical element culminates in a moral lesson teaching a love of Israel and a more universal humanism, namely: it is better for a man to descend into the fires of Hell to help a fellow man than to ascend to Paradise to enjoy alone the eternal splendor of heaven. Although in **"Hear O Israel"** the author attempts to break away from a realistic style in order to present his central character more vividly, it remains a mere narrative with a more oblique approach. The author increasingly subordinates the story to his eccentric theory that if a man's inner world is not endowed with conceptual thought purified from the mists of its origin, it is liable to "split the heavens." This idea dominates the story from the beginning, detracting from its intuitive quality and hence spoiling its literary effectiveness.

This point, which we made in connection with the stories in *The Voice of the People*, the high-point of Peretz's artistic achievement, is even more marked in some of the earlier collections of stories, such as *She*, containing **"The Dumb Girl," "Melodies of the Day,"** and **"Tales of the Moon,"** and *In a*

Vision, containing "Three Calls," "Thought and the Violin," and "A Mother's Vision," all of which deliberately sacrifice impressionism on the altar of intellectualism. The story is a sort of vignette, and was written quite deliberately for the purpose of conveying an intellectual idea. There the impressionism turns into an ironic allegory, and there is nothing more antagonistic to symbolism than allegory. (pp. 29-31)

In the hope of rescuring the modern Hebrew novel as well as his own works from the burden of allegory, Peretz turned to hasidic themes and styles, particularly to their lilting musicality. Through them, he felt he could realize his dream of achieving an impressionistic style that would eventually be transformed into symbolism. He deliberately imitated the language of the hasidic folktale, especially that of the Polish versions so close to his heart because of their musicality and allusiveness. Apart from listening to these folktales during his travels through the Polish townships, he also collected the moral teachings of the hasidic rabbis. He greatly admired the lively fashion in which they were phrased and modeled his own style on them, both in Yiddish and Hebrew, until it became more flexible, connotative, musically evocative of the inner world of the Jew, and, above all, redolent with allusions to a transcendent reality, to the mystery concealed within the visible world.

His collection entitled *Hasidism* may rightly be regarded as the focal point of this trend, not merely as far as Peretz's own literary efforts were concerned but for the Yiddish novel of his generation. In the same way that Shalom Aleikhem gave to the Jewish novel its literary realism, Peretz in his *Hasidism* provided the Yiddish (as opposed to the Hebrew) novel with a romanticism that deserted the harsh realism of the Jewish township and the urbanized Jews of the Polish cities. His technique in this book deserves particularly close examination, since on the surface it resembles that of Shalom Aleikhem's humorous tales. The stories in *Hasidism* tend to employ the monologue, the soliloquy of a single character through whom the story is told. In effect, the purpose here is the same as we noted in connection with Shalom Aleikhem: the monologue provides a deeper psychological insight into character. In the same way, then, as Shalom Aleikhem's use of the realistic monologue satisfied his aesthetic aims, so the impressionist monologue satisfied those of Peretz.

Not all of the stories in *Hasidism,* however, are written in the form of a monologue. A few, including "A New Melody," and "The Kabbalists," employ a straightforward narrative technique, and it is these that attain full stylistic expression with no extraneous purpose divorcing the plots from their realistic and deeply tragic background. . . . [When], in "A New Melody," the father and son are left in complete isolation and despair after the communal Blessing of the New Moon at the end of the Day of Atonement and the father teaches his son "a new melody" in order to ease his spiritual depression, the realism is so direct and vivid that it approaches Peretz's promised land in its symbolic yearning. Yet, in the impressionist monologue of most of the stories in *Hasidism,* with all the stylistic impression that accompanies them, we find the author struggling desperately to find a suitable mode of expression. For in these stories the intellectual allegory constantly ensnares him. (pp. 31-2)

Peretz's greatest effort, so obvious that it became part of his ideology, was to purify his work into an art form untouched by the external world, and its clearest instance can be seen in his drama *The Collapse of a Rabbi's House* (. . . the Yiddish version *Di Goldené Keyt* [*The Golden Chain*] is superior). (p. 35)

In this play, the characters are borrowed from Peretz's hasidic stories, in which the symbolic element battles with a more rationalized didacticism. The monologue is replaced by a dramatic dialogue that permits each character to come to life independently and to experience all its longings and suffering. As the monologue is reduced by the pressure of other speakers, each individual personality becomes more distinct. The central problem dealt with in this play is the same as that pulsating throughout the symbolist drama of Europe—how to find a satisfactory vehicle of expression for the individual listening to his own thoughts, absorbed in his intuitive knowledge, striving to uncover the sacred, aesthetic truth within his inner turmoil, and withdrawing from the hubbub of the "real" world outside.

Outwardly, the plot has a hasidic setting. The house is that of Reb Shlomo the tzaddik, and the action takes place late on a Saturday night. The "elders" and selected disciples of the tzaddik, together with the members of his household and a throng of followers who have come to lay their troubles before him and request his advice and blessing, are all waiting for the Rabbi to come out of his study and pronounce the havdalah blessing marking the end of the Sabbath. But the elderly Rabbi does not come out. The older hasidim and the disciples begin to fear that some catastrophe has occurred, and the hasidim outside are filled with dark foreboding. The atmosphere in the play becomes one of ominous pauses, of silences pregnant with emotion like those of Maeterlinck's symbolist plays or the poetic drama of Wyspianski, the Polish romantic. (p. 36)

[The] Rabbi will not answer his hasidim. He will not permit the Sabbath to end, even if the whole world of reality in all its pettiness should perish. He will ascend to the "pure marble" where splendor and glory shine, where one does not use wretched scales to weigh thought against action, good deeds against sins. The world of action is dead for him. . . . (pp. 37-8)

Eventually, the Rabbi's beadle, having failed to grasp the threatening catastrophe, rebels against his master and, turning to the mournful, depressed throng, announces in a loud voice: "A pleasant week—the Sabbath is over," thus breaking the spell of the sublime covenant of the "Sabbath Jews." The beauty of the "pure marble" is shattered, the glory dimmed, and the Rabbi expires.

This opening act of the play is sufficient to illustrate Peretz's attempt to bring a modernistic element into Yiddish and Hebrew literature. There can be no doubt that the heavy silences of the play approach the symbolism of Maeterlinck. The sense of something over and beyond the factual termination of the Sabbath and the ominous silence of the elders, the disciples, and the ordinary hasidim—all this suggests a mysterious mingling of life-in-death and death-in-life such as pervades *Pelléas et Mélisande, Les Aveugles,* and other plays by the great symbolist, Maeterlinck. The text of the opening scenes of Peretz's play, before the Rabbi comes out of his study, creates a vivid realism tinged with mystery, the first instance in the history of modern Jewish literature. Yet the climax of the play—the Rabbi's impassioned speech on the sublimity of the "pure marble"—destroys this atmosphere, making it mere pastiche. This fault is inherent in the gulf that the Rabbi creates between the "Sabbath News" and those who returned to their mundane tasks as soon as the Sabbath was technically over. This extreme aestheticism, personified by the author in Reb Shlomo, destroys that vital concern with the common people that was the motive force both of modern literature in general and of the symbolist and romantic schools in particular. (p. 38)

The beadle's "A pleasant week!" has in no way been prepared for in the play and forms no organic part of it; the author suddenly thrusts it upon us in the midst of the Rabbi's lofty meditations. If Peretz suddenly took pity on the poor creatures crowding at the Rabbi's door and hence brought in the beadle to cut the "golden chain" which bound them, he did so without any dramatic preparation. In this sense, the play is far inferior to Anski's *The Dibbuk,* with all its pseudo-mythology. The profane conquers the holy Sabbath—and the Rabbi dies. Here the author contradicts everything he struggled to achieve in his **The Voice of the People,** and it may well be that his indefinable feeling of despair, which accompanied Peretz in so much of his work, was responsible. Striking evidence of this may be seen in the fact that Peretz did not allow himself to close his play with a scene of the Rabbi's death. He moves from one individualistic extreme ("the pure marble") to another ("the completely innocent"), both of which show how far he was withdrawing from the popular traditions that had supplied him with the themes of his stories, namely the religious myths of the hasidim and their opponents, and how much his art depended on an intellectual didacticism. (p. 40)

After such literary efforts as these, whether in the drama or the short story, Peretz could no longer continue with the dark meditations of **Hasidism.** That form of expression, which he had so yearned for throughout his life and which he demanded from his colleagues and disciples, never found its fruition. Almost in despair, he turned from the beautiful musicality of his earlier writings to an expressionist fury that grew in force throughout the first decade of the twentieth century. This idealistic aesthete now began to prophesy the disintegration of the self. Man was no longer responsible for his actions, as nineteenth-century humanism had taught. Strange winds were blowing from all directions upon the human soul. . . . His drama **At Night in the Old Market Place,** with such characters as "the sinner," "the madman," and "shadows from the world of chaos," becomes enslaved to primitive techniques that contradict his frenzied outburst of strangled desires and frustrated visions. A fatal despair now destroys everything with its satanic beauty; everything mates, grows old, and dies. All the dramatic force disintegrates in a clownish laugh, as if to say that the entire universe is only an evil dream without hope of redemption.

Only in the simpler stories of **The Voice of the People** that are devoid of aesthetic or didactic purpose—such as **"Seven Good Years," "The Miracle Worker," "Treasure,"** and **"Golden Shoes"**—did Peretz really succeed. There the realism of the stories matched his inner dream, and out of the world of the "little man" is woven vividly realistic tales. These stories are free from all grandiose design, and man's inner beauty provides the motive force. The holy and the profane become combined in a fresh spontaneity that mingles light and shade as in the real world. In these Peretz remained close to his Jewish sources. (pp. 41-2)

> *Isaiah Rabinovich, "Hebrew Fiction in Search of a Hero," in his* Major Trends in Modern Hebrew Fiction, *The University of Chicago Press, 1968, pp. 1-42.**

CHARLES A. MADISON (essay date 1968)

[*A Russian-American literary critic and historian, Madison wrote such nonfiction works as* Critics and Crusaders *(1947) and* Book Publishing in America *(1966). In the following excerpt, he discusses Peretz's personal aesthetic and its influence upon his fic-*

STORIES AND PICTURES

BY

ISAAC LOEB PEREZ

TRANSLATED FROM THE YIDDISH BY

HELENA FRANK

PHILADELPHIA
THE JEWISH PUBLICATION SOCIETY OF AMERICA
1906

Title page of Stories and Pictures.

tional creations. Madison considers The Golden Chain *to be Peretz's best work, for it best represents the author's spirituality and idealism. For an opposing view of* The Golden Chain, *see the excerpt by Isaiah Rabinovich (1968).*]

In his journalistic writings Peretz was the serious and spirited social reformer. As a polemicist he exposed wrongs within the Jewish community and defended it from its overt and covert enemies. In this phase of his writing he was the inspired truth-seeker, hater of sham, contemner of servility, enemy of dead tradition, advocate of the living ideal, and the eloquent and effective Jewish leader.

Peretz was a publicist of necessity but an artist by inclination. Were he not living at a time when modern industry and liberated rationalism were bringing havoc and harassment to the Jews of Eastern Europe, so that their vicissitude became his vicissitude and their plight his plight, his writing might have assumed a gemlike wholeness instead of being sparklingly fragmentary. Consciously avoiding the seclusion of the ivory tower, however, he devoted his charged feelings to his didactic and polemical efforts. He also sought to achieve his purpose by fictional means, and provided a symbolic moral in a number of his stories.

In one sketch a garrulous furrier philosophizes about the *shtreimel*—the fur hat traditionally worn by many rabbis and Hasidim. He argues sarcastically, and brings up a number of pertinent incidents, to demonstrate that people respect the *shtreimel* rather than those wearing it. . . . (pp. 108-09)

Peretz championed the rights of the Jewish woman. Her lowly position in Jewish life—ignored as a girl and merely tolerated as wife and mother—seemed to him a barbaric condition not to be endured. In poem and story he wrote caustically of her role as sole provider, her forced meekness, and her work in the sweatshop. He was particularly incensed at the practice of keeping girls in poor homes without schooling, and of giving those in wealthier urban homes a completely non-Jewish education. . . . This situation is treated in **"The Outcast."** A girl is given lessons in foreign languages but not in either Hebrew or Yiddish. Ignored by her father and indulged by her mother, she gives her time to reading romances and dreaming of adventure. One day she is attracted to a Polish youth, elopes with him, and is converted. Her action drives her pious parents to a premature death. Years later she meets her brother and her mood is repentent yet accusatory. . . . The dangerous disparity between the pious gabardined youth and the sentimental Polonized girl worried him. At the end of the story he added this italicized coda: *Let her be judged by Him who is over nations and their complex bloody struggles."* (pp. 109-10)

[In such tales as **"The Outcast,"** **"The Anger of a Jewish Woman,"** and **"Mendel Breines"**] Peretz depicts the life of the orthodox Jews vividly and realistically, yet their traits, customs, and attitudes are seen from the point of view of the social reformer. Like Mendele, he speaks out vociferously against the blemishes and inadequacies he finds within the Jewish community; as a consequence he expresses himself artistically in a minor key.

Poverty being so egregiously prevalent among the Jews of his time, Peretz, like other Jewish writers, could not but deal with it at some length. And like them he stressed the Jews' ability to survive as a result of their spiritual faith and personal perseverance. Two of his best-known stories—**"The Messenger"** and **"Bontche Silent"**—are at once noteworthy and typically Peretzian. The first describes the death of an old messenger. (p. 112)

Here Peretz is primarily the artist. In its eleven pages this story gives us an unforgettable portrayal of a sturdy septuagenarian of simple and deep piety. The narrative is restrained, humorous, and persuasive, progressing with the sure strides of subtle art. In his death the docile, honest, and tenacious old man comes alive in the reader's imagination.

"Bontche Silent" presents another aspect of the same type of Jew. (p. 113)

Ostensibly the old messenger and Bontche are similar conceptions. Both are simple subservient creatures, ill abused, depicted with like sympathy. In the first story, however, the emphasis is on portrayal of character—the intuitive expression of the quintessence of a docile human soul. Bontche, on the other hand, becomes a springboard for social satire and religious irony. The meek porter's life is made a protest against man's abuse of man, an oppressed man's cry for human justice. There is something Christlike about Bontche. His abject suffering is dramatized to make him crushed, blood-stained, and forgiving. Yet Peretz also makes mock of his meekness, intimating that, in order to be heard, it is sometimes necessary to shout—especially on earth. As the Lord tells Bontche: "You yourself perhaps did not know that you could cry, and that your cry could have caused the wall of Jericho to tumble and collapse. You yourself did not know of your latent power. . . ."

Bontche's fatalistic attitude irritated Peretz because it symbolized the pious Jew's complete credence in life after death, his belief that suffering on earth would be compensated by pleasures in Paradise. Peretz knew only too well that the resulting meekness and self-abnegation were suicidal in an unconscionable world, especially as the faith that had kept the Jews alive for centuries was losing its hold upon them. Yet he loved the poor porter and the old messenger and sympathized with their naive piety, artless minds, and simple wholesomeness, and his portrayal made them memorable additions to Yiddish literature. (p. 115)

For all his rational European veneer, Peretz was deeply drawn to the beatitude of exalted revery, the splendor of the soul communing with the Godhead. Even in his mature years, in the presence of intimate friends, he would sometimes hum a Hasidic tune without words which repeated itself endlessly. To him song was not mere musical expression but symbolic of the loftiness of life. (p. 117)

To awaken this song within the soul of the modern Jew, Peretz eulogized the spiritual quality of Hasidism. **"Between Two Mountains"** contrasts the essential difference between the poeticized Hasid and the orthodox ritualist. The latter regards religion as a relationship between God and man. He prays alone and in silence even in the synagogue. His attitude is matter-of-fact: he believes that by faithfully performing his religious obligations he will gain Paradise. Not so the Hasid, to whom religion is an exciting, joyous experience. He envisages God not as a stern Jehovah but as a loving Father. In the synagogue he prays as a child amidst the children of the Almighty; he prays aloud, as to a father, waxing enthusiastic and forgetting his worldly self in spiritual ecstacy. In this story the ritualist rabbi is the older of the two, very learned, stern, cold, rigorous, zealous, and proud; the Hasid, equally learned, once a pupil of the other, is mild, warm, soft, sympathetic, and forgiving. (pp. 117-18)

Peretz was of course more interested in effect than in fact. He exaggerated the rapture of one and the rigor of the other to make the point more eloquently. For he is here presenting not so much the differing philosophies of two rabbis as he is his conception of them, imbuing Hasidism with romantic glamor because of its innate emotional appeal.

The rich folklore he uncovered—tales, legends, anecdotes—concerns largely wonder-working rabbis and secret saints who were endowed with supernatural powers which they often employed to right wrongs and reward the just. Pious Jews, Hasidim in particular, depend upon this intercession and ask for it in time of affliction or personal sorrow; the miraculous manner in which these requests are granted forms the basis of a number of his stories. In all of them man is judged not by his appearance but by his acts, and not so much by results as by intentions. Each folktale is told with great skill and verbal beauty. In each Peretz probes the deep recesses of human frailty, human goodness, and human greatness. Whether they treat of Hasidic miracles, incidents relating to humble yet lovable men and women, or flights of poetic nobility and folk fantasy, each adds to the quality and scope of his artistic achievement. (p. 119)

The bare bones of these stories impart not a whit of the poetic flavor and verbal beauty with which Peretz has fleshed them. These and other narratives of similar content possess a literary quality and imaginative depth found only in distinguished fiction. What heightens their worth to the Yiddish reader is the felicity with which Peretz treats the spiritual essence of Hasidism and Jewish folklore. (p. 122)

Peretz was most of all a poet: a lover of verbal beauty, a singer of the mystical and the loftiness in man. His first Yiddish poem, "**Monish**," gave the incipient literature a ballad whose beauty of thought and rhythm compared favorably with the best in current poetry in other languages. Monish was a most precocious youth, beautiful of body and incisive of mind—so pious and erudite as to endanger Satan's dominion. Fearful of his hold on mankind, the Evil One sends Lilith to lure the dangerous youth into sin. Her song and her pulchritude—symbolizing modern rationalism—are irresistible. Yielding to the advice of his Bad Angel rather than that of his Good Angel, Monish becomes Lilith's slave and victim. The poem was the first romantic ballad in Yiddish, wittily satirical, socially critical, with a mellifluent rhythm reminiscent of Heine but new to Yiddish verse.

He wrote numerous lyrics expressing his sympathy for the poor, indignation at injustice, and predilection to romance. His verse was wrought skillfully, possessed striking imagery, and was imbued with a rugged, if lofty, spirituality. Influenced early by Heine, he later regretted having emulated his "self-hatred." Peretz came to feel that satire in verse did not become the Yiddish poet. To Yehoash he wrote in 1907: "Let's be prophets, leaders, not clowns." This he assayed in his dramatic verse. *In Polish oif der Kayt (Expiation)* treats man's subjection to the world about him in lilting lines and inspired imagery. *Night in the Old Marketplace* is a tragedy of life and death, a work of philosophic fantasy symbolizing human striving and an innate yearning for salvation. Max Reinhardt, the famous German theatrical director, considered staging it and called it "a rare specimen of a universalist-symbolic play."

Peretz's greatest work is undoubtedly *The Golden Chain,* a poetic drama of romantic imagination and philosophic profundity. More than any of his other writings it expresses his idealistic insight into Jewish spirituality. A rabbinic family is presented dramatically unto the fourth generation, with each forming a distinct stage in the Hasidic movement. Its ecstatic apotheosis appears in the person of Reb Shlome; his son Pinkhos upholds its rigid fanaticism; the grandson Moshe embodies its spiritual diminuendo; and its pathetic disintegration is manifested in Leah, Moshe's daughter. The continuity of the golden chain, broken by Moshe's inner weakness, is dutifully taken up by his son Jonathan. Miriam, Moshe's wife, is wistfully prophetic, and comments on the fate of the family with the finality of a Greek chorus. (pp. 125-26)

In the final scene Jonathan, fervid in his faith and endowed with Shlome's imaginative vision, attempts to forge the golden chain anew.

Jonathan and Leah symbolize the two chief factions of Peretz's generation: one accepting the ancestral faith, obviously impaired, with anxious resolve; the other discarding it impulsively but uneasily for the rationalism of science. To Peretz the living truth was composed of both science and spirit, and of the two spirit was the more vital, for the spirit in man will not be denied. The laws of science have little power to succor man in emotional crisis, yet for modern man to ignore science could lead only to spiritual vacuity. These self-evident truths he stressed with poetic vigor and imaginative insight.

In *The Golden Chain* he presents with crystal clarity the essential nature of Hasidism: its ecstasy, idealism, fanaticism decadence, and belated poetic revival. The action is expressed

in exquisite poetry. With Goethian grandeur he creates a realm with a phrase and probes the human spirit with a word. With symbolic subtlety and artistic intuitiveness he delves into the depths of Judaism. And in the process the main characters perch lifesize on the fiery wings of dramatic creation.

Peretz was not so much a writer who happened to have been born a Jew as a Jew with the ability and urge to depict Jewish life profoundly and artistically. . . . Fully aware of the circumstances in which his people found themselves, of their particular qualities and failings, and of their spiritual status, he could not but assume the role of provocative polemicist and direct them toward social and religious insurgence. This part of his writing is always ethical, though not as obtrusively as Mendele's.

In his literary work he was a great experimenter. In prose and verse he essayed every form, rhythm, and style suited to his purpose. He was indeed more the inspired artist than any of his contemporaries—always writing with high seriousness; realizing from the first that he was one of the founders of a new literature, and in large part responsible for its character and growth. He therefore deliberately sowed the seeds of literary art. Endowed with the gift of versatility, he wrote in various genres. His innate delight in experimentation was stimulated by the new literary currents then prevailing among Western writers. He wrote in turn as a naturalist, a realist, a romanticist, a symbolist, and an impressionist, in each form creating an artistic pattern for younger Yiddish writers. He never lost his youthful suppleness, and continued to experiment and to encourage new writers to the end of his life. (pp. 130-31)

Although an ethicist in his thinking, in the expression of his subject-matter he was the genuine esthete. Once a theme ripened in his mind, he concentrated not so much on its content as on its form. His insistence on the exact word, the most effective image and phrasing, exercised with Flaubertian painstaking, gave his style a laconic pithiness. His frequent dots, indicating ellipses, so characteristic of his writing, often convey more than explicit statements. Although he was fully conscious of his great talent, and sometimes gave the impression of being conceited, he could never bring himself to regard his writings as finished products. *The Golden Chain,* for instance, was rewritten five times, and other works were revised again and again. In consequence he often achieved verbal brilliance along with genuine spontaneity of expression. For his ear was as sensitized as a fine photographic plate, and he heard and remembered the essence of folk speech. In all his stories, particularly the Hasidic and folk tales, he gave artistic form to the living language of the Polish Jews.

Because Peretz's style is dynamic in character, his dots assume the significance of unuttered gestures: the shrugs and eye movements of a person speaking, so subtly charged with overtones by the preceding words that the reader's imagination supplies the suggested nuances of meaning with the pleasure of a collaborator. Like the work of all thoughtful writers, his also possesses a three-dimensional connotation: his intent, while intelligible to the simple reader on a superficial level, sometimes eludes complete comprehension by even the sophisticated critic. (p. 132)

Charles A. Madison, "Isaak Laybush Peretz: Father of Modern Yiddish Literature," in his Yiddish Literature: Its Scope and Major Writers, *Frederick Ungar Publishing Co., 1968, pp. 99-133.*

IRVING HOWE AND ELIEZER GREENBERG (essay date 1974)

[*A longtime editor of the leftist magazine* Dissent *and a regular contributor to* The New Republic, *Howe is one of America's most respected literary critics and social historians. He has been a socialist since the 1930s, and his criticism is frequently informed by a liberal social viewpoint. Howe is widely praised for what F. R. Dulles has termed his "knowledgeable understanding, critical acumen and forthright candor." Howe has written: "Though I believe in the social approach to literature, it seems to me peculiarly open to misuse; it requires particular delicacy and care." Greenberg, a Yiddish poet and editor, has contributed to the popularizing of Yiddish literature in English. With Howe, he has coauthored* A Treasury of Yiddish Stories *(1969) and* A Treasury of Yiddish Poetry *(1969). In their introduction to* Selected Stories by Peretz, *the critics provide a brief biography and overview of Peretz's career. In the following excerpt from that introduction, Howe and Greenberg discuss the development of Peretz's unique style in the stories based on Hasidic folktales.*]

Concerned with the reconstitution of the Jewish community at the moment it seemed to be turning from the Divine Presence to a secular European outlook, Peretz wished to find mundane equivalents for those values that the sacred tradition could no longer sustain. His vision of "the good Jew," as it emerges from his writings, is similar in tone and quality to the late nineteenth-century idea of "the good European." Peretz spoke for a Yiddish version of that liberal humanism and secular idealism which characterized the best minds of Europe at the end of the nineteenth century. In doing so, however, he sharply attacked all tendencies toward assimilationism among Jews, insisting that the Jews bring to world culture their own spirit, their own uniqueness, as an equal among equals. That restlessness, that fever, that coil of problems which we associate with the nineteenth century, Peretz brought into Yiddish life and literature. But he brought them, in the main, not through a diffusion of contemporary ideas, nor through his role—a role every Yiddish writer had to undertake—of popular educator. He brought the qualities of the nineteenth century into Yiddish literature by going backward into the East European Jewish past.

In his earlier and weaker stories Peretz faced both ways: outward, toward the themes and methods of European literature, and inward, toward the folk heritage. As he developed his distinctive style, he broke away from the methods of Mendele and Sholom Aleichem. Peretz writes with the plastic rapidity, the transparent nervousness characteristic of a great many modern authors. He brought, as Niger remarks, "impact and hurriedness into the structure of the Yiddish story: short-breathed, staccato, and aphoristic prose." The rhythm of Mendele and even Sholom Aleichem is the rhythm of a sleepy *shtetl;* the rhythm of Peretz, even when writing about hasidic rabbis and old Yiddish legends, is the rhythm of Jewish Warsaw.

In the earlier stories, often colored by feelings of social indignation over Jewish suffering and the decay of Jewish communal life (see **"The Poor Boy,"** . . .), Peretz comes closer to individual characterization than most of his Yiddish contemporaries. He focuses upon what might be called *typical individuals,* though not yet the fully individualized characters that nineteenth-century European literature sought to achieve. His people stand somewhere between the archetype and the fully formed individual: a hopeless youth, as in **"The Mad Talmudist,"** torturing himself with his inadequacy, a pair of young lovers dreaming of happiness in a dismal Gorki-like cellar, as in **"The Cellar."**

In Peretz' later and stronger stories he reworks folk and hasidic materials in a way that appears to be folklike but is actually the product of a sophisticated literary intellect. The old properties, in their naïveté and charm, remain: Heaven is envisioned as a homely *beth din,* or rabbinical court, with an actual scale of justice, the legends contain "palaces" which testify to a poverty of imagination, or better, the imagination of poverty, and God Himself speaks out in anguish and impatience as if He were no more than a rabbi among rabbis. But together with the simple backgrounds and unadorned story lines, there is what Glatstein calls "an additional dimension of mind," with the "flavor of a modern story-teller added to their biblical clarity, so that they become neo-biblical moral fables" [see excerpt dated 1947]. As he retells and deepens these stories, Peretz, the writer who measures the distance between himself and the pieties to which he turns back, is always though unobtrusively in sight, sometimes through his rearrangement of materials, sometimes through no more than an ironic phrase at the end of a story. (pp. 13-14)

In the end Peretz must always part company with the hasidic wonder-workers and speakers of wisdom, for he cannot really share their oneness of vision, he can only offer variants and versions, completely honest in their approximation, which seek to break open the envelopes of doctrine in order to reach some fundamentals of wisdom. (pp. 14-15)

The most poised and complicated of Peretz' stories dealing with Hasidism is **"Between Two Peaks"** . . . in which the phalanxed ranks of rationalism and enthusiasm, Orthodoxy and Hasidism, are aligned through two formidable protagonists; and at the end Peretz can only hope for a measure of patience, or tolerance, but not for a genuine reconciliation. In this story there is a recognition of irreconcilables, an awareness that some issues of mind cannot be dissolved by a mere shuffling of words. Yet, if the pointer wavers a trifle in any direction, it is toward the warmth and democratism of the hasidic view, as when the Bialer Rebbe says to his orthodox antagonist: "Teacher, tell me! What do you have for the people? For the simple craftsman? For a woodchopper or butcher? For the ordinary man? Most of all, for a man who is sinful? Teacher, what do you give to those who are not scholars?"

From Hasidism Peretz tried to extract its life-strength, but without finally crediting the source. Peretz found there, in Glatstein's words, "what Christianity often claims for itself: sympathy for the lowest classes, for the silent and abject—the spirit of Dostoevsky and Tolstoy. He did not need to read anything into Judaism, he read it *out,* from the depths of our moral existence." He wanted, in short, to discover in Hasidism unbreakable qualities of Jewish strength, and he did so with enough ironic self-awareness to recognize that even if his attempt was doomed to intellectual failure, precisely in that failure might lie its literary reward. (pp. 15-16)

[To] our knowledge, there is nothing quite like his hasidic and folkloristic stories in Western literature. Perhaps the closest comparison—admittedly, not very close—is to be made with the stories of Hawthorne, also composed out of a quasi-allegorical intent, a heretical moral probing based on a lapsed religious orthodoxy, and some half-hidden, even sly touches of cleverness. Perhaps, too, there is a shade of comparison worth making with some of Kafka's shorter pieces. But in their essential qualities Peretz' stories seem to us unique: they have few points of similarity with the fictions we are likely to know in modern Western literature. (p. 16)

Peretz took . . . rudimentary but sturdy anecdotes and retold them through a range of strategies. There is little physical description, little provisioning of the social scene, and little effort at the psychic delineation of characters. The physical world is taken for granted—what matters is moral discovery, spiritual action, the location of hidden weaknesses in the soul, the search for new sources of strength. A few figures reappear in a number of the stories: for instance, Berl the tailor, a characteristic East European Jew, rebellious in his younger years against God and accepting in his later, but hardly individualized or rendered with the depth of, say, Sholom Aleichem's Tevye. There is also Rabbi Levi-Yitzkhok, the most tender and humane of all the hasidic rabbis, advocate of mankind before the gates of heaven; but he too appears in his typicality, we neither know nor need to know more about him than is required by a single line of action. Finally, Peretz stakes all on the anecdote and its unravelling of implication.

Sometimes, when moved by the charm or pathos of the original anecdote, Peretz changes very little—as in the story "**The Magician**" . . . , which preserves almost intact the original folk sentiment of gratitude and awe at the arrival of the Prophet Elijah bringing help to the poor at Passover, or in "**Devotion Without End**" . . . , where modes of love are blended into a pure act of self-sacrifice. It would be a depressing kind of sophistication that disabled us from appreciating the inherent loveliness of such tales, even when they are not speckled by Peretz' irony. As he renders them, Peretz uses an utterly simple, unadorned, and transparent prose, so as to efface his own presence. At other times, as in the story "**Three Gifts**" . . . , Peretz allows the legendary material to unfold in its own right, and then, at the very end, there occurs a sentence crushing in its irony: after the three gifts of selfless martyrdom have been delivered to heaven, "the Eternal Voice declared: 'Truly beautiful gifts, unusually beautiful. . . . They have no practical value, no use at all, but as far as beauty is concerned—unusual.'" This concluding sentence can make the head reel; it comes as a shock of dissociation, perhaps despair, regarding the very purities of martyrdom Peretz has celebrated. At still other times, as in "**The *Shabbes-Goy*"** . . . , a sardonic assault on traditional rationales for Jewish passivity, Peretz puts a heavy imprint of his own sensibility on the story.

Almost always, however, Peretz' telling or retelling is notable for its tact, with the perspective of ironic complication clearly separable from the anecdote itself, and often demurely tucked away in no more than a turn of phrase at the end of the story. What we have, then, in these versions of traditional material, is the past recaptured, the past untampered with, the past radically altered and recreated, in an ascending line of difficulty and ambivalence; so that for all their thinness of narrative line and fragility of substance, the hasidic and folk tales yoke together Jewish past and Jewish present in a bond of tense affection.

In the main, the voice dominating these stories is ironic, ambivalent, skeptical, a modern voice that knows enough not to be content with being merely modern. The skepticism is sharpest in Peretz' single most famous story, "**Bontsha the Silent.**" . . . Peretz—and here he does seem a little like Kafka—touches in this story on one of the major themes of modern literature: the radical, hopeless incommensurability between morality and existence, the sense of a deep injustice at the heart of the universe which even the heavens cannot remedy. (pp. 17-18)

In the hasidic and folklike stories we find, then, a whole range of perspective and tones, in their sum almost the totality of Jewish response to the Jewish situation. At their best, Peretz' stories ask to be read as "wisdom stories," pieces of fiction that evoke pleasure through a tacit engagement of mind, through oblique touches of cleverness, insight, commentary, through a sly negotiation of truth. What one hears, or overhears, in these stories is the Jewish mind at a certain point in its historical development, the Jewish mind engaged in self-reflection, self-argument, self-criticism, but most of all, self-discovery. The "wisdom story" is a fiction in which the pleasure resides not merely, perhaps not even mostly, in the matter itself, but rather in the conduit of argument that is established between the mind of the writer and the mind of the reader as both reflect—with the typical Jewish gesture of two fingers of one hand striking the palm of the other—on what the story can yield. It is a kind of fiction, to twist Robert Frost's remark about poetry, that begins in delight and ends in wisdom. (p. 19)

Irving Howe and Eliezer Greenberg, in an introduction to Selected Stories *by I. L. Peretz, edited and translated by Irving Howe and Eliezer Greenberg, Schocken Books, 1974, pp. 7-19.*

ELIE WIESEL (essay date 1974)

[*An American novelist and journalist, Wiesel was born in Sighet, Transylvania, and during World War II, at the age of fifteen, was taken with his family to the Auschwitz concentration camp, where he remained until his release two years later. After the war he entered journalism, became chief correspondent for the Tel Aviv daily* Yesioth Ahronot, *and later joined the staff of the New York Yiddish-language* Daily Forward. *In such early works as the autobiographical novel* Night (1958), *Wiesel recreated life in the concentration camp and examined the fate of the often guilt-ridden survivor. After a visit to the Soviet Union in 1965, Wiesel recalled his experiences and impressions in* Jews of Silence (1966). *While many of his early works question the role of religion and strive to forgive God for the world's horrors, later works concentrate on the affirmation of Jewish traditions.* Souls on Fire (1972), *a study of Hasidic folktales, grew out of Wiesel's lecture series at the Sorbonne. He has stated that Hasidism "offers not answers to the great questions which haunt mankind, but a way to live . . . in a world without answers. . . ." In the following excerpt from a review of Peretz's* Selected Stories, *Wiesel notes the musical quality of the stories, stating that they are "at once poetic and down-to-earth."*]

Do you know I. L. Peretz? You don't? Well that is regrettable but understandable. He did, after all, write in Yiddish, and Yiddish literature, begotten of suffering as a weapon against suffering, seems doomed to a tragic fate: not only is it little known—it is poorly known. . . .

Open this volume of **Selected Stories**. In it you will discover an admirable storyteller who weaves a melodious and evocative spell. His language is at once poetic and down-to-earth, lyrical and interspersed with wit. With one sentence, one image, he succeeds in restoring to us a Jewish world long since vanished, the world of the *Shtedtl*, with all its poverty and nostalgia. To read him is to follow him in his wanderings across Eastern Europe and to meet Jewish communities impossible to find anywhere else.

Peretz: maker of legends and himself legendary. . . . None other so thoroughly influenced both his peers and the beginners of this generation: his impact went beyond his work proper—a few volumes of essays, novellas and poetry.

Peretz: the *rebbe* of Yiddish literature. Small wonder then, that when he died at the age of 67, in 1915, a fervent crowd of 100,000 Jews gathered at his funeral. Recognizing itself in him, the Jewish people returned his love.

That is one of the salient aspects of his work: he loves the people of whom and for whom he writes; he loves all his characters. Rather than turn them into caricatures, monsters obsessed by sex or money, he shows their human vulnerability, their simplicity; he shows them as victims of society, victims of God, but victims always. Instead of judging them, he takes their defense. At their side, he fights the injustices that befall them—sometimes he even goes so far as to stand up on their behalf against the celestial powers, when they are unjust too.

This passionate desire to come to the aid of the poor inhabitants of the *Shtetl*, this brotherly love for the most wretched among them, reverberates in these 18 stories selected with reverence and intelligence by Irving Howe and Eliezer Greenberg. Hasidic tales, popular legends; some melancholy, some funny; they are all moving and disturbing, they all take place in a universe both near and far where, despite the sorrows and hazards of daily life, man proves capable of speaking his anger and singing his joy. (p. 26)

In all of Peretz's stories, the most humble, the most obscure character is always the winner. The author is forever on his side—sometimes he even glorifies him. Which explains why certain scholars stress the importance of social consciousness in Peretz's work. Rightly or wrongly, no matter; let us simply say that his consciousness is essentially Jewish, therefore sensitive to injustice in any form. His response: he loves the poor but not poverty, he admires the humble but he opposes submissiveness.

In his Hasidic tales, transcribed with humor and warmth, he praises only those Masters who use their powers to help man, even against God. The celebrated Levi-Yitzhak of Berditchev is to him an example: man may protest, must protest against evil and against the forces that beget it; man must plead for the victim.

This theme finds its deepest expression in the popular tale of Bontsha the Silent. Read it and you will not forget it. . . . Poor Bontsha: he doesn't even know what to yearn for, how to dream of something good, something beautiful. But—whose fault is that? Mankind's which has humiliated him too long, God's who did not intervene soon enough. Whatever shame there is in that tale, it is not Bontsha's but the others', all the others'.

This timeless story also reflects the Jewish condition of today: the generation that is mine could have shouted so loud that it would have shaken the world. Instead it but whispered content with its "buttered roll."

Oh yes, you should read Peretz. If only to hear his hymn to Jewish joy of yesteryear, to Jewish man of yesteryear. In his books you will discover a kingdom that vanished together with its sages and its beggars, its masters and their disciples; a beautiful kingdom set afire and erased from memory by countless assassins.

To read Peretz is to plunge into an ancient dream and the fervor it calls forth. You will emerge the richer for having done so. (pp. 26-7)

Elie Wiesel, "Victims of God," in The New Republic, *Vol. 171, No. 12, September 21, 1974, pp. 26-7.*

RICHARD J. FEIN (essay date 1980)

[*Fein, an American educator and essayist, has contributed to many national periodicals and is the author of* Robert Lowell *(1970). In the following excerpt, Fein examines* Sketches of a Provincial Journey, *which he credits with marking a significant change in Peretz's attitude—from a spirit of antagonism to one of sympathy—toward Jewish life, folktales, and speech.*]

About a year after publishing "**Monish**" (with its sniping at Yiddish), Peretz, jobless and prevented by the regime from practicing as a lawyer, joined the scheme of a Warsaw philanthropist to study and report on the life of the impoverished Jews in the *shtetlakh* of Poland. That trip (or return trip) to the Jewish life of small towns was to have a profound effect on Peretz's sense of Yiddish and its folk qualities. . . .

In *Sketches of a Provincial Journey,* he begins his interviews with a *maskil*-like faith that correct statistics will demonstrate that Jews are a productive people and that such statistics will support an effort to ameliorate the Jewish condition in the Pale. However, he ends up mocking the inefficacy of the information that he is gathering. (p. 146)

Rather than statistics and social improvements occupying his mind, he finds himself drawn to, and giving expression to, the "remedies" of the people: legends, folk beliefs, tales, multiple economic ventures, psychological and economic stealth. By the end of *Sketches* the mask of social scientist and reformer is dropped and there emerges the Jewish writer absorbing and exploiting the experience and tales of "the folk."

Not that Peretz is one with the folk whom he has come to study. His attitude toward his subjects is critical and sympathetic: critical but not carping, sympathetic but not sentimental, attached but not submissive. He is well aware of their political naivete. His comic description of the effort, by himself and two other men, to open a rabbi's dusty, putty-dried, sun-cracked window frame which had not been opened in fifteen years is an epiphany of his intrusion into the life of *shtetl* Jewry.

Peretz is aware that he appears as a stranger (sometimes not even as a Jew) to the Jews whom he is studying. More than once he remarks on the fear, the astonishment, even the shame (on the part of some of the women) as they see this stranger in their midst speaking Yiddish. (Peretz sometimes comes across as the visiting anthropologist who speaks the language of the natives, his own tribe re-visited.) To some of the Jews who peer at him, Peretz represents the blemished *goyish* world. This Jewish stranger among the Jews, this German-looking transcriber would come to memorialize their life.

By the end of the sketches Peretz has stopped describing himself as *der statistiker* and is himself listening more and more to the stories, the anecdotes, the legends that are being passed on to him. This shift in his approach to his informants supports Leo Wiener's observation that what makes *Sketches of a Provincial Journey* "particularly interesting is that it is written so that it will interest those very humble people about whom he is writing" [see excerpt dated 1899]. The book portrays Peretz's discovery of his relationship to his materials, as he absorbs the styles as well as the essence of his interviewees. If the purpose of the statistical expedition is to demonstrate that the Jews are a productive people (despite their handicaps), Peretz also discovers the story-telling productivity of these people who may hesitate or puzzle over being asked what their German name is, but who are quick to recite a story to the fact-gathering stranger or to reveal a scene or relay an anecdote which takes Peretz far beyond reportage and information-gathering. Peretz

himself becomes affected, if not transformed, by the very people and materials with whom he is coming into contact. He
gives himself up to their stories. (pp. 146-47)

Peretz at one point records the comments of the people rather
than the numerical information about them. Or, rather, his
informants create the pathos of their own statistics. Let them
be known by their own comments, Peretz indicates. Like ghostly
faces swimming before him in the air, the Jews whisper to him
their condition, the statistics initiating each statement of woe. . . .
Peretz realized that "the data" would best be revealed through
the speech of the people themselves. No one can read *Sketches
of a Provincial Journey* and not imagine that he is hearing at
first hand the accounts of impoverished Jews in Poland toward
the end of the nineteenth century.

At one point, unable to face the dilemma of his relationship
to his statistics, Peretz conjures up the kind of other-worldly
scene that he was later to perfect in several of his stories. He
dreams of two angels. The evil one appears to him holding the
promise of material wealth in one hand and potato peels in the
other. The good angel, appearing naked and carrying nothing,
is about to speak, but instead, a voice crying "Fire" awakens
Peretz. Tongues of fire stretch out toward him from nearby,
saying, "Don't be frightened, it's insured." The venture into
the impoverished *shtetlakh* is having such an impact on his
imagination that he finds himself waking from a dream into a
fantasy.

In the *Sketches* Peretz shows how fantastic and other-worldly
scenes are ways by which he can both verify and transcend the
poverty of Jewish life. Through such fantasies he interweaves
his despair and his sense of a Jewish condition not defined by
the sodden material terms alone. His fantasy confirms and yet
invigorates the impoverished Jewish situation, so that at certain
moments the sketch book realism, projecting a dour ethno-
graphical comedy, is metamorphosed to a dream-like obsession
with Jewish suffering in the Pale.

The impoverished life on which Peretz is gathering statistics
so impresses him that at one point he seems to be hallucinating
an interview. Toward the end of the *Sketches* the author has
returned to his lodgings, nervous and tired. Lying down on a
sofa, but before he can close his eyes, he is awakened by a
grimy looking madman climbing through the window into his
room, demanding that the recorder include him in his calcu-
lations. Affected by the unusual and fantastic appearance of
der meshugener who wants to be included in the figures, Peretz
feels himself possessed by the reality that he has come to study.
It has taken hold of him, rather than the other way around.
(Peretz, the inquiring gatherer of statistics, is a bit like the
prosecuting angel in **"Bontsha, the Silent"** in that, although
at first he calls for only the dry facts, he soon realizes the pity
surrounding those facts.) This interplay between reality and
fantasy in Peretz's work reflects his sense of such a desperate
Jewish condition that the realistic descriptions must occasionally be "transcended" in order for the reader to grasp the spirit
of the people within that condition, a recognition not attainable
through realism alone. At the same time, the escape into fantasy
sometimes allows Peretz to escape a sudden Jewish condition
which otherwise, in its sheer literalness, he fears he himself
will succumb to. (pp. 147-49)

To traditional Jewish belief Peretz is what Hawthorne was to
Puritanism—not a believer, but one who found its terms lodged
within him and useful to his art.

Unlike Heine or Babel, Peretz is able to capture the conversation of the Jews whom he visits. He captures their Yiddish
on the wing. We come into the middle of an inquiry about the
family of the respondent:

> "A wife?"
>
> "Et!"
>
> "What do you mean, 'et'?"
>
> "He wants to divorce her," answers someone
> else for him.
>
> "How many children?"
>
> He has to consider and start counting on his
> fingers:
>
> "From the first wife, mine—one, two, three;
> hers—one, two; from the second wife. . . ."
>
> He becomes bored of counting.
>
> "Nu, let it be six."
>
> " 'Let it be' isn't good enough. I need to know
> exactly."
>
> "Look here, 'exactly' isn't that simple. Ex-
> actly! What do you have to know exactly for?
> What are you, some kind of official? One has
> to count for you? Someone is going to come
> after you and check up on your figures? Ex—
> act—ly!"

The conversation goes on like this for four pages, Peretz showing how the evasions and grumbling and long-winded reckoning are all ways of responding to, yet keeping off, the prying
outsider. Indirectly and finally, Peretz as investigator finds out
the man's various strategies for earning a living. But what is
more important is that Peretz makes us feel that in the evasive
Yiddish of the respondent, along with his charges, interjec-
tions, and reciprocal questioning, there is a respectable and
ingenious self-defense going on. The rhythm of the Yiddish
hides and reveals the poverty of the speaker. On Peretz himself
this rhetorical decoy and revelation was not to be lost. The
passage illustrates Jacob Glatstein's description of Peretz "as
one seeking to gain the refined folk ear" [see excerpt dated
1947]. One can imagine Peretz *der shrayber* admiring what
Peretz *der statistiker* must formally object to, but whose objections force the continuation of the conversation that the other
half secretly relishes. Peretz came to the *shtetl* to ask questions
requiring only factual responses, but what struck him was the
total condition and the strategies of response. Here was "the
folk imagination" at work in answer to his very questions as
a social scientist. He had triggered more than what the questions
had imagined.

Thus, it is an immersion in the lives of these Jews of the Pale
that we witness in Peretz's travel sketches. His respect for,
and frustration with, their responses make up his total response.
Scornful as can be Mendele, the first great Yiddish novelist
(c. 1836-1917), in his descriptions of the impoverished conditions of the Jews of the Pale, Peretz can also indulge in the
famous legend of the Jews emigrating from Germany eastward,
deciding to rest at a certain place—*po-lin*, "here abide," thus
giving the country, Poland, its name. The intellectual and sophisticated mind attracted to folk material for literary purposes
is one of the great images of Peretz that emerges from *Sketches
of a Provincial Journey*.

The sketches end abruptly, with the story of a man who can't be helped because his insides are burnt out from too much drink. Not even the local *lamed-vovnik*, though he has the reputation of saving lives, could rescue this one from death. Perhaps Peretz is suggesting, in this last sketch, that no miracle work will save the worn-out condition of *shtetl* life. Neither will the gathering of statistics. Indeed, he comes to perceive that his very reporting of the extra-legal activities of the Jews (necessary for survival within the crevices of society) will threaten their livelihood.

In his trip to the interior of Jewish life Peretz had discovered the limits of reform at that historical moment. He registered the dismal, narrow life of *shtetl* Jewry that yet was touched by the folk: their legends, their speech, their gossip, their fears, their need to tell stories. . . . (pp. 151-52)

We discover in Peretz's *Sketches of a Provincial Journey* a work opposite from the *bildungsroman*, the story of the provincial young man who comes to the city and unexpectedly receives an education. Peretz's sketch book is about the intellectual, no longer young but still in his prime, who travels from the city to the provinces and discovers the connection between frustration and story-telling. The decay of Jewish life in the *shtetlakh* of Poland, along with the people's strategies in talking about their condition, left their impression on Peretz, for whom legend and fantasy were among the ways of exploring the Jewish condition. The historical moment told Peretz's imagination that what was intended to be social science and material for economic reform could only become literature. Peretz's sense of what his materials might be for the Yiddish literature that he would come to write and his attitude toward those materials were influenced by his frustrating, yet enriched, role as questioner and investigator of Jewish life. He found his material and its transmitters working on at a level that he had not anticipated. Going to the folk turned out to be more complicated and intriguing than he originally imagined. It was all a part of his own movement toward Yiddish. (p. 152)

> Richard J. Fein, "Peretz among the Jews," in *Judaism, Vol. 29, No. 2, Spring, 1980, pp. 146-52.*

RUTH ADLER (essay date 1980)

[*In the following excerpt, Adler discusses Peretz's sympathetic view of women and his mostly favorable portrayal of them in his fiction.*]

Though a number of Peretz's predecessors were sympathetic to women, Peretz added a new dimension in championing their rights. His personal quest for identity . . . allowed him to identify with woman in a unique way. Whereas others appeared to relate to a partial essence, Peretz saw woman in her totality. He saw and described her as wife, mother, daughter. His works are replete with characterizations of each of these types. . . .

Peretz penetrated the inner torment and estrangement of woman and revealed her conflicts and unutterable loneliness. He bemoaned the disparate and lonely fate of the Jewish wife who, even within her own home, stood visibly apart from her husband. . . . (p. 27)

Peretz utilized simple earthy types to convey self-evident truths. In his work **"An Idyllic Home,"** Hayim, an unlettered shtetl porter, is an eloquent advocate of women's rights. Notwithstanding his meager lot, Hayim is idyllically blessed with a loving, devoted wife. Her devotion is fully reciprocated by the humble porter. In querying the shtetl rabbi about the esoterics

of the "world to come," Hayim is told that such rewards are reserved for scholars, the just, and those who serve the learned. Women, he is told, can simply expect to serve as footstools for their husbands. Upon returning home, Hayim, nonetheless, assures his wife that there is room for two on the paradisical throne and that he will most assuredly seat her beside him. "I am certain," he exclaims, "that the Holy One Blessed Be He will undoubtedly agree to this." Through the simple porter, Peretz asserts the self-evident and natural truth of woman's right to equality, often distorted by the veneer of schooling. (p. 28)

Peretz is no less avid in his plea for the common man than he is in his defense of woman. In his essay **"Paths Leading Away from Judaism"** he condemns the shtetl brand of orthodoxy, which eschewed the simple beauty of the unlettered man and found no place for the woman. In talks at Czernowitz and Vilne, in the years 1908 and 1912 respectively, the equation between woman and the common man was most emphatically reiterated by Peretz. He credited both with contributing to the growth and spread of Yiddish language and literature. In a word, Peretz is the humanist concerned for the "outsider"— be it the exploited man or the disenfranchised woman.

Though Peretz's writings are essentially a plea for human dignity and parallel the works of his predecessors, Yalag and Mendele, in this respect, he differs significantly in his treatment of his characters. Perhaps most notable is his rather extensive use of shtetl women as protagonists. Whereas in the works of Mendele, Sholem Aleichem, and other of his predecessor-peers there is evident concern for woman, she rarely occupies a position of central importance in their narratives. She tends to appear either as a hapless but relatively unimportant personage, or, when assigned a position of significance, she is seen through the eyes of a male protagonist. In the works of Peretz, wife and daughter unequivocally appear as central characters in **"A Woman's Wrath," "The Mute," "A Disturbed Sabbath," "In the Basement,"** and others.

Another feature that distinguished Peretz from other raconteurs of the shtetl is the dearth of graphic detailed description of the shtetl populace salient in the works of Mendele and Sholem Aleichem. The reader is, for the most part, given only the barest hints of how Peretz's characters look and talk. Whereas the works of Mendele and Sholem Aleichem permit one to see the wart on the tip of the beadle's nose and hear the ring in his voice, the reader must content himself with a hazy or fragmented description of Peretz's heroes. Peretz's creative emphasis was invested in capturing "soul"—internal reality. The world of feelings, interrelationships, and psychological nuances was of paramount importance to him. (This is not to say that Sholem Aleichem and Mendele were indifferent to the realms of feelings and relationships or that Peretz was insensitive to externals. The difference between Peretz and the others is one of emphasis.)

In emphasizing the relationships among his characters, the roles of antagonist and protagonist, oppressed and oppressor, readily emerge. Into the fabric of these interrelationships the threads of pathos are elaborately woven. Villains and heroes are spun out of their mutual interaction. Significantly, it is the woman who often emerges as the protagonist, frequently abused by society, an oppressive husband, or father. Clearly, in the works of Peretz, woman and her travail are of central interest. It is Peretz who evolved the abstraction of the lonely Jewish wife into the character of **"Mrs. Hannah,"** deserted by her husband and exploited by her brother. In the person of the widow,

Grune, Peretz raised to classic heights the figure of the hapless mother who defied conventional shtetl morality in defense of her daughter. The alienation of the poor shtetl daughter is revealed in the description of **"The Three Seamstresses."** It is as if Peretz fulfilled a deep psychological need of his own in creating the tragic figure of rejected and forgotten woman. The role of the "outsider" is apparently one with which he could readily identify.

It has been suggested that Peretz's deemphasis of the external environment is attributable to his "outsider's" view of the shtetl. In contrast to Mendele and Sholem Aleichem, Peretz's perspective of the shtetl was that of the enlightened European. Albeit sympathetic to the milieu in which he was born and reared, he viewed it with the sobriety of a dispassionate clinical observer. Many of Peretz's works on shtetl life originated after his trek through the province towns of Poland in the role of census-taker. His census mission was carried out in Warsaw garb, strange and foreboding to the eye of the simple shtetl dweller. . . . Peretz chose to remain the "outsider," to be regarded as different, even odd. The census-taking orientation was retained in many of his subsequent accounts of shtetl life. These proved to be the accounts of a curious data gatherer concerned not with details of local color but with amassing facts in order to comprehend patterns and dynamics of interaction. Hence the emergence of a literary style lacking the folksy nuances of a Sholem Aleichem or a Mendele but replete with incisive insight into the psychological gears of shtetl life. As Roback has noted, Sholem Aleichem wrote "for the people" and Peretz, "about them."

A brief look at Peretz's childhood years is required to comprehend the essence of this curious identification with the outsider. In describing his childhood and adolescence in his memoirs, Peretz tells of his idiosyncratic behavior which earned him the appellation of "the crazy Leibush." . . . In several of his narratives Peretz clearly identifies with the half-crazed town recluse who is ignored and maligned by the "respectable" elements of the shtetl, but he is seen by Peretz as the only vestige of sanity in a world gone awry. Hence the role of outsider was a familiar one to Peretz. His own idiosyncratic needs inclined him to assert his right to be different, and in this role he encountered the ridicule and consternation of the underdog quite early in life. He could thus be expected to empathize readily with the aggrieved.

An author identifying with his character is a common literary occurrence. Critics such as Niger, Klausner, and Berdichevsky have indicated that this is especially true of Peretz. Particularly forceful and empathic portrayals of various characters have led numerous critics to suggest specific identification with these characters. Among others, he has been identified with the Litvak in **"If Not Higher,"** with the protagonist of **"The Death of the Musician,"** and with Hayim, the porter of **"An Idyllic Home."** If Peretz's identification with these characters can be inferred, his identification with woman is evident from his own word. In one of his essays he indeed draws a striking parallel between women and authors:

> Authors much as women have heretofore not been considered human. They have either been regarded as inferior and troublesome or else as ethereal and angelic. In either event, they have never been considered people. . . . This notion should be discarded! Woman is flesh and blood, no more no less, an author is also human, at least he should be.

The ever-restless Peretz, variously regarded as madcap, eccentric, and rebel, found an easy kinship with woman—the eternal outsider.

This curious facet of Peretz's personality, viewed in conjunction with his many strongly empathic statements about woman, demonstrate that Peretz was not merely sympathetic to woman but entered her consciousness by the process of identification. In addition to the *Zeitgeist* of Haskala and socialism that unquestionably exerted a liberalizing influence on Peretz's social outlook, his concern for woman appears to have been rooted, to a large degree, in his personal history. (pp. 28-32)

Peretz's treatment of woman is, in the main, a positive one—compassionate and empathic—but not without an element of contrasting detraction. The conflict reflected in the diversity of negative types can be seen as a manifestation of his ambivalence toward woman in her various roles of wife, mother, and daughter. . . .

As intellectual and social propagandist, Peretz allowed few aspects of Jewish life to escape his critical surveillance. The home, the shtetl, the religious hierarchy, and the like, all provided legitimate forums for analysis and critique. Traditionally an outsider as well as a vessel of new life, the woman provided the ideal means for mounting an offensive against decaying orthodoxies as well as for suggesting viable alternatives. As a neo-romanticist Peretz sought perfection in the marital relationship, in woman' genteelness and martyrdom, in the humanistic soul of Hasidism—and he portrayed them through idyllic, rose-colored spectacles. As a social critic he was at times harsh and unrelenting and painted with somber strokes.

Lord Dunsany once remarked that "psychologists, like roadmenders, go down only two inches, whereas poets, like miners, go down a mile." The contributions of Peretz, conceived with poetic lyricism and psychological incisiveness, notwithstanding literary license and partiality, cannot be overlooked as an invaluable social as well as literary document. (p. 119)

> *Ruth Adler, in her* Women of the Shtetl—Through the Eyes of Y. L. Peretz, *Fairleigh Dickinson University Press, 1980, 144 p.*

ADDITIONAL BIBLIOGRAPHY

Biletzky, Israel Ch. "Isaac Leibush Peretz." In his *Essays on Yiddish Poetry and Prose Writers of the Twentieth Century, Part I,* translated by Yirmiyahu Haggi, pp. 9-13. Tel-Aviv: I. L. Peretz Library, 1969.
Biographical sketch which examines Peretz's artistic philosophy.

Curley, Thomas. "One of the Greats of Yiddish Literature." *The Commonweal* LXXIII, No. 4 (21 October 1960): 98-9.
Review of *The Book of Fire.* Curley praises the stories, but finds the introduction by translator Joseph Leftwich confusing and superfluous.

Gittleman, Sol. "I. L. Peretz." In his *From Shtetl to Suburbia: The Family in Jewish Literary Imagination,* pp. 91-3. Boston: Beacon Press, 1978.*
Discussion of Peretz's concept of family. Peretz's stories are used to illustrate his concern for family problems and the family structure among Polish Jews, and Peretz's approach is compared with those of Mendele Sforim and Sholom Aleichem.

Goldberg, Fred. Introduction to *My Memoirs,* by Isaac Leib Peretz, translated by Fred Goldberg, pp. 9-19. New York: Citadel Press, 1964.
Biographical sketch and laudatory critical assessment. Goldberg places Peretz's works within the traditions of Yiddish and world

literature, crediting Peretz with experimentation in form and with fidelity to his personal beliefs and values.

Goldsmith, Emanuel S. "Yitzkhok Leybush Peretz." In his *Architects of Yiddishism at the Beginning of the Twentieth Century: A Study in Jewish Cultural History*, pp. 121-38. London: Associated University Presses, 1976.

Discussion of Peretz's influence at the Czernowitz Conference. Through Peretz's journalistic and poetic works, and his strong influence over the general attitude and formal doctrine at the Czernowitz Conference during the late 1890s, Goldsmith traces his growing radical Yiddishism and role as a national and international leader of the Yiddish cultural movement.

Leftwich, Joseph. Introduction to *The Book of Fire: Stories by I. L. Peretz*, by I. L. Peretz, translated by Joseph Leftwich, pp. 7-51. New York: Thomas Yoseloff, 1960.*

Biographical and critical sketch. Leftwich traces the historical origins of Jewish legends and folklore, and the various sources that blend to inform Peretz's folklorist tales with a wealth of cultural history. Peretz is compared to other writers in Jewish and world literature, and the assessments of his contemporaries are included throughout the introduction.

Levine, Stanley F. Review of *Selected Stories*, by I. L. Peretz. *Books Abroad* 49, No. 2 (Spring 1975): 342-43.

Assessment of Peretz's influence on modern Yiddish literature. Specifically, Peretz's Jewish world view, rejection of sentimentality and self-criticism, and break with European literary and cultural models are noted.

Liptzin, Sol. "Peretz and Sholom Aleichem." In his *A History of Yiddish Literature*, pp. 56-72. Middle Village, N.Y.: Jonathan David Publishers, 1972.*

Examination of Peretz's tales, his life, and his literary philosophy. Liptzin calls Peretz the "profoundest spokesman for the Yiddish intellectuals" who became their conscience and the interpreter of their ideals and disappointments.

Maisil, Nachman. "Isaac Leib Peretz." *Journal of Jewish Bibliography* II, No. 2 & 3 (April-July 1940): 42-6, 81.

Discussion of Peretz's contemporary and modern reputation. Maisil examines the growing legend of Peretz, and the improper appraisal of his contemporaries, who often found his works symbolically obscure, stylistically indistinct, and nonconformist. Maisil notes that as with many works of genius, Peretz's works today have a significance that extends beyond their author's original conception.

Miller, David Neal. "Y. L. Peretz' 'Bontsye Shvayg': Perspectives on Passivity." *Slavic and East European Journal* 18, No. 1 (Spring 1974): 41-6.

Critical discussion. Miller describes the controversy surrounding the meaning of the short story "Bontsha the Silent," which has been interpreted as both a work written in praise of passivity and as criticism of passivity. Miller examines the details of the story for clues to Peretz's somewhat ambiguous intention.

Niger, S. "The Legacy of I. L. Peretz." In *In This World and the Next: Selected Writings*, by I. L. Peretz, translated by Moshe Spiegel, pp. 371-77. New York: Thomas Yoseloff, 1958.

Discussion of Peretz's influence on Yiddish literature and importance as a modern inspiration to Jewish writers.

Trunk, J. J. "Peretz at Home: A Young Writer Meets the Great Yiddish Litterateur." *Commentary* 9, No. 3 (March 1950): 252-56.

Reminiscence. Trunk, who became one of Poland's leading pre-World-War-I Yiddish writers, discusses Peretz's benevolent attitude toward the young writers who sought out his advice and encouragement. Trunk acknowledges that it was Peretz who encouraged him to write in Yiddish rather than in Hebrew.

Waxman, Meyer. "Rise and Development of Yiddish Literature in the Nineteenth Century." In his *A History of Jewish Literature from 1880 to 1935, Part 1*, pp. 463-545. Rev. ed. New York: Thomas Yoseloff, 1960.*

Examines variety of tone, theme, and style in Peretz's short stories. Waxman accounts for the seeming contradictions in Peretz's short stories by noting the balance of such elements as the outspoken and symbolic, realistic and romantic, and the didactic and the amusing in his works.

Miklós Radnóti

1909-1944

Hungarian poet, translator, critic, essayist, and memoirist.

Radnóti is remembered as a tragically fated poet who in his last years, faced with a turbulent, death-ridden environment, expressed his deep faith in humanity through his poetry. Written while interned at a forced labor camp during World War II, these poems have inspired the admiration of critics for their superb craftsmanship and for their trenchant evocation of the poet's ongoing spiritual struggle. Radnóti is also recognized as a prolific, accomplished translator of works by numerous major writers.

Born in Budapest to Jewish parents, Radnóti lost both his mother and his twin brother at birth. The feelings of guilt, frustration, and remorse that arose from this tragic event are reflected in several of his poems and in his *Ikrek hava: napló a gyerekkorról* (''Under the Sign of Gemini: A Diary About Childhood''). Radnóti lived with his father until the elder Radnóti's death in 1921, at which time he was taken in by a maternal uncle. Radnóti's uncle, a successful textile dealer who planned to entrust his nephew with the business, enrolled him in secondary trade school. It was while studying there that Radnóti began writing poetry. The poems of these early years exhibit the influences of Hungarian poets Endre Ady and Dezso Kosztolányi, as well as the French Symbolist Paul Verlaine. Although he received further training in textiles in Reichenberg, Czechoslovakia, Radnóti finally abandoned what was an involuntarily chosen career and returned to Budapest in 1928 to pursue a career in letters. He eventually assumed the coeditorship of two literary periodicals, *Kortárs* and *1928,* and contributed to an anthology of works by younger writers, in effect joining modernists who opposed the conservative artistic ideals upheld by Hungary's most prestigious literary journal, *Nyugat,* and by its renowned editor, the poet Mihály Babits. In the fall of 1930—shortly after the publication of his first volume of poetry, *Pogány köszöntő (Pagan Salute),* which attracted national attention—Radnóti entered the University of Szeged to obtain a classical education, specializing in Hungarian and French literature. The following year Radnóti helped found a leftist student organization that held lectures on various political subjects, many antagonistic to the Hungarian régime of Admiral Miklós Horthy de Nagybánya. With the appearance of *Újmódi pásztorok éneke (Song of Modern Shepherds)* a revolutionary and spirited blend of proletarian idealism, risqué religious allusions, pastoral tributes, and earthy eroticism reminiscent of Walt Whitman, Radnóti was charged with offending public taste and inciting rebellion. The publication was seized, and Radnóti avoided expulsion from Szeged only through the aid of Sándor Sik, a Catholic poet and professor at the University of Szeged who appeased authorities with a supportive but apologetic letter.

Graduating from Szeged in 1934 after delivering a widely respected dissertation on Hungarian novelist Margit Kaffka, Radnóti married Fanni Gyarmati, who inspired him to write what are considered some of the most moving love poems in the Hungarian language. Unable to secure a teaching post, Radnóti worked as tutor, stenographic instructor, and translator while continuing to compose poetry. His fifth volume, *Járkálj csak,*

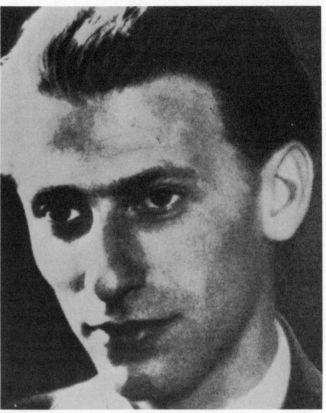

Courtesy of Ardis Publishers

halálraítélt! (Walk on, Condemned!), was published in 1936 under the imprint of *Nyugat* magazine. This apparent reversal in alliances was the result of a reconciliation with Babits, who had harshly reviewed one of Radnóti's earlier works, as well as by Radnóti's rising reputation among the Budapest literary establishment. Yet by this time Radnóti's personal outlook had become gravely serious and morbid due to Hungary's totalitarian rule and, particularly, to his profound identification with Spanish poet Federico García Lorca, the recent victim of a politically motivated assassination. *Walk on, Condemned!* represents Radnóti's apocalyptic vision of a once peaceful, natural world quickly disintegrating amidst widespread eruptions of fascism and nazism, which for him portended the coming of full-scale war. In 1938, two years after receiving the distinguished Baumgarten Prize in Poetry, Radnóti published *Meredek út (Steep Road),* the last collection of poems he compiled during his lifetime. From 1940 to 1944, while continuing to write a considerable amount of verse, Radnóti published prose works, including ''Under the Sign of Gemini'' and several children's books, edited the posthumous works of other Hungarian writers, and translated the works of such writers as Shakespeare, Guillaume Apollinaire, and Jean de la Fontaine. However, one of the countless victims in Eastern Europe during World War II, Radnóti spent a large portion of these years in Axis-controlled labor camps. In 1944 Radnóti's camp, then working in Yugoslavia, was forced to retreat due to advancing Russian troops. At the end of a long forced march back to Hungary the men were executed, not by the Germans but by noncommissioned officers of the Hungarian army. "These soldiers," as Emery George has explained, "tried twice to assign their prisoners to local hospitals near Gyor; due to crowded conditions, however, the patients were not accepted. The servicemen, who had to report back to their units that evening, did not wish to be considered absent without leave, and trained in existentialist ethics they were not." Radnóti was then buried in a mass grave near Abda. Two years later his body was exhumed and a notebook containing ten of his most artistically polished poems was discovered.

The most compelling aspect of Radnóti's poetic canon is a progression from early Whitmanesque optimism and idyllic settings to a morbid, mystical preoccupation with death to a final acceptance of fated death, balanced by a humanistic belief in the possibility of simple, harmonious existence. Nearly all critics agree that this last development, present in *Tajtékos ég (Clouded Sky)*, represents the pinnacle of Radnóti's achievement and insures his reputation as an important modern poet, particularly since Radnóti maintained a remarkably sane and orderly view of reality amidst his often chaotic surroundings. The photographic style in the cycle "Razglednicák" ("Picture Postcards"), written during the forced march, is representative of the serene stoicism that Radnóti arrived at in his art. Yet despite this objective stance, Radnóti is also described as a poet of the self who in his later work masterfully documented his troubled artistic consciousness, his awareness of the fact that he was a poet doomed to die prematurely. The "Eclogak" ("Eclogues"), his cycle of eight poems inspired by the classical pastorals of Virgil, are perhaps his most powerful expressions of this awareness, given their sharp contrast between an impersonal form and a tragic, personal content. The eighth eclogue—a dialogue between the poet and the Old Testament prophet Nahum—is viewed by Emery George, the translator of *Miklós Radnóti: The Complete Poetry*, as the worthiest piece in the collection, for in it "the poet's categorical self-imperatives, aesthetic, moral, philosophical, political, are transmuted into the highest kind of poetry known to the classical tradition: that of the *vates*, of prophecy." Empowered by his renewed faith in God following his conversion to Roman Catholicism during the war, and by his deep love for his wife, Radnóti lashes out at the wickedness of war as Nahum had done against the citizens of Nineveh. The poem closes with the prophetic affirmation that a new kingdom of God will soon be born and that Nahum, Radnóti, and Fanni will be there to join it.

Radnóti holds the distinction of being the modern Hungarian poet most often and most extensively translated into English, and his work has been well received by critics in England and the United States. His mature poetry in particular is considered a wellspring of ingenious metaphors, vibrant images, and unique insights. These works are valued as Radnóti's consummate expression of himself, his world, and his art, and firmly establish him as an important poetic witness to a violent and tragic period of modern history.

PRINCIPAL WORKS

Pogány köszöntő (poetry) 1930
    [*Pagan Salute* published in *Miklós Radnóti: The Complete Poetry*, 1980]

Újmódi pásztorok éneke (poetry) 1931
    [*Song of Modern Shepherds* published in *Miklós Radnóti: The Complete Poetry*, 1980]
Lábadozó szél (poetry) 1933
    [*Convalescent Wind* published in *Miklós Radnóti: The Complete Poetry*, 1980]
Újhold (poetry) 1935
    [*New Moon* published in *Miklós Radnóti: The Complete Poetry*, 1980]
Járkálj csak, halálraítélt! (poetry) 1936
    [*Walk On, Condemned!* published in *Miklós Radnóti: The Complete Poetry*, 1980]
Meredek út (poetry) 1938
    [*Steep Road* published in *Miklós Radnóti: The Complete Poetry*, 1980]
Ikrek hava: napló a gyerekkorról (memoir) 1940
    ["Under the Sign of Gemini: A Diary About Childhood," 1979; published in *The New Hungarian Quarterly*]
Naptár (poetry) 1942
    [*Calendar* published in *Miklós Radnóti: The Complete Poetry*, 1980]
Tajtékos ég (poetry) 1946
    [*Clouded Sky*, 1972; also published as *Sky with Clouds* in *Miklós Radnóti: The Complete Poetry*, 1980]
Bori notesz (poetry) 1970
Subway Stops: Fifty Poems (poetry) 1977
The Witness: Selected Poems (poetry) 1977
Forced March: Selected Poems (poetry) 1979
Radnóti Miklós művei (poetry, memoir, prose, and translations) 1979
Miklós Radnóti: The Complete Poetry (poetry) 1980

ISTVÁN SŐTÉR (essay date 1965)

[*In the following excerpt, Sőtér differentiates Radnóti's later works from his earlier ones, regarding his final poems as those that make him "a truly great poet" for their reaffirmation of humanity and recreation of an idyllic life in the face of absolute horror.*]

[If] Radnóti is now considered a poet of some significance, it is not on account of his martyrdom, which he shared with so many victims of the Second World War.

It is a strange paradox of fate that it was in the agonies of helplessness and humiliation that Radnóti created his purest poems, expressed his most profound message. How simple it seems to deduce from it the bitter and cynical argument that pure and authentic poetry could be fostered by nazism and barbarity. Yet the SS guards of *Lager Heideman* can hardly be regarded as muses of poetry; for Radnóti, their presence, their function in his life, and his encounter with nazism in general, were to decide only one thing—the necessity of creating in poetry the strongest possible repudiation of their world. Those who may have read the French versions of Radnóti's poems will be aware that the poet chose a human and even finer form of repudiation. These poems, written secretly in the *Lager* for himself, without any hope of—or aspiration to—publication, reveal not a hint of despondency or despair; nor, on the other hand, are these poems inspired by that militant political creed which, in an active anti-nazi struggle, might have supplied one of several answers for the poet.

The repudiation, the rejection, the counter-vision Radnóti chose was very different. That which is given expression in the *Lager* poems—and even in those which have been retrieved from the grave—is not the inferno of suffering in which the last year of the poet's life was spent; it is his love for his wife, images of his home, the orchards on the hill-slopes of Buda, evenings spent over a glass of wine in the company of friends, May Days—scenes of untarnished, natural joy. Among the poems recovered from the mass grave are four short poems which the poet entitled **Razglednicák** (*razglednica* is Serbian for picture postcard—Radnóti's forced labour battalion had been sent to work in the Bor mines in Serbia). The first of these strange poems, written under such tragic circumstances, contrasts the brightness of love with war; in the second, amidst burning houses, the poet concentrates on the image of the little shepherdess grazing her sheep; it is only in the third and the fourth of the *razglednica* that the terror of war finds expression—in the last poem, in a picture of one of the group being killed by a shot through the back of his head: this was barely a week before the poet's own death, as if a premonition of what was coming towards him. There is something surprising and terrifying about the objective, laconic style of the poem in which Radnóti jots down, as it were, the scene—the execution of the fellow next to him.

It is therefore a peculiar kind of poetry that came into being during this last period of his work—purified through the sufferings he endured. If by idyll we mean something else than a sentimental image; if we mean by it a real peace, the purity and profound joy of the spirit, the comfort and strength derived from the knowledge of the essential humanity of genuine morality, then the poetry of Radnóti, conceived in the inferno of the nazi camps, may be called idyllic poetry. How easy it might have been for him to escape from the Second World War in conventional idylls under more sheltered conditions. But the idyllic poetry of Miklós Radnóti acquires its poetic meaning and force precisely from the fact it was born in a world which was a helpless prey to barbarity. Only when set against the background of the *Lager Heideman* do the meaning and the values of these "idylls" make themselves felt. The "idyll" was both a repudiation and a revolt; poetic greatness appears in, and arises out of, the refusal of the victim to acquiesce in the fate forced on him. This kind of resistance is of at least as much value as resistance arms in hand; in this struggle the last word is spoken by poetry, and the murderers sustain their real defeat the very moment they commit the murder. By this act of poetry, by the creation of this rare idyll of his, Radnóti won freedom; the prisoner is more free than his jailers, and he bought his freedom not through the easy release of dreams, of fantasy, but by his power to transmute his happier past into the present, to extract the quintessential validity of a cleaner and better world from that past despite the horrors encompassing him, to bear witness to something his enemies had sought to take from him and the world alike. He built for himself not an ivory tower but a citadel of reality—a bulwark, a stronghold of the unvanquished heart. And the name of this bulwark, this stronghold, is poetry. It is when it stands invulnerable as a fortress that poetry comes into its own. (pp. 3-5)

Miklós Radnóti, even from behind the barbed wire of *Lager Heideman,* seems to me more essentially Hungarian than any of his poet contemporaries; the sense of his country, the vision of home, the Hungarian countryside, is as sharp and living in no other poet as it is in his poems of that time. None felt the callous inhumanity of war more keenly than he did. In his poem *I Cannot Know (Nem tudhatom),* he is distressed at the thought that the men of the allied bomber squadron overhead, fighting on his side, see only as an unrolled map the country which to him means home, the haunts of his boyhood, close and familiar people, the land of the poets who went before. In his poems Radnóti had the power to take back to himself what others tried to take away—his human dignity, his Hungarian personality. This re-assumption, this conservation, this re-creation was a major assertion of humankind in 1944. It made him a truly great poet. (p. 5)

The poems written during the last few years of his life reflect the different yet harmonious literary and ideological tendencies which had influenced him in the course of his life. There is evidence in these poems of a certain neo-classical discrimination in diction, as well as the effects of Apollinaire—and even vestiges of themes from folklore. All these elements had been variously and disjointedly present in Radnóti's earlier poems as experiments in diverse types of poetic diction—on occasion with certain mannerist effects. A comparison between Radnóti's final period and his earlier poetry shows a very substantial difference in quality.

The search for ancient folklore elements and allied themes sprang with the young Radnóti from the same urge as his desire for a return to classical verse-forms. The neo-classical tendencies in the poems of his early period now strike one as being dated; in his last poems however—as also in the **Seventh Eclogue**—it appears as a legitimate device which, through the classic purity of its form, still further accentuates the Kafkaesque unreason of the concentration camp. The perfect balance of proportion in these last poems came about independently of the classic forms occasionally employed; that is to say, the classic perfection of proportion was due as much to the influence of Apollinaire as to that of classical poetry. (p. 7)

Had [Radnóti] never written his last poems, his early period might be regarded as merely a reflection of a poetic manner. As it happened, however, this manner acquired real significance in his last period: his mastery of classical verse-forms was to be a decisive factor in the creation of the idyll set against the background of the *Lager Heideman.*

During his Szeged years, nonetheless, a new spirit, perhaps, on occasion, a new manner, emerged in Radnóti's poetry. (p. 9)

His growing awareness of social issues, the links which developed with the revolutionary movement, made themselves felt in an indirect rather than a direct manner, as a force shaping that attitude in him which helped to create the poems of his last period. Poetry admits of a good many varieties of Leftist progressive attitudes; views do not necessarily express themselves in militant poems: they may indeed find expression even in poems pitched in the "lowest key," or in the "most intimate" love lyrics. This is not to say, of course, that the poet's outlook on the world is a matter of complete indifference. It was precisely in the midst of the sufferings which lay ahead that Radnóti most needed the moral strength generated by his progressive views, his links with the working-class movement, his communist ideology.

Hence, also, the releasing effect of his brief stay in Paris in 1937. The period of the Civil War in Spain left a deep impression on his poetry and inspired the finest examples of Hungarian anti-fascist lyric poetry. (p. 10)

Anti-fascist views formed an essential element in Radnóti's poetry, but even this element asserted itself in a complex manner. From the 'thirties onwards, Death became the principal theme in Radnóti's lyric poems—expressed most effectively in his poem *Járkálj csak, halálraítélt (Stagger on, you doomed)*. In his last poems emerged a constant reiteration, an awareness, an expectation of death; if, in his earlier period, he had trifled with the theme of death as a young poet does, later on it achieved an oppressive predominance. Radnóti, who had translated Apollinaire, now produced translations of Hölderlin and Georg Trakl; Chénier took on a special significance for him, while Valéry Larbaud's ''Orient Express'' became the symbol of the unfulfilled expectations of an entire generation. Even his translations of La Fontaine were affected with deliberate inaccuracy, the occasional hints of death slip in—with stubborn consistency it appears in anything and everything he writes— looming behind the non-committal serenity and charm of the classic text. In his love lyrics the same voice is heard speaking, not of the death of a Tristan, but of a development anticipated with cool objectivity—death as the inevitable and logical consequence of the time and of his own position in his time. This cool, detached presence of the death-theme lacks romanticism, even stoicism of any kind. This is not the philosophy—no, not even the poetry—of death: for Radnóti, death is the characteristic of a whole era—the poet registers that fact as once he used to record an emotion, or experience a landscape. Death as the principal theme of poetic perception—that is Radnóti's testimony of his time. Is it acceptance? Is it meek acquiescence in the fate fascism has designed for him? Or is it a hastening towards one's fate, a haunted identification with the victim?

What Radnóti expresses is not the fear, but the fact, of death; all of his poetry is a process of knowing death, fraternizing with death, living daily with death. One period alone of his poetical work is devoid of the theme of death: the last. Of the poems he took with him into the grave, even the last *Razglednica* ends with a gesture—a gesture to life. Radnóti's poetry of death ended in the death-camp.

In *Lager Heideman*, his life seemed to begin again. *Forced March* expresses life-joy, peace and harmony, a spiritual equilibrium free from all unbalance, with an intensity not found in any of his earlier poems. A superficial observer might believe that Radnóti, who had lived in such awareness of death before, has now, at last, discovered a ''meaning in life.'' What, as a matter of fact, happened between *Stagger on, you doomed* (1936) and *Forced March* (15 September, 1944)?

In the last few months of his life—the period in which his poems rose to their supreme heights—Radnóti abandoned the miraculous, the fantasies that had once engrossed his attention as well as that of his entire generation. He became extremely clear-headed; summoning all the moral and physical strength he possessed, dependent only on his own resources, he rebuilt his ego, as it were; he re-created his poetry. This rebuilding, this re-creation of himself was a feat of such human greatness, an undertaking of such moral strength that it inevitably led to his greatest poetry. I have said already that the Radnóti of his last months seems to me to be a free man—none but a free man could have written poetry of the calibre of his last poems. This reborn consciousness stood impregnable before the face of horror and death. In a sense, he managed to overcome death. He assumed calmly that it was coming, and from then on lived as if it had arrived. It was this frame of mind that opened the new vistas of his last poetry. This renaissance equally meant that he shed all inessentials to retain the essential—memories, experiences, everything that had nourished him in earlier days. He must have been conscious of this process of transformation, for, in the poem *Letter to His Wife*, we find this profound

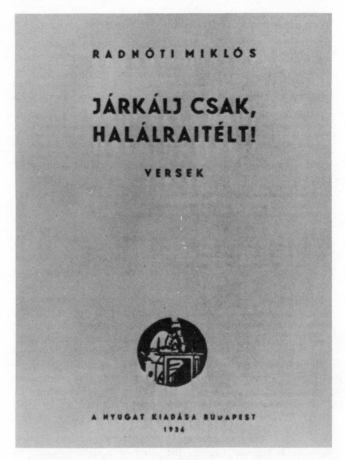

Cover of the first edition of Walk On, Condemned! *Courtesy of Ardis Publishers.*

sentence: *''Reality before, you have become a dream again.''* This sentence has come to assume a validity which holds good for his life as a whole. It was not Time which separated him from his former life; his *A la recherche* . . . , therefore, meant something different from what it means to those who set out to probe into their past in their heart and imagination. He had been torn away not from his Past but from his Present—and the separation took place, not in time, but in space, in his living body and mind. It brought to life, suddenly, all that had once put heart into him; his love now became a new love, and he found the power to speak of it with more deeper feeling, and with greater poignancy, than in his early love-poems. His admirable poetical craftsmanship no longer overburdened him— no longer needed to look for inspiration for its content; his whole being, his whole existence, was a splendid defiance to chaos. His world outlook, his anti-fascist views, now found an expression congenial to his temperament and spiritual nature; he gained his personal triumph over nazism by bringing all his moral strength to bear, by making himself impregnable, and by bringing his new poetry to life. This was the triumph of poetry—and for this very reason it is, in a sense, of more abiding value even than military victories. Little as this victory mattered for the few of his days, it matters today and will matter in times to come.

Miklós Radnóti became a great poet because, aided by the greatest emotional experience of his life, his education and his ideology and his morality, but left completely to his own resources, with none to help him, he rescued the human being in himself. He did so at a time when a large part of mankind was bent on destroying the human in themselves as well as in others. Human beings can, of course, be destroyed in a variety of ways. But to rescue the human being, to re-discover him, whether under conditions of tragedy and humiliation, or in happier, carefree days—is the only undertaking worthy of a poet. (pp. 11-13)

István Sőtér, "Miklós Radnóti, a Twentieth Century Poet," in The New Hungarian Quarterly, *Vol. VI, No. 18, Summer, 1965, pp. 3-13.*

B. S. ADAMS (essay date 1967)

[*In the following excerpt, Adams compares two cycles of Radnóti's "postcard" poems, the prewar "Cartes Postales" and the postwar "Razglednicák," and finds that the later poems possess a power not present in the earlier cycle.*]

How complete the contrast between Radnóti's two sets of short poems *Cartes Postales* and *Razglednicák*! Only six years separate them, but six years which had brought about some of the most sweeping and devastating changes that the world has known. The gentle happy life of pre-war Europe had given place to a continental battlefield, to concentration camps and the wholesale slaughter of man by man, while the gently idyllic style of Radnóti's pre-war verse had given place to a gentleness of quite a different nature. From the echoes of words and phrases of earlier writings in his later works we may hope to discover the nature of the change that took place within him. (p. 65)

Both are a series of literary glimpses; the one of a happy Radnóti in pre-war France, the other of a slave-labourer in devastated Serbia and Hungary. But in the ghastly record of human suffering in *Razglednicák* there is a power that *Cartes Postales* does not approach. *Cartes Postales* overflows with life, the play of young children, the eternal beauty of nature; *Razglednicák* is full of death and blood. 'Dobd el a rémes újságot' ['Throw away the horrible newspaper'], says *Cartes Postales*, referring presumably to the Spanish Civil War; *Razglednica* II forgets for a moment the horror of war in the picture of the little shepherdess and her sheep . . . and the pool at Cservenka is ruffled as is that at Versailles. But in *Cartes Postales* there is no personal element, while in *Razglednicák* Radnóti's love for his wife finds expression. Surely it is no mere coincidence that Radnóti should write two identically titled verses on two journeys, between which there can be no comparison. Radnóti, at the end of his strength and fully conscious of the imminence of the end, recalls in this obtuse way his former happiness.

Happy reminiscence is a startling innovation in Radnóti's verse, and is one of the most remarkable features of the Lager poems as a whole. Radnóti, in the main, is by no means a *laudator temporis acti*. He writes very little about his memories, and most of that little is of a mournful nature, contrasting strongly with his usual happy, idyllic poetry. The two main themes of his poetry of memory are the complex derived from the circumstances of his birth, and the occasional deaths of friends and other poets. In *Ikrek Hava* a few happy memories may be found, but the character of the work as a whole is sad. And yet here, amid conditions of the utmost squalor and vileness, this deeply sensitive man writes poetry of an allegorically happy and reminiscent nature. One might be tempted to dispute the fact that this is reminiscence at all, were it not for the explicit reminiscence of other Lager poems—the *Seventh Eclogue, Levél*

a Hitveshez, A la recherche, Erőltetett Menet. One cannot deny that happy memories play a significant part in the Lager verse, and that these memories are of two things—wife and poetry.

Radnóti's wife Fanni appears often in his poems, both by name and implication. An account of his love-poetry is beyond the scope of this article, but mention must be made of *Tétova Óda, Third Eclogue* and *Két karodban,* which rank among the greatest love-poems in the language. Even here, however, the omnipresent thoughts of death leave their traces. (pp. 66-7)

The more one reads of Radnóti, the more one becomes convinced that he was very well versed in what he himself had written. There is that Dostoyevskian characteristic about his work, that everything is interrelated, that a chance remark will find a sequel fifty pages on. Radnóti repeats words and phrases, uses the same imagery over and over again in so systematic a way that in a writer of his magnitude one cannot but interpret it as deliberate introversion. An example of this may be found in *Razglednica* I, which bears a certain resemblance to the *First Eclogue;* both speak of gunfire in the mountains, of crowds of refugees. But then they divide, the *Eclogue* into bitterness at the death of Lorca, the *Razglednica* into tender recollection. Similarly, the *Eclogue* has an echo in *Razglednica* II—the contrast of war and the pastoral scene. Again, the simile of the oak in the *Eclogue* is recalled in *Razglednica* IV. This relation of his last words to what he had previously written can only imply that the poet wished to regard his experiences at the time of writing as forming a continuity with his previous life. Expression of a sense of continuity is not limited to *Razglednicák* but may be detected in all the Lager poems, and in the continuous defiance that is the theme of the *Eclogues*. . . . [Radnóti's] militancy, centred in the *Eclogues,* his refusal to leave the fight unwon, his belief in the efficacy of his own message, his socialist leanings, all find their penultimate expression in *Gyökér.* Radnóti sees in his imminent martyrdom in the cause of freedom the goal of his life. The ripening for death, the theme of several earlier poems, is reaching its climax.

The final expression of this enmity to the world of cruelty and inhumanity is in the *Eighth Eclogue.* There is something about this poem that makes it seem rather contrived; it is as if Radnóti knew that his death was near and felt the need to clarify the enigmatic message of the *Eclogues.* The meaning of the poem is clear enough, but it lacks the poetic quality of the other *Eclogues* and of the rest of the Lager verse. But deliberately or not, this is Radnóti's last word on his purpose in life, and it is not without significance that he chooses to ally himself in it with an Old Testament prophet, in whose steps he has been following. (We may also recall here the last lines of *Töredék,* the conjectural *Sixth Eclogue,* with their reference to Isaiah.) There are a number of curious references to religious topics in Radnóti e.g. in *Arckép* and *Gyerekkor.* Gábor Tolnai maintains that these references are a sign of anticlericalism. But anticlericalism is not synonymous with irreligiousness; in our own literature we can point to Milton, Swift and others in proof of this. Radnóti was a Jew by birth, and as such unlikely to show marked Christian sympathies, but in his religion we find the same attitude as in his politics—no doctrinaire acceptance of any one creed, but rather an individualistic free-thinking prepared to include something among its tenets on merit, rather than on the dogmatic commands of some authority. As a Jew Radnóti could not accept Christ; as a socialist he could accept the social aspects of Christianity, the doing of good, the equality of all men in the sight of God. Is it possible that in his own life, with its quasi-miraculous beginnings and violent end, he

Miklós and Fanni Radnóti (right) with friends in Paris, 1939. Courtesy of Ardis Publishers.

saw a pale reflection of the life of Christ, and had faith that his work would live after him?

Thus it becomes clear that the poetic power of the Lager verse is based on Radnóti's happiness, a happiness derived not, as István Sőtér tells us [see excerpt dated 1965], from the rebuilding of his ego—when was that destroyed?—but from the satisfaction of seeing his life complete, drawing to the end that he had envisaged. It is the happiness of a man in love—in love with his wife, with his work, with humanity and with life itself. It is the happiness of a man who has lived life to the full, and who, looking back, has the satisfaction of seeing the good times and the bad fall into place, make sense. Above all, it is the sublime joy of the martyr who goes to the stake because he has no alternative, fearlessly joining the ranks of those who have gone before, rejoicing in his faith in the future of mankind. (pp. 68-70)

> B. S. Adams, "The Lager Verse of Miklós Radnóti," in Slavic and East-European Journal, Vol. 45, No. 104, January, 1967, pp. 65-75.

GEORGE GÖMÖRI AND CLIVE WILMER (essay date 1978)

[*Forced March is a selection of Radnóti's later poems that were initially translated by his countryman George Gömöri and then revised by British poet Clive Wilmer. In the following excerpt from the 1978 introduction to this edition, Gömöri and Wilmer*

discuss Radnóti as a poet who was overwhelmingly conscious of death, yet who remained spiritually idealistic.]

To read [Radnóti's] work chronologically is to follow something of the process whereby an individual talent is moulded by historical events; at the same time, it is to perceive that talent discerning meaning in the events, even as it is transformed by them. (p. 7)

The main influences on the early verse are fairly predictable: the French *avant-garde*, German Expressionism and a Hungarian version of Constructivism associated with the Socialist poet and theoretician, Lajos Kassák. His first book, *A Pagan Welcome* . . . , consists mainly of dithyrambic, Whitmanesque celebrations of life, nature and erotic love. The mature Radnóti is already in evidence in the more muted passages with their warmth and melancholy and certain gestures towards Christian symbolism. Around 1932, the vague, undirected rebelliousness he shared with so many of his contemporaries began to acquire a more concrete form: political protest became a feature of his poetry. At this stage in his life, Radnóti tended to think and write in categories of a somewhat nebulous Marxism. But he resisted orthodoxy. He refused to accept the aesthetic authority of the Soviet *Proletkult*. He was soon to become a close admirer of Sándor Sik, a Catholic poet-priest who taught at Szeged and whose influence on him was to prove both profound and lasting. Before long, the 'proletarian poet' stance had given way to a deeper concern with political developments at home and abroad.

The poet was gradually becoming a kind of seismograph, a sensitive instrument that registers even the slightest of the tremors that precede an earthquake.

Radnóti's response to the rise of Hitler was almost immediate. In a love poem dated September 1934, he wrote:

> You embrace her to protect her, while around you
> The world lies in wait for you
> To kill you finally with its long knives.

The allusion to Nazi terror is unmistakable. From now on, Radnóti saw himself as a doomed man. The danger of similar developments in Hungary was not yet so great, but he was not slow to register the force of the tremors reaching him from other lands. From all over Europe the enemy were closing in and Radnóti's convictions about his own fate became inextricably bound up with his compassion for those already suffering. His fifth book, published in the first year of the Spanish Civil War, bears the title, *Keep Walking, You, the Death-condemned!* . . . . He had solved the problem. The question was no longer 'Shall I die?' or 'May I die?' in the coming war, but '*How* shall I die?' 'And as for you, young man, what mode of death awaits you?' he asks in the poem which opens the present selection. For the eight years that remained to him, this *modus moriendi* was his central preoccupation.

This calm contemplation of violent death, which recurs throughout Radnóti's mature work, is remorseless almost to the point of morbid obsession. How exactly is it to be accounted for? Critics with a psychoanalytical bias have pointed to a latent guilt complex involving the poet's mother: the knowledge that it was his birth that had caused her death, goes the argument, filled him with a desire to atone, to offer himself as an expiating sacrifice. There is evidence of this anxiety in some of the poems—'**The Fourth Eclogue**' for example—but, as an explanation, it is plainly inadequate. There is little overt death-wish in the poems, nor any sense that he actually courted the fate he was only too justified in predicting for himself. The truth is rather that his work is steeped in an *awareness* of death. This awareness, based on presentiment, was rationally sustained by a variety of preoccupations: his Jewish origin, his developing interest in the Christian concept of sacrifice (he was converted to Roman Catholicism during the war), and his concern for the future of the European Humanist tradition at a time when the new barbarians were preparing to subdue the continent.

This is where [Spanish poet Federico García] Lorca appears as a figure of great symbolic importance. . . . In Radnóti's interpretation, Lorca *had* to die: because he was loved by the people and because, quite simply, he was a poet—that is, a spokesman for the forces of life. Behind his death there lay a simple equation: Fascism equals war equals death. It kills poets merely for being poets.

Once Radnóti had accepted this eventuality and seen it as part of his destiny, his whole sense of the physical world changed. Gone were the idyllic landscapes of *A Pagan Welcome*. He began to read omens in the clouds, to hear strange squeals and whimpers in the hushed garden, to watch the splendours of autumn with the eyes of a man to whom little of life remains. The generalised formulae of Expressionist imagery become sharper and more specific. They are more individually registered and with greater urgency. Joy and anxiety seem to become as tangible as the images that evoke them. (pp. 8-10)

The Radnóti of the late poems is basically a Christian Stoic. Survival was now of secondary importance: he had been called upon to bear witness in the grand trial that is history. In the last decade of his life, he seems to have been striving for what his contemporary, Attila József, called 'diamond consciousness': to focus all his spiritual and intellectual resources into one powerful beam of poetic energy. There is evidence in the poems of a growing preoccupation with the body/soul dichotomy, and speculation about the ways of the soul after death. The whole structure of his vision was now fundamentally Judaeo-Christian, with Socialism as the secular complement to his religion. When the Prophet Nahum, in '**The Eighth Eclogue**', invites Radnóti to join him in preaching 'the Kingdom about to be born', he is clearly referring to the Kingdom of God as promised by Jesus. Yet the phrase might also be interpreted historically and politically. Thus, the poem not only dramatises the continuity of the Jewish and Christian revelations; it also locates the roots of millenarian Socialism in the same tradition. Nor do the reconciliations stop there. The role of the prophet in the ancient world is equated with that of the poet in the new; and the language and teaching of the Bible are set in a poetic form whose origins are pagan and Classical. The poem thus brings together the different strands of that Humanist culture whose future had seemed so severely threatened. But the emphasis has changed. In the late 1930s, it had seemed inevitable that poets would 'disappear' as strangely as Lorca had—with maybe a few fragments of their work surviving for 'the curious who come after us'. In 1944, as Radnóti moved towards his death, to bear witness to the truth in verse had become much more than a gesture of defiance or self-defence; it had become a way of identifying himself with the values under threat and, thus, of sustaining them.

Commitment to such values involved commitment to the forms and language associated with them. By the mid-1930s, Radnóti's aim was no longer to provoke admiration or opposition; he wanted to express certain moods and to formulate certain ideas as clearly and exactly as possible. This involved a return to rhyme, regular stanzas and traditional metres. Although he remained spiritually attached to Romantic hopes and ideals, the forms through which he communicated were increasingly Classical. This retreat to classical metre and the adoption of a vocabulary not unfamiliar to readers of Virgil and Horace was more than a gesture towards a dying tradition. For a man writing at the very edge of survival, whose finest work flowered in conditions of intellectual darkness and moral anarchy, the expression of thought and feeling within the clear but flexible order of the classical hexameter came to seem a moral act. And it constituted a defensive bulwark against the uncertainty of the world.

His commitment to truth and form was—quite literally—ultimate. His '**Postcards**', more or less scribbled on the march west, are brief messages from Purgatory. They are unflinchingly realistic in their delineation of the horrors of war, yet never lose sight of the possibility of a better life. Against a background of villages on fire, he glimpses 'a tiny shepherdess' still going about her ordinary life and yet, in that setting, recalling to the reader's mind the rare fragility of a porcelain figurine. Then finally, a few days before the end, he anticipates the manner of his going with uncanny precision:

> Shot in the neck. 'This is how you will end,'
> I whispered to myself; 'keep lying still.
> Now, patience is flowering into death.'

(pp. 11-13)

Radnóti has often been referred to as a 'labour-camp' or 'anti-Fascist' poet, as if such phrases were sufficient to define his achievement. It is certainly relevant to an understanding of these poems to know that they tell the truth from experience about that most inconceivable phase of our history. What is still more relevant is the fact that their author was able to make great poems out of the experience, and that the courage their writing demanded was an essential feature of his creative impulse. The measure of Radnóti's achievement is that he remained articulate about the horrors of his time and transmuted them into poems of beauty and serenity. In the end, as his friend the poet István Vas has suggested, the moral and artistic perfection of Radnóti's work, the truth of it and its beauty, are quite inseparable. His poems, says Vas, are 'among the rare masterpieces that combine artistic and moral perfection . . . not just an exciting body of work, not just truly great poems, but also an example of human and artistic integrity that is as embarrassing and absurd as it is imperative'. (p. 13)

> *George Gömöri and Clive Wilmer, in an introduction to* Forced March: Selected Poems *by Miklós Radnóti, translated by Clive Wilmer and George Gömöri, Carcanet Press, 1979, pp. 7-13.*

MARIANNA D. BIRNBAUM (essay date 1979)

[*In the following excerpt, Birnbaum stresses that a concern with preparing for death is present throughout Radnóti's work and that his poems, for their richness of imagery and multiplicity of nuances, are the work of a truly great poet.*]

Miklós Radnóti, one of the most outstanding poets of twentieth-century Hungarian literature, lived merely thirty-five years but already his birth was darkened by tragedy. It cost the lives of his mother and twin brother as told in his only longer prose piece, **Gemini.** Grief and guilt feelings over the double tragedy accompanied Radnóti's entire creative life. In a poem written on his twenty-eighth birthday, he searches for his *raison d'être* by returning to the same event:

> An ugly, obstinate infant was I,
> my tiny, twin-bearing mother, your death!
> Whether my brother was stillborn or had
> five minutes of life, I do not know,
> but there, amidst blood, pain and screams
> I was lifted up toward the light, like
> a victorious little beast
> who has already shown its worth
> by leaving two dead bodies behind. . . .
>
> Little mother—you bleeding sacrifice,
> I have reached the age of men.
> The burning light is blinding me,
> send me a signal with your gentle hand
> that you know the truth, that it's all right,
> that there is a meaning to my life!
> [All translations by Marianna D. Birnbaum unless
> otherwise noted.]

His family's early disintegration is the topic of the **"Remembering Poem"** . . . in which he recalls the last minutes of his father.

Nothing would be easier than to show in his poetry that all through his life Radnóti was preparing himself for death. It was not the inevitability of passing that had occupied his mind, but the premonition that he would die a young man. This belief was, however not the decadent pose of the Symbolist of the

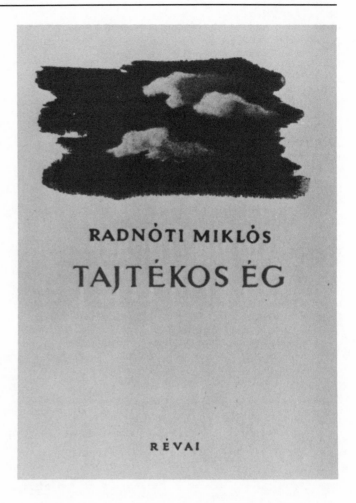

Cover of the first edition of Clouded Sky. *Courtesy of Ardis Publishers.*

fin-de-siècle, or of the post-Impressionists of the twenties, but the objective analysis of historical realities, their signals turning into a poetic scale of his life. Just as Kafka, Musil or Krleža presented us with a "preview" of alienation present in our world today, so did Radnóti progress in his poems on the road which ultimately came to an end at Abda.

Yet he was not a pessimistic poet; perhaps the most moving in his oeuvre is the pride and satisfaction with which he had collected and shaped into poems the rare minutes of happiness, those few moments of carefree joy that were granted him during his short life. (pp. 48-9)

His deep concerns for the fate of the world notwithstanding, Radnóti was primarily the poet of the individual, and thus his private experience gained equal significance in his poetry. In 1935 he married the only love of his life, Fanni, to whom some of the most beautiful love poems of modern Hungarian literature are addressed. Their texture is interlaced with ingenious metaphors whose most generous source is nature. Nature's images are simultaneously the medium in which Radnóti's social and moral messages are delivered. Colors, too, have a special role in his poetic world; their function, almost exclusively symbolic, is to separate feelings: the joyous from the sad, and ultimately to identify destruction and death. White and silver are Radnóti's colors for death, standing in significant opposition to gold, which consistently symbolizes life and happiness. Life's blessings are frequently portrayed in a 'golden synecdoche,' reducing them to Fanni's golden curls, or the sun's rays falling on her body. (pp. 50-1)

Consequently, as the years turn darker, silver and white become his predominant colors, forcing gold into the outer fringes of his imagination, to his occasional description of a cherished but unattainable humane future. In addition to the ones he most frequently used, Radnóti assigned symbolic meanings to practically every color of the spectrum. In his recapitulation of the world, nature is broached and its images transferred into various social and ethnic concepts, appearing in metaphorical metonymies such as "the trees rebel crimson flowers," or "two poppies demonstrate loyalty." Emblematic expressions showing the convertability of images and issues are frequent in his political poetry of the early thirties. Similarly, in a synaesthetic perception, people and objects live, suffer, fear and rejoice together. Their differences washed away by intricately interwoven adjectives and predicates, man and things together create a magic world of pananimism in which their convergence alone is sufficient to prove them isomorphs, as in the **"Naive Song to the Wife"**:

> As she enters, the door greets her with a clink
> and the flowerpots break into a pat,
> a sleepy patch wakes in her blonde hair
> like a startled sparrow, chirruping.
>
> The old electric cord utters a scream
> hulking its lazy body toward hers, and
> all is swirling, so fast, I cannot write it down.
> She just arrived, absent the entire day,
> a tall cornflower in her hand;
> with that she'll drive my death away.
>
> (pp. 51-2)

From 1938 on Radnóti's preparation for death intensifies:

> ... Among my memories I lie prostrated,
> a pupil, maturing speedily for death ...

He is, however, less afraid of biological death than of having to stop working. The fear that he would not be able to complete his poetic work, that he would die and be judged by a "torso" rather than the full oeuvre, caused him the greatest pain. Writing his own 'epitaph,' he anxiously asks "... but tell me, will what I've written, survive? ..." The poems focusing on death become more and more numerous, there are only a few pieces in which neither the word nor its symbolic colors appear. He turns to a new genre, the eclogue (a deliberate misnomer), which achieves its greatest evocative power by the sharp conflict between its form and its content. Radnóti soon abandons the bucolic voice and the traditional dialogue of shepherds: the streaming, pounding message demands a change in structure. His defiant rejection of form and rhyme of the earlier years is now replaced by the lucid language and style of neoclassicism. The rebellion of the Modernists had been directed against an overorganized universe, and in the face of a world gone mad, in Radnóti's poetry purified form, tightly composed lines have become the substitute for lost reason. His hexameters do not reach back to the Latin models. He turns to the Hungarian poets of the 18th and 19th centuries instead, to the verse of Dániel Berzsenyi and János Arany. Choosing them at that new juncture of his life, Radnóti sought out the only cultural community in which he could still feel at home.

Amazingly, some of his last are patriotic poems, although of a special kind. Of these the best example is, **"I Cannot Know,"** in which he, the potential victim, identifies himself with his land, its nature, its history and its present guilt as well. ... His is not a naive patriotism: Radnóti does not close his eyes to reality, and he is filled with revulsion about the world surrounding him. ... And all along he was sharply aware of his own, unavoidable fall:

> Inside myself I live through everything that is still to
>   come.
> I don't look back. I know, not even memory, no
> magic will save me—there's evil in the sky.
> Friend, if you see me, shrug your shoulders and turn
>   away.
> Where the angel with the sword stood before,
> now, maybe no one's there.
>   (Trans. by S. Polgar, S. Berg and S. J. Marks)
>   (pp. 53-4)

Radnóti never wrote his "Ars poetica," but it is easy to gather from his poems that his work was his reason for living, "... For I am worth no more than the value of the word / in my poem ...," he confessed to his wife in the **"Hesitant Ode,"** in which he also wrote:

> ... And I still can't tell of the full extent
> of what it means to me, while I'm working
> to feel your protective gaze over my hand.

In his persistent concern with every detail of his poems, in his constant striving for the best, the most subtle expression of his true thoughts, Radnóti put his entire intellectual and moral responsibility into every word he left behind.

Even when facing immediate death, the paramount, gnawing question on his mind was not how to save himself but how to assure that his poems in the small notebook would not perish with him.

His poems survived and the following generations have been reading them ever since. They know them by heart, they teach them in the high schools and universities of Hungary. Scholars have been analyzing his verse and rediscovering each piece with each new reading. There is still a hitherto unnoticed fine metaphor, a particularly successful harmony between sound and meaning that may surface with another close reading of the text. Additional ties between his work and that of his contemporaries are discovered by scrutinizing his vocabulary and the micropoetic components of his language. Like all great poets he is as inexhaustible for the interested reader as he is for the scholar. He perished young but he achieved what he had desired most—he has become an inalienable part of Hungarian literature. And as the years pass, he is more and more recognized on a European scale as a significant poetic witness to our time, ranking with the late Paul Celan and with the Polish poet, Zbigniew Herbert. (pp. 55-6)

Marianna D. Birnbaum, "In Memoriam: Miklós Radnóti (1909-1944)," in The Canadian-American Review of Hungarian Studies, *Vol. VI, No. 1, Spring, 1979, pp. 47-57.*

DICK DAVIS (essay date 1980)

[*In the following excerpt from a review of* Forced March, *Davis praises Radnóti's affirmation of traditional humane values, as well as the poet's adherence to classical prosody amidst the chaos of war.*]

Miklós Radnóti was executed, after serving four years in forced labour battalions, in 1944. The poems he wrote during and shortly before this period . . . are perhaps the finest witness that has come down to us of the devastation that then engulfed Europe. As a Hungarian he was the inheritor of a major poetic tradition (Miklós Vajda has pointed out that in countries like Britain literary energy is diffused in many forms, in Hungary it is concentrated almost entirely in poetry) and in a position to see at first hand what Nazi government meant: as a Jew (he became a Catholic during the war) he was not only a natural victim, but also the inheritor of another tradition—that of the Old Testament prophets—which proved a lasting influence on his poetry.

His themes are what we would expect; the immensity of destruction, the fragility of human life and of humane values caught up in the maelstrom, the imminence of death. (p. 126)

[Yet a] clinging to the known and human, the location of sustaining values in the traditional and private realms of agriculture and love (whereas the massive destruction he witnessed is seen as monstrous and inhuman—supernatural like the angel or with the dehumanized and simplifying perspective of the bomber-pilot) is at the centre of Radnóti's poetry: it is, to be awkwardly blunt, his 'message'. In the midst of the violation of humane values he clung to those values the more passionately—he refused to be brutalized.

Perhaps the most vivid evidence of this is, as his translators point out in their introduction [see excerpt dated 1978], his use of traditional form. The poems that deal with the harshest realities of the war are a series of **'Eclogues'** and the implicit evocation of pastoral peace and Virgilian order is not *merely* ironic—it is the assertion of civilized values, the values that European literature has striven to embody, against barbarism.

The American critic Yvor Winters referred to the idea that poetry must be chaotic in order to represent or deal with chaos as 'the fallacy of imitative form'. Since the Second World War an allied theory has gained currency that we might call the 'fallacy of brutal form'. The idea implies that our literary reactions to violence must be violent; that only a numbed and fractured syntax, a disordered and savage language and a disregard for metre will adequately express our reaction to the horrors perpetrated in this century. Further: the use of syntax that discriminates rather than merely states, of a language that attempts to understand rather than bludgeon the reader with emotion, is seen as either inauthentic ('artificial') or as a failure of sympathy with suffering—a withdrawal to aestheticism. Radnóti, who assuredly suffered far more than any of those who propound such theories, is proof that this is simply not so. For Radnóti the reaction to horrific violence was to discriminate more, not less; it was a more vigorous assertion of those values he saw threatened. His witness is like that of the Polish Franciscan Maximilian Kölbe who died in Auschwitz in another man's place: as their surroundings became progressively more brutal so they held the more tenaciously to those humane values that their disciplines—of poet and priest—demanded of them.

If form is a bastion against chaos, the sign of a mind that resists rather than embraces disintegration, it can be a bastion offered in humble understanding (and not merely the aesthete's retreat): writing of men sustained through nightmare by their memories of normality, Radnóti calls such memories:

Islands and caves to them inside this hostile order

and it is such 'islands and caves', such places of refuge against insanity, that the poems propose and are. And though aware of death's omnipresence he clings vigorously, with stubborn despairing persistence, to life. . . . (pp. 127-28)

The story of those poems found a year later in the dead man's pocket is like a tragic image of Radnóti's own life—a descent into a common grave in which, miraculously, sanity and understanding were preserved. (p. 128)

> *Dick Davis, ''Islands and Caves,'' in* London Magazine, *Vol. 20, Nos. 1 & 2, April & May, 1980, pp. 126-28.*

EMERY GEORGE (essay date 1980)

[*George is the translator of* Miklós Radnóti: The Complete Poetry. *In the following excerpt from the introduction to that edition, George traces Radnóti's development, examining the poet's artistic influences, fusion of idyllic and realistic themes, and mature poetic conception in the* Bor Notebook—*a collection George esteems above the rest of Radnóti's canon.*]

Radnóti came into his inheritance in the midst of war; he spoke, and spoke his best, when writers so often opt for silence. He told of beauty and radiance, and of the joy of being alive—and of his not expecting to live for long. He may be said to have been a poet in the holocaust rather than of it. In his introductory essay to the facsimile edition of the *Bori notesz (Bor Notebook)*, the small Lager copybook into which Radnóti wrote his last poems, Gyula Ortutay makes a point in observing that in these documents the formal and ethical moments present so inseparable a unity that saying so will never take second place to analyzing the poems themselves. In attempts to understand the phenomenon of Miklós Radnóti the anthropologist and the literary critic must work side by side.

One aspect of the portrait that remains interesting to the student of Radnóti and of his achievement is the complex setting of the poet's tragedy and triumph. The details of the tragedy are by now well documented; but Radnóti's generation, the generation of Auden and Spender, of Sartre and Simone Weil (whose dates, 1909-1943, could hardly be much nearer Radnóti's own), was also a fortunate one. During the decade-and-one-half that Radnóti was given, the years beween 1928 and 1944, Europe was in the wake of the great complex of modernisms pioneered by contemporaries of the poet's parents. Radnóti embraced pre-World War I modernism and outgrew it; it has been said that he adopted and surpassed every literary movement introduced on the Hungarian scene by such leading poets of the time as Endre Ady (1877-1919), Lajos Kassák (1887-1967), Milán Füst (1888-1967), and the first generation of the writers clustered about the influential periodical *Nyugat* (West), founded in 1908. What seems amazing about Radnóti's particular mode of adoption and reformulation of the -isms is that the final, mature product reflects both versatility and universality. The definitive achievement blends styles, voices, forms; it retains the company of past and present, eschewing fad alone. It is no accident that the most consciously postmodernist Radnóti, who grapples with the toughest questions of ''openness'' and ''freedom'' in verse, also returns to the prosodic discipline of the ancients. Not incidentally to the question of the poet's need for a spiritual father, the mature Radnóti lets himself be guided by Vergil in a sense reminiscent of that in which Vergil imparts guidance to Dante. Of course we do not forget that Radnóti also has another literary ''father,'' one much nearer his time and condition; and we recall that in 1909, the year Radnóti was born, Guillaume Apollinaire finally saw published, in the *Mercure de France,* his poem "La Chanson du Mal-Aimé," the work that established his reputation. (pp. 13-14)

Miklós Radnóti is a classic, meaning one of the standard authors and one of the nation's great dead, but an objective view of his exemplary magnitude must involve a disinterested if painful separation of the suffering per se from what remains. It is the latter from which future art profits. (p. 14)

In [*Pogány köszöntő (Pagan Salute)*] the poet's deepest commitment is to the countryside: to simplicity and naturalness, healthy eroticism, and self-confidence that is never unmixed with shades of doubt and sorrow. (p. 27)

The five cycles of *Pagan Salute—Pagan Salute, Psalms of Rapture, Cry of Seagulls, Variations on Sadness, Days of Piety—* concentrate on love and on man's universal joy in a nature which he perceives as pure gift. Yet subjectivity is ever-present; the poems are a series of partial self-portraits. *Psalms of Rapture* celebrates hiding, finding, touching: "you see / my life's spirit is blown tight / on autumn bushes' swelling / berryclusters; I feel / burdens of ripe grainstalks"; there is vividly felt "flailing / embrace of yellow thrushes on a / ramifying bough of learned kisses." In this there is already a hint of the pious-cum-erotic which informs [*Újmódi pásztorok éneke (Song of Modern Shepherds)*]. In "psalm" 4 we hear tell of "abandoned skies," from where "without embrace our wondrously / beautiful heavenchild was conceived / into laps of deciduous leafy woods"; it is a reformulation of the Annunciation, reabsorption of myth into nature and primal feeling. The poet's intense preoccupation with himself in this opening collection is continued in the third cycle, *Cry of Seagulls.* Here we realize how formulaic even so beautiful a turn as "the translucent, clear dawn of sorrow" was ("psalm" 8). In the lines that open the title poem there is an almost Rilkean note of despair, reminding us of the opener of the first *Duino Elegy:* "If I cry out with a terrible cry of seagulls / no one will hear it."

If cheer and sadness set the tone of the opening of *Pagan Salute,* a mixture of piety and humor define the later cycle, *Variations on Sadness.* The poem "Peacefulness" is a vivid miniature in modern pictorial art; "Meditation" on musical experience (Beethoven, Schubert) and the contemplation of pure natural light ("O Light, Resplendence, Sun-Eyed Morning!") follow. These latter two poems are members of a pair; in both, art or aesthetic feeling serves the impulse to prayer (despite the fact that they belong to two different cycles). In the closing cycle, *Days of Piety,* "Evening: Woman, Child on Her Back" and "Advent: Late Customer" constitute yet another pair. Both depict people carrying burdens, whether, as in the former, the precious burden of the child or, as in the latter, the somewhat amusing burden of the Christmas tree. Both poems bespeak kindness, and end on "sounding" and "singing." We know for whom the mother fears, and the poet carries about inside him her "smiling heart." He also tries to understand the "poor guy," caught singing as he trudges home: "(Possibly, he's still a child, and fears for the / hark the herald)." But soon both humor and grotesquery vanish in the closing "Quiet Lines, Head Bowed," that poignant reminder of who the poet is, where he comes from, and what it will remain his task to sing. For now his only truly worthy subject remains the transition between death and life, between the abiding memory of dead parents and a new hope that rises as the poet and his beloved "start, we two, / toward the sunlight."

Nowhere do religious sensibility and disbelief, commitment and freedom, mix more convincingly in the young Radnóti's work than in his second collection, *Song of Modern Shepherds.* A healthy and talented young man awakens both to the beauty of nature and to the legitimate demands of his own maturing sexuality. Sex is not "sin," and "taste" does not require that reference to it be either veiled or avoided. Yet nowhere, in this second offering, is there prurience, any more than there is prudishness.... In Radnóti eroticism and nature are and remain an occasion for unabashed and untainted joy. Consider only "A Little Duck Bathes," based on an image of a lovably grotesque gift of nature, the more delightful for all the grotesquery of the transformation that the old folk song itself undergoes. The moment of eros in *Song of Modern Shepherds,* no less than the deep, happily married love depicted in the mature "Fanni" poetry is, in fact, one of the levels in Radnóti's work that most successfully defy and deny the tragic moment.

Next to the palpable similarities between the first two collections—free verse at times not free from self-conscious mannerisms, expressionistic intensity of imagery, the concern with religion and with love—there is one very important difference. And that is that *Song of Modern Shepherds* begins to be concerned with others. The first important recording of the lives of people in their natural settings is "Tápé, Old Evening"; in the subsequent cycle, *Elegies and Laments,* five major poems: "Elegy on the Death of a Hobo," "Dawn Elegy," "Elegy, or Icon, Nailless," "My Dear One Is Ill," and "Italian Painter" deliver on the promise, made in the first-named piece, that the poet will expand his vision of humanity. To be sure Radnóti seems attracted to the life of the derelict as a symbol for the flouting of convention; in actuality both convention and symbol provide support to the poet's "modern, pastoral, and rebellious" *ars poetica.* Already in the short "Spring Poem" "the trees rebel crimson flowers / at night, and cheerful hoboes embrace / now under bushes with cracking branches." ... Man returns to nature, "according to law," as Radnóti was to say much later, on the occasion of the death of the poet and novelist Dezső Kosztolányi ("Song about Death"); this insight is to be repeated in a number of configurations and variations throughout the oeuvre. (pp. 27-9)

As were *Pagan Salute* and *Song of Modern Shepherds,* [*Lábadozó szél (Convalescent Wind)*] and [*Újhold (New Moon)*] are again, as it were, twins. They are books of continuation and deepening, but also of renewal. Most striking in *Convalescent Wind*—besides the news-item poetry of the cycle *Male Diary* . . .—is the allegorization of nature; more, that this allegorizing takes place before any attempt is made to endow nature with anthropomorphic qualities. Attempts to identify natural with human phenomena are made already in "Elegy on the Death of a Hobo" where, in the closing stanza, the dead hobo hugs the poet in the form of a tree. But in the third book something new happens—the poet is at work on an imagery that enables him to put up his symbolic fight against the system without risking a repetition of the legal row from which he is candidly showing himself as recovering. There is quick retrenchment—again the persona is provoking a probably not forever-patient gendarmerie, censor's office, law court: "my words / march, in the distance, raising / dust among cockfeathers!" and he continues, invoking nature (untitled invocation to *Male Diary*):

> Perhaps a storm is coming: with surfacing fish
> the tousled water smooths out;
> silence has spread its legs
> over the road, and with rowdy
> noises it readies for a scuffle!

Scuffle, wrestling; breeze, wind; storm, knife; the imagery of fighting and of nature's participation in the fight become important. (p. 30)

The feeling that poetry may justifiably depict struggle, or sorrow over the lack of opportunity for it, haunts especially the next two cycles in *Convalescent Wind: Love Lament* and *Quince*. In these two cycles, which immediately precede the great ballad, **"Song of the Black Man Who Went to Town,"** we hear repeatedly that "a tufted / cloud now sits above the trees"; "get ready . . . / for the fight: for the wind is coming!'"; "'I'll / go shine, like the sun, off to India, where / on white streets, in the mornings, rebellion runs." . . . (p. 31)

If there is a big early break in Radnóti's poetry it comes, strangely enough, not between his second and third collections, but between the third and fourth. After the predictably scant attention that the confiscated second collection had received (only five reviews of it had appeared), Miklós decided to rescue from it ten poems, over to the new volume. Little wonder that in his 1933 review of *Convalescent Wind* in *Nyugat* . . . the conservative Babits saw fit to write: "In this poetry *Kraftausdrücke* ["vulgarities"] substitute for strength, slovenliness for spontaneity, peasant birth for the sense of vocation, and daredeviltry for talent." . . . No matter how angry Radnóti was at first, he had to admit that Babits had a point. . . . How much the "daredevil" who wrote *Convalescent Wind* benefited from Babits's needling we may see in a perceptible maturation of vision and diction in his fourth collection, *New Moon*. Outwardly there are both important differences and similarities. Starting with *New Moon* the poems are no longer grouped in cycles; like its immediate predecessor the new book does, however, open and close on strong framing statements. The continuing dialectic of self and other determines an artistic vision which from this point on undergoes deepening rather than radical change.

It is of the greatest significance that, as did *Convalescent Wind*, *New Moon* too opens on a major statement on the poet's self and—without the faintest apology—on his maleness. It is no accident that [biographer Dezső] Baróti devotes to **"Like a Bull"** an analysis of seventeen pages . . . , something he does not do for any other work. The poem is an icon of the monolith that Radnóti himself is, a poem at work with the central image of a strong, quiet animal who senses both his own strength and the danger in which he finds himself. (pp. 31-2)

In *New Moon* we witness the beginning of a rich love poetry: **"Accounting," "Poppy," "Evening in the Garden," "October, Afternoon,"** and the two closing paeans, **"Love Poem on Istenhegy"** and **"Love Poem in the Forest."** (p. 32)

As *Convalescent Wind* ended on the hymn about awakening and rebelling tribal peoples, so *New Moon* closes on that unmistakable manifesto poem, a personal declaration of mission, **"Into a Contemporary's Passport."** (p. 33)

It is not known exactly when Radnóti completed his first translation of a poem, but it may well have happened before the Szeged years. We know that by 1936 he had done translations of such French contemporaries as Cocteau, Duhamel, Jacob, and Larbaud, as well as of Transylvanian German poets. From then until the appearance of *In Orpheus' Footsteps* (1943) we see Radnóti translating prodigiously from Greek and Latin authors, and from almost all the important traditions of three major European languages: English, French, and German. By whom, among translated old masters, Radnóti was influenced the strongest, the overt indications in his own rapidly devel-

oping craft do not always reveal. Conversely, demonstrable influence often goes beyond the poets we see translated in the 1979 edition of his works. (p. 34)

How do we know that Radnóti's "translation work builds itself organically into his oeuvre?" . . . First, there are the visible signs, preeminent among them prosody. Even outside the "Eclogues" a number of poems in strict classical meters pay their homage to authors whom Radnóti translated: **"In a Restless Hour"** to Horace, **"End-of-October Hexameters"** to Tibullus (and, probably, to Goethe), **"From the Flowers of Disgust"** and **"To a Poetaster"** to Martial. Nor need there be doubt when Radnóti, in a poem that opens on a line from a sonnet by Ronsard, speaks of mortality, and then does so in evocative Alexandrines. A very considerable body of poems in this latter meter is known by Radnóti, slightly over the number of those he wrote in hexameters; some of the most moving poems in [*Tajtékos ég (Sky with Clouds)*] also show the logical and highly effective combination of Alexandrines with the *Nibelungenlied* line (e.g. **"As, Imperceptibly,"** or **"Second Eclogue"**). The love of stylistic blend and mystification also invites the poet to alternate Nibelungen lines with lines of looser structure (**"Flames Flicker . . ."**); and Pléïade sensibility may be expressed also in the form of a modified Shakespearean sonnet (**"O Peace of Ancient Prisons"**). Finally, in **"Á la recherche . . ."** we have a combination of homages and allusions that includes Vergil (meter), Proust (title, background), and Apollinaire (subject and general situation). In all, Radnóti is interested in the particular, complex form that his subject demands. The result, especially in *Sky with Clouds,* is an astonishing variety in which almost all the traditions with which Radnóti was acquainted, whether translated from or not, are touched upon. (pp. 34-5)

In the fall of 1938 Radnóti was approached for contributions to two new publications involved in the then burgeoning revival of classical antiquity. . . . Radnóti responded by translating Tibullus' "Detestatio belli" (*Elegies* 1.10) for the magazine and Vergil's *Ninth Eclogue* for the anthology. Thus was born, in Radnóti, the idea of writing a series of "Eclogues," in response to Vergil's vision of the poet's threatened situation in a time of war and civil turbulence. It is as if Radnóti, who by 1938 had created a great body of verse imitating his own threatened condition and state of fear and sorrow, had decided that a series of major poetic statements in the Vergilian tradition was the fulfillment of his desire to make a truly strong, resistant poetry. . . .

It has seemed reasonable to view the **"Eclogue"** opus from the vantage point of Radnóti's lifelong interest in the bucolic. I would here like to suggest that the "Eclogues" may also have been Radnóti's answer to his need for the inter-generic, most specifically for the dramatic. If this seems too strong a claim to make for so pure a poet, then we need but reflect that a poet who wrote his dissertation on the novel and whose last activity as a civilian was the translation of a play, may well have entertained notions of artistic purity that did not include generic self-limitation. Indeed we know that, as did Delmore Schwartz not much later, Radnóti wrote stories as well as poems, and that scenes from Ben Jonson and Shakespeare figure among his translations. No matter how clearly the "Eclogues" are indebted to Vergil, they may profitably be seen also as Radnóti's opportunity to do justice to yet another master of his mature years, La Fontaine. (p. 37)

As did La Fontaine for the *Fables,* so Radnóti saw to it that the "Eclogues" incorporate subtle formal changes and twists

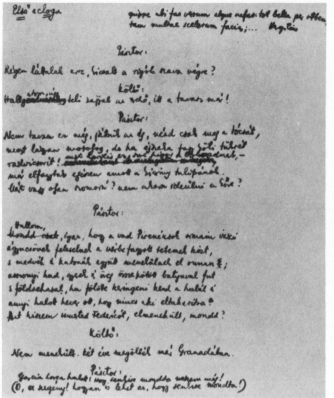

Holograph copy of the first edition of Radnóti's "First Eclogue." Courtesy of Ardis Publishers.

to heighten dramatic effect. . . . As regards external form, the dual requirements of classical prosody and dialogue, the **"First"** and **"Eighth"** are decidedly the most canonically Vergilian in the series; after them come the dramatically broken, and to that extent already stylized, **"Third"** and **"Fifth."** These latter are monodramas despite themselves, yet the invitation implied in each is accepted by the "absent" counterpart in the end—the poems achieve closure. Most tense dramatically, and most truly theatrical, is undoubtedly **"Second Eclogue,"** where we experience a genuine change in tone, pace, and overall emotional impact from first to last. Here too is where the poet performs his most decidedly sensitive, La Fontaine-like, stylistic légerdemain. . . . One last feature that may remain inconspicuous is the almost complete surrender, in the second half of **"Fourth Eclogue,"** of the dialogue form. . . . Despite this the freshness, the brightness of the dramatic closure are no more distant in this **"Eclogue"** than they are in **"Second,"** where too a low number of exchanges articulate the text.

Yet what assigns the **"Eclogues"** their near-central position in Radnóti's oeuvre, what makes them "a fitting memorial to a good and gentle man," [see the excerpt by B. S. Adams dated 1965] is their keen sense of mission, the force with which they define the poet's vocation. . . . Undoubtedly the most selfless, and thus worthiest, piece is the majestic keystone to the series, the **"Eighth Eclogue."** Here the poet's categorical self-imperatives, aesthetic, moral, philosophical, political, are transmuted into the highest kind of poetry known to the classical tradition: that of the *vates,* of prophecy.

If ever there was art that moves beyond the naturalistically faithful documentation of life that it appears to be providing, it is the poems of the *Bor Notebook.* To be sure we have no

reason not to accept at face value some of the conditions the poems depict, or—nearly so—some of the statements they represent a man as making. That the poet misses Fanni and that he hopes to make superhuman attempts to return to her (**"Seventh Eclogue," "Letter to My Wife," "Forced March"**), that in the solitude of his brutish exile he is consoled by his thoughts (**"Letter to My Wife," "Eighth Eclogue"**), that in the midst of his own predicament he is thinking of the many who have already met their fates in one form or another (**"À la recherche . . ."**), even the plain medical fact that on the tortuous march the men are suffering from kidney disease (**"Picture Postcards,"** no. 3)—all this is present and available in these seven last texts. What may still need our attention is secrets of the poems not revealed by the images alone. There are in particular four less-explored aspects of this poetry deserving of comment.

First, Radnóti's ambition that he end his life's work worthily is fulfilled in his completing the cycle of **"Eclogues."** Since **"Seventh"** and **"Eighth"** are two of the best pieces in this layer of the total oeuvre, it is significant that **"Eclogues"** and the Bor corpus are—to borrow a figure from **"Second Eclogue"**—siamese twins. The poet's question whether there is anyone left back home to appreciate the hexameter line (**"Seventh"**) recalls questions concerning the survival of the poetry itself (as in **"Hesitant Ode," "In a Restless Hour," "Third Eclogue," "Not Memory, Nor Magic"**). Everywhere we hear it asserted that the poet will not survive but that the work will, and that it is thus the poet's duty to go on working for as long as he possibly can. Vergil is, so to speak, behind barbed wire; the idyll is threatened beyond belief but not yet demolished.

Second, the Bor works bear some strong ties to earlier poetry that does not look like conventional poetry at all. I am thinking of imitations of postcards, letters, diary entries, newspaper reportage, expansions of the parameter of poetic expression that parallel concrete and three-dimensional poetic happenings in our time. The **"Razglednici"** do not merely continue the "postcard" poetry of the cubists, or of Radnóti himself. With **"Cartes Postales"** we never get a sense that they could not also be describing that other "poem," the photograph on the reverse side of an actual card. No such assurance is available for **"Razglednici."** I doubt whether Lager cards themselves amounted to *razglednici.* What would they have illustrated? At the same time the last **"Picture Postcards"** imply that the full blank side of the Lager card is being left empty; each of the four thumbnail poems can be accommodated on the left-hand half of the address side. Crammed full of images as Radnóti's poems usually are, the tiny poem-snapshots thus double for both sides of the card; they suggest a three-dimensional poetry, and an impossible one, topologically speaking! To polish off the neo-surrealist grotesquery, Radnóti himself wrote his last poem not directly into his square-ruled notebook but on the reverse side of an X-ray photograph—of a hand.

The third salient aspect of the Bor canon is its creation of a new mythology. We may understand this to be either a new "kingdom of the spirit" (as in **"Eighth Eclogue"**), or one of withdrawal, of life among "savage men," where "sobriety's $2x2$" is as comforting to the poet as philosophy is to imprisoned Boethius. . . . It has been said that what Radnóti ultimately owed even to such a symbolist as Ady is the invention of a mythology, the combined senses of revolt and apocalypse, the capacity to prophesy that a new order will come.

The fourth, and here final, aspect of the Bor poetry is its tones and skill, in a hardness and diamond-like perfection never before seen or heard in Radnóti's work. It has been said that those who wrote in the camps often did so in strict form, some in classical meters, as if tradition were a bulwark to which the psyche could cling. If this helps identify Radnóti's work as holocaust poetry, then its belonging to that body of twentieth-century writing only redounds to its credit. Ortutay is right: the tones are almost other-worldly; there is not one false note, not one word or syllable that could have been placed any other way. Stylistics could no doubt tell us a lot here. Let it suffice in the present connection to say that the poet was taken away from all that he loved—and found treasures. He came to an inner realm, of a *dolce stil nuovo* of his very own, to a competence and a purity he had never had the privilege of bringing forth before. (pp. 38-40)

> *Emery George, in an introduction to* Miklós Radnóti: The Complete Poetry *by Miklós Radnóti, edited and translated by Emery George, Ardis, 1980, pp. 13-46.*

JASCHA KESSLER   (broadcast date 1982)

[*In the following excerpt from a radio lecture, Kessler praises the artistic and human achievement represented by Radnóti's poems.*]

Radnoti, having been killed in his prime, is a poet's martyr, and also the most famous, *the* emblematic Hungarian poet of the Forties. . . . Radnóti's life and work symbolizes so very much of that country's tortured, and tortuous, history since 1918, that it would take hours to begin to introduce a notion of its complexity and importance. But, for Radnoti, obsessed during his late 20's and early 30's by death, which was part of his own peculiar psychological biography, and haunted by a fatalism that foresaw the coming horrors of European total war, and driven by his confidence in his own poetic gift and powers, what might have evoked mere despair in most others proved, perhaps paradoxically, to be the very source of his courage and creativity. (pp. 1-2)

Among many of the impressive poems during the war years from 1939 on, there remain to us 7 eclogues, modelled on the Virgilian pastoral poems, and Radnóti's *Eclogues* are written in classical "bound forms," as though the poet wanted to try to contain chaos and horror in the ancient and enduring vessels of poetic forms that symbolize detachment and calmness, as though saying that even the whirlwind has a form to the eye of the poet. One of Radnóti's greatest poems, the **"Seventh Eclogue,"** . . . is addressed to his [wife] Fanni. It almost seems to be that one lyric poem that all poets secretly hope to achieve, the poem that contains their own essence: their life, their time and their art, all fused, even alloyed, into one Monument. (pp. 3-4)

There are about 290 pages of poems in this first complete edition in English of Radnoti's work [Emery George's translation, *Miklos Radnóti: The Complete Poetry*], and although I have spoken of this brilliant poet in terms of his tragic ending, it should be said that there are many poems, from before 1939, that are full of high spirits, the clear vision of youth and love. I think Radnoti's love poems to his Fanni are fine pieces, sensual and passionate; they are not so much romantic as attempts to voice desire and its fulfillment in a sort of natural, that is "pagan" mode, as if Radnoti thought he could relive and reevoke the ways of loving of Sappho or Catullus, for example. And, there are many poems that are simply gorgeous, often metaphysically witty and original descriptions of Hungarian landscapes and countryside at all seasons, deeply and accurately engraved by this poet's eye during the years of his exuberant youth. . . . Radnoti had lived in Paris, and he knew what he was taking from modern poetry: a directness and simplicity of imagery, and a freedom of metaphor, complete metaphor though based on intimate and unpretentious speech. (p. 5)

It would not be an exaggeration to say of Miklos Radnoti that he is one of those poets who has come to be ranked among the very best of the 20th Century. The pity of it is that he lost his life so very early. The outlines of a rich poetic life were laid down early, and his technical skills were achieved in time for a complex personality to be expressed in terms of the brutality and warfare and horror of his times, so that he has left a record of his consciousness and of his judgment on our world, a record that it is most important for us all to study, if we hope to know what we are, and to know what is possible to achieve for ourselves. [*The Complete Poetry*] offers us such a record. . . . I would say that it's a book that should be known by poets and readers of poetry everywhere. (p. 6)

> *Jascha Kessler, "Miklos Radnoti: 'The Complete Poetry',*" *in a radio broadcast on KUSC-FM—Los Angeles, CA, August 11, 1982.*

ADDITIONAL BIBLIOGRAPHY

Adams, B. S. "The Eclogues of Miklós Radnóti." *The Slavonic and East European Review* 43, No. 101 (June 1965): 390-99.
 Places Radnóti's eclogues at the core of his oeuvre for their forceful documentation of the poet's nascent struggle to maintain hope while confronted with overwhelming adversity.

Berg, Stephen. "On Finding and Translating Radnóti Together." *Delos*, No. 1 (1968): 145-46.
 A brief discussion on translating Radnóti's works. Berg, one of three translators of *Clouded Sky*, labels Radnóti's vivid evocation of labor camp life a "calm innocent heroism of speech."

Gitlin, Todd. "Radnóti: Returning to Himself." *The Nation* 216, No. 22 (22 May 1973): 695-98.
 Discusses Radnóti's self-conscious yet objective stance in his poetry. Gitlin considers the poems in *Clouded Sky* "deceptively simple, since they deal with elemental emotions, but they are rarely prosy, rarely flat, and hardly ever obscure. The confessions, the forlorn curses flung at an unheeding nation, could so easily be flattened into bleats, yet they are rich and original."

Gömöri, George. Review of *Miklós Radnóti: The Complete Poetry*, by Miklós Radnóti. *World Literature Today* 55, No. 4 (Autumn 1981): 706.
 Notes the "uneven, stylistically inconsistent" nature of much of Radnóti's early verse and questions the need for the translation of Radnóti's complete poems into English.

Middleton, David. "Beyond the Merely Modern: New Poetry from Britain." *The Southern Review* 17, No. 1 (January 1981): 214-24.*
 Reviews the translation *Forced March*. Middleton states: "More than a mere 'war poet,' Radnóti, in his life and in the poems that came from that life, reminds us of the wider significance of poetry as a vehicle for transmitting civil values."

Sanders, Ivan. "Training for the Forced March." *Commonweal* CIX, No. 18 (22 October 1982): 271-72.
 Contends that Radnóti's fusion of Judeo-Christian morality and classical aesthetics is what provides his poetry with timelessness and universal meaning.

(Alphonsus Joseph-Mary Augustus) Montague Summers

1880-1948

(Born Augustus Montague Summers) English historian, editor, essayist, critic, biographer, short story writer, and poet.

Summers is regarded as a leading authority in two specialized and disparate fields: the Restoration theater and the supernatural. He was long held to be the foremost expert of his era on late seventeenth-century drama and stagecraft, and his histories *The Restoration Theatre* and *The Playhouse of Pepys* are considered important early texts in this area of study. Summers's second literary reputation is based on his work as a scholar of the occult and supernatural. His approach to this topic—in such works as *The History of Witchcraft and Demonology, The Vampire: His Kith and Kin,* and *The Werewolf*—is marked by a strict religious orthodoxy and by his sincere conviction that these matters constitute a very real threat to the unwary.

Summers was the youngest of seven children born into a financially secure family. His father, a businessman and bank director who had known Anthony Trollope, constantly urged Trollope's novels upon Summers when the bookish youngster complained that he had exhausted his family's library. Rites of passage were often marked for Summers by his father's permitting him access to the locked bookcases that held the works of such paternally proscribed authors as Henry Fielding, always with the caveat that they be kept from his sisters. In his autobiography *The Galanty Show,* Summers recalled the times spent in this library as among the happiest of his life. His favorite boyhood amusement, however, was a toy stage, or "miniature theatre," with which he spent hours reenacting abridged versions of seventeenth-century dramas. Frail and sedentary, Summers avoided athletic competition both at the private academy that he attended and later at Clifton College. He is said to have escaped his classmates' derision because of an impudent willingness to talk back to his schoolmasters. In 1899 Summers entered Oxford as an honors student in the school of theology. He went from Oxford to Lichfield Theological College as a candidate for holy orders, taking his Bachelor of Arts degree in 1905 and his Masters degree a year later. In 1908 he was ordained as a deacon and appointed curate of a small Bristol parish. He left this post after he and another deacon were prosecuted on charges of pederasty. While the other man was found guilty, Summers was acquitted. In 1909 Summers converted to Roman Catholicism. He studied for the priesthood while concurrently holding various teaching jobs, working as a teacher intermittently from 1911 until 1926. He may have eventually received holy orders and become a priest, possibly in Italy. No proof of this exists, however, and even his biographer, Brocard Sewell, admits uncertainty as to Summers's ecclesiastical standing. Nevertheless, after 1913, and until his death, Summers referred to himself as a priest and habitually wore full clerical vestments.

Summers spent years studying every aspect of Restoration-period theater. His first work as an editor was a comprehensive edition of Aphra Behn's writings, comprising the first modern collection of the works of this seventeenth-century female novelist, dramatist, and poet. He also edited the complete works of the seventeenth-century dramatists William Congreve, William Wycherley, Thomas Otway, Thomas Shadwell, and John

Dryden. As one of the founders of The Phoenix theater society, a group devoted to his maxim that "the real test of the worth of dramatic literature is performance in the theater," Summers was closely involved with the production of little-known and rarely performed works by Restoration dramatists. In 1924, for instance, The Phoenix presented the first public performance of Wycherly's *The Country-Wife* since 1748. Summers greatly enjoyed the theater work and broke with the group only after repeated difficulties with wealthy patrons who were willing to underwrite productions only in exchange for leading roles. His devotion to late seventeenth-century drama culminated in two complementary volumes of Restoration stage history. The first, *The Restoration Theatre,* was widely praised as an informed and comprehensive background to theater production in the latter half of the seventeenth century. In this work Summers detailed the practical workings of the theaters of the era, from the first advertisements of a new play through the handling of the audiences as well as the mechanics of actual play production. In his second volume of theater history, *The Playhouse of Pepys,* Summers examined the lives and careers of many Restoration dramatists. To the frequent criticism that an inordinate amount of space was devoted to minor dramatists while important writers were scanted, he answered that extensive criticism on the major authors was already available. In *The Playhouse of Pepys* he hoped to provide the first adequate accounts of some of the lesser-known Restoration dramatists.

Summers was deeply interested and widely read in certain areas of the supernatural, particularly witchcraft and demonology. The appearance of *The History of Witchcraft and Demonology* in 1926 attracted some notice—though it probably did not elicit quite the response that Summers extravagantly claimed, writing in his autobiography that the edition sold out in a few days as "men awoke to the danger still energizing and active in their midst." Reviews of the book tended to scoff at Summers's subject matter, though most noted that he seemed extremely knowledgeable in matters of the supernatural and presented his material in a lively and interesting way. Critical recognition of Summers's erudition in the field of occult studies continued with the appearance of subsequent books about witchcraft, vampirism, and lycanthropy—*The Vampire: His Kith and Kin, The Vampire in Europe,* and *The Werewolf.* While none denied the thoroughness of Summers's research, some critics did question the validity of many of his sources. Summers tended to treat any description of an encounter with the supernatural as irrefutable proof that diabolic forces were at work in the world, consistently refusing to consider the possibility of either willful fraud or self-delusion. Consequently, a frequent point of critical comment is the extent of Summers's own credulity regarding his arcane subject matter. He steadfastly claimed to believe that the Devil put in regular appearances at coven meetings, that satanic influence enabled some men and women to transform themselves into wolves, and that under certain circumstances corpses sought the blood of the living. While D. J. Enright has written that it is precisely this "strength of conviction" that gives Summers's studies of the supernatural their effectiveness, other critics maintain that Summers's ostensible belief was part of a literary pose. It has also been noted that most critics of Summers's works on supernatural and occult topics do not doubt that he sincerely believed in the existence of the phenomena that he described in his books.

Summers remains a perplexing and enigmatic figure even within the specialized circles of scholarship where he is highly regarded. His histories of the Restoration theater and, to a lesser extent, his study *The Gothic Quest: A History of the Gothic Novel,* are considered important but uneven, reflecting his personal prejudices by devoting an inordinate amount of space to those writers and works that he especially liked. Critics agree, however, that when Summers was personally engrossed in his topic, his scholarship was meticulous and the resultant work often became a definitive study. Summers also aroused controversy because of his literalist approach to supernatural topics—most particularly because he condemned the modern trend toward spiritualism as just another form of the black arts, an essentially evil practice. Although he retains a following among devotees of the occult and students of the supernatural, the tendency of many contemporary critics is to dismiss Summers as a mountebank: an amiable fraud who dabbled in obscure corners of literary scholarship and who prided himself on his ability to shock readers with his studies of the occult. He is respected, however, for the solid body of work he contributed to the study of the Restoration theater—some of which has been superceded by more modern and less subjective work, but most of which still stands as a notable pioneering effort in a long-neglected field.

PRINCIPAL WORKS

Antinous, and Other Poems (poetry) 1907
The Works of Aphra Behn. 6 vols. [editor] (dramas, poetry, and novels) 1915

The Complete Works of William Congreve. 4 vols. [editor] (dramas) 1923
The Complete Works of William Wycherley. 4 vols. [editor] (dramas) 1924
The History of Witchcraft and Demonology (nonfiction) 1926
The Complete Works of Thomas Otway. 3 vols. [editor] (dramas) 1927
The Complete Works of Thomas Shadwell. 5 vols. [editor] (dramas) 1927
The Geography of Witchcraft (nonfiction) 1927
The Vampire: His Kith and Kin (nonfiction) 1928
The Vampire in Europe (nonfiction) 1929
Dryden: The Dramatic Works. 6 vols. [editor] (dramas) 1931-32
The Supernatural Omnibus [editor] (short stories) 1931
Victorian Ghost Stories [editor] (short stories) 1933
The Werewolf (nonfiction) 1933
The Restoration Theatre (history) 1934
A Bibliography of the Restoration Drama (bibliography) 1935
The Playhouse of Pepys (history) 1935
The Grimoire [editor] (short stories) 1936
A Popular History of Witchcraft (nonfiction) 1937
The Gothic Quest: A History of the Gothic Novel (criticism) 1938
A Gothic Bibliography (bibliography) 1940
Witchcraft and Black Magic (nonfiction) 1946
*The Galanty Show (autobiography) 1980

*This work was written in 1948.

LYNN THORNDIKE (essay date 1927)

[*In the following excerpt from a review of* The History of Witchcraft and Demonology, *Thorndike comments on Summers's "fairly readable style," but notes the lack of a coherent organization of his material. Thorndike also questions the "impression of considerable erudition" that is partially engendered by the book's extensive footnotes and bibliography, finding that many questionable assertions within the text are unsupported.*]

"It is quite impossible to appreciate and understand the true lives of men and women in Elizabethan and Stuart England, in the France of Louis XIII and his son, in the Italy of the Renaissance and the Catholic Reaction—to name but three countries and a few definite periods—unless we have some realization of the part that witchcraft played in those ages amid the affairs of these kingdoms." With this attitude of the author [of *The History of Witchcraft and Demonology*] one may essentially agree, as also with his view that the Elizabethan dramatists were believers in the reality of witchcraft and magic. Overdrawn, but containing a certain amount of truth, is his identification of persons accused of witchcraft with social pests and parasites, poisoners, blackmailers, charlatans, bawds, abortionists, and other ministers to vice. One could wish that he had presented more specific evidence in support of this view.

But the Reverend Montague Summers goes much farther. He believes that among the persons who were burned as witches—or who should have been, in his opinion, but escaped detection or punishment—were "devotees of a loathly and obscene creed . . . members of a powerful secret organization inimical to church and state.'' He holds that ''satanists yet celebrate the black mass in London, Brighton, Paris, Lyons, Bruges, Berlin, Milan, and alas! in Rome itself. Both South America and Canada are thus polluted.'' Although admitting the existence of manifold deception and imposture, he nevertheless finds a large element of truth in the evidence that was accumulated during the period of the witchcraft delusion. He is willing to grant that women did not actually fly to the witches' sabbats on broomsticks, but he believes in the possibility of levitation. He maintains the existence, both past and present, of witches, sabbats, contracts with Satan, and cases of diabolic possession. (p. 43)

''Angels and ministers of grace defend us!'' appears to be the attitude of this book, with its mention in the dedication of ''all the Italian and French madonnas at whose shrines we have worshiped.'' It would restore the days of the witchcraft delusion and put us back into the mental attitude of the church fathers. And like them it is determined not to be ''culpably prudish'' in detailing the abominations of witches, ''the filth and foulest passions of the age.'' The author further gives us to understand, although he may be ill-advised in this, that his position is that of the Roman Catholic church today. . . .

The book is not a history in the sense of connected chronological narrative. Rather the following topics are treated: The witch as a heretic and anarchist, worship of the witch, demons and familiars, the sabbat, the witch in Holy Writ, diabolic possession and modern spiritism, and the witch in dramatic literature. Even within the chapters the discussion is discursive and confusing. The author has a fairly readable style but lacks constructive ability in the development of a theme and jumps from one period or thing to another in a most disconcerting manner. And he keeps arguing in season and out of season for the reality of witchcraft. ''The lady protests too much, methinks.''

At first glance the book gives the impression of considerable erudition, with its equipment of footnotes and long bibliography. But my experience in reading it has been that whenever I came to an interesting assertion of fact or a doubtful asseveration and looked for a means of verification or a reference to the original source, none was given. Moreover, such references as these from page 78 are entirely inadequate, giving no page or even no title:

33. Philip Schaff, ''History of the Christian Church.''

34. Matthew Paris, ''Chronica Minora.''

35. J. P. Kirsch.

A protest must be uttered against the relegating of the notes to the close of each chapter, thereby wasting the reader's time and giving him endless trouble and annoyance, especially since the name of the author of a work cited is often not given in the note, making it the more difficult to connect it with the text. Little evidence is given of new research by the author or of new ideas on his part, and it is hard to see how the volume adds anything to the previous works in the field. The views of Manicheans, Waldensians, and Albigensians are grossly misrepresented. It is asserted that the charge against the Templars of celebrating a blasphemous mass was ''established beyond any question or doubt''! In short, except for a few useful titles in the bibliography, it does not appear that any serious historical use can be made of this farrago from the literature of witchcraft, while it is to be hoped that it may not come to prurient and

superstitious ears, though they, too, would probably be disappointed in it. Finally, surprise and regret must be expressed that such a work should appear in a series on the history of civilization and under the consulting editorship, if not the aegis, of a student of intellectual history. (pp. 43-4)

> *Lynn Thorndike, ''A Welter of Witches,'' in* The Nation, *Vol. CXXIV, No. 3210, January 12, 1927, pp. 43-4.*

H. L. MENCKEN   (essay date 1927)

[*From the era of World War I until the early years of the Great Depression, Mencken was one of the most influential figures in American letters. His strongly individualistic, irreverent outlook on life and his vigorous, invective-charged writing style helped establish the iconoclastic spirit of the Jazz Age and significantly shaped the direction of American literature. As a social and literary critic—the roles for which he is best known—Mencken was the scourge of evangelical Christianity, public service organizations, literary censorship, boosterism, provincialism, democracy, all advocates of personal or social improvement, and every other facet of American life that he perceived as humbug. In the following excerpt from his review of* The History of Witchcraft and Demonology, *Mencken sardonically concurs with Summers that acceptance of the Christian faith implies a belief in the existence of witches, demons, and demonic possession.*]

This tome [*The History of Witchcraft and Demonology*] is learned, honest and amusing. Its author, an English clergyman—his full name is the Rev. Alphonsus Joseph-Mary Augustus Montague, M.A.—wastes no time trying to reconcile religion and science, a folly that has brought so many American scientists, including the eminent Dr. Robert Andrews Millikan, to grief. He is in favor of religion, not of science, and with it, in the manner of a true believer, he goes the whole hog. Does Exodus XXII, 18, say flatly that witches exist, and that it is the duty of every righteous man to butcher them when found? Then Dr. Summers accepts the fact and the duty without evasion, and proceeds to elaborate on both. He can't imagine a Christian who refuses to believe in demoniacal possession, and no more can I. Marshaling an array of proofs that must shake even an atheistic archbishop, he demonstrates with fine eloquence and impeccable logic that the air is full of sinister spirits, and that it is their constant effort to enter into the bodies of men and women, and so convert good Christians, made in God's image, into witches, sorcerers, spiritualists, biologists, and other such revolting shapes. The Bible is the rock of his argument, but he also makes frequent and very effective use of the revelations vouchsafed to Holy Church. There has never been a time in Christian history, he shows, when its chief experts and wiseacres did not believe in demons. The Roman rite, accepting their existence as indubitable, provides elaborate machinery for their scotching to this day. (p. 123)

Dr. Summers is . . . honest, and I think he deserves all praise for being so. Most ecclesiastics, when they write upon such subjects, try to evade the clear issue. They seem to be convinced—on what ground I don't know—that the old belief in demons is now dying out in the world, and to be afraid that they will be laughed at if they confess to it. All I can say is that that is a poor way to get into Heaven *post mortem*. Such duckers and skulkers, you may be sure, will have extremely unpleasant sessions with St. Peter when they reach the Gates, and Peter will be well justified in razzing them. Either the Christian religion involves a belief in disembodied powers, good and evil, or it doesn't. If it doesn't, then its Sacred

Caricature of Summers by Matthew Sandford (ca. 1925). Mary Evans Picture Library.

Scriptures are a mass of nonsense, and even its Founder was grossly misinformed. If it does, then everyone adhering to it ought to confess the fact frankly, and without ignominious equivocation. This is what Dr. Summers does. In detail, his colleagues in theology may sometimes reasonably challenge him, as when, for example, he lays down the doctrine that the heaving of tables at spiritualist seances is performed by demons from Hell. But his fundamental postulates stand beyond refutation. If he is wrong, then the whole science of theology is an imposture—something which no right-thinking, law-abiding, home-loving American, I am sure, will want to allege. I rejoice to find a holy man so forthright and courageous, and so irresistibly convincing. He has rescued demonology from its long neglect, and restored it to its old high place among the sacred sciences. What a knock-out he would be on an American lecture tour! I offer him $1,000 in advance for his Jackson, Miss., house, with an offer of the fattest pastorate in the town thrown in. (pp. 124-25)

> *H. L. Mencken, "The Powers of the Air," in* American Mercury, *Vol. XI, No. 41, May, 1927, pp. 123-25.*

THE SATURDAY REVIEW, LONDON (essay date 1927)

[*In the following excerpt an anonymous reviewer of* The Geography of Witchcraft *questions the value of the work as a survey of witchcraft, stating that Summers possessed "inadequate data, an insufficient knowledge of method and a far too limited view of his subject."*]

If the author of [*The Geography of Witchcraft*] aimed at producing an entertaining work he has beyond question succeeded; there is here unrolled before our eyes a volume of data relating to witchcraft in Western Europe, intermingled with stories of werwolves, poltergeists, ghosts and the like, which have some relation to the main subject, and, side by side with them, remarks on the eating of human corpses, human sacrifice, pagan cults, the morals of a Pope, and the Faust legend, the connexion of which with witchcraft remains obscure. But if Mr. Summers wished to produce a real survey of witchcraft he has set about his task with inadequate data, an insufficient knowledge of method and a far too limited view of his subject. He defends himself in the preface against the criticism that he deals with only a small portion of the earth's surface. But an author who writes in a series dealing with the history of civilization cannot circumscribe his outlook in this way; in the first place the witchcraft of Greece and Rome, with which the opening chapter is concerned, is not the beginning of sorcery, any more than Greek and Latin are the original tongues of the human race or even of Greece and Italy. The prologue to a history of witchcraft must be the examination of the allied phenomena all the world over. (pp. 707-08)

The arrangement of the work is primarily geographical, secondarily chronological; but this does not prevent the author from dragging in the supposed worship of Satan in modern Berlin, upon the authority of a daily paper, when he is giving a dissertation upon the misdeeds of the Roman Emperor Maxentius. The author's mania for the quotation of inapposite data is, in fact, the bane of the work; if Jane Shore is charged with sorcery on wholly imaginary grounds, Mr. Summers must needs tell us what Richard of Gloucester said when he accused her. . . . The author's anti-Protestant bias leads him to interpolate inept remarks at the slightest excuse . . . ; if a Puritan or a Calvinist sends a witch to the stake or the gallows, she is the victim of "blood lust and ignorant rage," but no such epithets are hurled at the Inquisitors. Not content with these efforts Mr. Summers tells a story of how Cromwell secured the victory at the battle of Worcester by making a pact with the devil, who appeared as a grave elderly man with a parchment in his hand. Mr. Summers does indeed tell us that he disbelieves it and justifies the presence of the story in a work on witchcraft by pleading that a fairy tale may be morally although not literally true. These futilities may make amusing reading even for those who do not share the author's views, but they do not suggest that he is either logical or prudent. If the space wasted on irrelevant data had been devoted to a more extended study of really important facts the book might have done something to justify its title.

It would be unjust to the author to imply that he has not been industrious; he has accumulated a mass of material and his notes at the end of the chapters number over seven hundred; but the majority of them are rather literary than scientific. . . .

The index, occupied almost solely by proper names, is hopelessly inadequate for those who are interested in facts. The work itself, if it does not leave the reader with any very clear ideas, provides a variety of information on wholly unexpected matters. (p. 708)

> *"Midnight Hags," in* The Saturday Review, London, *Vol. CXLII, No. 3732, May 7, 1927, pp. 707-08.*

LOUISE MAUNSELL FIELD (essay date 1929)

[*In the following excerpt from a review of* The Vampire: His Kith and Kin, *Field discusses the work as the first serious, carefully documented study of the subject. She especially commends the chapter on "The Vampire in Literature."*]

Of all the many hideous fears which have haunted the imaginations of men there is none more horrible than that of the vampire, the living corpse which rises at night from its grave and goes forth to suck the blood of the living. Thereby it maintains its own dreadful life while inflicting on its victims a fate worse than death, since those sucked by a vampire are doomed to become, after death, vampires in their turn. And as the tradition of the vampire is one of the most gruesome ever known, so, too, is it one of the most widely spread and most persistent. . . .

Yet despite the antiquity and prevalence of the tradition, and though many writers have commented upon it (the bibliography here given covers no less than eight pages), Mr. Summers and his publishers claim that [*The Vampire*] is the first serious and carefully documented study of the subject. It is certainly a full and extremely interesting one. The author treats first of the origins, then of the generation, the traits and practices of the vampire. . . .

One of the most interesting chapters in the book is devoted to "The Vampire in Literature." Strangely enough, it was not until the latter part of the seventeenth and the beginning of the eighteenth century that the tradition appeared in this form; then it was used in poetry, romance and drama. Here in New York it was seen a little while ago in the dramatization of Bram Stoker's widely read novel, "Dracula." Into this subject, as into all those closely allied with his theme, the author delves energetically. Touching but lightly on the belief in the werewolf, with which he intends to deal elsewhere, he writes of necrophagy, necrophilia and necrosadism, the latter being, so he declares, the dominant motive in the famous case of Leopold and Loeb. The ghoul, the Callicantzaros and the loogaroo, are all near kin to the vampire, and near kin, too, are those who cannot rest in their graves because of a curse laid upon them. The documentary testimony collected by Mr. Summers is amazingly extensive. . . .

He discusses various hypotheses as to the manner in which the vampire leaves the tomb and the possibility of vampire entities making use of the octoplasm of the medium, his point of view being scarcely less curious and interesting than his book. The volume is a mine of out-of-the-way information full of unspeakable tales.

> *Louise Maunsell Field, "Origin and History of the Strange Vampire Tradition," in* The New York Times Book Review, *March 24, 1929, p. 6.*

E. M. FORSTER   (essay date 1931)

[*Forster was a prominent English novelist, critic, and essayist, whose works reflect his liberal humanism. His most celebrated novel,* A Passage to India *(1924), is a complex examination of personal relationships amid the conflicts of the modern world. Although some of Forster's critical essays are considered naive in their literary assessments, his discussion of fictional techniques in his* Aspects of the Novel *(1927) is regarded as a minor classic of literary criticism. The following excerpt is taken from a review of* The Supernatural Omnibus, *an anthology of horror fiction edited by Summers. Forster discusses Summers's conviction that ghost stories are best written and read by believers in the supernatural.*]

Mr. Montague Summers has certainly included some readable ghost stories among the thirty-eight that make up his anthology

[*The Supernatural Omnibus*]. Here are Dickens and Lefanu, and here is a writer named Vincent O'Sullivan, who does excellent work. But the volume as a whole suffers, I think, from two defects; dogmatism and capriciousness. In his introduction Mr. Summers tells us that he "believes" in ghosts, otherwise he would not collect them, and he holds, furthermore, that ghost stories can only be written or read properly by believers. The willing suspension of disbelief which contented Coleridge would not satisfy him. He must have active faith, and relying on its co-operation he has included some very silly stuff; there are, for example, no fewer than three stories from the pen of an obscure writer of ritualistic tendency who is completely incompetent, but who endorses a view of the unseen evidently congenial to Mr. Summers himself. Satanism, to speak more plainly, presides over too much of this anthology, and Satanism, like everything else, must be presented forcibly, or it becomes owlish. Not all who say "abracadabra" shall enter the kingdom of darkness, not all unfrocked priests and pagan emblems can lead us into paths of unrighteousness. . . . Mr. Summers is too apt to identify the spiritual element in ghost stories (which he rightly values) with the external accidents of a cult. He is at the same time too serious and not serious enough.

But it is, of course, very easy to complain of an anthology; everyone has his own theory. About half Mr. Summers' selection is worth reading, and his erudite introduction and bibliography are interesting.

> *E. M. Forster, "Ghosts Ancient and Modern," in* The Spectator, *Vol. 147, No. 5395, November 21, 1931, p. 672.**

LOUISE MAUNSELL FIELD   (essay date 1934)

[*In the following excerpt, Field offers a dispassionate review of* The Werewolf.]

For centuries the imaginations of men have filled the night and the darkness with hideous shapes of incarnate evil. Most dreadful of these was the vampire. . . . Only a little less terrible than the horrific figure of the vampire is that of his close kin, the werewolf. Belief in the one is very likely to accompany dread of the other, in some places the connection being so close that he who, living, stalks abroad as a werewolf after death becomes a vampire. Both, too, are creatures of dread and darkness, sworn servants of Satan. . . .

Mr. Montague Summers, who has already stated his belief that there is a foundation of truth underlying the tales concerning those vampires of whom he has written so interestingly, declares [in *The Werewolf*] that he is convinced that werewolfery is "a terrible and enduring fact" and that he believes that men really can be changed into beasts. This, of course, entirely apart from that well-known form of madness called lycanthropy, the victim of which believes himself to be a wolf, and howls and slavers like one. The devil, Mr. Summers says, can make a werewolf, because the werewolf is said to have no tail and is therefore an imperfect creation.

Women as well as men may be werewolves, though witches usually prefer to take the shape of cats. Our author insists that: "No thinking person can deny that these witches in the form of cats suck the blood of children and overlook them, and indeed not unseldom kill them by diabolical agency." In support of these theories of his he cites numerous authorities in English, French, German, Greek and Latin, many of them theologians, but some mere amateurs, like King James I or even pagans. . . .

Mr. Summers devotes a chapter of his book to "The Werewolf in Literature," citing a number of interesting tales, though he omits any mention of Guy Endore's horror story, "The Werewolf of Paris." His new book, like its predecessors, is packed with ancient and peculiar lore, which, whether the reader accepts or rejects his conclusions, is sure to be found extremely interesting by any one curious about the mental history of man.

> *Louise Maunsell Field, "The Horrendous Werewolf's History," in* The New York Times Book Review, *March 18, 1934, p. 12.*

RICHARD Le GALLIENNE   (essay date 1934)

[*Le Gallienne was an English poet, essayist, and novelist who was associated early in his career with the fin de siècle movement of literary aestheticism that is commonly referred to as the Decadent movement. The literature of the Decadents, which grew out of French aestheticism, displays a fascination with perverse and morbid states; a search for novelty and sensation (the frisson nouveau, or "new thrill"); a preoccupation with both mysticism and nihilism; and the assertion of an essential enmity between art and life implicit in the "art for art's sake" doctrine. In their writings the Decadents routinely violated accepted moral and ethical standards, often for shock value alone. Most of Le Galliene's poetry appeared in the journal* The Yellow Book, *the primary organ of the English Decadents, and he was a cofounder of the Rhymers' Club, an informal group of poets associated with the Decadent movement that included Ernest Dowson and W. B. Yeats. In the following excerpt from his review of* The Restoration Theatre, *Le Gallienne calls Summers the greatest living authority on Restoration drama. He especially praises Summers's ability to bring his subject to life by vividly recreating the era, the physical appearance of the theaters, the nature of the audiences, and other aspects of the theatergoing experience.*]

[*The Restoration Theatre*] is a fascinating book, and it is good news that it is but the first volume of a series which Mr. Montague Summers has in preparation, and is to be followed by three more volumes dealing respectively with the actors and actresses of the Restoration Theatre, with the minor dramatists, "men of one or two plays," and with a survey of politics and personalities in the theatre. It is perhaps hardly necessary to say that Mr. Summers is not only our greatest living authority on the Restoration Theatre but that in him are summed up, embodied, so to say, all its previous enthusiasts and editors from Charles Lamb to A. H. Bullen and Edmund Gosse. His Nonesuch edition of several of them—Dryden, Congreve, Wycherly, Otway, Shadwell and Aphra Behn—will remain definitely authoritative. . . . For forty years he has lived and breathed the Restoration Drama. It has been his life. Such single-minded devotion is inspiring, and gives Mr. Summers so lonely an eminence in his own field that, while there are some few scholars who can appreciate his achievement, he alone is qualified to be his own final critic.

In addition to all this mighty editorial activity, it was Mr. Summers who in 1919 founded the Phoenix Society, for the adequate presentation of the plays of the older dramatists, and it was under the auspices of this society that some very notable performances of plays by Dryden, Congreve, Wycherly, Otway and Buckingham were given, performances which have had great influence on subsequent productions in the popular theatre, and which fully justified a contention for which Mr. Summers had made a long fight. This contention was, in Mr. Summers's own words, that "the drama of the Restoration—and

for that matter any other drama, too—fully to be appreciated and understood must be seen upon the stage, and the plays, moreover, must be given as nearly the original production as modern methods and changed conditions will reasonably permit." . . .

[The] rich, exuberant Restoration drama . . . is not dead but only sleeping, in the old play-books, and needs only the magic wand of good acting, plus inspired stage management, to reawaken into vivid, glamourous life. And as much as a book can do toward that end Mr. Summers's book certainly does, for steeped as he is in all the lore of his subject, he most livingly reconstructs the times of which that drama was a part, and the mirror, the stage on which it was presented, and all the various histrionic as well as social conditions, and his picture of the audience to which it appealed, in "all its forms and presence," is particularly alive. . . .

In so brief a review as this it is impossible to do more than hint at the scope of Mr. Summers's learned and entertaining book. Particularly important to the appreciation of the Restoration drama are his chapters on "The Curtain; the Prologue, and Changes of Scene," or "Realism on the Stage; the Scenery," and "Costume."

> *Richard Le Gallienne, "The Rowdy Restoration Stage," in* The New York Times Book Review, *August 19, 1934, p. 2.*

ROSAMUND GILDER   (essay date 1935)

[*An American drama critic, editor, and author, Gilder worked on the staff of* Theatre Arts Monthly *for over twenty-four years, first as the journal's drama critic and eventually as its editor in chief. She is the editor of several theater anthologies and author of* Enter the Actress: The First Women in Theatre (1931). *In the following excerpt from her review of* The Playhouse of Pepys, *Summers's second volume of the history of the Restoration stage, Gilder praises the book warmly, noting that Summers has effectively combined exacting scholarship and meticulous research with his intense enthusiasm for his subject, producing a solid introduction to the theater of the Restoration period.*]

The title of the second volume of Mr. Montague Summers' history of the Restoration stage [*The Playhouse of Pepys*] is one to conjure with. The intense relish with which Samuel Pepys approached the theatre makes his playhouse and its denizens alive today even though nearly three hundred years have passed since the indefatigable diarist recorded his enthusiasms. The theatre in all its aspects was to him an irresistible delight. . . .

Mr. Summers' second volume gives us the solid background of that theatre, fills in the crevices of our knowledge of the body of Restoration playwriting, records in minutest detail all the facts that have been preserved concerning the work of minor playwrights, the dates of production, the cast of the plays. The first volume was devoted to the physical aspect of playhouse ways used in advertising, audiences, production methods, costuming and so forth. In the next we are promised a gallery of performers. This second of the projected three-volume history gives us the lives of the two Patentees, Davenant and Killigrew, and a vast amount of information concerning those gallants and wits, those dashing young blades or hard-driven poetasters who indulged in only a few dramas, good, bad and indifferent, which filled in the many nights between such high spots as *The Man of Mode* and *The Way of the World*. Congreve, Wycherley and the other great Restoration writers are treated but briefly here, since Mr. Summers' definitive editions of their works, with long biographical and critical introductions and notes, already cover these important subjects. Here are gathered the lesser lights of a period rich in playwriting but in which the theatre as an institution was in its permanent state of decadence and fine despair. (p. 879)

Mr. Summers' meticulously exact study of this period will inevitably take its place on the shelf of every serious library of theatre history. Its painstaking scholarship is relieved by the fine intensity of Mr. Summers' enthusiasm for his subject and his offensive and defensive warfare with other less erudite writers in the field whose 'nebulous inaccuracies' fill him with justifiable rage. No one could accuse Mr. Summers of the sin of inaccuracy but occasionally his delight in the possibilities of the English language leads him into a verbal nebulosity of his own. Certain of the words he restores to use should indeed be recaptured for the enrichment of the language. (p. 880)

> Rosamund Gilder, "A Stramash of Playwrights," in Theatre Arts Monthly, *Vol. XIX, No. 11, November, 1935, pp. 879-80.*

MONTAGUE SUMMERS   (essay date 1948)

[*The following excerpt is from* The Galanty Show, *an autobiographical work completed by Summers shortly before his death. Although his autobiography was written in 1948, the death of his secretary and literary executor, Hector Stuart-Forbes, left Summers's affairs in disarray, and the manuscript of* The Galanty Show *disappeared. It was located in 1956 by Brocard Sewell, who edited the manuscript for publication; Sewell also authored* Montague Summers: A Memoir *under the pseudonym Joseph Jerome. In the following excerpt, Summers explains the source of his interest in the occult and the supernatural.*]

I have been asked frequently, but I find it difficult precisely to give an adequate answer, how and why I first came to study the huge field of witchcraft. In the West of England a belief in witches and their machinations has always prevailed and has never been stupidly stifled or ignored as in some (though few) parts. When I stayed in our villages I often heard of wise-women who wrought cures or, as it might be, cast spells, and everybody accepted such facts, without question or argument. (p. 154)

We read the stern denunciations of magical practices and witchcraft in the Holy Scriptures; we read how our Blessed Lord cured 'such as were possessed by devils'; how he gave his disciples 'power over unclean spirits, to cast them out'; how Simon, 'who before had been a magician in that city', Samaria, 'had bewitched them with his magical practices'; how secondary relics of St. Paul were brought to the sick and possessed, 'and the diseases departed from them, and the wicked spirits went out of them.'

Faith, the Bible, actual experience, all taught that witchcraft had existed and existed still. There could be and there is no sort of doubt concerning this. (pp. 154-55)

I had long held that the facts, the actuality of witchcraft, the contemporary practice of necromancy (otherwise spiritism), the unbiassed history of the whole subject, ought to be put out before scholars and the public generally.

It was one day when we were lunching at the Royal Societies Club, that Mr. C. K. Ogden observed to me: 'We are going to do *A History of Civilisation*.' 'That sounds rather a tall order,' I remarked. 'Oh, it's going to be in a great many

volumes, of course. Kegan Paul are publishing them. I wish you would do something for us. Can I persuade you?' I thought a bit. 'What about a study of witchcraft?' I asked. 'The very thing,' Ogden replied.

The result of that talk over the luncheon table was that on October 13th 1926 Messrs. Kegan Paul published *The History of Witchcraft and Demonology*.

The edition sold out in two or three days. Within less than a week copies were at a premium. Men awoke to the danger still energizing and active in their midst. The evil which many had hardly suspected, deeming it either a mere historical question, long dead and gone, of no interest save to the antiquarian, or else altogether fabled, was shown to be very much alive, potent in politics, potent in society, corrupting the arts, a festering, leprous disease and decay.

France knew the foul thing, Satanism, and so did Italy, and other countries beside, but it was, perhaps, the first time there had been in English a *History of Witchcraft* since the days of the learned Glanvil, the philosophic More, and of Dr. Richard Boulton's *Compleat History of Magick*, which appeared in 1715. True, Dr. F. G. Lee had raised a solemn voice during the decade 1875-1885; but the hour proved unpropitious, and his warnings were largely unheeded.

Not so in 1926. Facts were facts. The sensation was immense.

Men realized that spiritism, so vaunted, so advertised, so mysteriously attractive, so praised and tenselled by such highly placed writers as Sir Oliver Lodge and Sir Arthur Conan Doyle was nothing else than demoniality in masquerade.

Portrait of Summers (ca. 1925). Mary Evans Picture Library.

A veritable bombshell exploded amid the anti-christian and nihilist rabblement. (pp. 156-57)

One reason, I think, why *The History of Witchcraft* carried invincible conviction was that it showed by a number of citations how in the past this enormous wickedness had been impartially investigated, had been argued, and proven by the keenest minds of the centuries, by theologians, jurists, philosophers, scientists, saints, and sages, whose immensely erudite works were here in England practically unknown, or at any rate unread. I quoted from such great men as Prierias, John Gerson, Sprenger, Trithemius, Lorenzo, Anania, Vair, Node, Guazzo, Bodin, Michaelis, Remy, Bossuet, Delrio, Dominic Schram, Johann Joseph von Görres, Paul M. Baumgarten, and many more.

In my researches extending over many years I had accumulated a vast quantity of material, and when I discussed my work on Witchcraft with Mr. W. Swan Stallybrass, the managing director of Messrs. Routledge, Kegan Paul, Trench, Trübner, he urged that instead of issuing the *History* in two volumes, there should be a couple of separate books. The first he named *The History of Witchcraft;* and the second he named *The Geography of Witchcraft*. I fell in with this suggestion, although I thought we might, perhaps, have found rather better titles. . . . [In *The Georgraphy of Witchcraft*] I treated witchcraft country by country. The book is very detailed, being nearly double the length of the *History*.

Studies of allied themes followed: [*The Vampire, His Kith and Kin; The Vampire in Europe;* and then *The Werewolf*]. . . . (p. 158)

There is room, there always will be, for studies of witchcraft, of hauntings, of the occult. We only ask that these books should be written seriously, and with knowledge. The ignorant may posture and pose as authorities upon art, upon poetry, upon literature generally, and there is no vital mischief done. True, they lower the standards of culture and of taste. This many will consider harm enough. But there the dilettante is not playing with the eternal issues of life and death. The amateurs, and alas! there are all too many of them, who invade the occult are awaking forces of which they have no conception.

The world invisible is infinite. How many there are whose sight is blindly bounded by their own horizons, the wall they have builded of the bricks of gross materialism and denial. If they but guessed what lay beyond that barrier and bourne! (pp. 163-64)

> *Montague Summers, in his* The Galanty Show: An Autobiography, *Cecil Woolf, 1980, 259 p.*

CHARLES RICHARD CAMMELL   (essay date 1951)

[*In the following excerpt from his biography of the English occult writer, poet, and novelist Aleister Crowley, Cammell briefly sketches his impression of Summers as an extraordinary man who was widely read in the diverse fields of Gothic romance, early English drama, and demonology.*]

With the Reverend Montague Summers I became acquainted in my editorial capacity in 1936 (I was then Associate Editor of *The Connoisseur,* to which magazine he contributed articles on rare books). Montague Summers, like Aleister Crowley, is one of those rare personalities to whom the epithet *extraordinary* may be applied without exaggeration. He was in every respect singular: in appearance, in manner, in his way of life, his interests, his attainments. (p. 171)

The published and privately printed works of Montague Summers comprise a series of studies unsurpassed, and not seldom unrivalled, in those fields of research and speculation which he had made peculiarly his own. He was a world-famous Demonologist. He had written books on Witches, Devils, Vampires, Werewolves; he had also written of Angels, Saints male and female, Seers and Sages. His thick, scarlet-bound volumes, *The Gothic Quest* and *The Gothic Bibliography,* are monuments as much to his industry as to his learning. He had written of all our early English dramatic poets, and had edited Dryden's dramas, among others, for The Nonesuch Press. He had published an edition of *The Rehearsal* by George Villiers, second Duke of Buckingham, a personage in whom, as in his great father, I am especially interested, and he had produced that brilliant farce and the Duke's other comedy *The Chances* at the Phoenix Theatre, in the inception and management of which he had been the moving spirit.

As a writer, Montague Summers' style is quite beautiful, at once pure, graceful and picturesque: he could be grave, witty, racy or richly descriptive; he had the gift of penetrating to the depths of the characters he described. His study of the Marquis de Sade in his book *Essays in Petto* is masterly in its profound insight. (pp. 172-73)

In Crowley he took a remarkable interest. . . . He admired his genius; he perceived the high quality of his best poetry. Crowley reciprocated the admiration: in Summers he recognised a Demonologist of deep knowledge, a man of copious learning and understanding. (pp. 174-75)

> *Charles Richard Cammell, in his* Aleister Crowley: The Man, the Mage, the Poet, *The Richards Press, 1951, 229 p.**

FELIX MORROW   (essay date 1960)

[*In the following excerpt from his introduction to* The Vampire: His Kith and Kin, *Morrow offers a general discussion of Summers's books on the supernatural.*]

You who open this book [*The Vampire: His Kith and Kin*] because you wish to read about vampires may very well wish to hurry past an introduction written by someone other than the author and so I must tell you in this very first sentence, before I lose you, that what you will read further on will be puzzling and startling to you unless you first listen to me. Just what will you make of the author's earnest advice concerning how to dispose of the body of a vampire? Or of his description of what the usual vampire looks like? Is he pulling your leg or does he really believe it? Nor is it a question merely of personal belief on his part. With vast erudition he summons up Holy Writ, early, medieval and later church fathers and theologians; and it becomes clear that he feels confident that he speaks for all true Roman Catholics and, indeed, for all true Christians. Side by side with this, however, he takes the most enormous delight in freezing our blood and standing our few hairs on end with the most dreadful but fascinating stories of endless evil done through the centuries. (p. xiii)

In 1956 I arranged for the first proper publication in the United States of the author's *The History of Witchcraft and Demonology.* Although I found the book fascinating, I found it necessary to write a foreword dissociating myself from the views of the author and contrasting them with another, more tenable theory of the nature of witchcraft. I found Summers' views valuable "precisely because they provide us in modern English with what is actually the best account of the Roman Catholic version of the history of witchcraft and the church's fight against it. It was his contention, and we are inclined to agree with him, that his account is not only the true story as it appeared to the Catholic church in the seventeenth and eighteenth centuries, but that this remains, in spite of what Catholic apologists may say in encyclopaedias and other public forums, the true position of the Roman Catholic Church today.'' In 1958, I also arranged for the publication of the author's *The Geography of Witchcraft.* In this book, much more than in the first, the author was careful to distinguish between genuine instances of demoniacal possession and those outbreaks of contagious hysteria that led to the sacrifice of many harmless lives. Thus when he writes of the Salem witch trials he puts the blame where it belongs, on the malicious adolescent girls who first denounced mumbling old women, and on the neurotic adults who encouraged them. Summers does name some few among the many tried and condemned to death in witchcraft trials who, he believes, actually were members of covens of witches. But he does acknowledge often enough the tragedy of the implication of innocent people. (pp. xiii-xiv)

The books divide into two main groups. One includes those already mentioned, plus a sequel to the present work entitled *The Vampire in Europe,* another *The Werewolf,* and a number of similar works.

The other group, for which the author is indeed far more famous, includes his masterly editing of the plays of Elizabethan and Restoration dramatists (Jonson, Wycherley, Congreve, Vanbrugh) and *The Gothic Quest,* which has become the standard history of the Gothic novel. (p. xv)

[The reader will] find an author vast in erudition, but unfair to his opponents, doing his Godly work with such gusto that we shiver with delight as he shivers with horror. In reality, of course, the old boy is having a great time raising his hands in holy horror. (p. xvi)

> Felix Morrow, *''The Quest for Montague Summers,''* in The Vampire: His Kith and Kin *by Montague Summers, University Books, 1960, pp. xiii-xx.*

TIMOTHY D'ARCH SMITH   (essay date 1963)

[*The following excerpt is taken from Smith's introduction (1963) to his* A Bibliography of the Works of Montague Summers, *the only attempt to provide a bibliography of Summers's published books as well as his contributions to periodicals. Smith notes the remarkable range of Summers's scholarship, from his studies of Restoration theater to his writings on the occult—all areas in which he has published what are often considered to be definitive studies.*]

It is not easy to state exactly why Summers embarked on a career as a man of letters nor what drove him so deeply to study the three subjects he chose as his special provinces: the drama of the Restoration, Witchcraft, and the Gothic Novel. He tells us that 'even when a mere lad at school I had always been writing essays, stories, poems, plays', but his life at Clifton College, however literary his bent, is not marked by any contribution to the school magazine. (p. 12)

What is immediately striking is the contrast between the slim blue book of verses published late in 1907 [*Antinous*] and the scholarly edition of the Duke of Buckingham's *Rehearsal* which appeared only seven years later. . . . *The Rehearsal* was quickly

followed by a six-volume edition of the works of Aphra Behn, and Summers's career as a man of letters had begun.

Considering that he was studying for the priesthood and, after that, was employed full-time as a schoolmaster, it is amazing that he should have found not only the energy but the time for obtaining the knowledge required for such a difficult editorial undertaking as an edition of Mrs Behn. Moreover, it is still more remarkable that, in 1926, having only recently discontinued his teaching career [and] been busy with The Phoenix . . . he switched his attentions to Witchcraft and produced *The History of Witchcraft and Demonology* which, as he himself says, 'caused a sensation'. Not content with these two fields of research, he had set to work on the Gothic Novel as early as 1913, and the fruit of his extensive study was published in 1938 as *The Gothic Quest.* At the time of his death he had turned his attentions to yet another subject and was hard at work on Victorian melodrama.

It is apparent, I think, that he had far too much to do to accomplish everything satisfactorily. He was forced, at times, to shuffle his published material round to make another book. For instance, there is little in [*A Popular History of Witchcraft* and *Witchcraft and Black Magic*] . . . which cannot be found in his pioneering [*History of Witchcraft and Demonology* and *The Geography of Witchcraft*]. . . . His six-volume edition of Dryden's dramatic works . . . left much to be desired and he laid himself open to such serious charges, not only of editorial carelessness and misrepresentation, but of plagiarism, that he never attempted a similar editorial undertaking again. A note of doubt of his own abilities—an unusual thing in Summers, confident as he usually was of his own accuracy and other scholars' bungling—appears in his Prefatory Note to the first volume of *Dryden: the Dramatic Works.* He asks indulgence for 'the sad tricks which ill-health, weariness, failing eye-sight, inability to read proofs with precision, will play with one's work'. One feels that the overwork was caused not by old age (he was 51) but by his having too many irons which were not even in the same fire.

Despite the fact that his output was considerable in all fields in which he was interested, Summers was not content to credit himself with just these published works. Time and again, both in his entries in biographical dictionaries such as *Who's Who,* and in his own books, he announced as published, works which he had planned, written, or merely dreamed of, none of which had, in fact, ever appeared. Whether he hoped that they might finally be published, or whether he was impishly misleading his readers, may never be known, nor have many of these unpublished books come to light in any form, either of notes or completed manuscripts. (pp. 12-13)

> Timothy d'Arch Smith, in an introduction to his A Bibliography of the Works of Montague Summers, *University Books, 1964, pp. 11-15.*

JOSEPH JEROME [PSEUDONYM OF BROCARD SEWELL]   (essay date 1965)

[*The following excerpt is taken from the only book-length memoir of Summers's life and career. Sewell, who edited* The Galanty Show, *was an acquaintance of Summers. In the following excerpt, he provides a survey of Summers's career.*]

[Summers's] first publication, *Antinous, and Other Poems,* [is] a small book of distinctly decadent verse, which appeared in 1907. . . .

The contents are a strange *mélange* of 'sacred' and 'satanic' which would well qualify for the baudelairean title of *Fleurs du Mal*. (p. 6)

At this time Summers's mind was much dominated by Swinburne, and also by Oscar Wilde, the first being admired as a poet, the second as a man. Perhaps, as Mr. Redwood-Anderson suggests, these morbid interests were a kind of 'defence mechanism' against the conditions under which he had been brought up: a challenge to the mediocrity and hypocrisy of contemporary Clifton society, and a protest against the autocratic *régime* in his home. (p. 8)

From 1911 to 1926 Summers was not only a hardworking schoolmaster, a full time job in itself for most men, but also an industrious and prolific author and editor. His career as a man of letters had begun in 1910, when he became acquainted with the distinguished Elizabethan scholar Arthur Henry Bullen, as whose guest he was to spend much time at Stratford-on-Avon, where Bullen had his Shakespeare Head Press. . . .

It was Bullen who launched Summers on his career as a man of letters. . . .

In 1914 appeared the first of a series of Restoration dramas edited by Summers: '*The Rehearsal* by George Villiers, Duke of Buckingham.' . . . (p. 30)

The Rehearsal was followed, in 1915, by *The Works of Aphra Behn*, edited by Montague Summers and published in six pleasing crown octavo volumes by the Shakespeare Head Press. This is the first, and still remains the only, collected edition of the works of Mrs. Behn. . . . (p. 31)

Buckingham's *Rehearsal* and the *Works* of Mrs. Behn are models of scholarly editing. Their perfection no doubt owes something to the surveillance of A. H. Bullen. It is a great pity that his partnership with Summers was not of longer duration; but Bullen died in 1920. It is no denial or denigration of Summers's remarkable achievements to say that had he been able to continue to work in association with Bullen he would probably have been able to avoid those charges of carelessness and laxity in scholarship to which, in later years, he sometimes exposed himself.

The editions of *The Rehearsal* and Mrs. Behn were the first fruits of Summers's unrivalled knowledge of and enthusiasm for the writers of the Restoration period. They were to be followed by his splendid editions for the Nonesuch Press, the first of which [was] his *Congreve*. . . . (p. 32)

Summers's Introductions to the old dramatists usually run to a hundred or more pages, and are perhaps the best things he ever wrote. Would that some enterprising publisher would rescue them from these scarce limited editions and reprint them in one volume. Masterpieces of stage history and of literary and dramatic criticism, they deserve to rank high among the prose writings of the present century. Some readers, perhaps, may not care for the occasionally mannered elegance of Summers's prose nor his fondness now and then for the archaic word; but even they will find it difficult not to be carried away by the writer's enthusiasm for his subject.

Montague Summers's defence of the Restoration drama against the wholesale condemnations of Jeremy Collier and the aspersions of Lord Macaulay is of permanent interest and value. His exact exposition of the nature of the comedy of manners has helped to a more intelligent appreciation of these old masterpieces of the stage. (p. 34)

Especially meritorious, in my opinion, is Summers's defence of Thomas Shadwell, the Orange Laureate, and his rescue of Shadwell's plays from the near-oblivion into which they had fallen: the more so as Shadwell's Whiggism and his feud with Dryden were exactly calculated to arouse Summers's dislike. (p. 35)

In 1919 Montague Summers was on the way to becoming a social figure in London as the result of the founding, principally at his suggestion, of The Phoenix, a society for the presentation of the plays of our older dramatists. The activities of The Phoenix took up a great deal of Summers's time and attention until the collapse of the society in 1925 owing to internal disagreement. (p. 37)

The research involved in getting up the theatrical history of the plays for the programmes of the productions, and which often indicated points of practical guidance for the producer, kept Summers for many hours at a time in the Reading Room of the British Museum, where he was working also on the preparation of his editions of the old dramatists. (p. 47)

Summers's studies in the history of the drama culminated in 1934 and 1935 with the publication of his two complementary volumes (a third was projected but never completed) *The Restoration Theatre* and *The Playhouse of Pepys*. These two books, running to some four hundred pages each, and beautifully illustrated, deal with every aspect of the London stage between 1660 and 1710.

The first deals with the playhouse itself, the methods of advertising and admission, the conduct of its audiences, stage mechanism, scenery and costume. The second begins his studies of the dramatists who have not been the subjects of modern editors and biographers; among them Davenant, Killigrew, the Howards, Flecknoe, Wilson, Porter, and others. The series was to have been continued in the unwritten third volume.

These books certainly rank among Summers's major achievements, and they received an excellent press. Some reviewers found the studied archaic style and vocabulary too rich for their taste; but to other readers these factors give an added charm to the work. It constitutes 'a monumental study of the Restoration stage', wrote Malcolm Elwin. . . . (pp. 47-8)

By 1926 Summers's reputation as the most eminent living authority on the Restoration drama had been established; and he was now earning enough money from his writings to be able to give up schoolmastering and devote his whole time to study and letters. He now began to publish his series of works on the history of witchcraft and demonology, and other aspects of the occult and arcane: subjects which had fascinated him for many years. The occult publishing world in England in 1926 had little new to offer either to the scholar or the dilettante. . . . [In] fact, students of these subjects had long since decided that the phenomena of the witches were to be considered as springing from sources which could be defined as either Freudian, hysterical, or political; or were the outcome of the merry frolics of peasants or the suspicions of superstitious clergy.

Scientists had already begun to exercise their talents in an attempt to discover a rational explanation for all supernatural happenings. . . . (p. 49)

[The] surprise caused when the large and reputable firm of Kegan Paul published in their scholarly 'History of Civilization' series, edited by C. K. Ogden, Montague Summers's *The History of Witchcraft and Demonology* was considerable. True, the author, as far as the general public was aware, was a Roman Catholic priest; but for a man living in the twentieth century to uphold to the letter the orthodox (possibly) but seldom stated tenets of the Faith, and to believe quite literally in a personal Devil, in possession, in fact in all the medieval superstitions which went to make up the subject of witchcraft, caused reviewers of the volume to boggle, and, having boggled, to sit down, rather shaken, and give the book a dilatory review. What else could they do? They could hardly agree with the author's views, but they could certainly not deny the facts of history which he presented; not, at least, without several months' research not only in the British Museum and the Bodleian but in the Vatican itself. They could only decry the book's unpleasantness and commend its scholarship.

It is, of course, an extraordinary volume. In his Introduction Summers warns the reader of the nastiness he may expect to find in its pages:

> One cannot write in dainty phrases of Satanists and the Sabbat. However loathly the disease the doctor must not hesitate to diagnose and to probe. . . .

He is not slow to define his thesis:

> I have endeavoured to show the witch as she really was—an evil liver; a social pest and parasite; the devotee of a loathly and obscene creed; an adept at poisoning, blackmail, and other creeping crimes; a member of a powerful secret organization inimical to Church and State; a blasphemer in word and deed . . . battening upon the filth and foulest passions of the age. . . .
>
> (p. 50)

A not unimportant section of the book is devoted to the cult of spiritualism, which Summers is quick to damn as modern witchcraft. This had already been done, in less sulphurous but just as certain terms, by J. Godfrey Raupert in his *New Black Magic* (1924); and it is unfortunate that Summers's condemnation should have been couched in such purple and violent prose. Sincere though it undoubtedly was, a less gaudy attack would have been more likely to receive the attention it deserved—and still does deserve.

A year later Summers issued his second and companion volume, *The Geography of Witchcraft,* which gives the history of the cult in Europe and America. It is as interesting a work as the first, and doubtless as sincere; but it is more apparent that Summers always has an ear for the diversion of his reader. This he achieves firstly by the use of archaic language, well-fitted to the subject, and secondly by delightfully well-placed but inaccurate statements such as can perhaps be found in only one other book, Baron Corvo's *Chronicles of the House of Borgia.* (p. 51)

His further volumes, [*The Vampire: His Kith and Kin, The Vampire in Europe,* and *The Werewolf*] . . . are marred by a lack of coherence and no proper division of text and notes, through faulty editing. By the time these volumes appeared the critics were no longer surprised that the author should believe to the letter the superstitions of vampirism and lycanthropy; but we find more and more Latin and Greek extracts, pages long at times, creeping into his chapters instead of taking their rightful place in the notes; and at the same time his English becomes in places virtually incomprehensible, as in this quaint passage from *The Werewolf:*

Portion of a handwritten letter by Summers. Reproduced by permission of Cecil Woolf Publishers.

> Whereon mine host, little minded to be made a meal of, in a sad fright bolted rous through the door, which he took good care to double lock and bar behind him, leaving his cloak to shift for itself. So the budge nims the togeman, and Prince Prig is off on his way to see more of the world. Moral: We must not believe everything we hear. . . .

The Vampire in Europe is of interest for the evidence it contains that Summers's researches were not done solely in libraries, but had included on-the-spot inquiry in places where belief in vampirism was still common. It appears that he was in Greece during 1906 and 1907, when he visited Crete and the island of Santorin, the most southerly of the Cyclades. As early as January 1985 he had heard oral traditions of vampires at Mandoudi in Euboea, and also at Kokkinimilia, 'a tiny thorp . . . which is reached by a mule'. (pp. 51-2)

It is ironic that the best criticism that can be applied to the two Vampire books and the Werewolf volume is that which he himself gave to George Lyman Kittredge's *Witchcraft in Old and New England:* 'It presents a series of unconnected essays, their unity being that the . . . chapters one and all relate to the same subject.' To be fair, however, his research was indefatigable, his memory prodigious, and his prose deep and sonorous. (p. 52)

In 1928 Summers published a translation, with a learned Introduction and copious notes, of *Malleus Maleficarum,* the classic treatise on witchcraft by two fifteenth-century German Dominicans, James Sprenger and Henry Kramer. (p. 53)

[He] followed up the *Malleus* with three other translations: Henry Boguet's *Examen of Witches (Discours des Sorciers)* and Guazzo's *Compendium Maleficarum* in 1929, and Rémy's *Demonolatry (Daemonolatreiae Libri Tres)* in 1930. Finally a reprint in folio of Reginald Scot's *Discoverie of Witchcraft* completed what was known as 'The Church and Witchcraft' series.

The success of the *Malleus Maleficarum* was rather less than Summers assumed, in spite of the interest it had aroused. (pp. 53-4)

Works on witchcraft, dealing as they do with the more perverse and curious aspects of man's behaviour, are liable to be eyed by the authorities with some degree of suspicion, and Summers unwittingly had the misfortune to have two of his translations confiscated by the police. They were Sinistrari's *Demoniality,* and *The Confessions of Madeleine Bavent.* Other titles from the same press suffered a like fate. It was a ridiculous and narrow-minded action, for none of the books (to the mind of a disinterested reader) was pornographic. (p. 54)

The first, Sinistrari's *Demoniality,* published in 1927, is a learned priest's treatise on the incubus and succubus legend, and the possibility of such demons copulating with humans. A translation from the original Latin had already appeared under Isidore Liseux's imprint in Paris in 1879, but this, according to Summers, was 'something worse than indifferent'. It is another very dull book; but it is not obscene. Neither is the second, *The Confessions of Madeleine Bavent,* the possessed nun of Louviers, which was published in 1933. It is a nauseating example of anti-cloistral literature, on a par with *Maria Monk* (though presumably its author did not intend it as such). Apart from its importance as a document of witchcraft (which also it was probably not intended to be) it is rather a puzzle why Summers published it at all. His other translation, *A Treatise of Ghosts* by the learned Capuchin father Noël Taillepied is uninteresting also, except for some of Summers's notes. His final, and posthumously published edition of Richard Bovet's *Pandaemonium,* however, is well worth while and contains one of Summers's most spirited Introductions.

As a translator Summers was guilty throughout of the fault of distortion, or at least of 'heightening' certain passages. (p. 55)

When we come to examine Summers's work, apart from its interest as a storehouse of the history of the macabre, we begin to wonder at his intense passion for the subject. The question is often asked: 'Why was Montague Summers so fascinated by black magic and necromancy?' As an orthodox Roman Catholic priest his damning blasts against the cult's practitioners might be justified; but if he were not such, could this weird delving into witchcraft be something more than a literary and historical essay in research, more than an exposition of sincere belief in witchcraft's evil and heresy? Might not Summers himself have indulged in the very acts he denounced so vehemently? (pp. 55-6)

The true answer will probably never be known. What is possible is that if the story of the Black Mass celebration of 1913 is to be believed Summers learned from it a tremendous lesson: the lesson that such practices are dangerous to a degree. It is possible that he experienced a terrible manifestation of the powers of evil he had sought to invoke, thus forcing him to

his continuous denunciations and obviously sincere loathing of the practice of witchcraft in all its guises.

We must, however, remember, where witchcraft ends and black magic begins. Summers was no magician; he tells us nothing of the lore and tradition of occultism; of the immense and tangled theories of qabalistic theurgy and ritual magic he has nothing to say, except to denounce them as impious. Were Summers ever guilty of the practice of the black arts it was on an amateur level. (p. 56)

With so complex a personality, however, there may well have been more than one motive behind Summers's concern with these dark matters. It would be unrealistic, perhaps, not to detect in his work at many points the factor known to theologians as *delectatio morosa.* In less technical language, it is reasonable to suggest that Summers gave so much time and attention to these themes because he enjoyed them. (p. 57)

In 1927 and 1928 there were published under Summers's editorship reprints of three celebrated Gothic romances: *Horrid Mysteries: a Story from the German of the Marquis of Grosse; The Necromancer: or, The Tale of the Black Forest, founded on facts: Translated from the German of Lawrence Flammenberg;* and *Zofloya, or The Moor* by Charlotte Dacre. Ten years later, in 1938, came Summers's **The Gothic Quest,** the first part of his projected history of the Gothic Novel. The **Quest** is a fascinating book which some readers will perhaps find more entertaining than the quaint old tales with which it is concerned. The reader's attention is held from the opening paragraph of the Introduction. . . . (p. 62)

'In the present volume' [*The Gothic Quest*], Summers says, 'I have elected to deal mainly with those aspects of Gothic Romance which in some sense find their fullest expression in the work of that most notable and significant figure, Matthew Gregory Lewis. To Lewis ('The Monk') he devotes over a hundred pages. Other writers dealt with at length are Francis Lathom, T. J. Horsley Curteis, and William Henry Ireland. The pages on Ireland—the author of the pseudo-Shakespeare play *Vortigern* . . . , are of extraordinary interest. (pp. 62-3)

In a sequel to **The Gothic Quest,** to be entitled *The Gothic Achievement,* Summers proposed to treat in detail the work of Mrs. Radcliffe, Mrs. Charlotte Smith, Mrs. Parsons, Mrs. Roche, Mrs. Meeke, Mrs. Helme, Mrs. Bennett, Godwin, Charlotte Dacre, Jane and Anna Maria Porter, Mrs. Shelley, Maturin, Robert Huish, Charles Lucas, Mrs. Yorke, Catherine Ward, and very many more, 'the central place being, of course, held by "the mighty magician of *The Mysteries of Udolpho*"'.

The Gothic Achievement, though not completed, seems to have been well advanced at the time of Summers's death, and the disappearance of the manuscript is much to be regretted. In 1940, however, the Fortune Press published *A Gothic Bibliography* by Montague Summers, copiously illustrated and uniform with the **Quest.** The **Bibliography** was compiled under hampering wartime conditions, and Summers was conscious that it was not as perfect as it might have been. (p. 63)

The Physical Phenomena of Mysticism, full of interesting and out-of-the-way lore as it is, is hardly one of Summers's best books. (p. 64)

From the beginning of 1943 until his death five years later Summers contributed some seventy articles to the popular weekly magazine *Everybody's;* but in most of them he took small pride. They were hack work, and some are hardly worthy of him, being undertaken simply to strengthen a war-strained purse.

They can by no means compare with his earlier periodical writings for *The Connoisseur* and *Light,* both edited at the time by Mr. C. R. Cammell, and for *Architectural Design and Construction* and *Argentor.* (p. 65)

'Setting aside the highest masterpieces of literature,' Summers writes in his Introduction to **Victorian Ghost Stories** . . . , 'there is nothing more difficult to achieve than a first-class ghost story.' It is only in the ghost story that we are able to judge, and then only by two examples, Summers's own ability as a writer of fiction. The two tales, **'The Grimoire'** and **'The Man on the Stairs'** both appear, the latter anonymously, in *The Grimoire and Other Supernatural Stories.* . . . They are tales one might expect from the pen of a scholar and a literary critic: lively enough, told in a rather antiquarian prose style with, in **'The Grimoire',** a scholar as the hero, a cathedral town as the setting and a rare book as the organ of evil influence. In fact Summers's ideas on the construction of ghost stories are put into practice in these two tales and they agree with those of Dr. Montague Rhodes James, another scholar noted as much for his tales of terror as for his meticulous cataloguing of ancient manuscripts. Summers indeed held the stories of Dr. James in high repute, calling him 'a skilled and profound master of the supernatural'. The terror, Dr. James has said, must be a mainly intellectual one and the ghost must needs be malevolent (there is no place in the true ghost story for the fairy or the mischievous sprite); and the writer must himself believe in ghosts if he is to convince his readers. Summers acknowledges all these tenets in his Introduction to *The Supernatural Omnibus* . . . , the most popular of his three anthologies. He there declares himself particularly admiring of the ghost-story of 'Victoria's formal middle time', tales by J. S. Le Fanu, Mrs. Riddell and Catherine Crowe especially appealing to him. Elsewhere he expresses his distaste for the writings of Edgar Allan Poe, calling him a 'vastly overrated' writer, and he was always quick to scorn any story which might depart from his accepted norm of construction and content, such as the detective story and science-fiction. Of his contemporaries, apart from Dr. James, he appreciated the tales of Algernon Blackwood and Vernon Lee (Violet Paget). (pp. 81-2)

Here and there Montague Summers's writings are marred by an occasional short passage of near-pornography, an outcrop, evidently, of his sexual abnormality. This amounts to nothing very much; but from time to time a page of fine scholarly writing is spoiled for the reader by an unpleasing, because unnecessary, sentence or paragraph. The intrusion of such matter in such a way is symptomatic of the irresponsibility which sometimes betrayed Summers into lapses of taste and judgement. (p. 83)

Another flaw in Summers's character was his quite unnecessary virulence in controversy. The kindest of men in his personal dealings, once the pen was in his hand he seemed unable to express with moderation his disagreement with the views of others. Often his strictures were justified; but their manner of expression too frequently passed the bounds of civility. And unfortunately, quick as he was to detect the errors and stupidities of others, his own work, especially in editing and commenting on old texts, was not always free from faults. (p. 84)

It has also been alleged against Summers that he was jealous of other writers who entered his own special fields. This is not true. There is abundant testimony to his kindness and generosity to young students who approached him seeking help and information; and he was a ready collaborator with the many scholars who consulted him from time to time. But he certainly

gave short shrift to those in whom he detected signs of conceit or presumptuousness, or whom he found pretending to a learning which they did not possess.

For scholarship which he thought greater than his own Summers always showed admiration and respect; but his judgements were not always balanced. He was sometimes unduly influenced by personal liking, as in his exaggerated estimate of the merits of Sir Edmund Gosse and of the quality of the works of his friend S. M. Ellis. Conversely, there was something fantastically disproportionate in his denial of all merit as an actor to John Gielgud, which came to amount to something of a phobia with him.

As he aged, these discordant elements in Summers's personality began to recede, though he could still be majestic in rebuke on occasion. (pp. 85-6)

Pen in hand Summers could be acid and virulent, in conversation caustic; but not a few even of the saints have had this failing. In his later life it was his true self, and not the artificial carapace of earlier days, that his friends saw. He sympathized deeply with those in trouble, as, indeed, he had always done. (p. 87)

Summers has a place, no doubt, in the history of our English eccentrics; but there is very much more to him than that. It is greatly to his credit that out of the failure of his career in the Church, and out of his humdrum years of schoolmastering, he built for himself a third career as a scholar and man of letters, and so made a magnificent recovery from near-shipwreck.

In the long run his best claim to remembrance will be the books that he wrote on the history of the Restoration drama, and his work in connection with The Phoenix. He loved the old drama; and by his contagious enthusiasm he made others love it too.

Here he was a real pioneer; and, in the words of Sir Edmund Gosse, he really did 'open the doors of the Restoration Theatre'. (pp. 89-90)

> *Joseph Jerome [pseudonym of Brocard Sewell], in his* Montague Summers: A Memoir, *Cecil & Amelia Woolf, 1965, 105 p.*

ARTHUR CALDER-MARSHALL   (essay date 1980)

[*In the following excerpt from a review of Summers's posthumously published autobiography, Calder-Marshall offers a brief overview of Summers's life and work.*]

The only thing these two rum volumes [*The Galanty Show: The Autobiography of Montague Summers* and *Letters to Frank Harris and Other Friends* by Enid Bagnold] share is histrionical mountebankery. Notorious in their obsolescence, Summers and Harris wore so many masks that their true features were visible only to God.

Rev. Alphonsus Joseph-Mary Augustus Montague . . . listed his recreations in *Who's Who 1948* as—travel; staying in unknown monasteries and villages in Italy; pilgrimages to famous shrines; the investigation of occult phenomena; ghost stories; talking to intelligent dogs; that is, all dogs; research in hagiology, liturgies, mysticism, the older English drama; late Latin literature.

Writing under the pseudonym of Joseph Jerome, Fr. Brocard Sewell . . . in *Montague Summers: a Memoir* . . . confessed uncertainty whether Summers ever obtained priest's orders, but in his postscript to **The Galanty Show,** he states unequivocally that his orders obtained in Italy, were "valid" though perhaps "irregular". He was possibly a diabolist, certainly a homosexual, the restorer of Restoration drama and a Cassandra-like prophet of the dangers of a revival of magical practices.

Arthur Calder-Marshall, "Peeps Behind the Masks of Mountebanks," in The Guardian Weekly, *Vol. 123, No. 11, September 7, 1980, p. 22.***

JOHN C. MORAN (essay date 1982)

[*An American essayist and critic, Moran is president of the F. Marion Crawford Memorial Society, which is devoted to study of Crawford's works and those of other nineteenth- and twentieth-century Romantic authors. In the following excerpt, Moran characterizes Summers as an eccentric but erudite scholar.*]

Most infrequently in the annals of literature is found an author whose life itself reads more like a Romantic novel than do these fictions themselves; one immediately thinks of Marlowe and Crawford. In the present debased century, among men of letters the Rev. Montague Summers . . . has had virtually no rivals to the title of "most original character." Walking the streets of London and Oxford attired in the garb of a seventeenth-century priest; making no attempt to refute gossip and rumors of early scandals involving diabolism; impaling "modern enlightened progressives" (especially Catholics of this ilk) upon the massive, awesome erudition and scholarship pervading his studies of witchcraft, diabolism, vampirism, and lycanthropy during the 1920's and 1930's; frustrating jealous academics with his pioneering scholarship in the Gothic novel (mid-1910's onward) and the ghost story along with his monumental studies of Restoration-era drama and his model Nonesuch editions of seventeenth-century dramatists such as Dryden, Congreve, Mrs. Behn, *et al*. . . . Msgr. Summers was a founder of The Phoenix (1919)—the society dedicated to the production of Restoration-era drama—and an authority on Mysticism having written especially on the Carmelite mystics and having edited a number of their works.

But, as Father Sewell points out in his Introduction [to *The Galanty Show*], Msgr. Summers was known by his friends as "a kindly and gentle man—though on occasions he could be majestic in rebuke of foolishness or presumption—a scholar of wide and unusual learning, and a gay companion of rare conversational brilliance." Noteworthy also is Montague Summers' unrivalled knowledge of the history of London's moral underworld of the past three centuries. . . .

[*The Galanty Show*] in part describes the author's youth and home-life at Clifton during the 1880's and 1890's, his life-long love of the theater, his labors on behalf of the seventeenth-century dramatists, and his friendship with fellow drama enthusiast-authority A. H. Bullen. It also contains a fascinating chapter on the ghost story and other equally fascinating chapters which in part deal with lesser-known (but not necessarily lesser) "Victorian" novelists such as John Frederick Smith, T. W. Speight, Mrs. Emma Marshall ("the famous Clifton authoress"), J. H. Shorthouse, Miss Braddon, and Mrs. Frances Trollope (whilst finding little of merit in the novels of her son).

Especially interesting and amusing is the plethora of critical strictures by Montague Summers in reference to such fashionable (then) authors as Miss Dorothy L. Sayers ("authority" on Dante who could not read Italian), Mr. Evelyn Waugh ("Mr. Yeats doesn't know who Evelyn Waugh is!" "Why on earth should he?" I replied.), Mr. Grahame Greene, and the

poet-Satanist Aleister Crowley ("one-quarter conjuror and three-quarters charlatan, and whole common-publicist").

One cannot overlook Msgr. Summers' denunciations of modern academic scholarship as exemplified by Professors A. Nicoll and F. S. Boas (who "have all the mistakes of the older men without a shadow of their wit and wisdom"). *The Galanty Show* contains many animadversions such as the just-cited examples too numerous to include in the brief confines of this review.

On the other hand, however, Montague Summers' autobiography is basically a positive remembrance wherein praise and commendation are much more common than criticisms. (p. 7)

If the present writer had to choose the sections of this completely informative and interesting book which most appealed to him, then the difficult answer would refer to those parts which describe Msgr. Summers' recollections of his childhood joys and thrills of obtaining volumes of John Dick's Penny Plays and sets of the Parlour Theater (miniature stage with texts) all described in fond detail; he in particular liked the Skelt editions.

Whilst mentioning Montague Summers' life-long love for the drama, one cannot help but wonder if this unique and enigmatic man was an actor at heart. The reader who has studied Montague Summers' life (especially Mr. Joseph Jerome's biography published in 1965) and pondered his varied works would no doubt suspect it; the initial chapters of the present autobiography almost confirm it. (p. 8)

John C. Moran, "Montague Summers' Autobiography: 'The Galanty Show'," in The Romantist, *Nos. 4 & 5, John C. Moran, Don Herron, Steve Eng, eds., The F. Marion Crawford Memorial Society, 1982, pp. 7-8.*

STEVE ENG (poem date 1982)

[*A fantasy poet and essayist, Eng provides a memorial verse about Summers.*]

Arcane collector of Gothic lore,
Immersed in luridness and gore,
 He wryly catalogued it all—
 The ivy-covered castle wall,
The dungeon and the secret door.

He studied witches and werewolves too,
And found the vampire tales were true;
 A throw-back to another age,
 He loved the Restoration stage
And smiled . . . as gossip 'round him grew.

Steve Eng, "Montague Summers (1880-1948)," in The Romantist, *Nos. 4 & 5, John C. Moran, Don Herron, Steve Eng, eds., The F. Marion Crawford Memorial Society, 1982, p. 31.*

ADDITIONAL BIBLIOGRAPHY

Enright, D. J. "Parson Believes in Witches." *The Listener* 104, No. 2669 (10 July 1980): 54-5.
 Review of *The Galanty Show*. Enright notes that Summers has a high reputation in two distinct areas: his writings on the Gothic

romance and Restoration theater, and his studies of occult subjects.

Machen, Arthur. "The Other Side." *The New Statesman and Nation* n.s. II, No. 38 (14 November 1931): xii-xiv.
    Discusses the question of credibility in the ghost story. In his review of *The Supernatural Omnibus*, Machen notes that Summers holds to M. R. James's famous dictum—that a ghost story should inspire the reader to think "If I'm not very careful, something of this kind may happen to me!" However, Machen disagrees with this position, maintaining that readers like to regard ghost stories as disquieting, "but not likely to fall into our own experience."

Riley, Woodbridge. "Learned Superstition: *The History of Witchcraft and Demonology.*" *New York Herald Tribune Books* (19 December 1926): 7.
    Stresses Summers's personal belief in the existence of his supernatural subject matter.

Sewell, Father Brocard. Foreword to *A Bibliography of the Works of Montague Summers*, by Timothy d'Arch Smith, pp. 7-10. New Hyde Park, N.Y.: University Books, 1964.
    Notes the difficulty of preparing a bibliography of Summers, who contributed prolifically to periodicals. Sewell writes that while it

is chiefly Summers's studies of witchcraft that are sought by modern collectors, Summers's finest works are his studies of the Restoration drama.

Review of *The Restoration Theatre*, by Montague Summers. *The Times Literary Supplement*, No. 1678 (29 March 1934): 227.
    Largely approbatory review of *The Restoration Theatre*. Fault is found, however, with Summers's intolerance of other writers in the field, and with his fondness for obscure terms and obfuscatory phrases.

"Gothic Books and Authors." *The Times Literary Supplement*, No. 2040 (8 March 1941): 120.
    Review of Summers's *A Gothic Bibliography*. The critic notes that the coverage of authors is very uneven and dependent upon Summers's degree of interest in the subject.

Wilson, A. N. "Shades of Purple." *The Times Literary Supplement*, No. 4035 (25 July 1980): 831-32.
    Review of Summers's posthumously published autobiographical work *The Galanty Show*. Wilson characterizes Summers as an eccentric and controversial figure who may have been a priest, a pederast, and a pornographer, but who was unquestionably a leading authority on Restoration drama and the Gothic novel.

Israel Zangwill

1864-1926

(Also wrote under pseudonyms of Baroness von S., J. Freeman Bell, and Marshallik) English novelist, dramatist, short story writer, essayist, critic, translator, lecturer, and poet.

Through his stories and novels depicting life in the Jewish ghettos of England, Zangwill emerged as the father of modern English-Jewish literature and enjoyed worldwide recognition in the late nineteenth and early twentieth centuries. In his ghetto works he demonstrated a vivid, often grave realism that was shocking to many for its straightforward documentation of squalid city life. However, he distinguished himself from the English realistic school of the nineties, which included George Gissing, Arthur Morrison, and George Moore, by tempering a naturalistic portrayal of impoverished districts with a blend of wry humor and undying optimism. Zangwill was equally prominent for his lectures, essays, and administrative work on behalf of various political and reform movements, including women's suffrage and the establishment of a Jewish state. His deep concern with these issues lent an overly didactic cast to many of his later writings, which in turn contributed to a general decline in his literary reputation.

Zangwill was born in the Whitechapel ghetto of London to East European immigrants. The family moved for a time to Bristol, where Zangwill began his education. He displayed an early talent for writing, and by the age of ten was composing stories of school life and circulating them among his classmates. Soon after, he began contributing verses and essays to various juvenile publications and at sixteen won first prize in a humorous short story competition. When he was eighteen he published his first work, a pamphlet entitled *Motza Kleis,* written with Louis Cowen, which depicted market days in the East End of London and represented the nucleus of his novel *Children of the Ghetto.* Zangwill wrote for various Jewish community periodicals and taught at the Jews' Free School until 1888, when he began writing a column for *The Jewish Standard.* The same year he again collaborated with Cowen and published his first book-length work, a fantasy modeled after Mark Twain's *The Prince and the Pauper* entitled *The Premier and the Painter.* In 1890 Zangwill founded the humorous paper *Ariel: The London Puck,* which he edited for the next two years. During this time Zangwill's first successful works, *The Bachelors' Club* (a collection of humorous stories) and *The Big Bow Mystery,* were published. Recognized as a fine representation, though a burlesque, of the mystery genre, the latter work was subsequently adapted to the screen, as were several of Zangwill's other works, including *Merely Mary Ann, We Moderns, Children of the Ghetto,* and *The Melting Pot.* In these early works, Zangwill employed a lavish amount of puns, hyperbole, and inverted epigrams—elements that he never completely abandoned in his later fiction. While his humorous works had been modest successes, in 1892 Zangwill received worldwide recognition for his *Children of the Ghetto,* which had been commissioned by the Jewish Publication Society of America. Through the widespread sympathy inspired by this authentic portrayal of London Jewish ghetto life, Zangwill is credited with preventing passage of anti-Jewish legislation by Parliament.

Culver Pictures, Inc.

In 1895 Zangwill met the Hungarian-born Jewish leader Theodor Herzl in North London; it is said that their first conversation symbolized the founding of modern Zionism, which sought to establish the region of Palestine as a permanent homeland for the Jewish people. Thenceforward, Zangwill followed two interdependent careers, one political and the other literary, which oftentimes became inextricably bound together. This combination of interests enabled Zangwill to acquire an astonishing group of friends and acquaintances, including Winston Churchill, David Lloyd George, Theodore Roosevelt, Bernard Shaw, H. G. Wells, Rudyard Kipling, G. K. Chesterton, Oscar Wilde, and John Galsworthy. Through his friendship with Herzl he emerged as one of the chief proponents of Zionism and for a time was caricatured as "Lord Zion" for his zealous devotion to the cause. But in 1905, in the wake of the Zionist Congress's rejection of Britain's offer of East Africa as a Jewish homeland (the Uganda Project), Zangwill withdrew his membership and formed the Jewish Territorial Organization (ITO) in hopes of negotiating a new deal with Parliament for the acquisition of this region. By 1908 he was so involved with his work as president of ITO that he told the *Jewish Chronicle* that he had ceased to be a writer. He further extended this "second career" through his devotion to the suffragist and pacifist movements, and to the Jewish Historical Society. Yet, despite his many political and social concerns, Zangwill published something in virtually every year until his death.

After the turn of the century, Zangwill concentrated his creative energies on drama. His first success, the dramatization of his short story "Merely Mary Ann," came in 1904, the year following his marriage to writer and suffragist Edith Ayrton. In all, he produced 17 plays between 1900 and 1926. Zangwill's most famous play, *The Melting Pot,* was widely celebrated in America and popularized the phrase coined by St. John de Crevecouer in 1782. Although the drama's advocacy of racial integration was somewhat controversial, it was superceded in this respect by *The Next Religion,* which was officially banned in England for its support of a new, international faith and for what was thought to be a derogatory portrayal of the Christian Church. During this period of intense productivity, Zangwill also published two collections of stories, a book of poetry, a translation of Hebrew verse, and a novel adapted from an earlier play, *Jinny the Carrier.* Zangwill's last years were trouble-ridden and unhappy. Poor health, diminishing literary fame, the failure to restage a number of his earlier plays, and the vituperative response to his speech "Watchman, What of the Night?"—in which he declared the death of political Zionism—eventually led to a nervous breakdown. In 1925 Zangwill produced *We Moderns,* his final play, which failed to please both critics and the public due to its cliché-ridden exploration of generational conflicts and its bitter attack upon modern art and psychology. He died the following year in Sussex.

Zangwill was profoundly influenced by the works of several established literary figures, but perhaps most importantly by those of Leo Tolstoy, particularly Tolstoy's philosophy that art should serve in the dissemination of moral truths. Like Tolstoy, he believed that his craft went beyond literature and entered the realm of evangelism. Although some of Zangwill's fiction has consequently been labelled didactic, idealistic, or overly dramatic, critics consider him more a realist and moralist than a romantic. He knew and admired George Gissing, a noted realistic writer of the era whose influence can be discerned in Zangwill's ghetto works. But the Jewish author's perception of the starker aspects of life differed from that of Gissing and other realists. He unhesitatingly documented deplorable living conditions yet tempered his tragic scenes with comedy and irony, as well as an ardent affirmation of tradition, family, religious faith, and man's innate ability to overcome life's most difficult obstacles.

It is generally agreed that Zangwill's best works were his writings about Jews and Jewish concerns. In so doing he presented his most interesting subjects, achieved the greatest degree of verisimilitude, demonstrated the deepest pathos, and addressed the most compelling issues. In the epic work *Children of the Ghetto,* Zangwill presented the Jewish inhabitants of London's Whitechapel ghetto, with both their virtues and imperfections laid bare. Until the publication of this novel, the literary public had little besides Shakespeare's Shylock, Charles Dickens's Fagin, and George Eliot's Daniel Deronda to refer to for an artistic portrayal of the English Jew. Until Zangwill's time most portrayals of Jewish people in English literature were severely and negatively one-dimensional and left the general reader dangerously unenlightened. Zangwill's work, however, clearly revealed the life and struggles of the Anglo-Jewish world. His love for his people, his penchant for detail, and his intimate knowledge of his subject insured the realistic, three-dimensional quality of his characters. Most scholars acknowledge that *Children of the Ghetto* is not a novel in the strictest sense, but rather an epic progression of scenes and portraits loosely organized around the author's most dominant theme—the conflict between old and new values within the Jewish

community, and the younger generation's need to choose between the constancy and security of tradition or the flexibility and uncertainty of the modern world. Though commended for his thoughtful treatment of this theme, Zangwill was often criticized for his overly discursive, fragmented style. This inability to excise the superfluous made for uneven prose in all his works and has led to a mixed critical reputation. For example, *The King of Schnorrers,* which is set in late eighteenth-century London and details the comical life of a dignified beggar, has been described as an excellent documentation of Jewish humor and an informed, ironic commentary on the gross imbalance of existing social systems. Yet the work has also been criticized for its effusion of Jewish esoterica and occasionally tiresome wit. Some critics complain that Zangwill's regular use of Hebrew and Yiddish terminology in these works hampers their readability. But Zangwill was convinced that the use of these idioms was essential to a true representation of the ghetto world.

If Zangwill ever avoided discursiveness, overabundant detail, and trying wit, critics agree that he did so within his short stories. The titles of his two collections—*Ghetto Tragedies* and *Ghetto Comedies*—are misleading, for Zangwill sought to disregard traditional distinctions between comedy and tragedy. Instead, he frequently merged the two types with startling effect, lending the comedies an unusually strong emotive power and the tragedies an endearing appeal. Critics contend that Zangwill's short stories are artistically successful because the genre imposed limitations of length and form that controlled the weaknesses demonstrated in his novels. Of his novels, only *The Master* is considered a significant artistic achievement, due to Zangwill's concentration on the spiritual and intellectual development of a single character.

Less important to the modern reader than Zangwill's fiction are his plays. Although popular with the theatergoing public during his lifetime, they are extremely dated and today have been virtually forgotten. Zangwill did enjoy two significant commercial successes, *The Melting Pot* and *Merely Mary Ann*—the latter more lucrative than all the ghetto works combined. Yet critics dismiss both as mediocre entertainments. *Merely Mary Ann* is regarded as an unexceptional melodrama and *The Melting Pot,* though at least historically important for its revolutionary promotion of ethno-synthesis, is considered an emotionally effective but overly exuberant example of late nineteenth-century idealism. Zangwill's political trilogy, which includes *The War God, The Cockpit,* and *The Forcing House,* is commonly viewed as his best dramatic work for its forceful denunciation of war, intolerance, and the duplicity of modern politics. But few others were successful either commercially or artistically. An overabundance of stock characters, melodramatic scenes, and unrealistic dialogue, coupled with Zangwill's belief that the stage existed primarily for promoting philosophic views, led to their failure.

In addition to his fiction and dramas, Zangwill was an accomplished essayist. In *The Voice of Jerusalem* and other works he displayed a remarkable depth of thought, feeling, and vision on a variety of topics, including pacifism, Zionism, social and economic injustice, and the predicament of a hitherto cloistered Jewish community faced with a rapidly changing and expanding world. A master polemicist, Zangwill was as widely known during his lifetime for the promulgation of his ideas as he was for his creative works.

Although his writings were inconsistent in quality, Zangwill's depiction of the Jewish ghettos of London are significant portraits of an important portion of English culture. The popularity and artistry of these works earned him such titles as the "Disraeli of modern letters" and the "Dickens of the ghetto." His numerous accounts of immigrant life also inspired many later novelists, including Louis Golding, Wolf Mankowitz, and Bernard Kops, which led to Zangwill's reputation as the father of modern English-Jewish literature. In addition, critics contend that he pioneered the fictional treatment of many themes developed by such modern American chroniclers of Jewish life as Henry Roth, Bernard Malamud, Philip Roth, and Saul Bellow. Undoubtedly the popularity of these authors has in part contributed to the revival of critical interest in Zangwill, but the continued survival of the ghetto works themselves attests to the appeal of Zangwill's vivid portrayal of a long-ignored segment of English society.

(See also *Contemporary Authors*, Vol. 109 and *Dictionary of Literary Biography*, Vol. 10: *Modern British Dramatists, 1900-1945*.)

PRINCIPAL WORKS

Motza Kleis [with Louis Cowen]   (essay)   1882
The Ballad of Moses   (poetry)   1882
The Premier and the Painter [with Louis Cowen, as J. Freeman Bell]   (novel)   1888
The Bachelors' Club   (short stories)   1891
The Big Bow Mystery   (novel)   1892
Children of the Ghetto: Being Pictures of a Peculiar People (novel)   1892
The Great Demonstration [with Louis Cowen]   (drama) 1892
The Old Maids' Club   (short stories)   1892
Ghetto Tragedies   (short stories)   1893
Merely Mary Ann   (short story)   1893
The King of Schnorrers: Grotesques and Fantasies   (novel) 1894
The Master   (novel)   1895
Without Prejudice   (essays)   1896
The Celibates' Club: Being the United Stories of the Bachelors' Club and The Old Maids' Club   (short stories)   1898
They That Walk in Darkness: Ghetto Tragedies   (short stories)   1899
The Mantle of Elijah   (novel)   1900
The Grey Wig: Stories and Novelettes   (short stories)   1903
Jinny the Carrier   (drama)   1905
Merely Mary Ann   (drama)   1905
Ghetto Comedies   (short stories)   1907
The Melting Pot   (drama)   1908
Italian Fantasies   (travel essays)   1910
The War God   (drama)   1911
The Next Religion   (drama)   1912
The Principle of Nationalities   (lecture)   1917
Jinny the Carrier   (novel)   1919
The Voice of Jerusalem   (essays)   1920
The Cockpit   (drama)   1921
The Forcing House; or, The Cockpit Continued   (drama) 1922
We Moderns   (drama)   1924
Speeches, Articles, and Letters of Israel Zangwill   (essays, lectures, and letters)   1937
Selected Works of Israel Zangwill   (novel and short stories) 1938

The Collected Works of Israel Zangwill. 14 vols.   (novels, short stories, dramas, essays, and poetry)   1969

THE ATHENAEUM   (essay date 1891)

[*In the following excerpt, the anonymous critic offers lukewarm praise for Zangwill's* The Bachelors' Club, *concluding that its excessive length mutes the effect of the humor.*]

It is only right to observe that [*The Bachelors' Club*] is a jocular book not by any means exclusively modelled on that form of American humour of which Mark Twain's earlier works are the type and every American comic paper an example. The author may, therefore, assert for himself a claim to originality, simply because he is not, as many recent English wits have been, a mere imitator of the American humourists of a class one or more degrees below the highest. If the author is himself an American he may assert his claim not less confidently and it shall be allowed not less freely. The fault to be found with the author is not that he is too funny, but that he is funny too much. His preface is good, so are some of his verses, and so are many of his casual remarks, but he runs into 338 pages. If he could have compressed his wit into the brevity of thirty, or fifty, or even one hundred pages, he would have earned a considerable measure of gratitude which might have warmed into admiration.

A review of "The Bachelors' Club," in The Athenaeum, No. 3327, August 1, 1891, p. 157.

JAMES ASHCROFT NOBLE   (essay date 1892)

[*In the following excerpt, Noble discusses* Children of the Ghetto *as a nearly sociological portrait of Jewish London, praising the detail and literary quality of the work, but noting that the plot is sometimes submerged by the portrait of Jewish life.*]

Mr. Zangwill's first three-volume novel proves that he has other endowments besides humour, either of the old or the new kind. Indeed, **Children of the Ghetto** is rather deficient in humour of any kind, the only episode with a genuine smile in it being the ineffectual love-making of a young Hebrew. . . . Of late years the Jew has been increasingly *en évidence* in English fiction. George Eliot in *Daniel Deronda*, and Mr. Hall Caine in *The Scapegoat*, have treated him from the outside in a romantic and idealising fashion. The author of *Violet Moses*, a clever but rather cynical book published some two years ago, seemed to write from the inside as one native and to the manner born; but in intimacy of knowledge and unrelenting realism of handling, Mr. Zangwill leaves his predecessors far behind him. Dutch painting has a method which is, when rightly employed, interesting and attractive; but its elaborate verisimilitude is apt to be wearisome when applied to the details of a life with which we are altogether unfamiliar, because the spectator's pleasure in homely realistic art depends very largely on his ability to compare the representation with the thing represented. Mr. Zangwill has hardly laid this consideration sufficiently to heart, and in many portions of **Children of the Ghetto** the wood of narrative is hidden by the leafage of information: we feel that what we are reading is hardly a novel, but a clever treatise on the minutiae of manner and custom among the Jewish poor of London, illustrated by sketches of imaginary typical characters. . . . [In] Mr. Zangwill's book the picture of Jewish life is the main thing, while the story is altogether subordinate. He has taken pains that the Hebraic effect shall not be weakened or confused by the introduction of an alien element. . . . [The] literary quality of Mr. Zangwill's novel . . . is decidedly good. His materials are not always well digested, but in the main he manages to achieve the effect at which he aims, and this is the really important thing.

James Ashcroft Noble, in a review of "Children of the Ghetto," in The Academy, Vol. XLII, No. 1077, December 24, 1892, p. 585.

M. C. BIRCHENOUGH (essay date 1893)

[*In the following excerpt Birchenough notes that* Children of the Ghetto *masterfully replicates life in the London Jewish ghetto, but concludes that occasionally obscure references and the over-use of unfamiliar Yiddish words detracts from its potential for greatness.*]

In turning over the pages of Mr. Zangwill's very remarkable book [*Children of the Ghetto*], certain echoes of Heine rise unbidden to the mind with haunting persistency. Here, it seems, in our midst is a strange people, practically unknown to all of us who are not Jews, and only a little better known to the greater number of their co-religionists in England. Exiles and refugees, driven out by persecution from their homes in Russia and Poland, they speak a strange language and live a strange exotic life of their own, entirely separated from the jostling crowds around them. The rites and ceremonies they practise are more abundant than those of any other worshippers, and, according to Mr. Zangwill, their lives are ordered with even greater rigidness than those of English Jews in a corresponding class, whom the exiles regard indeed as "link," *i.e.*, lax, almost "heathen," guilty of much falling from grace. But from time to time, out of the midst of this group of aliens, appears a figure familiar to us all. . . .

More often still the Heine echo is to be found in the brief completeness of a number of dramatic episodes, which are threaded like separate pearls on a string of dull intermediate pages in the first and second volumes. For unlike Heine, the new poet of the Ghetto is by no means always an artist.

But he knows how to strike the same human cry out of the inarticulate tragedy of clashing traditions, out of the anguish of jarring generations, of exile, of oppression from within and without. He points to fine gold buried in the dust-heaps, and to wisdom and learning hidden in the garrets. He shows how the strange figures, with their un-English faces and queer merchandise, can still weep when they remember their lost Zion, for all the hard bargains driven over the stalls in the narrow lanes off the Whitechapel Road. (p. 330)

Those who can speak with complete authority on the subject say that the picture is an absolutely true one in all respects. So it is merely with the literary and artistic aspect of the book that the critic is concerned, and with no question as to its photographic accuracy. (p. 331)

The *Children of the Ghetto* is a curiously unequal book! In reading it most people will be roused at times to an enthusiasm of admiration by the dramatic force of several of its situations, by the power and humour of the character sketches, and the true note of its pathos. At such moments they are prompted to exclaim that Mr. Zangwill has written a great book. And great in parts it undoubtedly is. But while this delightful conviction steals over the soul of his reader, while the writer is at his very

best—concentrated, terse, full of restrained power or sly humour, and working up finely to his crisis—there comes some soul-shattering interruption, or rather irruption of matter possessing no interest whatever to literature or humanity at large. The wretch Pinchas, for example, is amusing for a page, but he is always elbowing out much better company. In the long run he becomes a weariness to the flesh. The same remark applies to the Sons of the Covenant, the Jargon Players, and above all to the *Flag* newspaper, together with all its internecine squabbles. Whatever topical or local allusions these may contain are necessarily lost upon the outside world. Now this book belongs not to one section of the community, but to that avenging angel the general reader. Two more complaints has this dread personage to prefer against the book as a whole before passing on to an examination of its details.

"The book as a whole"; one pauses over the words themselves, for here at once is a slight stone of stumbling. It has come to us in three volumes, and under one title, but the volumes certainly comprise as many separate works. First from all points of view are those dramas in miniature. . ., episodes tragic, or humorous, or both, for there is a deal of human nature in the Ghetto, and its interpreter is not likely to overlook any of its phases. . . . These dramatic idylls (the name must be excused, for no other describes them) contain Mr. Zangwill's best work, and how good that is will be in itself a happy discovery. Interspersed with them are matters of different and quite inferior interest, such as those referred to above, together with some disquisitions which are not entertaining when they stray into a work of imagination. The internecine politics and journalistic quarrels may have their exact counterparts in the real Jewish world, but this does not make them either interesting or artistic as presented in *Children of the Ghetto*. (pp. 331-32)

Non-Jewish readers have one more subject of cavilling with regard to Mr. Zangwill's methods. By the constant introduction of Yiddish and other words strange to the world in general, he has unnecessarily added to the initial difficulties which beset our reading of his book. (p. 332)

[After] having grappled with these troubles more or less successfully, flesh and spirit rebel when conversation of an entirely lay nature is invaded by incomprehensible words of a barbarous appearance, and only an occasional family likeness to any of the languages generally included in a modern education. It may be replied that the sum of them is not large, but from the moment that they become troublesome, and at all baffling to those without special instruction, their introduction is an artistic mistake.

So much for general cavillings. Their very nature shows how strong is the interest which the book arouses, how keen is the resentment of all that interferes with its appointed course. We would all enjoy to the very utmost its artistic beauties, and indulge the friendly—entirely sympathetic—curiosity it arouses about those of whom it mainly treats, the poor, who are as widely separated from the ordinary inhabitants of Whitechapel as the East is from the West. (p. 333)

After all, can one not say it is a great book? It is so very nearly one! With ruthless expurgations, with a certain amount of pulling together, with greater care as to the writing, it would have reached high-water mark. (p. 337)

M. C. Birchenough, in a review of "Children of the Ghetto," in The Jewish Quarterly Review, Vol. V, No. 18, January, 1893, pp. 330-337.

THE BOOKMAN, LONDON (essay date 1893)

[*In the following review of* Ghetto Tragedies, *the critic discusses the artistic weaknesses of the work but finds in it burgeoning artistry that improves upon previous collections of popular fiction by Zangwill. For a contrasting opinion, see the excerpt from* The Athenaeum *(1893).*]

As an interpreter of the Jew to the Gentile, at once a naturalist painter of Hebrew speech and manners, and a revealer of Hebrew ideals, Mr. Zangwill is already known. In this field he has a magnificent opportunity and few rivals. The life of modern Jews, even in London, where they are more absorbed in the population than anywhere else, has recesses and sanctuaries which few Gentiles guess. . . . [A few of the pages of *Ghetto Tragedies*] almost convince us that his race has found a masterly interpreter in Mr. Zangwill, and the rest is pure disappointment. Of the four stories, "**Satan Makatrig**," "**The Diary of a Meshumad**," "**Incurable**," and "**The Sabbath Breaker**," the second and third deserve high praise, and now and again, in all of them, the inner life of Judaism, its exalted moments, its fervid domestic affections, the significance of its symbols, the pathos of its memories, are depicted in a way for which we have only the most sympathetic admiration. The religious ecstasy of Rivkoly, in the first story, the early racial instincts of the apostate, in the second—instincts triumphing over all the influences and the self-interest of his later life—the painful adherence to every possible letter of the law, even in its heroic breach, in "**The Sabbath Breaker**," are described with quiet force. But here hesitation comes in. In the first place, he has not proved that he can write a story; rather he has proved that he can markedly fail. "**Satan Makatrig**" is the most ambitious from a narrative point of view, but, with much good detail, it is a jumble of improbabilities, a heap of uncalled for exaggerations. It is a story of neither this world nor another, neither natural nor supernatural, striving after effect, yet ineffective. A study in religious fanaticism, and of blasphemous mania, it needed sobriety of treatment, for want of which it has little coherence and carries no conviction. It is difficult at first to say wherein lies Mr. Zangwill's defect, but we steal upon it in "**Incurable**." This sketch of life in an East-end Refuge has in it an incident very striking and truly pathetic. Sarah, the bed-ridden paralytic, has a faithless husband. She taxes him with his neglect and desertion, and he does not deny it, but excuses himself with shuffling, whining cowardice. His wife is not without a feeling of bitter indignation at her luckless fate and scorn for his weakness. But she will not have him live in sin, and so she commands him to bring her the Gett—the voluntary acceptance of which by the wife annuls a marriage. The episode is really sublime, but it is nearly spoilt by the accessories, by the heaping up of the agony of the surroundings, by a struggle for effect which overreaches itself. . . . The four tragedies are all remarkable, full of tender statement, and wrapped about by picturesque circumstance. But Mr. Zangwill is not yet an artist. His earlier literary sins have left him an unfortunate legacy. No one can write 'Bachelors' Clubs' and 'Old Maids' Clubs' with impunity. The popular success of such attempts is dearly bought by any one who aims at literature, and finds his hand subdued to the baser stuff it has worked in. Mr. Zangwill is by nature an idealist. He is an idealist who went astray for a time, but he is on the right track now. (pp. 183-84)

A review of "Ghetto Tragedies," in The Bookman, *London, Vol. IV, No. 24, September, 1893, pp. 183-84.*

THE ATHENAEUM (essay date 1893)

[*In the following excerpt, the critic discusses the artistry of the commonplace in* Ghetto Tragedies. *For a contrasting opinion, see the excerpt from* The Bookman *(1893).*]

It is a sincere pleasure to meet another of Mr. Zangwill's books about the Jews. He again shows—what indeed was evident in *The Children of the Ghetto*—that in this subject he has found his true sphere, and that, instead of being merely a purveyor of amusing stories and good jokes, he is also an artist. And the art displayed [in *Ghetto Tragedies*] is of a very high order—the art of revealing the beauty inherent in what at first sight is merely ugly or commonplace. For Mr. Zangwill's Polish Jews are certainly not obviously beautiful; they might almost be called repulsive in some aspects; they have associations of squalor and unintelligent superstition which it is difficult to overcome; and, indeed, Mr. Zangwill does not attempt to overcome them. He presents them in all their native ugliness, he glosses over nothing, he hides nothing, and yet he adds just the touch of beauty which raises the commonplace into a fitting subject for art. (pp. 450-51)

A review of "Ghetto Tragedies," in The Athenaeum, *No. 3440, September 30, 1893, pp. 450-51.*

[H. G. WELLS] (essay date 1895)

[*Wells is best known today, along with Jules Verne, as one of the fathers of modern science fiction and as a utopian idealist who correctly foretold an era of chemical warfare, atomic weaponry, and world wars. His writing was shaped by the influence of Arnold Bennett, Frank Harris, Joseph Conrad, and other contemporaries with whom he exchanged criticism and opinions on the art of writing. Throughout much of his career, Wells wrote and lectured on the betterment of society through education and the advance of scientific innovation. A Fabian socialist and student of zoologist T. H. Huxley, Wells was, until his last bitter years, a believer in the gradual, inevitable moral and intellectual ascent of humanity. Much of his literary criticism was written during the 1890s at* The Saturday Review, *under the direction of Harris. In the following excerpt, Wells calls* The Master *"unreadable" because of its excessive passages of unimaginative dialogue and verbose narration. He finds this regrettable because he believes that these problems destroy the basic quality of the novel.*]

[In *The Master*,] Mr. Zangwill has made a big book of what might have been a great one, and we will confess we are disappointed and exasperated by it. There is a certain strength about Mr. Zangwill, coupled with a certain perverse badness that perplexes and irritates the reviewer exceedingly. Mr. Zangwill inserts pages—or at least paragraphs—that Dickens might have written, between masses of tawdry notebook copy that Mr. Sala's understudy—if Mr. Sala has an understudy—would blush to have compiled, even in a hurry. Why does he do it? There are whole pages of the merest drivel in his last book, stuff such as a tired man might write in the early morning under a vow to get so much finished—at any cost; and hang the quality! . . .

The plain fact is he has not learnt how to manage dialogue. He is like a poor conversationalist, and falls to on the cigarettes, the whisky, and the weather. Half the conversation in the book is such, mere stopgap chatter. But he does worse things than that. For instance, one finds page after page of art-studio shop, the ordinary things the intelligent beginner hears, repeats, and has done with in the first year of his work, put into the mouths of distinguished artists and labelled "A Symposium." They gabble about ideals and the imagination in art, and the prospects of black and white work, and the Academy and so forth like suckling professional geniuses rather than capable men. . . . Still more terrible is Mr. Zangwill on the Beautiful . . . *a propos* of the Louvre and Venice. And Mr. Zangwill's research after humour has been just as industrious as his pursuit of art. (p. 656)

Imagine a good story that might have been effectively told in a hundred and fifty pages enjellied in a huge mass of this unmeaning or collected matter, and you will have a very good idea of the structural effect of Mr. Zangwill's book. It is, in fact, a story afflicted with elephantiasis—cumbered with the excrescences a weakly constitution begets. Or, to take another image, the story is like that remarkable and eccentric insect, the "Reduvius" bug, which covers itself up in a huge mass of dust particles, wisps of cobweb and corner sweepings, until at last it becomes a mere slowly crawling lump of rubbish. The object of the "Reduvius" bug is protection; but we have no doubt that Mr. Zangwill's collections will as effectively protect him from all but the most voracious reader.

The pity of it is that this present novel, stripped of its morbid accretions, is a good one. It is the story of an artist, of his boyhood in Canada among unsympathetic people, of his coming to London, of his almost hopeless struggles to obtain instruction and a footing as an artist, and of his final success—ideals being thrown to the wind—as a painter of sentimental pictures. If the reader will only have the patience to excavate this buried character from this journalism-smothered Pompeii of a book he will be surprised at its consistency and reality. . . . The incidental characters are all good, the taxidermist, "Ole Hey," Abner Preep, Coble, all move amusingly in the interstices of the padding. These four characters, indeed, it would be difficult to overpraise. Only it is hard work discovering these chinks and crannies, these occasional rich veins of story. A guide to the book, like a correspondence crammer's notes to his students, might avail perhaps; "read p. 72," for instance, "omit pp. 273-280." Failing such aid the book remains, in our opinion, unreadable. Its veins of rich ore only make its unworkableness a matter for regret.

The present reviewer would repeat that he is—though it may not be apparent so far—an admirer of Mr. Zangwill, or rather of Mr. Zangwill's possibilities. In his *Ghetto Tragedies,* in his story of **"Flutter-duck,"** he has displayed qualities that may yet place him in the front rank of living novelists. There was real humour, too, in his conception of the *King of the Schnorrers.* But he has a lax facility, a feminine fecundity, that threaten to destroy him. There seems, indeed, a kind of dualism about him; there is the talented Zangwill, who conceived the personality of the Master, and the industrious Zangwill, who incontinently went to work with the vulgarest energy, notebook in hand, sharp superficial eye glancing about him, intent upon the commercial value of studio claptrap and wordy expansion, who has ruined this book as a work of art, and whom (frankly) we detest. This latter "Zangwill" says reassuringly to its other half, "You are a very clever fellow, you will do your dozen novels, you will criticize, you will write plays, you will shine in the world, and do a lot of things. What if your dialogue is sloppy, what if your story is flung together: it is good enough for your master, the public." This element was sufficiently in evidence in the *Children of the Ghetto,* and it is far more apparent in this book. It may possibly overcome the better part of Mr. Zangwill altogether. We would warn him while there is yet time. We believe there must be an artistic conscience still left in him. He writes too fast, he writes too much. If he would escape the fate of a successful mediocrity, he must alter

his way. His previous works have been applauded for their promise more than for their performance, but he cannot continue to live on promises. He was a good prentice hand, but we still await his diploma work.

Our advice will possibly offend him, but it is our duty to give it, and we will. Let him publish no more for a year or two; let him study the art of dialogue—it is a mistake to take Meredith as a model for that . . .—let him consider his own commentary in the light of a leisurely revision of Dickens, Thackeray, and Meredith; and above all, let him think over Kipling's perfected terseness. And he should spend lazy meditative days—chiefly alone. (He might even abstain from writing for a twelvemonth in order to lose his present excessive familiarity with the pen.) After such a retreat Mr. Zangwill might even come back to interest his generation. In all probability such a retirement is impossible, and in ten years' time we shall doubtless be giving Mr. Zangwill's thirty-second amateurish novel a quarter of a column to review under the heading of "Fiction," along with the punctual Besants and Norrises of the year. (pp. 656-57)

[H. G. Wells], "Mr. Zangwill's 'Master'," in The Saturday Review, *London, Vol. LXXIX, No. 2064, May 18, 1895, pp. 656-57.*

GEORGE SAINTSBURY (essay date 1895)

[*Saintsbury has been called the most influential English literary historian and critic of the late nineteenth and early twentieth centuries. His studies of French literature, particularly his* History of the French Novel, *have established him as a leading authority on such writers as Guy de Maupassant and Honoré de Balzac. Saintsbury adhered to two distinct sets of critical standards: one for the novel and the other for poetry and drama. As a critic of novels, he maintained that "the novel has nothing to do with any beliefs, with any convictions, with any thoughts in the strict sense, except as mere garnishings. Its substance must always be life not thought, conduct not belief, the passions not the intellect, manners and morals not creeds and theories. . . . The novel is . . . mainly and firstly a criticism of life." As a critic of poetry and drama, Saintsbury was a radical formalist, who frequently asserted that subject is of little importance and that "the so-called 'formal' part is of the essence." René Wellek has praised Saintsbury's critical qualities: his "enormous reading, the almost universal scope of his subject matter, the zest and zeal of his exposition" and "the audacity with which he handles the most ambitious and unattempted arguments." In the following excerpt from a review of* The Master, *Saintsbury contends that although the novel has several defects, it is still an interesting and promising work of fiction.*]

It is very interesting to read a man's work for the first time, and to discover that it is quite different from the impression which you have, perhaps unintelligently, formed of if from the accounts of third persons. It so happens that the present writer had never come across anything of Mr. Zangwill's before *The Master,* and that he had somehow or other derived from reviews the idea that Mr. Zangwill was, so to speak, a *jeune* of the youngest sort—realist, impressionist, euphuist, and so forth. Imagine his relief at discovering that *The Master* is purely romantic: that it might, some differences in dialect excepted (it must be confessed that Mr. Zangwill doth a little incline to the modern mixture of non-naturalisms and over-embroideries in style), have been written at almost any time since the romantic novel was invented. Its division into three books coincides fairly well with an actual threefold division of story: the first telling of Matthew Strang's early Nova Scotian life; the second of his artistic ambition and suffering in London;

the third of his, for a time, double life as "the Master" and as the husband of Rosina Cole. The way in which this double life is, so to speak, made single again by a failure of a great passion is novel in its particular application, and the end of the story is entirely different from that which an average *jeune* would have permitted himself. Several things strike us about this novel; but perhaps what strikes us most is that it exhibits both the defects and the merits of a first book rather than of one with at least two or three predecessors. There is in particular that fault of the too much which is so constantly seen in first work of promise. *The Master* does not want "cutting," but it wants "thinning": it is not so much too long as too full. The various characters, outlined on the whole with remarkable strength, are rather blurred than cleared by the after-strokes. We should not be sorry to hear that Mr. Zangwill had written it, or had at least begun it, sometime ago. But whether he did this or not, it is unquestionably a book of no little promise and of some considerable performance: preaching a little too much, divagating a little too much; a little exuberant here and a little excessive there; but on the whole lacking neither in sanity nor in strength. (p. 541)

> *George Saintsbury, in a review of "The Master," in* The Academy, *Vol. XLVII, No. 1208, June 29, 1895, pp. 541-42.*

WILLIAM MORTON PAYNE (essay date 1898)

[*The longtime literary editor for several Chicago publications, Payne reviewed books for twenty-three years at* The Dial, *one of America's most influential journals of literature and opinion in the early twentieth century. In the following excerpt, Payne agrees with critics, represented by H. G. Wells (1895), who believe that Zangwill's early works were artistically inferior. However, with the publication of* Dreamers of the Ghetto, *Payne believes Zangwill has reached the level of serious artist.*]

Most readers who turn to Mr. Zangwill's **"Dreamers of the Ghetto"** will find themselves compelled to revise their earlier estimate of the writer's abilities. Heretofore, he has stood as the embodiment of a sort of commonplace cleverness, and most of his work has been so ill-planned and diffuse as to be impossible from any artistic point of view. Even when he has dealt with the customs and character of his own race, his view has seemed superficial, his method to single out the grotesque and the accidental rather than the essential and permanent aspects of Jewish life and tradition. Occasional flashes of insight have not, indeed, been wanting, but the most generous criticism could hardly have found in them the promise of such a book as the one now before us. In this series of sketches—half story and half philosophical disquisition—we have the very soul of the Jewry, the vital expression of its thought, its poetry, and its ideal aspirations. . . . The book is deeply significant, both as a richly sympathetic and imaginative interpretation of the Jewish ideal, and as an altogether unexpected revelation of the powers hitherto latent in its author. From now on, Mr. Zangwill must be taken seriously. (pp. 78-9)

> *William Morton Payne, in a review of "Dreamers of the Ghetto," in* The Dial, *Vol. XXV, No. 291, August 1, 1898, pp. 78-9.*

MAX BEERBOHM (essay date 1899)

[*Though he lived until 1956, Beerbohm is chiefly associated with the fin de siècle period in English literature, more specifically with its lighter phases of witty sophistication and mannered el-*

Drawing of Zangwill that appeared in Vanity Fair in 1897. Mary Evans Picture Library.

egance. His temperament was urbane and satirical, and he excelled in both literary and artistic caricatures of his contemporaries. "Entertaining" in the most complimentary sense of the word, Beerbohm's criticism for The Saturday Review—*where he was a long-time drama critic—everywhere indicates his scrupulously developed taste and unpretentious, fair-minded response to literature. In the following excerpt from a review of Zangwill's first play,* Children of the Ghetto, *Beerbohm dismisses him as being neither an accomplished novelist nor a skilled playwright. Beerbohm cites Zangwill's inability to create life-like stage characters as the primary reason for the failure of the play.*]

Mr. Zangwill is a successful author, but this fact was not nearly enough to make me assume that he could not write a good play. The evidence I accumulated last Monday at the Adelphi all goes to prove that he cannot write a good play. But there was not, I suggest, any *prima facie* case against him. Mr. Zangwill, despite his many books and many editions, has not, really, any claim to be regarded as a man of letters. Certainly, he has an intellect, and a personality, and a point of view. But all the books of his which I have tried to read have merely proved to me that literature is not the form through which he ought to express himself. Let me explain. There is all the difference in the world between writing and being a writer; though the inclusion of writing with reading and arithmetic in our schools' curriculum has induced a general delusion that anyone can be a writer. People think that anyone who has something to say and writes it on paper is a writer. He is not necessarily so. Writing is a means of expression, certainly; but so are painting, musical composition, dramaturgy. And the true writer must have a specific innate gift for writing, as has the painter for painting. . . . Mr. Zangwill has proved in his writings that he himself has no such gift. I am not, as you may suspect, unfair to him. I am not judging him by the coarse humours he evolved under the influence of Mr. Jerome K. Jerome. I am judging him by his later *causeries,* and by his studies in Jewish life—**"Dreamers of the Ghetto"** and other books. Here, surely, was a man striving, plodding, floundering in a medium he never was meant for. Here was a man with ideas which, when he tried to wing them with live words, he did but bury under piles of dead words, leaving us to disinter them if we could. Here was a man with an interesting and new subject-matter, which, for all his knowledge of it, and for all his love of it, he succeeded in making tedious. **"Dreamers of the Ghetto"** was worth reading, though it was a bore. Many blue-books are worth reading. They are suggestive, instructive, if one is strong enough not to mind being bored by them. But the compilers of them are not literary men. Nor is he who compiled those books about the Ghetto a literary man. Had I accepted him as one, I should have expected his play to be bad—so widely different are literature and drama. As it was, I thought that possibly he might have found in dramaturgy a medium through which he could express himself well, and could make, at last, good use of his admirable subject-matter. . . . If he had written a play about something in which he took but slight interest, then the badness of his play would not have been positive proof that he could not write a good play. But the badness of **"Children of the Ghetto"** moves me to advise him not to attempt other plays. I am sorry he cannot express himself through drama any more than he can through fiction. . . . I do not say this because he has no sense of construction, the whole of his first act being occupied with a little incident which ought to have been merely explained by one of the characters, in a very few words, as having previously occurred. Sense of construction may be acquired. It is because Mr. Zangwill has no power of making his puppets live that I advise him to leave dramaturgy alone. When the conflicts come— a conflict between a young man and the old man whose daughter he loves, a conflict between the young man and the girl— one does not care twopence about them because none of the conflicting characters has drawn one breath of life or contains one drop of blood. The young man, we know, is a millionaire and a lax Jew; the old man is a strict Rabbi; the girl accepts the hand of the young man. But that is all we know about them. Never for one moment does Mr. Zangwill make them live. They are not more human than the A, B and C at the corners of a triangle in Euclid. "Why," soliloquises the girl, forced to choose between her lover on one hand, her faith and her father on the other, "why is this terrible alternative forced on me?" That is Mr. Zangwill's notion of a heart-cry, and it is typical of all the writing in the play. Mr. Zangwill, knowing that it is the kind of thing dramatists are expected to do, devises a "terrible alternative" for the chief character; but he cannot make the chief character express such emotion as is produced by "terrible alternatives" in real life. He can make her see (what he sees) that she is in a dramatic position; but there his power ends; and, unfortunately, it is there that a dramatist's power begins. Many men can propound problems, contrive situations, manufacture puppets. But to live in the puppets, and so make them live for us, and so, too, make real for us the situations they appear in and the problems they illustrate— that is the test of the dramatist. (pp. 763-64)

Max Beerbohm, "'Children of the Ghetto'," in The Saturday Review, *London, Vol. LXXXVIII, No. 2303, December 16, 1899, pp. 763-64.*

HOLBROOK JACKSON   (essay date 1914)

[*An English essayist, editor, and literary historian, Jackson was closely associated with a number of London periodicals during his career, among them* The New Age, *T. P. O'Connor's* Weekly *and* Magazine, *and* To-Day, *his own pocket journal which contained contributions from prominent writers such as Walter de la Mare, John Drinkwater, T. S. Eliot, and Ezra Pound. However, he is best remembered for his* The Eighteen Nineties (1913), *a comprehensive study of late nineteenth-century arts and letters which is regarded as an invaluable documentation of that era. In the following excerpt Jackson discusses the best of Zangwill's works, concentrating on his characteristic themes and his compelling depiction of Jewish life in England.*]

Readers of Israel Zangwill's earliest books might have been forgiven if they had prophesied for him a dazzling career as a literary entertainer. It is not easy to find in English literature such abundant wit and humour, such unabashed delight in mental quips and cranks, puns and tricks of thought and phrase, as you find in **"The Premier and the Painter," "The Bachelors' Club"** and **"The Old Maids' Club."** These books gush with that intellectual cleverness which came to be known as "brilliant." Whistler invented it; Oscar Wilde translated it into literature; Bernard Shaw still wields it as a sword, and Gilbert Chesterton as a prestidigitator of Notre Dame. With Zangwill it was different. He seemed, in these early books, to be doing nothing more serious than having a good time. But the critic with half an eye might have detected a higher seriousness behind the exuberant merriment of **"The Premier and the Painter."** . . . (p. 67)

With the exception of a few early adventures Zangwill's wit is as purposeful as Shaw's. He baits his earnestness with merriment hoping to make you laugh, or rather, smile and grow wise. And if he himself is under no illusion as to the limitations of fun—"To start anything exclusively funny," he says, "is a serious mistake"—there are times when the readiness of his wit overbalances his sense of proportion. His cleverness verges on the prodigious and the prodigality of his wit is always astounding and often disturbing. He has put enough of it in **"The Premier and the Painter"** to make three reputations, but too much to make one. The mind can stand an orgy of anything but wit. Wit must be the salt, not the dish: Zangwill has made it the feast. In several of his earlier books and in the more recent volume of shrewd and wise essays and comments, **"Without Prejudice,"** you never feel safe for a moment, the most innocent of sentences may end in an explosion. The experience is like being perpetually awakened out of pleasant dreams by warning detonators. Perhaps that was Zangwill's intention, but I suspect he was just enjoying himself. At the same time he does not attempt to sustain the interest of his finest books by facile brilliance, he can be as proportionate and as reticent as Meredith, and his comic study (comic in the Meredithian sense) of a Hebrew beggar in **"The King of Schnorrers,"** is a masterpiece of comedy approaching humour, but too subtle to be labelled humorous, although you have to go back to such great humorous conceptions as Sir John Falstaff and Mr. Wilkins Micawber to find the equal of that luxuriously named mendicant, Manasseh Bueno Barzillai Azevedo da Costa. (pp. 67-8)

There is something fitting in this first flight of a Hebrew genius in his own world bearing inspired records of the tragic life of his people, for the outer happiness of the Jews is often the cloak of sorrow; their jests are masks. By writing in English Israel Zangwill has not only revealed the tragedy and the comedy of Jewry to the English speaking members of this race, he has also revealed it to a nation which still took its knowledge of the Jew from the *naïveté* of Shakespeare's Shylock and the stale buffoonery of the comic papers. . . .

The spiritual facts of Jewish history and of modern Jewish life have received their highest and most convincing expression in English, in such books as **"Children of the Ghetto," "Dreamers of the Ghetto," "The King of Schnorrers,"** and **"They that Walk in Darkness."** From the point of view of art his great achievement is the re-statement of the seemingly eternal tragedy of Israel in the light of modern experience and modern culture. And he has done this with fitting seriousness and a most gracious and refreshing sense of humour. (p. 68)

[Zangwill], having had the most intimate experience of Jews, and possessing both a sense of humour and a sense of fact, gives us a more convincing idea of his compatriots than we have yet had or are likely to have. But he does not give us only realistic portraiture, after the manner of the newer novelists of his early days; nor does he strive particularly to see the good and bad, and to apportion praise and blame, after the manner of pre-Meredithian novelists. He knows the Jew to be human, not only because he hath "hands, organs, dimensions, senses, affections, passions," but because he is capable of the same virtues and vices, the same splendours and the same littlenesses as other human beings; that he is in short compact of good and bad like the rest of us. But he does not commit the opposite folly of concluding therefore that the Jew is not different. That would have left us where Shakespeare and Dickens stood. He knows the Jew is different and that this difference is surmounted only by a genius for adaptability.

These differences are revealed in his Jewish studies, which have always astonished Gentiles by their fairness in recognising the evil as well as the good among Jews. But that is no more an example of fairness than similar qualities in English or Scotch novelists. It is simply the faculties of observation and visualisation crystallised in art. Israel Zangwill sees the Jew steadily and sees him whole. Any equally capable artist might have done the same; any equally capable artist in letters might have wrung our hearts with the pathos, or moved our souls with the tragedy of Jewry; just as any equally capable writer might have raised our eyebrows or our laughter by records of Jewish cunning or humour. Zangwill has done all of these things and more. He has realised the irony of the age-long drama of Israel in a world to which she has given inventors and scientists, philosophers and artists, poets and prophets and Gods, but without, as a race, providing herself with a place to lay her head. He draws the modern Jew in all his squalor, whether of poverty, in Whitechapel, or of luxury, in Park Lane (both squalors having sprung from like causes), on a background of race-splendour. He communicates to us his vivid consciousness of the tragedy of this dream-fed race which has poured into the world treasures of the spirit and the imagination, whilst forging the metal of its permanence in bondage, migration and oppression. (pp. 69-70)

The world is a melting-pot to-day, and the Hebrew no less than any other race, is in the crucible—but as a leavening medium. From causes such as these Israel Zangwill, son of a Russian Jew, has become an English Jew, not only interpreting his race to the English, but to the Jews; mastering English life and literature, and taking his place in English letters and controversy, whilst retaining his racial characteristics, and developing in himself and others a new chivalry of the Brotherhood of Man. His novels, **"The Master"** and **"The Mantle of Elijah,"** are English works holding their own in the great tradition of the English novel; as his practical sympathy with the demand for Women's Enfranchisement is in the tradition of English political evolution; whilst his plays **"The War God," "The Next Religion,"** and **"The Melting Pot,"** and his latest prose work **"Italian Fantasies,"** reveal the universalism of the prophet of world-peace, which long since ought to have won for him the Nobel Prize.

Books live not because of any knowledge they contain, for knowledge soon becomes outmoded; neither do they live by reason of exquisite finish of workmanship, for art dies when the thing it meant is no longer a human need. Longevity is no test of art; a work of art should fill its time whether that time be a moment, an hour, a year, a century, or any number of centuries. But a book has a greater chance of life if it is a work of art revealing some unfathomable source of human ecstasy or power. Race has nothing to do with this, neither has nationality, nor religion. The thing that make a work of art live is the same as that which determines the life of a race, or a nation, or a religion. It is spiritual power. Applying this test to the works of Israel Zangwill, and after making every allowance for what may be called the temporal delight one may glean from any or all of them, the laurels might be awarded to the following in the order named: **"They That Walk in Darkness," "Dreamers of the Ghetto," "The King of Schnorrers," "Children of the Ghetto,"** and **"Italian Fantasies."** Here are books drawn from the spiritual deeps; they reveal the soul of a people and the soul of a man. More, they add something tragic, something humorous, something carefully observed, and something honestly thought, to a literature already rich in these things, but not so rich as to be weary of receiving fresh treasures. There is equal art and fine intent in his other books, and they are as alive to-day as when they were first published, but the best things in them are better in the books named. . . . (pp. 72-3)

I have placed **"Italian Fantasies"** among his greater books because, in a welter of scholarship, observation, criticism, wit and wisdom, he reveals the processes of the mind which imagined, with so much Christian love, those Ghetto tragedies which express the fulness of his genius. This book, masquerading as a travel-book, is really a confessional, an autobiography, the record of a soul's adventures among master-ideas. Many years hence it will be read as we read Montaigne and Sir Thomas Browne. To-day it is a commentary on contemporary life; modern, yet ripe; conservative among the verities, yet abundant in provocation; generous to the past, yet lavishly seductive of the future. And over-glamouring every page there is an irony which answers many a crude hope by tickling the reader into charity with all men. These Italian fantasies are Israel Zangwill's apologia conceived, not in the spirit of contrition, but in the spirit of interpretation; he has used Italy as a lay-figure, and made her the symbol of the world's glory and folly—but, as in all his works, it is the glory that survives in promise of performance. (p. 73)

Holbrook Jackson, "Israel Zangwill," in The Bookman, *London, Vol. XLVI, No. 272, May, 1914, pp. 67-73.*

GEORGE JEAN NATHAN (essay date 1924)

[*Nathan has been called the most learned and influential drama critic the United States has yet produced. During the early decades of the twentieth century, Nathan was greatly responsible for shifting the emphasis of the American theater from light entertainment to serious drama, introducing audiences and producers to the work of Eugene O'Neill, Henrik Ibsen, and Bernard Shaw, among others. Nathan was a contributing editor to H. L. Mencken's magazine* The American Mercury *and coeditor of* The Smart Set. *With Mencken, Nathan belonged to an iconoclastic school of American critics who attacked the vulgarity of accepted ideas and sought to bring a new level of sophistication to American culture, which they found provincial and backward. Throughout his career, Nathan shared with Mencken a gift for stinging invective and verbal adroitness, as well as total confidence in his own judgments. In the following excerpt, Nathan attacks Zangwill's drama* We Moderns, *which he considers a ridiculous and clichéd diatribe against the immorality of the younger generation of the 1920s.*]

What was left over of the preposterous kicking and braying that were indulged in by the M. Israel Zangwill while he was over here a few months ago [Nathan refers to Zangwill's **"Watchman, What of the Night?"** speech given in New York] has been incorporated by him into the dramatic form and given the name **"We Moderns."** With a rapid percussion of miff and grumble, sulk and spleen, huff and bellyache, the M. Zangwill, who talks like a blackball, get up on his hind legs and opens his mouth wide on the novel subject of the Younger Generation. Doubtless under the belief that no one has thus far ever thought to point out certain weaknesses of the present Younger Generation, and jumping at the subject in high glee, he goes through the stale rigmarole with a perfectly straight face—always excepting the nose—and succeeds admirably, after three hours of indignant yowling and yammering, in saying less, and saying it more idiotically, than the youngest Princeton or Yale author who has written on the theme.

The play is a stilted, affected, and thoroughly ridiculous piece of bombast. The characters representing the current young of the species no more resemble actual human beings than do the Yellow Kid, Pore Li'l Mose, or the Enfants Katzenjammer. Zangwill's modern flapper, for example, though a cigarette-smoking, cocktail-drinking, wise-cracking cutie who frequents loose studio parties and the like, has her own night key and is up on the latest international Greenwich Village literature, is completely ignorant of sex, still imagines that babies are brought by the *Ephippiorhynchus senegalensis,* and believes that a kiss on the lips signifies physical defloration. I am not trying to be funny; I set down the literal fact. The other representatives of the Younger Generation are scarcely less piquant. They have illegitimate babies, climb down water-spouts and show their legs to enthusiastic crowds of onlookers, pose in the nude, take up the family servants as boon companions, make rendezvous with professional seducers in their own drawing-rooms, and never lie down without perching their feet on the tops of the couches. They also quote poetry on every possible occasion and tell their parents to go to hell. The net impression of all of which is of the Messrs. Scott Fitzgerald and Stephen Vincent Benét, both beautifully boozy, rolling downstairs with their arms around each other.

There are bad plays that are simply bad plays, and there are bad plays that, in addition to being bad, are irritating in their irascibility and contentiousness. **"We Moderns"** is in the latter category. Zangwill's indignation, which appears to embrace everything that Hilaire Belloc hasn't yet thought of and which,

in its American manifestations, covered everything from the Pennsylvania Railroad's habit of locking up the *cabinets d' aisances* while the train is stopping at Elizabeth, N.J., to Otto Kahn's failure to pay his hotel bill in advance for him—this wholesale indignation is spread over the play like so much sour dough. The characters are so many Atrocity Reports; the dialogue is a series of scare heads.

The exhibit, which failed before you could say Joe Leblang, constituted the most juvenile buffet of bosh that the theatre has put on view in several seasons. (pp. 116-17)

George Jean Nathan, in a review of "We Moderns," in American Mercury, Vol. II, No. 5, May, 1924, pp. 116-17.

MEYER WAXMAN (essay date 1941)

[*In the following excerpt, Waxman discusses Zangwill's realistic portrayal of ghetto life and examines his work as an apologist for Jewish customs and aspirations.*]

The establishment of a ghetto with its multi-colored but seething life in London as well as in other cities . . . infused new vigor into the old and staid English Jewry. As a result there arose greater interest in Jewish literature, for life demands expression, and where it is surging and flowing, changing in movement and color, its reflection in literature is bound to come, and before long the kaleidoscopic ghetto of Britain found its master artist and portrayer. This was Israel Zangwill. . . . (p. 618)

[After] writing several novels of a general character which made an impression in English literary circles by their quaint humor, he turned his attention to the world he knew best and began the series of Jewish novels and short stories which he continued to produce during the greater part of his life. Zangwill was a prolific writer and he distinguished himself not only as a novelist and story writer but also as a poet, dramatist, and essayist. He never relinquished his activity in general literature and continued to write short stories on themes drawn from English life and also a number of dramas which were produced, with varying success, on the stage. But his genius expressed itself primarily in novels and stories of Jewish life. (p. 619)

It often happens with prolific authors who express themselves in numerous works and who display great talent in diverse directions that their first work is the best, in spite of their comparative youth at the time of its composition, and so it is with Zangwill. He displays skill and talent in all successive works, but it is *The Children of the Ghetto* on which his fame rests. In this work he is not only the portrayer of the new ghetto, of Jewish life in transition, in flux, in the process of change, but also its poet. It is a forerunner of all his other works, for in it, we have comedy and tragedy, mirth and sorrow, and numerous other nuances and shades of life combined in one picture, the canvas of which is the Jewish quarter in London.

The Children of the Ghetto is not a novel in the proper sense of the word, but in reality a gallery of pictures drawn from life. The number of its characters is exceedingly large and they represent all groups. . . . All these portraits in which different characters play their parts are united by the hand of the master through diverse threads into one all-embracive panorama.

The work begins with a little tragedy, the breaking of a pitcher of soup, supplied by the free kitchen, by little Esther Ansel, at the very moment when five hungry mouths were watering at the thought of tasting that delicious food. The note of tragedy pervades the whole book, for scene after scene displays one phase after another of the grim life of the poor of the ghetto, full of struggle and of frustrated aspirations. The experiences of Esther and the Ansel family form a prominent part of the book, but not the whole of it. They serve more as a thread to unite the group of pictures than its backbone. Esther, though, typifies the indomitable spirit of the children of Israel which overcomes all obstacles, the patience to bear suffering, and the ever-rising aspiration to a higher and finer life. Side by side with tragedy there is comedy; numerous little comic incidents which a multi-colored life supplies by its very flow and complexity are masterfully interwoven in the narrative.

The great qualities of the book are its variety of portraits and the attitude of the author towards the world he describes. (pp. 619-20)

The attitude of the author is neither that of an apologist who sees all beauty and glory dressed in the garb of poverty and squalor, nor that of a preacher who points out the sore spots in that life and advocates improvement. He is both sympathetic and critical. He sees the dire results of poverty, ignorance, and superstition, but he sees still more the nobility of character, the purity of the religious belief and devotion, and the beauty of filial and parental love which are so prevalent in the ghetto. (p. 621)

Thus, the kaleidoscopic panorama passes before us with its lights and shadows in this masterful work, fully deserving its name, *The Children of the Ghetto*.

In the sequel called *The Grandchildren of the Ghetto*, we have another gallery of pictures, more limited in scope and drawn from the life of the upper circle of English Jewry and from that of the former dwellers of the ghetto who had emancipated themselves from its narrowness, poverty, and squalor, though not from the lure of its spirit of idealism which had followed them beyond its confines. Two of the earlier characters, Esther Ansel and the student, Strelitske, are reintroduced. . . . These characters, however, are not introduced merely as a bond of unity for the series of portraits, but for a different purpose, to contrast the mechanical piety and materialistic outlook of the aristocratic Jewish circles with the idealism of the ghetto which finds an outlet in the lives of some of its children. (p. 622)

In his *Ghetto Tragedies* and *Ghetto Comedies* Zangwill extended his canvas beyond the confines of London's East End to include episodes and incidents of Jewish life all over the world. English Jewry, though, both in its upper and lower strata is not left out and a number of stories portray the fundamental characteristics of the circles. As in *The Children of the Ghetto*, so in the other stories, the comic and the tragic are not separated in spite of the titles. . . . Yet they are comical by their incongruity with reality and the unexpectedness of the events they portray. Incongruity and unexpectedness are the very elements of humor, and since Jewish life, due to its peculiarity and abnormality is replete with such incidents, it is no wonder that it furnishes the writers with themes which are simultaneously tragic and comic. This trait is masterfully depicted by the writer in a number of stories included in *The Comedies*, but especially in the "**Jewish Trinity**" and "**Samooborona**" ("**Self Defense**"). (pp. 622-23)

In *The Tragedies*, the stories deal primarily with episodes in the life of the individuals which are tragic in their essence and in their conclusion, because they struggle against cruel fate or

destiny. . . . Both the suffering and the sacrifice are portrayed with sympathy and with fine insight.

In *The King of Schnorrers*, Zangwill again widens his horizon, not in space but in time, by portraying a type and section of life of eighteenth century Jewry. . . . The story is throughout permeated with a spirit of delightful humor.

While in all these stories Zangwill portrayed the reality of Jewish life, especially as reflected in the ghetto, he devoted his attention in his *Dreamers of the Ghetto* to its ideal aspect as reflected in the lives of distinguished individuals of the race in various lands and times. . . . The historic setting is not always drawn accurately, but there is much art in the presentation of their characters and special emphasis is laid upon the bond of idealism which unites them all in spite of the diversity of their personalities, environment, and aspirations.

Zangwill, as said, was a versatile writer, and distinguished himself also as an essayist. During the many years of his literary and Jewish activity, he wrote essays on a wide variety of problems. The best of these . . . [appeared in] *The Voice of Jerusalem*. The title was derived, as he tells us in his preface, from a phrase once used by him in a letter to the London Times in 1914 in which he objected to the characterization of the Times of an appeal for peace by Jacob Schiff as "a brief for Germany" and insisted that it was "the voice of Jerusalem" which spoke in that appeal. In reality that title is applied to the first series of short essays but is extended to the book as a whole, for it is in fact the voice of true loyalty to Jews and Judaism symbolized by Jerusalem which speaks through all of the essays. The book, as a whole, is one of the finest apologetic works in the entire Jewish literature. The writer is convinced of the tragic glory of Jewish history and of the effectiveness of the influence of the Jewish spirit upon the elevation of humanity during the ages in spite of all persecutions aiming to annihilate the people of Israel. The small still voice of Jerusalem was heard, *volens nolens*, not withstanding all attempts to deafen it. Furthermore, he believes that the voice still has some important message for humanity provided the opportunity be given to the Jewish people to proclaim it. . . . At times, [Zangwill] is polemic and condemns the European nations for their lust for war and conquest, the degradation of Christianity, the atrocities against the Jews; at other times he is apologetic, combating the numerous false theories of the character of Judaism put forth by thinkers and philosophers who claim objectivity, such as H. G. Wells and others. He attributes the cause of intellectual anti-Semitism partly to the unconscious sense of indebtedness felt by the Christian world to Judaism, and in many more ways defends Jews and Judaism against their maligners. Zionism and the fate of the Jewish people in the post-War world occupy a prominent part in this series. Curiously enough, writing only a year or two after the issuance of the Balfour Declaration, Zangwill foresaw the difficulties in the way of the realization of the Jewish homeland with remarkable clearness, especially the Arab opposition. He, therefore, expresses dissatisfaction with the Declaration and even suspects the leaders of the English government, who succeeded Balfour, of insincerity. He boldly labels the promised Jewish state a mirage, for in his opinion a Jewish minority cannot have a home amidst a majority of Arabs. He suggests either a mass emigration of Arabs to other countries, or if this is impossible, the surrender of the government of Palestine to a Jewish minority for the purpose of converting them to a majority. Otherwise, he claims, the Declaration is meaningless. Unfortunately, his forebodings have come true. As a result of his analysis of Zionism he still advocates in these essays the territorialist idea that he championed in the decade before the War, though he offers little of a definite solution in that direction.

The second series [*The Legend of the Conquering Jew*] is a splendid defense of the Jews against anti-Semitism which was at the time showing its ugly head or rather heads in numerous books, ranging from quasi-scientific works to the notorious *Protocols of Zion* which were issued in 1920 under the title *The Jewish Peril*. He reduces *ad absurdum* the stock phrases, "the conquering Jew" or the "formidableness of the Jews" constantly repeated in the anti-Semitic works of all types. With remarkable irony he points out that the titles are justified only in two ways, namely, the Jew can be called a conqueror, inasmuch as he conquered all persecution and attacks, and his formidableness is expressed in the imposing mass of contributions to science, philosophy, art, politics, and other fields of civilization.

The essays undoubtedly bear the signs of the times in which they were written, yet many of them, due to the scholarship, the logical way of thinking, the deep pathos, the fine ironic humor by which they are distinguished, and above all by their splendid style, have permanent value. Zangwill's contribution to Jewish apologetics thus does not fall far behind his great contribution to belles-lettres. (pp. 624-27)

> Meyer Waxman, "Jewish Literature in European Languages," in his A History of Jewish Literature: From 1880-1935, Vol. IV, *1941. Reprint by Thomas Yoseloff, 1960, pp. 566-629.*

MILTON HINDUS (essay date 1954)

[*In the following excerpt, Hindus disagrees with Bernard N. Schilling's positive appraisal of* The King of Schnorrers *(see excerpt dated 1965—reprinted from the introduction to the 1953 Shoe String Press edition of the novel). Hindus finds little humor in this supposedly humorous book and concludes that Zangwill, though an attractive personality and occasionally interesting artist, is not worthy of a high place in English literary history.*]

I began *The King of Schnorrers* with an anticipation based on a misty recollection of an old reading of Zangwill. The letdown I experienced was commensurate with my hopes. Perhaps to one who is more of an "outsider," *The King of Schnorreres* may seem, as Professor Bernard N. Schilling says in his introductory essay, "an extremely funny book" [see excerpt dated 1965]. I find this hard to believe, however. Not that I think it a bad book, but it seems a good deal more humorous in intention than in fact.

And yet Zangwill has some solid literary virtues which are still discernible. He knew his Jewish subjects from within. If his tone occasionally suggests that he is writing with an eye to the quaintness which appeals to tourists, it is the Jewish tourist whom he has in mind as well as the Gentile. Zangwill's Jewish knowledge is authentic, but I am afraid that it does not go too deep. It is a kind of journalistic smattering which seeks to impress the reader with a loose sprinkling of supposedly esoteric facts and colorful foreign words.

Zangwill possesses a sense of literary form which makes him scrupulous about connecting the beginning of his story with its end; he has an inventiveness of comic detail which, while not of the highest order, is distinctly above the mediocre; and best of all he cultivates a conciseness of expression which

makes his style, if not classical, at least "studious of brevity." His style gives us the feeling of his being thoroughly at home in the English language; this, in spite of the greater example of Disraeli before him, was as flattering as it was surprising to the sensibilities of his fellow Jews in England in the last decade of the 19th century. What must have been doubly pleasing to them was the fact that he had used his sensitive ear for English not to make his way in the Gentile world, but had brought his gift "home" with him and used it for Jewish purposes.

His limitations as an artist appear most clearly when we compare him with Sholom Aleichem. Though the finer points of Sholom Aleichem's original Yiddish text defy the best-intentioned efforts to recapture them in any other idiom, yet even in the awkward gabardine of translation English he is distinctly funnier that Zangwill. It is perhaps a paradox that Sholom Aleichem, composing in a language which was accessible to Jews only, should have achieved a greater measure of universality than Zangwill did. I shan't attempt to say why this is so beyond remarking that Sholom Aleichem is never in doubt about his identity or his point of view, while Zangwill (in spite of an almost ostentatious feeling of ease in his English environment) betrays such doubts. Sometimes he is the Jew whom he is writing about, sometimes he is only one of the onlookers, and sometimes he falls between the two.

To those Jews whose native language is English, the name of Zangwill will always evoke a feeling of respect. This feeling (the experiment of the current reprint suggests) is probably based on an exaggeration of his actual merits. We tend to forget that while he brought his Jewish interests to the very border of English literary history, he never really took them across the line. The better part of his reputation lies in his attractive qualities as a person. He deserves his place in our pantheon, but it is not altogether without misgivings that we see his work being dusted off once more and offered to critical inspection. (pp. 308-10)

> Milton Hindus, "Does Zangwill Still Live?" in Commentary, *Vol. 17, No. 3, March, 1954, pp. 308-10.*

WOLF MANKOWITZ (essay date 1954)

[*In the following excerpt, Mankowitz discusses Zangwill's desire to overcome anti-Semitism by educating his readers about Jewish life, noting that, in his inability to perceive the irrational roots of hatred, Zangwill displayed his shortcomings as a creative writer.*]

Zangwill's generation believed that evil has its source in ignorance—that it was, in consequence, a disease which could be cured. To this therapy Zangwill applied himself.

The political problem for the Jew is simpler than for others. The enemy is always, whatever else, an anti-semite. For the Jewish writer the prejudice against the adjective he was born carrying is a reality which he quickly recognises and accepts. He may decide to fight this prejudice specifically, or he may set out, as Zangwill did, to eradicate it by educational means— at least to expound the character of what has been so unquestioningly rejected. So Zangwill systematically wrote up the East End, wrote up the characteristics and customs and recent history of the Jews, not for a moment as an apologist, but as a nineteenth-century idealist believing that the prejudiced are so because they have been deprived of educational opportunities which he, the devoted educationist, now strives to make good. . . .

Zangwill belonged to the rationalist pre-Freudian age; he believed that to argue convincingly could convince. If he had examined, for example, the case of his quite literate contemporary, G. K. Chesterton, he might have perhaps realised that ignorance is not entirely the source of racial prejudice; though Chesterton's sheer ignorance of what a Jew was like is in itself an indication of the educational necessity of Zangwill's work. Except, of course, that our bluff Chestertonian rolling in what he calls his 'innocence,' has no wish to disburden himself of his prejudices. He finds what Chesterton calls the 'negro vitality and vulgarity' of the Jew distasteful—and presumably objects to Negroes for their Jewish vulgarity and vitality. Chestertonian Jews speak stage cockney, are dressed like racecourse touts, and are not Christian. His Negroes are coons with banjos, pop-eyes, and striped trousers; they are Christian. But religion as such has nothing to do with the prejudice which Zangwill attempted to eradicate. For the Chestertonian—never vulgar enough perhaps to state it in bald terms—Negro and Jew are equally members of inferior races, celebrants of degenerate cultures. His beery afflatus never lifts him to Dr. Alfred Rosenberg's pinnacle of distaste. Your innocent Chesterton does not propose the extermination of the mongrel descendants of Shem and Ham. The burbling Gargantua of the surburbs just feels a chronic distaste, that's all, and (alas for the efforts of educationists!) he has a taste for his distaste.

It is by his failure to realise in his work such aspects of human irrationality that Zangwill betrays his limitations as an artist. His characters in *The King of Schnorrers*. . . , the aristocratic Mannasseh, the cunning Yankele, the benevolent Grobstock, have a two-dimensional quality. Zangwill's writing and dialogue only very occasionally capture the accent and rhythm of the language of the people he is observing, and even he resorts to stage tricks ('If you vas me vat vould you marry?') to get comic effects at a music-hall level. Zangwill's careful historical construction, his humour, and his detailed understanding of Jewish culture cannot entirely save his work from the clinical detachment which characterises a teacher making instructional points. He remains all the time aware of the serious intentions behind the entertainment, so that in reading his Ghetto stories one becomes conscious of a gap between the writer and his subject.

> *Wolf Mankowitz, "Israel Zangwill," in* The Spectator, *Vol. 193, No. 6581, August 13, 1954, p. 205.*

JOSEPH LEFTWICH (essay date 1957)

[*Leftwich was an English essayist who wrote widely on Jewish affairs. He was a close friend of Zangwill's during the last ten years of Zangwill's life and wrote the only biography of him, in part to defend his friend's reputation and importance as a writer. Leftwich's book focuses primarily on Zangwill's life and how his works reflect events in that life, particularly as they demonstrate his attitudes toward Judaism. In the following excerpt from that work, Leftwich discusses Zangwill's vision of literature and social commitment, the autobiographical aspects of his work, and his place in English literature.*]

"Why a writer of his quality should have ceased to find readers surpasses my understanding," St. John Ervine wrote to me about Zangwill. "*Children of the Ghetto, King of Schnorrers,* and all the rest of the books Zangwill wrote about his people, seemed to me to be overflowing with life. But it wasn't only about his own people that he could write. The last novel by him I read was entitled *Jinny the Carrier,* and it convinced me

that his sense of the Gentile in East Anglia was as sound as his sense of the Jews in the East End."

Ludwig Lewisohn came to the conclusion that Zangwill's "books have sunk from sight partly because he shared certain attitudes and emotions with the minor Victorians." He was speaking in an American radio discussion about Zangwill. "Although an immigrant Jew and brought up in Whitechapel and all that," he said, "much of his writing is typically Victorian." Maurice Samuel, who took part in that broadcast, added, however, that Zangwill "should have written as finely as he did, in spite of his (Victorian) handicaps, is perhaps the measure of a certain type of greatness that we haven't yet acknowledged."

Zangwill was, of course, a Victorian. He was born in Queen Victoria's reign, and lived two-thirds of his life under her reign. He lived long enough into the 1920s, when it had become fashionable to sneer at the Victorians, to accept the fashion as the judgment of the new generation. In 1925, the year before he died, he spoke of his books as belonging "to the despised Victorian era," and contented himself with "the gratifying fact" that they had survived so long "the annual avalanche of myriads of new books and the distractions of an age increasingly oblivious of yesterday." But Zangwill was not unaware of the ideas that made Lewisohn and others dismiss him, and those of his generation. "I do resent Mr. Lewisohn's intolerant assumption," he wrote, "that I must share his sex view, and that I am sinning against the light because I am doubting the quality of his. The romantic circles Mr. Lewisohn admires I find heavy with heartbreak and egotism."

Nor was Zangwill ignorant of Freud, whom Lewisohn invoked. Before he wrote *Children of the Ghetto,* a young man in Fleet Street, editing his comic paper *Ariel,* he shared lodgings with his cousin, Dr. Eder, who was a disciple of Freud's. Freud said of Eder: "He was the first and for a time the only doctor to practise the new therapy in England. I was proud to count him among my pupils." Eder supplied Zangwill with the medical information in his work. Zangwill said so in his diaries: "Saw Eder about my medical facts." There was a novel published recently turning on a medical point, using an idea Zangwill had employed in a short story more than fifty years before. I mentioned this story once to Zangwill, because of its cleverness and oddity. Zangwill smiled and said: "Yes, that's the sort of thing I wrote when I was young."

Zangwill stopped writing that sort of clever plot story, with ingenious twists and turns, as he showed once in *The Big Bow Mystery* that he could write detective thrillers, and then stopped. He studied Freud, but he concluded that "Freud ruined a good case by obscene over-statement." (pp. 11-12)

Yet Zangwill did not overlook the importance of modern psychology in literature. "We must go still deeper into Psychology," he wrote. He spoke of "our sub-consciousness" as "a tossing ocean of thoughts which feeds the narrow little fountain of consciousness. It holds," he said, "all our memories, the traces of vanished generations. In our sub-conscious are stored up all the voices and sounds we have ever perceived, and to all these reminiscences of our own are added the shadows of our ancestors' sensations—episodes that perchance we experience only in dreamland—so that part of the vivid vision of Genius may be inherited Memory." "All novels are written from the novelist's point of view," he said. "They are his vision of the world. Life, large, chaotic, inexpressible, not to be bound down by a formula, peeps at itself through the brain of each artist. All the novelists supplement one another, and relatively-true single impressions of life go to make up a picture of 'Life.' The artist selects, he studies tone and composition; he does not photograph real life. A good novel may be made of bad psychology; indeed, this is what most novels are made of.'' It is revealing of Zangwill's aims in literature that his "great novelists are Fielding, Cervantes, Flaubert, Thackeray.''

Perhaps Sholem Asch got nearest to describing Zangwill when he called him in a talk with me, a folk-writer. Zangwill took his stories, indeed, from the folk; he repeated in his own way the tales he heard, which had come from the common stock of Jewish folk-literature. Zangwill is the genius who in his Jewish work has retold in English literature the stories that were handed down by generations of Jews in the old Jewish Pale of Russia and were brought to England by the immigrants. It is not only their lives that he re-created, their struggles to adjust themselves in their new home in England, but also their heritage of story and song and legend, of wit and humour and piety. He translated it and transmuted it, and made it part of English literature. (p. 13)

It would be wrong not to emphasise . . . that Zangwill was not only a writer. To perhaps a greater extent than any other writer of his period Zangwill devoted years of his life to causes; most of all to the cause of the Jews. More than Shaw or Wells to Socialism he gave up years of his literary life to help his fellow-Jews. When Mrs. Zangwill wrote to Shaw about Zangwill, and suggested: "You probably feel that his earlier literary work was his best," she went on to say: "But the reason it is best is rather splendid. He felt that the prime purpose of his life was the helping of the underdog, and he quite consciously gave up his literary career to this end. He deliberately gave up his literary career at the height of his power in order to work for the suffering Jewish people, his own people.'' But she added: "He laboured not for Jews as Jews but as oppressed human beings. I remember his telling me more than once that had the Jews been as prosperous and powerful as the British'' (he was thinking at that time of the millions of Jews living in poverty and oppression in the lands of the Russian Czar) "he would not have spent himself for them, but for others who stood more in need. He cared more for humanity as a whole and less for himself than anyone I ever met. This was the greatest thing in him. His work as a writer was only a small part of him, and his work for the Jewish people was only a small part of him. He felt that the prime purpose of his life was the helping of the underdog.'' (p. 15)

[Zangwill's writings] are autobiographical because they are drawn from the scenes and people that he knew. He wrote with his own early life in mind. He pictured himself repeatedly in his characters. He wove his own thoughts into theirs. Till the end of his life he kept coming back to the ideas and emotions and the hopes and ideals which had seized his imagination as a child, as a small boy at the Jews' Free School, in his pious father's poor home, and in the little Whitechapel Synagogue to which he had accompanied him every day, whose poetry remained with him always, colouring all his later experiences and thoughts, so that however far he went away from that life, its sights and its sounds were forever in his eyes and ears. All his thinking and writing was founded on it, in affirmation or in denial, which usually ended in reaffirmation. It was the essence of everything he said and did. It was his vision of life.

Zangwill brought his father Moses Zangwill into *Children of the Ghetto* as Disraeli brought his father into *Vivian Grey*, as Wells said that in all his books he was writing his autobiog-

raphy, as Hardy was always drawing on his memories of his Wessex boyhood. "You are Joseph the dreamer of dreams,'' Hardy says of Jude. Zangwill was a Joseph the dreamer. And being a dreamer his people are more than real; they are symbolic, a type and a symbol. That is why Zangwill's London Jews of the 1890s did not die when their originals were lowered into their graves, but still live.

Of course, Zangwill as a writer has faults. Those who complain of his faults are not wrong. It is not difficult to pick any writer to pieces. . . . I have no wish to make Zangwill out to be a greater writer than he is. I am certainly not going to claim for him a faultlessness from which greater writers are not free. But his work is such that we can keep coming back to it with interest, with curiosity, with admiration, with a feeling that we are meeting in his pages living people, a rich company of characters who remain in the memory, some of them great comic creations like Melchitzedek Pinchas in *Children of the Ghetto* and Manasseh da Costa, the King of Schnorrers. His people overflow with life. They are Jews, Jews living in England; they are credible living human beings. Zangwill has more than anyone else working in this field painted a true and convincing picture from the inside of a group of people, with their struggles and hopes, their beliefs, their toil, their suffering, their humour, their separateness and their universal human oneness.

The life he painted was his own life, the life of the people he knew, whose experiences had so moved and shaken him that they were emotionally his own experiences. He had such rich and inexhaustible stores of childhood memories that he could forever draw on them, and transmute them through his imagination, through his vision. . . . Zangwill had another quality—his childhood memories, though harsh and full of the experiences of bitter poverty, had not made him bitter. His work was not drab and pessimistic, twisted and tormented. He had learned that the life of the poor is not necessarily drab or tortured life. It had humour and contentment and cheeriness. (pp. 297-98)

Yet the memory of his childhood poverty had impressed itself on him unforgettably. (p. 298)

Children of the Ghetto contains Zangwill's imaginative reconstruction of his life and background, his experiences and emotions, the life in which he grew and which shaped him. It is a story, or rather several stories, spun by a true yarn-spinner; but it is also an authentic social study of a part and a period of London life. (p. 300)

I don't think it is possible to take the Jewish life out of *Children of the Ghetto* without destroying the book. That is perhaps the greatest thing about it, that it is so completely of one piece. (p. 304)

Recently I sat with several writers in a public discussion on certain aspects of literature, and Zangwill's name came up. One of my colleagues said that Zangwill is no Shakespeare nor Dostoevsky nor James Joyce. Nor is he, I agree, Milton or Goethe, Tolstoy or Cervantes, Homer or the writer of the Book of Job. I have never understood this passion for having the world peopled only by giants. It is as though no mountain could command respect unless it towers to the height of Everest or at least of Mont Blanc. I have a very healthy respect for the much smaller mountains of the Derby Peak, and I see no reason to despise the Surrey Downs. The world would be poorer without these lesser hills. If Zangwill is no Everest and no Mont Blanc, he reaches nevertheless a very impressive height, and is worth an ascent. There is wonderful country to be viewed. We meet people in his country who are worth knowing.

The important thing about Zangwill is that in his own field he conveys a sense of reality, of genuineness, of truth. He has it all, the life of it, the sunshine and the shadow, the comedy and the tragedy, the humour and the grimness. He paints the life of the humble with its joy; he does not overlook its suffering and its pity. His people are not onesided, neither all sweetness, nor all acid. They are human, compounded of all the human qualities. Poverty does not degrade them, and nobility does not cloy. Not all Zangwill's work is of equal merit. Every author produces books that do not last. Only the student of literature makes it his business to read the entire body of work of an author. But I can name a dozen of Zangwill's books that should and I believe will live. They have truth enough and genius enough to justify his continuing place in English literature. If people will only read him, they will, I am sure go on reading him. (pp. 305-06)

> *Joseph Leftwich, in his* Israel Zangwill, *Thomas Yoseloff, 1957, 306 p.*

JOHN GROSS   (essay date 1964)

[*Gross is an English literary scholar and editor who wrote the highly regarded critical study* The Rise and Fall of the Man of Letters *(1969), in addition to studies on James Joyce and Rudyard Kipling. He is currently an editor of* The New York Times Book Review. *In the following excerpt, Gross maintains that Zangwill's verbose style is an insurmountable barrier to appreciation of his work, concluding that Zangwill was more important for his example than for his writings. Gross also contends that Zangwill's personal conflict between traditional Judaism and assimilation with English society was the motivating factor behind his best works.*]

Zangwill was a brave, shrewd, and intensely serious man, but judged by respectable standards he was not a very good writer, and though his personal qualities are apparent from his work he can hardly be said to survive on his literary merits alone. The style—at once florid, wordy, and slightly facetious—is as insurmountable barrier. (p. 54)

Zangwill might have done better if there had been a more distinguished literary tradition directly at hand, but as it was he began his writing career in the world of the sentimental cockney journalism of the 1880's: the best-known of his early literary friends was Jerome K. Jerome of *Three Men in a Boat.* In such an atmosphere there was very little inducement to think hard about the art of the novel, and the style of *Children of the Ghetto* is matched by the plot, a loose melodramatic affair full of "strong" situations and wild coincidences.

It says much for Zangwill's seriousness of purpose that the book is nevertheless still worth reading as a slice of social history, and that for all the staginess it has an underlying authenticity. Zangwill knew his raw material through and through, and if his characters are generally over-drawn or over-simplified they are almost never travestied out of existence. The range is much wider, too, than anyone knowing the book only through hearsay would be led to suppose: it encompasses West End as well as East End, early Zionism as well as the *Shulchan Aruch,* stockbrokers as well as sweatshop laborers. Some of the characters are taken straight from life, others are representative types; and there is a fair stab at explaining customs and attitudes which even well-educated English novel-readers of the day must have found almost totally unintelligible. The

general tone is, of course, sympathetic, but certainly not sugary: there is far more satire and far less idealization than in, say, the Jewish parts of *Daniel Deronda.* As a picture of Jewish life in London during the period of the mass-immigrations from Eastern Europe it is unrivaled, and, indeed, unique, for only fleeting and often unfriendly glimpses are to be found in the work of other English writers of the period. Those who doubt that Zangwill was performing an important service in trying to dispel mysteries should remind themselves of the prejudice against which he had to contend by looking up a novel like Hilaire Belloc's *A Change in the Cabinet,* where the hero inadvertently strays into the East End, and the same area as the one described in the first half of *Children of the Ghetto* is presented as a kind of sinister bedlam. . . . [Zangwill's] plays and novels sound like classic instances of good sentiments making bad literature. For the most part they appear to be heavy-handed and lifeless allegories advocating humanism, idealism, pacifism, and love, with a dash of 19th-century-style nationalism. The prevailing atmosphere can be gauged from one play, *The Next Religion,* where the last act takes place in a temple with stained-glass windows showing three saints of the "next religion": Emerson, Mazzini, and Swinburne.

All this is as dead as mutton today, but no one could doubt that Zangwill was in earnest when he wrote. . . . In a recent article in *Commentary* Dan Jacobson [see Additional Bibliography] characterized Zangwill the novelist as "a purveyor of exotica." In reality he was more ambitious than that would suggest, but it might have been better for him if he had stuck to his exotica: at least he would have been cultivating the territory which he knew best. As it is, to look at a list of his works is to be struck by how few of them are on Jewish themes. He began with comic novels like *The Celibates' Club,* and ended with his plays: the four or five "ghetto" books (with one minor exception) were written in his late twenties and early thirties, but though they alone keep his reputation alive, in a sense they represent a detour. For whatever his other loyalties, from first to last the main drive behind his career was to turn himself into a successful English man of letters, and by and large he managed to conform to the pattern of his period, right down to the olde-worlde Sussex village where he spent the last twenty years of his life.

Zangwill was in fact far less caught up in Jewish culture, and far more ambivalent about being a Jew, than the popular legend suggests. He was a man of cosmopolitan breadth (among his own books his particular favorite was a set of travel sketches, *Italian Fantasies*), but there is nothing in his work to indicate that he was a contemporary of either Bialik or Sholem Aleichem. . . . Yet he tended to think that religion was the only possible justification for Jewish separatism—and he made it clear that by religion he meant "not a seat in a synagogue and a grave in a Jewish cemetery, but a faith like that which made our fathers sit Shivah for faithless children." In one of his last speeches he quoted Charles Lamb: "Why keep up a form of separation when the life of it is dead?"

This was a question to which Zangwill, like countless other newly emancipated Jews, was unable to find a satisfactory answer. Liberated once and for all from traditional Orthodoxy, he was nevertheless anxious to maintain some kind of cultural continuity (of a positive kind, as opposed to a mere defensive reaction to anti-Semitism). As a result, his attitude was a mass of inconsistencies. Nothing could altogether uproot the tenderness and respect which he felt for the religion of his childhood, yet there were times when the whole subject clearly gave him claustrophobia, and he wished he could escape from it for good. He was less explicit about this than he was when the opposite mood was on him, and he spoke about preserving Jewish values, but the urge to escape underlies much of his work. As a political philosophy, the internationalism of his plays is hopelessly vague; in practice it means assimilation. (The hero of *The Melting Pot,* who foreshadows the ideal world-citizen of the future, is described as "a handsome youth of the finest Russo-Jewish type," and as a further guarantee that he is basically a sound chap he is given the Sephardic-sounding name of David Quixano.) At one moment Judaism is seen as a priceless heritage, at the next as a millstone round the modern Jew's neck.

A common enough conflict over the past hundred and fifty years; in Zangwill's case it was doubtless intensified by the example of his parents. His father, whom he deeply admired, was a model of traditional piety; his mother, whom he is supposed to have taken after in character, was a hard-headed "pagan" who had no patience with her husband's ineffectualness in worldly matters, and eventually refused to accompany him when he set out to end his days in Jerusalem. To a considerable extent the son can be seen as living out the parents' conflict; and if he often found this oppressive, it also gave him his true subject as a writer. But unfortunately it was a subject which generally proved too much for him. Only once did he really come to grips with it—in *Dreamers of the Ghetto,* which is his most rewarding book (of those I have read, at least), and still deserves to be kept in circulation. (pp. 55-6)

It is an excellent introduction to Jewish history for an imaginative child, doing the same kind of job Kipling's Puck of Pook's Hill books do for English history. But it also has a unity and depth which only the adult reader is likely to grasp. All the "dreamers"—and they range from Uriel Acosta and Solomon Maimon to Heine and Lassalle—are rebels who are unable to find peace either inside or outside the ghetto. The dream is of "the first emancipation"; and as the subtitle of the book makes clear, in Zangwill's eyes it is "a dream which has not come true." There is a vein of pessimism, indeed anguish, running through these stories which redeems the usual flowery style; one sees how it was possible for the French poet André Spire to feel that the course of his entire life had been changed by reading them, and that they had been enough in themselves to set him on the path from assimilation to Zionism.

Near the end of *Dreamers of the Ghetto* there is an account of the First Zionist Congress at Basel, which had been held only some two years previously. By including the Zionist idea in the book there is an implication that it, too, is yet another dream destined not to come true. But Zangwill had actually been won over by Herzl at their first meeting, one foggy evening in 1895 at his house in the North London suburb of Kilburn, and he was the most influential of Herzl's early English supporters. He was as inconsistent in his attitude to Zionism, however, as he was to everything else Jewish. As long as Herzl was alive he remained loyal to the official movement; but immediately after Herzl's death came the final split over the Uganda scheme and the formation of ITO. Zangwill's wisdom in breaking away from the main body of Zionism is open to question, but the whole debate now looks very remote, since in the end, after twenty years of fruitless investigations in Cyrenaica, Angola, and elsewhere, Territorialism came to nothing. This does not necessarily prove that Zangwill was wrong, of course. He foresaw trouble with the Arabs long before most of his colleagues; and who knows how many lives

might have been saved if he had succeeded in establishing the *Nachtasyl,* the temporary refuge which he regarded as a more urgent necessity than the resettlement of Palestine? For he was severely practical in his approach to Zionism, and convinced that any port would serve in the gathering storm. He had a strong premonition of calamites to come, even if he saw the chief source of danger—not unreasonably—as Czarist Russia rather than Germany. . . . This was the vision which lay behind Zangwill's political work; and if Territorialism eventually proved a lost cause, it was not an unworthy one. Zangwill can also take most of the credit for the one successful offshoot of Territorialism, the Galveston Project, which brought several thousand European refugees across the Atlantic.

In the end, Zangwill's importance lies outside literature: one honors the writer, and puts aside his books. Yet if his example continues to haunt one, it is as something more than a public worthy or a valuable source for the social historian. He was ultimately a tragic figure: a wanderer between two worlds, unable to give lasting expression to his dilemma. (pp. 56-7)

> *John Gross, "Zangwill in Restrospect," in Commentary, Vol. 38, No. 6, December, 1964, pp. 54-7.*

MAURICE WOHLGELERNTER (essay date 1964)

[*Wohlgelernter's* Israel Zangwill *is the most detailed thematic study of Zangwill's writing. In his book, Wohlgelernter examines the relationship of Zangwill's works to his life, his relationship to the literary trends of his time, his political activities, and his aesthetic and spiritual philosophies. In the following excerpt, Wohlgelernter examines those fictional depictions of the Jewish ghetto on which Zangwill's reputation is founded, detailing their thematic unity as well as what they reveal of Zangwill's personal philosophy.*]

It is certain that Zangwill deserves serious study when we recall that in the generation of famous writers including Shaw, Chesterton, and Belloc, he was considered their equal. And if today we are somewhat less sure of him, enough of value still remains in his works to warrant judicious review. To be sure, one must inevitably conclude that Zangwill is to be grouped with the lesser literary figures of his age; he is no Joyce or Yeats or Hopkins. But the literary world, we know, is not inhabited by giants only; men of smaller stature also walk there. Some of these men, also worth knowing, must be given attention. (p. viii)

Zangwill, seeking to depict life in London's ghetto, . . . introduced facts in his most famous novel, *Children of the Ghetto,* with a realism similar to that of Gissing, Moore, Morrison, Maugham, and Whiteing. But his sense of fact is highly modified by his predilection for the picturesque, the humorous, the faith, the sentimentality, and the romantic melancholy that are central to ghetto life. (p. 49)

Realism at the end of the nineteenth century was an attempt on the part of some novelists to see life steadily and, if possible, whole. Influenced by the realism of Flaubert and the naturalism of Zola, they based their "sense of fact" on the science of Darwin and Claude Bernard, "who applied the laws of matter to the study of creatures, and the positivism of Auguste Comte, who applied physical science to the study of man in society." Literature illustrated the laws of cause and effect. Hence, these novelists thought, the life, character, and environment of the protagonist in fiction must be carefully observed, selected, and presented with aloof impartiality. Realists contented themselves with "average reality."

And suddenly she remembered with a fresh pang the one woman who had a right to share her grief, nay to call him — in no figurative sense — 'Son'; the wrinkled old Jewess, palsied & deaf & peevish, who lived on bereft in a world of his splendid fighting strength, of his superb visionings.

Holograph copy of a fragment of the manuscript of Dreamers of the Ghetto.

Naturalism, an exaggerated form of realism, was the method Zola used (or, at least, professed) in his novels to analyze the brutality, ugliness, and degradation of life. "By naturalism," he said, "I mean analytical and experimental methods based on facts and human documents. There must be agreement between the social movement which is the cause, and literature which is the effect." Social mores, especially imperfect ones, must be dissected in order to achieve reform.... To show experimentally how a passion responds in a certain social condition, Zola as naturalist found it necessary to gather all the facts, even those that "decorum hitherto concealed."... Confining himself to analysis and demonstration, Zola was usually content to state the facts.

That Zangwill disapproved of Zola's method, feeling indifferent to its results and indisposed to incorporate it into his *Children of the Ghetto,* is certain.... What Zangwill demanded of the novelist . . . was not documentation but interpretation. Facts alone, he claimed, do not sufficiently stimulate the imagination; and environment, which admittedly plays a great role in the lives of all the children of the ghetto, cannot by itself provide all the necessary material for fiction. Zangwill understood that "Zola's science was pseudo-science and his faith in it was premature."

Moreover, Zangwill concluded . . . that, except for Da Vinci, "art and science have not been able to lodge together." If science is to become "the magnified, magical maid-of-all-work," she must allow will and emotion to supplement reason. "For the human consciousness, our sole instrument for apprehending the world, is trinitarian. I should say we have three antennae—Reason, Will, Emotion—wherewith to grope into our environment." To apply the methods of science to art would, he continues, be unreal and false. Lacking will and emotion, the world of the artist is incomplete.... To the "sense of fact" introduced into the novel at the close of the nineteenth century Zangwill added the forces of emotion and will in the observer.

Hence when he agreed to write *Children of the Ghetto* Zangwill found himself more in the realistic than in the naturalistic tradition, more like Gissing than like Zola. Both by choice and by temperament Zangwill could not be the "complete realist" that Wilson Follett describes:

> He escapes all prejudices by respecting all opinions, and rejecting all. He has the open and

inquiring mind, the steeled heart. He believes in everything as an evidence, but in nothing as a proof. His mind is a sympathetic and submissive recording instrument for the actual; for every experience, thought, memory, dream. He sympathizes with all, because his philosophical conscience tells him that whatever exists is worthy of sympathetic understanding. In short, his unremitting effort is to get outside himself, his own likes and dislikes, and finally to get outside the world, outside everything, for it is possible to see *through* everything. Likes and dislikes become relatively meaningless in a world conceived as an evolutionary unit in which we are all necessary parts of each other.

Though Zangwill possessed an open and inquiring mind, he did not have a "steeled heart." He could never be impersonal about what he was writing, least of all about the ghetto that he knew and loved so well. Moreover, it is well to remember that one of Zangwill's motives for writing *Children of the Ghetto* was to dispel, possibly forever, "the conception of a Jew in the mind of the average Christian as a mixture of Fagin, Shylock, Rothschild and the caricatures of the American comic papers." Hence it was necessary for him not only to depict the squalor of London's East End ghetto but also to record with admiration the heroic survival, despite adverse conditions, of these unfortunate immigrants. To escape all bias was for Zangwill impossible. Not only was he sympathetic to the inhabitants of the ghetto but, as will be seen, he was often nostalgic about them.

Furthermore, Zangwill was not a "complete realist," because he felt that the novelist must also include the absolutely essential quality of humor in his work. "Leave out humor," he said, "and you may get art and many fine things, but you do not get the lights and shadows or the 'values' of life." (pp. 50-3)

Though Zangwill considered himself in many ways unlike the realists of his day, he did not fail to appreciate their efforts. (p. 53)

[But what] is true of the other realists is true of Zangwill: given an evil environment, misery, the keynote of modern life, will follow.

Moreover, on reading the realistic novels of the nineties, one inevitably reaches the conclusion that in addition to the death, degradation, insolence, idiocy, murder, and misery common to all, there is yet something else central to them. These novels seem to be saying that some inexorable doom awaits anyone whose misfortune it is to land in the slums. Escape is impossible except, of course, by death, jail, or the gallows. Gissing, for one, attributes the cause of this entrapment to the callous indifference of an uninterested world. . . . Moore, for another, claims that fate predestined these people, despite their occasional attempts to escape into a decent life, to remain stuck in the mud of their environment. (p. 62)

[Yet] Zangwill, . . . careful to concede that environment influences character, would also insist that heredity plays an equal, if not greater role, in the life of his people. When Esther, for example, decides to return to the ghetto, it is not only because, like Jane Snowdon [Gissing's protagonist in *The Nether World*], she is moved by a desire to be of service to mankind but also, significantly, because of the influence of her parents and their faith. She yearns for the simple life of her parents and their abiding religious convictions centered on divine love. . . .

And it is this feeling for religious tradition, more than anything else, that distinguishes Zangwill from the other realists writing at the close of the nineteenth century. . . . Nowhere in Zangwill's ghetto do we find the flaunting vice, the rowdiness, or drunkenness that are indigenous to the other slums—because, Zangwill argues, there was a strong tendency among the children of the ghetto to abide by the faith of their fathers. (p. 63)

Central to *Children of the Ghetto* is the powerful influence that the home wields on the inhabitants of the ghetto. And religion and family are one. As indicated, Zangwill, like so many other students of history, understood that the one sustaining force in the survival of the Jewish race, in all ages and all ghettos, was the home. Hence, at the height of the two major crises of the novel—Hannah's decision not to follow her lover into exile, but to remain at home, and Esther's decision to heed her natural instincts and return to the ghetto—each heroine is moved by "the faces of her father and mother eloquent with the appeal of a thousand memories." Seated at the Passover *(Seder)* table, they recognize that it represents not merely a place where a series of rituals are observed but a center where each participant finds indissoluble links being forged for him with his race. . . . (pp. 64-5)

Hence, whereas Gissing's desire to champion the cause of the poor "was nothing more nor less than disguised zeal on behalf of [his] starved passions," Zangwill's resulted from an abiding admiration and identification with them. When the publication of *Workers in the Dawn* brought no financial relief, Gissing was subjected to continued poverty, which robbed him of "that natural sweetness of mind," which Dickens, for example, never lost. Submerged in the squalor and misery he saw about him, Gissing confessed to a hatred for the victims of the slums. (pp. 65-6)

On the other hand, Zangwill rarely set himself apart from the poor children of the ghetto and chose deliberately not to lose his "sweetness of mind." And if, like Esther, Zangwill suffered hardships and privations in early life, he never looked with contempt on the ghetto dwellers, but, on the contrary, attempted through varied political activity . . . to alleviate their troubled lot. (p. 66)

But Esther may be more than just a portrait of the artist as a Jew, or even the mouthpiece of her creator. She may, in effect, be a fictionalized symbol of her entire race. As Raphael Leon,

the Oxford don, says when offering her his hand in marriage: "I have come to conceive your life as an allegory of Judaism, the offspring of a great and tragic past with the germs of a rich blossoming, yet wasting with an inward canker." Esther refuses his hand, not out of caprice but because of an inner conviction that so long as her people languish in a ghetto, without a place of their own, without a national home where life can be lived in peace, she cannot lead a meaningful existence with him. Not in vain, therefore, does Esther consider herself "the grey spirit of the Ghetto which doubts itself." The question arises: Can a people so long enforced to live in squalor ever extricate itself? Esther's decision would seem to indicate the negative. . . . If happiness is to be denied her and her people, then what of the future? What must she do?

Whatever the solution, Esther feels that she cannot proceed alone apart from her race, or, for that matter, all mankind. Her race is her immediate identity; an attempt at happiness without the genuine happiness of all her people, as well as all peoples, would be futile. The ghetto, therefore, demands her sacrifice; but it also provides her with strength, the knowledge that her plight binds her in an eternal alliance with all the children of the ghetto. Unlike Gissing's Jane Snowdon and Sidney Kirkwood, who, standing in Abney Park Cemetery, see only defeat and sorrow ahead, and whose "lives would remain a protest against those brute forces of society which fill with wreck the abysses of the nether world," Zangwill's Esther joins her people in worship on the Day of Atonement, when the fate of *all* mankind is sealed. Not with bitterness or sorrow does she stand in the synagogue on the ground floor of No. 1 Royal Street but with a conviction that "the shadows of a large mysterious destiny seemed to hang over these . . . lives she knew so well in all their everyday prose, and to invest the unconscious shuffling sons of the ghetto with something of tragic grandeur." . . . Zangwill understood that brotherhood demands sacrifice, the sacrifice of self. . . . Thus, by sacrificing herself to Royal Street, Esther points to the right path in the future: one can leave the ghetto only by taking the ghetto, in some sense, along. Although he revised and later repudiated this notion, Zangwill does imply, at least in so far as Esther is concerned, that true progress cannot be achieved by abandoning unity and continuity of tradition.

Zangwill may have written his own critique of *Children of the Ghetto*. After the publication of Esther's pseudonymous novel, Zangwill has one of the Goldsmiths say to her:

> I say there is more actuality in it than in *Daniel Deronda* and *Nathan der Weise* put together. It is a crude production, all the same; the writer's artistic gift seems handicapped by a dead weight of moral platitudes and highfalutin, and even mysticism. He not only presents his characters but also moralizes over them—actually cares whether they are good or bad, and has yearnings after the indefinable—it is all very young. Instead of being satisfied that Judea gives him characters that are interesting, he actually laments their lack of culture. Still what he has done is good enough to make one hope his artistic instinct will shake off his moral.

And because Esther, as heroine, really represents Zangwill, he not only sentimentalizes about her but also about all his characters.

An excess of morality and sentimentality may perhaps have contributed chiefly to the gradual decline of the popularity of

Children of the Ghetto since the nineties when "it woke all England to applause." The sentimental spirit, we know, is basically a compound of "self" plus "emotion." So much "self" and "emotion" went into the writing of this novel that Zangwill could not allow himself to depict any character as immoral or indecent. Because sentimentality is also interpenetrated with optimism, Zangwill seems to be saying: "See how much nicer the ghetto is than the dismal world outside its boundaries, whose problems are never solved. Here all is good, brave, kind, noble and heroic." The world of the ghetto that Zangwill has given us may be and undoubtedly is "truth," but so much sentimentality is employed that the work is often full of platitudes.

But we dare not forget that to be moral and sentimental was Zangwill's deliberate choice. He wrote *Children of the Ghetto* with a specific purpose in mind: to offset, if possible, the blind medieval hatred of the chosen people that, in England, lingered till the mid-seventeenth century or later. And even in England, the most tolerant of European countries, complete freedom for the Jew was not fully attained till the close of the nineteenth century. Hence the sentimentality. (pp. 66-9)

[One] is nevertheless forced to conclude, on careful reading of *Children of the Ghetto,* that Zangwill's goal is a little too large for his novel. Since Zangwill has linked Esther's life with that of her entire people, it appears that he was, in fact, attempting to write an epic, something a little beyond his reach. Since he encompasses all aspects of the ghetto, we get, instead of a smooth and concise novel, a sprawling series of vignettes of ghetto characters, strung together on a thin thread of plot that must be tied together again at every breaking point. So large a canvas of life requires, if not many hands, then at least many volumes. Zangwill's attempt to comprehend all of it in one volume led only to excessive wordiness. (pp. 69-70)

But whatever his defects, they do not detract from the magnitude of the task. *Children of the Ghetto* surpasses by far Morrison's *A Child of the Jago,* Whiteing's *No. 5 John Street,* and Maugham's *Liza of Lambeth.* One might safely conclude that it even surpasses in some ways Gissing's *The Nether World,* the most significant of these realistic novels. . . . Conditioned by heredity and environment to look beneath the surface of the ghetto he investigated, Zangwill saw, unlike Gissing, that human life has more than artistic significance. Hence Zangwill envisaged the ghetto as the place not only of *a* people but of *all* people, of mankind. What he described, in short, was the totality of life, the life of tragedy and comedy, the *real* life. (p. 70)

"Over all Zangwill's work, even the *King of Schnorrers,*" writes the British poet, anthologist, and personal friend of Zangwill, Thomas Moult, "broods tragedy—tragedy in the Greek, the truer sense. It was instinctive in him to feel tragedy pressing everywhere." This brooding sense of tragedy, added to the comic spirit, reveals itself most clearly in the many short stories and novelettes included in *Ghetto Tragedies, Ghetto Comedies, The Celibates' Club, The Grey Wig,* as well as the play *Too Much Money* and the comic tale *The King of Schnorrers.* To balance these significant forces of tragedy and comedy and to show everywhere that they are closely related was Zangwill's ultimate aim in these stories. (p. 71)

Analyzing tragedy as a literary form, Aristotle says:

> A tragedy is the imitation of an action that is serious, complete, and also of a certain magnitude; in language embellished with each kind

of artistic ornament, each kind brought in separately in the parts of the work; in the form of action, not of narrative; through pity and fear affecting the proper purgation of these emotions.

What must be made unmistakably clear is that this definition of tragic, further elucidated in the *Poetics,* does not apply in every detail to Zangwill's work. What does apply, however, is the meaning of the Aristotelian term "serious" as regards character, the necessity of tragic conflict, and the reconciliation of the opposed and powerful influences of pity and fear.

Consider, for example, the character of the protagonists in the eleven stories that make up *Ghetto Tragedies* . . . and you will find that all are simple people. . . . But if they do not conform to the accepted view that tragedy must concern itself with a character well above the common level, they are nevertheless tragic. For, in harmony with his theory of art as an "imitation," Aristotle held that the gratification of art comes first of all from "recognition." If so, then Zangwill would believe that there is a place in tragedy for the simple, ordinary man.

And Zangwill is anxious to impress us with the fact that, given the stifling, suffocating nether world of the ghetto, the struggles and sufferings of its inhabitants will provide us with tragic exultation, not because they are eminent but because they epitomize man's own lack of eminence. For tragedy, Aristotle insists, involves "pity *and* fear," namely, as Gassner writes, "our capacity to feel for others and fear for ourselves, too, knowing that we share in their humanity and that they share in ours, which rules out the possibility of our ever dismissing humane considerations concerning other members of the species." And that is precisely what Zangwill wanted to do: to arouse in all his readers that feeling of pity, of being able to experience the tragedy that rests at the heart of the ghetto. Throughout *Ghetto Tragedies,* then, we find ourselves experiencing a pity, or the profound going out of the spirit, in response to unmerited suffering in the futile attitude of bewildered grief. The struggles of these unfortunate victims of circumstance must be our struggles as well.

Moreover, it is not only from witnessing their struggles that we derive tragic exultation but more significantly from their triumph over these struggles that we are ennobled. For we must never forget that tragedy, essentially, is not an expression of despair but of triumph over despair and of confidence in the value of human life. . . . Though these inhabitants of the ghetto suffer, they do not despair; they transcend their suffering with dignity, showing themselves to be people, if not above the common in social status, then certainly of uncommon significance and value.

What, then, does Zangwill consider "the tragic flaw" in each of the characters in *Ghetto Tragedies*? What basic error leads to the catastrophic end? What mistake is committed that brings on the lurking enemy in the dark, ready and eager to spring and only waiting for a chance? A careful reading of these stories will reveal that each protagonist suffers from substituting trust in man for trust in God. This is not to say that Zangwill would deny that a belief in the greatness of man is not a prerequisite for the noble life; on the contrary, he readily admits it. But what he does deny is that such a faith is sufficient unto itself. Without an equal, if not greater, faith in God, the traditional God of the ghetto, faith in man will disintegrate. (pp. 71-3)

If in *Ghetto Tragedies* Zangwill appears rhapsodic by comparison with Aristotle's matter-of-fact notations, he is nevertheless "allied to the man-centered point of view in the *Poetics*." For, as Gassner has correctly stated, "tragic art predicates the *special* universality of man's capacity for greatness of soul and mind in spite of his *hamartia* or the flaw in his nature." Central to all of these stories is a belief that tragedy is "a poetry of man":

> The individual is exemplified by the highest reaches of his humanity in erring and bearing the consequences, willing and suffering, groping and arriving at decisions, collaborating in his destiny (becoming its dupe when necessary but never its puppet), and affirming his personality even in defeat and dissolution.

And every one of these eleven children of the ghetto affirms his personality by recognizing that it is better to lose the world than one's soul; better to suffer torture than fail to collaborate with destiny; better to die than to live ignominiously. (pp. 75-6)

Albeit of common birth, these ghetto dwellers have an uncommon, heroic destiny, because Zangwill the artist found himself "capable of considering and of making us consider that his people and their actions have that amplitude and importance which make them noble." Fully aware of the calamities of life, these natives of the ghetto, like Zangwill, were supremely confident in the greatness of man. Hence over this, as over Zangwill's other works, there broods tragedy "in the Greek, the truer, sense."

But tragedy, we know, was not the only aspect of the ghetto that interested Zangwill; he was no less absorbed in its comic spirit and humor. He was convinced that both the comic spirit and humor, which always existed in the gloomy alleys of the ghetto, abetted the unconquerable faith that sustained his people in their struggle for survival. For, paradoxically, both the comic spirit and humor came out of a background of sorrow and evil and the need to accept them. Tragedy and comedy were, in fact, complementary aspects of ghetto life.

What, precisely, is the comic spirit? In his highly revealing "Essay on Comedy," Meredith tells us:

> Whenever they [men] wax out of proportion, overblown, affected, pretentious, bombastical, hypocritical, pedantic, fantastically delicate; whenever it sees them self-deceived or hoodwinked into vanities, congregating in absurdities, planning short-sightedly, plotting dementedly whenever they are at variance with their professions, and violate the unwritten but perceptible laws binding them in consideration one to another; whenever they offend sound reason, fair justice; are false in humility or mined with conceit, individually or in the bulk; the Spirit overhead will look humanely malign, and cast an oblique light on them, followed by volleys of silvery laughter. That is the Comic Spirit.

To be sure, Zangwill uses the term "humor" instead of "comedy" when he wishes to civilize the ghetto inhabitants by revealing the nature of their intellect. But, though "comedy" and "humor" are admittedly different in form, their ultimate interest, according to Zangwill, is the same. Both are interested in the influence of the social world upon the characters of men; both are less concerned with beginnings or endings or surrounding than with what men are now doing; both, in fact, laugh through the mind. Moreover, both contain a philosophic

attitude that says, "whenever a man laughs humorously there is an element which, if his sensitivity were sufficiently exaggerated, would contain the possibility of tears. He is a man who has suffered or failed of something. And although in the humor of art he usually arrives at something else, in the humor of everyday life he frequently arrives at nothing at all." Since the children of the ghetto arrived nowhere at all, humor became for them, Zangwill believed, an adroit and exquisite device by which their nerves outwitted the stings and paltry bitternesses of life. (pp. 76-7)

The tragic writer always produces a one-sided work because "he can only show one side of life at a time; the humorist alone can show both."

Desiring, therefore, to show both sides of life, Zangwill wrote comic stories and tales, notably such works as *The King of Schnorrers* and *Ghetto Comedies*. . . . By blurring the usual distinction between comedy and tragedy Zangwill was trying to say that comedy, like humor, should not necessarily be equated with raucous laughter, and that the "humorist" and the "funny man" are two distinct and separate people. The joy of Zangwill's comedy is thoughtful; its laugh is not noisy but "of the order of the smile, finely tempered, showing sunlight of the mind, mental richness rather than noisy enormity." (pp. 78)

And where but in the ghetto were there so many men to whom failure was as interesting as success? Where, too, but in the ghetto, were "good and bad" so finely interwoven as to produce a fabric of life at once intricate and absorbing? Fortunately Zangwill, more than any other writer of his day, was better equipped to show both the tragic and comic sides of life in London's East End. First, because he knew intimately and at first hand the tragedy inherent in the lives of the children of the ghetto. And, second, we will remember, that Zangwill began his career as one of the "new humorists" who rallied around Jerome K. Jerome's *The Idler*, in which *The King of Schnorrers* was first published serially. These humorists, in the words of Zangwill, believed that "life was Janus-faced, and the humorist invests his characters with a double-mask; they stand for comedy as well as for tragedy." . . . Because he was thus personally involved in the tragic and comic aspects of his life and times, Zangwill's *Ghetto Comedies*, like his other comic works, contains a mental richness rather than a noisy laughter, a finely tempered smile rather than a loud guffaw.

Read carefully, everyone of the fourteen stories in *Ghetto Comedies* . . . will show that its mirth is subdued; in fact, many of them lack any traces of humor at all. Why? Because Zangwill felt that comedy teaches us to look at life exactly as it *is*. It teaches us to be responsive, to be honest, to interrogate ourselves and correct our pretentiousness. Through the medium of comedy Zangwill chastened the children of the ghetto for their foolishness, stubbornness, self-deception, and failure to recognize the realities of life. This criticism, of course, was not the result of any rancor, for Zangwill, we know, had an abiding kinship with and affection for his people. He was able to ridicule those he loved without loving them less; he chastened without hating. (pp. 79-80)

Surveying, therefore, the social impact of the ghetto on its inhabitants, Zangwill's "comic spirit" mocked the Jew for failing to understand the two basic needs for his survival: recapturing the true image of himself and heeding the call to action. (p. 80)

To be a Jew, Zangwill believed, one must be "spotless as the dove." Only thus can the Jew be worthy of his suffering.

For the Jew to be worthy of suffering meant something more than just being kind, gracious, hospitable, and benevolent; he must be willing "to live and die with his own people." Even when success in the arts, sciences, and professions brings the Jew into close contact with the world beyond the ghetto walls, he dare not ever forget his past and its associations. (p. 81)

Of far greater evil than this failure to seek identification with one's people was the failure to seek salvation. Zangwill was firmly convinced that the Jew, if he is to survive his hostile environment and its pogroms, must resort to the only course open to him: action. (pp. 81-2)

Zangwill was firmly convinced that if the Jew in the ghetto would "drift into vanities, congregate in absurdities, plan shortsightedly," and refuse to unite in self-defense, the comic spirit must look with "humane malignity" at him and in the end bring "the peace of the devil." (p. 83)

In *Ghetto Comedies* the humorist Zangwill took a long look at the ghetto and found that it was filled with tragedy, which consisted either of an escape by some into the waiting arms of Christianity, or the refusal of others . . . to heed the call to action, allowing themselves to be slaughtered wantonly. In both instances the Jew was doomed to extinction. This, Zangwill, like all other believers in Jewish survival, wanted desperately to prevent. Hence, when he saw that the Jew in the ghetto refused to face reality, he invoked the comic spirit in order to cast an oblique eye upon him. . . . Zangwill hoped with these tales to clarify those issues that, he felt, were preventing the ghetto dwellers from achieving their freedom and felicity. Only the comic spirit could help Zangwill in his task. . . . (pp. 83-4)

The person who best typified the comic spirit was the ghetto *schnorrer,* immortalized by Zangwill in *The King of Schnorrers.* This short work is a vivid and humorous portrayal of a fictitious character—one Menasseh Bueno Barzilai Azevedo da Costa—who lords it in the London ghetto at the close of the eighteenth century. He is a Sephardic mendicant who has developed begging to a fine art and who combines with his audacious effrontery unfailing resourcefulness and ready repartee. (p. 84)

Surely Zangwill meant to do more in this book than relate some simple episodes in the life of a beggar. As Bernard Schilling has already indicated, "the whole seems an ironic comment upon the absurdity of all human arrangements." Beggary, the subject of this tale, implies a long history of poverty, injustice, and degradation, to which the Jew in the diaspora has been subjected. To offset the grim realities of the ghetto, there arose from the soil of Jewish life a determination to self-criticism that Freud called "tendency-wit." Humorous tales, subtle comments, witty anecdotes were directed, at times, against oneself or "against a person in whom one takes interest, that is, a composite personality such as one's own people." These stories, invented by Jews themselves, mocked Jewish peculiarities and shortcomings and thus provided much psychic relief for the downtrodden of the ghetto. "From death and beggary themselves the Jews extracted the ludicrous." Social stability, then, was achieved in the ghetto through "wise laughter."

And wisdom is the key to the understanding of Menasseh's life and mind. Faced with the absurdities of the ghetto in which he, a learned man, is considered inferior, Menasseh exagger-

ates his value in order to build up his position among men who, for the moment, appear vastly superior. In this effort to achieve prominence he uses his intellect, which, because of his close study and vast knowledge of the Talmud, has been sharpened to deal ingeniously with all the vexing problems confronting him. Being more learned, Menasseh refuses to recognize any difference between master and servant, and insists, as Freud also recognized, "that the rich man gives him nothing, since he is obligated by [religious] mandate to give alms, and strictly speaking must be thankful that the schnorrer gives him an opportunity to be charitable." Such arguments, at once audacious and humorous, offered psychic relief for all those anxious mendicants who, like Menasseh, roamed the streets of the ghetto in search of help.

The King of Schnorrers, therefore, underscores that special quality of Jewish humor that cures folly with folly, and, like the comic spirit, makes game of "serious" life. (pp. 86-7)

Comedy heightened Zangwill's consciousness of the tragic in ghetto life. If, for example, Menasseh acts absurdly, it is only because he reflects the absurdity of his environment; if he has to use his mental skill to overpower his adversaries, it is only because these adversaries need to be overpowered; if, in short, his antics make us laugh, they also make us cry. Why? Because within the narrow radius of the ghetto reside a group of people who, as a result of the vicissitudes of migration and worship, and in spite of their tradition, worship the gruff, pompous, parsimonious financiers instead of the learned, the scholars, the intellectuals. Second, these very people who bear the cross of discrimination gain the dubious distinction of discriminating against their own brethren by forbidding, for example, a Sephardi to marry a Tedesco. And, finally, what seems far worse, we find Menasseh, who refuses himself to distinguish between master and servant, looking with disfavor on Yankele, a fellow mendicant, until the latter proves his worth as a *schnorrer.* It is this theme—disunity among Jews in the face of adversity, and their loss of a sense of values—that preoccupied so much of Zangwill's mind and that he often returned to in his writing. . . . (p. 88)

Maurice Wohlgelernter, in his Israel Zangwill: A Study, *Columbia University Press, 1964, 344 p.*

BERNARD N. SCHILLING   (essay date 1965)

[*In the following excerpt, Schilling analyzes the protagonist of* The King of Schnorrers, *Manasseh Bueno Barzillai Azevedo da Costa. He also discusses the background of Jewish community tradition and presents theories on the development of Jewish humor in an informed portrait of the schnorrer character. For a disagreement about the quality of humor in* The King of Schnorrers, *see the excerpt by Milton Hindus (1954).*]

A certain form of comic insight seems more marked in Jews than in other men. Everyone who discusses Jewish humor remarks how the sombreness of this people's history has given a special tone to what it sees as funny. The Jews have loved life certainly; they have a will to endure, to survive when everything is done to make life intolerable for them, when everything is regularly taken away but life itself. We all have to accept the realities no matter how grim they are and laughter through tears is common enough; but this endurance is doubly imposed on the Jews who must accept the repudiation and abuse of other men.

If the comic view of life is needed to help us endure what we see, so is it needed to make things easier and sweeter especially for those who have to suffer at the hands of others. When we think what a monstrous and unspeakable joke has been played on the Jews, we can see why they have developed a rueful comic view the better to endure it. Their humor emerges from a background of sorrow and evil and the need to accept them; one stands such things better by making jokes which give a certain relief and perspective. (pp. 145-46)

This tendency to joke recalls the numerous stories of miracles in Jewish history. Miracles show rescue from defeat, triumph through unexpected reversals of fortune, divine help in hopeless situations. So also the joke that overcomes apparent disaster or defeat at the last minute. The miracle is typical of men facing adversity not to be borne without divine aid; so is the Jewish joke natural for those whose actual lives contain so much agony.

Closely related is the fact that if a Jew resents something he can't do anything about it. He can talk, however, or imagine what he would do if he could. People in exile or otherwise physically helpless cannot defend themselves; hence the Jews are such a convenient object of persecution. But words they have, and a kind of defense by verbose invective, comic exaggeration, and absurd insults which give vent to frustration at other levels.

So the comedy of insult flourishes, especially when there is no chance to carry out a threat in action. As in the scolding of small boys or the barking of little dogs, the noise made is ludicrously out of proportion to the offense first, and secondly to any chance that action will come of it. (p. 147)

These elementary thoughts about Jewish humor came to mind in the search for some example that would be typical but not too obvious. Freud has included some very amusing jokes in his study of wit, among them a series dealing with the *schnorrer,* a name for what was at one time an accepted institution in the Jewish community, a professional beggar who received the alms that were demanded of everyone as part of one's religious duty. This pathetic, absurd figure was given a kind of literary immortality by Israel Zangwill in a highly amusing book, *The King of Schnorrers.* . . .

Not only do we get some hilarious incongruities here, but we see a form of Jewish humor which so often springs from their tragedy. Leaving aside the lot of common humanity and what it demands of one man toward another, the most preposterous comedy emerges from misery and want. Never mentioned is what these people must have endured in sorrow and exile before the need to beg of one another arose in the first place. Once more these things are inseparable from the Jewish human lot and they are better endured if accepted and treated comically. If begging is a permanent necessity, why not use it as a commentary on the absurdity of human arrangements which seem to reward a lucky few and to condemn others without a chance?

So we have an incongruous picture of a beggar who so behaves as to seem superior to the very people from whom he begs; it is they who must defend themselves for their actions and their high place in the world and to show cause why, in actual fact, the beggar is not more to be praised than the man who just happens to have the money.

Now the *schnorrer* arose from two facts in Jewish history and belief. There was a religious requirement that charity be given as part of one's service to God. Then too a persecuted and homeless people, wandering much in exile and often uprooted or disinherited by sudden visitations, produced many penniless and needy persons who had to get their living as best they could. Each wave of massacres turned up fresh hordes of the destitute. The two facts are of course allied. Because charity was so much needed, it became a religious requirement. . . . Charity is a human duty since all men are equally of God; it is especially a Jewish obligation since philanthropy is demanded of those who have endured so much exile and oppression. Victims themselves they must never forget the sorrows of others, so that as a man and as a Jew one has to give. This compulsion cannot be overstressed; anyone who wants to obey God and be righteous *must* give charity.

Now, of course, such a high moral code is bound to encourage the cynical and the lazy who always exist and who see a chance to profit from society at no expense to themselves. It was easy for some *schnorrers* to abandon any pretense of work and simply to live off their communities. In the ghettos they could go from door to door and never be seen by gentiles, thus exploiting a religious and social privilege; they would not disgrace other Jews and would help them satisfy a religious duty. In earlier times the *schnorrer* might serve a useful purpose as a bearer of news. When his regular beat was confined he might, among other semi-useful activities, publish the day's obituary by going about the ghetto with a pyx, or money box; if one heard the rattle of this box one might ask the *schnorrer* who was dead today, and give him something for his information. Before the days of newspapers, the peripatetic *schnorrer* carried news about politics, discoveries, important developments of various kinds in business. Later he was the repository of anecdotes, humorous stories, and proverbial wit; indeed his name was derived from the Yiddish word for this kind of material.

But Zangwill's story is set in late 18th-century London under somewhat special conditions. There had been no Jewish community of any size in England after the expulsion under Edward I in 1290, and it was not until 1656 that the tiny group of Jews in London was openly accepted as within the law. In the course of time immigration to England from the continent became very cheap and easy; this encouraged the victims of any new persecutions to seek refuge where they would be unmolested.

Among hordes of abject and homeless fugitives, especially after the horrible Polish massacres in the mid-17th century, many were reduced to beggary and the number of *schnorrers* greatly increased. These were not only refugees from eastern Europe, but some who had fled the rigors of the Spanish inquisition, a more select and aristocratic group. The last of such large influxes came after the continental persecutions of 1768 when the English Jewish community more than doubled in size in thirty years. In time with the aid of the French revolutionary wars this large immigration stopped; the Jewish poor in London levelled off, and ceased to be a problem calling for the creation of a special class with its own name and function.

Now the great *schnorrer* whose exploits we are about to enjoy flourished at a time when a large pauper class had been imposed on the established Jews in London. Keep in mind that the oldest Jewish families were of Spanish-Portuguese origin called Sephardim, as distinguished from those of eastern Europe, the Ashkenazim or Tedescos. Our hero never lets anyone forget that he is a Sephardi, and it is worthwhile to emphasize that, along with their great antiquity and distinction in many other ways, the Sephardim were noted for generosity. Thus, the king of *schnorrers* finds himself at home in a charitable context. He is used to living with generous men, he is of their kind in birth and blood; he is therefore naturally placed toward charity which, as it happens, he receives instead of gives. He bears the proudest of all Sephardic names in addition, a name remarkable also for philanthropy. By birth, by association, by name he comes to his high expectation that charity will and should be bestowed upon him. His disdain of *schnorrers* with a mere Tedesco origin we will find among his most amusing traits as he proceeds on his parasitical way. (pp. 147-51)

As an example of Jewish humor the *schnorrer* arises from a tragic context of absolute human need to beg in order to live; from a consequent religious usage which enabled him to beg in order to create an opportunity of virtue in others; from, in turn, his own exploitation of the chance to live off a community, generous by custom and conviction; which finally persuades him that his way of life is entirely justified and indeed required for one so lofty and dignified, so learned and aristocratic as he.

Let us now make his acquaintance; he is presented by Israel Zangwill in a series of episodes which taken together become a minor classic of absurdity. The great philanthropist of London, Joseph Grobstock, is pleased one day to disburse from a large canvas bag a great many coins, each of which is separately wrapped in paper. Obviously well-known to a band of *schnorrers*, Grobstock is overwhelmed by customers for his bounty, each of whom receives one coin.

His bag still not empty, Grobstock comes upon a figure which could be nothing but that of a *schnorrer* but which has about it none the less something imposing and distinguished. The philanthropist reaches into the bag and offers one of the folded packets. Expecting some sign of gratitude, Grobstock is suddenly overwhelmed by a torrent of abuse. He has included one empty package in the whole sack, which it was his misfortune to bestow upon a man of regal deportment and a fierce sense of his own superiority in providing a chance for those who have money to display the virtue for the proper worship of God. Poor Grobstock does not escape from the encounter without paying a considerable sum for which he is thanked with dignity.

In answer to a question as to his name, the *schnorrer* gives this astounding reply: "I am Manasseh Bueno Barzillai Azevedo da Costa," a sonorous combination of some of the greatest of all Sephardic names. Poor Grobstock is reminded that Manasseh is indeed a Sephardi, even as it is written all over his own face that he is nothing but a Tedesco. He feels ever smaller and more inferior, as Manasseh establishes his towering intellect and aristocratic lineage above one who is clearly an upstart immigrant, a pitiful refugee from the ghettos of eastern Europe, whereas everyone knows the Sephardim have been in England for generations.

Grobstock can say or do nothing right as Manasseh maneuvers him into gifts of money and clothes, gets the better of him in an absurd contest as to who shall have the last good salmon in the fish-market, and loftily invites himself to have supper with Grobstock on the following Friday evening. To this supper he has the impudence to invite his friend Yankelé ben Yitzchok, and to speak with condescension of the food, while urging Yankelé to "make yourself at home—remember, you're my guest!" (pp. 151-53)

Zangwill has been content to assemble [his] episodes around three main contests: Manasseh against Grobstock, against Yankelé, and against the Sephardic authorities. In each case what seems to be inferior actually wins out over something higher and greater than itself. As Manasseh outwits and overwhelms both Grobstock and the Mahamad who are vastly above him in society, so in turn Yankelé prevails over a far mightier man than he. But Manasseh wins out by arrogance and a display of force from his natural superiority, while Yankelé prevails by flattery and insinuation and pretending to seem inferior.

This theme of incongruous victory unifies the story at one level and gives the episodes more continuity than the overall action calls for. . . . Here too a serious profession is made out of a piece of absurd quackery, and we are entertained by ludicrous deception and vanity in a world which seems to make no sense or to pretend to justice anyway. We end with the cynical assumption that all activities are not really what they seem to be, that they are based on some form of cheating, until outright fraud becomes defensible as being only a question of degree.

But the materials before us are much too funny to depress us by their sadder implications. They center largely upon Manasseh, of course, who is a loose combination of aristocracy, intellect, and religion. In varying degrees he entertains us by displays of arrogance, shrewdness, parasitism, vanity, and ingenious self-justification. Most of these qualities emerge at the outset when we hear his name: Manasseh Bueno Barzillai Azevedo da Costa, an original literary construction of his own, we are sure.

The mellifluous words sound the note of incongruity for Manasseh throughout. We see the ludicrous contrast between what he is and what his name implies: all that Manasseh is not in the eyes of the world. Certainly these elaborate and euphonious words contrast sharply with the harsh consonants of Joseph Grobstock. This is solid and crude, a piece of common wood, like the uncultivated homeliness of what the man does for a living. The word Grobstock says directly what he is about and is done with it. Da Costa the aristocrat is not about anything

"'YOU ROGUE! HOW DARE YOU BUY SALMON!'"

Illustration from an early edition of The King of Schnorrers.

and can take all the time necessary to say what his name is. (pp. 154-55)

A glamorous, romantic Spaniard of remote and ancient origins makes pitiful the homely German Grobstock, vulgarized by trade and the coarse associations of the market-place which have never besmirched the aristocratic culture of da Costa. The very length of this name implies ease and leisure—not the hurried, bare functionalism and practicality of Joseph Grobstock. Its complexity suggests also the noble or royal figures who have to include a series of various units in what they are called so as to take into account their complicated origins, branches, and ancestral obligations. The preposition "da" carries similar hints of being of or from an ancient place, whereas again a meagre single name like Grobstock seems to come from an occupation of some kind like miller, smith, or clerk. If one's name describes the work one does, or implies work of any kind, all is revealed and there is no concealing a plebeian origin. Da Costa therefore allows nothing to suggest that work was ever done or should be done; this becomes central to his own professional outlook. It all breathes an air of command, of privilege, of high expectation, of taking for granted the homage, the labor, and tribute of lesser men.

The names of the two antagonists then are keys to their worlds. Da Costa is a hellenist, a child of light and ideas; Grobstock has little discernment, taste, or delicacy, no metaphysical adroitness able to make remote connections, no skill to phrase them until they seem inevitable. A routine fellow without ideas, he has only wealth, respectability, and worldly success to compensate for his dullness. And who would have these at the price of being so devoid of taste and fluency? Not Manasseh Bueno Barzillai Azevedo da Costa certainly. This superbly constructed name is borne by a professional beggar, and creates a delightfully comic incongruity.

Manasseh's appearance goes not with his name, however, but with his profession, and thus appearance leads directly to a most amusing episode when poor Grobstock hopes to change it for the better by the offer of some clothes. (pp. 156-57)

[The] first encounters with Grobstock show how inseparable one from the other the three main lines of Manasseh's character are. His aristocracy, learning and intellect, and religious devotion are all involved one with another; in the end we will find that they cannot be separated from his beggary. A man of such overwhelming perfections cannot take a place among ordinary men in the world, and he persuades us that he has no choice but to beg from a society controlled by people so vastly inferior to him. (pp. 161-62)

Now Manasseh's generosity in providing an outlet for charity has another sanction. Not only is he poor, he is also learned. He can thus profit both from the Jewish law of charity and from a respect for intellect as well. (p. 171)

His grasp of the Jewish intellectual inheritance becomes one of his strongest weapons in the constant fight he wages to establish his superiority over other men and hence his right to beg from them. For clearly Manasseh must be superior in mind and attainment, not through being rich and powerful. He must be superior in the only way one can be without external means. His scholarship must therefore be impeccable if Manasseh is to meet his own terms. In the Jewish world which he inhabits, the scholar is honored as being and possessing on a high level what everyone would want or would get as his own if he could. The scholar is and has what everyone wants to be and have; hence it is that people like Grobstock who are and have only

tangible and material things must recognize Manasseh's real superiority, must suspect that after all he may be right to patronize them. For he has studied the *Torah* and the *Talmud;* he knows the *law,* as he is constantly pointing out, and indeed must know it if he is to seem higher than other men and rightly to demand their deference and charity for his learning as well as for his poverty. (p. 172)

So it is left to an aristocratic beggar to uphold what others are becoming too weak, too worldly, too unJewish to sustain. Manasseh, the real aristocrat deeply rooted by blood, learning, and religion in the past, would not think of following the likes of Grobstock and besmirching himself in the concerns of the outside world. He never forgets that he is Jewish nor ever shows a sign that it even occurs to him to be otherwise. Here his devotion becomes practical once more, because in any other context he would have to give up being a *schnorrer*. His whole life, character, and mode of living depend on his remaining in the Jewish scheme of things, where alone the assumptions he makes are conceivable. In some ways he seems urbane and cosmopolitan, superior to any label or classification, but only by clinging to his especially intensified Jewishness can he go on combining his fabulous talents with profitable beggary.

And his ingenious defense of professional *schnorrerism*, which makes Grobstock feel uncertain and inferior, at times is so persuasive that we have to wonder whether it might not contain some truth after all. Manasseh shows that their positions, that the one has money and the other begs, are only passing material accidents, and if society refuses to assign value to the beggar's role he will have to assert some value for it. It is of course incongruous that one in so low a social state should adopt a superior attitude, and this becomes very funny. But there is nothing laughable in the long history of poverty, injustice, and degradation that beggary implies; yet the beggar too is a man and must have his dignity, which ought to be higher and clearer than it is among other men.

To make it better, the *schnorrer* exaggerates and turns it completely around to make his human point. He builds up his position to equalize it with another's which is for the moment vastly superior. Some way has to be found to put Grobstock in the wrong and Manasseh in the right on human grounds, when clearly society and life in the world have greatly elevated one and depressed the other. The world's assumptions have to be upset to put down a rich and successful man below a wretched tramp. This is done by making the beggar enormously superior in all the ways that are supposed to suggest that one man is actually better than another, while at the same time showing that such superiority has nothing to do with worldly success, that in fact such success may well be achieved by men who have not a fraction of Manasseh's genius.

The whole becomes an ironic commentary on the absurdity of all human arrangements; one becomes almost persuaded that Manasseh is right, that his parasitical impudence and refusal to work for what he extorts from the sober, reasonable, and industrious pedestrians who have money and run the world— that this is in fact justified and is no more absurd than the actual nature of things. (pp. 192-93)

Bernard N. Schilling, "Aristocracy and the King of Schnorrers" and "Manasseh's Learning and Triumph," in his The Comic Spirit: Boccaccio to Thomas Mann, *Wayne State University Press, 1965, pp. 145-70, 171-93.*

ELSIE BONITA ADAMS (essay date 1971)

[Adams's Israel Zangwill *is the most thorough study to date of Zangwill's career. In this work, Adams examines all of Zangwill's writing in a genre by genre approach, including extensive plot summaries and commentaries particularly useful for those works by Zangwill that are not readily available. In the following excerpt, Adams surveys Zangwill's essays, novels, short stories, dramas, and poetry.]*

Like numerous other end-of-the-century Realists, Zangwill divided his time between journalism and fiction. (p. 25)

In his earliest journalistic work Zangwill was associated with the New Humor of Jerome K. Jerome, Robert Barr, Barry Pain, and others who have disappeared from even the footnotes of literary history. Beginning in February, 1892, Zangwill wrote for *The Idler*, edited by Jerome and Barr. A perusal of the pages of this magazine reveals that the humor was not new, nor was it even always amusing. Zangwill's contributions include several short stories which were later included in collections.... Illustrative of his efforts for "The Idlers' Club" are a criticism of Oscar Wilde couched in Wildean epigrams and reversals ("You are much too important to be discussed seriously"); the ironic defense of "Somewhere Else" as "the ideal resort"; or a parody of a Renaissance defense of tobacco in "Zangwill reasoneth with ye monarch." For the most part, Zangwill's essays in *The Idler*, though sometimes clever, are seldom distinguished in content or style.

His column, "Men, Women and Books," for *The Critic* (September, 1894—December, 1896) is of interest because of its sound, often witty, and very readable literary criticism. An example of Zangwill's technique as literary critic is his review of *Marcella*, a three-volume novel by the popular writer, Mrs. Humphrey Ward. Zangwill shows in this review an appreciation for Mrs. Ward's "talent and industry" in anatomizing a segment of English life, but he perceives her major weaknesses: tedium and pseudointellectualism. He describes precisely the feelings one has in reading Mrs. Humphrey Ward: "One rises from a novel of hers distinctly older. In the middle of the second volume one wonders vaguely how many aeons ago one was reading the first, and what infinities are to traverse before one will emerge from the third." Other reviews in "Men, Women and Books" are equally incisive in their critical judgments and imaginative in expression.

The essays in *The Critic* are also of interest because they, along with those which Zangwill was writing at the same time in [his monthly column for *The Pall Mall Magazine*] "Without Prejudice," contain his theory of art, a theory which places his own fiction, drama, and poetry outside the *fin-de-siècle* school of "art for art's sake" and within the stream of art for life's sake. To Zangwill, art was realistic (though not without elements of romance), serious (though necessarily touched by humor), and large. In a review of Turgenev's *Daughter of Joy* he comments on the nature of art: to him, "merely artistic" renderings of incident are not great art; for "A work of art that has no general relation to reality is only a toy, a luxury, and the maker thereof is veritably a 'Daughter of Joy.'"

Reality, however, to Zangwill consists of more than the external world of the senses; life is, he says in an essay in *Without Prejudice*, "large, chaotic, inexpressible, not to be bound down by a formula." Expressing in criticism a theory that he gave full expression in his novel *The Master*, Zangwill insists always on the artist's need to grasp the mystery, the romance, of everyday reality. (pp. 26-28)

Many of the essays [in *Italian Fantasies*] invite an analogy between the prose fantasies and musical form: the opening essay is **"A Rhapsody"**; the second, a **"Fantasia"**; the third, **"A Capriccio"**; later essays are entitled **"Intermezzo"** and **"Variations on a Theme."** With few exceptions, the essays with musical titles exemplify Zangwill at his worst: they are associative in organization, informal in tone, whimsical in content, and, as one critic complained, "shockingly overwritten." The style is indeed "rhapsodic," utilizing repetition, exclamations, many questions, interruptions, involuted sentences, and archaisms; the humor is often labored and lame.

Fortunately, most of the essays in the collection are serious explorations of artistic, social, and religious problems, and in these Zangwill is at his best. For example, the third essay, **"The Carpenter's Wife: A Capriccio,"** avoids the "neo-Carlylese" of the opening essays and pointedly comments on the failure of institutionalized religion. (p. 29)

The evils of nationalism was one of Zangwill's most persistent themes; and, during and after World War I, most of his artistic energies were directed to decrying the nationalism which he felt was destroying the world. In *Italian Fantasies* he attacks the "disease" of nationalism, calling for an "Intensive Imperialism" based on brotherhood and love and producing "the highest life per square mile." ... In **"The Gods of Germany"** (*The War for the World*. . .), he attacks superpatriotism, a nationalism so intense that we "worship each our own national spirit, to the exclusion even of whatever God transcends humanity." He develops a similar idea in *The Principle of Nationalities* ..., where he says that nationality has become God and replaced Christianity. Admitting the difficulty of defining nationality, Zangwill says that men are more accurately divided "into first-class and third-class passengers" than into national types. He finally pleads for men to realize "their common humanity" and "to maintain the virtues of tribalism without losing the wider vision."

The replacement of humane ideals by national goals led, Zangwill believes, to the disaster of World War I. In *The War for the World* Zangwill analyzes the world struggle that he had dramatized in *The War God*.... The title of the collection of essays means that conflicting forces struggle for control of the world and that, in a changing world, especially one at war, "no liberty is so old-established as to be safe." ... In the opening essay of the volume, he accuses England of a "growing passion for Prussianism" in suppressing plays and books. In a climate of wartime fear and suspicion, he maintains, England "has temporarily ceased to exist.".... His fear is that the war and war politics will destroy the very liberties that the war is supposed to safeguard. (pp. 32-3)

Those essays in *The War for the World* which are not on the war are on the Suffragette movement or on Russia and the Jewish question. Zangwill sees the world struggle as threefold; encompassing all struggles is the European war, while at the same time women are fighting for equality and minority groups are struggling for equal rights. (p. 34)

The question of what to do about the persecution of world Jewry is the subject of Zangwill's last collection of essays, *The Voice of Jerusalem*.... It was a subject about which Zangwill had written all his life: his best fiction treated it; his problem dramas alluded to it; his essays and speeches frequently dwelled on it. His work with Herzl and the Jewish Territorial Organization made him a prominent figure in the Zionist movement. Though the validity of his opinions about

Palestine and Zionism may still be debatable, the fact that he spent most of his life seeking an answer to the problem of Jewish homelessness and protesting the mistreatment of Jews throughout the world is not.

Commentators on Zangwill's opinions about world Jewry often stress the ambivalence which he felt toward Judaism. It is true that in *Children of the Ghetto,* as well as in Zangwill's personal life, there is a pulling away from orthodox Judaism. But it is also true that from his earliest works he recognized in Judaism a morality capable of leading the world, and in this opinion he wavered little during his lifetime. One of his early essays, **"The Position of Judaism,"** ... speaks of the failure of Christianity because of its otherworldliness to answer the needs of modern man; on the other hand, Judaism, with its acceptance of the sensuous world (in fact, its ability to make religion relevant to virtually every facet of life in that world), its emphasis on family and community, and its tendency "to unification" is peculiarly suited to the modern spirit. (p. 35)

The Voice of Jerusalem ends with a bleak prediction: "But humanity has not suffered enough, and doubtless we have to undergo still grimmer experiences before our almost incorrigible hearts are chastened, and our gun-deafened ears turned and attuned to the still small voice of Jerusalem." ...

The Zangwill of this passage seems a different man from the clever wit writing items for "The Idlers' Club" in 1892: one is an entertainer; the other, a prophet. However, the seeds of the later seriousness are in Zangwill's earliest work, notably in his ghetto fiction and in his social criticism of the 1890's. If his essays ceased to entertain as he turned his attention to Zionism, war politics, and programs of world community, they show no loss of literary power. In fact, the early, trivial essays now seem most dated in ideas and technique; but the social criticism remains interesting and effective. (p. 38)

Zangwill's earliest published novels were a political satire, *The Premier and the Painter* ... , and two humorous works, *The Bachelors' Club* ... and *The Old Maids' Club.* ... These early works show promise but suffer from a self-conscious display of wit, overabundant detail, and a labored style. Though Zangwill began as a humorist, he soon moved to the serio-comic (or tragi-comic) view characteristic of his best work, such as *Children of the Ghetto* ... and *The King of Schnorrers.* ... Of his other novels, *The Master* ... deserves a place among the "portrait of the artist" stories at the end of the century, but *The Mantle of Elijah* ... , an attack on modern politics, is best forgotten. Toward the end of a long career as novelist, short-story writer, dramatist, poet, and essayist, Zangwill produced his last novel, *Jinny the Carrier* ... , which deliberately escapes from the twentieth century by turning to a subject and technique of an earlier and simpler day. (p. 39)

The theme of political disorder [in *The Premier and the Painter*] is introduced in the opening words of the book, for a newsboy shouts news of dissension in the premier's cabinet. In the opening chapter, Conservative premier Arnold Floppington (popularly called "Floppy") finds his double in a Radical working man, a sign painter, Jack Dawe. By the end of the chapter, the two have changed places; and the rest of the book depicts the results of this change by contrasting the character of the self-assured, dynamic, but Philistine painter turned premier with that of the philosophical, indecisive, but moral premier turned painter. Ironically, the sign painter is an eminently successful politician, and the premier is a failure not only in politics but also in work and in love. (p. 40)

The Premier and the Painter presents a pessimistic view of human nature: the well-intentioned, kindhearted Floppington is unsuited for a world which is too corrupt for him to cope with; and the aggressive, ruthless, worldly wise Dawe, eminently suited to rule, can never, except by a subterfuge, achieve ruling power. ... [The] folly of both men is caused by their being thrust into roles not in keeping with their natural inclinations. In an absurd society the man of action is denied power, and the man of thought is forced to act. (p. 41)

One of the book's most startling characteristics is its length; a contemporary critic, complaining of its inordinate length, asserted that "probably no human being could read, without generous omissions, its five hundred closely printed pages." The critic was wrong about the possibility of such human effort, but he was right to complain about the excessive length of the book. However, if we are willing to make the effort, we discover that the next most startling characteristic of the work is the range and potency of its satire. Having conceived the device of putting a Radical worker at the head of the Tory aristocracy, Zangwill found a rich vein of satire open to him. (pp. 42-3)

In spite of its merits—and they overshadow its faults—*The Premier and the Painter* was not a popular success; but success arrived with Zangwill's next book [*The Bachelors' Club*]. ... *The Bachelors' Club* was followed ... by *The Old Maids' Club,* and both works were collected to form *The Celibates' Club.* ... Both are exercises in playful irony concerning the adventures of miscellaneous individuals united by a common purpose—to remain single. The form is a series of sketches, and the pattern followed in narrative is similar: in *The Bachelors' Club,* the fall from grace of one bachelor after another; in *The Old Maids' Club,* the failure of successive candidates to qualify as old maids. (pp. 46-7)

In each tale [in *The Bachelors' Club*], the bachelor is first characterized—his background, his present situation, and his peculiarities; then he is confronted by a problem, which demands for its solution his marriage; finally, a short epilogue states the ironic outcome of the marriage. (p. 47)

The tales, whimsical studies in human absurdity, ignore realistic probability. Occasionally, a satirical intention is evident, but the satire is never harsh. A number of the tales satirize the literary world, enough so that criticism of the follies of that world constitutes a minor theme of the book. (p. 48)

The satiric range of *The Old Maids' Club* is much wider than that of *The Bachelors' Club.* In addition to the satire on the literary world is Zangwill's satire of the man who has achieved social success by doing nothing. ... Zangwill also satirizes contemporary advertising ... and domestic servant-master relations. ... (pp. 49-50)

The primary target of Zangwill's satire is, however, womankind; and he includes almost every kind of woman. ...

But the wide range of satire in this book is unfortunately at the expense of formal neatness. *The Old Maids' Club* lacks the structural control of *The Bachelors' Club,* which moves surely, chapter by chapter, to the end—the dissolution of the club. However, *The Old Maids' Club* does move inevitably, though not so precisely, to a similar end. (p. 50)

As we would expect, *The Bachelors' Club* and *The Old Maids' Club* complement each other. The theme of both is marriage; more specifically, both books suggest that no amount of rules, resolutions, and organization can or should overrule the natural inclination of man (and woman) to marry. Finally, there are no members of the Celibates' Club. In the development of this theme lies Zangwill's comic force, and the humor which is most successful involves the comic irony of would-be celibates falling before Cupid. (p. 51)

Children of the Ghetto was published . . . by the newly founded Jewish Publication Society in Philadelphia, which commissioned Zangwill to write "a Jewish *Robert Elsmere*." The result was considerably more than a Jewish version of Mrs. Humphrey Ward's popular novel dealing with the problems of faith in the modern world. . . .

Children of the Ghetto, set in late nineteenth-century London, is divided into two books: *Children of the Ghetto*, depicting life in the Whitechapel ghetto, and *Grandchildren of the Ghetto*, showing middle-class Jewry outside the ghetto. The first book, with its unforgettable characters set in a milieu in which traditional values are collapsing but have not yet completely done so, is superior to the second book, in which essentially flat characters are placed in discursive rather than dramatic situations.

Book I is a panorama of life in the ghetto, consisting of character sketches and stories of the struggle to survive. In depiction of character, Zangwill is free from sentimentalism and avoids the stereotype. This objectivity is evident even in his portraits of minor characters. . . . (p. 52)

In creating his characters Zangwill combines apparent objectivity with actual sympathy to produce the effect described in the Proem to *Children of the Ghetto*, where he says that "the rose of romance" can bloom "in the raw air of English reality." . . .

The novel abounds in scenes characteristic of ghetto life. . . . Behind all the activities of the ghetto is the Jewish religion—the customs, stories, jokes, songs, and rituals of Judaism, which provide not only the background but the basis of conflict in Book I. (p. 53)

The central conflict in *Children of the Ghetto* is that of youth versus age: specifically, of child versus parent. Zangwill finds in the break from orthodox Judaism a metaphor for this universal conflict. The children of the ghetto are beginning to doubt and distrust the religion of their fathers. (p. 54)

The conflict between father and child is continued in *Grandchildren of the Ghetto*. . . . (p. 58)

The chapter of the reconciliation, entitled "The Prodigal Son," is the next-to-last chapter in *Grandchildren of the Ghetto;* and it serves as the final statement of the theme unifying both *Children of the Ghetto* and its sequel. Both children and grandchildren drift away from Judaism, but both return to it in moments of crisis. (p. 60)

Grandchildren of the Ghetto suggests that a step toward solution lies in acceptance of a common heritage: Strelitski tells Esther, "we are both Children of the Ghetto." . . . *Children of the Ghetto* offers the possibility of a union of old and new, perhaps in an acceptance of the "common heritage" without the ceremonial forms. The orthodoxy rejected in *Grandchildren of the Ghetto* is that of the hypocritical West End Jews and the orthodoxy accepted is that of the struggling ghetto, where religion was not merely a form but a part of everyday life cementing the family of man.

Zangwill's best long work and perhaps the best of all his work is *The King of Schnorrers*. . . . (p. 63)

[It] seems to me that the best way to understand the comic brilliance of *The King of Schnorrers* is not by regarding it exclusively as an example of Jewish humor [as does Bernard N. Schilling (see excerpt dated 1965)] but by placing it in its English comic tradition. *The King of Schnorrers* is a comedy about a confidence man, in the tradition of Chaucer's "Canon's Yeoman's Tale" and of Ben Jonson's *Alchemist* or *Volpone*. The comedy in the novel depends not only on the incongruity between the beggar-hero's rags and his regal manner but also on his thwarting folly, not with folly, but by playing, Volpone-fashion, on the weaknesses and foibles of others. (pp. 63-4)

The theme of the novel is . . . the comic discomfiture of fools and knaves. Like Ben Jonson's Subtle or Volpone, Manasseh is the intellectual superior of the people he cheats. But Manasseh lacks the criminality of Jonson's Alchemist; Manasseh always operates within the law; indeed, he does not even approve of telling lies to get money. He is—as the title of the book says—regal. . . .

Manasseh is able to rule because he finds himself in a kingdom of fools and knaves. The world cheated by Manasseh is worse than he—worse intellectually and morally. (p. 67)

Zangwill's next novel, *The Master* . . . , departs from the comic and also from Jewish subject matter. A long novel, it traces an artist's life from boyhood to artistic maturity in late middle age, and it contains tedious sections; nevertheless, it is a notable contribution to late nineteenth-century Realistic literature depicting the artist as a young man. In this novel Zangwill seems to be following the advice of George Gissing's realist in *New Grub Street* (1891), who wishes to show "the fateful power of trivial incidents." Part of the tedium of *The Master* arises from Zangwill's conviction that life is an accumulation of tedious, exhausting events which assume significance only if an artist shows their purpose and poetry. A man's character, Zangwill believes, is made up of trivial events. . . . In the novel, we see the "episodes and uniformities" that create a master painter, Matthew Stang. Like Gissing's *New Grub Street* and other artist stories at the end of the century, *The Master* explores the artist's life in London, where an artistically ignorant public allows talent to starve and artistic glibness to prosper. (pp. 68-9)

After *The Master*, Zangwill's next novel, *The Mantle of Elijah* . . . , is a disappointment. Though its theme, the corruption of modern politics, was one about which Zangwill felt strongly, his treatment of it in *The Mantle of Elijah* resulted in the least effective of all his novels. The novel lacks adequate character and plot development; it lectures when it should dramatize; and the world view expressed in it lacks coherence. In this novel Zangwill seems to be groping for values; the book seems hastily thought through and just as hastily put together. Strangely, the abundant detail that critics object to in his other novels is needed in this one. We are left uninterested in the leading characters and unconvinced that they have solved any problems. (p. 75)

The novel also suffers from the omission of incident. In *The Master*, Zangwill focuses on a few characters for over five hundred pages of small print; in *The Mantle of Elijah*, he attempts to trace the lives of a profusion of characters in a book about half the size. (p. 77)

This is not to deny that some merit exists in the novel. There is some potent political satire, especially on Jingoistic patriotism. . . . There are some excellent bon mots: "Politics is only inconsistency reduced to a career." . . . *The Mantle of Elijah* was the last novel Zangwill wrote for many years. After the turn of the century Zangwill turned his attention to political and social questions and his creative energies to the drama. His last novel, *Jinny the Carrier,* . . . is based on his three-act play of the same name. . . . This last novel, though not without faults, shows an ability to capture atmosphere and to create character that makes us regret the years that Zangwill wrote drama instead of novels. As it stands, *Jinny the Carrier* is an anachronism, showing no evidence of having been written in the twentieth century. Set in rural England in the middle of the nineteenth century, the novel, in its reversion to a literary art reflecting that leisurely, slow-paced life, recaptures the life of that day. Zangwill's Epistle Dedicatory, addressed to his "dear Aunt by adoption," says that he has written a "bland" novel, "one to be read when in bed with a sore throat." And *Jinny the Carrier* is a remarkable example of that genre—remarkable because of its deliberate exclusion of any hint of the twentieth century with its Great War, its alienated youth, and its avant-garde art.

On an "elaborate canvas," with "slowness and minuteness of . . . method," Zangwill attempts "to seize the essence of Essex" in an admittedly romantic tale. Zangwill also describes the "bland" novel: "Such a novel must, I conceive, begin with 'once upon a time' and end with 'they all lived happy ever after,' so that my task is simply to fill in the lacuna between these two points, and supply the early-Victorian mottoes, while even the material was marked out for me by Dr. Johnson's definition of a novel as 'a story mainly about love'." . . . The novel does indeed begin "Once upon a time," and it ends with Jinny's belief that they will "all live—wherever they all lived—happy ever after." In between these points are over six hundred pages devoted partially to the love story of Jinny and Will Flynt but primarily to a re-creation of the Essex countryside and its inhabitants in a more idyllic day. (p. 79)

Zangwill's major weakness as a novelist was in his failure to trim his all too prolific narratives. One critic's complaint (reflecting almost every Zangwill critic's complaint) about *The Master* applies to most of Zangwill's novels: "it is not so much too long as too full" [see the excerpt by George Saintsbury dated 1895]. When there is not too much going on, as in *The Mantle of Elijah,* there is too much detail about the little going on, as in *Jinny the Carrier.* In his best works, however, the abundance of detail contributes to the effect of Realism, as in *Children of the Ghetto* or in *The Master;* and in his worst novel, *The Mantle of Elijah,* it is precisely the lack of detail and plot development that is most missed.

Another major weakness of Zangwill as novelist is a tendency toward a "rhapsodic" style, which usually fails because of stilted diction, an overuse of apostrophe, and overelaborate sentence patterns. Zangwill is also guilty occasionally of lapses into nineteenth-century pedantic diction and sentence structure at its worst. . . . Furthermore, Zangwill cannot resist epigrams and puns; favorite puns, like "Methodism in his madness" or "let sleeping dogmas lie," appear more than once. On the other hand, his humor at its best appears in his style in the form of reversals of clichés (as, the veterinarian had "a good styside manner") and in thematic epigrams (such as those cited from *The Mantle of Elijah*). Most of the time, he writes a clear, vivid, though undistinguished, style.

His strength as novelist lay in the depiction of character and in the suggestions of beauty in a real, oftentimes ugly, world. Like the artist of *The Master,* Zangwill is at his best when he is showing us ordinary life—whether that life is of the London ghetto, London art circles, or rural Essex. Into his Realistic

milieu he characteristically places not the heroes and heroines of romance but people we might actually meet. . . . Notable in Zangwill's characterization is the fact that he seldom creates a wholly despicable character (Bob Broser in *The Mantle of Elijah* is an exception); he usually reveals the spiritual strength, the intellectual agility, the unexpected kindness, or the sincere piety of even the meanest of mankind—in short, he finds a trace of human dignity in even the weakest of men.

Though Zangwill's best novels deal with life in the ghetto, the novels he wrote on non-Jewish themes show an ability to deal with a wide range of subjects and themes, including the absurdity of political life (*The Premier and the Painter*), the disillusioning pursuit of an ideal (*The Master*), the ruthlessness of modern politics (*The Mantle of Elijah*), and the simple lives and blind routine of rural life (*Jinny the Carrier*). We are impressed not only with the variety of themes but of forms. . . . (pp. 82-4)

"A single one of these tales is worth a dozen 'Masters,'" a reviewer remarked of Zangwill's collection of short stories entitled *They that Walk in Darkness.* Though the critic underestimated *The Master,* he was certainly right to recognize in Zangwill's ghetto stories the work of a master. Some critics think that Zangwill is at his best in the short-story form; and, if *Children of the Ghetto* is viewed not as a novel but as "a gallery of pictures drawn from life," as one critic has described it [see the excerpt by Meyer Waxman dated 1941] and his *King of Schnorrers* is considered a long short story, as its appearance in a volume of short stories would suggest, we would have to agree. A significant number of Zangwill's stories reveal the subtle characterization, controlled structure, and world view of a sensitive and skilled artist. (p. 85)

With only a few exceptions, Zangwill's greatest skill lay in depicting Jewish life, seen as neither unremittingly tragic or comic, as the titles of two collections suggest, but as tragicomic, encompassing both the joy and sadness of life. The ghetto stories are not simply local-color stories. Some implicitly plead for tolerance and brotherhood; others show the ironic or tragic effects of loss of faith and tradition; still others analyze the failure of Jews to realize (or even to recognize) common goals. The scope of the stories is large, ranging from the effects of a broken engagement to the devastation of a pogrom. (pp. 85-6)

Many of Zangwill's stories with religious themes are concerned with the collapse of orthodox Judaism, which represents in the stories, as it does in *Children of the Ghetto,* not only religious rigidity and formalism but also family stability and piety; therefore, the gradual collapse of orthodoxy becomes symbolic of an adjustment to a new society and of a weakening of old values. Invariably, Zangwill reveals in his stories that the price of adjustment, of "Anglicization," as the title of one story has it, is high. Often the doubter or the convert to Christianity returns to Judaism because of childhood memories or familial affection. (p. 92)

In generalizing about Zangwill's achievement as a short-story writer, one must agree with the critic who said that "When Mr. Zangwill writes about his own people, though it be only to scourge or ridicule, he discards that air of jaunty flippancy which he deems appropriate to discussion of the rest of the universe." If at times he abandons the "jaunty flippancy" to show us two lonely old women in Paris, or two stubborn, loving sisters, or an ugly woman made beautiful by the tenderness of unrequited love, if at times he gives us glimpses of the power of love, the beauty of self-sacrifice, or the perversion of ambition, too often in discussing "the rest of the universe" Zangwill uses techniques that are convention-worn, themes that are stale, or characters that have no life. Even the humor is different. It is illuminating to contrast the farcical action of "**The Semi-Sentimental Dragon**" with the hilarious version of *Hamlet* in "**A Yiddish** *Hamlet.*" . . . Zangwill is unquestionably at his best when he follows the advice in his story "**The Hirelings**" and sings a song of Israel. Like the Jewish pianist who wins recognition for his "synagogue medley," Zangwill deserves greatest praise for his ghetto stories.

These stories together form an integrated view of world Jewry. To achieve the effect of coherence, Zangwill frequently provides in a story allusions to characters or events in other stories. (p. 105)

As we read these stories, we are increasingly aware of the fact that we are reading a single story—one work in which physically scattered people live in one world, united in character and mutual suffering. The effect of coherence in the stories does not depend solely on reference to mutual characters and incidents. The coherence derives also from Zangwill's accumulative portrayal of the complexity of Jewish character—its capacity for love, sacrifice, suffering, and, at times, guile. And it derives from the repeated exploration of the nature of Jews in a Gentile world, where values disintegrate in spite of the force and appeal of tradition and unity. (p. 106)

At its worst, Zangwill's drama contains melodramatic scenes, stock characters, awkward dialogue, and inflated diction. But at its best, it is a serious and often forceful treatment of important themes. Concerning Zangwill's themes, a recent commentator about Zangwill says, "All this is dead as mutton today" [see the excerpt by John Gross dated 1964]. But Zangwill's dramatic themes are as topical today as they were when Zangwill wrote them: the conflicting values of youth and age, the problems of war and peace, the effect of bigotry, the problem of racial assimilation, the fact of religious fanaticism and pious hypocrisy, or the failure of state socialism are topics still worthy of dramatic exploration. (p. 107)

Zangwill's first notable success in the theatre came . . . with a dramatization of his short story "**Merely Mary Ann.**" . . . It is undoubtedly Zangwill's least artistic major play. . . . The plot of *Merely Mary Ann*—in both the short story and the play—concerns a sensitive and somewhat priggish young artist's increasing love for a lovely, simple serving girl. The dangers of sentimentalism and over-simplification inherent in such a plot Zangwill avoids in the short story by focusing on a secondary conflict—the temptation of the poor artist to prostitute his musical genius by writing songs for the popular market—and by having the lovers part at the end of the story; in the play, Zangwill either could not, or did not, avoid the dangers.

The faults of the play are painfully obvious when it is compared to the short story. The story is divided into three sections, which furnish the essential matter for three acts of the play. (p. 108)

The play follows the story more or less faithfully for three acts, though it introduces many more characters, most of them

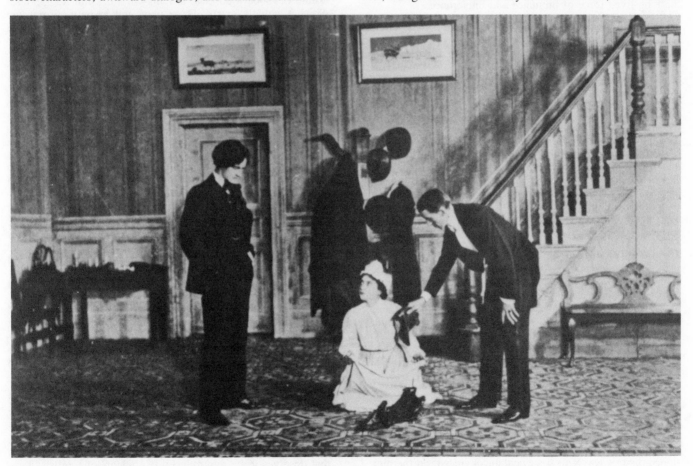

Scene from the 1904 London production of Merely Mary Ann.

dispensable.... [While] the story relies on a rather subtle presentation of the pain attending the love of the mismatched pair, the drama exploits the melodramatic and sentimental possibilities of the story.... (pp. 108-09)

The play does contain some successful dramatic effects; but most of them are obscured by sentimental excesses. (p. 109)

The dramatic weaknesses of *Merely Mary Ann* Zangwill was not always able to avoid in his future work, but his late drama always escapes superficiality of theme. In fact, the seriousness of theme of Zangwill's most famous drama, *The Melting Pot*, brought him severe criticism from many sides: from Jews horrified by Zangwill's thesis of race assimilation, from equally horrified Christians, from drama critics opposed to the theatrically passionate declamation of the thesis. The criticism of the play was not all hostile, however; it ranged from Theodore Roosevelt's "That's a great play, Mr. Zangwill" at the opening-night performance, to a condemnation of *The Melting Pot* as "Irish stew." (p. 110)

A modern reader of *The Melting Pot* feels vaguely embarrassed by the sentiments expressed in extravagantly rapturous speeches in the play. The play seems dated, and the hero's enthusiasm for America as "God's crucible" seems, if I may use a dated term, "corny." But to say that the play is out of date because Zangwill's dream for America has not been realized is to criticize society's failure, not Zangwill's. Therefore, if we are to judge the play fairly, it should be on its merits as a drama, not on its failure to anticipate the extent of modern cynicism and the long-lived force of prejudice and intolerance.

The play, in four acts, explores the range and results of racial hatred. The plot focuses on the love of a young musician, David Quixano, a Russian-Jewish immigrant to America, and a Russian-Christian immigrant, Vera Revendal.... David wishes to express in his music the spirit of America, "the great Melting-Pot where all the races of Europe are melting and re-forming" into a greater mankind, "perhaps the coming superman." (pp. 110-11)

The theme of the power of love to build a Kingdom of God on earth is presented primarily through the love story of David and Vera. Vera has to overcome anti-Semitic feelings when she first calls on David; but she overcomes her prejudice in her love for David, so much so that she faces the opposition of her outraged father, explaining, "Surely, father, all religions must serve the same God—since there is only one God to serve." ... (p. 112)

The forces of unchanging intolerance are represented in the play by the Revendals—a Russian baron and his aristocratic French wife—and Quincy Davenport, a millionaire American cultivating European ways. To counter these examples of Old World failure are the new Americans: a Russian Christian (Vera), Russian Jews (the Quixanos, especially David), an Irish servant (Kathleen), and a German musician (Herr Pappelmeister). This counterpointing of characters illustrating the forces of prejudice and love could still, no doubt, rouse an audience to an increased concern for the brotherhood of man.

This is not to say that the play does not have faults: it has all the dramatic weaknesses of *Merely Mary Ann*. It has the stage Irishman (here, Irish girl) and the stage German; its climax depends on the coincidence which no amount of foreshadowing (and there is some) can make us believe; and David's impassioned rhetoric leaves us somewhat unconvinced. Furthermore, the play is more "Jewish" than the theme will bear; that is,

in a play advocating the assimilation of all races and creeds, Zangwill seems impelled—possibly unconsciously—to slant the statement to favor the Jews. The Christians in the play are for the most part a bad sort.... The two "good" Christians in the play—Kathleen and Vera—adopt Jewish ways.... Though the Jews in the play are prejudiced, they do no harm.... (p. 113)

Finally, we detect in the play a note of desperation: it is a dramatization more of Zangwill's hope than of his conviction. In his 1914 afterword to the play, he writes, "To suppose that America will remain permanently afflicted by all the old European diseases would be to despair of humanity, not to mention super-humanity." ... The play was an alternative to despair. Zangwill was perfectly aware of the potential failure of America to realize his dream; Quincy Davenport is the only native-born American in the play; and he is, David notes, "killing my America".... Nevertheless, the play remains an eloquent, even if somewhat strained, expression of turn-of-the-century idealism. (pp. 113-14)

Zangwill's most famous play, *The Melting Pot*, though not his best, deserves a place in the history of English and American drama as an early, impassioned hope for the triumph of love and brotherhood in the American character. Zangwill's best plays are those constituting a political trilogy: *The War God*, affirming the eventual triumph of love and nonviolence over hatred and war, is Zangwill's expression of what ought to be; *The Cockpit* and *The Forcing House*, realistically facing the failure of modern politics, is Zangwill's pessimistic appraisal of what actually exists. These plays will remain current and meaningful as long as hypocrisy, ambition, intolerance, and violence trouble the world. (p. 132)

Zangwill, who was not a good poet, wrote and published poems in dozens of magazines and journals.... But in few of his poems does he achieve the stature of even a good minor poet. Perhaps one critic's recommendation that "the best thing to do with his [Zangwill's] sonnet on Theodore Herzl is to keep it decently out of sight" ought to be applied to all Zangwill's poetry....

Zangwill's comments on the relative difficulty of poetry and prose suggest why his poetry lacks artistic merit. In an 1894 column for *The Critic*, he maintains that prose is a more difficult art than poetry: "The swing and rush of verse compensate for reason, and it is wonderful how far a little sense will fly when tricked out with fine feathers." It should be no surprise that an author who believes that the trappings of verse can substitute for precision of thought writes bad poetry. (p. 133)

Zangwill's present obscurity can be attributed to the fact that at the turn of the twentieth century he abandoned his exceptional talent for writing short stories and novels and turned instead to writing essays and dramas analyzing and offering solutions to social, political, and religious ills. Thus, his reputation in the twentieth century rested on his journalistic prose and his dramatic offerings, and his strength as an artist was in neither of these.

But to read Zangwill's early fiction today is to discover again the genius that made him famous in the 1890's, a genius for the creation of unforgettable, living characters and for the depiction of scenes and incidents calling up the sordidness, pain, and wonder of everyday reality. In this fiction there is much that deserves to be reintroduced to students of English literature, especially in the ghetto works, *Children of the Ghetto*,

The King of Schnorrers, and numerous short stories from *They that Walk in Darkness* and *Ghetto Comedies.*

Given the popularity of modern American Jewish writers such as Bernard Malamud, Edward Wallant, Philip Roth, or Saul Bellow, it is ironic that Zangwill has not enjoyed a revival of interest. For we find in the characters, situations, and themes of these writers much that Zangwill treated with equal artistry sixty or seventy years earlier. (p. 145)

> *Elsie Bonita Adams, in her* Israel Zangwill, *Twayne Publishers, Inc., 1971, 177 p.*

NEIL LARRY SHUMSKY (essay date 1975)

[*In the following excerpt, Shumsky disagrees with such critics as Elsie Bonita Adams (1971) who contend that* The Melting Pot *is Zangwill's expression of a simple belief that Americans can create a homogeneous culture. Instead, Shumsky believes that Zangwill examined the myriad stumbling blocks to such a result, and finally resolved the situation by expressing a belief that a truly homogeneous culture would be found when racial and cultural heritage was abandoned in favor of a universal religion or system of belief.*]

[A] careful reading shows *The Melting Pot* to be much more complex than the simple notion that Americans can create a homogeneous culture. To begin with, the character of David is ambiguous. Some elements of the play imply that he is not wholly persuaded by his own statements and is deeply divided between his ideas about the melting pot on the one hand and a strong attachment to tradition and heritage on the other. At times he seems unable to decide whether the melting pot is either feasible or desirable. Rather than being an outspoken advocate of the melting pot theory, it is possible to argue that David symbolizes a dilemma which must have been felt by millions of immigrants—how to reconcile the past with life in America. At the same time, the "message" of the play is as difficult to comprehend as is David. An analysis of other characters, the dramatic action, and other works by Zangwill may leave one wondering whether the play really does propose the melting pot as traditionally interpreted. At the very least, it seems possible to suggest that Zangwill envisioned a melted America in which Judaism survived. An even more radical reading would intimate that Zangwill foresaw Judaism as the future religion of all Americans.

These questions of interpretation emerge if we consider *The Melting Pot*'s concept of Americanization. On one level the play implies that an immigrant must reject his traditional culture and identity before he can become an American. David is the principal spokesman for this idea and frequently articulates the desire to abandon his heritage. He consciously thinks that the immigrant must reject the past in order for the melting pot to work. But the play also shows that David cannot abandon the past or cut off his roots. Moreover, he is ambivalent about doing so. The past contains elements which are too valuable and which he cannot afford to lose.

On several occasions David argues that he and his family should cast off their Judaism. Once he berates his Uncle Mendel for maintaining the old ways, and another time wonders whether "that is the secret of our people's paralysis—we are always looking backward." David's own alienation seems to have preceded his arrival in America. As a boy in Russia he had neglected the Sabbath. Now in New York, he disdains Purim. Perhaps the early beginning of David's disaffection helps explain his apparent willingness to Americanize and argue in favor of the melting pot. One Sabbath in particular, David asks

where his uncle is going. Mendel, on the way to give dancing lessons, replies sarcastically that he is going to the synagogue, and David chastises him for "hankering after those old things!" Mendel responds "tartly" that he is sorry to see the Jewish people falling apart. David, whose conscious idea of Americanization implies the disappearance of ethnic differences, then asks why Mendel came to America if he wants to maintain Judaism: the essence of Americanization is the rejection of the past, and David thinks that his uncle must abandon the old ways. (pp. 30-1)

David believes he must reject the past in order to become an American. Nevertheless, *The Melting Pot* also implies that he cannot abandon his heritage and that his feelings about doing so are ambivalent. He seems more committed to his heritage than he realizes and has a strong attachment to his native culture. There is a split between his conscious and his unconscious thoughts and between his thoughts and his actions. Throughout the play David is torn between one feeling that he should forget the past and another of devotion to it. At one point he tries to persuade Kathleen, his family's Irish housekeeper, not to quit her job. As he talks to her he romanticizes his grandmother's past and sentimentalizes the hardships of the old woman's life. In the midst of this rhapsody, he recalls the pleasures that she, and his heritage, have offered him. (pp. 32-3)

David never stopped longing for that taste or the heritage that it represented. During the argument about David's impending marriage to Vera, Mendel finally says to "go out and marry your gentile and be happy." David, who has just been proclaiming the need to abandon the past by "forgetting all the nightmare of religions and races," replies with dismay, "You turn me out?" As the curtain falls upon the act, the audience sees a "tableau of DAVID in his cloak and hat, stealing out of the door . . . casting a sad farewell glance at the old woman [his grandmother] and at the home which has sheltered him."

The portrayal of David's grandmother, Frau Quixano, is also inconsistent with David's notion of the melting pot. She is a pious old woman who keeps kosher, observes the Sabbath and celebrates the holidays faithfully. She speaks only Yiddish and seems like a person whose way of life will be irrelevant in the melting pot. She symbolizes everything that David is trying to reject. At the beginning of the play, her piety causes a problem. One Saturday an important letter arrives for David, and Frau Quixano hides it. She does not want him to profane the Sabbath by opening mail. Then later, she forgets to give it to him. Thus at the outset, her behavior seems outdated. But as the play progresses, she is portrayed differently. She becomes a matriarchal figure who is tenderly drawn. At one point David praises her life and its hardships. At another, after he had decided to marry Vera, David hides his determination in order to spare the old woman's feelings. (p. 33)

This incident can be understood in several ways. For one, it may simply reflect David's love and affection for his grandmother; he does not want to hurt her. For another, he may realize that she is too old and too set in her ways to change; he accepts her as she is and makes no attempt to modify her behavior.

A third way of interpreting the conversation is that David's own feelings about rejecting the past are ambiguous and not as clear-cut as they seem. After all his grandmother conducts her life little differently from her own grandmother. And yet throughout the play, David treats her lovingly and affectionately. If he believed wholeheartedly in rejecting the past, he might well have treated Frau Quixano differently. He might have ignored her or ridiculed her way of life. He might have tried to change her. In any case, it appears unlikely that he would have been so responsive to a woman who symbolized everything he seems to oppose. One possible conclusion is that David's commitment to the past is stronger than some of his speeches suggest.

The realization that David cannot forget the past sustains this conclusion. (p. 34)

David's recognition that he cannot escape the past forces him to reevaluate the melting pot, and he admits that the idea was only an illusion. In the play's climactic final scene, David tells Vera that he cannot obliterate the past. . . . At the ultimate moment, David's belief in the melting pot is inadequate. Vera has pledged her love, and he cannot accept it. He is unable to eradicate the past and wants to go home. The melting pot is only a dream.

One could logically argue that *The Melting Pot* should end at this point. Its hero has admitted the futility of his dream and recognized that it cannot come true; but the play continues. It has a second conclusion which seems contrived and appears to contradict much of the play's development. In this anticlimax, David and Vera have finally realized that their futures lie apart and seem reconciled to that fact. Then suddenly, and for no apparent reason, David begs her to stay. He claims to be cured of hallucinations and says that she has the first place in his life. Vera falls into his arms, and the curtain drops on the reunited lovers seeing the vision of the melting pot.

These two endings, the climax and the anticlimax, further support the conclusion that the play's ideas about the past and the melting pot are ambiguous and contradictory. David cannot escape the past; its hold is unbreakable. Moreover, he is not ready to abandon it. Parts of the past are too valuable and must be preserved. Throughout the play, David has trouble reconciling his thoughts and feelings with his words, or his thoughts, feelings and words with his actions. He preaches the melting pot, but some of his behavior suggests a different set of beliefs altogether.

The inconsistencies in the depiction of David are not the only ambiguities in *The Melting Pot.* There is also a contradiction between the portrayal of David and that of the other characters. For at the same time that David is consciously trying to reject Judaism, other figures are praising or adopting it. For example, Herr Pappelmeister, the German conductor who introduces David's symphony, regrets that he does "haf not de honour" to be a Jew. Moreover, almost all of his musicians are Jews.

Kathleen O'Reilley, the Quixano's Irish housekeeper, does more than regret not being a Jew. She actually seems to become one. At the beginning of *The Melting Pot,* Kathleen is markedly anti-Semitic, but her attitudes have clearly changed by the start of the second act. It is Purim, and she is wearing the traditional false nose used to celebrate the holiday. (pp. 34-5)

Vera Revendal, David's Russian Christian fiancée, experiences a change similar to Kathleen's. She also begins the play with anti-Semitic attitudes, loses them as the play continues, and ultimately seems to identify with Judaism. Vera first appears as a visitor to the Quixano house and is admitted by Kathleen who thinks she is Jewish. "I, a Jewess! How dare you!" screams Vera. Stunned by the discovery of David's religion, she decides to leave but changes her mind when she realizes how much she likes him. David and Vera soon fall in love.

But, instead of seeing their marriage as an opportunity to further the melting pot (as we would expect in this play), Vera feels that she should assume David's cultural heritage. (p. 36)

Consequently, while David advocates abandoning Judaism, other characters identify with it. This inconsistency, as well as David's own ambivalence about Judaism and the past, shows *The Melting Pot* to be much more complex than is usually argued; the play does not merely present the melting pot theory. It is much more difficult to understand than scholars have suggested. How, then, are we to interpret the play? If it does not simply plead the romantic notion of the melting pot, what does it say? What are we to make of the inconsistencies and contradictions which *The Melting Pot* seems to contain?

There are many ways of answering these questions, but some are more intriguing and thought-provoking than others. One is to say that Zangwill himself was a divided man and that the play reflects his own inner conflicts. According to one of Zangwill's biographers, "consistency was not one of his virtues, except, perhaps, that he was consistently inconsistent" [see the excerpt by Maurice Wohlgelernter dated 1964]. He loved peace but also admired Napoleon. He followed Tolstoy's theories of aesthetics but was also attracted to Pater and the French symbolists. He was a Zionist but admitted that his dedication to the movement wasted his life. "Suffice it to say that for Zangwill 'convex things are equally concave, and concave things convex.'" According to this interpretation, Zangwill was a man whose mind and spirit were filled with "'violent contraries,'" and we can understand *The Melting Pot* in these terms. It reflects Zangwill's divided self.

Another way to understand the play's inconsistencies is to contend that Zangwill was trying to depict the reality of the immigrant mind. It is almost certainly true that millions of immigrants experienced the same tension as David. They wanted to become Americans, but they were unwilling or unable to reject the past. They desired to become a part of their new home, to learn from it and to contribute to it, but they also valued their traditions and heritage. They were torn between the past and the present, the desire to Americanize and the need for the security of familiar forms and traditional institutions. Seen in this context, the conflicts within David reveal Zangwill's insight into immigrant psychology.

One particularly troublesome aspect of the immigrants' dilemma was the conflict between generations. As children grew up in the new society and learned new ways, they changed and became different from their parents. They saw new possibilities and began to question their parents' ways of doing things. As a result, conflict was almost inevitable, and parents and children fought about the proper conduct of life. Relationships became strained, and there were two possible solutions other than total break: either one generation had to accept the ways of the other, or both generations had to accept each other as people while not necessarily accepting each other's ways. This theme of conflict and reconciliation between generations is clearly present in *The Melting Pot.* As we have seen, David and Mendel frequently argue but ultimately make peace. So do David and his grandmother. However, the question is whether the generations accept each other as people only or whether one generation accepts the ideas and beliefs of the other. What is the basis of the reconciliation within the play?

There is evidence to support both sides. On the one hand, David becomes reunited with his family but also marries Vera. The implication is that he can love his relatives and still reject their religion. He can be committed to people without being committed to their ways. On the other hand, this interpretation leaves unresolved the inconsistency between David's seeming rejection of Judaism and its acceptance by Vera and Kathleen. Why would Zangwill have David reject Judaism while he has other characters adopt it? An examination of external evidence, especially Zangwill's other writings, provides some tentative answers to all these questions and also suggests a radically new reading of *The Melting Pot*. One of Zangwill's early novels, *Children of the Ghetto,* also focuses on the conflict between generations. Although it is set in the London ghetto and does not deal with immigrants, the book nevertheless deals with the problems of the Jew in the modern world. It describes and analyzes the struggle between old and new, ghetto and outside, parents and children. (pp. 36-7)

In *Children of the Ghetto,* Zangwill seems to be saying that the conflict between generations is the same as the conflict between old and new. Moreover, the former cannot be resolved without the resolution of the latter.

If these are indeed Zangwill's ideas, we would expect them to be restated in *The Melting Pot*. We would expect David's reconciliation with his uncle and grandmother to be based on his reaffirmation of Judaism and his rejection of Vera. However, David seems to have had the best of both worlds, his family and Vera too. We are again left with several explanations of the dilemma. On the one hand, it can be argued that the two works are not comparable. Zangwill wrote *Children of the Ghetto* seventeen years before *The Melting Pot;* perhaps he changed his mind during the interim. Or perhaps in Zangwill's mind, England and America were different and produced different behavior. Maybe he thought the conflict would be resolved differently in the two countries. On the other hand, Zangwill's conception of the melting pot need not necessarily mean the disappearance or rejection of Judaism in America. Perhaps he thought it possible for David to believe in the melting pot and retain his Judaism at the same time. Such an explanation would account for the concurrence of David's marriage to Vera, his reconciliation with his family, and the conversion of Vera and Kathleen.

Once again, Zangwill's other writings provide insights into his thinking. It is important to realize that Zangwill distinguished between the "Jewish race" and the Jewish religion. He perceived Judaism as a distinct group of people and also as a set of moral and ethical precepts. Moreover, he argued that the "racial" aspects of Judaism, those which separated Jews from other men, should be abandoned and that Jews should cease to exist apart. (pp. 38-9)

Zangwill's distinction between racial and religious Judaism suggests a way of interpreting *The Melting Pot* which resolves all of the inconsistencies and contradictions. It is possible that David's rejection of Judaism reflects Zangwill's own rejection of Judaism as a separate group of people, and Kathleen and Vera's acceptance of Judaism represents Zangwill's notion of Judaism as a universal religion. There is then no contradiction within the play; there is only an implicit difference being drawn between two ideas about Judaism. This interpretation of the play is also consistent with Zangwill's conception of America and his notion of exactly how the melting pot would work. . . . A logical conclusion, and one which can be seen in *The Melting Pot,* is that Judaism will survive in the melting pot of America and will be accepted there when its racial aspects, those which keep Jews apart, have been abandoned. The play may be seen

as advocating the conjunction of Judaism's spiritual message with the sectarian message of America.

This interpretation also fits with the "Afterword" added by Zangwill to the 1914 edition of *The Melting Pot*. In this brief essay, Zangwill explains how the melting pot will actually work. It will not, he says, produce an amalgamation on every possible level. That is, the ultimate language of America will not be a conglomerate of every language spoken there. The ultimate physical appearance of Americans will not be a mixture of every racial group. Instead, the melting pot will presumably join together the best existing language with the best existing physical type.

It seems reasonable to assume that Zangwill also believed there was, in addition, a best religion—Judaism—to complement the best language and physical type. As Zangwill saw it, the melting pot and the Jewish religion were not inconsistent with each other. The melting pot and Judaism could exist in America at the same time. (pp. 39-40)

Of course this interpretation of *The Melting Pot* is radically different from any previously set forth. It rests almost entirely on circumstantial evidence and is clearly not the only way of understanding the play. It does, however, resolve several ambiguities within the work. But perhaps more important than the particular interpretation is the realization that the play contains much more than historians and sociologists have traditionally recognized. It is the complex product of a complex mind, and however we read the play, we must take care not to oversimplify. (pp. 40-1)

> *Neil Larry Shumsky, "Zangwill's 'The Melting Pot':*
> *Ethnic Tensions on Stage," in* American Quarterly,
> *Vol. XXVII, No. 1, March, 1975, pp. 29-41.*

ADDITIONAL BIBLIOGRAPHY

Adcock, A. St. John. "Israel Zangwill." In his *Gods of Modern Grub Street: Impressions of Contemporary Authors,* pp. 313-19. New York: Frederick A. Stokes Co., 1923.
> Commends Zangwill for his masterful, comprehensive depictions of London Jewry and also compliments him for his devotion to unpopular humanitarian causes.

Angoff, Charles. "Zangwill's Humor and Satire." *Congress Weekly* 21, No. 21 (31 May 1954): 19.
> Praises *The King of Schnorrers* for its satiric vision and knowledge of turn-of-the-century Jewish life.

Baker, Ernest A. "Aesthetes and Eclectics." In his *The History of the English Novel: The Day Before Yesterday,* pp. 203-42. London: H. F. & G. Witherby, 1938.*
> Considers Zangwill's expertise in local color fiction the foremost reason why he has contributed so greatly to Jewish literature. As Baker says, "Zangwill was not a creative artist; but he knew his people as intimately as his master Dickens knew his."

Bensusan, S. L. "Israel Zangwill." *The Quarterly Review* 247, No. 490 (October 1926): 285-303.
> Surveys Zangwill's most important works. Bensusan contends that Zangwill "will come to his own very slowly but surely, because when our descendants turn to the history of the struggle for great causes they will find his name writ large, and when they turn to consider the Jewish question . . . they will find that Judaism had one champion who was not satisfied to defend, who was not afraid to attack."

Bentwich, Norman. "Israel Zangwill: Man of Letters and of Action." *The Contemporary Review* 205, No. 1176 (January 1964): 39-42.
Surveys Zangwill's literary and political careers, particularly his involvement with the Zionist movement.

Burgin, G. B. "Israel Zangwill: Dramatist and Novelist." *Harper's Weekly* XXXVIII, No. 1954 (2 June 1894): 508.
Biographical summary. Burgin prophesies: "What [Zangwill] will be in another ten years, if he continues to develop at the rate of the last three, passes comprehension."

Cahan, Abraham. "Four Novels of Some Importance: I. Zangwill's *The Mantle of Elijah*." The Bookman, New York XII, No. 5 (January 1901): 481-84.
Highly favorable review of *The Mantle of Elijah*. Cahan regards Zangwill's novel as the obverse of Kipling's poem "The White Man's Burden"—instead of glorifying imperialism and war as means toward an ordered world, *The Mantle* denounces these as trappings of ethnocentric domination.

Calisch, Edward N. "Jewish Literary Activity." In his *The Jew in English Literature: As Author and as Subject*, pp. 152-98. Richmond, Va.: Bell Book and Stationery Co., 1909.*
Short survey. Calisch contends that Zangwill's works will assure him a high place in literary annals.

Garland, Hamlin. "Zangwill." *The Conservative Review* II, No. II (November 1899): 404-12.
Relates various encounters with Zangwill and praises him as a major novelist, comparable in stature to Thomas Hardy.

Golding, Louis. "Zangwill the Man." *The Fortnightly Review* n.s., No. DCCXXIV (1 April 1927): 519-28.
A reminiscence of Zangwill focussing on his qualities as a great man. Golding, who first met Zangwill after writing him requesting criticism of his poetry, objectively defines the artistic, political, and social aspects of his personality.

Jacobson, Dan. "Jewish Writing in England." *Commentary* 37, No. 5 (May 1964): 46-50.
Discusses the contribution of Anglo-Jewish writers to English literature. Jacobson, a South African novelist of Jewish heritage, considers Zangwill one of England's most important Jewish authors, yet concludes that as a fiction writer "he was a purveyor of exotica," a task which many other Jewish writers "have been tempted to perform" but which "even when the Jews were really a strange and unfamiliar people in England" was "a self-limiting one."

Kennard, Joseph Spencer. "Joseph the Dreamer." In his *The Friar in Fiction: Sincerity in Art and Other Essays*, pp. 137-46. New York: Brentano's, 1923.
Discussion of the novel *Joseph the Dreamer* that focusses on Zangwill's realistic portrait of Jewish character.

Leftwich, Joseph. "Israel Zangwill: On the Threshold of His Centenary." In *Jewish Book Annual*, Vol. 21, pp. 104-16. New York: Jewish Book Council of America, 1963.
Centenary appraisal of Zangwill's reputation. Leftwich contends that Zangwill's importance is attested to by constant critical comparisons made between new Jewish writing and Zangwill's work.

Lewis, Sinclair. "Did Mrs. Thurston Get the Idea of *The Masquerader* from Mr. Zangwill?" *The Critic* XLVI, No. 6 (June 1905): 551-54.*
Explores similarities between Thurston's novel, a best-seller at the time, and Zangwill's *The Premier and the Painter*, which preceded it by several years.

Mann, Arthur. "*The Melting Pot*." In *Uprooted Americans: Essays to Honor Oscar Handlin*, edited by Richard L. Bushman, Neil Harris, David Rothman, Barbara Miller Solomon, and Stephan Thernstrom, pp. 288-318. Boston: Little, Brown and Co., 1979.
Discusses performance history and popular and critical reactions to Zangwill's drama. Mann notes that Zangwill's work deserves the credit for popularizing the concept of America as a melting pot.

Modder, Montagu Frank. "The Old Order Changeth. . . ." In his *The Jew in the Literature of England: To the End of the 19th Century*, pp. 310-46. New York and Philadelphia: Meridian Books and The Jewish Publication Society of America, 1960.
Discusses Zangwill's portrayal of Jewish people and their lives.

"Israel Zangwill." *The Nation* CXXIII, No. 3188 (11 August 1926): 118.
Obituary that praises Zangwill's novels and his merits as a public figure but characterizes him as an interpreter of Jewish life, not as spokesman for the Jewish race.

Oliphant, James. "Rudyard Kipling and I. Zangwill." In his *Victorian Novelists*, pp. 229-48. 1899. Reprint. New York: AMS Press, 1966(?).
Discusses the extra-literary qualities of Zangwill's depictions of Jewish life, calling them the work of a first-rate novelist who opens an alien world to his readers. Oliphant also declares that: "Mr. Zangwill's poetic temperament and his well-rounded theory of life are vividly reflected in the idiosyncrasies of his style, which not only has the flexibility that fits it to every opportunity of description and dramatic speech, but is capable of rising to the highest eloquence under the stress of strong emotion."

Philipson, David. "Zangwill's *Children of the Ghetto* and Others." In his *The Jew in English Fiction*, rev. ed., pp. 161-207. New York: Bloch Publishing Co., 1927.*
Compares Zangwill's works to those of Leopold Kompert, an apologetic, somewhat sentimental portrayer of Jewish ghetto life, and contends that Zangwill's presentation of negative as well as positive aspects of the ghetto makes him the greater chronicler of this world.

Rubin, Philip. "Dusting Off the Bookshelf." *Congress Weekly* 17, No. 25 (16 October 1950): 14-16.
Discussion of *Dreamers of the Ghetto*, which Rubin believes will be read longer than any of Zangwill's other works. According to Rubin, this collection of fictional sketches about historic Jewish figures would have been more aptly called "Rebels Against the Ghetto," for most of those discussed in the volume rebelled in some manner against physically or spiritually stifling ways of life. Rubin concludes: "That Zangwill believed that those 'dreamers' or 'rebels' had a universal message for all mankind, not only for Jews, is evident."

[Warner, Charles Dudley]. "Editor's Study." *Harper's New Monthly Magazine* LXXXVI, No. DXIV (March 1893): 635-40.*
Criticizes the Naturalistic school of writers in vogue at the time who portrayed the baseness of life. Warner congratulates Zangwill on the more objective form of realism displayed in *Children of the Ghetto*, in which the ideals of hope, love, and pride are not lost.

Winehouse, Bernard. "Israel Zangwill's *Children of the Ghetto*: A Literary History of the First Anglo-Jewish Best-Seller." *English Literature in Transition* 16, No. 2 (1973): 93-117.
Discusses the composition, publishing history, and critical reaction to Zangwill's most popular novel.

Appendix

The following is a listing of all sources used in Volume 16 of *Twentieth-Century Literary Criticism*. Included in this list are all copyright and reprint rights and acknowledgments for those essays for which permission was obtained. Every effort has been made to trace copyright, but if omissions have been made, please let us know.

THE EXCERPTS IN TCLC, VOLUME 16, WERE REPRINTED FROM THE FOLLOWING PERIODICALS:

The Academy, n.s. v. XXII, October 7, 1882; v. XLII, December 24, 1892; v. XLVII, June 29, 1895.

Accent, v. XII, Winter, 1952.

American Mercury, v. XI, May, 1927./ v. II, May, 1924 for a review of "We Moderns" by George Jean Nathan. Copyright 1924, renewed 1952, by American Mercury Magazine, Inc. Reprinted by permission of Associated University Press, Inc., for the Estate of George Jean Nathan./ v. XIX, February, 1930 for "Confessional" by H. L. Mencken. Copyright 1930, renewed 1958, by American Mercury Magazine, Inc. Used by permission of The Enoch Pratt Free Library of Baltimore in accordance with the terms of the will of H. L. Mencken.

American Quarterly, v. XXVII, March, 1975 for "Zangwill's 'The Melting Pot': Ethnic Tensions on Stage" by Neil Larry Shumsky. Copyright 1975, Trustees of the University of Pennsylvania. Reprinted by permission of the publisher and the author.

The American Scholar, v. 53, Autumn, 1984. Copyright © 1984 by Donna Rifkind. By permission of the publishers, the United Chapters of Phi Beta Kappa.

The Arena, Boston, v. XXXVI, December, 1906.

The Athenaeum, n. 3327, August 1, 1891; n. 3440, September 30, 1893; n. 4651, June 20, 1919; n. 4698, May 14, 1920.

The Atlantic Monthly, v. 201, March, 1958 for "The Perceptions of James Joyce" by John V. Kelleher. Reprinted by permission of the author.

Blackwood's Edinburgh Magazine, v. CLXI, April, 1897.

Book World—The Washington Post, January 11, 1981. © 1981, *The Washington Post*. Reprinted by permission.

The Bookman, London, v. IV, September, 1893; v. XLVI, May, 1914.

The Bookman, New York, v. XLIV, November, 1916.

Adams, Elsie Bonita. From *Israel Zangwill*. Twayne, 1971. Copyright 1971 by Twayne Publishers. All rights reserved. Reprinted with the permission of Twayne Publishers, a division of G. K. Hall & Co., Boston.

Adams, Robert M. From *James Joyce: Common Sense and Beyond*. Random House, 1966. Copyright © 1966 by Random House, Inc. All rights reserved. Reprinted by permission of the publisher.

Adler, Ruth. From *Women of the Shtetl—Through the Eyes of Y. L. Peretz*. Fairleigh Dickinson University Press, 1980. © 1980 by Associated University Presses, Inc. Reprinted by permission.

Avins, Carol. From *Border Crossings: The West and Russian Identity in Soviet Literature, 1917-1934*. University of California Press, 1983. Copyright © 1983 by The Regents of the University of California. Reprinted by permission of the University of California Press.

Barksdale, Richard, and Keneth Kinnamon. From a headnote to "Two Black Women Serve and Observe: From 'Journal of Charlotte Forten'," in *Black Writers of America: A Comprehensive Anthology*. Edited by Richard Barksdale and Keneth Kinnamon. Macmillan, 1972. Copyright © 1972, The Macmillan Company. All rights reserved. Reprinted with permission of Macmillan Publishing Company.

Bechhofer, C. E. From *The Literary Renaissance in America*. William Heinemann Limited, 1923.

Becker, George J. From *D. H. Lawrence*. Ungar, 1980. Copyright © 1980 by Frederick Ungar Publishing Co., Inc. Reprinted by permission.

Beyer, Edvard. From *Ibsen: The Man and His Work*. Translated by Marie Wells. Souvenir Press (E & A) Ltd., 1978. Translation copyright © 1978 by Souvenir Press and Marie Wells. All rights reserved. Reprinted by permission.

Billington, Ray Allen. From an introduction to *The Journal of Charlotte L. Forten*. The Dryden Press, Publishers, 1953.

Booth, Wayne C. From *The Rhetoric of Fiction*. University of Chicago Press, 1961. © 1961 by The University of Chicago. Reprinted by permission of The University of Chicago Press and the author.

Brandes, Georg. From *Henrik Ibsen, Bjornsterne Bjornson*. Edited by William Archer, translated by Jessie Muir. William Heinemann Limited, 1899.

Brooks, Van Wyck. From an introduction to *History of a Literary Radical and Other Essays*. By Randolph Bourne, edited by Van Wyck Brooks. Huebsch, 1920. Copyright 1920 by B. W. Huebsch. Copyright renewed 1947 by The Viking Press, Inc. Reprinted by permission of Viking Penguin Inc.

Cammell, Charles Richard. From *Aleister Crowley: The Man, the Image, the Poet*. The Richards Press, 1951.

Casey, John. From *The Language of Criticism*. Methuen, 1966. © 1966 by John Casey. Reprinted by permission of Methuen & Co. Ltd.

Cassavant, Sharron Greer. From *John Middleton Murry: The Critic As Moralist*. University of Alabama Press, 1982. Copyright © 1982 by The University of Alabama Press, University, Alabama 35486. All rights reserved. Reprinted by permission.

Chambers, Jessie. From *D. H. Lawrence: A Personal Record*. Jonathan Cape, 1935.

Downs, Brian W. From *A Study of Six Plays by Ibsen*. Cambridge at the University Press, 1950.

Durbach, Errol. From *"Ibsen the Romantic:" Analogues of Paradise in the Later Plays*. Macmillan, 1982. © Errol Durbach. All rights reserved. Reprinted by permission of Macmillan, London and Basingstoke.

Eisinger, Erica M. From "'The Vagabond': A Vision of Androgyny," in *Colette: The Woman, the Writer*. Edited by Erica Mendelson Eisinger and Mari Ward McCarty. Pennsylvania State University Press, University Park, 1981. Copyright © 1981 by The Pennsylvania State University. All rights reserved. Reprinted by permission.

Eliot, T. S. From a foreword to *Katherine Mansfield, and Other Literary Studies*. By J. Middleton Murry, edited by Mary Middleton Murry. Constable, 1959. © 1959 by Mary Middleton Murry. Reprinted by permission of Faber & Faber Ltd.

Ellis, Havelock. From *The New Spirit*. G. Bell & Sons, 1890. Reprinted by permission of Bell & Hyman.

Cumulative Index to Authors

This index lists all author entries in the Gale Literary Criticism Series and includes cross-references to other Gale sources. References in the index are identified as follows:

AITN: *Authors in the News*, Volumes 1-2
CAAS: *Contemporary Authors Autobiography Series*, Volume 1
CA: *Contemporary Authors* (original series), Volumes 1-113
CANR: *Contemporary Authors New Revision Series*, Volumes 1-13
CAP: *Contemporary Authors Permanent Series*, Volumes 1-2
CA-R: *Contemporary Authors* (revised editions), Volumes 1-44
CLC: *Contemporary Literary Criticism*, Volumes 1-32
CLR: *Children's Literature Review*, Volumes 1-7
DLB: *Dictionary of Literary Biography*, Volumes 1-37
DLB-DS: *Dictionary of Literary Biography Documentary Series*, Volumes 1-4
DLB-Y: *Dictionary of Literary Biography Yearbook*, Volumes 1980-1983
LC: *Literature Criticism from 1400 to 1800*, Volume 1
NCLC: *Nineteenth-Century Literature Criticism*, Volumes 1-9
SATA: *Something about the Author*, Volumes 1-38
TCLC: *Twentieth-Century Literary Criticism*, Volumes 1-16
YABC: *Yesterday's Authors of Books for Children*, Volumes 1-2

Arnow, Harriette (Louisa Simpson)
    1908-..................CLC 2, 7, 18
    See also CA 9-12R
    See also DLB 6

Arp, Jean 1887-1966...............CLC 5
    See also CA 81-84
    See also obituary CA 25-28R

Argueta, Manlio 1936-............CLC 31

Arquette, Lois S(teinmetz)
    See Duncan (Steinmetz Arquette), Lois
    See also SATA 1

Arrabal, Fernando 1932-.....CLC 2, 9, 18
    See also CA 9-12R

Arrick, Fran......................CLC 30

Artaud, Antonin 1896-1948.......TCLC 3
    See also CA 104

Arthur, Ruth M(abel)
    1905-1979....................CLC 12
    See also CANR 4
    See also CA 9-12R
    See also obituary CA 85-88
    See also SATA 7
    See also obituary SATA 26

Arundel, Honor (Morfydd)
    1919-1973....................CLC 17
    See also CAP 2
    See also CA 21-22
    See also obituary CA 41-44R
    See also SATA 4
    See also obituary SATA 24

Asch, Sholem 1880-1957.........TCLC 3
    See also CA 105

Ashbery, John (Lawrence)
    1927-..... CLC 2, 3, 4, 6, 9, 13, 15, 25
    See also CANR 9
    See also CA 5-8R
    See also DLB 5
    See also DLB-Y 81

Ashton-Warner, Sylvia (Constance)
    1908-1984.....................CLC 19
    See also CA 69-72
    See also obituary CA 112

Asimov, Isaac
    1920-........ CLC 1, 3, 9, 19, 26
    See also CANR 2
    See also CA 1-4R
    See also SATA 1, 26
    See also DLB 8

Aston, James 1906-1964
    See White, T(erence) H(anbury)

Asturias, Miguel Ángel
    1899-1974...............CLC 3, 8, 13
    See also CAP 2
    See also CA 25-28
    See also obituary CA 49-52

Atheling, William, Jr. 1921-1975
    See Blish, James (Benjamin)

Atherton, Gertrude (Franklin Horn)
    1857-1948................... TCLC 2
    See also CA 104
    See also DLB 9

Atwood, Margaret (Eleanor)
    1939-.........CLC 2, 3, 4, 8, 13, 15, 25
    See also CANR 3
    See also CA 49-52

Auchincloss, Louis (Stanton)
    1917-.................CLC 4, 6, 9, 18
    See also CANR 6
    See also CA 1-4R
    See also DLB 2
    See also DLB-Y 80

Auden, W(ystan) H(ugh)
    1907-1973........ CLC 1, 2, 3, 4, 6, 9,
                                    11, 14
    See also CANR 5
    See also CA 9-12R
    See also obituary CA 45-48
    See also DLB 10, 20

Auel, Jean M(arie) 1936-.........CLC 31
    See also CA 103

Austen, Jane 1775-1817.......... NCLC 1

Avison, Margaret 1918-......... CLC 2, 4
    See also CA 17-20R

Ayckbourn, Alan 1939-.......CLC 5, 8, 18
    See also CA 21-24R
    See also DLB 13

Aymé, Marcel (Andre)
    1902-1967....................CLC 11
    See also CA 89-92

Ayrton, Michael 1921-1975.........CLC 7
    See also CANR 9
    See also CA 5-8R
    See also obituary CA 61-64

Azorín 1874-1967..................CLC 11
    See also Martínez Ruiz, José

Azuela, Mariano 1873-1952....... TCLC 3
    See also CA 104

"Bab" 1836-1911
    See Gilbert, (Sir) W(illiam) S(chwenck)

Babel, Isaak (Emmanuilovich)
    1894-1941................TCLC 2, 13
    See also CA 104

Babits, Mihály 1883-1941........ TCLC 14

Bacchelli, Riccardo 1891-..........CLC 19
    See also CA 29-32R

Bach, Richard (David) 1936-.......CLC 14
    See also CA 9-12R
    See also SATA 13
    See also AITN 1

Bagnold, Enid 1889-1981.........CLC 25
    See also CANR 5
    See also CA 5-8R
    See also obituary CA 103
    See also SATA 1, 25
    See also DLB 13

Bagryana, Elisaveta 1893-.........CLC 10

Baillie, Joanna 1762-1851 .... NCLC 2

Bainbridge, Beryl
    1933-....CLC 4, 5, 8, 10, 14, 18, 22
    See also CA 21-24R
    See also DLB 14

Baker, Elliott 1922-................CLC 8
    See also CANR 2
    See also CA 45-48

Baker, Russell (Wayne) 1925-......CLC 31
    See also CANR 11
    See also CA 57-60

Bakshi, Ralph 1938-..............CLC 26
    See also CA 112

Baldwin, James (Arthur)
    1924-......CLC 1, 2, 3, 4, 5, 8, 13, 15,
                                            17
    See also CANR 3
    See also CA 1-4R
    See also SATA 9
    See also DLB 2, 7, 33

Ballard, J(ames) G(raham)
    1930-..................... CLC 3, 6, 14
    See also CA 5-8R
    See also DLB 14

Balmont, Konstantin Dmitriyevich
    1867-1943...................TCLC 11
    See also CA 109

Balzac, Honoré de 1799-1850 ..... NCLC 5

Bambara, Toni Cade...............CLC 19
    See also CA 29-32R

Banks, Lynne Reid 1929-...........CLC 23
    See also Reid Banks, Lynne

Banville, Théodore (Faullain) de
    1832-1891..................... NCLC 9

Baraka, Imamu Amiri
    1934-.......... CLC 1, 2, 3, 5, 10, 14
    See also Jones, (Everett) LeRoi
    See also DLB 5, 7, 16

Barbey d'Aurevilly, Jules Amédée
    1808-1889.................... NCLC 1

Barbusse, Henri 1873-1935 .... TCLC 5
    See also CA 105

Barea, Arturo 1897-1957 .... TCLC 14
    See also CA 111

Barfoot, Joan 1946-................CLC 18
    See also CA 105

Baring, Maurice 1874-1945 .... TCLC 8
    See also CA 105
    See also DLB 34

Barker, George (Granville)
    1913-........................CLC 8
    See also CANR 7
    See also CA 9-12R
    See also DLB 20

Barker, Pat 19??-.................CLC 32

Barnes, Djuna
    1892-1982......... CLC 3, 4, 8, 11, 29
    See also CA 9-12R
    See also obituary CA 107
    See also DLB 4, 9

Barnes, Peter 1931-.................CLC 5
    See also CA 65-68
    See also DLB 13

Baroja (y Nessi), Pío
    1872-1956...................... TCLC 8
    See also CA 104

Barondess, Sue K(aufman) 1926-1977
    See Kaufman, Sue
    See also CANR 1
    See also CA 1-4R
    See also obituary CA 69-72

Barrett, William (Christopher)
    1913-........................CLC 27
    See also CANR 11
    See also CA 13-16R

Barrie, (Sir) J(ames) M(atthew)
    1860-1937.................... TCLC 2
    See also CA 104
    See also YABC 1
    See also DLB 10

Author Index

Campbell, (Ignatius) Roy (Dunnachie)
1901-1957................... TCLC 5
See also CA 104
See also DLB 20

Campbell, (William) Wilfred
1861-1918................... TCLC 9
See also CA 106

Camus, Albert
1913-1960...... CLC 1, 2, 4, 9, 11, 14, 32
See also CA 89-92

Canby, Vincent 1924-.............CLC 13
See also CA 81-84

Canetti, Elias 1905-......... CLC 3, 14, 25
See also CA 21-24R

Cape, Judith 1916-
See Page, P(atricia) K(athleen)

Čapek, Karel 1890-1938......... TCLC 6
See also CA 104

Capote, Truman
1924-1984........ CLC 1, 3, 8, 13, 19
See also CA 5-8R
See also obituary CA 113
See also DLB 2
See also DLB-Y 80

Capra, Frank 1897-.............CLC 16
See also CA 61-64

Caputo, Philip 1941-.............CLC 32
See also CA 73-76

Cardenal, Ernesto 1925-..........CLC 31
See also CANR 2
See also CA 49-52

Carey, Ernestine Gilbreth 1908-
See Gilbreth, Frank B(unker), Jr. and
  Carey, Ernestine Gilbreth
See also CA 5-8R
See also SATA 2

Carleton, William 1794-1869...... NCLC 3

Carman, (William) Bliss
1861-1929................... TCLC 7
See also CA 104

Carpentier (y Valmont), Alejo
1904-1980................ CLC 8, 11
See also CANR 11
See also CA 65-68
See also obituary CA 97-100

Carr, John Dickson 1906-1977......CLC 3
See also CANR 3
See also CA 49-52
See also obituary CA 69-72

Carrier, Roch 1937- ....CLC 13

Carroll, Lewis 1832-1898......... NCLC 2
See also Dodgson, Charles Lutwidge
See also CLR 2
See also DLB 18

Carroll, Paul Vincent
1900-1968...................CLC 10
See also CA 9-12R
See also obituary CA 25-28R
See also DLB 10

Carruth, Hayden
1921-................CLC 4, 7, 10, 18
See also CANR 4
See also CA 9-12R
See also DLB 5

Carter, Angela 1940-...........CLC 5
See also CANR 12
See also CA 53-56
See also DLB 14

Carver, Raymond 1938-...........CLC 22
See also CA 33-36R

Cary, (Arthur) Joyce
1888-1957................... TCLC 1
See also CA 104
See also DLB 15

Casares, Adolfo Bioy 1914-
See Bioy Casares, Adolfo

Casey, John 1880-1964
See O'Casey, Sean

Casey, Michael 1947- ....CLC 2
See also CA 65-68
See also DLB 5

Casey, Warren 1935-
See Jacobs, Jim and Casey, Warren
See also CA 101

Cassavetes, John 1929-...........CLC 20
See also CA 85-88

Cassill, R(onald) V(erlin)
1919-.................... CLC 4, 23
See also CAAS 1
See also CANR 7
See also CA 9-12R
See also DLB 6

Cassity, (Allen) Turner 1929- ....CLC 6
See also CANR 11
See also CA 17-20R

Castaneda, Carlos 1935?-..........CLC 12
See also CA 25-28R

Castro, Rosalía de 1837-1885 ..... NCLC 3

Cather, Willa (Sibert)
1873-1947................ TCLC 1, 11
See also CA 104
See also SATA 30
See also DLB 9
See also DLB-DS 1

Causley, Charles (Stanley)
1917-........................CLC 7
See also CANR 5
See also CA 9-12R
See also SATA 3
See also DLB 27

Caute, (John) David 1936-.........CLC 29
See also CANR 1
See also CA 1-4R
See also DLB 14

Cavafy, C(onstantine) P(eter)
1863-1933................. TCLC 2, 7
See also CA 104

Cavanna, Betty 1909- ....CLC 12
See also CANR 6
See also CA 9-12R
See also SATA 1, 30

Cayrol, Jean 1911- ....CLC 11
See also CA 89-92

Cela, Camilo José 1916-........ CLC 4, 13
See also CA 21-24R

Celan, Paul 1920-1970 .... CLC 10, 19
See also Antschel, Paul

Céline, Louis-Ferdinand
1894-1961........ CLC 1, 3, 4, 7, 9, 15
See also Destouches, Louis Ferdinand

Cendrars, Blaise 1887-1961........CLC 18
See also Sauser-Hall, Frédéric

Césaire, Aimé (Fernand)
1913-................... CLC 19, 32
See also CA 65-68

Chabrol, Claude 1930-............CLC 16
See also CA 110

Challans, Mary 1905-1983
See Renault, Mary
See also CA 81-84
See also obituary CA 111
See also SATA 23
See also obituary SATA 36

Chambers, James 1948-
See Cliff, Jimmy

Chandler, Raymond
1888-1959................. TCLC 1, 7
See also CA 104

Chaplin, Charles (Spencer)
1889-1977....................CLC 16
See also CA 81-84
See also obituary CA 73-76

Chapman, Graham 1941?-
See Monty Python

Chapman, John Jay
1862-1933................... TCLC 7
See also CA 104

Char, René (Emile)
1907-.................. CLC 9, 11, 14
See also CA 13-16R

Charyn, Jerome 1937- .... CLC 5, 8, 18
See also CAAS 1
See also CANR 7
See also CA 5-8R
See also DLB-Y 83

Chase, Mary Ellen 1887-1973 ....CLC 2
See also CAP 1
See also CA 15-16
See also obituary CA 41-44R
See also SATA 10

Chateaubriand, François René de
1768-1848................... NCLC 3

Chatterji, Saratchandra
1876-1938................. TCLC 13
See also CA 109

Chatwin, (Charles) Bruce
1940-........................CLC 28
See also CA 85-88

Chayefsky, Paddy 1923-1981.......CLC 23
See also CA 9-12R
See also obituary CA 104
See also DLB 7
See also DLB-Y 81

Chayefsky, Sidney 1923-1981
See Chayefsky, Paddy

Cheever, John
1912-1982...... CLC 3, 7, 8, 11, 15, 25
See also CANR 5
See also CA 5-8R
See also obituary CA 106
See also DLB 2
See also DLB-Y 80, 82

Cheever, Susan 1943- ....CLC 18
See also CA 103
See also DLB-Y 82

Author Index

Author Index

Haywood, Eliza (Fowler)
    1693?-1756....................LC 1

Hazzard, Shirley 1931-............CLC 18
    See also CANR 4
    See also CA 9-12R
    See also DLB-Y 82

H(ilda) D(oolittle)
    1886-1961...........CLC 3, 8, 14, 31
    See also Doolittle, Hilda

Head, Bessie 1937-...............CLC 25
    See also CA 29-32R

Headon, (Nicky) Topper 1956?-
    See The Clash

Heaney, Seamus (Justin)
    1939-...............CLC 5, 7, 14, 25
    See also CA 85-88

Hearn, (Patricio) Lafcadio (Tessima Carlos)
    1850-1904...................TCLC 9
    See also CA 105
    See also DLB 12

Heat Moon, William Least
    1939-......................CLC 29

Hébert, Anne 1916-.........CLC 4, 13, 29
    See also CA 85-88

Hecht, Anthony (Evan)
    1923-.................CLC 8, 13, 19
    See also CANR 6
    See also CA 9-12R
    See also DLB 5

Hecht, Ben 1894-1964.............CLC 8
    See also CA 85-88
    See also DLB 7, 9, 25, 26, 28

Heidegger, Martin 1889-1976......CLC 24
    See also CA 81-84
    See also obituary CA 65-68

Heidenstam, (Karl Gustaf) Verner von
    1859-1940...................TCLC 5
    See also CA 104

Heifner, Jack 1946-...............CLC 11
    See also CA 105

Heilbrun, Carolyn G(old)
    1926-......................CLC 25
    See also CANR 1
    See also CA 45-48

Heine, Harry 1797-1856
    See Heine, Heinrich

Heine, Heinrich 1797-1856.......NCLC 4

Heiney, Donald (William) 1921-
    See Harris, MacDonald
    See also CANR 3
    See also CA 1-4R

Heinlein, Robert A(nson)
    1907-............. CLC 1, 3, 8, 14, 26
    See also CANR 1
    See also CA 1-4R
    See also SATA 9
    See also DLB 8

Heller, Joseph 1923-.... CLC 1, 3, 5, 8, 11
    See also CANR 8
    See also CA 5-8R
    See also DLB 2, 28
    See also DLB-Y 80
    See also AITN 1

Hellman, Lillian (Florence)
    1905?-1984....... CLC 2, 4, 8, 14, 18
    See also CA 13-16R
    See also obituary CA 112
    See also DLB 7
    See also AITN 1, 2

Helprin, Mark 1947-.....CLC 7, 10, 22, 32
    See also CA 81-84

Hemingway, Ernest (Miller)
    1899-1961...... CLC 1, 3, 6, 8, 10, 13,
                            19, 30
    See also CA 77-80
    See also DLB 4, 9
    See also DLB-Y 81
    See also DLB-DS 1
    See also AITN 2

Henley, Beth 1952-...............CLC 23
    See also Henley, Elizabeth Becker

Henley, Elizabeth Becker 1952-
    See Henley, Beth
    See also CA 107

Henley, William Ernest
    1849-1903.................. TCLC 8
    See also CA 105
    See also DLB 19

Hennissart, Martha
    See Lathen, Emma
    See also CA 85-88

Henry, O. 1862-1909? .... TCLC 1
    See also Porter, William Sydney

Hentoff, Nat(han Irving) 1925-.....CLC 26
    See also CLR 1
    See also CANR 5
    See also CA 1-4R
    See also SATA 27

Heppenstall, (John) Rayner
    1911-1981...................CLC 10
    See also CA 1-4R
    See also obituary CA 103

Herbert, Frank (Patrick)
    1920-.................... CLC 12, 23
    See also CANR 5
    See also CA 53-56
    See also SATA 9, 37
    See also DLB 8

Herbert, Zbigniew 1924- ....CLC 9
    See also CA 89-92

Herder, Johann Gottfried von
    1744-1803.................. NCLC 8

Hergesheimer, Joseph
    1880-1954................. TCLC 11
    See also CA 109
    See also DLB 9

Herlagñez, Pablo de 1844-1896
    See Verlaine, Paul (Marie)

Herlihy, James Leo 1927-...........CLC 6
    See also CANR 2
    See also CA 1-4R

Herriot, James 1916-..............CLC 12
    See also Wight, James Alfred

Hersey, John (Richard)
    1914-....................CLC 1, 2, 7, 9
    See also CA 17-20R
    See also SATA 25
    See also DLB 6

Herzog, Werner 1942- ....CLC 16
    See also CA 89-92

Hesse, Hermann
    1877-1962...... CLC 1, 2, 3, 6, 11, 17,
                           25
    See also CAP 2
    See also CA 17-18

Heyen, William 1940-..........CLC 13, 18
    See also CA 33-36R
    See also DLB 5

Heyerdahl, Thor 1914-.............CLC 26
    See also CANR 5
    See also CA 5-8R
    See also SATA 2

Heym, Georg (Theodor Franz Arthur)
    1887-1912................... TCLC 9
    See also CA 106

Heyse, Paul (Johann Ludwig von)
    1830-1914................... TCLC 8
    See also CA 104

Hibbert, Eleanor (Burford)
    1906-.......................CLC 7
    See also CANR 9
    See also CA 17-20R
    See also SATA 2

Higgins, George V(incent)
    1939-...............CLC 4, 7, 10, 18
    See also CA 77-80
    See also DLB 2
    See also DLB-Y 81

Highsmith, (Mary) Patricia
    1921-...................CLC 2, 4, 14
    See also CANR 1
    See also CA 1-4R

Highwater, Jamake 1942-..........CLC 12
    See also CANR 10
    See also CA 65-68
    See also SATA 30, 32

Hill, Geoffrey 1932-..........CLC 5, 8, 18
    See also CA 81-84

Hill, George Roy 1922-.............CLC 26
    See also CA 110

Hill, Susan B. 1942- ....CLC 4
    See also CA 33-36R
    See also DLB 14

Hilliard, Noel (Harvey) 1929- ......CLC 15
    See also CANR 7
    See also CA 9-12R

Himes, Chester (Bomar)
    1909-....................CLC 2, 4, 7, 18
    See also CA 25-28R
    See also DLB 2

Hinde, Thomas 1926- ....CLC 6, 11
    See also Chitty, (Sir) Thomas Willes

Hine, (William) Daryl 1936- ....CLC 15
    See also CANR 1
    See also CA 1-4R

Hinton, S(usan) E(loise) 1950-......CLC 30
    See also CLR 3
    See also CA 81-84
    See also SATA 19

Hippius (Merezhkovsky), Zinaida
    (Nikolayevna) 1869-1945 ..... TCLC 9
    See also Gippius, Zinaida (Nikolayevna)

Hiraoka, Kimitake 1925-1970
    See Mishima, Yukio
    See also CA 97-100
    See also obituary CA 29-32R

Author Index

L'Amour, Louis (Dearborn)
1908-.........................CLC 25
See also CANR 3
See also CA 1-4R
See also DLB-Y 80
See also AITN 2

Lampedusa, (Prince) Giuseppe (Maria Fabrizio) Tomasi di
1896-1957................. TCLC 13
See also CA 111

Landis, John (David) 1950-.......CLC 26
See also CA 112

Landolfi, Tommaso 1908-.........CLC 11

Landwirth, Heinz 1927-
See Lind, Jakov
See also CANR 7

Lane, Patrick 1939-..............CLC 25
See also CA 97-100

Lang, Andrew 1844-1912....... TCLC 16
See also SATA 16

Lang, Fritz 1890-1976 ....CLC 20
See also CA 77-80
See also obituary CA 69-72

Lanier, Sidney 1842-1881........ NCLC 6
See also SATA 18

Larbaud, Valéry 1881-1957....... TCLC 9
See also CA 106

Lardner, Ring(gold Wilmer)
1885-1933............... TCLC 2, 14
See also CA 104
See also DLB 11, 25

Larkin, Philip (Arthur)
1922-........... CLC 3, 5, 8, 9, 13, 18
See also CA 5-8R
See also DLB 27

Larson, Charles R(aymond)
1938-........................CLC 31
See also CANR 4
See also CA 53-56

Latham, Jean Lee 1902-...........CLC 12
See also CANR 7
See also CA 5-8R
See also SATA 2
See also AITN 1

Lathen, Emma ....CLC 2
See also Hennissart, Martha
See also Latsis, Mary J(ane)

Latsis, Mary J(ane)
See Lathen, Emma
See also CA 85-88

Lattimore, Richmond (Alexander)
1906-1984....................CLC 3
See also CANR 1
See also CA 1-4R
See also obituary CA 112

Laurence, (Jean) Margaret (Wemyss)
1926-.................... CLC 3, 6, 13
See also CA 5-8R

Lavin, Mary 1912-............ CLC 4, 18
See also CA 9-12R
See also DLB 15

Lawrence, D(avid) H(erbert)
1885-1930.............TCLC 2, 9, 16
See also CA 104
See also DLB 10, 19, 36

Laxness, Halldór (Kiljan)
1902-........................CLC 25
See also Gudjonsson, Halldór Kiljan

Laye, Camara 1928-1980..........CLC 4
See also CA 85-88
See also obituary CA 97-100

Layton, Irving (Peter) 1912- .... CLC 2, 15
See also CANR 2
See also CA 1-4R

Lazarus, Emma 1849-1887 .... NCLC 8

Leacock, Stephen (Butler)
1869-1944.................. TCLC 2
See also CA 104

Lear, Edward 1812-1888 .... NCLC 3
See also CLR 1
See also SATA 18
See also DLB 32

Lear, Norman (Milton) 1922- ......CLC 12
See also CA 73-76

Leavis, F(rank) R(aymond)
1895-1978....................CLC 24
See also CA 21-24R
See also obituary CA 77-80

Lebowitz, Fran 1951?- ....CLC 11
See also CA 81-84

Le Carré, John
1931-............. CLC 3, 5, 9, 15, 28
See also Cornwell, David (John Moore)

Le Clézio, J(ean) M(arie) G(ustave)
1940-........................CLC 31

Leduc, Violette 1907-1972 ....CLC 22
See also CAP 1
See also CA 13-14
See also obituary CA 33-36R

Lee, Don L. 1942-.................CLC 2
See also Madhubuti, Haki R.
See also CA 73-76

Lee, (Nelle) Harper 1926-..........CLC 12
See also CA 13-16R
See also SATA 11
See also DLB 6

Lee, Manfred B(ennington) 1905-1971
See Queen, Ellery
See also CANR 2
See also CA 1-4R
See also obituary CA 29-32R

Lee, Stan 1922- ....CLC 17
See also CA 108, 111

Lee, Vernon 1856-1935.......... TCLC 5
See also Paget, Violet

Leet, Judith 1935-................CLC 11

Le Fanu, Joseph Sheridan
1814-1873................... NCLC 9
See also DLB 21

Leffland, Ella 1931-...............CLC 19
See also CA 29-32R

Léger, (Marie-Rene) Alexis Saint-Léger
1887-1975
See Perse, St.-John
See also CA 13-16R
See also obituary CA 61-64

Le Guin, Ursula K(roeber)
1929-.................. CLC 8, 13, 22
See also CLR 3
See also CANR 9
See also CA 21-24R
See also SATA 4
See also DLB 8
See also AITN 1

Lehmann, Rosamond (Nina)
1901-.......................CLC 5
See also CANR 8
See also CA 77-80
See also DLB 15

Leiber, Fritz (Reuter, Jr.)
1910-.......................CLC 25
See also CANR 2
See also CA 45-48
See also DLB 8

Leithauser, Brad 1953-............CLC 27
See also CA 107

Lelchuk, Alan 1938- ....CLC 5
See also CANR 1
See also CA 45-48

Lem, Stanislaw 1921- .... CLC 8, 15
See also CAAS 1
See also CA 105

L'Engle, Madeleine 1918-.........CLC 12
See also CLR 1
See also CANR 3
See also CA 1-4R
See also SATA 1, 27
See also AITN 2

Lennon, John (Ono) 1940-1980
See Lennon, John (Ono) and McCartney, Paul
See also CA 102

Lennon, John (Ono) 1940-1980 and **McCartney, Paul** 1942- ....CLC 12

Lenz, Siegfried 1926- ....CLC 27
See also CA 89-92

Leonard, Elmore 1925-............CLC 28
See also CANR 12
See also CA 81-84
See also AITN 1

Leonard, Hugh 1926- ....CLC 19
See also Byrne, John Keyes
See also DLB 13

Lerman, Eleanor 1952-............CLC 9
See also CA 85-88

Lermontov, Mikhail Yuryevich
1814-1841................... NCLC 5

Lessing, Doris (May)
1919-........CLC 1, 2, 3, 6, 10, 15, 22
See also CA 9-12R
See also DLB 15

Lester, Richard 1932-.............CLC 20

Levertov, Denise
1923-.........CLC 1, 2, 3, 5, 8, 15, 28
See also CANR 3
See also CA 1-4R
See also DLB 5

Levin, Ira 1929-................ CLC 3, 6
See also CA 21-24R

Author Index

Author Index

Ribman, Ronald (Burt) 1932- ....CLC 7
  See also CA 21-24R

Rice, Elmer 1892-1967 ....CLC 7
  See also CAP 2
  See also CA 21-22
  See also obituary CA 25-28R
  See also DLB 4, 7

Rice, Tim 1944-
  See Rice, Tim and Webber, Andrew Lloyd
  See also CA 103

Rice, Tim 1944- **and Webber, Andrew
    Lloyd** 1948- ....CLC 21

Rich, Adrienne (Cecile)
    1929- .... CLC 3, 6, 7, 11, 18
  See also CA 9-12R
  See also DLB 5

Richard, Keith 1943-
  See Jagger, Mick and Richard, Keith

Richards, I(vor) A(rmstrong)
    1893-1979............. CLC 14, 24
  See also CA 41-44R
  See also obituary CA 89-92
  See also DLB 27

Richards, Keith 1943-
  See Richard, Keith
  See also CA 107

Richardson, Dorothy (Miller)
    1873-1957.................. TCLC 3
  See also CA 104
  See also DLB 36·

Richardson, Ethel 1870-1946
  See Richardson, Henry Handel
  See also CA 105

Richardson, Henry Handel
    1870-1946.................. TCLC 4
  See also Richardson, Ethel

Richardson, Samuel 1689-1761 ...... LC 1

Richler, Mordecai
    1931-............. CLC 3, 5, 9, 13, 18
  See also CA 65-68
  See also SATA 27
  See also AITN 1

Richter, Conrad (Michael)
    1890-1968...................CLC 30
  See also CA 5-8R
  See also obituary CA 25-28R
  See also SATA 3
  See also DLB 9

Richter, Johann Paul Friedrich
  See Jean Paul

Riding, Laura 1901- .... CLC 3, 7
  See also Jackson, Laura (Riding)

Riefenstahl, Berta Helene Amalia 1902-
  See Riefenstahl, Leni
  See also CA 108

Riefenstahl, Leni 1902- ....CLC 16
  See also Riefenstahl, Berta Helene Amalia

Rilke, Rainer Maria
    1875-1926................ TCLC 1, 6
  See also CA 104

Rimbaud, (Jean Nicolas) Arthur
    1854-1891.................. NCLC 4

Ritsos, Yannis 1909- .... CLC 6, 13, 31
  See also CA 77-80

Rivers, Conrad Kent 1933-1968 .....CLC 1
  See also CA 85-88

Robbe-Grillet, Alain
    1922-.........CLC 1, 2, 4, 6, 8, 10, 14
  See also CA 9-12R

Robbins, Harold 1916- ....CLC 5
  See also CA 73-76

Robbins, Thomas Eugene 1936-
  See Robbins, Tom
  See also CA 81-84

Robbins, Tom 1936- .... CLC 9, 32
  See also Robbins, Thomas Eugene
  See also DLB-Y 80

Robbins, Trina 1938- ....CLC 21

Roberts, (Sir) Charles G(eorge) D(ouglas)
    1860-1943.................. TCLC 8
  See also CA 105
  See also SATA 29

Roberts, Kate 1891- ....CLC 15
  See also CA 107

Roberts, Keith (John Kingston)
    1935-....................CLC 14
  See also CA 25-28R

Robinson, Edwin Arlington
    1869-1935.................. TCLC 5
  See also CA 104

Robinson, Jill 1936-...............CLC 10
  See also CA 102

Robinson, Marilynne 1944- ....CLC 25

Robinson, Smokey 1940- ....CLC 21

Robinson, William 1940-
  See Robinson, Smokey

Roddenberry, Gene 1921- ....CLC 17

Rodgers, Mary 1931- ....CLC 12
  See also CANR 8
  See also CA 49-52
  See also SATA 8

Rodgers, W(illiam) R(obert)
    1909-1969...................CLC 7
  See also CA 85-88
  See also DLB 20

Rodriguez, Claudio 1934-.........CLC 10

Roethke, Theodore (Huebner)
    1908-1963......... CLC 1, 3, 8, 11, 19
  See also CA 81-84
  See also DLB 5

Rogers, Sam 1943-
  See Shepard, Sam

Rogers, Will(iam Penn Adair)
    1879-1935.................. TCLC 8
  See also CA 105
  See also DLB 11

Rogin, Gilbert 1929- ....CLC 18
  See also CA 65-68

Rohmer, Eric 1920-...............CLC 16
  See also Scherer, Jean-Marie Maurice

Roiphe, Anne (Richardson)
    1935-.................... CLC 3, 9
  See also CA 89-92
  See also DLB-Y 80

**Rolfe, Frederick (William Serafino Austin
    Lewis Mary)** 1860-1913..... TCLC 12
  See also CA 107
  See also DLB 34

Romains, Jules 1885-1972 ....CLC 7
  See also CA 85-88

Romero, José Rubén
    1890-1952.................. TCLC 14

Rooke, Leon 1934-................CLC 25
  See also CA 25-28R

Rosa, João Guimarães
    1908-1967....................CLC 23
  See also obituary CA 89-92

Rosenberg, Isaac 1890-1918...... TCLC 12
  See also CA 107
  See also DLB 20

Rosenblatt, Joe 1933- ....CLC 15
  See also Rosenblatt, Joseph
  See also AITN 2

Rosenblatt, Joseph 1933-
  See Rosenblatt, Joe
  See also CA 89-92

Rosenthal, M(acha) L(ouis)
    1917-....................CLC 28
  See also CANR 4
  See also CA 1-4R
  See also DLB 5

Ross, (James) Sinclair 1908- ....CLC 13
  See also CA 73-76

Rossetti, Christina Georgina
    1830-1894.................. NCLC 2
  See also SATA 20
  See also DLB 35

Rossetti, Dante Gabriel
    1828-1882.................. NCLC 4
  See also DLB 35

Rossetti, Gabriel Charles Dante 1828-1882
  See Rossetti, Dante Gabriel

Rossner, Judith (Perelman)
    1935-....................CLC 6, 9, 29
  See also CA 17-20R
  See also DLB 6
  See also AITN 2

Rostand, Edmond (Eugène Alexis)
    1868-1918.................. TCLC 6
  See also CA 104

Roth, Henry 1906-........... CLC 2, 6, 11
  See also CAP 1
  See also CA 11-12
  See also DLB 28

Roth, Philip (Milton)
    1933-......CLC 1, 2, 3, 4, 6, 9, 15, 22,
                                        31
  See also CANR 1
  See also CA 1-4R
  See also DLB 2, 28
  See also DLB-Y 82

Rothenberg, Jerome 1931-..........CLC 6
  See also CANR 1
  See also CA 45-48
  See also DLB 5

Rourke, Constance (Mayfield)
    1885-1941.................. TCLC 12
  See also CA 107
  See also YABC 1

Rovit, Earl (Herbert) 1927-........CLC 7
  See also CA 5-8R

Rowson, Susanna Haswell
    1762-1824.................. NCLC 5
  See also DLB 37

Roy, Gabrielle 1909-1983...... CLC 10, 14
  See also CANR 5
  See also CA 53-56
  See also obituary CA 110

Różewicz, Tadeusz 1921- .... CLC 9, 23
  See also CA 108

Ruark, Gibbons 1941-..............CLC 3
  See also CA 33-36R

Rubens, Bernice 192?- .... CLC 19, 31
  See also CA 25-28R
  See also DLB 14

Rudkin, (James) David 1936- ......CLC 14
  See also CA 89-92
  See also DLB 13

Rudnik, Raphael 1933-..............CLC 7
  See also CA 29-32R

Ruiz, José Martínez 1874-1967
  See Azorín

Rukeyser, Muriel
  1913-1980..........CLC 6, 10, 15, 27
  See also CA 5-8R
  See also obituary CA 93-96
  See also obituary SATA 22

Rule, Jane (Vance) 1931-..........CLC 27
  See also CANR 12
  See also CA 25-28R

Rulfo, Juan 1918- ....CLC 8
  See also CA 85-88

Runyon, (Alfred) Damon
  1880-1946................. TCLC 10
  See also CA 107
  See also DLB 11

Rushdie, (Ahmed) Salman
  1947-.................... CLC 23, 31
  See also CA 108, 111

Rushforth, Peter (Scott) 1945-......CLC 19
  See also CA 101

Russ, Joanna 1937-................CLC 15
  See also CANR 11
  See also CA 25-28R
  See also DLB 8

Russell, George William 1867-1935
  See A. E.
  See also CA 104

Russell, (Henry) Ken(neth Alfred)
  1927-.........................CLC 16
  See also CA 105

Ruyslinck, Ward 1929-............CLC 14

Ryan, Cornelius (John)
  1920-1974.....................CLC 7
  See also CA 69-72
  See also obituary CA 53-56

Rybakov, Anatoli 1911?- ....CLC 23

Ryga, George 1932-...............CLC 14
  See also CA 101

Sabato, Ernesto 1911-......... CLC 10, 23
  See also CA 97-100

Sachs, Nelly 1891-1970............CLC 14
  See also CAP 2
  See also CA 17-18
  See also obituary CA 25-28R

Sackler, Howard (Oliver)
  1929-1982.....................CLC 14
  See also CA 61-64
  See also obituary CA 108
  See also DLB 7

Sade, Donatien Alphonse François, Comte de
  1740-1814.................. NCLC 3

Sadoff, Ira 1945- ....CLC 9
  See also CANR 5
  See also CA 53-56

Safire, William 1929- ....CLC 10
  See also CA 17-20R

Sagan, Carl (Edward) 1934- ....CLC 30
  See also CANR 11
  See also CA 25-28R

Sagan, Françoise 1935-.....CLC 3, 6, 9, 17
  See also Quoirez, Françoise

Sainte-Beuve, Charles Augustin
  1804-1869.................. NCLC 5

Sainte-Marie, Beverly 1941-
  See Sainte-Marie, Buffy
  See also CA 107

Sainte-Marie, Buffy 1941- ....CLC 17
  See also Sainte-Marie, Beverly

Saint-Exupéry, Antoine (Jean Baptiste Marie
  Roger) de 1900-1944 .... TCLC 2
  See also CA 108
  See also SATA 20

Saki 1870-1916.................. TCLC 3
  See also Munro, H(ector) H(ugh)

Salama, Hannu 1936-..............CLC 18

Salamanca, J(ack) R(ichard)
  1922-.................... CLC 4, 15
  See also CA 25-28R

Salinger, J(erome) D(avid)
  1919-..............CLC 1, 3, 8, 12
  See also CA 5-8R
  See also DLB 2

Salter, James 1925-................CLC 7
  See also CA 73-76

Saltus, Edgar (Evertson)
  1855-1921.................. TCLC 8
  See also CA 105

Samarakis, Antonis 1919-...........CLC 5
  See also CA 25-28R

Sánchez, Luis Rafael 1936- ....CLC 23

Sanchez, Sonia 1934-..............CLC 5
  See also CA 33-36R
  See also SATA 22

Sand, George 1804-1876.......... NCLC 2

Sandburg, Carl (August)
  1878-1967............CLC 1, 4, 10, 15
  See also CA 5-8R
  See also obituary CA 25-28R
  See also SATA 8
  See also DLB 17

Sandoz, Mari (Susette)
  1896-1966....................CLC 28
  See also CA 1-4R
  See also obituary CA 25-28R
  See also SATA 5
  See also DLB 9

Saner, Reg(inald Anthony)
  1931-.........................CLC 9
  See also CA 65-68

Sansom, William 1912-1976...... CLC 2, 6
  See also CA 5-8R
  See also obituary CA 65-68

Santos, Bienvenido N(uqui)
  1911-........................CLC 22
  See also CA 101

Sarduy, Severo 1937- ....CLC 6
  See also CA 89-92

Sargeson, Frank 1903-1982.......CLC 31
  See also CA 25-28R
  See also CA 106

Sarmiento, Felix Ruben Garcia 1867-1916
  See also CA 104

Saroyan, William
  1908-1981............CLC 1, 8, 10, 29
  See also CA 5-8R
  See also obituary CA 103
  See also SATA 23
  See also obituary SATA 24
  See also DLB 7, 9
  See also DLB-Y 81

Sarraute, Nathalie
  1902-...........CLC 1, 2, 4, 8, 10, 31
  See also CA 9-12R

Sarton, (Eleanor) May
  1912-.................... CLC 4, 14
  See also CANR 1
  See also CA 1-4R
  See also SATA 36
  See also DLB-Y 81

Sartre, Jean-Paul
  1905-1980...... CLC 1, 4, 7, 9, 13, 18,
                                         24
  See also CA 9-12R
  See also obituary CA 97-100

Saura, Carlos 1932-...............CLC 20

Sauser-Hall, Frédéric-Louis 1887-1961
  See Cendrars, Blaise
  See also CA 102
  See also obituary CA 93-96

Sayers, Dorothy L(eigh)
  1893-1957................ TCLC 2, 15
  See also CA 104
  See also DLB 10, 36

Sayles, John (Thomas)
  1950-.................. CLC 7, 10, 14
  See also CA 57-60

Schaeffer, Susan Fromberg
  1941-.................. CLC 6, 11, 22
  See also CA 49-52
  See also SATA 22
  See also DLB 28

Scherer, Jean-Marie Maurice 1920-
  See Rohmer, Eric
  See also CA 110

Schevill, James (Erwin) 1920-.......CLC 7
  See also CA 5-8R

Schisgal, Murray (Joseph)
  1926-.........................CLC 6
  See also CA 21-24R

Schmitz, Ettore 1861-1928
  See Svevo, Italo
  See also CA 104

Schneider, Leonard Alfred 1925-1966
  See Bruce, Lenny
  See also CA 89-92

Schnitzler, Arthur 1862-1931 ..... TCLC 4
  See also CA 104

Schorer, Mark 1908-1977 ....CLC 9
  See also CANR 7
  See also CA 5-8R
  See also obituary CA 73-76

Author Index

Stout, Rex (Todhunter)
1886-1975......................CLC 3
See also CA 61-64
See also AITN 2

Stow, (Julian) Randolph 1935- .....CLC 23
See also CA 13-16R

Stowe, Harriet (Elizabeth) Beecher
1811-1896..................... NCLC 3
See also YABC 1
See also DLB 1, 12

Strachey, (Giles) Lytton
1880-1932.................. TCLC 12
See also CA 110

Strand, Mark 1934-............ CLC 6, 18
See also CA 21-24R
See also DLB 5

Straub, Peter (Francis) 1943- ......CLC 28
See also CA 85-88

Strauss, Botho 1944-..............CLC 22

Straussler, Tomas 1937-
See Stoppard, Tom

Streatfeild, Noel 1897- ....CLC 21
See also CA 81-84
See also SATA 20

Stribling, T(homas) S(igismund)
1881-1965.....................CLC 23
See also obituary CA 107
See also DLB 9

Strindberg, (Johan) August
1849-1912................. TCLC 1, 8
See also CA 104

Strugatskii, Arkadii (Natanovich) 1925-
See Strugatskii, Arkadii (Natanovich) and
Strugatskii, Boris (Natanovich)
See also CA 106

Strugatskii, Arkadii (Natanovich) 1925-
and Strugatskii, Boris (Natanovich)
1933-......................CLC 27

Strugatskii, Boris (Natanovich) 1933-
See Strugatskii, Arkadii (Natanovich) and
Strugatskii, Boris (Natanovich)
See also CA 106

Strugatskii, Boris (Natanovich) 1933- and
Strugatskii, Arkadii (Natanovich) 1925-
See Strugatskii, Arkadii (Natanovich) and
Strugatskii, Boris (Natanovich)

Strummer, Joe 1953?-
See The Clash

Stuart, (Hilton) Jesse
1907-1984............CLC 1, 8, 11, 14
See also CA 5-8R
See also obituary CA 112
See also SATA 2
See also obituary SATA 36
See also DLB 9

Sturgeon, Theodore (Hamilton)
1918-......................CLC 22
See also CA 81-84
See also DLB 8

Styron, William
1925-............ CLC 1, 3, 5, 11, 15
See also CANR 6
See also CA 5-8R
See also DLB 2
See also DLB-Y 80

Sudermann, Hermann
1857-1928.................. TCLC 15
See also CA 107

Sue, Eugène 1804-1857........... NCLC 1

Sukenick, Ronald 1932- ...... CLC 3, 4, 6
See also CA 25-28R
See also DLB-Y 81

Suknaski, Andrew 1942-..........CLC 19
See also CA 101

Summers, Andrew James 1942-
See The Police

Summers, Andy 1942-
See The Police

Summers, Hollis (Spurgeon, Jr.)
1916-.......................CLC 10
See also CANR 3
See also CA 5-8R
See also DLB 6

**Summers, (Alphonsus Joseph-Mary Augustus)
Montague** 1880-1948 .... TCLC 16

Sumner, Gordon Matthew 1951-
See The Police

Susann, Jacqueline 1921-1974.......CLC 3
See also CA 65-68
See also obituary CA 53-56
See also AITN 1

Sutcliff, Rosemary 1920- ....CLC 26
See also CLR 1
See also CA 5-8R
See also SATA 6

Sutro, Alfred 1863-1933.......... TCLC 6
See also CA 105
See also DLB 10

Sutton, Henry 1935-
See Slavitt, David (R.)

Svevo, Italo 1861-1928 .... TCLC 2
See also Schmitz, Ettore

Swados, Elizabeth 1951-............CLC 12
See also CA 97-100

Swados, Harvey 1920-1972 ....CLC 5
See also CANR 6
See also CA 5-8R
See also obituary CA 37-40R
See also DLB 2

Swenson, May 1919-........... CLC 4, 14
See also CA 5-8R
See also SATA 15
See also DLB 5

Swift, Jonathan 1667-1745.......... LC 1
See also SATA 19

Swinburne, Algernon Charles
1837-1909................... TCLC 8
See also CA 105
See also DLB 35

Swinnerton, Frank (Arthur)
1884-1982.....................CLC 31
See also obituary CA 108
See also DLB 34

Symons, Arthur (William)
1865-1945.................. TCLC 11
See also CA 107
See also DLB 19

Symons, Julian (Gustave)
1912-................. CLC 2, 14, 32
See also CANR 3
See also CA 49-52

Synge, (Edmund) John Millington
1871-1909................. TCLC 6
See also CA 104
See also DLB 10, 19

Syruc, J. 1911-
See Miłosz, Czesław

Tabori, George 1914-.............CLC 19
See also CANR 4
See also CA 49-52

Tagore, (Sir) Rabindranath
1861-1941.................. TCLC 3
See also Thakura, Ravindranatha

Tamayo y Baus, Manuel
1829-1898.................. NCLC 1

Tanizaki, Jun'ichirō
1886-1965............ CLC 8, 14, 28
See also CA 93-96
See also obituary CA 25-28R

Tarkington, (Newton) Booth
1869-1946................. TCLC 9
See also CA 110
See also SATA 17
See also DLB 9

Tate, (John Orley) Allen
1899-1979...... CLC 2, 4, 6, 9, 11, 14,
24
See also CA 5-8R
See also obituary CA 85-88
See also DLB 4

Tate, James 1943-........... CLC 2, 6, 25
See also CA 21-24R
See also DLB 5

Tavel, Ronald 1940- ....CLC 6
See also CA 21-24R

Taylor, C(ecil) P(hillip)
1929-1981...................CLC 27
See also CA 25-28R
See also obituary CA 105

Taylor, Eleanor Ross 1920- ....CLC 5
See also CA 81-84

Taylor, Elizabeth
1912-1975.............. CLC 2, 4, 29
See also CANR 9
See also CA 13-16R
See also SATA 13

Taylor, Kamala (Purnaiya) 1924-
See Markandaya, Kamala (Purnaiya)
See also CA 77-80

Taylor, Mildred D(elois) ....CLC 21
See also CA 85-88
See also SATA 15

Taylor, Peter (Hillsman)
1917-................ CLC 1, 4, 18
See also CANR 9
See also CA 13-16R
See also DLB-Y 81

Taylor, Robert Lewis 1912-........CLC 14
See also CANR 3
See also CA 1-4R
See also SATA 10

Teasdale, Sara 1884-1933........ TCLC 4
See also CA 104
See also SATA 32

Tegnér, Esaias 1782-1846........ NCLC 2

Teilhard de Chardin, (Marie Joseph) Pierre
1881-1955................... TCLC 9
See also CA 105

Author Index

Cumulative Index to Nationalities

Cumulative Index to Critics

Critic Index

Critic Index

Critic Index

Critic Index

Critic Index

Nevins, Allan
  Ring Lardner 2:327
Nevius, Blake
  Edith Wharton 3:566
Newberry, Wilma
  José Echegaray 4:104
Newcombe, Josephine M.
  Leonid Andreyev 3:29
Newton, Nancy A.
  Antonio Machado 3:314
Nicholls, Roger A.
  Heinrich Mann 9:322
Nichols, Wallace B.
  Alfred Noyes 7:508
Nicoll, Allardyce
  Maurice Baring 8:33
  Henrik Ibsen 2:228
  Eugene O'Neill 1:391
  Bernard Shaw 3:395
  August Strindberg 1:450
Nietzsche, Friedrich
  Friedrich Nietzsche 10:354
  August Strindberg 8:405
Nieuwenhuys, Rob
  Louis Couperus 15:47
Niger, Shmuel
  Sholom Aleichem 1:20
Nilsson, Nils Ake
  Osip Mandelstam 6:257
Nin, Anaïs
  D. H. Lawrence 2:348
Nissenson, Hugh
  Ivan Bunin 6:54
Noble, David W.
  F. Scott Fitzgerald 1:264
Noble, James Ashcroft
  Israel Zangwill 16:439
Nock, Albert J.
  Bret Harte 1:341
Nolin, Bertil
  Georg Brandes 10:71
Noon, William T., S.J.
  James Joyce 16:237
Nordau, Max
  Friedrich Nietzsche 10:357
Nordon, Pierre
  Arthur Conan Doyle 7:226
Noreng, Harald
  Bjørnstjerne Bjørnson 7:114
Norman, Henry
  F. Marion Crawford 10:138
  Olive Schreiner 9:393
Norman, W.H.H.
  Akutagawa Ryūnosuke 16:18
Normand, Guessler
  Henri Barbusse 5:19
Norris, Frank
  Stephen Crane 11:123
Norris, Margot
  James Joyce 3:281
Norton, David L.
  René Daumal 14:91
Novak, Barbara
  A. A. Milne 6:313

Noyes, Alfred
  William Ernest Henley 8:103
  Algernon Charles Swinburne
    8:431
Noyes, Henry
  Alfred Noyes 7:515
Nozick, Martin
  Miguel de Unamuno 2:568
Nugent, Robert
  Paul Eluard 7:257
Nye, Russel
  L. Frank Baum 7:15
  Zane Grey 6:182
Oates, Joyce Carol
  Géza Csáth 13:149
  Henry James 11:340
  Thomas Mann 2:441
  Andrei Platonov 14:411
  Virginia Woolf 1:540
  William Butler Yeats 1:582
O'Brien, James
  Dazai Osamu 11:180
O'Brien, Justin
  André Gide 12:157
  Valéry Larbaud 9:197
  Marcel Proust 7:528
O'Casey, Sean
  Bernard Shaw 3:399
O'Connor, Frank
  A. E. 3:8
  Anton Chekhov 3:161
  A. E. Coppard 5:180
  Lady Gregory 1:336
  Thomas Hardy 4:168
  James Stephens 4:416
O'Connor, Patricia Walker
  Gregorio Martínez Sierra and
    María Martínez Sierra 6:282,
    284
O'Connor, Ulick
  Oliver St. John Gogarty 15:110
O'Connor, William Van
  Joyce Cary 1:145
  Wallace Stevens 3:464
  Mark Twain 12:443
O'Conor, Norreys Jepson
  Standish O'Grady 5:353
O'Donnell, J. P.
  Bertolt Brecht 1:116
O'Faolain, Sean
  A. E. 3:8
  George Moore 7:482
  Leo Tolstoy 4:461
O'Hagan, Thomas
  John Millington Synge 6:431
O'Hara, John
  Robert Benchley 1:78
Ohlin, Peter H.
  James Agee 1:10
Okeke-Ezigbo, Emeka
  Paul Laurence Dunbar 12:127
Olgin, Moissaye J.
  Leonid Andreyev 3:21
  Konstantin Dmitriyevich
    Balmont 11:31
  Aleksandr Kuprin 5:297

Oliphant, Margaret
  Thomas Hardy 4:150
  Andrew Lang 16:251
Oliver, Edith
  Maxim Gorky 8:93
Olivero, Federico
  Emile Verhaeren 12:460
Olsen, Tillie
  Rebecca Harding Davis 6:153
Olson, Elder
  Dylan Thomas 1:470
Olson, Paul R.
  Juan Ramón Jiménez 4:218
Olson, Stanley
  Elinor Wylie 8:537
O'Neill, Eugene
  Mark Twain 12:439
O'Neill, Tom
  Giuseppe Tomasi di Lampedusa
    13:312
Orage, A. R.
  A. E. 10:14
  Ernest Dowson 4:87
O'Reilly, Robert F.
  André Gide 12:168
O'Rell, Max
  Paul Bourget 12:64
Ornstein, Robert
  F. Scott Fitzgerald 1:250
O'Rourke, David
  F. Scott Fitzgerald 14:184
  Thomas Wolfe 13:493
Orr, John
  Henrik Ibsen 16:193
Ortega y Gasset, José
  José Ortega y Gasset 9:334
  Marcel Proust 7:536
  Ramón del Valle-Inclán 5:479
Ortiz-Vargas, A.
  Gabriela Mistral 2:475
Orwell, George
  Arturo Barea 14:44
  D. H. Lawrence 2:354
  George Orwell 15:298, 301
  Jules Verne 6:491
  H. G. Wells 6:533
Osborne, Charles
  Thomas Hardy 10:223
  Francis Thompson 4:411
O'Sheel, Shaemas
  Lady Gregory 1:333
Ossar, Michael
  Ernst Toller 10:491
O'Sullivan, Susan
  Gabriel Miró 5:337
Oswald, Victor A., Jr.
  Hugo von Hofmannsthal 11:297
Ouida
  F. Marion Crawford 10:140
Ouimette, Victor
  José Ortega y Gasset 9:354
Ould, Hermon
  Rudolf Steiner 13:437

Overmyer, Janet
  Saki 3:371
Ozick, Cynthia
  Bruno Schulz 5:424
Pacey, Desmond
  Bliss Carman 7:145
  Frederick Philip Grove 4:140
  Charles G. D. Roberts 8:319
  Duncan Campbell Scott 6:393
Pachmuss, Temira
  Zinaida Hippius 9:160, 166
  Franz Werfel 8:475
Pacifici, Sergio
  Vitaliano Brancati 12:90
  Giuseppe Tomasi di Lampedusa
    13:320
  Giovanni Verga 3:545
Pack, Robert
  Wallace Stevens 3:455
Painter, George D.
  Marcel Proust 7:537
Pal, Bepin Chandra
  Annie Besant 9:15
Palamari, Demetra
  Emile Zola 6:569
Palamas, Kostes
  Kostes Palamas 5:377
Palmer, Nettie
  Henry Handel Richardson 4:375
Panek, LeRoy
  E. C. Bentley 12:22
Paolucci, Anne
  Luigi Pirandello 4:356
Parker, Alexander A.
  Miguel de Unamuno 2:565
Parker, Dorothy
  See also **Reader, Constant**
  Theodore Dreiser 10:174
Parker, H. T.
  Karl Čapek 6:82
Parks, Edd Winfield
  Edna St. Vincent Millay 4:310
Parrington, Vernon Louis
  James Branch Cabell 6:63
  Hamlin Garland 3:193
Parrot, Louis
  Paul Eluard 7:249
Parrott, Cecil
  Jaroslav Hašek 4:189
Parry, I. F.
  Franz Kafka 13:263
Parry, Idris
  Rainer Maria Rilke 1:422
Parry, M.
  Antoine de Saint-Exupéry 2:524
Parsons, Ian
  Isaac Rosenberg 12:310
Partridge, Ralph
  Josephine Tey 14:449
Pasternak, Boris
  Vladimir Mayakovsky 4:298
  Marina Tsvetaeva 7:558
Pater, Walter
  Arthur Symons 11:426
  Oscar Wilde 1:495

Critic Index

Solovyov, Vladimir
Valery Bryusov 10:77

Sonnerfeld, Albert
Georges Bernanos 3:120, 123

Sontag, Susan
Antonin Artaud 3:56
Cesare Pavese 3:338

Sorensen, Otto M.
Bertolt Brecht 13:50

Sorley, Charles Hamilton
Rupert Brooke 7:120

Soskin, William
Marjorie Kinnan Rawlings
4:360

Sőter, István
Miklós Radnóti 16:409

Southerington, F. R.
Thomas Hardy 10:225

Southworth, James Granville
Hart Crane 2:117
Thomas Hardy 4:166
Elinor Wylie 8:530

Spacks, Patricia Meyer
Charles Williams 1:524

Spalek, John M.
Franz Werfel 8:482

Spalter, Max
Karl Kraus 5:283

Spangler, George M.
Kate Chopin 5:154

Spann, Meno
Franz Kafka 13:282

Spanos, William V.
Dorothy L. Sayers 2:534

Speaight, Robert
Pierre Teilhard de Chardin
9:491

Spear, Allan H.
James Weldon Johnson 3:246

Spears, Monroe K.
Hart Crane 2:119

Spector, Ivar
Leonid Andreyev 3:25

Speir, Jerry
Raymond Chandler 7:179

Spell, Jefferson Rea
Mariano Azuela 3:76

Spencer, Benjamin T.
Sherwood Anderson 1:61

Spencer, Theodore
William Butler Yeats 1:554

Spender, Natasha
Raymond Chandler 1:176

Spender, Stephen
Wolfgang Borchert 5:106
Robert Bridges 1:131
C. P. Cavafy 2:93
Henry James 2:253
James Joyce 3:277
Franz Kafka 13:257
D. H. Lawrence 2:369
Wyndham Lewis 2:385
Malcolm Lowry 6:238
Wilfred Owen 5:361
Bernard Shaw 3:393

Dylan Thomas 8:451
Charles Williams 11:484
William Butler Yeats 1:555

Sperber, Murray
George Orwell 6:353; 15:317

Spettigue, Douglas O.
Frederick Philip Grove 4:138,
143, 144

Spilka, Mark
D. H. Lawrence 16:289

Spiller, Robert E.
Henry Adams 4:11
Hamlin Garland 3:195

Spinner, Jonathan Harold
Jack London 15:255

Spitteler, Carl
Carl Spitteler 12:334

Spivey, Ted R.
Oscar Wilde 8:501

Sprague, Claire
Edgar Saltus 8:352
Virginia Woolf 1:545

Sprague, Rosemary
Sara Teasdale 4:431

Sprinchorn, Evert
Henrik Ibsen 16:191

Spring, Powell
Rudolf Steiner 13:442

Squire, J. C.
See also **Eagle, Solomon**
Maurice Baring 8:32
Robert Bridges 1:125
G. K. Chesterton 6:97
W. H. Davies 5:201
Walter de la Mare 4:72
A. E. Housman 1:353
D. H. Lawrence 9:212
Katherine Mansfield 8:275
Alice Meynell 6:297
Bernard Shaw 3:385
William Butler Yeats 1:553

Stafford, Jean
Anthony Comstock 13:96

Stafford, John
Joel Chandler Harris 2:211

Stahl, E. L.
Rainer Maria Rilke 1:411

Stallman, Robert Wooster
Stephen Crane 11:137
F. Scott Fitzgerald 14:158

Stamm, Rudolf
Eugene O'Neill 1:390

Stanford, Derek
Havelock Ellis 14:130
Alfred Noyes 7:515
Arthur Symons 11:446
Dylan Thomas 8:455

Stanford, W. B.
Nikos Kazantzakis 2:314

Stanislavski, Constantin
Anton Chekhov 10:101

Stansbury, Milton H.
Jean Giraudoux 2:155

Stanton, Edward F.
Federico García Lorca 7:298

Stanton, Ruth
José Rubén Romero 14:433

Starck, Taylor
Stefan George 14:193

Starkie, Enid
André Gide 12:163

Starkie, Walter
Jacinto Benavente 3:97
Vicente Blasco Ibáñez 12:40
Federico García Lorca 1:317
Gregorio Martinez Sierra and
Maria Martinez Sierra 6:277

Starr, Nathan Comfort
Charles Williams 11:488

Starrett, Vincent
Ambrose Bierce 7:89
Arthur Conan Doyle 7:220
Arthur Machen 4:278

Stavrou, C. N.
Nikos Kazantzakis 5:261

Stearns, Harold
John Reed 9:382

Stearns, Monroe M.
Thomas Wolfe 13:474

Steele, Elizabeth
Hugh Walpole 5:502

Steen, Marguerite
Hugh Walpole 5:499

Steene, Birgitta
August Strindberg 8:413

Stegner, Wallace
Willa Cather 1:167
Bret Harte 1:343
Thomas Wolfe 13:477

Stein, Allen F.
Ring Lardner 2:340

Stein, Gertrude
F. Scott Fitzgerald 14:149
Henry James 2:261

Stein, Paul
Jack London 9:278

Steinbrink, Jeffrey
F. Scott Fitzgerald 14:179

Steiner, George
Ford Madox Ford 1:288
Henrik Ibsen 8:148
Leo Tolstoy 4:467

Steiner, Marie
Rudolf Steiner 13:442

Steiner, Rudolf
Friedrich Nietzsche 10:358
Rudolf Steiner 13:438

Steiner, T. R.
Nathanael West 14:488

Steinmann, Martin Jr.
T. F. Powys 9:369

Stempel, Daniel
Lafcadio Hearn 9:129

Stender-Petersen, Adolph
Władysław Stanisław Reymont
5:390

Stenerson, Douglas C.
H. L. Mencken 13:390

Stephen, James Kenneth
H. Rider Haggard 11:240

Stephens, Donald
Bliss Carman 7:147

Stephens, James
A. E. 10:17
William Butler Yeats 11:525

Stephensen, P. R.
Aleister Crowley 7:210

Sterling, George
Ambrose Bierce 7:88, 91

Stern, Alfred
José Ortega y Gasset 9:341

Stern, Guy
Bertolt Brecht 13:62

Stern, J. P.
Jaroslav Hašek 4:186
Thomas Mann 2:438
Friedrich Nietzsche 10:394
Rainer Maria Rilke 1:424

Stern, Philip Van Doren
Arthur Machen 4:279

Stevens, Wallace
Harriet Monroe 12:220
Wallace Stevens 12:357
Paul Valéry 4:494

Stevenson, Lionel
Gertrude Atherton 2:16
John McCrae 12:209
M. P. Shiel 8:364
May Sinclair 11:412

Stewart, Allegra
Gertrude Stein 1:434

Stewart, Donald Ogden
Robert Benchley 1:78
Robert W. Service 15:400

Stewart, J.I.M.
James Joyce 3:274
Rudyard Kipling 8:197
D. H. Lawrence 2:368
William Butler Yeats 1:569

Stewart, Joan Hinde
Colette 16:129

Stewart, Lady Margaret
Antoine de Saint-Exupéry 2:518

Still, William
Frances Ellen Watkins Harper
14:255

Stillman, Linda Klieger
Alfred Jarry 14:285

Stine, Peter
Franz Kafka 6:232

Stirling, Monica
Colette 1:191

Stock, Irvin
André Gide 12:154

Stock, Michael O. P.
Pierre Teilhard de Chardin
9:484

Stockinger, Jacob
Colette 16:118

Stone, Albert E., Jr.
Mark Twain 6:471

Stone, Geoffrey
Roy Campbell 5:117
Oscar Wilde 8:499

Critic Index

Critic Index